# TEXAS WRITE SOURCE

## Teacher's Edition

Grade 10

Authors
**Dave Kemper, Patrick Sebranek, and Verne Meyer**

Consulting Author
**Gretchen Bernabei**

Illustrator
**Chris Krenzke**

GREAT SOURCE®

HOUGHTON MIFFLIN HARCOURT

www.hmheducation.com/tx/writesource

Printed in USA

ISBN-13 978-0-547-39484-8


3 4 5 6 7 8 9 10  0914  19 18 17 16 15 14 13 12 11


4500305895            B C D E F G

# TEXAS WRITE SOURCE

## Reviewers

**Kim Brody**
Lindale Independent School District
Lindale, Texas

**Laurie Coker**
Round Rock Independent School District
Austin, Texas

**Rita Curington**
Athens Independent School District
Athens, Texas

**Sandy Emmerson**
Midland Independent School District
Midland, Texas

**Paula Jay**
Fort Bend Independent School District
Missouri City, Texas

**Lou Ann Kemper**
Lewisville Independent School District
Flower Mound, Texas

**Shelli Shaw**
Katy Independent School District
Katy, Texas

**Valerie Taylor**
Eanes Independent School District
Austin, Texas

Table of contents

# Program Overview

# Teacher Resources

# The Writing Process

## USING THE WRITING PROCESS

# The Forms of Writing

## NARRATIVE WRITING

## EXPOSITORY WRITING

## PERSUASIVE WRITING

## INTERPRETIVE RESPONSE

## CREATIVE WRITING

Table of Contents

# How Does *Texas Write Source* Work?

*T*exas Write Source is a complete language arts curriculum focused on writing and grammar in print and digital formats.

**With writing instruction at the core, all TEKS and ELPS are taught in an authentic writing context.**

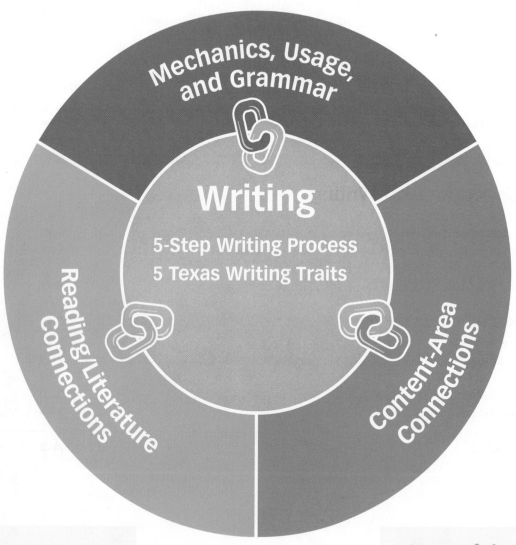

**Texas Traits**

**The Texas Traits**

- Focus and Coherence
- Organization
- Development of Ideas
- Voice
- Conventions

**Steps of the Writing Process**

- Prewrite
- Draft
- Revise
- Edit
- Publish

**Introduce the writing form:**

- Analyze a model paragraph.

- Preview the form by responding to questions about the model or by writing a new paragraph.

 Students reflect on how revising for the Texas traits and editing for **mechanics, usage, and grammar** can improve their writing.

**Each core writing unit follows the same instructional path— a consistent writing curriculum across all grade levels.**

**\* Explore the writing form:**

- Analyze a model essay or story.

 Students see how the author of the model essay or story uses the steps of the writing process.

- Use the writing process to write an essay or story.

 Students revise their work using the Texas traits and edit for **mechanics, usage, and grammar.**

*\* Repeat these steps based on an additional writing model as an enrichment activity.*

**Write for Assessment**

- Write a piece in the same writing form for assessment.

 Students read authentic, real-world essays and responses that model the appropriate form.

**Writing Across the Curriculum**

 Write in a variety of forms across the major content areas—Science, Social Studies, Math, and the Arts.

*Texas Write Source* prepares students for success in the 21st century.

# How is *Texas Write Source* Organized?

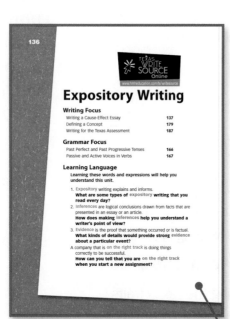

## The Forms of Writing

The core units focus on instruction in the following writing forms:

- Narrative Writing
- Expository Writing
- Persuasive Writing
- Interpretive Response
- Creative Writing
- Research Writing

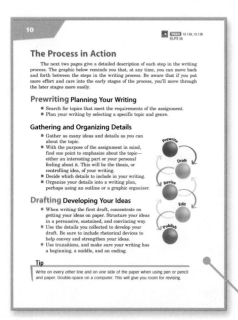

## The Writing Process

This unit introduces students to the steps in the writing process and integrates instruction on the five Texas traits of writing.

# Writing Across the Curriculum

This section helps students prepare for writing assignments in other content areas.

## The Tools of Language

This unit provides targeted support for English language learners in all the core areas taught in *Texas Write Source*.

## Basic Grammar and Writing

This section covers the fundamental building blocks of writing: words, sentences, and paragraphs.

## A Writer's Resource

This section is a reference tool with information about development and presentation of writing.

## Proofreader's Guide

This section address punctuation, mechanics, spelling, usage, sentence structure, and parts of speech.

---

**459**

### Writing in Social Studies

No two human beings are the same, and no two human societies are either. Social studies focuses on this diversity. As a student of social studies, you may need to survey a variety of documents (speeches, graphs, maps, photos, reports, and so on) and respond to them in writing. You'll need to analyze the documents, summarize and organize the information, and create a response that [...]

This chapter models two types of writi[...] your social studies classes. It addresses wri[...] responding to a series of documents.

■ Writing Guidelines: Descriptive Repo[...]
■ Writing Guidelines: Report on Social [...]

"History will be kind to me, for I intend to write it."
—Winston Churchill

---

**540**    ELPS 2C, 2I, 2J, 3E, 3G, 3H

### Reading the Expository Model

**What Do You Know?**

Next you will read a sample expository essay about Charlemagne. Have you ever heard of Charlemagne? What do you already know about him? When and where did he live? What did he do? Talk to a partner about what you know and where you learned it.

**Build Background**

Charlemagne, or "Charles the Great," was an emperor in Europe during the Middle Ages. He is famous for bringing together many nations into one great empire—the Holy Roman Empire. Charlemagne is known for stabilizing the European economy by balancing trade and commerce. He is also known for his efforts to promote education and learning ac[...]

**Listening**

Listen as your teacher or a classmate reads[...] listen, make a note about the thesis statement. [...] questions below.
**1.** What are two pieces of background infor[...]
**2.** According to the writer, why did Charlem[...]
**3.** With what final thought does the writer [...]

**Key Words**

| | |
|---|---|
| ability | by the sword or the[...] |
| in order to | peace |
| trust | when |

Look at the words and phrases in the box. Y[...] read the writing model. With a partner, discuss [...] **or the cross** mean. Use the other words to talk[...] event in history or the effects of an event in your[...] curfew.

---

**576**    ELPS 3E

### Adjectives Making a Precise Point

Some writers use adjectives like frosting, slathering their nouns as if the adjectives will make them tastier. You will do better to consider how adjectives subtract from a noun, rather than adding to it, by limiting its meaning and making it more precise.

> **DON'T Write**
> I had a big, beautiful **party.**
> (The adjectives do not make *party* more precise.)
> **DO Write**
> I had a sweet-sixteen birthday **party.**
> (The adjectives tell precisely what *kind* of party.)

### Adjective Phrases and Clauses

Phrases and clauses that function as adjec[...]

The house rocked like a dryer filled with shoes.[...]
(The phrase *filled with shoes* tells precisely[...]

We played a game of truth or dare that resulted[...]
(The phrase *of truth or dare* and the claus[...]
tell exactly what kind of game.)

**Try It!**

Think of a special event that you have att[...] related to it. Add one adjective and one [...] would make the noun's meaning more precise.[...] a paragraph about the event, using some [...] your list. Share and discuss your paragr[...]

| Nouns | Adjectives |
|---|---|
| pool | above-ground |
| diving board | squeaky |
| dives | ridiculous |
| belly flop | blistering |

---

**618**    TEKS 10.13A

### Finding a Topic

Searching for a topic can be a challenge even if the teacher provides a general writing subject. For example, you might be asked to write about the westward development of the United States in the 1800s. This subject is too broad to cover well in one paper. It would be necessary to narrow the focus to find a manageable topic. Here are some ideas to help you.

### Using a Cluster Diagram

A cluster diagram can help you identify a topic. Place the general subject in the center and then break it down into categories. Break each category into yet smaller topics. Choose one that has enough information and is the most interesting to you.

Conestoga wagons · war with Mexico · gold rush · Oregon trail · Lewis & Clark · California · 49ers · Louisiana Purchase · Westward Growth of the United States in the 1800s · Indian wars · Oklahoma land rush · Sooners · Transcontinental railroad · relocation of Indian Tribes · frontier open[...]

### Trying Freewriting

Freewriting can help you identify a topic. T[...] you can remember about a general subject. Incor[...] occur to you as you write. The freewriting belo[...] the relocation of Native American tribes.

The book Bury My Heart at Wounded Knee [...] knew that people came from other countries to [...] that the transcontinental railroad made it much[...] to settlement. But why couldn't Native Americ[...] land? The ownership of land seemed to make coo[...] reservati[...] the only answer? How long did it ta[...]

---

**698**    TEKS 10.19
ELPS 5C

### Spelling Rules

**698.1 Write *i* before *e***

Write *i* before *e* except after *c*, or when sounded like *a* as in *neighbor* and *weigh*.

relief  receive  perceive  reign  freight  beige

**Exceptions:** There are a number of exceptions to this rule, including these:
neither, leisure, seize, weird, species, science.

**698.2 Words with Consonant Endings**

When a one-syllable word (*bat*) ends in a consonant (*t*) preceded by one vowel (*a*), double the final consonant before adding a suffix that begins with a vowel (*batting*).

sum — summary    god — goddess

**NOTE:** When a word with more than one syllable (*control*) ends in a consonant (*l*) preceded by one vowel (*o*), the accent is on the last syllable (*con trol'*), and the suffix begins with a vowel (*ing*), the same rule holds true: double the final consonant (*controlling*).

prefer — preferred    begin — beginning
forget — forgettable    admit — admittance

**698.3 Words with a Silent *e***

If a word ends with a silent *e*, drop the *e* before adding a suffix that begins with a vowel. Do not drop the *e* when the suffix begins with a consonant.

state — stating — statement    like — liking — likeness
use — using — useful    nine — ninety — nineteen

**Exceptions:** judgment, truly, argument, ninth

**698.4 Words Ending in *y***

When *y* is the last letter in a word and the *y* is preceded by a consonant, change the *y* to *i* before adding any suffix except those beginning with *i*.

fry — fries — frying    hurry — hurried — hurrying    lady — ladies
ply — pliable    happy — happiness    beauty — beautiful

When *y* is the last letter in a word and the *y* is preceded by a vowel, do not change the *y* to *i* before adding a suffix.

play — plays — playful    stay — stays — staying    employ — employed

**Important reminder:** Never trust your spelling even to the best spell-checker. Use an online or print dictionary to determine or check the spelling of words your spell-checker does not cover.

# What are the main components in Texas Write Source?

**Texas Assessment Preparation** provides a pretest, progress tests, a post-test, and Texas assessment preparation.

The **Daily Language Workouts** build student grammar skills through quick, daily editing and proofreading activities.

The *Texas Write Source* **Student Edition** reflects the latest research on writing instruction. The **Teacher's Edition** has all the support you need to help students master the TEKS and ELPS.

The **SkillsBook** helps students practice and improve mechanics, usage, and grammar skills.

## Write Source Online
www.hmheducation.com/tx/writesource

- Discover the power of writing instruction with **Net-text**, an interactive, collaborative online worktext.

- Engage students in grammar through **GrammarSnap**, the grammar practice web application.

- Transform writing instruction through high-functioning **Interactive Whiteboard** presentations.

- Support instruction with a searchable teacher resource **File Cabinet**.

- Score essays accurately and efficiently with online **Essay Scoring**.

# How does the Teacher's Edition support instruction?

The Teacher's Edition has all the support you need to help students master the **TEKS and ELPS**.

**Differentiated Instruction** for struggling learners and advanced learners appears throughout the core instructional units.

The Teacher's Edition provides support for **English-language learners at all proficiency levels**.

**Conventions Connections** support grammar, usage, and mechanics instruction.

## Additional Resources

- Texas Standards Correlations
- Yearlong Timetable
- Professional Development
- Language Transfer Support
- Reading–Writing Connection
- Benchmark Papers
- Copy Masters Resources

# Texas Essential Knowledge and Skills for English Language Arts

The English Language Arts and Reading TEKS specify the skills students need to master by the end of English II. To remind you what is required of your students, we have provided a list of the skills you will cover during this school year. The second column shows where these TEKS are addressed in this program. As students master the TEKS, they will also practice and apply the Texas Career and College Readiness Standards that are listed in the third column.

**Texas Career and College Readiness Standards**

**★ (TEKS) 10.13 Writing/Writing Process**

Students use elements of the writing process (planning, drafting, revising, editing, and publishing) to compose text. Students are expected to:

**ENGLISH/LANGUAGE ARTS STANDARDS**

Writing:

A  plan a first draft by selecting the correct genre for conveying the intended meaning to multiple audiences, determining appropriate topics through a range of strategies (e.g., discussion, background reading, personal interests, interviews), and developing a thesis or controlling idea;

pages 4, 5, 9, 10, 15, 80, 85–88, 124, 131, 138, 143–148, 182, 184, 189, 198, 202, 238, 240, 256, 260, 264, 306, 307, 313, 315, 322, 328, 329, 337, 338, 372, 381, 382, 384, 385, 391, 450, 452, 456, 460, 462, 464, 472, 474, 476, 484, 486, 492–494, 496. 604, 611, 618–623, 630

1. Determine effective approaches, forms, and rhetorical techniques that demonstrate understanding of the writer's purpose and audience.
2. Generate ideas and gather information relevant to the topic and purpose, keeping careful records of outside sources.

B  structure ideas in a sustained and persuasive way (e.g., using outlines, note taking, graphic organizers, lists) and develop drafts in timed and open-ended situations that include transitions and the rhetorical devices used to convey meaning;

pages 9, 10, 18, 19, 21, 92–96, 100, 101, 126, 131–133, 148, 150–154, 163, 180, 181, 183, 184, 189–191, 196, 197, 199, 200, 203, 206–210, 214, 224, 236, 237, 247–249, 257, 258, 266–270, 273, 274, 276, 304, 306, 309, 314–317, 341, 392, 405, 414, 415, 450–452, 456, 457, 460, 464, 465, 467–470, 472, 474–476, 478–481, 484–486, 488, 489, 492, 496, 497, 499, 500, 506–513, 600–605, 607–611, 613, 614, 624–629, 631, 632, 636, 637

3. Evaluate relevance, quality, sufficiency, and depth of preliminary ideas and information, organize material generated, and formulate a thesis.
4. Recognize the importance of revision as the key to effective writing. Each draft should refine key ideas and organize them more logically and fluidly, use language more precisely and effectively, and draw the reader to the author's purpose.

C  revise drafts to improve style, word choice, figurative language, sentence variety, and subtlety of meaning after rethinking how well questions of purpose, audience, and genre have been addressed;

pages 9, 11, 22–25, 98, 99, 102–105, 110, 111, 127, 134, 156–163, 185, 186, 192, 212–219, 224, 226, 243, 244, 250, 272–279, 284, 286, 302, 310, 318, 330, 343, 351, 355, 357, 411–413, 416–419, 424, 456, 460, 466, 472, 474, 476, 477, 484, 487, 492, 498, 506, 509, 510, 512, 513, 579, 584, 587, 604, 611, 615
pages 74, 91, 118, 126, 127, 172, 175, 176, 221, 224

5. Edit writing for proper voice, tense, and syntax, assuring that it conforms to standard English, when appropriate.

**CROSS-DISCIPLINARY STANDARDS**

D  edit drafts for grammar, mechanics, and spelling; and

pages 9, 11, 26, 27, 108, 109, 112, 128, 134, 166, 167, 169, 170, 186, 192, 222, 223, 225, 226, 244, 250, 282, 283, 285, 286, 310, 318, 330, 343, 351, 355, 357, 422, 423, 456, 460, 466, 472, 474, 476, 477, 480, 484, 487, 492, 498, 506, 509, 510, 512, 513, 604, 615, 640, 641

Foundational Skills B:

1. Write clearly and coherently using standard writing conventions.
2. Write in a variety of forms for various audiences and purposes.

E  revise final draft in response to feedback from peers and teacher and publish written work for appropriate audiences.

pages 9, 11, 28–30, 50, 53, 54, 70–72, 75–77, 113, 128, 159, 171, 186, 227, 244, 287, 310, 428, 476, 611

3. Compose and revise drafts.

*Page References in *Teacher's Edition*
*Page References in *SkillsBook*

## ⭐ TEKS 10.14 Writing/Literary Texts

Students write literary texts to express their ideas and feelings about real or imagined people, events, and ideas. Students are responsible for at least two forms of literary writing. Students are expected to:

**A** write an engaging story with a well-developed conflict and resolution, interesting and believable characters, a range of literary strategies (e.g., dialogue, suspense) and devices to enhance the plot, and sensory details that define mood or tone;

pages 3, 81–89, 93–96, 98, 99, 102, 104, 105, 126, 133, 135, 323–329, 611, 636, 637

**B** write a poem using a variety of poetic techniques (e.g., structural elements, figurative language) and a variety of poetic forms (e.g., sonnets, ballads); and

pages 3, 348–357

**C** write a script with an explicit or implicit theme and details that contribute to a definite mood or tone.

pages 3, 334, 336–346, 452–455, 502

## ⭐ TEKS 10.15 Writing/Expository and Procedural Texts

Students write expository and procedural or work-related texts to communicate ideas and information to specific audiences for specific purposes. Students are expected to:

**A** write an analytical essay of sufficient length that includes:
  - (i) effective introductory and concluding paragraphs and a variety of sentence structures;
  - (ii) rhetorical devices, and transitions between paragraphs;
  - (iii) a thesis or controlling idea;
  - (iv) an organizing structure appropriate to purpose, audience, and context;
  - (v) relevant evidence and well-chosen details, and
  - (vi) distinctions about the relative value of specific data, facts, and ideas that support the thesis statement;

pages 140–148, 150–154, 156–163, 169, 170, 180–184, 190, 191, 236–238, 240, 241, 257, 258, 262–264, 266, 270, 272, 274–276, 304, 306–310, 360, 362, 363, 373, 378, 391, 395, 401, 406, 414, 415, 417, 450, 451, 477, 486–489, 582, 590, 605, 628, 629, 631, 636, 637

**B** write procedural or work-related documents (e.g., instructions, e-mails, correspondence, memos, project plans) that include:
  - (i) organized and accurately conveyed information;
  - (ii) reader-friendly formatting techniques; and
  - (iii) anticipation of readers' questions;

pages 3, 506–513, 607

**C** write an interpretative response to an expository or a literary text (e.g., essay or review) that:
  - (i) extends beyond a summary and literal analysis;
  - (ii) addresses the writing skills for an analytical essay and provides evidence from the text using embedded quotations; and
  - (iii) analyzes the aesthetic effects of an author's use of stylistic or rhetorical devices; and

pages 253, 255, 257, 258, 261–264, 266, 268–270, 272, 274–277, 299–301, 304–309, 315–317, 373, 414–417, 636, 637

**D** produce a multimedia presentation (e.g., documentary, class newspaper, docudrama, infomercial, visual or textual parodies, theatrical production) with graphics, images, and sound that conveys a distinctive point of view and appeals to a specific audience.

pages 171, 430–434, 437–441, 452, 455, 501, 503

---

## 🌟 Texas Career and College Readiness Standards

### ENGLISH/LANGUAGE ARTS STANDARDS

Writing:
1. Determine effective approaches, forms, and rhetorical techniques that demonstrate understanding of the writer's purpose and audience.

### CROSS-DISCIPLINARY STANDARDS

Foundational Skills B:
2. Write in a variety of forms for various audiences and purposes.

### ENGLISH/LANGUAGE ARTS STANDARDS

Writing:
1. Determine effective approaches, forms, and rhetorical techniques that demonstrate understanding of the writer's purpose and audience.

### CROSS-DISCIPLINARY STANDARDS

Key Cognitive Skills B:
2. Construct well-reasoned arguments to support positions.
3. Gather evidence to support arguments, findings, or lines of reasoning.

Foundational Skills B:
2. Write in a variety of forms for various audiences and purposes.

### CROSS-DISCIPLINARY STANDARDS

Foundational Skills E:
3. Use technology to communicate and display findings in a clear and coherent manner.
4. Use technology appropriately.

---

## ⭐ TEKS 10.16 Writing/Persuasive Texts

Students write persuasive texts to influence the attitudes or actions of a specific audience on specific issues. Students are expected to write an argumentative essay to the appropriate audience that includes:

| | | |
|---|---|---|
| A | a clear thesis or position based on logical reasons supported by precise and relevant evidence; | pages 196, 197, 199, 200, 203, 207, 209, 210, 212, 214, 216–218, 236, 237, 239, 240, 248, 249, 476–478, 630 |
| B | consideration of the whole range of information and views on the topic and accurate and honest representation of these views (i.e., in the author's own words and not out of context); | pages 199, 200, 204, 206, 209, 213, 214, 219, 238, 240, 247, 476–479 |
| C | counter-arguments based on evidence to anticipate and address objections; | pages 200, 204, 206, 209, 210, 213, 237, 241, 242, 247–249, 476, 477 |
| D | an organizing structure appropriate to the purpose, audience, and context; | pages 197, 199, 200, 206, 215, 236, 237, 476–479 |
| E | an analysis of the relative value of specific data, facts, and ideas; and | pages 197, 199, 200, 209, 215, 236, 237, 241, 248, 249, 477–479 |
| F | a range of appropriate appeals (e.g., descriptions, anecdotes, case studies, analogies, illustrations). | pages 242, 477, 478 |

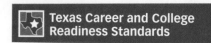

### Texas Career and College Readiness Standards

#### ENGLISH/LANGUAGE ARTS STANDARDS

Writing:

1. Determine effective approaches, forms, and rhetorical techniques that demonstrate understanding of the writer's purpose and audience.
2. Generate ideas and gather information relevant to the topic and purpose, keeping careful records of outside sources.
3. Evaluate relevance, quality, sufficiency, and depth of preliminary ideas and information, organize material generated, and formulate a thesis.

#### CROSS-DISCIPLINARY STANDARDS

Key Cognitive Skills B:

1. Consider arguments and conclusions of self and others.
2. Construct well-reasoned arguments to support positions.
3. Gather evidence to support arguments, findings, or lines of reasoning.

Foundational Skills B:

2. Write in a variety of forms for various audiences and purposes.

★ **Texas Career and College Readiness Standards**

## ★ TEKS 10.17 Oral and Written Conventions/Conventions

Students understand the function of and use the conventions of academic language when speaking and writing. Students will continue to apply earlier standards with greater complexity. Students are expected to:

**A** use and understand the function of the following parts of speech in the context of reading, writing, and speaking:

   (i)   more complex active and passive tenses and verbals (gerunds, infinitives, participles);

   (ii)  restrictive and nonrestrictive relative clauses; and

   (iii) reciprocal pronouns (e.g., each other, one another);

pages 46, 109–111, 166–170, 223, 282, 283, 310, 422, 423, 477, 487, 590, 734, 736, 737

pages 14, 15, 85, 88, 95–98, 101, 106, 129, 130, 134, 206, 211, 214, 222

**B** identify and use the subjunctive mood to express doubts, wishes, and possibilities; and

pages 222, 226, 286, 752, 753

pages 104, 105

**C** use a variety of correctly structured sentences (e.g., compound, complex, compound-complex).

pages 46, 47, 112, 128, 170, 186, 192, 224, 244, 250, 284, 310, 318, 424, 456, 460, 466, 472, 474, 476, 477, 480, 484, 487, 492, 498, 506, 509, 510, 512, 513, 587–593, 596, 604, 615, 764–767, 772–777, 784–787

pages 126–128, 136–138, 140–145, 161–171, 175, 176, 219–221, 224

**ENGLISH/LANGUAGE ARTS STANDARDS**

Writing:

5. Edit writing for proper voice, tense, and syntax, assuring that it conforms to standard English, when appropriate.

## ★ TEKS 10.18 Oral and Written Conventions/Handwriting, Capitalization, and Punctuation

Students write legibly and use appropriate capitalization and punctuation conventions in their compositions. Students are expected to:

**A** use conventions of capitalization; and

pages 46, 112, 128, 170, 186, 192, 226, 244, 250, 286, 310, 318, 456, 460, 466, 472, 474, 476, 477, 480, 484, 487, 492, 498, 506, 509, 510, 512, 513, 520, 570, 615, 640, 641, 682–687

pages 5, 6, 39–44, 69, 70, 195, 196, 200–202, 227

**B** use correct punctuation marks including:

   (i)   comma placement in nonrestrictive phrases, clauses, and contrasting expressions;

   (ii)  quotation marks to indicate sarcasm or irony; and

   (iii) dashes to emphasize parenthetical information.

pages 46, 112, 128, 169, 170, 186, 192, 225, 226, 244, 250, 285, 286, 310, 318, 425, 456, 460, 466, 472, 474, 476, 477, 480, 484, 487, 492, 498, 506, 509, 510, 512, 513, 582, 592, 604, 615, 640, 641, 643–681

pages 3–38, 69, 70, 161, 162, 166, 167, 169, 189, 190–195, 202, 220, 225–227, 229–232

**ENGLISH/LANGUAGE ARTS STANDARDS**

Writing:

5. Edit writing, assuring that it conforms to standard English, when appropriate.

**CROSS-DISCIPLINARY STANDARDS**

Foundational Skills B:

1. Write clearly and coherently using standard writing conventions.

## ⭐ (TEKS) 10.19 Oral and Written Conventions/Spelling

Students spell correctly. Students are expected to spell correctly, including using various resources to determine and check correct spellings.

pages 46, 112, 128, 170, 186, 226, 244, 250, 286, 310, 318, 425, 456, 460, 466, 472, 474, 476, 477, 480, 484, 487, 492, 498, 506, 509, 510, 512, 513, 520, 604, 615, 640, 641, 688–691, ,698–703, 710–729
pages 49–70, 197, 199–203, 227

## ⭐ (TEKS) 10.20 Research/Research Plan

Students ask open-ended research questions and develop a plan for answering them. Students are expected to:

A brainstorm, consult with others, decide upon a topic, and formulate a major research question to address the major research topic; and

pages 380, 382, 383, 462, 494

B formulate a plan for engaging in research on a complex, multi-faceted topic.

pages 362–370, 372, 380, 384, 462, 494

## ⭐ (TEKS) 10.21 Research/Gathering Sources

Students determine, locate, and explore the full range of relevant sources addressing a research question and systematically record the information they gather. Students are expected to:

A follow the research plan to compile data from authoritative sources in a manner that identifies the major issues and debates within the field of inquiry;

pages 360–370, 374–377, 379, 380, 385, 404, 463, 495

B organize information gathered from multiple sources to create a variety of graphics and forms (e.g., notes, learning logs); and

pages 362, 363, 367, 381, 383–386, 390, 392, 393, 463, 495

C paraphrase, summarize, quote, and accurately cite all researched information according to a standard format (e.g., author, title, page number).

pages 374, 375, 379, 387–389, 396, 403, 404, 456, 463, 472, 473, 492, 493, 495, 633

---

### Texas Career and College Readiness Standards

#### ENGLISH/LANGUAGE ARTS STANDARDS

Writing:
5. Edit writing, assuring that it conforms to standard English, when appropriate.

#### ENGLISH/LANGUAGE ARTS STANDARDS

Research A:
1. Formulate research questions.
2. Explore a research topic.
3. Refine research topic and devise a timeline for completing work.

#### CROSS-DISCIPLINARY STANDARDS

Foundational Skills C:
1. Understand which topics or questions are to be investigated.
2. Explore a research topic.

#### ENGLISH/LANGUAGE ARTS STANDARDS

Research B:
1. Gather relevant sources.
2. Evaluate the validity and reliability of sources.

#### CROSS-DISCIPLINARY STANDARDS

Key Cognitive Skills F:
3. Include the ideas of others and the complexities of the debate, issue, or problem.

## ⭐ TEKS 10.22 Research/Synthesizing Information

Students clarify research questions and evaluate and synthesize collected information. Students are expected to:

**A** modify the major research question as necessary to refocus the research plan;

pages 394, 400, 464, 496

**B** evaluate the relevance of information to the topic and determine the reliability, validity, and accuracy of sources (including Internet sources) by examining their authority and objectivity; and

pages 376, 377, 394, 397–399, 464, 496

**C** critique the research process at each step to implement changes as the need occurs and is identified.

pages 400, 416, 417, 464, 466, 496, 498

### ⭐ Texas Career and College Readiness Standards

#### ENGLISH/LANGUAGE ARTS STANDARDS

Research B:
3. Synthesize and organize information effectively.
4. Use source material ethically.

#### CROSS-DISCIPLINARY STANDARDS

Key Cognitive Skills F:
2. Evaluate sources for quality of content, validity, credibility, and relevance.

Foundational Skills C:
3. Refine research topic based on preliminary research and devise a timeline for completing work.
4. Evaluate the validity and reliability of sources.
5. Synthesize and organize information effectively.

## ⭐ TEKS 10.23 Research/Organizing and Presenting Ideas

Students organize and present their ideas and information according to the purpose of the research and their audience. Students are expected to synthesize the research into a written or an oral presentation that:

**A** marshals evidence in support of a clear thesis statement and related claims;

pages 401–406, 430–433, 435, 437, 465, 467–469, 497, 499, 500

**B** provides an analysis for the audience that reflects a logical progression of ideas and a clearly stated point of view;

pages 402–406, 430–433, 435, 437, 465, 467, 468, 497, 499, 500

**C** uses graphics and illustrations to help explain concepts where appropriate;

pages 72, 374, 430, 432–436, 465, 473, 497, 638, 639

**D** uses a variety of evaluative tools (e.g., self-made rubrics, peer reviews, teacher and expert evaluations) to examine the quality of the research; and

pages 403, 466, 469, 498

**E** uses a style manual (e.g., *Modern Language Association, Chicago Manual of Style*) to document sources and format written materials.

pages 396, 403, 404, 407–410, 432, 433, 465, 467, 470, 493, 497, 499, 500

#### ENGLISH/LANGUAGE ARTS STANDARDS

Research C:
1. Design and present an effective product.
2. Use source material ethically.

#### CROSS-DISCIPLINARY STANDARDS

Key Cognitive Skills F:
1. Attribute ideas and information to source materials and people.

Foundational Skills C:
6. Design and present an effective product.
7. Integrate source material.
8. Present final product.

Foundational Skills E:
3. Use technology to communicate and display findings in a clear and coherent manner.
4. Use technology appropriately.

*Page References in *Teacher's Edition*
*Page References in *SkillsBook*

# English Language Proficiency Standards

The English Language Proficiency Standards (ELPS) outline expectations for students who are learning English. The chart below includes descriptions of activities and interactions that will help students develop their knowledge of English. It also provides you with information on where these skills are specifically addressed in this program.

## ⭐ ELPS 1 Cross-curricular Second Language Acquisition/Learning Strategies

The ELL uses language learning strategies to develop an awareness of his or her own learning processes in all content areas. In order for the ELL to meet grade-level learning expectations across the foundation and enrichment curriculum, all instruction delivered in English must be linguistically accommodated (communicated, sequenced, and scaffolded) commensurate with the student's level of English language proficiency. The student is expected to:

**A** use prior knowledge and experiences to understand meanings in English;

pages 6, 31, 35, 61, 77, 78, 89, 136, 145, 163, 167, 183, 201, 237, 243, 281, 355, 361, 370, 379, 381, 401, 405, 419, 431, 435, 446, 448, 458, 470, 474, 490, 494, 504, 534, 540, 544, 546, 550, 552, 558, 564,

**B** monitor oral and written language production and employ self-corrective techniques or other resources;

pages 47, 103, 113, 117, 128, 147, 149, 155, 169, 177, 185, 193, 244, 247, 285, 309, 343, 346, 275, 391, 421, 425, 428, 429, 439

**C** use strategic learning techniques such as concept mapping, drawing, memorizing, comparing, contrasting, and reviewing to acquire basic and grade-level vocabulary;

pages 5, 12, 17, 19, 23, 59, 83, 91, 107, 143, 145, 151, 153, 157, 161, 169, 173, 183, 189, 193, 197, 215, 237, 239, 241, 243, 251, 267, 361, 367, 381, 399, 409, 419, 423, 425, 444, 507, 523, 545, 710–729

**D** speak using learning strategies such as requesting assistance, employing non-verbal cues, and using synonyms and circumlocution (conveying ideas by defining or describing when exact English words are not known);

pages 12, 140, 167, 178, 187, 205, 229, 251, 259, 346, 397, 407, 413, 417, 428, 442, 517, 518

**E** internalize new basic and academic language by using and reusing it in meaningful ways in speaking and writing activities that build concept and language attainment;

pages 6, 12, 23, 27, 39, 48, 67, 73, 89, 95, 101, 136, 140, 141, 147, 149, 151, 153, 157, 159, 161, 163, 168, 185, 193, 194, 197, 205, 209, 215, 217, 239, 241, 244, 251, 252, 265, 294, 309, 313, 319, 320, 327, 345, 349, 351, 358, 361, 363, 367, 369, 375, 377, 381, 387, 389, 393, 397, 399, 405, 407, 409, 413, 419, 423, 425, 428, 431, 433, 442, 514, 515, 521, 546, 551, 557, 568, 616, 642, 721, 727

**F** use accessible language and learn new and essential language in the process;

pages 141, 145, 147, 153, 155, 159, 169, 201, 231, 237, 243, 251, 361, 363, 375, 377, 381, 405, 409, 415, 417, 421, 423

**G** demonstrate an increasing ability to distinguish between formal and informal English and an increasing knowledge of when to use each one commensurate with grade-level learning expectations; and

pages 128, 151, 165, 169, 185, 218, 219, 227, 231, 249, 340, 365, 419, 427, 431, 439, 504, 536, 542, 548

**H** develop and expand repertoire of learning strategies such as reasoning inductively or deductively, looking for patterns in language, and analyzing sayings and expressions commensurate with grade-level learning expectations.

pages 38, 39, 143, 147, 153, 167, 185, 201, 309, 358, 363, 377, 403, 409, 415, 423, 704–709

### ELPS 2 Cross-curricular Second Language Acquisition/Listening

The ELL listens to a variety of speakers including teachers, peers, and electronic media to gain an increasing level of comprehension of newly acquired language in all content areas. ELLs may be at the beginning, intermediate, advanced, or advanced high stage of English language acquisition in listening. In order for the ELL to meet grade-level learning expectations across the foundation and enrichment curriculum, all instruction delivered in English must be linguistically accommodated (communicated, sequenced, and scaffolded) commensurate with the student's level of English language proficiency. The student is expected to:

**A** distinguish sounds and intonation patterns of English with increasing ease;

pages 105, 117, 127, 153, 175, 194, 197, 201, 219, 252, 335, 341, 346, 353, 367, 369, 415, 429

**B** recognize elements of the English sound system in newly acquired vocabulary such as long and short vowels, silent letters, and consonant clusters;

pages 143, 157, 169, 201, 353, 358, 545

**C** learn new language structures, expressions, and basic and academic vocabulary heard during classroom instruction and interactions;

pages 6, 25, 40, 48, 57, 61, 75, 78, 105, 109, 111, 131, 136, 137, 139, 143, 151, 153, 157, 161, 168, 169, 171, 178, 181, 183, 189, 194, 201, 215, 217, 223, 225, 227, 237, 251, 252, 269, 320, 332, 333, 337, 340, 345, 358, 361, 363, 367, 369, 379, 388, 389, 393, 397, 419, 423, 425, 442, 444, 514, 516, 518, 524, 525, 528, 533–535, 539, 540, 546, 547, 551–553, 556–559, 562, 563, 564, 568, 616, 642, 704–709, 757, 771

**D** monitor understanding of spoken language during classroom instruction and interactions and seek clarification as needed;

pages 48, 51, 159, 171, 173, 177, 187, 285, 313, 333, 385, 397, 504, 513, 516–519, 524, 525, 527, 531, 533, 534, 539

page 86

**E** use visual, contextual, and linguistic support to enhance and confirm understanding of increasingly complex and elaborated spoken language;

pages 89, 91, 93, 140, 141, 161, 163, 167, 171, 173, 181, 231, 237, 251, 265, 269, 325, 357, 361, 369, 373, 381, 397, 444, 447, 475, 484, 490, 493, 495, 504

**G** understand the general meaning, main points, and important details of spoken language ranging from situations in which topics, language, and contexts are familiar to unfamiliar;

pages 29, 48, 51, 54, 61, 105, 140, 175, 181, 187, 198, 203, 224, 231, 251, 265, 269, 285, 313, 373, 385, 397, 429, 441, 444, 447, 534, 535, 540, 546, 547, 552, 553, 558, 559, 564, 565, 567

**H** understand implicit ideas and information in increasingly complex spoken language commensurate with grade-level learning expectations; and

pages 37, 48, 51, 61, 171, 181, 231, 385, 389, 419, 423, 441, 444, 446, 537, 543, 549, 555, 561, 567

| | |
|---|---|
| **I** demonstrate listening comprehension of increasingly complex spoken English by following directions, retelling or summarizing spoken messages, responding to questions and requests, collaborating with peers, and taking notes commensurate with content and grade-level needs. | pages 3, 48, 51, 63, 64, 68, 70, 109, 140, 166, 167, 171, 175, 187, 189, 193, 203, 223, 231, 251, 260, 265, 313, 319, 344, 346, 365, 369, 389, 393, 407, 411, 415, 419, 423, 427, 429, 439, 441, 444, 446, 455, 461, 489, 516–520, 525, 527–529, 531–535, 537–540, 542, 543, 546, 547, 552, 553, 556, 558, 559, 564, 565, 721, 751, 757, 771 |

## ⭐ ELPS 3 Cross-curricular Second Language Acquisition/Speaking

The ELL speaks in a variety of modes for a variety of purposes with an awareness of different language registers (formal/informal) using vocabulary with increasing fluency and accuracy in language arts and all content areas. ELLs may be at the beginning, intermediate, advanced, or advanced high stage of English language acquisition in speaking. In order for the ELL to meet grade-level learning expectations across the foundation and enrichment curriculum, all instruction delivered in English must be linguistically accommodated (communicated, sequenced, and scaffolded) commensurate with the student's level of English language proficiency. The student is expected to:

| | |
|---|---|
| **A** practice producing sounds of newly acquired vocabulary such as long and short vowels, silent letters, and consonant clusters to pronounce English words in a manner that is increasingly comprehensible; | pages 32, 68, 97, 101, 103, 117, 139, 143, 153, 155, 157, 172, 174, 189, 194, 217, 252, 353, 358, 363, 369, 370, 389, 391, 403, 409, 411, 421, 527, 531, 533, 539, 545, 551, 557, 563 |
| **B** expand and internalize initial English vocabulary by learning and using high-frequency English words necessary for identifying and describing people, places, and objects, by retelling simple stories and basic information represented or supported by pictures, and by learning and using routine language needed for classroom communication; | pages 1, 5, 6, 11, 68, 75, 83, 97, 136, 153, 181, 183, 194, 209, 215, 221, 243, 244, 252, 320, 349, 358, 369, 370, 381, 385, 397, 399, 401, 403, 405, 417, 437, 439, 441, 442, 475, 482, 490, 495, 501, 514, 533, 539, 545, 551, 557, 563, 568, 616, 642, 727, 757 |
| **C** speak using a variety of grammatical structures, sentence lengths, sentence types, and connecting words with increasing accuracy and ease as more English is acquired; | pages 1, 47, 53, 68, 97, 103, 166, 167, 173, 175, 176, 177, 203, 205, 237, 265, 283, 285, 365, 370, 397, 425, 437, 485, 524, 533, 543, 545, 561, 567, 757 |
| **D** speak using grade-level content area vocabulary in context to internalize new English words and build academic language proficiency; | pages 9, 12, 21, 32, 136, 137, 140, 141, 145, 151, 155, 157, 159, 163, 175–178, 189, 193, 194, 217, 251, 252, 259, 269, 283, 294, 319, 320, 358, 370, 373, 375, 385, 399, 403, 405, 411, 419, 421, 435, 437, 442, 501, 514, 527, 529, 531, 532, 545, 568, 616, 642 |

**E** share information in cooperative learning interactions;

pages 2, 3, 5, 6, 8, 9, 11, 14, 15, 20, 21, 22, 24, 26, 36, 42, 48, 50, 52, 53, 60, 68, 73, 78, 94, 102, 105, 109, 125, 135, 136, 143, 145, 147, 149, 155, 157, 163, 166, 167, 175, 193, 194, 197, 209, 217, 222, 223, 226, 240, 243, 246, 251, 252, 254, 265, 267, 271, 283, 285, 294, 319, 320, 323, 325, 327, 341, 355, 357, 358, 363, 375, 377, 389, 391, 393, 399, 403, 405, 419, 421, 423, 425, 435, 441, 442, 445, 450, 451, 452, 455, 461–465, 470, 475, 476, 481, 485, 489, 490, 495, 497–499, 501, 503, 504, 509, 511, 513, 514, 517, 518, 520, 521, 525, 52–529, 531–533, 535, 537–541, 543–547, 549–552, 555–558, 561–564, 566–568, 576, 608, 616, 642, 721, 727, 733, 751, 757

**F** ask and give information ranging from using a very limited bank of high-frequency, high-need, concrete vocabulary, including key words and expressions needed for basic communication in academic and social contexts, to using abstract and content-based vocabulary during extended speaking assignments;

pages 1, 11, 32, 50, 68, 74, 89, 97, 103, 140–142, 145, 159, 163, 171, 173, 177, 178, 187, 193, 197, 199, 205, 209, 229, 234, 251, 261, 269, 320, 361, 363, 365, 370, 399, 411, 413, 417, 435, 437, 439, 441, 470, 485, 493, 507, 521, 525, 532, 535, 556, 558, 733, 751, 757

**G** express opinions, ideas, and feelings ranging from communicating single words and short phrases to participating in extended discussions on a variety of social and grade-appropriate academic topics;

pages 1, 2, 5, 9, 11, 12, 21, 31, 52–54, 60, 72, 78, 114, 118, 120, 131, 145, 151, 156, 163, 173, 181, 187, 193, 205, 209, 217, 223, 226, 227, 232, 233, 240, 244, 261, 265, 269, 293, 294, 323, 337, 348, 370, 373, 375, 399, 413, 417, 435, 437, 439, 441, 454, 455, 470, 482, 490, 503, 517, 518, 527, 529, 531, 533, 536, 537, 539, 540, 542, 543, 545, 546, 548, 549, 552–555, 560–562, 564, 566, 567, 733, 751

page 88

**H** narrate, describe, and explain with increasing specificity and detail as more English is acquired;

pages 21, 48, 53, 60, 63, 68, 89, 92, 97, 103, 145, 151, 159, 173, 209, 215, 217, 244, 269, 323, 329, 395, 413, 417, 437, 439, 441, 454, 455, 482, 501, 503, 517, 518, 527, 531, 533, 536, 537, 539, 540, 543, 545, 549, 555, 560–562, 566, 567, 608, 721, 727, 751, 757

**I** adapt spoken language appropriately for formal and informal purposes; and

pages 42, 128, 169, 218, 219, 244, 365, 437, 439, 447, 453, 454, 536, 542, 548, 554, 560, 566

**J** respond orally to information presented in a wide variety of print, electronic, audio, and visual media to build and reinforce concept and language attainment.

pages 1, 87, 120, 137, 161, 198, 261, 439, 441

*Page References in *Teacher's Edition*
*Page References in *SkillsBook*

## ⭐ ELPS 4 Cross-curricular Second Language Acquisition/Reading

The ELL reads a variety of texts for a variety of purposes with an increasing level of comprehension in all content areas. ELLs may be at the beginning, intermediate, advanced, or advanced high stage of English language acquisition in reading. In order for the ELL to meet grade-level learning expectations across the foundation and enrichment curriculum, all instruction delivered in English must be linguistically accommodated (communicated, sequenced, and scaffolded) commensurate with the student's level of English language proficiency. For kindergarten and first grade, certain of these student expectations apply to text read aloud for students not yet at the stage of decoding written text. The student is expected to:

**A** learn relationships between sounds and letters of the English language and decode (sound out) words using a combination of skills such as recognizing sound-letter relationships and identifying cognates, affixes, roots and base words;

pages 21, 62, 123, 127, 128, 139, 153, 169, 189, 197, 201, 335, 343, 353, 358, 363, 409, 421, 521, 533, 702

**B** recognize directionality of English reading such as left to right and top to bottom;

pages 534, 540, 546, 552, 558, 564

**C** develop basic sight vocabulary, derive meaning of environmental print, and comprehend English vocabulary and language structures used routinely in written classroom materials;

pages 6, 15, 17, 27, 35, 39, 43, 45, 46, 48, 57, 59, 65, 67, 77, 78, 81, 83, 87, 101, 107, 109, 111, 123, 131, 161, 166, 167, 193, 197, 211, 218, 221–225, 243, 251, 265, 269, 283, 332, 361, 377, 381, 391, 399, 403, 409, 415, 429, 435, 445, 479, 492, 520, 521, 524–527, 530, 531, 533–535, 539–541, 545–547, 551, 553, 557, 559, 563, 565, 571, 578, 581, 583, 586–589, 591, 605, 606, 636, 637, 710–729, 732, 734–787
pages 61–68, 70, 199

**D** use prereading supports such as graphic organizers, illustrations, and pretaught topic-related vocabulary and other prereading activities to enhance comprehension of written text;

pages 19, 43, 65, 67, 99, 119, 149, 233, 293, 315, 322, 339, 387, 389, 399, 445, 448, 490, 525, 534, 538, 540, 544, 546, 565

**E** read linguistically accommodated content area material with a decreasing need for linguistic accommodations as more English is learned;

pages 17, 35, 75, 120, 234, 251, 315, 387, 473

**F** use visual and contextual support and support from peers and teachers to read grade-appropriate content area text, enhance and confirm understanding, and develop vocabulary, grasp of language structures, and background knowledge needed to comprehend increasingly challenging language;

pages 6, 15, 17, 19, 35, 37, 43, 57, 65, 73–75, 77, 83, 91, 97, 99, 101, 109, 111, 115, 119, 120, 143, 189, 193, 197, 201, 211, 213, 221, 223, 225, 229, 233, 243, 251, 252, 255, 258, 265–267, 269, 271, 275, 277, 283, 288, 289, 291, 293, 297, 305, 309, 310, 313–315, 317, 319, 322, 326, 332, 337, 343, 358, 367, 370, 373, 375, 384, 387, 403, 411, 415, 417, 421, 442, 448, 451, 458, 473, 477, 481, 489, 492, 493, 497, 507, 511, 513, 525, 534, 540, 546, 564, 565, 741

**G** demonstrate comprehension of increasingly complex English by participating in shared reading, retelling or summarizing material, responding to questions, and taking notes commensurate with content area and grade level needs;

pages 6, 11, 17, 35, 36, 37, 50, 60, 65, 73–75, 78, 114, 115, 137, 139, 145, 173, 189, 193, 194, 196, 200, 211, 213, 229, 233, 234, 251, 252, 263, 265, 271, 277, 293, 309, 319, 320, 327, 336, 337, 358, 369, 370, 373, 375, 387, 388, 407, 413, 421, 442, 445, 446, 456, 457, 463, 469, 472, 473, 480, 485, 489, 493, 495, 507, 514, 519, 527, 531, 533–535, 539, 541, 545–547, 552, 553, 558, 559, 563–565, 568, 598, 600–603, 609, 614, 616, 642, 699, 741, 771

**H** read silently with increasing ease and comprehension for longer periods;

pages 35, 54, 60, 90, 115, 118, 211, 229, 271, 289, 291, 373, 375, 405, 421

**I** demonstrate English comprehension and expand reading skills by employing basic reading skills such as demonstrating understanding of supporting ideas and details in text and graphic sources, summarizing text and distinguishing main ideas from details commensurate with content area needs;

pages 17, 122, 149, 173, 189, 211, 213, 234, 370, 373, 375, 387, 397, 401, 403, 405, 411, 445, 446, 448, 456, 457, 469, 472, 493, 520, 535, 541, 547, 553, 559, 565, 598, 600–603, 609, 612, 614

**J** demonstrate English comprehension and expand reading skills by employing inferential skills such as predicting, making connections between ideas, drawing inferences and conclusions from text and graphic sources, and finding supporting text evidence commensurate with content area needs; and

pages 45, 48, 99, 142, 213, 233, 256, 257, 269, 271, 275, 293, 297, 316, 317, 375, 385, 387, 405, 413, 457, 464, 467, 469, 475, 493, 499, 500, 535, 541, 547, 550, 553, 559, 600, 614

**K** demonstrate English comprehension and expand reading skills by employing analytical skills such as evaluating written information and performing critical analyses commensurate with content area and grade level needs.

pages 19, 25, 31–33, 44, 60, 64, 65, 80, 83, 84, 90, 94, 99, 119, 130, 172–177, 181, 189, 191, 193, 199, 200, 213, 228, 229, 233, 236, 237, 255, 257, 258, 260, 263, 273, 275, 277, 289, 291, 293, 296, 297, 305, 309, 316, 317, 319, 322, 327, 370, 375, 35, 405, 413, 464, 535, 540, 541, 547, 553, 555,  559, 612

## ⬛ ELPS 5 Cross-curricular Second Language Acquisition/Writing

The ELL writes in a variety of forms with increasing accuracy to effectively address a specific purpose and audience in all content areas. ELLs may be at the beginning, intermediate, advanced, or advanced high stage of English language acquisition in writing. In order for the ELL to meet grade-level learning expectations across foundation and enrichment curriculum all instruction delivered in English must be linguistically accommodated (communicated, sequenced, and scaffolded) commensurate with the student's level of English language proficiency. For kindergarten and first grade, certain of these student expectations do not apply until the student has reached the stage of generating original written text using a standard writing system. The student is expected to:

**A** learn relationships between sounds and letters of the English language to represent sounds when writing in English;

pages 171, 185, 191, 367, 385, 409, 433, 499

**B** write using newly acquired basic vocabulary and content-based grade-level vocabulary;

pages 2, 6, 10, 23, 27, 39, 52, 95, 144, 146, 148, 149, 159, 165, 176, 183, 185, 189, 191, 194, 197, 239, 241, 266, 279, 301, 307, 309, 313, 339, 341, 351, 358, 369, 381, 383, 387, 391, 393, 395, 397, 403, 407, 427, 433, 453, 461, 470, 479, 515, 523, 533, 539, 545, 551, 557, 558, 563–565

pages 85–87, 117, 178

**C** spell familiar English words with increasing accuracy, and employ English spelling patterns and rules with increasing accuracy as more English is acquired;

pages 11, 45, 46, 112, 113, 128, 134, 165, 170, 171, 176, 177, 186, 192, 221, 226, 244, 250, 286, 287, 302, 310, 318, 407, 409, 427, 433, 456, 457, 466, 467, 472, 474, 476, 477, 480, 484, 487, 492, 498, 499, 506, 509, 510, 512, 513, 604, 615, 640, 641, 698–703, 710–729

**D** edit writing for standard grammar and usage, including subject-verb agreement, pronoun agreement, and appropriate verb tenses commensurate with grade-level expectations as more English is acquired;

pages 11, 26, 45, 46, 66, 67, 77, 84, 108, 109, 112, 113, 116, 128, 134, 165, 166, 167, 170, 175–177, 186, 192, 221, 226, 230, 244, 250, 279, 281–283, 286, 287, 302, 310, 318, 330, 331, 355, 427, 467, 477, 487, 498, 509, 513, 529

**E** employ increasingly complex grammatical structures in content area writing commensurate with grade level expectations, such as:
(i)     using correct verbs, tenses, and pronouns/antecedents;
(ii)    using possessive case (apostrophe -s) correctly;
(iii)   using negatives and contractions correctly;

pages 25, 45, 46, 108, 109, 112, 128, 165–167, 169–171, 176, 177, 186, 191, 222–224, 226, 230, 244, 249, 250, 261, 282, 283, 286, 287, 306, 393, 395, 397, 407, 419, 423, 467, 477, 487, 498, 513, 571–573, 578, 586, 594–596, 640, 641, 734–755, 758–769, 772–787

**F** write using a variety of grade-appropriate sentence lengths, patterns, and connecting words to combine phrases, clauses, and sentences in increasingly accurate ways as more English is acquired; and

pages 3, 23, 25, 41, 47, 59, 67, 71, 85, 88, 95, 110, 111, 123, 133–136, 147, 148, 151, 153, 165, 169–171, 185, 191, 192, 207, 224–226, 249, 250, 255, 261, 267, 274, 279, 284, 286, 301, 302, 307, 310, 313, 318, 331, 393, 395, 401, 417, 424, 451, 466, 474, 477, 484, 485, 487, 497, 498, 512, 513, 571, 572, 578, 587–592, 596, 613, 615, 628, 629, 736, 764–767, 772–777, 784–787

**G** narrate, describe, and explain with increasing specificity and detail to fulfill content area writing needs as more English is acquired.

pages 4, 5, 31, 37–41, 44, 47, 48, 51, 57, 59, 67, 78, 81–83, 85, 93, 103, 119, 125, 126, 133–136, 144, 148, 151, 157, 160, 161, 163, 184, 185, 191, 219, 233, 239, 241, 249, 258, 261, 293, 320, 325, 327, 329, 332, 349, 351, 357, 395, 447, 450–453, 456, 457, 460, 461, 463–465, 469, 472, 473, 476, 479, 481, 485, 486, 493, 497, 506, 508, 509, 511, 514, 515, 523, 527, 528, 533, 539, 545, 551, 557, 563, 571, 572, 574, 575, 577, 600–602, 611

pages 8, 24, 31, 52, 85, 87, 99, 101, 126, 127

*Page References in *Teacher's Edition*
*Page References in *SkillsBook*

# Yearlong Timetable

This suggested yearlong timetable presents one possible sequence of writing and language skills units based on a five-days-per-week writing class. There is a logical sequence of units and lessons built into the timetable. This logical sequence from personal to more challenging forms can also support an existing writing curriculum or integrated reading/language arts program.

## First Six Weeks

| Week | Writing Lessons | *Write Source* | Grammar and Writing Skills |
|---|---|---|---|
| 1 | Getting-Started (page TE A-64) **Why write?** | 1–5 | Nouns, pronouns, prepositions, commas |
| | **Understanding the Writing Process** | 6–12 | |
| | **One Writer'sProcess** | 13–32 | |
| 2 | **Understanding the Traits of Writing** | 33–48 | Verb, adjectives, adverbs |
| | **Peer Response** | 49–54 | |
| | **Evaluating Your Writing** | 55–68 | |
| | **Publishing Your Writing** | 69–77 | |
| 3 | **Using Words Effectively** | 569–584 | Word choice, capitalization, abbreviations, numbers, using the right word, verbs |
| | **Understanding Sentence Style** | 585–596 | |
| | **Writing Effective Paragraphs** | 597–615 | |
| 4 | **Writing a Narrative Paragraph** | 79–81 | Parallelism, using the right word, verbs |
| | **Writing a Phase Autobiography** (Model, Prewriting, Drafting) | 82–96 | |
| 5 | **Phase Autobiography** *(cont'd)* (Revising, Editing, Publishing, Evaluating) | 97–120 | Pronouns, commas, verbals |
| 6 | Portfolio Review *SkillsBook* Posttests | | |

## Second Six Weeks

| Week | Writing Lessons | *Write Source* | Grammar and Writing Skills |
|---|---|---|---|
| 1 | **Writing an Expository Paragraph** | 136–139 | Parallelism, wordiness and deadwood, clauses, rambling sentences, compound and complex sentences |
| | **Writing a Cause-Effect Essay** (Model, Prewriting, Drafting) | 140–154 | |
| 2 | **Cause-Effect Essay** *(cont'd)* (Revising, Editing, Publishing, Evaluating) | 155–178 | Apostrophes, comma splices and run-on sentences, capitalization |
| 3 | **Responding to Expository Prompts** | 187–193 | Commas with introductory phrases and clauses, pronoun-antecedent agreement |
| 4 | **Interpretive Response: Analyzing a Theme** (Model, Prewriting, Drafting) | 256–270 | Figures of speech, misplaced and dangling modifiers, pronouns (relative, indefinite, interrogative, demonstrative) |
| 5 | **Analyzing a Theme** *(cont'd)* (Revising, Editing, Publishing, Assessing, Reflecting) | 271–294 | Tense shifts, punctuating compound and complex sentences, punctuating quotations, end punctuation |
| 6 | **Writing a Historical Narrative** (Model, Prewriting, Drafting)<br><br>Portfolio Review<br>*SkillsBook* Posttests | 121–128 | Direct quotations Complete sentences (fragments), sentence types, adverbs, adjectives |

# Third Six Weeks

| Week | Writing Lessons | *Write Source* | Grammar and Writing Skills |
|---|---|---|---|
| 1 | **Responding to Narrative Prompts** | 129–135 | Transitions, conjunctions, pronouns (review), end punctuation, using the right word |
| 2 | **Writing a Persuasive Paragraph** | 194–197 | Pronoun shifts, commas (appositives, in a series, to separate adjectives) |
| | **Writing and Argumentative Essay** (Model, Prewriting, Drafting,) | 198–210 | |
| 3 | **Writing and Argumentative Essay** (Revising, Editing, Evaluating) | 211–234 | Verbs, modeling sentences, sentence problems, subject-verb agreement |
| 4 | **Responding to Persuasive Prompts** | 245–251 | Sentence problems (comma splices, run-ons, fragments), commas |
| 5 | **Writing Stories** (Model, Prewriting, Drafting, Revising, Editing) | 322–329 | Punctuating dialogue, conjunctions and interjections, nonstandard language |
| 6 | **Writing Stories** *(cont'd)* (Revising, Editing) | 330–332 | Brackets, ellipses, colons, semicolons, parentheses, and other forms of punctuation |
| | Portfolio Review *SkillsBook* Posttests | | |

# Fourth Six Weeks

| Week | Writing Lessons | *Write Source* | Grammar and Writing Skills |
|---|---|---|---|
| 1 | **Responding to Prompts about Literature** | 311–319 | Prepositions, prepositional phrases, parts of speech (review), adverbs, basic sentence patterns, phrases, spelling, commas (review) |
| 2 | **Expository Writing: Defining a Concept** (Model, Prewriting, Drafting, Revising, Editing, Publishing) | 179–186 | Comma rules (review), sentence problems (review), pronoun-antecedent agreement, subject-verb agreement, using the right word, shifts in construction |
| 3 | **Persuasive Writing: Editorial** (Model, Prewriting, Drafting, Revising, Editing, Publishing) | 235–244 | Sentence combining, adjectives, using the right word |
| 4 | **Writing Scripts** (Model, Prewriting, Drafting, Revising, Editing, Publishing) | 333–343 | Nonstandard language, interjections, pronouns |
| 5 | **Writing Scripts** *(cont'd)* (Radio Script Model, Prewriting, Drafting, Revising, Editing, Publishing) | 344–346 | Active and passive verbs, mood of verbs, word choice, commas (in a series, to set off appositives, to separate adjectives), sentences (review) |
| 6 | **Writing Across the Curriculum** (Teacher's Choice) | 442–513 | Brackets, ellipses, colons, semicolons, parentheses, and other forms of punctuation (review) |
| | Portfolio Review *SkillsBook* Posttests | | |

## Fifth Six Weeks

| Week | Writing Lessons | *Write Source* | Grammar and Writing Skills |
|------|-----------------|----------------|----------------------------|
| 1 | **Analyzing a Poem** | 303–310 | Figurative language, interjections, pronouns, end punctuation (review) |
| 2 | **Writing Poetry: Free Verse** (Model, Prewriting, Drafting, Revising, Editing, Publishing) | 347–351 | Specific nouns, sentence variety, subject-verb agreement |
| 3 | **Writing Poetry: Special Techniques and Other Types of Poems** (Model, Prewriting, Drafting, Revising, Editing, Publishing) | 352–357 | Spelling, hyphens and dashes, tenses (irregular verbs) |
| 4 | **Freestyle Writing Project** (Student 's/Teacher's Choice) | | Pronoun-antecedent agreement, subject-verb agreement, using the right word |
| 5 | **Writing Across the Curriculum** (Teacher's Choice) | 442–513 | Prepositions, prepositional phrases, adverbs, basic sentence patterns |
| 6 | **Responding to Nonfiction** (Model, Prewriting, Drafting, Revising, Editing, Publishing) | 295–302 | Figures of speech, misplaced and dangloing modifiers, compound and complex sentences |
| | Portfolio Review *SkillsBook* Posttests | | |

# Sixth Six Weeks

| Week | Writing Lessons | *Write Source* | Grammar and Writing Skills |
|------|-----------------|----------------|----------------------------|
| 1 | **Research Skills** | 358–370 | Tense shifts, punctuating compound and complex sentences, punctuating quotations, end punctuation (review) |
| 2 | **Writing an MLA Research Report** (Model, Prewriting) | 371–394 | Apostrophes, comma splices and run-on sentences (review) |
| 3 | **Writing an MLA Research Report** *(cont'd)* (Drafting) | 395–410 | Commas with introductory phrases and clauses, pronoun-antecedent agreement (review) |
| 4 | **Writing an MLA Research Report** *(cont'd)* (Revising, Editing, Publishing) | 411–428 | Direct quotations Complete sentences (fragments), sentence types, adverbs, adjectives (review) |
| 5 | **Making Presentations** (Planning, Practicing, Delivering, Evaluating) | 429–437 | Transitions, conjunctions, end punctuation, using the right word (review) |
| 6 | **Making Presentations** *(cont'd)* (Multimedia) | 438–441 | Active and passive verbs, mood of verbs, word choice, commas (in a series, to set off appositives, to separate adjectives) (review) |
|  | Portfolio Review *SkillsBook* Posttests | | |

# TEXAS WRITE SOURCE

Authors
**Dave Kemper, Patrick Sebranek, and Verne Meyer**

Consulting Author
**Gretchen Bernabei**

Illustrator
**Chris Krenzke**

## GREAT SOURCE®

 HOUGHTON MIFFLIN HARCOURT

Copyright © 2012 by Houghton Mifflin Harcourt Publishing Company

Printed in the U.S.A.

ISBN-13   978-0-547-39497-8

2 3 4 5 6 7 8 9 10  0914  19 18 17 16 15 14 13 12 11

450000000000          B C D E F G

# Quick Guide

# A Quick Tour of *Texas Write Source*

*Texas Write Source* contains many key features that will help you improve your writing and language skills. Once you become familiar with this book, you will begin to understand how helpful these features can be.

**Checklists** serve as effective revising and editing guides within the writing units.

**Writing guidelines** help you, step-by-step, to complete different forms of writing.

A **holistic scoring guide** will keep you on track and help you evaluate your finished pieces of writing.

Contents

The **writing samples** will stimulate you to write your own effective essays.

**Graphic organizers** show you how to organize your ideas for writing.

**Links to the traits** help you appreciate the importance of different traits at different points in the writing process.

contents

# The Writing Process

# The Forms of Writing

## NARRATIVE WRITING

viii

contents

## EXPOSITORY WRITING

# PERSUASIVE WRITING

x

## contents

### INTERPRETIVE RESPONSE

## CREATIVE WRITING

xii

contents

## RESEARCH WRITING

# WRITING ACROSS THE CURRICULUM

# The Tools of Language

# Basic Grammar and Writing

xvi

# A Writer's Resource

# Proofreader's Guide

contents

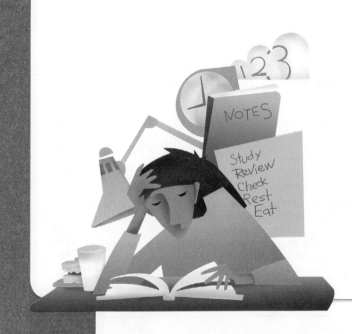

# Why Write?

Wouldn't it be nice if each of your writing assignments meant something to you personally . . . if each one helped you make sense of your life? Unfortunately, that is not the case. You are often asked to summarize facts, recall and interpret information, and explore topics in research papers. These assignments are important for academic reasons. However, they seldom get at your heartbeat—what makes you who you really are.

There is a type of writing that you can control, though, a type of personal writing that will help you explore your cares and concerns. This chapter will help you learn more about this valuable form of writing.

- **Purposes for Writing**
- **Getting Started**
- **Using a Writer's Notebook**

"All glory comes from daring to begin."

—Eugene F. Ware

## Why Write?

Ask students if they write for personal reasons—keeping a journal, writing songs, poems, or short stories, and so on. Invite them to tell why they write. ↙ **DIFFERENTIATE INSTRUCTION**

Show students the *New York Times* online archive of the "Writers on Writing" column (www.nytimes.com/books/specials/writers.html), in which famous writers were asked to consider why writing is important to them and to tell why they write. Have students read one or more of the essays.

Afterward, ask the following:

- Which essay(s) did you read? Why?
- Did the essay provide a clear account of why that author writes? What is the reason?
- If the essay didn't directly address the question "Why write?" could you read between the lines to find the answer? What is it?
- Did the essay discuss other important aspects of writing? What are they?

 **ELPS** 3J

---

## Differentiated Instruction: English Language Learners

**ELPS** 1C, 3B, 3C, 3F, 3G

| ELP Level **Beginning** | ELP Level **Intermediate** | ELP Level **Advanced/Advanced High** |
|---|---|---|
| Using pictures, gestures, and other supports, define journals, poems, and short stories. Have students repeat explanations in their own words, using supports as needed. | Discuss with students the reasons they like to write or topics they might like to write about. Allow students to use simple, routine language and provide sentence prompts as necessary. | Discuss with students the reasons they like to write or topics they might like to write about. Encourage students to use increasingly complex sentences in their comments. |

**ELPS 1C** Use strategic learning techniques to acquire basic and grade-level vocabulary; **3B** Expand vocabulary/learning and using high-frequency words for identifying and describing/ retelling information supported by pictures/learning and using routine language for classroom communication; **3C** Speak using a variety of grammatical structures and sentence lengths and types with increasing accuracy and ease; **3F** Give information/ranging from using a limited high-frequency vocabulary to using abstract and content-based vocabulary during speaking; **3G** Express opinions and feelings ranging from communicating short phrases to participating in discussions; **3J** Respond orally to information presented in a variety of media to build and reinforce concept and language attainment

## Purposes for Writing

**Writing helps you . . .**

Ask your class if anyone has ever written for one of these reasons before. Discuss their experiences.

⭐ ELPS 3G

### Tip

Compare writing to other skills or hobbies that students may have (playing music, athletics, etc.). Ask what would happen to their skills if they only practiced them once or twice a year.

**Learn to observe.** Allow students to begin making their observations in class. Tell them to dedicate pages in a notebook or journal to the activity, and encourage them to record their observations outside class over the next several days. Let them know that they might be asked to share selected observations with the class. DIFFERENTIATE INSTRUCTION ↘

⭐ ELPS 5B

When students have finished the activity, have them read selected observations and share their insights. Focus the discussion on students' writing experiences:

- Did they enjoy recording their observations?
- Did the activity help them to focus on their surroundings?
- Did they make any surprising observations? What were they? DIFFERENTIATE INSTRUCTION ↘

⭐ ELPS 3E

**ELPS 3E** Share information in cooperative learning interactions; **3G** Express opinions, ideas, and feelings ranging from communicating short phrases to participating in discussions; **5B** Write using newly acquired basic and content-based grade-level vocabulary

---

## Purposes for Writing

Experienced writers have their own reasons for writing. Some write in order to sort out their thoughts, while others write simply because it makes them happy. Whatever the reason, writing has a special meaning to them. The following thoughts may help you more fully appreciate the value of personal writing.

### Writing helps you . . .

**Learn more about yourself.**

Writing lets you look deep within yourself, sometimes with surprising results. When you keep a writer's notebook of your thoughts and feelings, you may, as you read your entries later, see yourself in a whole new light.

**Learn more about your world.**

By recording observations of the world around you (what you hear and see and sense), you can learn from the events that shape you. Your observations also serve as a fascinating record of your time in history. Finally, writing about your classes helps you remember and make sense of what you are learning.

**Share your ideas and insights.**

Sometimes writing is the best way to share your thoughts with others. Your writing could have many different readers, or audiences. Writing gives you time to decide exactly what you want to say before your audience "hears" it.

**Express what you know.**

Writing actually helps you become a better thinker. It lets you review what you already know, reflect on it, use new vocabulary words, and add new thoughts. Think of writing as exercise for your mind.

### Tip

Remember, writing is a skill. As with all other skills, the more you practice, the better you will become.

 **Learn to observe.** Take a minute to look around you. Write freely for 5 minutes about your surroundings, recording details about the sights and sounds in this setting. Try this activity in a variety of places. Did you make any surprising observations? Discuss your observations with a classmate.

---

⭐ TEKS 10.14A, 10.14B, 10.14C, 10.15B
ELPS 3E, 2I

Process

# Getting Started

Think of writing as a skill. Just as you set aside time to improve your musical or athletic skills, do the same with writing. Exercise your mind as well as your body. Your writing will improve if you make an honest effort.

## Where should I write?

**Write in school.** Here are ways you can write throughout your day:

- Listen carefully during your classes and take notes.
- Keep a learning log in each of your classes.
- Complete writing assignments and papers.

**Write at home.** Writing in your spare time can help you gain fluency—the ability to write quickly and easily. Here are some types of writing or genres you might want to try for fun or in your spare time:

- Write e-mail messages and letters.
- Keep a writer's notebook. (See pages 4–5.)
- Create short stories and poems. (See pages 320–357.)

**Write wherever you are.** Write in a car, on the bus, in a park, or in a coffee shop. In her book *Writing Down the Bones,* Natalie Goldberg suggests that you write wherever you feel comfortable.

## What should I write about?

You can write about anything and everything. The more you write, the more you learn. Here are just a few things you can write about:

- **Observations:** What is happening around you right now? What do you think about what is happening?
- **Memories:** What was the best moment of your day? Your week? Your year? What was the worst moment?
- **Hopes and dreams:** What do you want in life? What do you wish for your future?
- **People:** What person means the most to you? What person do you admire? What sort of person do you not understand?
- **Places:** Where are you right now? Where do you wish you were? Where do you never want to be again?
- **Things:** What is your favorite possession? Your least favorite? What one invention would you like to outlaw, and why?

 **Find inspiration.** Write for 5 to 10 minutes about your favorite place. What did you discover through your writing? Discuss your ideas with a partner.

---

# Getting Started

## Where should I write?

Remind students not to try and emulate their idea of the "typical writer." There is no typical writer! Some can write in noisy coffee shops while others need the silence of a midnight office. It's an individual preference.

## What should I write about?

Although the ideas presented here cater to a journal or diary, remind students that the same concepts can be worked into other forms of writing such as poems and short stories.

Suggest that students try several writing strategies, giving themselves time to practice a method. Suggestions include the following:

- Try writing at the same time every day so that it becomes a habit. Choose a time that you routinely have free, such as first thing in the morning, during your commute, or at the end of the day.
- Keep a record of the titles and authors' names of appealing books, poems, articles, and songs, and reflect on interesting words and phrases from favorite lines. Later, these can serve as inspirations or models for your own work.
- Use writing tools you enjoy. Try creating an electronic journal on a computer, or use a favorite pen and an unlined notebook. In other words, make your daily writing time pleasurable.

⭐ TEKS 10.14A, 10.14B, 10.14C, 10.15B

**Find inspiration.** Remind students that during freewriting they should be most concerned with expressing their ideas in creative ways. Make sure students focus their discussion on their discoveries, rather than on what they have written. ✓ DIFFERENTIATE INSTRUCTION

⭐ ELPS 2I, 3E

---

**Differentiated Instruction:
English Language Learners**                    ⭐ ELPS 5F

| ELP Level **Beginning** | ELP Level **Intermediate** | ELP Level **Advanced/Advanced High** |
|---|---|---|
| Allow students to express ideas by combining pictures and short, simple words or phrases. You may also want to provide sentence stems such as *I like. . . because. . . .* | Allow students to express their ideas in a combination of pictures and simple sentences. Encourage students to use descriptive language. | Encourage students to experiment with longer, more complex sentences and to include descriptive language in their writing. Challenge them to use more advanced vocabulary. |

 **TEKS 10.14A** Write a story with a conflict, a resolution, interesting and believable characters, and literary strategies and devices; **10.14B** Write a poem using poetic techniques and forms; **10.14C** Write a script with an explicit/implicit theme and details that contribute to the mood and tone; **10.15B** Write procedural and work-related documents; **ELPS 2I** Demonstrate listening comprehension in increasingly complex spoken language/following directions, summarizing spoken messages, responding to questions, collaborating with peers, and taking notes; **3E** Share information in cooperative learning interactions; **5F** Write using a variety of grade-appropriate sentence lengths and patterns/ combine in increasingly accurate ways

## Using a Writer's Notebook

If you will require students to turn in their writer's notebooks for your review, inform students how you will evaluate them. Some options follow:

- Collect all notebooks at the same time, or allow students to turn them in at a time of their choosing, say twice per grading period.
- Provide comments or assign participation grades based on their choice of topics and use of language and conventions.

Also consider how to approach entries that students might want to keep private. For example:

- Require students to date all entries for in-class writing, and check only for participation.
- Assure students that you will not read pages that are earmarked, such as by folding the page in half vertically.
- Have students write in loose-leaf notebooks and remove private entries before turning in their writing.

### Ensuring Success

Remind students that even the most enthusiastic writers experience writer's block. There will be days when writing is more difficult than usual. During these times, it is often helpful to just start writing, even if students don't feel it is "good" or "interesting." Getting words on paper can help ease the writer into the flow of the task and potentially generate ideas and inspiration.

**TEKS** 10.13A; **ELPS** 5G

---

## Using a Writer's Notebook

Your most powerful writing tool can be a notebook reserved exclusively for daily writing. A **writer's notebook** (also called a *journal*) is a place to record your thoughts on any topic. As you write regularly in your notebook, you will make countless discoveries about your world.

In his book *Breathing In, Breathing Out: Keeping a Writer's Notebook*, Ralph Fletcher compares a writer's notebook to a compost heap. Over time, all the cuttings and leftovers that a gardener composts turn into rich fertilizer. In the same way, you can use your notes to determine and select topics that you want to write about. Your notes will guide you as you write your thesis statement or controlling idea about your chosen topic. Your notes should also help you pick the best genre for the topic and plan your first draft.

### Ensuring Success

To make sure that your writer's notebook is a success, consider the quantity, quality, and variety of your entries. Also follow the rules on this page.

- **Quantity:** Teachers often require a certain number of pages or entries per grading period. Know your teacher's requirements for your notebook.
- **Quality:** Approach each entry with a high level of enthusiasm and interest. Develop your ideas fully with strong supporting details. Try to create vivid images that have sensory appeal.
- **Variety:** Write some of your entries from different points of view. For example, after an argument with a friend, write about it from your friend's point of view, or from the perspective of someone who overheard the argument.

### Rules for a Writer's Notebook

- **Date each entry.** The date helps you find an entry and puts those thoughts into perspective with other entries.
- **Write freely.** Don't worry about producing perfect copy. Just get your ideas on paper.
- **Write regularly.** Develop the habit of writing daily.
- **Reflect on your work.** Reread your entries. Consider what you have written and look for ideas for future writing topics.

---

**TEKS** 10.13A
**ELPS** 3E, 3G, 5G

Why Write?   **5**

Process

## Taking it Personally

Here is a page from a student writer's notebook. This entry focuses on an old lunch box.

### Sample Notebook Entry

April 9, 2011

Last week, Dad announced that it was time for spring-cleaning. As I dug through the garage, I found my old lunch box. Most kids had lunch boxes featuring the latest toys, cartoon characters, or comic-book heroes. My lunch box was different.

My lunch box looked like a pirate's chest. Bright splatters covered the surface because my grandpa used the lunch box when he was a painter. I would look at the paint, trying to imagine each color on an entire house. Mint green was the worst, I thought.

Even though I secretly loved that lunch box, it was so embarrassing to see kids pointing at me and laughing. I remember being relieved when everyone started using brown bags for lunch. Grandpa's lunch box was put on a shelf where it gathered dust.

After wiping the dirt and cobwebs off the lunch box, I realized that it would make a perfect container for my art supplies at school. The funny thing is, now my friends think Grandpa's lunch box is cool.

This notebook entry captures a time in the writer's life. It . . .

- starts with a "seed idea" (an old lunch box),
- describes the object's appearance and uses, and
- reflects on its importance.

**Remember:** Keeping a writer's notebook lets you look at ordinary things in new ways, describe your feelings, choose good descriptive words, and practice writing until you feel confident.

 **Write a quick reflection.** Think about an object that was once very important to you. Write freely for 5 to 10 minutes about that object. Discuss with a friend what it meant and still means to you.

## Taking It Personally

Note that writing topics can be very simple, mundane things. Brainstorm with students about other possible "seed ideas." Possibilities could include favorite childhood toys, holiday gifts, a favorite song, their second grade teacher, and so on.

**TEKS** 10.13A; **ELPS** 3E

**Write a quick reflection.** As an alternative to reflecting on an old possession, have students focus on something they may want to acquire in the future, such as a car, a sound system, or a special article of clothing.

Before students begin writing, ask them to pause for a minute or so to concentrate on the sensory details they can use in their freewriting. To help them visualize the details, have them imagine describing their object to someone who is not familiar with it. How would they describe the following:

- the colors, textures, or other characteristics that appeal to the senses
- its use, purpose, or function
- any special maintenance or storage requirements **☑ DIFFERENTIATE INSTRUCTION**

**ELPS** 3G, 5G

✳ For more about sensory details, see SE page 87.

---

**Differentiated Instruction:
English Language Learners**          **ELPS** 1C, 3B, 5G

| ELP Level **Beginning** | ELP Level **Intermediate** | ELP Level **Advanced/Advanced High** |
|---|---|---|
| Choose an object in the classroom and practice descriptive language with students (color, size, shape, etc.). | Have students create a word web for their object. With a partner's help on vocabulary, fill in the web with descriptive words and phrases. | Have students create a word web for their object with descriptive words and phrases. Challenge students to use similes and metaphors in their descriptions. |
| | Use page 624 | Use page 624 |

**TEKS** 10.13A Plan a first draft by determining topics through strategies; **ELPS** 1C Use strategic learning techniques to acquire basic and grade-level vocabulary; 3B Expand vocabulary by learning and using high-frequency words for identifying and describing; 3E Share information in cooperative learning interactions; 3G Express opinions, ideas, and feelings ranging from communicating short phrases to participating in discussions; 5G Narrate/describe/explain with increasing specificity and detail

# The Writing Process

## ⭐ UNIT TEKS

**10.13A** Plan a first draft; **10.13B** Structure ideas and develop drafts; **10.13C** Revise drafts; **10.13D** Edit drafts; **10.13E** Revise final draft and publish work; **10.14A** Write an engaging story; **10.14B** Write a poem; **10.14C** Write a script; **10.15Bi** Write procedural and work-related documents/convey information; **10.15Bii** Write procedural and work-related documents/include formatting; **10.15Biii** Write procedural and work-related documents/anticipate questions; **10.17A(i)** Use and understand tenses and verbals; **10.17C** Use correctly structured sentences; **10.18A** Use capitalization; **10.18B(i)** Use commas; **10.19** Spell correctly; **10.23C** Synthesize research into a presentation/use graphics and illustrations

## ⭐ UNIT ELPS

**1A** Use prior knowledge and experiences; **1B** Monitor oral/written language; **1C** Use learning techniques; **1D** Speak using learning strategies; **1E** Internalize new language/speaking and writing; **1F** Use and learn new language; **1H** Develop and expand repertoire of learning strategies such as reasoning inductively or deductively, looking for patterns in language, and analyzing sayings and expressions commensurate with grade-level learning expectations; **2C** Learn new structures, expressions, and vocabulary; **2D** Monitor understanding/seek clarification of spoken language; **2G** Understand spoken language/situations are familiar to unfamiliar; **2H** Understand ideas/information in spoken language; **2I** Demonstrate listening comprehension of spoken language; **3A** Practice sounds of new vocabulary; **3B** Expand and internalize initial vocabulary; **3C** Speak with increasing accuracy and ease; **3D** Speak using content-area vocabulary; **3E** Share information; **3F** Ask for and give information; **3G** Express opinions, ideas, and feelings; **3H** Narrate, describe, and explain/increasing specificity; **3I** Adapt spoken language appropriately for formal and informal purposes; **3J** Respond orally to information; **4A** Learn relationships between and decode sounds; **4C** Develop sight vocabulary/derive meaning of environmental print/comprehend written classroom materials; **4D** Use prereading supports; **4E** Read with decreasing need for linguistic accommodations; **4F** Use visual/contextual support and support from peers/teachers; **4G** Demonstrate comprehension of language/shared reading, summarizing, responding to questions, taking notes; **4H** Read silently with increasing ease; **4I** Employ and expand reading skills; **4J** Demonstrate English comprehension and expand reading skills by employing inferential skills such as predicting, making connections between ideas, drawing inferences and conclusions from text and graphic sources, and finding supporting text evidence commensurate with content area needs; **4K** Employ analytical skills; **5B** Write using new vocabulary; **5C** Spell and employ spelling patterns/rules with increasing accuracy; **5D** Edit writing for grammar and usage; **5E** Employ complex grammatical structures; **5F** Write using a variety of sentence lengths/patterns/connecting words; **5G** Narrate, describe, and explain with increasing specificity/content-area writing

## Why Write? (pages 1–5)

Students learn about the value of personal writing and are introduced to the concept of a writer's notebook.

## Understanding the Writing Process (pages 7–12)

Students are introduced to the steps in the writing process: prewriting, drafting, revising, editing, and publishing.

## One Writer's Process (pages 13–32)

Students watch student writer Nakeisha Williams follow the steps in the writing process to develop a persuasive essay about saving murals in her community.

## Understanding the Traits of Writing (pages 33–48)

Students learn the five traits of writing.

## Peer Response (pages 49–54)

Students share their writing with their peers and receive their classmates' feedback on their writing.

## Evaluating Your Writing (pages 55–68)

Students familiarize themselves with the Holistic Scoring Guide and begin using it to evaluate their writing.

## Publishing Your Writing (pages 69–77)

Students prepare their writing for publication.

### 🔗 Technology Connections

 **Write Source Online** www.hmheducation.com/tx/writesource
- **Net-text**
- **Writing Network**
- **Portfolio**
- **GrammarSnap**
- **File Cabinet**

 **Interactive Whiteboard Lessons**

# The Writing Process Unit Scope and Sequence

| Day | Writing and Conventions Instruction | Write Source Student Edition | | | Daily Language Workouts | Skills-Book | Write Source Online |
| | | Core Unit | Tools of Language | Resource Units | | | |
|---|---|---|---|---|---|---|---|
| 1–2 | **Why Write?** | 1–5 | TL 523–529 | | 6–9 | | |
| 3–5 | **Understanding the Writing Process** | 6–12 | | | | | |
| 6 | **One Writer's Process** Previewing the Texas Traits | 13–14 | TL 526–529 | | 10–13 | | |
| | Prewriting | 15–17 | | WR 620–627 | | | |
| 7 | Drafting | 18–19 | | WR 628–633 | | | |
| 8 | Revising | 20–25 | | WR 638–639 | | | |
| 9 | Editing | 26–27 | | | | | |
| | Publishing | 28–30 | | | | | |
| 10 | Assessing the Final Draft | 31 | | | | | |
| | Reflecting on Your Writing | 32 | | | | | |
| 11–12 | **Understanding the Traits of Writing** | 33–48 | TL 530–531 | | 14–17 | | |
| 13 | **Peer Response** | 49–54 | | | | | |
| 14 | **Evaluating Your Writing** | 55–68 | | | | | |
| 15 | **Publishing Your Writing** | 69–77 | | | | | |

Week 1 — Week 2 — Week 3

 **Resource Units** referenced above are located in the back of the *Student Edition* and *Teacher's Edition*
TL *"The Tools of Language"*  BGW *"Basic Grammar and Writing"*  WR *"A Writer's Resource"*  PG *"Proofreader's Guide"*

## Writing Focus

- Understanding the Writing Process
- One Writer's Process
- Understanding the Traits of Writing
- Peer Response
- Evaluating Your Writing
- Publishing Your Writing

## Grammar Focus

- Sentence Variety

## Learning Language

Read aloud the basic and academic terms, as well as the descriptions and questions. Model for students how to read one question and answer it. For example, *It says that something is persuasive when it convinces you to take a certain course of action. On TV, a Pepsi commercial is persuasive because it tries to convince you to buy Pepsi.* Have partners monitor their understanding of the terms by working through the meanings and questions together. `DIFFERENTIATE INSTRUCTION ↘`

 **ELPS** 1E, 2C, 3B, 3D, 3E, 4F, 4G

## Minilessons

| Dancing | Understanding the Writing Process |
| --- | --- |

- **FREEWRITE** about how the writing process graphic on SE page 10 resembles a pattern for a dance. **EXPLORE** the idea of your writing process as a dance. **NAME** and **DESCRIBE** that dance.

| My Thesis Is . . . | One Writer's Process |
| --- | --- |

- **READ** the model of the first draft on SE pages 18–19. **IGNORE** any errors. Then **WRITE** a thesis statement that opposes the writer's position. **SHARE** your statement with a classmate and **DISCUSS**.

**ELPS** 2C, 3B, 3D, 3E

---

**ELPS** **1A** Use prior knowledge to understand meanings; **1E** Internalize new basic and academic language by using and reusing it/speaking; **2C** Learn new expressions and basic/academic vocabulary heard during classroom instruction/interactions; **3B** Expand vocabulary by learning and using high-frequency words for identifying and describing/use routine language for classroom communication; **3D** Speak using grade-level content area vocabulary/new words and academic language proficiency; **3E** Share information in cooperative learning interactions; **4C** Comprehend vocabulary used in written classroom materials; **4F** Use support from peers/teachers to enhance and confirm understanding and develop vocabulary; **4G** Demonstrate comprehension of increasingly complex English/responding to questions; **5B** Write using content-based grade-level vocabulary

---

 **ELPS** 1E, 2C, 3B, 3D, 3E, 4G

www.hmheducation.com/tx/writesource

# Using the Writing Process

## Writing Focus

## Grammar Focus

## Learning Language

Working with a classmate, read the definitions below and discuss your answers to each question.

1. Something is persuasive when it convinces you to take a certain course of action.
   **What on TV could be described as persuasive?**
2. A writer's voice is the way a piece of writing sounds.
   **What does an author's voice reveal about her attitudes on a topic?**
3. A logical opinion is one that is sound and makes sense.
   **How can you tell if an argument is logical?**
4. A counter-argument presents an opposing idea.
   **What is one counter-argument to the idea of year-round school?**

---

**Differentiated Instruction: English Language Learners**     **ELPS** 1A, 1E, 4C, 4F, 5B

| ELP Level **Beginning** | ELP Level **Intermediate** | ELP Level **Advanced/Advanced High** |
| --- | --- | --- |
| Students write out each term. Then have them use descriptive or synonymous words from their first language to complete a word web for each word. | Students write out each term and, with the help of a partner, complete a word web for each word using more familiar English vocabulary. | Students may make a graphic organizer to plan their responses. They can also write a cohesive paragraph that uses all of the words. |
| Use page 624 | Use page 624 | Use page 624 |

# Understanding the Writing Process

The writing process begins before you put pen to paper. In fact, the writing process begins the day you think your first thoughts, and it never really stops. You are subconsciously involved in the writing process every day of your life. Each of your experiences becomes part of what you know, what you think, and what you have to say. Writing is the process of capturing those thoughts and experiences on paper.

The steps in the writing process discussed in this book include *prewriting, drafting, revising, editing,* and *publishing.* All of these steps are equally important. If you follow the process for each writing project, you (and your audience, your readers) will be pleased with the results.

- ■ **Building Good Writing Habits**
- ■ **Understanding the Writing Process**
- ■ **The Process in Action**
- ■ **Focusing on the Texas Traits**

"Don't think and then write it down. Think on paper."

—Harry Kemelman

# Understanding the Writing Process

### Objectives
- build good writing habits
- understand the five steps in the writing process
- connect the five traits of effective writing to the writing process

Explain to students that they are likely to find the stages of the writing process familiar. The process described on the following pages breaks down the act of writing into a series of manageable tasks. In the past, they may have given little thought to how writing connects to their lives. Identifying the steps by name and focusing on when and how to use them will help them to write better in all their classes.

The five traits of effective writing, covered in this unit, may also be familiar. Point out that all readers subconsciously use these traits to evaluate what they read. Identifying the characteristics of the traits provides students with a writer's vocabulary to use when discussing and improving their writing.

## Resources

### Copy Masters (see Appendix)

- Time Line
- 5W's Chart
- T-Chart
- Venn Diagram
- Sensory Chart
- Details Chart
- Quick List

## Building Good Writing Habits

Note that these tips are geared toward helping to inspire a writer. Some students may think that the imposition of writing tasks dampens **inspiration**. Encourage students to notice that the stages of writing allow ample opportunity for creativity—in fact, the structure inherent in the process may even promote it.

Discuss the concept of inspiration. Invite students to talk about the times they have felt inspired while doing something such as writing a poem, composing a song, practicing an instrument, working on a math problem, even doing chores. Ask the following questions:

- What was the task?
- What triggered your inspiration?
- Did you share your ideas?
- Do you look for ways to improve the time you spend on tasks?

Encourage students to stay alert for factors that inspire them while writing and working.

**Write about a quotation.** Invite volunteers to share their work with the class. Allow time for classmates to respond to each reading. Cover as many of the quotations as possible. **DIFFERENTIATE INSTRUCTION ↘**

 **ELPS** 3E

---

 ELPS 3E

## Building Good Writing Habits

Writing success begins with good writing habits. Follow the tips below and you will see real improvement in your writing.

### When to Write

Set aside time each day to write. Regular writing will help you develop fluency—the ability to write quickly and easily.

"Write about it by day, and dream about it by night."
—E. B. White

### Where to Write

Write in school and at home. Write on the bus or in a coffee shop. Just keep writing wherever you can.

"I write anywhere, but I still like cafes."
—J. K. Rowling

"Write in a place that you feel safe."
—Georgia Heard

### What to Write

Write about anything and everything that interests you—personal experiences, current events, music, books, or sports. Write in a variety of genres: stories, poems, plays, television or movie scripts, and nonfiction.

"If a story is in you, it has got to come out."
—William Faulkner

### How to Write

Relax and let the words flow. Share your true feelings and, before long, your distinctive writing voice will develop.

"The beautiful part of writing is that you don't have to get it right the first time, unlike, say, a brain surgeon."
—Robert Cormier

"There are a thousand ways to write, and each is as good as the other if it fits you."
—Lillian Hellman

Read the quotations above and pick one that stands out. Write for 5 to 10 minutes about what this quotation means to you. Discuss with a classmate.

---

**Differentiated Instruction: Advanced Learners**

Challenge students to use their freewriting as a springboard for developing an original quotation about writing. Tell students that their quotations may or may not relate to the quotations they chose for the activity. Have students share and explain their quotations.

**TEKS** 10.13A–E
**ELPS** 3E, 3G

# Understanding the Writing Process

Before a piece of writing is ready to share, it should have gone through a series of steps called the *writing process*. Each step is briefly described below.

## The Steps in the Writing Process

### Prewriting

The first step in the writing process is planning. It involves selecting a specific topic, developing a thesis, and gathering and organizing details to support the writer's position. The writer must also determine who the audience will be and what genre will work best for the topic.

### Drafting

The writer completes the first draft using the prewriting plan as a guide. This is a writer's *first* chance to get everything on paper. When drafting, the writer should attempt to include transitions and rhetorical devices such as analogies or repetition to convey meaning.

### Revising

During revising, the writer reviews the draft for key traits: *focus and coherence, organization, development of ideas, and voice.* The writer checks that the genre is appropriate for the topic and audience and that the purpose of the writing is clear. Improvements should also be made in style, word choice, use of figurative language, and subtlety of meaning.

### Editing

Check the revised draft for *conventions*—grammar, mechanics, and spelling. Proofread the final copy.

### Publishing

The final step in the writing process is publishing. It is an opportunity for the writer to share work and to respond to additional feedback.

## Understanding the Writing Process

Recap the sentence on SE page 7 (paragraph 2, sentence 2) stating that the authors feel all steps in the writing process are equally important. Conduct a classroom discussion about students' past experiences with using a writing process. Tell students that they are free to disagree or to change their minds after they've learned more. Also note that some types of writing—such as journals, personal e-mails, or text messages—do not require all five steps. ✔ **DIFFERENTIATE INSTRUCTION**

Point out that Publishing means all forms of sharing one's written work with others, not just work that is sold to magazine or book publishers.

**TEKS** 10.13A, 10.13B, 10.13C, 10.13D, 10.13E; **ELPS** 3E

---

### Differentiated Instruction: English Language Learners

**ELPS** 3D, 3E, 3G

| ELP Level **Beginning** | ELP Level **Intermediate** | ELP Level **Advanced/Advanced High** |
|---|---|---|
| Have students demonstrate an understanding of drafting and revising by practicing on a paragraph that they write in their first language. | Encourage students to explain the difference between drafting and revising to a partner or the teacher. Ask: *Why are they both important?* | Ask students to analyze the processes of drafting and revising, explaining to partners why each step is vital to producing a polished, interesting finished product. |

---

 **TEKS** **10.13A** Plan a first draft/selecting genre, determining topics, and developing a thesis; **10.13B** Structure ideas in a sustained and persuasive way/develop drafts in timed and open-ended situations that include transitions and rhetorical devices; **10.13C** Revise drafts/improve style, word choice, figurative language, sentence variety, and subtlety of meaning and rethink how purpose, audience, and genre have been addressed; **10.13D** Edit drafts/grammar, mechanics, and spelling; **10.13E** Revise the final draft to feedback from peers and teacher/publish written work; **ELPS** **3D** Speak using grade-level content area vocabulary/new words and academic language proficiency; **3E** Share information in cooperative learning interactions; **3G** Express opinions, ideas, and feelings ranging from communicating short phrases to participating in discussions

## The Process in Action

### Prewriting
#### Planning Your Writing

Emphasize the importance of students selecting topics that interest them. They will enjoy the writing process more if they are engaged by a topic, and their interest will show in their writing.

#### Gathering and Organizing Details

Encourage students to make and follow a writing schedule and to record new ideas and information about their topics in their notebooks. They can revisit their notes for future projects. Also, graphic organizers such as those in the TE Appendix can help students organize their ideas.

**TEKS** 10.13A

### Drafting
#### Developing Your Ideas

Remind students not to try for perfection in a first draft. Good writing requires experimentation, and keeping an open mind allows students to take risks and expand their writing repertoire. At this point in the writing process, the overall structure and flow of the piece is more important than grammar and spelling.

**TEKS** 10.13B; **ELPS** 5B

✱ For information about Writing Great Beginnings, see SE page 631.

#### Tip

Review any specific guidelines you have for student drafts. Encourage students to experiment with drafting on paper and on the computer to find their most productive method.

---

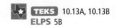 **TEKS** 10.13A, 10.13B
**ELPS** 5B

## The Process in Action

The next two pages give a detailed description of each step in the writing process. The graphic below reminds you that, at any time, you can move back and forth between the steps in the writing process. Be aware that if you put more effort and care into the early stages of the process, you'll move through the later stages more easily.

### Prewriting Planning Your Writing

- Search for topics that meet the requirements of the assignment.
- Plan your writing by selecting a specific topic and genre.

### Gathering and Organizing Details

- Gather as many ideas and details as you can about the topic.
- With the purpose of the assignment in mind, find one point to emphasize about the topic—either an interesting part or your personal feeling about it. This will be the thesis, or controlling idea, of your writing.
- Decide which details to include in your writing.
- Organize your details into a writing plan, perhaps using an outline or a graphic organizer.

### Drafting Developing Your Ideas

- When writing the first draft, concentrate on getting your ideas on paper. Structure your ideas in a persuasive, sustained, and convincing way.
- Use the details you collected to develop your draft. Be sure to include rhetorical devices to help convey and strengthen your ideas.
- Use transitions, and make sure your writing has a beginning, a middle, and an ending.

#### Tip

Write on every *other* line and on *one* side of the paper when using pen or pencil and paper. Double-space on a computer. This will give you room for revising.

---

Process

## Revising Improving Your Writing

- Set aside your first draft for a while so you can return to it with a fresh perspective.
- Read your first draft slowly and critically.
- Use these questions as a revising guide:
  · Is my topic interesting, and did I use the correct genre?
  · Are my style and word choice appropriate?
  · Are the ideas in order and easy to understand?
  · Have I included enough details to support my controlling idea?
  · Does the ending leave the reader with something to think about?
  · Have I varied my sentence structure?
  · Are the nouns specific and the verbs active?
  · Have I used figurative language and is it clear?
  · Does the piece read smoothly and convey subtlety of meaning?
- Ask another person to review your writing and give suggestions.
- Review for word choice and sentence variety. Make as many changes as necessary to improve your writing.

## Editing Checking Grammar, Mechanics, and Spelling

- Check for errors in grammar, punctuation, capitalization, and spelling.
- Have at least one other person check your writing for errors.
- Prepare a neat final copy.
- Proofread the final copy before publishing it.

## Publishing Sharing Your Writing

- Ask a classmate to review the final copy, and respond to the feedback.
- Consider submitting your writing to a newspaper or other publication. You may wish to include it in a portfolio of your writing.

**Learning Language** Reread the last two pages. Discuss the writing process with a classmate, and work together to summarize the steps. Remember, *summarize* means "to say again briefly."

## Revising
### Improving Your Writing

Show an understanding of students' reluctance to return to their writing after having worked hard on their first drafts. Then explain that successful writers do not allow themselves to "fall in love" with their first thoughts. Rereading and reviewing a piece of writing is a necessary part of the writing process.

⭐ **TEKS** 10.13C

✱ For information about Developing Great Endings, see SE page 632.

## Editing
### Checking Grammar, Mechanics, and Spelling

Admit that some people are better at focusing on conventions than others—but with practice all writers can improve their editing and proofreading skills.

⭐ **TEKS** 10.13D; **ELPS** 5C, 5D

## Publishing
### Sharing Your Writing

Suggest that students read a piece of writing aloud to a partner to get helpful feedback. Constructive criticism will help them improve as writers. ✔DIFFERENTIATE INSTRUCTION

⭐ **TEKS** 10.13E; **ELPS** 4G

**Learning Language.** Have students discuss the writing process with a partner. Explain that summarizing is a good way to review information quickly. Model summarizing of Prewriting: *Choose a topic to write about, and brainstorm details that could be included in your writing. Decide on a thesis and organize your details into a basic outline.*

⭐ **ELPS** 3E, 4G

---

## Focusing on the Texas Traits

Before students explore the page, have them turn to SE page 34 and read the introduction to the traits.

Then ask them to notice that each question on this page demonstrates how to connect the traits to the steps of the writing process.

### Try It!
#### Answers

Complete this activity as a class discussion, modeling responses as necessary. Possible responses:

The most important trait is focus and coherence because if readers find the ideas interesting and well-connected, they will want to read on even if there are some problems with it.

The most important trait is organization because if the piece isn't well organized, readers won't be able to understand the ideas.

Voice is quite important because without it the writing lacks individual character and sounds boring or trite. DIFFERENTIATE INSTRUCTION ↘

---

**12**

# Focusing on the Texas Traits

Writing is complicated, so don't try to focus on everything at once. For example, don't check your punctuation while considering the effectiveness of your beginning and ending paragraphs. Using the writing process will help you focus on each trait of good writing at the appropriate time. (See pages **33–48**.)

## Connecting the Traits to the Writing Process

### Prewrite

| | |
|---|---|
| **Focus and Coherence** | Is my writing focused on the prompt? Have I clearly stated my thesis, or controlling idea? Do all parts of my writing support my thesis statement? |
| **Organization** | How should I organize my writing? Which graphic organizer should I use for my planning? |
| **Voice** | What is my attitude about the topic? |

### Draft

| | |
|---|---|
| **Organization** | How do I want to arrange my ideas? |
| **Ideas** | What do I want to say? How can I best convey my purpose for writing? |
| **Voice** | How do I want to sound? |

### Revise

| | |
|---|---|
| **Organization** | Do my beginning, middle, and ending work well? |
| **Ideas** | Are my ideas clear and complete? |
| **Voice** | Have I created an appropriate tone? Have I chosen specific nouns and active verbs? Are my sentences varied? Do they read smoothly? |

### Edit

| | |
|---|---|
| **Conventions** | Have I used correct grammar, punctuation, capitalization, and spelling? |

### Publish

| | |
|---|---|
| **All Traits** | What do you think of my work? |

### Try It!

Reflect on the traits. When you develop a piece of writing, do you consider all of the traits listed above? Are some traits more important than other ones? Explain.

---

## Differentiated Instruction: English Language Learners

ELPS 1C, 1D, 1E, 3D, 3G

| ELP Level **Beginning** | ELP Level **Intermediate** | ELP Level **Advanced/Advanced High** |
|---|---|---|
| Have students list the traits in order of importance (their opinion). Next to each trait, they should define the trait using pictures or their first language. | Have students list the traits in order of importance. Next to each trait, they should explain its ranking using pictures or their first language as necessary. | Have students compare and discuss their rankings with a partner, defending their ranking decisions. Students may want to write out an explanation of their rankings. |

**ELPS 1C** Use strategic learning techniques to acquire basic and grade-level vocabulary; **1D** Speak using learning strategies/request assistance, employ non-verbal cues, and convey ideas by defining or describing; **1E** Internalize new academic language by using and reusing it/speaking and writing; **3D** Speak using grade-level content area vocabulary/new words and academic language proficiency; **3G** Express opinions and ideas ranging from communicating short phrases to participating in discussions

**13**

# One Writer's Process

Although every individual snowflake is different, all snowflakes are formed by the same natural process. In the same way, although every writer has a unique style, the best writers approach writing with the same writing process. Moving through the process, step-by-step and often back and forth, allows writers to express their ideas clearly, meaningfully, and accurately.

This chapter shows how student writer Nakeisha Williams used the writing process to develop a persuasive essay about saving murals in her community. As you follow her work, you'll see how she shaped her initial ideas into a convincing essay.

- **Previewing the Texas Traits**
- **Prewriting**
- **Drafting**
- **Revising**
- **Editing**
- **Publishing**
- **Assessing the Final Draft**
- **Reflecting on Your Writing**

"Write, write, and write some
  more. Think of writing as a muscle
  that needs lots of exercise."

—Jane Yolen

# One Writer's Process

One Writer's Process

## Objectives
- examine the goals for persuasive writing
- analyze one writer's work, step-by-step, through the writing process
- review one writer's final essay and self-assessment

Remind students that persuasive writing is a form in which the goal is to persuade, or convince, the reader of something. Note that they will study persuasive writing in more detail later and that they can apply the information in this section to any form of writing.

✱ For information about persuasive writing, see SE pages 194–251.

## Resources

**Copy Master (see Appendix)**

- Quick List

## Previewing the Texas Traits

Ask students to point out key words and ideas in the writing traits and to explain their importance. Some examples might be:

- *that you care about*—The topic should interest them personally.
- *appropriate for the. . . audience*—Who are they writing to? Who are they trying to persuade?
- *call for action*—The essay involves readers by asking them to do something.
- *balances facts and feelings*—While their arguments needs to be based on reason, they should not be afraid to show emotion in their writing as well. After all, they've chosen a topic that they really care about!

### Try It!
#### Answers

1. She should select a topic that interests her and that she has a definite opinion about.
2. She should state her opinion in the beginning, support it with facts and examples in the middle, and provide a call to action at the end.
3. Her voice should be confident and balanced between facts and feelings.

**ELPS** 3E

---

## Previewing the Texas Traits

The goal of persuasive writing is to defend a position in a well-organized way. Before Nakeisha began writing, she looked over the writing traits shown below. Nakeisha also looked over the holistic scoring guide on pages **60–61**. Considering these points and reminders helped her get started.

### Texas Writing Traits

- **Focus and Coherence**

  Select a topic that you care about. Create a thesis statement, or controlling idea. Connect ideas to the thesis statement and to each other. The introduction and conclusion add depth to the writing.

- **Organization**

  Use an organizational pattern that is appropriate for the topic and audience. Create a beginning that states your opinion, a middle that uses facts and examples to support your opinion, and an ending that makes a call for action. Use meaningful transitions.

- **Development of Ideas**

  Develop your ideas thoroughly. Connect all your ideas to the thesis statement and to each other. Use specific details to support your position.

- **Voice**

  Use a confident voice that balances facts and feelings, and use a tone that is appropriate and engaging for your topic and audience.

- **Conventions**

  Use grammar, capitalization, punctuation, sentence structure, and spelling properly.

### Try It!

Answer the following questions about the goals of Nakeisha's assignment, then discuss your answers with a classmate.

1. What must Nakeisha remember when selecting a topic?
2. What should Nakeisha remember about organization?
3. How should she sound (voice) in her essay?

**TEKS** 10.13A
**ELPS** 3E

# Prewriting Selecting a Topic

Nakeisha's teacher wrote this persuasive writing prompt on the board.

> Write a persuasive essay about a controversy at school or in our community. Choose a current, important issue that you feel strongly about. Your topic should be specific enough to cover in a few paragraphs.

Nakeisha used sentence starters to help her think of controversies. Sentence starters are one of a range of strategies a writer can use to choose a topic and explore ideas. Nakeisha put an asterisk next to her chosen issue.

## Sentence Starters

> People at my school disagree about . . .
> • banning food and drinks in study hall.
> • renovating the school theater.
>
> People in my community disagree about . . .
> • more lighting in the skate park.
> • eliminating the downtown murals.*

## Reflecting on the Topic

Nakeisha did some freewriting to explore her ideas on her chosen topic.

## Freewriting

> Mom said that the city council is discussing removing the murals because they are chipped and faded. I think the murals should be repaired, maintained, and saved. Hawkins students are proud of the work they did to create those murals. The unity, diversity, and creativity themes are still important today. Too much time and effort were put into this project . . .

### Try It!

Complete the two sentence starters above. Write at least two endings for each. Choose one issue that you feel strongly about from your list. Discuss your choice with a classmate and describe your feelings on the issue.

Process

# Prewriting

## Selecting a Topic

Review the meaning of the terms *writing prompt* and *sentence starter*:

- A writing prompt describes a task, whether for an assessment, a writing assignment, or a research project. Students should always read a prompt very carefully to be sure they understand what they are being asked to do.
- A sentence starter is an open-ended sentence that the writer finishes by filling in her or his own idea about a topic.

✱ For more about writing prompts and sentence starters, see SE pages 138 and 238.

## Reflecting on the Topic

Remind students that freewriting is the practice of quickly capturing ideas on paper, without pausing to plan their words. Freewriting on topics might include what students already know about topics, what they've heard others say about them, what they want to find out about them, or just their feelings about them—whether supported by facts or not.

**TEKS** 10.13A

✱ For more about freewriting, see SE page 618.

## Try It!

Remind students to use Nakeisha's sentence starters as examples, but to create their own unique ideas to complete the sentences. Prompt them with questions if they have trouble: *What ideas do people have about how students should dress?* ✔ DIFFERENTIATE INSTRUCTION

**ELPS** 3E, 4C

---

## Differentiated Instruction: English Language Learners

**ELPS** 4C, 4F

| ELP Level **Beginning** | ELP Level **Intermediate** | ELP Level **Advanced/Advanced High** |
|---|---|---|
| Students should copy the entire sentence starter before adding simple, one-word endings, then discuss their endings with a partner to ensure that they are spelled correctly. | Students should develop and complete an additional sentence starter about global controversies. Discuss them with a partner to ensure that they are appropriate. | Have students develop and complete two sentence starters on an additional prompt. Topics could include persuasive essays about political issues, healthy living, etc. |

**TEKS** 10.13A Plan a first draft by determining topics through strategies; **ELPS** 3E Share information in cooperative learning interactions; **4C** Comprehend language structures used in written classroom materials; **4F** Use support from peers and teachers/read grade-appropriate text, enhance and confirm understanding, and develop vocabulary and grasp of language structures

## Prewriting
### Gathering Details

Note that the student writer . . .

■ fills in complete information about her reading sources,

■ uses quotation marks to show that something is a quotation rather than just a general note or paraphrase, and

■ clearly labels each quotation with its source.

Making accurate research notes helps a writer avoid plagiarism and mistakes in the finished essay. It also eliminates the time wasted to track down the complete information needed for a resource later on.

✱ For more about plagiarism, see SE page 389.

### Try It!

Provide students with relevant newspapers and magazines or allow them to use the school's library. Warn students that articles found on the Internet are not always accurate; they should always check the reliability of any source before using it in an essay. **DIFFERENTIATE INSTRUCTION** ↘

## Prewriting  Gathering Details

It's important to gather details that support your position. Nakeisha went to the library to find information about the downtown murals. She looked through newspapers, magazines, and Internet sources.

### Sources of Information

To keep track of her research, Nakeisha recorded complete source information on note cards.

### Sample Source Notes

Stellpflug, Olivia. "Mural Masterpiece." Hawkins City Herald. 3 May 2008: A1

Edmund Burke School. "Community Service Program Overview." Our Programs. Edmund Burke School. n.d. Web. 10 April 2011.

Corporation for National & Community Service. "Benefits of Volunteering". About Us and Our Programs. Corporation for Natl. & Community Service. 8 April 2011. Web. 9 Apr. 2011.

### Quotations

During her research, Nakeisha recorded quotations from interviews. Nakeisha's teacher asked students to use quotations from at least two sources.

### Sample Quotations

Interview with a Hawkins student:
"Even though I was only a freshman, I made many friends as we all worked together."
"I thought, wow, these themes are real!"
"It was fun, not work."
Source: Keri Ellings

Interview with a Hawkins teacher:
"The after-school art club could take on the responsibility of restoring and preserving the downtown murals. The city would not have to pay anything."
Source: Ms. Larson, art teacher

### Try It!

Look for information about the issue you chose. Find one informative newspaper article and list two people that you could interview.

### Differentiated Instruction: Advanced Learners

Challenge students to create a modified outline that lists the points that a city council member might make about the Hawkins High murals. Have students use Nakeisha's outline as a basis to generate opposing arguments.

## Developing a Thesis

Once Nakeisha had enough information, she was ready to write a thesis statement for her essay. In persuasive writing, the thesis statement expresses an opinion. It consists of two parts: a specific topic and a particular feeling or an opinion about it.

**A specific topic** + **a particular feeling** = **an effective opinion statement.**

### Nakeisha's Opinion Statement

> The Hawkins High murals (specific topic) should be saved because they showcase important themes and quality work by students in their own community (particular feeling).

## Organizing the Essay

Next, Nakeisha organized her information (main points and supporting details) in a modified outline.

### Nakeisha's Modified Outline

> Thesis statement: The Hawkins High murals should be saved because they showcase important themes and quality work by students in their own community.
>
> Pride students have about murals
> - Quotation from Corporation for National & Community Service
> - Entire student body involvement (planning, designing, painting)
> - Student interview, Keri Ellings
>
> Sense of importance in community that murals give students
> - Teenagers feeling unheard and unseen
> - Murals as a positive form of expression
> - Destroying murals upsetting to students
>
> Important themes of the murals
> - Unity
> - Diversity
> - Creativity
>
> City's concern about expense of maintaining murals
> - Teacher interview, Ms. Larson
> - Art Club plan

**Process**

### Developing a Thesis

Point out two key words in the formula for writing a thesis statement (specific and particular). Emphasize that students must avoid writing a thesis statement that is vague or too general. Vagueness dilutes the impact of a thesis statement. Students should choose a topic of interest and express a well-reasoned opinion that captures the reader's attention. ✔ **DIFFERENTIATE INSTRUCTION**

⭐ **ELPS** 4C

### Organizing the Essay

Tell students that as they work through the book, they will learn other ways of organizing the details they include in their writing. While an outline is an easy-to-use list, some students may prefer other methods for organizing their ideas. A Quick List (see TE Appendix) is one choice. Another useful graphic organizer for a persuasive essay is the line diagram. Demonstrate on a board how the sample outline could be presented in line-diagram format.

⭐ **ELPS** 1C

✱ For an example of a line diagram, see SE page 625.

---

### Differentiated Instruction: English Language Learners

⭐ **ELPS** 4C, 4E, 4F, 4G, 4I

| ELP Level **Beginning** | ELP Level **Intermediate** | ELP Level **Advanced/Advanced High** |
|---|---|---|
| Provide a prearranged topic and one linguistically accommodated source. Supplement with images where necessary. | Provide a prearranged topic and several linguistically accommodated sources. Students should work through the sources with the help of a partner. | With teacher guidance, students should work with a partner to find and read appropriate sources for a topic of their choice. |

⭐ **ELPS 1C** Use strategic learning techniques to acquire basic and grade-level vocabulary; **4C** Develop basic sight vocabulary/comprehend vocabulary and language structures used in written classroom materials; **4E** Read linguistically accommodated content area material with a decreasing need for linguistic accommodations as more English is learned; **4F** Use visual/contextual support and support from peers/teachers to read grade-appropriate text, enhance understanding, and develop vocabulary, grasp of language structures, and background knowledge; **4G** Demonstrate comprehension of increasingly complex English/participating in shared reading; **4I** Demonstrate comprehension by employing basic reading skills

## Drafting

### Developing Your Ideas

After students have read through the sample draft, review each paragraph and have them identify the topic sentence, body sentences, and closing sentence for each paragraph in the essay. Ask the following questions:

- Is the topic for each paragraph clearly stated?
- Do the body sentences all support the topic?
- Does the closing sentence in each paragraph refer back to the topic, summarize the paragraph, or act as a transition to the paragraph that follows?

Students should, in general, agree that the sample essay is structured effectively, including topic sentences, supporting body sentences, and a closing sentence that summarizes the paragraph or acts as a transition to the next paragraph. **DIFFERENTIATE INSTRUCTION ⬊**

★ **TEKS** 10.13B

✱ For more about the parts of a paragraph, see SE pages 598–599.

---

## Drafting   Developing Your Ideas

Nakeisha referred to her outline as she wrote her first draft. She wanted to get all her ideas on paper. She also wanted to structure her ideas in a persuasive and convincing way so she could sustain her argument throughout the essay.

### Nakeisha's First Draft

> #### Save Our Murals from Sandblasting
>
> Its been nearly three years since students painted the downtown murals. In a suprising move, the city council recently proposed removing the art. The murals have begun to fade and peel The Hawkins High murals should be saved because they showcase important themes and quality work by students in their own community.
>
> The students are proud of the murals. "Pride, satisfaction, and a sense of accomplishment" are valuable benefits of volunteerism, according to the Corporation for National & Community Service. Everybody in the school had a chance to submit possible themes for the murals. Then the art teachers chose twenty of the best ideas for a schoolwide vote. The entire student body voted to choose the themes of unity, diversity and creativity. Three art classes made designs that the school then approved. For an entire month, students volunteered after school to complete the murals. Teachers and parents were impresed by how well students pull together. A student who work on the murals said that she really enjoyed painting.
>
> Allowing the murals to remain would give students a sense of importance in their community. All too often, adults don't realize that teenagers can feel unheard and unseen. If noticed by an adult, some teenagers feel that anything they do or say is negatively viewed. Their music is too loud or their hair is a weird color. The mural project allowed students to express themselves in a positive way. Many schools across the country agree that getting involved gives "student volunteers a sense of community" along with "increased self-esteem and a clearer sense of identity"

Sidebar notes:

- The first paragraph states the issue and ends with the opinion statement.
- Each middle paragraph covers one part of the issue.
- Nakeisha uses a transitional sentence to link the information in this paragraph to her opening paragraph.

---

### Differentiated Instruction: Struggling Learners

Help students find the strong note in Nakeisha's ending paragraph. Point out the word *prove* in the last sentence. Explain that Nakeisha uses it to convince the reader that her arguments are valid and mentions the 500 signatures to support this idea.

---

 **TEKS** 10.13B Structure ideas in a sustained and persuasive way/develop drafts in open-ended situations that include transitions

Process

> **Persuasive essays require evidence.** Nakeisha sustains her argument with quotations that support her position. She provides her source in parentheses.

> **By providing a counter-argument, a type of rhetorical device, and addressing that viewpoint,** Nakeisha sustains her own position and continues to persuade her audience.

> **The ending paragraph sums up the issue** and closes on a strong note.

("Edmund Burke School"). If the city sandblasts the murals, students at Hawkins could think that their voice doesn't matter.

A reason to save the murals is the message each one conveys. Every day thousands of people drive through downtown. Before the murals, commuters and shoppers had nothing to look at but brick walls and billboards. Now people can find inspiration in the themes expressed in the murals. Unified Universe shows teenagers. Divine Diversity presents costumed children. Creative Culture features young people. If the city removes the murals, it's saying that these issues aren't important.

The city says the reason for removing the murals is the estimated expense of maintenance. Art club students have already planned a yearly schedule for fund-raising and maintenance. Since painting will be done after school, any interested students will be encouraged to join in. In response, one of the Hawkins High art teachers, Ms. Larson, said, "The after-school art club will take on the responsibility of restoring and preserving the downtown murals. The city won't have to pay anything." With that kind of support from the school, the city shouldn't remove the one piece of public art created by the students of Hawkins High.

The murals give teenagers a sense of pride and belonging, while also sharing a good message with all who pass. In addition, maintaining the murals wouldn't cost the city a single penny, since students would do all of the work. Last weekend, students took petitions to downtown businesses and residential neighborhoods. The 500 signatures prove that the community has united with students at Hawkins.

## Try It!

Look through Nakeisha's first draft. Then answer these questions: Does Nakeisha's first draft contain all the information that she outlined (page 17)? Does she add any new details? If so, what are they? What else might she have included? Try to name at least one idea.

## Try It!
### Answers

1. Yes
2. New details:
   - Paragraph 1: when the murals were made, their current condition, that the city council proposes to remove them
   - Paragraph 2: how long it took to paint the murals, how students impressed parents and teachers
   - Paragraph 3: ways adults perceive teens negatively, a quotation from the Edmund Burke School
   - Paragraph 4: how the murals have improved the appearance of downtown
   - Paragraph 6: how students have collected signatures on a petition
3. Possible answers:
   - a more specific quotation or response from an involved student—the opinion cited is too general
   - more detailed descriptions of the murals
   - a clearer call to action, telling readers how they can help save the murals

   ✔ **DIFFERENTIATE INSTRUCTION**

TEKS 10.13B

---

## Differentiated Instruction: English Language Learners

ELPS 1C, 4D, 4F, 4K

| ELP Level **Beginning** | ELP Level **Intermediate** | ELP Level **Advanced/Advanced High** |
|---|---|---|
| Review the parts of a paragraph with students. Have students describe these three parts in pictures and/or their first language. | Have students read through the first paragraph of Nakeisha's essay with a partner and write out the three distinct parts of the paragraph in a graphic organizer. | Give students a copy of Nakeisha's essay. With the help of a partner, they should read the essay and highlight the three parts of each paragraph in different colors. |
| | Use pages 624–625 | |

 **TEKS** **10.13B** Structure ideas in a sustained and persuasive way/develop drafts in open-ended situations that include rhetorical devices; **ELPS 1C** Use strategic learning techniques to acquire basic and grade-level vocabulary; **4D** Use prereading supports to enhance comprehension of written text/graphic organizers, illustrations, and topic-related vocabulary; **4F** Use visual/contextual support and support from peers/teachers to develop grasp of language structures; **4K** Demonstrate comprehension and expand reading skills by employing analytical skills/evaluating written information and performing critical analyses

## Revising

### Focusing on Ideas

Point out that instead of jumping right in to rewrite her draft, Nakeisha paused to devise a revising strategy. Remind students of the graphic on SE page 10 showing the recursive nature of the writing process. While creating her strategy, Nakeisha briefly revisits the prewriting stage.

### Try It!
### Answers

**Possible Answers**

- **Organization:** The importance of the murals should be highlighted as the most significant reason for saving them. Also, more transitions could be added and some could be moved in order to increase their effectiveness. For example, the third sentence could be reordered to provide more of a transition: *Recently, in a surprising move, the city council proposed* . . .

- **Development of Ideas:** The description of the mural planning process could be a little less detailed. This would provide room for details about the murals themselves.

- **Voice:** The voice could be strengthened in some places. Occasionally, it sounds uninspired, as in the use of *stated* in the first line of revision text.

⭐ ELPS 3E

---

## Revising  Focusing on Ideas

After Nakeisha completed her first draft, she set aside her essay for a day. Then she rechecked the traits on page **14** and reviewed her first draft. Nakeisha's thoughts below reveal the changes she planned to make.

### Organization

Use an appropriate organizational pattern. Create a beginning that states your opinion, a middle that uses facts and examples to support your opinion, and an ending that calls for action.

> "I need smoother transitions between sentences and paragraphs."

### Development of Ideas

Create a thesis statement and connect all your ideas to it and to each other. Develop your ideas thoroughly, and use specific details.

> "Some of my details don't fit my opinion statement. I need to add more information from the student interview."

### Voice

Use a confident voice that balances facts and feelings and a tone that is appropriate and engaging for your topic and audience.

> "I need an opening that sets the right tone (the need for action) for my essay."

### Try It!

With a classmate, review and discuss the changes in Nakeisha's first revision on page **21**. What other changes in ideas, organization, or voice would you make to Nakeisha's essay? Name two.

---

One Writer's Process **21**

## Nakeisha's First Revision

Here are the revisions that Nakeisha made in the first part of her essay. As you read, think about how well Nakeisha's draft addresses her purpose, her audience, and the genre in which she is writing.

Process

> **Using a quotation strengthens the voice in the opening.**
>
> **A transition helps link two paragraphs.**
>
> **The specific words from a student worker are added.**

"Powerful murals painted by students of Hawkins High School have brought new life to downtown," stated the Hawkins City Herald in a front-page article (Stellpflug A1).

Its been nearly three years since ~~students painted the~~ that article praised the ~~downtown~~ murals. In a suprising move, the city council recently proposed removing the art. The murals have begun to fade and peel The Hawkins High murals should be saved because they showcase important themes and quality work by students in their own community.

First of all,
The students are proud of the murals. "Pride, satisfaction, and a sense of accomplishment" are valuable benefits of volunteerism, according to the Corporation for National & Community Service. Everybody in the school had a chance to submit possible themes for the murals. Then the art teachers chose twenty of the best ideas for a school-wide vote. The entire student body voted to choose the themes of unity, diversity and creativity. Three art classes made designs that the school then approved. For an entire month, students volunteered after school to complete the murals. Teachers and parents were impresed by how well students pull together. Keri Ellings, ~~A student~~ who worked on the murals said ~~that she really enjoyed painting.~~ "Even though I was only a freshman, I made many friends as we all worked together. I thought, wow, these themes are real!"

## Nakeisha's First Revision

Review the editor's marks used on the revision copy with the students. Explain that these symbols can be helpful when there are lots of changes in a text. As the symbols are used by nearly all writers, students should become familiar with them.

After students have read the editorial changes marked on the first revision, have them discuss the side notes to make sure they understand exactly where the changes have been made. Have them connect the notes to the actual changes in the text and discuss how each change improves the essay. ✔DIFFERENTIATE INSTRUCTION

**TEKS** 10.13B, 10.13C

✳ For information about revising and editing a response, see SE page 192.

---

**TEKS** 10.13B Develop drafts in open-ended situations that include transitions; 10.13C Revise drafts to improve style; ELPS 3D Speak using grade-level content area vocabulary/new words and academic language proficiency; 3E Share information in cooperative learning interactions; 3G Express opinions ranging from communicating short phrases to participating in discussions; 3H Explain with increasing specificity and detail; 4A Sound out words using a combination of skills

## Revising
### Using a Peer Response Sheet

Ask students to focus on the way the peer responder worded his questions and comments about the draft. Note that the tone is constructive and polite. He expresses his suggestions in a positive way by asking questions or using phrases that soften the comment. For example, he says *"Could you sound more direct"* instead of *"you weren't direct."* This way, he avoids putting the writer on the defensive and leaves the specific solution to the problem up to the writer.

✳ For more guidance about constructive peer responding, have students look ahead at the information on SE pages 51–53.

### Try It!
### Answers

1. Possible answers:
   - It's most important to provide details about the murals because the descriptions are too general for readers to get a sense of why the art is worth saving.

2. Possible student discussion answers:
   - Consider revising the last sentence of paragraph 4. It could be seen as using false logic: An opponent could say that removing them doesn't mean the city doesn't care about those values, only that it doesn't believe the murals express them effectively.
   - Clarify whether the art club created the plan before or after the city council made its intentions public. Before, it sounded as if the art club plan already existed. Once the Larson quotation is moved, it sounds as if the club acted after hearing the news. DIFFERENTIATE INSTRUCTION ↘

TEKS 10.13C; ELPS 3E

---

TEKS 10.13C
ELPS 3E

## Revising  Using a Peer Response Sheet

Mario evaluated Nakeisha's essay using the holistic scoring guide on pages **60–61**. His suggestions on the response sheet below showed Nakeisha where she could make additional improvements.

### Peer Response Sheet

Writer: <u>Nakeisha Williams</u>    Responder: <u>Mario Rodriguez</u>

Title: <u>Save Our Murals from Sandblasting</u>

What I liked about your writing:
- Your development of each idea helped me understand the issue and your position on it.
- Your writing is authentic. I can tell you care about this issue.
- You used specific details and gave background information.

Changes I would suggest:
- Wouldn't a transition make the beginning of the fourth paragraph stronger?
- Could you provide more details about the murals?
- Could you use Ms. Larson's quotation earlier in the essay?
- Could you sound more direct at the end of the fifth paragraph?

### Try It!

Review Mario's suggestions for improvement. Which suggestion seems to be most important? Explain why. With a classmate, discuss at least one new suggestion to improve Nakeisha's writing. Look at the explanation of organization, ideas, and voice on page **20** to help you make a suggestion.

---

**Nakeisha's Revision Using a Peer Response**

Discuss the side notes and edits, referring back to the peer response sheet. Demonstrate how Nakeisha responded to feedback from a peer.

⭐ TEKS 10.13C

---

⭐ TEKS 10.13C

**Nakeisha's Revision Using a Peer Response**

Using Mario's comments, Nakeisha revised her essay again. The changes she made in two middle paragraphs are shown here.

**A topic sentence is strengthened.** This change improves the style, and the author clearly states her opinion.

**Specific details are added.**

**A quotation is moved for greater impact.** This change also enhances the author's subtlety of meaning.

**Voice is made clearer and stronger.** The reader becomes even more engaged in the argument.

> Perhaps the most important
> ∧ A reason to save the murals is the message each one conveys. Every day thousands of people drive through downtown. Before the murals, commuters and shoppers had nothing to look at but brick walls and billboards. Now people can find inspiration in the themes expressed in the murals. Unified Universe shows teenagers, supporting the earth from around the world Divine Diversity presents artists, musicians, and dancers costumed children. Creative Culture features young people. If the city removes the murals, it's saying that these issues aren't important.
>
> The city says the reason for removing the murals is the estimated expense of maintenance. Art club students have already planned a yearly schedule for fund-raising and maintenance. Since painting will be done after school, any interested students will be encouraged to join in. In response, one of the Hawkins High art teachers, Ms. Larson, said, "The after-school art club will take on the responsibility of restoring and preserving the downtown murals. The city won't have to pay anything." With that kind of support from the school, the city shouldn't remove the has no excuse to remove the one work one piece of public art created by the students of Hawkins High.

---

## Differentiated Instruction: English Language Learners

⭐ ELPS 1C, 1E, 5B, 5F

| ELP Level **Beginning** | ELP Level **Intermediate** | ELP Level **Advanced/Advanced High** |
|---|---|---|
| Using Mario's peer responses, have students create a word web for "Likes" and "Suggestions." They should use single English and/or first language words to complete the web. | Using sentence stems from Mario's Peer Response Sheet, have students write one additional compliment and one additional suggestion. | Have students write one additional compliment and two additional suggestions. Encourage students to experiment with different wording and sentence structures. |

⭐ TEKS **10.13C** Revise drafts/improve style and the subtlety of meaning; ELPS **1C** Use strategic learning techniques to acquire basic and grade-level vocabulary; **1E** Internalize new basic and academic language by using and reusing it/writing; **5B** Write using content-based grade-level vocabulary; **5F** Write using a variety of grade-appropriate sentence lengths and patterns in increasingly accurate ways

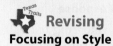

## Revising
### Focusing on Style

Review Nakeisha's thoughts about voice and conventions. Explain to students that developing the ability to look critically at one's own writing will make them better writers.

### Try It!
#### Answers

1. Possible answers:
   - To avoid repeating *article* in the second sentence, perhaps rephrase the sentence: *It's been three years since the students received this praise.*
   - In the second paragraph, try substituting words such as *teens* or *painters* for *students.*
   - The phrase *valuable benefits of volunteerism* is vague. Does *the rewards of volunteering* sound better?
   - To avoid overusing *vote/voted* in paragraph 2, perhaps rephrase the fourth sentence: *The entire student body chose the themes of . . .*

2. Possible answers:
   - Add a transition to the last sentence of paragraph 1 to emphasize the writer's opposition to the city's stance. For example: *Nevertheless, the Hawkins High murals should be . . .*
   - Vary the beginnings and lengths of the body sentences in paragraph 2. Most are declarative statements and are about the same length.

**TEKS** 10.13C; **ELPS** 3E

---

**TEKS** 10.13C
**ELPS** 3E

## Revising Focusing on Style

Nakeisha also reviewed her writing for its voice and sentence structure. Her thoughts below tell you what changes she planned to make.

### Voice

Use a confident voice that balances facts and opinion. Your voice should be appropriate for the topic. Explain important terms that may be unfamiliar to your audience.

> "I should find appropriate replacements for overused words (mural). I also want to add more exciting verbs and modifiers."

### Conventions

Write clear, complete sentences with varied beginnings. Use grammar, capitalization, punctuation, and spelling properly.

> "I should combine some of my short sentences to create a better flow in the text."

### Try It!

With a classmate, review Nakeisha's improved essay on page 25. What other improvements in voice could she make? Name one or two. What other changes in sentence structure could she make? Name one.

---

Process

## Nakeisha's Improvements in Voice

Here are the changes in word choice and sentence structure Nakeisha made in the first part of her essay.

> Sentences are combined to improve sentence structure.

> Changes in word choice improve voice.

"Powerful murals painted by the students of Hawkins High School have brought new life to downtown," ~~stated~~ proclaimed the Hawkins City Herald in a front-page article (Stellpflug A1). Its been nearly three years since that article praised the murals. In a suprising move, the city council recently proposed ~~removing the art~~ which has. The murals have begun to fade and peel The Hawkins High murals should be saved because they showcase important themes and quality work by students in their own community.

First of all, students are proud of ~~the murals~~ their efforts. "Pride, satisfaction, and a sense of accomplishment" are valuable benefits of volunteerism, according to the Corporation for National & Community Service. Everybody in the school had ~~a chance~~ an opportunity to submit possible themes for the murals. before Then the art teachers ~~chose~~ selected twenty of the best ideas for a schoolwide vote. The entire student body voted to choose the themes of unity, diversity and creativity. created lively Three art classes ~~made~~ designs that the school then approved. For an entire month, students volunteered after school to complete the ~~murals~~ work. Teachers and parents were impresed by how well students pull together of all ages and abilities. Keri Ellings, assisted who ~~worked~~ on the murals said, "Even though I was only a freshman, I made many friends as we all worked together. . . ."

---

**Nakeisha's Improvements in Voice**

To remind students of the variety of sentence types and patterns available to a writer, review additional sentence styles and patterns that the writer could have used when making her revisions. Provide examples of each strategy. For example:

- Use phrases and clauses to combine short sentences: . . . *proposed removing the art, <u>which is now fading and peeling.</u>*
- Use short sentences to create drama and emphasis: . . . *proposed removing the art, which has begun to fade and peel. <u>This is the wrong approach.</u> The Hawkins High murals should be saved . . .*
- Use coordinating conjunctions to create compound sentences: *Three art classes created lively designs, and the school approved them.* ✔ DIFFERENTIATE INSTRUCTION

TEKS 10.13C; ELPS 5E, 5F

✱ For more information about sentence style, see SE pages 585–596.

---

TEKS **10.13C** Revise drafts/improve word choice, sentence variety, and the subtlety of meaning; ELPS **2C** Learn new language structures heard during classroom instruction/interactions; **4K** Demonstrate comprehension and expand reading skills by employing analytical skills/evaluating written information and performing critical analyses; **5E** Employ increasingly complex grammatical structures in content area writing such as using correct verbs, tenses, and pronouns/possessive case/negatives and contractions; **5F** Write using a variety of grade-appropriate sentence lengths, patterns, and connecting words/combine in increasingly accurate ways

## Editing

### Checking for Conventions

Remind students that in addition to reading through their own essays, it is always a good idea to have others proofread them. Often an error doesn't stand out to the writer. Encourage students to double-check anything they aren't absolutely sure of—the more vigilant they are, the more problems they will be able to catch.

Challenge students and find all eight convention errors in the selection on SE page 25, not just the four or five asked for in the **Try It!** activity.

Students may have difficulty seeing the change from *twenty* to *20* as a correction. Remind students that the numbers one through ten are spelled out, but numbers above ten are written as numerals.

**TEKS** 10.13D

**Try It!**

See the changes indicated on SE page 27.

**ELPS** 3E, 5D

---

## Editing  Checking for Conventions

Finally, Nakeisha was ready to edit her essay. She checked her work for grammar, punctuation, capitalization, and spelling errors.

### Conventions

Follow rules of grammar, punctuation, capitalization, and spelling.

> "I'll check my essay and correct any errors in grammar, punctuation, capitalization, and spelling."

For help with conventions, Nakeisha used the "Proofreader's Guide" in the back of her *Write Source* textbook and the checklist below.

**GRAMMAR**

_____ 1. Do I use proper tense and voice for my verbs?

_____ 2. Do my subjects and verbs agree in number?

_____ 3. Do my pronouns clearly agree with their antecedents?

**PUNCTUATION**

_____ 4. Do I use punctuation correctly?

_____ 5. Do I use commas correctly?

_____ 6. Do I correctly italicize or use quotation marks for titles?

_____ 7. Do I use apostrophes correctly?

**CAPITALIZATION**

_____ 8. Have I capitalized all the proper nouns and adjectives?

**SPELLING**

_____ 9. Have I spelled words correctly?

_____ 10. Have I used the spell-checker on my computer?

_____ 11. Have I double-checked words my spell-checker may have missed?

### Try It!

With a classmate, find four or five errors in Nakeisha's revised draft on page 25. Did you find the same errors as Nakeisha found on page 27?

---

**TEKS** **10.13D** Edit drafts for grammar, mechanics, and spelling; **ELPS** **3E** Share information in cooperative learning interactions; **5D** Edit writing for standard grammar and usage/subject-verb and pronoun agreement and appropriate verb tenses

## Nakeisha's Editing for Conventions

## Nakeisha's Editing for Conventions

Here are Nakeisha's edits in the first part of her essay. See page **641** or the inside back cover of this book for common editing and proofreading marks.

> The title of the newspaper is marked for italics.

> Punctuation, spelling, and number errors are corrected.

> A verb-tense error is corrected.

"Powerful murals painted by the students of Hawkins High School have brought new life to downtown," proclaimed the Hawkins City Herald in a front-page article (Stellpflug A1). It's been nearly three years since that article praised the murals. In a ~~suprising~~ *surprising* move, the city council recently proposed removing the art, which has begun to fade and peel⊙ The Hawkins High murals should be saved because they showcase important themes and quality work by students in their own community.

First of all, the students are proud of their efforts. "Pride, satisfaction, and a sense of accomplishment" are valuable benefits of volunteerism, according to the Corporation for National & Community Service. Everybody in the school had an opportunity to submit possible themes for the murals before the art teachers selected ~~twenty~~ *20* of the best ideas for a schoolwide vote. The entire student body voted to choose the themes of unity, diversity, and creativity. Three art classes created lively designs that the school then approved. For an entire month, students volunteered after school to complete the project. Teachers and parents were ~~impresed~~ *impressed* by how well students of all ages and abilities pull~~ed~~ together. Keri Ellings, who assisted . . .

Process

## Nakeisha's Editing for Conventions

Review verb tense and voice.

- The tense of a verb tells when an action takes place (past, present, or future). The verb may be used alone (simple tenses) or with a form of *to be* or *to have,* indicating completed action (perfect tenses) or ongoing action (continuous tenses).
- The voice tells whether the subject performed the action of the verb (active voice) or had that action performed on it (passive voice). ✔ DIFFERENTIATE INSTRUCTION

Challenge students to find examples of tense and voice in the sample. (The future tense is not represented on the page.)

For example:

- simple present tense: . . . *they* <u>showcase</u> *important themes*. . .
- simple past tense: . . . *that article* <u>praised</u> *the murals*
- active voice: . . .*students* <u>volunteered</u> *after school*. . .
- passive voice: . . .*murals* <u>should be saved</u>. . .

✱ For more about verb tenses and voice, see SE pages 746–750.

---

 **TEKS** **10.13D** Edit drafts for grammar, mechanics, and spelling; **ELPS** **1E** Internalize new basic language by using and reusing it/writing; **4C** Comprehend language structures used in written classroom materials; **5B** Write using newly acquired basic vocabulary

## Publishing
### Sharing Your Writing

Note that in addition to her own name, the student wrote the teacher's name, the class, and the date on her final draft. This not only helps the teacher keep papers from different classes organized, but it also is useful for the writer after she has added her essay to a portfolio.

Discuss with students the benefits and drawbacks of handwritten versus computer copies. Let them know whether you have a specific preference, but keep in mind that students might need additional time to complete assignments if they have limited access to computers.

**TEKS** 10.13E

## Publishing   Sharing Your Writing

Nakeisha used the information below to produce a clean final draft of her essay.

### Tips for Handwritten Copies

- Use blue or black ink and write clearly.
- Write your name according to your teacher's instructions.
- Skip a line and center your title on the first page; skip another line and begin your essay.
- Indent each paragraph and leave a one-inch margin on all four sides.
- Place your last name and the page number on each page after the first.

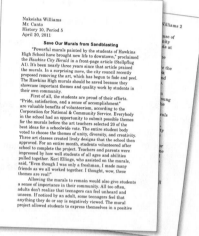

### Tips for Computer Copies

- Use an easy-to-read font set at 12-point type size.
- Double-space the text and set your margins so that you have a one-inch space around the outside of each page.

★ TEKS 10.13E

## Nakeisha's Final Draft

Nakeisha proudly presented a printed draft of her essay to Mr. Canto and volunteered to share her writing about the downtown murals with the class.

Process

Nakeisha Williams
Mr. Canto
History 10, Period 5
April 20, 2011

### Save Our Murals from Sandblasting

"Powerful murals painted by the students of Hawkins High School have brought new life to downtown," proclaimed the *Hawkins City Herald* in a front-page article (Stellpflug A1). It's been nearly three years since that article praised the murals. In a surprising move, the city council recently proposed removing the art, which has begun to fade and peel. The Hawkins High murals should be saved because they showcase important themes and quality work by students in their own community.

First of all, the students are proud of their efforts. "Pride, satisfaction, and a sense of accomplishment" are valuable benefits of volunteerism, according to the Corporation for National & Community Service. Everybody in the school had an opportunity to submit possible themes for the murals before the art teachers selected twenty of the best ideas for a schoolwide vote. The entire student body voted to choose the themes of unity, diversity, and creativity. Three art classes created lively designs that the school then approved. For an entire month, students volunteered after school to complete the project. Teachers and parents were impressed by how well students of all ages and abilities pulled together. Keri Ellings, who assisted on the murals, said, "Even though I was only a freshman, I made many friends as we all worked together. I thought, wow, these themes are real!"

Allowing the murals to remain would also give students a sense of importance in their community. All too often, adults don't realize that teenagers can feel unheard and unseen. If noticed by an adult, some teenagers feel that anything they do or say is negatively viewed. The mural project allowed students to express themselves in a positive way. Many schools across the country agree that getting

---

## Nakeisha's Final Draft

After students finish reading, discuss the fact that the writer presented the details in the order that best supports her opinion:

- She gives three reasons for her opinion in reverse order of importance, building up to the most important one.
- She addresses an opposing opinion—maintaining the murals is too expensive—and counters it with information that decisively solves the problem.

Point out that this structure is a good way to help convince people to support your point of view. Nakeisha started by presenting good reasons, and saved the best for last. This strategy leads the audience to respond to the writer's call for action.

★ TEKS 10.13E

✳ For more about the order of reasons in persuasive writing, see SE page 208.

Look back at Nakeisha's first draft on SE pages 18–19. Discuss with students the benefits of the five steps in the writing process and how each one helped lead to the final, polished essay. Ask students: *What are the most significant improvements between the first and final drafts? Could Nakeisha have improved her essay further?* ⟋ DIFFERENTIATE INSTRUCTION

---

## Differentiated Instruction:
## English Language Learners

★ ELPS 2D, 2G

| ELP Level **Beginning** | ELP Level **Intermediate** | ELP Level **Advanced/Advanced High** |
|---|---|---|
| Select simple sentences from Nakeisha's final draft (e.g., 2nd sentence). Read aloud and discuss meaning with students. Monitor understanding and provide clarification. | Select sentences of varying difficulty from the final draft. Preteach difficult vocabulary and then read aloud. Discuss meaning, monitor understanding, and provide clarification. | Have students take turns reading selections from the final draft aloud. While listening, students note unfamiliar words or concepts. Discuss these and provide clarification. |

★ TEKS **10.13E** Revise the final draft in response to feedback from teacher; ELPS **2D** Monitor understanding of spoken language during classroom instruction/interactions and seek clarification as needed; **2G** Understand the general meaning, main points, and important details of spoken language/topics, languages, and contexts are familiar to unfamiliar

Have students look back at the sample first draft on SE pages 18–19 and compare it with the completed essay to assess how the student writer revised her draft during the writing process. Note that she kept fairly close to her original outline as she revised. Although she did not add new paragraphs, reorder the original paragraphs, or substantially change any of the topic sentences, she did alter text. Discuss how being willing to make larger kinds of changes is not uncommon during the revision process. Remind students that revising is their opportunity to add, subtract, and move text around to improve their writing.

⭐ **TEKS** 10.13E

Williams 2

involved gives "student volunteers a sense of community" along with "increased self-esteem and a clearer sense of identity" ("Edmund Burke School"). If the city sandblasts the murals, students at Hawkins could think that their voice doesn't matter.

Perhaps the most important reason to save the murals is the message each one conveys. Every day thousands of people drive through downtown. Before the murals, commuters and shoppers had nothing to look at but brick walls and billboards. Now people can find inspiration in the themes expressed in the paintings. *Unified Universe* shows teenagers supporting the earth. *Divine Diversity* presents costumed children from around the world. *Creative Culture* features young artists, musicians, and dancers. If the city removes the murals, it's saying that these issues aren't important.

The city says the reason for removing the murals is the estimated expense of maintenance. In response, one of the Hawkins High art teachers, Ms. Larson, said, "The after-school art club will take on the responsibility of restoring and preserving the downtown murals. The city won't have to pay anything." Art club students have already planned a yearly schedule for fund-raising and maintenance. Since painting will be done after school, any interested students will be encouraged to join in. With that kind of support from the school, the city has no excuse to remove the one work of public art created by the students of Hawkins High.

The murals give teenagers a sense of pride and belonging, while also sharing a powerful message with all who pass. In addition, maintaining the murals wouldn't cost the city a single penny, since students would do all the work. Last weekend, students took petitions to downtown businesses and residential neighborhoods. The 500 signatures prove that the community has united with students at Hawkins to voice their opinion loud and clear: "Save the murals!" Because the experience of the students working together on the original mural project was so positive, maybe Hawkins High should replace one of the three murals every four years so that more students have a chance to create a mural sometime during their high school years.

Process

# Assessing the Final Draft

The teacher used a scoring guide like the one found on pages **60–61** to assess Nakeisha's final draft. Based on this guide a **4** is the very best score that a writer can receive. Nakeisha's teacher included comments under each trait.

---

### Score = 4

○ **Focus and Coherence**
The composition is focused on the topic, and you clearly state your opinion in your thesis statement. Your writing contains specific ideas and details that support your thesis.

**Organization**
Your ideas are organized in a fairly logical pattern and are mostly effective. You state your position, offer good support for it, and you make a call for support in the ending.

○ **Development of Ideas**
Your ideas are fully developed, and you have included strong supporting details. Your ideas are connected to each other and to the main idea.

**Voice**
You obviously care about this issue. Your voice conveys a sense of concern that fits the topic and the audience.

**Conventions**
Word choice could be stronger. You could use a wider variety of sentences. The writing could flow more smoothly from one idea to another. Your writing follows the rules of grammar, punctuation, capitalization, and spelling.

---

**❓ Review the assessment.** Do you agree with the holistic score and the comments made by Nakeisha's teacher? Why or why not? In a brief paragraph, discuss your reaction to Nakeisha's essay and how you would assess it.

---

## Assessing the Final Draft

Have students review the holistic scoring guide on SE pages 60–61 before reading the teacher's score and comments for the essay. Encourage them to look back at Nakeisha's final draft to refresh their memory if necessary.

**❓ Review the assessment.** Discuss students' assessments before they write their paragraphs. The paragraph should include an explanation for their own score as well as why they did or did not agree with the teacher's score. Encourage students to use specific examples from the text of Nakeisha's essay. ✔ DIFFERENTIATE INSTRUCTION

★ ELPS 3G, 4K

---

**Differentiated Instruction:**
**English Language Learners**

★ ELPS **1A, 5G**

| ELP Level **Beginning** | ELP Level **Intermediate** | ELP Level **Advanced/Advanced High** |
|---|---|---|
| Explain the scoring guide in terms of something more familiar (5-star movie ratings or Olympic diving scores). Students then explain the score of 4 using their first language. | Students choose one trait from the scoring guide and describe it in their own words for each possible score. They should write their description with the help of a partner. | Students should complete the "review the assessment" paragraph with a partner. Teacher should model and prompt appropriate sentence structures as necessary. |

★ **ELPS 1A** Use prior knowledge and experience to understand meanings; **3G** Express opinions ranging from communicating short phrases to participating in discussions; **4K** Demonstrate comprehension and expand reading skills by employing analytical skills/ evaluating written information and performing critical analyses; **5G** Explain with increasing specificity and detail/writing

## Reflecting on Your Writing

Emphasize that taking time to reflect helps students to plan for future writing. Writing a reflection also helps them analyze their experience. Rereading their reflections reminds them of what they learned and how they might improve.

Discuss the benefits of each item on the reflection sheet. For example:

**Item 1:** Reminds the writer of a successful part of the essay so that he or she can refer to it as a model for future work.

**Item 2:** Alerts the writer to take extra care with a particular facet of writing the next time.

**Item 3:** Reminds the writer to use a strategy again in the future.

**Item 4:** Provides a sense of what parts of the process require more time so that students can schedule accordingly.

**Item 5:** Helps in choosing a future persuasive essay topic.

**Item 6:** Gives students something to investigate next time.

⭐ **ELPS** 4K

⭐ **ELPS** **3A** Practice producing sounds of newly acquired vocabulary; **3D** Speak using grade-level content area vocabulary/new words and academic language proficiency; **3F** Give information/ranging from using a limited high-frequency vocabulary to using abstract and content-based vocabulary during speaking; **4K** Demonstrate comprehension and expand reading skills by employing analytical skills/evaluating written information and performing critical analyses

# Reflecting on Your Writing

After completing her essay, Nakeisha filled out a reflection sheet. This helped her think about the assignment and plan for future writing.

Nakeisha Williams
Mr. Canto
History 10, Period 5
April 20, 2011

Persuasive Essay: Save Our Murals from Sandblasting

1. The best part of my essay is . . .
   my introduction. It uses a powerful quotation to support a solid opinion statement.

2. The part that still needs work is . . .
   my word choice. I should avoid overusing certain words.

3. The most important part of my prewriting and planning was . . .
   exploring the history of the murals and interviewing people who were involved in creating them. That gave me the details I needed to support my position.

4. During revising, I spent a lot of time . . .
   developing better transitions between sentences and between paragraphs.

5. The thing I've learned about this type of essay is . . .
   that it's very important to choose a topic that I care about. If I don't care, it will be difficult to convince others to support my opinion.

6. Here is one question I still have about direct quotations . . .
   How do I handle them if the person I'm quoting wants to remain anonymous?

## Differentiated Instruction: English Language Learners

⭐ **ELPS** 3A, 3D, 3F

| ELP Level **Beginning** | ELP Level **Intermediate** | ELP Level **Advanced/Advanced High** |
|---|---|---|
| Have students say the five traits aloud to a partner. Repeat until they can pronounce the vocabulary consistently and confidently. | Remind students about the basic meanings of the five traits as covered earlier. Prompt students to complete definition stems aloud: *A writing's voice describes. . .* | Have students review the traits and then give a definition of each aloud and in their own words. Students may want to write down their definitions before speaking. |

**33**

# Understanding the Traits of Writing

An effective piece of writing is like a good stew. Many ingredients combine to create something nourishing and tasty. The ingredients in a piece of writing are known as **traits**, and they include *focus and coherence, organization, development of ideas, voice,* and *conventions.* Only with a proper balance or combination of these traits will you create a piece of writing worth sharing.

The next page in this chapter introduces you to the traits of writing. The pages that follow give writing samples that show the traits in action. Learning about the traits of writing—and putting them into practice— will help you write better in all your classes, whether you are writing a personal narrative, a book review, or a persuasive essay. Think of this chapter as your guide to good writing.

- ■ **Introducing the Traits**
- ■ **The Traits in Action**
- ■ **Understanding the Traits**
- ■ **Guide for Effective Writing**

"When I write . . . it's like driving a team of horses and giving them the lead but not letting them run away in a totally different direction."
—Monica Hughes

## Resources

**Copy Masters (see Appendix)**

- Venn Diagram
- Details Chart

# Understanding the Traits of Writing

### Objectives
- understand each of the five traits of effective writing
- learn about specific concepts related to the traits
- practice the concepts in short writing exercises

Encourage students to begin actively applying the knowledge they gain from the following pages to whatever they read, either for pleasure or for school. As they do this, they'll see that every piece of writing can be assessed by identifying these traits. The more students explore how different writers address these traits, the more likely they will be to connect the traits to their own work. ◢ DIFFERENTIATE INSTRUCTION
★ ELPS 4K

 **ELPS 4K** Demonstrate comprehension and expand reading skills by employing analytical skills/evaluating written information and performing critical analyses

**Introducing the Texas Traits**

Ask students to share passages that provide good illustrations of at least one of the first four traits. The passages may come from any source and should be fairly short—two paragraphs at most. The selections can be fiction or nonfiction, and students might find them anywhere—for example, in

- books they are currently reading,
- newspapers or magazines,
- assigned school readings,
- letters, or
- advertisements.

After each student reads and identifies the trait in her or his passage, invite others to comment. If possible, make sure that the class examples cover the first four traits. **DIFFERENTIATE INSTRUCTION ↘**

**FYI**

Discuss with students anything that might negatively affect the presentation of a piece they turn in for class. Examples might be messy handwriting (for a handwritten final draft), paragraphs that are hard to distinguish because they lack indentation, or a font size that is too small to read comfortably (for a final draft prepared using a computer).

---

# Introducing the Texas Traits

The following chart identifies the important traits of effective writing. Write with these traits in mind, and you will be pleased with the results.

---

**Traits of Writing**

- **Focus and Coherence**

  Strong writing presents a clear focus. It contains specific, connected ideas that support the thesis, and it does not contain unrelated information. Each paragraph adds depth to the writing.

- **Organization**

  Effective writing creates a meaningful whole—with interesting and distinct beginning, middle, and ending parts. The supporting details are arranged in the best order for the topic and audience. The writing flows smoothly from sentence to sentence and paragraph to paragraph.

- **Development of Ideas**

  Good writing contains thoroughly developed ideas that are clearly supported with appropriate details. This type of development helps the reader appreciate and understand the writer's message.

- **Voice**

  Writing that has voice reflects the writer's personality. It is engaging and appropriate for the topic and audience and contains strong words, including specific nouns, verbs, and modifiers.

- **Conventions**

  Strong writing follows the rules for grammar, sentence structure, capitalization, punctuation, and spelling. It is carefully edited to be free of errors.

---

**FYI**

Also consider *presentation*. An effective final copy follows the accepted guidelines for margins, indenting, spacing, and so on. The writing's appearance affects the reader's overall impression. (See pages 72–74.)

## The Texas Traits in Action

The following excerpt from an essay by Kendall McGinn displays an effective use of the traits of writing.

Process

---

### Buffalo Nation

Before the Europeans came to North America, the native people of the plains and the buffalo were one *Pte Oyate,* or Buffalo Nation. The big bull *tatanka* was life itself. The Native Americans followed the herds and used the buffalo for food, clothing, shelter, and medicine. A Lakota leader summed up this unity between human and animal: "When the Creator made the buffalo, he put power in them. When you eat the meat, that power goes into you, heals the body and spirit" (qtd. in Hodgson 69).

During the expansion of the United States, however, Europeans nearly eliminated the North American buffalo through a senseless slaughter of the animal. The population of 100 million buffalo in 1700 had, in fact, been reduced to 1,000 by 1889. But surprisingly, the buffalo has made a comeback (Allen 100).

In recent years, the number of buffalo has increased to nearly 400,000. Cable Network News owner Ted Turner raises almost 10,000 buffalo on his Montana and New Mexico ranches. "I guess I've gone buffalo batty," Turner says. He supports the raising of buffalo as an excellent source of low-fat meat (Hodgson 75).

Buffalo ranchers are learning that raising buffalo is more cost-effective and more environmentally safe than raising cattle. Here are four reasons why:

- Buffalo don't overeat.
- Their sharp hooves loosen hard soil.
- Buffalo improve grass crops.
- They adapt to any climate.

Buffalo living in Florida seem just as happy as those living in Alaska. In Hawaii, they even survived a hurricane. Hawaiian rancher Bill Mowry recalls how the buffalo "loved every minute of it" (qtd. in Allen 105).

*Side notes:*

The thesis for the essay is clearly stated. The writing focuses on the topic.

The passage is arranged chronologically.

Ideas are well developed, and the included details support the thesis.

The writer sounds interested in the topic.

Varied sentences and word choice add interest. Writing conventions are followed.

---

### The Texas Traits in Action

Have students read the essay silently, looking for examples that illustrate the side notes. Then, have students discuss as a class, or in small groups, what they found. For example, for supporting details, they may mention . . . *the big bull* tatanka *was life itself.* . . and . . . *raising buffalo is more cost-effective and more environmentally safe than raising cattle.*

⭐ ELPS 4H

---

## Differentiated Instruction: English Language Learners

⭐ ELPS 1A, 4C, 4E, 4F, 4G

| ELP Level **Beginning** | ELP Level **Intermediate** | ELP Level **Advanced/Advanced High** |
|---|---|---|
| Explain the word *trait* in terms of the traits of a friend (honest, kind, etc.). Choose one writing trait and discuss why it is an important quality of good writing. | Prepare a linguistically adapted news article that demonstrates one or more of the writing traits and is supplemented by pictures. Students read the passage and identify the traits. | Preselect an article that demonstrates all five writing traits. Have students work with a partner to read and identify the traits. Students may point out traits that could be improved. |

⭐ **ELPS 1A** Use prior knowledge and experience to understand meanings; **4C** Comprehend vocabulary used in written classroom materials; **4E** Read linguistically accommodated content area material with a decreasing need for linguistic accommodations as more English is learned; **4F** Use visual/contextual support and support from peers/teachers to read grade-appropriate text, enhance/confirm understanding, and develop grasp of language structures; **4G** Demonstrate comprehension of increasingly complex English/participating in shared reading; **4H** Read silently with increasing ease and comprehension for longer periods

## Understanding Focus and Coherence

Explain that focus and coherence begin with a strong thesis. Everything in the essay should clearly connect to that thesis.

### Establishing Focus and Coherence

When students have problems establishing a focus for a topic, suggest that they ask themselves questions such as:

- Why do I want to write about this topic?
- What is the most important or interesting thing about my topic?

The answers they provide may lead them to their focus for the piece.

 **Respond to the reading.** The paragraph focuses on Robinson's athletic ability. Details include: ran tremendously fast, stole 29 bases his first year, stole home 19 times in his career, played three different infield positions, batted .311, was named Rookie of the Year in 1947, won MVP in 1949, helped his team win the pennant in both seasons.

⭐ **ELPS** 3E, 4G

---

# Understanding Focus and Coherence

Strong writing engages the reader and sustains that feeling of engagement by remaining focused on key ideas and making sense throughout. A good thesis hooks the reader. Details (*facts, examples, quotations,* etc.) support the thesis and help create a sense of completeness and coherence.

## Establishing Focus and Coherence

Your writing would go on and on if you tried to say everything about a topic. That is why it is important to establish focus and coherence in your writing. Your focus may be based on your main feelings about a topic or on a special part you wish to emphasize. An effective focus gives you a starting point and directs your writing in a coherent manner—that is, in a way that makes sense.

### Sample Paragraph

Carefully read the following paragraph, paying close attention to the topic, the focus, and the specific details.

> **Not to Be Denied**
>
> Jackie Robinson's personal attributes allowed him to break major league baseball's color barrier in 1947. When Brooklyn Dodgers president Branch Rickey brought him up to play for the major league club, Robinson courageously faced racism and verbal abuse. Determined and proud, he had the discipline to play through these challenges. Tremendously fast on the base paths, Robinson stole 29 bases his first year. Over his career, he stole home no fewer than 19 times! His excellent defensive skills made him a stellar infielder, playing three different positions during his career. An intelligent and disciplined hitter, he batted .311 for his career. In 1947 he was named Rookie of the Year, and in 1949 won the Most Valuable Player award. His competitive nature helped his team win the pennant in both seasons. His legacy lives on today, as he is the only player to have his number retired by all major league baseball franchises.

 **Respond to the reading.** What is the focus of the paragraph? What details support this focus? Name two. Discuss your choices with a classmate.

# Supporting the Focus

Writing has **coherence** when all the supporting details in it are related. Below is a list of types of details you can use to support the focus of your writing.

## Types of Details

- **Facts** are details that can be proven.
- **Statistics** present numerical information.
- **Examples** illustrate a main point.
- **Quotations** are direct statements from other people.

## Sample Paragraph

Read the paragraph below and note the types of details that it includes.

---

### Hypersonic Travel

The X-15 rocket plane was the most successful and innovative experimental aircraft ever to take to the skies. A total of three X-15's flew 199 missions between 1959 and 1968. The plane looked futuristic with its black color, long, sleek fuselage, and stubby wings and tail. It didn't take off from the ground. Instead, the X-15 was dropped at high altitude from the wing of a B-52 bomber, gliding until the pilot fired a rocket engine that could be throttled up and down like a jet. This was the first rocket with so much pilot control. Unlike any other aircraft, the X-15 was steered by rockets in the plane's nose! According to an expert at the Smithsonian, the X-15 flew "so high that it functioned more as a spacecraft than an airplane." Over its years of service, the X-15 blew away all existing speed and altitude records and pioneered hypersonic technology that aided NASA's Gemini, Apollo, and space shuttle programs. Now retired, the two surviving X-15's are preserved in museums in Washington, D.C., and Dayton, Ohio.

---

## Try It!

Write a paragraph about a topic of your choice. Do some research and use at least three of the four types of details listed above. Be sure your details support the focus of your paragraph.

Process

---

## Supporting the Focus

Note that statistics are numerical facts. Explain that sometimes the clearest way to present statistics is in charts or tables.

✳ For more about types of details, see SE pages 605–606.

✳ For more about graphic elements, see SE pages 638–639.

### Try It!
#### Answers

Remind students that when they use a quotation, they need to tell their audience who the speaker is. They also need to take care to represent the speaker's words exactly as he or she said them and to enclose the words in quotation marks. Discuss the phrase "putting words in my mouth" and how a writer might abuse a quotation so as to say something that the speaker never intended. ☑ **DIFFERENTIATE INSTRUCTION**

ELPS 2H, 5G

---

## Differentiated Instruction: English Language Learners

ELPS 4F, 4G, 5G

| ELP Level **Beginning** | ELP Level **Intermediate** | ELP Level **Advanced/Advanced High** |
|---|---|---|
| Help students choose a familiar topic. Students then create a word web of supporting details. They can supplement their English with illustrations where necessary. | Have students choose a familiar topic and create a Details Chart using phrases to describe supporting details. At least two types of details should be included. | Students work with a partner to research a topic, taking notes on supporting details. Then they should write a paragraph together, using at least two of the four types of details. |

 **ELPS 2H** Understand implicit ideas in increasingly complex spoken language; **4F** Use support from peers/teachers to read grade-appropriate text, enhance/confirm understanding, and develop background knowledge; **4G** Use support from peers/teachers to read grade-appropriate content area text; **5G** Describe with increasing specificity and detail/writing

## Understanding Organization

Discuss the Donald Murray quote in the SE. Then have students consider organization from the audience's point of view. Take a well-written paragraph and reorder the sentences. Have students work with a partner to reorganize the paragraph so that it flows smoothly from idea to idea.

 **ELPS** 1H

### Connecting the Ending to the Beginning

Explain that while the sample on the page is a single paragraph, the information can also apply to closing longer works of writing, such as essays or research papers.

**Respond to the reading.** The topic is how far a great white shark traveled for several months while scientists tracked it. The closing sentence adds information about the surprising discovery scientists made by conducting the study mentioned in the first sentence.

 **ELPS** 5G

---

# Understanding Organization

Writer Donald Murray says that strong writing stems from "the solid construction of thoughts." A clear plan of organization gives writing unity, which makes it easy to follow from one point to the next. When you're planning the structure of a piece of writing, think in terms of the three main parts—the beginning, the middle, and the ending. There is a logical flow in the writing, and transitions help the reader move from one idea to the next. Each sentence moves the composition forward and helps the reader understand your ideas.

## Connecting the Ending to the Beginning

To close a piece of writing efficiently, remind the reader about the focus, the thesis statement, that was introduced in the beginning. Making this connection brings the writing full circle and helps put everything in perspective.

### Sample Paragraph

Pay close attention to the first and last sentences in this paragraph.

> **Long-Distance Swimmer**
>
> A few years ago, a group of scientists hoped to gain insight into the roaming patterns of sharks. To conduct their study, they attached a satellite tracking device to the tail of Nicole, a female great white shark they had located in the Indian Ocean. The tag started recording data in November 2003. It was set to break off, float to the surface, and transmit its recorded information to a satellite in February 2004. Shark experts expected Nicole to migrate a thousand miles or so up the coast of Africa. When the device broke loose and beamed up its report, the marine biologists couldn't believe what they discovered. Nicole had made her way some 7,000 miles (11,265 kilometers) across the Indian Ocean, all the way to Australia! With the device gone, researchers could no longer track Nicole. However, a zoologist in South Africa had collected photo records of the dorsal fin markings of Nicole and many other sharks. Six months later, the zoologist recognized Nicole off the Cape of Good Hope, right back where she had started. This shark had traveled a total of 14,000 miles (22,531 kilometers)! That a marine animal had such an expansive roaming pattern took the scientists completely by surprise.

 **Respond to the reading.** What is the topic of this paragraph? How does the closing sentence connect with the beginning?

---

 **ELPS** **1H** Develop learning strategies/reasoning, looking for patterns in language, and analyzing sayings and expressions; **5G** Explain with increasing specificity and detail/writing

**ELPS** 1H, 5G

Process

> "If I can write everything out plainly, perhaps I will myself understand better what has happened."
>
> —Sherwood Anderson

## Connecting the Supporting Ideas

Transitions can be used to connect one sentence to another sentence or one paragraph to another paragraph. The type of transitions you use depends on the organization of your writing. Some transitions show time, others compare, still others add information, and so on.

### Sample Paragraph

In the following paragraph the transitions (highlighted) help organize the writing chronologically.

---

**Technical Precision**

Every time a driver turns the ignition key of a car, he or she puts into action an amazing mechanical sequence. First, the starter motor spins the engine's crankshaft. Immediately, valves open in one cylinder, allowing the perfect mixture of gasoline and air to enter the combustion chamber above the piston. Then that piston rises, compressing the combustible mixture. Next, the car's electrical system discharges power to the spark plug at exactly the right time, and the spark triggers a very powerful explosion in the air-fuel combination. The resulting force drives the piston down. Meanwhile, the process of injection and spark is repeated for the next piston in the firing order, and as that one is propelled downward, the reaction brings the first one up. Finally, the rising piston forces the fumes left from the explosion into the exhaust system. All of the pistons quickly undergo this four-step action. The process is repeated over and over, many times per second, and when it works well, the engine runs so smoothly that the driver doesn't even have to think about what is occurring under the hood.

---

**Respond to the reading.** What is the topic of this paragraph? How do the transitions help organize the details?

### Try It!

Write a paragraph that describes a process that you understand well. Use transitions as needed. (See pages **628–629** for a list of transitions.)

## Connecting the Supporting Ideas

Note that although each transition in the sample paragraph consists of only one word, transitions may consist of a phrase or a clause. It is also not necessary for the transitional words to occur at the beginning of a sentence. Challenge students to provide alternative transitions for the paragraph. For example:

■ *To begin, the starter motor spins . . .*
■ *This is the cue for the car's electrical system to* *spring into action. It discharges power to the* *spark plug . . .*
■ *The valves in one section open immediately,* *allowing the perfect . . .*  **DIFFERENTIATE INSTRUCTION**

**Respond to the reading.** The topic is how a car engine works. The transition words clarify the chronological sequence of the actions described.

### Try It!

Encourage students that their process does not need to be as technical as the one given in the text. If they are having trouble thinking of an idea, prompt them with some general processes such as brushing their teeth, getting ready for school in the morning, or watching a parade.

**ELPS** 1H, 5G

---

## Differentiated Instruction: English Language Learners

**ELPS** 1E, 1H, 4C, 5B

| ELP Level **Beginning** | ELP Level **Intermediate** | ELP Level **Advanced/Advanced High** |
|---|---|---|
| Provide short sentences about an event (*Joe threw the ball. Fido chased the ball.*). Have students add transitional words from a word bank and place the sentences in order. | Explain brainstorming. With a partner, have students brainstorm transitional words. They should come up with five or six examples not shown in the text. | Students should imagine a parade. Writing simple sentences, have them describe the event using transitional words and phrases to link the sentences. |

 **ELPS 1E** Internalize new basic language by using and reusing it/writing; **1H** Expand learning strategies/reasoning, looking for patterns in language, and analyzing sayings and expressions; **4C** Develop basic sight vocabulary/comprehend vocabulary in written classroom materials; **5B** Write using newly acquired basic vocabulary; **5G** Explain with increasing specificity and detail/writing

## Understanding Development of Ideas

Compare development of ideas with focus and coherence. Explain that while these two traits are related, focus and coherence centers on the main thrust of the writing and the big ideas that will support it. Development of ideas centers on developing those big ideas with specific details.

### Including Facts

Use the Venn Diagram from the TE Appendix to explain the differences and similarities between what's included in the terms *facts* and *statistics*. Facts are verifiable; they can be proven. Statistics—at least good ones—are also facts, but they are facts that specifically include numerical information. Have students pick out several facts and several statistics from the paragraph on cyclones. A fact might be: *Hurricanes can wipe out whole neighborhoods and level huge trees.* A statistic might be: *The winds surrounding the eye of a hurricane can reach 155 mph.*

⚡ **ELPS** 2C

### Try It!

Remind students that facts are provable. Students can certainly express their opinions in what they write, but they need to include facts as well. Facts are very important to supporting and developing an idea. **DIFFERENTIATE INSTRUCTION** ↘

⚡ **ELPS** 5G

---

⚡ ELPS 5G

# Understanding Development of Ideas

The thesis statement, or controlling idea, for your composition should be clearly stated, and you should approach the topic from your own perspective. Each idea should be thoroughly developed, and you should include specific details to help the reader understand and appreciate your ideas. As you have already read, there are different ways to develop your ideas and there are different types of details. These include facts, statistics, examples, and quotations.

## Including Facts

Verifiable facts will strengthen your composition. They will show the reader you have done your research and understand the topic.

### Sample Paragraph

The writer sounds serious and sincere and wants his audience to act.

> **Categorical Fury**
>
> Tropical cyclones regularly carve destructive paths across our planet. Called hurricanes when they strike the Americas, these massive storms are rated from category one (weakest) to five (strongest) on the Saffir-Simpson Scale. Category-five hurricanes unleash more energy than the combined blast of hundreds of nuclear weapons. The distinctive "eye" of the storm is an area of very low barometric pressure. The winds surrounding this eye can reach speeds greater than 155 mph. Should a category-five hurricane hit land, it can hurl a surge of water 18 to 20 feet high, devastating low-lying areas far inland. Howling winds rip the roofs from buildings, wipe out neighborhoods, and level huge trees. In addition, torrential rains flood vast regions of land. These mighty storms terrify us as few other natural occurrences can.

### Try It!

Write freely for 8 to 10 minutes about something powerful and dramatic that you have witnessed. It could be an accident, a storm, a sporting event, or so on. Afterward, underline the facts that you have used in the development of your ideas.

---

 **ELPS 2C** Learn academic vocabulary heard during classroom instruction/interactions; **5G** Describe with increasing specificity and detail/writing

Understanding the Traits of Writing **41**

Process

## Using Quotations

Using quotations in your writing can help the reader understand the points you are making. They can support your ideas and emphasize your perspective. When you use quotations, you must be careful to cite the source and be accurate with the words.

### Sample Paragraph

In the following paragraph, the quotations emphasize the point the writer is making.

---

**Television and Toddlers**

One of the most serious problems with television is that it slows social and language development in toddlers. Toddlers need to spend more time playing and less time watching. They need to spend time interacting with their parents. The American Academy of Pediatrics has reinforced this idea. The academy has stated, ". . . research on early brain development shows that babies and toddlers have a critical need for direct interactions with parents and other significant caregivers for healthy brain growth and the development of appropriate social, emotional, and cognitive skills." According to a recent survey, most children under the age of 6 spend about two hours a day watching television or videos, and they watch every day (Kaiser Family Foundation). The Parents as Teachers National Center says that young children need to "explore, move, manipulate, smell, touch, and repeat as they learn." Studies have found that toddlers who are watching TV do none of these things. Parents need to be aware of the dangers of too much TV. They need to take action. They need to turn off the television. They need to take time to play with and talk to their children.

---

 **Respond to the reading.** Reread the paragraph. Write the main idea on your own paper, and then copy the quotations. Discuss with a partner the ways in which the quotations help develop the main idea of the paragraph.

### Using Quotations

Explain that writers can add the weight of experts to their arguments by using quotations. Even though the writer might not be a scientist or researcher, by quoting one they bring that person's expertise to bear on their argument.

 **Respond to the reading.** After students have discussed the quotations, bring them back as a class to analyze why the quotes from specific organizations were so important to this paragraph. Would the argument have been as impressive if the writer had quoted parents or teachers instead?

## Understanding Voice

Discuss the John Jakes quote. Ask students why it will be easier to implement the quote if they write about topics that interest or excite them.

### Knowing Your Purpose and Your Audience

Note that the idea of adjusting your voice to suit your purpose and audience is likely to be familiar to students. They probably use a more informal voice when they are with their friends than they use with older individuals in positions of authority. Compare this spoken change of voice to adapting their writing voice to the purpose and audience.

 ELPS 3I

 **Respond to the reading.** Students should generally agree that the voice is appropriate. Students may discuss the fact that the sober, urgent tone matches the importance and serious nature of the paragraph's subject matter.

ELPS 3E

---

 ELPS 3E

# Understanding Voice

Voice is that special quality that makes writing your own. Novelist John Jakes emphasizes the importance of voice when he says, "Be yourself. Above all, let who you are, what you are, what you believe shine through every sentence you write, every piece you finish."

## Knowing Your Purpose and Your Audience

Always know why you are writing—your *purpose*. Are you sharing information, arguing for or against something, or explaining a process? Also consider your reader—your *audience*. How much do they know about your subject? How can you gain and hold their attention? When you understand your purpose and audience, it's much easier to know how you should sound.

- For example, if you're writing a personal narrative, you probably want to sound friendly and personable.
- Or, if you're writing a persuasive letter to your school board, you will want to sound respectful, sincere, and concerned.

### Sample Paragraph

> **Save a Life!**
>
> Last June, while driving her son home from a baseball game, Pam Withers lost control of her car on wet pavement and skidded into a tree. Her son was unhurt, but Mrs. Withers was rushed to the hospital, bleeding from several deep cuts. Her condition was listed as critical as her family gathered at the hospital. Doctors stitched her wounds, and after a number of transfusions, she finally stabilized. The fully recovered Mrs. Withers is my mother. She is very thankful for the many generous blood donors. Without them, my mother may not have lived. Next week, there will be a blood drive at Northside High School. Please make time to stop in the gymnasium between 8:00 a.m. and 3:00 p.m. and give blood. Your donation could help save a life.

**Respond to the reading.** Does the voice seem appropriate for the purpose and intended audience of the writing? Discuss your response with a classmate.

---

### Differentiated Instruction: Advanced Learners

Discuss with students why the title "Fever Pitch" is a play on words. After completing the **Try It!** activity on SE page 43, have students think of a clever title for their freewrite. Have students consider the following literary devices to create their titles:

- oxymoron
- idiom
- metaphor
- irony
- pun

Refer students to the Index to find more information about these devices.

Process

> "You have to write a million words before you find your voice as a writer."
>
> —Henry Miller

## Knowing Your Topic

Your writing voice will hold the reader's attention if you are interested in and knowledgeable about your topic. To sound interested, be sure to choose a topic that you have strong feelings about. To sound knowledgeable, be sure to learn as much as you can about the topic before you start writing.

### Sample Paragraph

In this sample, the writer shares knowledge about a topic that clearly interests her.

---

#### Fever Pitch

Backpacking into a remote area can be both thrilling and rewarding. However, a trip can be marred for a backpacker who ignores certain important considerations. When pitching a tent, always place it in a spot clear of looming rotten limbs or loose rocks that could be knocked down by wind or rain and crush your shelter. In avalanche country, beware of snowfields or cornices on higher terrain and keep your tent out of any prospective slide paths. The ground under the tent should be dry, of course, but it should also be a little higher than the surrounding area. Otherwise, a sudden rainstorm could leave you sleeping in a puddle. Also, be sure that you securely stake out the corners of your tent and attach a good rain fly. Finally, do not camp on or near an animal trail. Hang food from a tree and always keep food out of your tent. With a little attention to these details, you will minimize any potential risks and maximize your enjoyment of the wilderness experience.

---

 **Respond to the reading.** What details reveal the writer's knowledge of the topic? Name three. How does she communicate her interest?

### Try It!

Write freely for 10 minutes about a topic that truly interests you. When you finish, underline at least four or five ideas that demonstrate your interest in and knowledge about the topic.

## Knowing Your Topic

Draw students' attention to the quotation by Henry Miller and discuss the idea that voice develops over time as a writer practices the craft. Invite students to talk about their experiences with other endeavors that involve extended effort. Artists face a similar challenge developing their own style, as do athletes.

 **Respond to the reading.** Knowledgeable details include the following: Place tents away from falling objects and out of the path of avalanches. For protection from rain, pitch a tent on high, dry ground and use the rain fly. Stay away from animal trails and keep food safe by hanging it in a tree.

The writer communicates interest by using specialized language such as *snowfields, cornices, slide paths, rain fly.* She uses positive-sounding words and phrases such as *thrilling, rewarding, maximize your enjoyment.* ✔ DIFFERENTIATE INSTRUCTION

## Try It!

If students are having trouble coming up with a topic, suggest hobbies, sports, movies, or music. Remind students that for a freewrite, they should not be worried about conventions or organization. They are simply putting ideas down on paper. ✔ DIFFERENTIATE INSTRUCTION

---

## Using Metaphors

Discuss with students what is meant by the metaphor in the example. What ideas does the metaphor add that weren't present in the basic idea?

 **ELPS** 4K

### Tip

Explain that it is sometimes hard to know whether a phrase has been overused. Suggest that, as students revise, they remember to watch out for anything that sounds as if they might have heard it used before. If they're not sure, the Internet can help identify clichés. Simply enter *cliché* into a search engine, or type the phrase itself into a search engine and examine the results.

To continue the discussion of extended metaphors, mention a related issue—the "mixed metaphor." Mixed metaphors result from combining different images. The result is often a confusing rather than a clear, evocative image.

**Respond to the reading.** The metaphor is expanded by continuing the imagery of a tapestry throughout the rest of the paragraph. Metaphorical words and phrases include *at loose ends, torn, frayed,* and *mended.*

### Try It!

If students have trouble extending metaphorical language throughout their paragraph, have them complete a Details Chart (see TE Appendix) of images and characteristics that describe their initial metaphor. Encourage them to refer to this list for ideas when writing their paragraph.

**DIFFERENTIATE INSTRUCTION** ⬦

**ELPS** 5G

---

 **ELPS** 5G

> "The best metaphors are spontaneous, arising naturally out of the writer's imagination. Some metaphors, though, have become clichés and lost whatever power they once had."
> —Scott Rice

## Using Metaphors

A metaphor compares an idea or an image in your writing to something new and brings the idea to life for your reader.

- **To Create a Picture** In the example that follows, note how the basic idea becomes a powerful picture when it is stated metaphorically.

   **Basic Idea:** My presentation was a real disappointment.

   **Metaphor:** My presentation was a real choke sandwich, all peanut butter and no jelly.

### Tip

Avoid overused words or phrases and metaphors such as "The sun was a ball of fire." They have become clichés.

- **To Expand an Idea** An extended metaphor can unify ideas in a series of sentences. Note how the metaphor (comparing family relationships to fabric) is extended in the following passage.

   **Metaphor:** My family is a rich tapestry of personalities.

   **Extended:** My family is a rich tapestry of personalities. We were at loose ends last summer, at least until the reunion in August. Whatever feelings had been torn over my brother's divorce and whatever emotions had frayed over my grandmother's illness were mended at the county park.

 **Respond to the reading.** How is the idea of rich tapestry expanded in the example above? Identify specific metaphoric words and phrases used.

### Try It!

Write a basic metaphor about someone or something that you know well. Then try to extend that metaphor in a short passage. Use the examples above as a guide.

---

### Differentiated Instruction: Struggling Learners

Allow students who have difficulty with conventions to focus on one or two from each category, particularly ones they need to practice. If students do not have access to a spell-checker, suggest that they partner with a volunteer who is a proficient speller.

After their partner has read through the paper and identified misspelled words, have students correct the mistakes and add these words to a spelling notebook or card file for future reference.

---

 **ELPS** **4K** Demonstrate comprehension and expand reading skills by employing analytical skills/evaluating written information and performing critical analyses; **5G** Describe with increasing specificity and detail/writing

**TEKS** 10.17A, 10.17C, 10.18A, 10.18B, 10.19
**ELPS** 5C, 5D, 5E

Understanding the Traits of Writing    **45**

Process

# Understanding Conventions

Effective writing is easy to follow because, among other things, it adheres to the conventions of grammar, sentence structure, punctuation, capitalization, and spelling. Writer and editor Patricia O'Conner summarizes the importance of punctuation in this way: "When you write, punctuation marks are the road signs that guide the reader, and you wouldn't be understood without them."

## Knowing the Basic Rules

The English language is always growing; it includes more words than any other "living" language. It stands to reason then that there are a lot of rules for using English. The checklist below can guide you as you check your writing for conventions. Also see the "Proofreader's Guide" (pages **642–787**).

### Conventions

**GRAMMAR**

_____  **1.** Do I use correct forms of verbs (*had eaten*, not *had ate*)?

_____  **2.** Do I use the correct word (*their, there, they're*)?

_____  **3.** Do my subjects and verbs agree in number (*the car races* and *the cars race*)?

**SENTENCE STRUCTURE**

_____  **4.** Do I use a variety of correctly structured sentences?

**MECHANICS (Punctuation and Capitalization)**

_____  **5.** Do I use end punctuation after all my sentences?

_____  **6.** Do I use commas and semicolons correctly?

_____  **7.** Do I use quotation marks and italics correctly?

_____  **8.** Do I use apostrophes to show possession (*that girl's keys* and *those girls' keys*)?

_____  **9.** Do I start each sentence with a capital letter?

_____  **10.** Do I capitalize the proper names of people and places?

_____  **11.** Do I avoid improper capitalization (*my mom*, not *my Mom*)?

**SPELLING**

_____  **12.** Have I checked my spelling using a spell-checker?

_____  **13.** Have I also checked my spelling with a dictionary?

## Understanding Conventions

Use the metaphor of the road signs to help students understand better the importance of conventions. Some students may supply examples in which well-known writers break conventions. Remind students that knowing and applying conventions correctly is a best practice. Good writers might break conventions rules to achieve a specific effect, but they know the rules and the reason for breaking them in a specific instance.

### Knowing the Basic Rules

Review the conventions checklist. Have students check the following pages in the Proofreader's Guide for information on checklist items:

- end punctuation, 643–644
- commas and semicolons, 646–656
- possessives, 664–666
- quotation marks and italics, 668–672
- capitalization, 682–686
- using the right word, 710–728
- nouns, 731–733
- forms of verbs (tense), 746–750
- irregular verbs, 748
- subject-verb agreement, 778–780

Answer students' questions about the basic rules and conventions as needed. Point out that some conventions are easy to master and others require more practice.  **DIFFERENTIATE INSTRUCTION**

**TEKS** 10.17A, 10.17C, 10.18A, 10.18B, 10.19; **ELPS** 5C, 5D, 5E

---

## Differentiated Instruction: English Language Learners

**ELPS** 4C, 4J

| ELP Level **Beginning** | ELP Level **Intermediate** | ELP Level **Advanced/Advanced High** |
|---|---|---|
| Give further explanation for the term "metaphor" with simple examples (e.g., *He was a real mountain.*) Discuss metaphors used in the student's first language. | Give several examples of simple metaphors (e.g., *He was lightning fast.*) and have students explain to each other what image or idea the metaphor is meant to convey. | Students take a cliché (e.g., *soupy fog*) and develop unique metaphors that convey a similar idea. Students can write a paragraph that extends this metaphor. |

**TEKS** **10.17A** Use and understand tenses and verbals; **10.17C** Use a variety of correctly structured sentences; **10.18A** Use conventions of capitalization; **10.18B** Use correct punctuation marks; **10.19** Spell correctly using resources to determine and check correct spelling; **ELPS** **4C** Comprehend vocabulary used in written classroom materials; **4J** Demonstrate comprehension and expand reading skills by employing inferential skills/predicting, making connections between ideas, drawing conclusions from text, and finding supporting evidence; **5C** Spell familiar words with increasing accuracy; **5D** Edit writing for standard grammar and usage/subject-verb agreement and verb tenses; **5E** Employ increasingly complex grammatical structures in content area writing such as using correct verbs, tenses, and pronouns/possessive case/negatives and contractions

## Showing Emphasis

One way students can think about using commas to add emphasis is to regard them as cues to pause slightly while reading for meaning. What follows a comma receives a little extra attention as the reader continues. Invite a volunteer to read the sample paragraph aloud for the class, paying special attention to pausing at the commas. **DIFFERENTIATE INSTRUCTION** ↘

**Respond to the reading.**

The commas

- set off appositives: *Frodo, the reluctant hero; Sam, the best friend ever; masterpiece,* The Lord of the Rings
- separate items in series: *Gandalf, and Aragorn, and Legolas, and Gimli; friendship and courage, betrayal and sacrifice; morality, legacy, and history*
- separate clauses: *I recently finished . . . , and it was the best . . . ; Tolkien's descriptions . . . are stunning, and the way . . .*
- separate a prepositional phrase from the main clause: *history, at a level . . .*

The semicolons join a series of independent clauses: *terror turns to triumph; opportunities . . . disaster; ultimate evil . . . good.*

**TEKS** 10.17A, 10.17C, 10.18A, 10.18B; **ELPS** 4C

## Try It!

If students are struggling with how to use commas correctly, direct them to page 646–654 of the Proofreader's Guide for more information about comma use.

**ELPS** 5C, 5D, 5E

---

**TEKS** 10.17A, 10.17C, 10.18A, 10.18B, 10.19
**ELPS** 5C, 5D, 5E

"Don't take commas for granted. They're like yellow lights. If you ignore one, you could be in for a bumpy ride."
—Patricia T. O'Conner

## Showing Emphasis

Carefully selected punctuation—especially commas, semicolons, and colons—can be used to emphasize certain words or ideas.

### Sample Paragraph

Notice how the commas, semicolons, and a colon are used to add emphasis in the following paragraph.

**High Adventure**

1  Who can forget Frodo, the reluctant hero? What about Sam, the
2  best friend ever? Remember Gandalf, and Aragorn, and Legolas, and
3  Gimli! These are just some of the heroes who make up the wonderful
4  fellowship in J. R. R. Tolkien's masterpiece, *The Lord of the Rings.*
5  For some individuals, the epic trilogy provides the best reading they
6  have ever experienced. The three books tell a magnificent story of
7  friendship and courage, betrayal and sacrifice. Tolkien's descriptions
8  of his imaginary world are stunning, and the way he takes the
9  reader to the very edge of doom before pulling him back embodies
10 the essence of high adventure. The tale includes many instances of
11 heart-pounding excitement: terror turns to triumph; opportunities
12 are born from disaster; ultimate evil threatens everything that is
13 good. But the "Rings" trilogy is so much more than an adventure
14 story. Throughout these fantastic books, Professor Tolkien addresses
15 issues of morality, legacy, and history, at a level of depth and
16 breadth that few storytellers have ever attained.

 **Respond to the reading.** How are commas and semicolons used to emphasize certain ideas in the paragraph? Identify specific examples from the writing.

### Try It!

Write a brief paragraph about a person you admire. Use punctuation to emphasize the traits and qualities this person exhibits.

---

 **TEKS** **10.17A** Use and understand the functions of parts of speech; **10.17C** Use a variety of correctly structured sentences; **10.18A** Use conventions of capitalization; **10.18B** Use correct punctuation marks; **ELPS 4C** Comprehend language structures used in written classroom materials; **5C** Spell familiar words with increasing accuracy; **5D** Edit writing for standard grammar and usage/subject-verb agreement and verb tenses; **5E** Employ increasingly complex grammatical structures in content area writing

**TEKS** 10.17C
**ELPS** 5F, 5G

## Checking for Sentence Variety

Use the following strategy to ensure sentence variety in your writing.

- **Vary sentence beginnings.** In one column on a piece of paper, list the opening words of each sentence in a piece of writing. (Do you need to vary some of your sentence beginnings?)
- **Vary sentence lengths.** In another column, write the number of words in each sentence. (Do you need to change the length of some sentences?)

Process

### Sample Paragraph

Read the following sample paragraph, paying attention to the sentence structure. Note the different ways the writer begins various sentences. Also note how the lengths of the sentences are different.

---

**Rite of Passage**

The vast marsh seethed with movement, as if a living carpet covered the ground. Wings rustling, heads bobbing, and feathers extended, thousands of Canada geese claimed this wetland for the night. With the new day, they will continue on their journey north, a flight repeated year after year after year. As the sun crests the horizon, several geese will honk. Here and there, a few will take to the air, powerful wing strokes thrashing the waters. More geese will join the chorus in a growing crescendo. Suddenly, hundreds of the big birds will take wing pulling the rest of the flock with them, as all the birds explode into the spring sky.

---

 **Respond to the reading.** On a piece of paper, analyze the sample paragraph for sentence variety using the strategy above as a guide.

### Try It!

Write freely for 10 minutes about animals (wild or domestic) in action. Check your sentence variety using the strategy above.

## Checking for Sentence Variety

Students who write using a computer can employ computer tools to help check for variety.

- Have students use the highlighting function to highlight sentence beginnings so they stand out on the page.
- Show students how to determine how many words are in a sentence by selecting the whole sentence with the cursor and using the word count function.

**Respond to the reading.**

| Beginnings | Words |
|---|---|
| *The vast marsh seethed* | 14 |
| *Wings rustling,* | 17 |
| *With the new day,* | 19 |
| *As the sun crests* | 10 |
| *Here and there,* | 16 |
| *More geese will join* | 10 |
| *Suddenly,* | 26 |

There is good variety in the sentence beginnings. There is some variation in lengths, but there could be more.

**Try It!**

Students should monitor their writing to see whether they have too many similar sentence beginnings or sentence lengths. Encourage them to revise their paragraph to add variety as needed. If necessary, prompt them with alternative sentence beginnings and help them combine shorter sentences for variety.

**TEKS** 10.17C; **ELPS** 1B, 5F, 5G

---

### Differentiated Instruction: English Language Learners

**ELPS** 3C

| ELP Level **Beginning** | ELP Level **Intermediate** | ELP Level **Advanced/Advanced High** |
|---|---|---|
| Have students draw the symbols for several punctuation marks (comma, period, etc.). Provide them with a word bank and have them connect the symbols to the proper terms. | Write several simple sentences with commas (*The boy, whose name was Joe, had a dog.*). Have students read these sentences aloud, being sure to pause at each comma. | Have students take turns reading the paragraph aloud, pausing appropriately for the punctuation marks. Discuss the difference between pausing for commas and periods. |

**TEKS** 10.17C Use a variety of correctly structured sentences; **ELPS** 1B Monitor written language and employ self-corrective techniques or other resources; 3C Speak using a variety of grammatical structures and sentence lengths/types with increasing accuracy and ease; 5F Write using a variety of grade-appropriate sentence lengths, patterns, and connecting words/combine in increasingly accurate ways; 5G Describe with increasing specificity and detail/writing

## Guide for Effective Writing

Ask students to use the Guide for Effective Writing to evaluate a piece of writing of their choice—perhaps a brief magazine or newspaper article. Invite several students to share their articles and evaluations with classmates and to discuss strengths and weaknesses they found in the writing.

## Learning Language

Model a description of one of the traits in your own words. Then monitor students' explanations and identify areas of difficulty. Students may refer to the chart for ideas, but they should describe the traits in their own words. Prompt students with questions if they continue to struggle: *What does organization say about starting and ending your writing? Whose personality is reflected by a writing's voice? What part does a thesis play in focus and coherence?* DIFFERENTIATE INSTRUCTION ↘

⭐ **ELPS** 1E, 2C, 2D, 2G, 2H, 2I, 3D, 3E, 3H

🔲 **TEKS** **ELPS** **1B** Monitor oral and written language production and employ self-corrective techniques or other resources; **1E** Internalize new academic language by using and reusing it/speaking; **2C** Learn academic vocabulary heard during classroom instruction/interactions; **2D** Monitor understanding of spoken language during classroom instruction/interactions and seek clarification as needed; **2G** Understand the general meaning of spoken language/topics are familiar to unfamiliar; **2H** Understand information in increasingly complex spoken language; **2I** Demonstrate listening comprehension in increasingly complex spoken language by collaborating with peers; **3D** Speak using grade-level content area vocabulary/academic language proficiency; **3E** Share information in cooperative learning interactions; **3H** Describe with increasing specificity and detail

⭐ **ELPS** 1E, 2C, 2D, 2G, 2H, 2I, 3D, 3E, 3H

### Guide for Effective Writing

If a piece of writing meets the following standards, it exhibits the traits of effective writing. Check your work using these standards.

■ **Focus and Coherence**

*The writing . . .*

_____ maintains a clear, specific focus or purpose. The thesis, or controlling idea, is clearly stated.

_____ presents interesting details that support the focus.

■ **Organization**

_____ includes a clear beginning, middle, and ending.

_____ arranges the details in the best order for the topic.

_____ flows smoothly from sentence to sentence and paragraph to paragraph, and includes transitions to connect ideas.

■ **Development of Ideas**

_____ develops each idea thoroughly, and leaves out no important information.

_____ supports each idea with appropriate details.

■ **Voice**

_____ reflects the writer's personality.

_____ engages the audience effectively.

_____ contains strong words, including specific nouns, verbs, and modifiers.

■ **Conventions**

_____ adheres to the rules of grammar, punctuation, capitalization, and spelling.

_____ follows established guidelines for presentation.

### Learning Language

Take turns with a classmate describing each of the traits of effective writing. When you are listening, ask your partner to clarify any part of the description you don't understand.

### Differentiated Instruction: English Language Learners

⭐ **ELPS** 1B, 2D, 4C, 4J, 5G

| ELP Level **Beginning** | ELP Level **Intermediate** | ELP Level **Advanced/Advanced High** |
|---|---|---|
| Write simple phrase definitions or descriptions for each of the five traits (*beginning, middle, end* or *writer's personality*). Have students match the phrases to the terms. | Have students write simple definitions or descriptions for each of the five traits. They should read these to classmates and ensure that they have been clear. | On a separate sheet of paper, mix up the descriptions of each trait given on SE page 48. Have students match each description with its appropriate trait. Discuss any errors and clarify. |

# Peer Response

Once you've written and revised a paper, you may be quite pleased with the result. You probably made some improvements and even found and corrected a number of mistakes. However, you still may wonder how to make your writing even better. What else can you do?

One of the best things you can do is ask someone else for an opinion. Having one or more classmates read and react to your work is called *peer response*. Often, another person will notice details that you missed. A new point of view can improve your whole approach to a description, an explanation, or an argument.

Peer response works best as a shared project. You read other students' papers, and they read yours. At first, you may find it difficult to offer and receive constructive criticism. Once you try this approach, however, you'll discover the benefit it holds for you as a writer.

- ■ **Peer-Response Guidelines**
- ■ **Using the Texas Traits to Respond**
- ■ **Sample Peer Response Sheet**

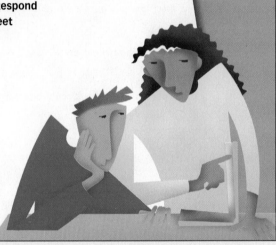

"The best advice on writing I've ever received was, 'Rewrite it.' A lot of editors said that. They were all right."
—Robert Lipsyte

## Peer Response

### Objectives
- understand the roles of the author and of the responder in peer response
- learn how to give helpful responses using the traits
- practice using a peer response sheet

Ask students to focus on the last two sentences on the page, which acknowledge that peer response may be difficult at first. Emphasize that it takes time to
- ■ look for traits in writing,
- ■ figure out how to phrase response questions and comments effectively, and
- ■ gain confidence in sharing work with peers.

Also explain that, ideally, students will work with the same classmates over a period of time, learning one another's strengths and weaknesses and how to be helpful reviewers in the process.

Urge students not to be discouraged if they don't feel comfortable with peer response right away. Once learned, the skill is invaluable—and will improve their overall writing abilities.

**TEKS** **ELPS** **4C** Comprehend vocabulary used in written classroom materials; **4J** Demonstrate comprehension and expand reading skills by employing inferential skills/predicting, making connections between ideas, drawing conclusions from text, and finding supporting evidence; **5G** Describe with increasing specificity and detail/writing

## Peer-Response Guidelines

### The Author's Role

Ask students to note the order of the bulleted items on the page. They are presented in the order in which they should be addressed during small group or one-on-one sessions.

Explain that writers should keep their introduction brief and not use it to explain problems they may be encountering with the writing. A responder's comments may address the very problems the writer is struggling with, or responders may identify different issues that, when resolved, eliminate the writer's original concerns.

 **TEKS** 10.13E

### Asking for Constructive Criticism

Emphasize that students are seeking *constructive* criticism. No one likes to be criticized, but everyone wants to improve their writing. Sometimes its hard to hear about things in your writing that don't work well, but everyone's goal—both responder and writer—is to make the writing better. When students ask for constructive criticism, they are really just asking for advice on how they can improve their work. **DIFFERENTIATE INSTRUCTION ↘**

**ELPS** 3E, 3F, 4G

---

 **TEKS** 10.13E
**ELPS** 3E, 3F, 4G

## Peer-Response Guidelines

Use the following guidelines to help you conduct an effective response session. Start by working with one other person or in a small group.

### The Author's Role

Bring a meaningful piece of writing to the session and provide one copy for each responder. Keep an open mind and consider all comments. Follow this procedure:

- **Introduce your writing.** Briefly explain the goal of your writing. Tell the group if you have already done some revising and editing.
- **Read your writing aloud.** Alternately, you can ask each group member to read the piece silently.
- **Ask for comments.** Listen to the responses. You don't have to make every suggested change, but keep an open mind.
- **Take notes.** Write comments on your copy where the changes need to be made.
- **Ask for help.** If you are having trouble with a specific part of the writing, ask for suggestions, ideas, and advice from your peers.

#### Asking for Constructive Criticism

Here are some questions that can produce useful information and create a cooperative relationship between you and the responders. The answers to "Why?" and "How?" give you specific ways to improve your writing.

**First ask . . .**

What do you like about my writing? Why?

**Then ask . . .**

What parts do you think could be improved? How?

---

### Differentiated Instruction: Advanced Learners

Invite students to write a public service announcement about the importance of a peer responder. Have students review the tips and choose those they feel are the most important. Have them write their own tips and include them in the PSA as well. Have students share their announcements with the class.

---

Process

## The Responder's Role

Respond honestly, but be careful of the author's feelings. Be sure that your comments are constructive, not destructive. Follow these tips.

- **Listen (or read) carefully.** Peer response only works if you pay attention to the writing and monitor your own understanding of the writer's words and ideas.
- **Take notes.** Write comments directly on your copy of the writing to show the author exactly where revisions are needed.
- **Start with positive feedback.** Find something good in the writing and make specific comments about what you liked.
- **Ask questions.** Don't hesitate to ask the author about parts that need clarification. Be specific and polite.
- **Avoid "piling on."** Allow one responder to finish before commenting.
- **Make suggestions.** When you point out a problem, try to include a possible solution. (See the chart below.)

| Giving Constructive Criticism | |
|---|---|
| **Don't give commands . . .** "You should make the beginning grab my attention." | **Do give suggestions . . .** "Wouldn't the beginning be stronger with a different hook?" |
| **Don't focus on the writer . . .** "You don't follow any logical order." | **Do focus on the writing . . .** "Is the order of your ideas clear?" |
| **Don't focus on the problem . . .** "There aren't enough details to make your main point." | **Do focus on the solution . . .** "More details would help me understand your main point." |
| **Don't give general comments . . .** "I thought it was boring." | **Do give specific advice . . .** "Could you use a personal story to support your main point?" |

### Try It!

Rewrite the unhelpful comments below to make them more constructive.

1. You don't sound like you really believe in your opinion.
2. Your closing sentence doesn't work.
3. I don't understand your solution.

## The Responder's Role

Some students may have experienced the kinds of negative criticism shown in the "Don't" examples. Point out that practicing polite, constructive communication can help them in many life situations, not only in responding to writing. Challenge students to try these methods wherever possible. Invite them to talk about what happened when they concentrated on giving constructive criticism.

### Giving Constructive Criticism

Ask the class why they would prefer to receive responses from the right column rather than the left column. Encourage them to provide the same types of constructive criticism to others as they would prefer to receive themselves. Have students include the Dos and Don'ts list in their notes to reference as they are providing feedback on future writing assignments. ✔ **DIFFERENTIATE INSTRUCTION**

ELPS 2D, 2G, 2H, 2I

### Try It!
#### Answers

#### Possible Answers

1. Consider revising so that your voice sounds confident and expresses your opinion more strongly.
2. Have you thought about tying your ending to your introduction to help the reader see the connection?
3. Adding more explanatory details or statistics might make your solution easier to understand.

ELPS 5G

---

**TEKS** ELPS **2D** Monitor understanding of spoken language during classroom instruction/interactions and seek clarification of spoken language as needed; **2G** Understand the general meaning of spoken language/topics and languages are familiar to unfamiliar; **2H** Understand implicit ideas and information in increasingly complex spoken language; **2I** Demonstrate listening comprehension in increasingly complex spoken language by collaborating with peers and taking notes; **5G** Explain with increasing specificity and detail/writing

## Using the Texas Traits to Respond

**Addressing Focus and Coherence, Organization, and Development of Ideas**

Note that whenever students aren't sure how to phrase their feedback for a peer response, they can look through the list on SE pages 52 and 53 for ideas. In many cases, they will find an example sentence starter to use.

**Try It!**

Alternately, use newspaper articles or other sources of writing. Monitor to ensure that student responses are *constructive* criticism and not simply criticism. DIFFERENTIATE INSTRUCTION ↘

⭐ **ELPS** 3E, 3G, 5B

---

 ELPS 3E, 3G, 5B

# Using the Texas Traits to Respond

When you respond, you are trying to help the author improve his or her writing by rethinking, refocusing, or revising. It can be useful to consider the traits of writing as you respond. Start by thinking about *focus and coherence, organization*, and *development of ideas*.

## Addressing Focus and Coherence, Organization, and Development of Ideas

**Focus and Coherence: Help the author maintain focus throughout the writing**.
- How would you state the main idea of your writing?
- I think you're trying to say . . . . Is that right?
- Is . . . the main idea in your writing?
- Do all the ideas support the main idea, the thesis statement?
- Does the writing work together as a whole and have a sense of completeness?
- I got the impression you want the reader to feel . . . . Is that right?

**Organization: Help the author focus on organization**.
- Which sentence is your thesis statement (or controlling idea)?
- I liked the way you got my attention by . . .
- Did you organize your paragraphs by . . . ?
- What main point do these details support?
- Could you make a smoother transition between these two paragraphs?
- What are you trying to say with this ending?

**Development of Ideas: Help the author develop ideas thoroughly**.
- You have developed most of your ideas thoroughly.
- The most important details, to me, are . . .
- Could you give a few more details about . . . ?
- Are you being fair to both sides in this paragraph?

### Try It!

Read one of the essays in this book. Write down one or two responses to the essay for each of these traits: *focus and coherence, organization*, and *development of ideas*. Then discuss your response with a classmate.

---

**ELPS 3E** Share information in cooperative learning interactions; **3G** Express opinions and ideas ranging from communicating short phrases to participating in discussions; **5B** Write using content-based grade-level vocabulary

**TEKS** 10.13E
**ELPS** 3E, 3G

Process

## Addressing Voice and Conventions

Later in the response process, try to address the author's *voice* and *use of writing conventions*. Here are some suggestions for doing this.

**Voice: Help the author focus on voice.**
- I can see your personality in this sentence: . . . .
- You really reveal how you feel about this topic when you . . .
- What audience are you trying to reach with the writing?
- Do you think you might sound too formal (or informal) in this paragraph?
- The writing makes me feel . . . about the topic.

**Conventions: Help the author focus on the conventions of writing.**
- Do you have too many sentences beginning with . . . ?
- In the middle paragraphs, could you combine some short sentences into longer sentences for variety?
- I noticed you used the word . . . three times. Maybe you can find a synonym.
- Did you check for errors in grammar, punctuation, capitalization and spelling?

### Try It!

Using the same essay you reviewed on page **52**, write down one response for *voice* and one or two for *conventions*. Discuss your responses with a classmate.

### Tip

> Listen carefully to your peers' comments, but remember that you don't have to make every change that they suggest. You should weigh the value of each comment and proceed accordingly. The following tips can help you use peer responses effectively.
>
> - Trust your own judgment about your writing.
> - Think about which issues are most important to you.
> - Pay special attention to comments made by more than one responder.
> - Seek another opinion if you are not sure about something.
> - Ask questions if you are not sure what a responder means.
> - Be patient. Focus on one problem area at a time.

## Addressing Voice and Conventions

Explain that sometimes a piece of writing may have many areas that need improvement. It can be discouraging and overwhelming for a writer to receive so much constructive criticism, even if it is presented in a very positive way. As a responder in these situations, it may be best to focus on the most significant points of improvement. The rest might be able to be addressed at a later revision.

**TEKS** 10.13E

### Try It!

Remind students that part of peer response is providing positive feedback as well as constructive criticism. If students have addressed a specific trait well, make sure you tell them! It will be encouraging to them as well as helpful in their future writing.

**ELPS** 3E, 3G

### Tip

Discuss the information in the tip box to emphasize that the decision whether to use feedback is always up to the writer. Provide additional hints such as the following:
- Remember that as the writer, you have been thinking about the topic and how to write about it for some time and are more familiar with the topic than the peer responder.
- Remember that readers may have different impressions or interpretations. As the writer, you may wish to investigate why they responded as they did.
- Don't rule out the possibility that readers' comments might inspire you to take an entirely different approach from what anyone has suggested. You must choose the best approach. **✔ DIFFERENTIATE INSTRUCTION**

---

**TEKS** **10.13E** Revise the final draft in response to feedback from peers; **ELPS 1B** Share information in cooperative learning interactions; **3C** Speak using a variety of grammatical structures with increasing accuracy and ease; **3E** Share information in cooperative learning interactions; **3G** Express opinions and ideas ranging from communicating short phrases to participating in discussions; **3H** Describe with increasing specificity and detail

## Sample Peer Response Sheet

Emphasize the importance of reading an essay all the way through a few times to get an overall feel for the piece before responding. Rereading will often answer questions that arose in the first reading. Note that students may

- take notes on a separate sheet of paper as they read essays the first time and then refer to those notes, especially their questions, as they read them a second time;
- read the essays once and then take some time to form their impressions before doing a second reading; or
- decide to read the essays through more than twice. **DIFFERENTIATE INSTRUCTION ↘**

⭐ **ELPS** 4G

Require the reader to date the peer response sheet. This will help the writer to remember exactly when they collected the comments (some may choose to have the same peer reader review more than one draft).

⭐ **TEKS** 10.13E

### Try It!

Encourage students to make their suggestions as specific as possible. Rather than making a general statement (*I think you could develop your ideas better.*), it is much more helpful to point out specific instances where change is needed (*Could you support . . . in the second paragraph with more details?*).

## Sample Peer Response Sheet

Use a response sheet like the one below to make comments about one of your classmate's essays. (The example includes sample responses.)

---

### Peer Response Sheet

Writer: *Veronica Gomez*    Responder: *David James*

Title: *Compromise: Let's Meet in the Middle*

What I liked about your writing:
- *I liked how you related the topic to history and to everyday life.*
- *The questions in the first paragraph really got me thinking about your topic.*
- *The folk saying was kind of funny.*
- *I'm glad you showed that compromises don't always work.*

Changes I would suggest:
- *Could you give a specific example about compromising between students and teachers?*
- *Do you really need to mention that compromise can be a noun and a verb? Does that fact give any insight about your topic?*
- *"Human social interaction" seems like a complicated phrase. Can you say that another way?*

---

### Try It!

Exchange a recent piece of your writing for a classmate's work.

1. Read the paper once to get an overall feel for it.
2. Read it again, paying attention to its strengths and weaknesses.
3. Fill out a response sheet like the one above.
4. Try revising your work using some of your classmate's suggestions.

---

### Differentiated Instruction: English Language Learners

⭐ **ELPS** 2G, 3G, 4H

| ELP Level **Beginning** | ELP Level **Intermediate** | ELP Level **Advanced/Advanced High** |
|---|---|---|
| Choose an adapted text to read aloud. Complete a response sheet together, allowing the students to communicate through words, gestures, and pictures. | Choose an adapted text. Read it aloud before students read it silently. Complete a response sheet with a partner. Teacher may prompt students with sentence stems as necessary. | Read a text aloud before students read it silently. Fill out a response sheet together, allowing the students to discuss with a partner proper phrasing and restate comments. |

# Evaluating Your Writing

Learning how to evaluate writing is one of the best ways to become a stronger writer. Evaluating writing helps you think like a professional writer and take on the responsibility of making meaningful changes in your work. You learn to evaluate writing by using a scoring guide, which lists the main traits for an effective piece of writing. As you gain more experience with scoring guides, you will come to better understand and appreciate the qualities inherent in effective writing.

Scoring guides aren't just for evaluating completed pieces of writing. They can also direct your early writing and provide specific suggestions for making improvements. By using a scoring guide throughout the writing process, you can expect to produce a quality piece of writing. In this chapter, you will learn about the uses of a scoring guide and you will familiarize yourself with the Write Source Holistic Scoring Guide—the specific evaluation tool that you will be using throughout this book.

- **Understanding Holistic Scoring**
- **Reading a Holistic Scoring Guide**
- **Getting Started with a Holistic Scoring Guide**
- **Understanding the Write Source Holistic Scoring Guide**
- **Evaluating an Essay**

"Rubrics help students and teachers define quality."
—Heidi Goodrich

## Evaluating Your Writing

### Objectives
- demonstrate the score points on the Write Source Holistic Scoring Guide
- learn how to read a scoring guide
- use a scoring guide to revise, edit, and assess writing

Explain that the Write Source Holistic Scoring Guide can be used for any type of writing. The scoring guide helps evaluate the five writing traits generally and does not need to be changed for different genres, such as narrative, expository, or persuasive writing.

**Resources**

**Copy Master (see Appendix)**

- Quick List

## Understanding Holistic Scoring

To increase students' familiarity with holistic scoring, work as a class to create a scoring guide for something other than writing.

- Decide whether five traits can be used to rate the chosen topic or if more or fewer traits are needed. For example, the traits for a movie might be *story, dialogue, acting, sets and costumes,* and *music.*
- Have the group brainstorm descriptions for each score point while you write the traits on the board.
- Practice using the new scoring guide on several items from your chosen category (movies every student has seen, for example).

### Score Points

If desired, have volunteers create a poster of the holistic scoring guide. Post it in the classroom. Explain that the scoring guide can be used by both peer responders and writers because it describes the characteristics of highly effective pieces of writing. DIFFERENTIATE INSTRUCTION ↘

# Understanding Holistic Scoring

Have you ever rated the quality of something on a scale of 1 (not so good) to 10 (fantastic)? Writing can also be rated on a scale. A **scoring guide is a tool used to evaluate and rate a written composition.** With a **holistic scoring guide**, the quality of any piece of writing can be evaluated for its overall impression. The reader does not focus on any individual writing characteristic, but looks at the overall effectiveness of the composition.

The basis of the scoring guide that you will see in this chapter is the five Texas writing traits: *focus and coherence, organization, development of ideas, voice,* and *conventions.* Writing conventions include grammar, usage, capitalization, punctuation, sentence structure, and spelling.

## Score Points

The holistic scoring guide in this book uses a 4-point system to evaluate writing. Below, you see a brief description of the score points used. Scores of 4 or 3 indicate strong levels of mastery in most aspects of writing. Scores of 2 or 1 show that the writer has not yet mastered any aspects of writing.

 A **4** means that the writing is **highly effective.** It shows an overall mastery of the five writing traits.

 A **3** means that the writing is **generally effective.** It shows some mastery of most of the five traits.

 A **2** means that the writing is **somewhat effective.** It shows that the writer has little mastery of most traits.

 A **1** means that the writing is **not effective.** It shows that the writer needs to work to master most of the traits.

# Reading a Holistic Scoring Guide

The scoring guide in this book is based on a four-point scale. At each score point, writing is described in terms of the five traits: *focus and coherence, organization, development of ideas, voice,* and *conventions.* The entire guide is shown on pages **60–61**.

Process

## Color-Coded Scoring Guide

Writing at this score point is highly effective.

**Focus and Coherence**
Maintains focus throughout the writing; all ideas clearly connect to each other and to the main idea. Includes a meaningful introduction and conclusion that add depth to the composition.

**Organization** Employs an effective organizational pattern for the purpose and audience. Has a smooth and logical flow; transitions help the reader move from one idea to the next.

Writing at this score point is generally effective.

**Focus and Coherence**
Maintains focus, with minor lapses; most ideas are clearly connected to each other and to the main idea. An introduction and conclusion add some depth to the composition.

**Organization** Uses an organizational pattern that is mostly effective for the purpose and audience. Generally flows but could use a few more transitions.

## Guiding Your Writing

A scoring guide helps you . . .

- **plan your work**—knowing what is expected;
- **create a strong first draft**—maintaining *focus and coherence, organization,* and *development of ideas;*
- **revise and edit your work**—considering each trait; and
- **assess your final draft**—rating the whole piece of writing in terms of the traits.

 **Think about the scoring guide.** Think about the level-4 descriptions above. According to these descriptions, how does a writer maintain focus? What characterizes the organization of a score-4 paper?

## Reading a Holistic Scoring Guide

Have students read and compare the descriptions for *focus and coherence* at a score of 4 and a score of 3. As a class, identify the key words and phrases that separate the two scores (*throughout the writing, clearly, most ideas, some depth,* etc.). Discuss how these subtle differences can mean the difference between an essay that is "highly effective" and one that is "generally effective."

 **ELPS** 2C, 4C

### Guiding Your Writing

We most often think of a scoring guide as something used to assess a completed piece of writing. Explain how it can also be used by the writer before and during the writing process.

 **Think about the scoring guide.** Possible answers: All ideas clearly connect to each other and to the main idea; organizational pattern effectively matches the purpose and audience; smooth and logical flow; and good transitions from one idea to the next.

---

## Writing with Scoring in Mind

Encourage students to read through the descriptions of each trait at a score of 4 on the scoring guide before beginning to write. Thinking through these traits and what a quality piece of writing will look like will help the students even as they are formulating their first draft.

# Writing with Scoring in Mind

Each of the writing units in this book includes a page like the one below. This page, which shows the Texas traits of writing, explains the main requirements for developing the composition in the unit. Notice how it also suggests that you refer to the scoring guide as part of your writing process.

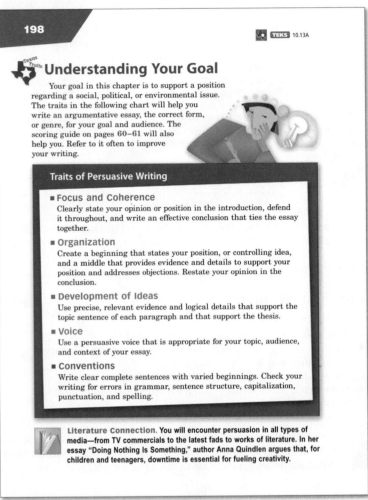

**198**  TEKS 10.13A

## Understanding Your Goal

Your goal in this chapter is to support a position regarding a social, political, or environmental issue. The traits in the following chart will help you write an argumentative essay, the correct form, or genre, for your goal and audience. The scoring guide on pages 60–61 will also help you. Refer to it often to improve your writing.

**Traits of Persuasive Writing**

- **Focus and Coherence**
  Clearly state your opinion or position in the introduction, defend it throughout, and write an effective conclusion that ties the essay together.

- **Organization**
  Create a beginning that states your position, or controlling idea, and a middle that provides evidence and details to support your position and addresses objections. Restate your opinion in the conclusion.

- **Development of Ideas**
  Use precise, relevant evidence and logical details that support the topic sentence of each paragraph and that support the thesis.

- **Voice**
  Use a persuasive voice that is appropriate for your topic, audience, and context of your essay.

- **Conventions**
  Write clear complete sentences with varied beginnings. Check your writing for errors in grammar, sentence structure, capitalization, punctuation, and spelling.

**Literature Connection.** You will encounter persuasion in all types of media—from TV commercials to the latest fads to works of literature. In her essay "Doing Nothing Is Something," author Anna Quindlen argues that, for children and teenagers, downtime is essential for fueling creativity.

ELPS 5G

Evaluating Your Writing **59**

Process

## A Closer Look at Understanding Your Goal

The following steps will help you get an overview of the assignment in each writing unit.

1. **Read through the Texas traits chart** to familiarize yourself with the unit's goals.
2. Concentrate on *focus and coherence, organization,* and *development of ideas* at the start of the project, when you are prewriting. As you work on your draft, also think about *voice* and *conventions*. These traits form the foundation of good writing.
3. **Identify specific requirements** for each trait (such as "supporting your opinion with logical reasons" and "sounding persuasive and respectful").
4. **Consult the Write Source Scoring Guide** to see how each trait relates to the four score points.

## A Special Note About the Traits

Different traits are important at different stages of the writing process. The following chart shows when the specific traits are important.

> During **prewriting**, pay attention to *focus and coherence, organization,* and *development of ideas.* Concentrate on these traits during **drafting** also, but think about *voice* as well.
>
> During **revising**, continue to concentrate on *focus and coherence, organization, development of ideas,* and *voice.* (For some assignments, your teacher may ask you to pay particular attention to one or two of these traits.)
>
> During **editing** and proofreading, concentrate on *conventions*—grammar, sentence structure, capitalization, punctuation, and spelling.
>
> When you, a peer, or your teacher is **assessing** or **reviewing** your final draft, consider all five traits.

### Exercise

Review the goals on page **58** and the scoring guide on pages **60–61.** Then write a persuasive paragraph defending your solution for a school-related problem. Keep the traits in mind as you write.

---

## A Closer Look at Understanding Your Goal

Encourage students to flag this page with a sticky note and revisit it whenever they begin new writing.

## A Special Note About the Traits

After students have read the note, have them look back at the diagram on SE page 10, which shows how their process through the stages may involve looping back one or more times along the way. Explain that as they continue to write throughout the year, they will become more familiar with each step along this writing journey—even if the path is a winding one.

### Exercise
### Answers

You may need to brainstorm possible topics with students if they are having trouble coming up with their own. Remind them that choosing a topic that they are truly interested in is very important; their writing will reflect how much they care about the subject. ✔ DIFFERENTIATE INSTRUCTION

ELPS 5G

---

**ELPS 1C** Use strategic learning techniques to acquire basic and grade-level vocabulary; **4C** Comprehend vocabulary and language structures used in written classroom materials; **5F** Write using a variety of grade-appropriate sentence lengths and patterns in increasingly accurate ways; **5G** Explain with increasing specificity and detail/writing

**Write Source Holistic Scoring Guide**

This is a good time for students to get a preliminary idea of how the scoring guide will work. Choose a piece of writing (newspaper article, sample student essays, etc.), and distribute a copy to each student. Have students read the article silently and assign it a score. Encourage them to refer often to the trait descriptions in the scoring guide on SE pages 60 and 61 as they make their decision. When everyone is finished, compare scores and see whether there was a general consensus. Discuss any disagreements as to what score the writing should receive. Students should be free to share their reasons for choosing the score they did, but be sure to clarify any misconceptions or misunderstandings they had about the process. **DIFFERENTIATE INSTRUCTION ↘**

**★ ELPS** 3E, 3G, 3H, 4G, 4H, 4K

**60**

 *Write Source* **Holistic Scoring Guide**

Use the descriptions at each score point to evaluate your own writing or that of your peers.

 Writing at this score point is highly effective.

**Focus and Coherence** Maintains focus throughout the writing; all ideas clearly connect to each other and to the main idea. Includes a meaningful introduction and conclusion that add depth to the composition.

**Organization** Employs an effective organizational pattern for the purpose and audience. Has a smooth and logical flow; transitions help the reader move from one idea to the next.

 Writing at this score point is generally effective.

**Focus and Coherence** Maintains focus, with minor lapses; most ideas are clearly connected to each other and to the main idea. An introduction and conclusion add some depth to the composition.

**Organization** Uses an organizational pattern that is mostly effective for the purpose and audience. Generally flows but could use a few more transitions.

 Writing at this score point is somewhat effective.

**Focus and Coherence** Is somewhat unfocused, but the reader can understand how ideas are related. Some ideas do not contribute to the writing as a whole. The introduction and conclusion are superficial.

**Organization** The flow of the ideas is not always clear. The organizational pattern may not suit the purpose and audience. Wordiness and repetition may interfere with the flow of ideas.

 Writing at this score point is not effective.

**Focus and Coherence** Lacks focus; includes a substantial amount of information not connected to the main idea. Is missing an introduction and/or conclusion.

**Organization** Has no clear organizational pattern or logical flow of ideas. Lacks transitions. Repetition or wordiness may interfere with the progression of ideas.

**ELPS 3E** Share information in cooperative learning interactions; **3G** Express opinions and ideas ranging from communicating short phrases to participating in discussions; **3H** Explain with increasing specificity and detail; **4G** Demonstrate comprehension of increasingly complex English/summarizing material; **4H** Read silently with increasing ease and comprehension for longer periods; **4K** Demonstrate comprehension and expand reading skills by employing analytical skills/evaluating written information and performing critical analyses

**Development of Ideas**
Ample support and specific details allow the reader to appreciate the writer's points. A novel approach to the topic may add to the overall quality of the writing.

**Voice** Engages the reader throughout the writing. Sounds authentic and original; expresses the writer's unique perspective.

**Conventions** Shows a strong command of conventions, allowing the reader to focus on the writer's message.

**Development of Ideas**
Supports all ideas, but some need to be developed more thoroughly. The presentation of ideas may be thoughtful but may not reflect a novel approach to the topic.

**Voice** Engages the reader for most of the writing. Sounds somewhat authentic and original, and expresses the writer's unique perspective.

**Conventions** Includes only minor errors in conventions; errors do not interfere with the reader's ability to understand the writer's message.

**Development of Ideas**
Ideas may be developed only superficially. Some information may be missing. The reader's ability to appreciate the writer's points is compromised.

**Voice** Engages the reader occasionally. Sounds authentic and original in only a few sections. Does not express a unique perspective.

**Conventions** Errors reflect a limited command of writing conventions and interfere with the flow of ideas in the writing.

**Development of Ideas**
Support is lacking or is only general and vague. Important information may be left out. The reader has difficulty understanding the writer's points.

**Voice** Does not engage the reader. Shows little or no evidence of the writer's individuality or unique perspective.

**Conventions** The writing shows major problems with conventions, which interferes with the reader's ability to understand the message.

---

## Differentiated Instruction: English Language Learners

⭐ ELPS 1A, 2C, 2G, 2H

| ELP Level **Beginning** | ELP Level **Intermediate** | ELP Level **Advanced/Advanced High** |
|---|---|---|
| Teach basic assessment vocabulary by helping students associate other descriptive words (*poor, fair, good, best,* etc.) with the scores in the scoring guide. | Recite general phrases from the scoring guide (*highly effective, major problems*). For each phrase, students should guess from which score point it most likely came. | Read sentences from the scoring guide (*Engages the reader occasionally.*). Students identify to which trait and which score point each sentence most likely belongs. |

**ELPS 1A** Use prior knowledge to understand meanings; **2C** Learn basic vocabulary heard during classroom instruction/interactions; **2G** Understand the details of spoken language/topics and languages are familiar to unfamiliar; **2H** Understand information in increasingly complex spoken language

## Evaluating an Essay

Have students find examples from the essay that demonstrate well the first four writing traits. Refer students to the side notes to help narrow their search. See examples below:

- **Focus and coherence:** The first paragraph clearly identifies the topic and focus of the essay.
- **Organization:** After identifying why the rain forest is important, the writer transitions nicely to a paragraph on the causes of rain forest destruction.
- **Development of ideas:** The writer gives many statistical details to support his or her point.
- **Voice:** The writer shows genuine interest in the topic through sentences like this one: *At that rate, there may be no more rain forests in another 40 years!* DIFFERENTIATE INSTRUCTION ↘

As they read, encourage students to sound out any unknown vocabulary and use context to determine its meaning.

**⊕ ELPS** 4A

# Evaluating an Essay

The essays that follow are examples of writing for each score point on the holistic scoring guide. Study these essays and the notes with them to better understand how to evaluate a written composition. **(Essays will contain errors.)**

**Writing that fits a score of 4 is highly effective.**

**4**

### CONSERVING RAIN FORESTS

Every time a tree in the Amazon rain forest is cut down for its wood, or another acre burnt to make way for crops, the earth's climate becomes a little more unbalanced. Rain forests are crucial because they absorb carbon dioxide and release oxygen into the atmosphere. Without rain forests, too much carbon dioxide may lead to climate change, which can affect the whole world.

Rain forests are being destroyed at a rate of 1½ acres per second. At that rate, there may be no more rain forests in another 40 years (Raintree 6)! Besides the effect on climate, many unique plants and animals will become extinct when they are no longer protected by the rain forests' fragile ecosystems. Today, a typical four-square-mile patch of tropical rain forest contains as many as 1,500 flowering plants, 750 species of trees, 400 species of birds and 150 species of butterflies (Nature Conservancy). Tropical rain forests provide us with favorite foods such as coffee, cocoa, and many types of fruits and nuts. Pharmaceutical companies use plants found only in rain forests to create many medicinal and cosmetic products. There are, for example, more than 2000 plants with properties that are used to fight cancer or that might even lead to a cure.

The main causes of rain forest destruction are logging, agriculture, and mining. Of these, illegal logging causes the most problems. Over 105,000 miles of roads have been illegally cut through the Amazon to reach mahogany and other expensive woods that sell for a lot of money on the world market (Wallace). Rain forest wood is also sent to other countries for fuel, charcoal, and paper production. The roads create more illegal activity by

The thesis is clearly stated. Writer uses expressive details to create a distinct voice.

Middle paragraphs build upon the thesis. Writer shows knowledge of topic.

Content is arranged from general to specific examples, engaging the reader.

opening areas to ranching, farming, and land speculation. People then burn more trees to create more open land.

Normally, the Amazon produces half of the water it needs, but all the clearing has reduced the amount of moisture released into the atmosphere, causing remaining trees to dry and die out (Wallace 132). This leads to drought and fires. Also, once an area has been cleared, it's very unlikely that it will grow again or recreate the ecosystem that it once supported.

Stopping the destruction of the Amazon will be difficult. Many of the problems are due to poverty and greed at all levels. People want free or cheap land to feed their families and to make money growing crops like soybeans or raising cattle. Rich countries like the United States and Japan want to import cheap wood for building and furniture and paper. The governments of countries with rain forests want the money provided by exports and land development and do little to encourage conservation or restrict destructive activities. They also don't have the money to manage and protect their resources.

It's clear that wealthier countries must cooperate with poorer tropical countries to save the rain forests. The United States can do its part by making it more profitable for countries like Brazil to conserve its forests instead of cutting them down. There are a number of ways to do this. One way is to show how more money can be made from the tropical plants that grow naturally in rain forests than from crops and cattle raised on cleared land. According to experts such as Dr. Robert Mendelsohn, an economist at Yale University, and Dr. Michael Balick, Director of the Institute of Economic Botany at the New York Botanical Gardens, there are hundreds of new drugs that could be discovered in rain forests, valued at billions of dollars (Raintree 63).

Much of the destruction of the world's rain forests cannot be reversed, but it's not too late to conserve what we have now. The future of our planet may depend upon it.

**Ideas are well developed, and details add interest.**

**Varied sentences create a smooth flow. Ideas are linked.**

**Conclusion provides sense of completeness.**

Draw students' attention to similarities between the introduction and conclusion. Discuss how the conclusion draws the reader back to the main focus and brings the essay to a tight conclusion. Ask students to reread the last several paragraphs of the essay but to eliminate the concluding paragraph. What feeling is the reader left with when the essay doesn't end with this connection to the main idea?

## Differentiated Instruction: English Language Learners

⭐ **ELPS** 2I, 3H

| **ELP Level** Beginning | **ELP Level** Intermediate | **ELP Level** Advanced/Advanced High |
|---|---|---|
| Ask students what the information in parentheses indicates (e.g., *Raintree 6*). Allow them to discuss with classmates before answering. Clarify and explain as needed. | Direct students to read the first paragraph of the essay, looking specifically for the focus of the writing. Ask them to identify it and explain their answer. | Ask students to identify three statistics and three facts in the essay. Allow them to work with a partner. Discuss the importance of both types of details. |

 **ELPS** **2I** Demonstrate listening comprehension in increasingly complex spoken language by following directions and responding to questions; **3H** Describe and explain with increasing specificity and detail

After reading the essay, have students express their overall impressions of the essay and its score. What parts of the essay stood out to them as needing improvement? How did its *organization* and *development of ideas* compare with the essay that scored a 4? Which of the traits were done well enough to make the essay generally effective?

Remind students that although spelling and grammatical errors often stand out in a piece, they do not automatically mean that the essay will score a 1 or a 2. In holistic scoring, the entire writing is taken into consideration when assigning a score. Even though this essay had some *conventions* errors, it was still generally effective.

⭐ ELPS 2I, 4K

**Writing that fits a score of 3 is generally effective.**

The beginning paragraph clearly introduces the thesis.

Details show knowledge of topic and support thesis. Minor grammar and spelling errors do not detract from the message.

### Getting Off the Grid

People today are finally becoming more aware of the impact they have on the environment. They are beginning to see that we need to conserve our non-renewable resources in order to save the planet for our children. Electricity is a resource that must be conserved. While electricity itself is not a non-renewable resource, it is often created from non-renewable resources. The use of electricity has gone up a lot because of computers and other new technology, so we have to become more efficient in the ways we create it and use it.

Think of our lives without electricity. We couldn't do much at night because there'd be no electric lights. Food would spoil without refrigeraters to store our food. We couldn't use our computers or watch TV. We'd swelter in the summer without air conditioning. Every time our electricity fails and there's a blackout, we get angry and frustrated. Important information gets lost. Important tasks don't get done. We are completely dependent on it. In 1940, electricity production accounted for 10 % of the energy used in the United States. In 1970, 25% of energy was used to produce electricity. Today it is 40%. Yet, even though our use of electricity is going up, construction of new electric plants have gone down. This situation makes it more likely to have major problems like power outages, poor power quality, and higher bills (Dept. of Energy).

Over 50% of electric power is created by burning coal, which is non-renewable and create a lot of carbon emissions. This is terrible for the environment and adds to global warming. Another 21% is from nuclear power, which is clean energy, but it's also non-renewable and could be dangerous because of the radiation. Only 7% of electric power is from hydroelectric dams and 2% from other renewable sources (Greenpeace). This has to change if we are going to reduce carbon by using cleaner energy.

Some of the renewable energies that we can use are water power, wind power, and solar power. Hydroelectric power is created by damming rivers and using the water to turn turbines.

⭐ **ELPS 2I** Demonstrate listening comprehension in increasingly complex spoken language by responding to questions; **4K** Demonstrate comprehension and expand reading skills by employing analytical skills/evaluating written information and performing critical analyses

Process

> **Idea could have been better developed.**

It is a clean and effective way to create electricity, though sometimes damming a river can cause problems. Wind power is becoming more popular. It costs more than fossil fuels, but it is expected to go to 5% by 2020 (Environmental Literacy Council). Solar power is not as efficient as fossil fuels for large electric plants, but people can use it in there own homes to reduce electricity use. Maybe one day they'll be able to use it to generate power plants.

> **Writer presents solution to problem.**

If we cut down our own use of electricity, there wouldn't be as much need to increase production. There are a lot of ways to do this. First, people should start using low energy appliances, especially their refrigerators, which use a lot of electricity. They can use florescent light bulbs. Florescent bulbs cost more than regular bulbs, but they last longer and use less energy. Turning off lights and appliances can also save electricity. Most people don't realize that even unplugging electric cords that their not using can help, for example, you're using electricity when your phone chargers plugged in even when the phone is not charging. In the future, more people might start using solar panels on their own houses to generate a lot of their electricity. That's a lot cheaper than paying the electric company! New kinds of electric meters that monitor usage in real time will help electric companies match supply and demand better, and people can change their usage habits (Dept. of Energy). If people waited to use appliances like their washing machines and dishwashers during non-peak times, there would be less strain on the system and their own costs would go down.

> **Writer engages the reader with distinct voice.**

If there was less need for electricity, there would be less dependence on fossil fuels like coal. There would be less carbon spewing into the atmosphere. By changing our own habits in our homes, we do a lot to conserve electricity and protect the environment.

Review the descriptions for *development of ideas* in the scoring guide. Have students reread the paragraph beginning *Some of the renewable energies*. . . . Students should analyze this passage, looking for the ideas the writer presents. Discuss the ways the author failed to fully develop some of the ideas. Take suggestions from the students on how this paragraph could be improved. ⤣ **DIFFERENTIATE INSTRUCTION**

⭐ **ELPS** 4K

---

### Differentiated Instruction: English Language Learners

⭐ **ELPS** 4C, 4D, 4F, 4G

| ELP Level **Beginning** | ELP Level **Intermediate** | ELP Level **Advanced/Advanced High** |
|---|---|---|
| Prepare pictures to go along with the various types of renewable energies (solar power, wind power, etc.). Use these supports to teach this vocabulary. | Preteach renewable energy vocabulary using pictures before students read the essay. They may refer to these supports when taking turns reading the essay aloud with a partner. | Have students read the paragraph with a partner. Encourage them to seek clarification on renewable energy vocabulary and to use this vocabulary when suggesting changes to the paragraph. |

 **ELPS** **4C** Comprehend vocabulary used in written classroom materials; **4D** Use prereading supports to enhance comprehension of written text/graphic organizers, illustrations, and topic-related vocabulary; **4F** Use visual/contextual support and support from peers/teachers to read grade-appropriate text, enhance and confirm understanding, and develop vocabulary and background knowledge; **4G** Demonstrate comprehension of increasingly complex English/participating in shared reading; **4K** Demonstrate comprehension and expand reading skills by employing analytical skills/evaluating written information and performing critical analyses

Challenge students to locate the errors in writing conventions in this essay. Some examples include:

1. *Resources* is spelled *resourses* in line 8.
2. The last sentence in the second paragraph has several problems. It should not start with the word *and*. It also sounds as if the market is reused, not the bags.
3. *Their* in line 15 should be *they're*.
4. *Live* should be *life* in line 21.
5. *Its* is missing an apostrophe in line 21.

⭐ **ELPS** 5D

There are other errors as well. Although these types of simple errors in writing conventions are not as important in the first few drafts of an essay, by the final copy they should be corrected.

66

**Writing that fits a score of 2 is somewhat effective.**

**2**

### Recycling

Americans are very wasteful. Everyday we throw out tons and tons of paper, glass, and plastic. We use 25 million plastic water bottles alone (http://www.reusablebags.com/facts.php?id=18). This goes into landfills, where it stays forever. Eventually we will run out of places to put all of our garbage! Recycling is the only way to avoid being buried by piles of junk.

Recycling is also important because without it we will use up our natural resourses. Eventually there won't be any trees left for making paper. Today alot of paper products are from recycled paper. Plastic can be reused again and again so there's no need to manufacture it from oil. It can even be turned into clothing! And people are beginning to take cloth bags to the market which can be reused over and over again insted of asking for plastic bags.

Sometimes dangerous items can get put into landfills if their not recycled. For example, computers and cellphones. They have toxic metals in them. Its called e-waste. There are companies that will fix them so they can be donated and reused. Or they take them apart and reuse the good parts and destroy the toxic parts (http://pages.ebay.com/rethink/faq.html#4).

Recycling is getting more common and is becoming a way of live for a lot of lots of people. Its easy to do. Many communities have recycling programs and all you have to do is put your bottles and cans and old newspapers into a special bin then a truck takes it away, just like the regular garbage. Supermarkets often has recycling centers where they even pay you for your bottles.

There is no excuse for people to recycle. They should feel guilty when they throw out a plastic bottle or newspaper. By recycling, they stop creting huge landfills, stop using natural resources, and stop the waste.

**Topic is not clearly stated.**

**Ideas are not well developed and are not well connected.**

**There are many errors in writing conventions throughout the essay.**

Evaluating Your Writing    **67**

Process

Writing that fits a score of 1 is not effective.

### Turn Off the Tap!

Its very important to save water these days because we're using up our supply too fast. Water concervation is something we should all think about when we brush our teeth or wash our hands. Its not good to leave the water tap on while you do those things because your just waisting water. You don't have to keep the water running it can save galons of water. And water is expensive.

What are some other ways to concerve water. Don't keep watering your lawn all the time, make sure that water is hitting the grass and plants and not just going on the sidewalk, use a broom to clean your driveway, instead of washing it down with a hose. Just doing little things like that can help alot.

It may seems like we have alot from rain and rivers but its not enough. There are too many people and theres climate change. Those things make it hard to have enough water for everyone even if it rains all the time. Some of the water isn't clean enough to drink, it has to be prosessed first.

Toilets are one of the biggest waisters of water. So use low flush tolets or don't flush all the time. And make sure your toilet isn't leaking because that also waists water.

In conclusion don't assume theirs enough. You can save water by doing a few simple. Like turning off the tap when you brush your teeth. Its easy and its right.

**Thesis is not clearly stated.**

**Errors in conventions make the essay difficult to understand.**

**Essay lacks organization. The examples are not clear. Writing does not engage the reader.**

Challenge students to rewrite the introductory paragraph for this essay. Remind them to consult the trait descriptions in the scoring guide—especially for focus and coherence—before beginning. Besides bringing some focus and clarity to the introductory paragraph, they should clean up the writing conventions as well. ☑ DIFFERENTIATE INSTRUCTION

⭐ ELPS 5D

---

## Differentiated Instruction: English Language Learners

⭐ ELPS 1E, 4C, 4D, 5D, 5F, 5G

| ELP Level **Beginning** | ELP Level **Intermediate** | ELP Level **Advanced/Advanced High** |
|---|---|---|
| Preteach necessary vocabulary. Help students create a topic sentence using a sentence stem that you provide (*It's important to save water because. . .*). | Preteach necessary vocabulary before students rewrite the introductory paragraph with a partner. Encourage students to make the paragraph no longer than three sentences. | Preteach necessary vocabulary before students rewrite the paragraph. Encourage students to consider the ideas presented later in the essay as they write the introduction. |

 **ELPS 1E** Internalize new basic and academic language by using and reusing it/writing; **4C** Comprehend vocabulary used in written classroom materials; **4D** Use prereading supports to enhance comprehension of written text/graphic organizers, illustrations, and topic-related vocabulary; **5D** Edit writing for standard grammar and usage/subject-verb and pronoun agreement and appropriate verb tenses; **5F** Write using a variety of grade-appropriate sentence lengths in increasingly accurate ways; **5G** Describe and explain with increasing specificity and detail to fulfill content area writing needs

## Evaluation Practice

Encourage students to review the trait descriptions in the scoring guide on SE pages 60 and 61 before reading the essay.

### Exercise
#### Answers

You may want to allow students to complete this assignment in pairs. Students should each write their own assessment sheet and assign their own score but should be allowed to collaborate and share ideas regarding the strengths and weaknesses. **DIFFERENTIATE INSTRUCTION ↘**

 **ELPS** 3E

## Evaluation Practice

Read the essay below, focusing on its strengths and weaknesses. Then follow the directions at the bottom of the page. **(The essay contains errors.)**

### Music and the Arts Make Education Complete

Funding for music and art programs in schools across the country have been cut or greatly reduced (VH1). This is an unfortunate trend. Music and the arts should be supported because they are critical for a well-rounded education.

Persoally, I think music and arts are not so important as other subjects, but studies have proven the positive affect of music and the arts in school. Students who participate in music and arts programs are four times more likely to be recognized for academic achievement. (Hills 65). Other studies reveal that music and the arts help develop critical thinking, cognitive development, and a positive self-esteem.

For most students school is the only place they can get instruction in music and the arts because private lessons are very expensive ("Americans"). Students should not miss out on the benefits of music and the arts just because of their economic status.

Schools support sports programs because sports encourage teamwork. Studies also show that students in sports get better grades. Both of these things are true for music and arts students though, too (Blair and Bruhn 17). Besides, not everyone can shoot hoops well enough to make the basketball team. At the same time, not everyone can play an instrument well enough to be first chair in a jazz band, or sketch a life-like drawing, but anyone with the desire can still participate. I guess we should all have the opportunity.

Music and the arts requires discipline, practice, and studying just like any other subject. They also develop creativity, encourage self-expression, and teach students how to work in a group. A program that can do all of those things should probably be part of every student's education.

### Exercise

Assess the persuasive essay you have just read, using the holistic scoring guide on pages **60–61** for reference. To get started, create an assessment sheet like the one on page **31**. Remember: After rating each trait, write at least one comment about a strength and one comment about a weakness.

**ELPS** **2I** Demonstrate listening comprehension in increasingly complex spoken language by responding to questions; **3A** Practice producing sounds of newly acquired vocabulary; **3B** Expand vocabulary by learning and using high-frequency words for identifying and describing; **3C** Speak using a variety of grammatical structures and sentence lengths and types with increasing accuracy and ease; **3E** Share information in cooperative learning interactions; **3F** Give information/ranging from using a limited high-frequency vocabulary to using abstract and content-based vocabulary during speaking; **3H** Describe and explain with increasing specificity and detail

| Differentiated Instruction: English Language Learners | | ELPS 2I, 3A, 3B, 3C, 3F, 3H |
|---|---|---|
| **ELP Level** **Beginning** | **ELP Level** **Intermediate** | **ELP Level** **Advanced/Advanced High** |
| Begin practicing presentation skills by having students pronounce key writing vocabulary terms (e.g., *the five traits*). Model pronunciation as needed. | Begin practicing presentation skills by having students answer simple questions (e.g., *Where do you live?*) aloud and in complete sentences. Model as necessary. | Practice presentation skills by having students describe things in their house (e.g., *dog, bedroom*) aloud and in complete sentences. Model complex sentences as necessary. |

# Publishing Your Writing

You've written many essays, articles, and reports since you've started high school. Many of these pieces were probably read by an audience of one, the teacher who made the assignment. But what if the size of your audience was greatly expanded, and included all of your classmates? How would that affect your feelings about writing? More than anything else, it would help you feel part of a writing community, which makes the process of writing a very meaningful and satisfying experience.

Of course, not everything you write is meant to be shared with an audience. You may not want to open up your journal to the world, but you could take a story idea from your journal, develop it, and then post it on your Web page or submit it to a magazine. You might want to finish a poem you started in your personal writing and recite it at an open-mike night at a coffee house.

This chapter will help you with all of your publishing needs—from preparing a piece for publication to launching your own Web site.

- **Preparing to Publish**
- **Publishing Ideas**
- **Designing Your Writing**
- **Publishing Online**
- **Creating Your Own Web Site**
- **Finding Places to Publish**

"No piece of writing, regardless of how much you polish and fuss with it, comes out exactly as you want it to."

—Tom Liner

## Publishing Your Writing

### Objectives
- learn how to format and design writing for publication
- learn about publishing online
- learn about creating a Web site

Some students may have already published their writing in a school publication, on their own Web site, or in a local or national magazine. Some may have presented their work to their peers or parents, others may have written scripts that have been performed. Invite these students to talk about their experiences. Ask them the following questions:

- How did you prepare for publication or your presentation?
- Did publishing make you feel part of a writing community (as the chapter text says)?
- Have you felt the same as Tom Liner, author of the quotation? ✓ **DIFFERENTIATE INSTRUCTION**

 **ELPS** 2I

## Preparing to Publish

In order to practice all of the steps for preparing a piece for publication, you may want to put together a single-issue class magazine in which each student contributes an article or a story.

### Publishing Tips

Point out that good writing takes time! There is no shortcut to producing a publishable piece. Even the best and most successful writers put hours and hours (and sometimes years) into crafting their finished product. They will perform some steps in the writing process many times in order to get every word just right.

### Try It!

Give adequate time for partners to read each other's writing aloud. Point out the usefulness of hearing what you have written. Discuss what students learned when they heard their work read aloud.

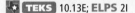 **TEKS** 10.13E; **ELPS** 2I

---

 **TEKS** 10.13E

# Preparing to Publish

Your writing is not ready to share until you have taken it through all the steps in the writing process. The tips below will help you prepare your writing for publication.

## Publishing Tips

- **Take advantage of peer response sessions and feedback from your teacher.**
  Make sure that you have addressed the important concerns identified by your teacher and classmates.
- **Check for the traits of writing.**
  Focus and coherence, organization, development of ideas, voice, and conventions are all important in your writing. (See pages 33–48.)
- **Put forth your best effort.**
  Continue working until you feel good about your writing from start to finish.
- **Save all drafts for each writing project.**
  Then you will be able to double-check the changes you have made.
- **Seek editing help.**
  Ask at least one trusted editor to check your work for conventions. Another person may spot errors that you miss.
- **Prepare a neat final copy.**
  Use a pen (blue or black ink) and one side of the paper if you are writing by hand. Select a font that is easy to read if you are using a computer. (Always use a computer when you submit your writing to outside publishers.)
- **Consider different publishing options.**
  There are many ways to publish writing. (See page **71**.)
- **Follow all publishing guidelines.**
  Each publisher has certain requirements for publishing. Be sure to follow their guidelines exactly.

### Try It!

Prepare to publish. Follow the tips above to get your next piece of writing ready to publish. Before submitting your work, have a friend read your writing out loud. Listen carefully. Does your writing say everything you'd like it to say? Does your personal voice come through in your writing?

---

Process

# Publishing Ideas

The simplest way to publish your writing is to share it with a friend or classmate. Other publishing ideas, such as entering a writing contest, take more time and effort. Try a number of these publishing ideas during the school year. All of them will help you grow as a writer.

## Self-Publishing
- Newsletter
- Greeting Cards
- Personal Book
- Web Site
- Blog

## Performing
- Sharing with Classmates
- Reading to Other Audiences
- Multimedia Presentation
- Open-Mike Night

## Sending It Out
- Local Newspaper
- Magazines
- Web Sites or E-zines
- Writing Contests
- Young Writers' Conferences

## Sharing in School
- Literary Magazine
- Writing Portfolio
- Classroom Collection
- School Newspaper/Yearbook

## Posting
- Bulletin Boards
- Display Cases
- Business Windows
- Literary/Art Fairs

**Think about publishing.** How many of these publishing ideas have you tried since you've been in high school? Which other ones would you like to try? Why? Which ones would you not like to try? Why not?

## Publishing Ideas

Promote the idea of publishing writing throughout the school year.
- Encourage students to inform classmates if something of theirs is going to be published or performed.
- Create a bulletin board in the room to keep the class informed of student Web sites or Web logs (blogs) of students who work on the school paper or literary magazine, and other related publishing news.
- Help sponsor open-mike nights and contests.
- Invite members of the school newspaper or yearbook staff to speak to the class, explaining what the work is like and how students can get involved.
- Invite professional writers to speak in the class and describe both the challenges and the rewards of writing. ✔ **DIFFERENTIATE INSTRUCTION**

**?** **Think about publishing.**

Share your own publishing experiences with the class, including any relevant details that they might find helpful or interesting. What were the challenges of your experience? What were the rewards?

★ **TEKS** 10.13E

**TEKS** 10.13E Publish written work; **ELPS** 5F Write using a variety of grade-appropriate sentence lengths and patterns in increasingly accurate ways

## Designing Your Writing

### Selecting an Appropriate Font

Students may enjoy the look of many display fonts. Remind students that, although they may be attractive, these fonts are not appropriate for many forms of publication. Give students the names of several fonts typically used for submitting work for publishing (Times New Roman, Arial, etc.). Explain the importance of following publishers' guidelines, including the choice of fonts, when submitting work to be published. **DIFFERENTIATE INSTRUCTION ↘**

### Using Consistent Spacing and Margins

Although students may want to adjust these standard page settings and layout rules, explain that many publishers will not allow the writer to decide these aspects of a finished copy. Unless publishers provide alternate requirements, it is best to stick with the standards.

**★ TEKS** 10.13E

### Including Graphic Elements

Graphics can range from charts and graphs to family photos. For more on using graphic elements, see SE pages 638–639.

### Try It!

Ask students to bring in an example of a publication that they especially like in terms of design. This can be a trade magazine, a book, or a CD booklet—as long as it has a reasonable amount of text.

Invite students to share their examples of good design. What do they find appealing? Is the text especially attractive and easy to read? Are the graphic elements helpful and interesting? How does the design support the content?

**★ TEKS** 10.23C; **ELPS** 3G

---

**★ TEKS** 10.13E, 10.23C
**ELPS** 3G

# Designing Your Writing

Always focus first on the content of your writing. Then consider its design, or appearance. For most types of publishing, you'll want to use a computer for your final copy. These guidelines will help you to design your writing.

## Selecting an Appropriate Font

- **Choose an easy-to-read font.** In most cases, a serif font is best for the text, and a sans serif style works for headings.

  The letters of **serif** fonts have "tails"—as in this sentence.

  The letters of **sans serif** fonts are plain, without tails—as in this sentence.

- **Include a title and headings.** Use the title to introduce your paper and use headings to guide the reader through the text. Headings break a long report into readable parts.

## Using Consistent Spacing and Margins

- **Set clear margins.** Use a one-inch margin (top, bottom, left, and right).
- **Indent paragraphs.** Use a half-inch indent.
- **Use one space after every period.** This will improve the readability of your paper.
- **Avoid awkward breaks.** Don't leave a heading or the first line of a paragraph at the bottom of a page or a column. Never split a hyphenated word between pages or columns.

## Including Graphic Elements

- **Use lists if appropriate.** Use numbered lists if your points have a clear number order. Otherwise, use bulleted lists (like the ones on this page).
- **Include graphics.** Use tables, charts, or illustrations to help make a point. Keep graphics small within the text. If a graphic needs to be large, display it on its own page.

### Try It!

Working with a classmate, compare and discuss the design features of chapters from two different textbooks. How are the design features the same? How are they different? With your partner, decide which design is the most effective, based on the text's audience and purpose.

---

**TEKS** **10.13E** Publish written work; **10.23C** Synthesize research into a presentation that uses graphics and illustrations to explain concepts; **ELPS** **3G** Express opinions ranging from communicating short phrases to participating in discussions

## Effective Design in Action

The following two pages show a well-designed student essay. The side notes explain the design features.

Process

> The title is 16-point sans serif type, centered.

> Centered subheadings (14-point sans serif type) identify main sections.

> The body text is 12-point serif type, double-spaced.

Juan Castillo
Mr. Rodriquez
Computer Technology
Nov. 18, 2011

### Warning for Computers: It's Flu Season

How can a computer act "sick"? Maybe its applications aren't working correctly, or it's crashing and restarting every few minutes. If so, a computer might be infected with a virus. Unfortunately, chicken soup and a lot of rest won't do any good. To ensure that a computer remains up and running, users should understand computer viruses so they can protect their computers in the future.

#### The Culprits

The Internet is an amazing but dangerous tool. With the click of a mouse, a user can communicate with people all over the world. That's also what makes it so dangerous for a computer. On the Internet, everyone is a neighbor, even the computer hacker with criminal intentions. These harmful hackers design destructive software programs called viruses.

#### The Viruses

Like human viruses, a computer virus can make a copy of itself. Then it spreads from one host to another. Since computer viruses are programs, they have the ability to delete files, format hard drives, or change home pages.

Computer viruses can be spread through floppy discs, CD's, e-mail attachments, and downloads. However, most viruses are spread through e-mail attachments. Once the attachment is opened, the virus activates, and infects a computer. Then the virus can send a copy of itself to everyone in a user's e-mail address book. Since a familiar e-mail address is the sender, friends open the attachment, and the whole process repeats itself. So how can an individual avoid these hidden dangers?

---

## Effective Design in Action

To demonstrate how good design improves the appearance of a published work, print and distribute a selection of sample pages that are hard to read.

Have students discuss the distracting features and offer suggestions to correct the distractions.

---

 **ELPS 1E** Internalize new academic language by using and reusing it/speaking

Further discuss using lists in published writing. For example:

- Note that students have a choice of numbering items in a list, as in the sample, or using bullets.
- Explain that numbers are generally used when sequence and order is important, such as the steps to complete a process.
- Explain that, for clarity, lists are indented at left (and sometimes at the right).
- Discuss the appropriateness of using lists. They work well in essays about scientific topics such as computers. They are less likely to be right for literary topics, such as analyses (although this depends on the ideas and organization of the essay).

**Learning Language**

Explain the directions and then model a summary of the first paragraph. For example, say, *Computer viruses can cause computers to act sick, just like real viruses can make people sick. A 'sick' computer may crash and restart often. It's important for people to understand computer viruses so they can protect their computers.* Encourage students to use a graphic organizer such as a Quick List, a Time Line, a 5 W's Chart, a T-Chart, or a Details Chart (see TE Appendix) to analyze their assigned section.

**DIFFERENTIATE INSTRUCTION ⇘**

⬛ ELPS 3F, 4F, 4G

74

### Protect Your Computer

Just like human viruses, there's no 100-percent-sure way to protect a computer. Following the steps below improve the odds.

A numbered list helps the reader digest related information.

1. **Install an anti-virus program from a trusted source.**
   New viruses are discovered every day, so it is important to stay current with all the updates.

2. **Also install firewall software.**
   Without a firewall, hackers can find a way to take control of a computer. Then they rent a "zombie" computer to criminals who want to send spam or attack other computers without having it traced back to them.

3. **Never open spam or unexpected e-mail attachments.**
   Suspicious files should be deleted. Files from a trusted friend can be saved and then opened.

4. **Keep software updated.**
   Over time, "holes" may be discovered in software programs. Download update "patches" from the program's Web site.

### Remove a Virus

If a computer does become infected, it should be disconnected from the Internet to keep from infecting others. It's like staying home from school when having the flu. Then run a virus scan and use the removal tool to get rid of the virus. If that doesn't work, get help from a "doctor"—your program's software support.

Don't let the threat of computer viruses keep you from enjoying the World Wide Web. Install anti-virus programs, stay updated, and use caution. A little effort can help keep a computer healthy all year long.

## Learning Language

A well-designed essay is often easier to read than a poorly written one. Even so, if the topic is complicated, the essay may still be difficult to understand. Work with a small group of students to reread the essay. Break it into sections and have each student take a section. Then have each student in the group retell or summarize the information in the assigned section. Listen carefully, take notes, and ask questions to clarify the information. If you need help, ask your teacher.

**ELPS 3F** Give information/ranging from using a limited high-frequency vocabulary to using abstract and content-based vocabulary during speaking; **4F** Use visual and contextual support and support from peers and teachers to read grade-appropriate text/use support from peers and teachers to enhance and confirm understanding and develop vocabulary and background learning; **4G** Demonstrate comprehension of increasingly complex English/participating in shared reading, summarizing material, responding to questions, and taking notes

Process

# Publishing Online

The Internet offers many publishing opportunities, including online magazines and writing contests. The information below will help you submit your writing for publication on the Net. (At home, always get a parent's approval first. In school, follow all guidelines established by the administration.)

## Checking Local Sites

Ask your teacher whether your school has a Web site where students can post work. Also check with local student organizations to see if any of them have Web sites that accept submissions.

## Finding Other Sites

Use a search engine to find sites that publish student work. Pay special attention to online magazines for young adults. If you don't have any luck with getting published, consider creating your own Web site. (See pages 76–77.)

## Submitting Your Work

Follow these tips for submitting your work.

- **Understand the publishing guidelines for each site.** Be sure to share this information with your teacher and your parents.
- **Become familiar with each site's audience.** Are the site's visitors an appropriate audience for your writing?
- **Send your writing in the correct form.** Some sites have online forms. Others will ask you to send your writing by mail or e-mail. Always explain why you are sending your writing.
- **Provide contact information.** Don't give your home address or any other personal information unless your parents approve.
- **Be patient.** Within a week or so, you should receive a note from the publisher verifying that your work has been received. It may take many weeks for a decision about publishing it.

### Try It!

Select a piece of writing that you would like to publish online. Find at least two Web sites that publish this type of student writing. Follow the guidelines, note each site's particular audience, and submit your writing.

# Publishing Online

## Checking Local Sites

Consider developing a class Web site where students can post their writing during the school year.

## Finding Other Sites

Explain that finding a publisher can sometimes be hard work. There are hundreds of journals, magazines, newspapers, etc., but only a fraction of them may be interested in a specific topic or type of writing. The Internet is a great help in overcoming this challenge.

## Submitting Your Work

Remind students to familiarize themselves with a Web site before submitting work. Students need to get a good idea of the works published there. The best way to decide whether a piece is suitable for a site is to read the site regularly.

## Try It!

Note that Web sites may not accept "simultaneous submissions," that is, the submission of a work that is under consideration by another publication at the same time. Students should check the guidelines carefully. If this is the case with the sites a student has chosen, they may wish to submit different works to the two sites.

Acknowledge that students may receive rejections from both of their chosen sites. Explain that this is very normal; some very famous writings were rejected many times before finally having their writing accepted for publication. Encourage them to submit pieces to different Web sites to increase the chances that one will be published.

TEKS 10.13E

**TEKS 10.13E** Publish written work; **ELPS 2C** Learn new expressions and basic vocabulary heard during classroom instruction/interactions; **3B** Expand vocabulary by retelling information represented or supported by pictures; **4E** Read linguistically accommodated content area material with a decreasing need for linguistic accommodations as more English is learned; **4F** Use visual and contextual support to enhance/confirm understanding; **4G** Demonstrate comprehension of increasingly complex English/summarizing material

## Creating Your Own Web Site

Mention the increasingly popular alternative to personal Web sites: the Web log (or blog). A blog is an online publication made up of ongoing entries, like a journal. Many people publish blogs—which can contain text and pictures—about their interests or experiences. A special link at the end of each entry invites readers to add their own comments. There are sites that host blogs free of charge.

A successful blog is updated often because the goal is to build a community of readers. Emphasize that, for both blogs and Web sites, students must observe Internet safety precautions. Review basic privacy practices and explain plagiarism and copyright violations. Refer students to your school's Internet policies for more information.

Invite students who are already familiar with blogs to share their own blogs or recommend favorites. Bookmark a selection of blogs on the class computer for students to explore.

★ **TEKS** 10.13E

### Try It!

As they design their own site, encourage students to think about Web sites that they visit often. What do they like about the design of these Web sites. What makes them easy (or hard) to use?

## Creating Your Own Web Site

To create a Web site on your home computer, check with your Internet service provider to find out how to get started. If you are using a school computer, ask your teacher for help. Then follow these steps.

### Planning Your Site

Begin by answering the following questions:
- What will be the purpose of this site, and who will be my audience?
- How are my favorite sites set up?
- How many pages will I include?
- How will my pages be linked together?

### Creating the Pages

First plan your pages by sketching them out. Then create each page as a text file. Most word-processing programs let you save a file as a Web page. If yours doesn't, you will have to add hypertext markup language (HTML) codes to format the text and make links to graphics and other pages. You can find instructions about HTML on the Internet.

### Testing Your Pages

Use your browser to open your first page. Then follow any links to make sure they work correctly. Finally, check the content and the look of all pages.

### Uploading the Site

Ask your Internet provider how to upload your finished pages. (If you're working at home, make sure to get your parents' approval first. If you're using school equipment, work with a teacher.) When you complete this step, visit your site to make sure it still works.

### Publicizing the Site

Once your site is up, e-mail your friends and tell them to visit it. Ask visitors to your site to spread the word to other people they know.

### Try It!

To create a personal Web site, start planning and sketch out your pages.

**TEKS** 10.13B

Publishing Your Writing **77**

Process

# Finding Places to Publish

The suggestions below will help you research places you can publish your writing. Before you submit writing anywhere, however, be sure you understand the conditions of the publication and share this information with your parents.

## School Days

If you have written about a topic that interests or affects others in your age group, school publications provide some good publishing options. Your school's newspaper is a good choice for expository or persuasive writing about school-related topics. A student literary magazine or journal offers publishing opportunities for a variety of writing forms, but especially for narrative writing, literary criticism, and poetry. There may even be a page for student writing on your school's Web site. If there isn't, perhaps you should be the one to start it!

## Your Own Backyard

The people in a community generally share some interests or background—that's what brought them together as a community in the first place. As a result, ideas that draw your attention may also appeal to your community as a whole. You may find that local publications, such as a local newspaper or neighborhood newsletter, are interested in publishing your writing.

## Explore the Possibilities

If you have a favorite national or regional magazine, it may accept writing from outside writers on certain topics. There are also writing contests that accept submissions; many of these contests are even geared toward young writers. A librarian can help you research the possibilities. You can also look in *Writer's Market*—available in most libraries—for more places to publish.

Thanks to modern technology, there are publishing options such as blogs that were not available in the past. By posting comments, readers can interact with other writers on a blog. Additionally, authors—including best-selling authors—have self-published their work for many years, but advances in technology have opened up many new possibilities. Enter "self publishing" into a search engine to investigate whether it has potential for you as a writer.

### Tip

Before submitting your work to a publication, check the submission guidelines to be sure your writing is in an acceptable form and style. Include a self-addressed stamped envelope when submitting your work to help ensure that you receive a response, as well as your returned work if it is not published.

## Finding Places to Publish

Note that any writer who submits work for publication will receive rejections. Remind students not to be discouraged by this and to discuss ways to deal with it. Have students:

- check magazines and Web sites to keep up with what's being published and to find publishing opportunities,
- look for a possible reason a submission was rejected (perhaps the piece needs more work), and
- consider it an encouraging sign to get a personal letter of rejection (this means the editor thought the piece was worth a personal response).

**TEKS** 10.13E

### Try It!

Have students research a specific publication or contest to find the writer's guidelines and submission procedures. ✔ **DIFFERENTIATE INSTRUCTION**
✔ **DIFFERENTIATE INSTRUCTION**

---

## Differentiated Instruction: English Language Learners

**ELPS** 1A, 4C, 4F, 5D

| ELP Level **Beginning** | ELP Level **Intermediate** | ELP Level **Advanced/Advanced High** |
|---|---|---|
| Model the written form of an address and have students practice by writing their own. Explain unfamiliar items like the P.O. Box and various abbreviations (*St.*, *Rd.*, etc.). | Help students understand the publication information on this page. *Which part is the title? What is meant by "forms?" Where does it say who can submit?* | With a partner's help, have students research a publication or contest to which they would like to submit work. Encourage students to prepare a manuscript and submit it! |

**TEKS** 10.13E Publish written work; **ELPS 1A** Use prior knowledge to understand meanings; **4C** Comprehend vocabulary and language structures used in written classroom materials; **4F** Use support from peers/teachers to read grade-appropriate text and enhance understanding and to develop grasp of language structures and background knowledge; **5D** Edit writing for standard grammar and usage/verb tenses

# Narrative Writing

## UNIT TEKS

**10.13A** Plan a first draft; **10.13B** Structure ideas and develop drafts; **10.13C** Revise drafts; **10.13D** Edit drafts; **10.13E** Revise final draft and publish work; **10.14A** Write an engaging story; **10.17Ai** Use and understand parts of speech; **10.17Aiii** Use and understand reciprocal pronouns; **10.17C** Use correctly structured sentences; **10.18A** Use conventions of capitalization; **10.18Bi** Use commas; **10.19** Spell correctly

## UNIT ELPS

**1A** Use prior knowledge and experiences; **1B** Monitor oral/written language; **1C** Use learning techniques; **1E** Internalize new language/speaking and writing; **1G** Distinguish between formal and informal English; **2A** Distinguish sounds and intonation patterns; **2C** Learn new structures, expressions, and vocabulary; **2D** Monitor understanding/seek clarification of spoken language; **2E** Use visual, contextual, and linguistic support to enhance understanding; **2F** Listen to and derive meaning from media; **2G** Understand spoken language/situations are familiar to unfamiliar; **2I** Demonstrate listening comprehension of spoken language; **3A** Practice sounds of new vocabulary; **3B** Expand and internalize initial vocabulary; **3C** Speak with increasing accuracy and ease; **3E** Share information; **3F** Ask for and give information; **3G** Express opinions, ideas, and feelings; **3H** Narrate, describe, and explain/increasing specificity; **3I** Adapt spoken language; **3J** Respond orally to information; **4A** Learn relationships between and decode sounds; **4C** Develop sight vocabulary/derive meaning of environmental print/comprehend written classroom materials; **4D** Use prereading supports; **4E** Read with decreasing need for linguistic accommodations; **4F** Use visual/contextual support and support from peers/ teachers; **4G** Demonstrate comprehension of language/ shared reading, summarizing, responding to questions, taking notes; **4H** Read silently with increasing ease; **4J** Employ inferential skills; **4K** Employ analytical skills; **5B** Write using new vocabulary; **5C** Spell and employ spelling patterns/rules with increasing accuracy; **5D** Edit writing for grammar and usage; **5E** Employ complex grammatical structures; **5F** Write using a variety of sentence lengths/patterns/connecting words; **5G** Narrate, describe, and explain with increasing specificity/content area writing

## Writing a Phase Autobiography (pages 79–120)

Students write about an extended life-changing experience.

## Historical Narrative (pages 121–128)

Students write about an important historical moment in the form of a historical narrative.

## Responding to Narrative Prompts (pages 129–135)

Students learn about the process of responding to narrative prompts.

 **Technology Connections**

 **Write Source Online**
www.hmheducation.com/tx/writesource
- **Net-text**
- **Writing Network**
- **Portfolio**
- **GrammarSnap**
- **Essay Scoring**
- **File Cabinet**

 **Interactive Whiteboard Lessons**

## Narrative Writing Unit Scope and Sequence

| Day | Writing and Conventions Instruction | Write Source Student Edition | | | Daily Language Workouts | Skills-Book | Write Source Online |
|---|---|---|---|---|---|---|---|
| | | Core Unit | Tools of Language | Resource Units | | | |
| **WEEK 1** 1–5 | **Writing a Phase Autobiography** Narrative Writing Warm-Up | 79–84 | **TL** 532–537 | | 18–21 | | Interactive Whiteboard Lesson |

 **Resource Units** referenced above are located in the back of the *Student Edition* and *Teacher's Edition*
**TL** *"The Tools of Language"*   **BGW** *"Basic Grammar and Writing"*   **WR** *"A Writer's Resource"*   **PG** *"Proofreader's Guide"*

| Day | Writing and Conventions Instruction | Write Source Student Edition | | | Daily Language Workouts | Skills-Book | Write Source Online |
|---|---|---|---|---|---|---|---|
| | | Core Unit | Tools of Language | Resource Units | | | |
| **WEEK 2** 6–10 | Prewriting | 85–90 | TL 526–529 | WR 618–627 | 22–25 | | Net-text |
| | Drafting | 91–96 | | WR 628–633 | | | Net-text |
| | Revising | 97–106 | | WR 634–637 | | | Net-text |
| | Skills Activities:<br>•Tone (Transitive and Intransitive Verbs) | | | | | 99 | GrammarSnap |
| **WEEK 3** 11–13 | Editing | 107–112 | TL 526–529 | | 26–29 | | Net-text |
| | Skills Activities:<br>•Adjectives: Positive, Comparative, and Superlative | | | BGW 576 | | 109 | GrammarSnap |
| | •Reflexive and Reciprocal Pronouns | | | PG 742–749 | | 87–88 | GrammarSnap |
| | •Commas after Introductory Phrases and Clauses | | | PG 648–649 | | 9–10 | GrammarSnap |
| | •Punctuating Dialogue | | | PG 654–655, 676–677 | | 31–33 | GrammarSnap |
| | •Pronoun–Antecedent Agreement | | | PG 742–749 | | 152 | GrammarSnap |
| | •Spelling and Plurals | | | PG 696–699, 706–711 | | 51–58 | |
| | Publishing | 113 | | | | | Net-text |
| 14–15 | Assessing and Reflecting | 114–120 | | | | | Net-text |
| **WEEK 4** 16–20 | **Writing a Historical Narrative**<br>Sample | 121–123 | TL 526–529 | | 30–33 | | Net-text |
| | Prewriting | 124–125 | | WR 618–627 | | | Net-text |
| | Drafting, Revising | 126–127 | | WR 628–637 | | | Net-text |
| | Editing, Publishing | 128 | | | | | Net-text |
| **WEEK 5** 21 | **Responding to Narrative Prompts** | 129 | TL 526–529 | | 34–37 | | Net-text |
| 22 | Prewriting | 130–131 | | | | | Net-text |
| 23 | Drafting | 132–133 | | | | | Net-text |
| 24 | Revising, Editing | 134 | | | | | Net-text |
| 25 | Narrative Writing on Tests | 135 | | | | | Net-text |

**Resource Units** referenced above are located in the back of the *Student Edition* and *Teacher's Edition*
TL *"The Tools of Language"*   BGW *"Basic Grammar and Writing"*   WR *"A Writer's Resource"*   PG *"Proofreader's Guide"*

## Writing Focus

- Writing a Phase Autobiography
- Historical Narrative
- Responding to Narrative Prompts

## Grammar Focus

- Reflexive and Reciprocal Pronouns

## Learning Language

Read aloud the basic and academic terms, as well as the descriptions and questions. Model for students how to read one question and answer it. For example, *It says that a narrative tells a story, either fiction or nonfiction. It's asking what nonfiction story I've read lately. Recently, I read the story of the writing of the Declaration of Independence.* Have partners monitor their understanding of the terms by working through the meanings and questions together. DIFFERENTIATE INSTRUCTION ↘

⭐ ELPS 2C, 2D, 3E, 3G, 4C, 4G

## Minilessons

### A Big Splash
Writing a Phase Autobiography

- **READ** the paragraph on SE page 81. **NOTICE** the last line. Can you list sports for which that sentence has been true for you? **TALK** with a classmate about the paragraph.

⭐ ELPS 3E, 3G, 4C, 4G

### Business As Usual
Writing a Historical Narrative

- **STUDY** the history of a business in your community. **DEVELOP** a plan for a historical narrative based on an interesting event or a significant period in the history of the business.

⭐ **ELPS 1A** Use prior knowledge and experience to understand meanings; **2C** Learn new language structures/expressions and basic/academic vocabulary heard during classroom instruction/interactions; **2D** Monitor understanding of spoken language during classroom instruction/interactions and seek clarification of spoken language as needed; **3E** Share information in cooperative learning interactions; **3G** Express opinions ranging from communicating short phrases to participating in discussions; **4C** Comprehend vocabulary used in written classroom materials; **4G** Demonstrate comprehension of increasingly complex English/responding to questions; **5G** Describe with increasing specificity and detail/writing

---

⭐ ELPS 2C, 3E, 3G

# Narrative Writing

## Writing Focus

## Grammar Focus

## Learning Language

Working with a classmate, read the definitions below and discuss possible answers to each question.

1. A narrative tells a story. It can be fiction or nonfiction. **What nonfiction narratives have you read recently?**
2. A simile is a comparison of unlike things, using "like" or "as." **Using a simile, what could you compare to a thunderstorm?**
3. Sensory details are details that refer to the five senses. **The words "crash" and "bang" appeal to which sense?**
4. To shed light on something is to give information about it. **How might you shed light on an accident you observed?**

---

| Differentiated Instruction: English Language Learners | | ⭐ ELPS 1A, 4C, 5G |
|---|---|---|
| **ELP Level**<br>**Beginning** | **ELP Level**<br>**Intermediate** | **ELP Level**<br>**Advanced/Advanced High** |
| Give simple examples to help students understand similes (e.g., *cold as ice*). Help students develop their own similes using sentence stems (*Hot as a. . . ., He was like a. . .*). | Compare and contrast similes and metaphors. Provide students with examples of each that they must identify. | Have students write a paragraph describing something (a baseball game, a car, a place) and use at least three similes. Challenge students to use a metaphor as well. |

## Narrative Writing
# Writing a Phase Autobiography

A phase autobiography re-creates an extended period in your life that changed you. This type of narrative writing invites the reader to experience what you experienced, and it illustrates the lessons you learned from it. If a reader says, "That was an inspiring story. You shed light on the topic, and I know just what you went through," the writer should know that he or she has succeeded.

For this chapter, you will share an extended life-changing experience, such as caring for a sick relative, campaigning for student council president, or surviving summer camp. Your phase autobiography will hold the reader's interest if it includes four key elements: action, sensory details, dialogue, and personal reflection.

### Writing Guidelines

Subject: **A period that changed you**
Purpose: **To share a life-changing time in your life**
Form: **Phase autobiography**
Audience: **Classmates**

"We all have big changes
in our lives that are more
or less a second chance."
—Harrison Ford

### Objectives

- understand the purpose, content, and form of a phase autobiography
- choose a topic (a life-changing experience) to write about
- plan, draft, revise, and edit a phase autobiography

Some students may not recognize periods that have changed them in significant ways. Explain that the experiences they choose to write about in their **phase autobiographies** don't have to be ones that completely redirected their lives. The experiences might be ones that helped them change their attitudes or feelings toward themselves or other people. They might be experiences that changed their minds about something they thought or believed. Share personal experiences (a college professor; an unexpected trip; the death of a pet) that changed your life in major or minor ways to help students develop an understanding of the range of experiences they can share.

### Resources

**Copy Masters (see Appendix)**

- Time Line
- Sensory Chart
- Details Chart

**Benchmark Papers (see Appendix)**

**Narrative Writing Warm-Up: Being Selective**

As you review the sample details list, provide the following questions to help students distinguish between important and unimportant details.

Does the detail. . .

- describe my thoughts and feelings before the experience?
- help re-create what I thought or felt during or after the experience?
- explain how I changed as a direct result of the experience?

Explain that if they ask these three questions about each detail and their answer to each question is "no," then the detail is probably not important enough to include.

**Try It!**

Before beginning this activity, work with students to select several possible topics for their narrative paragraphs. Because students will be writing about life-changing experiences in both a paragraph and in a lengthier phase autobiography, they will benefit from brainstorming multiple topics. Have students ask themselves the following questions to generate ideas:

- What times in my life do I often talk about with family and friends? Why do I recall these times? How did I change or what did I learn from these experiences?
- What photographs or souvenirs do I treasure from specific times in my life? Why do I treasure these items? How did I change or what did I learn during these times?

 **TEKS** 10.13A, 10.14A; **ELPS** 4K

---

 **TEKS** 10.13A, 10.14A

## Narrative Writing Warm-Up: Being Selective

When you write a phase autobiography, it's important to include specific details. However, you don't want to overwhelm the reader with too much information—after all, your life-changing experience could extend over several months. You need to be selective. Choose specific details that build a story to share and shed light on the main focus of your experience.

A writer compiled the list of details below for a narrative paragraph. After reading through his list, he crossed out the ideas that weren't important enough to include.

### Sample Details List

**Water Skiing**

- A friend asked me to go water skiing with him.
- ~~It was Memorial Day weekend.~~
- I was hoping my parents would say no.
- I didn't want to look silly.
- ~~Even my friend's kid sister can ski.~~
- The boat had 150 hp motor.
- ~~The skis were huge.~~
- ~~My friend's cousins showed up.~~
- My first attempt left me with a mouth full of water.
- I finally got up on the skis and sailed across the lake.
- There was no wind and the water was like glass.
- I even crossed the wake without falling.
- ~~I pulled and leaned so that I was running parallel to the boat.~~
- ~~I waved to people on the shore.~~
- I was so pleased, and my friend celebrated with me.
- After a rest, I was ready to go again.

**Note**: This final list of details guided the writer as he wrote a paragraph about the experience that changed him. (See the next page.)

### Try It!

Think of an experience that changed you. List the details related to the experience. Then review your list and cross out any unimportant ideas. Remember, you don't need to share every detail, just a good story.

---

 **TEKS** **10.13A** Plan a first draft/determining topics through a range of strategies, and developing a thesis; **10.14A** Write a story with a conflict, a resolution, interesting and believable characters, and literary strategies and devices to enhance the plot; **ELPS** **4K** Demonstrate comprehension and expand reading skills by employing analytical skills/evaluating written information and performing critical analyses

# Writing a Narrative Paragraph

A narrative paragraph shares an important experience. Remember that a paragraph has three main parts:

- The **topic sentence** introduces the experience.
- The **body sentences** share details that re-create the experience.
- The **closing sentence** reflects on the experience and how it changed the writer.

## Sample Narrative Paragraph

In the following narrative paragraph, the writer shares an experience that changed him—water skiing for the first time.

Narrative

---

The **topic sentence** introduces the experience.

The **body sentences** share the important details.

The **closing sentence** reflects on the experience.

**Ready to Go Again**

**I was always a bit nervous about my athletic ability until a friend asked me to go water skiing with him.** At first, I hoped my parents would say no because I was afraid of looking silly, but they thought it was a great idea. I got more worried when I saw the massive 150 hp motor on the back of the boat waiting next to the dock. Bill went first to show me what to do. He sliced through the water, leaped over the wake, and sailed off the ski jump, landing perfectly. All too soon, it was my turn. I jumped in the water, pulled on the skis, and signaled I was ready. The boat surged forward, catching me off guard; I swallowed half the lake. Bill's dad stopped the boat. Patiently, Bill and his dad showed me once more how to use my arms and legs. This time I was ready, and I suddenly found myself standing on skis zipping over the water. The water looked like glass because there were no waves or wind that day. I yelled, "Yahoo!" Carefully, I made my way across the wake, and I didn't fall! When we returned to the dock, I laughed and celebrated. Bill and his relatives shouted, "You were great!" After others had their turns, I was ready to go again. **I suddenly realized that I didn't have to be an expert to enjoy a sport.**

---

 **Write your narrative paragraph.** Review the three parts of a paragraph (top of page) and what they do. Then use your details list from page **80** to write a narrative paragraph about an experience that changed you.

## Writing a Narrative Paragraph

Review the three main parts of the sample paragraph. Have students identify the details in each part that helped the writer fulfill the purpose of the piece.

✻ For more about writing strong paragraphs, see SE pages 597–615.

## Sample Narrative Paragraph

Explain that using vivid, colorful language makes it easier for readers to visualize and connect with a writer's experience. Explain that when readers connect with the experience, they can better understand why it changed the writer. Have students point out examples of vivid language that helps them visualize the writer's experience in the sample paragraph. For example, they may point out

- active verbs such as *sliced, leaped, sailed,* and *surged,* and
- figurative language, such as *swallowed half the lake* and *the water looked like glass.*

**Write your narrative paragraph.** In writing their own narrative paragraphs, remind students that they should be able to show how each main part of their writing succeeds in fulfilling its purpose. ✔DIFFERENTIATE INSTRUCTION

TEKS 10.14A; ELPS 5G

---

TEKS **10.14A** Write a story with a conflict, a resolution, interesting and believable characters, and literary strategies and devices to enhance the plot; ELPS **4C** Comprehend vocabulary and language structures used in written classroom materials; **5G** Narrate/describe/explain with increasing specificity and detail to fulfill content area writing needs

## Understanding Your Goal

The first four traits—focus and coherence, organization, development of ideas, and voice—relate directly to the development of content and form. They are important for students to address during prewriting, drafting, and revising.

The remaining trait—conventions—will be an important focus during the editing process.

❋ The scoring guide on SE pages 60–61 is based on these traits.

Remind students that writing is a skill. As with any skill, learning and applying appropriate techniques can lead to proficiency.

Refer students to the traits chart as you work through the sample essay on SE pages 83–84.

**TEKS** 10.14A

### Learning Language

Provide a Sensory Chart (TE Appendix) to help students organize their ideas. Give students examples to demonstrate the power of sensory details and dialogue. For example, have students compare the following two sentences : *I hit a home run.* and *I blasted the ball high into the cloudless sky as the crowd roared, "Home run!"*

Discuss the reasons that the second sentence is much more effective for drawing the reader into the story. **DIFFERENTIATE INSTRUCTION** ↘

**ELPS** 5G

---

**TEKS** 10.14A
**ELPS** 5G

## Understanding Your Goal

Your goal in this chapter is to write about a period in your life that changed you. The traits in the following chart can help you plan and write your phase autobiography.

### Traits of Narrative Writing

■ **Focus and Coherence**

Share an important extended time in your life. Focus on that event. The narrative should tell a story about your life, and the reader should understand how the event you write about changed your life.

■ **Organization**

Develop a clear beginning, middle, and ending that together form a meaningful whole. Use a logical organizational pattern and transitions to move the reader from one idea to the next.

■ **Development of Ideas**

Make sure that each specific event adds to the overall story. Choose sensory details that create a rich description. Consider how storytelling devices such as suspense and conflict can add to your narrative.

■ **Voice**

Use a personal, interested voice appropriate for your topic.

■ **Conventions**

Write sentences of varied length and structure. Check for errors in grammar, punctuation, capitalization, and spelling.

**Learning Language** As you write, remember that your narrative should show why this was an important event in your life. Using sensory details and dialogue, you can make the event come alive for your reader.

---

**TEKS** **10.14A** Write a story with a conflict, a resolution, interesting and believable characters, and literary strategies and devices to enhance the plot; **ELPS** **5G** Describe and explain with increasing specificity and detail to fulfill content area writing needs

# Phase Autobiography

In this phase autobiography, the student writer tells about volunteering at an animal shelter. The side notes explain key parts of the essay.

Narrative

**Beginning**
The writer starts in the middle of the action and introduces the situation.

### In the Doghouse

The first time I met Mugsy, I smelled him before I even saw him. He'd just been brought to the animal shelter after getting sprayed by a skunk, and now it was my job to bathe this furry stink bomb. It was only my second day volunteering at the shelter, and I wasn't sure what to do.

The second Mugsy saw me, he wanted to be my best friend. He was an ordinary-looking mutt, about six years old, as big as a shepherd, with long brown matted fur. He bounded toward me, yapping happily, tail wagging like a windshield wiper on hyperspeed. If he hadn't been tethered, I would have had his large skunk-scented muddy feet all over me.

**Middle**
Descriptive details pull the reader into the experience.

I tried to spray him with the hose, but Mugsy played with the water, running through it, ducking, and generally making me look very incompetent when my supervisor Elena walked by. She quickly grasped the situation. "You're going to have to hold him firmly while you wash him," she said. She looked at me in a way that showed she expected me to do this myself and to do it right.

This was my chance to prove to Elena that she'd made a good choice when she agreed to let me work for her. I was younger than most of the other volunteers, but I'd told her I was ready for the responsibilities of caring for these animals. One day I plan to become a veterinarian, so I thought this would be great preparation. Now I already faced a challenge that I didn't feel ready for. "No problem," I said, hoping that I seemed confident.

**Middle**
Details about the dog make him a believeable character.

I grabbed Mugsy's collar and managed to soap him down. I was surprised to see how skinny he was. One ear was chewed up and he had a sore spot on his hind leg. His life was as a stray must have been really tough. Still soaking wet, Mugsy decided to play again. He jumped up on me, tried to lick my face, and I started laughing. I finally got him clean, but I was a mess. When Elena came back, she looked pleased. "If you want to be successful here, don't try to stay clean," she said with a smile.

---

## Phase Autobiography

Work through the sample phase autobiography with the class, pointing out the elements that make it a good piece of narrative writing. Focus on the following traits, and encourage students to identify specific details that support each point.

### Focus and Coherence

- The writer shares an important life-changing experience.
- The writing clearly shows how the experience changed the writer.

### Organization

- There are strong beginning, middle, and ending parts that explain how the experience changed the writer.
- The writer uses good transitions to move the reader from one event to the next.

### Development of Ideas

- Each idea helps support the writer's reflection in the ending.
- Dialogue adds interest and realism.
- Sensory details help re-create the experience.
- Suspense creates interest in the reader.

### Voice

- The writer uses a natural, honest voice.
- Dialogue helps reveal the writer's personality and thoughts.

TEKS 10.14A; ELPS 4K

---

## Differentiated Instruction:
## English Language Learners

ELPS 1C, 3B, 4C, 4F, 5G

| ELP Level **Beginning** | ELP Level **Intermediate** | ELP Level **Advanced/Advanced High** |
|---|---|---|
| Define the five senses (sight, sound, etc.). Students should draw pictures representing each sense and practice saying the terms aloud after the teacher models pronunciation. | List the five senses on the board. Brainstorm with students to come up with descriptive words for each sense (*hot, loud, bright,* etc.). | Have students write a short description of an event, such as a parade or baseball game, including at least three of the senses. Challenge students to use all five if possible. |

**TEKS** 10.14A Write a story with a conflict, a resolution, interesting and believable characters, and literary strategies and devices to enhance the plot; **ELPS 1C** Use strategic learning techniques to acquire basic vocabulary; **3B** Expand vocabulary by learning and using high-frequency words for identifying and describing; **4C** Comprehend vocabulary used in written classroom materials; **4F** Use visual/contextual support and support from peers/teachers to develop vocabulary; **4K** Demonstrate comprehension and expand reading skills by employing analytical skills/evaluating written information and performing critical analyses; **5G** Describe with increasing specificity and detail/writing

Remind students that a successful phase autobiography explains how an experience changed the writer. Have students point out phrases and sentences in the last two paragraphs that fulfill the writer's purpose.

 **TEKS** 10.14A

 **Respond to the reading.**

#### Focus and Coherence

1. Students should generally agree that the events do work well together.

#### Organization

2. Chronological. Students should generally agree that the events are not hard to follow.

#### Development of Ideas

3. Examples may include: *furry stink bomb; ordinary-looking mutt; big as a shepherd; long brown matted fur; windshield wiper on hyperspeed; large skunk-scented muddy feet; skinny; the big "no" in their eyes; large, soft head.*

#### Voice

4. Students should generally agree that the narrator does sound interested. Examples that might demonstrate this include: *I wasn't sure what to do. This was my chance to prove to Elena. . . . I desperately hoped that someone would adopt Mugsy. I took a deep breath and hoped. . . .*

#### Conventions

5. Students should generally agree that there are few, if any, errors in writing conventions or pronoun usage.

**ELPS** 4K, 5D

**Middle**
Dialogue moves the story along.

Over the next few months, I hosed down cages and fed and bathed dogs, cats, rabbits, and even snakes that were left at the shelter. My favorite job was helping people find the right pet. I desperately hoped that someone would adopt Mugsy, but during all that time nobody was interested in an ordinary old mutt, no matter how friendly he was. They wanted puppies or purebreds or small dogs or cute dogs. It broke my heart to see families walk right by his cage. Whenever I could, I'd spend time with Mugsy. "Don't worry," I'd say, as I petted him, "Someone will see how special you are." But Mugsy would just lie down. He'd lost his happy goofiness.

One day Elena told me that Mugsy was being sent to a different shelter. They needed his space for more adoptable dogs. I knew I had to do something, so that night, I took Mugsy home with me. My parents took one look at him and I could see the big "no" in their eyes. They didn't want a dog.

**Ending**
The writer reflects on how the experience has changed him.

I took a deep breath and hoped they could see the new responsible me. "I promise you, I'll take care of him, no matter what. Mugsy needs me." I explained his situation at the shelter. Mugsy seemed to understand that this was his big chance. He walked over to where my dad was sitting, laid his large, soft head on my dad's lap and looked up. Instinctively, my dad petted him, and Mugsy's tail came to life. I knew then that Mugsy had a home. Taking care of Mugsy became the highlight of my day. Having Mugsy and working at the shelter has helped to make my future clearer. I now know without a doubt that I want to become a veterinarian one day.

**Respond to the reading.** Answer the following questions.

**Focus and Coherence** (1) Do all the events in the essay work well together? **Organization** (2) What is the organizational pattern? Are any events out of sequence or hard to follow? **Development of Ideas** (3) What kinds of sensory details are used? **Voice** (4) Does this writer sound interested? Explain. **Conventions** (5) Did you find any errors in writing conventions? Were pronouns used correctly?

**TEKS** 10.14A Write a story with a conflict, a resolution, interesting and believable characters, and literary strategies and devices to enhance the plot; **ELPS** 4K Demonstrate comprehension and expand reading skills by employing analytical skills/ evaluating written information and performing critical analyses; **5D** Edit writing for standard grammar and usage/subject-verb and pronoun agreement and appropriate verb tenses

**TEKS** 10.13A, 10.14A

# Prewriting

Your phase autobiography will be about a period of time in your life that changed you. In your prewriting, you will plan your first draft by choosing a specific period, listing the details that capture the phase, and organizing your ideas for writing.

Narrative

### Keys to Effective Prewriting

1. Think about extended periods of time in your life when you went through important changes.

2. Choose one of those periods to write about.

3. List the key events that occurred during this time.

4. Collect sensory details and personal thoughts related to this phase.

5. Consider how you can engage your audience.

6. Organize your ideas in chronological order for writing.

## Prewriting
### Keys to Effective Prewriting

The Keys to Effective Prewriting on this page explain the process that students are guided through on SE pages 86–90.

A phase autobiography is by definition personal and potentially revealing. Some students, however, may consider experiences that are inappropriate for sharing. As students begin to list topics for their phase autobiographies, remind them that they will be sharing their writing with you and their classmates. To help students choose appropriate topics, have them submit their writing ideas in advance for your approval. Doing so also gives you the opportunity to check for understanding and to help students develop their topics. **✓ DIFFERENTIATE INSTRUCTION**

**TEKS** 10.13A, 10.14A

### 🐭 Writer's Craft

The activities in the prewriting, drafting, revising, and editing sections of this chapter can serve as minilessons for whole-group instruction, small-group work, or independent work time.

---

**TEKS** **10.13A** Plan a first draft/selecting genre and determining topics through a range of strategies; **10.14A** Write a story with interesting/believable characters and literary strategies/devices to enhance the plot; **ELPS 5F** Write using a variety of grade-appropriate sentence lengths and patterns in increasingly accurate ways; **5G** Describe with increasing specificity and detail/writing

## Prewriting
### Planning Your Writing

Work with the class to compile a list of categories that may suggest life-changing experiences for students. For example:

- sports
- school clubs or extracurricular activities
- summer vacations
- volunteer events and part-time jobs
- family events, such as moving or a new baby

Remind students to review the topics list they generated before writing their narrative paragraph.

**Complete the sentence starter.** Even if students already know what they want to write about, encourage them to list several options. These other topics may be useful for future writing assignments.

### Reflecting on Your Topic

Remind students that freewriting enables them to write their first thoughts about a topic without unduly worrying about writing conventions. Point out that freewriting is a way for them to generate ideas and details about their topic.

**Collect your first thoughts.** Remind students that some of the details they write now will be cut later. For freewriting, however, they shouldn't worry about which details will be included and which will not.

★ **TEKS** 10.13A, 10.14A

---

## Prewriting Planning Your Writing

To think of life-changing periods of time, Sarah completed the sentence starter "I experienced an important change when I . . ." in three different ways. She put an asterisk next to the one that she wanted to write about.

**Sentence Starter**

> I experienced an important change when I . . .
>      overcame homesickness when my family moved.
>      practiced four hours a day to make the soccer team.
> *helped build sets for the school musical.

**Complete the sentence starter.** Finish the sentence in at least three different ways. Put an asterisk (*) next to the period of time you will choose.

## Reflecting on Your Topic

To gather her initial thoughts, Sarah wrote freely about her topic. Then she underlined details that seemed important.

**Freewriting**

> Being on the tech crew for school plays taught me more than construction skills—I also learned patience and how to be part of a team. You had to work your way up to certain jobs. We spent 3 weeks building a fence for "West Side Story." Mr. Morales had built a frame out of pipe, and my job was to cut fencing and attach it to the frame. My arms got scratched up because I wouldn't wear long sleeves—it was too warm in the theater.
> When the fence was done, we had to paint a fake brick wall on wooden flats. We drew chalk lines to look like bricks, then painted them red.
> But we were running out of time. Opening night was only a week away. Luckily, we made it! I really felt proud when the audience applauded. I had learned how to work with people who had different talents and ideas.

**Collect your first thoughts.** Write freely for 5 to 10 minutes to gather your initial thoughts about your life-changing period. Underline key details that you could use in your story.

## Gathering Details

An effective phase autobiography, one that captures the essence of the time, contains three types of details: actions, sensory details, and personal thoughts.

- **Specific actions or events** move the story forward.
- **Sensory details** show what you saw, felt, heard, smelled, or tasted.
- **Personal thoughts** reveal your feelings and insights at that time.

Sarah completed the following details chart to gather ideas for her story.

### Details Chart

| Actions or events | Sensory details | Thoughts |
|---|---|---|
| Scratched arm on fencing | Sore arm | I'm too hot to cover up with a sweatshirt. |
| Cutting fencing | Aching arms and hands | Grandpa's voice: "Stick with it!" |
| Saw other kids goofing off | Annoyed at the goof-offs | I'll just ignore them and keep doing my job. |
| Had to keep repainting fake brick wall | Frustration about having to repaint | I'm learning patience. |
| Finished scenery by opening night | Sound of opening night applause | I'm proud of my work and of getting along with everyone. |

**Prewrite**

**Create a details chart.** To gather details for your writing, complete a details chart like the one above.

**Texas Traits**

⭐ **Focus on the Texas Traits**

**Development of Ideas** Actions can keep the reader interested in your story, but be sure to develop your ideas fully. Sensory details and thoughts will make the reader feel part of your experience.

*Narrative*

## Gathering Details

Direct students' attention to the word *essence* in the first sentence. Have students generate a list of synonyms, such as *spirit, core, heart, soul,* and *meaning*. These words should help students better understand the types of details they need to use.

⭐ TEKS 10.13A, 10.14A

**Create a details chart.** Provide photocopies of the reproducible details chart (TE Appendix) for students to use as they gather their details. ✓ **DIFFERENTIATE INSTRUCTION**

⭐ **Focus on the Texas Traits**

**Development of Ideas**
Ask students why including their thoughts and feelings in their phase autobiography is important. Responses may include the following:

- Although readers may not have had the exact same experience as the writer, they probably have had similar reactions, thoughts, and feelings about something in their own lives. This similarity helps them connect with the writing.
- When a reader thinks, "I would have reacted the same way," the writer has connected with the reader. The reader is then probably more interested in what the writer has to communicate.

---

⭐ **TEKS** **10.13A** Plan a first draft/selecting genre and determining topics through a range of strategies; **10.14A** Write a story with interesting/believable characters and literary strategies/devices to enhance the plot; **ELPS** **2F** Listen to and derive meaning from a variety of media to build and reinforce concept attainment; **3J** Respond orally to information presented in a variety of media to build and reinforce concept and language attainment; **4C** Comprehend vocabulary used in written classroom materials

## Prewriting
### Building Narrative Suspense

Make sure students understand that the word *conflict* in the context of "Start with a conflict" refers to the problems that they face. Among other things, the conflict may be something that the students don't think they will enjoy doing, but need to do. To reinforce this understanding, refer students back to the sample phase autobiography on SE page 83–84. Have them identify the conflict in this piece (living up to new responsibilities).

**Create a plot line.** Remind students that their phase autobiography should only have one main conflict and one main climax. Details that don't correspond to either of these may not be necessary. DIFFERENTIATE INSTRUCTION ↘

★ TEKS 10.13A, 10.14A

---

## Prewriting Building Narrative Suspense

A compelling phase autobiography is suspenseful; it makes the reader want to know what happens next. Here's how to build suspense into your story:

**Start with a conflict**—a task to be accomplished or a problem to be solved. The conflict in Sarah's narrative is the challenge to build sets for a musical.

**Respond to the conflict.** Sarah does a number of things to address her challenge—working on the fence, ignoring the goof-off kids, repainting the "slipping" brick wall. Each action builds suspense.

**Build toward the climax or high point.** The climax is the most exciting part of the story. It's the point at which the writer does or does not master the challenge. Sarah's narrative builds to opening night.

### Focus on the Texas Traits

**Organization** An effective phase autobiography should follow the classic plot line. The beginning gets the reader's attention and introduces the conflict, or challenge. Then a series of actions builds suspense. (Include at least two or three key actions.) At the climax, the writer either does or does not master the challenge. The ending tells how the writer's life is changed.

### Plot Line

 **Create a plot line.** Plan the main actions of your phase autobiography in a plot line like the one above. Use your details chart from page 87.

Prewrite

---

### Differentiated Instruction: Struggling Learners

Some students may have difficulty moving the action along naturally with dialogue. Provide opportunities for practice by generating sentences without dialogue and having volunteers rewrite the sentences using dialogue. Examples:

I told Roy that we should leave the park quickly.

"Let's get out of this park fast!" I yelled to Roy.

Anna said that I had never seen a movie I didn't like.

"Dude, you rave about every flick you see!" Anna exclaimed.

★ ELPS 5F

---

★ TEKS **10.13A** Plan a first draft/selecting genre and determining topics through a range of strategies; **10.14A** Write a story with a conflict and a resolution; **ELPS 5F** Write using a variety of grade-appropriate sentence patterns in increasingly accurate ways

**TEKS** 10.14A

> "Of all the subjects available to you as a writer, the one you know best is yourself."
>
> —William Zinsser

Narrative

## Adding Dialogue

Dialogue enriches a phase autobiography by moving the action along, by revealing aspects of the speakers' personalities, and by simply adding information. The chart below shows how Sarah can present the same information without and with dialogue. (The dialogue examples are taken from the model on pages 93–96.)

|  | **Without Dialogue** | **With Dialogue** |
|---|---|---|
| **Show a speaker's personality** | As the piece of fencing scratched my arm, I began to question why I had joined the tech theater crew. | "Ouch!" I yelped as the piece of fencing scratched my arm, making marks like animal tracks. "Are we having fun yet?" |
| **Keep the action moving** | We decided to ask for more help. | "Please give us more help," we begged Mr. Morales. |
| **Add information** | My grandpa told me to always do my best work. | I could hear my grandpa's voice in my head: "You don't want your name on anything you're not proud of." |

 **Consider dialogue for your phase autobiography.** For practice, write some realistic dialogue that would be appropriate near the beginning of your story. (See page 654 for information about punctuating dialogue.)

Prewrite

## Adding Dialogue

Give students more practice in discerning the difference between straight narrative text and dialogue. To emphasize the difference, ask students to imagine a movie in which a narrator tells the entire story and the characters perform their different actions without dialogue. (If students have seen any silent films, have them share their reactions to them.) ✔ **DIFFERENTIATE INSTRUCTION**

Encourage students to look at the key details that they underlined in their freewriting from SE page 86 and at the ideas in their details chart from SE page 87 to identify ideas that they could present with dialogue.

**TEKS** 10.14A

### Writer's Craft

**Speech patterns:** Impressionists adopt the speech patterns of famous people, such as politicians or movie stars. Through vocal imitation, the impressionist seems to become the person. That's because the way a person speaks reveals his or her personality.

Dialogue should do the same. By creating distinctive speech patterns, writers make characters come to life.

---

## Differentiated Instruction: English Language Learners

**ELPS** 1A, 1E, 2E, 3F, 3H

| ELP Level **Beginning** | ELP Level **Intermediate** | ELP Level **Advanced/Advanced High** |
|---|---|---|
| Use the plot line to visually support student understanding of key vocabulary (rising, climax, action, etc.). | Using the plot line and basic vocabulary for support, have students explain the meaning of key terms (rising, climax, action, etc.). | Have students identify the key plot points from a well-known movie or book. Students should use key terms (rising, climax, action, etc.) in their descriptions. |

**TEKS** 10.14A Write a story with interesting/believable characters and literary strategies to enhance the plot; **ELPS** 1A Use prior experiences to understand meanings; 1E Internalize new academic language by using and reusing it/speaking; 2E Use visual and linguistic support to enhance and confirm understanding of increasingly complex spoken language; 3F Give information/ranging from using a limited high-frequency vocabulary to using abstract and content-based vocabulary during speaking; 3H Explain with increasing specificity and detail

## Prewriting

### Reviewing Features of a Narrative

Have students first read the excerpt for enjoyment. Then have them read it again, looking for the narrative features. Point out that some of these narrative features overlap. For example, the last sentence of the second paragraph, which begins with *I loved rubbing my fingers . . .*, contains sensory details and expresses a personal thought.

Suggest that students create a four-column chart to list examples of each narrative feature that they find in the excerpt.

 **On your own paper**

**Possible Answers**

- **action details:** The captain began barking orders. The boat rocked back and forth . . .
- **sensory details:** golden orange sky, flecked with purple clouds; brisk wind; polished oak decks; smelled of salt and varnish
- **personal thoughts:** I imagined myself living in a time . . . , It was odd to look back and see . . .
- **dialogue:** "Break down the sails!" "Where are you, Pete?" [DIFFERENTIATE INSTRUCTION ↘]

⬛ **ELPS** 4H, 4K

## Prewriting Reviewing Features of a Narrative

Read the following excerpt from a phase autobiography, watching for action details, sensory details, personal thoughts, and dialogue.

### From "Charting a New Course"

The sixth day dawned with a golden orange sky, flecked with purple clouds. The sea was calm, and a brisk wind filled the sails.

We had been onboard the *John Gray Williamson*, a 64-foot sailing yacht, for nearly a week. Our crew of 12—four adult leaders and eight boys aged 14 to 17—were part of a Boy Scout expedition to the Bahamas. I imagined myself living in a time when sailors relied on wind rather than oil for power. I loved rubbing my fingers along the polished oak decks, which smelled of salt and varnish.

Then I noticed the leaders gazing off the starboard side at a massive cloud formation. Its base melted into the sea in dark columns.

The captain began barking orders: "Break down the sails!" he yelled to three of us standing near him. We had just barely untied the last knot to bring the sail down when the wind began roaring, and we got pelted with rain. I couldn't see my friend. I cried out, "Where are you, Pete?" Then I saw him struggling toward me. The boat rocked back and forth, making it hard to keep firm footing, and the boom swung around wildly. Just before the boom grazed over our heads, I screamed, "Watch out!" and tackled Peter.

Then a tremendous gust of wind struck the starboard side of the ship, tipping it dramatically. "I'm going over!" I shouted. Two scouts called out, "Hold on!" and grabbed my arm to keep me from sliding into the waves. I flopped down on the deck and grabbed a mast, frightened but relieved.

Thirty-five minutes later, we emerged from the storm into bright, blue sky and afternoon sunshine. The captain said that the storm was classified as a "white squall" because of the blinding torrent of rain it produces. It was odd to look back and see the black sky with occasional flickers of lightning. We'd made it!

 On your own paper, identify at least one example of each narrative feature—*action details, sensory details, personal thoughts,* or *dialogue*—in the sample above. Be sure to use similar elements in your phase autobiography.

**Differentiated Instruction: Advanced Learners**

Have students work with partners to choose the most effective words to convey the speaker's thoughts and feelings in their autobiographies.

 **ELPS 4H** Read silently with increasing ease and comprehension for longer periods; **4K** Demonstrate comprehension and expand reading skills by employing analytical skills/evaluating written information and performing critical analyses

# Drafting

With your planning in place, you're ready to write your first draft. This is your first opportunity to put the key elements in place: the beginning, middle, and ending of your story.

*Narrative*

### Keys to Effective Writing

1. Use the details you gathered and organized as a general guide.

2. Don't tell every detail about this phase in your life. Include just the details that allow the reader to appreciate the essence of this time; otherwise, your writing will go on and on.

3. Avoid getting "stuck" as you write the first draft by not fretting over each word.

4. Build suspense in the middle part of your story to keep the reader interested.

5. Use sensory details and dialogue to help the reader experience the events.

## Drafting
### Keys to Effective Writing

The Keys to Effective Writing explain the process students will be guided through on SE pages 92–96.

To help students focus on the important details related to their topics, suggest that they write the end of their narrative—in which they explain what they learned and how they changed—first. Then, they can address the beginning and middle parts of their drafts and select details that will logically lead to the ending.

If students have trouble expressing a specific idea, tell them to highlight the space or use an asterisk to mark the place and then move on. They will have several opportunities during the revising stage to fill in these spots. ✔ **DIFFERENTIATE INSTRUCTION**

### Writer's Craft

One key concept of teaching writing is to model writing for your students. On a board, draft several opening sentences. Create a few sentences of description or dialogue. By modeling the drafting process, you embolden your students to write as well—and you foster the creation of a writing community in your class.

---

## Differentiated Instruction:
### English Language Learners

⭐ **ELPS** 1C, 2E, 4F

| ELP Level **Beginning** | ELP Level **Intermediate** | ELP Level **Advanced/Advanced High** |
|---|---|---|
| Prepare four alternate sentences, each demonstrating a narrative feature. Preteach new vocabulary and help students read to identify the features. | Provide an adapted text that contains one example of each narrative feature. After preteaching new vocabulary, work through the piece with students to identify the features. | Allow students to identify the narrative features in the text with a partner. Challenge students to read troublesome sentences aloud and discuss unfamiliar words or concepts. |

**ELPS 1C** Use strategic learning techniques to acquire basic and grade-level vocabulary; **2E** Use contextual support to enhance and confirm understanding of increasingly complex spoken language; **4F** Use visual and contextual support to read grade-appropriate text and enhance/confirm understanding

## Drafting

### Getting the Big Picture

Encourage students to refer to this chart as they read the sample autobiography on SE pages 93–96. Discuss how the organization reflects the big picture of the essay. Suggest that when students have finished their first drafts they return to this page and fill in a similar chart, using the parts of their narratives. If they have used their prewriting notes and followed the steps presented on SE pages 93–96, they should see their own "big picture" emerge. As an added benefit, this activity can call attention to any gaps in the drafts. Students can then fill in these gaps as they revise. **DIFFERENTIATE INSTRUCTION ↘**

**TEKS** 10.13B; **ELPS** 3H

---

## Drafting Getting the Big Picture

The chart below shows how the parts of a phase autobiography work together. (The examples are from Sarah's essay on pages **93–96**.)

| **Beginning** | **Opening Paragraphs** |
|---|---|
| The **beginning** gets the reader's attention and identifies the topic of the writing—in this case, a phase. | "Ouch!" I yelped to my best friend, Angela, as the piece of fencing scratched my arm, making marks like animal tracks. "Are we having fun yet?" <br><br> This was my first musical as part of the Riverside High School tech crew. And I was determined, and excited, to help with the backdrops. |

| **Middle** | |
|---|---|
| The **middle, or body,** paragraphs use details, description, and dialogue to develop the phase. | At first, I had been disappointed not to be assigned to the carpentry crew. <br><br> Mr. Morales, who taught our sixth-hour stagecraft class, had his rules for technical crews. <br><br> So for three weeks, day after day, we cut the fencing and attached it, cut and attached. . . . |

| **Ending** | **Closing Sentences** |
|---|---|
| The **ending** explains the importance of this time in the writer's life. | Working with more than 100 people with different skills and personalities taught me how to get along with others, even some people I didn't especially like. And I had high hopes for being on the carpentry crew for the next show. |

---

**TEKS** 10.13B, 10.14A

## Starting Your Phase Autobiography

Once you've planned the main parts of your phase autobiography, you're ready to write your first draft. An effective opening should do these things:

| Beginning |
| --- |
| Middle |
| Ending |

- Grab the attention of the reader.
- Include relevant background information.
- State the topic, or phase, that you will write about.

### Beginning Part

The writer grabs the reader's attention.

> "Ouch!" I yelped to my best friend, Angela, as the piece of fencing scratched my arm, making marks like animal tracks. "Are we having fun yet?"
>
> "Well, you could wear long sleeves," she said smugly, looking down at her own protected, sweat-shirted arms.
>
> "Nah," I said. "It's too hot in here." Then I picked up the tools and went back to work.

Background information is given.

> Angela and I were working side by side with two other kids, building the fence that would be the backdrop for one of the scenes in our high school musical, <u>West Side Story</u>. Our tech director, Mr. Morales, had welded the frame for the fence out of 1 ½-inch pipe. It was our job to cut the fencing—the kind you see in people's yards—and attach it to the frame with cable ties.

The phase is identified.

> This was my first musical as part of the Riverside High School tech crew. And I was determined, and excited, to help with the backdrops.

Draft

**Write your beginning.** On your own paper, write the beginning part of your phase autobiography. Use transitions to connect your ideas.

| Transition Words and Phrases |
| --- |
| To shift time: **later, before, then** |
| To shift location: **between, across, at the edge** |
| To create a contrast: **however, on the other hand, even so** |
| To show cause and effect: **because, as a result, due to** |
| To add information: **in addition, in fact, also** |

Narrative

### Starting Your Phase Autobiography

Point out to students that using lively dialogue to begin their phase autobiographies, as shown in the sample, is an effective way to grab the readers' attention. There are other ways, however, to create an effective beginning. For additional strategies for beginning phase autobiographies, have students turn to SE page 102 and examine the strategies listed under **Does the beginning lead logically to the ending?**

**Write your beginning.** As you review the transition words and phrases, remind students that writers use transitions to link ideas between sentences in a paragraph and to connect ideas from one paragraph to the next.

**TEKS** 10.13B, 10.14A

✱ For a more extensive list of transitions, have students turn to SE pages 628–629.

---

| ELP Level **Beginning** | ELP Level **Intermediate** | ELP Level **Advanced/Advanced High** |
| --- | --- | --- |
| Demonstrate the three parts of an essay by drawing a visual representation of the autobiography's structure (e.g., as a train with an engine, cars, and a caboose). | Have students label a visual representation of the autobiography's three-part structure (e.g., as a train) with key descriptive phrases (gets attention, provides details, etc.). | Have students add sentences from their autobiography to a visual representation of its three-part structure. Encourage students to experiment with compound sentences. |

 **TEKS** **10.13B** Structure ideas in a sustained way/develop drafts in open-ended situations that include transitions; **10.14A** Write a story with a conflict, a resolution, and literary strategies/devices to enhance the plot; **ELPS** **2E** Use visual support to enhance and confirm understanding of increasingly complex spoken language; **5G** Narrate with increasing specificity and detail/writing

## Drafting
### Developing the Middle Part

Have students form four groups.

- Assign each group one tip.
- Have group members work together to find details in the sample middle paragraphs that show how the writer applied the tip.
- Have groups share their results.

Example answers might include:

- **Key actions:** cut the fencing; worked silently; I yelled; step back and look
- **Sensory details:** hands and arms ached; hear my grandpa's voice; signs like graffiti
- **Personal thoughts:** disappointed; just wanting to get the job done; made me mad; ignored them; "Cut it out, you guys!"
- **Maintain suspense:** challenge of building the set despite difficulties; responding to the challenge by "listening to her grandpa," ignoring the goof-offs, and persevering despite physical pain

⭐ **ELPS** 3E, 4K

Students should recognize that the bulleted items in the SE overlap. For example, personal thoughts and dialogue may include sensory details and may be used to describe key actions or maintain suspense.

⭐ **TEKS** 10.13B, 10.14A

---

## Drafting Developing the Middle Part

The middle part, or body, of your phase autobiography shares the important information about your experience. *Remember:* Your goal is to tell a good story and hold the reader's interest. Use the tips below as a guide to your writing.

Beginning
Middle
Ending

- **Include the key actions,** showing how you tackled your challenge. (See pages 87–88 for help.)
- **Add sensory details** to create vivid images in the reader's mind.
- **Share your personal thoughts** and feelings; use dialogue to show speakers' personalities as appropriate.
- **Maintain suspense!** (See page 88.)

### Middle Paragraphs

> The writer includes her personal thoughts and feelings.
>
> At first, I had been disappointed not to be assigned to the carpentry crew. I love working with wood, ever since I was ten and my grandpa helped me build a small chair.
>
> But Mr. Morales, who taught our sixth-hour stagecraft class, had his rules for the technical crews. "You have to work your way up to certain jobs," he told us. "But don't worry—by the end of high school, you'll have done a little of everything."
>
> So for three weeks, day after day, we cut the fencing and attached it, cut and attached. Though my hands and arms ached, I could hear my grandpa's voice in my head: "You don't want your name on anything you're not proud of." As a result, I tried to measure and cut the pieces carefully. Angela and I usually worked silently—that's the kind of friends we are — just wanting to get the job done.
>
> The writer's descriptions and dialogue make the scene believable.
>
> At first, it made me mad when other kids goofed off, like when the boys started squirting glue at each other. Turning to them with a scowl, I yelled, "Cut it out, you guys!" They just laughed and kept playing around. Since they ignored me, I just ignored them, too.
>
> Sensory details create effective imagery.
>
> Although it took about three weeks, we could finally step back and look at the finished fence. It was huge—almost 35 feet wide and 15 feet tall!—so it would look real to the audience. Someone else painted signs like graffiti to hang on it. Then the big moment: five or six of us lifted the fence on a pipe, called a fly

---

⭐ **TEKS** **10.13B** Structure ideas in a sustained way; **10.14A** Write a story with a conflict, a resolution, interesting and believable characters, and literary strategies and devices to enhance the plot; **ELPS** **3E** Share information in cooperative learning interactions; **4K** Demonstrate comprehension and expand reading skills by employing analytical skills/evaluating written information and performing critical analyses

Narrative

rail, so it could be moved around. Then Jon, our "fly man," moved it slowly on stage. It really looked like a fence!

> But there was still more to be done. Our next assignment was to paint a fake brick wall made out of three large wooden flats covered in muslin. If I thought building the fencing had been tedious, that was nothing compared to painting the wall. We spent days drawing chalk lines to look like bricks, then painting them red and adding gray edges for mortar. If we made a mistake, we'd have to whitewash it and start over. "I guess we're learning patience," I sighed.

> And as we added more "layers" of brick, the bottom chalk line slipped on the diagonal, making it look like the building was leaning. So we'd erase it and start over, trying to make everything look straight. But time was running out. Opening night was only a week away, and we still had half of the wall to finish. "Please give us more help," we begged. Mr. Morales assigned two of the boys who had played around with the glue—not the most diligent workers. Then we persuaded the janitor to let us stay late, and we asked our teachers for extensions on our homework.

> By opening night, the wall was upright and in place, and it looked, well, almost straight. Angela and I were exhausted. At the end of the opening night show, the audience applauded the cast and musicians long and hard. Backstage, the rest of us who made the show happen—the painters, prop people, electricians, sound people, stage managers, costumers, and, of course, we scenery builders—high-fived each other.

**Side notes (left margin):**
- Each new action builds suspense.
- Other key actions build to the climax.
- The writer presents a resolution of the conflict as she describes how the situation turned out.

**Draft**

**Write your middle paragraphs.** Use your prewriting notes to guide your writing. Keep the following drafting tips in mind.

## Tip

- Remember that your purpose is to tell about a period that changed you.
- Don't worry about having everything correct in the first draft. Relax and let your ideas flow. If necessary, leave blank spaces and fill them in later.
- Add important ideas that occur to you as you're writing.

---

## Writer's Craft

**Pacing and transitions:** In a phase autobiography, you can't cover every event that happened over an extended time period. You have to pick and choose, leaping from one event to another. This ability to manipulate pacing is a key to effective writing.

Writers have the power of time travel. They can begin a sentence in the current moment and end it in the deep past:

> I straighten the page before me, set my pencil tip to the whiteness, and scrawl out an equation that tells what happened at the Big Bang.

They can leap over hundreds of days to arrive at a precise moment:

> I thought my humiliation was complete when Dad arrived at school in a Santa outfit, but four months later, he hopped up the steps as a six-foot-tall bunny.

Each transition word or phrase functions like the settings on a time machine, carrying the reader wherever (and whenever) the writer wants to take them. Encourage students to experiment with their transitions, taking the reader to the most crucial moments in the best order. ◣ DIFFERENTIATE INSTRUCTION

**Write your middle paragraphs.** Point out that students can also make notes to themselves in the margin of their draft copy. Notes such as "add more detail here" or "could the time I did such and such fit here?" will remind them of ideas they had during the draft writing but were unsure about. This can be a big help during revision or the writing of a second draft.

⭐ TEKS 10.13B, 10.14A

---

## Differentiated Instruction: English Language Learners

⭐ ELPS 1E, 5B, 5F

| ELP Level **Beginning** | ELP Level **Intermediate** | ELP Level **Advanced/Advanced High** |
|---|---|---|
| Practice numerical transitions by having students order them from a word bank (first, second, etc.) Then, have students add the correct word to a series of simple sentences. | Reinforce transitions by having students write three simple sentences about something they've done, beginning with the words *first, then,* and *finally*. | Have students practice transitions by describing a familiar event with steps (e.g., brushing teeth). Encourage students to write with complex and compound sentences. |

**TEKS** **10.13B** Structure ideas in a sustained way; **10.14A** Write a story with a conflict, a resolution, interesting and believable characters, and literary strategies and devices to enhance the plot; **ELPS 1E** Internalize new basic language by using and reusing it/writing; **5B** Develop basic sight vocabulary used in written classroom materials; **5F** Write using a variety of grade-appropriate sentence lengths, patterns, and connecting words/combine in increasingly accurate ways

## Drafting
### Ending Your Phase Autobiography

Make sure students understand the concept of "come full circle" before asking them to write their own endings. Invite a volunteer to explain the connection between the beginning and ending in the samples. Point out that the phrase *blood, sweat, and tears* in the ending connects to the beginning of the essay where the writer describes the jagged piece of metal that scratched her arm.

**Write your ending and form a complete first draft.** Suggest that students who keep a writer's notebook or journal look back at any entries they may have made about the experience they are describing. They may have already written about the importance of the experience, how it changed them, and what they learned from it. If so, they may want to incorporate these earlier reflections into their endings. `DIFFERENTIATE INSTRUCTION ↘`

⭐ **TEKS** 10.13B, 10.14A

### Tip

Remind students that the change does not have to be a major life-altering event (although it certainly can be). Often, it will be a smaller change in attitude, understanding, or belief. These life-phases are important, however, and have made them who they are today.

---

 ⭐ **TEKS** 10.13B, 10.14A

## Drafting Ending Your Phase Autobiography

Beginning
Middle
**Ending**

The ending is your opportunity to reflect on the experience and summarize for the reader what you learned about yourself. Be truthful and sincere. Coming full circle is one idea for an effective ending. You can "come full circle" if you connect the ending with the beginning.

- **Key idea in the beginning**
  "Ouch!" I yelped to my best friend, Angela, as the jagged piece of fencing scratched my arm, making marks like animal tracks. "Are we having fun yet?"

- **Key idea in the ending**
  I'd put blood, sweat, and tears into building those sets, but I got even more out of the experience.

### Ending Paragraph

In the conclusion, the writer reflects on how she has grown.

I'd put blood, sweat, and tears into building those sets, but I got even more out of the experience. I learned how to stick with a job until it's finished, and I learned about teamwork. Working with more than 100 people with different skills and personalities taught me how to get along with others, even some people I didn't especially like. And I had high hopes for being on the carpentry crew for the next show.

 Draft

**Write your ending and form a complete first draft.** Complete your phase autobiography by telling what you learned during that period of your life. Put together a complete copy of your story, double-spacing on the computer or writing on every other line so you have room to revise.

### Tip

If you have trouble with the ending, put your writing aside for a while. This will give you time to reflect on the importance of the experience. Or ask friends or family members how they saw you change as a result of your experience.

---

# Revising

Your first draft gets the basic story of your phase onto the page. During the revising step, you improve your first draft by reorganizing, rewriting, adding to, or deleting different parts as needed. Concentrate on *focus and coherence, organization, development of ideas,* and *voice.*

Narrative

### Keys to Effective Revising

1. Set your first draft aside for a day or two, if possible, before you begin revising.

2. As you review your draft, think about your purpose, your audience, and the genre, or form, of your writing.

3. Be sure each main part—the beginning, the middle (or body), and the ending—works well.

4. Revise any parts that seem confusing. Add more details to any parts that seem incomplete.

5. Pay special attention to your writing voice. Do you sound interested and sincere?

6. Be sure you have chosen the right words to describe your experience.

---

# Revising

## Keys to Effective Revising

Remind students that the revising stage is a writer's opportunity to make improvements to the first draft.

The Keys to Effective Revising explain the process students will be guided through on SE pages 98–106.

Students are frequently advised to put their writing aside for a day or two before revising so that they can look at it with "fresh eyes." Too often, however, students do not follow this advice because either the schedule doesn't allow for it or students put off writing until the last minute. To encourage this beneficial practice, consider making this step mandatory by incorporating it into your schedule and by having students turn in their drafts for you to keep for one or two days before they revise.

Prior to revision, have students read and respond to each other's drafts. A constructive peer response helps students pinpoint the traits that need revision. Remind students how to do a beneficial peer response by referring them to SE pages 50–54. On the following pages, students can find the specific strategies that will most improve their writing. **☑ DIFFERENTIATE INSTRUCTION**

---

## Differentiated Instruction: English Language Learners

**⚡ ELPS** 3A, 3B, 3C, 3F, 3H, 4F

| ELP Level **Beginning** | ELP Level **Intermediate** | ELP Level **Advanced/Advanced High** |
|---|---|---|
| Model sentences about change. Explain unfamiliar vocabulary and help students verbalize these sentences, paying special attention to pronunciation. | Using sentence stems (*I learned that* . . . , etc.), students should verbalize how they changed, using gestures and occasional reference to their first language for support. | Model complex sentences about change. Students then verbalize how they changed. Encourage students to experiment with complex sentences. |

**ELPS 3A** Practice producing sounds of newly acquired vocabulary; **3B** Expand vocabulary by learning and using routine language needed for classroom communication; **3C** Speak using a variety of grammatical structures and sentence lengths/types with increasing accuracy and ease; **3F** Give information/ranging from using a limited high-frequency vocabulary to using abstract and content-based vocabulary during speaking; **3H** Describe and explain with increasing specificity and detail; **4F** Use support from peers/teachers to develop vocabulary and grasp of language structures

## Revising for Focus and Coherence

This is a good time to point out why so little attention is given to conventions during the first draft. Explain that there's no sense spending lots of time and effort polishing spelling and grammar when some sections may be rewritten or eliminated entirely!

### Have I included only necessary events?

Students may hesitate to remove events that they find especially interesting or exciting, even if they don't relate directly to the controlling idea. Remind them that these details will detract from the overall emphasis of their writing and may distract the reader.

### Exercise
### Answers

Complete the **Exercise** together. Have students explain why weeks 3 and 7 should be eliminated (they are not essential to the narrative) and why the remaining items are important. Students might also correctly suggest that item 11 doesn't move the story along, but that it could work in the ending. **DIFFERENTIATE INSTRUCTION ↘**

**Review the events in your phase autobiography.** Have students create a time line, such as the one shown in the **Exercise**, for their own phase autobiographies, or provide photocopies of the reproducible time line (TE Appendix) for them. Have students share their lists with partners before eliminating any details. Articulating each point with a classmate can help identify which points should be removed.

 **TEKS** 10.13C, 10.14A

---

## Revising for Focus and Coherence

When you revise your phase autobiography for *focus and coherence,* be sure that you have introduced the controlling idea in your first paragraph and that your introduction will grab the reader's attention. In addition, you want to cover only the events that relate directly to the controlling idea.

As you begin your revision, look back at the topic and details charts you put together as you planned your phase autobiography. Remember the audience and purpose for your writing. If your essay sticks to your purpose and all the events relate to the controlling idea, your essay will have focus and coherence.

### Have I included only necessary events?

You have included only necessary events if each event covers a critical experience during the phase. As you read each event, ask yourself, "What's the point?" If you can't think of the point, cut the event from your narrative.

### Exercise

Read through the following time line to get a sense of the total phase. Then reread each event and ask yourself, "What's the point?" Decide which events do not move the narrative along.

| Week 1 | Aunt Marisa lost her job. |
| Week 2 | My cousin Anna moved in to share my tiny bedroom. |
| Week 3 | Anna and her boyfriend broke up. |
| Week 4 | I caught Anna wearing my favorite sweater. |
| Week 5 | I put a tape line across our bedroom. |
| Week 6 | My favorite sweater was missing, and I accused Anna. |
| Week 7 | Anna and her boyfriend got back together. |
| Week 8 | I found my sweater in the bottom of my locker and apologized. |
| Week 9 | Anna and I made up. We had a good week. |
| Week 10 | Anna's mom got a new job, and Anna moved out. |
| Week 11 | Anna and I get together on weekends. |

 **Review the events in your phase autobiography.** Ask yourself, "What's the point?" for each event. Remove events that do not move the narrative along.

Revise

---

**Differentiated Instruction: Struggling Learners**

Some students may have difficulty understanding why weeks 3 and 7 do not move the narrative along. Tell students to think of each event as a scene in a movie. Explain that the point of the movie is to find out if Aunt Marisa will find another job and if the writer and Anna will learn to get along.

Point out that the events in the other weeks move the plot of the "movie" along, whereas Anna's breaking up with her boyfriend (week 3) and getting back together with him (week 7) do not. These events actually interrupt the action because they introduce irrelevant issues.

---

**TEKS** **10.13C** Revise drafts/improve the subtlety of meaning and rethink how well the purpose and genre have been addressed; **10.14A** Write a story with a conflict and a resolution

## Does my narrative sustain its focus in each paragraph?

Each paragraph in your phase autobiography should communicate, either by restating or suggesting, the focus of your essay. Each paragraph should contain details that support and extend your controlling idea so that the reader will understand and appreciate your viewpoint. The paragraphs should work together to support and sustain your purpose for writing.

**Revise**

As you revise for focus and coherence, answer each of the following questions. **They will help guide your revision and ensure that the focus of the narrative is sustained.**

1. What is the controlling idea or conflict that is introduced in the beginning of the essay?
2. How do the main points of each middle paragraph help sustain the narrative's focus?
3. How do these points relate to the controlling idea?
4. How do the details in each paragraph relate to the main idea of the paragraph?
5. How do the details help sustain the narrative's focus?
6. Does the conclusion add meaning and reinforce the writing?

**Tip**

The conclusion of your phase autobiography should help the reader put the event into perspective. You should leave the reader with something to think about and an understanding of why and how this particular event affected your life.

Narrative

## Does my narrative sustain its focus in each paragraph?

Just as individual details sometimes had to be removed from the first draft, occasionally a writer will decide that an entire paragraph is irrelevant to the controlling idea. Students should not be discouraged if they have to remove a whole paragraph from their original draft; cutting unnecessary sections helps tighten the writing and hone its focus.

TEKS 10.13C, 10.14A

**As you revise for focus and coherence, answer each of the following questions.** It may be helpful to model this questioning process for students using a sample essay. ✔DIFFERENTIATE INSTRUCTION

**Tip**

Explain to students that a reader should know them better after reading their phase autobiography. The conclusion is the section that brings this new insight into clear focus.

---

### Differentiated Instruction: English Language Learners

ELPS 4D, 4F, 4J, 4K

| ELP Level **Beginning** | ELP Level **Intermediate** | ELP Level **Advanced/Advanced High** |
|---|---|---|
| Complete the activity with students using an adapted list. Use and preteach several vocabulary words in all relevant events to link them together clearly. | Students complete the activity with a partner using an adapted list. Preteach any key vocabulary. | Preteach any unfamiliar vocabulary for the activity. Have students complete the activity with a partner and summarize the controlling idea. |

TEKS **10.13C** Revise drafts/improve the subtlety of meaning and rethink how well the purpose and genre have been addressed; **10.14A** Write a story with a conflict and a resolution; ELPS **4D** Use prereading supports to enhance comprehension of written text/graphic organizers, illustrations, and topic-related vocabulary; **4F** Use support from peers/teachers to read grade-appropriate text, enhance understanding, and develop vocabulary; **4J** Demonstrate comprehension and expand reading skills by employing inferential skills/predicting, making connections between ideas, drawing conclusions from text, and finding supporting evidence; **4K** Demonstrate comprehension and expand reading skills by employing analytical skills/evaluating written information and performing critical analyses

**Revising for** Organization

## Is my organization scheme clear to my reader?

One reason peer response is so important has to do with organizational scheme. Explain to your students that, as the writer, they already have a clear understanding of the events in their phase autobiography and in what order they occurred. Often, they may have trouble identifying problems with their organization because they are putting the pieces together in their mind even when they are not organized clearly on the paper. Another reader, with no knowledge of the event, will have a much easier time pointing out confusing organization and helping the writer correct it.

### Exercise
### Answers
The correct order is: 2, 7, 5, 6, 1, 3, 8, 4

**Reread your phase autobiography.** If students are having trouble organizing the details in their essay, encourage them to write their details out in single sentences like in the **Exercise** activity. Have them order the details and then compare this list to the way their phase autobiography is organized. If there are differences, those areas might need to be restructured in the autobiography.

 **TEKS** 10.13B

---

 **TEKS** 10.13B

 **Revising for** Organization

When you revise for *organization*, check to see that your writing has a clear beginning, middle, and ending. It is also important to use a variety of transitions that lead the reader logically through the narrative.

## Is my organization scheme clear to my reader?

A well organized composition is easy for readers to follow. The order in which the ideas are presented is logical and usually sequential. There may be some details from a memory or past event, but they should fit smoothly into the flow of the narrative. The reader should easily be able to understand why these details were included. Transitional words and phrases connecting sentences and paragraphs help the reader understand the action and the flow of ideas.

### Exercise

Put the following sentences in a logical, sequential order so that the reader can identify the beginning, the middle, and the ending.

1. Mugsy, who had come into the shelter the day before, had matted fur and needed a bath.
2. I volunteered at the animal shelter because I want to become a veterinarian.
3. My family did not have a dog; in fact, we did not have any pets.
4. I decided that I do want to pursue a career working with animals.
5. It was my job to clean cages and help feed the animals.
6. Lots of dogs arrived at the shelter, and most of them needed loving care and attention.
7. I was surprised that I was the youngest volunteer.
8. It looked like no one would adopt Mugsy, but I hoped that my family would agree to take him in.

 **Reread your phase autobiography. Are your ideas logically and sequentially organized? Can your reader easily follow the flow of ideas? If not, rearrange the paragraphs and the details.**

Revise

---

**TEKS** **10.13B** Structure ideas in a sustained way and develop drafts in open-ended situations that include transitions and rhetorical devices

## Have I used effective transition words and phrases?

Your transitions will be most effective if you use a variety of them in your writing. Using only transitions that indicate time can become tedious. *First* one thing happened, *then* another thing happened, *next* a third thing happened, etc. A variety of transitions will help you indicate not just the order of events but also their *meaning* and importance to the events of the narrative.

> Most of the people taking the lifesaving course were members of the swim team. I wasn't on the team, though, and I'd actually taught myself to swim. In the pool, my inexperience showed. As a result, I struggled to swim 12 feet down, put on a mask, and fill it with air. I also gasped as I towed classmates using the cross-chest carry. Because I was the slowest swimmer, I often was still swimming laps after the other students were gone. Usually, my goggles leaked, so my eyes burned with chlorine. Everybody told me I should give up, but I didn't.

*Narrative*

### Exercise

For each blue transition above, write whether it indicates time, location, contrast, cause and effect, or added information.

**Check your transitions.** Review your phase autobiography, underlining transition words or phrases. Decide whether they help to better organize your writing. Revise as necessary.

Revise

**Organization**
The writer uses a variety of transitions.

> So for three weeks, day after day,
> ^We cut the fencing and attached it, cut and attached. ^My    Though
>
> hands and arms ached I could hear my grandpa's voice in my
>               ^
> head: "You don't want your name on anything you're not proud
>      As a result,
> of." I tried to measure and cut the pieces carefully. Angela and I
>
> usually worked . . .

## Have I used effective transition words and phrases?

Point out to students that although *first, then,* and *next* are sometimes the most logical transitions, frequently they are overused. Have students brainstorm a list of other transition words and phrases that could be used in place of these words. Challenge students to avoid using *first, then,* and *next* whenever possible and to use more expressive phrases to give their writing greater variety.

TEKS 10.13B

* For more information about transitions, see SE pages 628–629.

### Exercise
**Answers**
- **though**—contrast
- **As a result**—cause and effect
- **also**—added information
- **Because**—cause and effect
- **Usually**—time
- **so**—cause and effect  ✔ DIFFERENTIATE INSTRUCTION

**Check your transitions.** Have students count how many times they repeat the same transition words or phrases in their essays. If they repeat any transition more than two times or if they use only one kind of transition, they should revise to add variety.

TEKS 10.13B

 TEKS **10.13B** Develop drafts in open-ended situations that include transitions; ELPS **1E** Internalize new basic language by using and reusing it/writing; **3A** Practice producing sounds of newly acquired vocabulary; **4C** Comprehend vocabulary and language structures used in written classroom materials; **4F** Use visual and contextual support to develop vocabulary

## Revising for Development of Ideas

### Does the beginning lead logically to the ending?

Students do not necessarily have to use one of these strategies, but they are very useful suggestions, especially if a student is having trouble connecting their beginning to their ending on their own. The specific examples shown here can also be helpful for demonstrating what is meant by "connecting the beginning to the ending" to students who may be struggling with this concept.

**Reread your beginning and your ending.** Have students explain to a partner how their beginning and ending parts connect. If students cannot explain a clear and obvious connection, have them experiment with each of the strategies (question and answer, challenge and outcome, and foreshadowing) to revise their beginnings, endings, or both. They can then choose the strategy they think works most effectively in their phase autobiographies. Partners can also offer specific suggestions for using one of the strategies to connect the beginning with the ending.

⭐ **TEKS** 10.13C, 10.14A; **ELPS** 3E

---

⭐ **TEKS** 10.13C, 10.14A

## Revising for Development of Ideas

When you revise for *development of ideas,* you want to be sure that you have covered only the necessary events that relate to the topic. Be sure, however, that you have included enough details to make the narrative clear. Each event should be fleshed out completely and illustrate, or "show," the event.

### Does the beginning lead logically to the ending?

The beginning of your phase autobiography connects with the ending if the two parts work together to show how the phase changed you. Here are three strategies for connecting the beginning with the ending.

- Use a question and answer.
  **Beginning:** When Mom asked me to walk the Appalachian Trail with her, I thought, "Do I really want to do this?"

  **Ending:** Mom and I looked back over the 400 miles we'd hiked together, and I knew that it was the best thing I'd ever done.

- Use a challenge and an outcome.
  **Beginning:** I sat shivering, staring at the high school pool, and thought I'd never be strong enough to become a lifeguard.

  **Ending:** All the chlorine and swallowed water was worth it when I got my lifesaving certificate.

- Use foreshadowing.
  **Beginning:** When I showed up at my best friend's house on the first day of summer, I should have noticed how pale he looked.

  **Ending:** We were just kids when that horrible summer began, but as John fought—and beat—cancer, we both grew up.

**Reread your beginning and your ending.** If they do not clearly connect, use one of the strategies above to make them work together. If your ending still does not clearly relate to the beginning, reread your narrative and try to see where the connection is lost. Does some event or detail described in the middle part of the narrative interrupt the chain of connections or lead the narrative off course? If so, ask yourself, is this event or detail really important to *this particular* narrative? If I take it out, does my narrative make more sense?

---

### Differentiated Instruction: Struggling Learners

Break down the task of checking for sensory details in the **Exercise** paragraph for students who are having difficulty. Have them read through the paragraph several times, each time looking only for details that pertain to a particular sense. After each reading, have them jot down what they found before rereading the paragraph.

**TEKS** 10.13C, 10.14A
**ELPS** 5G

## Have I included enough sensory details?

You have included enough sensory details if the reader can truly experience the sights, sounds, and smells associated with the phase. (Depending on your topic, you may or may not cover all of the senses.) Sensory details will also help you define the mood or tone of your narrative.

### Exercise

Read the following paragraph from a phase autobiography. Then, on your own paper, list one or two sights, sounds, and smells. Then, briefly describe how those sensory details help define the narrative's mood or tone.

> It was so hot that we could feel the scorching sand through our thin sandals. Still, we were very glad to be at the beach. Younger children splashed in the waves, but my brother Pedro and I wandered to a cove about 100 yards from the main beach where we discovered a treasure trove of seashells. Some were creamy colored, but many others were tinted pink, lilac, blue, and pale green. We quickly filled two plastic sacks with a rainbow of shells and made plans to give them to friends as gifts. We hurried back to the main beach, placed the sacks carefully on our towels, and ran off to cool in the water. When it was time to go home, we gathered sandy towels, wet shirts, and our big picnic cooler and dumped everything in the trunk of our car. Every time we went around a corner on the way home, we heard a curious crunching sound. We thought there was something wrong with the car. When we got home, we discovered the source of the sound. Our treasure trove of shells were underneath the cooler, crushed to tiny colorful shell smithereens.

Revise

**Check your details.** Review your narrative to be sure that you have included sensory details. If not, add some.

**Development of Ideas**
Sensory details make the experience vivid.

But there was still more to be done. Our next assignment
~~made out of three large flats covered in muslin~~
was to paint a fake brick wall. If I thought building the fence had
∧
been boring, . . .

---

## Have I included enough sensory details?

Besides using details that describe sights, sounds, and smells, students may include those that describe touch and taste. As an example, point out that in the sample excerpt on SE page 90, the writer appeals to the sense of touch (or feeling) and the sense of smell in the sentence, *I loved rubbing my fingers along the polished oak decks, which smelled of salt and varnish.*

### Exercise
**Answers**
**Possible Answers**

- **sights**—younger children splashed in the waves; creamy colored; tinted pink, lilac, blue, and pale green; rainbow of shells; tiny colorful shell smithereens
- **sounds**—splashed, curious crunching sound
- **textures**—feel the scorching sand, cool in the water ✔ **DIFFERENTIATE INSTRUCTION**

**Check your details.** Encourage students to appeal to more than just one or two of the senses. A wide variety of sensory details will help the reader become more involved in the story.

**TEKS** 10.13C, 10.14A

### Writer's Craft

**Sensory details:** Sensory words have power. The word *sour,* for instance, almost makes us pucker. The word *grating* makes us cringe. The word *rumble* makes us shake. Sensory words have an impact on readers because they let readers see, smell, hear, taste, and touch what is being described. ✔ **DIFFERENTIATE INSTRUCTION**

**ELPS** 5G

---

**TEKS** **10.13C** Revise drafts to improve style, figurative language, and subtlety of meaning; **10.14A** Write a story with sensory details that define the mood or tone; **ELPS** **1B** Monitor oral language and employ self-corrective techniques or other resources; **3A** Practice producing sounds of newly acquired vocabulary; **3C** Speak using a variety of grammatical structures and sentence lengths with increasing accuracy and ease; **3F** Give information/ranging from using a limited high-frequency vocabulary to using abstract and content-based vocabulary during speaking; **3H** Narrate/describe with increasing specificity and detail; **5G** Narrate with increasing specificity and detail/writing

## Revising for Voice

Voice is probably the most difficult writing trait for students to check. Encourage them that with practice they can gain confidence in writing with voice.

### Is my voice appropriate for the topic?

Have students select an adjective from the highlighted box that they believe best matches the attitude or feeling that they have about their topic and jot it down. When they complete the **Check your voice** activity, they should keep the adjective in mind or think of another adjective that more aptly describes the voice in their writing. **DIFFERENTIATE INSTRUCTION ↘**

### Exercise
#### Answers
**Possible Answers**

1. timid, hesitant
2. grateful, appreciative
3. embarrassed, humorous
4. scared, tentative

**Check your voice.** In evaluating their voice, it may be helpful for students to ask themselves questions such as: *Does the experience sound important to me? Is my story believable? Do the feelings I express match the experiences I've written about?*

**TEKS** 10.13C, 10.14A

### ★ Conventions Connections

**Grammar: Tone**
- *Proofreader's Guide* pages 744–745
- *Write Source* page 575
- *SkillsBook* pages 99–100

---

## Revising for Voice

When you revise for *voice*, be sure that your voice matches your feeling about the topic and shows your interest. You should state your position clearly so that the reader can recognize your viewpoint. If you do this, you will sound authentic, and the reader will understand your perspective. Your success at conveying your attitude may depend on your choice of words.

### Is my voice appropriate for the topic?

Your voice is appropriate for the topic if it matches your attitude or feeling about the phase in your life. Here are adjectives that can describe attitude.

| | | | | | |
|---|---|---|---|---|---|
| friendly | smart | silly | enthusiastic | bitter | sarcastic |
| know-it-all | timid | humorous | anxious | sad | flip |

Here are some examples of voice:

**Sarcastic:** Sure, I can wash the dishes. I've got nothing to do tonight except practice the piano, clean my room, and do three hours of homework.

**Sad:** I wailed, as any seven-year-old would, after finding my goldfish floating upside down.

**Enthusiastic:** Our student trip to Belize includes a fantastic trek through the rain forest. I can hardly wait!

### Exercise

For each sentence, write an adjective that describes the attitude.

1. When we moved to our new neighborhood last summer, I sat on the porch a lot, hoping new friends would simply appear.
2. You are so kind to take time to visit me in the hospital.
3. After rolling down the hill, flattening a marker flag or two, I stood up quickly, like a feline who's fallen from the back of a chair, stretched, and assumed a nonchalant pose.
4. I stepped weakly onto the swaying rope bridge, shaky, eyeing the swollen creek below.

**Check your voice.** Read your narrative out loud and think of an adjective to describe your voice. Is that adjective appropriate for the phase?

Revise

---

## How can figurative language add to my writing?

Figurative language creates an imaginative comparison between things that are not usually compared to each other. When you use figurative language, you grab the reader's attention and make your writing come alive for the reader. Figurative language helps engage the reader because the reader experiences your unique perspective on events as reflected in your language. There are several different types of figurative language.

A **simile** is a comparison using the words *like* or *as*: *Her hair swished like a velvet curtain.*

A **metaphor** is a comparison of two things in which no word of comparison (*as* or *like*) is used: *He's a bolt of lightning.*

**Personification** is a literary device in which the author speaks of or describes an animal, object, or idea as if it were a person: *My bicycle was happy to be washed.*

**Onomatopoeia** is the use of a word whose sound suggests its meaning, as in *clang, buzz,* and *twang*: *The whirring of the buzz saw.*

> **Caution:** Be as original as you can. Avoid cliches like *busy as a bee, on his merry way, the spitting image of his father,* and *right off the bat.*

### Exercise

On your own paper, write an example for each figure of speech. Be original!

1. Simile:
2. Metaphor:
3. Personification:
4. Onomatopoeia:

 **Use figurative language in your writing.** Read through your writing and look for places where you can add an example of figurative language to make your writing come alive.

*Revise*

### How can figurative language add to my writing?

Find some additional examples in popular short stories, novels, or other forms of writing and share these with the class. If you can find any, also point out examples that would be considered clichés.

### Exercise Answers

Before students complete the activity on their own, have them work together to create additional examples for each figure of speech given.

**Possible Answers**

1. **Simile:** He arranged the food on the plate like an artist composing a still life.
2. **Metaphor:** Math had become a mountain I had to climb and conquer.
3. **Personification:** The night sky wraps itself in a twinkling blanket of stars.
4. **Onomatopoeia:** Each loud thud of the pick in the hard dirt was accompanied by a low growl from the dog.

TEKS 10.13C, 10.14A; ELPS 3E

**Use figurative language in your writing.** Also, students should be aware of clichés that have accidentally slipped into their writing. Encourage them to replace these with original figurative language.

### ★ Conventions Connections

**Grammar: Figures of Speech**
- *Proofreader's Guide* pages 704–709
- *Write Source* pages 352, 580, 636–637

Narrative

---

### Differentiated Instruction: English Language Learners

ELPS 2A, 2C, 2D, 2G

| ELP Level **Beginning** | ELP Level **Intermediate** | ELP Level **Advanced/Advanced High** |
| --- | --- | --- |
| Recite simple sentences (e.g., *I love cleaning!*) both sarcastically and sincerely, and encourage students to identify which is which. | Preteach several of the adjectives in the box. Then read simple sentences that exemplify each of them. Students identify which adjective goes with each sentence. | Read short paragraphs that exemplify an adjective from the box. Allow students to seek clarification before identifying which adjective goes with each paragraph. |

TEKS **10.13C** Revise drafts to improve style and figurative language; **10.14A** Write a story with interesting and believable characters; ELPS **2A** Distinguish intonation patterns with increasing ease; **2C** Learn basic vocabulary heard during classroom instruction/interactions; **2D** Monitor understanding of spoken language during classroom instruction/interactions and seek clarification of spoken language as needed; **2G** Understand the general meaning of spoken language/topics and contexts are familiar to unfamiliar; **3E** Share information in cooperative learning interactions

## Revising
### Using a Checklist

**Check your revising.** Remind students that using a final revising checklist is a very useful tool for a writer. They should give themselves enough time before a deadline to answer the checklist questions thoughtfully.

**Make a clean copy.** The editing process is easier with a clean draft. Undoubtedly, the copy that has been used for revision is marked with many notes, proofreading marks, etc. These can make for a messy page and can be a distraction during editing.

## Revising Using a Checklist

**Check your revising.** On your own paper, write the numbers 1 to 11. Put a check by the number if you can answer "yes" to that question. If not, continue revising that part of your phase autobiography.

### Revising Checklist

#### Focus and Coherence

_____ 1. Have I focused on an extended period of time that changed me?

_____ 2. Does each action or event add to the phase autobiography?

_____ 3. Does my conclusion explain the importance of the event?

#### Organization

_____ 4. Do I have a clear beginning, middle, and ending?

_____ 5. Does the ending connect with the beginning?

_____ 6. Do I use a variety of transition words and phrases?

#### Development of Ideas

_____ 7. Does each action or idea add to the phase autobiography?

_____ 8. Have I used sensory details and dialogue to help develop my ideas?

#### Voice

_____ 9. Is my voice appropriate for the topic?

_____ 10. Do I sound interested in my topic?

_____ 11. Have I clearly explained my perspective or viewpoint?

**Make a clean copy.** When you've finished revising your story, make a clean draft to edit.

Writing a Phase Autobiography **107**

# Editing

Once you've made your revisions, you should edit your writing for conventions: grammar, sentence structure, capitalization, punctuation, and spelling.

Narrative

### Keys to Effective Editing

1. To guide your corrections, refer to a dictionary, a thesaurus, and the "Proofreader's Guide" in the back of this book.

2. Watch for any words or phrases that may be confusing to the reader.

3. Check your phase autobiography for the correct use of grammar, sentence structure, capitalization, punctuation, and spelling.

4. Use the editing and proofreading marks inside the back cover of this book.

5. Edit on a computer printout and then enter your changes into the computer.

## Editing

### Keys to Effective Editing

The Keys to Effective Editing list explains the process students will be guided through on SE pages 108–112. ✔ DIFFERENTIATE INSTRUCTION

To ensure that students do their final edit on a printout (item 5), require them to submit it with their final copy.

---

**Editing** for Conventions

## Grammar

Review with students the basic grammatical terms (noun, verb, adjective, etc.).

### Have I used adjective forms correctly?

Before students begin the **Grammar Exercise** activity on their own, produce several more examples of adjective forms together. Draw a chart on the board similar to the one on the page and fill it in with additional examples. Include one or two exceptions to the normal rules, such as the forms of happy (happy is a two-syllable word but follows the form typical for shorter words).

**TEKS** 10.13D; **ELPS** 5D, 5E

✳ For more on forms of adjectives, see SE page 756.

---
#### Grammar Exercise
#### Answers
- *badder*—worse
- *most late*—latest
- *perfectest*—most perfect

**Edit for adjective forms.** Encourage students to check with you if they are having trouble with a specific adjective. The exceptions to the typical rules can be tricky!

### ⭐ Conventions Connections

#### Grammar: Adjectives
- *Proofreader's Guide*  pages 756–757
- *Write Source*  page 576
- *SkillsBook*  page 109

⚡ *Write Source Online*  **GrammarSnap**

---

**108**  **TEKS** 10.13D
**ELPS** 5D, 5E

 **Editing** Checking for Conventions

When you edit for *conventions*, you should check for grammar, sentence structure, punctuation, capitalization, and spelling.

## Grammar

Grammar refers to how language is put together. It also refers to the rules for writing sentences correctly. As you check for grammar errors, be sure to look for correct usage of parts of speech, including nouns, verbs, adjectives, adverbs, and pronouns.

### Have I used adjective forms correctly?

You have used adjective forms correctly if you have used the positive form to describe a single noun or pronoun, the comparative form to compare two nouns or pronouns, and the superlative form to rank three or more.

| Positive | Comparative | Superlative |
|----------|-------------|-------------|
| hard | harder | hardest |
| difficult | more difficult | most difficult |
| good | better | best |

### Grammar Exercise

For many short adjectives, the comparative form is created by adding *-er*, and the superlative form by adding *-est*. For longer adjectives, the comparative form is created by using the word *more* or *less*, and the superlative form by using *most* or *least*. Some adjectives have irregular forms: *bad, worse, worst*.

Find the adjective-form errors and indicate how each should be corrected.

My desire to get a job was badder than ever. I checked the most late classified ads, I made phone calls, and I set up interviews. But I couldn't land a job, and I was more frustrated than ever. Then I heard about the perfectest job, working as an assistant to the athletic director at the local community center. Believe it or not, the athletic director hired me right after my interview! I couldn't have been happier.

**Edit for adjective forms.** Check the adjectives in your narrative and be sure to use the adjective forms correctly.

---

## Do I Use Reflexive and Reciprocal Pronouns Correctly?

A reflexive pronoun refers to the subject of a sentence. First-person reflexive pronouns are *myself*, which refers to the subject pronoun *I*, and *ourselves*, which refers to the subject pronoun *we*. The second-person reflexive pronouns are *yourself* and *yourselves*. Third-person reflexive pronouns are *himself, herself, itself,* and *themselves.*

**Examples:**

I cut myself with that sharp knife. (The reflexive pronoun *myself* refers to the subject pronoun *I*.)

Cecilia let herself in through the back door. (The reflexive pronoun *herself* refers to the subject, *Cecilia*.)

You need to make that decision by yourself. (The reflexive pronoun *yourself* refers to the subject pronoun *you*.)

They chose costumes for themselves. (The reflexive pronoun *themselves* refers to the subject pronoun *they*.)

A reciprocal pronoun expresses a mutual action or relationship, one that moves or works in each direction. The reciprocal pronouns *each other* and *one another* refer to the individual members of a plural subject.

**Examples:**

The children exchanged gifts with one another.

Julio and Pedro laughed at each other's jokes.

### Grammar Exercise

Rewrite the following sentences, using the correct reflexive or reciprocal pronouns. Your rewrites should eliminate wordiness.

1. Larry gave Natalie a present, and Natalie gave Larry a present. (Rewrite with *each other.*)
2. I bought that bike for me, not for someone else. (Rewrite with *myself.*)

**Check your use of pronouns.** Look for places where you could make your sentences flow better by using reflexive or reciprocal pronouns.

**Learning Language** Work with a partner to create additional example sentences to show correct use of reflexive and reciprocal pronouns.

*Narrative*

---

**Do I use reflexive and reciprocal pronouns correctly?**

Have students practice using both reflexive and reciprocal pronouns by referring to themselves and their classmates aloud (e.g., *John is wearing his blue jacket today. Jill and Pedro are sitting next to each other.*). After making a statement, require that students identify which type of pronoun they used and, if applicable, whether it was in first, second, or third person. ✔DIFFERENTIATE INSTRUCTION

#### Grammar Exercise
**Answers**

1. Larry and Natalie gave each other a present.
2. I bought that bike for myself.

**Check your use of pronouns.** Remind students that, in addition to using the wrong pronoun, a common mistake is using unclear pronouns. Explain that each pronoun must clearly relate back to its referent (e.g., *Jill told Maria that she was flying to Texas. Who's flying to Texas? Jill or Maria?*).

TEKS 10.13D, 10.17A(iii); ELPS 2C, 5D, 5E

**Learning Language** Model partner work by working with the class to create additional examples of each type. State these new examples verbally and write them on the board before students work with their partner.

ELPS 2C, 2I, 3E

 **Conventions Connections**

**Grammar: Reflexive and Reciprocal Pronouns**

- *Proofreader's Guide* pages 734–735, 736–737
- *SkillsBook* page 87–88

✦ *Write Source Online* **GrammarSnap**

---

TEKS **10.13D** Edit drafts for grammar; **10.17A(iii)** Use and understand reciprocal pronouns; **ELPS 2C** Learn basic vocabulary heard during classroom instruction/interactions; **2I** Demonstrate listening comprehension in increasingly complex spoken language by collaborating with peers; **3E** Share information in cooperative learning interactions; **4C** Develop basic sight vocabulary used in written classroom materials; **4F** Use support from peers/teachers to develop grasp of language structures; **5D** Edit writing for standard grammar and usage/pronoun agreement; **5E** Employ increasingly complex grammatical structures in content area writing such as using correct verbs, tenses, and pronouns/possessive case/negatives and contractions

## Sentence Structure

### Have I varied my sentence beginnings?

Have volunteers read aloud the two sample paragraphs so that students can hear how the addition of phrases and clauses at the beginning of sentences can improve sentence fluency.

✳ For more on phrases and clauses, see SE pages 590–591.

#### Exercise
**Answers**

**Answers will vary. Possible answer:**

I turned to see the 100-year-old farmhouse with its wooden clapboards and wraparound porch. While the cat was weaving through the spindles of the porch rail, Grandma sat in her rocker watching the wheat wave. Used to living in sunny, mild San Diego, I wondered if I could survive the windy hot summers and the stinging cold winters of the plains. Without a doubt, I'd go stir-crazy. **DIFFERENTIATE INSTRUCTION ↘**

⚝ **TEKS** 10.13C, 10.17A

**Edit for varied sentence beginnings.** To help students vary their sentence beginnings, have them list the first three words of each sentence in their narrative. Doing so will help them see where they can improve sentence fluency.

**ELPS** 5F

 **Conventions Connections**

**Grammar: Sentence Structure**
- *Proofreader's Guide* pages 764–777
- *Write Source* pages 585–594

---

 **TEKS** 10.13C, 10.17A
**ELPS** 5F

## Sentence Structure

When you edit for *sentence structure,* be sure that you have a variety of sentence beginnings and lengths. As you edit, ask yourself if your sentences will hold the reader's interest. Use different types of phrases and clauses to start your sentences. In addition, use both complex and compound sentences.

### Have I varied my sentence beginnings?

You have varied your sentence beginnings if some sentences begin with the subject, some with a phrase, and some with a clause. Also, avoid starting too many sentences with "I." Note how repetitive this paragraph sounds.

> I stepped out of my grandfather's car and looked at the farm fields. I saw unending shafts of golden wheat extending to the edge of the world. I could see grain silos standing on the horizon ten miles away. I was used to living in canyons of glass and steel. I wondered if I'd be able to survive out here on the wide-open plains.

Here are the same ideas with varied beginnings.

> I stepped out of my grandfather's car and looked at the farm fields. Unending shafts of golden wheat extended to the edge of the world. On the horizon, I could see grain silos. Used to living in canyons of glass and steel, I wondered if I would I be able to survive out here on the wide-open plains.

### Exercise

Rewrite the following paragraph to vary the sentence beginnings.

> I turned to see the 100-year-old farmhouse with its wooden clapboards and wraparound porch. I could see Grandma sitting on the rocker there, watching the wheat wave. I noticed her cat, weaving through the spindles of the rail. I thought that life here would be tough during the windy hot summers and the stinging cold winters. I would probably go stir-crazy.

Edit

**Edit for varied sentence beginnings.** Check your phase autobiography for varied sentence beginnings. Begin some sentences with phrases and clauses, and avoid repetitive "I" sentences.

---

**Differentiated Instruction: Struggling Learners**

Help students with the extensive punctuation section of the Proofreader's Guide by focusing on a short section, such as SE pages 643–645. Walk students through the rules and examples. Pay particular attention to the use of commas after longer introductory word groups and in compound and complex sentences. ⚝ **ELPS** 5F

---

**TEKS** 10.13C, 10.18B(i)
**ELPS** 5F

# Mechanics: Punctuation

Using correct punctuation is important. If there are errors in punctuation, the reader will have difficulty following your essay and may not be able to understand your message.

## How should I punctuate introductory phrases and clauses?

Place a comma after longer introductory phrases and all introductory clauses.

**No comma:** Soon I decided I couldn't live someone else's life.

**Longer introductory phrase:** During the summer before my junior year, my weird haircut grew out.

**Introductory clause:** When stores would take back the clothes or music, I returned them.

### Exercise

Indicate where commas should be placed in the following paragraph.

No matter what my friends thought Mr. Foyle was not a control freak. As a matter of fact he gave me a lot of responsibilities right away. I started by setting up the teams for the spring youth basketball league. Then I had to plan a practice schedule for all of the teams. When I finished the scheduling my next task was to help Mr. Foyle set up the league games. Then he had me help him interview people interested in running a concession stand at the games and I learned a lot about the kinds of questions you need to ask in an interview. After my first weekend on the job I knew I was going to like this job.

 **Edit for correct punctuation.** Reread your phase autobiography. Check for punctuation inside your sentences and at the end the end of each sentence. Make sure you have used commas appropriately after introductory phrases and clauses.

*Narrative*

## Mechanics: Punctuation

### How should I punctuate introductory phrases and clauses?

Point out to students that commas are often used where pauses occur naturally in speech. To reinforce this concept, read aloud the paragraph at the bottom of SE page 111, pausing where commas appear or have been inserted.

### Exercise
**Answers**
- No matter what my friends thought,
- As a matter of fact,
- When I finished the scheduling,
- . . . running a concession stand at the games,
- After my first weekend on the job,

**Edit for correct punctuation.** Refer students to SE pages 646–654 to learn more about comma use, including rules having to do with separating adjectives, separating items in a series, and setting off dialogue. **✓ DIFFERENTIATE INSTRUCTION**

**TEKS** 10.13C, 10.18B(i); **ELPS** 2C

### ⭐ Conventions Connections

**Mechanics: Commas after Introductory Phrases and Clauses**
- **Proofreader's Guide** pages 648–649
- **SkillsBook** pages 9–10

---

**TEKS** **10.13C** Revise drafts to improve sentence variety; **10.18B(i)** Use commas in nonrestrictive phrases, clauses, and contrasting expressions; **ELPS** **2C** Learn new language structures heard during classroom instruction/interactions; **4C** Comprehend vocabulary used in written classroom materials; **4F** Use support from peers/teachers to develop grasp of language structures; **5F** Write using a variety of grade-appropriate sentence patterns and connecting words/combine in increasingly accurate way

## Editing
### Using a Checklist

**Check your editing.** Refer students to the Proofreader's Guide (SE pages 642–787) for their final edits. Explain to them that throughout the year, they can refer to the instruction, rules, and examples there to edit and resolve questions about mechanics, usage, and grammar.  **DIFFERENTIATE INSTRUCTION ⤵**

⭐ **TEKS** 10.13D, 10.17C, 10.18A, 10.18B(i), 10.19; **ELPS** 5C, 5D, 5E

### Creating a Title

Encourage students to try all three strategies for creating a title. Other title ideas for their narrative may come from:

- the lesson they learned during the phase;
- the setting in which the experience occurred;
- an expression that often comes to mind when they recall the phase; or
- a key word, phrase, or piece of dialogue in the narrative.

### ⭐ Conventions Connections

**Mechanics: Punctuating Dialogue**
- *Proofreader's Guide* page 654–655, 668–671
- *SkillsBook* pages 31–33

**Grammar: Pronoun-Antecedent Agreement**
- *Proofreader's Guide* pages 734–741, 782–783
- *SkillsBook* page 152

⚡ *Write Source Online* **GrammarSnap**

**Spelling: Spelling and Plurals**
- *Proofreader's Guide* pages 688–691, 698–699
- *SkillsBook* pages 51, 53–54

---

 **TEKS** 10.13D, 10.17C, 10.18A, 10.18B(i), 10.19
**ELPS** 5C, 5D, 5E

 ## Editing Checking for Conventions

 **Check your editing.** On a piece of paper, write the numbers 1 to 11. Put a check by the number if you can answer "yes" to that question. If not, continue to edit your narrative for that convention.

### Editing Checklist

#### Conventions

**GRAMMAR**
_____ **1.** Do I use correct forms of verbs (*had gone*, not *had went*)?
_____ **2.** Do my pronouns agree with their antecedents?
_____ **3.** Have I used reflexive and reciprocal pronouns correctly?

**SENTENCE STRUCTURE**
_____ **4.** Do I use a variety of correctly structured sentences that don't sound repetitive?

**MECHANICS (Capitalization and Punctuation)**
_____ **5.** Do I start all my sentences with capital letters?
_____ **6.** Do I capitalize all proper nouns?
_____ **7.** Do I use end punctuation after all my sentences?
_____ **8.** Do I use commas after longer introductory word groups?
_____ **9.** Do I punctuate my dialogue correctly?

**SPELLING**
_____ **10.** Have I spelled all my words correctly?
_____ **11.** Have I consulted a dictionary to check the spellings of words my spell-checker would have missed (*were, we're; to, too, two; its, it's*)?

### Creating a Title

- Focus on the tone of your narrative: **Behind the Scenes**
- Give the words rhythm: **Cut and Attach, Draw and Paint**
- Play with words: **Go Along to Get Along**

---

**TEKS** **10.13D** Edit drafts for grammar, mechanics, and spelling; **10.17C** Use a variety of correctly structured sentences; **10.18A** Use conventions of capitalization; **10.18B(i)** Use commas in nonrestrictive phrases, clauses, and contrasting expressions; **10.19** Spell correctly using resources to determine and check correct spelling; **ELPS 5C** Spell familiar words with increasing accuracy; **5D** Edit writing for standard grammar and usage/subject-verb and pronoun agreement and appropriate verb tenses; **5E** Employ increasingly complex grammatical structures in content area writing such as using correct verbs, tenses, and pronouns/possessive case/negatives and contractions

**TEKS** 10.13E

# Publishing

## Sharing Your Phase Autobiography

After you have completed revising and editing, you can make a neat final draft of your story to share. You might ask your teacher or classmates for feedback so that you can make a few final improvements (see pages **72–74**). Consider publishing ideas such as recording your narrative, presenting it on a class Web site, or reading it aloud to an audience. (See the suggestions below.)

**Make a final copy.** When you write your final draft, follow your teacher's instructions or use the guidelines below. Create a clean copy of your phase autobiography and carefully proofread it.

## Focusing on Presentation

- Use blue or black ink and write neatly.
- Write your name in the upper left-hand corner of page 1.
- Skip a line and center your title; skip another line and begin your essay. Double-space your narrative.
- Indent every paragraph and leave a one-inch margin on all four sides.
- Write your last name and the page number in the upper right-hand corner of every page after the first one.

### Make a recording
Record your phase autobiography. Be sure to use an expressive voice. Give the recording and a printed copy of it to someone as a gift.

### E-mail your story
E-mail your phase autobiography to a small group of friends and relatives not associated with your school. Ask for feedback. Also ask them to share a few details about a period of time that changed them.

### Share with a younger audience
Ask if you and several classmates could read your phase autobiographies to younger students. When each author is finished, ask the students what they liked about the story, and why. If you're feeling brave, ask what they didn't like, and why.

---

## Differentiated Instruction: English Language Learners

**ELPS** 1B, 5C, 5D

| ELP Level **Beginning** | ELP Level **Intermediate** | ELP Level **Advanced/Advanced High** |
|---|---|---|
| Give students a sample paragraph that shows errors of one type only, such as capitalization. Have students correct the paragraph, then review the revisions as a group. | Give each student a worksheet with ten or twenty sentences. Each sentence should contain an error. After students have completed the sheet, review the corrected sentences as a group. | Give students a sample paragraph that contains multiple errors. Have students work in pairs to correct the paragraph, then review the revisions as a group. |

---

## Publishing

### Sharing Your Phase Autobiography

The following suggestion can be used in addition to the publishing ideas on SE page 113:

- Encourage students to incorporate two or three photographs from the period covered into their narrative.
- Have students assemble their narratives in a class publication. Suggest an organizational plan for the publication. For example, they can arrange the phase autobiographies alphabetically by the author's name or by title.
- Then have volunteers create a cover page and table of contents for the publication.
- Students can display it in the school library.

**Make a final copy.** Encourage students to take great care on this final step in the writing process. The temptation can sometimes be to rush this step as all the "important" and "hard" work is already completed. However, remind students how powerful first impressions can be, and after all the time and effort they have put into writing their phase autobiography, the last thing they want is for sloppy presentation to tarnish their finished product before people even get a chance to read it.

 **TEKS** 10.13E

### Focusing on Presentation

Brainstorm with students about other creative ways to publish their work. Examples could include a large in-class display, public readings at a special after-school event, or the exchange of phase autobiographies with international "pen-pals."

### Technology Connections

- Write Source Online Portfolio
- Write Source Online Essay Scoring

 **TEKS** 10.13E Revise the final draft in response to feedback from peers and teacher/publish written work; **ELPS 1B** Monitor written language and employ self-corrective techniques or other resources; **5C** Spell familiar words/employ spelling patterns and rules with increasing accuracy; **5D** Edit writing for standard grammar and usage/subject-verb and pronoun agreement and appropriate verb tenses

## Evaluating a Narrative

After reading the narrative once, have students reread the first two paragraphs, looking especially for the controlling idea and the conflict. Then have students try to sum these up in one sentence each. An example for the controlling idea might be *I want to be a rock and roll star.* An example for the conflict might be *My parents expect me to be a classical musician, but I want to be a rock star.*

⭐ ELPS 4G

Ask students whether they agree with the score given to this narrative. In general, students should agree that it deserved a score of 4. Discuss disagreements, being sure to emphasize how well the writer addressed the five writing traits.

⭐ ELPS 3G

## Evaluating a Narrative

As you read the narratives that follow, focus on the writers' strengths and weaknesses. Then read the student self-assessment on page **127**. **(The essays contain errors.)**

**Writing that fits a score of 4 is highly effective.**

### Roll over Beethoven

I would watch the second hand on the clock as I practiced piano. Every minute seemed so slow, and an hour of practice seemed to take forever. "You want to go to a good music school, don't you?" my mom would pointedly remark. "Don't you want to play with a symphony orchestra?" asked my dad—though he wasn't really asking. "Sure," I'd reply. Then I'd start practicing my Bach fugue with a bit more dedication, hiding my deep dark secret from my parents. You see, what I really wanted was to be a rock and roll star.

> The controlling idea is introduced and clearly states the writer's position.

Both of my parents are classical musicians, as were all four of my grandparents. So, of course, I was expected to carry on the family tradition, especially since I'd won awards for my piano playing since I was five years old. Then I turned thirteen. Suddenly all my friends were listening to music that we never played in my house. I heard keyboards being used in ways that Beethoven never dreamed of. It was loud. It was frenzied. Rock musicians looked like they were having fun when they played. Audiences went wild. It was not like performing to a polite audience in a symphony hall.

> The conflict is explained logically and descriptively.

When my school announced a music talent night, everyone expected me to perform a complicated classical piece that would make every parent wish his or her child could play the piano. Only my friends knew that I was competing as part of a band called Slam the Doors. We were going to cover songs by the sixties band The Doors. As the day of the talent competition approached, my parents kept asking me what piece I was going to play. I should have just told them the truth, but I didn't have the nerve. I was

> Writer shows strong command of writing conventions.

Narrative

sure I would let them down if I told them I was playing "Light My Fire" instead of Mozart's Sonata in C Major. I went ahead and bought them tickets. Even my grandfather was excited about coming to hear me play. I started to feel sick.

On the day of the show, I threw up. My mom was concerned because I'd never had stage fright before. "Is something wrong?" she kept asking. "No . . . yeah . . . no," I'd vaguely reply. As soon as I could, I left the house for our sound check and a final rehearsal. The electric keyboard I was playing was an old rickety one, and I was sure it would collapse on me, if I didn't collapse first.

I avoided my parents when they arrived because I knew they'd wonder where my name was on the program. As I listened to the other performers before us, I got more and more nervous. They all sounded so good. I was sure we couldn't compare. Worse, my parents would be out there, judging me, furious with me, disappointed in me.

It was our turn. My bandmates and I went out on stage. I fiddled with the keyboard to avoid looking at the audience. Then Pete, the lead singer, signaled to me and I started the keyboard intro to "Light My Fire." I could feel the audience react to the melody, and I dared to look up and could see the principal nodding along, smiling in recognition. I felt a surge of joy and energy, and suddenly Slam the Doors was really rocking!

The applause was thunderous when we finished. At least, it seemed thunderous to me. We came in second place. The winner was a girl who played a Bach Two-Part Invention on the guitar. Triumphant, I finally was ready to face my parents. Before I could apologize, my grandfather ran over. "I saw The Doors play in Dallas," he said gleefully, "and your version of 'Light My Fire' was better." My mom and dad were smiling. I took a deep breath and went to face my newest fans.

**Specific examples and details add tension to the story.**

**The reader can understand and appreciate the writer's feelings.**

**Meaningful conclusion adds a sense of completeness.**

---

Have students list five to ten details from the story. Refer to the controlling idea and conflict that the students identified on TE page 114 and discuss how each detail relates to the focus of the narrative. ✔ DIFFERENTIATE INSTRUCTION

Have students label each detail that they listed as one of the three types of details from SE page 87 (actions or events, sensory details, and thoughts).

- Examples of actions or events might include *watch the second hand on the clock, bought them tickets,* and *I threw up.*
- Examples of sensory details might include *Slam the Doors was really rocking* and *the applause was thunderous.*
- Examples of thoughts might include *I didn't have the nerve, I was sure it would collapse on me,* and *I got more and more nervous.*

---

## Differentiated Instruction: English Language Learners

🌟 ELPS 4F, 4G, 4H

| ELP Level **Beginning** | ELP Level **Intermediate** | ELP Level **Advanced/Advanced High** |
|---|---|---|
| Provide students with adapted sentences from the narrative, supported by pictures. Students read silently and with a partner underline details that they find in the reading. | Provide students with an adapted paragraph from the narrative, supported by pictures. Students read silently and with a partner take notes on details that they find in the reading. | Students read the narrative silently and with a partner take notes on details that they find in the reading. Encourage students to differentiate between the types of details. |

🌟 **ELPS 4F** Use visual/contextual support and support from peers/teachers to enhance/confirm understanding; **4G** Demonstrate comprehension of increasingly complex English/ taking notes; **4H** Read silently with increasing ease and comprehension for longer periods

Have students identify the writer's use of dialogue in this narrative. Model examples for the students—in writing—of how the same ideas could have been conveyed without the dialogue. Discuss how dialogue added interest, humor, and variation to the narrative. **DIFFERENTIATE INSTRUCTION ↘**

Have students identify as many errors in writing conventions as they can. Examples might include:

- The sentence in the first paragraph beginning with *Over the summer . . .* is long and confusing. The sentence should be broken up into smaller sentences.
- In the third full paragraph, *disappointed* is misspelled.
- The second sentence in the third full paragraph should read *. . . and I said yes to five more jobs.*
- In the second paragraph on page two, *exhausted* is misspelled.
- The second to last sentence needs to be restructured. Either break it into two sentences or eliminate the comma and add the word *and*.

**✛ ELPS** 5D

116

**Writing that fits a score of 3 is generally effective.**

> ### Get Rich Quick?
>
> For my buddy Enrique and me, the beginning of tenth grade was the worst. We were too young to get a work permit or to drive. And we NEVER had enough money to buy the stuff we wanted. Over the summer, we had thought about starting a lawn mowing service, but our parents were too busy to drive us to the jobs, and our neighborhood was spread out, so it wasn't practical to wheel the mowers around. Then, in late September, we hit on the idea of a raking and snow shoveling service. We could easily walk or bicycle around town with the equipment.
>
> "Get rich quick!" said Enrique.
>
> "Video games, here we come!" I said.
>
> So E&M Raking & Snow Shoveling Services was born. We made a professional-looking flyer that listed our rates and even included my next door neighbor as a reference. Then we posted it on some community boards at church and at our local market. We also put flyers in people's mailboxes. By the end of the week, we had six jobs scheduled. The first one, on Monday, was for Mrs. Garcia, a nice, retired school teacher who even brought out cookies while we worked. "I have a bad back, or I'd do this myself," she said. "I'm so happy you boys are here." She had a big lawn, with several trees on the side. It took about three hours, and we split the $20. We congratulated each other over our big success.
>
> Monday night, there was a big storm, and lots of leaves blew to the ground. The phone started ringing, and I say yes to five more jobs. Tuesday, it rains hard all day, so we had to postpone our next job. But Mr. Edgars didn't understand. He called Tuesday night. "I'm disapointed you boys didn't show up," he yelled. "Better be here tomorrow." So we had to do two jobs on Wednesday and didn't get home until after dark. We got only $12 from Mr. Edgars, even though he made us drag brush out to the street in addition to the raking. He also walked around the yard, pointing to the few leaves that were left. "There's a leaf, there's a leaf," he

**The topic is set forth in the introductory paragraph.**

**Dialogue adds interest and humor.**

**Essay contains minor errors in writing conventions.**

**Narrative**

cried, while Enrique and I took turns picking them up. I hoped he wouldn't call back.

**Examples build on each other.**

It rained again both Thursday and Friday, so on Saturday we had to rush around doing three jobs. The leaves were soggy and our arms ached. And the five people who called on Monday night all called back, demanding to know when we would be there. I started dreading the sound of the phone. I asked my dad to help us on Saturday. "Sure, just this once," he growls. "But this business was your idea—you've got to figure out how to manage it."

It was only mid November. I wanted to quit but my dad said I couldn't until all the raking jobs were handled. "You can eliminate the snow shoveling," he said, "but you've got to follow through on what you promised people." So even though Enrique and I were exausted, behind in our homework, and tired of being "the boss," we stuck with it. By the time all of the trees were bare, Enrique and I had made $250 each. We were pleased about the money, but glad the work was over.

**Writer sounds sincere and has engaged the reader.**

Once the pressure was off, I realized that my favorite part of the job was advertising the business and negotiating with customers. It made me realize that I might like a career in business or marketing. Now I'm planning to take some econ courses in high school, maybe major in business at college. My almost disastrous job helped me see a future for myself.

Have students identify points in the narrative that the author does a good job conveying his voice. Examples might include:

- *We NEVER had enough money to buy the stuff we wanted.*
- *"Video games, here we come!"*
- *So we had to do two jobs on Wednesday and didn't get home until after dark.*
- *"There's a leaf, there's a leaf," he cried. . .*
- *I hoped he wouldn't call back.*
- *We were pleased about the money, but glad the work was over.*

Review the adjectives listed on SE page 104. Discuss with students which of these adjectives, or others that they can think of, best describe the narrative's voice.

---

## Differentiated Instruction: English Language Learners

⭐ **ELPS** 1B, 2A, 3A

| ELP Level **Beginning** | ELP Level **Intermediate** | ELP Level **Advanced/Advanced High** |
|---|---|---|
| Teach unfamiliar vocabulary in the narrative's title and model the title aloud, being careful to give it the right intonation. Students practice reading the title aloud. | Preteach unfamiliar vocabulary in the narrative's dialogue. Have students practice reading the sentences aloud, paying special attention to proper intonation. | Have students read the narrative aloud, paying special attention to proper intonation. Students should monitor themselves for correct pronunciation and intonation. |

**ELPS** **1B** Monitor oral language and employ self-corrective techniques or other resources; **2A** Distinguish intonation patterns with increasing ease; **3A** Practice producing sounds of newly acquired vocabulary

Have students read the narrative silently. Discuss with them what effect the errors in writing conventions had on their reading. Did the errors make it difficult to understand what the writer meant in some places? How did they distract from the author's message? What overall impression did the errors leave them with? Emphasize the importance of editing their own writing in order to avoid similar distractions.

⭐ **ELPS** 4H

Ask students if they agree with the score given to this narrative. In general, students should agree that it deserved a score of 2, although some may argue for one score point higher or lower. Discuss disagreements, being sure to emphasize how the writer failed to address the five writing traits effectively. **DIFFERENTIATE INSTRUCTION ↘**

⭐ **ELPS** 3G

**Writing that fits a score of 2 is somewhat effective.**

### A Different Life

Last year my parents decided they want to visit Guatemala where they grew up. I didn't want to go. It was summer and I wanted to spend it with my friends plus I'd have to speak Spanish all the time because no one spoke English there. Also there wouldn't be my favorite TV shows and they didn't have internet service or even a computer! It sounded terrible.

Once we get to Guatemala, it took us three hours to get to my grandparents' house, which was in a small village way out in the country. My heart sunk when we got there. There was nothing to do. No movies, no stores, and not close to any interesting places. It looked like the most intresting thing to do was pick the fruit that was growing everywhere.

Everyone was really happy to see us. They all hugged each other. They all started speaking to me in fast Spanish and when I spoke back they laughed and said I had an American accent! "Great," I thought, "They're going to make jokes about my Spanish the hole time I'm here." But then they started telling me how great it was that I could speak Spanish.

I had to sleep with two of my cousins in a small room. At first it really bugged me, but then we started to talk. I told them about america and they told me they wanted to go to america one day, but they also loved Guatemala. I started meting there friends and we started going out all the time. It was fun and actually a lot less stressful than America. I found out you didn't need to play videogames or talk on cell phones or buy new CDs to have fun with friends.

When I got back I really miss my life in Guatemala. I want to go back son and I've been working hard to improve my Spanish. I found out that life in Guatemala is different from here, but its just as good in its own way.

**The controlling idea is unclear. Writing lacks a clear focus.**

**Fragments and other errors in conventions interefere with the message.**

**Detailed descriptions would have added interest.**

**Ideas are not fully developed, so reader cannot appreciate the writer's position.**

Writing that fits a score of 1 is not effective.

**1**

No clear, controlling idea is presented.

The many errors in conventions interfere with understanding.

Passage lacks variety in sentence structure.

Scene lacks description and does not engage the reader.

Narrative

### Team Runt

When I was in middle school I was pretty small for my age. I really like sports though but no one ever picked me for there teams cause I was so small.  In PE I was always the last one.

I new that I was a good player even though I was small. But I am always put in the outfild for softball and in soccer no one ever kicked the ball to me. When we played basketball or flag football I would just sit on the bench it was really humilating.

One day we got a new PE teacher who's rule was that everyone plays. That made the kids that got me on there basketball team really mad and they figured if I played they would lose so the teacher made me one of the starters. The other team laughed.

I play basketball all the time with my brothers and dad. I was actually a good shot and could get in close to the basket. I was also good shooting from the fall line. And I'm fast.  I guess they didn't know that. I don't think they cared.

When we started playing the big kids thought it was funny to block me and no one would pass me the ball. But once there was a lose ball and I got it. I dribled the ball around the bigger players went up for the shot and scored! Nobody could believe it. They thought it was a one time thing. But after I made a few more baskets they started passing the ball to.

After that basketball game people started picking me for their basketball teams. And me I also grew! Now I play junior varsity basketball and other sports and I'm one of the biggest kids but I'm always nice to the smaller kids!

Have students work in pairs to rewrite the opening paragraph. Encourage them to keep the basic idea of the narrative but to work especially on improving focus and coherence and writing conventions. Refer students to SE pages 98, 99, and 108–112 to refresh their memory on these two writing traits.

Discuss with students what types of sensory details could be added to the fifth paragraph to make this action-packed scene really come alive. Brainstorm phrases and sentences that could be worked into the paragraph, and encourage students to include figurative language when possible.

---

### Differentiated Instruction: English Language Learners

ELPS 4D, 4F, 4K, 5G

| ELP Level **Beginning** | ELP Level **Intermediate** | ELP Level **Advanced/Advanced High** |
|---|---|---|
| Provide students with the short, adapted opening paragraph of another narrative. Preteach vocabulary and read together. Discuss whether it presents a controlling idea. | Provide students with an adapted, mini-narrative. Students should read it with a partner and assign it a score point, focusing on only one or two of the traits. | Students read another narrative with a partner and assign it a score point. Students should write a paragraph explanation of their score. |

 **ELPS 4D** Use prereading supports to enhance comprehension of written text/graphic organizers, illustrations, and topic-related vocabulary; **4F** Use support from peers/teachers to enhance and confirm understanding and develop vocabulary; **4K** Demonstrate comprehension and expand reading skills by employing analytical skills/evaluating written information and performing critical analyses; **5G** Explain with increasing specificity and detail/writing

## Evaluating and Reflecting on Your Writing

Encourage students to keep a folder or a computer file of their past evaluation/reflections. Tell students to date their evaluation/reflections so that they can compare them and monitor their progress as writers.

Now that students have completed their phase autobiography, you may want to hold a class discussion on the writing process as a whole. Prompt students to express their opinions, ideas, and feelings about the process. What parts did students find most difficult? Most rewarding? What parts did they enjoy the most? The least?

⭐ ELPS 3G

# Evaluating and Reflecting on Your Writing

You've worked hard to write a phase autobiography that your classmates will enjoy. Now take some time to score your own narrative and think about your writing experience. To score your narrative, use the scoring guide on pages **60–61** and refer to the examples on pages **114–119**. On another sheet of paper, finish each of the sentence starters below. Reflecting on your writing will help you see how you are growing as a writer.

### My Phase Autobiography

1. The focus of my phase autobiography, which I express in my introduction, is . . .

2. My phase autobiography has a logical organizational pattern because . . .

3. One idea I could develop more clearly and completely is . . .

4. In my next personal writing, I would like to . . .

5. One improvement in grammar, usage, or sentence structure that I need to work on is . . .

---

### Differentiated Instruction: English Language Learners

⭐ ELPS 3J, 4E, 4F

| ELP Level **Beginning** | ELP Level **Intermediate** | ELP Level **Advanced/Advanced High** |
|---|---|---|
| Define "historical narrative" using pictures and the student's first language as needed. Discuss examples that students are familiar with (*The Right Stuff*, etc.). | Explain adapted versions of the three characteristics, using pictures and other supports. Give examples from well-known historical narratives (*The Right Stuff*, etc.). | Explain the three characteristics, using pictures and other supports as needed. Watch a clip from a historical movie, and help students identify the characteristics in a class discussion. |

**ELPS 3G** Express opinions, ideas, and feelings ranging from communicating short phrases to participating in discussions; **3J** Respond orally to information presented in a variety of media to build and reinforce concept attainment; **4E** Read linguistically accommodated content area material with a decreasing need for linguistic accommodations as more English is learned; **4F** Use visual/contextual support and support from peers/teachers to read grade-appropriate text, enhance understanding, and develop vocabulary

# Narrative Writing
# Writing a Historical Narrative

Writer Grace Paley advises that "you write from what you know, but you write *in* what you don't know." This advice is especially helpful when it comes to writing a historical narrative, which re-creates a significant event or experience from the past. While it's important to share accurate details about the event, you were not an eyewitness and so cannot know everything. That's when you need to "expand" the narrative with details that make sense within the context of the story.

This chapter begins with a sample historical narrative based on an event involving Louis Pasteur and one of his patients. The rest of the chapter provides guidelines that will help you write your own historical narrative.

## Writing Guidelines

**Subject:** An important historical moment
**Purpose:** To share a significant event from the past
**Form:** Historical narrative
**Audience:** Classmates

"Tell me facts and figures
and you touch my mind,
but tell me a story and
you touch my soul."
—Anne McCaffrey

---

### Objectives
- choose a topic for a historical narrative
- create a time line with which to organize the narrative
- write, revise, and edit a historical narrative

Have students share their experiences reading and writing **historical narratives**. Work with them to list the characteristics of a historical narrative.

- The central characters in the story lived in the past.
- The main events in the story really happened. Significant dates are accurate and true.
- The general setting is real, although specific minor details about the setting may be fictitious. ✔ **DIFFERENTIATE INSTRUCTION**

---

## Resources

**Copy Master (see Appendix)**

- Time Line

**Benchmark Papers (see Appendix)**

## Sample Historical Narrative

Have students read the sample historical narrative for enjoyment and information. Tell them to think about the following as they read:

- Details that reflect historical data were probably gathered through research.
- The writer enriched the story with appropriate "made-up" details.

Historical narratives often include dates and other significant details that contain numbers. Have students skim the narrative to find examples of details that show numbers written as words, numerals, and dates. Possible choices include *1885, nine years old, July 4, 300 miles, 10 days,* and *thousands.* Ask students to infer the rules for writing numbers by studying how they are used in this sample. They should be able to determine the following:

- Write numbers from one to nine as words.
- Write numbers 10 and above as numerals.
- Write numbers in dates and statistics as numerals. **DIFFERENTIATE INSTRUCTION ↘**

**ELPS** 4I

✱ For more about using numbers, see SE page 692.

## Sample Historical Narrative

A historical narrative shares a significant experience from the past. In the following sample, DaShawn Mathews shares a lifesaving experience in the life of Joseph Meister, who received the first rabies vaccine from Louis Pasteur. The narrative is told from the point of view of Joseph as a 16-year-old.

**Beginning**
The first paragraph sets the scene.

**Middle**
The second paragraph jumps right into the action.

Descriptive words bring the story to life.

### Lurking in the Shadows

In the summer of 1885, I was nine years old, living with my family in the Alsace region of Germany. On the morning of July 4, I was walking alone on the road that led to school. I never even saw the dog lurking in the shadows of the butcher shop.

The snarling beast leapt from nowhere, slamming me to the ground. Pain seared through my body as the huge dog ripped at my arms and legs. "Help! Help!" I shouted. Foam and saliva from the dog's mouth splattered onto me, and blood stained my clothes.

Suddenly, I heard a voice yell, "Someone save little Joseph from that rabid dog!" The vicious attack finally ended when strong hands pulled me to safety. That evening, I screamed in agony as Dr. Weber poured carbolic acid on my wounds to clean them.

Two days later, after traveling nearly 300 miles, my mother and I arrived at the Paris office of Louis Pasteur, who was working on a rabies vaccination. Mother knew that rabies causes seizures, paralysis, and eventually death, so she pleaded with Pasteur to save me. I struggled to stand, because the deep bites on my legs were incredibly painful. Pasteur seemed hesitant, but Mother convinced him to examine me.

Several men in white coats peered down at me as I lay on a cold table. "Due to the severity and number of bites, it's almost inevitable that this boy will come down with rabies and die," whispered a gruff voice.

Pasteur looked uneasy and concerned. He ushered the men over to his desk and explained that he would try a rabies vaccine treatment, even though it hadn't been tried on humans. I heard Pasteur say, "Joseph will be given a series of shots for at least 10 days."

Terrified, I screamed and tried to sit up.

Pasteur quickly came to my side and gently explained that the shots wouldn't hurt much. "Just a tiny sting," he promised. Pasteur's eyes were warm and friendly. His whiskery beard reminded me of my grandfather's beard. I decided that I could trust this man.

For the next 10 days, I received shots of the rabies vaccine. Pasteur grabbed my skin just below my rib cage and pinched it into a fold. I didn't watch as he pushed the needle into my skin. Thankfully, the injections weren't very painful. I didn't understand how the vaccination worked, but I did know that I wasn't getting sick.

My mother was so excited to see me every morning. Pasteur's face drooped with concern because he was so afraid that I would get sick with rabies and die.

Pasteur shouldn't have worried because I never developed rabies. Less than a month after I was attacked, Pasteur decided that I was healthy enough to go home. Newspapers declared that my amazing recovery was the result of Pasteur's miraculous rabies vaccination. In the months and years ahead, rabies vaccinations were used to treat thousands of people around the world. I was the first of many.

**Dialogue adds** realism and makes the characters more interesting.

**Ending**
The final paragraph explains the significance of the story.

Narrative

 **Respond to the reading.** Answer the following questions about the historical narrative you have just read.

**Focus and Coherence** (1) What is the controlling idea of the narrative? (2) How does the conclusion add to the essay? **Organization** (3) What transitions does the writer use to help organize the narrative? **Development of Ideas** (4) What specific facts about this experience does the writer share? Name at least three. **Voice** (5) Does the writer create a believable firsthand experience? **Conventions** (6) How might the writer improve sentence variety? Explain.

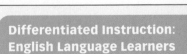

Ask students to consider how a strictly factual account of Pasteur's first use of the rabies vaccine would differ from this historical narrative.

 **Respond to the reading.**

**Answers**

**Focus and Coherence**
1. Possible controlling idea: The first successful use of the rabies vaccine saved the life of a young boy.
2. The conclusion shows how the event was historically significant and affected far more than just one nine-year-old boy.

**Organization**
3. Possible choices: *In the summer of 1885, on the morning of, Suddenly, That evening, Two days later, For the next 10 days, Less than a month after*

**Development of Ideas**
4. Possible choices: the place and date where Joseph was attacked by the dog; the traveling distance and visit to Louis Pasteur; the decision to treat Joseph with the rabies vaccine; the fact that Joseph didn't get rabies

**Voice**
5. Students should generally agree that the writer creates a believable firsthand experience. The vivid description of the attack, the concern of his mother and doctors, and the dialogue add realism.

**Conventions**
6. Many sentences, especially on the second page, are of similar length and structure. Students may suggest combining some of these short sentences to add variety.

## Differentiated Instruction: English Language Learners

| ELP Level **Beginning** | ELP Level **Intermediate** | ELP Level **Advanced/Advanced High** |
| --- | --- | --- |
| Provide students with a word bank of numbers written out as words (one, two, etc.). Help students sound out the words and match them to the correct numeral. | Provide students with simple sentences that write numbers incorrectly. Students must write out the sentences correctly by applying the three rules for number writing. | Students write a short paragraph (topic of their choice) that demonstrates all three rules for number writing. Provide complex sentence stems as needed. |

 **ELPS 4A** Sound out words using a combination of skills; **4C** Develop basic sight vocabulary used in written classroom materials; **5F** Use visual/contextual support to read grade-appropriate content area text and enhance understanding

## Prewriting
### Planning Your Writing

In addition to paging through their history books to find topics, students can:

- look through their reading log to recall biographies and essays they have read;
- recall historical documentaries and movies with plots that center around historical events and characters; and
- ask teachers in other curriculum areas for ideas.

**Choose your topic.** Remind students that the narrator is the person through whose eyes the story will be told. Note that the narrator doesn't always have to be a famous person. In DaShawn's examples, they range from Thomas Jefferson to a nameless factory worker.

### Gathering Details

Emphasize that students should use several reliable sources to gather historically accurate details. If students think of ideas that will make their narratives come alive as they prepare their note cards, they should highlight them on note cards that are used specifically for creative and imagined details.

**TEKS** 10.13A, 10.14A

**Gather details.** Note that many of DaShawn's notes didn't make it into the story directly. However, a broad understanding of the topic helped him write in a believable way.

---

## Prewriting Planning Your Writing

After paging through his history book, DaShawn created a chart of possible topics (events) for his historical narrative. He listed only topics that were brief and specific. With each topic, DaShawn chose a specific narrator.

### Topics Chart

| TOPIC (Specific Events) | NARRATOR |
|---|---|
| Signing the Declaration of Independence | Thomas Jefferson |
| Louis Pasteur's first human trial with his rabies vaccine * | Joseph Meister, first person treated with the vaccine |
| A day in an 1800s tenement sweatshop | Girl working in garment sweatshop |

 **Choose your topic.** Create a chart, listing historical events and possible narrators. Put an asterisk next to the event that you would like to write about.

### Gathering Details

The next step is to research your topic and take careful notes. Remember that you are writing from the perspective of someone who personally experienced this moment in time. DaShawn used note cards to organize his research. He will use these notes to help him choose a controlling idea for his narrative.

### Sample Notes

Pasteur, Louis
- says that germs affect fermentation
- proves his theory
- says that germs cause diseases
- develops anti-rabies vaccine
- treats Joseph Meister with vaccine in 1885
- story of Louis Pasteur pages 8–10

Meister, Joseph
- lives in Meissengott in Alsace
- attacked by a rabid dog while walking to school
- bitten badly, rescued by a local bricklayer
- first person treated for rabies with vaccine
- www.sciencefounder.net/Rabies.htm

 **Gather details.** Research your topic, using a variety of sources to find information for your narrative. Take careful notes.

---

## Organizing Your Details

Historical narratives are usually written in chronological order. DaShawn used a time line to organize the information he had gathered. Above the line, he listed specific dates from the story; below the line, he listed the details.

### Sample Time Line

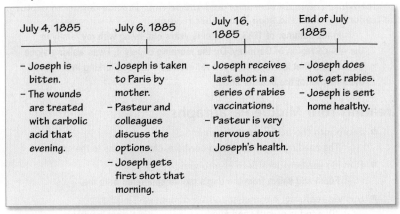

| July 4, 1885 | July 6, 1885 | July 16, 1885 | End of July 1885 |

- Joseph is bitten.
- The wounds are treated with carbolic acid that evening.

- Joseph is taken to Paris by mother.
- Pasteur and colleagues discuss the options.
- Joseph gets first shot that morning.

- Joseph receives last shot in a series of rabies vaccinations.
- Pasteur is very nervous about Joseph's health.

- Joseph does not get rabies.
- Joseph is sent home healthy.

**Organize your details.** Create a time line, listing dates or specific times above the line and details below it. The following types of details will make your story engaging.

- **Historic details:** facts about *Who? What? When? Where?* and *Why?*
- **Sensory details:** what your character may have seen, heard, smelled, tasted, or touched
- **Reflective details:** what your character may have thought or felt
- **Actions:** what your character may have done or experienced
- **Dialogue:** what your character may have said or heard

### Focus on the Texas Traits

**Voice** The narrative on pages **122–123** is written from the first-person perspective of a character remembering the experience. This personal voice pulls the reader into the action.

---

## Organizing Your Details

Use the organization and details in the sample time line to illustrate that, like any narrative, a historical narrative has:

- a beginning (July 4, 1885), a middle (July 6 and 16, 1885), and an ending (end of July 1885);
- a main character (Joseph) who faces a problem or has a goal; and
- a plot, with a series of events organized chronologically.

**Organize your details.** Provide photocopies of the reproducible time line (TE Appendix) for students to use as they organize their own details for their historical narrative. ✔DIFFERENTIATE INSTRUCTION

✱ For more about using chronological order and a time line, see SE pages 607.

Also, to ensure that your students understand the distinctions between the detail types (historic, sensory, etc.), you may want to go back to DaShawn's narrative and have them find examples of each type.

### Focus on the Texas Traits

**Voice**
Ask students how the voice of the narrative on SE pages 122–123 would have been different if the narrative had been told from Pasteur's point of view. (The voice would have been more objective.)

---

### Differentiated Instruction: English Language Learners

ELPS **3E, 5G**

| ELP Level **Beginning** | ELP Level **Intermediate** | ELP Level **Advanced/Advanced High** |
|---|---|---|
| Allow students to complete their time line using a combination of English (provide short, simple sentence stems), pictures, and their first language. | Provide students with sentence stems to help them complete their time line. Allow them to supplement unfamiliar vocabulary with pictures as needed. | Allow students to complete their time line with the help of a partner. Partners should help express difficult concepts by aiding with vocabulary and sentence structure. |

 **ELPS 3E** Share information in cooperative learning interactions; **5G** Narrate/describe/explain with increasing specificity and detail to fulfill content area writing needs

## Drafting

### Writing Your Beginning Paragraph

Note that by including action in the beginning paragraph, students can create suspense from the start. This technique acts as a hook to draw their readers into the rest of the story. **DIFFERENTIATE INSTRUCTION ↘**

### Creating Your Middle Paragraphs

As students write their first drafts, emphasize that each paragraph in their historical narratives should contain a combination of factual and lively, creative details.

**ELPS** 5G

✱ For more on writing narrative paragraphs, see SE page 600.

### Developing a Strong Ending Paragraph

Note that the ending paragraph should leave few, if any, unanswered questions. Most significantly, the main conflict should be brought to a satisfying conclusion.

**Write your first draft.** If, as students write, they discover that they are missing an important date or other piece of factual information, suggest that they leave a place marker in the draft and continue writing. They can research the date and fill in any gaps later.

**TEKS** 10.13B, 10.14A

**TEKS 10.13B** Structure ideas in a persuasive way; **10.14A** Write a story with a conflict, a resolution, interesting and believable characters, and literary strategies and devices to enhance the plot; **ELPS 5G** Narrate with increasing specificity and detail/writing

---

## Drafting

After gathering and organizing your details, read the following tips. They will guide you as you write your first draft.

Beginning
Middle
Ending

### Writing Your Beginning Paragraph

Introduce the main character and the setting. Provide details to capture the reader's interest and keep him or her reading.

> In the summer of 1885, I was nine years old, living with my family in the Alsace region of Germany. On the morning of July 4, I was walking alone on the road that led to school. I never even saw the dog lurking in the shadows of the butcher shop.

### Creating Your Middle Paragraphs

- Jump into the action of the moment.
  > The snarling beast leapt from nowhere, slamming me to the ground.
- Provide sensory details to create vivid imagery.
  > Foam and saliva from the dog's mouth splattered onto me.
- Include realistic, natural-sounding dialogue.
  > "Due to the severity and number of bites, it's almost inevitable . . . "
- Add thoughts, feelings, and explanations as needed.
  > Pasteur's face drooped with concern because he was so afraid that I would get sick with rabies and die.

### Developing a Strong Ending Paragraph

Share the resolution of the conflict and why it was significant.

> Pasteur shouldn't have worried because I never developed rabies. Less than a month after I was attacked, Pasteur decided that I was healthy enough to go home. Newspapers declared that my amazing recovery was the result of Pasteur's miraculous rabies vaccination. In the months and years ahead, rabies vaccinations were used to treat thousands of people around the world. I was the first of many.

**Write your first draft.** Use your time line (page 125) and the tips to guide your writing. Get all of your ideas on paper and don't worry about mistakes.

Draft

---

### Differentiated Instruction: Advanced Learners

Challenge students to begin their first drafts with the second or third event listed on their time lines. Have them weave the prior events into their stories as flashbacks. Model this technique for students using DaShawn's middle paragraph on SE page 122 as the beginning of the narrative. Have volunteers suggest sentences that help make smooth transitions back to earlier events, such as "While I waited for the vaccine to take effect, I thought about how this summer had begun like any other."

**TEKS** 10.13B

Historical Narrative **127**⁰

 **TEKS** 10.13C

## Revising Improving Your Writing

Think about your purpose, your audience and the genre, or form, of the writing you have just done. Then use this checklist to improve your writing.

Narrative

### Revising Checklist

**Focus and Coherence**

_____ **1.** Have I clearly communicated my purpose for writing?
_____ **2.** Do all my ideas relate to the topic?

**Organization**

_____ **3.** Does my beginning introduce the main character?
_____ **4.** Do the middle paragraphs convincingly re-create the event?
_____ **5.** Does the ending explain the significance of the event?

**Development of Ideas**

_____ **6.** Have I thoroughly explained the significance of the topic?
_____ **7.** Are my facts, such as names and dates, accurate?
_____ **8.** Are all my ideas connected to each other, and can the reader understand the connection?

**Voice**

_____ **9.** Does the story sound like a realistic firsthand experience?
_____ **10.** Do I use dialogue effectively?

## Creating a Title

- Be clever or humorous: **Vaccine Vanquishes Villain**
- Use an expression or common saying: **A Shot in the Dark**
- Use a line from the narrative: **Lurking in the Shadows**

**Revise your first draft.** Use the checklist above to review and make changes to your first draft. Then add a title.

Revise

### Revising
**Improving Your Writing**

If students are concerned about the accuracy of any fact or detail, suggest that they return to their original notes or to the original source to verify the information.

**Creating a Title**

Note that it's important to make sure that a title reflects the purpose, audience, and genre of the writing. For example, a humorous title would probably not be appropriate for a story whose purpose is to describe the horrors of the holocaust.

**Revise your first draft.** If students have difficulty thinking of satisfactory titles, suggest that they share their narratives with two or three classmates and ask them to suggest several possible titles from which to choose.

☑ DIFFERENTIATE INSTRUCTION
**TEKS** 10.13C

---

### Differentiated Instruction: English Language Learners

**ELPS** 2A, 4A

| ELP Level **Beginning** | ELP Level **Intermediate** | ELP Level **Advanced/Advanced High** |
| --- | --- | --- |
| Explain the term *alliteration*. Help students practice the concept by completing sentence stems (e.g., *Bill broke the _____.*) and saying them aloud. | Explain the term *alliteration*. Have students work with a partner to create an alliterative title for their historical narrative. Prompt students with helpful words as necessary. | Explain *alliteration*. Have students work with a partner to create several alliterative titles for their narrative. Challenge students to use difficult letters (e, j, o, etc.). |

**TEKS** 10.13C Revise drafts/improve style, word choice, and subtlety of meaning and rethink how well the purpose, audience, and genre have been addressed; **ELPS** 2A Distinguish sounds with increasing ease; 4A Learn relationships between sounds and letters

## Editing
### Checking for Conventions

Aside from consulting the Proofreader's Guide, encourage students to ask you if they have a question about a specific grammatical or mechanical rule. As students ask questions, bring areas of frequent confusion before the whole class.

**Correct your narrative.** Suggest that students first read through their narratives looking only for mistakes in punctuation. Emphasize especially the correct use of apostrophes to show possession. For additional examples, have students find possessives on SE page 123 (grandfather's beard, Pasteur's face, Pasteur's miraculous rabies vaccination). Students can then reread their narratives to check for errors in capitalization, spelling, and grammar.

**TEKS** 10.13D, 10.13E, 10.17C, 10.18A, 10.18B, 10.19; **ELPS** 5C, 5D, 5E

## Publishing
### Sharing Your Writing

**Share your historical narrative.** Schedule a Historical Perspective Day during which students can read their narratives aloud to the class. Encourage students to incorporate appropriate music and art to enhance their readings. DIFFERENTIATE INSTRUCTION ↘

**TEKS** 10.13E

### Technology Connections

⚡ *Write Source Online* **Portfolio**

⚡ *Write Source Online* **Essay Evaluation**

**TEKS** 10.13D Edit drafts for grammar, mechanics, and spelling; **10.13E** Revise the final draft in response to feedback from peers and teacher/publish written work; **10.17C** Use a variety of correctly structured sentences; **10.18A** Use conventions of capitalization; **10.18B** Use correct punctuation marks; **10.19** Spell correctly using resources to determine and check correct spelling; **ELPS 1B** Monitor oral language and employ self-corrective techniques or other resources; **1G** Demonstrate increasing ability to distinguish between formal/informal English and an increasing knowledge of when to use each one; **3I** Adapt spoken language for formal and informal purposes; **4A** Learn relationships between sounds and letters/sound out words using a combination of skills; **5C** Spell familiar words with increasing accuracy; **5C** Spell familiar words with increasing accuracy; **5D** Edit writing for standard grammar and usage/pronoun agreement and appropriate verb tenses; **5E** Employ increasingly complex grammatical structures in content area writing such as using correct verbs, tenses, and pronouns/possessive case/negatives and contractions

---

**TEKS** 10.13D, 10.13E, 10.17C, 10.18A, 10.18B, 10.19
**ELPS** 5C, 5D, 5E

## Editing Checking for Conventions

After making revisions, you're ready to edit your writing for grammar, sentence structure, punctuation, capitalization, and spelling errors. The following checklist can help you with this step. (See the "Proofreader's Guide" for more about writing rules.)

### Editing Checklist

#### Conventions

**GRAMMAR**

_____ **1.** Do I use the correct tenses and forms of verbs (*had gone*, not *had went*)?

_____ **2.** Do my subjects and verbs agree in number (*She was running*, not *She were running*)?

_____ **3.** Do I use the right words (*too, to, two*)? Remember, a computer grammar checker does not catch all usage errors.

**SENTENCE STRUCTURE**

_____ **4.** Do I use a variety of correctly structured sentences that clearly communicate my ideas?

**MECHANICS (PUNCTUATION, CAPITALIZATION, AND SPELLING)**

_____ **5.** Do I use end punctuation correctly after all sentences?

_____ **6.** Do I use apostrophes to show possession (*Pasteur's beard*)?

_____ **7.** Do I use end commas correctly?

_____ **8.** Do I capitalize all proper nouns?

_____ **9.** Have I used a dictionary to check for spelling errors?

**Correct your narrative.** Use the checklist above to find and correct any errors. Also ask a classmate, friend, or teacher to check your work. Then create a neat final draft and proofread it again.

## Publishing Sharing Your Writing

Take time to share your work with classmates and family members.

**Share your historical narrative.** If you read your narrative to the class, practice first. Then read it clearly and with feeling. Consider using a prop or costume appropriate for the story.

---

### Differentiated Instruction: English Language Learners

**ELPS** 1B, 1G, 3I, 4A

| ELP Level **Beginning** | ELP Level **Intermediate** | ELP Level **Advanced/Advanced High** |
|---|---|---|
| Model how to introduce yourself in a formal way before giving a presentation. Students practice introducing themselves. | Help students practice reading their essay aloud, providing help—including modeling—with pronunciation and decoding. Then have students read it aloud to the class. | Students read their essay aloud and monitor their speech, employing self-corrective techniques as necessary. Encourage students to use proper intonation. |

# Writing for Assessment
# Responding to Narrative Prompts

In one section of his autobiography *Good Old Boy,* Willie Morris states, "Almost every afternoon when the heat was not too bad my father and I would go out to the old baseball field behind the armory to hit flies." Morris's father would hit ball after ball into the outfield, and the author, then a young boy, would try to catch them. Because of all this practice, Morris became a skilled center fielder.

You, too, have learned many skills during your lifetime. You may, for example, have learned how to ride a bike or swim or knit or play the guitar. Narrative writing prompts on assessments often ask you to recall such a learning experience. To respond effectively, you must share the key details related to the experience and tell why it was (or is) important to you. This chapter will guide you through the process of responding to narrative writing prompts.

## Writing Guidelines

**Subject:** Narrative prompt
**Form:** Response to a prompt
**Purpose:** To demonstrate competence
**Audience:** Instructor or test evaluator

"Pain is temporary. It may last a minute, or an hour, or a day, or a year, but eventually it will subside and something else will take its place. If I quit, however, it lasts forever."
—Lance Armstrong

# Responding to Narrative Prompts

## Objectives
● use STRAP questions to analyze and plan a response to a narrative prompt
● apply what has been learned about narrative writing when responding to a narrative prompt

If your students take school, district, or TAKS assessments this year, focus on the writing form on which they will be tested.

Call attention to Lance Armstrong's quotation at the bottom of the page.
■ Ask students to discuss a time when something they were trying to accomplish or learn became so difficult that they wanted to quit.
■ Have students recall and share details about these experiences and what they learned about themselves.
■ Remind students that the most meaningful experiences in their lives are usually the ones that they can recall most vividly. As a result, such experiences can be the ones that are the easiest to describe. Students should keep this in mind when responding to narrative prompts.

## Prewriting
### Analyzing a Narrative Prompt

Explain to students that working efficiently is an important part of taking any timed assessment test. Making sure that they understand the prompt is an important first step when taking a writing assessment test.

### Using the STRAP Questions

Make sure students understand that the ideas given in parentheses in the STRAP questions are provided as examples of possible responses. **DIFFERENTIATE INSTRUCTION** ↘

### Try It!
**Answers**

**Possible Answers**

1. **Subject**: learning to type; **Type**: autobiographical article; **Role**: student; **Audience**: teacher; **Purpose**: inspire
2. **Subject**: top ranking in class; **Type**: personal narrative; **Role**: student; **Audience**: younger students; **Purpose**: illustrate
3. **Subject**: help build a skateboard track; **Type**: personal essay; **Role**: friend; **Audience**: classmates; **Purpose**: share

⭐ **ELPS** 4K

### Tip

For example, prompt number one in the **Try It!** activity didn't specify the type, role, audience, or purpose, but the answers given will work well and help the writer understand the prompt.

---

## Prewriting Analyzing a Narrative Prompt

A prompt is a set of directions that tells you what to write. For example, a narrative prompt is one that tells you to write about a significant personal experience. To effectively respond to the prompt, you must first understand it. The **STRAP questions** below will help you to analyze a narrative prompt.

## Using the STRAP Questions

**Subject:** What specific experience (memorable, life changing, challenging, inspiring) should I write about?

**Type:** What type of writing (personal narrative, personal essay, autobiographical article) should I create?

**Role:** What role (student, son or daughter, friend, community member) should I assume as the writer?

**Audience:** Who (principal, parent, city official, classmates) is the intended reader?

**Purpose:** What is the goal (share, re-create, entertain, illustrate, inspire) of my writing?

### Try It!

Analyze these prompts, answering the STRAP questions for each one.

1. You often hear the phrase "Learn by doing." Recall how you learned a skill, and explain how the skill has benefited you.
2. Think about a time when you wanted something very badly and were not able to obtain or achieve it. What did you learn from the experience? Your response will appear in a booklet for younger students in your school district.
3. "The only way to help yourself is to help others." Share a personal experience that reveals the truth of these words.

### Tip

Some prompts do not contain key words for every STRAP question. Use your best judgment to find answers for all the questions.

---

⭐ **ELPS 4K** Demonstrate comprehension and expand reading skills by employing analytical skills/evaluating written information and performing critical analyses

## Planning Your Response

Once you understand a prompt thoroughly, you can plan your response. The following graphic organizers can help you complete your planning.

### Narrative Graphic Organizers

Narrative

 **Reread the narrative prompts on page 130.** Choose one prompt to respond to, and create a graphic organizer like one of those above to plan your response.

Prewrite

### Tip

Be sure to use your time wisely. For example, if you have 45 minutes to respond to a prompt, consider using the first 5 to 10 minutes to analyze the prompt and plan your response, and the last 5 minutes to revise and edit it. That leaves 30 to 35 minutes for writing your response.

---

### Planning Your Response

Students are probably familiar with most or all of the graphic organizers shown and understand how and when to use each one. To be sure of this, however, ask students to explain which organizer(s) they would use to prepare their response to the prompts in the **Try It!** activity on SE page 130. (Possible responses: Prompt 1: Cluster, 5 W's Chart; Prompt 2: Before-After Chart, Specific Details Chart; Prompt 3: Cluster, Before-After Chart)

**Reread the narrative prompts.** You may want to provide photocopies of the reproducible time line, 5 W's chart, and details chart (TE Appendix) for students to use for organizing their responses. Remind students, however, that in an on-demand writing situation, they will probably not be given premade graphic organizers to fill out. Students need to become familiar with using and creating their own graphic organizers in a testing situation.

TEKS 10.13A, 10.13B

### Tip

To prepare students for real test situations, set a timer for 10 minutes and have them try to analyze and organize their responses while being timed.

---

TEKS **10.13A** Plan a first draft/selecting genre and determining topics through a range of strategies; **10.13B** Structure ideas in a sustained way; ELPS **2C** Learn basic vocabulary heard during classroom instruction/interactions; **3G** Express ideas ranging from communicating short phrases to participating in discussions; **4C** Comprehend vocabulary used in written classroom materials

## Drafting

### Responding to the Prompt

Review the characteristics of narrative writing. Ask students to look for these elements as they read the sample response:

- a strong beginning that introduces the topic,
- middle paragraphs that help explain the topic,
- transitions that connect ideas,
- literary devices like dialogue and suspense, and
- a strong ending that reflects on the experience.

**TEKS** 10.13B

---

## Drafting Responding to the Prompt

After planning your response, it's time to begin writing. Student writer Ari Marks chose to respond to prompt number 1 on page 130. Ari plans to use dialogue and rich sensory details to make the characters and situations in her narratiive interesting and realistic. Her response to the prompt is below.

### Sample Response

> The **beginning** introduces the writer's focus (underlined).

> Each **middle** paragraph presents details about the experience. There is a logical organizational pattern, and ideas are well developed.

> The writer has an authentic voice, and details add interest.

#### Eleanor Roosevelt Teaches Me to Knit

"Knit one, purl two," I whispered to myself as I rubbed the textured yarn between my fingers. The needles dipped in and out, forming a neat row of stitches along the edge of the scarf. <u>The process of knitting, even for just a few minutes, made me feel happy and confident.</u>

I learned to knit the summer after seventh grade, when I begged my grandmother to teach me. Gran (and she is a very hip gran, by the way) had been knitting since she was in college, and she always wears the most beautiful handmade things. She is known for her elegantly fringed scarves and boldly patterned sweaters. And she always looks content when she knits. "It's the world's greatest relaxer," she says.

At first, I thought I'd never get the hang of it. I fumbled with the needles. I tangled up the yarn. I kept "dropping a stitch" by letting the yarn slip off the needle by mistake. Then, five or six rows later, I would notice a hole, and I'd have to ask Gran to fix it. Every time, she patiently used a crochet hook to work the dropped stitch back up and onto the needle.

Even when I finally mastered the stitches, my first projects weren't always successful. One sweater was too short. The vest I made for my dad was uneven on the bottom. He wore it anyway, mostly when he walked the dog.

The following summer I almost gave up knitting for good. I wanted to knit something spectacular, so I saved my allowance and bought some expensive wool to make a poncho. I used small

---

### Differentiated Instruction: Advanced Learners

Have students share what they know about Eleanor Roosevelt. Explain that the title arouses curiosity because the reader does not know how Eleanor Roosevelt fits into the story until the middle of the second page. Finally, have students come up with and discuss possible themes for the response, such as "persistence pays off."

needles to work the intricate design. When it was time for school to start again, I was really discouraged because I had only finished a piece about 14 inches square!

But Gran's encouragement kept me knitting. She quoted her idol, former First Lady Eleanor Roosevelt. "Eleanor said, 'You must do the thing you think you cannot do,'" Gran said. "I think that applies to knitting as well as to anything else."

I took Gran's advice and continued to knit. But I decided to wait with the poncho. Instead, I perfected my skills on easier patterns that used large needles. Two of my favorite pieces included a silky choker and a backpack made out of a multicolored rayon and cotton. A lot of my friends really liked my backpack. Some people even asked me where I bought it!

Any frustrations I may have had with learning how to knit were well worth it. Knitting helped me become even closer to Gran. It also helped me learn more about fabrics, colors, and design. Most importantly, it built up my self-confidence and taught me not to be afraid to try new things, even if that meant "dropping a stitch" every now and then.

The **ending** tells what the writer learned from the experience.

**Write your own response.** Look over the prompt you chose on page **130** and look over the planning you did. Then write a response in the amount of time provided by your teacher.

Draft

---

Point out the similarities between the phase autobiographies they wrote and the sample response on SE pages 132–133.

When they wrote their phase autobiographies, their goal was to explain how a meaningful time in their lives changed them.

- They introduced their experiences in an engaging way.
- They used chronological order to present important events in the middle paragraphs.
- They used dialogue and sensory details to make their stories memorable.
- They wrote endings that connected to the beginnings and explained how they changed as a result of their experiences.

Similarly, in the sample narrative, the writer's goal is to explain how learning a skill changes her (or him) for the better.

- The writer grabs the reader's attention with engaging dialogue.
- The writer uses chronological order to present story events in the middle paragraphs.
- Dialogue and sensory details make the experience real for the reader.
- In the ending, the writer recalls the frustration she described in the beginning and explains what she learned.

TEKS 10.13B, 10.14A

**Write your own response.** Give your students a time limit that closely reflects testing situations that students will encounter during the school year. ✔ DIFFERENTIATE INSTRUCTION ✔ DIFFERENTIATE INSTRUCTION

---

TEKS **10.13B** Structure ideas in a sustained way/develop drafts in timed situations that include transitions and rhetorical devices; **10.14A** Write a story with a conflict, a resolution, interesting and believable characters, and literary strategies and devices to enhance the plot; ELPS **5F** Write using a variety of grade-appropriate sentence lengths and patterns in increasingly accurate ways; **5G** Narrate/describe/explain with increasing specificity and detail to fulfill content area writing needs

## Revising
### Improving Your Response

Stress the importance of taking the time *before* beginning a response to answer the STRAP questions and to organize ideas as thoroughly as possible. Explain to students that if they do so, the revisions they may need to make when they return to the STRAP questions should be minor.

**Improve your work.** Remind students to keep the first four writing traits in mind as well. Does their response have a clear controlling idea? Does it have a well-organized beginning, middle, and end? Does it include sensory details? Does their personal voice come through in the writing?

⭐ **ELPS** 5G

## Editing
### Checking for Conventions

Have students refer to SE page 128 for a more detailed conventions checklist.

**Check for conventions.** Students make more careless mistakes when they are under the pressure of time. Common mistakes often involve subject-verb agreement and using the correct form of words, such as *there, they're,* or *their.* Tell students to proofread carefully to identify and correct these types of mistakes.

⭐ **TEKS** 10.13C, 10.13D; **ELPS** 5C, 5D

### ⭐ Conventions Connections

**Grammar: Nouns**
- *Proofreader's Guide* pages 731–732
- *SkillsBook* pages 74–79
- *Write Source Online GrammarSnap*

**Grammar: Conjunctions**
- *Proofreader's Guide* pages 762
- *SkillsBook* pages 117–120
- *Write Source Online GrammarSnap*

**Grammar: End Punctuation**
- *Proofreader's Guide* pages 643–644
- *SkillsBook* pages 5–6
- *Write Source Online GrammarSnap*

**Grammar: Using the Right Word**
- *Proofreader's Guide* pages 710–728

## Revising Improving Your Response

Most writing tests allow you to make changes to your response, but be sure you know the number and kinds of changes that are allowed.

### Using the STRAP Questions

Return to the STRAP questions to guide your revisions.

> **Subject:** Does my response focus on a specific experience related to the prompt?
>
> **Type:** Have I written the appropriate type of response (personal narrative, essay, article)?
>
> **Role:** Have I assumed the role indicated in the prompt (student, friend, son or daughter, community member)?
>
> **Audience:** Have I kept my intended audience in mind and used language appropriate for that audience?
>
> **Purpose:** Does my response accomplish the goal called for by the prompt (share, re-create, entertain, illustrate, inspire)?

**Improve your work.** Review your response, using the STRAP questions as a guide. Make any changes neatly in the time allowed.

## Editing Checking for Conventions

Finally, it is a good idea to read through your draft again to check for punctuation, capitalization, spelling, and grammar errors.

### Conventions

_____ 1. Do my subjects and verbs agree?
_____ 2. Have I used a variety of correctly structured sentences?
_____ 3. Have I checked for spelling errors?
_____ 4. Have I used commas and end punctuation correctly?
_____ 5. Have I capitalized proper nouns and the first words of sentences?

**Check for conventions.** Review your response and correct errors in grammar, sentence structure, punctuation, capitalization, and spelling.

- *SkillsBook* pages 62–67
- *Write Source Online GrammarSnap*

**Grammar: Pronoun Shifts**
- *Write Source* pages 573
- *SkillsBook* pages 180–181
- *Write Source Online GrammarSnap*

⭐ **TEKS** 10.13C Revise drafts to improve sentence variety; **10.13D** Edit drafts for grammar, mechanics, and spelling; **ELPS** 5C Spell familiar words with increasing accuracy; **5D** Edit writing for standard grammar and usage/subject-verb agreement; **5G** Narrate/describe/explain with increasing specificity and detail to fulfill content area writing needs

# Narrative Writing on Tests

The following tips will guide you whenever you are asked to write a response to a narrative prompt.

Narrative

## Before you write . . .

- **Understand the prompt.**
  Use the STRAP questions and remember that a narrative prompt asks you to share or re-create an experience.
- **Plan your response.**
  Spend several minutes planning your response. Use an appropriate graphic organizer to help you. (See page **131**.)

## As you write . . .

- **State the focus of your response in the beginning.**
  Keep your purpose *(to share, to illustrate)* in mind as you write.
- **Be mindful of time.**
  If you have 45 minutes total, you should spend only 30 to 35 minutes drafting.
- **Demonstrate good writing skills.**
  Use dialogue, as well as literary and rhetorical devices (irony, metaphors, and so on), to make your experience interesting. Include transitions that indicate the passage of time, such as "The following summer" in the sample response.
- **End in a meaningful way.**
  Tell why the experience has been important to you.

## After you've written your first draft . . .

- **Check for completeness and correctness.**
  Use the STRAP questions to revise your work. Then check for errors in conventions.

## Narrative Prompts

- In a personal narrative, share a time in your life when you learned to do something for yourself. Your audience is your classmates.
- In an article for your school newspaper, describe an accomplishment that made you really proud. Make the experience come alive with vivid details and dialogue.

## Narrative Writing on Tests

Explain to students that the tips on this page will help them use the test time efficiently and successfully. During assessments, they may not order their thoughts as well as they do in non-timed situations. Remind them to include transitions to make the sequence of events clear in their narrative.

Consider using one or both of these prompts for further practice. Allow students the same amount of time to plan and write their response essay as they will be allotted on high stakes assessments. Break down each part of the process into clear chunks of time. For example:

- 10 minutes for note taking and planning,
- 30 minutes for writing, and
- 5 minutes for editing and proofreading.

**✔ DIFFERENTIATE INSTRUCTION**

**TEKS** 10.13B, 10.14A

Tell students when time is up for each section. Start the assignment at the top of the hour or at the half-hour to make it easier for students to keep track of the time.

If your state, district, or school requires students to use and submit a graphic organizer as part of their assessment, have students draw their own copies.

Organize students into groups and have groups review one set of the tips. Have them make a poster to help their classmates remember the tips.

**ELPS** 3E

---

## Differentiated Instruction:
### English Language Learners

**ELPS** 5F, 5G

| ELP Level **Beginning** | ELP Level **Intermediate** | ELP Level **Advanced/Advanced High** |
|---|---|---|
| Help students write a short response supplemented by pictures and their first language. Give students extended or unlimited time and guide them through each step. | Help students write a short response using pictures and their first language occasionally. Give students extended or unlimited time to work through each step. | Students write a response with a partner. Allow extended time for students to complete each step, and challenge students to practice complex sentence structures. |

**TEKS** **10.14A** Write a story with a conflict and a resolution; **ELPS** **3E** Share information in cooperative learning interactions; **5F** Write using a variety of grade-appropriate sentence lengths and patterns in increasingly accurate ways; **5G** Narrate/describe/explain with increasing specificity and detail to fulfill content area writing needs

# Expository Writing

## ★ UNIT TEKS

**10.13A** Plan a first draft; **10.13B** Structure ideas and develop drafts; **10.13C** Revise drafts; **10.13D** Edit drafts; **10.13E** Revise final draft and publish work; **10.15A** Write an analytical essay; **10.15D** Produce a multimedia presentation; **10.17A(i)** Use and understand tenses and verbals; **10.17A(ii)** Use and understand clauses; **10.17C** Use correctly structured sentences; **10.18A** Use capitalization; **10.18B(i)** Use commas; **10.19** Spell correctly

## ★ UNIT ELPS

**1C** Use learning techniques; **1D** Speak using learning strategies; **1F** Use and learn new language; **1G** Distinguish between formal and informal English; **1H** Develop and expand learning strategies; **2A** Distinguish sounds and intonation patterns; **2B** Recognize elements of English sound system in vocabulary; **2E** Use visual, contextual, and linguistic support to enhance understanding; **2F** Derive meaning from media; **2G** Understand spoken language/situations are familiar to unfamiliar; **2H** Understand ideas/information in spoken language; **3G** Express opinions, ideas, and feelings; **3H** Narrate, describe, and explain/increasing specificity; **3I** Adapt spoken language; **3J** Respond orally to information; **4A** Learn relationships between and decode sounds; **4C** Develop sight vocabulary/derive meaning of environmental print/comprehend written classroom materials; **4D** Use prereading supports; **4I** Employ and expand reading skills; **5A** Learn relationships between sounds and letters; **5D** Edit writing for grammar and usage

## Cause-Effect Essay (pages 137–178)

Students write a cause-effect essay of sufficient length to discuss an important historical event or time.

## Defining a Concept (pages 179–186)

Students write an expository essay of definition, one that shows their understanding of a concept and its importance.

## Writing for Assessment: Responding to Expository Prompts (pages 187–193)

Students learn how to write explanations in response to expository prompts in time-limited situations.

 **Literature Connections**

- *Meltdown: A Race Against Nuclear Disaster at Three Mile Island* by Wilborn Hampton

 **Technology Connections**

 *Write Source Online*
www.hmheducation.com/tx/writesource
- *Net-text*
- *Writing Network*
- *Portfolio*
- *GrammarSnap*
- *Essay Scoring*
- *File Cabinet*

 *Interactive Whiteboard Lessons*

# Expository Writing Unit Scope and Sequence

| | Day | Writing and Conventions Instruction | Write Source Student Edition | | | Daily Language Workouts | Skills-Book | Write Source Online |
| --- | --- | --- | --- | --- | --- | --- | --- | --- |
| | | | Core Unit | Tools of Language | Resource Units | | | |
| **WEEK 1** | 1 | **Cause-Effect Essay** Model <br>🎬 Literature Connection <br>*Meltdown: A Race Against Nuclear Disaster at Three Mile Island* by Wilborn Hampton | 137–142 | 🔲 538–543 | | 30–33 | | Interactive Whiteboard Lesson |
| | 4–5 | Prewriting | 143–148 | | WR 616–627 | | | Net-text |
| **WEEK 2** | 6–8 | Drafting | 149–154 | TL 526–529 | WR 630–633 | 34–37 | | Net-text |
| | 9–10 | Revising | 155–164 | | | | | Net-text |
| | | Skills Activities: <br>• Adverbs | | | PG 766–767 <br>BGW 578–579 | | 111–114 | GrammarSnap |

 **Resource Units** referenced above are located in the back of the *Student Edition* and *Teacher's Edition*
TL *"The Tools of Language"*   BGW *"Basic Grammar and Writing"*   WR *"A Writer's Resource"*   PG *"Proofreader's Guide"*

| Day | Writing and Conventions Instruction | Write Source Student Edition | | | Daily Language Workouts | Skills-Book | Write Source Online |
| --- | --- | --- | --- | --- | --- | --- | --- |
| | | Core Unit | Tools of Language | Resource Units | | | |
| **Week 3** 11–13 | Editing | 165–170 | TL 526–529 | | 38–41 | | Net-text |
| | Skills Activities:<br>• Complex Verb Tenses: Past Perfect and Past Progressive | | | PG 750–763 | | 97 | GrammarSnap |
| | • Passive versus Active Voice | | | PG 750–751 | | 95 | GrammarSnap |
| | • Sentence Structure: Restrictive and Nonrestrictive Clauses for Combining Sentences | | | BGW 582–583<br>PG 650–651, 770–771 | | 14–15, 17, 136–137 | GrammarSnap |
| 14 | Publishing | 171 | | | | | Net-text |
| 15 | Assessing and Reflecting | 172–178 | | | | | Net-text |
| **Week 4** 16 | **Defining a Concept** | 179–181 | TL 526–529 | | 42–45 | | Net-text |
| 17 | Prewriting | 182–183 | | WR 616–627 | | | Net-text |
| 18 | Drafting | 184 | | WR 630–633 | | | Net-text |
| 19 | Revising | 185 | | | | | Net-text |
| 20 | Editing and Publishing | 186 | | | | | Net-text |
| | Skills Activities:<br>• Subject–Verb Agreement | | | BGW 595<br>PG 746–747, 766–767, 778–779, 780–781 | | 147–149 | |
| **Week 5** 21–25 | **Writing for Assessment: Responding to Expository Prompts** | 187–193 | TL 526–529 | | 46–49 | | |

**Resource Units** referenced above are located in the back of the *Student Edition* and *Teacher's Edition*
TL *"The Tools of Language"*   BGW *"Basic Grammar and Writing"*   WR *"A Writer's Resource"*   PG *"Proofreader's Guide"*

# Writing Focus

- Writing a Cause-Effect Essay
- Defining a Concept
- Responding to Expository Prompts

# Grammar Focus

- Past Perfect and Past Progressive Tenses
- Passive and Active Voices in Verbs

# Learning Language

Read aloud the basic and academic terms, as well as the descriptions and questions. Model for students how to read one question and answer it. For example, *it says that expository writing explains and informs. One example of expository writing that we could read every day is a newspaper. It informs us of what happens in our world each day.* Have partners monitor their understanding of the terms by working through the meanings and questions together.

**ELPS** 1E, 2C, 3B, 3D, 3E

# Minilessons

### Rube Goldberg Revisited
Writing a Cause-Effect Essay

- **READ** about Rube Goldberg's whimsical inventions. **WRITE** a description of your own cause-effect machine designed to accomplish a simple task.

**ELPS** 5G

### Defining Moment
Defining a Concept

- **THINK** of an experience, a moment, an anecdote that you would call a "defining moment." In other words, the moment defines you, another person, or a situation in your life. **SHARE** the example with a partner or the class. **ASK** them to name the word your illustration "defines."

**ELPS** 1E, 2C, 3B, 3D, 3E

**ELPS** **1A** Use prior knowledge and experience to understand meanings; **1E** Internalize new basic and academic language by using and reusing it/speaking and writing; **2C** Learn basic and academic vocabulary heard during classroom instruction/interactions; **3B** Expand vocabulary by learning and using routine language needed for classroom communication; **3D** Speak using grade-level content area vocabulary/new words; **3E** Share information in cooperative learning interactions; **5F** Write using a variety of grade-appropriate sentence patterns in increasingly accurate ways; **5G** Explain with increasing specificity and detail/writing

---

www.hmheducation.com/tx/writesource

# Expository Writing

## Writing Focus

## Grammar Focus

## Learning Language

Learning these words and expressions will help you understand this unit.

1. Expository writing explains and informs.
   **What are some types of expository writing that you read every day?**
2. Inferences are logical conclusions drawn from facts that are presented in an essay or an article.
   **How does making inferences help you understand a writer's point of view?**
3. Evidence is the proof that something occurred or is factual.
   **What kinds of details would provide strong evidence about a particular event?**
4. A company that is on the right track is doing things correctly to be successful.
   **How can you tell that you are on the right track when you start a new assignment?**

---

## Differentiated Instruction: English Language Learners

**ELPS** 1A, 1E, 2C, 3D, 3E, 5F

| ELP Level **Beginning** | ELP Level **Intermediate** | ELP Level **Advanced/Advanced High** |
|---|---|---|
| Have students draw and label causes, such as *rain* or *being ill*, and effects, such as *puddles* and *sneezing*, drawing arrows from each cause to the effect. | Have students think-pair-share common cause and effect relationships, e.g., lack of fuel causes a stalled car, too much rain causes flooding, etc. | List five causes and five effects on the board. Have students write five sentences combining one cause and one effect in each. Have students share two sentences each. |

# Expository Writing
# Cause-Effect Essay

You studied thoroughly for your geometry test, so you feel confident that you are on the right track and will do well. You worked hard at swim practice, so you know that you'll be sore tomorrow. Life is a series of actions and reactions, causes and effects. When you reflect upon these actions, you gain a better understanding of your life, and the bigger world around you. That is why keeping a writer's notebook or personal journal can be so enlightening.

In the same way, you can better understand history if you reflect upon the circumstances surrounding important events. What caused the Black Plague to spread across Europe? What effect did Gutenberg's printing press have on literacy and learning? In this chapter you will write a cause-effect essay of sufficient length to discuss an important historical event or time. As you think and write about your topic, you will see how it connects with other times and events.

## Writing Guidelines

**Subject:** A historical event
**Purpose:** To make connections
**Form:** Cause-effect essay
**Audience:** Classmates

"The cause is hidden, but the result is known."

—Ovid

## Resources

### Copy Masters (see Appendix)

- 5 W's chart (TE p. 139)
- Quick list (TE p. 148)
- Time line (TE p. 153)
- Venn diagram (TE p. 169)

### Benchmark Papers
### (see Appendix)

## Cause-Effect Essay

### Objectives

- understand that a cause-effect essay is a form of expository writing
- understand the purpose, form, and content of a cause-effect essay
- plan, draft, revise, edit, and publish a cause-effect essay

Review the general purpose of expository writing (it is writing that explains something). Then have students tell the purpose of a cause-effect essay (it explains the causes of a particular situation and/or the significance of the resulting effects).

Read aloud the quote by Ovid. Point out that the opposite might also be true. With this in mind, have a volunteer read aloud the two questions at the beginning of the second paragraph. Have students discuss the different focus of the questions.

- What caused the Black Plague to spread . . . ?
- What effect did Gutenberg's printing press have . . . ?

Explain that these are two different ways of thinking about potential topics for a cause-effect essay.  DIFFERENTIATE INSTRUCTION

 **ELPS** 2C, 3D, 3J, 4G

### Technology Connections

Use the Interactive Whiteboard lessons to introduce expository writing.

*Interactive Whiteboard Lesson*

**TEKS** **ELPS** **2C** Learn basic vocabulary heard during classroom instruction/interactions; **3D** Speak using grade-level content area vocabulary/new words; **3J** Respond orally to information presented in a variety of media to build and reinforce concept and language attainment; **4G** Demonstrate comprehension of increasingly complex English/responding to questions

## Expository Writing Warm-Up: Focusing on a Specific Topic

Explain to students that the expository paragraph they are about to write will share information about a specific topic. Students should understand that the purpose of writing the paragraph is to practice narrowing a general subject to a manageable topic and explaining something about the topic.

Point out, however, that writing the expository paragraph can be a good way to prepare for the cause-effect essay. A writer can use the paragraph to explore one aspect of the topic in more detail. Invite students to choose a topic that could be expanded into a cause-effect essay, if they wish to.

**Try It!**

You may wish to model narrowing the topic on the board for one or two of the general subjects listed to make the concept clearer to students.

**TEKS** 10.13A

**Writing Your Topic Sentence**

Remind students that the topic sentence should not only identify the specific topic, feeling, or feature, but should also capture the audience's interest.

**Try It!**

Using the model topics from above, have students volunteer to write topic sentences on the board. Then comment and revise the sentences with help from the class.

**TEKS** 10.13A

---

## Expository Writing Warm-Up: Focusing on a Specific Topic

Teachers usually base their writing assignments on a general subject that you are studying. For example, your science teacher could ask you to write about the space program in the United States. Before doing any writing, you would have to narrow or limit the subject to a specific topic suitable for the assignment.

Here's how one student narrowed the general subject—the United States space program—to a specific topic suitable for an expository paragraph.

**Narrowing a Subject**

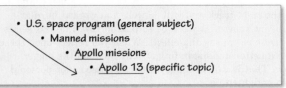

- U.S. space program (general subject)
  - Manned missions
    - Apollo missions
      - Apollo 13 (specific topic)

**Try It!**

Narrow one of the general subjects listed below until you identify a specific topic suitable for an expository paragraph. (Afterward, research the topic if you don't know a lot about it.)

**General subjects:** community life, current medicine, high school athletics, weather, movie industry, automobiles, security issues

## Writing Your Topic Sentence

Think of the topic sentence as the engine that powers the rest of a paragraph. A topic sentence should identify the specific topic and identify a particular feeling or feature about it that you want to emphasize.

The Apollo 13 spaceflight (specific topic) **nearly ended in disaster** (a particular feature).

**Try It!**

Write a topic sentence about your specific topic using the sample above as a guide. (Refer to page **599** for more information.)

---

**TEKS** **10.13A** Plan a first draft by determining topics through a range of strategies and developing a theme or thesis

Cause-Effect Essay **139**

## Writing an Expository Paragraph

An expository paragraph shares information about a specific topic. The paragraph may present facts, give directions, define terms, explain a process, or so on. The following paragraph explains the causes of the *Apollo 13* disaster. Remember that a paragraph has three main parts:

- The **topic sentence** identifies what the paragraph is about.
- The **body sentences** support the idea expressed in the topic sentence.
- The **closing sentence** reminds the reader of the topic or summarizes the paragraph.

**Expository**

**Topic Sentence**

### "Houston, We Have a Problem"

The *Apollo 13* spaceflight on April 17, 1970, nearly ended in disaster. The problem—an oxygen leak and loss of electricity—was first noted by astronaut Jack Swigert. He calmly informed the mission control center in Houston of the situation. A NASA investigation later determined that the cause of the problem stemmed from inadequate thermostatic switches that somehow were not noticed during the safety inspections. The switches malfunctioned when they overheated, igniting the insulation surrounding the oxygen tank and causing an explosion. The crew had

**Body**

to move from the command module into the smaller lunar module, which was not designed to hold three people. There was limited water and heat in this module, and condensation on the walls created the fear of short circuits. Four tense days passed before the crew landed safely in the Pacific Ocean. As a result of the mission, safety checks of space modules have become more rigorous. In addition, NASA discovered that astronauts were very well prepared

**Closing Sentence**

to handle such emergencies. More importantly, they learned that respect and teamwork between astronauts and ground control were invaluable.

 **Draft**

**Write your own expository paragraph.** Use your planning from page 138 and the paragraph above as a guide for your writing.

---

## Writing an Expository Paragraph

Have students read aloud the topic sentence, the body, and the closing sentence. Remind students that the body sentences should address the five W's and H questions (*Who? What? When? Where? Why?* and *How?*) while supporting the topic sentence.

Have students explain how each sentence of the body supports the topic sentence and what makes the closing sentence effective.

**✓ DIFFERENTIATE INSTRUCTION**

✳ For more about Writing Effective Paragraphs, see SE pages 597–604.

**Write your own expository paragraph.** You may decide to allow students to use a graphic organizer for paragraph structure and/or reproduce the 5 W's chart (see TE Appendix) to plan their paragraphs before drafting.

### ⭐ Conventions Connections

**Grammar: Sentence Structure**
- ***Student Edition*** pages 597–604; ***Proofreader's Guide*** pages 764–771
- ***SkillsBook*** pages 125–128

---

### Differentiated Instruction: English Language Learners

⭐ **ELPS** 2C, 3A, 4A, 4G

| ELP Level **Beginning** | ELP Level **Intermediate** | ELP Level **Advanced/Advanced High** |
|---|---|---|
| Read the paragraph aloud to students, listing new or difficult words on the board. Have students repeat each new word several times. | Have students take turns reading the paragraph aloud, stopping to correct pronunciation and to summarize each sentence. | Have students read text aloud with a partner and then summarize the body, explaining how it supports the topic sentence. |

**ELPS 2C** Learn academic vocabulary heard during classroom instruction/interactions; **3A** Practice producing sounds of newly acquired vocabulary; **4A** Sound out words using a combination of skills; **4G** Demonstrate comprehension of increasingly complex English/participating in shared reading and summarizing material

**Understanding Your Goal**

Four traits relate to the development of the content and the form. They provide a focus during prewriting, drafting, and revising.

- **Focus and Coherence**
- **Organization**
- **Development of Ideas**
- **Voice**

The final trait becomes the primary focus of editing. Review the traits listed on the SE page and the holistic scoring guide, emphasizing the importance of all the traits.

- **Conventions**

✱ The scoring guide on SE pages 60–61 is based on these traits.

After students review the goals and the scoring guide, explain that all the traits must be solidly in place for their expository writing to be considered highly effective.

**TEKS** 10.15A(i), 10.15A(ii), 10.15A(iii), 10.15A(iv)

### Learning Language

Conduct one-on-one conferences with each student, discussing and listing possible essay topics. Ask pertinent questions about the student's chosen topics and encourage them to use newly learned vocabulary in responding to your questions. **DIFFERENTIATE INSTRUCTION ↘**

**ELPS** 1D, 1E, 2E, 2G, 2I, 3D, 3F

---

 **TEKS** 10.15A(i)–10.15A(iv)
**ELPS** 2G, 3F

  **Understanding Your Goal**

Your goal in this chapter is to write a well-organized expository essay about a historical event that has a clear cause-and-effect relationship. The traits listed in the chart below will help you plan and write your essay. Keep in mind your purpose, audience, and context for writing.

> **Traits of a Cause–Effect Essay**
>
> - **Focus and Coherence**
>   Select an interesting historical event. Clearly state your controlling idea and the direction your writing will take in your introduction. Plan an essay of sufficient length to cover the topic.
>
> - **Organization**
>   Include a strong beginning that creates interest and states your thesis. In the middle, support your thesis with reliable, well-researched information. Tie all of your main points together in the conclusion. Be sure to use transitions to connect ideas.
>
> - **Development of Ideas**
>   Develop your ideas by establishing and sustaining the cause-and-effect relationship related to the event. Support your ideas with researched evidence and carefully thought-out supporting details.
>
> - **Voice**
>   Sound knowledgeable about and interested in your topic. Use rhetorical devices and vocabulary appropriate to your audience.
>
> - **Conventions**
>   Use correct grammar, a variety of sentence structures, correct capitalization, punctuation, and spelling.

### Learning Language

Review the scoring guide on pages **60–61**. Then using newly acquired vocabulary, discuss possible topics for your essay with your teacher. Ask questions, and listen carefully to the responses.

---

**TEKS** **10.15A(i)** Write an analytical essay that includes an introductory and concluding paragraph and a variety of sentence structures; **10.15A(ii)** Write an analytical essay that includes rhetorical devices and transitions; **10.15A(iii)** Write an analytical essay that includes an idea or thesis; **10.15A(iv)** Write an analytical essay that includes a structure appropriate to the purpose, audience, and context; **ELPS 1D** Speak using learning strategies/request assistance, employ non-verbal cues, and convey ideas by defining or describing; **1E** Internalize new academic language by using and reusing it/speaking; **2E** Use contextual/linguistic support to enhance and confirm understanding of increasingly complex spoken language; **2G** Understand the general meaning of spoken language/topics, languages, and contexts are familiar to unfamiliar; **2I** Demonstrate listening comprehension in increasingly complex spoken language by responding to questions; **3D** Speak using grade-level content area vocabulary/new words and academic language proficiency; **3F** Ask for and give information/ranging from using a limited high-frequency vocabulary to using abstract and content-based vocabulary during speaking

# Cause-Effect Essay

In the following expository essay, the writer identifies the effects of Charlemagne's unification of Europe. The notes in the left margin explain the key parts of the essay. The writer considered audience, purpose, and context.

**Beginning**
The first paragraph introduces the topic and gives the thesis statement (underlined).

**Middle**
The middle paragraphs provide background information and discuss three effects. Writer has considered the relative value of data, facts, and ideas that support the thesis. Transitions link paragraphs.

### Charlemagne

"By the sword or the cross," proclaimed Charles the Great, one of the most fearless and colorful leaders of the Middle Ages. Better known as Charlemagne, this leader utilized both the sword and the cross to become the first crowned emperor of the Holy Roman Empire, a political area including most of Western and Central Europe. During his 32-year rise to power, he was able to unify the nations of that area into a strong, single entity. Charlemagne's unification of Europe brought peace to all the people, stabilized the European economy, and promoted education.

Charles was the son of Pippin, king of the Franks, whose title he inherited in 768. With this responsibility, Charles developed the leadership and management skills he eventually used to rule much of Europe. He gained control of European lands by political maneuvering and by waging war, also spreading Christianity to unite the people under a common religion. Charles earned the reputation of being a fair-minded, diplomatic leader (Judd 75). In the year 800, Pope Leo III crowned Charles as Emperor *Carolus Magnus*. That Latin name translates to *Charlemagne* in Old French. Charlemagne brought about solidarity among kingdoms and unified continental Europe.

One of Charlemagne's greatest gifts was his skillful peacemaking ability. Prior to his reign, civil uprisings erupted continually as peasants grew weary of funding military campaigns by paying heavy taxes or forfeiting their land. Charlemagne organized the resources of each region to avoid heavy taxing. He started by collecting tolls, custom duties, and tributes from conquered peoples and distributing the funds to the regions where they were most needed (Judd 92). Charlemagne endeared himself to his subjects when he showed mercy to captured invading troops. When peasant and nobleman alike realized that they were being treated fairly, a feeling of trust and peace spread throughout Europe.

Expository

## Cause-Effect Essay

Work through this sample essay with the class, pointing out the elements that make it a good cause-effect essay.

### Focus and Coherence

- The topic is about a historical event.
- The writer clearly states the controlling idea and explains the essay's direction.
- The essay is of sufficient length.

### Organization

- The beginning creates interest by starting with a quote and clearly stating the theme.
- The middle paragraphs provide well-researched details that support the thesis.
- The ending provides a final overview of Charlemagne's achievements and refers to the opening.

### Development of Ideas

- The topic is interesting.
- The writer explains the connections between Charlemagne's actions and the improvements that resulted.

### Voice

- The voice sounds interested and knowledgeable.
- The vocabulary used is appropriate for the topic and the audience.

★ **TEKS** 10.15A(i), 10.15A(ii), 10.15A(iii), 10.15A(iv), 10.15A(v), 10.15A(vi)

**Respond to the reading.**

**Answers**

**Focus and Coherence 1.** how Charlemagne improved conditions in Europe during his time as emperor **2.** The writer rephrases the thesis statement and reuses the same quote to underscore the focus.

**Organization 3.** The thesis says that Charlemagne unified Europe, brought peace, stabilized the economy, and promoted education. The middle paragraphs address each of these points in that order.

**Development of Ideas 4.** Yes, ideas are developed thoroughly and logically and based on research as evidenced by the internal citation.

**Voice 5.** enthusiastic and interested in topic; Students may cite the following details as evidence: *one of the most fearless and colorful leaders; skillful peacemaking; cherished the written word; it is difficult to imagine how Europe . . .*

**TEKS** 10.15A(i), 10.15A(ii), 10.15A(iv), 10.15A(v); **ELPS** 3F, 4J

## Literature Connections

**Mentor text:** The sample cause-effect essay focuses on a man who held Europe together in a time of crisis. Students may wish to write an essay that focuses on a person, or they may prefer to write about an event or a technological development.

To inspire students to write this second type of essay, read excerpts from the amazing book *Meltdown: A Race Against Nuclear Disaster at Three Mile Island*. The writer, Wilborn Hampton, starts with the first nuclear tests in New Mexico in 1945, and then traces the chain of causes and effects that led to the near-meltdown at Three Mile Island in 1979.

 TEKS 10.15A(i), 10.15A(ii), 10.15A(vi), 10.15A(v)

> The writer uses facts, paraphrases, and rhetorical devices such as quotations to develop and support the thesis.

In order to maintain peace, Charlemagne soon realized that he needed to stabilize the economy in the entire region. He divided larger parcels of land into more manageable estates that were self-contained and administered by a steward or caretaker. Each estate had a bustling center of commerce surrounded by a market, church, guilds, and public buildings. The remaining land was rented to the farmers who produced the crops that fed the people living on the estate. In return, the stewards provided protection and administered justice. The changes instituted by Charlemagne created an intricately balanced system of commerce and trade and stabilized the European economy (Sullivan 115).

With peace and a more stable economy in place, Charlemagne was then able to concentrate his efforts on education. He assembled the greatest minds of the entire region into an "academy" whose members traveled with and advised Charlemagne. Artists, scientists, and teachers, who were educated at the monasteries, were sent to other regions to share their knowledge. Due to Charlemagne's efforts, education was promoted and learning flourished throughout his empire.

> **Ending**
> The final paragraph ties all the key points together and connects with the thesis statement. It also contains sentences of varying length and complexity.

Charlemagne died in 814 at the age of 72. During his reign as king of the Franks and as emperor, he succeeded in unifying Europe, leaving behind a legacy of peace, economic stability, and an appreciation for the value of education. He cherished the written word and preserved the rich culture of his era. Although historians may judge Charlemagne as a foreign invader rather than a hero, it is difficult to imagine how Europe would have developed without the influence of this dynamic leader who lived "by the sword or the cross."

 **Respond to the reading. Answer the following questions.**

**Focus and Coherence (1)** What is the primary focus of this essay? **(2)** How does the conclusion tie the essay together? **Organization (3)** How does the thesis statement help structure this cause-effect essay? **Development of Ideas (4)** Are the conclusions logical, based on the evidence and research presented? **Voice (5)** What effect does the variety of sentence structures have on the writer's voice? Explain.

**TEKS** **10.15A(i)** Write an analytical essay that includes a concluding paragraph and a variety of sentence structures; **10.15A(ii)** Write an analytical essay that includes rhetorical devices and transitions; **10.15(iv)** Write an analytical essay that includes a structure appropriate to the purpose, audience, and context; **10.15A(v)** Write an analytical essay that includes relevant evidence and details; **ELPS** **3F** Give information/ranging from using a limited high-frequency vocabulary to using abstract and content-based vocabulary during speaking; **4J** Demonstrate comprehension and expand reading skills by employing inferential skills/predicting, making connections between ideas, drawing conclusions from text, and finding supporting evidence

**TEKS** 10.13A, 10.15A(i), 10.15A(iii)

# Prewriting

During the initial step in the writing process, you will plan your first draft by selecting a specific topic, gathering details, developing a thesis or controlling idea, and creating a basic structure for your writing.

**Expository**

---

### Keys to Effective Prewriting

1. Choose a specific historical event to write about.

2. Refer to a variety of sources and gather information about your topic. Consider relevant quotations, explanations, and facts.

3. Write a thesis statement that identifies a specific cause-effect relationship related to the topic.

4. Identify the key points that support the thesis statement.

5. Keep in mind your essay's purpose, audience, and context.

6. Organize your details using an outline or another graphic organizer.

---

## Prewriting

### Keys to Effective Prewriting

Remind students of the purpose of the prewriting stage in the writing process: It is when the writer selects a topic, gathers details, and decides how to organize those details.

The Keys to Effective Prewriting list explains the process students will be guided through on SE pages 144–148.

Point out to students that expository writing is the form of writing they are asked to use in most of their course work. Explain that during the prewriting step, they will gather details from different sources, analyze them, and decide how to organize ideas and information. Point out that good prewriting lays the groundwork for writing their essays. Also explain to students that as they spend time gathering information about their topics, they will naturally begin to form ideas about what they want to say and how to focus their writing (the thesis statement). ✔ DIFFERENTIATE INSTRUCTION

**TEKS** 10.13A , 10.15A(i), 10.15A(iii)

### Writer's Craft

Use the activities in this section as minilessons in your writing workshop. Each activity introduces and models a key skill and helps students apply the skill to their own writing.

---

**TEKS 10.13A** Plan a first draft by selecting the correct genre and determining topics through a range of strategies; **10.15A(i)** Write an analytical essay that includes an introductory paragraph; **10.15A(iii)** Write an analytical essay that includes an idea or thesis; **ELPS 1C** Use strategic learning techniques to acquire basic and grade-level vocabulary; **1H** Expand learning strategies/reasoning, looking for patterns in language, and analyzing sayings and expressions; **2B** Recognize elements of the English sound system in new vocabulary/long and short vowels, silent letters, and consonant clusters; **2C** Learn new expressions and academic vocabulary heard during classroom instruction/interactions; **3A** Practice producing sounds of newly acquired vocabulary; **3E** Share information in cooperative learning interactions; **4F** Use support from peers/teachers to enhance understanding and develop vocabulary, grasp of language structures, and background knowledge

## Prewriting

### Planning Your Writing

Note that Mark, the student writer, began his topic search by focusing first on his own interests. He was not concerned with causes and effects at this point.

**Start your topic search.** Mark waited until he had generated a general categories list to consider causes and effects. Encourage students to use this strategy for selecting their topics.

**Choose your topic.** Ask students to suggest factors to take into account once they have filled out their Topics Charts and are ready to choose topics.

- Preference: If one topic interests them more than another, they should probably choose it as the topic for their writing.
- Time limitations: If a topic is complicated, it could take too long to research.
- Lack of information: If little information is readily available about a topic, they should make another choice.

**TEKS** 10.13A, 10.15A(iv); **ELPS** 5B, 5G

### Writer's Craft

**Two-part organization:** Cause-effect essays can be challenging. That's because there are a number of different types of causal chains:
- one cause and one effect
- one cause and many effects
- many causes and one effect
- many causes and many effects

Help students select a topic that won't be too complex to explore fully.

---

**TEKS** 10.13A, 10.15A(iv)

## Prewriting Planning Your Writing

Mark Santos started his topic search by thinking about periods of history that he enjoyed reading about and that he thought would be of interest to his audience. After choosing the Middle Ages, he listed a few general categories, or subjects, related to this time. He starred the two categories in this list that interested him the most.

### General Categories List

| Middle Ages | | |
|---|---|---|
| natural disasters | invasions | discoveries |
| economy | religion | famous individuals |
| *government | the Crusades | *medicine |

 **Start your topic search.** Think of a period in history that you enjoy learning about. Then create a general categories list to identify various subject areas. (If necessary, use some of the categories listed above.) Place an asterisk next to the categories that interest you the most.

Next, Mark created a chart in which he listed possible cause-and-effect topics for each category that he starred. After reviewing his chart, Mark decided to write about the Black Plague in Europe.

### Topics Chart

 **Choose your topic.** In a topics chart, list potential cause-and-effect topics related to the categories that you starred in your general categories list. Then circle the specific topic that you would like to write about.

---

## Gathering Your First Thoughts

To gather his initial thoughts about the Black Plague, Mark did the following freewriting. He recorded what he knew about the topic and asked some interesting questions.

### Freewriting

> The Black Plague pretty much devastated Europe during the 1300s. I read that about a third of the population died. Anyone infected died a horrible, painful death, usually within three days. I know it was spread by fleas on ship rats. That means port cities were probably hardest hit. What about the countryside? Did the farmers get the plague? That must have affected how much food there was. What about the clergy? What happened to religion and education back then? What about the culture of the time? What kinds of treatments were available? Did any of them work, or did the doctors die? Is it still possible to catch the plague today? I think there is an inoculation and a cure.

**Freewrite on your topic.** To get started, write down everything you already know about your topic. Write for 5 to 10 minutes.

*Prewrite*

## Listing Your Sources

As you gather your information, keep track of the sources you use so that you can correctly cite them in your essay. You will need the following information.

- **Book:** Author's name. Title. City: Publisher, Copyright year.
- **Magazine:** Author's name. Article title. Magazine title. Date published: Page numbers.
- **Newspaper:** Author's name. Article title. Newspaper title. Date published: Section and page numbers.
- **Internet:** Author's name (if listed). Page title or description of document. Site title. Date posted or copyright date (if listed). Site sponsor. Date of access.
- **DVD or video file:** Title. Format. Distributor or Web site, date.

**List your sources.** Keep a list of your sources and include the information shown above. Whenever you find a new source, add it to your list.

*Prewrite*

Expository

## Gathering Your First Thoughts

Point out to students that the freewriting they do at this stage is an opportunity to explore their topics.

**Freewrite on your topic.** Point out that Mark's freewriting is 15 sentences long and lists facts, asks questions, and poses theories (*That means port cities . . . That must have affected how much food . . . ; I think there is an inoculation . . .*).

TEKS 10.13A, 10.15A(i), 10.15A(iii)

## Listing Your Sources

This is a good place to emphasize to students the importance of keeping accurate source information. It's an easy step to forget.

**List your sources.** Encourage students to learn the rules for formatting source information and to follow them from the start. Doing so can save them time in the revision stage.

✔ DIFFERENTIATE INSTRUCTION

✱ For more about formatting sources, see SE pages 407–410.

---

### Differentiated Instruction: English Language Learners

ELPS 1A, 1C, 1F, 3D, 3E, 3F, 3G, 3H, 4G

| ELP Level **Beginning** | ELP Level **Intermediate** | ELP Level **Advanced/Advanced High** |
|---|---|---|
| Write the word *source* on the board and ask students what other definitions the word has, providing examples as necessary. | Have a class discussion on other meanings of *source*, such as sources of food, etc. Have students explain how these sources are alike/different. | Have students think-pair-share about what is meant by *source* and why citing sources is important. Then discuss answers as a class. |

TEKS **10.13A** Plan a first draft by selecting the correct genre and determining topics through a range of strategies; **10.15A(i)** Write an analytical essay that includes an introductory paragraph; **10.15A(iii)** Write an analytical essay that includes an idea or thesis; **ELPS 1A** Use prior knowledge and experience to understand meanings; **1C** Use strategic learning techniques to acquire basic and grade-level vocabulary; **1F** Use accessible language and learn new and essential language in the process; **3D** Speak using grade-level content area vocabulary/academic language proficiency; **3E** Share information in cooperative learning interactions; **3F** Give information/ranging from using a limited high-frequency vocabulary to using abstract and content-based vocabulary during speaking; **3G** Express ideas ranging from communicating short phrases to participating in discussions; **3H** Explain with increasing specificity and detail; **4G** Demonstrate comprehension of increasingly complex English/responding to questions

## Prewriting

### Collecting and Organizing the Details

Discuss with students how to tell whether identifying a source is necessary.

- No source is identified on the first sample note card because the details listed are commonly known facts about the plague.
- On the second sample card, the source is cited because the information is a direct quotation.
- On the third sample card, the source is cited because the idea stated is not the writer's but that of a particular author.

**Collect and organize your information.** Have students begin creating their gathering grids and writing their questions. Also suggest to students to use color-coded note cards to easily organize them.

⭐ **TEKS** 10.13A, 10.15A(iii); **ELPS** 5B

✳ For information about avoiding plagiarism, see SE page 389.

### Writer's Craft

**Elaboration:** Make sure that students gather a variety of details, including paraphrases, quotations, explanations, statistics, anecdotes, and so forth. By gathering a rich set of details, writers can move beyond a simple listlike structure to create paragraphs that deeply elaborate the comparisons and contrasts.

---

## Prewriting Collecting and Organizing the Details

A gathering grid (see page 383) is an effective way to collect and organize details for an essay. However, sometimes you need more space to record a quotation, to paraphrase important information, or to list important details. In these cases, you should use note cards.

Number each new card and identify the question or main point that the card covers. Then write your notes. If you used a source, identify it at the bottom of the note card.

### Sample Note Cards

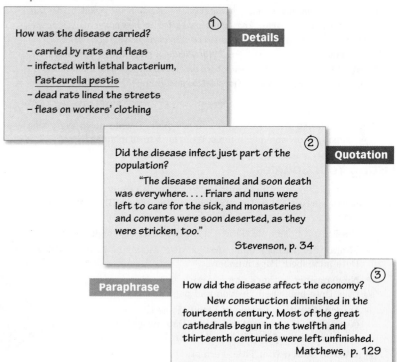

**Collect and organize your information.** Use a gathering grid and note cards to collect information for your essay.

Prewrite

---

## Focusing on Causes and Effects

Once you complete your research, find the cause-and-effect relationship in your topic. A cause-effect organizer can help you complete this step. The essays in this chapter put forth one main cause (stated in the thesis) and follow with its effects. However, this is not the only way to develop a cause-effect essay. You can also start with one main effect and follow with its causes.

### Cause-Effect Organizer

**Focus your efforts.** Use the graphic organizer above (or on page 624) to identify the cause-effect relationship related to your historical event.

## Writing a Thesis Statement

The thesis statement of your essay should establish the focus or direction of your writing. Mark's thesis statement covers the main points included in his cause-effect organizer.

**Write your thesis statement.** Use the model above to create a thesis statement for your essay. Try different versions until you are satisfied.

Expository

### Focusing on Causes and Effects

Note that organizers can be displayed in different ways. For example, some initial effects may serve as causes of later effects. In the sample, the writer could have expressed the economic devastation as the result of the population loss. The chart would have looked like this:

✳ For more about cause-effect organizers, see SE page 624.

**Focus your efforts.** Have students try a variety of different graphic organizers to see which style works for their topic and style of writing.

### Writing a Thesis Statement

Look at the model with students and emphasize the useful equation: cause + effects = a strong thesis statement.

**Write your thesis statement.** Ask students to use the formula to write two or three possible thesis statements. Then have them share their ideas with a partner to choose and refine one. ☑ DIFFERENTIATE INSTRUCTION

⭐ TEKS 10.13A , 10.15A(iii)

⭐ **TEKS 10.13A** Plan a first draft/selecting genre, determining topics through a range of strategies, and developing a thesis; **10.15A(iii)** Write an analytical essay that includes an idea or thesis; **ELPS 1B** Monitor oral/written language and employ self-corrective techniques or other resources; **1E** Internalize new basic and academic language by using and reusing it/speaking and writing; **1F** Use accessible language and learn new and essential language in the process; **1H** Develop and expand learning strategies/reasoning, looking for patterns in language, and analyzing sayings and expressions; **3E** Share information in cooperative learning interactions; **5F** Write using a variety of grade-appropriate sentence lengths and patterns/combine in increasingly accurate ways

**Differentiated Instruction: English Language Learners**          ⭐ **ELPS** 1B, 1E, 1F, 1H, 3E, 5F

| ELP Level **Beginning** | ELP Level **Intermediate** | ELP Level **Advanced/Advanced High** |
|---|---|---|
| Provide students with a word bank of historically significant causes and events. Have them practice writing and sounding out the words with a partner. | Using sentence strips of significant historical causes and effects, have students combine the phrases into a short thesis statement. Model as necessary. | Provide students several thesis statements as models. Working with a partner, students should write their own thesis statements. |

## Prewriting

### Outlining Your Essay

Talk with students about their experiences using outlines. Assure them that taking the time to plan ahead will make the drafting stage easier. Use the following to provide helpful suggestions:

- Students might try a topic outline, which uses notes and phrases rather than full sentences (see SE page 626).
- Have students look ahead to SE page 150 and examine how the writer used his outline's main points as topic sentences.
- Point out to students that their outline is a guide for organizing their details and that they should adjust it to accommodate their research.

**TEKS** 10.13A

**Prepare a sentence outline.** You may want to reproduce the quick list (see TE Appendix) for students to use in writing their outlines. Students may need to add to the list to complete their outlines. **DIFFERENTIATE INSTRUCTION ↘**

**TEKS** 10.13A, 10.13B, 10.15A(iii); **ELPS** 1G, 5B, 5F, 5G

---

## Prewriting Outlining Your Essay

Before you write your first draft, you should outline the main information you will use to develop your thesis. (Not all of the specific details need to be included in your outline.) Below is the first page of Mark's sentence outline. (See pages **626–627** for more about outlining.)

> Thesis Statement: The Black Plague, caused by poor sanitary conditions, destroyed one-third of Europe's population and devastated its economy.
>
> *[Background information about cause listed first.]*
>
> I. Poor sanitation fostered conditions that were perfect for the spread of the disease.
>    A. Rats and fleas carried the microbe called Pasteurella pestis.
>    B. Dead rats lined the streets where children played.
>    C. The fleas from rats got on the clothing of workers.
>    D. Touching the dead bodies of plague victims was common.
>    E. The disease infected multiple family members.
>
> *[The first effect is explored.]*
>
> II. Once the outbreak took hold, the disease spread uncontrollably.
>    A. The first symptoms of the plague were similar to those of a common cold.
>    B. Then more-extreme symptoms would set in.
>    C. Once individuals started shaking uncontrollably, death would soon follow.
>    D. Proper medical care did not exist.
>    E. Some resorted to bleeding; others used astrology to prescribe "cures."
>    F. Apothecaries and peddlers sold quack remedies.
>
> III. The disease did not discriminate.
>    A. The loss of life was greatest in big cities.
>    B. In London, more than 100,000 lives were lost.
>    C. An average of 1,000 people died weekly in England.

**Prewrite**   **Prepare a sentence outline.** Begin with your thesis statement. Then include the main points (I., II., III.) and supporting details (A., B., C.). You do not need to include every detail in your outline.

---

**TEKS** **10.13A** Plan a first draft/selecting genre, determining topics through a range of strategies, and developing a thesis; **10.13B** Structure ideas in a sustained way; **10.15A(iii)** Write an analytical essay that includes an idea or thesis; **ELPS** **5B** Write using newly acquired basic and content-based grade-level vocabulary; **5F** Write using a variety of grade-appropriate sentence lengths in increasingly accurate ways; **5G** Explain with increasing specificity and detail/writing

## Drafting

Now that you have completed your prewriting, you are ready to compose your first draft. As you write, refer to your outline and your research notes.

Keys to Effective Drafting

1. Get all of your ideas down on paper in your first draft.

2. In the first paragraph, state your thesis, identifying a significant cause and its major effects. The middle paragraphs should clarify the cause and discuss the key effects.

3. Include well-reasoned, relevant supporting details in each paragraph.

4. Use smooth transitions to connect your ideas.

5. Write on every other line or double-space to leave room for notes and changes.

Expository

## Drafting

### Keys to Effective Drafting

Remind students that the writing stage is when they get to write, or draft, their ideas on paper.

The Keys to Effective Drafting list explains the process students will be guided through on SE pages 150–154.

To demonstrate how much students accomplished during the prewriting stage, ask the following questions:

- Item 1: Do you know enough about your topic to write an essay about it?
- Item 2: Do you have a thesis statement? Have you written topic sentences for your middle paragraphs?
- Item 3: Have you collected a fair number of details in your research notes and organized them in your outline?

If students have followed the steps in the prewriting pages, they should be ready to begin writing their expository essays.

###  Writer's Craft

Make sure to model your own writing in front of your students. After all, you aren't just an instructor: you're also a writer. Use an overhead or the board to create your own beginning sentences or explanations of causes and effects—and you'll help to create a writing community.

---

### Differentiated Instruction: English Language Learners

**ELPS** 1B, 1E, 3E, 4D, 4I, 5B

| ELP Level **Beginning** | ELP Level **Intermediate** | ELP Level **Advanced/Advanced High** |
|---|---|---|
| Provide a word bank of causes and effects, review unfamiliar words, and then have students complete a cause-effect organizer using the words provided, offering guidance as needed. | Provide a quick list graphic organizer (see TE Appendix) and have students work with a partner to complete it. Students can use words instead of phrases if needed. | Students should work in groups to help each other use complete sentences for writing their outline, using a graphic organizer if necessary. |
| Use page 624 | Use pages 624–625 | Use pages 624–625 |

 **ELPS** **1B** Monitor written language and employ self-corrective techniques or other resources; **1E** Internalize new basic and academic language by using and reusing it/writing; **3E** Share information in cooperative learning interactions; **4D** Use prereading supports to enhance comprehension of written text/graphic organizers, illustrations, and topic-related vocabulary; **4I** Demonstrate comprehension by employing basic reading skills; **5B** Write using newly acquired basic and content-based grade-level vocabulary

## Drafting
### Getting the Big Picture

Review the structure of a good essay. Focus on the overall organization and how each part builds on the parts that precede it.

Point out to students that they have already planned the first two sections of the diagram. The last section refers to the ending, a section they have yet to focus on.

Assure students that they do not yet need to know how to conclude their essays. Explain, however, that as they write, they may think of ideas for the ending. Encourage them to record these ideas for later reference.

★ **TEKS** 10.13A, 10.15A(i), 10.15A(iii), 10.15A(iv), 10.15A(v)

## Drafting Getting the Big Picture

The graphic that follows shows how the parts of your essay should fit together. (The examples come from the student essay on pages 151–154.)

**Beginning**

The **introductory paragraph** provides both the topic and the thesis.

> **Thesis Statement**
> The Black Plague, caused by poor sanitary conditions, destroyed one-third of Europe's population and devastated its economy.

**Middle**

The organization and structure of the **middle** paragraphs is appropriate for purpose, audience, and context. Ideas sustain the thesis. Relevant evidence and details provide information and support the thesis.

> **Topic Sentences**
> Poor sanitation fostered conditions that were perfect for the spread of the disease. **(Background about cause)**
>
> Once the outbreak took hold, the disease spread uncontrollably, killing millions. **(Effect)**
>
> The disease did not discriminate. **(Effect)**
>
> The plague had a devastating impact on the European economy. **(Effect)**

**Ending**

The **conclusion** ties all the information together. The essay ends with a memorable final sentence.

> **Closing Sentences**
> Today, medicines are available to combat most infectious diseases. Still, the specter of diseases like the Black Plague continues to motivate researchers striving to avert other plagues.

★ **TEKS** 10.13A Plan a first draft/selecting genre, determining topics through a range of strategies, and developing a thesis; **10.15A(i)** Write an analytical essay that includes an introductory and concluding paragraph; **10.15A(iii)** Write an analytical essay that includes an idea or thesis; **10.15A(iv)** Write an analytical essay that includes a structure appropriate to the purpose, audience, and context; **10.15A(v)** Write an analytical essay that includes relevant evidence

## Starting Your Essay

The introductory paragraph of your essay should effectively capture the reader's interest, introduce your topic, and state your thesis. Here are some ways to start your essay.

- **Set up a scenario.**
  *Imagine a disease that killed millions of people who had no way to defend themselves.*

- **Ask a question.**
  *What was it really like during the Black Plague?*

- **Use rhetorical devices, such as a quotation.**
  *"Black Plague brought death and devastation," wrote Boccaccio, "and nary a whimper could be heard."*

- **Present unusual or surprising information.**
  *During the Middle Ages, the Black Plague descended, and, after only five years, one-third of Europe's people had died.*

### Beginning Paragraph

Mark starts his beginning paragraph with a *scenario*. He uses a transition phrase and follows the first sentence with information that leads to his thesis statement. The paragraph flows smoothly from the scenario to the thesis because it contains a variety of sentence structures.

> The writer captures the reader's interest and leads up to the thesis statement (underlined).

Imagine a disease that killed millions of people who had no way to defend themselves. At its height, from 1348 to 1351, the bubonic plague, better known as the "Black Plague" because of the black spots it caused on the skin, brought Europe to its knees. In The Decameron, Giovanni Boccaccio observed, "Almost everyone expected death. . . . And people said, 'This is the end of the world.'" The Black Plague, caused by poor sanitation, destroyed one-third of Europe's population and devastated its economy.

**Write your introduction.** Try one of the suggestions above to capture your reader's attention. Then add information that leads to your thesis statement. Be sure to vary the structure of your sentences.

---

### Starting Your Essay

Have students turn to SE page 631 and compare the beginning strategy formula described there to the sample paragraph on this page. Discuss the similarities and differences.

Review various strategies for beginning the essay. If possible, provide other examples from published works or previous student work. ✔ **DIFFERENTIATE INSTRUCTION**

**Write your introduction.** Encourage students to experiment with at least two strategies for starting their essays. Then have them select the strategy that works best for them and their topic.

Remind students that their introductory paragraph should include their thesis statement. Also encourage them to use transitions effectively in their introductory paragraph and throughout their essays.

⭐ **TEKS** 10.13B, 10.15A(i), 10.15A(iii)

---

## Differentiated Instruction: English Language Learners

⭐ **ELPS** 1C, 1E, 1G, 2C, 3D, 3G, 3H, 5F, 5G

| ELP Level **Beginning** | ELP Level **Intermediate** | ELP Level **Advanced/Advanced High** |
|---|---|---|
| Have students choose unfamiliar words from the model beginning paragraph and sound them out with a partner. Use gestures and pictures to help students understand and internalize meaning. | Have students give their own examples of the four ways to start their essays. Share and discuss with the class what makes their examples effective. | Have students compose their introduction with guidance from you and a peer, then share paragraphs aloud with a group for feedback on formal English usage. |

⭐ **TEKS** **10.13B** Structure ideas in a sustained way/develop drafts in open-ended situations that include transitions; **10.15A(i)** Write an analytical essay that includes an introductory paragraph; **10.15A(iii)** Write an analytical essay that includes an idea or thesis; **ELPS 1C** Use strategic learning techniques to acquire basic and grade-level vocabulary; **1E** Internalize new academic language by using and reusing it/speaking and writing; **1G** Demonstrate increasing knowledge of when to use formal/informal English; **2C** Learn academic vocabulary heard during classroom instruction/interactions; **3D** Speak using grade-level content area vocabulary/new words and academic language proficiency; **3G** Express opinions and ideas ranging from communicating short phrases to participating in discussions; **3H** Explain with increasing specificity and detail; **5F** Write using a variety of grade-appropriate sentence lengths, patterns, and connecting words/combine in increasingly accurate ways; **5G** Explain with increasing specificity and detail/writing

## Drafting

### Developing the Middle Paragraphs

Discuss the order in which the writer presents the information.

- The writer begins by describing the plague. This is important because all of the details that follow rely on the reader knowing this basic information.
- Some information is presented in chronological order; for example, the process of the disease's spread in the first and second paragraphs. This order provides a clear explanation of what happened.
- Information is also presented in order of broadening scope. The writer begins with the microbe that causes the plague and ends with the impact the disease had on Europe. This structure dramatically parallels the impact of the disease.

⭐ **TEKS** 10.13B, 10,15A(i), 10.15A(ii)

---

 **TEKS** 10.13B, 10.15A(i), 10.15A(ii)

# Drafting Developing the Middle Paragraphs

Refer to your outline and select an organizational pattern that fits the topic and the audience. Expand on key ideas with specific details and evidence. Be sure to include transitions.

Beginning
▶ Middle
Ending

## Middle Paragraphs

> Rhetorical devices engage the reader. Carefully chosen details and relevant evidence make the cause clear and support the thesis.

> Transitions link sentences and paragraphs.

> The first effect is discussed. Logical inferences are made. A variety of sentence structures sustain interest.

How could one disease travel so quickly? Poor sanitation fostered conditions that were perfect. Rats and fleas carried the microbe called <u>Pasteurella pestis</u>, the lethal bacterium that spread the disease. Dead, infected rats lined the streets like people lining up to watch a parade, and the rats lay within inches of places where little children played. The fleas got on the clothing of workers who then brought the plague into their homes. The fleas spread easily, infecting people through their bites. Since few people understood the nature of diseases, touching the dead bodies of plague victims was a common practice; unfortunately, it was not common practice to wash one's hands afterward. After one family member became infected, it wasn't long before other family members would become sick, too. Cleanup crews often found houses containing several dead—a husband and wife, two or three brothers, a father and a son, and the like (Matthews 87).

Once the outbreak took hold, the disease spread uncontrollably, killing millions. The first symptoms of the plague were similar to those of a common cold, and most people ignored the chills, fever, and coughs. Tragically, this was the period when the disease was most contagious. Then more-extreme symptoms would set in. Victims' bodies would become mottled with blackish spots and swelling boils. Once individuals started shaking uncontrollably, death would soon follow. No one had ever encountered an epidemic as destructive as the Black Plague; as a result, proper medical care did not exist. The most common treatment was bleeding, and many doctors used astrology to prescribe "cures" based on the position of the planets (Matthews 102). Pope Clement VI sat between two fires, which probably saved him, as heat could kill the germs (Cline 67), but this was

---

### Differentiated Instruction: Struggling Learners

Provide students with a word bank of transitional words and phrases. Working with a partner, have them incorporate the transitions into their paragraphs.

⭐ **TEKS** 10.13B, 10.15A(ii)

---

⭐ **TEKS** **10.13B** Develop drafts in open-ended situations that include transitions and rhetorical devices; **10.15A(i)** Write an analytical essay that includes a variety of sentence structures; **10.15A(ii)** Write an analytical essay that includes rhetorical devices and transitions

**TEKS** 10.13B, 10.15A(i), 10.15A(ii), 10.15A(v)

not understood at the time. Apothecaries and peddlers sold quack remedies, and desperation created a market for anything that offered hope. However, nothing worked, and the death rate soared.

> A quotation is included.

As people continued to die, it became clear that the disease did not discriminate. An unknown author stated, "The disease remained and soon death was everywhere.... Friars and nuns were left to care for the sick, and monasteries and convents were soon deserted, as they were stricken, too" (Stevenson 34 ). The loss of life was greatest in the big cities where overcrowding allowed the disease to spread more quickly. John Baker explains that in London alone, more than 100,000 lives were lost. Of 28 monks in Westminster Abbey, 27 died of the plague. An average of 1,000 people died weekly in England, and survivors buried bodies by the hundreds in mass graves (215–216).

> The second effect is explored. The writer continues to use transitions and rhetorical devices. Paragraphs are logically organized.

With so many deaths, what was the effect on Europe's economy? By 1363, the plague had affected nearly all business and commerce in Europe. Building came to a halt as workers died or fled. New construction diminished in the fourteenth century, and most of the great cathedrals begun in the twelfth and thirteenth centuries were left unfinished (Matthews 129). Without a source of labor, business people tried to import workers from other countries by offering them financial incentives. The remaining healthy workers, however, were too fearful to accept the offers. With fewer workers available, wages became inflated and most business owners could no longer afford to keep their workers. The cost of goods rose, too. Farmers died because of the plague, decreasing the amount of food available. In turn, food prices skyrocketed. It was not until the late Renaissance, a period of intellectual and artistic revival ending in the 1600s, that most countries began to recover some of the population and economic ground that was lost due to the plague.

> Relevant details and solid evidence are offered to explain the effect.

Expository

**Write your middle paragraphs.** Follow your outline and use transitions to connect your thoughts and paragraphs. Ideas should flow in a logical order and relate to one another. Evidence should support your thesis.

Draft

---

**Write your middle paragraphs.** Have students point out and discuss examples of the transitions used to make the ideas in the middle paragraphs flow smoothly. Possible responses:

- (first middle paragraph, SE page 152) . . . *touching the dead bodies . . . was a common practice; unfortunately, it was not common practice to wash one's hands afterward.* A contrasting transition word and repetition (*common practice*) link two causes that spread the disease.
- (second middle paragraph, SE page 152) *Once the outbreak took hold . . .* A time transition is used to begin the second middle paragraph.
- (second middle paragraph, SE page 152) . . . *as a result, proper medical care did not exist.* The transition helps draw a conclusion (no one had experience with the plague; therefore, no treatments had been developed).
- (last middle paragraph, SE page 153) *In turn, food prices skyrocketed.* The transition phrase connects rising costs with information about food availability in the previous sentence.

✔ **DIFFERENTIATE INSTRUCTION**  ✔ **DIFFERENTIATE INSTRUCTION**

**TEKS** 10.13B, 10.15A(i), 10.15A(ii), 10.15A(v)

✷ For more about transition words, see SE pages 628–629.

**TEKS** **10.13B** Develop drafts in open-ended situations that include transitions and rhetorical devices; **10.15A(i)** Write an analytical essay that includes a variety of sentence structures; **10.15A(ii)** Write an analytical essay that includes rhetorical devices; **10.15A(v)** Write an analytical essay that includes relevant evidence and details; **ELPS 1C** Use strategic learning techniques to acquire basic and grade-level vocabulary; **1E** Internalize new basic language by using and reusing it/speaking and writing; **1F** Use accessible language and learn new and essential language in the process; **1H** Develop learning strategies/reasoning, looking for patterns in language, and analyzing sayings and expressions; **2A** Distinguish sounds with increasing ease; **2C** Learn basic and academic vocabulary heard during classroom instruction/interactions; **3A** Practice producing sounds of newly acquired vocabulary; **3B** Expand vocabulary by learning and using high-frequency words for identifying and describing/learning and using routine language for classroom communication; **4A** Learn relationships between sounds and letters/sound out words using a combination of skills; **5F** Write using a variety of grade-appropriate connecting words in increasingly accurate ways

---

## Differentiated Instruction: English Language Learners

✷ **ELPS** 1C, 1E, 1F, 1H, 2A, 2C, 3A, 3B, 4A, 5F

| ELP Level **Beginning** | ELP Level **Intermediate** | ELP Level **Advanced/Advanced High** |
|---|---|---|
| Have students underline transitional words and phrases in the model essay dealing with time. Students should take turns sounding out the words with a partner. | Have students use transitional words and phrases to map out or draw the events of the essay in order on a time line. Reproduce the time line (see TE Appendix) as needed.<br><br>**Use page 624** | Have students write and share a paragraph about their morning routine using transitional words and phrases like those found in the essay. |

## Drafting

### Ending Your Essay

Ask students to identify the new information the writer included in the ending. Possible responses:

- No one knows for sure why the plague disappeared.
- Today medicines can combat most diseases.
- Researchers still work to be prepared for new plagues.

Now that students have examined each part of the sample essay, have them go back and read it as a whole. Have them discuss what they find most effective about it and what they think could be improved during the revision stage. Possible responses:

- The writer provides many solid details to explain the plague and its effects. (Development of Ideas)
- The writer clearly explains the plague's causes and their effects. (Organization)
- The writer's knowledgeable voice engages the reader's interest in the topic. (Voice)
- There is some repetition. For example, the writer associates the idea of devastation with the economy three times. (Focus and Coherence) **DIFFERENTIATE INSTRUCTION ↘**

**Write your conclusion.** Remind students that the conclusion should sound natural and not forced, following the style of the introduction, thesis, and supporting paragraphs.

**TEKS** 10.13B, 10.15A(i)

**TEKS 10.13B** Structure ideas in a sustained way; **10.15A(i)**
Write an analytical essay that includes a concluding paragraph;
**10.17C** Use a variety of correctly structured sentences

---

 **TEKS** 10.13B, 10.15A(i)

## Drafting Ending Your Essay

Your conclusion should contain important last thoughts for the reader. Here are some examples of rhetorical devices you can use to clearly convey meaning and create an effective ending.

Beginning
Middle
**Ending**

- **Reflect on your topic and convey its importance with figurative language, such as a metaphor.**
  *Still, the specter of diseases like the Black Plague continues to motivate researchers striving to avert other plagues.*
- **Use repetition for emphasis**
  *The horror of the Black Plague, the fear of the Black Plague, and the enormous death toll of the Black Plague continue to motivate researchers seeking to find a cure.*
- **Provide an effective quotation.**
  *"How many valiant men, how many fair ladies, breakfasted with their kinfolk and the same night supped with their ancestors."*

### Ending Paragraph

The writer refers to the thesis and includes figurative language, in this case, a metaphor.

> Unsanitary conditions made the Black Plague one of the worst natural disasters ever to affect Europe. The effects were felt in cities and rural areas alike. Families in both areas were torn apart. The loss of a third of the population had a devastating impact on the European economy, and it took many years to recover. The plague eventually ceased, after having lingered on for almost 300 years. No doubt improved sanitation and an emphasis on personal hygiene helped, but no one knows for sure why the plague ended. Today, medicines are available to combat most infectious diseases. Still, the specter of diseases like the Black Plague continues to motivate researchers striving to avert other plagues.

Draft

**Write your conclusion.** Write the conclusion, the final paragraph of your essay, using one or more of the rhetorical devices above.

"The writing itself has been as important to me as the product. I have always been somewhat indifferent as to whether I have been working on a solemn novel or an impertinent paragraph."
—Sinclair Lewis

### Differentiated Instruction: Advanced Learners

Students should pay attention to sentence structure throughout the essay and attempt to employ a variety of correctly structured sentences (e.g., compound, complex, compound-complex).

**TEKS** 10.15A(i), 10.17C

# Revising

When you revise, you improve your writing. You add relevant details, delete unnecessary ideas, rewrite unclear parts, and reorder passages as needed.

Keys to Effective Revising

1. If possible, set your first draft aside for a day or two before you do any revising.

2. As you look over your draft, always keep your purpose, your audience, and the genre, or form, of your writing in mind.

3. Check your opening paragraph, your introduction. Have you effectively introduced your topic and clearly stated your thesis?

4. Review your middle paragraphs to be sure that they explore the causes and effects related to the topic.

5. Check your ending paragraph, your conclusion. Have you effectively connected with your thesis and provided a memorable final idea?

6. Be sure that you have developed and maintained a knowledgeable, interested voice.

*Expository*

## Revising
### Keys to Effective Revising

Remind students that the revising stage is an opportunity for writers to make improvements to their first drafts. At this stage, students can think about refinements they might not have considered as they were drafting.

The Keys to Effective Revising list explains the process students will be guided through on SE pages 156–164.

Listening to and considering the input of a peer at this point will help students look at their writing more objectively as they revise. In addition, scheduling instructor conferences can further motivate students to work thoughtfully as they revise.

Ask students to read and review each other's first drafts. Peer response is a crucial yardstick with which students can measure their work. Constructive peer responses can help students determine which revision strategies can make the largest difference for their writing. ✔ DIFFERENTIATE INSTRUCTION

## Differentiated Instruction: English Language Learners
⭐ ELPS 1B, 1F, 3A, 3D, 3E

| ELP Level **Beginning** | ELP Level **Intermediate** | ELP Level **Advanced/Advanced High** |
|---|---|---|
| Have students read aloud the Keys to Effective Revising with an English-proficient partner, making adjustments to their pronunciation. | Have students work with a partner, reading aloud and summarizing each Key to Effective Revising. | Have students discuss the meaning of each point after reading each Key to Effective Revising aloud. |

**ELPS 1B** Monitor oral language and employ self-corrective techniques or other resources; **1F** Use accessible language and learn new and essential language in the process; **3A** Practice producing sounds of newly acquired vocabulary; **3D** Speak using grade-level content area vocabulary/new words and academic language proficiency; **3E** Share information in cooperative learning interactions

## Revising **for** Focus and Coherence

Clarify for students that the idea expressed in "each effect carries equal weight" applies specifically to the thesis statement.
**DIFFERENTIATE INSTRUCTION ↘**

### Does my thesis statement provide the proper focus?

Remind students that the thesis statement should identify the cause and focus on two or three major effects. Emphasize, however, that including minor effects as supporting details in the middle paragraphs is certainly appropriate.

**Review your thesis statement.** Students may work with a partner to review the effectiveness of their thesis statements. Encourage students to focus on the meaning of each word in the thesis statement. Students should revise the statements as needed to convey their precise ideas. **DIFFERENTIATE INSTRUCTION ↘**

**TEKS** 10.13C, 10.15A(iii); **ELPS** 3G

---

## Revising **for** Focus and Coherence

When you revise for *focus and coherence,* check your thesis statement to see if it shows a clear cause-effect relationship. The controlling idea of your essay must be clearly stated. Also be sure that all your ideas are logically presented. They should clearly connect to each other and support your thesis statement. The effects included in your essay should carry equal weight, meaning that they are of equal importance. In addition, be sure that each paragraph contains relevant evidence and enough supporting detail. Your conclusion should tie the essay together and bring the reader back to the thesis statement.

### Does my thesis statement provide the proper focus?

Your thesis statement provides the proper focus if it clearly establishes a cause-effect relationship. In the sample essays in this chapter, the thesis identifies one main cause plus two or three resulting effects. (Each effect carries equal weight.)

**Charlemagne's unification of Europe** *(cause)* **brought peace to all the people** *(effect)*, **stabilized the European economy** *(effect)*, **and promoted education** *(effect)*.

**The Black Plague, caused by poor sanitary conditions** *(cause)*, **destroyed one-third of Europe's population** *(effect)* **and devastated its economy** *(effect)*.

Revise

**Review your thesis statement.** Answer these questions to check the effectiveness of your thesis statement. Revise your thesis as needed.

1. Does the first part of my thesis statement identify the historical event? If so, what is it?

2. Does the second part of my thesis statement identify the main effects? If so, what are they?

3. Do the ideas in the middle paragraphs all relate to and support my thesis statement?

4. Do the details and supporting evidence in the paragraphs relate to and support my thesis statement?

5. Could I state my controlling idea more effectively? Write another version to find out.

---

**Differentiated Instruction: Struggling Learners**

Students should work with a partner to review the effectiveness of their thesis statements. You may want to provide a graphic organizer that students can use as they analyze each question on SE page 156.

---

## Do my body paragraphs maintain the focus set by my thesis statement?

The body of your essay, the middle paragraphs, should show knowledge of and interest in the topic. These paragraphs should work together to show and support the cause-effect relationship you established in your introduction. Your essay should contain sufficient information and be of sufficient length to support your thesis. The effects should be clearly explained and presented logically so that your reader can follow your ideas. The chain of ideas should lead the reader to the conclusion.

### Exercise

Read this thesis statement: The community service requirement for graduation benefits both the student and the community.

Then rewrite the following paragraph topic sentences so that each one shows a direct and logical link to the thesis statement.

1. This is a new requirement.
2. Walking dogs at an animal shelter takes a lot of time.
3. People find homeless animals every day.
4. I used a lot more math than I expected at the animal shelter.

Revise

**Check your paragraph topic sentences.** Do they clearly convey the point of each paragraph and maintain the focus of the thesis statement?

**Focus and Coherence**

Topic sentences relate directly to the thesis statement.

Once the diesase took hold, the disease spread uncontrollably, killing millions.
It seemed like a lot of people got sick. The first symptoms of
∧
the plague were similar to those of a common cold, and most

people ignored the chills, fever, and coughs. ~~The plague had a devastating effect on the European economy.~~
Many workers died and this affected business. No one
∧

expected this to happen. By 1363, the plague had affected

nearly all business and commerce in Europe.

Expository

---

## Do my body paragraphs maintain the focus set by my thesis statement?

Review with students each of the changes made in the paragraph at the bottom of SE page 157. Discuss the specific way each change improves the paragraph.

⭐ **TEKS** 10.13C

### Exercise
**Answers**

Sentences will vary but should resemble the following:

1. Although this is a new requirement, the benefits for the student and the community will be great.
2. Many community members don't have the time to devote to walking the dogs at the animal shelter.
3. Since people find homeless animals every day, this requirement will ensure a steady stream of volunteers for the animal shelter.
4. Working at the animal shelter provided me with opportunities to improve my math skills.

**Check your paragraph topic sentences.** Encourage students to use the skills they learned in the exercise above in revising their own topic sentences.

⭐ **TEKS** 10.15A(iii); **ELPS** 5G

---

**Differentiated Instruction: English Language Learners**                    ⭐ **ELPS** 1C, 1E, 2B, 2C, 3A, 3D, 3E, 5G

| ELP Level **Beginning** | ELP Level **Intermediate** | ELP Level **Advanced/Advanced High** |
|---|---|---|
| Write the words *focus* and *coherence* on the board. Help students identify long and short vowel sounds while they pronounce the words. | Have students draw and label pictures to illustrate the meaning of *focus* and *coherence*, and then use each in a short phrase. | Discuss the meanings of *focus* and *coherence*. Have students work with a partner to analyze and revise their thesis statements to provide a clear focus. |

⭐ **TEKS** **10.13C** Revise drafts to improve the subtlety of meaning; **10.15A(iii)** Write an analytical essay that includes an idea or thesis; **ELPS** **1C** Use strategic learning techniques to acquire basic and grade-level vocabulary; **1E** Internalize new academic language by using and reusing it/speaking and writing; **2B** Recognize elements of the English sound system in new vocabulary/long and short vowels, silent letters, and consonant clusters; **2C** Learn academic vocabulary heard during classroom instruction/interactions; **3A** Practice producing sounds of newly acquired vocabulary; **3D** Speak using grade-level content area vocabulary/academic language proficiency; **3E** Share information in cooperative learning interactions; **5G** Explain with increasing specificity and detail/writing

## Revising for Organization

Suggest to students that as they evaluate their ending paragraphs, they concentrate on the idea of crafting a decisive closing. The essay doesn't necessarily have to "end with a bang," but it shouldn't just fizzle out, either. The reader shouldn't be left wondering, "Is that it?"

**TEKS** 10.13C, 10.15A(iv)

**Does my ending paragraph, my conclusion, work well?**

Find samples of good endings in newspaper or magazine articles or in other student essays and read them to the class. Discuss why they are strong endings.

**Evaluate your ending.** As students work, help individual students label their closing paragraphs and give suggestions for revision.

---

## Revising for Organization

To revise for *organization,* you should first re-read your essay to make sure that the cause-effect pattern that you have chosen is appropriate for the purpose, the audience, and the context of your essay. The reader should be able to see a clear connection from one idea to the next, from the cause to the effects. Check to see that the introduction, middle parts, and conclusion work well together. Also make sure that you have used transition words and phrases to connect the paragraphs in your essay.

### Does my ending paragraph, my conclusion, work well?

Your conclusion works well if it helps the reader understand the importance or value of the information presented in the main part of your essay. An effective ending may often do these three things:

- remind the reader of your thesis,
- summarize the important points that you covered, and
- leave the reader with a final thought about the topic.

| The thesis is restated. | Unsanitary conditions made the Black Plague one of the worst natural disasters ever to affect Europe. The effects were felt in cities and rural areas alike. Families in both areas were torn apart. The loss of a third of the population had a devastating impact on the European economy, and it took many years to recover. The plague eventually ceased, after having lingered on for almost 300 years. No doubt improved sanitation and an emphasis on personal hygiene helped, but no one knows for sure why the plague ended. Today, medicines are available to combat most infectious diseases. Still, the specter of diseases like the Black Plague continues to motivate researchers striving to avert other plagues. |
| --- | --- |
| Main points are highlighted. | |
| The closing adds a final thought. | |

**Evaluate your ending.** As you review your final paragraph, label the different parts, using the information above as a guide. Did you restate your thesis, summarize the main points, and leave the reader with a final thought? Revise as needed.

---

**Differentiated Instruction: Struggling Learners**

Help students identify the transitions or key words that link the paragraphs in the sample essays in this unit. Then demonstrate for students how to check for and, if necessary, add transitions in a sample essay that you display on an overhead. Refer students to SE pages 628–629 for more examples of transitions.

**TEKS** **10.13C** Revise drafts/rethink how well the purpose, audience, and genre have been addressed; **10.15A(iv)** Write an analytical essay that includes a structure appropriate to the purpose, audience, and context

**TEKS** 10.13C, 10.13E, 10.15A(i)

Cause-Effect Essay **159**

## Are the paragraphs of my essay clearly connected?

When the paragraphs of an essay are organized so that they connect and relate to the thesis statement, the writer has created a strong, logical organizational pattern that has both focus and coherence. When you selected the organizational pattern for your essay, you may have also decided on logical ways to link the paragraphs. The paragraphs of your essay will be clearly connected and lead the reader from one idea to the next if you have effectively used either or both of these linking strategies:

- Choose a key word or phrase from one paragraph and repeat it in the next.
- Start a new paragraph with a transition word or phrase such as *in addition, more importantly,* and so on.

In the sample below, a key word (shown in red) from one paragraph is repeated in the next.

> . . . When peasant and nobleman alike realized that they were being treated fairly, a feeling of trust and peace spread throughout Europe.
>
> In order to maintain peace, Charlemagne soon realized that he needed to stabilize the economy in the entire region.

 **Revise**

**Check the coherence and organization of your essay.** Review your writing to make sure that you have effectively linked your paragraphs. Make changes as needed. Make sure that your conclusion ties the essay together.

Expository

**Organization**
A key phrase is repeated to connect the paragraphs.

> . . . The Black Plague, caused by poor sanitation, destroyed one-third of Europe's population and devastated its economy.
>
> Poor sanitation
> ∧ The way of life fostered conditions that were perfect for the spread of the disease. Rats and fleas carried the microbe called Pasteurella pestis, the lethal bacterium . . .

**Are the paragraphs of my essay clearly connected?**

Suggest that students have partners read their essays and do the following:

- Circle key words and phrases. Do these words provide clear connections from one paragraph or sentence to the next?
- Check the transitional phrases used at the beginnings of sentences. Would it be helpful to add more? (Students should use a variety of transitions so that the same words or sentence patterns aren't repeated too often.)

✔ DIFFERENTIATE INSTRUCTION  ✔ DIFFERENTIATE INSTRUCTION

**Check the coherence and organization of your essay.** Discuss how using the key phrase "Poor sanitation" adds organization and cohesiveness to the sample essay.

**TEKS** 10.13C, 10.13E , 10.15A(i)

---

**Differentiated Instruction:**
**English Language Learners**

**ELPS** 1B, 1E, 1F, 2D, 3D, 3F, 3H, 5B

| ELP Level **Beginning** | ELP Level **Intermediate** | ELP Level **Advanced/Advanced High** |
|---|---|---|
| Have students practice using basic transition words from a word bank in simple phrases using basic classroom vocabulary; partners should monitor understanding. | Using transition words from a word bank, have students compose simple sentences with a partner, explaining how to prepare a favorite food. | Have students work with a partner to insert and correctly use basic and abstract transition words and phrases within their essays. |

**TEKS** **10.13C** Revise drafts to improve the subtlety of meaning; **10.13E** Revise the final draft in response to feedback from peers; **10.15A(i)** Write an analytical essay that includes an introductory and concluding paragraph; **ELPS** **1B** Monitor oral/written language and employ self-corrective techniques or other resources; **1E** Internalize new basic and academic language by using and reusing it/ speaking and writing; **1F** Use accessible language and learn new and essential language in the process; **2D** Monitor understanding of spoken language during classroom instruction/interactions; **3D** Speak using grade-level content area vocabulary/new words and academic language proficiency; **3F** Give information/ranging from using a limited high-frequency vocabulary to using abstract and content-based vocabulary during speaking; **3H** Explain with increasing specificity and detail; **5B** Write using newly acquired basic vocabulary

## Revising **for** Development of Ideas

Remind students to be cautious of using logical fallacies and circular reasoning in their essays.

**Does my essay illustrate a clear cause-effect relationship?**

Complete the following exercise as a class and discuss answers.

### Exercise
### Answers

1. Not relevant; this sentence does not support the controlling idea that Charlemagne's unification of Europe brought peace.
2. Not relevant; this sentence does not support the controlling idea that the unification of Europe promoted education, only that scholars were brought to one location.
3. Not relevant; this sentence does not logically support any of the controlling ideas.
4. Relevant; this sentence logically supports the controlling idea that Charlemagne's unification of Europe helped to stabilize the economy.
5. Not relevant; although the sentence mentions his renown as peacemaker, it does not logically explain or justify how his actions brought peace.
6. Not relevant; although the sentence mentions the impact on France's economy, the facts do not support the controlling idea that Charlemagne was responsible.

**Revise for development of ideas.** Have students peer-edit each other's essays to answer these questions: Does it make sense? Is it relevant? Are the inferences valid? Does it logically support the controlling paragraph?

**TEKS** 10.13C, 10.15A(iv), 10.15A(v); **ELPS** 5G

---

**TEKS** 10.13C, 10.15A(iv), 10.15A(v)
**ELPS** 5G

## Revising **for** Development of Ideas

When you revise for *development of ideas,* be sure that all your ideas are clearly stated and that enough information is provided to support your thesis. Each paragraph should have a topic sentence that shows an aspect of the cause-effect relationship, and the paragraphs should expand upon your controlling idea. The evidence and supporting details in each paragraph should relate to and support the paragraph's topic sentence. Be sure that inferences you have drawn from your own research are logical. Check to make sure that the reader is also led to make valid inferences from the information in your essay. Check again to make sure that you have chosen the correct genre for the writing.

### Does my essay illustrate a clear cause-effect relationship?

Your thesis statement provided the focus for your essay. The body of your essay must make the cause-effect relationship clear. To do this, you will need to provide sufficient evidence and relevant details about each effect.

#### Exercise

Consider the controlling idea that Charlemagne's unification of Europe brought peace, stabilized the economy, and promoted education. Read the following statements; then label each one relevant or not relevant to the thesis statement. Explain your answers.

1. Charlemagne greatly expanded the territory under his rule by both war and political maneuvering.
2. Charlemagne brought scholars from all over Europe to France.
3. France is now a republic.
4. Charlemagne provided funds to regions that truly needed more resources.
5. Charlemagne was known both as a warrior and as a peacemaker.
6. France is now part of the European Union, which has had a major impact on its economy.

**Revise for Development of Ideas.** Carefully review your essay to make sure that each idea is well developed. Be sure that you have provided sufficient evidence to support the controlling idea. Verify that any inferences you have made from the evidence you gathered for your essay are valid. If not, be sure to correct them, and revise your essay as needed.

---

**TEKS** **10.13C** Revise drafts/rethink how well the genre has been addressed; **10.15A(iv)** Write an analytical essay that includes a structure appropriate to the purpose and context; **10.15A(v)** Write an analytical essay that includes relevant evidence; **ELPS** **5G** Explain with increasing specificity and detail/writing

**TEKS** 10.13C,
10.15A(iv), 10.15A(v)
**ELPS** 5G

## Have I included enough detail?

When you look at the details you have included in your essay, remember the genre you have chosen, a factual cause-effect essay. You have already chosen an organizational pattern that is appropriate for the purpose, audience, and context. Be sure that your essay is long enough to adequately cover the topic. It is important to keep those basics in mind as you begin to examine the details you have chosen to include. You have included enough detail if the body sentences in each paragraph clearly and completely support the topic sentence. A well-written paragraph often contains three levels of detail.

**Level 1:** **Topic sentence:** In order to maintain peace, Charlemagne soon realized that he needed to stabilize the economy in the entire region.

**Level 2:** **Clarifying sentence:** He divided larger parcels of land into more manageable estates that were self-contained and . . .

**Level 3:** **Completing sentence** *(an explanation, a quotation, or a paraphrase)*: Each estate had a bustling center of commerce surrounded by a market, church, guilds, and public buildings.

**Note:** Most paragraphs include at least two clarifying sentences, each one usually followed by one or two completing sentences.

Revise

**Check for levels of detail.** As you read through your essay, try putting a *1* next to each topic sentence, a *2* next to each clarifying sentence, and a *3* next to each completing sentence. Then decide if you have included enough detail.

**Development of Ideas**
A completing detail is added.

> . . . The first symptoms of the plague were similar to those of a common cold, and most people ignored the chills, fever, and coughs. Then more-extreme symptoms would set in. Victims' bodies would become mottled with blackish spots . . .
>
> Tragically, this was the period when the disease was most contagious.

*Expository*

---

## Have I included enough detail?

Point out the example of the revision to add detail on the bottom of this page and then, as a group, discuss the distinction between clarifying sentences and completing sentences.

- A clarifying sentence provides information that builds on, or elucidates, the idea stated in the topic sentence.
- A completing sentence can add a final piece of information to the details that have been presented in the clarifying sentence.

**TEKS** 10.13C, 10.15A(iv), 10.15A(v); **ELPS** 5G

**Check for levels of detail.** Students should complete the activity first on their own and then switch papers with a partner and discuss any disparities in their labels. ✔DIFFERENTIATE INSTRUCTION

---

## Differentiated Instruction:
## English Language Learners

**ELPS** 1C, 1E, 2C, 2E, 3J, 4C

| ELP Level **Beginning** | ELP Level **Intermediate** | ELP Level **Advanced/Advanced High** |
|---|---|---|
| Write the word *detail* on the board and model pronunciation. Have students find main ideas and details using environmental print. | Using a photograph or environmental print, have students take turns pointing out and naming details using phrases and sentences. | Have students work in pairs on the activity, then revise their paragraphs to include two of each type of sentence. |

 **TEKS** **10.13C** Revise drafts/rethink how well the genre has been addressed; **10.15A(iv)** Write an analytical essay that includes a structure appropriate to the purpose and context; **10.15A(v)** Write an analytical essay that includes relevant evidence; **ELPS** **1C** Use strategic learning techniques to acquire basic and grade-level vocabulary; **1E** Internalize new basic and academic language by using and reusing it/speaking and writing; **2C** Learn basic and academic vocabulary heard during classroom instruction/interactions; **2E** Use visual support to enhance and confirm understanding of increasingly complex spoken language; **3J** Respond orally to information presented in a variety of media to build and reinforce language attainment; **4C** Derive meaning of environmental print; **5G** Explain with increasing specificity and detail/writing

## Revising for Voice

**Have I used the proper voice in my essay?**

After students have completed the exercise, discuss specific elements that can create a "too personal" voice. Refer to examples on the page as needed.

- Using second-person pronouns (exercise sentence 1) makes it sound as if the writer is directing the essay toward one person instead of a broader audience.
- Using first-person pronouns (exercise sentence 3) inserts the writer's personality into the work. By convention, expository writing should be objective.

✱ For more about the person of pronouns, see SE page 738.

### Exercise
### Answers

1. TCP
2. PD
3. TCP
4. PD
5. TCP

**Revise for voice.** Have students work in pairs or groups to complete this activity. If they work in groups, have the writer read one paragraph aloud while the group members take notes on suggested changes for voice. Then have students revise the remainder of their essay on their own.

**TEKS** 10.13C, 10.15A(v)

---

## Revising for Voice

When you revise for *voice*, be sure that you use the proper informational voice and that you sound knowledgeable and confident. Try to maintain this same knowledgeable, engaging voice throughout your essay. Your writing should engage the reader, and your writing should express your own perspective or viewpoint. Look carefully at the writing style you have used.

### Have I used the proper voice in my essay?

If you've "kept your distance," then you've probably used the proper voice. The purpose of a cause-effect essay is to inform the reader, not to get too close and personal with the reader. You'll be right on track if your essay engages the reader with plenty of interesting and relevant facts and draws valid inferences from the evidence you have presented.

> **Too close and personal:** I've learned about the early battles during the Civil War. Now I know about the Battle of Gettysburg, especially when Pickett's men made their final charge. It was unbelievable.

> **Proper distance:** The Union troops on Cemetery Ridge destroyed the ranks of Pickett's men, which meant not only the end of the battle, but also the eventual collapse of the Confederate army.

### Exercise

Read the following statements; then label each one TCP (too close and personal) or PD (proper distance).

1. If you'd been a passenger on that voyage across the Atlantic, you'd have been blown away by the ship's incredible speed.
2. On April 14, 1912, the largest ship ever built, the *Titanic,* collided with an iceberg just before midnight.
3. If I had been scrambling around the deck of the *Titanic,* I would have been scared to death.
4. Tragically, over 1,500 people lost their lives when the ship sank.
5. Can you believe that the *Titanic* only had enough lifeboats for about half the people on board the ship?

**Revise for voice.** Carefully review your essay for voice, making sure that you have engaged the reader and kept the proper distance. Check for word choice and proper use of rhetorical devices. Revise as needed.

---

## Does my voice sound confident in my essay?

The style of your essay and the voice you choose should be appropriate for the purpose, the audience, and the context. Well-placed and carefully thought-out rhetorical devices, such as quotations, show your research and knowledge; they also help engage the reader. You'll sound confident in your cause-effect essay if you have a clear and thorough understanding of your topic. Simply put, there is a direct link between your knowledge of a topic and the level of confidence in your voice. In the following samples, it's clear which writer is confident and which is not.

**Not confident:** When the *Hindenburg* crashed in 1937, many people died. The great airship caught fire, which probably caused the explosion.

**Confident:** When the German zeppelin *Hindenburg* caught fire and crashed on May 6, 1937, 36 people lost their lives. Some people thought the crash occurred on the zeppelin's maiden voyage, but the *Hindenburg* had already made 17 round-trip excursions across the ocean, including 10 trips to the United States and 7 to Brazil.

 **Revise** **Check for the confidence in your voice.** Carefully review your essay, looking for parts where you don't speak with the proper level of authority. Research and revise as needed.

> **Voice**
> An idea is changed because it is "too close and personal."

Imagine a disease that killed millions of people who had no
~~I've had pneumonia and bronchitis, but I've never had to~~
way to defend themselves. ~~deal with an incurable disease like the bubonic plague.~~ At its height, from 1348 to 1351, the bubonic plague, better known as the "Black Plague" because of the black spots it caused on the skin, brought Europe to its knees. In <u>The Decameron</u>, Giovanni Boccaccio observed, "Almost everyone expected . . ."

*Expository*

---

**Does my voice sound confident in my essay?**

Ask students to discuss why the first sample does not sound confident, whereas the second one does.

First sample:
- The language is too general (in 1937; many people).
- The writer states a fact (the great airship caught fire) without seeming to know important details about it. As a consequence, the writer has to use the qualifier *probably*.

Second sample:
- The writer provides more explanation and specific details (the German zeppelin *Hindenburg*; May 6, 1937; 36 people lost their lives).
- The writer corrects a common misunderstanding (that the *Hindenburg* was on its maiden voyage) and gives solid statistics to support the statement.

TEKS 10.13B, 10.13C, 10.15A(ii)

**Check for confidence in your voice.** Discuss how the revision changed the voice in the example paragraph. Then have students read their essays aloud to a partner who will point out areas that lack authority and confidence in voice.

✏ **DIFFERENTIATE INSTRUCTION**

---

**Differentiated Instruction:**
**English Language Learners**            ★ **ELPS** 1A, 1E, 2E, 3D, 3E, 3F, 3G, 5G

| **ELP Level** **Beginning** | **ELP Level** **Intermediate** | **ELP Level** **Advanced/Advanced High** |
| --- | --- | --- |
| Help students create a word web for the word *confident*. | Have students interview each other about what makes them feel confident and enumerate ways they show their confidence in their written work. | Have students work in groups to find qualifying words in their essays and then revise the words to show more confidence. |

Use page 624

 **TEKS** **10.13B** Develop drafts in open-ended situations that include rhetorical devices; **10.13C** Revise drafts/improve style and rethink how well the audience has been addressed; **10.15A(ii)** Write an analytical essay that includes rhetorical devices; **ELPS 1A** Use prior knowledge and experience to understand meanings; **1E** Internalize new basic language by using and reusing it/speaking and writing; **2E** Use contextual/linguistic support to enhance and confirm understanding of increasingly complex spoken language; **3D** Speak using grade-level content area vocabulary/new words and academic language proficiency; **3E** Share information in cooperative learning interactions; **3F** Give information/ranging from using a limited high-frequency vocabulary to using abstract and content-based vocabulary during speaking; **3G** Express opinions, ideas, and feelings ranging from communicating short phrases to participating in discussions; **5G** Explain with increasing specificity and detail/writing

## Revising
**Improving Your Writing**

**Revise your essay.** Discuss students' thoughts about the revision process after they used the checklist.

- Did using the checklist help you to focus on the part(s) of your essay that still need work? Which ones?
- Did you enlist the aid of another reader during the revising process?
- Did you find that you enjoyed the revising process more than you had expected? Why or why not?
- What was the biggest challenge you faced during revision?
- What was a helpful strategy that you would probably employ again?

**Make a clean copy.** Remind students that revising and editing, although similar, are really two distinct processes.

 **Conventions Connections**

### Grammar: Adverbs
- **Student Edition** pages 578–579;
  **Proofreader's Guide** pages 758–759
- **SkillsBook** pages 111–113

**Write Source Online GrammarSnap**

---

## Revising **Improving Your Writing**

 **Revise your essay.** On a piece of paper, write the numbers 1 to 10. If you can answer "yes" to a question, put a check mark after that number. If not, continue to revise that part of your essay.

### Revising Checklist

#### Focus and Coherence

_____ 1. My thesis statement establishes a clear, strong cause-effect relationship.

_____ 2. The body paragraphs effectively support my thesis.

_____ 3. My conclusion reminds the reader of the thesis statement and ties my essay together.

#### Organization

_____ 4. I have closely followed my outline.

_____ 5. I have a distinct introduction, middle parts, and an effective conclusion.

_____ 6. I use strong transitions to connect ideas and paragraphs.

#### Development of Ideas

_____ 7. My ideas are relevant to the thesis, well developed, and sustain the cause-effect relationship.

_____ 8. Researched evidence and sufficient details show the importance of each effect in the essay.

#### Voice

_____ 9. My voice sounds knowledgeable and is appropriate for the purpose, audience, and context of the essay.

_____ 10. My voice sounds confident.

 **Make a clean copy.** When you've finished revising, make a clean copy of your essay for editing.

Cause-Effect Essay **165**

Prewrite · Draft · Revise · Edit · Publish

## Editing

Once you have completed your revisions, you are ready to edit your essay for grammar, sentence structure, capitalization, punctuation, and spelling. These aspects of written English are called *conventions*.

Expository

### Keys to Effective Editing

1. Edit your essay using a dictionary, a thesaurus, and the "Proofreader's Guide." (See pages 642–787.)

2. Check your writing for grammar, sentence structure, capitalization, punctuation, and spelling errors.

3. Also have a trusted classmate or your teacher check your writing for errors. (Writers usually work with an editor.)

4. If you're using a computer, edit on a printout of your essay. Then enter your changes on the computer.

5. Use the proofreading marks located inside the back cover of this book.

## Editing

### Keys to Effective Editing

Remind students that the editing step is their opportunity to find and correct errors.

The Keys to Effective Editing page explains the process students will be guided through on SE pages 166–170.

Expand on the list as appropriate for your students. For example:

- Emphasize the importance of consulting references, such as the Proofreader's Guide in this book. Note that professional writers constantly consult resources and work with editors.
- Remind students that they must remain vigilant and investigate anything that *might* be wrong.
- Encourage students to use the grammar checkers and spell-checkers on their computers, but also remind them to evaluate each suggestion before making a change. (Point out to students that neither feature is infallible.)
- Instruct students to read their drafts several times, focusing on different items each time (say, once for punctuation, once to check spelling, and so on). ✓ **DIFFERENTIATE INSTRUCTION**

⭐ **ELPS** 5B, 5C, 5D, 5E, 5F

---

### Differentiated Instruction: English Language Learners

⭐ **ELPS** 1G, 5B, 5C, 5D, 5E, 5F

| ELP Level **Beginning** | ELP Level **Intermediate** | ELP Level **Advanced/Advanced High** |
|---|---|---|
| Have students write several short phrases using newly acquired basic vocabulary, then work with a partner to edit the writing for spelling and formal English use. | Have students peer-edit their essays, concentrating on spelling, standard grammar and usage, and formal English use. | Have students peer-edit their essays concentrating on spelling, standard grammar and usage, variety of sentence structure, verb tense, and clarity. |

**ELPS 1G** Demonstrate increasing ability to distinguish between formal/informal English and an increasing knowledge of when to use each one; **5B** Write using newly acquired basic and content-based grade-level vocabulary; **5C** Spell familiar words/employ spelling patterns and rules with increasing accuracy; **5D** Edit writing for standard grammar and usage/subject-verb and pronoun agreement and appropriate verb tenses; **5E** Employ increasingly complex grammatical structures in content area writing such as using correct verbs, tenses, and pronouns/possessive case/negatives and contractions; **5F** Write using a variety of grade-appropriate sentence lengths, patterns, and connecting words/combine in increasingly accurate ways

Editing **for** Conventions

## Grammar

Provide several examples of the proper use of verb tenses when writing about historical events. Also, give students sample sentences written in passive voice and have them work with a partner to restate them in active voice.

 **ELPS** 2I, 3C, 3E, 4C

### How do I know when to use more complex verb tenses?

Remind students to use a variety of past verb tenses to express past actions correctly.

#### Grammar Exercise
**Answers**

1. Rats and fleas were spreading the plague.
2. Children were playing near dead rats.
3. Peddlers were selling quack remedies.

**TEKS** 10.13D, 10.17A(i)

**Check verb tenses.** You may wish to remind students to be sure they don't switch from past tense into present or future unless it is logically necessary to do so.

**ELPS** 5D, 5E

---

⭐ **Conventions Connections**

**Grammar: Complex Verb Tenses**
- **Proofreader's Guide** pages 748–749, 750–751
- **SkillsBook** pages 96–97

✸ **Write Source Online GrammarSnap**

---

 Editing **for** Conventions

# Grammar

When you edit for *grammar,* you make sure that you have used all parts of speech, including verbs and verb tenses, correctly. For example, your cause-effect essay will show relationships related to a particular historical event. Because it is a historical event, most of the verbs you use will be in a past tense. As you write, aim for the active voice, not the passive. Remember that in the active voice, the subject commits the action. The sentence *John hit the ball* is written with an active voice. The sentence *The ball was hit by John* is written in the passive voice. The subject (in this case *the ball*) receives the action.

## How do I know when to use more complex verb tenses?

You are already familiar with simple present, past, and future tenses. When you write your cause-effect essay, you will be using more complex verb tenses. To express an action that occurred in the past, there are several complex verb tenses you can use, including past perfect and past progressive.

- To express an action in the past that occurred before another past action, use the past perfect tense.

  **After I had completed my homework, I met some of my friends at the mall. My parents had given me a gift certificate.**

- To express an action that was happening at a certain time in the past and continued in the past, use the past progressive tense. This is also called the past continuous tense.

  **The car engine was making very odd noises. We were traveling on the train.**

### Grammar Exercise

Rewrite the following sentences, changing the simple past to past progressive tense.

1. Rats and fleas spread the plague.
2. Children played near dead rats.
3. Peddlers sold quack remedies.

 **Check verb tenses.** Review your essay to be sure you have correctly used past perfect and past progressive verb tenses. Edit for tense and consistency.

---

**TEKS** **10.13D** Edit drafts for grammar; **10.17A(i)** Use and understand more complex passive tenses; **ELPS** **2I** Demonstrate listening comprehension in increasingly complex spoken language by collaborating with peers; **3C** Speak using a variety of grammatical structures with increasing accuracy and ease; **3E** Share information in cooperative learning interactions; **4C** Comprehend language structures used in written classroom materials; **5D** Edit writing for standard grammar and usage/subject-verb agreement; **5E** Employ increasingly complex grammatical structures in content area writing such as using correct verbs, tenses, and pronouns/possessive case/negatives and contractions

**TEKS** 10.13D, 10.17A(i)
**ELPS** 2I, 3C, 3E, 4C, 5D, 5E

## When is it appropriate to use the passive voice?

When writing about actual events, try always to use the active voice. In some cases, however, you will need to use the passive voice. For example, in the sentence *Artists, scientists, and teachers were sent from monasteries to other regions to share their knowledge,* we do not know who sent these people. Therefore, the writer correctly used passive voice. We do know that *Charlemagne divided large parcels of lands into more manageable estates,* so that sentence is written in active voice. Just as there are complex active voices, there are also complex passive voices.

- The past perfect in the passive voice is similar to the past perfect in the active voice. It is used to express an action in the past that occurred before another past action.

   **Teachers had been sent to outlying regions to teach.**

- The past progressive tense in the passive voice is also similar to the past progressive in the active voice. It expresses an action that was happening at a certain time in the past and continued in the past.

   **At the same time that teachers were being sent to outlying regions, scientists were being sent away from monasteries to share their knowledge as well.**

### Grammar Exercise

Rewrite the following sentences, changing the verbs from passive to active voice.

1. Charlemagne was crowned emperor by the Pope.
2. Much of Europe was ruled by Charlemagne.

 **Check verb voice.** Review your essay for active and passive voice. When possible, change your verbs to active voice, and make sure you have used active and passive voices and complex tenses correctly.

### Learning Language

Tell a classmate what you did yesterday, what you are doing today, and what you plan to do tomorrow. Use active voice. Have your classmate repeat each sentence, changing the verb from active to passive voice.

Expository

## When is it appropriate to use the passive voice?

Explain to students that they do not have to replace every passive verb—just those that slow the essay down or disrupt its flow. Some verbs are more naturally expressed in the passive voice (*Abraham Lincoln was born on February 12, 1809*). Sometimes the focus is not on who or what performed the action (*More than 100,000 men were killed in battle during the Civil War*).

**TEKS** 10.17A(i)

✱ For more about the Voice of a Verb, see SE page 750.

### Grammar Exercise
#### Answers

1. The Pope crowned Charlemagne emperor.
2. Charlemagne ruled much of Europe.

**Check verb voice.** Encourage students to use the skills they learned in the exercise above in revising their essays.

**TEKS** 10.13D; **ELPS** 5D, 5E

### Learning Language

Encourage students to listen as they change voice and form an opinion about which they think is more appropriate for the sentence.

**⬆ DIFFERENTIATE INSTRUCTION**

**ELPS** 2I, 3C, 3E, 4C

---

 **TEKS** **10.13D** Edit drafts for grammar; **10.17A(i)** Use and understand more complex passive tenses; **ELPS** **1A** Use prior knowledge and experience to understand meanings; **1D** Speak using learning strategies/request assistance, employ non-verbal cues, and convey ideas by defining or describing; **1H** Develop and expand learning strategies/reasoning, looking for patterns in language, and analyzing sayings and expressions; **2E** Use visual and contextual support to enhance and confirm understanding of increasingly complex spoken language; **2I** Demonstrate listening comprehension in increasingly complex spoken language/following directions, summarizing spoken messages, responding to questions, and collaborating with peers; **3C** Speak using a variety of grammatical structures/sentence lengths and types with increasing accuracy and ease; **3E** Share information in cooperative learning interactions; **4C** Comprehend language structures used in written classroom materials; **5D** Edit writing for standard grammar and usage/ subject-verb agreement and verb tenses; **5E** Employ increasingly complex grammatical structures in content area writing such as using correct verbs, tenses, and pronouns/possessive case/negatives and contractions

## Sentence Structure

**Do I need to combine or expand any of my sentences?**

Have students complete the exercise and then share answer sentences on the board. Have volunteers underline the restrictive and nonrestrictive clauses. As a class, discuss how restrictive clauses limit and nonrestrictive clauses describe the noun they modify. Circle commas and point out that the meaning of the sentence is not changed when the words between commas are taken out.

**TEKS** 10.17A(ii); **ELPS** 2C

---

### Exercise
### Answers

Answers will vary, but each sentence should contain a common relative pronoun, and nonrestrictive clauses should be set apart by commas.

**Check for short, choppy sentences.** Students may read their essays aloud to a partner to check for short, choppy sentences and then revise on their own.

**ELPS** 1E

---

**TEKS** 10.15A(i), 10.17A(ii)

# Sentence Structure

Remember, your essay should include a variety of sentence structures. Using short, simple sentences can help you emphasize important points, such as your thesis statement or the last sentence in your conclusion, but you should include longer, complex sentences as well. To edit for *sentence structure,* look for choppy sentences that you can combine or expand.

## Do I need to combine or expand any of my sentences?

One way to combine sentences is to use restrictive and nonrestrictive clauses. A restrictive relative clause is essential to the meaning of the sentence. Without the restrictive clause the reader would not understand what the sentence is about. A nonrestrictive clause is not essential to the meaning of the sentence as a whole. In other words, it could be deleted, and the meaning of the sentence would not change.

These clauses are often joined to the independent clause with the relative pronouns *who, whom, whose, that* and *which.* The relative pronoun *which* is used in nonrestrictive clauses.

**Restrictive Clauses:** The man who is reading the newspaper is my uncle. The book that I read last night was fascinating.

The words ***who is reading the newspaper*** and ***that I read last night*** are essential to the meaning of the sentences because they identify the subject.

**Nonrestrictive Clauses:** Tennis, which is a popular sport, is not difficult to learn. This novel, which is a best-seller, is about a daughter and her mother.

The words ***which is a popular sport*** and ***which is a best-seller*** are not essential to the meaning of the sentences.

### Exercise

Combine the following sentences using a relative pronoun.

1. I want to attend our local university. It has outstanding teachers.
2. My goal is to become a systems analyst. It is a profitable career.
3. I want to buy a new book. I want a book about Austin, Texas.
4. My uncle is an engineer. You met him last night.

 **Check for short, choppy sentences.** Review your first draft for series of short, choppy sentences. Rewrite these sentences as needed, adding restrictive and nonrestrictive clauses.

---

**TEKS** **10.17A(ii)** Use and understand restrictive and nonrestrictive relative clauses; **ELPS** **1E** Internalize new basic and academic language by using and reusing it/writing; **2C** Learn new language structures and expressions heard during classroom instruction/interactions

# Mechanics: Punctuation

To edit for *mechanics*, you check for correct use of capitalization and punctuation. Be sure to check both end punctuation and punctuation within a sentence. As you know, commas have multiple uses within sentences.

- Commas are used to separate items in a series.
  **I bought lettuce, tomatoes, cucumbers, and bell peppers.**
- Commas set off participial phrases. For example:
  **Panting heavily, the dog flopped onto the cool tile floor.**
- Commas are used to separate independent clauses in a sentence.
  **I bought a sweater, and my sister bought a jacket. I wanted to go to the movies, but my friends wanted to go bowling.**

## How do I punctuate restrictive and nonrestrictive phrases and clauses?

- Because nonrestrictive clauses are not essential to the meaning of a sentence, they are set off with commas.
  **Pope Clement VI sat between two fires, which probably saved him, as heat could kill the germs. The Black Plague, which was deadly to humans, also killed many farm animals.**
- Restrictive clauses are essential to the meaning of a sentence, and they are not separated by commas.
  **This method works for people who want to improve their listening skills. Adults who cannot drive often have trouble finding jobs. She accepted all of the suggestions that were practical.**

**Check for comma use.** Review your essay to be sure that you have used commas correctly to set off nonrestrictive clauses.

### Grammar Exercise

Decide which of the following sentences have restrictive or nonrestrictive clauses. Add commas as appropriate.

1. The person whom I wanted most to meet could not come to the meeting.
2. My backpack which I left at my friend's house had all my schoolwork inside.
3. The house which was once blue needs painting.
4. The boy who sat next to me did not say a word.

Expository

## Mechanics: Punctuation

Review the various uses of commas. Provide additional examples as needed.

### How do I punctuate restrictive and nonrestrictive phrases and clauses?

After reading each example sentence aloud in its complete form, read each sentence aloud, skipping both the nonrestrictive and the restrictive clauses. As a class, discuss whether and how this changed the sentences' meanings. Also have students offer answers to the question: *Why do we need commas to set apart nonrestrictive clauses?* ✓ **DIFFERENTIATE INSTRUCTION**

TEKS 10.13D, 10.15A(i), 10.17A(ii), 10.18B(i)

**Check for comma use.** Suggest that students underline each restrictive and nonrestrictive clause and decide whether it limits or describes the noun it modifies. They should then add or delete commas as necessary.

TEKS 10.13D; ELPS 5E, 5F

### Grammar Exercise
**Answers**

1. Restrictive, no commas necessary.
2. My backpack, which I left at my friend's house, had. . .
3. The house, which was once blue, needs painting.
4. Restrictive, no commas necessary.

TEKS **10.13D** Edit drafts for mechanics; **10.15A(i)** Write an analytical essay that includes a variety of sentence structures; **10.17A(ii)** Use and understand more complex active and passive tenses; **10.18B(i)** Use commas in nonrestrictive phrases and contrasting expressions and in clauses; ELPS **1B** Monitor oral language and employ self-corrective techniques or other resources; **1C** Use strategic learning techniques to acquire basic and grade-level vocabulary; **1F** Use accessible language/learn new and essential language in the process; **1G** Demonstrate increasing ability to distinguish between formal/informal English and an increasing knowledge of when to use each one; **2B** Recognize elements of the English sound system in new vocabulary/long and short vowels, silent letters, and consonant clusters; **2C** Learn basic vocabulary heard during classroom instruction/interactions; **3I** Adapt spoken language for formal and informal purposes; **4A** Learn relationships between sounds and letters/sound out words using a combination of skills; **5E** Employ complex grammatical structures in content area writing such as using correct verbs, tenses, and pronouns/possessive case/negatives and contractions; **5F** Write using a variety of grade-appropriate sentence lengths and connecting words/combine in increasingly accurate ways

## Editing

### Checking for Conventions

**Check your editing.** Give students a few moments to look over the Proofreader's Guide (SE pages 642–787). Throughout the year, they can refer to the instructions, rules, and examples to clarify any checklist items or to resolve questions about their own writing. **DIFFERENTIATE INSTRUCTION ↘**

**DIFFERENTIATE INSTRUCTION ↘**

**TEKS** 10.13D, 10.15A(i), 10.17A(i), 10.17C, 10.18B(i), 10.19

Explain to students that they should usually include page numbers with their citations. Circumstances in which they do not need to do so are

- when the information comes from a Web site or other source that does not have numbered pages, and
- when the reference in the essay sums up an overall idea expressed in the source.

✱ Refer students to SE page 379 for a model Works Cited page.

### Creating a Title

Review the suggestions with students, adding that sometimes authors use a word or phrase from the writing itself as a title.

**ELPS** 5C, 5D, 5E, 5F

---

### ⭐ Conventions Connections

**Grammar: Restrictive/Nonrestrictive Clauses for Combining Sentences**
- *Proofreader's Guide* pages 650–651
- *SkillsBook* pages 14–15

✴ *Write Source Online* **GrammarSnap**

---

**TEKS** **10.13D** Edit drafts for grammar, mechanics, and spelling; **10.15A(i)** Write an analytical essay that includes a variety of sentence structures; **10.17A(i)** Use and understand more complex active and passive tenses; **10.17C** Use a variety of correctly structured sentences; **10.18A** Use conventions of capitalization; **10.18B(i)** Use commas in nonrestrictive phrases and contrasting expressions and in clauses; **10.19** Spell correctly using resources to determine and check correct spelling; **ELPS 5C** Spell familiar words with increasing accuracy; **5D** Edit writing for standard grammar and usage/verb tenses; **5E** Employ increasingly complex grammatical structures in content area writing such as using correct verbs, tenses, and pronouns/possessive case/negatives and contractions; **5F** Write using a variety of grade-appropriate sentence patterns and connecting words in increasingly accurate ways

---

**TEKS** 10.13D, 10.15A(i), 10.17A(i), 10.17C, 10.18A, 10.18B(i), 10.19
**ELPS** 5C–5F

## Editing Checking for Conventions

**Check your editing.** On a piece of paper, write the numbers 1 to 9. If you can answer "yes" to a question, put a check mark after that number. Continue editing until you can answer "yes" to all the questions.

### Editing Checklist

#### Conventions

**GRAMMAR**
_____ **1.** Have I correctly used passive and active voice and more complex verb tenses?
_____ **2.** Have I used the right words *(there, their, they're)*?

**SENTENCE STRUCTURE**
_____ **3.** Do I correctly use restrictive and nonrestrictive relative clauses to combine sentences?

**MECHANICS (Capitalization and Punctuation)**
_____ **4.** Do I begin every sentence with a capital letter?
_____ **5.** Have I capitalized proper nouns and adjectives?
_____ **6.** Do I punctuate restrictive and nonrestrictive phrases, clauses, and contrasting expressions correctly?
_____ **7.** Have I correctly cited my sources? (See pages **396** and **407–410**.)

**SPELLING**
_____ **8.** Have I spelled all my words correctly?
_____ **9.** Have I consulted a dictionary to determine or check the spellings of words my spell-checker may have missed?

### Creating a Title

When you write informational essays and reports, it's important to engage your reader with an attention-getting title. Here are some ideas:

- Establish the proper tone: **A Plague for the Ages**
- Catch the reader's attention: **The "Wee-Beasties" of Death**

---

### Differentiated Instruction: Struggling Learners

Remind students that reading the essay aloud one last time is an effective way to check for editing conventions. For example, when pausing at the end of a sentence, check for a period, a question mark, or an exclamation point and make sure the next sentence begins with a capital letter.

**TEKS** 10.18A

# Publishing

## Sharing Your Essay

After editing your essay, make a neat final draft, proofread it, and share it. Ask your teacher or your classmates for feedback so that you can make a few final improvements (see pages **49–54**). Then, consider publishing ideas such as posting it on a Web site, submitting your writing for publication, or turning your writing into a multimedia presentation. (See the suggestions below.)

**Make a final copy.** Follow your teacher's instructions or use the guidelines below to format your essay. (If you are using a computer, see pages **72–74**.) Create a clean final copy of your essay and carefully proofread it.

## Focusing on Presentation

- Use blue or black ink and write neatly.
- Write your name in the upper left corner of page 1.
- Skip a line and center your title; skip another line and start your writing.
- Indent every paragraph and leave a one-inch margin on all four sides.
- Write your last name and the page number in the upper right corner of every page after page 1.

### Ideas for Publishing

**Post Your Essay on a Web Site**
Upload your paper to a school or personal Web site. Add graphic elements, sounds, and images that will appeal to your audience, show your point of view, and enhance your essay.

**Submit Your Essay**
Submit your essay to a school publication or create a class anthology.

**Create a Multimedia Presentation**
Use the information and same point of view in your essay to create a multimedia presentation. Include visual aids, graphics, images, and sounds that will appeal to your audience.

*Expository*

---

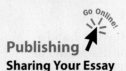

# Publishing

## Sharing Your Essay

Suggest having a classmate who has not read the student's essay read it for a final check to identify any remaining errors. Remind students not to forget the importance of **careful proofreading** when preparing their final copies. As students proofread for conventions, have them look for errors that are easy to miss:

- numerical errors and omissions in citations,
- using the wrong word (*their* for *there; to* for *too*), and
- simple misspellings (*be* for *me; my* for *by*).

TEKS 10.13E

**Make a final copy.** Review formatting for both handwritten and computer formatting.

### Focusing on Presentation

Show students a correctly formatted model essay for visual reinforcement.

TEKS 10.15D

## Technology Connections

- *Write Source Online* **Portfolio**
- *Write Source Online* **Essay Scoring**

---

## Differentiated Instruction: English Language Learners

ELPS 2C, 2D, 2E, 2H, 2I, 3F, 5A, 5C, 5E, 5F

| ELP Level **Beginning** | ELP Level **Intermediate** | ELP Level **Advanced/Advanced High** |
|---|---|---|
| Write *there, their,* and *they're* on the board. With the help of a partner, have students practice role-playing its meaning. | Read several sentences using homographs aloud. After each sentence, students hold up the card with the correct word/spelling used. | Have students edit independently, but encourage them to ask you or an English-proficient student for clarification or help if needed. |

TEKS **10.13E** Revise the final draft in response to feedback from peers and teacher/publish written work; **10.15D** Produce a multimedia presentation with graphics, images, and sound; **ELPS 2C** Learn new language structures and basic vocabulary heard during classroom instruction; **2D** Monitor understanding of spoken language during classroom instruction; **2E** Use visual/contextual/linguistic support to enhance understanding of increasingly complex spoken language; **2H** Understand implicit ideas in increasingly complex spoken language; **2I** Demonstrate listening comprehension in increasingly complex spoken language by following directions; **3F** Ask for information/ranging from using a limited high-frequency vocabulary to using abstract and content-based vocabulary during speaking; **5A** Learn relationships between sounds and letters to represent sounds when writing in English; **5C** Spell familiar words/employ spelling patterns and rules with increasing accuracy; **5E** Employ increasingly complex grammatical structures in content area writing; **5F** Write using a variety of grade-appropriate sentence lengths, patterns, and connecting words/combine in increasingly accurate ways

## Evaluating a Cause-Effect Essay

Instruct students to cover up the left-hand column with a piece of paper or their hand as they read the example essay. Then ask them to list reasons why they believe this essay received a score of 4. At the end of each page, have them compare their answers with the side notes.

As they read, encourage students to sound any unknown vocabulary and use context to determine its meaning. DIFFERENTIATE INSTRUCTION ↘

⭐ ELPS 3A, 4K

**172**

# Evaluating a Cause-Effect Essay

To learn how to evaluate a cause-effect essay, you will use the scoring guide on pages **60–61** and the essays that follow. These essays are examples of writing for each score on the scoring guide (1–4).

Notice that the first essay received a score of 4. Read the description for a score of 4 on page **60**. Then read the essay. Use the same steps to study the other examples. As you read, concentrate on the overall quality of the writing in each example.

**Writing that fits a score of 4 is highly effective.**

The **beginning** introduces the writer's focus. (underlined)

Thesis is clear and establishes cause-effect relationship.

Each **middle** paragraph presents details about the experience.

Nonrestrictive clauses add sentence variety. Quotations add interest and come from a reliable source.

### A Famine That Crushed a Nation

Ever since 1600 when the potato was successfully introduced in Ireland, the Irish had depended upon it for food. In September 1845, an airborn fungus found in the holds of ships traveling from North America to England, created a blight that destroyed crops throughout Ireland. <u>From 1845 to 1850, the Irish potato famine ravaged the country, leading to over a million deaths from starvation and disease and forcing over two million people to emigrate to the United States and Canada.</u>

The five year blight had not only caused crop failure and low food supplies, but it had also driven prices beyond the reach of the poor and destroyed the source of income for small farmers. With the widespread starvation, diseases such as typhus, dysentery, and scurvy began to weaken and kill people of all ages. One man told the British House of Commons in 1847 "a quarter of [Ireland's] population will perish unless you come to her relief" (NBE). Yet many in England, which governed Ireland, did not fully understand the scope of the disaster or even care to help the Irish. Many, like Lord Trevelyan, the British Treasury Secretary, believed that Irish misery was caused by their own "inferior" way of life, and he considered the famine a "sharp but effectual remedy by which the cure is likely to be effected." (Donnelly 6)

Much of the responsibility for the poor was placed on the shoulders of the English landlords, who owned large estates in Ireland and rented small plots of land to tenant farmers. Some

Expository

**Writer stays on topic as ideas are developed. Specific examples develop ideas and add interest. All ideas are relevant to the topic and evidence is well-documented.**

**Transitions connect paragraphs and ideas within paragraphs.**

**Each paragraph presents details about the experience.**

**Conclusion effectively summarizes the causes and effects of the famine.**

landlords attempted to do their part, but often they did not care about their Irish renters, especially when rents had not been paid because of the blight. Many landlords did not want the expense of caring for tenants. Also, since their potato crops had been destroyed, they could make more money by using the land for sheep or cattle. Landlords had tenants arrested and their families thrown out of their homes. In 1850, over 104,000 people were evicted, and "one landlord, the Earl of Lucan, evicted 187 families (913 people) in 18 months." (NBE) Starving, homeless families roamed the countryside, often having only grass and weeds to eat.

The potato blight continued and after a few years, the famine had ruined the economy. Ireland could not handle all of the unemployed poor. Left without choices, thousands began to emigrate to England, but most went to Canada or the United States. Landlords often paid for their tenants to emigrate just to get rid of them. Hundreds of families were crammed onto ships. Conditions on the ships were terrible and many of the people who made the voyage were weak and sick. The ships became known as "coffin ships" because so many passengers died on board. Things weren't much better when they arrived. The sick often died waiting to get into their new coutries, which didn't have the facilities to handle the thousands who arrived.

The potato famine of 1845 to 1850, turned a delicate balance of government policies, economic conditions, and single-crop dependency into a terrible crisis. First, the crop loss and starvation created horrible suffering. Then, England's government failed to grasp the scope of the disaster or come up with policies to help the people. The famine increased Britain's power, which made it possible for self-serving landlords to evict their tenants and forced many people to leave Ireland under terrible conditions. Although the mass migration brought a new mix of people to North America, the huge loss of its population crippled Ireland. Many years passed before the country was able to recover from the damage done to its economy, the food supply, and its people.

After reading the essay, have students express their overall impressions of the essay and its score. Sample comments could include:

**Focus and Coherence:** The first paragraph clearly focuses on the Irish potato famine and directs the reader to follow a cause-and-effect relationship.

**Organization:** The thesis is clearly stated and supported throughout each paragraph.

**Development of Ideas:** The writer develops the cause-and-effect relationship and stays on topic.

**Voice:** The writer shows genuine interest in and knowledge of the topic through sentences such as: *Yet many in England, which governed Ireland, did not fully understand the scope of the disaster or even care to help the Irish.*

**Conventions:** Use of nonrestrictive clauses (first sentence in paragraph 3) adds variety to sentence structure and makes the essay interesting to read.

 **ELPS** 3C, 4K

---

**Differentiated Instruction:
English Language Learners**

 **ELPS** 1C, 2D, 2E, 3F, 3G, 3H, 4G, 4I

| ELP Level **Beginning** | ELP Level **Intermediate** | ELP Level **Advanced/Advanced High** |
|---|---|---|
| Show pictures that illustrate relevant words such as *famine, blight, starvation* and have students practice speaking/writing them. | Use echo reading to read the essay. Then have students draw and label pictures summarizing the essay. | Have students describe specific examples in each paragraph of the highly effective writing strategies mentioned in the side notes boxes. |

**ELPS 1C** Use strategic learning techniques to acquire basic and grade-level vocabulary; **2D** Monitor understanding of spoken language during classroom instruction/interactions; **2E** Use visual support to enhance and confirm understanding of increasingly complex spoken language; **3C** Speak using a variety of grammatical structures/sentence lengths and types/connecting words with increasing accuracy and ease; **3F** Give information/ranging from using a limited high-frequency vocabulary to using abstract and content-based vocabulary during speaking; **3G** Express opinions, ideas, and feelings ranging from communicating short phrases to participating in discussions; **3H** Explain with increasing specificity and detail; **4G** Demonstrate comprehension of increasingly complex English/summarizing material; **4I** Demonstrate comprehension by employing and expanding basic reading skills/understanding of supporting ideas and details, summarizing text, and distinguishing main ideas from details; **4K** Demonstrate comprehension and expand reading skills by employing analytical skills/evaluating written information and performing critical analyses

Again instruct students to cover up the left-hand column with a piece of paper or their hand as they read the example essay. Then ask them to list reasons why they believe this essay received a score of 3. At the end of each page, have them compare their answers with the side notes.

As they read, encourage students to sound any unknown vocabulary and use context to determine its meaning. **DIFFERENTIATE INSTRUCTION ↘**

⭐ **ELPS** 3A, 4K

**Writing that fits a score of 3 is generally effective.**

**3**

The **introduction** presents the controlling idea. Cause-effect relationship is stated.

### Sugar and the Slave Trade

Today we don't think much about the sugar we put into coffee, but from the 17th to 19th centuries it was a precious substance, bought with the blood and labor of many African slaves. Sugar and slaves are two sides of whats called the Triangle Trade. "Slaves of the Caribbean sugar plantations produced molasses that was transported to New England for distillation into rum that was shipped to Africa in exchange for the slaves who would endure the final leg of the triangle, the horrific Middle Passage to the sugar islands." (Westfield 69)

Each **middle** paragraph continues to develop the thesis statement.

Sugar was grown and processed in the Caribbean in the 1500s by the Spanish. English and French colonies also started producing it by the 1600s. By 1700, thousands of slaves were being used to grow the sugar cane. It was very hard and difficult work, and it required a lot of slaves to plant it, harvest it, and grind it. Then the sugar cane had to be boiled to produce sugar. The leftover liquid from this process was molasses.

Molasses was used to produce rum. Merchants in New England bought the molasses cheaply to make rum, which cost very little to produce. "Tiny Rhode Island had more than 30 distilleries, 22 of them in Newport. In Massachusetts, 63 distilleries produced 2.7 million gallons of rum in 1774." (Hooper 72) They would then use the rum to buy slaves. "Slaves costing the equivalent of £4 or £5 in rum or bar iron in West Africa were sold in the West Indies in 1746 for £30 to £80." (Hooper 76) Slave traders from Newport alone had 150 slave ships and traded rum for over 106,000 slaves.

Specific examples add interest and support the thesis. Researched, relevant evidence supports thesis and shows writer's knowledge of topic.

The slave trade was so profitable that it affected the whole economy of New England. "When the British in 1763 proposed a tax on sugar and molasses, Massachusetts merchants pointed out that these were staples of the slave trade, and the loss of that would throw 5,000 seamen out of work in the colony and idle almost 700 ships." (Hooper 94) Many of the important families of New England were involved in the slave trade. For example, the founders of Brown University owned slave ships and used slaves in their factories. Boat makers also became wealthy.

The demand for sugar kept the triangle trade going. Slaves were brought in to work on the sugar plantations,. The plantations sent the molasses to New England to make rum, and then the rum was used to trade for more slaves to be sent to the plantations. There were lots of people who thought slavery was immoral and wanted to end it, but the abolition movement really had not become strong enough. In any case, people did not stop buying sugar. Eventually there were so many planatations, though, that there was too much sugar on the market and eventually prices dropped, and plantations went out of business.

Even after slavery had ended in the north (in the late 1700s), the slave trade continued. "Some 156,000 slaves were brought to the United States in the period 1801-08, almost all of them on ships that sailed from New England ports that had recently outlawed slavery." (Hooper 105) Most of the slaves were now sold in the American South.

The sugar industry also led to the first independent nation ruled by former slaves. Haiti was a French colony that was one of the biggest producers of sugar. There were over half a million slaves there by 1789. The American and French revolutions inspired the slaves to revolt in 1791, and they burned down plantations. Even though Napoleon sent troups to the island, the slaves led by Toussaint Louverture, declared independence in 1804.

The production of sugar was one of the major reasons that the slave trade became so important. It created a triangle trade that ended up taking millions of people to work as slaves on sugar plantations in the Caribbean. This, in turn, led to the production of rum in New England, which was traded for more slaves in Africa. The slave trade affected the whole American economy and eventually led to the Civil War.

**Occasional lapses in organization and non-developed ideas detract.**

**Each middle paragraph contains relevant supporting evidence. Errors in conventions may lead to confusion.**

**Conclusion effectively sums up the thesis and adds an additional effect, the Civil War.**

Expository

After reading the essay, have students express their overall impressions of the essay and its score. Ask: What parts of the essay stood out to them as needing improvement? How did its organization and development of ideas compare with the essay that scored a 4?

Remind students that although spelling and grammatical errors often stand out in a piece, they are only one part of the scoring component. In holistic scoring, the entire writing is taken into consideration when assigning a score. Even though this essay had several conventions errors, it was still generally effective because it has strengths in many of the traits.

 **ELPS** 3C, 3D, 4K

## Differentiated Instruction: English Language Learners

**ELPS** 2A, 2F, 2G, 2I, 3E, 5D

| ELP Level **Beginning** | ELP Level **Intermediate** | ELP Level **Advanced/Advanced High** |
|---|---|---|
| Read the essay aloud and have students keep track of when they hear dates, references to countries, and vocabulary such as *sugar, slave, slavery,* etc. | Read the text aloud and have students use a graphic organizer to identify the main idea and supporting details of each paragraph. | Have students read the text with a partner and circle or underline errors in English conventions (*prescious, whats,* etc.). |
|  | Use pages 624–625 |  |

**ELPS** **2A** Distinguish sounds with increasing ease; **2F** Listen to and derive meaning from a variety of media to build and reinforce concept and language attainment; **2G** Understand the general meaning, main points, and important details of spoken language/topics, languages, and contexts are familiar to unfamiliar; **2I** Demonstrate listening comprehension in increasingly complex spoken language by taking notes; **3C** Speak using a variety of grammatical structures/sentence lengths and types/connecting words with increasing accuracy and ease; **3D** Speak using grade-level content area vocabulary/new words and academic language proficiency; **3E** Share information in cooperative learning interactions; **4K** Demonstrate comprehension and expand reading skills by employing analytical skills/evaluating written information and performing critical analyses; **5D** Edit writing for standard grammar and usage/subject-verb and pronoun agreement and appropriate verb tenses

Again instruct students to cover up the left-hand column with a piece of paper or their hand as they read the example essay. Then ask them to list reasons why they believe this essay received a score of 2. At the end of each page, have them compare their answers with the side notes.

After reading the essay, have students express their overall impressions of the essay and its score. Ask: *How did the errors in conventions and lack of organization affect your ability to gain meaning from the essay?*

As a class, discuss and write on the board a clear thesis statement for this essay. Then working in small groups, have students revise the three middle paragraphs for organization and consistency of verb tense.

**ELPS** 3C, 3D, 4K, 5B, 5C, 5D, 5E

**Writing that fits a score of 2 is somewhat effective.**

The **introduction** does not present a clear thesis or show a cause-effect relationship.

**Middle** paragraphs are in chronological order, but organization does not support cause-effect relationship.

Misspellings and errors in verb tenses impede understanding. Sentences do not relate to each other or to the thesis.

Essay lacks **conclusion.** Paragraphs read more like lists than developed ideas.

### The Conquest of Mexico

In 1519, Hernán Cortés sailed from Cuba to Mexico with a fleet of 11 ships and 550 men. In three years he manages to defeat the native tribes who lived in the country, including the powerful Aztecs. He did it by a combination of luck and bravery and skill.

Cortés comes to Mexico because he was looking for gold. His first bit of good luck was finding people who can translate the native languages for him so that helped him make friends with smaller tribes who hated the Aztecs. He also scares the natives by showing them horses and powerful weapons like his cannons. Before going to meet the Aztecs in Tenochtitlán, Cortés burns all his ships so that his men wouldn't dessert him.

Cortés didn't know about his next bit of luck that the Aztec king Moctezuma had omens that something bad was going to happen, and he thought Cortés might be the god Quetzalcoatl who was supposed to return and reclaim his kingdom. So Moctezuma didn't want to fight Cortés at first. He sent gifts instead hoping that would satisfy Cortés. But the gold gifts just made the Spanish want more gold.

When the Spanish gets to Tenochtitlán Cortés took Moctezuma captive, which he thought this would keep the outnumbered Spanish safe. After eight months, though Cortés has to leave the city to fight some Spanish who had come to arrest him for disobeying the governor of Cuba. Cortés defeats the Spanish, but when he got back to Tenochtitlán, things were a mess. Cortés had left someone in charge, but he didn't do a good job and the Aztecs began to rebel.

Many Spanish were killed but they were able to escape from the city. Cortés was lucky once again. While he was gone, the Aztecs came down with smallpox, which was brought by the Spanish. Many of them died. Cortéz returned after about six months. He had more Indian allies. The Aztecs fought for 80 days, but Cortés finally defeated them. (Wood)

 **ELPS 3C** Speak using a variety of grammatical structures/ sentence lengths and types/connecting words with increasing accuracy and ease; **3D** Speak using grade-level content area vocabulary/new words and academic language proficiency; **4K** Demonstrate comprehension and expand reading skills by employing analytical skills/evaluating written information and performing critical analyses; **5B** Write using newly acquired basic and content-based grade-level vocabulary; **5C** Spell familiar words/employ spelling patterns and rules with increasing accuracy; **5D** Edit writing for standard grammar and usage/subject-verb and pronoun agreement and appropriate verb tenses; **5E** Employ increasingly complex grammatical structures in content area writing such as using correct verbs, tenses, and pronouns/possessive case/ negatives and contractions

Writing that fits a score of 1 is not effective.

**1**

The **introduction** presents a vague thesis, but ideas are not connected. Incorrect punctuation, grammar errors, and problems in sentence structure distract the reader.

### The Silk Road

The Silk Road is one of the worlds oldest trade routes. It goes from China to the Mediteranean. People have traveled on it since around 150 BC, though China stopped using it around 1400 AD and it wasn't just used for silk even though thats what its called. It brought Chinese products and inventions all the way to Europe and visa versa. Religion also spread.

Other things from China besides silk. Spices, paper and gunpowder for example. Eurapean traitors brought Eurapean things back to China too, like glass, ivory and perfume. Many ideas went back and fourth. Religion was very important. Buddism started in India and then it was brought to China.

Around 1 AD silk made it all the way from China to Rome, Italy. No one could figure out how it was made, but everyone in Rome liked to. No one could figure it out until around 400 AD when a princess smuggled silkworms out of China. By the next century they were able to grow silkworms in Europe so it wasn't as important to trade silk anymore.

Most traitors didn't travel over the whole, complete entire road they would just travel over part of the road like the part in there own country and then they would trade off with someone in the next country who would trade with the next county and so on and so on. In 1271 though, Marco Polo travelled from Italy all the way to China. He didn't go home for 24 years! When he got back he wrote a popular book and so he could describe what he had seen on his trip.

Of import for the world's development were the inventions and ideas shared between east and west as the result of the increased trade and communication. Can we underestimate the impact that inventions like the plow, paper or movable type had on the development of the west? Similarly, China was immeasurably enriched by the introduction of Buddism from India.

Organization is not evident. Paragraphs are out of order. Examples are listed, not developed. No evidence is presented to support ideas.

**Conclusion** is ineffective and does not tie essay together.

*Expository*

After they read, discuss students' expression of their overall impressions of the essay and its score. Point out that, although the essay is written using third person point of view, word choice and lack of organization detract from an interested and confident voice.

Challenge students to locate the conventions errors in the first two paragraphs. Some examples include:

1. The third sentence is a run-on sentence.
2. The apostrophe is missing in the word "it's" on line 4.
3. "Vice versa" is misspelled in line 6.
4. The first two sentences in paragraph 2 are incomplete.
5. "Traders" is misspelled in sentence 3 of paragraph 2. ✏ **DIFFERENTIATE INSTRUCTION**

🔷 **ELPS** 3C, 3D, 4K, 5D, 5E

---

## Differentiated Instruction: English Language Learners

🔷 **ELPS** 1B, 2D, 2F, 3C, 3F, 5C, 5D

| ELP Level **Beginning** | ELP Level **Intermediate** | ELP Level **Advanced/Advanced High** |
|---|---|---|
| Choral read several sentences, stopping after each to have students practice asking questions for clarification, using model questions from the board. | Have students role play writer and reader of the essay, taking turns asking questions for clarification. | Using a copy of the essay, have students practice using editing/proofreader's marks for the last three paragraphs, focusing on spelling and grammatical errors. |

**ELPS 1B** Monitor oral/written language and employ self-corrective techniques; **2D** Monitor understanding of spoken language during classroom instruction and seek clarification of spoken language as needed; **2F** Listen to and derive meaning from a variety of media to build and reinforce concept and language attainment; **3C** Speak using a variety of grammatical structures/sentence lengths and types/connecting words with increasing accuracy and ease; **3D** Speak using grade-level content area vocabulary/new words and academic language proficiency; **3F** Ask for and give information/ranging from using a limited high-frequency vocabulary to using abstract and content-based vocabulary during speaking; **4K** Demonstrate comprehension and expand reading skills by employing analytical skills/evaluating written information and performing critical analyses; **5C** Spell familiar words/employ spelling patterns and rules with increasing accuracy; **5D** Edit writing for standard grammar and usage/subject-verb and pronoun agreement and appropriate verb tenses; **5E** Employ increasingly complex grammatical structures in content area writing such as using correct verbs, tenses, and pronouns/possessive case/negatives and contractions

## Evaluating and Reflecting on Your Writing

Students should complete the activity, finishing each of the sentence starters. Encourage students to add any additional thoughts they have about their essay to the reflection.

Suggest that students keep their reflections (along with all their planning notes, drafts, and the final version of the essay) in files in case they need to refer to them when compiling a portfolio.

## Evaluating and Reflecting on Your Writing

After you have completed your cause-effect essay, take a few moments to reflect on your writing experience. On your own paper, finish each of the sentence starters below. To score your writing, refer to the scoring guide on pages 60–61 and the examples you just read. Evaluating and reflecting on your writing will help you see how you are growing as a writer.

**My Cause-Effect Essay**

1. The introduction and conclusion work together because . . .

2. The prewriting activity that worked best for me was . . .

3. The ideas that need better development are . . .

4. I need to use a more confident voice or show more evidence in . . .

5. Reviewing the sentence structure I used and mechanics, in my next cause-effect essay, I would like to . . .

6. One question I still have about writing a cause-effect essay is . . .

---

**Differentiated Instruction:**
**English Language Learners**

ELPS 1D, 2C, 3D, 3F

| ELP Level **Beginning** | ELP Level **Intermediate** | ELP Level **Advanced/Advanced High** |
|---|---|---|
| Give students a list of concepts and review their meanings. Have students place a check mark next to words with positive connotations. | Have the students create a chart listing 15–20 words, then labeling the words' connotations, placing a check mark under either +, neutral, or –. | Using only concepts, play a game like Twenty Questions; have students take turns asking questions of the answerer/teacher. |

**ELPS 1D** Speak using learning strategies/request assistance, employ non-verbal cues, and convey ideas by defining or describing; **2C** Learn new expressions and academic vocabulary heard during classroom instruction/interactions; **3D** Speak using grade-level content area vocabulary/academic language proficiency; **3F** Ask for information/ranging from using a limited high-frequency vocabulary to using abstract and content-based vocabulary during speaking

# Expository Writing
## Defining a Concept

What is the real meaning of freedom? How do you explain love, health, or strength? What does it mean to compromise, enjoy, communicate, or celebrate? While you can look up these words in a dictionary, each of them represents a concept that extends far beyond any single definition.

In this chapter, you'll read a sample expository essay that presents a detailed definition of compromise, going well beyond the basic definition of the term. After that, you'll be asked to choose another interesting term and write your own expository essay of definition—one that shows your understanding of the concept and its importance.

### Writing Guidelines

Subject: **A complex term**
Purpose: **To define the concept**
Form: **Essay of definition**
Audience: **Classmates**

"A concept is stronger than a fact."
—Charlotte P. Gillman

## Defining a Concept

### Objectives
- understand that an essay of definition is a form of expository writing
- use what has been learned about expository writing to create an essay defining a concept
- plan, draft, revise, edit, and share an essay of definition

Briefly discuss what developing an extended definition entails. For example:
- Dictionary definitions can be difficult to understand without additional explanations and examples.
- The *denotation* of a word is its dictionary meaning. The *connotation* of a word is the meaning or feeling it suggests beyond its dictionary definition. When writing an essay of definition, students must focus a great deal of attention on a word's connotation—what the word means to the writer, what it means to other people, and so on.

### Writing Guidelines
Remind students to use vocabulary fitted to their audience. ✔ DIFFERENTIATE INSTRUCTION

### Resources

#### Copy Masters (see Appendix)

- T-chart (TE p. 183, 189)
- Quick list (TE p. 189)
- Time line (TE p. 189)
- Venn diagram (TE p. 189)

#### Benchmark Papers
#### (see Appendix)

## Essay of Definition

Review the structure of the essay before having students read it. After they have read the essay, ask questions about the writer's thesis and the evidence and details the writer uses to support her thesis. Also have students identify the rhetorical devices the writer uses.

The essay can also be used for a review of prepositions. Note that prepositions help a writer express the relationship of one word or idea to another. Challenge students to point out prepositional phrases in the sample and to explain how they function in the essay. Possible responses:

- Paragraph 1: *to arrive at common ground*—The phrase helps express the idea of two people working together toward a common goal.
- Paragraph 2: *In terms of usage, compromise is used*—The transition leads to a discussion of the topic word's grammatical aspects.
- Paragraph 6: *from maintaining friendships to conducting business*—The prepositions help to explain the range of activities that involve compromise.

**TEKS** 10.13B, 10.15A(i), 10.15A(ii), 10.15A(iii), 10.15A(iv), 10.15A(v)

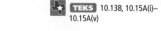
## Essay of Definition

In the following essay, Veronica Baban explains a concept that is valuable in all aspects of life.

### Compromise: Let's Meet in the Middle

**Beginning**
The beginning introduces the topic and presents the thesis statement, which is clearly stated (underlined).

Do people have to work hard in order to reach an agreement? Do the parties involved often give up something to arrive at common ground? If so, they know what it means to compromise. They understand that they can't always get everything they want in every situation, that life often involves as much "giving" as it does "taking." In fact, the concept of the compromise lies at the very heart of social interaction.

**Middle**
Each middle paragraph presents relevant evidence and well chosen details that support the thesis statement. Rhetorical devices, questions and quotations, help sustain reader interest. The voice and word choice is appropriate for the audience, purpose and context.

First, to understand the concept of compromise, we need to understand the meaning of the word. The dictionary defines compromise as "a settlement of differences in which each side makes concessions." In terms of usage, compromise is used as a verb or a noun: When someone compromises (*a verb*), he or she reaches an agreement or a compromise (*a noun*). The modern word *compromise* comes from the Latin word *compromissum*, meaning "mutual promise." Common synonyms for compromise include "settlement," "agreement," "bring to terms," "strike a balance," and "resolve." The opposite of compromising is to act unilaterally, without thinking about the other side.

There is an old saying, "A compromise is an agreement where nobody's happy." As in all sayings, this one has a grain of truth. In a compromise both sides must give up something. Of course, a compromise can be influenced by the relative power of the two sides. For example, an employer or a teacher has more power than an employee or a student, which may affect the eventual agreement. Still, working out compromises is essential in both work- and school-related situations.

Moreover, compromise has played a key role throughout history. The Magna Carta, signed in England in 1215 by King John and his chief nobles, may be the most famous historical compromise. The king had to renounce certain royal powers, respect key legal procedures, and accept that the will of the king could be bound by law. The United States Constitution, framed in the 1700s, is another masterpiece of compromise. This

**TEKS** **10.13B** Structure ideas in a sustained way; **10.15A(i)** Write an analytical essay that includes an introductory paragraph and a variety of sentence structures; **10.15A(ii)** Write an analytical essay that includes rhetorical devices; **10.15A(iii)** Write an analytical essay that includes an idea or thesis; **10.15(iv)** Write an analytical essay that includes a structure appropriate to the purpose; **10.15A(v)** Write an analytical essay that includes relevant evidence and details

**TEKS** 10.13B, 10.15A(i) –10.15A(vi)
**ELPS** 4K

Expository

document established the balance of power between the executive, legislative, and judicial branches of government, a critical compromise that is a foundation of American life.

Most agreements between countries or regions represent compromise. Because of deception or different values, these agreements may not always succeed. The Missouri Compromise is a famous agreement in United States history. Northern states allowed the new state of Missouri to be a slave state with the understanding that no other slave states would be admitted to the Union. The compromise lasted for more than 30 years, but slavery was a polarizing issue that eventually led to the Civil War.

Finally, the ability to compromise is critical in all aspects of life—from maintaining friendships to conducting business. It is especially useful within a family. A husband may enjoy professional sports, while his wife may enjoy attending concerts. In a strong marriage there would be a compromise, each partner occasionally sharing in the other partner's interest. Or a teenage son may want more use of the family car. His parents suggest that he work a little harder around the house; in return they will free up the car more often. The son agrees with the compromise, and everyone is satisfied.

In many ways, compromise makes free societies work. Whatever the situation, the two sides must determine what is most important to them and what they will be willing to give up. Then, and only then, the give and take of ideas can take place until a compromise is reached. British statesman Edmund Burke identified the value of compromise best when he stated: "All government—indeed, every human benefit and enjoyment, every virtue and every prudent act—is founded on compromise and barter."

**Middle**
Transitions between sentences and paragraphs connect ideas and details. The essay expands the definition from historical to personal, showing the relative value of the ideas, data, and facts presented.

**Ending**
The conclusion puts the concept in perspective and ties the essay to the thesis statement.

**Respond to the reading.** Answer the following questions.

**Focus and Coherence** (1) How does the conclusion support the thesis statement? **Organization** (2) How is the essay structured? (3) How does the writer show the relative value of ideas, facts, and data that support the thesis? **Development of Ideas** (4) What parts of the definition stand out? Explain your answer to a classmate. **Voice** (5) How would you describe the writer's voice (comical, personal, interested, informative)? Explain your choice to a classmate.

**Respond to the reading.**

**Answers**

**Focus and Coherence 1.** It refers back to the idea that *compromise lies at the very heart of social interaction*, which is part of the thesis statement in the first paragraph.

**Organization 2.** The essay's focus moves from specific definition and grammar usage to more general description and application. **3.** by expanding the idea of compromise from historical to personal examples

**Development of Ideas 4.** Possible responses:
- the idea that both sides give up something in a compromise—it is interesting that both sides sacrifice in order to gain
- the historical example of the Magna Carta—it is interesting that a king was willing to compromise for the good of his country
- the historical example of the U.S. Constitution—it is interesting that the precepts of the Magna Carta are still in effect today
- the interpersonal examples of family compromise—the idea is applied to familiar situations that might interest the reader personally

**Voice 5.** Interested and informative. The writer gives a variety of examples to support her ideas about the importance of compromise. ✔ **DIFFERENTIATE INSTRUCTION**

**TEKS** 10.13B, 10.15A(i), 10.15A(ii), 10.15A(iii), 10.15A(iv), 10.15A(v), 10.15A(vi); **ELPS** 4K

---

**Differentiated Instruction: English Language Learners**

**ELPS** 2C, 2E, 2G, 2H, 3B, 3G, 4K

| **ELP Level** Beginning | **ELP Level** Intermediate | **ELP Level** Advanced/Advanced High |
|---|---|---|
| Have students draw pictures of a time they made a compromise, labeling relevant images in English or their first language. | Have students role-play a disagreement and how they came to a compromise. Have them define *compromise*. | Discuss the phrase *A compromise is an agreement where nobody's happy.* Form teams and debate the topic. Guide students to use formal English. |

 **TEKS** 10.13B Structure ideas in a sustained way; **10.15A(i)** Write an analytical essay that includes a concluding paragraph and a variety of sentence structures; **10.15A(ii)** Write an analytical essay that includes rhetorical devices; **10.15A(iii)** Write an analytical essay that includes an idea or thesis; **10.15A(iv)** Write an analytical essay that includes a structure appropriate to the purpose; **10.15A(v)** Write an analytical essay that includes relevant evidence and details; **10.15A(vi)** Write an analytical essay that includes distinctions about specific data, facts, and ideas; **ELPS 2C** Learn basic and academic vocabulary heard during classroom instruction; **2E** Use visual and contextual support to enhance understanding of increasingly complex spoken language; **2G** Understand the general meaning, main points, and important details of spoken language/topics, languages, and contexts are familiar to unfamiliar; **2H** Understand implicit ideas/information in increasingly complex spoken language; **3B** Expand vocabulary by learning and using high-frequency words; **3G** Express opinions, ideas, and feelings ranging from communicating short phrases to participating in discussions; **4K** Demonstrate comprehension and expand reading skills by employing analytical skills

## Prewriting

### Planning Your Writing

Work as a group to brainstorm abstract concepts to add to the concepts list.

**TEKS** 10.13A, 10.15A(i), 10.15A(iii)

### Focusing Your Topic

Invite students to choose a few concepts from the list the class compiled to begin their own lists. (Students who choose to write about the same concept will interpret it differently and use different examples.) Then have them freewrite for 5 to 10 minutes about one or two of their chosen concepts.

**Create your own concepts list.** Have students use the available lists as a starting point for their own brainstorming. Remind them to cross out topics that are too broad or too narrow, giving more examples of each as necessary. **DIFFERENTIATE INSTRUCTION ↘**

---

**TEKS** 10.13A, 10.15A(i), 10.15A(iii)

## Prewriting Planning Your Writing

In your expository essay, you will be defining a complex, abstract term. (An *abstract term* is one you can think about but not see or touch.) Your essay needs to be long enough to adequately cover the topic with evidence and details to support your thesis statement. Before writing her essay, Veronica brainstormed possible topics. She started with one word, *freedom*, and added others as quickly as they came to mind. Here is her list.

### Concepts List

| | | | | |
|---|---|---|---|---|
| freedom | compromise | love | humor | enemy |
| conflict | anger | sadness | friendship | failure |
| disappointment | happiness | disagreement | weakness | success |
| liberty | confusion | strength | tragedy | satisfaction |

## Focusing Your Topic

The topic should be broad enough to discuss in a multiparagraph essay—examining what the term means, how it is important historically, how it relates to real life, and so on. After brainstorming, Veronica looked over her list. She crossed out topics that were either too broad or too narrow. From the remaining words, she chose the one that she wanted to write about and put an asterisk next to it.

| | | | | |
|---|---|---|---|---|
| ~~freedom~~ | *compromise | ~~love~~ | ~~humor~~ | enemy |
| conflict | ~~anger~~ | ~~sadness~~ | friendship | failure |
| ~~disappointment~~ | ~~happiness~~ | ~~disagreement~~ | weakness | success |
| ~~liberty~~ | ~~argument~~ | strength | tragedy | ~~satisfaction~~ |

Prewrite

**Create your own concepts list.** Brainstorm a list of possible topics to define. Begin with a term that interests you and quickly write down other concepts that come to mind after that. Then look over your list, crossing out concepts that you feel will not give you the right amount of material for an essay. Finally, put an asterisk next to the topic that interests you the most. You may also want to consider the terms in Veronica's list.

---

**TEKS** 10.13B, 10.15A(iii), 10.15A(iv)

## Gathering and Organizing Details

After choosing your topic, consider what the term means, how it is important in history and in everyday life, how it is used in sayings or quotations, and so on. As Veronica researched her term, she took notes.

### Notes

> **Dictionary definition:** *a settlement of differences; both sides make concessions*
>
> **Parts of speech:** *noun and verb*
>
> **Word history:** *comes from* <u>compromissum</u>*, meaning "mutual promise"*
>
> **Synonyms:** *settlement, agreement, bring to terms, strike a balance, resolve*
>
> **Saying:** *"A compromise is an agreement where nobody's happy."*
>
> **Historical importance:** *Magna Carta, Constitution, Missouri Compromise*
>
> **Quotation:** *"All government—indeed, every human benefit and enjoyment, every virtue and every prudent act—is founded on compromise and barter."*
>
> —Edmund Burke

**Note:** Even though you may not use the exact dictionary definition in your essay, it is important to your understanding of the concept.

 **Prewrite**

**Gather and organize your details.** Research your term, taking notes as you go along. Keep in mind your audience, the purpose, and context for your writing. Begin with a dictionary definition; then include your own ideas about the term as well as examples of its historical and everyday importance. Use the information above as a guide. Remember that when you begin your draft, you will need to structure your ideas in a sustained way.

## Writing a Thesis Statement

Your thesis statement should introduce the topic and explain its importance. Veronica used this formula to write her thesis statement.

| topic | + | the topic's importance | = | thesis statement |
|---|---|---|---|---|
| Compromise | | lies at the heart of social interaction | | The concept of the compromise lies at the very heart of social interaction. |

 **Prewrite**

**Write a thesis statement.** Use the formula above to shape your thesis statement for your essay.

*Expository*

## Gathering and Organizing Details

Note that the Web site www.bartleby.com provides access to many traditional library reference books—dictionaries, thesauruses, encyclopedias, quotation books— as well as electronic versions of classic literature. The Web site is a helpful place to begin gathering details.

**Gather and organize your details.** Remind students to consider the validity of their sources as they gather information on the Internet, in magazines, etc.

**TEKS** 10.13B

## Writing a Thesis Statement

Encourage students to jot down all ideas for thesis statements that occur to them while they research their topic. They can choose the best statement after they've finished.

**Write a thesis statement.** Remind students to choose a final thesis statement that they can easily support with facts and details that fit their purpose and relate to their audience.

**TEKS** 10.15A(iii), 10.15A(iv)

---

**TEKS** **10.13B** Structure ideas in a sustained way; **10.15A(iii)** Write an analytical essay that includes an idea or thesis; **10.15A(iv)** Write an analytical essay that includes a structure appropriate to the purpose, audience, and context; **ELPS** **1A** Use prior knowledge and experience to understand meanings; **1C** Use strategic learning techniques to acquire basic and grade-level vocabulary; **2C** Learn academic vocabulary heard during classroom instruction/interactions; **3B** Expand vocabulary/learning and using high-frequency words for identifying and describing/retelling information supported by pictures/learning and using routine language for classroom communication; **5B** Write using newly acquired basic and content-based grade-level vocabulary

## Drafting
### Developing Your Ideas

Guide students through the drafting tips on the page.

### Beginning Paragraph

Have students write one of each type of attention-getting strategy for their topic, choosing the most effective. Remind them a clearly developed and stated thesis statement is imperative to the rest of the essay's organizational structure and development of ideas. If they have trouble supporting their thesis, they should consider revising it right away.

### Middle Paragraphs

Have students include *at least* three middle paragraphs in their first drafts. Remind students that a good essay presents paragraphs in the order that explains or supports the thesis statement most clearly. Encourage students to think about this before they begin writing their drafts and not to hesitate to move things around after they get started, if doing so strengthens their definitions.

### Ending Paragraph

Students should try a variety of closing strategies to find the one that works in coherence with their essay's voice. Remind students to engage the reader and maintain proper distance.

**Write your first draft.** Before students write their first drafts, display and review the five writing traits, highlighting traits with which students have had trouble. **DIFFERENTIATE INSTRUCTION ⬎**

⭐ **TEKS** 10.13A, 10.13B, 10.15A(i), 10.15A(ii), 10.15A(iv), 10.15A(v), 10.15A(vi); **ELPS** 5G

---

⭐ **TEKS** 10.13A, 10.13B, 10.15A(i), 10.15A(ii), 10.15A(iv)–10.15A(vi) **ELPS** 5G

## Drafting Developing Your Ideas

The tips below can guide your writing of each part of the essay.

## Beginning Paragraph

An effective **introduction** should get the reader's attention, give some background, and include the thesis statement, your controlling idea. Your organization should be appropriate for the audience, the purpose, and the context of the essay. Here are some strategies for starting out.

- **Provide a personal story.** My mom and I reached a compromise about the weekend. If I did the laundry, I could go to the movies.
- **Ask a challenging question.** Do people have to work hard in order to reach an agreement? Answer the question in your essay.
- **Refer to a well-known issue.** Many teenagers in El Paso wanted a skate park, but the city officials planned for a picnic area. They compromised by putting some skateboard ramps in one corner.

## Middle Paragraphs

The **middle** paragraphs should explain the concept. Be sure to structure your ideas in a sustained way. Consider these directions as you write.

- Develop a paragraph for each part of your definition.
- Write a topic sentence for each paragraph. Consider the relative value of the data, facts, and ideas you plan to include.
- Include plenty of accurate, specific details to explain each part. Be sure to include an appropriate variety of sentence structures.
- Use transitions to link ideas and rhetorical devices for interest.

## Ending Paragraph

An effective **conclusion** wraps up the definition and reminds readers of the concept's importance. Use these strategies.

- **Write a summary.** Compromise makes free societies work.
- **Suggest that the reader use the concept.** The next time your parents say "No!" ask them if they will compromise.
- **Give the reader something to think about.** If things aren't going your way, a little compromise may provide a solution.

 **Write your first draft.** Use your prewriting work (pages 182–183), the sample essay, and these suggestions. Add interesting details and examples.

Draft

---

⭐ **TEKS** **10.13A** Plan a first draft by developing a thesis or idea; **10.13B** Structure ideas in a sustained way/develop drafts in open-ended situations that include transitions and rhetorical devices; **10.15A(i)** Write an analytical essay that includes an introductory and concluding paragraph and a variety of sentence structures; **10.15A(ii)** Write an analytical essay that includes rhetorical devices; **10.15A(iv)** Write an analytical essay that includes a structure appropriate to the purpose, audience, and context; **10.15A(v)** Write an analytical essay that includes relevant evidence and details; **10.15A(vi)** Write an analytical essay that includes distinctions about specific data, facts, and ideas that support the thesis; **ELPS** **5G** Explain with increasing specificity and detail/writing

**TEKS** 10.13C

# Revising Improving Your Writing

Think about your purpose, your audience, and the genre, or form, of the draft you have written. Then use the checklist below to help you improve your essay.

## Revising Checklist

### Focus and Coherence

_____ 1. Are my introduction and conclusion effective?
_____ 2. Have I clearly stated my thesis statement?
_____ 3. Do all my ideas connect to the thesis statement?

### Organization

_____ 4. Do I include a strong introduction, middle, and conclusion?
_____ 5. Are my details in a logical order?
_____ 6. Does each paragraph have a topic sentence?
_____ 7. Have I used transitions to connect my ideas?

### Development of Ideas

_____ 8. Have I defined the concept clearly?
_____ 9. Have I included interesting examples, well thought-out details, and relevant evidence that support my thesis?
_____ 10. Have I used rhetorical devices to sustain reader interest?

### Voice

_____ 11. Does my voice fit the topic, the audience, and the purpose?
_____ 12. Do I show enthusiasm for the topic?
_____ 13. Does my word choice adequately convey subtlety of meaning?

 **Improve your first draft.** Use the checklist above as you review your first draft and make changes. If possible, ask a classmate to review your work.

*Expository*

## Revising
**Improving Your Writing**

Encourage students to use the following techniques while revising:

■ Make revision notes using a pen or pencil that is a different color from the writing in the draft.
■ Underline the thesis statement (beginning paragraph), each topic sentence (middle paragraphs), and the closing statement (last paragraph).
■ Circle the transitions to make them stand out.
■ Underline at least three or four general words in the draft. Would replacing some or all of these words improve the writing?
■ Put brackets around technical terms. Are all the terms defined for the reader?

 **TEKS** 10.13C

Have students exchange essays and read each other's draft aloud. Remind students to listen for voice and sentence fluency. Finally, have students work on their revision independently.

**Improve your first draft.** Have students write the numbers 1–13 on a piece of paper and place a check mark next to the numbers to which they can answer *yes*. Challenge them to revise for any numbered items without check marks.

## Differentiated Instruction: English Language Learners

**ELPS** 1B, 1E, 1G, 1H, 5A, 5B, 5F, 5G

| ELP Level **Beginning** | ELP Level **Intermediate** | ELP Level **Advanced/Advanced High** |
|---|---|---|
| Amend the length of the essay to a paragraph with a topic sentence, at least three supporting sentences (or phrases), and a concluding sentence. | Have students write at least an introduction, one middle paragraph, and a conclusion, focusing on using clear and effective transitions. | Challenge students to write a complete essay, focusing on formal English usage and employing a variety of sentence structures. |

 **TEKS** 10.13C Revise drafts/improve style, word choice, and subtlety of meaning and rethink how well the purpose, audience, and genre have been addressed; **ELPS 1B** Monitor written language and employ self-corrective techniques or other resources; **1E** Internalize new basic and academic language by using and reusing it/writing; **1G** Demonstrate increasing ability to distinguish between formal/informal English and an increasing knowledge of when to use each one; **1H** Develop and expand learning strategies/reasoning, looking for patterns in language, and analyzing sayings and expressions; **5A** Learn relationships between sounds and letters to represent sounds when writing in English; **5B** Write using content-based grade-level vocabulary; **5F** Write using a variety of grade-appropriate sentence lengths, patterns, and connecting words/combine in increasingly accurate ways; **5G** Explain with increasing specificity and detail/writing

## Editing

### Checking for Conventions

As needed, review any of the conventions that your students find difficult. For instance, review subject and verb agreement with sample sentences.

**\*** For more about the agreement of subject and verb, see SE page 595.

**Edit your essay of definition.** Provide two-sided copies of this checklist to students, who should use one side for editing their own draft and the other for having a peer edit their draft.

**TEKS** 10.13C, 10.13D, 10.13E, 10.17C, 10.18A, 10.18B, 10.19; **ELPS** 5C, 5D, 5E

## Publishing

### Sharing Your Writing

Set aside time for students to read their essays aloud in writing groups. Have the group provide feedback after each reading. **DIFFERENTIATE INSTRUCTION ↘**

### Conventions Connections

**Grammar: Subject-Verb Agreement**
- **Student Edition** page 595;
  **Proofreader's Guide** pages 746–747, 766–767, 778–779, 780–781
- **SkillsBook** pages 126, 147–149

### Technology Connections

**↖ Write Source Online Portfolio**

**↖ Write Source Online Essay Scoring**

---

**186**

 **TEKS** 10.13C–10.13E, 10.17C, 10.18A, 10.18B, 10.19 **ELPS** 5C–5E

## Editing Checking for Conventions

When you have completed your revising, it's time to edit your paper for grammar, sentence structure, capitalization, punctuation, and spelling.

### Editing Checklist

#### Conventions

**GRAMMAR**

_____ 1. Do my verbs and subjects agree in number *(they were,* not *they was)*?

**SENTENCE STRUCTURE**

_____ 2. Do I use a variety of correctly structured sentences that clearly communicate ideas?

**MECHANICS (Capitalization and Punctuation)**

_____ 3. Did I capitalize all proper nouns and proper adjectives?

_____ 4. Did I capitalize the first word in each sentence?

_____ 5. Have I used end punctuation correctly?

_____ 6. Have I used commas correctly, especially in phrases and clauses?

**SPELLING**

_____ 7. Did I double-check my spelling and look for errors my spell-checker might miss?

_____ 8. Did I use a dictionary to double-check the spelling of any special terms?

 **Edit your essay of definition.** Use the checklist above as you review your work for errors. Ask a partner to check your work, too. Discuss suggested edits, and incorporate feedback from your teacher or peers. Then write a neat final copy and proofread it.

## Publishing Sharing Your Writing

After completing your essay and giving it an interesting title, be sure to share it with a number of different audiences. You can also post your work on a personal Web site.

---

**TEKS** **10.13C** Revise drafts to improve sentence variety; **10.13D** Edit drafts for grammar, mechanics, and spelling; **10.13E** Revise the final draft in response to feedback from peers and teacher/publish written work; **10.17C** Use a variety of correctly structured sentences; **10.18A** Use conventions of capitalization; **10.18B** Use correct punctuation marks; **10.19** Spell correctly using resources to determine and check correct spelling; **ELPS** **5C** Spell familiar words with increasing accuracy; **5D** Edit writing for standard grammar and usage/subject-verb agreement; **5E** Employ increasingly complex grammatical structures in content area writing

# Writing for Assessment
# Responding to Expository Prompts

When you explain or inform in a longer piece of writing, you're developing an expository essay. Effective expository writing begins with your complete understanding of a topic, and it ends with a written piece that shows your ability to share this knowledge clearly with your reader. What happens in between is all of the planning, drafting, and revising you do to produce your essay.

On assessment tests, you may be asked to write explanations in response to expository prompts. Of course, your time is limited for this type of expository writing, so you must make the best use of every available minute. This chapter will show you how to complete such a response, adapting the writing process as you work against the clock.

## Writing Guidelines

**Subject:** Expository prompt
**Form:** Response essay
**Purpose:** To demonstrate competence
**Audience:** Instructor

"Good writers are those who keep the language efficient. That is to say, keep it accurate, keep it clear."

—Ezra Pound

## Responding to Expository Prompts

### Objectives
- understand the elements of an expository prompt
- practice analyzing an expository prompt, and then plan, write, revise, and edit a response
- practice writing for assessment

Explain that expository writing prompts are the most common form of prompts found on assessments.

Point out that the Ezra Pound quotation is generally good advice for any type of writing and is especially appropriate for expository writing on timed assessment tests.

Acknowledge that taking tests can produce anxiety, but assure students that learning and practicing the techniques on the following pages will improve their performance on writing assessments.

## Differentiated Instruction:
## English Language Learners

**ELPS** 1D, 2D, 2G, 2I, 3F, 3G

| ELP Level **Beginning** | ELP Level **Intermediate** | ELP Level **Advanced/Advanced High** |
| --- | --- | --- |
| As students finish sharing their paragraphs aloud, encourage their peers to ask questions and provide positive feedback. Provide model sentences as needed. | Review how to ask for information and clarification. After sharing essays aloud, have students ask clarifying questions about each other's essays. | Encourage students to give positive feedback in both formal and informal English, discussing when it is appropriate to use each. |

 **ELPS 1D** Speak using learning strategies/request assistance, employ non-verbal cues, and convey ideas by defining or describing; **2D** Monitor understanding of spoken language during classroom instruction/interactions and seek clarification of spoken language as needed; **2G** Understand the general meaning, main points, and important details of spoken language/topics, languages, and contexts are familiar to unfamiliar; **2I** Demonstrate listening comprehension in increasingly complex spoken language by responding to questions; **3F** Ask for and give information/ranging from using a limited high-frequency vocabulary to using abstract and content-based vocabulary during speaking; **3G** Express opinions, ideas, and feelings ranging from communicating short phrases to participating in discussions

## Prewriting
### Analyzing an Expository Prompt

Direct students' attention to the tip at the bottom of the page. Explain to students that certain STRAP elements may not appear in every prompt. For example, the prompt may not specify a role for them to assume as the writer. Explain that when this occurs, they may assume whatever role best suits their purpose and audience.

Stress that deciding how to answer each of the STRAP questions will make their writing stronger and clearer.

### Try It!
### Answers

**Possible Answers**

1. **Subject:** the concept of *happiness*; **Type:** essay of definition; **Role:** will depend on the explanatory examples chosen; **Audience:** teacher; **Purpose:** define
2. **Subject**: a good part-time job; **Type**: essay; **Role**: student; **Audience**: teacher or potential employer; **Purpose**: analyze and explain
3. **Subject**: two classes; **Type**: letter; **Role**: friend; **Audience**: friend; **Purpose**: compare and contrast DIFFERENTIATE INSTRUCTION ↘

## Prewriting Analyzing an Expository Prompt

Most writing tests ask you to respond to a prompt. A prompt is a set of directions that tells you what to write. It's crucial for you to analyze the prompt carefully so that you write a response that fits the requirements of the test. When you analyze a prompt, answer the following **STRAP questions:**

<u>S</u>ubject: What subject (school, schedule, homework policy, healthy living, friendships) should I write about?

<u>T</u>ype: What form (essay, letter, announcement, report, article) of writing should I create?

<u>R</u>ole: What position (student, community member, son or daughter, friend) should I assume as the writer?

<u>A</u>udience: Who (classmates, teacher, principal, parents, city council) is the intended reader?

<u>P</u>urpose: What is the goal (inform, explain, evaluate) of my writing?

These key words are often found in **expository** prompts: *explain, analyze, compare and contrast, outline,* and *define.*

### Try It!

Analyze these prompts by answering the five STRAP questions above.

1. Aristotle once said, "Happiness depends upon ourselves." Everyone knows the word "happiness," but most of us have a different idea of what it means to be happy. Define the word "happiness" and include two or three clear examples.
2. Many high school students have part-time jobs. Students often choose jobs that are based on economic factors and personal preferences. Identify a part-time job that you would like to have, analyze the duties involved, and explain why you believe the job would suit you.
3. In a letter to a friend, compare and contrast two classes that you are currently taking. In your letter, explain the positive and negative aspects of each class.

### Tip

Some prompts do not contain key words for every STRAP question. You will have to use your best judgment to answer these questions.

### Differentiated Instruction:
### Struggling Learners

Students may prefer certain graphic organizers above others. They may not, however, understand that the organizers they prefer may not work well with every prompt. Point out that identifying the T in STRAP (Type) will lead students to the graphic organizer that best matches the type of writing.

## Planning Your Response

Once you have answered the STRAP questions, you should quickly plan your response. The following graphic organizers can help.

### Graphic Organizers

**Quick List (Any Essay)**

1. First Point
   —Detail 1
   —Detail 2
2. Second Point
   —Detail 1
   —Detail 2
3. Third Point
   —Detail 1
   —Detail 2

**Cluster (Definition/Classification)**

Topic

**Prewrite**

**Reread the expository prompts on page 188. Choose one prompt and use one of the graphic organizers above to quickly organize a response to the prompt.**

## Drafting Using Transitions in Timed Situations

For this exercise you will have 45 minutes to respond. In the 30 minutes you allot for drafting, your response should still maintain the features of good writing. As you develop your draft, remember to include transitions (for example, *first, next, therefore, finally*) to better convey your meaning by connecting the ideas within your paragraphs and by linking ideas from paragraph to paragraph. Using transitions will improve your organization and make your response more coherent.

### Tip

Manage your time wisely. Allow enough time for prewriting, revising, and editing. For example, if you have 45 minutes to respond, use 5 to 10 minutes to analyze the prompt and plan your response, 30 to 35 minutes for writing, and the last 5 minutes for revising and editing.

Expository

## Planning Your Response

Provide photocopies of the reproducible quick list, time line, T-chart, and Venn diagram (see TE Appendix) for students to choose from as they organize their responses. Remind students, however, that in an on-demand writing situation, they will probably not be given premade graphic organizers to fill out. Students need to become familiar with using and creating their own graphic organizers in a testing situation.

TEKS 10.13A, 10.13B

**Reread the expository prompts.** Have students use graphic organizers to organize their response to writing prompts. With practice, students will know which organizer will work best and how to adapt it quickly during a timed writing assessment. ✔ DIFFERENTIATE INSTRUCTION

✱ For more about graphic organizers, see SE pages 624–625.

### Drafting Using Transitions in Timed Situations

Help students use the 45 minutes of the test efficiently. As they draft their responses, they should focus on connecting ideas and paragraphs with transitions to convey meaning. Break down each part of the process into clear units of time. For example:

- 10 minutes for analyzing and planning,
- 25 minutes for writing, and
- 10 minutes for editing and revising.

### Tip

After students have read the tip, encourage them to use this practice to figure out a schedule that best suits their own writing habits. For example, if they can write very quickly, they could spend more time planning their responses.

---

TEKS **10.13A** Plan a first draft by selecting the correct genre and determining topics through a range of strategies; **10.13B** Structure ideas in a sustained way; ELPS **1C** Use strategic learning techniques to acquire basic and grade-level vocabulary; **2C** Learn new language structures/expressions and basic/academic vocabulary heard during classroom instruction/interactions; **2I** Demonstrate listening comprehension in increasingly complex spoken language by following directions and collaborating with peers; **3A** Practice producing sounds of newly acquired vocabulary; **3D** Speak using grade-level content area vocabulary/academic language proficiency; **4A** Learn relationships between sounds and letters; **4F** Use visual/contextual support and support from peers/teachers to read grade-appropriate text, enhance understanding, and develop vocabulary, grasp of language structures, and background knowledge; **4G** Use visual and contextual support to develop vocabulary and grasp of language structures; **4I** Demonstrate comprehension by employing and expanding basic reading skills; **4K** Demonstrate comprehension and expand reading skills by employing analytical skills; **5B** Write using content-based grade-level vocabulary

## Writing
### Responding to the Prompt

Remind students that the main goal in this type of writing is to provide clear explanations and solid support for their ideas.

Instruct students to read the sample response, paying special attention to the information in the side notes. Review the sample response's structure, thesis, supporting evidence, and use of rhetorical devices.

**TEKS** 10.13B, 10.15A(i), 10.15A(ii), 10.15A(iii), 10.15A(iv)

---

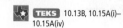 **TEKS** 10.13B, 10.15A(i)–10.15A(iv)

## Drafting Responding to the Prompt

After using a graphic organizer to plan your response, it's time to begin writing. After analyzing the prompt, Victoria Moreno decided that an expository essay was the best genre to discuss the concept of loyalty. She chose expository because its purpose is to explain and inform, a good match to the prompt.

### Sample Response

**The Good and the Bad of Loyalty**

> Loyalty is a slippery concept. It can be considered an outstanding quality to have in a friend, as in this quote from Woodrow Wilson: "Loyalty means nothing unless it has at its heart the absolute principle of self-sacrifice." Loyalty, however, can also be seen as a quality that can be manipulated, as implied in an old Irish proverb: "The best way to keep loyalty in a man's heart is to keep money in his purse."

> The dictionary defines loyalty without any sort of good or bad associations. It is merely "faithfulness to commitments or obligations." (Random House) When is loyalty something to be praised and when should it be condemned?

> Few people would question the security of having friends and family who are loyal to them. It is reassuring to know that there are certain people you can always count on no matter what you do or in times of need. Loyalty goes beyond bonds with people though. Sports fans can be loyal to a particular team. Soldiers are loyal to the military and to their country. There are even those who are loyal to particular brands of merchandise, like computers or soda.

> Sometimes loyalty is so strong that it can become a problem. People might become so loyal to a product that they refuse to use anything else. Imagine, for example, how difficult that could become when you want to eat out with a friend who will only go to one particular fast-food chain. Further, people sometimes become so loyal to a cause, a job, or an organization that it takes over their lives. These people begin to see life in a very limited way

*The **introduction** clearly states the thesis and engages the reader's attention.*

*Rhetorical devices, like questions, show knowledge and support the thesis. Ideas in the **middle** paragraphs are structured in a sustained way.*

---

 **TEKS** **10.13B** Structure ideas in a sustained way/develop drafts in timed situations that include transitions and rhetorical devices; **10.15A(i)** Write an analytical essay that includes an introductory paragraph; **10.15A(ii)** Write an analytical essay that includes rhetorical devices and transitions; **10.15A(iii)** Write an analytical essay that includes an idea or thesis; **10.15A(iv)** Write an analytical essay that includes a structure appropriate to the purpose

**TEKS** 10.13B, 10.15A(i)–
10.15A(iv)

Responding to Expository Prompts **191**

**Each middle** paragraph sustains the thesis. Transitions link ideas from paragraph to paragraph and within paragraphs.

because their faithfulness to these particular commitments become more important than anything else.

This leads to the concept of "blind" loyalty. The Merriam-Webster Dictionary defines this as "unquestioning." Does loyalty have to be unquestioning? The fact that the word "blind" has to be put in front of the word implies that loyalty by itself is not unquestioning. So even though a loyal person is faithful, it does not mean that he or she doesn't question that faithfulness from time to time.

Blind loyalty can happen when someone has gotten so used to supporting a person or an organization or even an idea that he or she just keeps supporting it. The object of loyalty, which might be a person or an object, might change into something that's unpleasant, cruel, or corrupt; still the person continues the support. In such cases, blind loyalty may not be such a good quality.

Loyalty can also be bought, as described in the Irish proverb. Loyalty doesn't necessarily have to be bought with money, though plenty of loyalty is. Many people will overlook bad qualities when they are profiting from a relationship. Loyalty can also be bought by fear. You may stay loyal to an organization because your friends all belong to it, and you don't want to look different. Many employees won't blow the whistle on an employer because they are afraid of being fired.

**Effective conclusion** ties essay together.

Are blind loyalty and bought loyalty the real thing? Most people consider a faithful dog to be the true example of loyalty. Dog love, though, can certainly be blind. If that is the case, then pure, unadulterated loyalty is a special quality that should be reserved for the deserving.

Expository

**Now write your own response.** Look over the planning you did for the prompt on page 189, including your use of a graphic organizer. Then write a response to the prompt in the amount of time your teacher gives you.

Draft

---

Ask students to discuss the sample response. Does it meet the goals for an expository essay, given on SE page 140? Focus on the first four traits.

- **Focus and Coherence**—The first sentence and use of quotations engage the reader's attention. All paragraphs directly support the thesis.
- **Organization**—Ideas are presented clearly (order of importance) and strong transitions connect ideas naturally (*This leads to the concept. . .* and *Loyalty can also be bought. . .*).
- **Development of Ideas**—The topic is strong and supported with vivid layers of details, using both clarifying sentences (*Loyalty goes beyond the bonds with people though*) and completing sentences (*Sports fans can be loyal to a particular team*).
- **Voice**—The third person voice is lively and interesting. The use of rhetorical devices (*Does loyalty have to be unquestioning?*) shows knowledge and reflection on the topic and supports the thesis statement.

**TEKS** 10.13B, 10.15A(i), 10.15A(ii), 10.15A(iii), 10.15A(iv); **ELPS** 4K

**Now write your own response.** This exercise is designed for a timed-writing practice. Although students have already completed their planning, remind them about the importance of structuring their time wisely, so they have time to plan, draft, and revise their work.

**◢ DIFFERENTIATE INSTRUCTION**

---

**Differentiated Instruction: English Language Learners**

**ELPS** 5A, 5B, 5E, 5F, 5G

| ELP Level **Beginning** | ELP Level **Intermediate** | ELP Level **Advanced/Advanced High** |
|---|---|---|
| Have students write an organized and focused paragraph instead of longer essay format. Writing time may also be extended. | Have students write the entire essay, with extended time, focusing on coherence, organization, and development of ideas. | Have students write the full essay in the allotted time, allowing for some errors in conventions and voice. |

**TEKS** **10.13B** Structure ideas in a sustained way/develop drafts in timed situations that include transitions and rhetorical devices; **10.15A(i)** Write an analytical essay that includes an introductory and concluding paragraph; **10.15A(ii)** Write an analytical essay that includes transitions; **10.15A(iii)** Write an analytical essay that includes an idea or thesis; **10.15A(iv)** Write an analytical essay that includes a structure appropriate to the purpose; **ELPS** **4K** Demonstrate comprehension and expand reading skills by employing analytical skills/ evaluating written information and performing critical analyses; **5A** Learn relationships between sounds and letters to represent sounds when writing in English; **5B** Write using newly acquired basic and content-based grade-level vocabulary; **5E** Employ increasingly complex grammatical structures in content area writing such as using correct verbs, tenses, and pronouns/possessive case/negatives and contractions; **5F** Write using a variety of grade-appropriate sentence lengths, patterns, and connecting words/combine in increasingly accurate ways; **5G** Explain with increasing specificity and detail/writing

## Revising
### Improving Your Response

Point out and discuss the quote at the bottom of the page. How accurate is George V. Higgins's assessment of writing/editing?

Encourage students to familiarize themselves with the proofreader's marks in the back cover of their books. Using these marks will help students make neat, legible corrections.

**Improve your work.** Remind students to use the STRAP questions. If they will be writing with pencils, remind students to have additional sharpened pencils and erasers on hand.

**TEKS** 10.13C

## Editing
### Checking Your Response

Suggest that students pay careful attention to the conventions whenever they do any writing. The errors that they make should decrease over time.

**TEKS** 10.13D, 10.17C, 10.18A, 10.18B(i)

**Check your conventions.** Remind students to pay attention to the time so they will be able to make their corrections without rushing.

**ELPS** 5C, 5D, 5F

---

**TEKS** 10.13C, 10.13D, 10.17C, 10.18A, 10.18B(i)
**ELPS** 5C, 5D, 5F

## Revising Improving Your Response

Most writing tests allow you to make corrections to improve your work, though you should find out ahead of time how many are allowed. Always make changes and corrections as neatly as possible. If the test allows revising and editing, use the STRAP questions to guide your changes.

> **Subject:** Does my response focus on the topic in the prompt? Do my main points support my thesis?
> **Type:** Have I followed the correct form (essay, letter, article)?
> **Role:** Have I assumed the position indicated in the prompt?
> **Audience:** Have I used the right level of language for my audience?
> **Purpose:** Does my writing accomplish the goal set forth in the prompt?

**Revise**

**Improve your work.** Reread your response, asking yourself the STRAP questions above. Make neat changes in the time your teacher allows.

## Editing Checking Your Response

Check your response for punctuation, capitalization, spelling, and grammar errors. Careless errors can confuse the reader.

### Conventions

_____ 1. Have I used end punctuation for every sentence?
_____ 2. Have I capitalized all proper nouns and the first word of each sentence?
_____ 3. Have I checked my spelling?
_____ 4. Do my subjects and verbs agree (*it does*, not *it do*)?
_____ 5. Have I used the right word (*there*, *they're*, *their*)?

**Edit**

**Check your conventions.** Review your response for punctuation, capitalization, spelling, and grammar errors. Make neat corrections in the time your teacher allows.

> "If you can read your writing to yourself without wincing, you have probably gotten it right."
> —George V. Higgins

---

**TEKS** **10.13C** Revise drafts to improve style, word choice, figurative language, sentence variety, and subtlety of meaning after rethinking how well questions of purpose, audience, and genre have been addressed; **10.14D** Edit drafts for grammar, mechanics, and spelling; **10.17C** Use a variety of correctly structured sentences (e.g., compound, complex, compound-complex); **10.18A** Use conventions of capitalization; **10.18B** Use correct punctuation marks; **10.18B(i)** Comma placement in nonrestrictive phrases, clauses, and contrasting expressions; **ELPS 5C** Spell familiar words with increasing accuracy; **5D** Edit writing for standard grammar and usage/subject-verb agreement; **5F** Write using a variety of grade-appropriate sentence patterns in increasingly accurate ways

# Expository Writing on Tests

Use the following tips as a guide whenever you respond to an expository writing prompt.

### Before you write . . .

- **Understand the prompt.**
  Review the STRAP questions listed on page 188.
  Remember that an expository prompt asks you to *explain*.
- **Plan your time wisely.**
  Spend several minutes making notes and planning before starting to write. Use a graphic organizer. (See page 189.)

### As you write . . .

- **Decide on a focus or thesis for your response.**
  Keep your main idea or purpose in mind as you write.
- **Be selective.**
  Use examples and explanations that directly support your focus.
- **End in a meaningful way.**
  Remind the reader about the importance of the topic.

### After you've written a first draft . . .

- **Check for completeness.**
  Use the STRAP questions on page 192 to revise your work.
- **Check for correctness.**
  Check your punctuation, capitalization, spelling, and grammar.

Prewrite

**Plan and write a response.** Analyze one of the prompts below, using the STRAP questions. Then plan and write a response. Complete your work in the time your teacher gives you.

### Expository Prompts

- Good parents or guardians demonstrate many valuable qualities. Choose three qualities of a good parent or guardian and write an essay that includes examples to support your choices.
- The German poet Johann Wolfgang von Goethe said, "There is nothing insignificant in the world. It all depends on the point of view." Explain why it is important to see a situation from another person's point of view.

*Expository* (side tab)

## Expository Writing on Tests

Point out that students must approach writing-on-demand assignments with a clear writing strategy in mind.

Have students read aloud the Before you write, As you write, and After you've written. . . tips and reflect on how well they've used each step in their last writing practice.

**Plan and write a response.** Remind students to use the STRAP questions as they plan their responses.

### Expository Prompts

Allow students the same amount of time to write their response essays as they will be allotted on school, district, or state assessments. Break down each part of the process into clear chunks of time. For example, you might give students

- 10 minutes for note taking and planning,
- 20 minutes for writing, and
- 10 minutes for editing, revising, and proofreading.

Tell students when time is up for each section. Start the assignment at the top of the hour or at the half-hour to make it easier for students to keep track of the time.

If your state, district, or school requires students to use and submit a graphic organizer as part of their assessment, refer students to SE pages 624–625. ✔ DIFFERENTIATE INSTRUCTION

ELPS 1C, 1E, 2I, 3D, 3E, 3F, 4C, 4F, 4G

---

**ELPS 1C** Use strategic learning techniques to acquire basic and grade-level vocabulary; **1E** Internalize new basic and academic language by using and reusing it/writing; **2I** Demonstrate listening comprehension in increasingly complex spoken language by summarizing spoken messages and taking notes; **3D** Speak using grade-level content area vocabulary/academic language proficiency; **3E** Share information in cooperative learning interactions; **3F** Give information/ranging from using a limited high-frequency vocabulary to using abstract and content-based vocabulary during speaking; **3G** Express opinions and ideas ranging from communicating short phrases to participating in discussions; **4C** Comprehend vocabulary used in written classroom materials; **4F** Use support from peers/teachers to enhance understanding and develop vocabulary; **4G** Demonstrate comprehension of increasingly complex English/participating in shared reading

# Persuasive Writing

## Writing an Argumentative Essay (pages 195–234)

Students write an argumentative essay about an issue that affects many people.

## Writing an Editorial (pages 235–244)

Students read a sample editorial, then write their own editorial that expresses their opinion about a recent issue or event.

## Writing for Assessment: Responding to Persuasive Prompts (pages 245–251)

Students learn how to use the writing process to create a clear, effective persuasive response in a timed situation.

### Literature Connections

- *"Doing Nothing Is Something"* by Anna Quindlen
- *"Abolishing the Penny Makes Good Sense"* by Alan S. Blinder

### Technology Connections

 *Write Source Online*
www.hmheducation.com/tx/writesource

- *Net-text*
- *Writing Network*
- *Portfolio*
- *GrammarSnap*
- *Essay Scoring*
- *File Cabinet*

 *Interactive Whiteboard Lessons*

# Persuasive Writing Unit Scope and Sequence

| | | Write Source Student Edition | | | Daily Language Workouts | Skills-Book | Write Source Online |
|---|---|---|---|---|---|---|---|
| Day | Writing and Conventions Instruction | Core Unit | Tools of Language | Resource Units | | | |
| **1–5** WEEK 1 | **Writing an Argumentative Essay** Model ▶ Literature Connection *"Doing Nothing Is Something"* by Anna Quindlen | 195–200 | **TL** 544–549 | | 50–53 | | Interactive Whiteboard Lesson |
| | Skills Activities: •Direct Quotation | | | | | 32 | |
| | •Shifts in Verb Tense | | | | | 94–96 | |

 **Resource Units** referenced above are located in the back of the *Student Edition* and *Teacher's Edition*
**TL** *"The Tools of Language"* **BGW** *"Basic Grammar and Writing"* **WR** *"A Writer's Resource"* **PG** *"Proofreader's Guide"*

| Day | Writing and Conventions Instruction | Write Source Student Edition | | | Daily Language Workouts | Skills-Book | Write Source Online |
| | | Core Unit | Tools of Language | Resource Units | | | |
|---|---|---|---|---|---|---|---|
| **WEEK 2** | | | | | | | |
| **6–7** | Prewriting | 201–204 | **TL** 526–529 | **WR** 618–627 | 54–57 | | Net-text |
| **8–10** | Drafting | 205–210 | | **WR** 628–633 | | | Net-text |
| **WEEK 3** | | | | | | | |
| **11–12** | Revising | 211–220 | **TL** 526–529 | | 58–61 | | Net-text |
| | Skills Activities: • Fragments | | | **BGW** 594–595 **PG** 772–773 | | 161–165 | |
| | • Adverbs | | | **BGW** 578–579 **PG** 766–767 | | 111–114 | GrammarSnap |
| **13–14** | Editing and Publishing | 221–227 | | | | | Net-text |
| | Skills Activities: • Subjunctive and Indicative Mood | | | **PG** 752–753 | | 104–105 | GrammarSnap |
| | • Verbals: Gerunds, Infinitives, and Participles | | | **PG** 762–763 | | 101 | GrammarSnap |
| | • Sentence Types for Variety: Declarative, Interrogative, Imperative, and Exclamatory | | | **BGW** 584–591 **PG** 780–785 | | 140 | GrammarSnap |
| | • Dashes | | | **PG** 684–685 | | 24 | GrammarSnap |
| **15** | Assessing and Reflecting | 228–234 | | | | | Net-text |
| **WEEK 4** | | | | | | | |
| **16–20** | **Writing an Editorial** Model ⓛ Literature Connection *"Abolishing the Penny Makes Good Sense"* by Alan S. Blinder | 235–237 | **TL** 526–529 | | 62–65 | | Net-text |
| | Prewriting | 238–240 | | **WR** 618–627 | | | Net-text |
| | Drafting | 241 | | **WR** 628–633 | | | Net-text |
| | Revising | 242–243 | | | | | Net-text |
| | Editing | 244 | | | | | Net-text |
| **WEEK 5** | | | | | | | |
| **21–25** | **Writing for Assessment: Responding to Persuasive Prompts** | 245 | **TL** 526–529 | | 66–69 | | Net-text |
| | Prewriting | 246–247 | | **WR** 618–627 | | | Net-text |
| | Drafting | 248–249 | | **WR** 628–633 | | | Net-text |
| | Revising and Editing | 250–251 | | | | | Net-text |

**Resource Units** referenced above are located in the back of the *Student Edition* and *Teacher's Edition*
**TL** *"The Tools of Language"*   **BGW** *"Basic Grammar and Writing"*   **WR** *"A Writer's Resource"*   **PG** *"Proofreader's Guide"*

## Writing Focus

- Writing an Argumentative Essay
- Writing an Editorial
- Responding to Persuasive Prompts

## Grammar Focus

- The Subjunctive Mood
- Verbals (Gerunds, Infinitives, and Participles)

## Learning Language

Read aloud the basic and academic terms as well as the descriptions and questions. Model for students how to read one question and answer it. For example, *It says that an argument is a discussion in which different opinions are expressed, and it's asking for an example of an argument I've had with a friend. Last Sunday, I argued with a friend over who the best football team is. I think it's the Giants, but he favors the Steelers.* Have partners monitor their understanding of the terms by working through the meanings and questions together.

**DIFFERENTIATE INSTRUCTION ⇘**

⭐ **ELPS** 1E, 2C, 3B, 3D, 3E, 4G

## Minilessons

### Goldilocks Principle   Writing an Argumentative Essay

- **STUDY** your list of potential topics for an argumentative essay on a social, a political, or an environmental issue. Then **WRITE** topics into one of three columns: "Too Big," "Too Small," or "Just Right." **DISCUSS** your results with a partner.

### Ironclad Argument    Writing an Editorial

- **THINK** of an issue that you feel very strongly about. **CREATE** a brief outline that lists a topic sentence and three main arguments. **FIND** a classmate who would take the opposite side of the issue and discuss. **WRITE** a brief outline of your counterargument.

⭐ **ELPS** 3E, 5B

⭐ **ELPS 1E** Internalize new basic and academic language by using and reusing it/speaking; **2A** Distinguish sounds with increasing ease; **2C** Learn new language structures, expressions, and basic/academic vocabulary heard during classroom instruction/interactions; **3A** Practice producing sounds of newly acquired vocabulary; **3B** Expand vocabulary by learning and using routine language and high-frequency words; **3D** Speak using grade-level content area vocabulary/new words and academic language proficiency; **3E** Share information in cooperative learning interactions; **4G** Demonstrate comprehension of increasingly complex English/responding to questions; **5B** Write using newly acquired basic and content-based grade-level vocabulary

---

⭐ ELPS 1E, 2C, 3B, 3D, 3E, 4G

www.hmheducation.com/tx/writesource

# Persuasive Writing

## Writing Focus

## Grammar Focus

## Learning Language

Learning these words and expressions will help you understand this unit.

1. A mood is a set of verb forms that tells the writer's attitude about the factuality or possibility that something will occur. **When do you think you would use the indicative mood?**

2. An argument is a discussion in which different viewpoints or opinions are expressed. **Describe a recent argument that you had with a friend.**

3. Something that is precise is exact and clearly expressed. **Why do you need to be precise when you give directions to a particular location?**

4. Loaded language consists of words that have a strong negative or positive connotation and that are intended to influence the reader. **Describe an advertisement you have seen or heard recently that uses loaded language.**

---

### Differentiated Instruction: English Language Learners

⭐ ELPS 1E, 2A, 3A, 3D, 5B

| ELP Level **Beginning** | ELP Level **Intermediate** | ELP Level **Advanced/Advanced High** |
|---|---|---|
| Model pronunciation of the vocabulary words. Then, pronounce each word correctly and incorrectly in a sentence. Have students identify the correct pronunciation. | Model pronunciation of the vocabulary words. Then, have students practice pronouncing them correctly, both individually and in a sentence. | Have students practice developing and saying aloud sentences that use each word correctly. Challenge students to write a paragraph that uses all four vocabulary words. |

195

## Persuasive Writing
# Writing an Argumentative Essay

People have different opinions and take different positions on issues, both big and small. Big issues might include global warming, child labor, or ways to improve education in the United States. Local issues might include whether or not dogs should be allowed in parks. People often disagree over the seriousness of issues, about the consequences, and about the ways to resolve issues that confront them every day.

You are sure to encounter issues that you feel strongly about—topics that are worth debating. Perhaps your school board is deciding whether to eliminate funding for after-school sports or for school bands. Perhaps city leaders are deciding whether or not overnight parking should be allowed in public lots and on public streets. How can you present your ideas and convince others to agree with you?

Persuasive writing helps you address a difference of opinion. By clearly stating a position and defending it with facts and logical reasons, you can convince others to agree with you. In this chapter, you will write an argumentative essay about an issue that affects many people.

## Writing Guidelines

**Subject:** A social, political, or environmental issue
**Purpose:** To defend a position
**Form:** Argumentative Essay
**Audience:** Classmates and community members

"Opinions are made to be be changed
or how is truth to be got at?"
—Lord Byron

---

# Writing an Argumentative Essay

## Objectives
- understand that an argumentative essay is a form of persuasive writing
- understand the purpose, form, and content of an argumentative essay
- plan, draft, revise, edit, and publish an argumentative essay

Remind students that persuasive writing is writing intended to *persuade* the reader to agree with the writer's opinion about something.

Note that creating an argumentative essay is a good way to sharpen persuasive writing skills because it forces the writer to provide effective details to support his or her position rather than just opinion and personal feelings.

### Technology Connections

Use the Interactive Whiteboard lessons to introduce persuasive writing.

 *Interactive Whiteboard Lesson*

---

## Resources

### Copy Masters (see Appendix)

- T-chart (TE p. 203)
- Details chart (TE p. 224)

### Benchmark Papers  (see Appendix)

## Persuasive Writing Warm-Up: Using Support

Remind students of the difference between facts and statistics. The difference is the inclusion of numbers. Statistics have to include numbers while facts do not. Compare the examples given about child labor to make this point.

Explain that the best persuasive essay will contain a variety of types of precise and relevant evidence. A combination of facts, statistics, and quotations will build on one another to make a strong argument. For example: without statistics, quotations can just appear to be a bunch of people's opinions. But without quotations, statistics can be hard to interpret or seem divorced from the human element.

**TEKS** 10.13B, 10.16A

### Try It!

Take a trip to the school library to allow students to do some basic research. Before going, however, model how to choose a topic and take notes by demonstrating with a topic of your choice.

**ELPS** 4G

---

## Persuasive Writing Warm-Up: Using Support

When you write a persuasive paragraph or essay, it is important to include effective supporting details. You will need to include a range of appropriate appeals: facts, statistics, and case studies that support your position and help persuade your audience. These are considered precise, relevant evidence. Quotations from leading experts on the topic are also considered to be relevant evidence. You may wish to include appropriate anecdotes or analogies as well.

The notebook page below shows evidence and supporting details that one student used to support her position on child labor.

> **Fact:** Worldwide, one in six children aged 5 to 14 is engaged in child labor.
> **Fact:** Girls often work as domestic servants.
>
> **Fact:** Children who work are not able to attend school.
> **Fact:** Child labor exists in developed countries.
> **Statistic:** According to the UN, in Sub-Saharan Africa, approximately 69 million children work.
>
> **Statistic:** Worldwide, approximately 158 million children work.
> **Statistic:** Sixteen percent of children in developing countries work.
> **Quotation:** "Children deserve basic human rights" U.S. Senator Barbara Boxer
> **Quotation:** "Child labor is the bane of modern existence and should be outlawed." Society Against Child Labor
>
> The **solution** is . . .                              moderate people should stand up and take charge.
>
> The **problem** with the world today is . . . limited access to school.
> The **solution** is . . .                              make it easier for children to attend.
>
> The **problem** with the world today is . . . third-world countries can't compete.
> The **solution** is . . .                              third-world debt relief.
> The **problem** with the world today is . . . globalization causes child labor.
> The **solution** is . . .                              enforce the UN rules on the rights of the child.

### Try It!

On your own paper, express an opinion about an important environmental, social, or political problem. Then find precise details and evidence: facts, statistics, and a quotation to support your position. List these appeals.

---

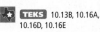

# Writing a Persuasive Paragraph

A persuasive paragraph expresses an opinion about a specific topic and contains logical reasons and precise, relevant evidence to support the position. The ideas are structured to sustain the topic sentence and to persuade the audience. A persuasive paragraph has three parts:

- The **topic sentence** states the position or opinion.
- The **body sentences** support the position.
- The **closing sentence** revisits the position or opinion.

## Sample Persuasive Paragraph

Martin wrote the following paragraph about child labor. In his paragraph he considered the relative value of the information he decided to include.

The **topic sentence** names the problem and solution.

The **body sentences** present evidence and details to support the opinion.

The **closing sentence** revisits the opinion.

> ### Certain Inalienable Rights
>
> As globalization sends more children into sweatshops and dangerous factories, it's time for the United States to ratify the United Nations Conventions on the Rights of the Child (CRC). This piece of legislation was created in 1989 to protect those under the age of 18 against bonded labor (slavery) and labor that is dangerous or that interferes with education. Today, one in six children between the ages of 5 and 14 endures forced labor, curtailing any possibility for education and ensuring a life of poverty. Children are forced to work in mines, in fields, and with dangerous machinery. Girls frequently become domestic servants at the age of 5. Such forced labor "crushes the right to normal physical and mental development" (UNICEF Child info), and as U.S. Senator Barbara Boxer has argued, "Children deserve basic human rights." Child labor exists all over the world, in Africa, South Asia, Central Europe, and in the Commonwealth of Independent States (CIS). The United States should ratify the CRC and work with other nations and international groups to stop this practice.

 **Write a persuasive paragraph.** Review the three parts of a paragraph (top of page) and what they do. Then present your opinion and details from page **196** on the topic you selected.

---

## Writing a Persuasive Paragraph

Discuss the sample paragraph. Ask students: *Why do you think the paragraph is effective?* Possible responses:

- The opening sentence presents a clear position or opinion.
- The second through fifth sentences provide facts and statistics that clearly support the opinion.
- The sixth sentence provides quotations that clearly support the position.
- The seventh and eighth sentences revisit the position. ✔ **DIFFERENTIATE INSTRUCTION**

 **TEKS** 10.13B, 10.16A, 10.16D, 10.16E

**Write a persuasive paragraph.** After writing, encourage students to exchange papers with a partner. Students should read through their partner's paragraph, paying special attention to the evidence that's been provided. Partners should then ask for and give information about the relevance of the supports that were given.

**ELPS** 3E, 3F

### ⭐ Conventions Connections

**Grammar: Direct Quotations**
- ***Proofreader's Guide*** pages 668–669
- ***SkillsBook*** page 32
- ⚡ *Write Source Online* **GrammarSnap**

**Grammar: Shifts in Verb Tense**
- ***Proofreader's Guide*** pages 746–747
- ***SkillsBook*** page 94
- ⚡ *Write Source Online* **GrammarSnap**

---

## Differentiated Instruction: English Language Learners

**ELPS** 1C, 1E, 2A, 4A, 4C, 4F, 5B

| ELP Level **Beginning** | ELP Level **Intermediate** | ELP Level **Advanced/Advanced High** |
|---|---|---|
| Identify unfamiliar vocabulary in the paragraph. Have students identify and decode words by focusing on sound/letter relationships. Model as needed. | Identify unfamiliar vocabulary in the paragraph. Guide students in writing definitions using pictures and their first language as necessary. | Identify unfamiliar vocabulary in the paragraph. Using a bilingual dictionary, have students find and write definitions. Challenge students to use each new word in a sentence. |

 **TEKS** 10.13B Structure ideas in a sustained and persuasive way; **10.16A** Write an argumentative essay supported by precise and relevant evidence; **10.16D** Write an argumentative essay that includes a structure appropriate to the purpose; **10.16E** Write an argumentative essay that includes analysis of specific data, facts, and ideas; **ELPS** **1C** Use strategic learning techniques to acquire basic and grade-level vocabulary; **1E** Internalize new academic language by using and reusing it/writing; **2A** Distinguish sounds/intonation patterns with increasing ease; **3E** Share information in cooperative learning interactions; **3F** Ask for and give information/ranging from using a limited high-frequency vocabulary to using abstract and content-based vocabulary during speaking; **4A** Learn relationships between sounds and letters/sound out words using a combination of skills; **4C** Comprehend vocabulary used in written classroom materials; **4F** Use visual and contextual support to develop vocabulary; **5B** Write using content-based grade-level vocabulary

## Understanding Your Goal

Four traits relate to the development of the content and the form. They provide a focus during prewriting, drafting, and revising.

- **Focus and Coherence**
- **Organization**
- **Development of Ideas**
- **Voice**

The other trait relates only to form. It is primarily considered during the editing process.

- **Conventions**

**TEKS** 10.13A

### Literature Connections

Watch a TV commercial with students. Explain how the ad tries to persuade the audience. Then show several other commercials and have students analyze them. Can the students identify the main focus of the ad? The facts and statistics used? The voice of the ad?

**ELPS** 2F, 2G, 3J

---

**198**

 **TEKS** 10.13A

## Understanding Your Goal

Your goal in this chapter is to support a position regarding a social, political, or environmental issue. The traits in the following chart will help you write an argumentative essay, the correct form, or genre, for your goal and audience. The scoring guide on pages **60–61** will also help you. Refer to it often to improve your writing.

### Traits of Persuasive Writing

- **Focus and Coherence**

  Clearly state your opinion or position in the introduction, defend it throughout, and write an effective conclusion that ties the essay together.

- **Organization**

  Create a beginning that states your position, or controlling idea, and a middle that provides evidence and details to support your position and addresses objections. Restate your opinion in the conclusion.

- **Development of Ideas**

  Use precise, relevant evidence and logical details that support the topic sentence of each paragraph and that support the thesis.

- **Voice**

  Use a persuasive voice that is appropriate for your topic, audience, and context of your essay.

- **Conventions**

  Write clear complete sentences with varied beginnings. Check your writing for errors in grammar, sentence structure, capitalization, punctuation, and spelling.

 **Literature Connection.** You will encounter persuasion in all types of media—from TV commercials to the latest fads to works of literature. In her essay "Doing Nothing Is Something," author Anna Quindlen argues that, for children and teenagers, downtime is essential for fueling creativity.

---

**TEKS** **10.13A** Plan a first draft by selecting the correct genre; **ELPS** **2F** Listen to and derive meaning from a variety of media to build and reinforce concept and language attainment; **2G** Understand the general meaning, main points, and important details of spoken language/topics, languages, and contexts are familiar to unfamiliar; **3J** Respond orally to information presented in a variety of media to build and reinforce concept and language attainment

**TEKS** 10.13B, 10.16A, 10.16B, 10.16D, 10.16E

# Argumentative Essay

An argumentative essay clearly states where you stand on an issue. By stating and defending your position, you may be able to convince others to agree with you. In this sample essay, the student writer clearly defends his position.

**Beginning**
The beginning introduces the controlling idea and clearly states the opinion (underlined).

**Middle**
The first middle paragraph uses precise factual evidence to support the position.

The second, third, and fourth middle paragraphs add more evidence and logical reasons. Ideas are structured according to their relative value.

### Conserve Energy and Prevent an Oil Crisis

Gasoline continues to become more and more expensive. The reason is simple—the world's oil supply is slowly being used up. People are using more oil than ever without thinking of the consequences. In fact, many economists believe that an oil crisis is inevitable. When the crisis hits, prices of gasoline, home heating oil, and many other products will rise quickly. People will struggle to heat their homes and buy gas for their cars. Businesses will slow production—or even close down. It is time to address this serious issue and prevent an oil crisis—we must begin conserving oil.

The world's appetite for oil is huge. In 2010, people in the United States used more than 22 million barrels of oil per day to fuel cars, heat homes, and make plastics, clothing, and paint (Cummings 83). The United States government estimates current trends show world wide energy usage will rise to about 98 million barrels a day by 2015. Unless people learn how to conserve, the demand for oil will soon exceed the supply. To avoid a crisis, we must all do our best to conserve oil.

Oil conservation makes sense for many reasons. First of all, oil conservation will help to preserve a valuable resource. In 2008, the average passenger vehicle in the United States got about 22 miles per gallon (Reynolds 3). Today's fuel-efficient vehicles can get more than 30 miles per gallon (Staunton 15). If everyone chose a hybrid, cut out unnecessary car trips, and took public transportation whenever possible, the United States would save millions of barrels of oil every day. That, in turn, would help the nation's oil supply last longer.

Persuasive

## Argumentative Essay

Work through this sample with the class, pointing out the elements that make it an effective argumentative essay.
**DIFFERENTIATE INSTRUCTION**

### Focus and Coherence
- The thesis statement presents the opinion clearly.

### Organization
- The beginning states the position in general terms.
- The middle paragraphs contain specific supporting details.
- The last middle paragraph answers an objection.
- The ending restates the opinion.

### Development of Ideas
- The writer uses facts, statistics, and reasoning that support his argument.

### Voice
- The voice is natural and persuasive.
- The writer uses language that expresses his concern for the topic, such as *we must all do our best, if people don't act now, everyone can help,* and *everyone can play a part.*

**TEKS** 10.13B, 10.16A, 10.16B, 10.16D, 10.16E

---

**Differentiated Instruction:**
**English Language Learners**  **ELPS** 3F, 4K

| ELP Level **Beginning** | ELP Level **Intermediate** | ELP Level **Advanced/Advanced High** |
|---|---|---|
| Use strategies such as employing non-verbal cues and using synonyms to discuss how a persuasive essay should be organized. | Use strategies such as employing non-verbal cues and using synonyms to discuss how the essay is organized. | Have students explain how a persuasive essay should be organized. Have them check their paragraph from SE page 197 and make necessary organizational changes. |

 **TEKS 10.13B** Structure ideas in a sustained and persuasive way; **10.16A** Write an argumentative essay supported by precise and relevant evidence; **10.16B** Write an argumentative essay that includes the range of information and views on the topic and an accurate/honest representation of views; **10.16D** Write an argumentative essay that includes a structure appropriate to the purpose, audience, and context; **10.16E** Write an argumentative essay that includes analysis of specific data, facts, and ideas; **ELPS 3F** Give information/ranging from using a limited high-frequency vocabulary to using abstract and content-based vocabulary during speaking; **4K** Demonstrate comprehension and expand reading skills by employing analytical skills/evaluating written information and performing critical analyses

Ask students if they can think of ways the writer could improve his essay. Possible responses include the following:

- Add an interesting or powerful quotation or two.
- Address the possibility of inventing new technology to replace gasoline.

 **TEKS** 10.13B, 10.16A, 10.16B, 10.16C, 10.16D, 10.16E

**Respond to the reading.**

**Answers**

**Focus and Coherence 1.** It restates the position (we must begin conserving oil) and reinforces it by calling the readers to action.

**Organization 2.** the first middle paragraph **3.** the last middle paragraph

**Development of Ideas 4.** *oil conservation will help to preserve a valuable resource; conserving oil also helps to protect the environment;* and *conserving oil can save consumers money.*

**Voice 5.** Yes. He supports his opinion with facts and statistics, answers an objection, and uses an authoritative voice.

 **ELPS** 4G, 4K

---

**200**

 **TEKS** 10.13B, 10.16A–10.16E
**ELPS** 4K

**Middle**
paragraphs show an analysis of the relative value of data, facts, and ideas.

Conserving oil also helps to protect the environment. Automobiles, home oil burners, and other oil-consuming technologies contribute to air pollution and global warming. When oil and gasoline are burned, polluting gases are released into the atmosphere. One of these gases, carbon dioxide, is a leading cause of global warming. Using less oil for transportation and home heating will reduce air pollution and the effects of global warming.

Finally, conserving oil can save consumers money. Conservation decreases demand for oil, which causes prices of gasoline, heating oil, and other petroleum-based products to drop, or at least to increase at a slower rate. Conservation also saves consumers money directly. At $3 per gallon, using 10 fewer gallons would save $30. Decreased usage increases savings.

The last middle paragraph addresses an objection.

Some people say that the best way to prevent an oil crisis is to drill more oil wells (Miller 86). This is a short-term solution that has its own environmental problems. No one knows how much oil is left, but we do know that the supply is limited. Conservation is smarter. It makes the most of the available oil supply.

**Ending**
The conclusion restates and reinforces the position stated in the introduction.

Gasoline is expensive now, but in the future it could cost $7 per gallon or more. If people don't act now to conserve oil, these prices will soon be here. Conserving oil not only stretches oil supplies and saves consumers money but also cuts pollution. Everyone can help. Drivers can avoid gas-guzzling SUV's and opt for more fuel-efficient hybrid cars. Homeowners can insulate their homes and turn down their thermostats in the winter. Everyone can play a part in preventing an oil crisis.

 **Respond to the reading. Answer the following questions. Discuss your ideas with a classmate. Focus and Coherence (1) How does the conclusion support the thesis statement? Organization (2) Which paragraph explains the problem in detail? (3) Which paragraph answers an objection? Development of Ideas 4) What are three logical reasons the writer gives for conserving oil? Voice 5) Does the writer sound knowledgeable and persuasive? Explain.**

---

**Differentiated Instruction: Struggling Learners**

When it comes time to select a problem, have students consider one that

- affects their age group,
- has been publicly debated, so that both sides are well known, and
- will be easy to research.

---

**TEKS** 10.13B Structure ideas in a sustained and persuasive way; **10.16A** Write an argumentative essay supported by precise and relevant evidence; **10.16B** Write an argumentative essay that includes the range of information and views on the topic and an accurate/honest representation of views; **10.16C** Write an argumentative essay that includes counter-arguments to anticipate and address objections; **10.16D** Write an argumentative essay that includes a structure appropriate to the purpose, audience, and context; **10.16E** Write an argumentative essay that includes analysis of specific data, facts, and ideas; **ELPS** 4G Demonstrate comprehension of increasingly complex English/participating in shared reading/responding to questions; **4K** Demonstrate comprehension and expand reading skills by employing analytical skills/evaluating written information and performing critical analyses

# Prewriting

In your prewriting for your argumentative essay, you will select a social, political, or environmental issue, and then gather reasons and details to support your position. It is important to organize your ideas in a sustained, persuasive way. Careful prewriting makes persuasive writing easier and more effective.

### Keys to Effective Prewriting

1. Choose a social, political, or environmental topic that interests you. Think about the topic, and decide what your position is.

2. Write a clear position statement to guide your research and your writing.

3. Gather the most logical reasons and the best evidence to support your position. Rank the reasons according to their relative value, 1 for the most important, 2 for the next most important, etc.

4. Address an important objection.

5. Create a list or an outline as a planning guide.

Persuasive

## Prewriting
### Keys to Effective Prewriting

Remind students of the purpose of the prewriting stage in the writing process: The prewriting stage is when the writer selects a topic, gathers details, and decides how to organize those details. ✔ DIFFERENTIATE INSTRUCTION

The Keys to Effective Prewriting list explains the process students will be guided through on SE pages 202–204.

To launch the students' prewriting, ask them whether they have read any articles about current issues (local, state, national, or global). List some of these issues on the board for discussion. Consider the various positions that people take on each issue. Encourage students to take notes during the discussion. These notes might yield useful ideas as they decide what to write about.

 **Writer's Craft**

The activities in prewriting can function as minilessons in your writing workshop. Use them to introduce, model, and teach specific strategies to the whole class, to small groups, or to individual students. You'll find similar minilesson materials in the drafting, revising, and editing steps.

---

## Differentiated Instruction: English Language Learners

⭐ **ELPS** 1A, 1F, 1H, 2A, 2B, 2C, 4A, 4F

| ELP Level **Beginning** | ELP Level **Intermediate** | ELP Level **Advanced/Advanced High** |
|---|---|---|
| Identify relationships between sounds and letters by explaining the meaning of *pre* in *prewriting* and having students pronounce it and other words with the same prefix. | Identify relationships between sounds and letters by explaining the meaning of *pre* in *prewriting*. Identify other words with this prefix and help students predict their meanings. | Present various prefixes (*pre-, re-, anti-*) as they are used in familiar words. Help students predict the meaning of each by comparing the meanings of the words. |

**ELPS 1A** Use prior knowledge to understand meanings; **1F** Use accessible language and learn new and essential language in the process; **1H** Develop and expand learning strategies/reasoning, looking for patterns in language, and analyzing sayings and expressions; **2A** Distinguish sounds with increasing ease; **2B** Recognize elements of the English sound system in new vocabulary/long and short vowels, silent letters, and consonant clusters; **2C** Learn academic vocabulary heard during classroom instruction/interactions; **4A** Learn relationships between sounds and letters/sound out words using a combination of skills; **4F** Use support from peers/teachers to develop vocabulary

## Prewriting
### Planning Your Writing

Caution students that some issues they may consider writing about are too complex to address in a typical essay. Explain that often complex issues can be narrowed to identify a topic that is the correct size for an essay.

**Choose an issue.** Remind students that a topic need not be dramatic and global in scope to be suitable. For example, they could write about the problem of the large amount of waste produced in the school cafeteria.

**TEKS** 10.13A, 10.16A

### Focus on the Texas Traits

**Focus and Coherence**
Suggest that students use an evaluation-collection grid, reasons chart, or other graphic organizer to collect their evidence and supporting details.

---

## Prewriting Planning Your Writing

Controversies and differing opinions are a part of life. To find a writing topic, student writer Marcela Andrade answered two key questions about important, interesting issues that had been in the news recently. After reviewing her answers, she marked the issue that she would like to write about with an asterisk. Then she stated the position she would take on the issue.

### List of Issues

What issues have been covered in the news recently?
- global warming and its damage to the environment
- the increasing cost of health care
- the growth of hunger in the United States *
- a decline in the number of people who vote

What social, environmental, or political issues have we discussed in class?
- increased crime in our state and nation
- the reemergence and spread of tuberculosis
- a lack of good jobs for factory workers

Position statement about hunger in the United States: I believe that the best way to address the hunger crisis in the United States is to support local food banks.

**Choose an issue.** On your own paper, answer each of the questions above in two or three different ways. Then put an asterisk next to the issue that you feel most strongly about. Also write a sentence that states your position or opinion on the issue and the reasons for your choice.

### Focus on the Texas Traits

**Focus and Coherence** Choose an issue that you can discuss clearly with your audience. You may have to do some research before you can write your thesis, or opinion, statement. You can then select relevant evidence and precise details to defend your position.

---

### Differentiated Instruction: Struggling Learners

Have students evaluate the supporting details for each reason in their charts. Instruct them to consider not only the number of details but also their strength. Point out that the reason supported by the greatest number of strong details is most likely the strongest reason.

**TEKS** 10.16A

---

**TEKS** 10.13B, 10.16A, 10.16F

# Gathering Reasons to Support Your Position

After you have you have chosen your topic and stated your opinion, you need to use a range of appeals—facts, data, case studies, anecdotes—to convince your audience. Marcela used a chart to gather and list reasons and evidence.

## Reasons Chart

Position: The best way to solve this country's hunger crisis is to support local food banks.

| Logical Reasons | Supporting Evidence |
|---|---|
| Food banks do a great job of getting food to the people who need it. | – 36 million served in 2011<br>– food banks know local situation<br>– many people work with food banks<br>– food banks deliver food |
| Food banks help businesses and the environment. | – accept food from restaurants, grocery stores, other businesses<br>– save businesses money every year<br>– keep food out of waste stream |
| Food banks are economically efficient. | – in Texas alone, people volunteer more than 200,000 hours each year<br>– don't require fancy offices or tons of paperwork |

**Prewrite**

**Create a reasons chart. Create your own logical reasons and evidence chart. List a range of appeals, identifying at least three reasons to support your position. Include precise, factual data and logical details that support each reason.**

**Texas Traits**

## Focus on the Texas Traits

**Organization** Persuasive essays are often organized by order of importance and relative value of the information. After you have finished your chart, consider ranking your appeals in order of importance. This will help you plan your essay.

## Gathering Reasons to Support Your Position

Encourage students to use more than one source when gathering supporting evidence. The more varied the experts, studies, and organizations that they refer to, the stronger their argument will be.

**Create a reasons chart.** Reproduce the T-chart (see TE Appendix) for students to use as their reasons chart. Students could also use index cards to make notes as they research their topics, labeling each card at the top with the main reason and listing supporting details below. ⬆ **DIFFERENTIATE INSTRUCTION**

**TEKS** 10.13B, 10.16A, 10.16F

✳ For more about creating note cards, see SE page 432.

### Focus on the Texas Traits

**Organization** Have students meet in small groups to discuss their ranking of the evidence. Have classmate evaluate the ranking and suggest changes or reasons that require additional evidence.

## Literature Connections

**Mentor texts:** Often, professional writers pile up reasons to strengthen their arguments. Inspire students to find a variety of types of support for their position by reading to them excerpts from persuasive literature that is loaded with many reasons:

*You Can Save the Animals: 251 Simple Ways to Stop Thoughtless Cruelty* by Ingrid Newkirk

*101 Reasons to Love the Red Sox: And 10 Reasons to Hate the Yankees* by David Green

*50 Ways to Save the Ocean* by David Helvarg, Philippe Cousteau, Jim Toomey

*Ultimate Weight Solution for Teens: The 7 Keys to Weight Freedom* by Jay McGraw and Phil McGraw ⬆ **DIFFERENTIATE INSTRUCTION**

**TEKS** **10.13B** Structure ideas in a sustained and persuasive way; **10.16A** Write an argumentative essay supported by precise and relevant evidence; **10.16F** Write an argumentative essay that includes a range of appeals; **ELPS** **2G** Understand the general meaning and main points of spoken language/topics, languages, and contexts are familiar to unfamiliar; **2I** Demonstrate listening comprehension in increasingly complex spoken language by summarizing spoken messages; **3C** Speak using a variety of grammatical structures and sentence lengths with increasing accuracy and ease

**Persuasive**

## Differentiated Instruction: English Language Learners

**ELPS** 2G, 2I, 3C

| ELP Level<br>**Beginning** | ELP Level<br>**Intermediate** | ELP Level<br>**Advanced/Advanced High** |
|---|---|---|
| Read a short, adapted section from one of these books. Have students demonstrate listening comprehension by summarizing material using short phrases and their first language. | Have students read a short section from one of these books with a partner. Have students summarize the material using short phrases and applicable supports. | Have students read a section from one of these books. Then have students demonstrate listening comprehension by summarizing material using increasingly complex sentences. |

## Prewriting
### Gathering Objections

Students may decide to address more than one objection if that is the best way to make their argument. However, students should usually select only one objection, perhaps the strongest one, to counter.

**Gather objections.** Explain the meaning of a straw man argument (an opposing argument that is misrepresented so as to make it easy to defeat), and encourage students to avoid using them. Any objection students address should be strong and accurately represented. By dealing with the true objections of those who oppose their view, students can strengthen their position much more than they would by defeating straw men.

 **TEKS** 10.16B

### Countering an Objection

Remind students that when presenting counter-arguments, they should be sure to focus their reasons on the opposing view. Unrelated reasons should be located elsewhere in their essay.

**Counter an important objection.** Have pairs of students exchange their lists of counter-arguments. Have each student rate the strength of his or her partner's ideas. What counter-argument seems the most convincing? Are there other ways to counter the argument?

Ask students to consider their partner's feedback as they decide how to address the objection in their essay.

 **TEKS** 10.16C

---

 **TEKS** 10.16B, 10.16C

## Prewriting Gathering Objections

As you gather reasons and evidence that support your position, it is wise to gather evidence that will enable you to defend your opinion against at least one strong objection that readers might pose. Addressing objections honestly and accurately can make your position even more persuasive. How can you anticipate and address the objections? Start with a little research.

- Read local newspapers and monitor local television and radio news reports to find arguments that both support and oppose your position.
- Think of class discussions. Recall any opposing arguments and how they were addressed.
- Ask the opinions of your friends and family. Try to debate positions that differ from yours, and listen carefully during the discussion.

Marcela found the following three objections and put an asterisk next to the strongest one.

> – Food banks already have plenty of support.
> – Government programs like food stamps provide all the help people need. ✳
> – Not many people in the United States use food banks.

 **Gather objections.** Use the strategies above to gather and list three objections to your position. Put an asterisk next to the strongest objection.

## Countering an Objection

Countering an objection means arguing against it. Marcela listed three reasons that she could support with evidence to disagree with the objection she chose to address.

> **Objection:** Government programs like food stamps provide all the help
>     people need. ✳
>
> 1. Even with food stamps, the hunger problem has grown.
> 2. Despite government help, millions of people still visit food banks.
> 3. Applying for food stamps takes time. Some people need food right away.

 **Counter an important objection.** Write down the strongest objection to your argument. List several logical reasons why you disagree with it.

---

**TEKS** **10.16B** Write an argumentative essay that includes the range of information and views on the topic; **10.16C** Write an argumentative essay that includes counter-arguments to anticipate and address objections

## Drafting

You have chosen an issue, stated your position, developed support for it, and identified an objection to address. You are ready to begin your draft.

Keys to Effective Drafting

1. Write on every other line or double-space on the computer to make room for changes later on.

2. Introduce the issue and state your position in the first paragraph.

3. Provide background information, specific logical reasons, and supporting evidence in the middle paragraphs.

4. Include precise details to support your reasons.

5. Address an important objection.

6. In the conclusion, reemphasize your position and summarize the support for your position.

*Persuasive*

## Drafting
### Keys to Effective Drafting

Remind students that the drafting stage is when they are able to connect their ideas on paper.

The Keys to Effective Drafting list explains the process students will be guided through on SE pages 206–210.

Lead students through each item on the list. The first is a simple matter of form. All of the other items are about content, which students should have thought about during prewriting.

Encourage students to consult their graphic organizers or planning notes as they write. Tell them that checking off the important points on their reasons chart or in their notes as they mention them in the draft is helpful.

### Writer's Craft

Use an overhead or the board to compose sample sentences of your own so that your students can see you writing. It's crucial that they see you not just as an instructor, but as a writer as well. This is one key strategy for creating a writing community in your classroom. ✔ DIFFERENTIATE INSTRUCTION

---

## Differentiated Instruction: English Language Learners

⭐ ELPS 1D, 1E, 3C, 3F, 3G

| ELP Level **Beginning** | ELP Level **Intermediate** | ELP Level **Advanced/Advanced High** |
|---|---|---|
| Ask students to state their position aloud. Model sentence stems and learning strategies such as nonverbal cues, requesting assistance, etc. | Ask students to present several of the reasons for their position using newly learned vocabulary. Model sentence stems as needed. | Have students discuss their positions and related objections in groups. Encourage students (through modeling) to speak using a variety of sentence lengths, sentence types, and connecting words. |

**ELPS 1D** Speak using learning strategies/request assistance, employ non-verbal cues, and convey ideas by defining or describing; **1E** Internalize new basic and academic language by using and reusing it/speaking; **3C** Speak using a variety of sentence lengths/types and connecting words with increasing accuracy and ease; **3F** Give information/ranging from using a limited high-frequency vocabulary to using abstract and content-based vocabulary during speaking; **3G** Express opinions and ideas ranging from communicating short phrases to participating in discussions

## Drafting
### Getting the Big Picture

Review the basic structure of an argumentative essay using the beginning, middle, ending diagram on SE page 206. Discuss the importance of developing the ideas to build a persuasive case for their position on the issue.

Before students begin their first drafts, consider having them organize their planning notes into an outline. This helps them see how everything will fit together.

＊ For more about outlines, see SE pages 626–627.

Remind students that outlines and other planning notes are only guides. As students create their drafts, they may think of new details to add and better ways to organize the information. Also stress to students the importance of forming an effective thesis statement to guide their writing. Remind students that their thesis should state their position on the issue. A helpful formula for creating a thesis statement for an argumentative essay is:

An issue + A specific position on the issue = An effective thesis statement

Students may want to try several different thesis statements before proceeding with writing their drafts. **DIFFERENTIATE INSTRUCTION ↘**

**★ TEKS** 10.13B, 10.16B, 10.16C, 10.16D

＊ For more about thesis statements, see SE page 630.

---

## Drafting Getting the Big Picture

The graphic below shows how the parts of your argumentative essay should fit together. Be sure that your organizational pattern is appropriate for the purpose, audience, and context of your essay. Use this graphic and your prewriting plan to guide the writing of your first draft. (The examples are from the student essay on pages **207–210**.)

**Beginning**

The **introduction** states the writer's position about the chosen issue.

> **Position Statement**
> People can help end hunger in this country by supporting local food banks.

**Middle**

The **middle** paragraphs explain the issue and supply logical reasons and evidence supporting the writer's position. The objection shows an honest representation of the opposing viewpoint. Ideas are structured in a sustained and persuasive manner.

> **Topic Sentences**
> Hunger affects people in the United States, and the problem is worsening.
>
> First and foremost, food banks deserve support because they know how to put food in the hands of the people who need it.
>
> In addition, food banks operate in a very efficient way.
>
> Lastly, food banks serve the environment well.
>
> Some people argue that food banks are not necessary.

**Ending**

The **conclusion** sums up the writer's position on the issue and offers a final important thought.

> **Closing Sentence**
> After all, everyone deserves at least one good meal a day.

---

**TEKS** **10.13B** Structure ideas in a sustained and persuasive way; **10.16B** Write an argumentative essay that includes the range of information and views on the topic and an accurate/honest representation of views; **10.16C** Write an argumentative essay that includes counter-arguments to anticipate and address objections; **10.16D** Write an argumentative essay that includes a structure appropriate to the purpose, audience, and context

# Starting Your Essay

The beginning paragraph of your essay should capture the reader's attention, introduce the topic, and state your position. Here are some examples of rhetorical devices you can use to convey meaning and create an effective introduction.

> **Beginning**
> Middle
> Ending

- **Capture the reader's attention.**
  Use a rhetorical device, such as a question, a quotation, or repetition.
  *What is it like to be hungry? How does it feel?*

- **Introduce the topic, and appeal to the reader's sympathy.**
  A rhetorical device, such as an appeal to sympathy, adds to the effectiveness of your argument.
  *Sadly, millions of men, women, and children in this country face hunger every day.*

- **State your position.**
  Your position statement is your thesis statement for the entire essay. You can also use a rhetorical device, such as parallelism or irony, to support your thesis.
  *People can help end hunger in this country by supporting local food banks.*

## Beginning Paragraph

> The topic is introduced.
>
> Ideas are structured in a persuasive way. Position statement is presented (underlined).

> Every day, needless hunger devastates families in the United States. What is it like to be hungry? How does it feel? Initially, the stomach starts to rumble, and the mouth waters. Then thoughts of food fill the mind. It becomes hard to concentrate. Most people head for the kitchen or the cafeteria, find some food, and the hunger is history. Now what if there is no food in sight? Sadly, millions of men, women, and children in this country face hunger every day. <u>People can help end hunger in this country by supporting local food banks.</u>

**Write an introduction.** Use dramatic, engaging language or rhetorical devices to introduce the topic, state your position, and provide necessary background information.

Draft

---

**Differentiated Instruction: English Language Learners**

ELPS 5F

| ELP Level **Beginning** | ELP Level **Intermediate** | ELP Level **Advanced/Advanced High** |
|---|---|---|
| Have students complete the thesis statement formula for a topic of their choice using simple phrases. Allow students to supplement with drawings and their first language. | After students complete the issue and position portions of the thesis formula on a topic of their choice, have them craft a simple thesis sentence with a partner's help. | Have students write an effective thesis statement using the thesis formula. Provide vocabulary and sentence structure modeling when needed. |

---

# Starting Your Essay

Acknowledge that coming up with the right opening is challenging. Suggest that students experiment with two or three different openings before choosing the one that seems to work best.

✷ For more about writing great beginnings, see SE page 631.

**Write an introduction.** Have students read the quote by Gloria D. Miklowitz at the bottom of the page. Discuss what it means to "write visually" and why such writing serves to engage the reader (it appeals to their senses). Also ask students, *What does it mean to 'make every word count?'* Explain that eliminating unnecessary, superfluous words or sentences from their writing gives their work a greater impact.

TEKS 10.13B, 10.16A

 **TEKS 10.13B** Structure ideas in a sustained and persuasive way; **10.16A** Write an argumentative essay supported by precise and relevant evidence; **ELPS 5F** Write using a variety of grade-appropriate sentence lengths and patterns in increasingly accurate ways

Persuasive

## Drafting

### Developing the Middle Part

Have students take a few minutes to review the order in which they plan to present their ideas. While there are general rules for the best order in which to present reasons and details, there are certainly exceptions. The key is to present them in the order that provides the strongest support for their thesis statement.

### Using Transitions

Tell students that appropriate transitions should create an essay that flows very naturally from idea to idea. They help the reader move from one thought to the next and see the connection between them. If, while reading their work, students find that some paragraphs don't seem to fit with those before and after, the problem may be poor transitions. Encourage them to experiment with the transition examples on this page to restore the flow of their writing.

⭐ **TEKS** 10.13B

---

## Drafting Developing the Middle Part

The middle part of your essay provides the main reasons, relevant evidence, and precise details that support your position. Refer to your reasons and evidence chart. Begin each paragraph with a topic sentence, and then add details that support it. Also address an objection in the last middle paragraph.

## Using Transitions

Transitions move your essay smoothly from one paragraph to the next. They can also show the order of importance of your ideas. The following chart includes transitions that could connect your middle paragraphs, depending upon the organizational pattern that you have chosen.

| Paragraph 1 | Paragraph 2 | Paragraph 3 |
|---|---|---|
| First of all ⟶ | Also ⟶ | Another reason |
| One reason ⟶ | Another reason ⟶ | Most importantly |
| First and foremost ⟶ | In addition ⟶ | Lastly |

### Middle Paragraphs

> Facts and precise statistical data support the position.

> A topic sentence introduces each middle paragraph (underlined). Transitions link ideas.

Hunger affects people in the United States, and the problem is worsening. In 2007, about 33 million Americans did not know how or where they would get the food they needed to stay healthy ("Current News"). By 2011, that number had grown to 36 million. Hunger affects people in many ways. Children who are hungry have a harder time learning, and they may experience delays in physical development. Hunger affects the health of grown-ups, too, and makes it harder for them to work and care for their families (Workman 82).

First and foremost, food banks deserve support because they know how to put food in the hands of the people who need it. In 2010, one food bank in Texas collected, stored, and distributed enough food to provide over 12 million meals ("East Texas Food Bank"). Feeding the hungry is a massive effort that has been going on for years. Because food banks are local, they often know where to locate and how to reach out to people who need food. People often

---

Argumentative Essay   **209**

feel more comfortable visiting a local food bank than they do applying for assistance from a government agency.

In addition, food banks operate in a very efficient way. Because they rely largely on donations and the work of volunteers, food banks keep their costs low. Thousands of people donate hundreds of thousands of hours every year to food banks. That means money donated to a food bank isn't wasted. For example, the Davis City Food Bank uses 90 cents of every dollar donated to buy food for hungry men, women, and children.

Lastly, food banks serve the environment well. Every day, grocery stores, restaurants, and other businesses throw out tons of unneeded food or food beyond its expiration date. The food is safe and edible but often ends up in landfills. Many food banks now collect this food and redistribute it. This process keeps this food from being wasted and filling landfills. Businesses save money, too. Instead of paying a trash hauler, businesses can have the food bank pick up the food for free. There are federal tax incentives for donating, and laws have been passed to protect businesses that donate food.

Some people argue that food banks are unnecessary. They think that government programs such as food stamps are enough to ease hunger. However, not all the people in need qualify for government programs, and applying for help can take time. Hungry people need to be fed, and food banks do just that. Also, even with government help, the hunger problem has escalated. Without food banks, the problem will only keep getting worse.

> **Each middle paragraph provides logical reasons, relevant evidence, and details to support the position.**

> **The fifth middle paragraph counters an objection.**

**Draft**

**Write your middle paragraphs.** Create persuasive middle paragraphs that promote your position and give reasons that support it. Start each paragraph with a topic sentence and follow with precise, relevant evidence and details. Your final middle paragraph should respond to a significant objection.

## Tip

- Structure your essay so that the most important reasons come first, and use transitions between paragraphs to show order of importance.

- Support reasons with relevant facts, statistics, and quotations from experts. Respond to a significant objection with solid facts and reasons.

Have students respond to the middle paragraphs by asking them whether the paragraphs fulfill the writing goals on SE page 206. (Students should agree that they do.) *What could be improved?* Possible responses include the following:

- Consider putting the most important reason last. This may be more convincing.
- Include quotations that provide expert support for the topic.
- Make sure there are enough details. For example, readers may not know that using 90 cents per dollar on food means that food banks have very low administration costs.

**Write your middle paragraphs.** If you are allowing flexibility in how many middle paragraphs students write, explain that although there is no set number of middle paragraphs required for an argumentative essay, several points deserve consideration. Too few ideas leave the position undersupported; the audience won't be persuaded to the writer's point of view. Too many ideas may lose the readers' interest or cause them to miss the argument's big picture. The example essay that contains five middle paragraphs is a good example of balancing these two extremes. Depending on the audience and purpose, students may want to write more or less.

TEKS 10.13B, 10.16A, 10.16B, 10.16C, 10.16E

If students have trouble determining which of their reasons are most important, have them consult a partner. Another person's insight is often very helpful. ☑ **DIFFERENTIATE INSTRUCTION**

**ELPS** 3E, 3F

**Persuasive**

---

## Differentiated Instruction: English Language Learners

**ELPS** 1E, 3B, 3F, 3G, 3H

| **ELP Level** **Beginning** | **ELP Level** **Intermediate** | **ELP Level** **Advanced/Advanced High** |
|---|---|---|
| Model the words *most* and *least* in explaining the importance of several ideas. Then, have students use these words to describe their own ideas. | Have students order their ideas from most to least important. Prompt students with sentence stems and basic vocabulary to help them explain why they ordered the ideas as they did. | Have students order their ideas from most to least important. Prompt students with complex sentence stems and academic vocabulary to help them explain their order. |

TEKS **10.13B** Structure ideas in a sustained and persuasive way/develop drafts in open-ended situations that include transitions; **10.16A** Write an argumentative essay supported by relevant evidence; **10.16B** Write an argumentative essay that includes the range of information and views on the topic and an accurate/honest representation of views; **10.16C** Write an argumentative essay that includes counter-arguments to anticipate and address objections; **10.16E** Write an argumentative essay that includes analysis of specific data, facts, and ideas; **ELPS 1E** Internalize new basic and academic language by using and reusing it/speaking; **3B** Expand vocabulary by learning and using routine language needed for classroom communication; **3E** Share information in cooperative learning interactions; **3F** Ask for and give information/ranging from using a limited high-frequency vocabulary to using abstract and content-based vocabulary during speaking; **3G** Express opinions ranging from communicating short phrases to participating in discussions; **3H** Explain with increasing specificity and detail

## Drafting
### Ending Your Essay

Point out that an important strategy for writing a successful closing paragraph is reviewing or reemphasizing information from the essay while making it sound fresh. One way to do this is to avoid the ineffective repetition of words.

**Write your ending paragraph and prepare a complete first draft.** Note that writers will often include a call to action in their ending paragraph. Explain that a call to action is something writers ask readers to do in response to their essay. This can be an effective way to bring an argument to a close.

### Try It!

Further analysis may also be helpful. For example, students may want to underline all of their logical reasons and circle the relevant evidence that goes with each. This will allow students to see at a glance whether each middle paragraph contains a single topic supported by sufficient evidence.

**★ TEKS** 10.13B, 10.16A, 10.16C

---

## Drafting Ending Your Essay

The main part of your essay should have stated your position and supported it with solid, logical reasons and relevant evidence. With that information in place, you are ready to write your ending. Your conclusion should do all of the following:

> Beginning
>
> Middle
>
> ▶ **Ending**

- Restate your position and add a final insight.
- Summarize the main reasons that support your position.
- Leave the reader with an important final insight.

### Ending Paragraph

| | |
|---|---|
| The solution is restated. | <u>Supporting local food banks is the best way to help ease the hunger problem.</u> Individuals can provide support by volunteering their services or by donating money or food. In either case, hungry people get the food they need, and surplus food gets used. Concerned citizens should contact their local food banks today and offer their help because government programs can't do enough. By backing food banks, people can help to alleviate hunger in this country. After all, everyone deserves at least one good meal a day. |
| A final persuasive call is made. | |
| A final insight is provided. | |

Draft

**Write your ending paragraph and prepare a complete first draft.** Use the ideas listed above as a guide to develop your final paragraph. Then prepare a copy of your entire essay. Write on every other line or double-space on the computer. This will give you room for revising.

### Try It!

If you have followed the traditional persuasive essay structure, your first draft should have turned out well. That structure includes four parts:

1. Introduce the topic and state your opinion.
2. Support your opinion with logical reasons and relevant evidence.
3. Answer an objection.
4. Wrap up your argument.

To make sure that your essay is complete, mark each paragraph with the correct number—a 1 next to your opening paragraph, a 2 next to each supporting paragraph, and so on.

---

# Revising

Revising is the process of improving a first draft. When you revise, you add or delete details, rearrange parts of your writing, and work on developing a more convincing, persuasive voice. You also check your word choice and sentence fluency to make sure you have communicated your ideas effectively.

Argumentative Essay **211**

**Keys to Effective Revising**

1. As you begin to revise, read your essay to get a feeling for how well it works as a whole. As you begin your revision, keep in mind your purpose, your audience, and the genre, or form, of the writing.

2. Be sure you have clearly stated your position.

3. Check your paragraphs. They should have topic sentences followed by supporting details in logical order, according to their relative value.

4. Be sure you've used an authoritative, respectful voice.

5. Check your writing for precise nouns and direct, active verbs.

6. Be sure you have used different kinds of sentences with varied beginnings.

Persuasive

# Revising

**Keys to Effective Revising**

Remind students that the revising stage is when writers have an opportunity to make improvements to their first drafts. At this stage, they can think about refinements they might not have considered when they were drafting.

The Keys to Effective Revising list explains the process students will follow on SE pages 212–220.

As students work on their revisions, schedule brief conferences to discuss the improvements they plan to make. ✔ DIFFERENTIATE INSTRUCTION

---

**Differentiated Instruction: English Language Learners**

⭐ **ELPS** 4C, 4F, 4G, 4H, 4I

| ELP Level **Beginning** | ELP Level **Intermediate** | ELP Level **Advanced/Advanced High** |
|---|---|---|
| Have students demonstrate comprehension by summarizing the example ending paragraph (adapted) after shared reading. Students use pictures and their first language as needed. | Have students demonstrate comprehension by summarizing the example ending paragraph (adapted) after silent reading. Students work with a partner for help with basic vocabulary. | Have students demonstrate comprehension by summarizing the example ending paragraph after reading it silently. Students work with a partner for help with academic vocabulary. |

 **ELPS** **4C** Develop basic sight vocabulary and comprehend vocabulary used in written classroom materials; **4F** Use support from peers/teachers to read grade-appropriate text, enhance understanding, and develop vocabulary; **4G** Demonstrate comprehension of increasingly complex English/participating in shared reading and summarizing material; **4H** Read silently with increasing ease and comprehension for longer periods; **4I** Demonstrate comprehension by employing basic reading skills

**Revising for Focus and Coherence**

Remind students that the essay structure discussed during the drafting step is designed specifically for an argumentative essay. Other genres, like narrative or expository essays, will be organized in their own ways to meet the specific goals of that form.

⭐ **TEKS** 10.13C, 10.16A

**Have I focused on one major issue throughout the essay?**

Similar to what happens when writing other genres, remind students that there may be very good details that are not directed toward the central idea and must be cut. This may include removing anything from a simple phrase to an entire paragraph. **DIFFERENTIATE INSTRUCTION ↘**

### Exercise
**Answers**

**Possible Answer**

Providing food for food banks doesn't even have to cost money. Every day, grocery stores and restaurants throw out unwanted food (sometimes their waste can be as high as 40%!). This food is perfectly good and safe. What a terrible waste! Rather than being sent to a landfill, this food can be donated to food banks and used to feed the hungry. Often, businesses can even save money on their taxes by making these charitable donations. It's a win for the environment, a win for the business, and, most of all, a win for those who need this food the most.

**Check your thesis statement and topic sentences.** Students may want to use a graphic organizer to visualize the connections between the topic sentences and the thesis statement and between the body sentences in each paragraph and their corresponding topic sentence.

---

 **Revising for Focus and Coherence**

When you revise for *focus and coherence*, be sure you have clearly explained the issue and convincingly argued your position. Remember, your job is to convince the audience. Your entire essay should be directed toward this goal. Check your choice of genre. Have you chosen the appropriate form for the writing? If not, you will need to change the genre.

### Have I focused on one major issue throughout the essay?

An argumentative essay focuses on one major issue. Your introduction should describe and state your position on that issue. The middle paragraphs should provide more information and give relevant evidence, precise details, and logical reasons to convince your audience. Your conclusion should restate your position and tie the essay together.

- **Review the following thesis statement.**
  Food banks are working together to help solve the problem of hunger in America.

- **The following topic sentences focus on the thesis statement.**
  Hunger affects about 36 million people in the United States, and the problem is worsening. Food banks operate very efficiently.

- **The following topic sentences do not seem to focus on the thesis statement.**
  Our community food bank is running out of food. People in Africa and South America are going hungry, too.

### Exercise

Read the paragraph below. How would you revise the paragraph to add focus and coherence?

1     Food banks also serve the environment well. Every day, grocery stores,
2 and restaurants throw out unwanted food. They want to attract customers, so
3 they run ads with specials in the papers. This unwanted food is safe to eat,
4 but it ends up in landfills. This creates another problem, not enough room to
5 store our trash. Everyone can recycle. Businesses are encouraged to donate to
6 food banks, and many do donate. It saves them money in several ways.

 **Check your thesis statement and topic sentences.** Re-read your essay to make sure that your topic sentences focus on the thesis statement and that the other sentences support each paragraph topic sentence.

---

## Is my position consistent?

As you re-read your essay and revise it, look carefully to make sure that you have convincingly and consistently argued for your position. As you revise, check to make sure that you accurately explored the issue and considered a wide range of views on the topic. This includes identifying at least one major objection and developing counter-arguments to address it. Be careful not to use loaded language. Check to make sure that your reasons are logical, well documented with factual evidence, and that they support your thesis. The following exercise can help you decide if your position is consistent.

### Exercise

Use the following checklist to ensure that you have consistently supported your position.

_____ **1.** After reading the essay, do I still believe in my position? Explain.

_____ **2.** Do I have three compelling reasons that consistently support my position? Underline them in your essay.

_____ **3.** Have I given an honest accounting of views on the issue?

_____ **4.** Do I accurately, logically, and honestly counter a main objection? Circle that part.

_____ **5.** Have I included ideas that do not relate to the main issue? If so, delete them.

**Check your essay.** Revise to make sure that your position is consistent.

Writer supports the thesis with relevant evidence.

like food stamps are enough to ease the hunger problem.
Some people think that government programs help.

However, not all people qualify for government programs.

Hungry people need to be fed when they are hungry, and food

banks do just that. Also, even with government programs, the

hunger problem has escalated.

## Is my position consistent?

Note the emphasis on accuracy, logic, documentation, and truthfulness. Many issues can evoke strong emotional reactions from those writing about them. While these feelings can be harnessed and used effectively in the writing, they must not replace precise, relevant, and accurate evidence.

### Exercise
### Answers

Tell students that as a writer explores an issue, it is not unusual for her or his perspective or position to change. If that is the case with any of your students, encourage them to use the reasons that changed their mind as they revise their essay to reflect their new position. If these reasons were convincing enough to persuade them, then they'll be convincing enough to persuade others as well!

 **TEKS** 10.13C, 10.16B, 10.16C

**Check your essay.** Students may find it difficult to assess the consistency of their arguments. After they have worked through the checklist, have partners check their work as well. If possible, partners should suggest ways in which the arguments could be made more consistent. Remind students to always keep their comments polite and constructive.

**TEKS** 10.13C Revise drafts/rethink how well the purpose, audience, and genre have been addressed; **10.16B** Write an argumentative essay that includes the range of views on the topic and an accurate/honest representation of views; **10.16C** Write an argumentative essay that includes counter-arguments to anticipate and address objections; **ELPS** **4F** Use support from peers/teachers to enhance and confirm understanding; **4G** Demonstrate comprehension of increasingly complex English/participating in shared reading, summarizing material, and taking notes; **4I** Demonstrate comprehension by employing basic reading skills; **4J** Demonstrate comprehension and expand reading skills by employing inferential skills/predicting, making connections between ideas, drawing conclusions from text, and finding supporting evidence; **4K** Demonstrate comprehension and expand reading skills by employing analytical skills/evaluating written information and performing critical analyses

## Differentiated Instruction:
## English Language Learners

**ELPS** 4F, 4G, 4I, 4J, 4K

| ELP Level **Beginning** | ELP Level **Intermediate** | ELP Level **Advanced/Advanced High** |
|---|---|---|
| Present an adapted persuasive paragraph from a magazine or newspaper. Read together to identify the thesis. Allow gestures and use of first language as needed. | Present an adapted persuasive essay from a magazine or newspaper. Have students work with a partner to identify and summarize the essay's thesis. | Have students read a persuasive essay from a magazine or newspaper with a partner, taking notes on the writer's position, reasons and supporting evidence. |

**Revising for** Organization

To help students check the organization of their essays as a whole, have them read their work aloud to a partner and ask for feedback. Afterward, have them ask themselves these questions:

- *Did my partner identify the issue, the position, and an objection?*
- *Could my partner follow my arguments? Were there gaps, or was any information out of order?*
- *Were there places where I stumbled or got confused?*

## Is my essay unified?

Sometimes, simply by reading through the essay silently, students can identify problems with unity. Whenever they feel a break in the flow or an idea seems disjointed, it is a good indication that the organization can be improved. In some cases, additional effective transitions can solve the problem. In other cases, rewriting or re-organization of parts of the essay may be needed.

**TEKS** 10.13B, 10.16A, 10.16B

## Exercise
### Answers
**Possible Answer**

Even on the best day, traffic rolls over the Elm Street Bridge very slowly. The bridge is only one lane wide with stoplights at either end. During rush hour, more than 4,000 cars travel over it. Last Thursday, a huge traffic jam on the bridge delayed commuters for four hours. The best solution to the problem would be to widen the Elm Street Bridge so that additional lanes can be added.

**Check for unity.** While specific words can help tie the parts of an essay together, remind students to watch for overused words (in the case of the Exercise paragraph, *traffic* and *bridge*) and replace them as needed.

**TEKS** 10.13C

---

 **TEKS** 10.13B, 10.13C, 10.16A, 10.16B

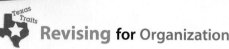 **Revising for** Organization

When you revise for *organization*, you check the structure of your essay. You make sure that the beginning, middle, and ending parts form a meaningful whole. Your paragraphs should be connected in a logical way, and the reasons you have given to support your position should be arranged by order of importance. Check to make sure that you have used transitions, both words and phrases, to link paragraphs and sentences within each paragraph. Once again, keep in mind the audience, purpose, and context for your writing.

## Is my essay unified?

Your essay is unified if all the parts work together. The introduction states your position and describes the issue. The middle paragraphs expand and explore the issue, provide evidence, and address objections. The conclusion and effective transitions tie the essay together. The following checklist will help you evaluate the unity in your essay.

_____ **1.** Does my first paragraph clearly state my position statement?

_____ **2.** Does the topic sentence of each middle paragraph give a key reason to support my position?

_____ **3.** Do the sentences in each paragraph support my position statement?

_____ **4.** Does my conclusion tie the essay together and sum up my position?

### Exercise

Rewrite the paragraph below, using transitions to tie the ideas together. Be sure to choose your transition words carefully.

> In rush hour, more than 4,000 cars travel down Elm Street. Some people say Elm Street should be closed. Others say it should be widened. The Elm Street Bridge could be widened so that additional lanes can be added. The bridge is only one lane wide with stoplights at either end. Last Thursday, a huge traffic jam on the Elm Street Bridge tied up traffic for four hours. Traffic rolls over the bridge very slowly.

 **Check for unity.** Revise your essay using the checklist above. Also check your essay for word choice that leads to unity. Make sure that you have used effective transitions to link ideas.

---

**TEKS** **10.13B** Develop drafts in open-ended situations that include transitions; **10.13C** Revise drafts to improve word choice and the subtlety of meaning; **10.16A** Write an argumentative essay supported by precise and relevant evidence; **10.16B** Write an argumentative essay that includes the range of information on the topic

## Do I present reasons in the best order?

As you revise for organization, it is important to think about the relative value of the ideas, facts, and data you have included in your essay. As you conducted the research for your essay, you probably noted which were the major arguments in support of your position and which were the major objections against your position. The arguments in your essay should be listed in order of importance. You can check for the order of importance by using the following checklist.

_____ **1.** Does the topic sentence of my first middle paragraph address the most (or least) important supporting reason? Revise as needed.

_____ **2.** Does the topic sentence of my second middle paragraph address the next most (or next least) important reason?

_____ **3.** Have I identified and addressed an objection with a logical counter-argument?

**Revise**

**Check for organization** Make sure you have correctly structured your essay. Rearrange paragraphs that are out of order.

**Persuasive**

**Organization**
A counter-argument is identified and addressed.

Ideas are logically arranged. Writer supports position.

> Some people argue that food banks are not necessary.
>
> They think that government programs such as food stamps
> Not all people qualify. People need to be fed when they are hungry.
> are enough to ease the hunger problem. A lot of money does
>
> go to government programs for feeding the hungry, and these
>
> programs are worthwhile. They actually work pretty well, but I
> Even with government programs, the hunger problem has escalated.
> don't think that they are a very good solution.

---

## Do I present reasons in the best order?

Although it is often suggested that writers use the least important argument first (see the **Tip** on SE page 209), remind your students that this is not mandated. They should feel free to experiment with starting with their most important argument as well. Remind students that the goal of an argumentative essay is to persuade their audience to support their position.

**✓ DIFFERENTIATE INSTRUCTION**

**TEKS** 10.13C, 10.16D, 10.16E

**Check for organization.** If students are revising on a computer, encourage them to make use of the cut-and-paste function to quickly rearrange their paragraphs. If they are revising on paper, they can still keep this technique in mind when they implement their changes on their computer copy after revision is completed.

## Revising for Development of Ideas

Remind students that even if they have excellent reasons and evidence for their position, if they don't present them clearly and develop them fully, they will not be persuasive.

### Have I effectively explained the issue?

Making details more specific to your readers can be effective. For example, rather than just saying *Volunteers give thousands of hours of time to food banks all across the country*, the writer specifies the statistics for one state—Texas. This make his argument more applicable to his audience—people who live in Texas.

★ **TEKS** 10.13C, 10.16A

### Exercise
### Answers
**Possible Answer**

Increased soda consumption is causing problems for kids across the country, and Centerville High is no exception. A 2004 study by the Center for Science in the Public Interest found that a lot of teens consume too many soft drinks; one in ten boys drinks almost six cans a day. Water, juice, and milk would all be healthier choices. Water quenches thirst without adding calories. Juice and milk provide important nutrients. An 8-ounce glass of orange juice contains 82 milligrams of vitamin C, more than a full day's allowance. An 8-ounce glass of milk has about a quarter of the bone-building calcium you need daily. The average soda, on the other hand, contains 30 to 40 grams of sugar. "It's pretty much just like sitting down and eating three tablespoons of sugar," says Ms. Barton, our school nurse.

**Make the issue clear.** Some students may need to conduct additional research. Consider giving students an extra day of research time during this revision step.

---

## Revising for Development of Ideas

When you revise for *development of ideas*, you make sure that you that you have clearly explained the issue. Further, you check to make sure that the arguments in support of your position are accurate, logical, and well defended. Be sure to check that evidence is relevant and that you have used precise, factual data. Your reasons should be logical, and you should have responded to at least one important objection. Remember your purpose: to convince your audience that your position is the best one. You may even compel your reader to take action and support you. Your word choice will be important as you convince your reader and convey your subtlety of meaning.

### Have I effectively explained the issue?

You have effectively explained the issue if the reader understands its importance. Make sure to use revealing facts and precise details in your explanation.

■ **Use facts and statistics to make sure the problem is clear and show its significance.**

In Texas alone, volunteers gave over 200,000 hours of time to food banks.

■ **Explain how the problem affects people.**

Children who are hungry have a harder time learning, and they may experience delays in physical development.

### Exercise

Read the paragraph below. How would you revise it so that it more effectively explains the problem of soda consumption?

Increased consumption of soda is causing problems for students at our high school. More and more kids are drinking soda. Not many kids are drinking water, juice, or milk. While milk and juice have important nutrients, soda does not. According to our school nurse, that is bad news for our health.

**Make the issue clear.** Read your essay carefully. If necessary add facts and statistics that help explain the issue and persuade the reader.

---

★ **TEKS** **10.13C** Revise drafts to improve the subtlety of meaning; **10.16A** Write an argumentative essay supported by precise and relevant evidence

# Have I convincingly argued for my position?

You have convincingly argued for your position if you have included compelling, persuasive reasons and adequate support for your thesis. Check to make sure that you have included logical reasons, relevant evidence, and precise data to support the topic sentence of each paragraph. Precise data is information that is exact, correct, and can be proved using reliable sources.

Use the following checklist to help you decide how well you supported your position.

_____ **1.** Do I still believe in my position? Explain.

_____ **2.** Does the supporting evidence clearly support my position?

_____ **3.** Have I used precise data, as well as compelling and persuasive language, in my essay? Circle examples.

_____ **4.** Do I effectively counter objections with relevant evidence, precise data, and logical reasons? Underline your counter-arguments.

 **Check your essay.** Answer the questions in the checklist. Continue to revise as needed. Make sure your language is persuasive.

Revise

Persuasive

> Relevant evidence is supported with precise details.

> A final persuasive sentence is added.

over twelve thousand          twelve
In Texas alone, a lot of volunteers serve meals to hungry

men, women, and children.  Food banks use money donations
Daly City City food bank uses 90 cents of every dollar to buy food.
very efficiently too. While it may be hard to get donations,

most of the money goes to purchasing food.
After all, everyone deserves at least one good meal a day.

## Have I convincingly argued for my position?

Discuss the following possible flaws that could undermine students' arguments.

- Rigid thinking: Remind students that no complex problem can be reduced to "always" or "never." Statements such as *If you drive a car, you don't care about the environment* would fall into this trap.
- Weak analogies: Beware of drawing unfair comparisons that do not fit the argument. For example: *Driving a car is like causing a Gold Coast oil spill.*
- Bandwagon: Point out that another fallacy of thinking is to appeal to everyone's sense of wanting to belong or be accepted. For example: *Since everyone drives a car, this form of transportation must not harm the environment.* ✔ DIFFERENTIATE INSTRUCTION

**Check your essay.** You may want students to practice peer response by having them exchange papers and complete the checklist for their partner's paper. Have them explain their evaluation verbally, using constructive, positive language. Encourage students to make revisions focusing on precision of evidence and of word choice.

 **TEKS** 10.13C, 10.16A; **ELPS** 3E, 3G, 3H

---

**TEKS** **10.13C** Revise drafts to improve figurative language; **10.16A** Write an argumentative essay supported by precise and relevant evidence; **ELPS** **1E** Internalize new academic language by using and reusing it/speaking; **2C** Learn new expressions and academic vocabulary heard during classroom instruction/interactions; **3A** Practice producing sounds of newly acquired vocabulary; **3D** Speak using grade-level content area vocabulary/new words and academic language proficiency; **3E** Share information in cooperative learning interactions; **3G** Express opinions and feelings ranging from communicating short phrases to participating in discussions; **3H** Explain with increasing specificity and detail

##  Revising **for** Voice

Give several more examples of when a formal tone is necessary (public speaking, cover letters for job applications, etc.). Model several sentences in both an informal and a formal tone so students can hear the difference. Students should practice identifying which is which. For example: *I really think you should hire me because I'm a great person and I work hard.* versus *I think I would be a great fit for your company. I bring excellent character and a diligent work ethic and will make a beneficial addition to your staff.* **DIFFERENTIATE INSTRUCTION ↘**

**TEKS** 10.13C; **ELPS** 1G, 3I

### Have I used an authoritative voice?

Have students note that nearly every sentence in the more authoritative sample contains at least one specific detail. While it may not always be possible to use details in every sentence, students should aim to work specific details into as many sentences as possible. **DIFFERENTIATE INSTRUCTION ↘**

**For more authority, add facts.** Students may discover that they don't have enough facts to effectively convey an authoritative, formal voice. Encourage them to do more research to gather additional precise and relevant evidence.

**TEKS** 10.16A

 **Writer's Craft**

**Etymology:** Point out to students the etymological connections between the following words:
- authoritative: from Latin *auctoritas,* meaning decision, power, opinion
- author: from Latin *auctor,* meaning promoter, originator, author
- authentic: from Greek *authentes,* meaning perpetrator, master

**ELPS** 4C

 **TEKS** **10.13C** Revise drafts to improve style; **10.16A** Write an argumentative essay supported by precise and relevant evidence; **ELPS 1G** Demonstrate increasing ability to distinguish between formal/informal English and an increasing knowledge of when to use each one; **3I** Adapt spoken language for formal purposes; **4C** Comprehend vocabulary used in written classroom materials

---

 **TEKS** 10.13C, 10.16A
**ELPS** 1G

 **Revising for** Voice

When you revise for *voice,* remember your purpose for writing this essay. In order to convince people to support your position, you need to use an authoritative, reasonable voice. Because this is an argumentative essay, your voice and word choice should also be more formal. Using a more formal tone will help you sound more authoritative. Think about the way that you speak with a classmate or friend and the way that you speak with a respected adult. With a friend, you are likely to speak informally, using simple vocabulary or slang. If you are discussing a serious issue with an adult, you are more likely to use vocabulary that is formal. It is the same when you write.

### Have I used an authoritative voice?

You have used an authoritative voice if you sound knowledgeable and focus on factual information in your essay. Your voice is not authoritative if you use weak, general statements. One way to improve your voice is to include plenty of specific, precise facts and relevant evidence in your essay. When you do this, you will have written with a more formal tone.

> **Less Authoritative Voice**
>
> When a supertanker spills oil, it damages the ocean. It damages beaches, too. The damage caused by an oil spill can last a long time. And it can cost a lot to clean up.

> **More Authoritative Voice**
>
> A supertanker accident can spill as much as 2 million barrels of oil into the ocean. Oil spills cause incredible damage. In 1989, the supertanker *Exxon Valdez* spilled 257,000 barrels of oil. The oil killed thousands of sea birds, hundreds of sea otters, and contaminated 1,300 miles of shoreline. Nine years later, much of that shoreline was still contaminated with oil. Exxon spent $2.1 billion on its cleanup efforts.

 **For more authority, add facts.** Review your essay. Does your voice sound authoritative? If it doesn't, replace weak, general statements with reliable, specific facts. Use vocabulary that is suited to the topic and audience.

"When your writing is filled with details, it has a lot more impact."
—Ivan Levison

---

### Differentiated Instruction: Struggling Learners

Have pairs practice revise for an authoritative voice by rewriting the following sentences so they include specific facts:
- The Constitution was written a few years after the Declaration of Independence (1787).
- The human body contains lots of bones (about 206, but can vary from person to person).
- A rainbow is made up of a spectrum of colors (seven: red, orange, yellow, green, blue, indigo, violet).
- Mount Rushmore depicts the faces of four U.S. presidents (Washington, Jefferson, Lincoln, T. Roosevelt).

## Do I treat my reader with respect?

You have treated your reader with respect if you don't use loaded, emotionally charged, or aggressive language. Using such language may make the reader feel as if he or she were being attacked. Inflammatory language does not serve your purpose for writing, nor does ridiculing people who oppose your position. Inflammatory language and ridicule are ways to lose an argument, not win it. Remember that your goal is to convince your reader. Therefore, treat your audience with respect.

When you revise your essay, look again to make sure that you have supported your position honestly and accurately and that you have considered a wide range of supporting and opposing arguments on the topic.

In the following paragraph, a writer uses an unreasonable, overly aggressive voice to propose a solution.

> Some people think the Elm Street Bridge doesn't need to be widened to four lanes. They must have rocks in their heads. Get a clue! If the bridge isn't widened, people will continue to sit in traffic forever. Widening the bridge is the only solution, and anyone with any sense knows it.

### Grammar Exercise

Rewrite the paragraph above so that it sounds respectful and reasonable. Trade papers with a classmate. Discuss each other's changes.

 **Check your voice for respect.** Review your essay, making sure that you don't sound too emotional, aggressive, or inflammatory. Revise as needed.

**Voice**
An aggressive sentence is deleted and an overemotional one is revised.

> Some people argue that food banks are not necessary. They think that government programs such as food stamps are enough to ease the hunger problem. That's ~~completely ridiculous.~~ However, not all the people who need food qualify for government programs, and applying for government help ~~takes~~ can take time. ~~forever!~~

---

**Do I treat my reader with respect?**

Have students identify the parts of the sample that sound extreme. For example:

- *They must have rocks in their heads* is slangy and insulting.
- *Get a clue!* is informal and slangy.
- *Continue to sit in traffic forever* is exaggerated language.
- *The only solution* is a broad generalization.

★ **TEKS** 10.13C

### Grammar Exercise
**Answers**
**Possible Answer**

Some people think the Elm Street Bridge doesn't need to be widened to four lanes, but traffic is already a problem. More and more drivers are using the bridge. If nothing is done, there will be even more and longer delays. Widening the bridge is the best solution.

**Check your voice for respect.** Remind students that some emotion—of the type that lets their readers know that the author is interested in the topic—is good. Too much emotional language, however, can detract from the argument, especially when it is aggressive or inflammatory.

★ **TEKS** 10.16B

---

| Differentiated Instruction: English Language Learners | | ★ ELPS 1G, 2A, 3I, 5G |
|---|---|---|
| **ELP Level**<br>**Beginning** | **ELP Level**<br>**Intermediate** | **ELP Level**<br>**Advanced/Advanced High** |
| Model simple formal and informal expressions (e.g., *Hey, dude!* versus *Hello.*). Have students identify which is which. Correct as needed. | Identify situations in which formal and informal language is easily distinguishable (greetings, invitations, etc.). Have students practice these both formally and informally. | Have students write two short letters describing an event in their life. One should be written to a peer (informally) and another to a respected adult (formally). |

 **TEKS** **10.13C** Revise drafts/improve word choice and rethink how well the audience has been addressed; **10.16B** Write an argumentative essay that includes the range of views on the topic and an accurate/honest representation of views; **ELPS 1G** Demonstrate increasing ability to distinguish between formal/informal English; **2A** Distinguish intonation patterns with increasing ease; **3I** Adapt spoken language for formal and informal purposes; **5G** Narrate and describe with increasing specificity and detail/writing

**Revising**

**Improving Your Writing**

Remind students that each item in the checklist is discussed in detail on the preceding pages.

**Check your revising.** Note that many important aspects of writing appear in the Basic Grammar and Writing section (SE pages 568–615). Some of these aspects can specifically help students with their argumentative essay and some are more general. Encourage students to refer to this section whenever necessary to improve their writing.

**Make a clean copy.** Remind students not to throw away old copies of their essays. They should keep them, both for reference as to what changes have been made and as a way to see their progress from beginning to end. Comparing their eventual finished draft with their first draft will reinforce the benefits of the writing process.

---

 **Revising** Improving Your Writing

 **Check your revising.** On a piece of paper, write the numbers 1 to 10. If you answer "yes" to a question, put a check mark next to that number. If not, continue to work on that part of your essay.

**Revising Checklist**

### Focus and Coherence

_____ 1. Do I clearly focus on one significant issue?

_____ 2. Do I use solid reasons and verifiable evidence to support my position?

_____ 3. Do my ideas consistently support my position?

### Organization

_____ 4. Have I structured my arguments in order of importance?

_____ 5. Does my essay have a sense of unity, with an introduction, a middle, and an effective conclusion?

### Development of Ideas

_____ 6. Have I adequately explained the issue?

_____ 7. Have I presented my argument with convincing details and persuasive language?

### Voice

_____ 8. Do I use an authoritative voice?

_____ 9. Do I treat the reader with respect?

_____ 10. Have I avoided overly emotional or inflammatory language?

**Make a clean copy.** When you are finished revising, make a clean copy of your essay to edit for conventions.

Prewrite → Draft → Revise → Edit → Publish

# Editing

When you have finished revising your argumentative essay, it is time to edit for conventions: grammar, sentence structure, capitalization, punctuation, and spelling.

### Keys to Effective Editing

1. Use a dictionary, a thesaurus, and the "Proofreader's Guide" in the back of this book to check your writing.

2. Check your writing for errors in grammar, sentence structure, capitalization, punctuation, and spelling.

3. Have a classmate edit your writing. You are too close to your writing to catch everything.

4. If you are using a computer, edit your essay on a printed copy and then key in the changes. Otherwise, write a new, final handwritten copy that includes the changes.

5. Use the editing and proofreading marks inside the back cover of this book.

*Persuasive*

## Editing

### Keys to Effective Editing

Remind students that during the editing stage, they will focus on finding and correcting errors in:

- sentence structure,
- capitalization,
- punctuation, and
- grammar.

Explain these terms and give examples as needed. ✔ **DIFFERENTIATE INSTRUCTION**

**ELPS** 4C

The Keys to Effective Editing list explains the process students will follow on SE pages 222–226.

---

## Editing for Conventions

## Grammar

### How and when do I use the subjunctive mood?

Students will likely need to see more examples to really get a handle on the indicative and subjunctive moods. Consider presenting a paragraph or longer piece of writing that contains both. Have students read through it with a partner and identify examples of both moods. Then go through it as a class to correct any confusion the students might have.

 **TEKS** 10.13D, 10.17B; **ELPS** 3E, 4C, 5E

### Grammar Exercise
#### Answers
**Possible Answers**

1. If it were up to me, I would go to the movies tonight.
2. If we were to get the principal's permission, we could organize a food drive at school.
3. If we were to plan the event, volunteers would need to work 10 hours a week.

**Check for subjunctive mood.** Students may also want to exchange papers with a partner and look for proper use of the indicative and subjunctive moods in each other's writing.

 **Conventions Connections**

**Grammar: Subjunctive and Indicative Mood**
- *Proofreader's Guide* pages 752–753
- *SkillsBook* pages 104–105

 *Write Source Online* **GrammarSnap**

---

**222**

 **TEKS** 10.13D, 10.17B
**ELPS** 4C, 5E

## Editing for Conventions

## Grammar

Editing for *conventions* means checking grammar, sentence structure, capitalization, punctuation, and spelling. Part of the grammar edit means looking carefully at the verb forms you have used.

### How and when do I use the subjunctive mood?

The mood of a verb indicates the attitude with which a statement is made. The indicative mood is used to state facts or to ask questions. The subjunctive mood is used to express a condition that is not necessarily a fact. It may be used to express doubts, wishes, or possibilities.

The subjunctive mood is often used in persuasive writing when possibilities and wishes are presented in the form of conditional statements. Conditional statements often begin with *if* clauses. (See pages **752–753** for more information.)

**Indicative Mood**

I finished my essay. Would you bring in the mail?
(Indicative mood is used for statements of fact and for questions.)

**Subjunctive Mood**

If I were to volunteer at a food pantry, what would I do?
(The subjunctive mood is used in conditional statements introduced with an *if* clause. )

I wish that I were going to the beach. Everyone would be surprised if our team were to win the game on Friday.
(The subjunctive mood is used to express wishes and possibilities.)

### Grammar Exercise

Rewrite the following sentences. Add a conditional *if* clause to express doubts, wishes, or possibilities. Use the subjunctive mood in the clause.

1. I want to go to the movies tonight.
2. We could organize a food drive at school.
3. Volunteers should plan to work 10 hours a week.

 **Check for subjunctive mood.** Read your essay carefully. Look for proper use of indicative and subjunctive mood. Correct any verb forms that are incorrect.

---

 **TEKS** **10.13D** Edit drafts for grammar; **10.17B** Identify and use subjunctive mood to express doubts, wishes, and possibilities; **ELPS** **3E** Share information in cooperative learning interactions; **4C** Comprehend language structures used in written classroom materials; **5E** Employ increasingly complex grammatical structures in content area writing such as using correct verbs, tenses, and pronouns/possessive case/negatives and contractions

**TEKS** 10.13D, 10.17A(i)
ELPS 2C, 2I, 3G, 3E, 4C, 5E

## Have I used verbals correctly?

A verbal is a word that is derived from a verb, but it acts as another part of speech. There are three different types of verbals. Often they make up part of a verbal phrase.

### Gerunds

A *gerund* is a verb form that ends in *ing* and is used as a noun.

Walking **provides good exercise.** Reading **is my favorite pastime.**

### Infinitives

An *infinitive* is a verb form that is usually introduced by the word *to*. Infinitives may be used as nouns, adjectives, or adverbs.

**Most people find it fun** to cook. To cook **a meal for twelve people, however, can be difficult. The desire** to cook **often comes from enjoying good food.**

### Participles

A *participle* is a verb form that ends in *ing* or *ed* that acts as an adjective.

**The men** eating lunch **must be very hungry. The** tired **workers went home.**

## Grammar Exercise

Rewrite these sentences using gerunds, infinitives, and participles.

1. After they leave the factory, the pollutants flow into the river.
2. The dogs were tired, and they stopped running.
3. The two men were very tired. They had waited at the airport for four hours.
4. The cleanup of the site was costly. It had to be done so that a park could be built.

 **Edit**

**Check for verbals.** Make sure that you have included verbals in your essay and used them properly.

## Learning Language

Remember that nouns are names of people, places, or things. Gerunds are also nouns, but they convey actions, like swimming, watching, or playing. Work with a partner to tell  about things you like and dislike using gerunds. Then use infinitives to explain how to do chores or everyday activities.

---

### Have I used verbals correctly?

Students may need additional examples to fully understand the use of these verbals. Present a paragraph or longer piece of writing that contains all three. Have students read through it with a partner and identify examples of all three types of verbals. Alternatively, give examples aloud and have students listen to identify which verbal you used. ✔ **DIFFERENTIATE INSTRUCTION**

### Grammar Exercise
**Answers**
**Possible Answers**

1. After they leave the factory, the pollutants empty from the pipes to flow into the river.
2. The tired dogs stopped running.
3. Waiting at the airport for four hours made the two men very tired.
4. Cleaning was costly, but it had to be done so the park could be built on the site.

**ELPS** 5E

**Check for verbals.** Have students highlight the verbals in their essays, using a different color for each type. In this way, they will know how many and what type of verbals they have used.

**TEKS** 10.13D, 10.17A(i)

### Learning Language

Model a conversation with a volunteer before students break into pairs to complete the activity. Tell students to reread SE page 223 for further explanation of the verbals as needed.

**ELPS** 2C, 2I, 3E, 3G, 4C

 **Conventions Connections**

**Grammar: Verbals: Gerunds, Infinitives, and Participles**
- ***Proofreader's Guide*** pages 754–755
- ***SkillsBook*** page 101

⚡ *Write Source Online* **GrammarSnap**

**TEKS** 10.13D Edit drafts for grammar; **10.17A(i)** Use and understand verbals (gerunds, infinitives, and participles); **ELPS 2C** Learn basic vocabulary heard during classroom instruction/interactions; **2I** Demonstrate listening comprehension in increasingly complex spoken language by collaborating with peers; **3E** Share information in cooperative learning interactions; **3G** Express opinions ranging from communicating short phrases to participating in discussions; **4C** Comprehend vocabulary used in written classroom materials; **4F** Use visual/contextual support and support from peers/teachers to read grade-appropriate text and enhance understating, grasp of language structures, and background knowledge; **5E** Employ increasingly complex grammatical structures in content area writing such as using correct verbs, tenses, and pronouns/possessive case/negatives and contractions

---

| **Differentiated Instruction:** **English Language Learners** | | **ELPS** 4C, 4F |
|---|---|---|
| **ELP Level** **Beginning** | **ELP Level** **Intermediate** | **ELP Level** **Advanced/Advanced High** |
| Give students adapted sentences that demonstrate the difference between nouns and verbs. Help students identify both parts of speech. | Give students an adapted paragraph that demonstrates the three types of verbals. As you point out each verbal, have students identify which type of verbal it is. | Give students a paragraph that demonstrates all three types of verbals. Have students work with a partner to identify all three types. |

Persuasive

## Sentence Structure

Demonstrate the effectiveness of varied sentences by reading a short paragraph with little sentence variety. Then read the same paragraph, only edited to improve sentence structure. Discuss with students why the second reading was more interesting than the first.

### Have I used a variety of sentence types effectively?

Have students note that most sentences in their essays or in any of the examples given in the text are declarative. Explain that declarative sentences are the essential building blocks of writing. The other types add variety and emphasis to certain parts of their writing.

**TEKS** 10.13B, 10.13C, 10.17C; **ELPS** 2G

#### Grammar Exercise
#### Answers

1. Declarative sentence: *Supporting the clean water initiative. . . . It is an intestinal disease. . . . If left untreated. . . . For people in many parts of the world. . . .*
2. Interrogative sentence: *What is cholera? How dangerous is it?*
3. Imperative sentence: *But you can help. . . . Support the clean-water initiative.*
4. Exclamatory Sentence: *But you can help. . . .*

Sentence variety helps keep the reader's attention and interest.

**Review your sentences.** Supply a details chart (see TE Appendix). Have students make a column for each type of sentence. As they read their essay, they should note how many of each type they use and include examples of each.

**ELPS** 4C, 5E, 5F

 **Conventions Connections**

**Grammar: Sentence Types for Variety**
- *Proofreader's Guide* pages 772–773
- *SkillsBook* page 140

**Write Source Online GrammarSnap**

**TEKS** **10.13B** Develop drafts in open-ended situations that include rhetorical devices; **10.13C** Revise drafts to improve sentence variety; **10.17C** Use a variety of correctly structured sentences; **ELPS 2G** Understand the general meaning of spoken language/topics, languages, and contexts are familiar to unfamiliar; **4C** Comprehend language structures used in written classroom materials; **5E** Employ increasingly complex grammatical structures in content area writing such as using correct verbs, tenses, and pronouns/possessive case/negatives and contractions; **5F** Write using a variety of grade-appropriate sentence patterns in increasingly accurate ways

 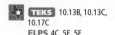

## Sentence Structure

When you edit for *sentence fluency*, you check to see that you have properly used different kinds of sentences and that they flow smoothly. As you edit, you want to make sure, too, that you have varied your sentence beginnings, and that your sentences spark the reader's interest in your position. (See pages 772–774 for more information about sentence types.)

### Have I used a variety of sentence types effectively?

You have used a variety of sentence types effectively if they help you develop your argument. Here are four different types of sentences that you can use. A declarative sentence makes a statement. The situation is worsening. An interrogative sentence asks a question. What does it feel like to be hungry? An imperative sentence makes a command. Imagine that you are hungry. An exclamatory sentence communicates strong emotion or surprise. It is time for us to help out!

#### Grammar Exercise

Identify each kind of sentence in the following paragraph. Explain how the sentence variety makes the paragraph more effective.

> Supporting the clean-water initiative will help solve the spread of cholera. What is cholera? It is an intestinal disease that is caused by bacteria in the water. How dangerous is it? If left untreated, cholera is deadly. But you can help, so take action! Support the clean-water initiative. For people in many parts of the world, clean water makes the difference between life and death.

 **Review your sentences.** Read your essay carefully. Check to make sure that you have used differerent kinds of sentences correctly and that your sentence starters engage the reader's interest.

Argumentative Essay **225**

**TEKS** 10.13D, 10.18B(iii)

## Mechanics: Punctuation

When you edit for *mechanics*, you check to make sure that you have followed the correct rules for capitalization and punctuation. You don't want mechanical errors to confuse or distract your readers.

## Have I correctly punctuated parenthetical information?

Parenthetical information explains or clarifies particular words or phrases. Dashes are one way to set off parenthetical information in your writing. Dashes serve other purposes as well. They can indicate a sudden break or change in a sentence. They can indicate interrupted speech. They can be used to emphasize a word, a series, a phrase, or a clause, and they can be used to set off an introductory series or list of items. (See pages **676–677** for more information.)

### Grammar Exercise

Read the following sentences. Rewrite them so that the appropriate words or phrases are correctly set off using dashes.

1. The members of the school board all of them agreed to the new schedule.
2. The text plus all of the supplementary material can be purchased at the bookstore.
3. A new bike and a helmet all that I needed to enjoy the day was waiting for me.
4. I was amazed when I saw the guitar the one that I had wanted for so long in my bedroom.
5. After years of hard work, my sister finally reached her goal, to go to college in Europe.

**Check for dashes.** Read your essay carefully. Make sure that you have used dashes correctly to set off parenthetical information, emphasize a word, or to set off an introductory series.

Persuasive

## Mechanics: Punctuation

Students can refer to SE pages 682–703 for detailed information on mechanics.

### Have I correctly punctuated parenthetical elements?

Parentheses can also be used to set off explanatory information or to add additional material that interrupts the sentence flow. Refer students to SE page 674 for information on using parentheses correctly.

**TEKS** 10.13D

### Grammar Exercise
**Answers**

1. The members of the school board—all of them—agreed to the new schedule.
2. The text—plus all of the supplementary material—can be purchased at the bookstore.
3. A new bike and a helmet—all that I needed to enjoy the day—was waiting for me.
4. I was amazed when I saw the guitar—the one that I had wanted for so long—in my bedroom.
5. After years of hard work, my sister finally reached her goal—to go to college in Europe.

**Check for dashes.** It is very likely that some students will not have used any dashes in their essay. Encourage them to experiment with sentence structures and to use dashes at least once or twice. ✔ **DIFFERENTIATE INSTRUCTION**

**TEKS** 10.18B(iii); **ELPS** 5F

### ★ Conventions Connections

**Mechanics: Dashes for Punctuating Parenthetical Elements**
- ***Proofreader's Guide*** pages 676–677
- ***SkillsBook*** page 24

➤ *Write Source Online* **GrammarSnap**

**TEKS** **10.13D** Edit drafts for mechanics; **10.18B(iii)** Use dashes to emphasize parenthetical information; **ELPS** **2C** Learn new language structures and academic vocabulary heard during classroom instruction/interactions; **4C** Comprehend vocabulary and language structures used in written classroom materials; **4F** Use support from peers/teachers to develop grasp of language structures; **5F** Write using a variety of grade-appropriate sentence lengths and patterns in increasingly accurate ways

## Editing

### Checking for Conventions

Give students a few moments to look over the Proofreader's Guide (SE pages 642–787). Throughout the year, they can refer to the instructions, rules, and examples to clarify any checklist items or to resolve other questions about their writing.

**Check your editing.** Encourage students to read their essay several times, focusing on specific conventions from the checklist each time. Assure students that many people need to repeatedly look up the rules for writing conventions when they are editing their work. Encourage students to flag and label key pages of the Proofreader's Guide that they refer to frequently. **DIFFERENTIATE INSTRUCTION ↘**

⭐ **TEKS** 10.13C, 10.13D, 10.17B, 10.18A, 10.18B(ii), 10.18B(iii), 10.19;
**ELPS** 5C, 5D, 5E, 5F

### Creating a Title

Good ideas for a title may come to students at any stage of the writing process. Encourage them to jot down all ideas in their planning notes for easy reference.

⭐ **TEKS** **10.13C** Revise drafts to improve sentence variety; **10.13D** Edit drafts for grammar, mechanics, and spelling; **10.17B** Identify and use subjunctive mood to express wishes; **10.18A** Use conventions of capitalization; **10.18B(ii)** Use quotation marks to indicate sarcasm and irony; **10.18B(iii)** Use dashes to emphasize parenthetical information; **10.19** Spell correctly using resources to determine and check correct spelling; **ELPS 3E** Share information in cooperative learning interactions; **3G** Express opinions, ideas, and feelings ranging from communicating short phrases to participating in discussions **5C** Spell familiar words with increasing accuracy; **5D** Edit writing for standard grammar and usage/subject-verb agreement; **5E** Employ increasingly complex grammatical structures in content area writing such as using correct verbs, tenses, and pronouns/possessive case/negatives and contractions; **5F** Write using a variety of grade-appropriate sentence patterns in increasingly accurate ways

---

 **TEKS** 10.13C, 10.13D, 10.17B, 10.18A, 10.18B(ii), 10.18B(iii), 10.19
**ELPS** 5C–5F

 **Editing** Checking for Conventions

 **Check your editing.** This checklist will help you edit your essay for conventions: grammar, sentence structure, capitalization, punctuation, and spelling. On a piece of paper, write the numbers 1 to 9. If you can answer "yes," put a check after that number. If you can't, continue to edit.

### Editing Checklist

#### Conventions

**GRAMMAR**

_____ **1.** Do I use the subjunctive mood correctly? (*I wish I were* not *I wish I was*)

_____ **2.** Do I use gerunds, infinitives, and participles correctly?

**SENTENCE STRUCTURE**

_____ **3.** Do I use a variety of sentence types for their appropriate purposes?

**MECHANICS (Capitalization and Punctuation)**

_____ **4.** Do I start all my sentences with capital letters?

_____ **5.** Do I capitalize all proper nouns and adjectives?

_____ **6.** Do I use end punctuation after all my sentences?

_____ **7.** Do I use dashes to set off parenthetical information?

**SPELLING**

_____ **8.** Have I spelled all words correctly?

_____ **9.** Have I consulted a dictionary to determine or check the spellings of words my spell-checker may have missed?

### Creating a Title

After your editing is complete, add a title that describes your essay and catches your reader's attention. Here are several ways to approach this task.

- Summarize the issue: **Food Banks Ease Hunger Pangs**
- Call to action: **Back Food Banks and Reduce Hunger**
- Hook the reader: **Help Put an End to Hunger**

---

### Differentiated Instruction: Struggling Learners

Have students read through their writing from beginning to end and circle the words they need to check for spelling. Afterward, have students exchange papers with partners. Partners should reread the essays to check for additional misspelled words.

⭐ **TEKS** 10.19; **ELPS** 3E

TEKS 10.13E
ELPS 3G

Prewrite → Draft → Revise → Edit → Publish

# Publishing

## Sharing Your Essay

After writing, revising, and editing your essay, make a neat final draft. Ask your teacher or your classmates for feedback and make final improvements. When that is done, it's time to share your essay. You can present your essay in a debate, publish it in a newspaper, or send it to an official who can help.

**Format your final copy.** To format a handwritten essay, use the guidelines below or follow your teacher's instructions. (If you are using a computer, see pages 72–74.) Make a clean copy and carefully proofread it.

## Focusing on Presentation

- Write neatly using blue or black ink.
- Write your name in the upper left corner of page 1.
- Skip a line and center your title; skip another line and start your essay.
- Indent every paragraph and leave a one-inch margin on all four sides.
- Write your last name and the page number in the upper right corner of every page after page 1.

### Stage a Debate

Invite a group of friends or family members who have differing viewpoints on the issue. Invite some people who have not yet formed an opinion to come and listen. Present and defend your idea. Then allow others to present and defend their ideas. Finally, ask the audience to form an opinion, based on the debate.

Persuasive

### Contact an Official

Identify an official who has authority to take action on your issue. Send your essay to that person along with a cover letter stating your position and asking for help. Remember to use a respectful tone in your letter, and to encourage the official to support your position.

### Publish a Letter

Reformat your essay as a letter to the editor of a local newspaper. Make sure your letter conforms to the newspaper's submission guidelines. Then e-mail your letter or send it through the postal service.

---

## Publishing

### Sharing Your Essay

In addition to debates and publishing a letter, you could arrange for students to publish their work in the school newspaper or on a class Web site.

Students could also send their essays to individuals who might take action. Assist students as needed in the process of discovering contact information for government officials on the Internet or in the library. Ask them to report any responses they receive. ✔ DIFFERENTIATE INSTRUCTION

**Format your final copy.** When students have finished their essays, set aside class time for a sharing session.

### Focusing on Presentation

Be sure to make your expectations clear for students' final drafts. If you have preferences that differ from those suggested here, make sure that students know what they are.

From the issues students addressed in their essays, select two or three for a classroom debate. Review the rules of debate, then encourage groups to plan their arguments using the reasons and arguments that have already been researched.

TEKS 10.13E; ELPS 3G

### Technology Connections

*Write Source Online* **Portfolio**

*Write Source Online* **Essay Scoring**

---

## Differentiated Instruction: English Language Learners

| ELP Level **Beginning** | ELP Level **Intermediate** | ELP Level **Advanced/Advanced High** |
|---|---|---|
| Explain and model basic components of a letter (heading, greeting, etc.). Have students add these components to a letter's body that you provide. | Explain and model basic components of a letter (heading, greeting, etc.). Have students write a letter to a friend with a partner's help for difficult concepts and vocabulary. | With a partner's help, have students turn their essay into a letter to a government official or other appropriate party, paying close attention to creating a formal tone. |

**TEKS** **10.13E** Revise the final draft in response to feedback from peers and teacher/publish written work; **ELPS 1G** Demonstrate increasing ability to distinguish between formal/informal English and an increasing knowledge of when to use each one; **2C** Learn basic vocabulary heard during classroom instruction/interactions; **3G** Express opinions, ideas, and feelings ranging from communicating short phrases to participating in discussions

## Evaluating an Argumentative Essay

Ask students whether they agree with the score given to this essay. Discuss whether there are any areas that could be improved in this essay. Students may comment that some of the sentences read a little awkwardly (such as *Workers who complain can be and have been fired.*) or suggest that there could be more facts and statistics to support some of the ideas. In general, however, they should agree with the score of 4.

See whether students can identify this essay's thesis statement (*However, it is possible to put a stop to sweatshops by boycotting the clothing made in them.*).

**ELPS** 4K

## Evaluating an Argumentative Essay

To learn how to evaluate an argumentative essay, you will use the holistic scoring guide on pages **60–61** and the essays that follow. These essays are examples of writing for each score on the scoring guide (1–4).

Notice that the first essay received a score of 4. Read the description for a score of 4 on pages **60–61.** Then read the narrative. Use the same steps to study the other examples. As you read, concentrate on the overall quality of the writing in each example.

**Writing that fits a score of 4 is highly effective.**

### Put a Stop to Sweatshops

**The beginning** introduces the writer's focus (underlined). Rhetorical question engages reader.

Why do people spend a lot of time choosing the clothes they wear, but little time worrying about where those clothes are manufactured? If people knew, they would be shocked. Many clothes are manufactured in sweatshops, which are factories where the owners treat workers unfairly. Sweatshops pay extremely low wages and demand long hours in conditions that are often unsafe. Workers who complain can be and have been fired (Harris 95). <u>However, it is possible to put a stop to sweatshops by boycotting the clothing made in them</u>.

Sweatshops are found around the world. Owners of sweatshops often treat workers badly. At one sweatshop, workers made sneakers for 16 cents an hour, and they were required to work more than 70 hours a week. Workers were fired if they refused to work extra hours even though they were never paid for them. At another factory, workers were paid 1.3 cents for every baseball cap they sewed. By any standard, this is outrageous! American manufacturers, though, buy goods from these factories because the labor is so cheap. They can sell these products at low prices and still make a good profit.

**Each middle** paragraph presents relevant evidence and precise details about the topic. Writer shows knowledge of topic.

Many people believe that clothes that say "Made in the USA" were not made in a sweatshop. Unfortunately, that is not true. If a garment is made in a U.S. territory like Guam, the label will says "Made in the USA," even though the workers there may work for low wages and are not protected by U.S. labor laws.

The **middle** paragraphs continue to build on and support the writer's position.

Boycotting sweatshop clothes—as well as any stores that sell them—will help eliminate sweatshops. Boycotts are effective because they directly affect the profits of clothing manufacturers and retailers. If people refuse to buy clothing made in sweatshops, the manufacturers will in fact lose money. (Anderson 45). It is easy to write to or call the headquarters of your favorite stores, and ask if all the workers who make their garments are treated fairly. If not, tell the stores that you and your friends will no longer buy their products. Do some Web research. A number of organizations are dedicated to opposing sweatshops, and they offer online resources.

Transitions link paragraphs and sentences within paragraphs.

Boycotting sweatshops will also help reward clothing manufacturers and retailers who sell "sweat-free" apparel. Sweat free means that the people who make the garments are paid a fair wage and are treated well. Many universities and colleges now will only sell apparel with their logos if the items come from sweat-free factories. Take a look on the Internet to find retailers and clothing manufacturers who sell sweat-free clothes ("Shop for Sweat Free" 28) Give them your business and your purchases will send a clear message: It pays to treat workers fairly.

Boycotting stores that sell sweatshop goods, and asking others to do the same, focuses media attention on the issue. People need to know that sweatshops abuse their workers. Publicity and coverage in the media that will help spread the word.

An objection is identified and addressed.

Some people insist that sweatshops provide necessary jobs to workers and help them build better lives. They argue that without sweatshops, these workers wouldn't have jobs at all. We all wish that this were true, but it isn't. Instead, companies make huge profits, while workers suffer. Companies could offer higher pay, safer working conditions, and still make a profit.

Effective **conclusion** restates position.

Taking action against sweatshops isn't difficult, and it can make a big difference. Boycott clothing made in sweatshops and, the next time you shop, choose sweat-free clothing and stores that sell it. Help clothing workers everywhere lead better lives.

Persuasive

Discuss the importance of the reasons chart (SE page 203). Emphasize that effort at that stage of the writing process pays off by making it much easier to structure the overall essay: in the example essay, each paragraph has a central reason and supporting evidence taken from the reasons chart. ✔DIFFERENTIATE INSTRUCTION

Have students compare the beginning and ending paragraphs. Note how the thesis statement is restated in a new, fresh way, which ties the essay together without sounding repetitious and boring.

## Differentiated Instruction: English Language Learners

⭐ ELPS 1D, 3F, 4F, 4G, 4H, 4K

| ELP Level **Beginning** | ELP Level **Intermediate** | ELP Level **Advanced/Advanced High** |
|---|---|---|
| Provide students with an adapted middle paragraph from the essay, supported by pictures. Have students read with a partner and identify the paragraph's central topic. | Provide students with an adapted middle paragraph from the essay. Have students read with a partner and underline the topic sentence and supporting evidence. | Have students read the essay silently and with a partner create a reasons chart. Encourage students to seek clarification on difficult concepts or vocabulary. |

**ELPS 1D** Speak using learning strategies/request assistance, employ non-verbal cues, and convey ideas by defining or describing; **3F** Ask for information/ranging from using a limited high-frequency vocabulary to using abstract and content-based vocabulary during speaking; **4F** Use visual/contextual support and support from peers/teachers to enhance understanding and develop vocabulary; **4G** Demonstrate comprehension of increasingly complex English/participating in shared reading; **4H** Read silently with increasing ease and comprehension for longer periods; **4K** Demonstrate comprehension and expand reading skills by employing analytical skills/evaluating written information and performing critical analyses

After reading the entire essay, have students focus on the third paragraph. Although it supports the essay's position and includes specific details, note that the paragraph's topic sentence is not clear and the information does not seem unified. Encourage students to suggest how the paragraph might be improved. Suggestions may include:

- New topic sentence: *Organ donations can be used to help people with a variety of medical problems.*
- Move information that comes after the word *kidneys* to the next paragraph. It seems to fit better with the details on how many people receive and are waiting for organs.
- Consider adding more details on how organs are used. **DIFFERENTIATE INSTRUCTION ↘**

Have students identify as many errors in writing conventions as they can. Examples might include:

- The second sentence in the second paragraph should read *Parks, schools, streets, and even a hospital were named after Nicholas.*
- In the fourth sentence in the second paragraph, *important* should be *importantly.*
- In the last sentence of the fourth paragraph, *heart surgery* is not something treated by tissue transplants. Perhaps it should be changed to *heart disease* or *heart problems.*
- There should be a comma between *survey* and *51 percent* in the first sentence of paragraph 7.
- The subjunctive mood is used incorrectly in the second sentence of paragraph 8. A possible change would be *Some people worry that if their doctor were to know that they are willing to donate their organs, he might not try as hard to save them.*

**✦ ELPS** 5D, 5E

---

**Writing that fits a score of 3 is generally effective.**

> The **beginning** paragraph clearly states the writer's position. Introducing the controlling idea with a story engages reader's interest.

> Each **middle** paragraph supports the position with precise and relevant evidence. Minor errors in conventions do not detract.

> Better transitions are needed. Paragraph topic sentences are not always clear.

### A Priceless Donation

In 1994, the Green family was traveling in Italy when a terrible tragedy struck. During a robbery, their seven year old son Nicholas was killed. Reg and Maggie Green were grieving, but they decided to donate his organs to Italians, even though they were American. Their act of kindness had unexpected positive effects.

The family and Nicholas were honored all over Italy for their donation. Parks, schools, and streets and even a hospital was named after Nicholas. The president and prime minister thanked the family in person. More important, it helped seven people and their families. Two were saved from blindness and others were on the brink of death. It also made Italians aware of how important it was to donate organs. Since Nicholas's death, organ donations in Italy have quadrupled from 4.2 per million people to 18 per million people. This doesn't seem like a lot, but it has saved the lives of thousands of people. (Greenwood 56)

If more people was to donate organs, I wonder how many sick people would be saved. People use transplanted corneas to see again. People who are on the brink of death can be saved by transplanted organs like hearts and livers and kidneys. Successful transplants have become pretty common, but there are not enough people who will donate organs. So people who are sick have to wait and wait, and sometimes they die while they wait.

In the United States, there are over 100,000 people waiting for organ donations and over a million waiting for donated tissues or corneas. In 2008, 28,000 people—people who might have died without help—had organ transplants. More than a million tissue transplants are performed each year for treating blindness, injuries, and heart surgery. (DLA)

Despite all the success of transplants, though, there are still not enough Americans signing up to donate organs. Many donations come from people who die suddenly and hadn't thought about donating. When that happens, family members may not want to donate. The family may not think of helping other people

---

**ELPS 5D** Edit writing for standard grammar and usage/subject-verb and pronoun agreement and appropriate verb tenses; **5E** Employ increasingly complex grammatical structures in content area writing such as using correct verbs, tenses, and pronouns/possessive case/negatives and contractions

Persuasive

when they were mourning. They may also have religious reasons for not donating. (Greenwood 61)

That's why health organizations are trying to get people who want to donate to sign up at a state donor registry. Most people signed up when they get a driver's license through their Department of Motor Vehicles. It's easy to do. At the end of 2008, over 38 percent of licensed drivers in the United States were enrolled in state donor registries, which is almost 80 million people. (DLA)

In a survey 51 percent of Americans said they wanted to donate organs or tissues. If a person enrolled in a donor registry program, they could make sure that their wish to donate was honored. I know that I would donate if I was asked. But why then are only 38 percent of people with driver's licenses or state ID enrolled in the program? What keeps people from enrolling?

Some of the problem is misinformation. Some people argue that their doctor won't try to save them if they know they want to be a donor. Others think there's an illegal black market in the United States where people can buy and sell organs. And still other people think they're too old or not healthy enough to become donors. None of those rumors are true. Anyone can donate, and donors are safe if that's what they choose.

A single person can donate tissue to help up to fifty people and organs to three people. People might get their sight back or even be able to do simple things without struggling. The lives of children and mothers and fathers could be saved so that families don't have to live in sadness.

Even though the Greens can't get Nicholas back, they have honored his memory by unselfishly donating his organs. They turned a tragedy into something that is beautiful, and it should be a lesson for all of us. Anyone who can should check "Yes" to donate when they get their driver's license.

**Research helps writer provide precise details and creates an authoritative voice.**

**An objection is identified and addressed.**

**Conclusion** ties essay together.

Ask students whether they feel that the author has conveyed an authoritative voice and why they feel this way. In general, students should agree that the author has an authoritative voice and cite the specific, precise facts and relevant evidence that are used. Students may complain, however, that at times the author seems too informal and that this weakens his or her voice.
**ELPS** 1G

## Differentiated Instruction: English Language Learners

**ELPS** 1F, 2E, 2G, 2H, 2I

| ELP Level **Beginning** | ELP Level **Intermediate** | ELP Level **Advanced/Advanced High** |
|---|---|---|
| Prepare an adapted version of the essay using high-frequency words and basic language whenever possible. Read aloud and ask students to summarize the author's position. | Prepare an adapted version of the essay using basic language mixed with some grade-level vocabulary. Read aloud. Have students summarize the author's position. | Read the essay aloud, providing support for unfamiliar vocabulary. Have students summarize the author's position. Encourage use of grade-level vocabulary. |

**ELPS** **1F** Use accessible language and learn new and essential language in the process; **1G** Demonstrate increasing ability to distinguish between formal/informal English and an increasing knowledge of when to use each one; **2E** Use contextual and linguistic support to enhance and confirm understanding of increasingly complex spoken language; **2G** Understand the main points of spoken language/topics, languages, and contexts are familiar to unfamiliar; **2H** Understand implicit ideas and information in increasingly complex spoken language; **2I** Demonstrate listening comprehension in increasingly complex spoken language by summarizing spoken messages

Have students take turns reading the essay aloud. Discuss with them what effect the errors in writing conventions had on their reading. Students should note that the errors made it difficult to understand what the writer meant in some places. Emphasize that they also distract from the author's argument. Use this example to remind students of the importance of editing their own writing to avoid similar distractions and confusion.

Ask students whether they agree with the score given to this argumentative essay. In general, students should agree that it deserved a score of 2, although some may argue for one score point higher or lower. Discuss disagreements, being sure to emphasize the problems with focus and coherence and with organization that run throughout the middle and ending paragraphs. **DIFFERENTIATE INSTRUCTION ↘**

**ELPS** 3G

**Writing that fits a score of 2 is somewhat effective.**

**The beginning** gives an idea of the thesis. Personal story adds interest.

Each **middle** paragraph connects somewhat to the position statement, but organization is lacking. Some evidence and general details are provided, but ideas are not developed.

Errors in conventions lead to confusion.

**Conclusion** does not sum up the essay or restate the position.

## BUY LOCALLY

My parents own a shoe store downtown and it's getting harder and harder for them to get business and stay in business, too. People in town really like the store, but my dad he thinks that even though they like the store they still go to big chain stores to buy their shoes. Other businesses downtown have the same problem. If people want to keep stores like ours open then they need to start buying from us and from other local stores.

There are alot of reason to buy locally. First, "for every $100 spent at a locally owned business, $45 stays in the local economy, creating jobs and expanding the city's tax base. For every $100 spent at a national chain or franchise store, only $14 remains in the community." (Portland) Local businesses put money back in the comunity, like giving to local charities. Our store supports a school baseball team.

My town has a really nice downtown with alot of independant stores. Thats what makes the downtown nice because we give people a lot of choices and people like shopping in that area. "Independent businesses, choosing products based on what their local customers need and desire, not a national sales plan, guarantees a more diverse range of product and service choices." (I Buy Austin)

Alot of people think that it cost way lots more to buy stuff in a small store instead of in a big chain. That just isn't true. To stay in business, small stores have to have competative prices. You also get better service at our small stores. The people who work at the stores give more personal service and know the merchendise plus they know the loyal customers and our customers know us so Its a much more pleasant place to shop.

If shoppers just would start shopping in our small stores instead of just window shopping and then going somewhere else to buy their things it could make a big difference. If everyone shifted only 10% of their shopping from chain stores to local stores, they would make a big difference to their local economy.

Writing that fits a score of 1 is not effective.

1

Thesis is vague, and is not supported or developed.

### Give Back to the Community

Nobody can graduate from highschool these days unless you have community service credit. I think this is a good thing. Many teenagers don't think of anyone but themselves. Community service makes you think of other peoples.

In my town most kids just want to have fun and don't think if they themselves can do anything for anyone else. Thats why its good that schools are going to make them do community service. At our school we have to do 20 hours in order to gradate. I did my service at a senior citisens center and it was very inspiring work but hard sometimes.

Essay lacks organization, evidence, and details. Errors in conventions make it difficult to understand. Writer never establishes clear voice.

At the center I would help the activities director set up activities and then I would help any of the seniors that had trouble with the activity because a lot of them couldn't here well or they had trubble keeping up or following along. If any of them was having trouble I would help because it was fun sometimes and the people were nice to me and happy to see me so it made me feel good.

My other jobs at the center weren't always so good. Sometimes I had to help clean up or help dress someone and I didn't like that so much. But it was good experience otherwise I might not of learned as much as I did.

The job at the senior center was good experence for other jobs too. It gave me an idea of what I'm good at and what I'm not. I found out I'm good with people and make them happy and also it will also look good when I apply for other jobs or if I apply for college.

Essay lacks **conclusion**.

Community service is good for highschool students. It makes them think about other people and its good experience for other jobs. They might even like what they do and feel good about helping others.

Persuasive

Have students work in pairs to rewrite the beginning paragraph. Prompt them that the position should be assumed to be that community service is a good graduation requirement for high school students. Remind students that the beginning paragraph should grab the reader's attention and contain a thesis statement. Refer students to SE pages 206 and 207 to refresh their memory on writing beginning paragraphs.

---

## Differentiated Instruction: English Language Learners

 **ELPS** 3G, 4D, 4F, 4G, 4J, 4K, 5G

| ELP Level **Beginning** | ELP Level **Intermediate** | ELP Level **Advanced/Advanced High** |
| --- | --- | --- |
| Provide students with an adapted beginning paragraph of another argumentative essay. Preteach vocabulary and read together. Discuss whether it presents a clear thesis statement. | Provide students with a short, adapted argumentative essay. Students should read it with a partner and assign it a score point, focusing on only one or two of the traits. | Have students read another argumentative essay with a partner and assign it a score point. Students should write a short explanation of their score. |

**ELPS 3G** Express opinions ranging from communicating short phrases to participating in discussions; **4D** Use prereading supports to enhance comprehension of written text/graphic organizers, illustrations, and topic-related vocabulary; **4F** Use support from peers/teachers to enhance and confirm understanding and to develop vocabulary; **4G** Demonstrate comprehension of increasingly complex English/participating in shared reading; **4J** Demonstrate comprehension and expand reading skills by employing inferential skills/predicting, making connections between ideas, drawing conclusions from text, and finding supporting evidence; **4K** Demonstrate comprehension and expand reading skills by employing analytical skills/evaluating written information and performing critical analyses; **5G** Explain with increasing specificity and detail/writing

## Evaluating and Reflecting on Your Writing

Set aside 5 or 10 minutes for students to reflect on their writing experiences. Suggest that they think of this as a freewriting exercise. Often, reflections such as this are easier to capture if writers let their ideas flow rather than stopping to ponder each thought.

After students finish their reflections, discuss the sentence starters on SE page 234 as a class.

**DIFFERENTIATE INSTRUCTION ↘**

**234**

# Evaluating and Reflecting on Your Writing

After you finish your argumentative essay, take some time to reflect on your essay and your writing experience. On your own paper, complete each of the sentences below. To score your writing, refer to the holistic scoring guide on pages **60–61** and the examples you just read. Evaluating and reflecting on your writing will reinforce what you learned from your writing experience and help you apply that knowledge to future assignments.

### My Argumentative Essay

1. The paragraphs that best focus on my thesis statement are . . .

2. The paragraphs that need better development are . . .

3. My introduction and conclusion are effective because . . .

4. I should have sounded more knowledgeable and authoritative in paragraphs . . .

5. Word choice that would have made me sound more confident is needed in . . .

6. One question I still have about writing a persuasive essay is . . .

---

**Differentiated Instruction:**
**English Language Learners**

**ELPS** 3F, 4E, 4G, 4I

| ELP Level **Beginning** | ELP Level **Intermediate** | ELP Level **Advanced/Advanced High** |
|---|---|---|
| Prepare an adapted version of the introduction on SE page 235. Encourage students to read silently, allowing for breaks as needed. Pose questions to check understanding. | Prepare an adapted version of the introduction on SE page 235. After students read silently, they should summarize the information to show understanding. | Have students read the introduction on SE page 235 silently. Pose questions to check understanding. Challenge students to summarize the information verbally. |

**ELPS 3F** Give information/ranging from using a limited high-frequency vocabulary to using abstract and content-based vocabulary during speaking; **4E** Read linguistically accommodated content area material with a decreasing need for linguistic accommodations as more English is learned; **4G** Demonstrate comprehension of increasingly complex English/summarizing material and responding to questions; **4I** Demonstrate comprehension by employing basic reading skills

## Persuasive Writing
# Writing an Editorial

In six weeks, your city will vote on whether or not to change the zoning regulations for schools. The new zoning would force you to go to a different high school. Do you think you could convince people to vote "no" to the zoning change? You could try—in an editorial for your city's newspaper. An editorial is a persuasive essay that presents your opinion about an important, timely topic and often includes a call for action.

In this chapter, you'll read a sample editorial about the writer's desire to see Valentine's Day celebrated differently at her school. Then you'll write your own editorial to express your opinion about a recent issue or event. Choose a topic that you feel strongly about. Your confidence and conviction will prompt the reader to agree with your point of view.

## Writing Guidelines

**Subject:** Opinion about a school-related issue
**Purpose:** To present an opinion about a timely and important topic
**Form:** Editorial
**Audience:** Classmates

"Sentences are sharp nails, which force truth upon our memories."
—Denis Diderot

### Resources

**Copy Master (see Appendix)**

• T-chart (TE p. 238)

**Benchmark Papers (see Appendix)**

# Writing an Editorial

### Objectives
• understand that an editorial is a form of persuasive writing
• use what has been learned about persuasive writing to create an editorial
• plan, draft, revise, edit, and publish an editorial

Explain that newspapers usually make a clear distinction between pieces written by their editors and those written by columnists and freelance writers. A page opposite to the regular editorial page ("op-ed") may contain writing by the last two groups. Show examples from local newspapers.

Encourage students to start reading their paper's editorial page. Bring a selection of editorials to share with the class. Many periodicals are also available online.

## Editorial

After reading the editorial, ask students whether they find it effective. (Most should agree that it is strong.) Have them point out parts that make it successful:

- Sentences vary in length. The two-word fragment that opens the essay grabs the reader's attention.
- All of the different sentence types are used.
  - ☐ declarative (*During the season of chocolates . . .*)
  - ☐ interrogative (*Does any other holiday . . . ?*)
  - ☐ imperative (*So let's love that special someone . . .*)
  - ☐ conditional (*Even if an individual can ignore these huge displays . . .*)
  - ☐ exclamatory ( *. . . bring on the Valentine's Day fund-raiser!*)
- Transitions are effective (*In middle school . . .* followed in the next paragraph by *Now that we're in high school . . .*).
- Use of the first-person pronoun *we* helps the reader feel involved.
- The middle paragraphs all support the thesis.

**DIFFERENTIATE INSTRUCTION ↘**

⭐ **TEKS** 10.13B, 10.15A(i), 10.15A(iii), 10.15A(iv), 10.16A, 10.16D, 10.16E; **ELPS** 4K

**TEKS** 10.13B, 10.15A(i), 10.15A(iii), 10.15A(iv), 10.16A, 10.16D, 10.16E

## Editorial

In the following editorial, Patricia presents her opinion that Valentine's Day should be celebrated differently at her school. Her editorial was printed in the school's February newsletter.

### Let Love Rule

**Beginning**
The beginning introduces the topic and presents the opinion statement (underlined).

Valentine's Day. Does any other holiday tap into the deepest emotions, bitter or sweet? During the season of chocolates, roses, cards, and stuffed animals, someone always gets left out. Nowhere is the sting more humiliating and unnecessary than at school. <u>At Benchfield High, students should be more sensitive about how they celebrate Valentine's Day.</u>

The first taste of Valentine's Day comes as soon as children can scribble their friends' names. They stuff valentines into decorated shoe boxes. The rules are simple: Students give a valentine to everyone in class. Of course, a student can always add a carefully chosen candy heart, or save the biggest card of the bunch for that special someone. It's impossible to make life completely fair, but at least teachers and parents try to make this situation as fair as possible.

**Middle**
Each paragraph supports Patricia's opinion.

Middle school students have the carnation fund-raiser: white for "friends," pink for "like," and red for "love." The rule, "all or none," no longer applies. Girls with armfuls of floral trophies giggle with valentine glee. Meanwhile, others can only hope that their lack of colorful carnations will just help them fade into the background.

In high school, the carnation parade is bigger than ever, but carnations alone just don't cut it. Now, on Valentine's Day, the pressure is on to do something extraordinary.

During class, the names of the lucky few are called over the intercom. They go to the office to pick up towering arrangements of flowers and balloons. Even if an individual can ignore these huge displays, they probably find themselves wondering, "Will someone special remember me? Will I be the only one without a valentine?" Talk about distracting, and depressing.

⭐ **TEKS** **10.13B** Structure ideas in a sustained and persuasive way; **10.15A(i)** Write an analytical essay that includes an introductory paragraph; **10.15A(iii)** Write an analytical essay that includes an idea or thesis; **10.15A(iv)** Write an analytical essay that includes a structure appropriate to the purpose, audience, and context; **10.16A** Write an argumentative essay supported by precise and relevant evidence; **10.16D** Write an argumentative essay that includes a structure appropriate to the purpose, audience, and context; **10.16E** Write an argumentative essay that includes analysis of specific data, facts, and ideas; **ELPS** **4K** Demonstrate comprehension and expand reading skills by employing analytical skills/evaluating written information and performing critical analyses

TEKS 10.13B, 10.15A(i),
10.15A(iii), 10.15A(iv),
10.16A, 10.16C–10.16E
ELPS 4K

**Patricia** considers an opposing viewpoint and provides a solution.

A student's love/hate relationship with Valentine's Day can easily change depending on whether or not he or she has a sweetie. Certainly students should show their special someone that they care. But when at school, can't students celebrate Valentine's Day in a way that doesn't flaunt popularity and make others feel excluded?

Introducing a Valentine's Day fund-raiser might be the answer. Instead of carnations, students could buy "Hearts of Hope." Each dollar gets a buyer a paper heart to post on the wall. Each wall represents a different charity. On Valentine's Day, the money would be split between the charities based on the number of hearts on each wall. The money could provide toys for needy children, help for the senior citizen center, and so on. Maybe people can't make life fair, but they can make it a little better?

**Ending** The ending leaves the reader with strong, final thoughts.

At its heart, Valentine's Day is about love; it's not a popularity contest. It's time for Benchfield High to put popularity on the bench and let love rule.

Persuasive

 **Respond to the reading.** Answer the following questions.

**Focus and Coherence** (1) What is the thesis statement? (2) How does the conclusion tie the essay together? **Organization** (3) How does Patricia organize the middle part of her editorial? **Development of Ideas** (4) What is the main point of Patricia's editorial? (5) How does she inspire the reader to take action? **Voice** (6) What words or phrases convey her feelings about the topic? Name three.

**Literature Connection:** You might enjoy reading another editorial, "Abolishing the Penny Makes Good Sense," by Alan S. Blinder.

Note how Patricia summarized her argument in a fresh way and included a positive closing statement that ties the entire editorial together.

 **Respond to the reading.**

**Answers**

**Focus and Coherence**

1. "At Benchfield High, students should be more sensitive about how they celebrate Valentine's Day."
2. It summarizes the argument that she's made throughout the editorial.

**Organization**

3. The first four middle paragraphs are in chronological order and describe how Valentine's Day was celebrated from elementary school to high school. The fifth middle paragraph answers an opposing viewpoint.

**Development of Ideas**

4. At school, Valentine's Day should be celebrated in a positive way that doesn't exclude people.
5. Create a program in school that uses the Valentine's Day idea to collect for charities.

**Voice**

6. Possible answers include: *Nowhere is the sting more humiliating and unnecessary than at school, students should be more sensitive . . . , Talk about distracting, and depressing, it's not a popularity contest, let love rule.*

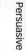 TEKS 10.13B, 10.15A(i), 10.15A(iii), 10.15A(iv), 10.16A, 10.16C, 10.16D, 10.16E; ELPS 4K

 **Literature Connections**

Alternatively, refer to local or national newspapers for additional editorials.

---

**Differentiated Instruction: English Language Learners**    ELPS 1A, 1C, 1F, 2C, 2E, 3C

| **ELP Level** **Beginning** | **ELP Level** **Intermediate** | **ELP Level** **Advanced/Advanced High** |
|---|---|---|
| Define declarative, interrogative, and exclamatory sentence types. Help students connect these with familiar punctuation marks (question mark, etc.) | Define the five sentence types. Present simple examples of each (e.g., *Are you hungry?*) and have students identify the sentence type. | Define the five sentence types. Present examples of each in a variety of sentence structures (including complex and compound). Have students identify the sentence types. |

TEKS **10.13B** Structure ideas in a sustained and persuasive way; **10.15A(i)** Write an analytical essay that includes a concluding paragraph; **10.15A(iii)** Write an analytical essay that includes an idea or thesis; **10.15A(iv)** Write an analytical essay that includes a structure appropriate to the purpose, audience, and context; **10.16A** Write an argumentative essay supported by precise and relevant evidence; **10.16C** Write an argumentative essay that includes counter-arguments; **10.16D** Write an argumentative essay that includes a structure appropriate to the purpose, audience, and context; **10.16E** Write an argumentative essay that includes analysis of specific data, facts, and ideas; **ELPS 1A** Use prior knowledge to understand meanings; **1C** Use strategic learning techniques to acquire basic and grade-level vocabulary; **1F** Use accessible language and learn new and essential language; **2C** Learn new language structures and academic vocabulary heard during classroom instruction/interactions; **2E** Use linguistic support to enhance and confirm understanding of increasingly complex spoken language; **3C** Speak using a variety of grammatical structures/sentence lengths and types/connecting words with increasing accuracy and ease; **4K** Demonstrate comprehension and expand reading skills by employing analytical skills

## Prewriting
### Planning Your Writing

Remind students that, like Patricia, it's not enough for them to simply have a strong opinion about something. They must also have—or be able to get—enough relevant evidence and details to support their opinion.

 **TEKS** 10.15A(iii), 10.15A(v), 10.16B

**Choose your topic.** Suggest that students who have difficulty coming up with topic ideas try the following:

- Think about conversations they have had with friends about school issues.
- Read the school paper—not just the current issue, but earlier ones—if possible.
- Use a concept web or other graphic organizer to gather ideas for possible topics.
- Brainstorm a selection of ideas with a group of classmates. **DIFFERENTIATE INSTRUCTION ↘**

### ⭐ Focus on the Texas Traits

**Development of Ideas**
Distribute photocopies of the reproducible T-chart (TE Appendix). Have students label one column on their charts *Opposing POV* and the other *Call to Action.* Students can then jot down two or three ideas for each. As they gather details and think about their essays, they can choose the most telling or important point from each column to incorporate into their essays.

⭐ **TEKS** 10.13A

---

 **TEKS** 10.13A, 10.15A(iii), 10.15A(v), 10.16B

## Prewriting Planning Your Writing

The purpose of your editorial is to express your opinion about a timely and important topic. To find a topic for her editorial, Patricia completed a sentence starter about several important issues at her school. After looking over her possible topics, she realized she didn't have enough information about some of the issues, and another matter wasn't up for vote for six months. She chose the Valentine's Day issue, which seemed to be perfect for the school paper.

### Sentence Starter

Students at my school are saying that . . .
- the online driver's ed course is a big help.
- Valentine's Day is a popularity contest.\*
- we might lose open-campus lunch if students keep skipping class.
- bathroom graffiti is becoming a problem.
- the possible school zoning change for next year is unfair.

 **Choose your topic.** Complete the sentence starter above in three or four different ways. Put an asterisk (\*) next to the topic that you would like to write about. Remember that you need a strong opinion in order to present a convincing editorial.

Prewrite

###  Focus on the Texas Traits

**Development of Ideas** An editorial is a form of persuasive writing. An effective persuasive essay includes specific examples that support your opinion. You should consider the whole range of arguments about your position. Your argument will also be more convincing if you do the following:

- **Address an opposing point of view.** Respectfully, honestly, and accurately address and counter objections.
  While it's true that plastic bags are convenient for shoppers, they are more than inconvenient for the environment.

- **Make a final call to action.** Encourage readers to agree with your opinion and take appropriate action.
  Urge friends and family to reuse more durable kinds of shopping bags.

---

## Gathering and Organizing Reasons and Evidence

After choosing your topic, you must gather supporting details to convince your audience. Patricia created a quick list of convincing supporting details. She knew that she would have to build a foundation for her thesis statement in order to convince other students. As you begin to think about your topic, develop a quick list like Patricia's, shown here.

### Quick List

> – People send flowers and gifts to school.
> – In grade school, everyone got a valentine.
> – We should do a fund-raiser for a charity.

Next, Patricia arranged her details in order. She knew that in order to convince her audience to support her, she would have to include relevant evidence in her editorial. As you consider ways to support your editorial, create a details chart that you can refer to. Remember your audience, purpose, and context.

### Details Chart

| | |
|---|---|
| early years in school | – stuffed valentines in boxes, all students get cards |
| middle school | – held carnation fund-raiser |
| | – popularity contest made some feel left out |
| high school | – continue carnations |
| | – give "special someones" bouquets or balloons |
| other viewpoint | – people with my opinion are just jealous |
| possible solution | – find another way to celebrate |

**Prewrite** **Gather ideas and build a logical foundation.** Using the list and chart above, gather logical and precise, relevant evidence for your position.

Persuasive

## Gathering and Organizing Reasons and Evidence

Encourage students to research their topics if they need to. This might involve:

- finding articles about them in the school or local newspapers or online;
- searching newspapers for articles about how other schools have dealt with the same issues; or
- interviewing teachers, school administrators, parents, or other students about the issues.

**Gather ideas and build a logical foundation.**
Although the school library is a great place to gather ideas, encourage students doing research to broaden their search to public libraries, reliable online sources, and respected adults who could contribute valuable information and ideas.

 **TEKS** 10.16A

**TEKS** 10.16A Write an argumentative essay supported by precise and relevant evidence; **ELPS** 1C Use strategic learning techniques to acquire basic and grade-level vocabulary; 1E Internalize new basic language by using and reusing it/writing; 5B Write using newly acquired basic vocabulary; 5G Describe and explain with increasing specificity and detail/writing

## Prewriting
### Planning Your Writing

### Writing an Opinion Statement

If students are having trouble writing opinion statements, suggest that they freewrite two or three sentences that express opinions on their topic. Once they have written them, they can choose one to work with. **DIFFERENTIATE INSTRUCTION** ↘

⭐ **TEKS** 10.13A

### Review Your Opinion Statement and Your Details Chart

If students answer *no* to any of these questions, they should go back and either revise their opinion statement, gather further evidence and precise details, or, potentially, choose another topic.

⭐ **TEKS** 10.15A(iii), 10.15A(v), 10.15A(vi), 10.16A, 10.16B

**Write your opinion statement.** Once students have written an opinion statement, have them exchange statements with a partner. Each student should answer the first two review questions from SE page 240 about their peer's thesis. Encourage positive, constructive feedback.

⭐ **ELPS** 3E, 3G

---

## Prewriting Planning Your Writing

### Writing an Opinion Statement

When you write your opinion statement for an editorial, it is critical to keep in mind your audience. For Patricia, the audience was students and administrators at the high school. If you are preparing an editorial for the local newspaper, your audience will be different. Therefore, your voice and the vocabulary that you use should be more formal. The following graphic organizer will help you develop a thesis statement. Also refer to the planning that you did on the previous page.

An editorial needs a strong opinion statement on a timely, important topic.

| timely and important topic | + | your opinion about the topic | = | a thesis statement |
|---|---|---|---|---|
| Valentine's Day | | Need to be more sensitive about how students celebrate | | At Benchfield High, students should be more sensitive about how they celebrate Valentine's Day. |

### Review Your Opinion Statement and Your Details Chart

After you have written your opinion statement, think about it carefully. Then look at your details chart to make sure that it includes logical reasons, relevant evidence, and precise details that you can use to support your opinion.

- Does your opinion statement express a single strong opinion?
- Does it accurately express your viewpoint?
- Can you support it sufficiently with relevant evidence and precise details?
- Can you identify a strong objection and counter it with a logical argument?

**Write your opinion statement.** Use your list and chart to write a strong statement that will engage your reader and that you can support throughout your editorial.

Prewrite

---

**TEKS** **10.13A** Plan a first draft/selecting genre, determining topics through a range of strategies, and developing a thesis; **10.15A(iii)** Write an analytical essay that includes an idea or thesis; **10.15A(v)** Write an analytical essay that includes relevant evidence and details; **10.15A(vi)** Write an analytical essay that includes distinctions about specific data that support the thesis; **10.16A** Write an argumentative essay supported by precise and relevant evidence; **10.16B** Write an argumentative essay that includes the range of information and views on the topic; **ELPS** **3E** Share information in cooperative learning interactions; **3G** Express opinions and ideas ranging from communicating short phrases to participating in discussions

# Drafting Creating Your First Draft

The following tips will help you write your editorial. Also refer to the planning that you did on the previous pages.

## Writing Your Beginning Paragraph

The beginning paragraph should introduce the topic in an interesting way and present your opinion statement. Here are strategies for capturing your reader's attention.

- Present a question or an interesting detail about the topic. *Does any other holiday tap into the deepest emotions, bitter or sweet?*
- Explain why the topic is important. *During the season of chocolates, roses, cards, and stuffed animals, someone always gets left out.*
- Share a quotation. *"To love and be loved is to feel the sun from both sides."*

## Writing Your Middle Paragraphs

The middle paragraphs should build your argument in a logical way, explain the opposing point of view, and offer a possible solution.

- Organize your points in a logical way with relevant examples, precise details, and illustrations. Consider the relative value of the data, facts, and ideas that you include.
- Avoid attacking others or preaching.
- Be brief and direct.
- Offer a reasonable solution.

## Writing Your Ending Paragraph

The ending paragraph should sum up the argument in a strong, convincing way. Use the tips below to create a powerful ending.

- Summarize your opinion. *At its heart, Valentine's Day is about love.*
- Put your spin on the opposing viewpoint. *It is not a popularity contest.*
- Create a memorable, positive closing statement. *It's time for Benchfield High to put popularity on the bench and let love rule.*

**Write your first draft.** Use your own prewriting work and the tips above to develop your editorial.

Persuasive

# Drafting
## Creating Your First Draft

### Writing Your Beginning Paragraph

Before students begin writing, have them collect quotations and interesting details that apply to their topics. Ask students to make room for one or two of these items in their beginning paragraph.

### Writing Your Middle Paragraphs

Remind students that every paragraph should have a topic sentence followed by supporting details and a closing sentence that acts as a transition or connection to the ideas in the next paragraph.

### Writing Your Ending Paragraph

Point out the pun in the closing statement (popularity on the *bench* at *Bench*field High). Remind students that this and various forms of figurative language (similes and metaphors) are helpful in drawing the reader's attention and creating interest.

**Write your first draft.** Remind students to focus on the first four of the writing traits (focus and coherence, organization, development of ideas, and voice). While they should certainly try to follow the rules of grammar, spelling, etc., writing conventions will be considered in detail during the editing process.

TEKS 10.15A(v), 10.16C, 10.16E

**TEKS** **10.15A(v)** Write an analytical essay that includes relevant evidence and details; **10.16C** Write an argumentative essay that includes counter-arguments to anticipate and address objections; **10.16E** Write an argumentative essay that includes analysis of specific data, facts, and ideas; **ELPS 1C** Use strategic learning techniques to acquire basic and grade-level vocabulary; **1E** Internalize new basic language by using and reusing it/writing; **5B** Write using newly acquired basic vocabulary; **5G** Describe and explain with increasing specificity and detail/writing

## Drafting
### Creating Your First Draft

#### Convincing Your Audience

Students may protest that they have been taught to avoid emotional appeals in their writing. Explain that they need to distinguish between writing that shows the *author's* emotion in aggressive, offensive, or confrontational ways and writing that uses language meant to engage the *reader's* emotions about the topic. The former should be avoided, but the latter is an effective technique that can be used in editorial writing. **DIFFERENTIATE INSTRUCTION ↘**

#### Addressing Objections

Encourage your students to be careful in discussing objections with others. They have chosen a topic that they have strong feelings about and, no doubt, those with objections have strong feelings as well. It is important to keep these discussions friendly and open; otherwise, confrontation and hurt feelings can result.

**Choose an appeal to use.** Encourage students to come up with an example for each of the four appeals given on this page, even if they don't plan to use them all.

★ **TEKS** 10.16C, 10.16F

---

## Drafting Creating Your First Draft

### Convincing Your Audience

There are many ways you can appeal to your audience, make a strong case for your position, and convince your readers to support your position.

■ **Emotional appeals try to create strong feeling in the reader.**

When you use an emotional appeal, you use words and phrases that evoke either positive or negative emotions. Consider adding descriptions, analogies, and illustrations that have emotional appeal in your editorial.

■ **A testimonial is a kind of appeal in which famous people endorse a product or a cause.**

The positive qualities of the famous person are transferred to the product or the cause. If you add quotations to your editorial, think about them as possible testimonials.

■ **The bandwagon technique persuades by convincing the reader that everyone else holds the opinion.**

The bandwagon technique invites readers to "join the winning team." It reinforces people's natural desire to be accepted and admired. Consider using descriptions, case studies, and anecdotes with the bandwagon technique to support your position and help convince your reader.

■ **Glittering generalities focus on highly valued concepts and beliefs, such as patriotism, peace, freedom, glory, and honor.**

The "glitter" and positive emotional appeal of these can cause readers to lower their guards and accept information inadequately supported by evidence. Try to avoid generalities that you cannot support with precise detail.

### Addressing Objections

In an editorial, it is important to consider a range of views. Identify and address objections to your position. You are trying to convince people to support your position, so you need to identify, describe, and counter objections.

■ **Talk to teachers, friends, and family about your position. Listen to what they have to say. Make a list of objections.**

■ **Choose at least one objection that you can address. Use counter-arguments in your editorial.**

Draft

**Choose an appeal to use.** Think of appeals you can make to your audience. Jot down descriptions, anecdotes, case studies, analogies, and illustrations you can use to support your position. Include them in your editorial.

---

Writing an Editorial **243**

 **TEKS** 10.13C

# Revising Improving Your Editorial

Once you complete your first draft, set it aside for a while. Then use the guidelines below to revise your editorial.

### Revising Checklist

## Focus and Coherence

_____ **1.** Have I clearly stated my opinion?

_____ **2.** Have I supported and defended my opinion?

## Organization

_____ **3.** Does my editorial have a strong introduction, middle, and conclusion?

_____ **4.** Have I organized my points in a logical way?

## Development of Ideas?

_____ **5.** Do I support my position with logical reasons, relevant examples, and precise details?

_____ **6.** Do I address the other side of the argument?

_____ **7.** Have I provided a reasonable call to action?

_____ **8.** Have I included an appropriate range of appeals?

## Voice

_____ **9.** Is my voice confident and convincing?

_____ **10.** Does my voice show my interest in the topic?

Revise

**Revise your first draft.** Use the checklist above as you revise your first draft. Ask a partner to read your editorial and make suggestions as well.

## Creating a Title

■ Ask a question: **Why Can't We Be Fair?**
■ State the topic: **Celebrate Valentine's Day in a New Way**
■ Call for action: **Let Love Rule**

*Persuasive*

## Revising

**Improving Your Editorial**

If the schedule allows, you may want students to set their writing aside for a day or two. Encourage students to work on other assignments during this time and not to think about their editorial or possible revisions they plan to make.

**Revise your first draft.** Have the partners pose additional objections to the writers' arguments. Challenge writers to answer these objections. Afterward, ask the writers to consider these questions:

■ *Did you see weaknesses in your reasoning that you didn't notice before?*
■ *Did you discover a new objection that might be more important to address than the one you first chose?*

**TEKS** 10.13C

## Creating a Title

Note that the readers of newspapers—where most editorials are found—often skim the headlines very quickly, stopping only at the ones that capture their interest. Challenge students to think of the most eye-catching titles possible for their editorials. For ideas and strategies, have students scan newspapers or blogs for headlines that grab their attention.

**TEKS** 10.13C

---

**Differentiated Instruction: English Language Learners**

**ELPS** 1A, 1C, 1F, 3B, 3E, 4C, 4F

| ELP Level **Beginning** | ELP Level **Intermediate** | ELP Level **Advanced/Advanced High** |
|---|---|---|
| Have students create a word web for the list of "glittering generalities" (peace, etc.). Help students use accessible language, pictures, and first language words to complete it. | Have students create a word web for the list of "glittering generalities" (honor, peace, etc.). Students work with a partner to complete the web. | Have students create a word web for the list of "glittering generalities" (honor, peace, etc.). Students work with a partner to complete the web. |
| Use page 624 | Use page 624 | Use page 624 |

 **TEKS** **10.13C** Revise drafts/improve style, word choice, and subtlety of meaning and rethink how well the purpose, audience, and genre have been addressed; **ELPS** **1A** Use prior knowledge to understand meanings; **1C** Use strategic learning techniques to acquire basic and grade-level vocabulary; **1F** Use accessible language and learn new and essential language in the process; **3B** Expand vocabulary by learning and using high-frequency words for identifying/describing and routine language needed for classroom communication; **3E** Share information in cooperative learning interactions; **4C** Comprehend vocabulary used in written classroom materials; **4F** Use support from peers/teachers to develop vocabulary and background knowledge

## Editing

### Checking for Conventions

Encourage students to read their editorials aloud. Often, hearing their writing will help them identify problems with grammar and sentence structure that they wouldn't have noticed otherwise.

**Edit your editorial.** Have students use the checklist to guide them as they edit their writing. Encourage them to read the editorial several times, looking for specific conventions errors each time.

 **TEKS** 10.13C, 10.13D, 10.17C, 10.18A, 10.18B(ii), 10.19; **ELPS** 5C, 5D, 5E

## Publishing

### Sharing Your Editorial

Have students share their finished editorials with classmates through public readings or organized classroom debates. Encourage them to keep up to date with the topics they wrote about, especially if they publish their editorials outside of the classroom. **DIFFERENTIATE INSTRUCTION**

**TEKS** 10.13E

### ★ Conventions Connections

**Grammar: Capitalization**
- *Proofreader's Guide* pages 682–687
- *SkillsBook* pages 41–43

**Grammar: Commas**
- *Proofreader's Guide* pages 646–655
- *SkillsBook* pages 7–16

✎ *Write Source Online* **GrammarSnap**

**TEKS** **10.13C** Revise drafts to improve sentence variety; **10.13D** Edit drafts for grammar, mechanics, and spelling; **10.13E** Revise the final draft in response to feedback from peers and teacher/publish written work; **10.17C** Use a variety of correctly structured sentences; **10.18A** Use conventions of capitalization; **10.18B(ii)** Use quotations marks to indicate sarcasm and irony; **10.19** Spell correctly using resources to determine and check correct spelling; **ELPS 1B** Monitor oral language and employ self-corrective techniques or other resources; **1E** Internalize new basic and academic language by using and reusing it/speaking; **3B** Expand vocabulary by learning and using high-frequency words for identifying and describing; **3G** Express opinions, ideas, and feelings ranging from communicating short phrases to participating in discussions; **3H** Explain with increasing specificity and detail; **3I** Adapt spoken language for formal purposes; **5C** Spell familiar words with increasing accuracy; **5D** Edit writing for standard grammar and usage/subject-verb and pronoun agreement and appropriate verb tenses; **5E** Employ increasingly complex grammatical structures in content area writing such as using correct verbs, tenses, and pronouns/possessive case/negatives and contractions

---

 **TEKS** 10.13C–10.13E, 10.17C, 10.18A, 10.18B(ii), 10.19
**ELPS** 5C–5E

## Editing Checking for Conventions

After you've revised your editorial, it's important to edit it. The following checklist can help you spot any errors in grammar, sentence structure, capitalization, punctuation, and spelling.

#### Editing Checklist

### Conventions

**GRAMMAR**
_____ **1.** Do I use the correct forms of verbs (*I went* not *I gone*)?
_____ **2.** Do my subjects and verbs agree in number?
_____ **3.** Have I used the right words (*there, their, they're*)?

**SENTENCE STRUCTURE**
_____ **4.** Have I correctly used a variety of sentence structures?

**MECHANICS (Capitalization and Punctuation)**
_____ **5.** Do I capitalize the first word in each sentence?
_____ **6.** Do I capitalize all proper nouns and proper adjectives?
_____ **7.** Have I ended my sentences with the correct punctuation?
_____ **8.** Have I used commas correctly?
_____ **9.** Have I punctuated quotations correctly?

**SPELLING**
_____ **10.** Do I spell all my words correctly?
_____ **11.** Have I double-checked for spelling errors that my spell-checker might miss?

 **Edit your editorial.** Use the checklist above to edit for conventions. Have a partner check your work, too. Then prepare a final copy and proofread it.

## Publishing Sharing Your Editorial

Share your timely editorial with friends and family as soon as possible. If appropriate, consider submitting your editorial to your school or city newspaper, a magazine, or a Web page. Let your voice be heard.

---

### Differentiated Instruction: English Language Learners

**ELPS** 1B, 1E, 3B, 3G, 3H, 3I

| ELP Level **Beginning** | ELP Level **Intermediate** | ELP Level **Advanced/Advanced High** |
|---|---|---|
| Help students prepare and present a short statement verbalizing their thesis. Students may use pictures, gestures, and other supports as necessary. | After you model an example, students work with a partner to prepare and present a short statement verbalizing their positions and arguments. | Have students participate in a formal debate to verbalize their positions and arguments. Students should monitor their language to ensure a formal tone. Correct as needed. |

245

## Writing for Assessment
# Responding to Persuasive Prompts

Developing a well-organized and convincing persuasive argument can take time. Sometimes, however, you don't have much time to convince people to agree with you. Let's say you're trying to get permission from your parents to spend Saturday night at a classmate's house, or you're trying to convince a friend to go to a concert with you. At times like these, you'll need to organize and present your argument quickly and effectively.

Responding to a persuasive prompt on a test presents a similar problem. Within a set time limit, you'll need to choose a position, structure your argument, and present it in a logical, effective manner. This chapter will show you how to use the writing process to create a clear, effective persuasive response in a timed situation.

### Writing Guidelines

**Subject:** Persuasive prompt
**Form:** Response essay
**Purpose:** To demonstrate competence
**Audience:** Instructor or test evaluator

"Good writing is clear thinking made visible."
—Bill Wheeler

### Resources

**Copy Masters (see Appendix)**

- T-chart (TE p. 247)
- Quick list (TE p. 247)

**Benchmark Papers
(see Appendix)**

# Responding to Persuasive Prompts

### Objectives

- understand the elements of a persuasive prompt
- practice analyzing a persuasive prompt; then plan, write, revise, and edit the response
- practice writing for assessment

Assure students that the more they practice persuasive writing, the less difficulty they will have when they encounter a persuasive writing prompt. They will become more adept at stating a position and supporting it with appropriate details.

Acknowledge that when time is short, it may not be possible to spend a lot of time thinking of the best argument. What is important in testing situations is that students choose a good, solid argument and support it competently.

## Prewriting
### Analyzing a Persuasive Prompt

Suggest that students develop a consistent way of marking up prompts to identify the STRAP answers. Students might

- circle and label each element accordingly, or
- devise their own set of symbols, such as using a single line under the Subject, a double line under Type, a triple line under Role, a circle around Audience, and parentheses around the Purpose.

### Try It!
### Answers

1. **Subject:** plan to double license fees for drivers under 18; **Type:** editorial; **Role:** person who will be affected by the increase; **Audience:** peers (readers of student newspaper); **Purpose:** persuade to support or oppose the decision
2. **Subject:** proposal to reduce the number of summer jobs provided by city council; **Type:** letter to the editor; **Role:** person who will be affected by the reduction; **Audience:** members of the community; **Purpose:** persuade to support or oppose the proposal

**DIFFERENTIATE INSTRUCTION ↘**

# Prewriting Analyzing a Persuasive Prompt

In order to respond effectively to a persuasive prompt, you must analyze it carefully, using the following **STRAP questions** as a guide.

| | |
|---|---|
| Subject: | What topic should I write about? |
| Type: | What form (essay, letter, editorial, article, report) of writing should I create? |
| Role: | What position (student, son or daughter, friend, employee, citizen) should I assume as the writer? |
| Audience: | Who (teacher, parents, classmates, employer, official) is the intended reader? |
| Purpose: | What is the goal (persuade, respond, evaluate, tell, describe) of my writing? |

## Sample Analyzed Prompt

Subject
Type
Role
Audience
Purpose

You are a resident of Bradford. The town's recreation director has announced a plan to close the recreation center during the summer months because not many kids use it. Write a letter to the director arguing for or against this decision.

### Try It!

Analyze these prompts by answering the STRAP questions. (Use your best judgment to form an answer for every question.)

1. Your state plans to double license fees for drivers under age 18. The money will be used to fund driver-education programs. Write an editorial for your student newspaper supporting or opposing this decision.
2. The city council is considering a proposal to reduce the number of summer jobs it provides for high school students each year. Write a letter to the editor supporting or opposing this decision.

### Differentiated Instruction: Struggling Learners

Have students work in small groups to complete a five-point STRAP chart, using a separate sheet of paper for each point. Have them discuss and analyze the **Try It!** prompts or practice with other prompts in the chapter. Assign a recorder, or have students take turns making notes based on their discussions. Point out that the STRAP strategy will make writing a strong persuasive paragraph easier.

**ELPS** 3E

## Planning Your Response

Once you have answered the STRAP questions, you should quickly plan your persuasive response. The following graphic organizers can help you.

## Considering Both Sides

The graphic organizers include space for both pro and con arguments because your response should consider both sides to see where the strongest position lies. In general, facts make the strongest argument, but a reasonable appeal to emotion can also provide strong support.

When planning a persuasive response, you should always present and respond to at least one main objection. By countering the objection, you will strengthen your own position. You will also demonstrate that you have considered both sides of an issue.

Prewrite

**Use a graphic organizer to plan a response.** Reread the persuasive prompts on page 246. Choose one prompt and use a graphic organizer to plan your response.

## Tip

In a timed writing test, plan carefully. Allow yourself time for planning before you write and for revising and editing after you write. For example, if you have 45 minutes to respond to a prompt, use the first 5 minutes to analyze the prompt and plan your response, the last 5 minutes to revise and edit your response, and the time in between to write your response.

Persuasive

### Differentiated Instruction: English Language Learners

**★ ELPS 1B**

| ELP Level **Beginning** | ELP Level **Intermediate** | ELP Level **Advanced/Advanced High** |
|---|---|---|
| Do not give students a time limit. Instead, focus on helping them convey their ideas using accessible basic vocabulary supplemented by their first language when necessary. | Do not give students a time limit. Focus on helping them convey their ideas using basic and grade-level vocabulary. Students should monitor their writing and correct as needed. | Give students extended time to convey their ideas using grade-level and academic vocabulary. Students should monitor their writing and correct as needed. |

## Planning Your Response

Encourage students to become familiar with many different types of graphic organizers so they can decide at a glance which one to use for a given prompt. Note that in this case the choice between the T-chart, quick list, and cluster is a matter of personal preference.

✱ For more graphic organizers, see SE pages 624–625.

### Considering Both Sides

Note that even if they aren't sure at this stage how they feel about a topic, they should proceed with listing the pros and cons. Once they have noted three or four of each, students can evaluate the overall effect. The side with the most convincing ideas will determine their position. The most convincing idea in the opposite column can be the objection they respond to in the essay.

**Use a graphic organizer to plan a response.** Distribute photocopies of the reproducible T-chart and quick list (see TE Appendix) for students to use. Suggest that they choose the organizer that works best for them. Remind students, however, that in an on-demand writing situation, they will probably not be given premade graphic organizers to complete. Students need to become familiar with using and creating their own graphic organizers in a testing situation.

Use a timer to mark off 10 minutes for planning a response. This will help students get a feel for how much time they have during a real testing situation. ✔DIFFERENTIATE INSTRUCTION

**TEKS** 10.13A, 10.13B, 10.16B, 10.16C

### Tip

Discuss as a class how students approach a writing prompt. Encourage students to share ideas of techniques, especially planning techniques, that work well for them.

**TEKS** **10.13A** Plan a first draft by determining topics through a range of strategies; **10.13B** Structure ideas in a sustained and persuasive way; **10.16B** Write an argumentative essay that includes the range of information and views on the topic; **10.16C** Write an argumentative essay that includes counter-arguments to anticipate and address objections; **ELPS 1B** Monitor written language and employ self-corrective techniques or other resources

## Drafting

### Responding to a Prompt

Point out that the writer of the sample correctly formatted his essay as a letter, starting it with the salutation *Dear Editor* and closing with *Sincerely.* This demonstrates that he carefully read the prompt and accurately determined the form of writing, a letter to the editor.

Some students may view letter writing much differently than writing an essay or an editorial (especially if they associate letter writing with e-mail). Note that even in a letter, students should apply the same basic techniques they've learned for other forms of persuasive writing (e.g., the first paragraph has a clear thesis statement).

⭐ **TEKS** 10.13B, 10.16A

---

## Drafting Responding to the Prompt

Once you have answered the STRAP questions and planned your response using a graphic organizer, you can begin writing. In this essay, the student writer chose to respond to the second prompt on page 246.

### Sample Persuasive Prompt

> *In an effort to save money, your city council is considering a proposal to reduce the number of summer jobs it gives to high school students each year. The jobs involve working in the recreation department maintaining the grounds of city parks. Write a letter to the editor of your local newspaper supporting or opposing this decision.*

### Sample Response

**Beginning**
The beginning paragraph leads up to the opinion (underlined).

Dear Editor:

When school lets out every summer, the city's high school students go out to look for jobs. For many students, these jobs are important. Summer jobs allow students to make the extra money they need to save for college, maintain a car, or even save for next year's school clothes. But this summer, students in our city might have a harder time finding work. The city council has decided to cut summer jobs in the recreation department. However, for the good of the city and its young people, these jobs should be restored.

**Middle**
Each middle paragraph presents a logical reason that supports the opinion. Transitions connect ideas.

One reason to restore the jobs is that they may actually end up helping the city and the recreation department save money. Every summer, student workers mow lawns, clean up litter, and help keep parks neat and clean. But they often get paid much less than full-time workers. So hiring a student is like getting a full-time worker for less than full-time pay. And that's a great deal for the city.

---

### Differentiated Instruction: Struggling Learners

For all students, but especially for struggling learners, the best way to prepare for a test is to practice under similar conditions. If your state assessment is administered in the library, for example, try to arrange a test prep experience in that setting. If students write on lined paper in an exam book, try to provide a similar-looking workspace for their practice writing.

---

⭐ **TEKS** **10.13B** Structure ideas in a sustained and persuasive way/develop drafts in timed situations that include transitions and rhetorical devices; **10.16A** Write an argumentative essay supported by relevant evidence

**Rhetorical devices add interest, and the appeal strengthens the position.**

In addition, students who work for the city in the summer are not only earning money, but continuing their education. They learn important job skills such as getting to work on time, following directions, using tools and equipment safely, and working as a team. Learning these skills will help students succeed at college and in their careers. So isn't spending money on summer jobs for students an investment that will pay off for everyone in the future?

Finally, students who work during the summer are less likely to become bored. If kids are busy, they are less likely to get into trouble. Students who work for the city are also more likely to have respect for the city and its property. This respect means that young people will take better care of city facilities.

**Objection**
**The final middle paragraph addresses an objection.**

Some people might argue that students hired by the city don't work hard enough for their money. Maybe some students don't work as hard as they could, but this is true for adults, too. The fact remains that most students will work hard and gladly contribute to making city parks better for everyone.

**Ending**
**The ending summarizes the argument and offers a final plea.**

Reducing the number of student summer jobs will not only result in bored students, but it may end up costing the city more in the end. The small amount of money the city pays to hire students for the summer is an investment. And that investment pays off not only in better city parks, but also in students having the skills they need to succeed in the years beyond high school. So please encourage the city council to maintain this program. Everyone in town will benefit.

Sincerely,

Angel Hernandez

*Persuasive*

**Respond to a persuasive prompt.** Review the prompt you chose on page 246, your answers to the STRAP questions, and your graphic organizer. Then write a response to the prompt your teacher gives you. Be sure to plan your time carefully.

---

Have students respond to the sample. *Does it answer the prompt?* (They should agree that it does.) *Do they have suggestions for improving it?* Possible responses:

■ The first middle paragraph is based on the assumption that if students don't do the work, full-time workers will. The writer could also address the possibility that the city might decide not to have anyone do the work.

■ The writer could sound a bit more interested in the topic. The voice is authoritative but slightly distant.

■ The writer uses fairly general adjectives; it might be good to substitute more vivid ones. For example, *better city parks* in the last paragraph could be changed to *greener, cleaner city parks*.

Have students reread the essay and identify the transitions and rhetorical devices the writer has used.

⭐ **TEKS** 10.16A, 10.16C, 10.16E

**Respond to a persuasive prompt.** Consider letting students know when each time interval is up (5 minutes for analyzing the prompt, 10 minutes for planning their response, etc.). Or, if this is the second or third practice response your students are writing, encourage them to keep track of the time themselves as they will have to do during a real testing situation. ✔ **DIFFERENTIATE INSTRUCTION**

✔ **DIFFERENTIATE INSTRUCTION**

⭐ **TEKS** 10.13B

---

⭐ **TEKS** **10.13B** Structure ideas in a sustained and persuasive way/develop drafts in timed situations that include transitions and rhetorical devices; **10.16A** Write an argumentative essay supported by relevant evidence; **10.16C** Write an argumentative essay that includes counter-arguments to anticipate and address objections; **10.16E** Write an argumentative essay that includes analysis of specific ideas; **ELPS** **1G** Demonstrate increasing ability to distinguish between formal/informal English and an increasing knowledge of when to use each one; **5E** Employ increasingly complex grammatical structures in content area writing such as using correct verbs, tenses, and pronouns/possessive case/negatives and contractions; **5F** Write using a variety of grade-appropriate sentence lengths and patterns in increasingly accurate ways; **5G** Describe and explain with increasing specificity and detail/writing

**Revising**

**Improving Your Response**

Encourage students to review the goals for persuasive writing on SE page 198 and talk about the ways they apply to the STRAP questions:

- Subject, type, and purpose apply mainly to the traits of focus and coherence and organization.
- Role and audience apply mainly to the development of ideas and voice used in the piece.
- Conventions ensure that the writer's answers to all of the STRAP questions are conveyed accurately and well.

**Improve your work.** Remind students that in a testing situation, their time will be limited. They should be sure to leave time for revision, but may not be able to make major changes.

 **TEKS** 10.13C

## Editing

**Checking Your Response**

Have students refer to SE page 226 for a more detailed conventions checklist.

**Check your conventions.** Remind students that they are more likely to make careless mistakes when they are under the pressure of time. That's why it is so important to plan their time well, leaving appropriate amounts of time for every step in the writing process. It is just as important, however, that they make a conscious effort to remain calm throughout the assessment. If they allow themselves to feel rushed and stressed, errors may multiply.

**TEKS** 10.13D, 10.17C, 10.18A, 10.18B(i), 10.19;
**ELPS** 5C, 5D, 5E, 5F

---

 **TEKS** 10.13C, 10.13D, 10.17C, 10.18A, 10.18B(i), 10.19
**ELPS** 5C, 5D, 5F

 **Revising** Improving Your Response

Before you begin a writing test, find out whether you will be allowed to make changes in your writing. If this is allowed, always make your revisions and edits neatly. The STRAP questions below can guide your revisions.

> **Subject:** Does my response focus on the topic of the prompt? Do my main points support the opinion stated in my first paragraph?
>
> **Type:** Have I used the form requested in the prompt (essay, letter, editorial, article, report)?
>
> **Role:** Have I assumed the position called for in the prompt?
>
> **Audience:** Have I used appropriate language for my audience?
>
> **Purpose:** Does my response accomplish the goal of the prompt?

 **Improve your work.** Reread your response, asking yourself the STRAP questions above. Make necessary changes to your response.

## Editing **Checking Your Response**

Read through your response one final time, checking for errors in grammar, sentence structure, capitalization, punctutation, and spelling.

**Editing Checklist**

### Conventions

_____ 1. Have I made sure my subjects and verbs agree?
_____ 2. Have I used the right words *(their, they're, there)*?
_____ 3. Have I correctly used a variety of sentence structures?
_____ 4. Have I capitalized all proper nouns and the first word of each sentence?
_____ 5. Have I used commas and end punctuation correctly?
_____ 6. Have I spelled all words correctly?

 **Check your conventions.** Read through your response one final time. In the time allowed, neatly correct any errors in conventions.

---

**TEKS** **10.13C** Revise drafts to improve word choice and sentence variety; **10.13D** Edit drafts for grammar, mechanics, and spelling; **10.17C** Use a variety of correctly structured sentences; **10.18A** Use conventions of capitalization; **10.18B(i)** Use commas in nonrestrictive phrases and contrasting expressions and in clauses; **10.19** Spell correctly using resources to determine and check correct spelling; **ELPS** **5C** Spell familiar words/employ spelling patterns and rules with increasing accuracy; **5D** Edit writing for standard grammar and usage/subject-verb and pronoun agreement and appropriate verb tenses; **5E** Employ increasingly complex grammatical structures in content area writing such as using correct verbs, tenses, and pronouns/possessive case/negatives and contractions; **5F** Write using a variety of grade-appropriate sentence lengths, patterns, and connecting words/combine in increasingly accurate ways

# Persuasive Writing on Tests

Use this guide when preparing to respond to a persuasive writing prompt.

## Before you write . . .

- **Analyze the prompt.**
  Use the STRAP questions. Remember that a persuasive prompt asks you to use facts and logical reasons to persuade or convince.
- **Plan your response.**
  Decide how much time you will spend on planning, writing, revising, and checking conventions. Use a graphic organizer to help you organize your response.

## As you write . . .

- **Clearly state your thesis and support your argument.**
  Keep your main idea or opinion in mind as you write. All your reasons should clearly support your opinion.
- **Answer an objection.**
  Make your argument stronger by answering a likely objection.
- **Use transitions to improve your organization.**
  In the 25 minutes you take to draft your response, remember to use transitions to better convey your meaning and support your position.
- **Craft a powerful ending.**
  In the final paragraph, summarize your opinion and supporting reasons and make a final plea to the reader.

## After you've written a first draft . . .

- **Revise and edit.**
  Use the STRAP questions to revise your response. Correct any errors in writing conventions.

## Try It!

Write a response to the prompt below. Use a graphic organizer to gather details and plan. Then draft, revise, and edit your response.

- Your school lunchroom wants to buy produce from local farmers. It is more expensive but pesticide free. Write a letter to the food service director expressing your support or objection to the plan.

## Learning Language

Work with a classmate to review this guide. Take turns reading each tip and then have your classmate retell the tip in his or her own words. If you have questions about any of the words or information, be sure to ask your teacher.

Persuasive

## Persuasive Writing on Tests

Remind students that they must approach writing-on-demand assignments differently from open-ended writing assignments.

## Try It!
### Answers

Allow students the same amount of time to write their response essays as they will be allotted on the school, district, or state assessments. As they draft their responses, students should remember to connect ideas and paragraphs with transitions to better convey their meaning. Break down each part of the process into clear units of time.

- 10 minutes for analyzing and planning,
- 25 minutes for writing, and
- 10 minutes for revising and editing.

Tell students when time is up for each section. Start the assignment at the top of the hour or at the half-hour to make it easier for students to keep track of the time.

If your state, district, or school requires students to use and submit a graphic organizer as part of their assessment, refer students to SE pages 624–625.

## Learning Language

Model this activity with one of your students. For example, have the student read the tip under **Analyze the prompt** and then say *This tip means to use the STRAP questions to understand the prompt and reminds us that the purpose of persuasive writing is to convince people using facts and reasons.* ✓ DIFFERENTIATE INSTRUCTION

 **ELPS** 1C, 1D, 1E, 1F, 2C, 2G, 2I, 3D, 3E, 3F, 4C, 4F, 4G

---

### Differentiated Instruction: English Language Learners

**ELPS** 2E, 4E

| ELP Level **Beginning** | ELP Level **Intermediate** | ELP Level **Advanced/Advanced High** |
|---|---|---|
| Complete the activity with the students, using an adapted guide. Prompt their summaries with simple sentence stems and basic vocabulary. | Complete the activity with the students, using an adapted guide. Provide contextual and linguistic support when reading the tips for them to summarize. | Complete the activity with the students. Provide linguistic support as needed when using academic language. Encourage students to use academic language in their summaries. |

**ELPS** **1C** Use strategic learning techniques to acquire basic/grade-level vocabulary; **1D** Speak using learning strategies; **1E** Internalize new academic language by using and reusing it/speaking; **1F** Use accessible language/learn new and essential language; **2C** Learn new language structures and basic/academic vocabulary; **2E** Use contextual/linguistic support to enhance understanding; **2G** Understand the general meaning of spoken language/topics, languages, and contexts are familiar to unfamiliar; **2I** Demonstrate listening comprehension in complex spoken language by collaborating with peers and taking notes; **3D** Speak using grade-level content area vocabulary/academic language proficiency; **3E** Share information in cooperative learning interactions; **3F** Give information/using a limited high-frequency vocabulary to using abstract and content-based vocabulary during speaking; **4C** Comprehend vocabulary used in written classroom materials; **4E** Read linguistically accommodated content area material with a decreasing need for linguistic accommodations; **4F** Use support from peers/teachers to enhance understanding and develop vocabulary; **4G** Demonstrate comprehension of increasingly complex English/participating in shared reading

# Interpretive Response

## Analyzing a Theme (pages 253–294)

Students analyze the theme of a novel by examining the interplay between the novel's characters, plot, setting, and symbols.

## Interpreting a Nonfiction Text (pages 295–302)

Students read an essay and a sample interpretation that presents a detailed analysis of the author's ideas, then they choose a nonfiction text and write their own interpretation of it.

## Analyzing a Poem (pages 303–310)

Students read a student analysis of a poem, then write their own poetry analysis.

## Writing for Assessment (pages 311–319)

Students learn to analyze various types of literary prompts, to use the writing process in a test situation, and to respond to fiction and nonfiction.

## UNIT TEKS

**10.13A** Plan a first draft; **10.13B** Structure ideas and develop drafts; **10.13C** Revise drafts; **10.13D** Edit drafts; **10.13E** Revise final draft and publish work; **10.15A** Write an analytical essay; **10.15C(i)** Write an interpretative response to expository/ literary text; **10.15C(ii)** Write an interpretative response to expository and literary text/address writing skills and provide evidence using quotations; **10.15C(iii)** Write an interpretative response to expository and literary text/analyze author's devices; **10.17A(i)** Use and understand tenses and verbals; **10.17A(ii)** Use and understand clauses; **10.17B** Identify and use the subjunctive mood; **10.17C** Use correctly structured sentences; **10.18A** Use capitalization; **10.18B(i)** Use commas; **10.19** Spell correctly

## UNIT ELPS

**1E** Internalize new language/speaking and writing; **2C** Learn new structures, expressions, and vocabulary; **2I** Demonstrate listening comprehension of spoken language; **3B** Expand and internalize initial vocabulary; **3C** Speak with increasing accuracy and ease; **3D** Speak using content-area vocabulary; **3E** Share information; **4C** Develop sight vocabulary/derive meaning of environmental print/comprehend written classroom materials; **4D** Use prereading supports; **4F** Use visual/contextual support and support from peers/teachers; **4G** Demonstrate comprehension of language/shared reading, summarizing, responding to questions, taking notes; **4H** Read silently with increasing ease; **4J** Employ inferential skills; **4K** Employ analytical skills; **5B** Write using new vocabulary; **5C** Spell and employ spelling patterns/rules with increasing accuracy; **5D** Edit writing for grammar and usage; **5E** Employ complex grammatical structures; **5F** Write using a variety of sentence lengths/patterns/ connecting words; **5G** Narrate, describe, and explain with increasing specificity/content-area writing

### Literature Connections

- *"Author Brings Back Memories of Not So Long Ago"* by Yvette Cabrera
- *Letter to His Mother, dated January 29, 1865, and "The Artilleryman's Vision"* by Walt Whitman

### Technology Connections

 *Write Source Online* www.hmheducation.com/tx/writesource

- *Net-text*
- *Writing Network*
- *Portfolio*
- *GrammarSnap*
- *Essay Scoring*
- *File Cabinet*

 *Interactive Whiteboard Lessons*

# Interpretive Response Unit Scope and Sequence

| Day | Writing and Conventions Instruction | Write Source Student Edition | | | Daily Language Workouts | Skills-Book | Write Source Online |
|---|---|---|---|---|---|---|---|
| | | Core Unit | Tools of Language | Resource Units | | | |
| **1–2** | **Analyzing a Theme** Model <br> ⓛ Literature Connection <br> *"Author Brings Back Memories of Not So Long Ago" by Yvette Cabrera* | 253–255 | ⓣⓛ 550–555 | | 70–73 | | Interactive Whiteboard Lesson |
| **3–5** | **Response Essay** <br> Response Essay Model | 256–258 | | | | | Net-text |
| | Prewriting, Drafting, Revising | 259–280 | | ⓦⓡ 618–639 | | | Net-text |
| | Editing, Publishing | 281–287 | | | | | Net-text |
| | **Skills Activities:** <br> • Third-Person Pronouns | | | ⓑⓖⓦ 573 <br> ⓟⓖ 742–748 | | 81 | GrammarSnap |
| | • Shifting Verb Tenses | | | ⓟⓖ 750–761 | | 96–97 | GrammarSnap |
| | • Split Infinitives | | | ⓑⓖⓦ 590 <br> ⓟⓖ 768–769 | | 101, 130 | GrammarSnap |
| | • Parallel Sentence Structure | | | ⓑⓖⓦ 586 <br> ⓟⓖ 776–777 | | 173–174 | GrammarSnap |
| | • Commas to Punctuate Interrupting Words and Phrases | | | ⓟⓖ 644–653 | | 12–13 | GrammarSnap |
| **6–7** | Assessing and Reflecting | 288–294 | ⓣⓛ 526–529 | | 74–77 | | Net-text |
| **8–10** | **Interpreting a Nonfiction Text** <br> Sample | 295–298 | | | | | Net-text |
| | Prewriting | 299–300 | | | | | Net-text |
| | Drafting, Revising, Editing | 301–302 | | ⓦⓡ 618–639 | | | Net-text |
| **11–13** | **Analyzing a Poem** <br> Sample <br> ⓛ Literature Connection <br> *Letter to His Mother, dated January 29, 1865, and "The Artilleryman's Vision" by Walt Whitman* | 303–305 | ⓣⓛ 526–529 | | 78–81 | | Net-text |
| | Prewriting | 306–307 | | | | | Net-text |
| | Drafting, Revising, Editing | 308–310 | | ⓦⓡ 618–639 | | | Net-text |
| **14–15** | **Writing for Assessment** | 311 | | | | | |
| | Prewriting | 312–315 | | | | | |
| | Drafting, Revising, Editing | 316–319 | | ⓦⓡ 618–639 | | | |

**Resource Units** referenced above are located in the back of the *Student Edition* and *Teacher's Edition*
ⓣⓛ *"The Tools of Language"*  ⓑⓖⓦ *"Basic Grammar and Writing"*  ⓦⓡ *"A Writer's Resource"*  ⓟⓖ *"Proofreader's Guide"*

## Writing Focus

- Analyzing a Theme
- Interpreting a Nonfiction Text
- Analyzing a Poem
- Responding to Prompts About Literature

## Grammar Focus

- Verb Tenses
- Infinitives

## Learning Language

Read aloud the terms, as well as the descriptions and questions. Model for students how to read one question and answer it. For example: *It says that annotating means to add commentary or notes, and it's asking why annotating a text can help you focus your reading. Annotating helps to focus your reading because it forces you to pay attention to the important elements of a story as you write them down.* Have partners monitor their understanding of the terms by working through the meanings and questions together.

**DIFFERENTIATE INSTRUCTION ↘**

 **ELPS** 1E, 2C, 3B, 3D, 3E, 4F, 4G

## Minilessons

### Searching for Themes
Analyzing a Theme

- **READ** the "Basics of Life" list on page 619 in your textbook. **THINK** of books or short stories that deal with general life concerns. **LIST** as many possible themes as you can related to short stories or books you have read. With several classmates, **DISCUSS** your results.

### Name that Theme
Responding to Prompts

- **THINK** back to the books you read or had read to you as a child. **LIST** three or four titles. **WRITE** a theme for each book. **SHARE** your work with a partner, then you and a partner try to **LIST** another theme for each title.

**ELPS 1E** Internalize new basic and academic language by using and reusing it/speaking; **2A** Distinguish sounds/intonation patterns with increasing ease; **2C** Learn new expressions and basic/academic vocabulary; **3A** Practice producing sounds of newly acquired vocabulary; **3B** Expand vocabulary by learning and using routine language; **3D** Speak using grade-level content area vocabulary/new words and academic language proficiency; **3E** Share information in cooperative learning interactions; **4F** Use support from peers/teachers to enhance understanding and develop vocabulary, grasp of language structures, and background knowledge; **4G** Demonstrate comprehension of increasingly complex English/responding to questions

---

**ELPS** 1E, 2C, 3B, 3D, 3E, 4G

www.hmheducation.com/tx/writesource

# Interpretive Response

## Writing Focus

## Grammar Focus

## Learning Language

Work with a partner. Read the definitions below and share your answers to the questions that follow.

1. Annotating a text means to add commentary or notes. **Explain why annotating a text can help focus your reading.**

2. Theme is the underlying message about life or human nature that a writer wants the reader to understand. **What do you think might be a common theme in adventure stories?**

3. When you interpret a piece of literature, you explain it. **Why do you think there could be different interpretations of a literary work?**

4. The idiom "hitting the bull's-eye" means getting something exactly right. **What do you think "missing the bull's-eye" means?**

---

**Differentiated Instruction:**
**English Language Learners**

**ELPS** 1E, 2A, 3A, 3D, 4G

| ELP Level **Beginning** | ELP Level **Intermediate** | ELP Level **Advanced/Advanced High** |
|---|---|---|
| Model pronunciation of the vocabulary words. Then, read a paragraph containing the words, pronouncing some incorrectly. Have students identify incorrect pronunciation. | Model pronunciation of the vocabulary words. Then, have students read simple sentences that contain the words, practicing correct pronunciation. | Have students complete the Learning Language activity in a group. Challenge students to use complete, complex sentences. Provide sentence stems as necessary. |

**TEKS** 10.15C(i)

## Interpretive Response
# Analyzing a Theme

When you tell someone what happens first, second, and third in a novel, you are describing its *plot*. When you talk about the author's message, you are explaining the *theme*. Although reading a compelling story is one of life's great pleasures, the real reward is the new perspective you gain by figuring out its theme. Quality novels are full of insights into life; they can help you think, act, dream, hope, learn, accept, appreciate, and on and on.

In order to understand the theme of a novel, you must examine the interplay between the characters, the plot, the setting, and the symbols. A novel may have one overall theme, or it may have several, each one a significant message and worthy of discussion.

### Writing Guidelines

**Subject:** A novel
**Purpose:** To analyze a theme
**Form:** Literary analysis
**Audience:** Classmates

"Each novel is a kind of voyage of discovery."
—Margaret Lawrence

### Resources

**Copy Masters (see Appendix)**

- T-chart (TE p. 288)
- Details chart (TE pp. 254, 260)
- Time line (TE p. 255)

**Benchmark Papers (see Appendix)**

# Analyzing a Theme

### Objectives

- understand the content and form of an essay that analyzes a literary theme
- understand how to write an essay that analyzes a theme
- plan, draft, revise, edit, and publish an analysis of a theme

Explain to students that a **literary analysis** is a type of essay that examines how the working parts of a piece of literature help to form a meaningful whole. Point out to students that analyzing a theme is a common form of literary analysis:

- The theme expresses a lesson or an insight about life.
- The theme may be stated directly by the narrator or may be implied.
- The author may use symbols and other figurative devices to convey theme.
- A novel may have more than one theme, although one is usually dominant.

**TEKS** 10.15C(i)

### Technology Connections

Use the Interactive Whiteboard lessons to introduce interpretive response to literature.

*Interactive Whiteboard Lesson*

 **TEKS** **10.15C(i)** Write an interpretive response to expository/literary text beyond a summary and literal analysis

## Writing Warm-Up: Subject vs. Theme

To emphasize the difference between the subject and the theme of a novel, explain that

- the **subject** tells what the main character experiences, and
- the **theme** is the lesson about life that the story communicates, usually as a result of what the main character experiences.

Tell students that first they are going to write a paragraph analysis and then an essay analysis of a novel. Explain to students that they can use the titles they list for their Subject vs. Theme Chart for both analyses.

### Try It!

Reproduce the details chart (see TE Appendix) for students to use to make their subject vs. theme charts. Have each student complete a chart. The partners should collaborate on the subject of the novels, but may write different themes on their charts.

 ELPS 3E

---

 ELPS 3E

## Writing Warm-Up: Subject vs. Theme

First, you need to understand the difference between the *subject* of the novel and its *theme*. The subject describes, in a general way, what the story is about; the theme is the message about life that the story suggests. Study the following chart to discern this difference.

### Subject vs. Theme Chart

| Novel | Subject | Theme |
|---|---|---|
| The Red Badge of Courage | This story is about an inexperienced young man who enlists to fight in the Civil War. | A young soldier learns that courage in war is defined by how a soldier reacts to fear, death, and failure. |
| A Christmas Carol | An old miserly man is hard-hearted and sees no meaning in Christmas, rejecting any involvement in the holiday. | A bitter old man learns that Christmas is a yearly reminder about the importance of love and the rewards of generosity and kindness toward one's fellow humans. |
| Fahrenheit 451 | This is a story about a society in which free expression is limited by a strong central government. | Government can only control the minds of people who allow themselves to become uninformed and thoughtless. |

### Try It!

Work with a classmate to create a chart like the one above. Try to list at least three novels that you both have read. For each novel, write a subject statement (what the book is about) and a theme statement (the book's message about life). Remember, a novel may have more than one theme.

> "He conceived persons with torn bodies to be peculiarly happy. He wished that he, too, had a wound, a red badge of courage."
> —Stephen Crane, *The Red Badge of Courage*

## Writing a Paragraph Analysis

You can analyze the theme of a novel in one paragraph by following these guidelines. Include rhetorical devices in your writing to engage your audience.

- In the **opening sentence**, include the title, author, and subject of the novel.
- In the **body sentences**, briefly describe the elements (character, plot, setting, symbols) of the novel and stylistic devices related to those elements that reveal the theme.
- In the **closing sentence**, state the theme of the novel.

### Sample Paragraph Analysis

The **opening sentence** introduces the title, author, and subject of the novel.

The **body sentences** describe the elements and devices in the novel that reveal the theme.

The **closing sentence** states the theme (underlined).

**Scrooge's Awakening**

In Charles Dickens's *A Christmas Carol,* the main character, Ebenezer Scrooge, is a hard-hearted man who sees no meaning in Christmas. Flashbacks reveal that he has become more and more focused on his business, shunning contact with friends and relatives. Scrooge is a character living in a cocoon of selfishness, blinded to the world beyond his counting house. One Christmas Eve Scrooge follows his usual holiday pattern—refusing requests for charity, berating his employee for wanting to take Christmas Day off, and rejecting the holiday dinner invitation of his only nephew. But as darkness falls, the setting shifts to mysterious images of deceased acquaintances, lost youth, and a prophecy of Scrooge's own cold and lonely death. What he sees horrifies him and ironically brings him to his senses. <u>Scrooge learns that Christmas is a yearly reminder about the importance of love and the rewards of generosity and kindness toward one's fellow humans.</u>

Response

**Write a paragraph analysis.** Using one of the novels you identified on the previous page, write a paragraph in which you briefly analyze a major theme of the novel. Include the three parts explained above.

Draft

## Writing a Paragraph Analysis

Review the three main parts of a paragraph and discuss their specific functions when analyzing the theme of a novel. Then have students identify details from the sample paragraph analysis that illustrate how these parts function.

⭐ **TEKS** 10.15C(iii)

✱ For more about writing effective paragraphs, see SE pages 597–615.

Students should have on hand the novels they plan to analyze for the paragraph analysis. Ideally, they should have their own personal copies of these books so that they can mark important passages. Self-stick tags are useful for identifying passages in library books.

⭐ **ELPS** 4K

**Write a paragraph analysis.** Suggest that students use a time line or other graphic organizers to help them plan their analyses. Reproduce a time line (see TE Appendix) for students to use in their planning. ☑ DIFFERENTIATE INSTRUCTION

✱ For more about using graphic organizers, see SE pages 624–625.

---

⭐ **TEKS** 10.15C(iii) Write an interpretive response to expository and literary text/analyze effects of author's stylistic and rhetorical devices; **ELPS 4F** Use support from peers/teachers to develop grasp of language structures; **4K** Demonstrate comprehension by employing analytical skills; **5F** Write using a variety of grade-appropriate sentence lengths in increasingly accurate ways

## Understanding Your Goal

Four traits relate primarily to the development of content and form of a literary analysis. These traits provide a focus during prewriting, drafting, and revising.

- **Focus and Coherence**
- **Organization**
- **Development of Ideas**
- **Voice**

The remaining trait is the primary focus of the editing stage of the writing process.

- **Conventions**

### Literature Connections

In the essay "Author Brings Back Memories of Not So Long Ago," the author models the components of the literary analysis that are described. Discuss this example with students, highlighting the five traits listed so that students can better understand them. **DIFFERENTIATE INSTRUCTION ↘**

---

 **TEKS** 10.13A

 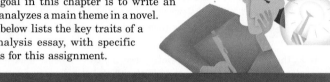

## Understanding Your Goal

Your goal in this chapter is to write an essay that analyzes a main theme in a novel. The chart below lists the key traits of a literary analysis essay, with specific suggestions for this assignment.

### Traits of a Response to Literature

- **Focus and Coherence**

  Select a novel. Write a thesis statement that explains your interpretation of the novel's theme. Support your interpretation by using relevant, logical evidence. Write an effective conclusion.

- **Organization**

  Include a clear introduction, middle part, and a conclusion. Use transitions to effectively connect sentences and paragraphs.

- **Development of Ideas**

  Use specific details and quotations from the text to support the thesis statement. Make sure each paragraph has a topic sentence and that sentences in the paragraph relate directly to the topic.

- **Voice**

  Show your interest in the novel and a thorough knowledge of its subject and theme. Use literary terms that reveal your understanding of the novel. Choose precise, vivid words to share your ideas.

- **Conventions**

  Correct all grammar, sentence structure, capitalization, punctuation, and spelling errors.

 **Literature Connection.** The essay "Author Brings Back Memories of Not So Long Ago" by Yvette Cabrera provides a literary analysis of the novel *The House on Mango Street* by Sandra Cisneros.

"No matter how disguised, in a certain sense, novel writing is autobiographical."

—Jan Slepian

---

### Differentiated Instruction: Advanced Learners

Challenge advanced learners to read the sample essay recommended in the Literature Connection. Ask them to identify the five traits described in the sample essay. Then encourage them to model their own essay after the example essay.

**TEKS** 10.13A; **ELPS** 4J

---

# Response Essay

Mary Shelley's novel, *Frankenstein,* tells about a scientist who creates a superhuman being. The model below analyzes two themes, revealing the more significant of the two in the thesis statement.

**Beginning**
The beginning names the author and novel and states the thesis (underlined).

**Middle**
The middle paragraphs trace the development of two themes. Writer analyzes author's use of stylistic devices. Ideas are structured in a sustained way.

### Monsters Are Made, Not Born

Mary Shelley's *Frankenstein* traces the plight of Victor Frankenstein, a scientist tortured by the thought that he is responsible for bringing into the world a hideously deformed, vicious creature. While *Frankenstein* clearly cautions readers about the dangers of science left unchecked, there is also a very strong message about the effects of mistreating outcasts. As the story develops, Shelley shows that those who are shunned may strike back in anger.

*Frankenstein* is really a set of linked stories, revealing the tragic lives of Frankenstein and his monster. The early chapters focus on a series of letters from a man named Walton to his sister. Walton recalls his voyage to the Arctic Circle, where he sees a huge figure traveling on a sled followed at a distance by Victor Frankenstein. Frankenstein's words dominate the next set of chapters as Walton records Victor's story, starting with his happy childhood and his interest in medieval science. In college, Victor had become very interested in human anatomy. As a result of his work, Victor claimed to have found "the cause of generation and life." But before continuing his story, Victor warns Walton that the "acquirement of knowledge is dangerous."

The tale becomes much darker when Victor tells of bringing a monster into being. He tells of fleeing from his apartment in terror and not returning until much later, when he is relieved to find that the monster has escaped. Many months later, Victor learns that his own brother has been brutally murdered, and his sister has been accused of the crime. Frankenstein, however, has the eerie feeling that his monster is the killer and that he himself is responsible because of his "unhallowed arts."

The narrator role then shifts to the monster. After Victor flees to the Alps to escape his shame, the monster catches up with him and forces Victor to hear the truth. The monster has nothing but contempt for Victor, who has doomed him to an unhappy existence. It becomes clear

Response

## Response Essay

Before reading the sample response essay, provide background information to aid students' comprehension. Work through this sample essay with the class, pointing out the following elements that make it a good response to literature. ✔ **DIFFERENTIATE INSTRUCTION**

### Focus and Coherence

- The writer clearly states the novel's themes and each paragraph builds support for the writer's analysis of the themes.

### Organization

- The opening identifies the title of the novel, the author, and two important themes.
- The middle paragraphs are organized chronologically according to action in the book.
- The ending revisits the two themes.

### Development of Ideas

- The thesis statement connects an element of the novel to a theme.
- The writer addresses several events from the book and analyzes how these events help reveal two themes.
- The writer examines the stylistic devices the author uses to convey the themes.

### Voice

- The writer maintains the third-person point of view throughout the essay.
- The writer's voice sounds knowledgeable and interested.
- The writer chooses words with the appropriate connotation.

---

## Differentiated Instruction:
## English Language Learners

 **ELPS** 4J, 4K

| ELP Level **Beginning** | ELP Level **Intermediate** | ELP Level **Advanced/Advanced High** |
|---|---|---|
| Allow students to use their first language to express their understanding of the structure of the interpretive response essay. | Have students summarize the structure of the interpretive response essay, using their first language as needed. | Working with a partner, have students identify the two themes analyzed and list the supporting evidence the writer uses to explain each theme. |

**TEKS** **10.13B** Structure ideas in a sustained way; **10.15A(i)** Write an analytical essay that includes an introductory paragraph; **10.15A(iii)** Write an analytical essay that includes an idea or thesis; **10.15A(iv)** Write an analytical essay that includes a structure appropriate to the purpose; **10.15C(ii)** Write a response to literary text that addresses writing skills for an analytical essay; **10.15C(iii)** Write a response to literary text that analyzes the effects of stylistic and rhetorical devices; **ELPS 4J** Demonstrate comprehension and expand reading skills by employing inferential skills/predicting, making connections between ideas, drawing conclusions from text, and finding supporting evidence; **4K** Demonstrate comprehension and expand reading skills by employing analytical skills/evaluating written information and performing critical analyses

**Respond to the reading.**

## Answers

**Focus and Coherence 1.** The thesis is introduced at the end of the first paragraph after the basic information of the story is provided. **2.** The conclusion ties the essay together by restating the themes outlined in the essay and supporting them with significant quotes from the text.

**Organization 3.** The details are presented chronologically as they occur in the story, with flashbacks that explain what happened to lead up to events that affect the development of the two themes.

**Development of Ideas 4.** People mistreat others at their own risk, or those who are shunned may strike back in anger. **5.** *There was none among the myriads of men that existed who would pity or assist me; and should I feel kindness toward my enemies?*

**Voice 6.** The writer sounds knowledgeable. The writer describes what happens to Victor and the monster with specific and sufficient detail. These details and well-chosen quotations show that the writer has a clear understanding of what happened to the characters and how that relates to the two themes. **DIFFERENTIATE INSTRUCTION ↘**

**TEKS** 10.13B, 10.15A(i), 10.15A(iv), 10.15C(ii), 10.15C(iii);
**ELPS** 4K

**TEKS** **10.13B** Structure ideas in a sustained way; **10.15A(i)** Write an analytical essay that includes a concluding paragraph; **10.15A(iv)** Write an analytical essay that includes a structure appropriate to the purpose; **10.15C(ii)** Write a response to literary text that addresses writing skills for an analytical essay and using embedded quotations; **10.15C(iii)** Write a response to literary text that analyzes the effects of stylistic and rhetorical devices; **ELPS 4F** Use support from peers/teachers to enhance and confirm understanding; **4K** Demonstrate comprehension and expand reading skills by employing analytical skills/ evaluating written information and performing critical analyses

---

**TEKS** 10.13B, 10.15A(i), 10.15A(iv), 10.15C(ii), 10.15C(iii)
**ELPS** 4K

> The detailed analysis is more than a summary, and the writer's insights about the novel extend beyond a literal analysis. Writer analyzes the author's use of rhetorical devices.

that the monster begins his existence as a gentle creature trapped in a frightening body. After escaping from Victor's apartment, he is ill treated by everyone he meets. He cannot understand why until one day he sees his reflection in a pool of water and realizes why people loathe him. Longing for companionship, he eavesdrops on happy lives and secretly helps others whenever he can. However, in an awful series of events, the monster is attacked by a mob he has tried to befriend and is shot by the companion of a girl he has saved from drowning. At that point, he declares war on all men, killing Victor's brother and framing his sister.

The monster's story makes it obvious that Victor's creation is vicious not because he is created that way, but because Victor abandons him and because others mistreat him. There is one last chance for Victor to ease the monster's loneliness—by creating another monster to keep him company. But Victor fails to take action. Walton encounters Frankenstein in the Arctic because Victor is chasing down his creation, intent on killing him. Finally, Walton's last report tells how Victor gets sick and dies before he can catch his monster, and the giant, satisfied that Frankenstein is dead, wanders off to perish on the ice.

> **Ending**
> The ending analyzes the two themes and expresses the importance of the second in quotations from the text.

Through *Frankenstein*, Mary Shelley expresses her fears that science left unchecked could be dangerous. However, in the end, that theme is not nearly as moving as the monster's message—mistreating others is risky. This theme becomes clear when he states, "There was none among the myriads of men that existed who would pity or assist me; and should I feel kindness toward my enemies?" It is the monster's plight that haunts the reader as the monster recalls that he sought shelter from the weather, but "still more from the barbarity of man," and no shelter was given.

 **Respond to the reading.** **Answer the following questions.**

**Focus and Coherence (1)** How is the thesis introduced? **(2)** How does the conclusion tie the essay together? **Organization (3)** How is the middle part of the analysis organized? **Development of Ideas (4)** What theme becomes the focus of this analysis? **(5)** Which key quotation from the novel supports this theme? **Voice (6)** Does the writer sound knowledgeable about the topic? Explain.

---

**Differentiated Instruction: Struggling Learners**

Have students read the essay aloud, by themselves or with partners, and take notes or highlight important sentences. They need to understand the words of the essay before they can begin to analyze the traits of the literary analysis at work within it.

**ELPS 4F**

# Prewriting

The writing process begins with prewriting—selecting a novel to analyze and planning what you will say about it. Always provide evidence from the novel to support your main ideas.

### Keys to Effective Prewriting

1. Select an interesting novel, one that you have recently read and enjoyed.

2. Identify the main theme of the novel.

3. Find the key elements of the novel that reveal the main theme.

4. Look also for the author's use of stylistic or rhetorical devices that make the writing distinctive and help illuminate the theme.

5. Write a clear thesis statement that states the theme.

6. Decide how to organize the information in your middle paragraphs.

7. Write a topic sentence for each middle paragraph.

*Response*

## Prewriting

### Keys to Effective Prewriting

Remind students that the purposes of the prewriting stage are to select a topic, gather details, and decide how to organize those details.

The Keys to Effective Prewriting list explains the process students will be guided through on SE pages 260–264.

Suggest that students consider choosing a novel from the subject vs. theme chart that they created on SE page 254. They should have already jotted down notes related to the subject and theme for each novel. ✔ **DIFFERENTIATE INSTRUCTION**

### 🖊 Writer's Craft

The activities in the prewriting pages can function as minilessons to teach selecting a topic, identifying a theme, gathering details, using direct quotations, writing a thesis statement, and organizing an essay. Use these minilessons for whole-group instruction, small-group instruction, or scaffolding for individual work time.

---

## Differentiated Instruction: English Language Learners

🇺🇸 **ELPS** 1D, 3D

| ELP Level **Beginning** | ELP Level **Intermediate** | ELP Level **Advanced/Advanced High** |
|---|---|---|
| Allow students to discuss their prewriting ideas in their first language. Encourage students to use drawings or a graphic organizer for their prewriting. | Allow students to discuss their ideas in their first language. Encourage the use of a graphic organizer for effective prewriting. | Encourage students to discuss their prewriting ideas in English. Support students in the development of details and specificity in their prewriting. |
| Use pages 624–625 | Use pages 624–625 | |

**ELPS** **1D** Speak using learning strategies/request assistance, employ non-verbal cues, and convey ideas by defining or describing; **3D** Speak using grade-level content area vocabulary/ new words and academic language proficiency

## Prewriting
### Planning Your Writing

Explain that in the topics chart, students are going to think of possible themes for the novels they have recently read. Also point out that the possible themes included in the sample topics chart are general concepts and have not yet been fully articulated. Elaborating on a general theme is their purpose for writing a literary analysis.

Provide photocopies of the reproducible details chart (TE Appendix) for students to use to plan their writing.
**TEKS** 10.13A

Some students may understand the theme of a novel but may not be able to articulate it concisely. Brainstorm a list of themes commonly found in literature. Some important themes that emerge from great literature include those in the sample topics chart, as well as the following:
- the power of fate or destiny
- the search for one's identity
- the destructive nature of cruelty (racism, bullying, abuse)
- staying optimistic in the face of adversity
- the individual vs. society (or nature)
- the benefits of friendship or family
- the importance of loyalty **DIFFERENTIATE INSTRUCTION ↘**

**Select a topic.** Have students work alone or in groups to complete a topics chart. You may wish to provide the list of novels to choose from.

**Reflect on your choice.** Students may struggle with explaining their choices, but this is a crucial step. If they cannot clearly articulate the reason for choosing a novel and clearly articulating one of its themes, they will likely struggle with writing an essay analyzing the novel. Encourage students to continue working until they have an explanation or suggest they consider a different novel or theme.

---

## Prewriting Planning Your Writing

Completing a topics chart like the one below allows you to list novels you have read recently, state what the novels are about, and record possible themes.

### Topics Chart

| Title and author of the novel | What the novel is about | Possible themes |
|---|---|---|
| Brave New World by Aldous Huxley | A future government controls life so that everyone is happy. | – government vs. the individual<br>– the "right" to happiness<br>– life's shortcomings |
| Things Fall Apart * by Chinua Achebe | A man experiences changes in his Nigerian village during the late 1800s. | – native culture<br>– manhood<br>– evangelism<br>– tradition vs. change |

 **Select a topic.** Make a topics chart like the one above. List at least two or three novels. Then put an asterisk next to the novel that you will analyze.

Prewrite

### Tip

Choose a novel you have read, understood, and enjoyed. You will find it much easier to analyze the theme of such a book.

I picked Things Fall Apart mostly because it's an amazing book. I identify with the main character. I have to struggle for everything I get, and things keep changing around me. I like the book because the main character struggles with the same issues that I struggle with.

 **Reflect on your choice.** As in the example above, write a few sentences that explain the reason for your choice.

Prewrite

### Differentiated Instruction: Advanced Learners

Have students work as a group to create a class topics chart bulletin board. Have them work together to list general themes and then correlate those themes with books they have read.
**ELPS** 2I, 4K

## Identifying a Main Theme

Your next challenge is to identify the theme you will analyze. Choose one of the possible themes you listed in your topics chart (previous page) or look further by using the three strategies that follow:

- **Look for clues in the title.**
  Paper combusts at 451 degrees Fahrenheit.
  —Ray Bradbury, *Fahrenheit 451*

- **Look in the novel for the author's statement about life.**
  "A man can be destroyed but not defeated."
  —Ernest Hemingway, *Old Man and the Sea*

- **Identify a life lesson that emerges in the novel.**
  Wang Lung sees that genuine happiness is living on the land.
  —Pearl S. Buck, *The Good Earth*

### Try It!

Search for a theme. Answer the following questions to find a main theme in your novel.

1. What clues does the title offer about a main theme? Explain.
2. What statements about life does the author make?
3. What lessons about life do the main character's actions reveal?
4. Are there any symbols that play a significant role in the novel? How do they relate to the main character's actions?

**Identify a main theme.** After answering the "Try It!" questions, complete the sentence below to identify a main theme of your novel.

**A main theme of my novel is** _____ .

### Focus on the Texas Traits

**Development of Ideas** Authors use stylistic or rhetorical devices to make their writing interesting. They also use them to convey ideas to the reader. Among these devices are figures of speech, such as *simile, metaphor, personification,* or *hyperbole.* Look for these figures of speech as you analyze your novel, since they often contain thematic ideas.

---

### Identifying a Main Theme

Before having students complete the **Try It!** activity, remind them that symbols are objects or characters in a novel that represent an idea or a quality. Explain that symbols usually suggest something about particular themes.

- In Charles Dickens's *A Christmas Carol,* which is the topic of the paragraph analysis on SE page 255, the images that appear to Scrooge are symbols of important traits that are missing in his present life. He must become aware of these missing traits before he can be happy.

- In Mary Shelley's *Frankenstein,* the topic of the response on SE pages 257–258, the monster is the symbol of many things, including the danger of science left unchecked.

### Try It!

Student answers will vary depending upon the novel they have chosen. Verify that they have adequately thought out the theme of their novels.

**Identify a main theme.** This simple sentence prompt should be easy for students to complete if they have done all of the other prewriting activities. If they struggle with this statement of the main theme, encourage them to review the prewriting steps again. ⟨ DIFFERENTIATE INSTRUCTION⟩

TEKS 10.15C(iii)

### Focus on the Texas Traits

**Development of Ideas**
Select appropriate examples of figures of speech from the novels students are analyzing or have students identify them, and discuss how each figure of speech reflects one of the novel's themes. Point out to students that symbols, discussed above, are considered figurative language for analysis purposes.

---

TEKS **10.15C(iii)** Write a response to literary text that analyzes the effects of stylistic and rhetorical devices; ELPS **2F** Listen to and derive meaning from a variety of media to build/reinforce concept and language attainment; **3F** Give information/ranging from using a limited high-frequency vocabulary to using abstract and content-based vocabulary during speaking; **3G** Express ideas ranging from communicating short phrases to participating in discussions; **3J** Respond orally to information presented in a variety of media to build and reinforce concept and language attainment; **5E** Employ increasingly complex grammatical structures in content area writing such as using correct verbs, tenses, and pronouns/possessive case/negatives and contractions; **5F** Write using a variety of grade-appropriate sentence lengths and patterns in increasingly accurate ways; **5G** Describe and explain with increasing specificity and detail/writing

---

## Differentiated Instruction: English Language Learners

ELPS 2F, 3F, 3G, 3J, 5E, 5F, 5G

| ELP Level **Beginning** | ELP Level **Intermediate** | ELP Level **Advanced/Advanced High** |
|---|---|---|
| Watch a film adaptation of a novel. After watching, work with students to verbalize the theme. Encourage them to request assistance and use gestures as needed. | Watch a film adaptation of a novel. After watching, have students write one or two sentences describing one of the novel's themes. Provide sentence stems and linguistic support as needed. | Watch a film adaptation of a novel. After watching, have students write several sentences describing at least two of the novel's themes. Challenge students to use complex sentences. |

## Prewriting
### Gathering Details

To create their plot charts, students can take handwritten notes, or they can use a computer to create a plot chart like that shown on SE page 262. Remind students that the purpose of the plot chart is to gather details that can later be used in their essays. The chart lists these details in chronological order.

Some students may have difficulty focusing on the main plot line. Have a partner review the plot chart and suggest revisions to either simplify the details or to add more details. Remind students to focus primarily on the actions of the main character(s).

**TEKS** 10.15A(v), 10.15C(ii)

## Prewriting Gathering Details

To gather details for your analysis, list the major actions and the significant thoughts and feelings of the main characters in the novel. A character's thoughts and feelings won't always be stated outright, so you may have to infer them. Focus on examples that reflect the theme. The chart below corresponds with the essay on pages 267–270. (The side notes reveal the writer's thoughts about various elements in the plot.)

### Plot Chart

| | **Novel Title:** Things Fall Apart |
|---|---|
| | **Theme:** Tradition vs. change |
| The wrestling match is not important to the theme. | – At 18, Okonkwo becomes famous for winning a wrestling match. |
| | – Okonkwo's father, Unoka, is irresponsible and constantly in debt, and Okonkwo is ashamed of him. |
| | – Okonkwo becomes a powerful, prosperous, respected man. |
| Tradition is a key idea. | – Tradition rules the village of Umuofia, and Okonkwo follows the rules, except when his temper gets him in trouble. |
| | – Okonkwo becomes a member of *egwugwu*, a powerful, secret cult that dispenses justice in Umuofia. |
| | – At the funeral of the clan's most respected elder, Okonkwo accidentally kills the elder's son and must go into exile for seven years as punishment. |
| The second part of the story starts when Okonkwo leaves Umuofia. | – Okonkwo goes to a village that his mother came from, and is accepted by her relatives. |
| | – His friend Obierika visits him and tells him about white men who wiped out a neighboring village. |
| | – Later, Obierika returns with stories of white missionaries who have converted many clan members in Umuofia, including Okonkwo's oldest son. |
| The traditions of the natives and the teachings of the missionaries conflict. | – After seven years, Okonkwo returns to find that life in Umuofia has changed much because of missionaries. |
| | – Europeans have set up a government and courts. |
| | – Mr. Brown, a kind and compassionate missionary, gets sick and is replaced by Rev. Smith, who causes trouble. |
| | – Okonkwo's aggressive ways end in tragedy. |

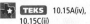 **TEKS** 10.15A(iv),
10.15C(ii)

## Using Direct Quotations

You can use quotations from the novel to emphasize important points about the theme. As you choose quotations, keep in mind the purpose and context of your essay. The student who analyzed *Things Fall Apart* gathered the following list of quotations. Note how each quotation relates to the theme.

### Sample Quotations

- "He had had no patience with his father." (A comment about Okonkwo)
- "Age was respected among his people, but achievement was revered." (The reason that Okonkwo was important in Umuofia)
- "The world has no end, and what is good among one people is an abomination with others." (The words of Okonkwo's uncle after the killing of the first white man)
- "The white man is very clever. He came quietly and peaceably with his religion. We were amused at his foolishness and allowed him to stay. Now he has won our brothers, and our clan can no longer act like one. He has put a knife on the things that held us together and we have fallen apart." (Obierika's words to Okonkwo)

### Try It!

Discuss how each quotation relates to the theme of tradition vs. change.

 **Gather quotations.** Search your novel to find direct quotations that relate to the theme you are analyzing.

Prewrite

### Focus on the Texas Traits

**Organization** To talk about the theme of a novel, you must also discuss the plot and the main characters. As you discuss the plot and characterization, your analysis will often be organized chronologically, but an analysis can also be organized by order of importance.

Response

## Using Direct Quotations

Emphasize the importance of selecting quotations that relate to the theme. Remind students to write and punctuate quotations correctly. ✓ **DIFFERENTIATE INSTRUCTION**

✱ For more about quotations, see SE pages 263 and 633.

### Try It!
### Answers

**Possible Answers**

- His father's irresponsibility causes Okonkwo to lose respect for his father.
- Okonkwo honored traditions by his actions.
- Traditions of different cultures can lead to clashes and change.
- If the outsiders are strong and smart enough, local traditions can be changed, or even cease to exist.

**Gather quotations.** Once students have selected sample quotations, have them review their selections and verify that each quotation relates to the theme.

 **TEKS** 10.15A(iv), 10.15C(ii)

### Focus on the Texas Traits

**Organization**
Students who use order of importance should arrange details from least to most important in order to build their connections to the theme.

**Differentiated Instruction:
English Language Learners**

**ELPS** 4G, 4K

| ELP Level **Beginning** | ELP Level **Intermediate** | ELP Level **Advanced/Advanced High** |
|---|---|---|
| Have students work with a partner to identify and note useful quotations and illustrate them with photos or pictures. | Have students select and note quotations on their own. Then work with students to assess whether the quotations they chose relate to the theme. | Encourage students to select and note quotations that relate to their theme. Then have them discuss, with a partner, how the quotation relates to their theme. |

 **TEKS** **10.15A(iv)** Write an analytical essay that includes a structure appropriate to the purpose and context; **10.15C(ii)** Write a response to literary text that addresses writing skills for an analytical essay and using embedded quotations; **ELPS 4G** Demonstrate comprehension of increasingly complex English/taking notes; **4K** Demonstrate comprehension and expand reading skills by employing analytical skills/evaluating written information and performing critical analyses

# Prewriting

## Writing a Thesis Statement

Point out to students that a strong thesis statement can guide and direct a whole essay. Schedule time to review students' thesis statements before having them proceed with their essays.

 **TEKS** 10.13A

**Form a focus.** Prompt students to use the formula provided. Encourage them to try different ideas if they are not able to develop an adequate thesis statement.

## Organizing the Middle Paragraphs of Your Essay

Before students write topic sentences for their middle paragraphs, they should separate the details in the plot charts they created on SE page 262 into sections corresponding to the middle paragraphs in their essays. Then they can reference the details to help them compose their topic sentences. To get students started:

- have them compare the sample plot chart on SE page 262 with the middle paragraphs on SE page 268–269, and
- show them where the writer could have drawn lines to create three groups of details for the three middle paragraphs (after *At the funeral of the clan's . . . as punishment* and after *Later, Obierika returns . . . Okonkwo's oldest son*).

 **TEKS** 10.15A(iv), 10.15C(ii)

**Plan your middle paragraphs.** Remind students that a graphic organizer may be a useful tool for planning their paragraphs.

✱ For more about graphic organizers, see SE pages 624–625.

---

 **TEKS** 10.13A, 10.15A(iv), 10.15C(ii)

## Prewriting Writing a Thesis Statement

Now that you have gathered details, you are ready to write your **thesis statement**. Your thesis statement should connect an element of the novel—usually character, setting, or action—to the theme.

| element (main character) | | theme (tradition vs. change) | | thesis statement |
|---|---|---|---|---|
| Okonkwo | **+** | becomes ensnarled in the clash of two cultures | **=** | As the novel progresses, Okonkwo becomes ensnarled in the clash of two cultures. |

**Form a focus.** Write a thesis statement for your response essay using the formula above.

## Organizing the Middle Paragraphs of Your Essay

Each middle paragraph should address a different stage in the explanation of the theme. The writer of the sample essay on pages 267–270 planned her middle paragraphs by writing a topic sentence for each one. Remember that your analysis is much more than a summary of the novel.

**Topic Sentence 1 (First middle paragraph)**
Okonkwo, the main character, is known far beyond the village of Umuofia for his personal achievements and extraordinary bravery and toughness.

**Topic Sentence 2 (Second middle paragraph)**
...although Okonkwo feels his exile is the worst thing that could happen to him, the coming of the Europeans proves to be a problem on a much larger scale.

**Topic Sentence 3 (Third middle paragraph)**
Obierika returns two years later with more stories about missionaries, churches, courts, and converts.

**Plan your middle paragraphs.** Review your plot chart from page 262. Add any important details you may have left out. Write a topic sentence for each middle paragraph of your essay. Then decide on the best order for your paragraphs.

---

**TEKS** **10.13A** Plan a first draft by developing a thesis or idea; **10.15A(iv)** Write an analytical essay that includes a structure appropriate to the purpose; **10.15C(ii)** Write a response to expository text that addresses writing skills for an analytical essay

Analyzing a Theme **265**

# Drafting

Once you have finished your prewriting, you are ready to write the first draft of your analysis. Your thesis statement, plot chart, quotations, and topic sentences will guide your writing.

### Keys to Effective Drafting

1. Write on every other line so that you have room to make changes later.

2. Use your thesis statement and topic sentences as a guide to organize your writing.

3. Support your topic sentences with specific details from the novel.

4. Refer to your plot chart and sample quotations for details, adding more if needed.

5. Get all of your thoughts on paper.

6. Tie your ideas together with transitions.

Response

## Drafting

### Keys to Effective Drafting

Remind students that the drafting stage is when they write or draft their ideas on paper.

The Keys to Effective Drafting list explains the process students will be guided through on SE pages 266–270. ✓ DIFFERENTIATE INSTRUCTION

Students who are working on a computer should double-or triple-space to allow for handwritten revisions.

 **Writer's Craft**

On the next five pages, you'll find minilessons that help writers develop a strong beginning, middle, and ending during individual work time. These minilessons can also provide small-group or whole-class instruction.

---

**Differentiated Instruction: English Language Learners**

➕ **ELPS** 1E, 2E, 2G, 2I, 3C, 3E, 3G, 4C, 4F, 4G

| ELP Level **Beginning** | ELP Level **Intermediate** | ELP Level **Advanced/Advanced High** |
|---|---|---|
| In shared reading, have students read the Keys to Effective Drafting aloud. Ask questions to assess comprehension of each item, using models such as a plot chart for visual examples. | Have students work with a partner to read the Keys to Effective Drafting aloud and to summarize each item using phrases or short sentences. | Have students read the Keys to Effective Drafting silently. Have them write a paragraph describing how they will use the information gathered during prewriting to help them draft their essay. |

**ELPS 1E** Internalize new basic and academic language by using and reusing it/speaking; **2E** Use linguistic support to enhance and confirm understanding of increasingly complex spoken language; **2G** Understand the main points of spoken language/topics, languages, and contexts are familiar to unfamiliar; **2I** Demonstrate listening comprehension in increasingly complex spoken language by following directions; **3C** Speak using a variety of grammatical structures and sentence lengths/types with increasing accuracy and ease; **3E** Share information in cooperative learning interactions; **3G** Express ideas ranging from communicating short phrases to participating in discussions; **4C** Comprehend vocabulary used in written classroom materials; **4F** Use support from peers/teachers to enhance and confirm understanding; **4G** Demonstrate comprehension of increasingly complex English/responding to questions

## Drafting

### Getting the Big Picture

If students have not yet planned and organized their paragraphs, suggest that they look back at their topic sentences and the details in their plot charts. Have them number the details in the order in which they plan to present them in each paragraph. If they are working on a computer, they should rearrange details to reflect their organization. **DIFFERENTIATE INSTRUCTION** ↘

Encourage students to skim SE pages 267–270 to see how the details in this chart reflect the big picture of the student response essay. Suggest that when students have finished their first drafts, they return to this page and fill in a similar chart, using the parts of their literary analyses. If they have used their prewriting notes and followed the steps presented on SE pages 267–270, they should see their own "big pictures" emerge. As an added benefit, this activity will call attention to gaps in their drafts, which they can fill in when they revise.

⭐ **TEKS** 10.13B, 10.15A(i), 10.15A(iv), 10.15C(ii)

## Drafting Getting the Big Picture

Remember that an essay includes three main parts—the beginning, the middle, and the ending. You are ready to begin drafting your response if you have . . .

- discovered the theme;
- written a clear thesis statement that ties the theme to the novel;
- planned and organized your paragraphs in a sustained way that is appropriate for your audience, purpose, and context.

The chart below shows how the three parts of a response-to-literature essay fit together. The examples are from the essay on pages **267–270**.

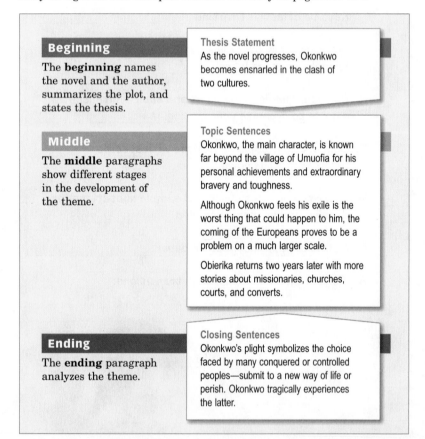

**Beginning**

The **beginning** names the novel and the author, summarizes the plot, and states the thesis.

**Thesis Statement**
As the novel progresses, Okonkwo becomes ensnarled in the clash of two cultures.

**Middle**

The **middle** paragraphs show different stages in the development of the theme.

**Topic Sentences**
Okonkwo, the main character, is known far beyond the village of Umuofia for his personal achievements and extraordinary bravery and toughness.

Although Okonkwo feels his exile is the worst thing that could happen to him, the coming of the Europeans proves to be a problem on a much larger scale.

Obierika returns two years later with more stories about missionaries, churches, courts, and converts.

**Ending**

The **ending** paragraph analyzes the theme.

**Closing Sentences**
Okonkwo's plight symbolizes the choice faced by many conquered or controlled peoples—submit to a new way of life or perish. Okonkwo tragically experiences the latter.

⭐ **TEKS** **10.13B** Structure ideas in a sustained way; **10.15A(i)** Write an analytical essay that includes an introductory and concluding paragraph; **10.15A(iv)** Write an analytical essay that includes a structure appropriate to the purpose, audience, and context; **10.15C(ii)** Write a response to literary text that addresses writing skills for an analytical essay; **ELPS** **4F** Use visual/contextual support and support from peers/teachers to develop grasp of language structures; **5B** Write using content-based grade-level vocabulary

### Differentiated Instruction: Struggling Learners

Review the beginning paragraph and the three elements listed at the top of the page. Then have students list the title and author, background information, and thesis statement before they write. Allow students to write the essay with a partner. Encourage the use of appropriate vocabulary.

⭐ **TEKS** 10.13B; **ELPS** 4F, 5B

Analyzing a Theme 267

TEKS 10.13B
ELPS 3E

## Starting Your Analysis

Your opening paragraph should set the scene for the rest of your analysis. It should include the following information:

- **the title and author of your novel,**
- **background information about the plot and characters, and**
- **your thesis statement.**

| Beginning |
| --- |
| Middle |
| Ending |

### Beginning Paragraph

> The first paragraph introduces the novel and gives the thesis statement (underlined).

<u>Things Fall Apart</u> by Chinua Achebe focuses on Nigeria in the late 1800s, a time of great change in Africa. Okonkwo, a leader in his village, is a commanding and merciless man deeply involved in the traditional life of his village, Umuofia. The first part of the novel follows Okonkwo's life to the point where an accident threatens to wipe out everything he has worked for. Unknown to Okonkwo, however, something even more disturbing is about to affect his people. White missionaries begin to travel throughout his homeland, bringing their religion. Soon, their laws and their government follow. These missionaries change everything in his village. <u>As the novel progresses, Okonkwo becomes ensnarled in the clash of two cultures.</u>

Draft

**Write your beginning.** As you develop your beginning, include the title of the novel and its author, a brief plot summary, and your thesis statement.

Response

## Tip

If you have trouble getting started, try one of these strategies.

- **Talk about your story with a classmate** before you begin to write.
- **Write freely** without trying to produce the perfect analysis right away.
- **Reread the sample on pages 257–258** to see how that writer started his analysis.
- **Think of someone you believe should read this book,** and write with that person in mind.

## Starting Your Analysis

Remind students that they are writing to analyze the theme of a novel. They are not writing a personal response to the novel or a book review. Point out and discuss with students the components of a literary analysis in the sample paragraph.

- In a literary analysis, the writer should maintain a third-person point of view.
- An analysis of a theme does not express the opinions or feelings of the writer.
- An analysis of a theme does not usually contain an evaluation of the author's style or a specific recommendation to readers.

✔ DIFFERENTIATE INSTRUCTION

TEKS 10.13B; ELPS 3E, 4F

**Write your beginning.** Students are often encouraged to write creative and engaging opening sentences that grab the reader's attention. Students can write a successful opening for an analysis simply by identifying the novel and its author and by telling a few details about the text. Suggest to students that they simply imitate the pattern (title, author, subject focus) of the first sentence of the sample paragraph.

## Tip

Share your own reflections on how you get started with a writing project. Encourage students to share ideas they have found helpful in beginning to draft an essay.

---

**Differentiated Instruction: English Language Learners**

 ELPS 1C, 5F

| ELP Level **Beginning** | ELP Level **Intermediate** | ELP Level **Advanced/Advanced High** |
| --- | --- | --- |
| Allow students to draw or to use their first language to outline their beginning paragraph. Provide simple, short, sentence stems for use in their beginning paragraph. | Allow students to use their first language to outline their beginning paragraph. Provide students with sentence stems, and encourage use of appropriate sentence lengths. | Provide students with complex sentence stems. Encourage students to model their paragraph after the sample provided, using appropriate sentence lengths and patterns. |

**TEKS 10.13B** Structure ideas in a sustained way; **ELPS 1C** Use strategic learning techniques to acquire basic and grade-level vocabulary; **3E** Share information in cooperative learning interactions; **4F** Use visual/contextual support and support from peers/teachers to develop grasp of language structures; **5F** Write using a variety of grade-appropriate sentence lengths and patterns in increasingly accurate ways

## Drafting

### Developing the Middle Part

Suggest to students that they review the sample middle paragraphs provided and model their paragraphs after these.

Discuss common literary terms that students may choose to use in their essays.

- **analogy:** a rhetorical device in which the writer makes point-by-point comparison of two things that are alike in some way; often using a familiar subject or idea to explain an unfamiliar one
- **conflict:** problem or clash between two forces in a story
- **flashback:** a technique in which a writer interrupts a story to go back and relive an earlier time or event
- **foreshadowing:** hints about what will happen later in a story
- **parallelism:** a rhetorical device in which similar grammatical structures are used to express ideas that are related or that are of equal importance
- **plot:** the events or actions that move the story along from start to finish
- **rhetorical device:** techniques used by writers to communicate their themes more effectively
- **setting:** place and time period in which a story takes place
- **symbolism:** the use of an object or character to represent an idea
- **theme:** the author's message about life

**DIFFERENTIATE INSTRUCTION ⇘**

★ **TEKS** 10.13B, 10.15C(iii)

✶ For more literary terms, see SE pages 634–637.

---

 **TEKS** 10.13B, 10.15C(iii)

## Drafting Developing the Middle Part

Each middle paragraph explores a stage in your explanation of the theme and how it is revealed in the novel. Your writing should focus on the elements of the novel and any stylistic or rhetorical devices that are important to the theme.

> Beginning
> **Middle**
> Ending

### Middle Paragraphs

> *The first middle paragraph summarizes the first part of the novel dealing with traditional life. Writer uses embedded quotations to support ideas.*

Achebe uses vivid imagery and figurative language to draw the reader into the setting, to describe the characters, and to develop the theme. Okonkwo, the main character, is known far beyond the village of Umuofia for his personal achievements and extraordinary bravery and toughness. The force that drives him is the fact that he "had no patience with his father," who was irresponsible and constantly in debt, preferring to drink and play the flute. Okonkwo thinks of his father as "effeminate" and is determined that no one will think of him in that way. Because "age was respected among his people, but achievement was revered," Okonkwo works harder than anyone to provide food for his family, reveres the words of the mystic oracles, kills without mercy, and obeys the priestess Chielo. Achebe describes in great detail how hard Okonkwo works and how prudent he is. As a result the reader empathizes with Okonkwo, and is happy when Okonkwo rises to the highest circle of Umuofia's powerful men. Okonkwo is a spiritual man, like his fellow clansmen, and he believes that the living and their ancestors move back and forth between life and death. Unfortunately, he makes a mistake at the funeral of the clan's elder, accidentally killing the elder's son. Knowing that he has done wrong, he immediately takes the step that tradition dictates, exiling himself from Umuofia for seven years.

> *The writer analyzes the development of the theme and the author's stylistic and rhetorical devices.*

Achebe develops the theme as he shows how although Okonkwo feels his exile is the worst thing that could happen to him, the coming of the Europeans proves to be a problem on a much larger scale. Again, Achebe uses vivid language to bring readers into the conflict and to make his point. This is particularly important in the scene where a friend Obierika visits Okonkwo in his village of exile two years later and brings news

---

⭐ **TEKS** 10.13B, 10.15C(iii)

Analyzing a Theme **269**

Each paragraph includes insights into the novel. Using an effective organizational pattern, the writer sustains her thesis and provides details relating to the theme.

that the Abame settlement has been wiped out by white men. This action was done in retaliation for the death of another white man who rode an "iron horse"—a bicycle—through a group of panicked villagers. They apparently attacked him because he did not reply to their questions. Okonkwo's wise uncle Uchendu feels the people of Abame were fools to kill the white man on the bicycle. He says, "Never kill a man who says nothing," for the man's silence holds an ominous secret, whereas "There is nothing to fear from someone who shouts."

Obierika return two years later with more stories about missionaries, churches, courts, and converts. In these scenes, Achebe continues to show the conflicts Okonkwo faces. The reader is drawn into these conflicts and sympathizes with Okonkwo. Achebe uses stylistic and rhetorical devices to emphasize the theme, including the proverb "Blessed is he who forsakes his father and his mother for my sake." Though Kiaga, Okonkwo's son finds it "blessed" to forsake the old ways, Okonkwo feels it is cursed.

**Draft**

**Write your middle paragraphs.** Use your topic sentences, plot chart, and sample quotation list to guide your writing. Try to include an example of a stylistic or rhetorical device to enhance the theme for the reader.

## Tip

Most literary analyses are organized chronologically, providing events in the order they appear in the novel. Use transition words and phrases that show time to connect your ideas.

**Transitions That Show Time**

| | | | |
|---|---|---|---|
| After | Before | In the end | That night |
| As soon as | During | Later | Then |
| At the start | Finally | Soon | When |

Other types of transitions are also useful for connecting ideas. The sample paper uses time transitions (*the first part of the novel, two years later, eventually*) as well as those that show cause and effect (*as a result, because*) and contrast (*however, unfortunately*).

*Response* (rotated side text)

After students have had a chance to read the sample middle paragraphs, ask volunteers to explain in their own words how the details in each paragraph support its topic sentence and how all of the paragraphs work together to support the thesis statement. Encourage students to strive for the same results as they write. Remind them, however, that they are primarily trying to get their best ideas down on paper right now. When they revise, they will make sure that all of their details in a paragraph support the topic sentence and that their paragraphs support their thesis.

⭐ **TEKS** 10.13B, 10.15C(iii); **ELPS** 4F

**Write your middle paragraphs.** Have students identify how the transitions identified in the **Tip** help to connect ideas in the sample paragraphs.

✱ Have students turn to SE pages 628–629 for more information on using transitions effectively.

---

**Differentiated Instruction:**
**English Language Learners**      ⭐ **ELPS** 1B, 2C, 2E, 2G, 3D, 3E, 3F, 3G, 3H, 4C, 4J

| **ELP Level** **Beginning** | **ELP Level** **Intermediate** | **ELP Level** **Advanced/Advanced High** |
|---|---|---|
| Model pronunciation of each literary term. Have students repeat the words. Encourage them to monitor and self-correct their pronunciations. | Give students a list of the literary terms and their definitions. Have students read the list aloud to a partner who corrects pronunciation as needed. | Give students a list of the literary terms and their definitions. Have students participate in a group discussion in which they discuss their chosen novel using one or more of the literary terms. |

⭐ **TEKS** **10.13B** Structure ideas in a sustained way; **10.15C(iii)** Write a response to literary text that analyzes the effects of stylistic and rhetorical devices; **ELPS** **1B** Monitor oral language and employ self-corrective techniques or other resources; **2C** Learn new expressions and basic/academic vocabulary heard during classroom instruction/interactions; **2E** Use linguistic support to enhance and confirm understanding of increasingly complex spoken language; **2G** Understand the main points of spoken language/topics, languages, and contexts are familiar to unfamiliar; **3D** Speak using grade-level content area vocabulary/new words and academic language proficiency; **3E** Share information in cooperative learning interactions; **3F** Give information/ranging from high-frequency vocabulary to content-based vocabulary during speaking; **3G** Express ideas ranging from short phrases to discussions; **3H** Narrate and explain with increasing specificity and detail; **4C** Comprehend vocabulary used in written classroom materials; **4F** Use visual/contextual support and support from peers/teachers to develop grasp of language structures; **4J** Demonstrate comprehension and expand reading skills by employing inferential skills/predicting, making connections between ideas, drawing conclusions from text, and finding supporting evidence

## Drafting
### Ending Your Analysis

Review the sample ending paragraph with students and discuss the ways that the writer brings the analysis to an effective close. If students choose to use a quotation in their ending, point out that they should:

- choose a quotation of reasonable length,
- make sure that the quotation clearly reflects the theme,
- copy the quotation accurately, and
- set off the quotation with quotation marks or, if it's a long quotation, indent it.

✱ For more about quotations, see SE page 633.

Tell students who plan to make predictions to make sure their predictions are logical and based on evidence in the book.

Tell students that a basic truth about life is one that has been frequently proven true. Have students state in their own words the basic truth in the sample ending paragraph (*many conquered or controlled people are forced to submit to a new way of life or perish*).

**Write your ending and form a complete first draft.** Encourage students to use the sample ending paragraph as a model, by clearly connecting back to the thesis and providing a concluding insight to complete the analysis.

**★ TEKS** 10.13B, 10.15A(i), 10.15C(i), 10.15C(ii)

---

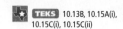
**★ TEKS** 10.13B, 10.15A(i), 10.15C(i), 10.15C(ii)

## Drafting Ending Your Analysis

Beginning
Middle
**Ending**

Your essay starts with a thesis statement that connects the theme to a key element (plot, character, setting) in the novel. In the middle paragraphs, you show how the theme develops during the course of the action. The ending is your final chance to comment on and analyze the theme. Here are some suggestions for this final part of your essay.

- Show how the character has changed because of the theme.
- Use a quotation from the story.
- Predict how the theme might affect the characters in the future.
- State the theme as a basic truth about life.

Theme can be shown through characters or conflict. Theme is a perception about life or human nature that the writer shares with the reader.

### Ending Paragraph

> Eventually, *Okonkwo serves his seven-year exile and returns to Umuofia, inflamed by Obierika's analysis of the situation:*
>
> > The white man came quietly and peaceably with his religion. We were amused at his foolishness and allowed him to stay. Now he has put a knife on the things that held us together, and we have fallen apart.

**A quotation sums up the fatal situation.**

> *Okonkwo takes up his role as a warrior against the invaders, and in a disastrous series of events, becomes a kind of disgraced martyr. Okonkwo's traditions have been ridiculed and insulted by some of the missionaries, but the damage goes far beyond religious issues. An entire society has been uprooted. The title of a book the English commissioner writes about his African adventures reveals the European attitude toward the natives:* The Pacification of the Primitive Tribes of the Lower Niger. *Okonkwo's plight symbolizes the choice faced by many conquered or controlled peoples—submit to a new way of life or perish. Okonkwo tragically experiences the latter.*

**The final ideas state the thesis as a basic truth.**

Draft

**Write your ending and form a complete first draft.** Develop the last paragraph using one or more of the suggestions above. Make a clean copy of your complete essay. Double-space or write on every other line to make room for changes.

---

**★ TEKS 10.13B** Structure ideas in a sustained way; **10.15A(i)** Write an analytical essay that includes a concluding paragraph; **10.15C(i)** Write a response to literary text that extends beyond a summary and literal analysis; **10.15C(ii)** Write a response to literary text that addresses writing skills for an analytical essay

Prewrite　　Revise　　Publish
Draft　　Edit

# Revising

Now that your first draft is complete, you are ready to begin the revision process. Concentrate on focus and coherence, organization, and other key traits to make changes that will improve your writing.

## Keys to Effective Revising

1. As you review your draft, consider your purpose, your audience, and the genre, or form, of your writing.

2. Read your essay aloud to see whether it makes sense from start to finish.

3. Check your thesis statement to be sure it includes the theme of the story.

4. Be sure that each middle paragraph supports and explains the thesis statement.

5. Check your ending. Have you given a final analysis of the theme you developed in your essay?

6. Check to see that your voice sounds knowledgeable.

Response

# Revising

## Keys to Effective Revising

Remind students that the revising stage is when they improve their first drafts. At this stage, they can refine their writing in ways they might not have considered when they were writing their first drafts. ✓DIFFERENTIATE INSTRUCTION

The Keys to Effective Revising list explains the process students will be guided through on SE pages 272–280.

Have students read and respond to each other's writing. For more on promoting constructive peer responses, see SE pages 49–54.

### Writer's Craft

Instead of assigning all of the revising activities, let the results of peer responses or self-assessments direct students to the activities they need most. As an alternative, use the activities as minilessons to workshop specific traits with small groups of writers.

---

## Differentiated Instruction: English Language Learners

ELPS 3E, 4F, 4G, 4H, 4J

| ELP Level Beginning | ELP Level Intermediate | ELP Level Advanced/Advanced High |
|---|---|---|
| Have students read an adapted form of the sample ending paragraph silently, requesting help and taking breaks as necessary. Ask basic questions to check for understanding. | Have students read the sample ending paragraph silently, requesting help as necessary. Then have students identify to a partner which of the bulleted points at the top of the page the writer used. | Have students read the sample ending paragraph silently, requesting help as necessary. Have students summarize what they have read orally to a partner. |

 **TEKS ELPS 3E** Share information in cooperative learning interactions; **4F** Use visual/contextual support and support from peers/teachers to develop grasp of language structures; **4G** Demonstrate comprehension of increasingly complex English/responding to questions; **4H** Read silently with increasing ease and comprehension for longer periods; **4J** Demonstrate comprehension and expand reading skills by employing inferential skills/predicting, making connections between ideas, drawing conclusions from text, and finding supporting evidence

## Revising for Focus and Coherence

Remind students of the importance of focus and coherence as they begin the revision process. Their essays should have a sense of unity from the beginning paragraph through the conclusion, and the thesis statement should relate directly to theme. You may wish to review the holistic scoring guide on pages 60–61 before students begin revising their essays.

### Is my thesis statement clear and complete?

For students to best assess the thesis statement, they need to state their theme and then ask themselves the questions provided regarding plot, characters, or setting.

**TEKS** 10.13C, 10.15C(i)

### Try It!
#### Answers

1. **Theme:** Happiness is possible even after terrible loss. **Key element:** characters—two young sharecroppers
2. **Theme:** Society's control over individuals is fragile. **Key element:** setting—isolated location of the island
3. **Theme:** Recognizing the true value of love can lead a person out of isolation and selfishness. **Key element:** plot—discovery of the baby sets in motion Silas Marner's (the main character) journey of self realization.

**DIFFERENTIATE INSTRUCTION ↘**

**Check your thesis and your conclusion.** After students complete the **Try It!** activity, encourage them to exchange their first drafts with partners and have them identify the theme and key element in each other's beginning and ending paragraphs.

**TEKS** 10,15A(i), 10.15C(ii)

**TEKS** **10.13C** Revise drafts to improve the subtlety of meaning; **10.15A(i)** Write an analytical essay that includes a concluding paragraph; **10.15C(i)** Write a response to literary text that extends beyond a summary and literal analysis; **10.15C(ii)** Write a response to literary text that addresses writing skills for an analytical essay

 **TEKS** 10.13C, 10.15A(i), 10.15C(i), 10.15C(ii)

## Revising for Focus and Coherence

When you revise for *focus and coherence,* you make sure that your essay has a sense of unity. The introduction presents a clear and complete thesis statement; the middle paragraphs flow smoothly from one to the next; and the conclusion sums up the points you have made in a final analysis of the theme. All the parts work together to form a whole that supports the thesis, and the reader understand the subtlety of meaning you are conveying.

When you write an interpretive response to a literary text, you are writing more than a summary or a literal analysis of the text. You are providing your reader insights into the author's purpose and theme.

### Is my thesis statement clear and complete?

Your thesis statement will be clear and complete if you state the theme and connect it with at least one element *(plot, character, setting)* of the novel. Here are some guidelines to help you evaluate how theme is revealed.

1. Does the **plot** seem to propel the characters? How do the events work together to create the theme? Remember that you are providing an analysis, not a plot summary.
2. Do the **characters** create the conflicts, problems, and solutions? Is there one central character? Be sure to go beyond a simple, literal analysis of the characters.
3. Is the **setting** an important and continuing presence in the novel? How does it impact the characters and their actions? How does the setting help establish the theme of the work?

### Try It!

In these thesis statements, identify the theme and the key element.

1. In the end, however, two young sharecroppers demonstrate the hope that happiness can eventually return after terrible loss.
2. The isolated location of the island creates an atmosphere that reveals the fragile nature of society's control over individuals.
3. The moment he discovered the baby on his doorstep, the reclusive Silas Marner began the journey out of isolation and greed, a journey that would reveal the true value of love.

Revise

**Check your thesis and your conclusion.** Does the thesis statement present a clear, controlling idea? Does the conclusion sum up your analysis of the theme? If not, revise as needed.

---

**Differentiated Instruction: Advanced Learners**

Challenge advanced learners to work with a partner to write a thesis statement containing the theme and key element for a novel they have both recently read.

**TEKS** 10.13C

★ **TEKS** 10.13B, 10.13C

## Is each paragraph of my analysis coherent?

Remember the meaning of the word *coherent*: orderly and logical. A paragraph will be coherent if the sentences within it flow smoothly, orderly, and logically from one to the next. *Unity* is a key characteristic of coherent paragraphs. It is best to delete any phrase or sentence that does not clearly support the topic of the paragraph.

When you begin revising your paragraphs for focus and coherence, use the following tips.

- **Use rhetorical devices.** Ask yourself how and where you might use rhetorical devices to make the paragraphs and sentences flow more smoothly from one to the next. Rhetorical devices can also help you focus on your thesis statement.
- **Examine your word choice.** Make sure you have used words that appropriately convey subtlety of meaning to the reader. Remember that your choice of words is critical as you support your ideas and share your insights in the essay.

### Try It!

Carefully read the following paragraph. Then decide which sentence should be eliminated to make the paragraph more coherent.

1     The novel is a lesson in how to raise a family. Marmee helps three
2 girls overcome teenage anxiety and tragedy by anchoring them in religion,
3 common sense, and love. Nowadays, people turn to counseling or
4 antidepressants. As adults, the girls carry Marmee's teachings into their
5 own productive lives as a pianist, an artist, and a writer.

 **Revise**   **Review your first draft for clear focus and coherence.** Be sure that each paragraph is unified, relates to the thesis, and conveys your meaning. Make sure that your paragraphs flow smoothly from one to the next. Revise any problems.

**Focus and Coherence**
A sentence is removed to make the paragraph more coherent.

This action was done in retaliation for the death of another white man who rode an "iron horse"—a bicycle—through a group of panicked villagers. ~~Some early bicycles were called velocipedes.~~  They apparently attacked him because he did not reply to their questions. Okonkwo's wise uncle . . .

*Response*

## Is each paragraph of my analysis coherent?

Students can be sure that their analyses are coherent and unified if

- all of the sentences in the paragraphs contain details that support the topic sentences of the paragraphs;
- sentences within the paragraphs flow logically from one to the next;
- all of the topic sentences support and help develop clearly stated thesis statements;
- each paragraph flows logically to the next paragraph, with appropriate transitions; and
- none of the details in the paragraphs distract readers.

★ **TEKS** 10.13B, 10.13C

### Try It!
**Answers**

Eliminate sentence 3: *Nowadays, people turn to counseling or antidepressants.*

**Review your first draft for clear focus and coherence.** Remind students to check that their paragraphs have flow and relate to the thesis.

---

**TEKS 10.13B** Develop drafts in open-ended situations that include rhetorical devices; **10.13C** Revise drafts to improve word choice and the subtlety of meaning; **ELPS 4K** Demonstrate comprehension and expand reading skills by employing analytical skills/ evaluating written information and performing critical analyses

## Revising **for** Organization

Students may feel that their paragraphs and thoughts flow smoothly from one to the next when, in fact, the connections may not be fully developed or clear to other readers.

**Do my paragraphs flow smoothly from one to the next?**

Most students will benefit from a peer evaluation.

- Have students ask partners to read their drafts for the sole purpose of identifying the connections between paragraphs.
- Partners should identify an explicit word or phrase that links the last sentence of one paragraph to the opening sentence of the next paragraph.
- Where no clear link exists, partners should suggest a possible revision.

 **TEKS** 10.13B, 10.13C, 10.15A(iv), 10.15C(ii); **ELPS** 5F

### Exercise
### Answers

1. The transition is *As the novel progresses.* This tells the reader that the coming text discusses content that is further into the novel.
2. The transition is *immediately.* This identifies the time when the action is taking place.
3. The transition is *although.* This sets up the contrast of the sentence.
4. The transition is *Again.* This establishes the comparison to a previous sentence.

**Review your first draft.** Students can revise based on their peer evaluation results.

---

 **TEKS** 10.13B, 10.13C, 10.15A(iv), 10.15C(ii)

## Revising **for** Organization

When you revise for *organization,* check the way you have arranged your ideas. Each paragraph should contain a topic sentence. All the sentences in the paragraph should support the topic sentence with insights and relevant evidence from the text. The paragraphs should flow smoothly from one to the next, and the ideas within each paragraph should also flow smoothly from one sentence to the next. As you begin your revision, remember that you are writing an analysis. Keep in mind that your organizational pattern should be appropriate for your purpose in writing the essay and for your audience.

### Do my paragraphs flow smoothly from one to the next?

Effective transitions will help your paragraphs flow smoothly from one to the next. Transitions can be used to show location, time, and to compare and contrast things. Transition words and phrases can also be used to emphasize a point, to clarify your meaning, and to add information.

### Exercise

Read the following sentences and identify the transitions. Explain how each transition works to move paragraphs smoothly from one to the next.

1. As the novel progresses, Okonkwo becomes ensnarled in the clash of two cultures.
2. Knowing that he has done wrong, he immediately takes the steps that tradition dictates, exiling himself from Umuofia for seven years.
3. ...although Okonkwo feels his exile is the worst thing that could happen to him, the coming of the Europeans proves to be a problem on a much bigger scale.
4. Again, Achebe uses vivid language to bring the readers into the conflict and to make his point.

 **Review your first draft.** Check each paragraph and decide if your paragraphs flow smoothly. The opening sentence should connect in some way with the previous paragraph. Then check for the effective use of transitions within paragraphs. Revise accordingly.

---

 **TEKS** **10.13B** Develop drafts in open-ended situations that include transitions; **10.13C** Revise drafts to improve word choice; **10.15A(iv)** Write an analytical essay that includes a structure appropriate to the purpose and audience; **10.15C(ii)** Write a response to literary text that addresses writing skills for an analytical essay; **ELPS** **5F** Write using a variety of grade-appropriate connecting words in increasingly accurate ways

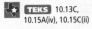 TEKS 10.13C,
10.15A(iv), 10.15C(ii)

## Is my organization appropriate for my purpose and audience?

In a literary analysis essay, you are writing about your viewpoint and insights about a particular piece of literature. It is important that you consider who your audience will be and write with appropriate tone and vocabulary. Also consider your purpose: you are not writing a summary or providing a literal analysis of the plot. Therefore, it is important to choose an organizational pattern that matches the purpose for your writing and works best for your readers.

### Exercise

Carefully read the following paragraph. Then rearrange the sentences into a logical pattern for the purpose and the audience.

1  In the poem "Fifteen," William Stafford creates a snapshot of the
2  dreams and realities of a teenager. The speaker describes a motorcycle
3  using human qualities. He then contrasts his dreams with a real accident.
4  The motorcycle is called "a companion, friendly." Its metal parts are called
5  "flanks," and its headlights are described as shy. After the accident, when
6  the adult rider gets back on the cycle, the boy is left with only his dreams.

 **Review your first draft for smooth flow and coherence.** Be sure that each paragraph is clear and unified. Revise any problems.

**Organization**
A sentence is moved to make the paragraph more coherent.

> Achebe describes in great detail how hard Okonkwo works and how prudent he is. As a result the reader empathizes with Okonkwo and is happy when Okonkwo rises to the highest circle of Umofia's powerful men. Okonkwo works harder than anyone to provide food for his family, reveres the words…

*Response*

## Is my organization appropriate for my purpose and audience?

Students can be sure their paragraphs are well organized if:
- one sentence flows logically into the next, and
- the last sentence of a paragraph is linked to the first sentence in the next paragraph.

 **DIFFERENTIATE INSTRUCTION**

TEKS 10.13C, 10.15A(iv)

### Exercise
**Answers**

**Possible Answer**

In the poem "Fifteen," William Stafford creates a snapshot of the dreams and realities of a teenager. He then contrasts his dreams with a real accident. The speaker describes a motorcycle using human qualities. The motorcycle is called "a companion, friendly." Its metal parts are called "flanks," and its headlights are described as shy. After the accident, when the adult rider gets back on the cycle, the boy is left only with his dreams.

**Review your first draft for smooth flow and coherence.** Remind students of the importance of coherence in a literary analysis. If students are still struggling with the concept of coherence, provide additional practice paragraphs.

TEKS 10.15C(ii)

---

**Differentiated Instruction:**
**English Language Learners**                    ELPS 4F, 4J, 4K

| ELP Level **Beginning** | ELP Level **Intermediate** | ELP Level **Advanced/Advanced High** |
|---|---|---|
| Read the sample paragraph aloud to students. Provide students with sentence strips so that they can work in groups to manipulate them into the correct order. | Provide students with sentence strips of the sample paragraph so that they can manipulate them to put them in correct order. Then have students rewrite the paragraph in correct order. | Have students read the first paragraph from the model essay on SE page 268 and discuss with a partner how the reorganization improved to the flow of the paragraph. |

 TEKS **10.13C** Revise drafts/rethink how well the purpose, audience, and genre have been addressed; **10.15A(iv)** Write an analytical essay that includes a structure appropriate to the purpose and audience; **10.15C(ii)** Write a response to literary text that addresses writing skills for an analytical essay; ELPS **4F** Use visual/contextual support and support from peers/teachers to develop grasp of language structures; **4J** Demonstrate comprehension and expand reading skills by employing inferential skills/predicting, making connections between ideas, drawing conclusions from text, and finding supporting evidence; **4K** Demonstrate comprehension and expand reading skills by employing analytical skills/evaluating written information and performing critical analyses

## Revising for Development of Ideas

The only way that students can be sure that they have not included irrelevant supporting details is to reevaluate them. Although this will take a little time, the results will produce a tightly organized, cohesive, incisive analysis.

### Does my analysis clearly reveal the theme?

To evaluate each detail, students should ask, "Does this detail help develop or reflect the theme?" If the answer is "not clearly," the detail does not belong in the essay.

### Exercise
#### Answers

In line 5: *transmitted by* ekwe, *a hollowed-out wooden instrument*

**Review your first draft for development of ideas.** Have students review their analyses and remove any details that do not help reveal their themes. Provide an opportunity for students to consult with you or their peers to discuss any details about which they are uncertain.

**TEKS** 10.13B, 10.13C, 10.15A(ii), 10.15C(ii)

---

 **TEKS** 10.13B, 10.13C, 10.15A(ii), 10.15C(ii)

## Revising for Development of Ideas

### Does my analysis clearly reveal the theme?

Your analysis will clearly reveal the theme if you support your ideas with details from the book. Focus on details that apply directly to the theme. The evidence from the text that you use to support your ideas must be relevant. Use quotations as appropriate to support your insights and to help the reader understand the points you are making. You may wish to use various rhetorical devices, including analogies and figurative language, to convey your insights about the theme.

- **Choose events related to the theme.**
  Knowing that he has done wrong, he immediately takes the step that tradition dictates, exiling himself from Umuofia for seven years.
  *not*
  Okonkwo had three wives.
- **Mention secondary characters only as they expand the theme.**
  Obierika returns two years later with more stories about missionaries.
  *not*
  Mr. Brown is a kind and compassionate missionary.

### Exercise

Read the paragraph below. Which detail does not apply to the theme?

1  Word spread that the white men had formed a court in Umuofia to protect
2  followers of their religion. The procedures were different from those used in
3  the natives' system of justice, resulting in anger and misunderstanding when
4  a villager was hanged for killing a missionary. News of the execution was
5  transmitted by *ekwe*, a hollowed-out wooden instrument.

 **Review your first draft for development of ideas.** Be sure that you have presented sufficent relevant evidence and details from the text to support your thesis.

---

**TEKS** **10.13B** Develop drafts in open-ended situations that include rhetorical devices; **10.13C** Revise drafts to improve word choice and the subtlety of meaning; **10.15A(ii)** Write an analytical essay that includes rhetorical devices; **10.15C(ii)** Write a response to literary text that addresses writing skills for an analytical essay

# Have I effectively used literary terms in my analysis?

You have effectively used literary terms if they reveal your understanding of the novel and help you to express yourself. Like science, history, and mathematics, literature has its own set of specialized terms (*conflict, theme, symbol,* and so on). As you discuss conflict, differentiate between internal and external conflicts. Use or identify figurative language, such as similes, metaphors, and hyperbole, that the author uses in the piece of literature. This will help show your understanding of the purpose of literary analysis. Using specific terms, as well as including key quotations from the piece, will help the reader understand your meaning and will also make you sound knowledgeable about the topic.

## Try It!

Read the paragraph below and explain how the underlined literary terms add meaning to the analysis.

In *Fahrenheit 451*, Bradbury's references to the natural world serve as <u>symbols</u> of reality. For example, Montag experiences the sensation of smell for the first time when he tries to escape down the river. The nomadic lifestyle also becomes a <u>metaphor</u> for returning to an unstructured, natural existence. Gradually, artificial, urban <u>settings</u> turn out to be less and less real for Montag.

 **Revise for literary terminology.** Review your analysis to be sure that you have used appropriate literary terms as needed.

Revise

**Development of Ideas**
The writer makes use of literary terms and gives an example of a rhetorical device.

In these scenes, Achebe continues to show the ~~problems~~ conflicts
Okonkwo faces. The reader is drawn into the ~~problems~~ conflicts and
sympathizes with Okonkwo. Acebe uses ~~good words~~ stylistic and rhetorical devices to
"Blessed is he who forsakes his father and his mother for my sake."
emphasize his point; he even uses a proverb.

Response

---

## Have I effectively used literary terms in my analysis?

Review with students the specialized literary terms and their meanings: *conflict, theme, symbol, metaphor, similes,* and *hyperbole*. Make sure they have a clear understanding of these terms.

TEKS 10.13C, 10.15C(iii)

✱ For more literary terms, see SE pages 634–637.

### Try It!
Answers

**Possible Answer**

The literary terms in the paragraph show that the writer understands the novel being analyzed on multiple levels beyond the literal events and circumstances. ✓ DIFFERENTIATE INSTRUCTION

**Revise for literary terminology.** Remind students of the literary terms you discussed on TE page 268. Have students review their drafts specifically for opportunities to include literary terminology where appropriate.

---

## Differentiated Instruction: English Language Learners

ELPS 4F, 4G, 4K

| ELP Level **Beginning** | ELP Level **Intermediate** | ELP Level **Advanced/Advanced High** |
|---|---|---|
| Read the **Try It!** paragraph aloud to students. Allow students to use their first language to aid understanding of the literary terms. | Read through the **Try It!** paragraph with students to make sure they understand the text. Have them write a definition of each literary term, using a bilingual dictionary as needed. | After students have read the **Try It!** paragraph silently, have them work with a partner to define the underlined literary terms and to develop an answer for the activity. |

TEKS **10.13C** Revise drafts to improve figurative language; **10.15C(iii)** Write a response to literary text that analyzes the effects of stylistic and rhetorical device; ELPS **4F** Use support from peers/teachers to enhance and confirm understanding; **4G** Demonstrate comprehension of increasingly complex English/participating in shared reading; **4K** Demonstrate comprehension and expand reading skills by employing analytical skills/evaluating written information and performing critical analyses

## Texas Traits

### Revising **for** Voice

Ask students why they think it is important to maintain a third-person point of view in their analyses. Students should recognize that the third-person point of view enables them to remain objective and sound more authoritative.

**Do I maintain a third-person point of view throughout?**

Alert students to the key pronouns (*he, she, it,* and *they*) that indicate third-person point of view as well as the first-person and second-person pronouns (*I, we,* or *you*).

### Try It!
#### Answers

**Possible Answer**

In *The Old Man and the Sea*, an old fisherman named Santiago is tested beyond human endurance. He goes out in his boat one morning and catches sight of a huge swordfish. Santiago hooks it, battles with it, and finally lashes it to his boat. Then he sees sharks all around his boat, eating pieces of the fish. Santiago must summon every ounce of strength in his struggle against the sharks, which shows that courage is not limited to young heroes. Santiago says, "Man is not made for defeat. A man can be destroyed, but not defeated." His actions reveal that he is a courageous man.

**Check for third-person point of view.** Students can exchange papers and check each other's drafts for a consistent point of view.

 **TEKS** 10.13C

---

**278**

 **TEKS** 10.13C

## Texas Traits

### Revising **for** Voice

When you revise for *voice,* pay attention to the way your writing sounds. This is an opportunity to improve the style of your writing. You should sound engaging and knowledgeable.

In a literary analysis, it is important to maintain the third-person point of view throughout. Point of view refers to the position or angle from which a story is told. Third-person point of view means that you are outside the story. As an outside observer, your tone should be objective and neutral.

### Do I maintain a third-person point of view throughout?

You have maintained a third-person point of view if you have consistently used third-person pronouns *(he, she, it, they)*. Avoid using first-person pronouns *(I, we)* or the second-person pronoun *(you)*.

### Try It!

The paragraph below sometimes drifts away from the third-person point of view. On your own paper, rewrite the paragraph so that the voice is consistently third person. In places, you will need to completely change the sentence structure to correct the point of view.

> In *The Old Man and the Sea*, an old fisherman named Santiago is tested beyond normal human endurance. He goes out in his boat one morning, and you catch sight of a huge swordfish. Santiago hooks it, and I thought he was never going to land it, but next thing you know, it's lashed to the boat. Then you see sharks all around, eating pieces of the fish. Santiago must summon every ounce of strength in his struggle against the sharks, and you realize that courage is not limited to young heroes. Santiago says, "Man is not made for defeat. A man can be destroyed but not defeated." You feel he is courageous because of his actions.

 **Check for third-person point of view.** Read your analysis to see whether you have maintained a third-person point of view throughout. Make any necessary revisions.

---

### Differentiated Instruction: Advanced Learners

Students may enjoy creating a humorous poster for the classroom or computer lab to remind writers to avoid flowery or wordy language. Ask volunteers to add examples as they find them in their own writing.

TEKS 10.13C

## Do I sound knowledgeable about the book?

Your voice will sound knowledgeable if you show a clear understanding of the theme and write with confidence about it. Use appropriate vocabulary when you write, and keep these tips in mind.

- **Be direct.** Use the fewest words possible to get your point across. Use figurative language appropriately, but avoid flowery or wordy language.
- **Avoid starting sentences with "It is" or "There is."** These constructions lack energy and direction.
- **Avoid waffle words** such as *kind of, sort of, in a way, maybe, might,* or *seemed like* that overly qualify what you write.
- **Your style should not be too casual.** Remember your audience. Do not include slang or sentence constructions that are not appropriate for an academic essay.

### Try It!

Rewrite the following sentence to make it sound more knowledgeable. Use the strategies given above.

It seems like Manolin wants to go along on the fishing trip with Santiago, but there is the problem that his parents think that maybe he shouldn't go because it seems to them that the old man might be bad luck.

 Revise

**Check your essay for voice.** Reread your essay, marking any places that do not sound knowledgeable. Revise as needed.

**Voice**
Waffle words are deleted.

The force that ~~kind of~~ drives him is ~~probably~~ the fact that he "had no patience with his father," who was ~~sort of~~ irresponsible and constantly in debt, preferring to drink and play the flute. Okonkwo thinks of his father as . . .

Response

---

## Do I sound knowledgeable about the book?

Point out to students that flowery or wordy language refers to the excessive overuse of modifiers. To illustrate this idea, write the sentence below on an overhead or the board. Have students compare the effective and knowledgeable-sounding first sentence of the **Try It!** passage on SE page 278 with the following:

*In the really wonderful novel* The Old Man and the Sea, *an unlucky and humble, but proud and stubborn, old fisherman named Santiago is tested way beyond normal human endurance.*

Check that students can identify the unnecessary words in the sentence above (*the really wonderful novel; an unlucky and humble, but proud and stubborn; way*).

Remind students to avoid writing sentences that begin with *It is, There is,* and *It seems that* or *It seems like.* Have them delete these phrases where they occur and rewrite the sentences. ✔DIFFERENTIATE INSTRUCTION

 TEKS 10.13C

### Try It!
### Answers

**Possible Answer**

Manolin wants to go fishing with Santiago, but Manolin's parents think that the old man is bad luck.

**Check your essay for voice.** Students should revise their drafts for voice, particularly avoiding flowery or wordy language. ✔DIFFERENTIATE INSTRUCTION

---

TEKS 10.13C Revise drafts/improve style and word choice and rethink how well the audience has been addressed; ELPS 5B Write using content-based grade-level vocabulary; 5D Edit writing for standard grammar and usage/subject-verb and pronoun agreement and appropriate verb tenses; 5F Write using a variety of grade-appropriate sentence patterns in increasingly accurate ways

## Revising
### Improving Your Writing

Encourage students to use each question in the checklist as a guide for a careful review of their essays. Explain that responding thoughtfully to the Revising Checklist will help them to improve their analyses.

**Check your revising.** Encourage students to work through the checklist point by point to identify specific areas of their analyses that may still need to be refined.

**Make a clean copy.** Explain to students that starting with a clean copy of their essays will allow them to edit them more productively because they will not be cluttered with all of the previous revisions.

### Conventions Connections

**Grammar: Third-Person Pronouns**
- ***Student Edition*** page 573;
  ***Proofreader's Guide*** pages 738–739
- ***SkillsBook*** page 81

⚡ *Write Source Online* **GrammarSnap**

---

**280**

## Revising Improving Your Writing

**Check your revising.** On a piece of paper, write the numbers 1 to 11. If you can answer "yes" to a question, put a check mark after that number. If not, continue to work with that part of your essay.

### Revising Checklist

**Focus and Coherence**

_____ 1. Is my thesis statement clear and complete?

_____ 2. Do my ideas develop the book's theme?

_____ 3. Does my entire essay present a coherent, unified analysis?

**Organization**

_____ 4. Have I written a clear introduction, middle, and conclusion?

_____ 5. Do my paragraphs flow smoothly from one to the next?

_____ 6. Is my organizational pattern appropriate for the audience, purpose, and context?

**Development of Ideas**

_____ 7. Are all my supporting details related to the theme?

_____ 8. Have I used key embedded quotations to support my thesis?

_____ 9. Have I used appropriate literary terms in the analysis?

**Voice**

_____ 10. Do I maintain a third-person point of view throughout?

_____ 11. Do I sound knowledgeable about the novel?

**Make a clean copy.** When you finish revising your essay, make a clean copy for editing.

# Editing

After you've finished revising your essay, it's time to edit for the following conventions: grammar, sentence structure, capitalization, punctuation, and spelling.

### Keys to Effective Editing

1. Use a dictionary, a thesaurus, and the "Proofreader's Guide" in the back of this book (pages 642–787).

2. Use quotation marks correctly for direct quotations.

3. Check all of your writing for correct grammar, sentence structure, capitalization, punctuation, and spelling.

4. If you use a computer, edit on a printout and then enter your changes on the computer.

5. Use the editing and proofreading marks inside the back cover of this book.

Response

---

# Editing

## Keys to Effective Editing

Remind students that during the editing stage, they will focus on finding and correcting errors in:

- grammar,
- sentence structure,
- capitalization,
- punctuation, and
- spelling.

The Keys to Effective Editing list explains the process students will be guided through on SE pages 282–286. **DIFFERENTIATE INSTRUCTION**

Share your own tips, hints, and tools for editing. Then ask students to share any effective strategies they have used. Have students list the editing ideas in their writing journals, and encourage them to refer to the list as they correct mistakes on their final copies.

---

## Differentiated Instruction: English Language Learners

**ELPS** 1A, 5D

| ELP Level **Beginning** | ELP Level **Intermediate** | ELP Level **Advanced/Advanced High** |
|---|---|---|
| Provide students with a bilingual dictionary (English and their first language). Practice using it with the students until they can look up words on their own. | Encourage students to use all tools available to them to assist with editing. Make sure they have access to dictionaries, including a bilingual dictionary, grammar texts, or a computer. | Encourage students to edit their work based upon what they know about English grammar and usage. Then, have students use available tools to assist with editing. |

**ELPS 1A** Use prior knowledge and experience to understand meanings; **5D** Edit writing for standard grammar and usage/ subject-verb and pronoun agreement and appropriate verb tenses

## Editing for Conventions

### Grammar

Remind students that good grammar is critical for readers to clearly understand your literary analysis.

#### When should I shift tenses in my analysis?

Make sure that students have a clear understanding of the more complex verb tenses. Review the tenses and remind students of key words they can look for that indicate different tenses.

**TEKS** 10.13D, 10.17A(i); **ELPS** 5D, 5E

✳ For more about verb tenses, see SE pages 746–751.

---

#### Grammar Exercise
**Answers**
**Possible Answer**

The narrator in the story starts thinking about the situation. He starts to look for the owner of the motorcycle and finds him lying in the grass. When the motorcycle rider "thanked the teenager" for his help, we see the contrast between the two characters. The narrator had been dreaming of being an adult. The adult can climb back on the motorcycle and take off for exciting adventures. The narrator, however, is still just a boy.

**Review your first draft.** Remind students that choosing tense sometimes has to be a conscious decision and that it is easy to slip from one tense to another. Encourage them to work with a partner to edit their work.

**Grammar: Shifting Verb Tenses**
- *Proofreader's Guide* pages 746–751
- *SkillsBook* pages 96–97

⚡ *Write Source Online* **GrammarSnap**

---

**TEKS** **10.13D** Edit drafts for grammar; **10.17A(i)** Use and understand more complex active and passive tenses; **ELPS** **5D** Edit writing for standard grammar and usage/subject-verb agreement; **5E** Employ increasingly complex grammatical structures in content area writing such as using correct verbs, tenses, and pronouns/possessive case/negatives and contractions

---

## Editing for Conventions

### Grammar

When you edit for *grammar*, especially in a literary analysis essay, check to make sure that you have used the correct verb tenses and that you have not shifted from one tense to another in your writing. As you edit, you should also check to make sure that subject and verb in the sentences agree and that your sentences flow smoothly.

#### When should I shift tenses in my analysis?

A simple rule to follow is that you should not shift tenses in your analysis unless there is good reason to do so. In a response to literature, including a literary analysis, you should usually write in the present tense. The plot unfolds in the same way each you time you read a story, so it makes sense to discuss the story in the present tense. Stories are written, however, in present and past tenses. When you include embedded quotes, you may need to shift to simple or complex past tenses.

- **Present tense (active voice):** Okonkwo works harder…
- **Present tense (passive voice):** Okonkwo is known…
- **Present perfect tense:** Okonkwo's traditions have been ridiculed…
- **Past tense (active voice)** He "had no patience"…

#### Grammar Exercise

Read the example below. Correct the shift in verb tenses

> The narrator in the story started thinking about the situation. He starts to look for the owner of the motorcycle and found him lying in the grass. When the motorcycle rider "thanked the teenager" for his help, we see the contrast between the two characters. The narrator had been dreaming of being an adult. The adult can climb back on the motorcycle and take off for exciting adventures. The narrator, however, is still just a boy.

**Review your first draft.** Read your essay and make sure that you have not shifted tenses without good reason.

**TEKS** 10.13D, 10.17A(i)
**ELPS** 3C–3E, 4C, 4F, 5E

## Should I always avoid split infinitives?

Remember that an infinitive is a verb form that includes the word *to*. The verbals *to write, to walk, to talk, to finish* are infinitives. Infinitives can be used as nouns, adjectives, or adverbs.

- **As a noun:** I want to win the race.
- **As an adjective:** Her desire to win is no stronger than mine.
- **As an adverb modifying an adjective:** People may think it is easy to win a race, but it requires hard work and practice.

The general rule in writing is that infinitives should not be split. In other words, avoid inserting words between the word *to* and the verb itself. The following are examples of split infinitives: *to easily win, to quickly walk, to sharply turn*. The rule about not splitting infinitives comes from Latin, in which infinitives are one word and cannot be split.

There are exceptions, and you will find times when it is almost impossible not to split an infinitive. For example, in the sentence *Economists expect the nation's output to more than double in the coming decade,* not splitting the infinitive would lead to a clumsy sentence.

### Exercise

Rewrite the following sentences, so that the infinitives are not split.

1. That loud music is going to certainly harm your hearing.
2. The loss of the game is bound to incredibly damage the team's prospects of winning the championship.
3. The severe drought is going to harmfully affect the crops, and it is going to really hurt the animals.

## Learning Language

Work with a partner. Take turns saying the present tense of a verb and have your partner change it into an infinitive. Then ask your partner to say a sentence using the infinitive form. Then say two short sentences and have your partner change them into one sentence using an infinitive. For example, say *He came to the house. He came to have dinner with us. He came to the house to have dinner with us.* Then do the same activity using gerunds. If you have difficulty or questions, ask your teacher for assistance. **Gerund:** a verb form that ends in *ing* and is used as a noun. **Infinitive:** a verb form that is usually introduced by *to* and that can be used as a noun, an adjective, or an adverb.

Edit

**Revise for split infinitives.** Check to work to make sure that you have used infinitives and infinitive phrases correctly.

Response

### Differentiated Instruction: English Language Learners

**ELPS** 4F, 5D

| ELP Level **Beginning** | ELP Level **Intermediate** | ELP Level **Advanced/Advanced High** |
| --- | --- | --- |
| Give students sample sentences that contain infinitives and gerunds. Have students underline the infinitive and circle the gerund in the sentences. | Give students a sample paragraph that contains infinitives and gerunds. Have students underline the infinitives, circle the gerunds, and revise the split infinitives. | Encourage students to underline the infinitives and circle the gerunds in their own essay. Prompt students to work with a partner to revise any split infinitives. |

## Should I always avoid split infinitives?

Remind students that the simple rule is that infinitives should not be split. They should review their essay looking for the word "to" in conjunction with a verb and make sure that they are not split. Any situations in which they are split should be intentional and unavoidable.

**TEKS** 10.13D, 10.17A(i)

### Exercise
**Answers**

1. That loud music is certainly going to harm your hearing.
2. The loss of the game is bound to damage the team's prospect of winning the championship.
3. The severe drought is going to affect the crops adversely, and it is going to hurt the animals.

### Learning Language

Encourage students to write their sentences, especially if one partner is having difficulty using any of the verbal forms correctly.

**DIFFERENTIATE INSTRUCTION**
**ELPS** 3C, 3D, 3E, 4C, 4F, 5E

**Revise for split infinitives.** Encourage students using computers to use the search or find function to search for the word *to* and then assess whether the word is being used as part of an infinitive. If so, have them check for split infinitives. Students can also work with a partner and review each other's work.

 **Conventions Connections**

**Grammar: Split Infinitives**
- ***Student Edition*** page 590; ***Proofreader's Guide*** pages 754–755, 768–769
- ***SkillsBook*** pages 101, 130

 *Write Source Online* **GrammarSnap**

**TEKS 10.13D** Edit drafts for grammar; **10.17A(i)** Use and understand verbals (gerunds, infinitives, participles); **ELPS 3C** Speak using a variety of grammatical structures with increasing accuracy and ease; **3D** Speak using grade-level content area vocabulary/new words and academic language proficiency; **3E** Share information in cooperative learning interactions; **4C** Comprehend language structures used in written classroom materials; **4F** Use support from peers/teachers to develop grasp of language structures; **5D** Edit writing for standard grammar and usage/subject-verb agreement and verb tenses; **5E** Employ increasingly complex grammatical structures in content area writing such as using correct verbs, tenses, and pronouns/possessive case/negatives and contractions

## Sentence Structure

Have students explain the parallel structure in the example sentences (three phrases acting as objects of the preposition *in*, all with the same verb tense; compound verb, both elements in the past tense).

### Are my sentences parallel?

To provide students with additional practice, have volunteers read sentences from their own drafts for the class to analyze for parallel structure.

### Grammar Exercise
**Answers**
**Possible Answers**

1. Thinking about her life made Granny feel like rolling up her sleeves and putting the whole place right again.
2. She remembered lighting the lamps, scrubbing the wooden floors, and caring for her little children.
3. Matthew wanted to volunteer at the community center tutoring younger children and playing outdoor games with older children.
4. The wind was howling, the lights were flickering, and the house creaked in the wind.

**Revise for sentence fluency and parallel construction.** Encourage students to read and analyze each sentence carefully. They should revise any sentences that do not have parallel construction and make other changes to improve sentence fluency.

⭐ **TEKS** 10.13C, 10.17C; **ELPS** 5F

⭐ **Conventions Connections**

**Grammar: Parallel Sentence Structure**
- **Student Edition** page 586;
  **Proofreader's Guide** pages 776–777
- **SkillsBook** pages 173–174

✦ **Write Source Online** **GrammarSnap**

**TEKS** **10.13C** Revise drafts to improve sentence variety; **10.17C** Use a variety of correctly structured sentences; **ELPS** **5F** Write using a variety of grade-appropriate sentence patterns and connecting words in increasingly accurate ways

---

⭐ **TEKS** 10.13C, 10.17C
**ELPS** 5F

## Sentence Structure

When you edit for *sentence structure,* be sure to look at each of your sentences for variety and for correct structure. Using a variety of correct sentence structures will add interest to your writing and engage the reader.

### Are my sentences parallel?

You should check each of your sentences to see if its parts are balanced. In other words, check to see if certain elements within each sentence are *parallel,* or stated in the same way. Study the following examples to see the difference that parallel structure can make. Besides adding balance to your sentences, parallel construction can be used as a rhetorical device to emphasize a point in a speech or in your writing.

| | |
|---|---|
| **Unparallel:** | Granny knew that her love could be seen in the food she cooked, her making all the clothes, and the gardens she liked growing. |
| **Parallel:** | Granny knew that her love could be seen in the food she had cooked, the clothes she had made, and the garden she had grown. |
| **Unparallel:** | Granny remembered her life and is preparing for dying. |
| **Parallel:** | Granny remembered her life and prepared for death. |

### Grammar Exercise

Revise the following unparallel sentences to make them parallel.

1. Thinking about her life made Granny feel like rolling up her sleeves and she could put the whole place right again.
2. She remembered lighting the lamps, the scrubbing of wooden floors, and how she cared for her little children.
3. Matthew wanted to volunteer at the community center tutoring younger children and he could play outdoor games outdoors with older children.
4. The wind was howling, and the lights began to flicker, and we heard noises as the house creaked in the wind.

 **Revise for sentence fluency and parallel construction.** Be sure that your sentences are balanced so that they read smoothly.

---

**Differentiated Instruction: Advanced Learners**

Point out that when interrupting words or phrases are used correctly, they help to make a statement, show contrast, give an example, qualify something, or draw a conclusion. As students complete the **Try It!** exercise, have them explain how each interrupting word functions.

# Mechanics

When you edit for *mechanics,* you check your punctuation and capitalization. Certain phrases and clauses need punctuation after them so that your reader can more easily understand your meaning. Interrupting words and phrases are words that provide detail, emphasis, and transitions. They need to be set off from the main idea of the sentence.

## How do I punctuate interrupting words and phrases?

You should place commas before and after any words or phrases that interrupt the flow of your sentences. If the interrupter is in the middle of a sentence, remember to enclose only the interrupting word or phrase in the commas. Common interrupting words and phrases include the following:

| | | | | |
|---|---|---|---|---|
| however | in fact | by contrast | of course | for example |
| true | as a rule | as a result | in response | after all |

### Try It!

Rewrite the following paragraph, inserting commas as needed for any interrupting words or phrases.

> Hobbits are as a rule peaceable people who aren't interested in adventure. When a Black Rider appears in the Shire however Frodo Baggins must journey from his comfortable home. He carries the one ring that can enslave the world. Frodo could use the ring to turn invisible, but doing so would in fact make him easier to detect by the Black Rider. Instead, Frodo and his companions flee across country. At an old watchtower, five Black Riders catch up to them, and Frodo is stabbed by a rider's blade. The tip breaks off in the wound and as a result Frodo becomes ill.

**Edit for punctuation of interrupting words and phrases.** Check your essay for words or phrases that interrupt the flow of your sentences. Make sure to set off these words or phrases with commas.

Revise

Response

## Mechanics

### How do I punctuate interrupting words and phrases?

Read aloud the list of common interrupting words and phrases. Write them on the board and clarify the meaning of each for students. Ask volunteers to suggest others to add to the list. You may wish to write several example sentences on the board and model for students where and when to place commas.

### Try It!
**Answers**

Hobbits are, as a rule, peaceable people who aren't interested in adventure. When a Black Rider appears in the Shire, however, Frodo Baggins must journey from his comfortable home. He carries the one ring that can enslave the world. Frodo could use the ring to turn invisible, but doing so would, in fact, make him easier to detect by the Black Rider. Instead, Frodo and his companions flee across country. At an old watchtower, five Black Riders catch up to them, and Frodo is stabbed by a rider's blade. The tip breaks off in the wound, and, as a result, Frodo becomes ill. ✔ **DIFFERENTIATE INSTRUCTION**

✔ **DIFFERENTIATE INSTRUCTION**

**Edit for punctuation of interrupting words and phrases.** Encourage students to stop at each mark of punctuation in their essays and ask themselves if it is being used properly.

TEKS 10.13D, 10.18B(i)

### ★ Conventions Connections

**Grammar: Commas to Punctuate Interrupting Words and Phrases**
- ***Proofreader's Guide*** pages 654–655
- ***SkillsBook*** pages 12–13

⚡ *Write Source Online* **GrammarSnap**

## Differentiated Instruction:
### English Language Learners

ELPS 1B, 2D, 2G, 3C, 3E

| ELP Level **Beginning** | ELP Level **Intermediate** | ELP Level **Advanced/Advanced High** |
|---|---|---|
| Post a list of common interrupting words and phrases in a visible location. Work with students to correctly identify and punctuate interrupting words in an adapted paragraph. | Have students read aloud the paragraph in the **Try It!** activity to a partner. Then have them complete the activity with a partner and re-read the paragraph, noticing the changes. | Have students attempt the **Try It!** activity on their own. Then have them read their revisions aloud to a partner, making changes as needed based on the partner's feedback. |

## Editing
### Checking for Conventions

Remind students to use the Proofreader's Guide (SE pages 642–787) as they edit for conventions. Throughout the year, they can refer to the instructions, rules, and examples in the guide to clarify checklist items or to resolve other questions.

**TEKS** 10.18A, 10.18B(i), 10.19

**Check your editing.** Explain to students that even great writers revise and rewrite many times. Also explain that all books go through multiple reviews by various editors before they ever get published. So, likewise, their work may take several revisions before it can pass the editing checklist.

**TEKS** 10.13C, 10.13D, 10.17B; **ELPS** 5C, 5D, 5E, 5F

### Creating a Title

Encourage students to be creative with their titles, but to make sure that they make sense in conjunction with their themes. Titles should not mislead. Readers will be disappointed or irritated if a title indicates a writing is about one thing when, in truth, it is about something entirely different.

---

## Editing Checking for Conventions

**Check your editing.** On a piece of paper, write the numbers 1 to 12. Put a check mark by the number if you can answer "yes" to that question. If not, continue to edit your essay for that convention.

### Editing Checklist

#### Conventions

**GRAMMAR**

_____ **1.** Have I used correct verb tenses throughout?

_____ **2.** Have I used correctly structured verbals, such as infinitives?

_____ **3.** Have I used the right words (*its, it's*)?

**SENTENCE STRUCTURE**

_____ **4.** Do I use a variety of correctly structured sentences to clearly communicate ideas?

**MECHANICS (Capitalization and Punctuation)**

_____ **5.** Do I start all my sentences with capital letters?

_____ **6.** Have I capitalized all proper nouns?

_____ **7.** Does each sentence have correct end punctuation?

_____ **8.** Have I used quotation marks correctly with direct quotations?

_____ **9.** Have I used commas to set off interrupting words and phrases?

_____ **10.** Do I use apostrophes to show possession (*in Poe's story*)?

**SPELLING**

_____ **11.** Have I spelled all my words correctly?

_____ **12.** Have I consulted a dictionary to determine or check the spellings of words my spell-checker may have missed?

### Creating a Title

- Focus on the theme: **Good Intentions and Bad Results**
- Refer to a character: **The Pacification of Okonkwo**
- Be creative: **When Cultures Clash, *Things Fall Apart***

---

**TEKS** **10.13C** Revise drafts to improve sentence variety; **10.13D** Edit drafts for grammar, mechanics, and spelling; **10.17B** Identify and use subjunctive mood to express wishes; **10.18A** Use conventions of capitalization; **10.18B(i)** Use commas in nonrestrictive phrases; **10.19** Spell correctly using resources to determine and check correct spelling; **ELPS** **5C** Spell familiar words with increasing accuracy; **5D** Edit writing for standard grammar and usage/verb tenses; **5E** Employ increasingly complex grammatical structures in content area writing such as using correct verbs, tenses, and pronouns/possessive case/ negatives and contractions; **5F** Write using a variety of grade-appropriate sentence patterns in increasingly accurate ways

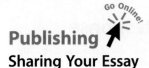

**TEKS** 10.13E

# Publishing

## Sharing Your Essay

Now that you've finished drafting, revising, and editing your essay, it is time to publish it. First, however, share your essay with your classmates. Ask for feedback. Then ask your teacher to review your essay. Make any needed final corrections. See the suggestions in the boxes below for a variety of ways to present your essay.

 **Make a final copy.** Follow your teacher's instructions or use the guidelines below to format your paper. (If you are using a computer, see pages 72–74.) Write a final copy of your essay and proofread it for errors.

## Focusing on Presentation

- Use blue or black ink and write neatly.
- Write your name in the upper left corner of page 1.
- Skip a line and center your title; skip another line and start your writing.
- Indent every paragraph and leave a one-inch margin on all four sides.
- Write your last name and the page number in the upper right-hand corner of every page after page 1.

**Publish in a Class Literary Magazine**

Set up your work in a multicolumn format, add headlines, and include photos or paintings of the author and characters. Consider adding "sidebar" graphics or comments.

**Make a Recording**

Read your analysis and record it on a CD or DVD. Consider including appropriate music, sound effects, and video clips.

**Post Your Essay on the Web**

Submit your work to a community, school, or class Web site or post it on a family Web site.

---

# Publishing

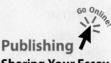

## Sharing Your Essay

Share with students of the usefulness of incorporating feedback from a small audience (i.e., classmates) before publishing their work for a broader audience. Review the technology available in your classroom and school as students explore different publishing ideas.

**TEKS** 10.13E

Students could produce a monthly or bi-monthly literary magazine, possibly via the school or class Web site. Online publishing allows students the option of providing links to other information. For example, for the publication of their literary analyses, they could add links to:

- author biographies and Web sites,
- lists of awards and prizes earned by the novels, and
- movies and plays based on the novels.

**Make a final copy.** Make sure students know your instructions for formatting of their final copy.

### Focusing on Presentation

Review the bullet points with students. Note that some of these apply regardless of whether the work is handwritten or keyed on a computer. Other items are specific to handwritten materials. Emphasize the importance of neatness and consistency. **DIFFERENTIATE INSTRUCTION**

 **Technology Connections**

Write Source Online **Portfolio**

Write Source Online **Essay Scoring**

---

## Differentiated Instruction: English Language Learners

 **ELPS** 5C, 5D, 5E

| ELP Level **Beginning** | ELP Level **Intermediate** | ELP Level **Advanced/Advanced High** |
|---|---|---|
| Have students work with a partner to edit their essays, focusing only on capitalization and spelling. | Have students work with a partner to edit their essays, focusing only on the mechanics and spelling portions of the editing checklist. Encourage students to use proper proofreading marks. | Have students use the editing checklist to edit their essays. Then have them review their edits with a partner, making changes as needed. |

**TEKS** 10.13E Revise the final draft in response to feedback from peers and teacher/publish written work; **ELPS** 5C Spell familiar words/employ spelling patterns with increasing accuracy; 5D Edit writing for standard grammar and usage/subject-verb and pronoun agreement and appropriate verb tenses; 5E Employ increasingly complex grammatical structures in content area writing such as using correct verbs, tenses, and pronouns/possessive case/negatives and contractions

## Evaluating an Interpretive Response

Refer students to the holistic scoring guide on SE pages 60–61 for use as they read the literary analyses essays on this and the following pages. Have students compare the criteria for each score with the essays provided.

Step through this essay with students and discuss what makes this a highly effective essay. Point out the strong use of the elements of writing. Ask students to evaluate if they see any areas where improvements can be made. Encourage students to model their own work after this sample. **DIFFERENTIATE INSTRUCTION ↘**

288

# Evaluating an Interpretive Response

To learn how to evaluate a literary analysis, you will use the holistic scoring guide on pages **60–61** and the essays that follow. These essays are examples of writing for each score on the scoring guide (1–4).

Notice that the first essay received a score of 4. Read the description for a score of 4 on pages **60–61**. Then read the literary analysis. Use the same steps to study the other examples. As you read, concentrate on the overall quality of the writing in each example.

**Writing that fits a score of 4 is highly effective.**

### Land Values

*The Good Earth*, by Pearl S. Buck, is the story of Wang Lung, a simple farmer who becomes a wealthy man by acquiring more and more land. As he does, he loses his traditional way of life and values. In the end, Wang Lung is haunted by the words he spoke as a young man: "Land is one's flesh and blood." The author sets up the conflict early in the novel, describing Wang Lung's <u>desire for prosperity and the importance of land in his life.</u> As the characters are developed and the plot unfolds, the conflict is fully developed for the reader.

The basic conflict of Wang Lung's life is foreshadowed when his father arranges for him to marry a young woman from the big city. O-lan is a servant girl working for a rich family, the House of Hwang. When Wang Lung goes to get his future bride to take her back to his father's farm, he is shocked by the high prices and the rude ways of the city. The House of Hwang, with its impersonal atmosphere and showy wealth, is a huge contrast to life in the village. When Wang Lung brings O-lan home however, she immediately fits in with the traditional ways of the farm.

Wang Lung's life with O-lan begins happily as they work the land and prosper. They have a son, save their money, and live by the traditional, old-fashioned values that have been in place for centuries. They are so successful, in fact, that Wang Lung buys land from the House of Hwang, although O-lan warns that they already have enough land. Wang Lung does not realize that he has

> **The beginning** gives the novel's title and the author. It also introduces the writer's focus. (underlined)

> Each **middle** paragraph supports the thesis with evidence and details from the text. Writer provides insights as the analysis is developed.

> Writer consistently uses correct verb tenses.

**Differentiated Instruction: Struggling Learners**

Reproduce a T-chart (see TE Appendix) to help students see the contrast between the main character as a simple farmer and then as a wealthy landowner. Discuss how each detail supports the writer's analysis of the theme that land is a man's flesh and blood, and true home.

✪ **ELPS** 4F

Have students compare the beginning and ending paragraphs. Discuss as a class how the writer connects the thesis and theme of the novel in these paragraphs. ✔ DIFFERENTIATE INSTRUCTION

**Middle**
paragraphs continue to support thesis with evidence from text. Sentences show correct use of infinitives.

**Conclusion**
adds a final analysis. Embedded quotations emphasize writer's point. Correct punctuation is used.

Response

begun to turn away from the traditional values toward something new—ambition.

Ambition is so satisfying to Wang Lung that over the years he buys much more land from the failing House of Hwang. One of the ironies in the novel is that, although land is the source of traditional life, obtaining more land leads him from that life. Wang is gradually overcome by lazy relatives, starving villagers, and spoiled children. Although he continues to gain land and wealth, he seems less and less satisfied with his life. Wang Lung goes to the city, seeking escape, and gets involved in fast living, forgetting the morals that he was raised with. At one point, he agrees to cut off his pigtail, a symbol of his traditional, rural background, because an attractive woman in the city laughs at him for wearing one.

Life back on the farm becomes more and more complicated, with huge tracts of land, numerous buildings, and many workers to manage. Because there is so much to keep track of, Wang Lung hires people to take care of business for him, and Wang Lung ends up with nothing to do all day but deal with his family troubles. In the ultimate irony of the novel, Wang Lung decides to move everyone to the old House of Hwang, which has been abandoned by its bankrupt owners. Wang Lung's family has become like the one he despised when he went to bring O-lan home.

Wang Lung doesn't have much to be happy about, but he does have one remaining comfort—when he picks up a hoe to work in the field, he says, "The land did again its healing work." As an old man, Wang Lung returns to live out his life on the old farm. He still loves the land, thinking, "It is the end of a family—when they begin to sell the land." Wang Lung sees that wealth is not everything; there is more happiness in living on the land—man's true home.

---

## Differentiated Instruction: English Language Learners

🔲 ELPS 4F, 4H, 4K

| ELP Level **Beginning** | ELP Level **Intermediate** | ELP Level **Advanced/Advanced High** |
|---|---|---|
| In shared reading, read the first and last paragraph of the essay aloud, correcting pronunciation as needed. Then have students identify the life lesson Wang Lung learns. | In shared reading, read the essay aloud, correcting pronunciation as needed. Then have students identify how the writer connects the ending paragraph to the thesis. | Have students read the essay silently. Then have students summarize the main points the writer uses to support his or her thesis. |

**ELPS 4F** Use support from peers/teachers to enhance and confirm understanding; **4H** Read silently with increasing ease and comprehension for longer periods; **4K** Demonstrate comprehension and expand reading skills by employing analytical skills/ evaluating written information and performing critical analyses

Point out that although this writer is analyzing the same novel as the student who wrote the essay on SE pages 288–289, he or she focuses on very different themes. Some students may point to this as the reason the essay scored a 3. Explain, however, that novels often have more than one theme and different writers will likely choose to analyze different themes. Discuss the weaknesses noted in the side notes as the reason that the essay received a score of 3.

Step through this essay with students and discuss what makes this a generally effective essay. Ask students to evaluate what writing elements were used and where improvements can be made. **DIFFERENTIATE INSTRUCTION ↘**

Writing that fits a score of 3 is generally effective.

### Living Off the Land

Pearl Buck has a lot of themes in *The Good Earth*, but she expresses them in a very interesting story that really keeps the reader's attention. As she tells the story of Wang Lung and O-lan, she brings up many of important issues like the way women are treated in China, how traditional ways in China are coming to an end, and how wealth can change a once humble man.

O-lan is not a pretty woman but she is a good wife for Wang Lung. She works side by side with him in the field and she takes care of him and his father at home. Like Wang Lung she is careful with money. Soon the couple's hard work pays off and Wang Lung starts to become wealthy. Money makes Wang Lung more aware of his status. Even though O-lan has done so much for him, Wang Lung starts to slowly feel ashamed of her, particularly her big feet. In China, women bound their feet so they would be tiny. Wang-Lung falls in love with Lotus, a pretty woman who has bound feet. Unlike O-lan, she couldn't work. She could barely walk. "She swayed upon her little feet and to Wang Lung there was nothing so wonderful...as her pointed little feet and her curling helpless hands." Even though he feels bad about what he's done to O-lan, now that Wang Lung doesn't have to work as hard, he is more concerned with Lotus's outer beauty than O-lan's inner beauty.

The richer Wang Lung gets, the less he is interested in traditional ways. Also, his sons are less traditional than he is. In the beginning of the book, Wang Lung lights incense for the gods of the earth. By the end, he stops being thankful to the gods. "Facing him were the small gods and...he noted how...of old he had been afraid of them, but now he was careless, having become prosperous and in no need of gods...." He cuts off his traditional braid to please Lotus. Also the duty and respect that he shows to older family members is corrupted when he gives his uncle opium. He himself is treated with disrespect by his own sons who plan to sell his land and lie to him about it. Selling the land is also the end of traditions. Farming is looked down on by Wang Lung's sons.

---

The **introduction** gives the title of the novel and the author. The introductory paragraph provides the thesis statement.

Each **middle** paragraph provides detail and support for the thesis statement. Writer occasionally uses transitions between paragraphs to link ideas. Flow could be smoother.

Writer uses embedded quotes to support ideas and advance the thesis statement. Most ideas are well developed.

Have students work in groups to rewrite the ending paragraph to focus on one theme, using supporting details from the other paragraphs to build a stronger ending to the essay.

**Organization is shown by use of transitions.**

Finally, the most important theme of the book is how wealth took Wang Lung from being a kind and humble man into the kind of people that he despised. When he first comes for O-lan at the rich home of the Hwangs, he feels humilated and embarrassed by his humble position. Then when he goes back to his farm, he feels comfortable again and he doesn't have to measure his worth by what he sees around him. As Wang Lung gets richer and richer, he moves away from seeing his value from within and begins to judge himself the way he thinks others view him. He begins to dress in fine clothes and spend more money. Finally he buys the Hwang's mansion, which they lost because of there decadent lifestyle. When O-lan, who never changed, dies, Wang Lung really looses his connection to his former self. However, whenever Wang Lung goes back to his farm and works on the land, he feels "healed." But it's too late for his sons to understand this feeling. Wang Lung's family is heading the same downward route as the Hwangs.

**Errors in conventions do not detract. Reader can understand meaning.**

The Good Earth was a fascinating story about the people of China, but beneath the story are universal themes about women and beauty, traditional and modern life, and wealth versus happiness. That's why this book won a Pulitzer Prize for the author and will stay a classic for all time.

**Conclusion does not effectively add to essay.**

Response

---

**Differentiated Instruction: English Language Learners**

⭐ **ELPS** 4F, 4H, 4K

| **ELP Level** **Beginning** | **ELP Level** **Intermediate** | **ELP Level** **Advanced/Advanced High** |
|---|---|---|
| Read the essay aloud as students follow along. Then have students work with a partner to identify two themes discussed in the essay. | Using shared reading, have the students read the essay aloud. Then have them identify the writer's thesis and the details in the middle paragraph that support the thesis. | Have students read the essay silently. Then have them work with a partner to analyze the side notes and summarize why the essay received a score point of 3. |

⭐ **ELPS 4F** Use support from peers/teachers to enhance and confirm understanding; **4H** Read silently with increasing ease and comprehension for longer periods; **4K** Demonstrate comprehension and expand reading skills by employing analytical skills/ evaluating written information and performing critical analyses

Ask students if they agree with the score given to this essay. In general, students should agree that it deserved a score of 2, although some may argue for one score point higher or lower. Discuss disagreements, being sure to emphasize how the writer failed to address the five writing traits effectively.

**292**

**Writing that fits a score of 2 is somewhat effective.**

### Real Love Versus Money

The beginning gives an idea of the thesis statement.

*The Good Earth*, by Pearl Buck, the main charcter Wang Lung has two loves, his land and his wife. By the end of the book he looses both of them. That is what the book is about, a man who gets rich and forgot what he came from and he suffers for it.

Wang Lung married an ugly woman named O-lan and he's upset because she has big feet. They weren't bound to be small, But Wang Lung began to soon appreciate O-lan she is quiet and she works hard in the house and also helps him in the field. He doesn't think he loves her, but he appreciates her and with her help, he begins to make money.

**Middle** paragraphs provide a summary, not an analysis. Writing is difficult to understand. Errors in conventions lead to confusion.

Then Wang Lung falls in love with a beautiful woman named Lotus and he feels embarressed about being a farmer. He begins to ignore O-lan to be with Lotus and finally brings her to the house to live. And he also starts to loose his felings for his land. He uses hired people to do the work for him and his family.

Wang Lung begins to change when he moved away from O-lan and land. Then he cuts off his pigtail and starts worrying about he looks to other people. But when O-lan got sick, he feels terrible because he probably cares for her. And when she died he understands what she really meant to him. Then O-lan dies, Wang Lung moves to a big house in the city. He lived like a rich man. His sons never had to work on the land and want to sell it.

Details are vague and do not support thesis.

The person who wrote the book showed me how Wang Lung used to appreciate humble pleasures when he was poor. He appreciated his good, but plain wife, and working hard on his land. Having money changed him for the worse Life back on the farm is hard but Wang Lung ends with nothing to do all day but deal with his family troubles. When he decides to move everyone to the old House of Hwang. Wang Lung's family has become like the one he despised when he went to bring O-lan home.

Essay lacks **conclusion**.

Wang Lung doesn't have much to be happy about, "The land did again its healing work." As an old man, Wang Lung returns to live out his life on the old farm. He still loves the land, "It is the end of a family—when they begin to sell the land."

Step through this essay with students and discuss why this essay is ineffective. Ask students to evaluate what changes they would suggest to address each of the writing traits. Focus especially on organization and development of ideas.  **DIFFERENTIATE INSTRUCTION**

Writing that fits a score of 1 is not effective.

The **beginning** does not provide a thesis. Author's name is misspelled.

**Middle** paragraphs provide confusing summary; no analysis provided. Errors throughout make the essay confusing for readers.

Essay lacks focus, coherence, and organization.

Response

### The Good Earth

*The Good Earth* is a book by Perl Buck. It's about some Chinese farmer who married a woman who's a slave. They had a family he made more and more money from his land. He became rich and lived in the mansion that was owned by the rich people where his wife was a slave but he isn't as happy as he was when he was poor.

The book starts off with Wang Lung' on his wedding day. He's poor so the only woman he can efford to marry is a slave. Her name is O-lan. He's unhappy that she's not pretty but his father wants him to marry a girl who will work in the fields and bare lots of kids. She is strong and helps Wang Lung in the field and she hardly even stops working to have her first baby. That impressed me and Wang Lung was happy.

Soon Wang Lung gets more money. Hes able to buy more land from the rich people. But then there's a drout and Wang Lng loses all his money. The family and him have to go live in a city so they won't starve. But Wang Lung wants go home. He ends up getting some silver and he's able to finally go home.

Wang Lung gets rich again and he bys more land so after a while he doesn't have to work anymore and then he hires people who can work. He gets a pretty young woman instead of O-lan and O-lan then gets unhappy but she still helps Wang Lung and is faithful. Even when she is sick and dying she thinks of him. And when she dies he feels her loss.

By the end of the book Wang Lung is so rich he bys the mansion of the rich people. But he's not the same man he was. He is more concerned about being rich than about his land and then finally he goes back to his first house at the end but its too late so after he dies his sons are going to sell the land

Life back on the farm gets harder, with lots of stuff to do and problems so Wang Lung hires people and he ends up with nothing to except family troubles. and decides to move everyone to an old mansion. Wang Lung is unhappy so he goes back to being a farmer.

---

## Differentiated Instruction: English Language Learners

**ELPS** 3G, 4D, 4F, 4G, 4J, 4K, 5G

| ELP Level **Beginning** | ELP Level **Intermediate** | ELP Level **Advanced/Advanced High** |
|---|---|---|
| Provide students with a short, adapted opening paragraph of an essay about the novel. Preteach vocabulary and read together. Discuss whether it presents a clear thesis. | Provide students with a separate, adapted one paragraph response essay about the novel. Students read it with a partner and assign it a score point, focusing on the first three traits. | Have students read another literary response essay with a partner and assign it a score point. Students should write a brief explanation of their score. |

**ELPS** **3G** Express opinions and ideas ranging from communicating short phrases to participating in discussions; **4D** Use prereading supports to enhance comprehension of written text/graphic organizers, illustrations, and topic-related vocabulary; **4F** Use support from peers/teachers to enhance understanding and develop vocabulary; **4G** Demonstrate comprehension of increasingly complex English/participating in shared reading; **4J** Demonstrate comprehension and expand reading skills by employing inferential skills/predicting, making connections between ideas, drawing conclusions from text, and finding supporting evidence; **4K** Demonstrate comprehension and expand reading skills by employing analytical skills; **5G** Explain with increasing specificity and detail/writing Use support from peers/teachers to enhance and confirm understanding

## Evaluating and Reflecting on Your Writing

Encourage students to read through their written reflections regularly to monitor their progress and to use them as a basis for setting new goals for their writing. **DIFFERENTIATE INSTRUCTION ↘**

**294**

# Evaluating and Reflecting on Your Writing

Reflect on and score your finished analysis of a theme by completing each starter sentence below. These comments will help you check your progress as a writer.

---

### My Response to Literature

1. The focus of my essay is the theme of the novel, and my thesis statement is . . .

2. The organizational pattern that I chose is appropriate for my purpose, audience, and context because . . .

3. The embedded quotes and relevant details from the text that I used as I developed my ideas emphasize . . .

4. The variety of sentence structures in my essay shows . . .

5. One question I still have about writing an analysis of a theme is . . .

6. Right now I would describe my writing ability as . . . (excellent, good, fair, poor)

---

**Differentiated Instruction:**
**English Language Learners**

**ELPS** 1E, 3D, 3E, 3G

| ELP Level **Beginning** | ELP Level **Intermediate** | ELP Level **Advanced/Advanced High** |
|---|---|---|
| Have students work with a partner to read and answer the first three questions about their own writing as well as their partner's. | Have students focus on the fourth question and check their writing for grade- and audience-appropriate sentence lengths and structures. | Prompt students to answer questions thoughtfully and accurately. Have them work with a partner to assess their own and each other's progress in writing well. |

**ELPS 1E** Internalize new basic and academic language by using and reusing it/writing; **3D** Speak using grade-level content area vocabulary/new words and academic language proficiency; **3E** Share information in cooperative learning interactions; **3G** Express opinions and ideas ranging from communicating short phrases to participating in discussions;

## Interpretive Response
# Interpreting a Nonfiction Text

Nonfiction texts include stories about the lives of real people, the exploration of real places, and descriptions of real events. Nonfiction is written to convey factual information, and you can learn a great deal from reading nonfiction texts. Writers of nonfiction, however, can shape information in accordance with their own views and attitudes. When you read nonfiction, you need to examine it carefully to detect biases, notice gaps in the information, and identify errors in logic. Nonfiction includes a diverse range of writing—newspaper articles, letters, essays, biographies, speeches, true-life adventure stories, and more.

In this chapter, you'll read an essay and a sample interpretation that presents a detailed analysis of the author's ideas. After that, you'll be asked to choose another nonfiction text and write your own interpretation of it.

## Writing Guidelines

**Subject:** Interpretation of nonfiction
**Purpose:** To analyze a writer's ideas
**Form:** Literary analysis
**Audience:** Classmates

"Literature adds to reality, it does not simply describe it."
—C. S. Lewis

### Resources

**Copy Masters (see Appendix)**

- T-chart (TE pp. 296, 299)
- Details chart (TE p. 296)

**Interpreting a Nonfiction Text**

### Objective

- apply what has been learned about interpreting literature to interpret a nonfiction text

Encourage students to note how writers of nonfiction shape the information they convey. Also, encourage students to keep a reading journal to record personal responses and thoughts about the selections.

## Sample Nonfiction Text

Work through the sample nonfiction text with the class. Suggest the following tips for analyzing a nonfiction work.

- Read the selection carefully, looking for details and ideas that can be used to write a literary analysis.
- Identify key words, phrases, and details.
- Use a T-chart, details chart, or other graphic organizer (see TE Appendix) to gather details.
- Identify the main theme of the text.
- Draft a thesis statement based on the theme and key ideas in the text.

⭐ ELPS 4K

## Sample Nonfiction Text

From "On Liars" by Michel de Montaigne

I know quite well that grammarians make a distinction between telling an untruth and lying. They say that to tell an untruth is to say something that is false, but that we suppose to be true, and that the meaning of lying is to go against one's conscience, and that consequently it applies to those who say the opposite of what they know; it is of them I am speaking. . . .

Now liars either invent the whole thing, or they disguise and alter an actual fact. If they disguise and alter, it is hard for them not to get mixed up when they refer to the same story again and again because, the real facts having been the first to lodge in the memory and impress themselves upon it by way of consciousness and knowledge, they will hardly fail to spring into the mind and dislodge the false version, which cannot have as firm or assured a foothold. . . .

Lying is indeed an accursed vice. We are men, and we have relations with one another by speech. If we recognized the horror and gravity of an untruth, we should more justifiably punish it with fire than any other crime. I commonly find people taking the most ill-advised pains to correct their children for their harmless faults and worrying them about heedless acts which leave no trace and have no consequences.

Lying—and in a lesser degree stubbornness—are, in my opinion, the only faults whose birth and progress we should consistently oppose. They grow with a child's growth, and once the tongue has got the knack of lying, it is difficult to imagine how impossible it is to correct it. Whence it happens that we find some otherwise excellent men subject to this fault and enslaved by it. I have a decent lad as my tailor, whom I have never heard to utter a single truth, even when it would have been to his advantage.

If, like the truth, falsehood had only one face, we should know better where we are, for we should then take the opposite of what a liar said to be the truth. But the opposite of a truth has a hundred thousand shapes and a limitless field.

There are a thousand ways of missing the bull's-eye, only one of hitting it. . . .

**ELPS 4K** Demonstrate comprehension and expand reading skills by employing analytical skills/evaluating written information and performing critical analyses

## Student Response

In the following essay, student Dominic Montano wrote a careful, detailed interpretation of Montaigne's essay "On Liars." Before he began to write his own essay, Dominic read Montaigne's essay carefully and analyzed each paragraph.

---

### "An Accursed Vice"

**Beginning**
The first paragraph builds up to the thesis statement (underlined).

Montaigne's essay "On Liars," brings up some interesting questions. Should we "more justifiably punish [lying] with fire than any other crime"? It seems as though Montaigne might be exaggerating the evils of lying until he defines it: "the meaning of lying is to go against one's conscience." If that is the definition of lying, then perhaps <u>Montaigne is right to believe that there is nothing more important than telling the truth.</u>

**Middle**
The middle paragraphs develop the writer's argument, using a personal anecdote and a reflection.

One of Montaigne's strongest points is his example of children. According to him, parents need to "consistently oppose" any signs of lying from a child, more than any other act. Whether trying to get out of trouble or to get a special treat, children quickly realize that lying can be in their best interest. That could lead to more serious consequences because lies "grow with a child's growth, and once the tongue has got the knack of lying, it is difficult to imagine how impossible it is to correct it.".

If a lie must go "against one's conscience," it's crucial for parents to explain why lying is wrong. Without understanding what is right and what is wrong, a child might not feel that pang of guilt when he tells a lie. Instead the child might feel gleeful that he got away with something that turned out to be beneficial for him. Montaigne is right when he says that that sort of behavior might be difficult to correct.

The real problem may be that repeated lying changes a person. Like Montaigne's tailor, a liar might

---

## Student Response

Ask students if they think the writer successfully interpreted the nonfiction text. (Most students will say *yes* because the writer clearly explains that he agrees with Montaigne's feelings about lying. The writer expresses his own feelings about liars and lying, using the first-person point of view to connect these feelings with a personal experience.) ✔ **DIFFERENTIATE INSTRUCTION**

⭐ **ELPS** 4J, 4K

---

## Differentiated Instruction: English Language Learners

⭐ **ELPS** 4F, 4J, 4K

| ELP Level **Beginning** | ELP Level **Intermediate** | ELP Level **Advanced/Advanced High** |
|---|---|---|
| Read the sample text and the sample student response as a group. Analyze each paragraph to ensure student comprehension. | Have students read the text and sample student response in small groups. Assist groups and provide needed vocabulary for their discussions about the effectiveness of the student response. | Encourage students to read the sample text and the student response on their own. Prompt them as necessary to ensure they comprehend the main ideas in each. |

 **ELPS 4F** Use support from peers/teachers to read grade-appropriate content area text and to enhance understanding; **4J** Demonstrate comprehension and expand reading skills by employing inferential skills/predicting, making connections between ideas, drawing conclusions from text, and finding supporting evidence; **4K** Demonstrate comprehension and expand reading skills by employing analytical skills/evaluating written information and performing critical analyses

**Respond to the reading.**

**Answers**

**Focus and Coherence 1.** The thesis statement is *There is nothing more important than telling the truth.* It is introduced with quotes about lying from the essay "On Liars."
**2.** The writer ties the conclusion back to the introductory paragraph with additional quotes about lying and truthfulness from the essay "On Liars."

**Organization 3.** The middle paragraphs relate to each other in that they each refer to a quote from the Montaigne essay, and the paragraphs are built around those quotes. **4.** Transition words and phrases include *According to him, Instead, Like, Worse, But,* and *Ultimately.*

**Development of Ideas 5.** The writer uses quotes as well as summaries of the ideas from the essay to support the thesis. **6.** The writer uses the following quotations: *more justifiably punish* [lying] *with fire than any other crime; the meaning of lying is to go against one's conscience; consistently oppose; grow with a child's growth, and once the tongue has got the knack of lying, it is difficult to imagine how impossible it is to correct it; horror and gravity of an untruth; If, like the truth, falsehood had only one face, we should know better where we are. . . . But the opposite of a truth has a hundred thousand shapes and a limitless field.* **7.** The quotations serve the purpose of illustrating that the idea of the thesis is not just the student's, but that it is supported by the essay. It brings validity to the student's essay.

**Voice 8.** The writer primarily uses a thesis obtained from the essay that is supported with quotes from the essay as well. These quotes are integrated and interwoven into the writer's own words so it flows smoothly and logically. **9.** Some of the literary terms that the writer uses to make his voice sound knowledgeable include *essay, definition, points,* and *metaphor.*

get so used to doing it, that he can't tell the truth even when it's to his advantage. That kind of person can never be trusted or taken seriously. Worse, constant liars might not have any conscience left to be concerned about the consequences of their lies. What Montaigne calls the "horror and gravity of an untruth," can lead to terrible behavior, like companies cheating customers, politicians deceiving their citizens, innocent people being killed.

   Montaigne clearly demonstrates the power of truthfulness when he states: "If, like the truth, falsehood had only one face, we should know better where we are....But the opposite of a truth has a hundred thousand shapes and a limitless field." His metaphor shows how many ways there are to lie, but how impossible it is to defend any of them. Ultimately the truth must always prevail.

> **Ending**
> The ending revisits the thesis and shares a final insight.

**Respond to the reading.** Answer the following questions about the student response.

**Focus and Coherence** (1) What is the thesis statement, and how is it introduced? (2) How does the student writer tie the conclusion back to the main point introduced in the introductory paragraph?

**Organization** (3) How do the middle paragraphs relate to each other? (4) What transition words and phrases does the writer use to link paragraphs and connect ideas?

**Development of Ideas** (5) What evidence from the Montaigne essay does the student writer use to support his thesis statement? (6) What quotations does the student writer use from Montaigne's essay? (7) What purpose do the quotations serve?

**Voice** (8) What rhetorical devices does the student writer use to emphasize his points and engage the reader? (9) What literary terms does the student writer use to make his voice sound knowledgeable?

# Prewriting Planning Your Writing

In your interpretation of a nonfiction text, you will be developing a critical analysis of the writer's ideas. Remember the meaning of *analysis*: the separation of a whole into its parts for individual study. The meaning of *interpret* is slightly different: to explain the meaning of something.

Your essay needs to be long enough to analyze and explain the selection. You will need to include sufficient evidence and details from the text to support your controlling idea thoroughly. As you choose your nonfiction text, keep in mind your audience, the purpose, and the genre, or form, your writing will take. It is also important to keep in mind the context of your writing, as well as the context of the nonfiction piece that you have chosen for interpretation. Keep in mind the following:

- **Choose a nonfiction text that interests you.**
  Your essay needs to show interest in the text, and you should convey both your interest and your understanding to your audience.
- **Decide on the genre of nonfiction that you want to analyze.**
  Remember that there are a variety of nonfiction genres. Essays, letters, magazine articles, biographies, and adventure stories are just some that you can choose from for your essay.

## Choosing a Topic

After thinking about the form of your essay, make a chart of possible topics. This will help you find a suitable text for analysis. Use a two-column chart or a simple outline like the one below to guide you.

- Magazine articles:
- Historical letters:
- Biographies:
- Essays:
- Adventure stories:

### Focus on the Texas Traits

**Development of Ideas** Remember that your analysis must go beyond a summary or literal analysis. As you plan your essay, make notes about the nonfiction piece you are analyzing. Identify its thesis statement or controlling idea. Note how the author supports his or her position and develops ideas. Look for errors in logic and for any biases that the author may have. Make note of any rhetorical devices the author uses.

*(Response)*

# Prewriting

## Planning Your Writing

Discuss various genres of nonfiction work with the class. Encourage students to select an appropriate nonfiction text. You may want to supply several suggested texts or plan for library time for students to identify appropriate nonfiction texts. Tell students that they should look for topics that interest them.

## Choosing a Topic

Provide students a T-chart (see TE Appendix) for their use in identifying a suitable topic. If students are having trouble choosing a topic, suggest that they freewrite for 5 to 10 minutes on possible topics of interest. ✓**DIFFERENTIATE INSTRUCTION**

**TEKS** 10.15C(i)

### Focus on the Texas Traits

**Development of Ideas**
Students may find it helpful to develop various graphic organizers to help them gather details for their literary analysis. Remind students that graphic organizers can take many shapes. Students may also organize information on note cards or in a sectioned notebook. To plan their analysis, they will want to gather useful quotations and examples of the author's use of rhetorical and stylistic devices.

---

## Differentiated Instruction: English Language Learners

**ELPS** 1A, 4F

| ELP Level **Beginning** | ELP Level **Intermediate** | ELP Level **Advanced/Advanced High** |
|---|---|---|
| Supply adapted nonfiction texts for students to analyze. Encourage them to use a graphic organizer for planning their writing. | Prompt students to choose a nonfiction text that they are comfortable reading. Encourage students to use a graphic organizer for planning their writing. | Encourage students to challenge themselves with their selection of a nonfiction text. Assist students in topic selection to ensure it is appropriate to their abilities. |
| Use pages 624–625 | Use pages 624–625 | |

**TEKS** **10.15C(i)** Write a response to expository text that extends beyond a summary and literal analysis; **ELPS** **1A** Use prior knowledge and experiences to understand meanings in English; **4F** Use visual and contextual support to develop grasp of language structures/use support from peers/teachers to read grade-appropriate content area text and develop grasp of language structures

## Prewriting
### Planning Your Writing

Remind students that all the steps that they take in prewriting are important and that they should use the materials they have gathered to draft their essay.

### Organizing Your Essay

Encourage students to take time to organize their ideas and conduct any needed research before they begin to write. As students develop their drafts they can analyze the details and order them in ways that will best support their theses. Remind students that using transitions in timed responses will improve the flow of their writing and help them more effectively convey their meaning.

### Analyzing Nonfiction Text

If students are having trouble getting started with their analysis, suggest that they freewrite answers to the questions given, focusing on the purpose of rhetorical and stylistic devices. They may initially have multiple answers to the questions but, as they read more or think more about it, certain answers will gain more clarity.

**TEKS** 10.15C(ii), 10.15(iii)

**Plan your essay.** Encourage students to use a graphic organizer when planning their essay. Students may also find it helpful to have a list of transition words on hand.

---

## Prewriting Planning Your Writing

The following tips will help you plan your interpretation. Also refer to the planning that you did on the previous page.

### Organizing Your Essay

In your interpretation, be sure to include relevant details and supporting evidence from the text that you have chosen. Citing relevant evidence will be critical as you develop your own analysis. If you find errors in logic or believe that the author shows bias, use quotations from the text to support your explanation. As you plan, be sure to consider the following elements.

- **Start with an effective introductory paragraph that presents your controlling idea. Your conclusion should revisit the thesis statement and tie the essay together.**
- **As you organize the details and relevant evidence from the text, consider the relative value of the specific ideas, facts, and data that you are going to include in your essay to support your thesis.**
- **Plan to include rhetorical devices, such as quotations or an analogy, to engage your reader.**
- **When developing your response in a timed situation, plan to use transitions to connect your ideas. Using transitions will improve the flow of your writing and help you convey your meaning.**

### Analyzing Nonfiction Text

When you plan your interpretation, you should carefully analyze the nonfiction text that you have chosen. First, look at the author's purpose for writing. For the most part, nonfiction text will not have characters, nor will it have a plot arc. Take notes as you read the text, and use them as you write. Look for the following, and answer these questions.

- How has the author structured his ideas?
- What rhetorical devices has the author used? What purpose do they serve?
- What stylistic devices has the author used? These would include metaphorical or figurative language, anecdotes, allusions, and irony.

**Plan your essay.** Use the prewriting tips above and from the previous page to plan and organize your essay. Decide which rhetorical and stylistic devices you are going to use and what kinds of transitions will best connect your ideas.

---

**TEKS** **10.15C(ii)** Write a response to expository text that addresses writing skills for an analytical essay and using embedded quotations; **10.15C(iii)** Write a response to expository text that analyzes the effects of stylistic and rhetorical devices

**TEKS** 10.15C(i)–
10.15C(iii)

## Drafting Creating Your First Draft

The following tips will help you write your interpretation. Also refer to the planning that you did on the previous pages.

### Writing Your Beginning Paragraph

The **beginning** paragraph should introduce the nonfiction text that you have chosen. Give both the title and the author of the piece. Present your controlling idea, the thesis statement, completely and clearly.

- **Explain why the topic is important.**
  *…then perhaps Montaigne is right to believe that there is nothing more important than telling the truth.*
- **Ask a rhetorical question or share a quotation.**
  *Should we "more justifiably punish [lying] with fire than any other crime"?*

### Writing Your Middle Paragraphs

The **middle** paragraphs should build your interpretation in a logical way. Consider the relative value of the ideas, facts, and data that you are going to include as you create an organizational pattern that is appropriate for your purpose and audience. Use transitions to connect sentences in your paragraphs and to move your essay smoothly from one paragraph to the next.

- **Organize your ideas in a logical, coherent way.**
- **Use relevant evidence and details from the text to support your position.**
- **As appropriate, use embedded quotations to emphasize your points.**
- **Identify faulty logic in the text and discuss why you believe the author introduced these errors.**
- **Identify and discuss any biases that you see in the text.**

### Writing Your Ending Paragraph

The **ending** paragraph should tie the essay together into a coherent whole.

- **Summarize your thesis and create a memorable closing.**
  *Ultimately, the truth must always prevail.*

Draft

**Write your first draft.** Use your prewriting work and the tips above to develop your essay.

*(side tab:)* Response

## Drafting

### Creating Your First Draft

Remind students as they begin writing that every paragraph should have a topic sentence followed by supporting details and a closing sentence that acts as a transition or connection to the ideas in the next paragraph.

### Writing Your Beginning Paragraph

Model for students simple formats for writing the beginning paragraph such as *The _____, written by _____, is about _____.* Explain that a simple sentence like this is a good way to start the writing process even though they will likely come back and change it later.

### Writing Your Middle Paragraphs

Make a list of the important elements for middle paragraphs and display it prominently so that students can continue to refer to it throughout their writing process. Emphasize the points about using evidence and quotations to build their points logically and completely.

### Writing Your Ending Paragraph

Share with students that they could begin their ending paragraph by simply restating their thesis. They can then build upon and rephrase this statement so that it is not redundant but does tie the beginning and the ending together.

 **TEKS** 10.15C(i)–10.15C(iii)

**Write your first draft.** Encourage students to refer to the prewriting work they have done while drafting to ensure that they do not get off topic. Remind students that the goal of drafting is to get their ideas on paper in a reasonably structured way. ☑ **DIFFERENTIATE INSTRUCTION**

---

**TEKS** **10.15C(i)** Write a response to expository and literary text that extends beyond a summary and literal analysis; **10.15C(ii)** Write a response to expository and literary text that addresses writing skills for an analytical essay and using embedded quotations; **10.15C(iii)** Write a response to expository and literary text that analyzes the effects of stylistic and rhetorical devices; **ELPS 5B** Write using newly acquired basic and content-based grade-level vocabulary; **5F** Write using a variety of grade-appropriate sentence lengths, patterns, and connecting words/combine in increasingly accurate ways

## Revising
### Improving Your Writing

Encourage students to address each of the writing elements separately, asking themselves the questions provided and rewriting if they have not adequately met the writing requirements. Have students exchange their essays and critique each other's work.

**Revise your work.** Remind students that incorporating feedback from others as well as evaluating their own work is an important step in revising.

⭐ **TEKS** 10.13C

## Editing
### Checking Your Writing

Tell students to make corrections on their response neatly and be sure to check carefully for grammar, punctuation, and spelling; and to use the conventions checklist. **DIFFERENTIATE INSTRUCTION** ↘

⭐ **TEKS** 10.13D; **ELPS** 5D

**Check your response.** Reassure students that even great writers revise and rewrite many times. So, likewise, their work may take several revisions before it is ready to be published.

⭐ **TEKS** **10.13C** Revise drafts/improve style, word choice, figurative language, sentence variety, and subtlety of meaning and rethink how well the purpose, audience, and genre have been addressed; **10.13D** Edit drafts for grammar, mechanics, and spelling; **ELPS 5C** Spell familiar words/employ spelling patterns and rules with increasing accuracy; **5D** Edit writing for standard grammar and usage/subject-verb and pronoun agreement and appropriate verb tenses; **5F** Write using a variety of grade-appropriate sentence lengths and patterns in increasingly accurate ways;

---

## Revising Improving Your Writing

Always review your writing. Make any changes and corrections neatly. Use the following questions to help you revise your response.

- **Focus and Coherence:** Does my introductory paragraph contain my controlling idea? Do the details and evidence support the thesis? Does the conclusion tie the essay together?

- **Development of Ideas:** Have I adequately analyzed the nonfiction text? Have I supported my ideas with relevant evidence, specific details, and embedded quotations?

- **Organization:** Have I included a beginning, a middle, and an ending? Does each paragraph have a focus? Have I used transitions so that paragraphs flow smoothly from one to the next?

- **Voice:** Do I sound clear in my thinking? Have I used literary terms to express my ideas? Do I sound knowledgeable about the selection that I have analyzed?

**Revise your work.** Answer the questions above and revise your work as needed.

## Editing Checking Your Writing

Check your final draft for grammar, sentence structure, capitalization, punctuation, and spelling.

### Conventions

_____ **1.** Have I used correct and consistent verb tenses?

_____ **2.** Have I correctly used a variety of sentence structures?

_____ **3.** Have I capitalized all proper nouns and first words of sentences?

_____ **4.** Have I put quotation marks around the exact words that I quoted from the selection?

_____ **5.** Have I checked the spelling in my work?

**Check your response.** Read over your work, looking for errors in conventions. Make any needed corrections neatly.

---

### Differentiated Instruction: English Language Learners

⭐ **ELPS** 5C, 5D, 5F

| ELP Level **Beginning** | ELP Level **Intermediate** | ELP Level **Advanced/Advanced High** |
|---|---|---|
| Encourage students to check their spelling carefully for accuracy and to employ spelling patterns and rules. | Have students edit their writing for correct grammar and usage. Encourage them to pay particular attention to verb tenses. | Have students check their writing to ensure they have used a variety of grade-appropriate sentence lengths and patterns. |

## Analyzing a Poem

303

### Objective
- apply what has been learned about interpreting literature to analyze a poem

Encourage students to note details in the selection that pertain to the aesthetic effects of stylistic and rhetorical devices used in poetry. Also, encourage students to keep a journal to record personal responses and thoughts about the reading selections.

## Interpretive Response
# Analyzing a Poem

A good poem can make us look at the world in a new way. After reading a poem, you may find yourself remembering images that "spoke" to you. When you read a poem closely and analyze it, you will discover how carefully it was crafted.

An analysis goes beyond a mere summary; it explains the way that a poem communicates experiences. You examine a poem's form, the way the words appear on the page. You might consider meter and rhyme. Much of the power of poetry depends upon rhythm—the pattern of syllables in each line. Poets use rhythm to emphasize ideas and to create a mood. Equally important is imagery in a poem—the use of words to create sensory experiences. Figurative language can convey meanings beyond the literal meaning of words. Through these devices and others, poets help us gain a deeper understanding of the beauty of the English language.

In this chapter, you'll read a student analysis of a poem. Then you'll be asked to write your own poetry analysis.

### Writing Guidelines

**Subject:** Analyzing a Poem
**Purpose:** To explain the aesthetic effects of stylistic and rhetorical devices of the poem
**Form:** Response to literature essay
**Audience:** Classmates

"The poet is a liar who always speaks the truth."

—Jean Cocteau

### Resources

**Copy Masters (see Appendix)**

- T-chart (TE p. 306)
- Quick list (TE p. 308)
- Details chart (TE p. 306)
- Venn diagram (TE p. 306)

## Analyzing a Poem

Review the sample analysis of a poem with students. Ask students how the writer used the writing traits in developing a highly effective analysis. Some suggestions include:

- The beginning and ending work well together.
- The writer clearly stated a thesis and coherently developed it.
- The writer chose an organizational pattern that is appropriate.
- The writer analyzed the stylistic and rhetorical devices used in the poem to develop its theme.
- The writer's analysis extended beyond a literal analysis.
- Quotations were effectively used to support the writer's thesis and main points.

Encourage students to use this as a model for their own analysis. **DIFFERENTIATE INSTRUCTION ⬐**

⭐ **TEKS** 10.13B, 10.15A(i), 10.15A(iii), 10.15A(v),10.15C(i)-10.15C(iii)

⭐ **TEKS** **10.13B** Structure ideas in a sustained way; **10.15A(i)** Write an analytical essay that includes an introductory and concluding paragraph; **10.15A(iii)** Write an analytical essay that includes an idea or thesis; **10.15A(v)** Write an analytical essay that includes relevant evidence and details; **10.15C(i)** Write a response to expository and literary text that extends beyond a summary and literal analysis; **10.15C(ii)** Write a response to expository and literary text that addresses writing skills for an analytical essay and using embedded quotations; **10.15C(iii)** Write a response to expository and literary text that analyzes the effects of stylistic and rhetorical devices

---

**TEKS** 10.13B, 10.15A(i), 10.15A(iii), 10.15(v), 10.15C(i)–10.15C(iii)

## Analyzing a Poem

In the following essay, student Gabriel Ferro wrote a detailed analysis of Walt Whitman's poem "O Captain, My Captain."

### Elegy for a President

> Student introduces poem and provides background information. Thesis is introduced.

Walt Whitman wrote "O Captain! My Captain!" after the assassination of Abraham Lincoln. This short, three-stanza poem expresses the deep grief the poet felt when he heard the news that the president had died. Whitman uses the metaphor of a ship and its captain to represent the country and the president. He then uses these strong visual images to create a moving homage to President Lincoln that is almost like watching a tragic film.

In the first stanza, Whitman sets up the metaphors that carry through until the end. The ship that "has weather'd every rack" is the United States, just recovering from the "fearful trip" of the Civil War. The next line describes the mood of the country after the war and the hope people feel now that the worst is behind them: "the prize we sought is won, The port is near, the bells I hear, the people all exulting." Then, after the first impression of triumph, Whitman expresses the shock of finding the ship's captain, Abraham Lincoln, "Fallen cold and dead."

> Embedded quotes support analysis of stylistic devices in the poem. Writer provides detailed analysis of structure and aesthetic effects of poetic, stylistic, and rhetorical devices.

Once the reader understands that the poem is about President Lincoln and the state of the country after the Civil War, the poem takes on a more tragic tone than it would if it were read without understanding the background. It is easy to picture the president who had been shot and was dying at Ford's Theatre when Whitman exclaims: "But O heart! heart! heart!/ O the bleeding drops of red,/ Where on the deck my Captain lies, Fallen cold and dead." Every time Whitman repeats "O Captain! my Captain!" his anguish gets deeper. The narrator cradles the fallen captain's head with his arm. He calls him "dear father." It's clear that Whitman feels that the country has lost a guiding caring leader.

Throughout the poem, Whitman contrasts the loud colorful celebration of the people on the shore with the still captain on the deck. He moves between the two different feelings by changing the rhythm and the rhyming scheme. The first four lines of each stanza rhyme every two lines. The last four lines have fewer beats and rhyme every other line. The first two stanzas start with the celebration on shore then abruptly change their rhythm and rhyme when Whitman turns to the fallen

---

### Differentiated Instruction: Advanced Learners

Challenge students to find out more about authors mentioned in this section by conducting library research or using the Internet. Invite them to share their findings in a creative way, such as making a poster or a presentation.

Analysis of aesthetic effects of poet's use of stylistic and rhetorical devices continues. Organizational pattern works well for purpose, audience, and context. Embedded quotations support analysis and show rhetorical devices used by poet.

Writer **concludes** analysis with a personal opinion.

leader. The last stanza is different because it begins with the image of the dead captain. Then when it changes style, it briefly moves back to the celebration, but ends again on the fallen captain.

Whitman structures the poem almost like scenes in a movie. First you watch the victorious ship entering the harbor: "While follow eyes the steady keel, the vessel grim and daring." This is followed by a quick cut to the horror on the ship of seeing their dead captain: "But O heart! heart! heart!" Next you see the people on shore excitedly waiting for their hero to emerge from the ship: "For you bouquets and ribbon'd wreaths—for you the shores a-crowding,/For you they call, the swaying mass, their eager faces turning." But then Whitman cuts back again to the sad scene on the deck: "It is some dream that on the deck,/You've fallen cold and dead." In the final scene, the focus is completely on the people grieving around their leader on the ship. The celebration is now in the background.

Whitman has created what looks like a simple poem on the surface. When you look at the symbolism behind it, though, it has a much greater impact. His imagery and techniques draw in the reader so that you feel like you are almost watching the action. I could feel the grief of the nation that was emerging from darkness of war only to be shattered by the tragedy of their leader's death.

*Response*

 **Respond to the reading.** Answer the following questions.

**Focus and Coherence** (1) How is the thesis statement introduced? **Organization** (2) How are the middle paragraphs structured? (3) How is the organization appropriate for the purpose, audience, and context of the essay? **Development of Ideas** (4) What purpose do the embedded quotes serve? (5) Do the examples from the poem support the thesis? **Voice** (6) What devices does the writer use to sound knowledgeable? (7) What imagery does the writer create in the analysis?

 **Literature Connection.** You may wish to read Walt Whitman's letter to his mother, dated January 29, 1865 and his poem "The Artilleryman's Vision."

**TEKS** 10.15C(i)–10.15C(iii)

---

 **Respond to the reading.**

## Answers

**Focus and Coherence 1.** The thesis statement is introduced as an element in the opening paragraph. The development of the thesis also begins in the introductory paragraph.

**Organization 2.** The middle paragraphs are structured in parallel to the poem itself, analyzing the lines of the poem in their sequential order. **3.** This organization works well because it is a logical analysis to support the thesis. Each segment of the poem can be addressed, in order.

**Development of Ideas 4.** The embedded quotes serve the purpose of supporting the ideas and thesis of the author. **5.** Most of the examples from the poem do support the thesis, though there are some that could be used to support a different thesis.

**Voice 6.** The writer provides specific and sufficient details from the poem as well as specific historical facts in order to sound knowledgeable. These details and well-chosen quotations show that the writer has a clear understanding of the poem. **7.** The writer uses the imagery of the poem being like scenes or images from a movie to create the analysis.

☑ **DIFFERENTIATE INSTRUCTION**

⭐ **TEKS** 10.15C(i)-10.15C(iii)

### Literature Connections

Reading other works by Walt Whitman will give students additional insight into the work of this famous American poet. It may be useful for them to read "O Captain, My Captain!" as well.

---

## Differentiated Instruction: English Language Learners

**ELPS** 4F, 4K

| ELP Level **Beginning** | ELP Level **Intermediate** | ELP Level **Advanced/Advanced High** |
| --- | --- | --- |
| Read the analysis of the poem aloud with students. Then, reread the analysis, pointing out the thesis, the organization, and the ways in which examples are used. | Have students read the analysis aloud to ensure comprehension first. Then, work with students to read it again and identify the traits that make the essay highly effective. | Have students read the analysis silently. Then, ask students to read it again and write an explanation of why the essay is highly effective. |

**TEKS** **10.15C(i)** Write a response to expository and literary text that extends beyond a summary and literal analysis; **10.15C(ii)** Write a response to expository and literary text that addresses writing skills for an analytical essay and using embedded quotations; **10.15C(iii)** Write a response to expository and literary text that analyzes the effects of stylistic and rhetorical devices; **ELPS** **4F** Use support from peers/teachers to enhance and confirm understanding; **4K** Demonstrate comprehension and expand reading skills by employing analytical skills/evaluating written information and performing critical analyses

## Prewriting
### Planning Your Writing

Encourage students to select a poet or a poem that they are familiar with. Have some poems available for students to choose from if they do not have their own preferences.

### Freewriting

Students should begin by writing whatever words and thoughts come to them as they read the poem. Students should not be concerned about grammatical correctness and should let their thoughts flow freely.

⭐ **TEKS** 10.13B

### Choose Your Topic

After reading a few poems and freewriting, one poem and topic will likely appeal to the student. If nothing strikes them, suggest rereading the poems and seeing if any other ideas occur.

### Gather and Organize Details

Have students review their freewriting for the poem and topic they chose. Review the meanings of rhythm, rhyme, repetition, and diction; suggest students consider which of these is at work in the poem chosen. Then have them assess how these might work into their own analysis of the poem.

⭐ **TEKS** 10.13A, 10.15A(ii), 10.15C(i), 10.15C(iii)

**Plan your analysis.** Students should use the tips given on the page to choose their poem and begin to plan their essay.

Supply graphic organizers including a T-chart, a details chart, and a Venn diagram (see TE Appendix) for student use. Encourage students to use graphic organizers to plan their analysis.

---

**306**

 **TEKS** 10.13A, 10.13B, 10.15A(ii), 10.15C(i), 10.15C(iii)
**ELPS** 5E

## Prewriting Planning Your Writing

The first step in planning your essay is to choose a poem. Find a poem that you like and that will work for an analysis. Look for a poem that has figurative language, vivid imagery, and language that establishes a mood or theme that you can use in your analysis.

## Freewriting

When Gabriel read the poem "O Captain! My Captain!" he began to write some of his ideas about the poem. *Turbulent time in the United States; imagery of the Civil War; United States is the ship at sea; President Lincoln is the captain; repetition of line "Fallen cold and dead."*

Gabriel also liked the poem "Fifteen" by William Stafford. He wrote the following notes about it.

*Teenager dreams of being an adult; sees motorcycle with engine running; wants to ride it; helps owner; teenager knows he is not yet an adult.*

## Choose Your Topic

After completing the freewriting exercise, Gabriel chose "O Captain! My Captain!" because the figurative language appealed to him, and the poetic devices would lend themselves well to an analysis of meter, figurative language, and other poetic devices.

## Gather and Organize Details

Gabriel made the following chart so that he could organize details for his essay. He wanted to include stylistic devices, such as rhythm and rhyme, and rhetorical devices, such as repetition of lines and phrases, and diction, which is the word choice.

**Rhythm** "The port is near, the bells I hear, the people all exulting,"

**Rhyme** "The arm beneath your head!...You've fallen cold and dead."

**Repetition** "But O heart! heart! heart!"

**Diction** "While follow eyes the steady keel, the vessel grim and daring;"

 **Plan your analysis.** Use the tips above to choose a poem and plan your essay.

---

⭐ **TEKS** **10.13A** Plan a first draft by determining topics through a range of strategies; **10.13B** Structure ideas in a sustained way; **10.15A(ii)** Write an analytical essay that includes rhetorical devices; **10.15C(i)** Write a response to expository and literary text that extends beyond a summary and literal analysis; **10.15C(iii)** Write a response to expository and literary text that analyzes the effects of stylistic and rhetorical devices

# Prewriting Writing a Thesis Statement

In your analysis, you will be developing a critical analysis of the ideas and theme in the poem. You will also be developing a detailed analysis of the aesthetics of the rhetorical and stylistic devices the poet has used. When you analyze a poem, be sure to look at all the stylistic and rhetorical devices. These include meter and rhyming patterns, the use of language, and the imagery.

Your essay needs to be long enough to analyze the poem you have chosen. You will need to include details and quotations from the poem to support your controlling idea thoroughly. As you choose a poem, keep in mind your audience, the purpose, and the genre, or form, your writing will take. It is also important to keep in mind the context of your writing.

## Developing Your Thesis Statement

Now that you have chosen your poem and gathered and organized the details and quotations that you want to include, you are ready to write your thesis statement.

| Element | | Theme | | Thesis Statement |
|---|---|---|---|---|
| Stylistic and rhetorical devices | **+** | Assassination of President Lincoln | **=** | The poet Walt Whitman uses the metaphor of a ship and its captain and strong visual images to create a moving homage to President Lincoln that is almost like watching a tragic film. |

Response

**Write your thesis statement.** Using the poem you have chosen, the planning guide from the previous page, and the formula above, write the thesis statement for your analysis. Then write your introductory paragraph.

Prewrite

### Focus on the Texas Traits

**Development of Ideas** Remember that your analysis must go beyond a summary, a paraphrase, or a literal analysis. As you plan your essay, make notes about what you want to say in each paragraph. Draft the topic sentence for each paragraph, and then choose quotations from the poem that support the thesis and the paragraph topic sentences.

## Writing a Thesis Statement

If students are having trouble writing thesis statements, suggest that they freewrite two or three sentences that express opinions on their topics. Once they have written them, they can choose one to work with.

## Developing Your Thesis Statement

Encourage students to think about the poem on several levels: first the stylistic and rhetorical devices used and then the overriding theme. These together can be used to build the thesis statement. ✔DIFFERENTIATE INSTRUCTION

TEKS 10.13A, 10.15A(iii), 10.15C(i), 10.15C(iii)

**Write your thesis statement.** Make sure students take the time to develop their thesis statement before they attempt to write their introductory paragraph. Explain that attempting to write the introductory paragraph without first refining the thesis statement will lead to a rambling and incoherent beginning, and the essay will likely follow suit.

### Focus on the Texas Traits

**Development of Ideas**
Encourage students to outline their paragraphs prior to beginning to write. Outlining will help them clarify their ideas, build upon their theses, and stick to the topics.

---

## Differentiated Instruction:
### English Language Learners

ELPS 5B, 5F

| ELP Level **Beginning** | ELP Level **Intermediate** | ELP Level **Advanced/Advanced High** |
|---|---|---|
| Allow students to work through thesis ideas using their first language. Provide students with a short, simple sentence stem for creating their thesis statements. | Allow students to discuss their thesis statements with a partner using their first language. Provide students with a simple sentence stem for creating their thesis statements. | Encourage students to use correct technical vocabulary and complex sentence structures in their thesis statements. |

**TEKS 10.13A** Plan a first draft by developing a thesis or idea; **10.15A(iii)** Write an analytical essay that includes an idea or thesis; **10.15C(i)** Write a response to expository and literary text that extends beyond a summary and literal analysis; **10.15C(iii)** Write a response to expository and literary text that analyzes the effects of stylistic and rhetorical devices; **ELPS 5B** Write using content-based grade-level vocabulary; **5F** Write using a variety of grade-appropriate sentence patterns in increasingly accurate ways

## Drafting

### Developing Your Ideas

Before students begin writing, have them collect evidence from the poem and note lines that they can use as supporting evidence for their analyses. Remind students that adding these kinds of supporting details will strengthen their analysis and show comprehension of the poem. **DIFFERENTIATE INSTRUCTION ↘**

### Writing Your Middle Paragraphs

Distribute photocopies of the reproducible quick list (see TE Appendix) and have students list their main points and supporting details on it.

Remind students as they begin writing that every paragraph should include a topic sentence that develops the writer's thesis. Each topic sentence must be supported with sufficient evidence, including quotations from the poem.

#### Focus on the Texas Traits

**Organization**
Remind students that they should not simply paraphrase the poem. Students should include an analysis of the theme and of the rhetorical and stylistic devices the poet used.

**Write your middle paragraphs.** Students should use the tips to begin drafting their middle paragraphs. Explain that the organizational pattern they choose should fit their analyses.

**TEKS** 10.15A(iv), 10.15A(v), 10.15C(i)–10.15C(iii)

---

 **TEKS** 10.15A(iv), 10.15A(v), 10.15C(i)–10.15C(iii)

## Drafting Developing Your Ideas

The middle paragraphs should build your analysis in a logical way. Refer to the exercises that you did on the previous pages. Your essay must be long enough to provide a detailed analysis. Remember to use relevant evidence and carefully chosen details to support your ideas.

### Writing Your Middle Paragraphs

Develop ideas in each middle paragraph so that you clearly convey your meaning. Be sure to include relevant evidence and well chosen details. The following tips will help you plan your middle paragraphs.

- **First, provide your readers with a brief summary.**
  *The ship that "has weather'd every rack" is the United States, just recovering from the "fearful trip" of the Civil War.*

- **Other paragraphs should focus on the poem's stylistic and rhetorical devices. Write one paragraph on rhythm, another about diction, another about imagery, and so on.**
  *He [Whitman] moves between the two different feelings by changing the rhythm and the rhyming scheme. The first four lines of each stanza rhyme every two lines.*

- **Begin each paragraph with a topic sentence and support it with evidence from the poem. Include examples to illustrate your point, and end each paragraph with a concluding statement.**
  *Whitman structures the poem almost like scenes in a movie. First you watch the victorious ship entering the harbor: "While follow eyes the steady keel, the vessel grim and daring." This is followed by a quick cut to the horror on the ship of seeing their dead captain: "But O heart! heart! heart!" In the final scene, the focus is completely on the people grieving around their leader on the ship. The celebration is now in the background.*

#### Focus on the Texas Traits

**Organization** Choose an organizational pattern in which you can analyze both the theme of the poem and the effects of the rhetorical and stylistic devices. Do not paraphrase the poem in your analysis.

**Write your middle paragraphs.** Use the prewriting tips above to draft your middle paragraphs.

---

**TEKS** **10.15A(iv)** Write an analytical essay that includes a structure appropriate to the purpose and context; **10.15A(v)** Write an analytical essay that includes relevant evidence and details; **10.15C(i)** Write a response to expository and literary text that extends beyond a summary; **10.15C(ii)** Write a response to expository and literary text that addresses writing skills for an analytical essay and using embedded quotations; **10.15C(iii)** Write a response to expository and literary text that analyzes the effects of stylistic and rhetorical devices

# Drafting Embedding Quotations in Your Essay

As you draft your analysis, be sure to use quotations from the poem to support your points. Choose quotations and lines that you feel best support the paragraph topic sentence and the controlling idea of your essay. The following tips will help you embed your quotations correctly.

- **If you are including more than one line of poetry, use a slash mark at the end of the line to show the line breaks.**
- **Be sure to use quotation marks correctly around the quotations or lines of poetry. You must also include any punctuation marks that appear in the quotations you are including.**
- **If the poem you are citing has line numbers, embed them in your essay along with the line or quotation.**

Remember, too, to use transitions so that your paragraphs flow smoothly from one to the next and from sentence to sentence within a paragraph.

## Writing Your Introductory and Concluding Paragraphs

The following tips will help you write beginning and ending paragraphs.

- **Present your controlling idea in an effective introductory paragraph that gives your reader essential background information about the poem. Be sure to cite the title of the poem and the author's name.**
- **End your essay with an effective conclusion. Revisit the thesis statement and give your own personal opinion about the poem and why and how it "spoke" to you. End with an insight about the poem and why it was important to you.**

Response

### Focus on the Texas Traits

**Organization** Choose an organizational pattern in which you can analyze both the theme of the poem and the effects of the rhetorical and stylistic devices. Do not paraphrase the poem in your analysis.

**Write your opening and closing paragraphs.** Use your prewriting work and the tips above to draft effective introductory and concluding paragraphs for your essay.

Draft

## Embedding Quotations in Your Essay

Caution students against trying to embed too many lines of poetry into their analyses. A few well-chosen lines from the poem can be more effective than a lot of lines following one after the other.

TEKS 10.15C(ii)

## Writing Your Introductory and Concluding Paragraphs

Encourage students to write their introductory and concluding paragraphs in parallel with each other and before the rest of the essay is written. Though they may need some revision after the middle paragraphs are written, the introductory and concluding paragraphs will serve as the parameters for the rest of the essay. Remind students of the importance of using transitions to connect ideas and to keep their analyses flowing well.

TEKS 10.13B, 10.15A(i), 10.15A(ii)

**Write your opening and closing paragraphs.** Students should use the work they've already done and the tips on the page to draft the opening and closing paragraphs of their essay.

### Focus on the Texas Traits

**Organization**
Remind students that they should not simply paraphrase the poem. Students should include an analysis of the theme and of the rhetorical and stylistic devices the poet used.

**TEKS** **10.13B** Develop drafts in open-ended situations that include transitions; **10.15A(i)** Write an analytical essay that includes an introductory and concluding paragraph; **10.15A(ii)** Write an analytical essay that includes transitions; **10.15C(ii)** Write a response to expository and literary text using embedded quotations; **ELPS 1B** Monitor written language and employ self-corrective techniques or other resources; **1E** Internalize new basic language by using and reusing it/writing; **1H** Develop and expand learning strategies/reasoning, looking for patterns in language, and analyzing sayings and expressions; **4F** Use support from peers/teachers to enhance and confirm understanding; **4G** Demonstrate comprehension of increasingly complex English/taking notes; **4K** Demonstrate comprehension and expand reading skills by employing analytical skills/evaluating written information and performing critical analyses; **5B** Write using content-based grade-level vocabulary

## Revising
### Improving Your Response

Encourage students to consider each writing trait separately, asking themselves the questions provided and revising if they have not adequately addressed the trait. Consider using peer review to help with the revising process.

**TEKS** 10.13C, 10.13E

**Revise your essay.** Encourage students to answer each question. If they answer *No* to any question, have them revise their essays until they can answer *Yes* to the question.

## Editing
### Checking Your Conventions

Tell students to begin with a clean copy of their essays before they begin editing.

**DIFFERENTIATE INSTRUCTION** ↘

**Check your response.** Provide students with a copy of the checklist so that they can address each question individually. Again, if they answer *No* to any question, have them edit until they can answer *Yes* to each question.

Consider supplying an expanded checklist to help students edit their drafts. Add items about proper use and punctuation of restrictive and nonrestrictive clauses, the correct punctuation of quotations of several lines from the poem being analyzed, and any other grammar and usage items that your students find challenging.

**TEKS** 10.13D, 10.15A(v), 10.17A(ii), 10.17C, 10.18A, 10.18B(i), 10.19A; **ELPS** 5C, 5F

**TEKS** **10.13C** Revise drafts/improve style, word choice, sentence variety, and subtlety of meaning and rethink how well the purpose has been addressed; **10.13D** Edit drafts for grammar, mechanics, and spelling; **10.13E** Revise the final draft in response to feedback from peers and teacher/publish written work; **10.15A(v)** Write an analytical essay that includes relevant evidence and details; **10.17A(ii)** Use and understand restrictive and nonrestrictive relative clauses; **10.17C** Use a variety of correctly structured sentences; **10.18A** Use conventions of capitalization; **10.18B(i)** Use commas in nonrestrictive phrases and in clauses; **10.19** Spell correctly using resources to determine and check correct spelling; **ELPS** **4F** Use support from peers/teachers to develop grasp of language structures; **5C** Spell familiar words with increasing accuracy; **5D** Edit writing for standard grammar and usage/subject-verb and pronoun agreement and appropriate verb tenses; **5F** Write using a variety of grade-appropriate sentence patterns in increasingly accurate ways

---

**310**

 **TEKS** 10.13C–10.13E, 10.15A(v), 10.17A(ii), 10.17C, 10.18A, 10.18B(i), 10.19  **ELPS** 5C, 5F

## Revising Improving Your Response

Always review your writing. Make any changes and corrections neatly. Use the following questions to help you revise your essay.

- **Focus and Coherence:** Does my introductory paragraph contain my controlling idea? Are my ideas well supported? Do they all relate to the thesis? Does the conclusion tie the essay together?

- **Organization:** Have I included a beginning, a middle, and an ending? Does each paragraph have a focus? Have I used transitions so that paragraphs flow smoothly from one to the next?

- **Development of Ideas:** Have I adequately analyzed the poem, including the rhetorical and stylistic devices? Have I used key quotations, relevant evidence, and well chosen details to support the thesis? Have I given the reader background information and explained the theme?

- **Voice:** Have I used literary terms to express my ideas? Do I sound knowledgeable about the poem that I have analyzed?

 **Revise your essay.** Answer the questions above and revise your work as needed.

## Editing Checking Your Conventions

Check your final draft for grammar, sentence structure, capitalization, punctuation, and spelling.

### Conventions

| | | |
|---|---|---|
| ____ | **1.** | Have I used correct and consistent verb tenses? |
| ____ | **2.** | Have I correctly used a variety of sentence structures? |
| ____ | **3.** | Have I capitalized all proper nouns and first words of sentences? |
| ____ | **4.** | Have I put quotation marks around the exact words that I quoted from the poem? |
| ____ | **5.** | Have I checked the spelling in my work? |

 **Check your response.** Read over your work, looking for errors in conventions. Make any needed corrections neatly.

---

**Differentiated Instruction:**
**English Language Learners**                                    **ELPS** 4F, 5D, 5F

| ELP Level **Beginning** | ELP Level **Intermediate** | ELP Level **Advanced/Advanced High** |
|---|---|---|
| Work with students to review their essays, looking at each of the writing conventions. Encourage them to strive for increasing accuracy in spelling. | Have students work with a partner to edit their essays focusing on verb tenses, punctuation, and spelling. | Encourage students to edit their essays using the checklist. Have students focus on including a variety of sentence lengths and patterns as well as appropriate connecting words. |

## Writing for Assessment
# Responding to Prompts About Literature

Some assessments require you to respond to prompts about literature. These prompts may focus on something you have read before the test, something you will read during the test, or a combination of the two. Your response should show how well you understand the literature and how clearly you can form your thoughts within a limited amount of time. To prepare for this type of writing, carefully read your assignments in English class and pay particular attention to terms related to literature, such as *theme, symbol, character, metaphor,* and *irony*.

This chapter will help you to develop responses to literary prompts. You will learn to analyze various types of prompts, to use the writing process in a test situation, and to respond to fiction and nonfiction.

### Writing Guidelines

**Subject:** Literature prompt
**Purpose:** To demonstrate competence
**Form:** Response to a prompt
**Audience:** Instructor or test evaluator

"The difficulty of literature is not to write, but to write what you mean."
—Robert Louis Stevenson

### Resources

**Copy Masters (see Appendix)**

- T-chart (TE p. 313)

# Responding to Prompts About Literature

### Objective
- apply what has been learned about interpreting literature to respond to a literature prompt

Strongly encourage students to complete all their reading assignments before they have to take assessment tests that require them to respond to prompts about literature. Also encourage them to note details in the selection that describe setting, character, plot, and theme. Remind students to keep a reading journal to record personal responses and thoughts about the reading selections.

## Prewriting
### Analyzing a Literature Prompt

Students need to understand what is meant by a literature prompt. Review the sample prompt with them and detail how to determine what is important to note.

### Try It!
### Answers

**Possible Answers**

1. In her essay "Border: A Glare of Truth," Pat Mora discusses her feelings about <u>moving to Ohio from El Paso, the place where she grew up.</u> <u>What is the "truth" that Mora learns about her early life in the border country of the Southwest?</u> Using specific examples from her essay, <u>prove how moving away from the border actually brought her closer to her heritage.</u> **Notes:** the author's feelings, her experiences growing up, and what she encountered in Ohio

2. The following excerpts from the <u>first chapter of Edith Wharton's novel *Ethan Frome*</u> describe the night Ethan walked to town and caught a glimpse of a <u>church dance.</u> Explain how Edith Wharton uses the <u>setting</u> to help you understand <u>Ethan's emotions.</u> <u>Cite specific examples</u> from the excerpts to support your thesis. **Notes:** details that describe the setting, understanding of Ethan's emotions, excerpts from the text

---

*"Literature is news that stays news."*
—Ezra Pound

## Prewriting Analyzing a Literature Prompt

Prompts about literature ask you to respond to specific characteristics of a story, a poem, a novel, or a nonfiction selection. In this chapter, you will be drafting a response to a selection your teacher provides. Look for key words that tell you exactly what the prompt requires. In the sample prompt below, key words and phrases are underlined. The word *analyze* (red) gives the main direction or focus for the response.

**Sample Prompt**

> In Joan Aiken's story "Searching for Summer," the <u>setting</u> and the <u>title</u> are <u>important clues</u> to the <u>theme.</u> <u>When</u> does the story take place? <u>What</u> are the characters really searching for? <u>How</u> does the story suggest a frightening possibility? <u>Analyze</u> <u>how the story serves as a warning about the dangers of present-day technology.</u>

### Try It!

Copy the following sample prompts on a sheet of paper. Underline key words and phrases for each prompt and make notes about the kinds of supporting information that you would need for your response.

1. In her essay "Border: A Glare of Truth," Pat Mora discusses her feelings about moving to Ohio from El Paso, the place where she grew up. What is the "truth" that Mora learns about her early life in the border country of the Southwest? Using specific examples from her essay, prove how moving away from the border actually brought her closer to her heritage.

2. The following excerpts from the first chapter of Edith Wharton's novel *Ethan Frome* describe the night Ethan walked to town and caught a glimpse of a church dance. Explain how Edith Wharton uses the setting to help you understand Ethan's emotions. Cite specific examples from the excerpts to support your thesis.

## Planning Your Response

Once you analyze and understand the prompt, you are ready to plan your response. If a reading selection is provided, examine it carefully for information related to the prompt. Choose the correct genre, form a topic sentence, and organize the details.

### Sample Prompt and Selection

> In this excerpt from A. Conan Doyle's "A Study in Scarlet," Sherlock Holmes explains the effective use of one's memory. In a paragraph, analyze how he makes his point with comparisons.
>
> "You see," he explained, "I consider that a man's brain originally is like a little empty attic, and you have to stock it with such furniture as you choose. A fool takes in all the lumber of every sort that he comes across, so that the knowledge which might be useful to him gets crowded out, or at best is jumbled up with a lot of other things so that he has a difficulty in laying his hands upon it. Now the skillful workman is very careful indeed as to what he takes into his brain-attic. He will have nothing but the tools which may help him in doing his work, but of these he has a large assortment, and all in the most perfect order.

> Comparisons are underlined.

Response

## Writing a Topic Sentence

After reading the prompt and selection, a student wrote this topic sentence.

> Sherlock Holmes thinks of the brain (specific topic) as an empty storage space, where care must be taken to avoid cluttering the memory with useless facts (particular focus).

## Creating a Graphic Organizer

The writer used a T-chart to organize the elements being compared.

| Comparisons | |
| --- | --- |
| Memory | Everyday Objects |
| – jumbled memory | – "takes in lumber of every sort" |
| – helpful memory | – "the tools which may help him" |

---

## Planning Your Response

Have students read the sample prompt and selection. Then invite students to point out key words in the prompt and explain the process they would use to form a topic sentence and organize details. ✔ **DIFFERENTIATE INSTRUCTION**

### Writing a Topic Sentence

Remind students that a topic sentence gives focus to the analysis. Challenge students to create a topic sentence in response to the prompt without looking at the sample. Have students compare their topic sentences to the sample. (Possible alternative topic sentence: *Holmes compares the human brain to an empty attic, which a person may fill unwisely with any sort of information or wisely with only important or useful information.*)

★ **TEKS** 10.13A

### Creating a Graphic Organizer

Distribute photocopies of the reproducible T-chart (see TE Appendix), and have students use it to organize details to respond to the sample prompt. Then for practice, ask students to write a response to the sample prompt, using their topic sentences and the details they organized.

---

### Differentiated Instruction: English Language Learners

☆ **ELPS** 1E, 2D, 2G, 2I, 4F, 5B, 5F

| ELP Level **Beginning** | ELP Level **Intermediate** | ELP Level **Advanced/Advanced High** |
| --- | --- | --- |
| Preteach vocabulary from the selection, then read the selection and sample topic sentence aloud. Have students to summarize the topic using their first language as needed. | Have students read the prompt and selection silently. Ask questions to assess comprehension. Provide a simple sentence stem for students to write their topic sentences. | Have students read the prompt, selection, and sample topic sentence silently. Provide students a complex sentence stem to use in creating their own topic sentences. |

★ **TEKS** 10.13A Plan a first draft by selecting the correct genre; **ELPS** **1E** Internalize new basic and academic language by using and reusing it/writing; **2D** Monitor understanding of spoken language during classroom instruction/interactions and seek clarification of spoken language as needed; **2G** Understand the main points of spoken language/topics, languages, and contexts are familiar to unfamiliar; **2I** Demonstrate listening comprehension in increasingly complex spoken language by summarizing spoken messages and collaborating with peers; **4F** Use visual and contextual support to develop grasp of language structures/use support from peers/teachers to read grade-appropriate text, enhance understanding, and develop grasp of language structures; **5B** Write using content-based grade-level vocabulary; **5F** Write using a variety of grade-appropriate sentence lengths, patterns, and connecting words/combine in increasingly accurate ways

## Drafting
### Responding to a Fiction Prompt

Ask students to read the sample prompt and the selection. Then, have them read the student's side notes and note the details that she underlined. Ask the following questions:

- *Why do you think the student underlined these particular details?* (Most of the details provide information about the setting. The prompt asks students to show how Wharton uses the setting to help readers understand Frome's emotions.)
- *Which other details would you have underlined?*
- *What do the writer's notes indicate about the setting?*
- *What other notes would you have added?*

 **TEKS** 10.13B

 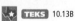
## Drafting Responding to a Fiction Prompt

The student writer of the sample essay chose to respond to the second prompt on page 312. The excerpt below shows how the student underlined words and phrases and added some notes on a copy of the selection to address the focus of the prompt (red). You will be responding to a prompt provided by your teacher.

### Sample Prompt and Selection

**The following excerpts from the first chapter of Edith Wharton's novel *Ethan Frome* describe the night Ethan walked to town and caught a glimpse of a church dance.** Explain how Edith Wharton uses the setting to help you understand Ethan's emotions.

From *Ethan Frome* by Edith Wharton

*Stillness, cold, shades of black and white except for yellow light from church basement*

The village lay under two feet of snow, with drifts at the windy corners. In a sky of iron the points of the Dipper hung like icicles and Orion flashed his cold fires. The moon had set, but the night was so transparent that the white house-fronts between the elms looked gray against the snow, clumps of bushes made black stains on it, and the basement windows of the church sent shafts of yellow light far across the endless undulations.

Young Ethan Frome walked at a quick pace along the deserted street. . . . [T]he church reared its slim white steeple. . . . As the young man walked toward it the upper windows drew a black arcade along the side wall of the building. . . .

At the end of the village he paused before the darkened front on the church. . . . The hush of midnight lay on the village, and all its waking life was gathered behind the church windows, from which strains of dance-music flowed with the broad bands of yellow light. . . .

*Heat, movement inside church contrast with cold outside.*

Seen thus, from the pure and frosty darkness in which he stood, it seemed to be seething in a mist of heat. The metal reflectors of the gas-jets sent crude waves of light against the whitewashed walls, and the iron flanks of the stove at the end of the hall looked as though they were heaving with volcanic fires. The floor was thronged with girls and young men. . . .

### Differentiated Instruction: Struggling Learners

Review the graphic organizer at the bottom of SE page 315 with students. Point out that the author uses images to create a setting that is dark, cold, and lonely. Read through each phrase in the first column and ask students whether the image is associated with something dark, cold, or lonely. For example:

- snow (cold)
- hush of midnight (lonely)

- sky of iron (cold)
- hung like icicles (cold)
- flashed cold fires (cold)
- black stains (dark)

**ELPS** 4F

> The guests were preparing to leave, and the tide had already set toward the passage where coats and wraps were hung, when a young man with a sprightly foot and a shock of black hair shot into the middle of the floor and clapped his hands. The signal took instant effect. The musicians hurried to their instruments . . . and the lively young man, after diving about here and there in the throng, drew forth a girl who had already wound a cherry-coloured "fascinator" about her head, and, leading her up to the end of the floor, whirled her down its length to the bounding tune of a Virginia reel.
>
> Frome's heart was beating fast. . . .

*A lively young man and a girl with colorful scarf dance.*

## Writing a Thesis Statement

After reading the excerpt and taking notes, the student wrote the following thesis statement for her response essay.

> **Wharton helps the reader understand the feelings of a man** (specific topic) **who sees through a church basement window a scene much different from his colorless world** (particular focus).

## Creating a Graphic Organizer

The writer created a T-chart to list important details about the setting.

| on the way to the church | in the church basement |
|---|---|
| "two feet of snow" | "shafts of yellow light" |
| "hush of midnight" | "strains of dance-music" |
| "sky of iron," constellations | "broad bands of yellow light" |
| "hung like icicles" | "seething in a mist of heat" |
| "flashed his cold fires" | "waves of light," "whitewashed walls" |
| "black stains" | "stove . . . heaving with volcanic fires" |
| "white steeple" | "cherry-coloured 'fascinator'" |

*Response*

**Differentiated Instruction: English Language Learners**

⭐ **ELPS** 4D, 4E, 4F

| ELP Level **Beginning** | ELP Level **Intermediate** | ELP Level **Advanced/Advanced High** |
|---|---|---|
| Provide an adapted prompt and selection and preteach vocabulary. Have students read it aloud with a partner. Work with students to plan and write a thesis for their analyses. | Have students read an adapted prompt and selection aloud with a partner. Provide a sentence stem for students to use in writing their thesis statements. | Have students work with a partner to develop a thesis statement and beginning paragraph. Encourage students to use both complex and compound sentences. |

## Writing a Thesis Statement

Have students explain how the student formulated a solid, effective thesis statement for her response. Students should recognize that the *specific topic* part of the thesis statement comes from the focus of the prompt, shown in red. The *particular focus* is based on the first part of the prompt and is expanded with details that show an understanding of the reading selection. Students should try to apply this same strategy to create thesis statements when they have to respond to prompts. ✓ **DIFFERENTIATE INSTRUCTION**

## Creating a Graphic Organizer

Remind students that they can create simple graphic organizers like the T-chart shown on SE page 315 to help plan their responses to prompts. Explain that the important thing is for them to organize the details they gather in a way that will make writing easier. They should not, however, waste precious test time drawing elaborate graphic organizers.
✓ **DIFFERENTIATE INSTRUCTION**

⭐ **TEKS** 10.13A, 10.13B, 10.15C(iii)

⭐ **TEKS** **10.13A** Plan a first draft by developing a thesis or idea; **10.13B** Develop drafts in timed situations that include rhetorical devices; **10.15C(iii)** Write a response to literary text that analyzes the effects of stylistic and rhetorical devices; **ELPS** **4D** Use prereading supports to enhance comprehension of written text/graphic organizers, illustrations, and topic-related vocabulary; **4E** Read linguistically accommodated content area material with a decreasing need for linguistic accommodations as more English is learned; **4F** Use visual/contextual support and support from peers/teachers to develop grasp of language structures

**Student Response**

After students read the student response, have them point out elements of the response that are similar to their earlier analyses. This should help them understand that they are well prepared to write such a response to a prompt. Students may point out similarities such as these:

- The beginning includes the title and author. It introduces the character, setting, and an important event.
- The thesis statement focuses and controls the direction of the essay.
- Each middle paragraph has a topic sentence that supports the thesis statement.
- Each middle paragraph addresses a different stage in the analysis (outside the window, inside the window) and helps reveal the setting.
- Transitions are used to provide a good flow to the essay.
- Quotations help emphasize important points about the setting.
- The ending explains how Frome has changed. It uses a quotation from the selection and makes a prediction about how the character may be affected in the future.

 **TEKS** 10.13B, 10.15C(i)–10.15C(iii); **ELPS** 4J, 4K

---

 **TEKS** 10.13B, 10.15C(i)–10.15C(iii)

## Student Response

In this student response to the excerpts from *Ethan Frome*, note how the student writer used details from the novel to support the thesis statement.

### Ethan Sees Red

**Beginning**
The first paragraph leads up to the thesis statement (underlined).

In this excerpt from *Ethan Frome*, Ethan walks into a village one cold winter night to get a glimpse of a dance in a church basement. He is definitely portrayed as an outsider in this passage. <u>Wharton helps the reader understand the feelings of this man who sees through a church basement window a scene much different from his colorless world.</u>

**Middle**
One paragraph focuses on the setting outside the church. Writer begins to analyze author's use of stylistic and rhetorical devices.

Ethan was out late at night, as "the hush of midnight lay on the village." Bleak images in shades of black and white mark his journey. He seems to be a part of the quiet landscape as he walks under a "sky of iron" filled with constellations "hung like icicles" or flashing "cold fires." The shadows cast by these night lights are "black stains" on the snow. As he approaches the church, the "white steeple" rises above the black walls of the building. He avoids those walls, attracted by something much different from the night that surrounds him.

The next paragraph focuses on the setting inside the church basement. Writer uses embedded quotes and specific evidence from the text to support thesis.

In contrast with the stark surroundings, the windows of the church basement send out inviting "shafts of yellow light." As Ethan looks in, "strains of dance-music" flow. Inside is a scene "seething in a mist of heat" with "waves of light" washing the walls and a stove, "heaving with volcanic fires." Suddenly, a young man dives into the throng of dancers and pulls out a girl with a "cherry-

---

 **TEKS** **10.13B** Structure ideas in a sustained way/develop drafts in timed situations that include transitions; **10.15C(i)** Write a response to literary text that extends beyond a summary and literal analysis; **10.15C(ii)** Write a response to literary text that addresses writing skills for an analytical essay and using embedded quotations; **10.15C(iii)** Write a response to expository text that analyzes the effects of stylistic and rhetorical devices; **ELPS 4J** Demonstrate comprehension and expand reading skills by employing inferential skills/ predicting, making connections between ideas, drawing conclusions from text, and finding supporting evidence; **4K** Demonstrate comprehension and expand reading skills by employing analytical skills/evaluating written information and performing critical analyses

TEKS 10.13B, 10.15C(i)–10.15C(iii)

Responding to Prompts About Literature    317

**Middle**
The middle paragraphs include details from the excerpts to support thesis. Transitions move ideas smoothly.

**Ending**
The closing summarizes the thesis.

coloured" scarf on her head. The young man and the girl whirl to the "bounding tune of a Virginia reel."
   Wharton shows a man as cold and gray as the snowy winter's night in which he finds himself. Then a warm room, snappy music, lively dancing, and a girl in a red scarf give Ethan an emotional wake-up call. As Wharton relates, "Frome's heart was beating fast." The contrast between the winter night and the party has had a dramatic effect on Ethan—an effect that could be important in the rest of the story.

 **Respond to the reading.** Answer the following questions about the student response.

   **Focus and Coherence** (1) How does the thesis statement respond to the focus of the prompt? **Organization** (2) How does the writer organize the middle two paragraphs in the response? (3) What kinds of transitions does the writer use? **Development of Ideas** (4) What types of details does the student use to support her thesis? **Voice** (5) List two words or phrases quoted from the novel that are particularly effective. (6) What kinds of rhetorical devices does the student use?

 Draft

**Now write your response to the prompt.** Use the questions above as a guide.

Response

---

 **Respond to the reading.**

**Answers**

**Focus and Coherence 1.** The thesis statement incorporates key words and ideas from the prompt (*Wharton helps the reader understand the feelings of a man*) and explains that the focus of the essay will be the contrast between Frome's colorless world and what he sees through a church basement window.

**Organization 2.** The writer organizes the two middle paragraphs as a comparison/contrast. The first middle paragraph describes the cold, bleak world outside the window. The details in the second middle paragraph contrast with those of the first middle paragraph. They describe the bright, warm, cheery world inside the church. **3.** The writer uses transitions that provide details about the setting.

**Development of Ideas 4.** The writer uses sensory details that emphasize the contrast in color, temperature, and emotions outside the window and inside the church.

**Voice 5.** Possible choices: *the hush of midnight lay on the village, sky of iron, black stains, seething in a mist of heat, heaving with volcanic fires, cherry-colored scarf.* **6.** The writer uses contrast as the primary rhetorical device. ⟋DIFFERENTIATE INSTRUCTION

TEKS 10.13B, 10.15C(i)–10.15C(iii)

**Now write your response.** Supply a quick list (see TE Appendix) and encourage students to use it to outline their response. After students write their response, they should use the questions on SE page 317 as they revise their work.

---

TEKS **10.13B** Structure ideas in a sustained way/develop drafts in timed situations that include rhetorical devices; **10.15C(i)** Write a response to expository text that extends beyond a summary and literal analysis; **10.15C(ii)** Write a response to expository text that addresses writing skills for an analytical essay and using embedded quotations; **10.15C(iii)** Write a response to literary text that analyzes the effects of stylistic and rhetorical devices; **ELPS 4F** Use support from peers/teachers to enhance and confirm understanding; **4J** Demonstrate comprehension and expand reading skills by employing inferential skills/predicting, making connections between ideas, drawing conclusions from text, and finding supporting evidence; **4K** Demonstrate comprehension and expand reading skills by employing analytical skills/evaluating written information and performing critical analyses

## Revising

### Improving Your Response

Review with students the four traits of writing that will be addressed during revising and encourage them to respond to each question as it pertains to their own essays.

**TEKS** 10.13C

**Improve your work.** Encourage students to take their time when revising their responses. Tell students that, if time allows, they should make one pass through their responses to address each of the key traits of writing.

## Editing

### Checking Your Response

Tell students to make corrections on their responses neatly and to be sure to follow the test guidelines for making neat, readable edits.

**TEKS** 10.13D, 10.17C, 10.18A, 10.18B(i), 10.19; **ELPS** 5C, 5D, 5F

**Check your response.** Students should review the entire response for each of the conventions on the checklist. Making several passes through their essays, if time permits, will increase the likelihood of catching errors.

---

**TEKS** 10.13C, 10.13D, 10.17C, 10.18A, 10.18B(i), 10.19
**ELPS** 5C, 5D, 5F

## Revising Improving Your Response

Always review your response at the end of a writing test. Make any changes and corrections as neatly as possible. Use the following questions to help you revise your response.

- **Focus and Coherence:** Does my thesis statement address the focus of the prompt? Do the details and conclusion support the thesis?
- **Organization:** Have I included an introduction, a middle, and an effective conclusion? Does each paragraph have a focus? Do I use transitions effectively to link ideas between paragraphs? Do my sentences flow smoothly from one to the next?
- **Development of Ideas:** Have I included relevant and precise evidence from the text to support my ideas? Have I included key quotations that support my thesis? Do I conclude with an insight about the literature selection?
- **Voice:** Do I sound clear in my thinking? Have I used correct literary terms? Do I sound confident and knowledgeable?

 **Improve your work.** Reread your practice response, asking yourself the questions above. Make any changes neatly.

## Editing Checking Your Response

In your final read-through, check for conventions: grammar, sentence structure, capitalization, punctuation, and spelling.

### Conventions

_____ 1. Have I used proper and consistent verb tenses?

_____ 2. Have I correctly used a variety of sentence structures?

_____ 3. Have I capitalized all proper nouns and the first words of sentences?

_____ 4. Have I put quotation marks around the exact words that I quoted from the selection?

_____ 5. Have I checked the spelling in my work?

 **Check your response.** Read over your work, looking for errors in conventions. Make needed corrections neatly.

---

**TEKS** **10.13C** Revise drafts/improve style, word choice, figurative language, and sentence variety and rethink how well the purpose, audience, and genre have been addressed; **10.13D** Edit drafts for grammar, mechanics, and spelling; **10.17C** Use a variety of correctly structured sentences; **10.18A** Use conventions of capitalization; **10.18B(i)** Use commas in nonrestrictive phrases and in clauses; **10.19** Spell correctly using resources to determine and check correct spelling; **ELPS** **5C** Spell familiar words with increasing accuracy; **5D** Edit writing for standard grammar and usage/subject-verb and pronoun agreement and appropriate verb tenses; **5F** Write using a variety of grade-appropriate sentence lengths in increasingly accurate ways

# Responding to Literature on Tests

Use the following tips as a guide whenever you respond to a prompt about literature. These tips will help you respond to both fiction and nonfiction selections.

## Before you write . . .

- **Be clear about the time limit.**
  Plan enough time for prewriting, writing, and revising.
- **Understand the prompt.**
  Be sure that you know what the prompt requires. Pay special attention to the key word that tells you what you need to do.
- **Read the selection with the focus of the prompt in mind.**
  Take notes that will help you form your thesis. If you're working on a copy of the selection, underline important details.
- **Form your thesis statement.**
  The thesis statement should identify the specific topic plus the particular focus of the prompt.
- **Make a graphic organizer.**
  Jot down main points and possible quotations for your essay.

## As you write . . .

- **Maintain the focus of your essay.**
  Keep your thesis in mind as you write.
- **Be selective.**
  Use examples from your graphic organizer and the selection to support your thesis.
- **End in a meaningful way.**
  Start by revisiting the thesis. Then try to share a final insight about the topic with the reader.

## After you've written a first draft . . .

- **Check for completeness and correctness.**
  Use the questions on page 318 to revise your essay. Then check for errors in grammar, sentence structure, capitalization, punctuation, and spelling.

### Try It!

Plan and write a response. Read a prompt your teacher supplies. Analyze it, read the selection, form a thesis statement, list ideas in a graphic organizer, and write your essay. Then revise and edit your response. Try to complete your work within the time your teacher gives you.

**Response**

## Responding to Literature on Tests

Point out to students that they must approach timed-writing assignments differently from open-ended writing assignments and that timed writing can create pressures not normally associated with open-ended writing.

Allow students the same amount of time to write their response essays as they will be allotted on school, district, or state assessments. Break down each part of the process into clear chunks of time. For example, you might give students

- 15 minutes for note taking and planning,
- 20 minutes for writing, and
- 10 minutes for revising and editing.

Tell students when time is up for each section. Start the assignment at the top of the hour or at the half-hour to make it easier for students to keep track of the time.

If your state, district, or school requires students to submit a graphic organizer as part of the assessment, refer students to SE pages 624–625 for ideas.

### Before you write. . ., As you write. . ., and After you've written a first draft. . .

Have students work with a partner to take turns reading the steps aloud. The student who is not reading should look away from the page and listen to the partner. The student who is reading should read one time and ask his or her partner a question about it. Circulate through the class during this activity to respond to questions and clarify points as needed.

ELPS 1E, 2I, 3D, 3E, 4F, 4G

### Try It!
### Answers

Answers will vary depending upon the prompt provided. Students should apply the prewriting, drafting, revising, and editing steps and supply both a finished essay and a graphic organizer.

✔ DIFFERENTIATE INSTRUCTION

---

**ELPS 1E** Internalize new academic language by using and reusing it/speaking; **2I** Demonstrate listening comprehension in increasingly complex spoken language by responding to questions and collaborating with peers; **3D** Speak using grade-level content area vocabulary/academic language proficiency; **3E** Share information in cooperative learning interactions; **4F** Use support from peers/teachers to enhance understanding and develop background knowledge; **4G** Demonstrate comprehension of increasingly complex English/participating in shared reading; **4K** Demonstrate comprehension and expand reading skills by employing analytical skills/evaluating written information and performing critical analyses

# Creative Writing

## Writing Stories (pages 321–332)

Students read a sample story and learn about plot, story-writing guidelines, story patterns, and important terms related to fiction.

## Writing Scripts (pages 333–346)

Students read a brief play script, then follow guidelines to develop their own script about an individual who learns a lesson about life.

## Writing Poetry (pages 347–357)

Students learn to write an autobiographical free-verse poem, and also learn about two special forms of poetry: the ballad and the lune poem.

## Technology Connections

↗ **Write Source Online**
www.hmheducation.com/tx/writesource
- **Net-text**
- **Writing Network**
- **Portfolio**
- **GrammarSnap**
- **Essay Scoring**
- **File Cabinet**

 **Interactive Whiteboard Lessons**

# Creative Writing Unit Scope and Sequence

| Day | Writing and Conventions Instruction | Write Source Student Edition | | | Daily Language Workouts | Skills-Book | Write Source Online |
| | | Core Unit | Tools of Language | Resource Units | | | |
|---|---|---|---|---|---|---|---|
| **1** | **Writing Stories** Model | 321–327 | **TL** 556–561 | | 82–85 | | Interactive Whiteboard Lesson |
| **2–3** | Prewriting | 328 | | | | | Net-text |
| | **Skills Activities:** •Prepositions | | | **BGW** 580–581 **PG** 768–769 | | 116 | GrammarSnap |
| **4–5** | Drafting | 329 | | | | | Net-text |

WEEK 1

 **Resource Units** referenced above are located in the back of the *Student Edition* and *Teacher's Edition*
**TL** *"The Tools of Language"*   **BGW** *"Basic Grammar and Writing"*   **WR** *"A Writer's Resource"*   **PG** *"Proofreader's Guide"*

| Day | Writing and Conventions Instruction | Write Source Student Edition | | | Daily Language Workouts | Skills-Book | Write Source Online |
|---|---|---|---|---|---|---|---|
| | | Core Unit | Tools of Language | Resource Units | | | |
| **6–7** (Week 2) | Revising and Editing | 330 | TL 526–529 | | 86–89 | | Net-text |
| | Skills Activities:<br>•Conjunctions and Interjections | | | BGW 582–583<br>PG 770–771 | | 117–120 | |
| | •Verbs | | | BGW 574–575<br>PG 750–761 | | 90–94 | GrammarSnap |
| **8–9** | Story Patterns | 331 | | | | | Net-text |
| **10** | Elements of Fiction | 332 | | | | | Net-text |
| **11** (Week 3) | **Writing Scripts**<br>Script Model | 333–336 | TL 526–529 | | 90–93 | | Net-text |
| **12** | Prewriting | 337–340 | | | | | Net-text |
| **13** | Drafting | 341 | | | | | Net-text |
| **14** | Revising | 342–343 | | | | | Net-text |
| | Skills Activities:<br>•Pronouns | | | BGW 572–573<br>PG 742–749 | | 80–89 | GrammarSnap |
| **15** | Editing | 343 | | | | | Net-text |
| **16** (Week 4) | **Writing Scripts**<br>Sample Radio Script | 344 | TL 526–529 | | 94–97 | | Net-text |
| **17–18** | Prewriting, Drafting | 345 | | | | | Net-text |
| **19–20** | Revising, Editing | 346 | | | | | Net-text |
| **21** (Week 5) | **Writing Poetry**<br>Sample Free-Verse Poem | 347–348 | TL 526–529 | | 102–105 | | Net-text |
| **22** | Prewriting | 349–350 | | | | | Net-text |
| **23** | Revising, Editing, Publishing | 351 | | WR 630–633 | | | Net-text |
| | Skills Activities:<br>•Adverbs | | | BGW 578–579 | | | |
| | Using Special Poetry Techniques | 352–353 | | | | | Net-text |
| **24** | **Writing Poetry**<br>Ballad, Prewriting | 354 | | | | | Net-text |
| | Drafting, Revising, Editing | 355 | | WR 630–633 | | | Net-text |
| **25** | **Writing Poetry**<br>Lunes<br>Prewriting, Drafting | 356 | | | | | Net-text |
| | Revising, Editing | 357 | | | | | Net-text |

**Resource Units** referenced above are located in the back of the *Student Edition* and *Teacher's Edition*
**TL** *"The Tools of Language"*   **BGW** *"Basic Grammar and Writing"*   **WR** *"A Writer's Resource"*   **PG** *"Proofreader's Guide"*

## Writing Focus

- Writing Stories
- Writing Scripts
- Writing Poetry

## Learning Language

Read aloud the words, their descriptions, and the questions as students follow along in their texts. Clarify terms students identify as difficult, such as *atmosphere*, *participate*, *exaggerated*, and *admiration*, before they answer. Model answering the first question for students: *The description says that mood is a feeling. A writer might describe a scary setting, or place, using words like **dark** and **stormy** to create a scary feeling.* Have partners take turns reading and answering questions.

**DIFFERENTIATE INSTRUCTION ➘**

⭐ **ELPS** 1E, 2C, 3B, 3D, 3E

## Minilessons

### Defining Moment
Defining a Concept

- **THINK** of an experience, a moment, an anecdote that you would call a *defining moment*. In other words, the moment defines you, another person, or a situation in your life.

- **SHARE** the example with a partner or the class. **ASK** them to name the word your illustration "defines."

**ELPS 1E** Internalize new basic/academic language by using and reusing it/speaking; **2C** Learn basic/academic vocabulary heard during classroom instruction/interactions; **3B** Expand vocabulary by learning and using routine language needed for classroom communication; **3D** Speak using grade-level content area vocabulary/new words and academic language proficiency; **3E** Share information in cooperative learning interactions; **3F** Give information/ranging from using a limited high-frequency vocabulary to using abstract and content-based vocabulary during speaking; **5G** Describe with increasing specificity and detail/writing

---

⭐ ELPS 1E, 2C, 3B, 3D, 3E, 4G

TEXAS
WRITE
SOURCE
Online
www.hmheducation.com/tx/writesource

# Creative Writing

## Writing Focus

## Learning Language

Learning these words and expressions will help you understand this unit.

1. Mood is the feeling or atmosphere that a writer creates for the reader.
   **What adjectives might a writer use to create a scary mood in a story?**

2. Characters are the individuals who participate in the action of a literary work.
   **Who is your favorite character in short stories or novels that you have read?**

3. Hyperbole is a figure of speech, an exaggerated statement that is used for humor or to emphasize a point.
   **Why is the statement "I am so hungry I could eat a horse," considered to be hyperbole?**

4. The expression to ooh and aah means to exclaim in wonder or admiration.
   **Why do you think people ooh and aah when they see babies?**

---

## Differentiated Instruction: English Language Learners

⭐ ELPS 1E, 2C, 3F, 5G

| ELP Level **Beginning** | ELP Level **Intermediate** | ELP Level **Advanced/Advanced High** |
| --- | --- | --- |
| Use expressions and gestures to express such moods as *sad*, *happy*, *funny*, and *scary*. Have students use these words to identify the mood of your expression. | Read question 1. Write on the board: *creepy, dark, sunny, breezy, windy, rainy*. Have partners discuss and identify the adjectives that could create a scary mood. | After students answer question 1, have them use their adjectives to write a sentence or a paragraph describing a setting or character that would create a scary mood. |

# Writing Stories

You are a born storyteller. You may find that talking about your experiences helps you to make sense out of your life. You may also enjoy making up stories, but that might not be as easy for you as it once was. It's no fault of your own. You're simply more focused on real-life experiences at this point in your life.

Here's the best way to feel inventive again: Sit down and start writing. Write simple stories, crazy stories, stories modeled after the ones you read now and the ones you read when you were younger.

This chapter will help you get started. It discusses the basic plot, offers a sample story and story-writing guidelines, and ends with a discussion of story patterns and important terms related to fiction.

## Writing Guidelines

**Subject:** A conflict within the main character
**Purpose:** To engage and entertain
**Form:** Short story
**Audience:** Classmates

"The only way to learn to write short stories is to write them, and then try to discover what you have done."

—Flannery O'Connor

## Resources

**Copy Master (see Appendix)**

• 5 W's chart (TE p. 328)

# Writing Stories

### Objectives
- understand the elements and structure of a short story
- choose a topic (a special experience that leads to inner conflict)
- plan, draft, revise, and edit a short story

A **short story** usually presents one main character with a conflict or problem to overcome.
- The exposition, or opening, introduces the characters, setting, and conflict.
- The rising action consists of a series of events or actions that lead to the climax, or high point.
- The falling action shows how the main character has changed, and it leads to the resolution—which brings the story to a satisfying end.

**Writing Guidelines.** Make sure students are clear about the assignment. Explain that the task will be to write a story for their classmates about a character facing and overcoming a problem.

### Technology Connections

Use the Interactive Whiteboard lessons to introduce creative writing.

*Interactive Whiteboard Lesson*

## The Shape of Stories

Have students freewrite for 5 or 10 minutes to explore two or three special experiences from their own lives that could provide inspiration for a fictional short story. Remind students that writers create stories out of what they know. When it is time for students to write their short stories, they may wish to base their stories on one of their own experiences.

**DIFFERENTIATE INSTRUCTION** ↘ **DIFFERENTIATE INSTRUCTION** ↘

⭐ **TEKS** 10.13A

Point out that many fiction writers believe a good short story is more difficult and challenging to write than a novel. Ask students why they think this could be true. Students may offer the following ideas:

- A novel has unlimited space. The writer can use long passages, even whole chapters, to describe settings and characters and to create subplots that enrich the main story line.
- A short story has limited space and must be focused. Every detail must contribute to the development of the characters and the plot.

### Beginning with the Plot

Have small groups of students work together to analyze two or three short stories that they have read in order to see how these stories follow the plot line.

⭐ **ELPS** 4K

### Exposition

Explain that the exposition tells readers where the story takes place (*setting*), who the story is about (*main character*), and what problem the characters will face (*conflict*). Read the sample story and have students work in pairs to identify the story's setting, main character, and conflict.

⭐ **ELPS** 4D, 4F

⭐ **TEKS** **10.13A** Plan a first draft by determining topics through a range of strategies; **ELPS** **4D** Use prereading supports to enhance comprehension of written text/graphic organizers, illustrations, and topic-related vocabulary; **4F** Use support from peers/teachers to enhance and confirm understanding; **4K** Demonstrate comprehension and expand reading skills by employing analytical skills/evaluating written information and performing critical analyses

---

## The Shape of Stories

Think of special experiences in your life: a key game, a family reunion, starting at a new school, getting your driver's license. These experiences build in excitement to a high point that really makes the event memorable. Fiction works in the same way. The story builds until the action reaches the climax, the most intense part of the plot.

### Beginning with the Plot

The plot refers to the events or actions that move a story along from start to finish. A plot has five parts: *exposition, rising action, climax, falling action,* and *resolution.* The plot line below shows how these parts work together.

**Plot Line**

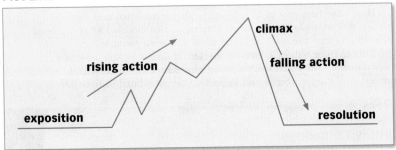

### Exposition

The *exposition* is the beginning part of a story. In it, the main character, the conflict, and the setting are introduced. The conflict is the problem that the main character faces. The setting is the place and the time of the action. The following example demonstrates the sort of information that you would share in the exposition.

> Marina is in her room, cuddling her cat, Feather. Feather is very old, has lost his eyesight, and has extreme difficulty moving around. The cat had once belonged to her beloved grandmother, who has since passed away. Marina's parents and the veterinarian have suggested that Feather be put to sleep, but Marina is resisting.

Writing Stories **323**

## Rising Action

In a short story, the *rising action* usually includes at least two or three important actions involving the main character and his or her problem. This builds suspense into the story.

**First Action:** Marina talks with her little sister Rosie about their ailing cat, Feather, especially how playful he used to be. Marina tries to play with the cat, but Feather shows no interest.

**Second Action:** Marina starts to tell Rosie stories about their grandmother. She talks about how much their grandmother had loved Feather.

**Third Action:** Rosie admits that she doesn't remember much about their grandmother because she was so little when their grandmother died. Marina accuses her sister of forgetting about this special person.

## Climax

The *climax* is the moment of truth, or the most exciting part, when the character confronts his or her problem head-on. All the action leads up to the climax. In the best stories, the main character is changed by the climax.

Marina's mother comes in, and Marina confesses that she wants to keep the cat alive because it is her connection with her grandmother. Marina is afraid that if the cat dies, so will her memories. Her mother assures her she won't forget her grandmother, and that it is cruel to make Feather suffer. Marina decides to let the veterinarian put Feather to sleep.

## Falling Action

The *falling action* involves the main character as he or she begins to deal with life after the moment of truth.

Marina declares that she will never forget her grandmother. Marina's mother assures her that anyone who is truly loved is never forgotten.

## Conflict

A well-developed *conflict* in a story is the struggle between two opposing forces. Almost every story has a major conflict—a conflict that is the story's focus. An *external conflict* involves a character pitted against an outside force, such as nature, a physical obstacle, or another character. An *internal conflict* is one that occurs within a character.

Marina is afraid that she will forget her grandmother. *(internal conflict)*
She quarrels with her sister about the cat. *(external conflict)*

*Creative Writing*

## Rising Action

Explain that to write an engaging story, an author must build suspense, or keep the readers guessing what will happen next. The actions that intensify the conflict must be thought out and believable. Have students read the sample and discuss what they think Marina will do.

## Climax

Explain that the outcome of a well-developed conflict is an exciting climax that leaves the main character changed as a result. Tell students that sometimes characters will make decisions and sometimes events will happen that change characters.

## Falling Action

Tell students that the falling action wraps up loose ends and leads to a resolution of a well-developed conflict. Sometimes characters move on or reflect on their personal changes.

## Conflict

Remind students that the conflict is the core of the plot, or story line. Often the main character experiences both internal and external conflict as a result of a particular situation. Encourage students to develop both kinds of conflict in their stories.

★ **TEKS** 10.14A

Make sure students understand the purpose of each part of a story's structure before moving on. Ask volunteers to explain each part in their own words.

---

## Differentiated Instruction:
## English Language Learners

★ **ELPS** 3E, 3G, 3H

| ELP Level **Beginning** | ELP Level **Intermediate** | ELP Level **Advanced/Advanced High** |
|---|---|---|
| Pair students and have them identify experiences using brief descriptions. Then have them complete the frame: *This experience made me feel . . .* | Have partners name experiences and provide brief descriptions of the conflicts they faced. Have partners finish the sentence: *This was important because . . .* | After students freewrite, have them share with partners and discuss the significance of the experiences and how they could be transformed into a fictional short story. |

**TEKS** **10.14A** Write a story with a conflict and a resolution; **ELPS** **3E** Share information in cooperative learning interactions; **3G** Express ideas and feelings ranging from communicating short phrases to participating in discussions; **3H** Explain with increasing specificity and detail

## Developing Believable Characters

Tell students that to create characters they should describe how the characters look, act, think, and feel. As writers, they control what their characters do and say as well as how characters respond to events and to other characters.

 **TEKS** 10.14A

## Types of Characters

### Main characters

Explain that main characters usually have complex personalities like real people. When students construct a main character, they need to think about his or her qualities and how someone with those qualities acts, thinks, and talks.

### Minor characters

Tell students that minor characters do not have the same depth as main characters. Often minor characters display only one personality trait or quality and do not change over the course of a selection.

### Dynamic and static characters

Explain that usually main characters are dynamic and minor characters are static. The point of a story is to explore how the main character faces an obstacle and changes as a result of the experience.

 **TEKS** 10.14A

---

**TEKS** 10.14A

## Developing Believable Characters

Characters are the people in your story. You can make them come alive through their actions and through the adjectives you use to describe them. Your characters should be believable, and they should be interesting to your readers. Most stories have more than one character. As you will see from the descriptions below, there are different types of characters. As you create your own story, remember that this is fiction, and your characters will become whatever you want them to be.

## Types of Characters

Like real people, characters display certain qualities, distinct characteristics that make them come alive. Characters develop and change over time, and they usually have motivations, or reasons for their behaviors.

### Main characters

The main character or characters are the most important ones in a story. Generally, especially in a short story, the plot focuses on one main character. A novel, however, may have several main characters.

### Minor characters

The less important characters in a literary work are known as minor characters. Their purpose is to support the plot. The story is not centered on them, but they help carry out the action and help the reader learn more about the main character.

### Dynamic and static characters

A dynamic character undergoes important changes as the plot unfolds. These changes can be good or bad. They occur because of the character's actions or experiences in the story.

A static character remains the same throughout the story. Static characters may experience events and interact with the other characters, but they do not change.

Alan, the main character in the sample story on pages **326–327**, has to work out his feelings toward Tiffany, which is an internal conflict. He is the main character, and he is a dynamic character.

---

**TEKS** 10.14A

Writing Stories **325**

## Resolution of the Plot

In a short story or a novel, the *resolution* brings the story to a natural, thought-provoking, or surprising conclusion. In some stories, it's hard to tell the difference between the falling action and the resolution because they are so closely related. As the falling action in a story begins, tensions ease. The final outcome of the story, however, has not yet been fully worked out. It is the events in the falling action that lead to the resolution. In the story about Marina and the cat Feather, the resolution is shown below.

> Marina's mother brings out a photo album.
>
> She and Marina sit down with Rosie to tell stories about Grandma.

### How the Resolution is Revealed

When you read a short story, you will see that in the resolution the author has revealed the final outcome and tied up any loose ends. In a fairy tale, the outcome is usually a happy one. In many stories, the conflict is resolved, and the characters live happily ever after.

When you write your own short story, ask yourself these questions as you develop the resolution.

1. How have the events and conflicts affected or engaged the characters?
2. How is the conflict resolved?
3. What message are you suggesting for your readers in the resolution?
4. What lesson has the main character learned from the experiences that occurred in the story?

Creative Writing

## Resolution of the Plot

Tell students that the resolution is the answer to the question "What happens in the end?" Explain that often the resolution reflects the results of the change the main character has undergone.

### How the Resolution Is Revealed

Tell students that the resolution does not always have to be directly described for the reader. Authors might describe characters' feelings, thoughts, or actions to suggest what will happen next without actually including "next" in the story.

Review the questions with students and clarify any confusion they have about the connection between the characters, conflict, theme, and resolution. ✔ **DIFFERENTIATE INSTRUCTION**

**TEKS** 10.14A

---

**Differentiated Instruction:
English Language Learners**

**ELPS** 2E, 3E, 5G

| ELP Level **Beginning** | ELP Level **Intermediate** | ELP Level **Advanced/Advanced High** |
|---|---|---|
| Simplify each question for beginning students. For example, ask: *What problem did the character face?* Have students work with partners to answer. | Have students orally summarize their stories for partners. Then, have partners work together to answer the questions for each story and collaborate on endings. | Have students write sentences explaining the message they want their stories to present. Students form small groups and discuss how the story can express their messages. |

**TEKS** 10.14A Write a story with literary strategies and devices to enhance the plot; **ELPS** 2E Use linguistic support to enhance and confirm understanding of increasingly complex spoken language; **3E** Share information in cooperative learning interactions; **5G** Explain with increasing specificity and detail/writing

## Sample Story

Work through this sample story with the class, pointing out the elements that make it a good short story.

### Focus and Coherence

- The main character is in conflict with himself over his feelings.
- Dialogue and actions reveal the personality of each character.
- The main character is changed at the end when he realizes his true feelings.

**TEKS** 10.14A; **ELPS** 4F

### Organization

- The beginning introduces the setting, two characters, and the main character's inner conflict.
- The events that lead to the climax build suspense about the main character's feelings.
- The ending shows how the main character has changed.

**TEKS** 10.14A; **ELPS** 4F

### Development of Ideas

- The conflict is well-developed.

### Voice

- The dialogue sounds real and natural.
- Sensory details show readers instead of telling them. For example, instead of saying, "Alan remembered Tiffany's perfume," the writer says, "Even now, her heady jasmine perfume seemed to fill his senses."

**TEKS** 10.14A; **ELPS** 4F

## Sample Story

Read and enjoy the sample story by Thea Karas. The side notes indicate how the story develops from the exposition to the resolution.

### Building Foundations

**Exposition**
The writer creates interesting, believable characters. She describes the setting and conflict.

Alan sniffed the fragrant blend of open earth, fresh cement, and new wood, almost forgetting how miserable he was feeling. The Construction Class students were actually building a house. As the students grouped around the site for Mr. Hanson's instructions, Alan's friend Sara sidled up and nudged him, her soft lily-of-the-valley cologne mingling pleasantly with the construction smells.

"So, what happened? I thought you were taking Tiffany to the dance," she whispered.

His agony returned. "She got a better offer."

Sara didn't say anything more as Mr. Hanson explained the day's activity: creating foundation walls.

**Rising Action**
Dialogue and details add to the suspense of the story. They also make characters more believable.

Working in teams, the students began building up the short walls of the crawl space that would serve to support the rest of the house. Alan and Sara worked side by side on the prepared footings, Sara slapping down mortar and Alan setting the cinder blocks.

"I'm sorry about Tiffany," Sara said softly as she tapped her trowel against the mortar bucket. "But why did you ask her to begin with?"

Alan thought about Tiffany, her glossy black hair and amber eyes. Even now, her heady jasmine perfume seemed to fill his senses. "She's just so pretty."

"Pretty boring," Sara snorted. "What do you two have to talk about?"

**Rising Action**
Additional action keeps the reader engaged and enhances plot development. Conflict is well developed.

Alan considered. What *did* they talk about? Tiffany was into international affairs. When they'd eaten lunch together on Friday, all she had talked about was how some country he had never even heard of was being repressed by another country he hadn't heard of! He had sat silent the whole time, just looking at those amber eyes.

"Here." Sara shoved the mortar bucket at him. "Let's switch jobs."

He began slapping the grainy gray mortar on top of the blocks.

> Writer continues to develop believable, interesting characters. She uses a variety of literary strategies and devices to enhance the plot.

"I love this class," Sara grunted as she hoisted a cinder block into place. "It's great to build something."

"Yeah, I can't wait to get to the real stuff—putting down the floors, putting up the walls, and fitting windows. This is kinda boring."

"It is pretty tedious," Sara admitted, "but think about it. If we don't do a good job on the foundation, the rest of the house could shift and even fall apart!"

Alan grinned at her enthusiasm. "You're not given to hyperbole, are you?"

Sara blushed, a blond wisp escaping from her hat and curling around her face. "I just think foundations are important." Alan tried to imagine Tiffany working next to him, but the picture wouldn't form. He admired how skillfully Sara skimmed her trowel along, cleaning off the excess mortar.

> **Climax**
> Writer creates a believable climax, revealing complex character traits.

"So how's your biology project coming?" he asked.

Alan almost forgot about Tiffany as they discussed genetics. When it was time to get back on the bus, Sara checked her watch. "Wow, time flies . . ."

" . . . when you're having fun!" Alan finished, and they both laughed.

A wayward curl dipped across Sara's eye, and Alan reached over to brush it away. Her eyes were green with little yellow flecks, and looking at them, Alan suddenly felt his knees go weak.

> **Falling Action and Resolution**
> With a well-developed resolution, the story comes to a satisfying end.

As they started up the bus steps, he looked back at the wall he and Sara had built together. *It's a good foundation,* he thought to himself. *It will support a good house.* Then he plopped down in the seat next to Sara and caught a delicate whiff of lily-of-the-valley cologne.

"Hey, Sara," he said, "about the dance . . ."

*Creative Writing*

 **Respond to the reading.** Review the story and answer these questions.

**Focus and Coherence** (1) What is the conflict? How is it introduced and developed? **Organization** (2) What main actions are included in the rising action? Name two. **Development of Ideas** (3) Who are the characters? (4) What details make them interesting and believable? (5) What details make the setting believable? **Voice** (6) How realistic does the dialogue sound? Explain.

---

Ask students to explain what makes Alan seem real. (Possible response: Alan is drawn to Tiffany's looks, but he isn't aware of his feelings for Sara.) Readers who can identify with the characters and make connections to their problems become more involved with a story.

⭐ **ELPS** 4K

 **Respond to the reading.**

**Answers**

**Focus and Coherence 1.** Alan asks Tiffany to go to the dance and she refuses. The conflict is introduced by Sara asking Alan what happened.

**Organization 2.** Possible answers:
- Alan and Sara work together building the foundation and discuss what happened.
- Alan recalls that he and Tiffany had nothing to talk about.
- Alan forgets about the time as he works with Sara.

**Development of Ideas 3.** Alan and Sara **4.** Possible answer: Their human feelings, realistic dialogue, and friendly connection makes them interesting and believable. **5.** Possible answer: The description of the class project and of the upcoming dance reflects real life.

**Voice 6.** The dialogue sounds realistic. When Alan says *She got a better offer,* and Sara says *Pretty boring,* it sounds like teenagers talking.

✔ **DIFFERENTIATE INSTRUCTION**

⭐ **TEKS** 10.14A

---

**Differentiated Instruction: English Language Learners**                    ⭐ **ELPS** 1E, 3E, 4G, 4K, 5G

| ELP Level **Beginning** | ELP Level **Intermediate** | ELP Level **Advanced/Advanced High** |
|---|---|---|
| Review academic vocabulary—*conflict, rising action, characters, setting, dialogue*—before students answer. Have students work with partners to answer the questions. | Have students think about the questions and jot down answers, additional questions, and notes. Then pair students to discuss and compare answers. | Have students use their answers to the questions to write a one-paragraph evaluation of the story. They should cite evidence from the text to support their opinions. |

⭐ **TEKS** 10.14A Write a story with a conflict, a resolution, interesting and believable characters, and literary strategies and devices to enhance the plot; **ELPS 1E** Internalize new academic language by using and reusing it/speaking; **3E** Share information in cooperative learning interactions; **4G** Demonstrate comprehension of increasingly complex English/responding to questions; **4K** Demonstrate comprehension and expand reading skills by employing analytical skills/evaluating written information and performing critical analyses; **5G** Explain with increasing specificity and detail/writing

## Prewriting

### Planning Your Writing

The quotations by C. S. Forester and William Faulkner highlight two important points for students to keep in mind when they write fiction.

- Writers have their own methods for developing story ideas. Students can follow the ideas suggested here, but as they become more seasoned writers, they may develop their own method for planning a story.

- Writers don't always know what's going to happen in a story. Students can plan what will happen, but they should remain open to the possibility the story will go in a different direction. **DIFFERENTIATE INSTRUCTION ↘**

### Creating Characters

Have students write a brief character sketch of their main characters. Encourage them to write one paragraph that describes the personality and appearance of a believable character. Students can describe minor characters in one or two sentences. **DIFFERENTIATE INSTRUCTION ↘**

⭐ **TEKS** 10.13A, 10.14A

### Considering a Conflict

Review internal and external conflict. Identify several literary strategies and devices, such as flashback, foreshadowing, suspense, and dialogue, before students begin. Have students consult their character sketches to think about problems their characters might face.

⭐ **TEKS** 10.14A

### Establishing a Setting

Remind students that a setting includes not only the place the action happens, but also the weather, the time period, and the customs or beliefs of that time and place.

### Thinking about the Action

Have students think about the conflicts they have chosen, how they want to resolve the conflict, and what events could lead up to the moment of truth when the conflict is resolved. Suggest students use a sequence of events chart to organize the story's action.

⭐ **TEKS** 10.14A

**Plan your story.** Have students organize all their information in a 5 W's chart (see TE Appendix) for quick reference.

**TEKS** **10.13A** Plan a first draft by determining topics through a range of strategies; **10.14A** Write a story with a conflict, a resolution, interesting and believable characters, and literary strategies and devices to enhance the plot

---

 **TEKS** 10.13A, 10.14A

## Prewriting Planning Your Writing

Fiction writers plan stories in different ways. For example, C. S. Forester thinks "first of something to be done and then . . . of an interesting character to do it." William Faulkner, on the other hand says he "begins with a character, usually, and once he stands up on his feet and begins to move, all I do is trot along behind." Another writer may start with a particular setting.

No matter how you start, just remember that your short story should include well-developed, interesting, believable characters. As you plan your story, identify at least the main character and his or her problem.

## Creating Characters

Who is the central person in your story? You can base the main character on someone you know, but don't embarrass a person by making the main character too much like him or her.

Also decide on one or two supporting, minor characters who will be involved in the action. Including too many characters, however, may make your story unnecessarily complicated. Review the information on types of characters as you plan your story.

## Considering a Conflict

For this assignment, your main character should be in conflict with him- or herself. Use a range of strategies to develop your plot. Think about literary strategies and devices you can use to enhance the plot. Consider a number of possible conflicts that your main character could deal with: his or her relationship with someone, peer pressure, stage fright, meeting expectations, and so on.

## Establishing a Setting

Your setting can be any place that allows your main character to deal with the conflict. Limit yourself, though, to one main location and a brief span of time. The sample story takes place at a construction site during one class.

## Thinking about the Action

The conflict requires the main character to act, so list two or three actions that could move your story along. Also consider the climax, or turning point.

**Plan your story.** Using the guidelines above, choose a main character, a conflict, and a setting. Then list actions that result from the conflict.

---

## Drafting Making Your Story Work

Stories are built with a few interesting characters, realistic dialogue, and believable action. Use a range of literary strategies and devices to develop your plot. Also consider the following points about story writing.

### Starting Your Story

To get the reader's attention, start your story in one of these ways.

- **Start in the middle of the action.**
  **Without slowing down, Zack artfully dodged the rock flung at his head.**
- **Begin with dialogue.**
  **"Never flown before, huh?" the flight attendant asked as I clutched the arms of my seat, preparing for takeoff and the end of my young life.**
- **Make an attention-grabbing statement.**
  **Everyone always oohs and aahs over my cute little brother, but I know the truth: He was sent from an alien planet to destroy the earth.**

In the exposition, establish a setting, introduce the characters, and identify the conflict. Once this background is set, write the middle part of your story.

### Developing the Action

Place your character in the first challenging action. Build suspense with each new action leading up to the climax.

- Create real, believable, and natural dialogue. Let the words reflect what the characters think and feel.
- Include sensory details and other stylistic and literary devices to enhance the plot.
- Show instead of tell. For example, instead of saying "Alan was sad," say "Alan slumped into his seat." Instead of "Sara felt embarrassed," write "Sara blushed."
- Build to a climax, when the main character confronts the problem.

### Bringing the Story to a Close

After the climax, end the story. Show how your character has been changed.

**Write your first draft.** Use your planning from page 328 plus the information above as a general guide.

*Creative Writing*

---

## Drafting

### Making Your Story Work

Tell students that they need to simply start writing during the drafting process. They will have multiple opportunities to revisit and improve their writing.

### Starting Your Story

Emphasize that the opening lines of the exposition should attract the reader's attention. But it should not reveal so much that readers have nothing to anticipate or imagine. To stimulate their imaginations, have students examine the three strategies for starting a story.

### Developing the Action

Remind students that good writers use language to "show" rather than "tell" readers what is happening as the action unfolds. One way writers do this is to use strong, specific verbs. For example, in the sample story on SE page 326, the writer says that Alan "plopped down in the seat." Readers can picture Alan plopping down—like a familiar friend who feels at ease—next to Sara.

TEKS 10.13A

### Bringing the Story to a Close

Review falling action and resolution with students. Remind students that the resolution is the end of the story.

**Write your first draft.** If students have difficulty getting started, review the plot line on SE page 322 and tell them to start by introducing the character, setting, and conflict. From there they can construct a well-developed plot by connecting actions that will lead to the climax and resolution.

TEKS 10.14A

---

## Differentiated Instruction: English Language Learners

ELPS 3H, 5G

| ELP Level **Beginning** | ELP Level **Intermediate** | ELP Level **Advanced/Advanced High** |
|---|---|---|
| Instead of writing a character sketch, have students fill out a chart that asks for the name, age, gender, appearance (height, hair color, etc.), and personality traits. | Have students describe their main characters to partners, using specific descriptions and details. Students tell everything they have imagined about their characters. | Have students review their character sketches and use a thesaurus to replace mundane words with vivid details. Tell students to check definitions so they can be as specific as possible. |

**TEKS 10.13A** Plan a first draft by determining topics through a range of strategies; **10.14A** Write a story with a conflict, a resolution, interesting and believable characters, and literary strategies and devices to enhance the plot; **ELPS 3H** Describe with increasing specificity and detail; **5G** Describe with increasing specificity and detail/writing

# Revising

## Improving Your Story

Have students use peer-responding groups to review their story drafts. Suggest that writers provide printed copies of their stories or upload them to the class Web site for students to read and review ahead of time. To help the writers improve their stories, peer reviewers should point out:

- dialogue and word choice that don't sound realistic or natural, or reflect what the characters think or feel;
- actions that do not build suspense or help to advance the plot; and
- details that lack subtlety of meaning; "tell" instead of "show" what is going on.

 **TEKS** 10.13C

**Revise your story.** If possible, plan a day or two break before students begin their revisions. Have students use the feedback from peers, as well as their own insights, to revise their stories.

# Editing

## Checking for Conventions

Tell students to read through their revised drafts several times. Each time they should check for and correct one type of error.

**DIFFERENTIATE INSTRUCTION ↘**

**TEKS** 10.13D; **ELPS** 5D

**Edit your story.** Have students check their stories for use of correct conventions.

### Conventions Connections

**Grammar: Appositives**
- ***Proofreader's Guide*** pages 768–769
- ***SkillsBook*** page 131

⚡ *Write Source Online* **GrammarSnap**

---

**330** **TEKS** 10.13C, 10.13D

## Revising **Improving Your Story**

Ask yourself the following questions when you revise your story.

### Focus and Coherence

_____ **1.** Do I introduce conflict, setting, and characters and describe them consistently throughout?

### Organization

_____ **2.** Have I included a well-developed plot?

### Development of Ideas

_____ **3.** Are the characters interesting and believable?

_____ **4.** Is my main character tested? Does my main character change during the story?

_____ **5.** Do all actions build toward the climax?

### Voice

_____ **6.** Do I show rather than tell? Do I use descriptive words, images, and figurative language to improve my writing?

 **Revise your story.** Use the information above to help you revise the first draft of your story.

## Editing **Checking for Conventions**

When you edit your revised story, check grammar, sentence structure, capitalization, punctuation, and spelling.

### Conventions

_____ **1.** Are my verb tenses consistent and correct?
_____ **2.** Have I correctly used a variety of sentence structures?
_____ **3.** Have I used correct capitalization, punctuation, and spelling?
_____ **4.** Have I punctuated dialogue correctly?

 **Edit your story.** Check your story for use of correct conventions.

---

 **TEKS** **10.13C** Revise drafts to improve style/word choice; **10.13D** Edit drafts for grammar/mechanics; **ELPS** **5D** Edit writing for standard grammar and usage/verb tenses

Writing Stories **331**

# Story Patterns

Many short stories follow a basic pattern. Here are brief descriptions of some popular short-story patterns.

### The Quest

The main character goes on a journey into the unknown, overcomes a number of obstacles, and returns either victorious or wiser. Heroic myths follow this pattern, but so do many modern stories.

**A young woman fights for the right to join an all-male sports team.**

### The Discovery

The main character follows a trail of clues to discover an amazing secret. Mystery and suspense novels use this pattern.

**A curious young man discovers that the bully at school is . . .**

### The Rite of Passage

A difficult experience changes the main character in a significant and lasting way. These stories are also called *coming of age* stories.

**A young soldier learns about responsibility while on the battlefield.**

### The Choice

The focus in this type of story is a decision the main character must make. Tension builds as the decision approaches.

**A young adult must decide to follow the crowd or follow her own conscience.**

### The Union

Two people fall in love, but they are held apart by a number of obstacles. Their struggle to come together only causes their love to grow stronger. Sometimes they succeed, and sometimes they fail.

**A young deaf man falls in love with a gifted violinist and then struggles to understand the music he can't hear.**

### The Reversal

In this pattern, the main character follows one course of action until something causes him or her to think or act in a different way.

**A young woman quits school, but then discovers her true love is painting and enrolls in an art school.**

*Creative Writing*

## Story Patterns

Review the list of story patterns and discuss their specific features. Point out that often a short story contains elements of different patterns, but usually one pattern is the most evident.

- Have students tell what pattern the sample story on SE pages 326–327 follows (reversal), as well as the pattern of the story they just wrote.
- Gather a list of short stories students have recently read in literature class. Invite volunteers to summarize the stories and tell what pattern each one follows.
- Read summaries of classic short stories by such writers as O. Henry, Edgar Allen Poe, and Nathaniel Hawthorne. Have students identify the patterns of those stories.

---

## Differentiated Instruction: English Language Learners

**ELPS** 5D, 5F

| ELP Level **Beginning** | ELP Level **Intermediate** | ELP Level **Advanced/Advanced High** |
|---|---|---|
| Review past, present, and future verbs. Have students circle each verb in their drafts and label each by tense. Work with small groups to correct tenses as needed. | Have students review their stories for verb tense, changing tenses for consistency. Tell students they can use the past tense in flashbacks to add depth to the narrative. | Review coordinating and subordinating conjunctions. Have students revise their stories by using connecting words to add variety to their sentences. |

 **ELPS 5D** Edit writing for standard grammar and usage/verb tenses; **5F** Write using a variety of grade-appropriate sentence lengths, patterns, and connecting words/combine in increasingly accurate ways

## Elements of Fiction

Review with students the academic vocabulary for elements of fiction and their definitions. Focus the discussion on those elements that students find difficult or challenging to identify. Provide clarification where needed, using literature samples and student writing as examples.

Suggest that students bookmark SE page 332 and use it as a reference whenever they are discussing or writing about works of fiction.

⭐ ELPS 2C

# Elements of Fiction

The following terms describe elements of literature. This information will help you discuss and write about novels, poetry, essays, and other literary works.

**Antagonist** The person or force that works against the hero of the story (See *protagonist*.)

**Character** A person or an animal in a story

**Conflict** A problem or clash between two forces in a story
- **Person vs. person** A problem between characters
- **Person vs. himself or herself** A problem within a character's own mind
- **Person vs. society** A problem between a character and society, the law, or some tradition
- **Person vs. nature** A problem with an element of nature, such as a blizzard or a hurricane
- **Person vs. destiny** A problem or struggle that appears to be beyond a character's control

**Mood** The feeling a piece of literature creates in a reader

**Narrator** The person or character who tells the story, gives background information, and fills in details between dialogue

**Plot, Plot Line** See pages 322–323.

**Point of View** The angle from which a story is told
- In **first-person point of view,** one character is telling the story.
- In **third-person point of view,** someone outside the story is telling it.
- In **omniscient point of view,** the narrator tells the thoughts and feelings of all the characters.
- In **limited omniscient point of view,** the narrator tells the thoughts of one character at a time.
- In **camera view** (objective), the narrator records the action from his or her own point of view without any other characters' thoughts.

**Protagonist** The main character or hero in a story (See *antagonist*.)

**Setting** The place and time period in which a story takes place

**Theme** The author's message about life or human nature

**Tone** The writer's attitude toward his or her subject (*angry, humorous*, and so on)

---

### Differentiated Instruction: English Language Learners

⭐ ELPS 4C, 4F, 5G

| ELP Level **Beginning** | ELP Level **Intermediate** | ELP Level **Advanced/Advanced High** |
| --- | --- | --- |
| Have students make a literary terms glossary. Have them write *play, script, theme, dialogue*. Practice pronunciation and provide definitions for glossaries. | Have students make a literary terms glossary using the Beginning words. Intermediate students work in pairs to determine meanings from the SE instruction. | Write this prompt on the board: *Name the parts of a script and describe each.* Have students respond in writing, either creating a glossary or explaining in a paragraph. |

**ELPS 2C** Learn academic vocabulary heard during classroom instruction/interactions; **4C** Comprehend vocabulary used in written classroom materials; **4F** Use visual and contextual support to enhance/confirm understanding/develop vocabulary; **5G** Explain with increasing specificity and detail/writing

# Writing Scripts

333

At one time or another, we have all felt that we were sure about something, only to learn that maybe we didn't know as much as we thought. A play is an excellent literary form for exploring such a theme, or underlying message, and for considering what a character might do when things don't work out in the expected way.

In a script for a play, you develop your story almost exclusively through dialogue. Each new exchange between characters moves the story toward the climax or high point of interest. The only other device that you have to work with is stage direction, which provides explanations about the characters' actions onstage.

In this chapter, you will read a brief play script about a student who "thinks" he knows all about the world of work. Then guidelines will help you develop your own script about an individual who learns a lesson about life.

## Writing Guidelines

Subject: **Learning a lesson about life**
Purpose: **To entertain and enlighten**
Form: **Brief script**
Audience: **Classmates**

"Drama is life with the
dull bits cut out."
—Alfred Hitchcock

## Writing Scripts

### Objectives

- understand the content and structure of a play, including stage directions and stage terminology
- choose a topic (a life-learning lesson) for a play
- write a radio script about a scene from real life

A **play** is a story told through the dialogue and movements of the characters. A play is usually organized into acts and scenes.

- A play has characters, a setting, and a plot, and is intended to be performed by actors on a stage in front of an audience.
- A play script contains a cast, or list, of characters; the dialogue; and the stage directions, which describe the character's actions and the stage setup for each scene.

**↙ DIFFERENTIATE INSTRUCTION**

**⊞ ELPS** 2C

### Writing Guidelines

Make sure students know they are to write an entertaining script for a play about learning a life lesson.

**⊞ ELPS** 2D

**ELPS 2C** Learn academic vocabulary heard during classroom instruction/interactions; **2D** Monitor understanding of spoken language during classroom instruction/interactions

## Sample Script

Many students will be familiar with plays, having read them in class, attended performances in school or the community, or acted in them. Have students compare the organization and style of plays they know to the organization and style of the sample play script on SE pages 334–336.

The abbreviations in the stage directions may be unfamiliar to some students.

- Before students read the sample play, have partners study the stage diagram on SE page 339 to become familiar with the acting areas on a stage and the abbreviation used to refer to each area. Emphasize that the acting areas are labeled from the point of view of the actors.
- Once students have a solid working knowledge of stage terminology, they can read the play without having to flip back to the diagram to check the shorthand. **DIFFERENTIATE INSTRUCTION** ↘

⭐ **TEKS** 10.14C

⭐ **TEKS** 10.14C

## Sample Script

In the following script by student writer Matt Holmes, the main character thinks he knows what it takes to get a job. The side notes identify key points in the development of the play. (See page **339** for an explanation of the abbreviations used in the stage directions.)

### Suiting Up

Characters: **Wesley**, a high school student seeking a job
**Luke**, his friend
**Tori**, another friend
**Mr. Hayes**, a potential employer
**Kyle**, a student

### Scene 1

**Stage Directions**
The stage setup and characters are described.

*(The only furniture on the stage is in the UC area—a desk with two chairs, one behind the desk, one in front. At the beginning, Mr. Hayes and Kyle are seated, frozen, in the dark UC area. Tori stands, frozen, in the dark DR area. As the curtain rises, the DL pool of light comes up, where Luke is bouncing a basketball. Wesley enters from DR and comes into the light. He is dressed casually, even a little sloppily, with shirttail untucked and shoelaces untied.)*

**Beginning**
The play starts right in the middle of the action. The theme is introduced.

| | |
|---|---|
| LUKE: | Hey, Wesley, you wanna shoot some hoops? |
| WESLEY: | Can't. I'm heading over to the Food Mart to interview for a job. |
| LUKE: | You joining the ranks of the employed? Cool. |
| WESLEY: | Yeah, I gotta start earning some bucks if I want to get a car. |
| LUKE: | A car? You can't get your license for another six months. |
| WESLEY: | I know, but it'll take me at least that long to get a down payment. |
| LUKE: | What kind of job? |
| WESLEY: | Stocking shelves. I figure a big, strong guy like me . . . |
| LUKE: | You think you look okay for a job interview? |
| WESLEY: | Sure. It's not an executive position, right? |
| LUKE: | Well, good luck, buddy. |
| WESLEY: | Thanks. Catch you later. |

*(The DL light goes down and Luke freezes as Wesley moves toward the DR section. The light comes up on Tori as Wesley crosses into her area.)*

TORI: Hey, Wesley. You seen Luke?

WESLEY: Hi, Tori. Yeah, he's at the park shooting hoops. See ya.

TORI: Where are you headed in such a hurry?

WESLEY: Job interview at Food Mart.

TORI: Er—shouldn't you go home and change first? You look like you just overhauled an engine or something.

WESLEY: Heck, it's only a stocking job. They won't care what I look like.

TORI: Don't you want to make a good impression?

WESLEY: My shining personality will win them over.

TORI: Right. Well, good luck!

*(The light goes down and Tori freezes as Wesley moves toward UC. The light comes up on Mr. Hayes and Kyle. Kyle rises, they shake hands, and Kyle turns and leaves.)*

MR. HAYES: Next! *(Wesley peeks in.)* Ah, Wesley Jones, isn't it? Come in, son.

WESLEY: Thank you, sir. *(Enters and extends his hand for a handshake, politely sits down.)*

MR. HAYES: *(Eyes Wesley's grungy clothes.)* Well. Let's see here. *(Looks over Wesley's application.)* Hmmm. Ah, you're on the basketball team. Well, we have other students involved in after-school activities. We can always work schedules around.

WESLEY: *(Politely)* Yes, sir.

MR. HAYES: Your grades are good, too.

WESLEY: Yes, sir, I can do that and hold a job.

MR. HAYES: Yes. Well, Wesley, I'll tell you. You seem like a pleasant young man. But I'm not going to give you the job.

WESLEY: *(Surprised)* Sir? But why?

MR. HAYES: There's a lot of competition in this world, Wesley. Did you see that young man who just went out?

WESLEY: Kyle? My grades are better than his!

---

**Middle**
Each new interchange advances the theme and adds tension. The mood is enhanced by figurative language.

**Writer continues** to develop the mood. The tone, the attitude the writer has toward the main character, is clearly revealed.

Creative Writing

---

Work through this sample play with the class, pointing out the elements that make it a good play.

### Focus and Coherence

- The main character has a believable problem that is introduced in the beginning. He wants to find a job.
- The dialogue helps to develop the characters, present the main conflict, build suspense, and contribute to a definite tone and mood.

TEKS 10.14C

### Organization

- The beginning introduces the characters and sets the scene.
- The stage directions are clearly set off from the dialogue and also help move the play along.

### Development of Ideas

- Each complication builds logically on the preceding one and leads to the climax.
- The dialogue moves the plot along while developing characters' personalities.
- The actions build to express an explicit theme, or message about life.

TEKS 10.14C

### Voice

- The characters use language that sounds natural and realistic for people their age.
- The dialogue flows naturally between characters.
- The writer uses proper stage terminology.

---

## Differentiated Instruction: English Language Learners

ELPS 2A, 4A

| ELP Level **Beginning** | ELP Level **Intermediate** | ELP Level **Advanced/Advanced High** |
|---|---|---|
| Echo read several lines of dialogue. Read aloud each sentence as students track the text. Then, have them repeat the sentence aloud to you. | Divide the class into two groups and assign one LUKE's lines and the other WESLEY's. Have the class follow your lead as they read their designated parts chorally. | Organize students into pairs; have each student assume the role of LUKE or WESLEY and read SE page 334 together. Then, have them switch parts and reread. |

TEKS **10.14C** Write a script with an explicit/implicit theme and details that contribute to the mood and tone; ELPS **2A** Distinguish sounds with increasing ease; **4A** Sound out words using a combination of skills

**Respond to the reading.**

## Answers

**Focus and Coherence 1.** The theme is introduced in the middle when Mr. Hayes says, "First impressions do count." **2.** Wesley's interactions with his friends foreshadow the theme to come.

`DIFFERENTIATE INSTRUCTION ↘`

**Organization 3.** The climax of the play happens in the middle, when Wesley has his interview and learns that he will not get the job because of the way he is dressed. **4.** Wesley learns his lesson and dresses up for his interview for another position at the Food Mart.

**Development of Ideas 5.** The action, which is expressed mostly through dialogue, advances the theme by setting up a situation in which a character will learn a life lesson. The tone, or attitude the writer takes toward the subject, is informal yet serious. The dialogue lends the informality to the tone while the theme contributes the seriousness.

**Voice 6.** The writer includes natural conversational elements, such as unfinished sentences, informal and colloquial language, and short comments. **7.** The writer adds specific details about the characters and their reactions that contribute to mood.

`★ TEKS 10.14C; ELPS 4G`

| | |
|---|---|
| MR. HAYES: | Maybe, but did you see the way he was dressed? |
| WESLEY: | Heck, I have a suit, too! |
| MR. HAYES: | But you didn't wear it, did you? He took the trouble to be well groomed. That shows me that he wants this job. Your clothes tell me you don't really care. |
| WESLEY: | But I do care! I'd work really hard for you! |
| MR. HAYES: | Maybe you would, Wesley, but I have to *see* that before I can hire you. I'm sorry, son. First impressions do count. |
| WESLEY: | Yes, sir. *(He rises to leave, then turns.)* Thank you, Mr. Hayes. |
| MR. HAYES: | Try again another time, Wesley. *(Wesley nods and goes right as the light goes down and Mr. Hayes exits left.)* |

*(The light goes up DC. Wesley appears from the right wearing a suit and tie. Luke and Tori move to the area and Luke whistles.)*

| | |
|---|---|
| LUKE: | Whoa, who died? |
| WESLEY: | There's another opening at the Food Mart. This time I'm going to get it. |
| TORI: | Ah— |
| WESLEY: | Don't say it, Tori. Okay, so you were right. |
| TORI: | *(Smiling)* I wasn't going to say a thing. |
| WESLEY: | Maybe this time Mr. Hayes'll get the chance to see my shining personality. |
| TORI: | I'm sure of it. After all, you're *suited up* for success! Good luck, Wesley. |

**Middle**
The main character realizes his mistake. The theme is explicit for the reader.

**Ending**
The main character sets a new course of action. The writer continues to show mood and tone throughout the script.

**Respond to the Reading** Answer these questions about the script.

**Focus and Coherence (1)** When and how is the theme introduced? **(2)** How is it developed? **Organization (3)** In what part of the play does the climax occur? **(4)** What happens after this point? **Development of Ideas (5)** How do the action and dialogue advance the theme and tone? **Voice (6)** How does the writer make the dialogue sound natural? **(7)** How does the writer create the mood?

# Prewriting Choosing Your Main Character

In a play script, the main character usually wants something, but faces a problem that keeps him or her from achieving it. As you start your planning, choose a main character and decide on something he or she wants.

The main character of the play is the **protagonist**. This person is changed in some way by the action. Matt decided to write about a teenage boy like himself. He named the character Wesley. Then Matt made a list of things Wesley might want, and starred the one he would write about.

### List of Wants

| | |
|---|---|
| Wesley wants . . . | to have a girlfriend<br>to earn high grades<br>to find a job  *<br>to buy a car |

**Choose your main character.** Decide on a main character for your play and make a list of things this person may want to achieve or obtain. Choose one that would make an interesting script. Think of how this character will help convey your tone and set a definite mood for your audience.

## Selecting a Conflict

The conflict occurs when something stands in the way of the main character. Matt compiled the following list before selecting a conflict. He starred the problem he thought was most interesting.

### Potential Conflicts

Things that could keep Wesley from finding a job

- His parents
- His attitude  *
- His grades
- His after-school activities

**List possible conflicts.** Be sure these conflicts are believable. Then place an asterisk beside the one that you will use in your play. Consider how your choice of conflict will help to illuminate the theme of your play.

*Creative Writing*

## Prewriting

### Choosing Your Main Character

Suggest that students make a list of things they or their friends have wanted to achieve or obtain in the last year. This will ensure that students select believable, realistic situations for the main story line of their plays.

**TEKS** 10.13A

**Choose your main character.** Tell students that the tone is the writer's attitude toward a subject. The mood is the feeling created by the action in the play. Tell students to think about what kind of tone and mood they want to express. Provide a details chart (see TE Appendix) for students to gather details about the characters. This can help them make connections between the character's words and actions and tone and mood.

**TEKS** 10.14C; ELPS 2C

### Selecting a Conflict

Students are likely to have chosen main characters who are based on themselves or people they know well. Since students will be presenting their plays to their classmates, remind them to consider the feelings of others as they choose conflicts and to think about how they will portray the way the main characters deal with the conflicts.

**TEKS** 10.13A

**List possible conflicts.** Take time to review students' topics and conflicts for their plays. Evaluate them for believability and appropriateness for presenting to the class.

---

### Differentiated Instruction: English Language Learners

**ELPS** 3G, 4F, 4G

Before reading the sample script, turn to the Tools of Language for additional support for the writing form.

| ELP Level **Beginning** | ELP Level **Intermediate** | ELP Level **Advanced/Advanced High** |
|---|---|---|
| Tell students that the Spanish cognate for *theme* is *tema*. Have them choose between *beginning, middle,* and *end* to answer question 1. | Ensure students understand question 1. Tell them the theme is directly stated in the text; have them read Mr. Hayes's third speech on page 336 to identify the theme. | After students answer question 1, have them discuss the theme of the selection with partners. Tell students to express the theme in their own words. |

**TEKS** **10.13A** Plan a first draft by determining topics through a range of strategies; **10.14C** Write a script with an explicit/implicit theme and details that contribute to the mood and tone; **ELPS 2C** Learn basic vocabulary heard during classroom instruction/interactions; **3G** Express ideas ranging from communicating short phrases to participating in discussions; **4F** Use support from peers/teachers to enhance and confirm understanding; **4G** Demonstrate comprehension of increasingly complex English/responding to questions

## Identifying Other Characters

While it is ideal for students to determine the function of each of the supporting characters in their plays ahead of time, they may discover as they write that one of their supporting characters is unnecessary or that supporting characters change roles. Remind students that, as they learned when planning their short stories (SE page 328), things won't always work out as they initially intended.

**List additional characters for your play.** Have students record character information in a three-column chart with the heads "Character's Name," "Description," and "Purpose." DIFFERENTIATE INSTRUCTION ↘

## Planning the Starting Point

Students may need to plan all the important events in their play before they can decide on the starting point. Suggest that after they make a list of background details to include in the early part of their plays, they plot the rest of the play's actions.

**Plan how to start your play.** Students can use a story map or a plot line (see SE page 322) to organize preliminary ideas and show the story line. Once again, remind students that they can always change the plan as they write, but that having a general idea of the story line is a good way to begin. Alternately, provide a time line (see TE Appendix) for students to use in their planning.

⭐ **TEKS** 10.13A, 10.14C

---

## Identifying Other Characters

Other characters serve specific purposes. They explain information or complicate the plot. They may help convey theme, either explicitly or implicitly. They can also help set the tone for the play. In the sample, Wesley wants to get a job. Each of the other characters contributes in some way to the action.

### Character List

> Wesley's friend Luke brings up the idea that Wesley may not be suitably dressed for a job interview.
> Wesley's friend Tori reinforces the idea that he is not dressed properly.
> Mr. Hayes also points out Wesley's mistake about his attire.
> Kyle presents a contrast, showing someone properly dressed for an interview.

**Prewrite**   **List additional characters for your play.** Explain what the function of each will be. (Limit yourself to a few additional characters.)

## Planning the Starting Point

Start your play right in the middle of the action. Work in any necessary background information in interchanges between the characters. Matt decided that the action would begin with a conversation between Luke and Wesley about the interview Wesley was going to. Matt also listed background information that he may need to work in early in the play. (Later, Matt crossed out ideas that were unnecessary.)

### Background Information

> **What the audience needs to know:**
> – Wesley is going on a job interview.
> – ~~He has just come from basketball practice.~~
> – He wants to work as a stocker at the Food Mart.
> – He needs to earn money to buy a car.
> – ~~His parents said they would cover his car insurance if he bought a car.~~

**Prewrite**   **Plan how to start your play.** Decide which action will begin your play. Also decide what your audience needs to know so they will be able to follow the story line. (Later, you may find that some of these ideas are unnecessary.)

---

⭐ **TEKS** **10.13A** Plan a first draft by determining topics through a range of strategies; **10.14C** Write a script with an explicit/implicit theme/with details that contribute to the mood and tone

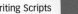
## Considering the Stage Directions

Because a play is a visual as well as an oral medium, the writer must plan the characters' movements onstage. **Stage directions** are the nondialogue parts of a play that identify where the characters are and what they are doing in each scene.

In Matt's play, the action moves smoothly from one location to the next. The opening stage descriptions describe the setup for each acting area that will be used. Remember that the setting and stage directions play a major role in establishing mood.

### Stage Directions

*(The only furniture on the stage is in the UC area—a desk with two chairs, one behind the desk, one in front. At the beginning, Mr. Hayes and Kyle are seated, frozen, in the dark UC area. Tori stands, frozen, in the dark DR area. . . .)*

**Plan your opening stage directions.** Describe where and how the opening action of your play takes place. Try to keep things simple.

Prewrite

## Using Proper Stage Terminology

Below is a diagram of the basic acting areas on a stage and the shorthand used to refer to each area. Use this shorthand in your stage directions.

### Stage Diagram

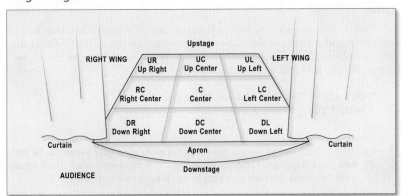

Creative Writing

## Considering the Stage Directions

Students should know in advance where they will present their play so that they can become familiar with its layout and the technology that is available to them. Stress the importance of keeping stage directions simple and brief.

Students can look back at the sample play on SE pages 334–336 to see more examples of simple stage directions.

**Plan your opening stage directions.** Have students describe simply where and how the opening action of their play takes place.

### Using Proper Stage Terminology

Emphasize again the importance of keeping stage directions simple. Tell students to minimize the use of different lighting and special effects, which will simplify the stage terminology. ☑ **DIFFERENTIATE INSTRUCTION**

**TEKS** 10.14C

## Developing Theme, Mood, and Tone

Begin discussion by asking students to explain their understanding of theme, mood, and tone, and how development of these three components can enhance their plays.

### Theme

Explain to students that theme is directly connected to the lesson the main character learns from facing a conflict. Clarify *explicit* and *implicit*, telling students that *explicit* means directly stated and *implicit* means implied.

⭐ **TEKS** 10.14C; **ELPS** 2C

### Mood

Tell students that the details they include—stage directions, word choice, imagery—all contribute to a definite mood. Have students consider details to include to support the mood, or feeling, of the script.

⭐ **TEKS** 10.14C

### Tone

Have students consider how they feel about the theme they want to express. Ask: *Do they think it is serious? Important? Ask them to think about how they want to approach the theme. Do they think that an audience would be more receptive if they used formal or informal language?* Remind students that just as with mood, the details they include directly contribute to the tone.

⭐ **TEKS** 10.14C; **ELPS** 1G

**Plan on a theme, mood, and tone.** Have students jot down ideas and then meet with partners to discuss their plans. Encourage students to incorporate the peer feedback in their drafts as appropriate. **DIFFERENTIATE INSTRUCTION ↘**

---

**340**

 **TEKS** 10.14C

## Developing Theme, Mood, and Tone

As you plan your script, keep in mind three key components: theme, mood, and tone. These components will influence the conflict, the staging and dialogue, and how you portray the characters in your play.

### Theme

Theme is the underlying message about life or human nature that a writer wants the reader to understand. In most cases, themes are not explicitly stated but are implied, so they must be inferred by the audience. A theme may imply how a person should live, but theme should not be confused with a moral. Universal themes are those that are found in the literature of all time periods.

Introduce your theme:

**"You think you look okay for a job interview?"**

### Mood

Mood is the feeling or atmosphere that the writer creates for the reader or audience. Descriptive words, imagery, and figurative language contribute to the mood of a play. If the stage is dark, with only a tree or two, and you hear a hooting owl, you can imagine that the mood of the play will be one of dread or fright. Dialogue, too, can convey the mood.

**"Well, Wesley, I'll tell you. You seem like a pleasant young man. But I'm not going to give you the job."**

### Tone

Tone is the attitude the writer takes toward the subject. Unlike mood, which is intended to shape the audience's emotional response, tone reflects the writer's feelings. Tone can be described by a single word, such as humorous, serious, formal, informal, ironic, sarcastic, and so on.

**"Don't say it, Tori. Okay so you were right."**
**"I wasn't going to say a thing."**

**Prewrite** **Plan on a theme, mood, and tone.** Decide what your theme will be and how you are going to establish the mood in the audience's mind. Think about ways to convey the tone you want to use toward your characters.

---

### Differentiated Instruction: Struggling Learners

If students have difficulty conceptualizing theme, provide additional instruction. Help students differentiate between *topic*, *theme*, and *moral* by providing this example: Topic: Friendship. Moral: Treat your friends right. Theme: True friends are priceless.

---

⭐ **TEKS** **10.14C** Write a script with an explicit/implicit theme and details that contribute to the mood and tone; **ELPS** **1G** Demonstrate increasing knowledge of when to use formal/informal English; **2C** Learn academic vocabulary heard during classroom instruction/interactions

⭐ **TEKS** 10.13B, 10.14C

Writing Scripts **341**

# Drafting Creating Your Script

Remember that the characters tell the story. Imagine what they will say and do in response to the play's conflict. Keep in mind that ideas in a script should be structured in a sustained, persuasive way.

### Beginning

- **Start right in the middle of the action** and work in the necessary background information. Introduce the theme, either explicitly or implicitly, and use details that will establish a definite mood. As you introduce the characters, include details that will contribute to a definite tone. (See page **340**.)

### Middle

- **Use dialogue and action to present the play's ideas.** Make sure the dialogue sounds natural.
- **Add complications (problems) to build suspense.** Don't let the character solve the problem too quickly.
- **Build to the climax.** This is the point where the character comes face-to-face with his or her problem and responds to it in some way.

### Ending

- **Bring your play to a close.** Show how your character has changed because of what he or she has learned.

## Developing Your Characters

1. **What does the character say and do?** From Wesley's words and actions, we learn that he doesn't think he needs to dress up for the interview. The stage directions tell us what he is doing.

    WESLEY:   My shining personality will win them over.
    WESLEY:   Thank you, sir. *(Enters and extends his hand for a handshake, politely sits down.)*

2. **What do others say to, or about, the main character?** Their thoughts can reveal personality traits of the character.

    TORI:   You look like you just overhauled an engine or something. . . .
    MR. HAYES:   Your clothes tell me that you don't really care.

**Write your first draft.** Use the tips above to write your first draft.

*Creative Writing*

---

Before reading the sample script, turn to the Tools of Language for additional support for the writing form.

| ELP Level **Beginning** | ELP Level **Intermediate** | ELP Level **Advanced/Advanced High** |
|---|---|---|
| Demonstrate tone by reading lines in an angry, lighthearted, and sad tone of voice. Have students identify a description of tone from a list of possibilities. | Help students plan details to include to create mood. Have students use a cluster diagram, writing the name of the mood in the center and specific details in the outlying circles. | Have students write their themes in their notebooks. Organize students into pairs and have them discuss how they will express the theme through details and events. |

---

# Drafting
## Creating Your Script

Remind students to keep the audience in mind as they write their draft.

- If the action is too slow, the audience will lose interest. If the action is too fast, the audience may have trouble following the story. By structuring ideas and events in a sustained way, writers maintain audience interest and slowly build a case for the theme.
- The audience knows only what it sees happening on the stage and what it hears the characters say. Although a few plays (for example, Thornton Wilder's *Our Town*) have narrators to provide background and commentary on the characters and their problems, most plays rely mainly on dialogue and stage actions to tell the story. The details included in dialogue contribute directly to mood and tone. A character may explicitly state the theme or imply it through conversation, actions, and reactions. ⟋ **DIFFERENTIATE INSTRUCTION**

⭐ **TEKS** 10.13B, 10.14C

## Developing Your Characters

Point out that playwrights use the same three methods of characterization that storytellers use to develop their characters: what the character says, what the character does, and what other characters in the story say to or about the character.

Provide students with a sensory chart (see TE Appendix) or another graphic organizer to help them explore each of their characters. This will help them see if they need to add any dimension to their characters.

**Write your first draft.** Tell students that now that they have a good idea about the content and direction of their scripts, they can express that information through dialogue and stage directions. Tell students to write what comes to them. They will have the opportunity to revise the writing later.

⭐ **TEKS** 10.14C

 **TEKS** **10.13B** Structure ideas in a sustained way/persuasive way; **10.14C** Write a script with an explicit/implicit theme and details that contribute to the mood and tone; **ELPS 2A** Distinguish intonation patterns with increasing ease; **3E** Share information in cooperative learning interactions; **5B** Write using content-based grade-level vocabulary

## Revising
**Improving Your Writing**

### Theme

Read aloud the questions and clarify meaning if needed. Tell students that if they cannot answer *yes* to the final two questions, they will need to revise dialogue and add or rearrange events.

### Mood

Provide student examples of a definite mood and figurative language used to express the mood. Have students consider these examples as they answer the questions about their own writing.

### Tone

Suggest that students write the adjective to describe tone at the top of their scripts and then highlight all the details that reinforce that tone.

**Revise for theme, mood, and tone.** Invite students to exchange papers with partners for review and to incorporate peer feedback into their revisions.

 **TEKS** 10.14C

---

 **TEKS** 10.14C

## Revising **Improving Your Writing**

Read your script again. Use these questions to help guide your revision.

### Theme

- How and when did you introduce the theme?
- Is the theme stated implicitly or explicitly?
- Can your audience infer the theme from the conflict and the actions or dialogue of the characters?
- Has your development of the theme been consistent throughout the script?

### Mood

- What feeling or atmosphere have you created?
- Have you used imagery and figurative language to convey the mood to the audience?
- Are the descriptions you have created believable and engaging?
- Does the mood change during the script? If so, how have you conveyed the change to your audience?

### Tone

- What is your tone toward the main character? What is your tone toward the other characters?
- What words and details have you used to reflect your feelings about the characters?
- What one adjective would you use to describe the tone? Have you adequately conveyed it to your audience?

Revise

**Revise for theme, mood, and tone.** Use the questions above to guide you as you revise your script for consistent theme. If necessary, add details that contribute to a definite mood and to a definite tone.

---

**TEKS** **10.14C** Write a script with an explicit/implicit theme and details that contribute to the mood and tone

**TEKS** 10.13C, 10.13D, 10.14C

## Revising Improving Your Writing

Read your script out loud or have someone else read it to you. Use this checklist to help with your revision.

### Focus and Coherence

_____ **1.** Have I adequately conveyed the theme, mood, and tone?

_____ **2.** Does the plot flow smoothly from beginning to end?

### Organization

_____ **3.** Does each complication build on the previous one?

_____ **4.** Is the climax easily recognized?

_____ **5.** Do stage directions help move the action along?

### Development of Ideas

_____ **6.** Is the main character's conflict believable?

_____ **7.** Does the action include complications (problems)?

_____ **8.** Does each character serve an important role within the play?

### Voice

_____ **9.** Does the dialogue sound natural and believable?

_____ **10.** Does the dialogue flow smoothly from character to character?

## Editing Checking for Conventions

Use the following checklist as a guide when you check your script for proper formatting and for conventions.

### Conventions

_____ **1.** Have I used correct and consistent verb tenses?

_____ **2.** Are the sentences in my dialogue structured correctly?

_____ **3.** Have I checked for correct capitalization and punctuation?

_____ **4.** Have I checked for spelling errors?

**Revise and edit your writing.** Use the checklists above as a guide when you revise and edit the first draft of your script.

*Creative Writing*

## Revising
### Improving Your Writing

Playwrights and directors often have table readings of a script. The actors gather in an informal setting to read their lines aloud. This gives everyone the opportunity to see if the dialogue works. Encourage students to gather in groups to read aloud their scripts. This will give them the opportunity to determine if:

- theme, mood, and tone are clearly conveyed,
- plot events are organized logically and build upon preceding events,
- the characters and events are engaging and believable, and
- the dialogue sounds natural and flows smoothly. ✔ **DIFFERENTIATE INSTRUCTION**

**TEKS** 10.13C, 10.14C

## Editing
### Checking for Conventions

Point out the various punctuation marks in the sample play on SE pages 334–336. For example, you could point out the comma that separates the character's name and his or her description in the character list; the colon following each speaker's name; and end marks, dashes, and ellipses within the dialogue itself.

**TEKS** 10.13D

---

**TEKS** **10.13C** Revise drafts to improve style/word choice/figurative language; **10.13D** Edit drafts for grammar, mechanics, and spelling; **10.14C** Write a script with an explicit/implicit theme and details that contribute to the mood and tone; **ELPS 1B** Monitor oral language and employ self-corrective techniques or other resources; **4A** Learn relationships between sounds and letters; **4F** Use support from peers/teachers to read grade-appropriate content area text

## Sample Radio Script

Encourage students to choose a contemporary topic most radio listeners can identify with, or tell them to imagine they are writing an ad for a particular radio station and tailor the ad to its audience.

Point out that the sample radio script is based on a pet peeve—waiting in line in the "express lane." Writers often use humor to express a pet peeve, as the writer of this radio script has done.

- Have students point out the elements of humor in the script. (Possible choices: when Gladys says, "This one's quicker" and the checker responds; when Gladys says her two-for-one stuff should count as one; when Gladys says she has forgotten her wallet.)
- Have interested students brainstorm other pet peeves they could use as a topic for their radio scripts (for example, cell phones ringing in restaurants, the price of movie tickets, girls or boys who talk only about themselves).

 TEKS 10.14C

### Try It!

Before writing, provide students with a greater sense of what is involved in performing a radio script.

---

## Sample Radio Script

In radio drama, your audience can only imagine the action. Radio scripts have theme, mood, and tone, just like plays.

---

**LIFE IN THE EXPRESS LANE**

(SCENE: A GROCERY STORE CHECKOUT LINE. WE CAN HEAR VOICES, THE DING OF THE SCANNER.)

LOUDSPEAKER: Manager to checkout three, please. Manager to three.

CHECKER: Er—ma'am, this is the express checkout. Eight items or less. You really should go to the regular line.

GLADYS: This one's quicker.

CHECKER: Yes, that's because people only have eight items or less. Usually.

GLADYS: So how many do I have? It's not that much more.

CHECKER: Ma'am, your cart is completely full.

GLADYS: They're big items.

MALE VOICE: Guess she didn't see the sign.

CHECKER: Really, ma'am, it's not fair to the others in line.

GLADYS: Some of my stuff is two-for-one. They should count as one.

FEMALE VOICE: Hey, is this really the express lane?

GLADYS: Next, I suppose you'll want to count each of the bananas in a bunch!

CHECKER: Okay, okay, ma'am. Let's just get going here. (SOUND OF SCANNER BEGINS.)

GLADYS: I'm a long-time customer. I don't need to be treated so poorly.

CHECKER: I'm very sorry, ma'am. That'll be $63.47, please.

GLADYS: Honestly, I don't need to be lectured about—er—oh, my.

CHECKER: Ma'am? Is there a problem?

GLADYS: Well, I seem to have forgotten my wallet.

MALE VOICE: Oh, man! You've got to be kidding!

CHECKER: (*Sighs.*) I'm sorry, I'll have to close for a few minutes.

VOICES: (*Background grumbling grows loud; then fades out.*)

---

### Try It!

Write a radio script about an interesting scene from your life.

---

# Prewriting Choosing Your Main Character

In a radio script you may have fewer characters, but there will still be a main character who faces conflict. As you start your planning for a radio script, choose a main character and decide how you want to portray him or her. Think about details you can use to convey tone.

## Selecting a Conflict

The conflict is the problem that the main character faces. In the sample script, the problem is that the checker sees Gladys in the express line with too many items. As you plan your own radio script, think about conflicts that your main character might realistically face. Choose a theme you want to address and details you will need to include to create a definite mood for your script.

## Considering Sound Effects

Instead of stage directions, in a radio script you will need to consider how to convey action. Think about possible sound effects that will convey the action so that your audience can "see" what is happening.

 **Plan how to start your radio script.** Decide on your characters and the conflict. Think about ways to effectively convey the action.

# Drafting Creating Your Script

Remember, in a radio script, the characters tell the story.

### Beginning
- Start your script in the middle of the action. Background should be provided in the dialogue between characters.

### Middle
- Use dialogue and sound effects to convey action.
- Add complications among characters to add tension.
- Build to the climax.

### Ending
- Bring your radio script to its conclusion.

 **Draft your radio script.** Use the tips above to help guide you as you draft your script.

*Creative Writing*

## Prewriting
### Choosing Your Main Character

Remind students that main characters should be dynamic; that is, they should be complex like real people and change as a result of the conflicts they face. Tell students that they can set the tone of the play through the words and actions of the main character.

**TEKS** 10.14C

### Selecting a Conflict

Remind students that the lesson the main character learns through facing a conflict is directly related to the script's theme. Tell students to decide whether their script will have an explicit or implicit theme and fashion the conflict and dialogue to express that theme.

**TEKS** 10.14C

### Considering Sound Effects

Tell students that they will have to set the scene using sound effects since a radio script is heard, not seen. Give students examples of sound effects, such as cars passing by on a busy street, sirens, or running water. Explain to students the connection between sound effects and mood. For example, the sound of thunder in the distance sets a mood of suspense or foreboding.

**TEKS** 10.14C

**Plan how to start your radio script.** After students choose characters and conflict, have them use a sequence of events chart to identify the main actions in the script. From this list students can choose the best place to begin.

## Drafting
### Creating Your Script

Remind students that like a story a radio script has a beginning, middle, and ending. Review the Plot Line on SE page 322 and tell students to use the diagram to structure their scripts.

**Draft your radio script.** Remind students to follow the same format as writing a script for a play. Tell students they will have the opportunity to revise their first drafts later.

**Revising**

**Improving Your Radio Script**

After students answer the questions in the checklist, discuss how to address any shortcomings in their scripts. Tell students they can re-order events, add information, take out information, or replace general words with vivid words.

**TEKS** 10.14C

## Editing

**Checking for Conventions**

Tell students to read through their scripts numerous times, looking for one error at a time. Have students focus on punctuation, making sure they have followed the script format and used punctuation properly within the stage directions and dialogue.

**Revise and edit your script.** Suggest that students read dialogue aloud in small groups before answering the questions on the Revising Checklist. Students can then hear the flow of their dialogue and incorporate peer feedback in their revisions. **DIFFERENTIATE INSTRUCTION** ⟶

**TEKS** 10.13D; **ELPS** 1B, 2I

 **Conventions Connections**

**Grammar: Prepositions**
- *Proofreader's Guide* pages 760–761
- *SkillsBook* page 116

✦ *Write Source Online* **GrammarSnap**

**TEKS** **10.13D** Edit drafts for grammar/mechanics; **10.14C** Write a script with an explicit/implicit theme and details that contribute to the mood and tone; **ELPS** **1B** Monitor oral language and employ self-corrective techniques or other resources; **1D** Speak using learning strategies/request assistance, employ non-verbal cues, and convey ideas by defining or describing; **2A** Distinguish sounds/ intonation patterns with increasing ease; **2I** Demonstrate listening comprehension in increasingly complex spoken language by collaborating with peers

---

## Revising Improving Your Radio Script

Ask yourself the following questions when you revise and edit your script.

### Focus and Coherence

_____ **1.** How have I conveyed the theme?
_____ **2.** What details have I included to create the mood of my radio script?
_____ **3.** What is the tone? What details have I used to set my script's tone?

### Organization

_____ **4.** Do the actions build toward the climax?
_____ **5.** Does the main character change after the climax?
_____ **6.** Do the sound effects help the audience "see" the action?

### Development of Ideas

_____ **7.** Do my characters talk and act like real people?
_____ **8.** Is my conflict believable?

### Voice

_____ **9.** Can I improve my style or word choice to make the characters seem more real?

## Editing Checking for Conventions

When you edit your revised script, check for correct grammar, sentence structure, capitalization, punctuation, and spelling.

### Conventions

_____ **1.** Have I checked for correct verb tenses and grammar?
_____ **2.** Have I structured my sentences and dialogue correctly?
_____ **3.** Have I capitalized proper nouns and first words in sentences?
_____ **4.** Have I correctly punctuated my script, including the dialogue?
_____ **5.** Have I used a print or online dictionary to check my spelling?

 **Revise and edit your story.** Use the information above to help you revise and edit the first draft of your radio script.

---

**Differentiated Instruction:**
**English Language Learners**                    **ELPS** 1D, 2A

| ELP Level **Beginning** | ELP Level **Intermediate** | ELP Level **Advanced/Advanced High** |
|---|---|---|
| Have students form pairs and practice correct intonation by reading aloud lines from the script on SE page 344. Emphasize lines punctuated with question marks or exclamation points. | Have students practice intonation as in the Beginning exercise, but also add nonverbal cues and facial expressions to help express the intended intonation. | Have students choose a line and say it aloud to a partner, emphasizing a different word each time they read it; then discuss how the meaning changed by varying intonation. |

# Writing Poetry

Have you ever read a poem and thought, "I know that feeling"? Part of the pleasure of reading poetry is that sense of connection between poet and reader. As Italian poet Salvatore Quasimodo put it, "Poetry is the revelation of a feeling that the poet believes to be interior and personal, which the reader recognizes as his own."

A poem reveals much about a poet's inner feelings, especially when it is an autobiographical poem. In this chapter, you will learn to write an autobiographical free-verse poem. You will also learn about two special forms of poetry: the ballad and the lune poem. No matter what form you work with, you will learn something new about yourself as you develop your thoughts and feelings.

## Writing Guidelines

**Subject:** Self-portrait
**Purpose:** To entertain
**Form:** Free-verse poem
**Audience:** Friends, family, and classmates

"I should not talk so much about myself if there were anybody else whom I knew as well."

—Henry David Thoreau

## Resources

### Copy Masters (see Appendix)

- Details chart (TE pp. 349, 350)
- Quick list (TE p. 350)
- Sensory chart (TE p. 349)

## Writing Poetry

## Objectives

- understand the content and structure of free-verse poems, ballads, and lunes
- choose a topic (a trait that reveals the writer's personality) to inspire an autobiographical free-verse poem
- use poetry techniques, including figures of speech and special sounds, in a poem
- plan, draft, revise, edit, and share a free-verse poem, a ballad, and a lune

## Writing Guidelines

Ask students to reflect on the quotation by Henry David Thoreau. Tell students that just like a self-portrait painting, a self-portrait poem reveals something about the subject.

## Sample Free-Verse Poem

Many students may feel hesitant about their ability to read and understand poetry.

**Respond to the reading.**

**Answers**

**Focus and Coherence 1.** Perfection comes from within, not from one's personal appearance.

**Organization 2.** Possible answers:
- Beginning: lines 1–2. These lines focus on the speaker's self-consciousness about his teeth.
- Middle: lines 3–6. These lines focus on how unaware the speaker was of his inner self.
- Ending: lines 7–11. These lines focus on the speaker's growing awareness that he is someone he would like to know better.

**Development of Ideas 3.** He was self-conscious about his appearance because of his imperfect teeth, until one day he saw himself in a mirror and liked what he saw.

**Voice 4.** The use of third person allows the speaker to remain detached from the moment of self-discovery, which can be uncomfortable for many people. **DIFFERENTIATE INSTRUCTION ↘**

**TEKS** 10.14B; **ELPS** 3G

---

**TEKS** 10.14B
**ELPS** 3G

## Sample Free-Verse Poem

Most traditional poetry follows a specific pattern of rhythm and rhyme, two major poetic devices. Free-verse poems, on the other hand, develop a structure of their own. This makes free verse ideal for an autobiographical poem. Eli Pulkkinen wrote the following free-verse poem to tell about a moment of self-discovery.

**Perfection**

His teeth were not perfect,
so only his lips smiled,
until one day,
laughing at a joke, he
glanced up to find a stranger
laughing with him–
a grin so inviting
that for a moment
he did not recognize
the mirror,
his own reflection.

—Eli Pulkkinen

**Respond to the reading.** On your own paper, reflect on the focus and coherence, organization, ideas, and voice of the free-verse poem above. Discuss your reflections with a classmate. Listen carefully to what your partner has to say, and ask questions using appropriate vocabulary.

**Focus and Coherence** (1) The central idea is about a moment of self-discovery. How does the title relate to the poem's message? **Organization** (2) If you were to divide this poem into three parts—beginning, middle, and ending—where would you divide it? Explain why. **Development of Ideas** (3) What does this poem reveal about the writer? **Voice** (4) Why do you think the poet used third-person pronouns (*his, he*) in this poem?

**Tip**

Some poems rely on many sensory details to build a mental picture. Others are more sparse, like the one above. In either case, the poet must carefully choose the best words to convey the poem's idea.

---

### Differentiated Instruction: Advanced Learners

After students have read the poem and discussed and answered the questions, challenge them to write a one-paragraph evaluation of the poem. They should evaluate the quality of the poem—discussing the focus and coherence, development of ideas, organization, and voice—not just their personal opinion of it. Tell students to be sure to cite examples from the text to support their opinions.

## Prewriting Choosing a Focus

When writing an autobiographical poem, you should focus on one particular idea, event, or feeling that reveals your personality. To choose that focus, you can use one of the following strategies.

### Looking in a Mirror

When artists draw a self-portrait, they use a mirror. Poets can do the same. Take time to examine your own face in a mirror and jot down notes about what you see. How would you describe each of your features? What personality do you see looking back at you? How do your features reveal that personality?

Think about poetic techniques you can use to convey these features. Sound devices include alliteration and assonance. Other common poetic devices include metaphors and similes, figurative language, and imagery. Be sure to include a variety of poetic techniques as you plan and write your poem.

### Making a Personality Cluster

Write your name in a circle; then list your personality traits around it. Expand your cluster to include ideas about how you reveal each trait.

### Reviewing Your Journal or a Photo Album

Browse through your journal to find interesting ideas or events. Or look through a family album for ideas. Eli chose an entry from his journal.

> Sept. 14, 2008
> Today at my part-time job, I was sweeping the break room when Rhoda said something that made me bust out laughing. When I looked up, I saw this other guy behind her with a big, amazing grin. For a minute, I didn't realize it was my own reflection in the break-room mirror. Seeing that grin, I don't think I'm going to be so self-conscious about my smile anymore.

Eli boiled down this memory to a purpose statement:

> I want to share the surprise of the moment when I realized the laughing stranger with the great smile was me.

 **Prewrite**

**Select a focus.** Use one of the techniques above to choose a specific feature, idea, or memory that reveals something about your personality. Then write a purpose statement to identify the focus of your poem.

*Creative Writing*

## Prewriting

### Choosing a Focus

Remind students that poetry is usually a succinct form of writing. Therefore, students need to narrow the focus to an idea that can be expressed in a few lines. To identify a specific focus, they can use a variety of strategies.

TEKS 10.13A

### Looking in a Mirror

Have students spend a few minutes looking in the mirror and responding to the questions in the SE. Alternately, supply a details chart of a sensory chart (see TE Appendix) for students to record their observations. Then review metaphor and simile and challenge students to come up with original comparisons to describe the traits they identified in the mirror. Students might include the imagery in the poem or use it as a starting point.

TEKS 10.14B

### Making a Personality Cluster

Draw a three-tiered cluster diagram on the board to demonstrate the process for students. In the center, write your name or a student's name. In the next circle, record a personality trait, such as *witty* or *funny*. In the next layer of circles, write examples, such as *love to tell jokes* or *always have a quick reply.* ✔ DIFFERENTIATE INSTRUCTION

### Reviewing Your Journal or a Photo Album

Allow students time to review journals or think about the events of their weeks. Help students make the connection between Eli's purpose statement and his journal entry.

**Select a focus.** Suggest that students try more than one strategy to see which is most productive for them. Before students write, explain that a purpose statement is a sentence that explains what they will do in their poem.

TEKS 10.13A

 **TEKS 10.13A** Plan a first draft by selecting the correct genre and determining topics through a range of strategies; **10.14B** Write a poem using poetic techniques and forms;
**ELPS 1E** Internalize new academic language by using and reusing it/ writing; **3B** Expand vocabulary by learning and using high-frequency words for identifying and describing; **5G** Describe with increasing specificity and detail/writing

## Prewriting
### Gathering Details

Students should notice that the language Eli used in the poem on SE page 348 is quite different from the language he used to gather details. Emphasize that during prewriting, students should focus on gathering details rather than deciding on word choice.

**Make a list.** Provide copies of the reproducible details chart or the quick list (see TE Appendix) for students to use to list essential details for their poem. DIFFERENTIATE INSTRUCTION ↘

## Drafting
### Developing Your Poem

Some students will benefit from going through the same evolutionary process that Eli did: a list of essential details, a sentence draft, a draft with line breaks, and finally the poem. Other students may find it easier to jump from their details list right into the poem.

### Using Poetic Techniques

Discuss the poetry techniques here, as well as the ones on SE pages 352–353.

Have students experiment with different line breaks in their own poem to see how the changes affect the sound and sense of the poem.

⭐ **TEKS** 10.14B

**Write your first draft.** Have students follow the steps outlined in the SE. Circulate around the room as students write to answer questions and provide feedback.

⭐ **TEKS** 10.14B

---

 **TEKS** 10.14B

# Prewriting Gathering Details

One of the best ways to gather details for a self-portrait poem is to make a list. Eli made the following list of essential details for his poem:

> 1. Feeling shy about my teeth
> 2. Laughing at Rhoda's joke
> 3. Noticing a stranger laughing
> 4. Being shocked that he was my own reflection

 **Make a list** of details to include in your poem. Put them in the order you want to use in your poem.

# Drafting Developing Your Poem

Many poets begin with sentences, focusing on ideas, sounds of words, and imagery. Then they break the sentences into shorter lines to set the rhythm, create rhymes, and make a poem. Eli started with this:

> I was shy about my teeth. Then one day, while laughing at a joke, I saw this stranger laughing, too. His smile was so surprising that for a moment I didn't realize it was my own reflection.

## Using Poetic Techniques

Rhythm is a special sound technique that separates prose from poetry. One way poets create rhythm is by breaking their writing into unique phrasing for a desired effect and meaning.

> I was shy about my teeth.
> Then one day,
> while laughing at a joke,
> I saw this stranger
> laughing, too.
> His smile was so surprising
> that for a moment
> I didn't realize
> it was my own reflection.

### Line Breaks

*Line breaks* help to set the pace and rhythm of a poem. They help control the poem and add emphasis to certain words.

 **Write your first draft.** Start with phrases or sentences that get across the idea. Then add line breaks to control the rhythm and add emphasis.

---

⭐ **TEKS** **10.14B** Write a poem using poetic techniques and forms

## Revising Focusing on the Traits

The first draft of a poem often comes in a rush of creativity. Revision is your chance to polish your work. In particular, look at the following traits.

- **Focus and Coherence**
1. Is my poem focused on my chosen subject?
- **Organization**
2. Do I use line breaks effectively to control the rhythm of my poem?
3. Have I used the correct poetic structure?
- **Development of ideas**
4. Have I used precise details, figurative language, and imagery to convey my meaning?
5. Do I show my feelings without telling the reader what to think?
- **Voice**
6. Does my poem show inventiveness and personality?

Compare the first draft of Eli's poem on page **350** to his final draft on page **348**. What changes did he make? Which version seems most effective to you?

 **Revise your poem.** Using the questions above as a guide, keep revising until your poem is the best that it can be.

## Editing Checking for Conventions

Because poems are shorter than most other types of writing, every word and punctuation mark is important. Careful editing is necessary.

- **Conventions** Is my poem free from errors in grammar, capitalization, punctuation, or spelling that could distract a reader?

 **Edit your poem.** Poems sometimes break the rules, but never by accident. Edit your poem for careless errors and make a neat final copy.

## Publishing Sharing Your Poem

When your poem is finished, share it with others.

- **Post it.** Put it on a bulletin board or a Web site.
- **Submit it.** Send your poem to a contest or magazine.
- **Perform it.** Read your poem to friends and family.

 **Present your poem.** Let other people read or hear what you have created.

Creative Writing

## Revising
### Focusing on the Traits

After revising, students should read aloud their poems to make sure they have the rhythm and meaning they desire.

**Revise your poem.** Suggest that students meet in small groups to read their poems aloud for feedback. After reading their poems, students can ask listeners for comments, using the questions shown in the text for each of the traits.

TEKS 10.13C, 10.14B

## Editing
### Checking for Conventions

**Edit your poem.** Point out that although poems sometimes break punctuation and capitalization rules, they usually don't break spelling rules, except for special emphasis.

TEKS 10.13D

## Publishing
### Sharing Your Poem

**Present your poem.** Set aside time for students to share their poems in class. Students may want to create an illustrated class album with photographs or self-portraits.

 **Technology Connections**

➤ *Write Source Online* **Portfolio**

➤ *Write Source Online* **Essay Scoring**

---

## Differentiated Instruction: English Language Learners

ELPS 1E, 5B, 5G

| ELP Level **Beginning** | ELP Level **Intermediate** | ELP Level **Advanced/Advanced High** |
|---|---|---|
| Provide sentence frames and basic answer choices for students to copy and complete in their detail charts. For example, *I felt (happy, sad, scared)*. | Point out that Eli's details are in time order. Have students decide how they will organize details, then record them in order in their charts. Provide transitions: *first, next, finally*. | Have students exchange details with partners. Have students ask questions and comment on details partners have chosen, then work on word choice to include vivid, sensory words. |

---

TEKS **10.13C** Revise drafts to improve style, word choice, and figurative language/rethink how well the genre has been addressed; **10.13D** Edit drafts for grammar, mechanics, and spelling; **10.14B** Write a poem using poetic techniques and forms; **ELPS 1E** Internalize new basic language by using and reusing it/writing; **5B** Write using newly acquired basic and content-based grade-level vocabulary; **5G** Describe with increasing specificity and detail/writing

## Using Special Poetry Techniques

Suggest that students look back at all of the creative writing that they have done in this unit, including the short story, play, radio script, and poems. Have them identify places in their prose and poetry where they used figures of speech to enhance their writing. Ask them to consider where they could have used one of the figures of speech shown on SE page 352 to improve their writing.

### Figures of Speech

Read each definition and example. Clarify any confusion for students. Have them solidify their understanding by writing examples of simile, metaphor, personification, and hyperbole. To direct the exercise, provide students with instructions: *Use a simile to describe a baseball player. Use a metaphor to describe a marching band. Personify a textbook. Use hyperbole to describe your homework.* **DIFFERENTIATE INSTRUCTION** ↘

 **TEKS** 10.14B

### Sounds of Poetry

Read aloud the definitions and have students read the examples chorally to hear the sound patterns. **DIFFERENTIATE INSTRUCTION** ↘

---

 **TEKS** 10.14B

# Using Special Poetry Techniques

Poets use a variety of special techniques in their work. This page and the next define some of the most important ones.

**Figures of Speech**

- A **simile** (*sĭm´ə-lē*) compares two unlike things with the word *like* or *as*.

  She twirled
  across the stage
  like a tornado.

- A **metaphor** (*mĕt´ə-fôr*) compares two unlike things without using *like* or *as*.

  An avalanche of books
  covered the stairs.

- **Personification** (*pər-sŏn´ə-fĭ-kā´shən*) is a technique that gives human traits to something that is nonhuman.

  Brown trees frowned all down the lane.

- **Hyperbole** (*hī-pûr´bə-lē*) is an exaggerated statement, often humorous.

  The test sheet landed
  on my desk
  with a thud.

**Sounds of Poetry**

- **Alliteration** (*ə-lĭt´ə-rā´shən*) is the repetition of consonant sounds at the beginning of words.

  A **b**right green **b**louse

- **Assonance** (*ăs´ə-nəns*) is the repetition of vowel sounds anywhere in words.

  It pl**ea**s**e** m**e** to s**ee**
  a tr**ee** l**ea**n in a br**ee**ze.

- **Consonance** (*kŏn´sə-nəns*) is the repetition of consonant sounds anywhere in words.

  abou**t** wha**t** **n**o**t** to wear

---

### Differentiated Instruction: Struggling Learners

Tell students that when they compare they look for the way things are alike. Explain that similes and metaphors are interesting because they compare things that seem as if they are not alike. By doing this, they create vivid images in readers' minds.

Read the example of simile. Ask what a tornado and a girl dancing, or twirling, across the stage might have in common. Help them understand that this comparison says that the girl was spinning quickly and powerfully across the stage.

---

- **Line breaks** help control the rhythm of a poem. The reader naturally pauses at the end of a line. There's also added emphasis on the last word in a line.

    laughing at a joke, he
    glanced up to find a stranger
    laughing with him

- **Onomatopoeia** (ŏn′ə-mät′ə-pē′ə) is the use of words that sound like what they name.

    Wind hissing on snow

- **Repetition** (rĕp′ĭ-tĭsh′ən) uses the same word or phrase more than once, for emphasis or for rhythm.

    You are not my mother.
    You are not my father.
    You are not my teacher.
    You are my friend.

- **Rhyme** (rīm) means using words whose endings sound alike.

    *End rhyme* happens at the end of lines.

    My style's not moderate.
    I've got a doctorate
    in "Color it!"

    *Internal rhyme* happens within lines.

    Brown trees frowned all down the lane.

- **Rhythm** (rĭth′əm) is the pattern of accented and unaccented syllables in a poem. The rhythm of free-verse poetry tends to flow naturally, like speaking. Traditional poetry follows a more regular pattern, as in the following example.

    I don't fear
    what I hear

**Try It!**

Write your own example of two or more of the special poetry techniques explained on these two pages. Then expand each of your examples into a complete poem.

*Creative Writing*

---

Hold an open discussion on the poetry techniques and how to apply them to writing.

Then ask students to read favorite poems that employ one or more of these techniques. Ask listeners to identify the different techniques used in the poems.

Invite students to revisit their free-verse poems and add various poetic techniques to enhance their writing.

**Try It!**
**Answers**

Suggest that students use both a figure of speech and a sound device in their poems.

⭐ TEKS 10.14B

---

| ELP Level **Beginning** | ELP Level **Intermediate** | ELP Level **Advanced/Advanced High** |
|---|---|---|
| Write: *Please pass the peas.* Explain that this shows both alliteration and assonance. Have students echo-read each word after you, enunciating initial *ps* and the long *e* sound. | Spanish speakers may have difficulty discerning /b/ and /v/. Show mouth formation of /b/, explaining that the lips are held together and /b/ is made by expelling air. | Write: *She cleans the seat. Larry laughed a long time.* Have students copy the sentences and identify the sound device for each, then underline repeated vowel and consonant sounds. |

⭐ TEKS **10.14B** Write a poem using poetic techniques;
**ELPS 2A** Distinguish sounds with increasing ease; **2B** Recognize elements of the English sound system in new vocabulary/long and short vowels, silent letters, and consonant clusters; **3A** Practice producing sounds of newly acquired vocabulary; **4A** Learn relationships between sounds and letters

## Ballad

Tell students that a ballad is a form of narrative poetry; that is, a ballad includes characters, has a plot and setting, and expresses a theme. Explain that as students approach writing a ballad, they will need to combine the steps of writing a story with writing a poem.

**TEKS** 10.14B

Review Sounds of Poetry on SE pages 352–353, focusing especially on rhythm and rhyme. If possible, play an audio recording of "Barbara Allen" and/or other popular ballads so students can get a sense of the rhythm and flow of the songs. **DIFFERENTIATE INSTRUCTION ↘**

### Prewriting
#### Planning Your Ballad

Tell students that as they plan their ballads, they should begin with a character, a conflict, a setting, and a theme. After they have the content and organization of the ballad recorded, they can then consider the structure, rhyme scheme, rhythm, and other poetic techniques they might use.

Suggest that students break their stories into stanzas, writing a paraphrase in prose of each stanza. When they draft, they can focus on word choice and techniques to express the ideas of each stanza clearly.

**TEKS** 10.14B

**Plan your ballad.** Students might use a Story Map to organize initial ideas for their ballads.

---

354     **TEKS** 10.14B

## Ballad

For centuries, people have composed ballads, stories told in song using the voice and language of everyday people. Ballads were composed orally, and singers often added or changed details to make the songs meaningful for their audience. The earliest ballads are known as folk ballads.

Ballads have characters, setting, and dialogue. Like songs, ballads use repetition and have regular rhyme and meter. A traditional ballad, like "Barbara Allen," consists of four-line stanzas with a simple rhyme scheme, and it narrates a single tragic event.

The ballad "Barbara Allen" has many variations. Several stanzas of the ballad are shown here. Song lyrics today continue to employ the medieval ballad form of poetry.

> **"Barbara Allen"**
>
> All in the merry month of May,
> When green buds they were swellin'
> Young William Grove on his death-bed lay,
> For love of Barbara Allen.
>
> He sent his servant to her door
> To the town where he was dwellin'
> Haste ye come, to my master's call
> If your name be Barbara Allen,
>
> So slowly, slowly got she up,
> And slowly she drew nigh him,
> And all she said when there she came:
> "Young man, I think you're dying!"
>
> He turned his face unto the wall
> And death was drawing nigh him.
> Good bye, Good bye to dear friends all,
> Be kind to Barbara Allen.

### Prewriting Planning Your Ballad

- **Select** a single, tragic event for your ballad. Create the characters.
- **Gather and organize details.** Make a list of the events that will be in your ballad. Then organize them in a logical flow. Most ballads are arranged in chronologically.
- Think about the structure and poetic techniques you will use. Most ballads are written in everyday language. Decide on a rhyme scheme and the figurative language you want to use. (Check a rhyming dictionary for help.) Work with the rhythm until the poem reads well aloud.

 **Plan your ballad.** Use the tips and the information about the structure and poetic techniques of a ballad as a guide for your prewriting.
Prewrite

---

### Differentiated Instruction: Struggling Learners

Because a ballad is such a structured form, struggling learners may have difficulty writing to its specifications. Suggest that students complete a frame for each stanza, beginning by imitating the rhyme scheme and rhythm of "Barbara Allen."
- Line 1: 9 syllables, rhyme a
- Line 2: 7 syllables, rhyme b
- Line 3: 9 syllables, rhyme a
- Line 4: 7 syllables, rhyme b

**TEKS** 10.14B

---

**TEKS** 10.13C, 10.13D, 10.14B

## Drafting Writing Your Ballad

Use the information about the structure of ballads, the information about poetic techniques, and the planning you did on the previous page to write your ballad. Structure your ideas in a sustained way, and develop a conflict or tragic event that will engage the reader.

## Revising Focusing on the Traits

Ask yourself the following questions when you review and revise the first draft of your ballad.

### Focus and Coherence

_____ **1.** Do I narrate a single tragic event in my ballad?

_____ **2.** Can the reader follow the flow of ideas from start to finish?

### Organization

_____ **3.** Is there an introduction, middle part, and a conclusion?

_____ **4.** Do I use line breaks to control the rhythm of the poem?

_____ **5.** Have I chosen an effective organizational pattern?

### Development of Ideas

_____ **6.** Do I use well-chosen, precise details?

_____ **7.** Do my characters seem real and the event believable?

_____ **8.** Can the reader follow the flow of ideas?

### Voice

_____ **9.** Have I used poetic techniques to convey my meaning?

## Editing Checking for Conventions

Edit your ballad for grammar, capitalization, punctuation, and spelling.

_____ **1.** Have I used correct verb tenses, and have I capitalized, punctuated, and spelled words correctly in my ballad?

**Revise and edit your ballad.** Use the information above to help you revise and edit the first draft of your ballad.

Revise

Creative Writing

## Drafting

### Writing Your Ballad

Have students work from the paraphrases of events for each stanza. Tell students that drafting a ballad may take considerably more time than free verse or prose due to all of the restrictions of the form. Allow students to discuss questions with you or partners if they get stuck during drafting. ✔ DIFFERENTIATE INSTRUCTION

**TEKS** 10.13B, 10.14B

## Revising

### Focusing on the Traits

Have students read and answer the questions independently. Then divide them into small groups and have group members answer the questions as students read their ballads aloud. When each member has read, students can gather feedback and incorporate it into their final drafts.

**TEKS** 10.13C; **ELPS** 3E

## Editing

### Checking for Conventions

Tell students to pay special attention to spelling, focusing on the end rhymes. Point out that words that rhyme are sometimes spelled differently.

**Revise and edit your ballad.** Tell students to read through their ballads several times, checking for a different kind of error each time.

**TEKS** 10.13D; **ELPS** 5D

**TEKS** 10.13B Structure ideas in a sustained way; **10.13C** Revise drafts to improve style, word choice, and figurative language/rethink how well the genre has been addressed; **10.13D** Edit drafts for grammar, mechanics, and spelling; **10.14B** Write a poem using poetic techniques and forms; **ELPS** 1A Use prior knowledge and experience to understand meanings; **3E** Share information in cooperative learning interactions; **5D** Edit writing for standard grammar and usage/subject-verb and pronoun agreement and appropriate verb tenses

## Lunes

Read and distribute examples of English haiku poems to students so that they can see and hear the difference between traditional haiku and the lunes shown here.

Try composing several lunes together as a class before asking students to compose lunes themselves.

- Display a photograph from a magazine.
- Have students study the photograph for a few moments to come up with two or three different topics.
- Then, using the sample lunes as models, work together to write a lune for each of the suggested topics.

### Prewriting
**Planning Your Lune**

Read the steps aloud and make sure students understand that the purpose of a lune is to capture a single image or feeling.

⭐ **TEKS** 10.14B

### Drafting
**Writing Your Lune**

Explain that students will be limited by the length of the poem, so they will need to choose their words carefully.

**Write a lune.** Have students use a thesaurus to choose the most vivid language to describe images. **DIFFERENTIATE INSTRUCTION ➘**

⭐ **TEKS** 10.14B

---

⭐ **TEKS** 10.14B

## Lunes

In the 1960s, Robert Kelly decided that the English haiku form (5–7–5 syllables) did not effectively represent the original Japanese form. The problem is that English words have fewer syllables than Japanese words, so an English haiku holds more words. He believed that a new form was needed.

Kelly invented a form with 13 syllables in three lines, in a pattern of 5, 3, and 5 syllables. Because its right edge reminded him of a crescent moon, he called his new form a "lune."

**When you're having fun
clocks run fast
not when you're waiting**

**Trotting by the fence
my new dog
keeps pace with our bus**

**In a doubtful world
I believe
in you and in me**

### Prewriting Planning Your Lune

- Select a single image or thought.
- Jot down vivid, descriptive adjectives, and figurative language.
- Think about structure and poetic devices you want to include.

### Drafting Writing Your Lune

Use the information about structure, poetic devices, and planning tips to write your lune. Structure your idea to fit the pattern of 5, 3, and 5 syllables.

Draft

**Write a lune.** Choose a topic from the list on page **619** and compose a lune about it.

---

★ **TEKS** 10.13C, 10.13D, 10.14B

## Revising Focusing on the Traits

Ask yourself the following questions when you review and revise the first draft of your lune. (Also see page **332**).

### Focus and Coherence

_____ **1.** Do I describe a single image, idea, or thought?

_____ **2.** Do all the adjectives relate directly to that image or thought?

### Organization

_____ **3.** Have I followed the structure for a lune?

_____ **4.** Have I carefully counted and arranged the words so that the 5, 3, 5 pattern of syllables is correctly followed?

### Development of Ideas

_____ **5.** Have I used vivid adjectives to describe the image or thought?

### Voice

_____ **6.** Can I improve my word choice or style of writing to better convey my meaning?

_____ **7.** Have I used figurative language to create a powerful image?

## Editing Checking for Conventions

When you edit your revised lune, check for correct conventions: grammar, capitalization, punctuation, and spelling.

_____ **1.** Is my lune grammatically correct?

_____ **2.** Have I capitalized proper nouns and the first word of each sentence?

_____ **3.** Have I used correct punctuation, including end punctuation?

_____ **4.** Have I checked my spelling?

**Revise**

**Revise and edit your lune.** Use the information above to help you revise and edit the first draft of your lune. Pay careful attention to the structure and poetic techniques you have used.

*Creative Writing*

## Revising

### Focusing on the Traits

Have students work with partners to answer the revising questions. Allow students time to incorporate revisions.

★ **TEKS** 10.13C, 10.14B

### Editing

#### Checking for Conventions

Explain to students that lunes often do not follow standard rules of grammar, capitalization, and punctuation. Use the examples on SE page 356 to demonstrate the lack of punctuation, the use of fragments, and the varied capitalization. Have students use capitalization, grammatical elements, and punctuation to support their imagery.

**Revise and edit your poem.** Emphasize that students should check for and use correct spelling in their lunes.

★ **TEKS** 10.13D

### Conventions Connections

**Spelling**
- ***Proofreader's Guide*** pages 698–703
- ***SkillsBook*** pages 53–58

---

### Differentiated Instruction: English Language Learners

★ **ELPS** 2E, 3E, 5G

| ELP Level **Beginning** | ELP Level **Intermediate** | ELP Level **Advanced/Advanced High** |
|---|---|---|
| Guide students through the process of planning and drafting by showing a picture, helping students choose words to describe it, and organizing syllables as 5-3-5. | Provide students with a picture as a starting point for writing. Have students work with partners to choose vivid details to describe the photograph and write a collaborative lune. | After students finish drafting, divide them into groups and have them read poems aloud. Invite student feedback and have students revise and present final drafts to their groups. |

★ **TEKS** 10.13C Revise drafts to improve style, word choice, and figurative language; **10.13D** Edit drafts for grammar, mechanics, and spelling; **10.14B** Write a poem using poetic techniques and forms; **ELPS** **2E** Use visual support to enhance and confirm understanding of increasingly complex spoken language; **3E** Share information in cooperative learning interactions; **5G** Describe with increasing specificity and detail/writing

# Research Writing

**10.13A** Plan a first draft; **10.13B** Structure ideas and develop drafts; **10.13C** Revise drafts; **10.13D** Edit drafts; **10.13E** Revise final draft and publish work; **10.15A** Write an analytical essay; **10.15C(ii)** Write procedural and work-related documents/ include formatting; **10.15D** Produce a multimedia presentation; Write procedural and work-related documents/anticipate questions; **10.17A(i)** Use and understand tenses and verbals; **10.17A(ii)** Use and understand clauses; **10.17C** Use correctly structured sentences; **10.18B(i)** Use commas; **10.19** Spell correctly; **10.20A** Brainstorm/consult/decide topic/ formulate research question; **10.20B** Formulate a plan for research; **10.21A** Follow a research plan; **10.21B** Organize information; **10.21C** Paraphrase/ summarize/quote/cite information; **10.22A** Modify the research question; **10.22B** Determine reliability/ validity/accuracy of sources; **10.22C** Critique research process; **10.23A** Support thesis statement and related claims; **10.23B** Reflect a progression of ideas/clearly state a point of view; **10.23C** Use graphics/illustrations; **10.23D** Use evaluative tools; **10.23E** Use a style manual

## ⬤ UNIT ELPS

**1A** Use prior knowledge and experiences; **1D** Speak using learning strategies; **2H** Understand information in spoken language; **3A** Practice sounds of new vocabulary; **3D** Speak using content-area vocabulary; **3I** Adapt spoken language; **4H** Read silently with increasing ease; **4I** Expand reading skills; **5A** Learn relationships between sounds and letters

## Research Skills (pages 359–370)

Students learn how to use the Internet and the library, as well as how to discern between reliable and unreliable sources.

## MLA Research Report
### (pages 371–428)

Students write an MLA research report about a great work of engineering that interests them.

## Making Presentations
### (pages 429–441)

Students learn how to prepare and give a presentation based on a research report they have written, and also how to turn their presentations into multimedia reports.

 **Technology Connections**

🔆 *Write Source Online*
www.hmheducation.com/tx/writesource

- *Net-text*
- *Writing Network*
- *Portfolio*
- *GrammarSnap*
- *Essay Scoring*
- *File Cabinet*

⬚ *Interactive Whiteboard Lessons*

# Research Writing Unit Scope and Sequence

| Day | Writing and Grammar Instruction | Core Unit | Tools of Language | Resource Units | Daily Language Workouts | Skills-Book | Write Source Online |
|---|---|---|---|---|---|---|---|
| | | | *Write Source Student Edition* | | | | |
| 1 | **Research Skills** | 359 | TL 562–567 | | 98–101 | | Interactive Whiteboard Lesson |
| 2 | Primary vs. Secondary Sources | 360 | | | | | Net-text |
| 3 | Evaluating Sources of Information | 361–363 | | | | | Net-text |
| 4 | Using the Internet | 364 | | | | | Net-text |
| 5 | Using the Library | 365–367 | | | | | Net-text |
| | Using Reference Books | 368–370 | | | | | Net-text |

 **Resource Units** referenced above are located in the back of the *Student Edition* and *Teacher's Edition*
TL *"The Tools of Language"*   BGW *"Basic Grammar and Writing"*   WR *"A Writer's Resource"*   PG *"Proofreader's Guide"*

| Day | Writing and Grammar Instruction | Write Source Student Edition | | | Daily Language Workouts | Skills-Book | Write Source Online |
|-----|-------|-----------|----------------|-------------|--------------|------------|------------|
| | | Core Unit | Tools of Language | Resource Units | | | |
| **6–7** | **MLA Research Report** Model | 371–379 | TL 526–529 | | 102–105 | | Net-text |
| **8–10** | Prewriting | 380–394 | | | | | Net-text |
| | Selecting a Topic Creating Note Cards | 381–389 | | WR 618–621 | | | Net-text |
| | Keeping Track of Your Sources | 390 | | WR 626–631 | | | Net-text |
| | Writing Your Thesis Statement | 391 | | | | | Net-text |
| | Outlining Your Ideas | 392–393 | | | | | Net-text |
| | Modifying Your Thesis | 394 | | | | | Net-text |
| | Evaluating Your Research | 394 | | | | | Net-text |
| **11–15** | Drafting | 395–400 | TL 526–529 | | 106–109 | | Net-text |
| | Starting Your Research Report | 401 | | | | | Net-text |
| | Developing the Middle Part | 402–405 | | | | | Net-text |
| | Ending Your Research Report | 406–410 | | | | | Net-text |
| **16–17** | Revising | 411–420 | TL 526–529 | | 110–113 | | Net-text |
| **18–19** | Editing | 421–427 | | | | | Net-text |
| | Skills Activities:<br>•Sentence Variety | | | BGW 592–593<br>PG 780–785 | | 139–142 | GrammarSnap |
| | •Passive Voice | | | PG 750–761 | | 95 | GrammarSnap |
| | •Restrictive/Nonrestrictive Phrases and Clauses | | | PG 644–653, 772–779 | | 14–15, 129–138 | GrammarSnap |
| | •Punctuating Quotations | | | PG 676–679 | | 31–37 | GrammarSnap |
| **20** | Publishing | 428 | | | | | Net-text |
| **21–25** | **Making Presentations** | 429–441 | TL 526–529 | | 114–117 | | Net-text |

(Left margin labels: Week 2, Week 3, Week 4, Week 5)

**Resource Units** referenced above are located in the back of the *Student Edition* and *Teacher's Edition*

TL *"The Tools of Language"*   BGW *"Basic Grammar and Writing"*   WR *"A Writer's Resource"*   PG *"Proofreader's Guide"*

## Writing Focus

- Research Skills
- MLA Research Report
- Making Presentations

## Grammar Focus

- Restrictive and Nonrestrictive Clauses
- Active and Passive Voice in Verbs

## Learning Language

Read aloud the basic and academic terms, as well as the descriptions and questions. Model for students how to read one question and answer it. For example, *It says that plagiarism is using someone else's ideas as my own, and it's asking why doing so is unacceptable. When someone has a great idea, he or she likes to receive credit for it, and if I take credit when the idea is not mine, it's like stealing the idea. Stealing in any form is unacceptable.* Have partners monitor their understanding of the terms by working through the meanings and questions together. **DIFFERENTIATE INSTRUCTION** ↘

**ELPS** 1E, 2C, 3B, 3D, 3E, 4F, 4G

## Minilessons

**The Plague of Plagiarism**   Defining a Concept

- **THINK** of a time when someone got credit for an idea you had.

  **WRITE** down the idea and how you felt when someone else received the credit.
  **SHARE** your writing with the class.

**ELPS 1E** Internalize new basic and academic language by using and reusing it/speaking; **1H** Develop learning strategies/reasoning, looking for patterns in language, and analyzing sayings and expressions; **2B** Recognize elements of the English sound system in new vocabulary/long and short vowels, silent letters, and consonant clusters; **2C** Learn new expressions and basic/academic vocabulary heard during classroom instruction/interactions; **3A** Practice producing sounds of newly acquired vocabulary; **3B** Expand vocabulary by learning and using routine language needed for classroom communication; **3D** Speak using grade-level content area vocabulary/new words and academic language proficiency; **3E** Share information in cooperative learning interactions; **4A** Learn relationships between sounds and letters/sound out words using a combination of skills; **4F** Use visual/contextual support and support from peers/teachers to read grade-appropriate text, enhance understanding, and develop vocabulary, grasp of language structures, and background knowledge; **4G** Demonstrate comprehension of increasingly complex English/responding to questions; **5B** Write using content-based grade-level vocabulary

---

**358**

**ELPS** 1E, 2C, 3B, 3D, 3E, 4F, 4G

www.hmheducation.com/tx/writesource

# Research Writing

## Writing Focus

## Grammar Focus

## Learning Language

Learning these words and expressions will help you understand this unit.

1. Plagiarism means passing off someone else's ideas as your own.
   **Explain why plagiarism is unacceptable.**
2. Something that is valid is accurate and has been correctly inferred or deduced from a premise.
   **Why is it important to check whether or not a source is valid?**
3. To cite a source means to give credit and to mention the source formally.
   **Why must you cite the sources you use in a research report?**
4. To be "plugged in" means to have access to modern technology.
   **What do you think it would be like to live in a village that was not "plugged in"?**

---

**Differentiated Instruction:
English Language Learners**          **ELPS** 1E, 1H, 2B, 2C, 3A, 3E, 4A, 4G, 5B

| ELP Level **Beginning** | ELP Level **Intermediate** | ELP Level **Advanced/Advanced High** |
|---|---|---|
| Have students practice sounding out and writing the words, identifying silent letters, long/short vowels, and consonant clusters after you demonstrate. | Have students use a word list you provide and work with a partner to create root-word word webs (*cite: citation, recite, incite; valid: validate, validity*; etc.). | Using the same word list, have students work in groups to identify affixes and root words and use each word in an original sentence. |

359

## Research Writing
# Research Skills

You can learn a lot simply by observing, but to gain an in-depth understanding of a subject, you must do research. Effective researching in any field of inquiry means knowing where to look for appropriate, reliable information from authoritative sources. The library is an excellent place to start, as is the Internet. While the Internet can make researching easy, however, not every Web site offers solid, verifiable information. You must be careful to use only trustworthy Web sites that post information from authoritative sources.

In this chapter, you will learn how to use the Internet and the library as well as how to discern between reliable and unreliable sources. Knowing how to research efficiently will help you now in school and in the future.

- ■ **Primary vs. Secondary Sources**
- ■ **Evaluating Sources of Information**
- ■ **Using the Internet**
- ■ **Using the Library**
- ■ **Using Reference Books**

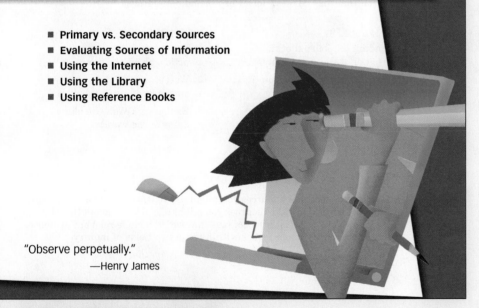

"Observe perpetually."
—Henry James

### Resources

**Copy Masters (see Appendix)**

- T-chart (A-93)
- Details Chart (A-96)

## Research Skills

### Objectives
- distinguish between primary and secondary sources
- learn to evaluate the accuracy of sources
- understand how to use the Internet to conduct research
- access and use library reference materials
- identify the elements of a dictionary page

Students often approach the writing of research reports with little enthusiasm. The reasons are varied.

- ■ Topics or topic areas, usually assigned, may not interest them.
- ■ Research is a long process that requires planning time, research skills, and attention to details.
- ■ The writing process is lengthy and requires the integration of information from a variety of reliable sources.
- ■ Specific formatting and citation guidelines are difficult to follow.

Ask students to share their experiences writing research reports. Use this opportunity to evaluate students' attitudes toward research writing and to determine which phase(s) of writing a research report requires most of your support.

## Primary vs. Secondary Sources

Access to primary sources—even observation and participation—requires planning. For example, students may need to make arrangements with a museum curator to view the diaries, journals, and letters of historic figures. They also have to schedule interviews—whether in person or by phone, mail, or e-mail—and allow time to produce and process surveys and questionnaires. DIFFERENTIATE INSTRUCTION ↘

TEKS 10.15A(v), 10.21A

Establish the importance of respecting an expert's time and privacy during one-on-one interviews.

- Show up at the scheduled time, or give sufficient notice that you will be late or have to reschedule.
- Confine questions to the research topic.
- Take careful notes. Obtain permission ahead of time to record the interview.

### Try It!
#### Answers

**Possible Answers**

- **Secondary sources:** American history textbook; DVD of *The North and the South,* a TV miniseries; encyclopedia entry
- **Primary sources:** diary entries from someone who was at the Alamo, artifacts from the Alamo on display in museums or at the site DIFFERENTIATE INSTRUCTION ↘

---

 TEKS 10.15A(v), 10.21A

# Primary vs. Secondary Sources

**Primary sources** are original sources that inform you directly, not through another person's explanation or interpretation. When doing research, use as much primary information as possible.

Primary sources include . . .

- **Diaries, Journals, and Letters** You can often find these in museums, in libraries, or at historic sites.
- **Presentations** An expert at a museum or a historic site can give you firsthand information, but be aware of the presenter's own interpretation of events.
- **Interviews** Talk to an expert about your research topic.
- **Surveys and Questionnaires** These tools help you gather a great deal of data from many people.
- **Observation and Participation** Your own observations of a person, a place, or an event provide excellent firsthand information. Participating in an event can give you insights that cannot be discovered through the reports of others.

**Secondary sources** are third-person accounts found in research done by other people. Much of the news (*television, radio, Internet, books, magazines*) is secondary information. Keep in mind that secondary sources represent filtered information that may contain biases or misunderstandings.

| Primary Sources | Secondary Sources |
|---|---|
| 1. Reading the journal of the designer of the Aswan High Dam | 1. Reading a magazine article about the dam |
| 2. Interviewing someone from Egypt who lived near the dam | 2. Watching a TV drama based on the building of the dam |
| 3. Watching a documentary with original film footage of the dam's construction | 3. Exploring a Web site about dams of the world |

### Try It!

List several secondary sources you might use to learn about the Civil War. Then list several primary sources you might use to learn about the Alamo. Be sure to cite authoritative sources that would include relevant evidence and that identify major issues within these two fields of inquiry.

---

**Differentiated Instruction: Struggling Learners**

Remind students about the importance of not using others' ideas as their own. Provide several written excerpts and have students think-pair-share with a partner which material is general knowledge and does not require citations and which information should be cited.

 **TEKS** 10.21A

# Evaluating Sources of Information

You may find a lot of information about your research topic. But before you use any of it, decide whether or not the information is dependable and comes from authoritative sources. Use the following questions as a guide.

## Is the source a primary source or a secondary source?

You can usually trust the information you've collected yourself, but be careful with secondary sources. Although many of them are reliable, they can contain outdated or incorrect information.

## Is the source an expert?

An expert knows more about a subject than other people. Using an expert's thoughts and opinions can make your paper more believable. If you aren't sure about a source's authority, ask a teacher or librarian what he or she thinks.

## Is the information accurate?

Sources that people respect are usually very accurate. Reputable newspapers (*New York Times* or *Chicago Tribune*) and credible Web sites (CNN or ESPN) are reliable sources of information. Sources that do not support their facts or that contain errors may not be reliable.

### Tip

Be especially cautious about the accuracy of information on the Internet. While there is an incredible amount of information available on the Net, there is also a lot of misinformation.

## Is the information fair and complete?

A reliable, authoritative source should provide information fairly, covering all the major issues within the field of inquiry and all sides of the subject. If a source presents only one side of a subject or has an identifiable bias, its information may not be accurate. To make themselves sound convincing, politicians and advertisers often present just their side of a subject. Avoid sources that are one-sided, and look for those that are balanced.

## Is the information current?

Usually, you want to have the most up-to-date information about a subject. Sometimes information changes, and sources can become outdated quickly. Check the copyright page in a book, the issue date of a magazine, and the posting date of online information.

Research

# Evaluating Sources of Information

Be sure students can identify experts.

- Using their social studies textbooks or a current issue of a periodical, suggest a broad topic, such as immigration.
- Then ask students to suggest five related questions suitable for research and list them on the board.
- Have students identify three or four experts they could consult and list them under the corresponding question.

**TEKS** 10.21A

### Tip

Especially on the Internet, biased or slanted information can be so subtle that students may not recognize it. Besides checking the posting date of online information to determine whether it is current, students need to check online sponsors. Political, social, and religious groups may have specific agendas. Students should probably not rely on information from such groups because they may interpret facts to promote their purposes.

**TEKS** **10.21A** Follow the research plan to compile data that identifies major issues; **ELPS** **1A** Use prior knowledge and experience to understand meanings; **1C** Use strategic learning techniques to acquire basic and grade-level vocabulary; **1F** Use accessible language and learn new and essential language in the process; **2C** Learn basic vocabulary heard during classroom instruction/interactions; **2E** Use visual/contextual support to enhance and confirm understanding of increasingly complex spoken language; **3F** Give information/ranging from using a limited high-frequency vocabulary to using abstract and content-based vocabulary during speaking; **4C** Comprehend language structures used in written classroom materials

## Authoritative Sources

As a class, read through the guidelines aloud, giving additional examples of both reliable and unreliable sources. Possible answers using the Battle of Gettysburg include:

- Reliable—a museum curator's account of the battle; Unreliable—a family member who retells stories that have been handed down through the generations.
- Reliable—a Civil War historian's article about causes of the battle; Unreliable—a historical novel detailing the causes (still too many elements of fiction).
- Reliable—an encyclopedia article listing events from both sides leading up to the battle; Unreliable—one soldier's journal entries (although a good primary source, it will present only a narrow perspective).
- Reliable—a noted historian; Unreliable—a Web site sponsored by a person/group with a specific agenda. **DIFFERENTIATE INSTRUCTION** ↘

**TEKS** 10.15A(v), 10.20B, 10.21A, 10.21B

## Compiling Data

Point out to students that the graphic organizer on this page only lists possible useful sources and describes them. To actually compile their information, data, and quotations, students can use both a details chart (see TE Appendix) and note cards.

---

 **TEKS** 10.15A(v), 10.20B, 10.21A, 10.21B

## Authoritative Sources

Select reliable and authoritative sources. Respected newspapers and magazines with articles written by experts are considered to be authoritative. Nonfiction books and documentaries are also generally good. The following guidelines will help you determine if a source is authoritative.

- **Is the author an expert on the subject?** Look at the author's credentials. Is the author an expert in the field?
- **What is the level of writing?** Look for scholarly material. A children's book would most likely not be authoritative.
- **Has the author presented complete information?** Look for discussion of all sides of the issue, including controversies or dissenting views. Not all primary and secondary sources present a full view of the issues or the major debates that surround a complex, multi-faceted topic.
- **Is the author unbiased?** Letters or diaries may not be fair. Secondary sources may only discuss one side of an issue.

## Compiling Data

After identifying your sources, compile your data. For her report on the Aswan Dam, Isabel consulted several sources and began a list of useful ones that she could consult and include.

| | Source | Description |
|---|---|---|
| CULTURAL & POLITICAL ISSUES | http://www.washingtonpost.com/wp-dyn/content/article/2006/11/02/AR2006110201657.html | analysis of cultural effects of Aswan High Dam; dam history; includes political issues |
| TECHNICAL ISSUES | http://www.jstor.org/pss/2010254 | "Technological Dimension of Decision Making: The Case of the Aswan High Dam." Johns Hopkins study on technical decisions by Egypt, World Bank, and U.S. about dam. |
| ECONOMIC ISSUES | http://www.us.sis.gov.eg/En/Pub/magazin/fall2001/110220000000000010.htm | Egyptian Information Service. Book Review of From High Dam to Toshka: The Nile and Man in Egypt between Legend and Reality. Financing; archaeological impact; environmental concerns. |

---

**TEKS 10.15A(v)** Write an analytical essay that includes relevant evidence and details; **10.20B** Formulate a plan for research on a complex, multi-faceted topic; **10.21A** Follow the research plan to compile data that identifies major issues and debates; **10.21B** Organize information from multiple sources to create graphics

TEKS 10.15A(v), 10.20B, 10.21A, 10.21B

## Major Debates

As you begin your research and formulate a plan, think about the issues that surround your topic. When Isabel began her research on the Aswan High Dam, she identified three major issues that surrounded the building of the dam: cultural issues or problems, technical issues, and economic issues.

There will also be major debates surrounding any complex, muti-faceted topic. Debates involve the two sides of the issue. For example, while building the Aswan Dam would protect Egypt from drought and flood, it would, and did, change the salinity of the soil, destroying the fertility of the fields surrounding the Nile forever. As a result, Egypt has had to greatly increase the use of chemical fertilizers, adding to environmental concerns.

As you compile data from authoritative sources, look for those that identify the major debates that exist within your chosen topic.

## Pros and Cons

As Isabel began to compile data, she made the following list of pros and cons, listing the major debates surrounding the Aswan High Dam.

| PROS | CONS |
|---|---|
| controls annual flooding and protects against drought | Egypt was forced to agree to using only Soviet engineers and equipment. |
| made more land available for agriculture | New lake covers irreplaceable archaeological treasures. |
| enabled urban development along the Nile | Thousands of people had to be relocated. |
| provides irrigation throughout year | Farmers have to use tons of chemical fertilizer. |
| provides 50% of Egypt's electricity | decrease in fish and shrimp populations |

### Try It!

Conduct preliminary research, compile data, and identify major debates that surround your chosen topic. Look for sources that provide information on both sides of the issue. List your sources in a table such as the one on the previous page. Then arrange specific information in a chart of Pros and Cons like the one above, or in another graphic organizer form.

Research

## Major Debates

In small groups, have students list three to five reasons they should look at both sides of the issues about their topics. Then, as a class, share and discuss their reasons. Possible answers:

- To write an unbiased research paper, one must have an understanding of all issues involved.
- Understanding issues about the topic will lead to forming more natural conclusions about the topic.
- Addressing some of the major debate points in the research paper is more likely to engage the reader and will make the writer sound more knowledgeable about the topic.

TEKS 10.15A(v), 10.20B, 10.21A, 10.21B

### Try It!

Encourage students to use charts like the samples or to create their own graphic organizers on which they can list sources and arrange their information.

 TEKS **10.15A(v)** Write an analytical essay that includes relevant evidence and details; **10.20B** Formulate a plan for research on a complex, multi-faceted topic; **10.21A** Follow the research plan to compile data that identifies major issues and debates; **10.21B** Organize information from multiple sources to create graphics; **ELPS 1E** Internalize new basic and academic language by using and reusing it/speaking; **1H** Develop and expand learning strategies/reasoning, looking for patterns in language, and analyzing sayings and expressions; **2C** Learn basic and academic vocabulary heard during classroom instruction/interactions; **3A** Practice producing sounds of newly acquired vocabulary; **3E** Share information in cooperative learning interactions; **3F** Ask for and give information/ranging from using a limited high-frequency vocabulary to using abstract and content-based vocabulary during speaking; **4A** Learn relationships between sounds and letters

## Using the Internet

Students may be so used to relying on a single search engine that they may not be aware of the great variety of search engines. To give students an idea of what else is available, suggest that they type the phrase *search engines* or *list of search engines* into the search box of their favorite search engine.

### Try It!

The **Try It!** activity shows the importance of narrowing a topic. If you have a classroom computer or can move the class temporarily to the computer lab or the library, do the **Try It!** activity together. Provide additional topics—from general to specific—and have pairs of students take turns searching them. Students will learn how to narrow their own topics on SE page 381.

⭐ **TEKS** 10.20B, 10.21A

---

**364** ⭐ **TEKS** 10.20B, 10.21A

## Using the Internet

You can access many resources by surfing the Web. Therefore, the Internet is a valuable research tool, especially as you formulate your plan and conduct research on a complex, multi-faceted topic. You can find government publications, encyclopedia entries, business reports, and firsthand observations on the Internet. Using reliable, authoritative sources, you can quickly identify the major debates and issues within your field of inquiry. When researching on the Internet, keep in mind the following points:

- **Use the Web wisely.** Sites that include *.edu, .org,* and *.gov* in the Web address are often reliable. These sites are usually from educational, nonprofit, or government agencies. If you have questions about a site, talk to your teacher. (Also see page **361**.)

- **Try several search engines.** Because there is an enormous amount of information on the Web, no one search engine can handle it all. So employ at least two search engines when you surf the Web. Enter keywords to start your research or enter specific questions to zero in on your topic, especially a complex, multi-faceted research topic.

  When you type a term into a search engine's input box, the search engine scans its database for matching sites. Then the engine returns recommendations for you to explore.

- **Take advantage of links.** When you read a page, watch for links to other sites. These may offer different perspectives on your topic.

- **Experiment with keywords.** Ask different questions or use different keywords to find the information you need. Check the date of the site to make sure the information is current.

- **Ignore Web sites that advertise research papers for sale.** Using these sites is dishonest. Teachers and librarians can recognize and verify when a paper is someone else's work.

- **Learn your school's Internet policy.** Using the computer at school is a privilege. To maintain that privilege, follow your school's Internet policy and any guidelines your parents may have set.

### Try It!

Open your favorite search engine and type in the word "Dams." How many sites are listed related to your search? Now type in the phrase "Aswan High Dam." How many sites are listed now? Finally, type in "Aswan High Dam History." How have the numbers changed by focusing your search?

---

# Using the Library

The Internet may be a good place to initiate your research, but a library is often a more valuable place to continue it. Most libraries contain a wide range of authoritative resources on a wide range of multi-faceted topics. Talk to the librarian as you plan your research and begin to compile data.

## Books

- **Reference** books include encyclopedias, almanacs, dictionaries, atlases, and directories, plus resources such as consumer information guides and car-repair manuals. Reference books provide a quick overview of research topics.
- **Nonfiction** texts are a good source of facts that can serve as a foundation for your research. Check the copyright dates to be sure you are reading reasonably up-to-date information. (Some libraries organize nonfiction using the Library of Congress system, but most libraries use the Dewey decimal system as shown on page 367.)
- **Fiction** can sometimes aid or enhance your research. For example, a historical novel can reveal people's feelings about a particular time in history. (Fiction books are grouped together in alphabetical order by the authors' last names.)

## Periodicals

Periodicals (*newspapers* and *magazines*) are grouped together in a library. Use the *Readers' Guide to Periodical Literature* to find articles in periodicals. (See page 370.) You will have to ask the librarian for older issues.

## The Media Section

The media section of your library includes DVD's, CD-ROM's, CD's, cassettes, and videotapes. These resources are valuable, but remember that directors and screenwriters may present events from their personal viewpoints.

## Computers

Computers are available in most libraries, and many are connected to the Internet, although there may be restrictions on their use.

### Try It!

Visit your school or public library. Which sections would you use if you were researching the origin of the moon's craters? Which sections would help you find material on the history of filmmaking? Are there any sections you would use for both topics? List them.

Research

## Using the Library

Libraries often provide patrons with direct access to many of their resources through the Internet. Students can use their library's resources without leaving home or school. Encourage them also to meet the reference librarian, if the library has one. ✓ DIFFERENTIATE INSTRUCTION

- A reference librarian has extensive knowledge of the library's resources and can usually access materials much faster than the average person.
- A reference librarian also has additional knowledge of and skill with searching the databases available on the library's computer network and is often more than willing to share that knowledge.

TEKS 10.20B, 10.21A

## Try It!

Encourage students to visit their library before they begin a research report to learn what reference resources are available only at the library.

## Differentiated Instruction: English Language Learners

ELPS 1G, 2I, 3C, 3F, 3I

| ELP Level **Beginning** | ELP Level **Intermediate** | ELP Level **Advanced/Advanced High** |
| --- | --- | --- |
| Prepare students for the library trip by providing some key phrases/questions. Practice by role-playing asking for items listed on this page and asking follow-up questions if needed. | Have students prepare for their trip to the library by instructing them how to ask questions using formal English and connecting words, and how to ask follow-up questions if needed. | Prepare for the library visit by having students practice asking questions in formal English, listening to the response, and taking notes. |

TEKS **10.20B** Formulate a plan for research on a complex, multi-faceted topic; **10.21A** Follow the research plan to compile data that identifies major issues and debates; ELPS **1G** Demonstrate increasing ability to distinguish between formal/informal English and an increasing knowledge of when to use each one; **2I** Demonstrate listening comprehension in increasingly complex spoken language by taking notes; **3C** Speak using a variety of grammatical structures and connecting words with increasing accuracy and ease; **3F** Ask for information/ranging from using a limited high-frequency vocabulary to using abstract and content-based vocabulary during speaking; **3I** Adapt spoken language for formal purposes

## Using the Computer Catalog

- Encourage students to learn what online services are available through their library's Web site and to use as many of these services as possible.
- Many libraries are part of larger networks that provide patrons with online access to the computer catalog for the entire network. This allows patrons to see what books and periodicals are available in the entire system, not just at their branch.
- Most library networks have an efficient procedure for requesting an interlibrary transfer of books and materials that are not available at the patron's branch. Patrons are usually notified by e-mail or phone when the requested materials arrive at their library. Remind students to plan ahead so the requested materials arrive in plenty of time to do their research.

⭐ **TEKS** 10.20B, 10.21A

## Using a Variety of Search Methods

Guide students in searching for the same book by the three methods described. Note the differences in the results screen, if any, and discuss reasons for the differences.

### Try It!

As students complete the **Try It!** activity, let them know it is sometimes a good idea to mix and match search methods, meaning that they might want to use their subject and search for it as a title search. Books' titles often contain the subject word, and sometimes the author of a book or article might be the same as the subject (Ben Franklin, Isaac Asimov, etc.).

⭐ **TEKS** 10.20B, 10.21A

## Using the Computer Catalog

Some libraries still use a card catalog located in a cabinet with drawers. Most libraries, however, have put their entire catalog on computer. Each system varies a bit, so ask for help if you're not sure how the system in your library works. A **computer catalog** lists the books held in your library and affiliated systems. It lets you know if a book is available or if you must wait for it.

## Using a Variety of Search Methods

When you are using a computer catalog, you can find information about a book with any of the following methods:

1. If you know it, enter the **title** of the book.
2. If you know the **author** of the book, enter the first and last names.
3. A general search of your **subject** will also help you find books on your topic. Enter either the subject or a related keyword.

### Sample Computer Catalog Screen

The key to the right identifies the types of information provided for a particular resource, in this case, a book. Once you locate the book you need, make note of the call number. You will use this to find the book on the shelf.

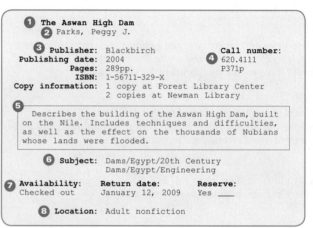

### Try It!

Look up a topic that interests you on a computer catalog. Identify two authoritative works on the topic and locate them in the library.

## Understanding Call Numbers

All nonfiction books are arranged in the library according to their **call numbers**. Call numbers are usually based on the **Dewey decimal classification** system, which divides nonfiction books into 10 subject categories:

| | | | |
|---|---|---|---|
| 000–099 | **General Works** | 500–599 | **Sciences** |
| 100–199 | **Philosophy** | 600–699 | **Technology** |
| 200–299 | **Religion** | 700–799 | **Arts and Recreation** |
| 300–399 | **Social Sciences** | 800–899 | **Literature** |
| 400–499 | **Languages** | 900–999 | **History and Geography** |

A call number often has a decimal in it, followed by the first letter of an author's name. Note how the following call numbers are ordered.

| 973 | 973.19 | 973.2 | 973.2 | 974 | 974 | 974.3 | 974.3 | 975 | 975.5 |
| M | D | De | Do | F | H | B | R | R | Ry |

## Identifying the Parts of a Book

Each part of a book provides valuable information. The **title page** includes the title of the book, the author's name, and the publisher's name and city. The **copyright page** follows with the year the book was published. The **preface**, **foreword**, or **introduction** comes before the table of contents and tells why the book was written. The **table of contents** lists the names and page numbers of sections and chapters in the book. At the end of the book, you may find at least one **appendix**, containing various maps, tables, or lists. Finally, the **index** is an alphabetical list of important topics and their page numbers in the book.

### Try It!

Select an authoritative nonfiction book on a topic that interests you. On a note card, write the book's title and call number, the publisher's name and city, and the year it was published. Then select a term related to your topic and find it in the index. Write down the page numbers given there.

Research

## Understanding Call Numbers

Check students' understanding of how call numbers are arranged and how students can use them to facilitate research. Use the following questions:

- *How do you find a book's call number?* (Search the computer catalog by title, author, or subject, or look at the spine of the book.)
- *How do you search for a nonfiction, biography, or reference book using its call number?* (Enter the whole number into the computer.)
- *What is the subject category of the books in the illustration? How do you know?* (The category is history and geography. All of the whole numbers are between 900 and 999.)

 TEKS 10.20B, 10.21A, 10.21B

## Identifying the Parts of a Book

Have students use their *Write Source* book or another textbook to practice identifying the parts of a book. ✔ DIFFERENTIATE INSTRUCTION

## Try It!

For more practice, create a BINGO-style game card on which you've written various page numbers that correspond to a list of terms you've prepared from the textbook's index. Call out terms randomly, and have students look up their page numbers and mark their game cards. The first student to correctly mark a game card with a horizontal, diagonal, or vertical row wins!

 **TEKS 10.20B** Formulate a plan for research on a complex, multi-faceted topic; **10.21A** Follow the research plan to compile data that identifies major issues and debates; **10.21B** Organize information from multiple sources to create forms; **ELPS 1C** Use strategic learning techniques to acquire basic and grade-level vocabulary; **1E** Internalize new academic language by using and reusing it/speaking and writing; **2A** Distinguish sounds with increasing ease; **2C** Learn academic vocabulary heard during classroom instruction/interactions; **4F** Use visual/contextual support and support from peers/teachers to develop vocabulary; **5A** Learn relationships between sounds and letters to represent sounds when writing in English

## Using Reference Books

School and small local libraries often lack the funds to update their print encyclopedias. As a result, these resources may contain dated information. However, publishers often offer annual yearbooks to supplement and update the information found in the original volumes. Students should check to see whether the library has purchased these supplemental volumes or whether updates are available online. Students should also find out whether the library provides access to online encyclopedias.

### Referring to Encyclopedias

Give students time to review the sample index. Then have them use it to tell the volume and page or pages where they would find the following information:

- an illustration of the Aswan Dam (volume A, page 852)
- an explanation of dams (volume D, pages 15–20)
- a list of articles related to the topic, the Aswan Dam (after the Egypt article in volume E, pages 118–132)

 10.20B, 10.21A

---

  10.20B, 10.21A

## Using Reference Books

A reference book is a special kind of nonfiction book that contains specific facts or background information. The reference section includes encyclopedias, dictionaries, almanacs, and so on. Usually, reference books cannot be checked out, so you must use them in the library.

### Referring to Encyclopedias

An encyclopedia is a set of books (or a CD-ROM, or a Web site) that contains basic information on topics from A to Z. Topics are arranged alphabetically. Here are some tips for using encyclopedias.

#### Tips for Using Encyclopedias

- **At the end of an article, there is often a list of related articles.** You can read these other articles to learn more about your topic.
- **The index can help you find out more about your topic.** The index is usually in a separate volume or at the end of the last volume. It lists every article that contains information about a topic. For example, if you look up "dams" in the index, you would find a list of articles—"Aswan Dam," "Hoover Dam," and so on—that include information on that topic. (See below.)
- **Libraries usually have several sets of encyclopedias.** Review each set and decide which one best serves your needs. (Always check with your teacher first to see if you can use an encyclopedia as a source for your research.)

#### Sample Encyclopedia Index

| | |
|---|---|
| **Encyclopedia volume** | **Aswan Dam** [A:] 852 with pictures |
| | Egypt **E: 118-132** |
| | Dams **D: 15-20** |
| **Page numbers** | Lake Nasser [L: 42] |
| | *See also the list of related articles in the Egypt article.* |
| **Related topics** | Abu Simbel, Temple of **A: 19** |
| | Ramsas II **R: 135** |
| | Amon-Re **A: 438** |
| | Nubia **N-O: 382** |
| | Delta **D: 147** |

---

TEKS 10.20B, 10.21A

## Consulting Other Reference Books

Most libraries contain a number of different kinds of reference books in addition to encyclopedias. You may find these very helpful as you plan your research and gather data.

### Almanacs

Almanacs are books filled with facts and statistics about many different subjects. *The World Almanac and Book of Facts* contains celebrity profiles; statistics about politics, business, and sports; plus consumer information.

### Atlases

Atlases contain detailed maps of the world, continents, countries, and so on. They also contain statistics and related information. Specialized atlases cover topics like outer space and the oceans.

### Dictionaries

Dictionaries contain definitions of words and their origins. Biographical dictionaries focus on famous people. Specialized dictionaries deal with science, history, medicine, and other subjects.

### Directories

Directories list information about groups of people, businesses, and organizations. The most widely used directories are telephone books.

### Periodical Indexes

Periodical indexes list articles in magazines and newspapers. These indexes are arranged alphabetically by subject.

- The *Readers' Guide to Periodical Literature* lists articles from many publications. (See page **370**.)
- The *New York Times Index* lists articles from the *New York Times* newspaper.

### Other Reference Books

Some reference books do not fit into any one category:

- *Facts on File* includes thousands of short but informative facts about events, discoveries, people, and places.
- *Facts About the Presidents* presents information about all of the presidents of the United States.
- *Bartlett's Familiar Quotations* lists thousands of quotations from famous people.

Research

## Consulting Other Reference Books

Remind students that it is important to take careful, thorough notes when using a reference source that cannot be borrowed. Point out that when it is time to write their reports and works-cited pages, students will have to rely on their notes. Students will learn more about taking notes on SE pages 386–390 in this unit.

✍ DIFFERENTIATE INSTRUCTION

TEKS 10.20B, 10.21A

---

### Differentiated Instruction: English Language Learners

ELPS 1E, 2A, 2C, 2E, 2I, 3A, 3B, 4G, 5B

| ELP Level **Beginning** | ELP Level **Intermediate** | ELP Level **Advanced/Advanced High** |
|---|---|---|
| Have each type of reference available. Say the name of each one, and have students repeat the name and point to the book. | After students look through each type of book, use a transparency with prepared questions, and have students name the book to use to find each answer. | Have students find answers to a prepared list of questions in scavenger-hunt style by using the various types of reference books. |

TEKS **10.20B** Formulate a plan for research on a complex, multi-faceted topic; **10.21A** Follow the research plan to compile data that identifies major issues and debates; **ELPS 1E** Internalize new academic language by using and reusing it/speaking; **2A** Distinguish sounds with increasing ease; **2C** Learn academic vocabulary heard during classroom instruction/interactions; **2E** Use visual support to enhance and confirm understanding of increasingly complex spoken language; **2I** Demonstrate listening comprehension in increasingly complex spoken language by responding to questions; **3A** Practice producing sounds of newly acquired vocabulary; **3B** Expand vocabulary by learning and using routine language needed for classroom communication; **4G** Demonstrate comprehension of increasingly complex English/responding to questions; **5B** Write using content-based grade-level vocabulary

## Using Periodical Guides

Tell students that when they find a listing for a topic in the *Readers' Guide to Periodical Literature,* they should write down the name and issue date of the publication and the title and page numbers of the article. Many libraries provide simple requisition slips for students to record this information. If the issue date of the magazine is recent and the library subscribes to it, they will find it in the periodical section of the library. Older issues are probably archived or available in microfilm files or digital archives.

### Tip

The library's policy may allow patrons to check out older issues of a magazine. If students cannot do this, they can take notes in the library or follow the procedure for copying resources.

⭐ **TEKS** 10.20B, 10.21A

---

 ⭐ **TEKS** 10.20B, 10.21A

## Using Periodical Guides

**Periodical guides** are located in the reference or periodical section of the library. These guides alphabetically list topics and articles found in magazines, newspapers, and journals. Some guides are printed volumes, some are CD-ROM's, and some are on library Web sites. Ask your librarian for help.

### Readers' Guide to Periodical Literature

The *Readers' Guide to Periodical Literature* is a well-known periodical reference source and is found in most libraries. The following tips will help you look up your topic in this resource:

- Articles are always listed alphabetically by author and topic.
- Some topics are subdivided, with each article listed under the appropriate subtopic.
- Cross-references refer to related topic entries where you may find more articles pertinent to your topic.

### Sample *Readers' Guide* Format

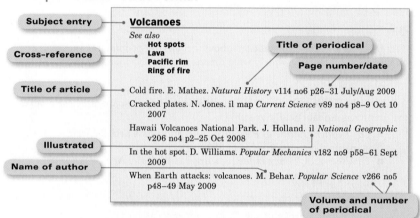

### Tip

The librarian will have a list of magazines in the library's collection. Check it for the magazine you seek. If you need an older issue, it might be in the archives. If so, ask the librarian to get it for you.

---

⭐ **TEKS** **10.20B** Formulate a plan for research on a complex, multi-faceted topic; **10.21A** Follow the research plan to compile data that identifies major issues and debates; **ELPS** **1A** Use prior knowledge and experience to understand meanings; **3A** Practice producing sounds of newly acquired vocabulary; **3B** Expand vocabulary by learning and using routine language needed for classroom communication; **3C** Speak using a variety of grammatical structures/ sentence lengths and types/connecting words with increasing accuracy and ease; **3D** Speak using grade-level content area vocabulary/new words and academic language proficiency; **3F** Give information/ranging from using a limited high-frequency vocabulary to using abstract and content-based vocabulary during speaking; **3G** Express opinions and ideas ranging from communicating short phrases to participating in discussions; **4F** Use support from peers/teachers to read grade-appropriate text and develop grasp of language structures and background knowledge; **4G** Demonstrate comprehension of increasingly complex English/responding to questions; **4I** Expand reading skills; **4K** Demonstrate comprehension and expand reading skills by employing analytical skills/evaluating written information and performing critical analyses

### Differentiated Instruction: English Language Learners

⭐ **ELPS** 1A, 3A-D, 3F, 3G, 4F, 4G, 4I, 4K

| ELP Level **Beginning** | ELP Level **Intermediate** | ELP Level **Advanced/Advanced High** |
|---|---|---|
| Explain differences in pronunciation and meaning between *polish* (from the quote) and *Polish.* Have students draw what the words say. Use their drawings to teach the concept of figurative language. | Read the quote with students, pointing out figurative language; students list other examples of figurative language they have seen and explain their meanings. | Discuss the quote with students and ask students to infer and support what Montaigne meant and why he chose these words. |

371

## Research Writing
# MLA Research Report

Thomas Carlyle, the Scottish essayist and historian, once wrote, "Man is a tool-using animal." He went on to explain, "Nowhere do you find him without tools; without tools he is nothing, with tools he is all." In nature, most creatures adapt to their environment. People, on the other hand, tend to use their tools to adapt the environment to meet their needs. Consider, for example, great works of engineering such as the Empire State Building, the Great Wall of China, or the Hoover Dam. Not only were these monuments built with tools, they are—in effect—tools themselves, helping humans change their environment.

This chapter will help you to write an MLA research report about a great work of engineering that interests you. (MLA is the most common documentation style for research writing.) In the process, you will learn why and how the work came to be, and what effect it has had on the world.

### Writing Guidelines

**Subject:** A great work of engineering
**Purpose:** To research and present accurate information
**Form:** MLA research report
**Audience:** Classmates

"It is good to rub and polish our brain against that of others."

—Michel de Montaigne

### Resources

#### Copy Masters (see Appendix)

- T-chart (A-93)
- Details chart (A-96)

# MLA Research Report

### Objectives

- understand what an MLA research report is
- understand the purpose of an MLA research report
- plan, draft, revise, edit, and publish an MLA research report

An **MLA research report** is a piece of writing that

- assimilates and synthesizes information from a variety of reliable resources;
- presents information in a clear, interesting, organized way; and
- uses standard MLA formatting to cite sources.

Students who have never used MLA standards to document sources may be concerned that these standards will affect their writing or their research. Assure them that, for the most part, following the MLA documentation style means giving credit for others' ideas in an easy-to-understand, common-sense way. All of the key features of the MLA style for citing sources are explained in this chapter.

Point out the quote by Michel de Montaigne and ask students how the quote may apply to the writing of research papers (learning from others during research, editing, etc.).

**⌐ DIFFERENTIATE INSTRUCTION**

## Title Page and Outline

Discuss the organization of information in the outline. Point out that the sample outline is an example of a sentence outline. Students will learn more about outlining on SE page 392.

**TEKS** 10.13A, 10.20B

**TEKS** 10.13A, 10.20B

# Title Page and Outline

After watching a PBS special about dams, Isabel Cotero became interested in Egypt's Aswan High Dam. She decided to write a research paper about that topic. Her paper starts on the next page. Below are the title page and outline of her paper. Some teachers require these additional pages. If your teacher requires them, follow any special instructions he or she may give you.

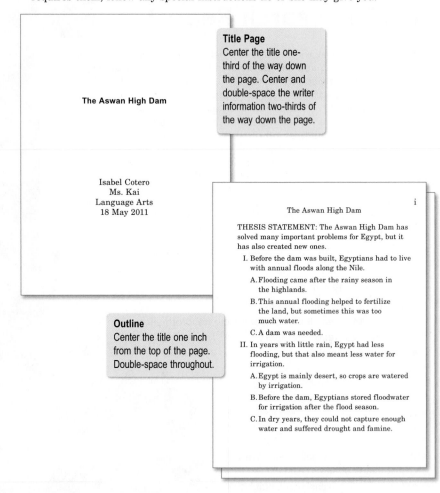

**Title Page**
Center the title one-third of the way down the page. Center and double-space the writer information two-thirds of the way down the page.

The Aswan High Dam

Isabel Cotero
Ms. Kai
Language Arts
18 May 2011

**Outline**
Center the title one inch from the top of the page. Double-space throughout.

i

The Aswan High Dam

THESIS STATEMENT: The Aswan High Dam has solved many important problems for Egypt, but it has also created new ones.

I. Before the dam was built, Egyptians had to live with annual floods along the Nile.

 A. Flooding came after the rainy season in the highlands.

 B. This annual flooding helped to fertilize the land, but sometimes this was too much water.

 C. A dam was needed.

II. In years with little rain, Egypt had less flooding, but that also meant less water for irrigation.

 A. Egypt is mainly desert, so crops are watered by irrigation.

 B. Before the dam, Egyptians stored floodwater for irrigation after the flood season.

 C. In dry years, they could not capture enough water and suffered drought and famine.

**TEKS** **10.13A** Plan a first draft by selecting the correct genre and determining topics through a range of strategies; **10.20B** Formulate a plan for research on a complex, multi-faceted topic

## Sample MLA Research Report

**TEKS** 10.15A(i)–
10.15(iv), 10.15C(ii), 10.21C

> **1/2"**
> Cotero 1 ← 1" →
>
> **↑1"**
>
> ← 1" →
>
> Isabel Cotero
> Ms. Kai
> Language Arts
> 18 May 2011
>
> ### The Aswan High Dam
>
> Humans have been building dams for thousands of years. One of the oldest examples is the Saad El Kafara, built in Egypt around 2700 B.C.E. Its main purpose was to stop catastrophic flooding during wet years, but its water storage also allowed for increased irrigation of croplands. While most dams have been built for these two purposes, huge new dams in the past century have provided the added benefit of hydroelectric power for the world's growing population. However, people are discovering that these large dams also have many detrimental effects on the environment. Egypt's High Dam at Aswan illustrates this critical trade-off. The Aswan High Dam has solved many important problems for Egypt, but it has also created new ones.
>
> ### Reasons for the Dam
>
> Before the dam was built, Egyptians had to live with annual floods along the Nile. Each year, after the rainy season, the river would spill over its banks onto the Egyptian countryside. While this annual flooding helped to fertilize the land, sometimes there was just too much water. For example, "between 1860 and 1880, there were four major floods that forced people to flee to higher ground" (Parks 12). They desperately needed a dam to help prevent this recurring damage.
>
> **↑1"↓**

**The entire report is double-spaced.**

**Beginning**
The writer introduces her topic and states her thesis (underlined).

**Middle**
The first middle section explains the historical background. Writer uses embedded quotes to support topic sentence, and she correctly cites researched information.

Research

---

## Sample MLA Research Report

Give students time to read the sample research report from beginning to end. Tell students to ignore the side notes for the time being and to concentrate on the content, style, and organization of the report. Tell them to keep these questions in mind as they read:

- What is the topic and thesis of this report?
- What does the writer want a reader to learn or understand about the topic?
- Is the information presented clearly and interestingly?
- Can a reader easily follow the ideas?
- Does the writer sound as if she cares about the topic? **✔DIFFERENTIATE INSTRUCTION**

**TEKS** 10.15A(i), 10.15A(ii), 10.15A(iii), 10.15A(iv), 10.15C(ii), 10.21C

---

## Differentiated Instruction: English Language Learners

**ELPS** 2E, 2F, 2G, 3D, 3G, 4F-4I

| ELP Level **Beginning** | ELP Level **Intermediate** | ELP Level **Advanced/Advanced High** |
|---|---|---|
| Prepare pictures and maps to go along with this essay. Use these supports as you read aloud or play a taped version of the essay. | Show a video of the Aswan Dam to build background knowledge of vocabulary/concept. Then use shared reading to have students summarize each paragraph. | Show a video of the Aswan Dam to reinforce concept/language attainment. Have students read the essay silently, then think-pair-share the above questions. |

**TEKS** **10.15A(i)** Write an analytical essay that includes an introductory paragraph and a variety of sentence structures; **10.15A(ii)** Write an analytical essay that includes transitions; **10.15A(iii)** Write an analytical essay that includes an idea or thesis; **10.15A(iv)** Write an analytical essay that includes a structure appropriate to the purpose; **10.15C(ii)** Write a response to expository and literary text using embedded quotations; **10.21C** Quote and accurately cite researched information; **ELPS 2E** Use visual support to enhance and confirm understanding of spoken language; **2F** Listen to and derive meaning from a variety of media; **2G** Understand the general meaning, main points, and important details of spoken language; **3D** Speak using grade-level content area vocabulary/academic language proficiency; **3G** Express opinions and ideas; **4F** Use visual/contextual support and support from peers/teachers to read grade-appropriate text, enhance understanding, and develop vocabulary, grasp of language structures, and background knowledge; **4G** Demonstrate comprehension of increasingly complex English/participating in shared reading, summarizing material, and responding to questions; **4H** Read silently with increasing ease and comprehension for longer periods; **4I** Demonstrate comprehension by employing basic reading skills

Review the sample research report with students from the beginning on SE page 373, using the side notes as a guide to analyze the content and form of the report and to discuss how the writer has applied the traits of writing (Focus and Coherence, Organization, Development of Ideas, Voice, and Conventions).

Use the following points to discuss focus and coherence in the report. Have students point out specific details when appropriate.

- The writer has chosen an interesting work of engineering, the Aswan High Dam in Egypt.
- The writer identifies the topic (the Aswan High Dam) and the focus of the report (the dam has solved problems and created problems for Egypt) in a clear thesis statement (SE page 373).
- The writer uses many interesting, informative details throughout the report to support the thesis.
- The writer uses both quotations and paraphrases from reliable sources.
- The writer makes sure to cite reference ideas accurately following the MLA documentation style. **DIFFERENTIATE INSTRUCTION** ↘

**TEKS** 10.21A, 10.21C

---

**TEKS** 10.21A, 10.21C

Cotero 2

In years with little rain, Egypt had less flooding, but that also meant less water for irrigation. Egypt is mainly desert, so crops grown there must be watered by irrigation. Before the dam was built, the Egyptians captured floodwater and stored it in pools for irrigation use during the rest of the year. In dry years, however, they could not capture enough water to last. The result was drought and famine (11).

By building a dam, the people of Egypt hoped to accomplish several things. A dam would help to stop catastrophic floods during wet years. It would also prevent Egypt from running out of water during dry years. In fact, it would store enough water to allow even more land to be irrigated. This was important because Egypt's population started to outgrow its crop production during the twentieth century (*Building Big: Dams*).

**Building the Dam**

The first Aswan Dam was built between 1898 and 1902, while Egypt was a colony of Great Britain. It was designed by William Willcocks, a British engineer who was very familiar with traditional Egyptian irrigation. Willcocks built a dam that would let the silt-laden water of each year's early rains pass through to fertilize the croplands below. The dam then stored later rainwater to be used for irrigation during the rest of the year (Pearce 50). Unfortunately, Willcock's dam didn't hold enough water to last through dry years, even after being raised twice, once in 1912 and again in 1933. Also, the dam almost overflowed in 1946, which happened to be a very wet year (Parks 14).

> The writer paraphrases and correctly cites a source of information (Parks, page 11). She addresses major issues in the middle paragraphs.

> Headings help guide the reader from section to section.

> The second middle section details how the dam came into existence, a major issue.

---

**TEKS** **10.21A** Follow the research plan to compile data that identifies major issues; **10.21C** Paraphrase researched information

Cotero 3

In 1952, Egypt became independent from Britain, and its new government decided to build a dam that could hold enough water for three years of irrigation. The project quickly became a touchy subject, because Egypt didn't want to hire British engineers to design the dam. As a gesture of friendship, Germany donated plans to the new government. In 1956, the World Bank, Great Britain, and the United States offered to fund the project, but they cancelled those plans when Egypt bought Soviet weapons to fight Israel (17–20). The Soviet Union agreed to fund the dam if Egypt agreed to use only Soviet engineers and equipment. By 1959, plans were complete and the project began ("Aswan Dam" 40).

First, the valley that the dam would flood had to be cleared. This meant moving more than 100,000 Nubian people to new lands. Also, the new lake would cover many ancient temples and other monuments. In 1960, the United Nations Educational, Scientific, and Cultural Organization (UNESCO) asked governments around the world to help move these monuments. In all, 23 were rescued before the reservoir was filled, though many more were lost (*Building Big: Dams*).

Next, preparations had to be made for the dam's actual construction. New roads and railroads had to be built to carry men and equipment to the construction site. In addition, an electrical station had to be built at the old Aswan Dam to supply power for the project. Also, the town of Aswan had to be prepared to host the thousands of workers that would be needed (Parks 27).

Once building began, the construction team faced very harsh conditions. The terrain was extremely

> **Page numbers alone (17–20) refer to the last source cited (Parks). Writer continues to cite and summarize information from authoritative sources concerning major debates about her topic.**

> **Each paragraph begins with a topic sentence, followed by relevant evidence and carefully chosen supporting details.**

Research

Use the following points to discuss the organization and development of ideas in the report. Have students point out specific details when appropriate.

- The writer grabs the reader's attention with an interesting fact about the oldest dams.
- Each paragraph contains a clear topic sentence and supporting details that help explain and expand on the thesis statement.
- Headings (Reasons for the Dam, Building the Dam, Effects of the Dam, Conclusion) help break up the report visually and tell readers what they can expect to learn in each section.
- The first three middle paragraphs provide a detailed explanation of the reasons that the Aswan Dam was built.
- The next group of middle paragraphs describes the history of the building of the Aswan Dam in chronological order, using specific dates to make the order clear.
- The last group of middle paragraphs discusses the positive and negative effects of the Aswan High Dam.
- The conclusion summarizes the main points and relates to the thesis by stating the writer's position on the responsibility people have to the environment.

⭐ **TEKS** 10.21A, 10.21C

**TEKS** **10.21A** Follow the research plan to compile data that identifies major issues and debates; **10.21C** Summarize researched information; **ELPS** **1E** Internalize new basic language by using and reusing it/speaking; **1F** Use accessible language and learn new and essential language in the process; **3D** Speak using grade-level content area vocabulary/new words; **3E** Share information in cooperative learning interactions; **3G** Express opinions and ideas ranging from communicating short phrases to participating in discussions; **4F** Use support from peers/teachers to read grade-appropriate text, enhance understanding, and develop vocabulary and grasp of language structures; **4G** Demonstrate comprehension of increasingly complex English/taking notes; **4H** Read silently with increasing ease and comprehension for longer periods; **4I** Demonstrate comprehension by employing and expanding basic reading skills; **4J** Demonstrate comprehension and expand reading skills by employing inferential skills; **4K** Demonstrate comprehension and expand reading skills by employing analytical skills

## Differentiated Instruction: English Language Learners

🔹 **ELPS** 1E, 1F, 3D, 3E, 3G, 4F–4K

| ELP Level **Beginning** | ELP Level **Intermediate** | ELP Level **Advanced/Advanced High** |
|---|---|---|
| Echo read one to two paragraphs on these pages, stopping to clarify pronunciation and word meaning. Encourage students to monitor their own understanding and seek clarification. | Have students work with a partner, taking notes on examples of focus and coherence, organization, and development of ideas. Use these notes to support discussion. | Have students reread the essay silently, analyzing it for focus and coherence, organization, and development of ideas. Use their analysis to support class discussion. |

Use these points to discuss how the writer achieved a knowledgeable and engaging voice in the report. Have students point out additional specific details in other parts of the report.

- The writer uses interesting facts and details (for example, the cost of $1 billion; 50,000 people worked on it; more than 17 times the materials used to build the Great Pyramid).
- The writer uses an interesting quotation about important benefits of the Aswan Dam (Michael Sorkin).
- The writer uses the first-person voice to make a personal call to action.

⭐ **TEKS** 10.21A, 10.22B

Cotero 4

rugged, rapidly wearing out tires on construction equipment. Daytime temperatures reached 135 degrees Fahrenheit in the shade, so most work had to be done at night. Under these conditions, the Soviet equipment broke down five times faster than expected. This caused expensive delays while replacement parts were shipped from the Soviet Union or equipment was sent back there for repair. In 1961, with little progress made, the Egyptian government brought in Egyptian construction experts to replace the Soviet engineers, and it began using equipment from Sweden and Great Britain (28–29).

The dam was finally completed in July 1970, ten years after the project began. It was by far the largest engineering work of its time, costing over $1 billion (*Building Big: Dams*). More than 50,000 people worked on the dam, using 17 times more material than was used to build the Great Pyramid. The finished dam stretches two miles wide and 364 feet high. The reservoir (holding the water) covers an area larger than the state of Delaware (Parks 35).

**Effects of the Dam**

The Aswan High Dam immediately helped control flooding. Before the Nile was dammed, floods sometimes forced evacuation of the Nile Valley and its delta, with a great loss of life and property. With the dam in place, however, flooding became a thing of the past. As a result, cities like Cairo, which used to be limited to high ground near the river, have expanded all the way to the Nile's banks. As Michael Sorkin puts it, "By stabilizing the river's banks, the dam not only rescued Egyptian

*Dates help the reader follow the development of the dam. By citing and comparing several sources, writer shows that she has considered the reliability, validity, and accuracy of sources she has used.*

*The third middle section explains the effects of the dam. Writer again considers major issues and debates about the dam.*

*Writer includes the source of a quotation (Michael Sorkin) in the text, and the page number (82) appears in parentheses.*

⭐ **TEKS** **10.21A** Follow the research plan to compile data that identifies major issues and debates; **10.22B** Evaluate the relevance of information to the topic/determine the reliability, validity, and accuracy of sources by examining their objectivity and authority

Cotero 5

agriculture from historic cycles of flood and drought, but enabled extensive urban development along the shore" (82).

The vast reservoir behind the dam makes more irrigation possible in Egypt. In the past, the people could grow crops only as long as their stored water lasted each year. Now the dam provides irrigation throughout the entire year. In fact, Egyptians are able to irrigate two million more acres of land than they could before the dam was built (Parks 41).

Also, the Aswan High Dam provides 50 percent of Egypt's electricity. Once the dam was built, thousands of villages that had never had electricity before were "plugged in." The power station has been important for the swelling populations in Egypt's larger cities (*Building Big: Dams*).

However, there are some significant environmental problems related to the dam. For one thing, without the annual deposit of silt to enrich their fields, Egyptian farmers now have to use tons of chemical fertilizers each year. This has changed the chemistry of the waterways, leading to an excess of waterweeds and a decrease in fish and shrimp. Even the nearby sardine population in the Mediterranean Sea has suffered. The loss of silt has also caused the Nile delta to erode severely (Parks 39–40). Furthermore, industrial building closer to the Nile itself has caused more water pollution. As a result, the soil of the Nile delta, whose crops feed 40 million people, is becoming dangerously contaminated with toxins such as heavy metals (Penvenne 17).

Because the irrigation canals no longer dry up each year, Egyptians suffer from more waterborne diseases than before. One example is schistosomiasis,

> Writer has abundance of material to choose from, but includes only relevant evidence to support the topic sentence.

> Negative effects of the dam are also discussed. Writer shows that she has considered both sides of the issue and is knowledgeable about major debates surrounding the topic.

> A technical term (schistosomiasis) is explained for the reader.

Research

Have students notice conventions that make the report informative and enjoyable to read. Have them point out additional examples in other parts of the report.

- In addition to adhering to rules of grammar, punctuation, and spelling, the writer has used a pleasing and appropriately varied mix of sentence lengths and patterns.
- The writer also uses specific nouns to help readers understand ideas. (For example, on this page, the following specific nouns help explain the negative effects of the dam: chemical fertilizers, waterweeds, fish and shrimp, sardine population, Nile delta, toxins, heavy metals, and schistosomiasis.)

**☑ DIFFERENTIATE INSTRUCTION**

TEKS 10.21A, 10.22B

## Differentiated Instruction: English Language Learners

**ELPS** 1E, 1F, 1H, 2A, 3E, 4C

| ELP Level **Beginning** | ELP Level **Intermediate** | ELP Level **Advanced/Advanced High** |
|---|---|---|
| Read the essay aloud. Have students raise hands when they hear a water word (*dam, flooding, river,* etc.). Then have them repeat each word after you, practicing distinguishing sound and intonation. | Have students work with a partner to list all nouns directly relating to the topic. Discuss why using specific nouns is important in this essay. | Review connotative/denotative meaning. Using a 3-column chart, have students identify each adjective and noun's connotative meaning as positive, neutral, or negative. |

TEKS 10.21A Follow the research plan to compile data that identifies major issues and debates; 10.22B Evaluate the relevance of information to the topic; ELPS 1E Internalize new basic language by using and reusing it/speaking and writing; 1F Use accessible language and learn new and essential language in the process; 1H Develop and expand learning strategies/reasoning, looking for patterns in language, and analyzing sayings and expressions; 2A Distinguish sounds/intonation patterns with increasing ease; 3E Share information in cooperative learning interactions; 4C Comprehend vocabulary used in written classroom materials

Ask students to explain how the writer uses the conclusion to express her thoughts and feelings about the building of the Aswan High Dam. (The writer recalls details presented earlier in the report to point out that while the dam has had many benefits, it's a reminder of the kinds of problems that occur when people change the environment. The writer reflects on this lesson in the final sentence.) DIFFERENTIATE INSTRUCTION ↘

 **TEKS** 10.15A(i), 10.15A(ii)

 **TEKS** 10.15A(i), 10.15A(ii)

Cotero 6

an intestinal and urinary disease transmitted by microscopic worms that live on snails in the waterways. Before the dam was built, these snails died every year during the dry season. Now they flourish year-round, making the disease seven times more common (Larrson 2). Besides the snails, there are more mosquitoes carrying malaria and other diseases in Egypt since the dam was built (Louria 3).

In addition, the dam continues to threaten some of Egypt's most important monuments. Year-round irrigation has led to rising groundwater, and this moisture is causing ancient structures like the temples of Luxor to crumble from the bottom up (Brown 22). If this problem isn't corrected, these historical treasures will be destroyed as surely as those that lie beneath the waters of the reservoir.

### Conclusion

No one can deny that the Aswan High Dam has benefited Egypt. Its flood control has prevented loss of life and property in wet years. Year-round irrigation and the expansion of croplands have helped supply food and other goods for Egypt's booming population. The electrical power it provides has helped the country to build and modernize. However, the dam also demonstrates that whenever humans change their environment, they introduce new problems that must be dealt with. The building of the Aswan High Dam teaches people that they have to learn to modernize with caution, and to predict and prepare for the consequences of their actions.

> **Transitions** such as "in addition" help link paragraphs. Writer effectively uses a variety of sentence structures to engage reader throughout the essay.

> **Ending**
> The closing summarizes the main points of the paper and leaves the reader with a final thought.

**Differentiated Instruction: Advanced Learners**

Have students do additional research on the Aswan High Dam and its effects on Egypt's environment and share their findings with the class. Discuss what information they may have added or left out if they had written the sample essay.

Cotero 7

## Works Cited

A separate page alphabetically lists the sources cited in the paper.

"Aswan Dam." *STC-Link*. University of Colorado at
    Denver, 15 Apr. 2004. Web. 7 May 2011.

Brown, Jeff. L. "Researchers Unravel Mystery of Eroding
    Egyptian Monuments." *Civil Engineering* 71.9
    (2007): 22. Print.

*Building Big: Dams.* WGBH Boston Video, 2006. VHS.

Larrson, Birgitta. "Aquaculture and schistosomiasis."
    *Three Overviews on Environment and Aquaculture*
    *in the Tropics and Sub-Tropics.* Food and
    Agriculture Organization of the United Nations,
    Dec. 1994. Web. 15 Apr. 2011.

Second, third, and additional lines are indented five spaces.

Louria, Donald B. "The Specter of Emerging and
    Re-Emerging Infection Epidemics." *Healthful Life*
    *Project.* The Healthcare Foundation of New Jersey,
    15 Dec. 2007. Web. 18 Apr. 2011.

Parks, Peggy J. *The Aswan High Dam.* San Diego:
    Blackbirch, 2008. Print.

Pearce, Fred. "Dammed Lies." *New Scientist* 175.2361
    (2006): 50–51. Web.

Penvenne, Laura Jean. "The Disappearing Delta." *Earth*
    Aug. 2004: 16–17. Print.

Sorkin, Michael. "Deciphering Greater Cairo."
    *Architectural Record* 189.4 (2007): 82–87. Print.

**Note:** This Works Cited page follows MLA documentation style. (See pages **407–410** for more information.)

Research

Give students a chance to look over the works-cited page and to flip back through the report to see how these works are cited in parentheses within the report.

Encourage students to refer to the Sample Research Report and the works-cited pages frequently as models for organization and presentation when they write their reports.

✔ DIFFERENTIATE INSTRUCTION

★ TEKS 10.21A, 10.21C

---

## Differentiated Instruction: English Language Learners

★ ELPS 1A, 2C

| ELP Level **Beginning** | ELP Level **Intermediate** | ELP Level **Advanced/Advanced High** |
|---|---|---|
| Have students draw the various meanings of the word *work(s)* that they know and instruct them how, in this case, the word can also mean *pieces of writing*. | Prepare strips of paper with one reference per strip. Have students practice arranging the strips in the correct alphabetic order. | Have students work with partners to find how and where each work is cited in the essay. Discuss how this page relates to the parenthetical documentation in the essay. |

★ **TEKS 10.21A** Follow the research plan to compile data that identifies major issues and debates; **10.21C** Accurately cite researched information; **ELPS 1A** Use prior knowledge to understand meanings; **2C** Learn basic and academic vocabulary heard during classroom instruction/interactions

## Prewriting

**Keys to Effective Prewriting**

Remind students of the purpose of the prewriting stage in the writing process: It is when the writer selects a topic, gathers details, and decides how to organize those details.

The Keys to Effective Prewriting list explains the process that guides students on SE pages 381–394. Review the importance of each step.

Discuss the schedule for planning, writing, and presenting research reports. Let students know

- how much time they have to select a topic and whether topics have to be approved beforehand;
- what materials they have to submit and when (for example, research notes, outlines, and first drafts);
- when writing conferences will be held;
- when different drafts should be submitted; and
- a final date for requesting deadline extensions, if necessary and permitted.

**TEKS** 10.20A, 10.20B, 10.21A

## Prewriting

Just as every work of engineering begins with a blueprint, every research report must start with some prewriting. Prewriting involves choosing a topic and researching it to gather and organize information for your report.

### Keys to Effective Prewriting

1. For your topic, brainstorm, consult with others, and decide on a topic. Choose a complex, multi-faceted, interesting example of a work of engineering.

2. Formulate major research questions you want to have answered about that topic.

3. Formulate a plan for your research. Use a gathering grid to organize your research questions and answers. Use note cards to keep track of longer answers. (See pages 383–386.)

4. Keep track of the sources of information you summarize or quote. You must correctly cite them in your report.

5. Gather plenty of details about your topic, including why and how the work of engineering was built and what the effects of the work have been. You should learn about and address major issues and debates about the topic.

**TEKS** **10.20A** Brainstorm, consult with others on, decide upon, and formulate a research question to a major research topic; **10.20B** Brainstorm, consult with others on, decide upon, and formulate a research question to a major research topic; **10.21A** Follow the research plan to compile data that identifies major issues and debates

## Selecting a Topic

To narrow a general subject to a specific topic, there are a range of strategies that you can use. One strategy is to brainstorm and then cluster. Isabel brainstormed and then made the following graphic organizer.

### Cluster Diagram

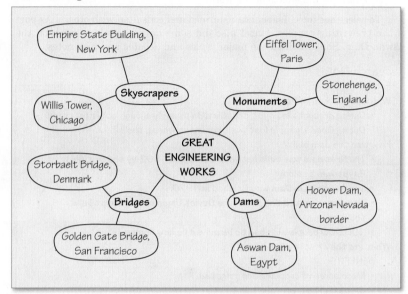

### Tip

Great works of engineering aren't limited to skyscrapers, monuments, bridges, and dams. Others include tunnels, cathedrals, pyramids, railways, and so on.

**Prewrite**

**Select a topic.** Create a cluster diagram like the one above to identify possible topics (great engineering works) for your research. If necessary, browse through your social studies or history text for ideas. Finally, select a topic from your cluster. (You may also choose one of the works of engineering in the cluster above.)

**Research**

---

### Selecting a Topic

Students can benefit from the interests and general knowledge of their classmates when trying to generate a list of possible topics for their cluster diagram. Be sure to point out the **Tip** below the example cluster diagram.

- Organize students into groups and have each group create a cluster diagram of great engineering works.
- Besides browsing through social studies and history texts for ideas, they can search the Internet for ideas.
- Have groups display their cluster diagrams so the entire class can get topic ideas from the clusters.

★ **TEKS** 10.13A, 10.21B

**Select a topic.** Remind students that their topic should be something that interests them. ☑ **DIFFERENTIATE INSTRUCTION**

✱ For more about using a cluster diagram, see SE page 618.

---

 **TEKS** 10.13A Plan a first draft by determining topics through a range of strategies; **10.21B** Organize information from multiple sources to create graphics; **ELPS** 1A Use prior knowledge and experience to understand meanings; **1C** Use strategic learning techniques to acquire basic and grade-level vocabulary; **1E** Internalize new basic language by using and reusing it/speaking and writing; **1F** Use accessible language and learn new and essential language in the process; **2E** Use visual support to enhance and confirm understanding of increasingly complex spoken language; **2F** Listen to and derive meaning from a variety of media to build and reinforce concept and language attainment; **3B** Expand vocabulary by learning and using high-frequency words for identifying and describing; **4C** Comprehend vocabulary used in written classroom materials; **5B** Write using newly acquired basic and content-based grade-level vocabulary

## Prewriting

### Selecting a Topic

Call attention to the bulleted items at the top of the SE page and make sure students understand that these bullets outline the objectives, or goals, of their report.

Then have students read the Research Notes to themselves. Suggest that they use Isabel's notes as a model as they do initial research to size up their own topic. Point out that these early notes can also provide them with a preliminary organizational plan for their reports. If they compare Isabel's notes with her report on SE pages 373–379, they will see that the notes serve as a rough outline for the organization of ideas in her report.

**★ TEKS** 10.13A

**Decide on your topic.** If students are having a difficult time choosing among topics, encourage them to freewrite about each topic. The topic that generates the most writing is usually the best one to choose. Also encourage students to use a graphic organizer such as a T-chart or a details chart (see TE Appendix) to list issues or debates about their topics.

**★ TEKS** 10.20A

## Prewriting Selecting a Topic

An effective research report about an important work of engineering should explain the following three things.

- Why was the work built?
- How was it built?
- What are the effects of the work?

To select her topic, Isabel brainstormed and consulted with others. As part of the prewriting process, Isabel also did some quick initial research on the Aswan Dam. She identified the major issues and debates and took notes.

### Research Notes

> **Why was the Aswan Dam built?**
> - During droughts in Egypt, the Nile didn't supply enough water for crops.
> - During floods, people lost their homes or, worse, their lives.
>
> **How was the dam built?**
> - The first dam was built between 1898 and 1902 by the British, when Egypt was a colony.
> - The Aswan High Dam was finished in 1970.
> - Germany donated the plans; the Soviet Union helped Egypt build the dam.
> - 100,000 people also had to be moved to new homes.
>
> **What are the effects of the dam?**
> BENEFITS
> - More acres of cropland are irrigated.
> - Crops can be grown all year.
> - Cities can build closer to the Nile.
>
> PROBLEMS
> - Crops need more chemical fertilizers.
> - The Nile delta is eroding.
> - Fish populations are decreasing.

From this initial research, Isabel could tell that there would be plenty to write about. What interested her most were the good and bad effects of the dam. She was confident that she could write about these issues.

 **Decide on your topic.** Brainstorm, consult with others, and do some initial research about your topic. List major issues and debates about the topic.

## Formulating a Research Question

Isabel made a gathering grid during her research about the Aswan Dam. Down the left side, she listed major research questions about the topic. Across the top, she listed sources she found to answer those questions. For answers too long to fit on the grid, Isabel used note cards. (See page **386**.)

### Gathering Grid

| ASWAN DAM | *Building Big: Dams* (video) | *The Aswan High Dam* (book) | "Aswan Dam" (Web site) | "Deciphering Greater Cairo" (magazine article) |
|---|---|---|---|---|
| 1. Why was the Aswan Dam built? | To provide year-round irrigation | | | British cotton mill owners wanted more cotton. |
| 2. How was the dam built? | | See note card #1. | All-local material Rock: 28.6 million cubic yards Sand: 20 million cubic yards Clay: 4 million cubic yards | |
| 3. What are the effects of the dam? | Doubled agricultural production Damage to environment | | Lake Nasser holds 1.99 trillion cubic yards of water. The lake is 6 miles wide and 310 miles long. | See note card #2. |

**Create a gathering grid.** List your research questions in the left-hand column of a grid or graphic that fits your topic. Across the top of a grid, list sources you will use. Fill in the rest of the grid or graphic with answers you find. Use note cards for longer, more detailed answers.

*Prewrite*

*Research*

---

### Formulating a Research Question

Have students look at Isabel's research notes on SE page 382 to see how they relate to the gathering grid.

★ TEKS 10.20A

**Create a gathering grid.** Suggest that students read the information on SE page 386 together to help them understand how note cards can be used to extend the usefulness of the gathering grid. ↙DIFFERENTIATE INSTRUCTION

★ TEKS 10.21B

---

★ TEKS **10.20A** Formulate a research question to the major research topic; **10.21B** Organize information from multiple sources to create graphics and forms; **ELPS 5B** Write using content-based grade-level vocabulary

## Formulating a Plan

Not all students will encounter the same complexities as Isabel did; however, as they conduct their research, they should begin to notice problems or issues about their topic coming to light as well. Remind students that graphic organizers are just that—visual/graphic ways to organize written information. Encourage students to

- use an organizer like the one Isabel chose,
- choose a graphic organizer in this textbook, or
- create an original graphic organizer to focus their research and help formulate a plan for writing. DIFFERENTIATE INSTRUCTION ↘

TEKS 10.13A, 10.20B, 10.21B; ELPS 4F

✳ For more samples of graphic organizers, see pages 624–625.

**Formulate a plan.** Point out to students that using a graphic organizer can provide them with a preliminary organizational plan for their reports.

---

 TEKS 10.13A, 10.20B, 10.21B

## Formulating a Plan

As Isabel continued the research for her paper, she realized that the Aswan Dam was a multi-faceted, complex topic. There were economic, political, social, and technical issues involved. The Aswan Dam was years in the making, and all kinds of controversies emerged, including debates over the planning, the financing, and the construction of the dam.

Using her research notes and questions, Isabel created the following graphic organizer so that she could focus her research and formulate a plan that would help her write an analysis that would cover the major issues and debates surrounding the dam.

 **Formulate a plan.** Formulate a plan for your research that will enable you to address the major issues and debates surrounding your topic. Then choose a graphic organizer that will help you organize the information about the various facets of the complex topic that you have chosen.

Prewrite

---

TEKS **10.13A** Plan a first draft by determining topics through a range of strategies; **10.20B** Formulate a plan for research on a complex, multi-faceted topic; **10.21B** Organize information from multiple sources to create graphics; **ELPS 4F** Use visual/contextual support to read grade-appropriate text, enhance understanding, and develop background knowledge

## Gathering Sources

From her initial research, Isabel realized that there were a variety of sources to choose from as she conducted her research. She wanted to be sure to use only highly reliable, authoritative sources. She wanted to use different types of printed materials, including books, magazines, journals, and newspapers that were available in her school and local public library. She also wanted to use online sources in her research. Isabel had learned that there was a video about the dam. Isabel's teacher also suggested that she contact Polly Lewis and try to conduct an interview. Isabel decided to pursue a personal interview, e-mailed Ms. Lewis and verified that she was an authority about the dam. Isabel was then able to incorporate the results of that interview in her research paper.

Isabel understood that to gather data about both sides of the issues and debates surrounding the dam, she would need a variety of authoritative sources. She wanted to be able to compare viewpoints and identify writers' biases. She also wanted to show that she had conducted sufficient research to support her viewpoint. Finally, Isabel knew it was critical to use a variety of print and online sources to show mastery of her topic.

## Compiling Data

| | |
|---|---|
| **PRINT** | Brown, Jeff. "Researchers Unravel Mystery of Eroding Egyptian Monuments." Civil Engineering 2007. Essay on erosion problems resulting from dam.<br><br>Parks, Peggy. The Aswan High Dam. Book about issues and controversies surrounding planning and building of dam.<br><br>Penvenne, Laura Jean. "The Disappearing Delta" Earth August 2004: pages 16–17. Discussion of environmental problems caused by dam. |
| **ONLINE** | Larsson, Birgitta. "Aquaculture and schistosomiasis." From "Three Overviews on Environment and Aquaculture in the Tropics and Subtropics." Food and Agriculture Organization of the United Nations. Dam's health issues.<br><br>"Aswan Dam." STC-Link. University of Colorado at Denver. Information about history, planning, and construction of dam. |
| **VIDEO** | Building Big: Dams. Detailed history of construction and financing controversies |

**Gather your sources and compile your data.** Create a graphic organizer to show the types and variety of sources that you are using and the kinds of data you will find in each source.

## Gathering Sources

Ask students to explain why using a variety of sources is important. Possible answers:
- to ensure finding enough specific details to support the thesis
- to sound knowledgeable and well-rounded about the topic
- to ensure the information you have is the most reliable and unbiased

## Compiling Data

Explain to students that they may wish to organize their grid differently depending on their focus and plan for writing. Remind them of the need to gather information about major issues and debates related to the topic.

TEKS 10.13A, 10.21A, 10.21B

**Gather your sources and compile your data.** Encourage students to learn the rules for formatting source information and follow them from the start. Doing so can save them time in the revision stage.

**TEKS** 10.13A Plan a first draft by determining topics through a range of strategies; **10.21A** Follow the research plan to compile data that identifies major issues and debates; **10.21B** Organize information from multiple sources to create forms; **ELPS** **2D** Seek clarification of spoken language as needed; **2G** Understand the general meaning, main points, and important details of spoken language/topics, languages, and contexts are familiar to unfamiliar; **2H** Understand implicit ideas and information in increasingly complex spoken language; **3B** Expand vocabulary by learning/using high-frequency words for identifying and describing and learning/using routine language for classroom communication; **3D** Speak using grade-level content area vocabulary/new words; **4J** Demonstrate comprehension and expand reading skills by employing inferential skills; **4K** Demonstrate comprehension and expand reading skills by employing analytical skills/evaluating written information and performing critical analyses; **5A** Learn relationships between sounds and letters to represent sounds when writing in English; **5B** Write using content-based grade-level vocabulary

## Prewriting
### Create Note Cards

Remind students that, if they choose, they can number their note cards with corresponding numbers from their grids or highlight them with corresponding colors. DIFFERENTIATE INSTRUCTION ↘

Point out that on this page, the writer has numbered the cards sequentially to keep them in order. The order probably reflects the order in which the writer came across the information while doing research.

⭐ **TEKS** 10.21B

**Create note cards.** Emphasize the importance of
- making neat, thoughtful, complete notes (this will ensure that the note cards are useful when it's time to write), and
- recording all source information accurately on each card (this will save time and avoid confusion when it's time to use the material in their reports and to create their works-cited pages). DIFFERENTIATE INSTRUCTION ↘

## Prewriting Creating Note Cards

A gathering grid or similar organizer allows you to see all your research at a glance, but sometimes you need more space for an answer. In that case, use note cards. Number each new card and write a question at the top. Then answer the question with a list, a quotation, or a paraphrase (see pages 387–389). At the bottom identify the source of the information (including a page number if appropriate).

Note cards

**Question** → How was the dam built? ①
To prepare:
**Answer (list)** →
- Thousands of workers had to be summoned and housed at Aswan.
- Roads and railroad lines had to be built to bring heavy equipment.
- For power, an electric station had to be added to the low dam.

...the Aswan High Dam.

pages 26–27 ← **Source**

What are the effects of the dam? ②
"By stabilizing the river's banks, the dam not only rescued Egyptian agriculture from historic cycles of flood and drought, but enabled extensive urban development along the shore."
Sorkin, Michael. "Deciphering Greater Cairo"
Architectural Record, April 2007:
page 82

**Answer (quotation)**

**Card number**

Why was the dam built? ③
The dam would make irrigation around the Nile more modern and much easier. It would allow Egypt to turn large areas of desert into new cropland.
Scientific American
January 2006: page 18

**Answer (paraphrase)**

**Prewrite** **Create note cards.** Make note cards like the examples above whenever your answers are too long to fit on your gathering grid or graphic.

## Paraphrasing

When you *paraphrase*, you restate ideas from a text in your own words. Paraphrasing is a useful tool when you are analyzing poetry. It is also very helpful when you are conducting research and analyzing the finer points of a major debate or issue. Paraphrasing will help you better understand difficult vocabulary and complex texts.

- A paraphrase should be about the same length as the original source
- should contain simpler language
- should contain all of the source's significant information.

Isabel found paraphrasing a useful tool as she conducted her research and compiled her data. For example, Isabel read this information written by Michael Sorkin.

"By stabilizing the river's banks, the dam not only rescued Egyptian agriculture from historic cycles of flood and drought, but enabled extensive urban development along the shore."

She then wrote this paraphrase.

> The dam stabilized the river's banks. It protected Egypt's farming from times of flood and times of drought. The dam also made it possible to build housing and create city life along the shore.

### Try It!

Read this excerpt from "To Preserve Egypt's Past." Then write a paraphrase of the selection.

> One reason Egypt's history is so well known is that it is so well preserved. Many of Egypt's most ancient monuments were protected for millennia by the dry desert sands that covered them. Unfortunately, in many places those sands are no longer so dry. The year-round irrigation made possible by the Aswan High Dam elevates the local groundwater, which in turn is eroding many standing monuments from the bottom up. No one knows what damage it may be causing to archaeological treasures as yet undiscovered.

Research

## Paraphrasing

Call attention to the bulleted items and emphasize that paraphrasing does NOT mean simply deleting or rearranging another person's words. Emphasize that to paraphrase, the student must

- read and understand the original text
- identify how the information will be useful in supporting the topic
- state the information in a new way, using the student's words
- state the information in words that are appropriate to the student's audience
- state the information in a way that shows the student is knowledgeable about the topic

TEKS 10.21C

### Try It!

Remind students that a paraphrase is restating the author's original thoughts in their own words. It is not a summary, which is explained on the next page.

---

**Differentiated Instruction:**
**English Language Learners**

ELPS 1E, 4D-4G, 4I, 4J, 5B

Help students find linguistically accommodated content material and visual supports. Assist with reading as needed.

| ELP Level **Beginning** | ELP Level **Intermediate** | ELP Level **Advanced/Advanced High** |
|---|---|---|
| Label note cards with one each of the 5 W's/H. Prepare labeled illustrations to support students in listing simple answers about their topics on each card. | Encourage students to write three questions about their topics on note cards and answer using one quote, one paraphrase, and one list. | Encourage students to use the three types of note cards for each of their ideas/paragraphs as practice, even if they won't use them all in the final paper. |

 TEKS **10.21C** Paraphrase, summarize, quote, and accurately cite researched information; ELPS **1E** Internalize new basic and academic language by using and reusing it/writing; **4D** Use prereading supports to enhance comprehension of written text/ graphic organizers, illustrations, and topic-related vocabulary; **4E** Read linguistically accommodated content area material with a decreasing need for linguistic accommodations as more English is learned; **4F** Use visual/contextual support to read grade-appropriate text, enhance understanding, and develop vocabulary and grasp of language structures; **4G** Demonstrate comprehension of increasingly complex English/taking notes; **4I** Demonstrate comprehension by employing basic reading skills; **4J** Demonstrate comprehension and expand reading skills by employing inferential skills/predicting, making connections between ideas, drawing conclusions from text, and finding supporting evidence; **5B** Write using content-based grade-level vocabulary

## Summarizing

Call attention to the difference in Isabel's summary and paraphrase. Ask students

- Besides being fewer words, how is it different?
- What is the main purpose of a summary?
- What is the main purpose of a paraphrase?

 **TEKS** 10.21C

### Try It!

Before students try this activity on their own, provide a few more example excerpts and model how to paraphrase and summarize, thinking aloud, using an overhead transparency.

**ELPS** 2C, 4G

---

## Summarizing

When you *summarize*, you restate the main or key ideas. A summary should only include information that appears in the original text. Like a paraphrase, a summary is written in your own words. Unlike a paraphrase, however, a summary is shorter than the original text.

Summarizing is an effective way to take a large amount of material, or a complex issue, and retell the key points in just a few sentences.

Isabel read the quote she had noted from Michael Sorkin and decided to summarize it.

> "By stabilizing the river's banks, the dam not only rescued Egyptian agriculture from historic cycles of flood and drought, but enabled extensive urban development along the shore."

Isabel's summary was shorter: *The dam protected Egypt's agriculture and made urban development possible.*

### Try It!

Refer to the excerpt from "To Preserve Egypt's Past" on the previous page. Read the excerpt again and write a summary of the information in the text. When you have finished, compare your summary to your paraphrase. Did your summary capture only the key points? Was it shorter than the paraphrase? If not, you may need to revise both your paraphrase and your summary.

---

**TEKS** **10.21C** Summarize and accurately cite researched information; **ELPS** **2C** Learn basic and academic vocabulary heard during classroom instruction/interactions; **4G** Demonstrate comprehension of increasingly complex English/summarizing material

**TEKS** 10.21C
**ELPS** 2C, 2I

## Avoiding Plagiarism

It's always important to give other people credit for their words and ideas. Not doing so is called *plagiarism,* and it is intellectual stealing. Here are two ways to avoid plagiarism.

- **Paraphrase:** Write in your own voice. Use your own words and simpler vocabulary. Always give credit to the source of the ideas.
- **Quote:** Use the exact words of a source to add authority to your paper. Enclose those words in quotation marks and give credit to the source.

### Paraphrase

> What are the effects of the dam? ④
> Heavy metals and other dangerous substances are polluting delta croplands and lagoons where Egypt grows a lot of its food.
>
> Earth, August 2004
> Disappearing Delta."
> page 17

### Quote

> What are the effects of the dam? ④
> "Thus, the biggest problem . . . is the increasing accumulation of salts, heavy metals, and other pollutants on the delta and in the lagoons where much of Egypt's food is grown."
>
> Earth, August 2004
> Penvenne, Laura. "The Disappearing Delta."
> page 17

## Learning Language

Take turns reading the excerpt from "To Preserve Egypt's Past" aloud to a classmate. Pause at the end of each sentence and have your classmate retell the sentence in his or her own words. When you have finished, read the entire excerpt aloud again and have your classmate summarize it in his or her own words. Be sure to listen carefully and ask clarifying questions if you do not understand the summary or any of the vocabulary used by your classmate. Ask your teacher for help if you do not understand the words in the excerpt or the vocabulary used by your classmate.

Research

## Avoiding Plagiarism

Plagiarism is stealing the words and ideas of others and claiming them as one's own. This is both illegal and unethical. To emphasize the seriousness of this crime, provide students with real examples from the publishing world of high-profile cases in which writers were accused of plagiarism, and discuss the consequences of those accusations. You can find stories about plagiarism cases in a newspaper's online archives or in the library's digital archives.

**TEKS** 10.21C

## Learning Language

You could provide an additional excerpt so each partner summarizes different text. Remind students to monitor their own understanding and to ask clarifying questions if necessary.

✓ **DIFFERENTIATE INSTRUCTION**

**ELPS** 2C, 2I, 3E

**TEKS** **10.21C** Quote and accurately cite researched information; **ELPS** **1E** Internalize new basic language by using and reusing it/speaking; **2C** Learn academic vocabulary heard during classroom instruction/interactions; **2H** Understand implicit ideas and information in increasingly complex spoken language; **2I** Demonstrate listening comprehension in increasingly complex spoken language by collaborating with peers; **3A** Practice producing sounds of newly acquired vocabulary; **3E** Share information in cooperative learning interactions; **4D** Use prereading supports to enhance comprehension of written text/graphic organizers, illustrations, and topic-related vocabulary

## Prewriting
### Keeping Track of Your Sources

Have students share with a partner the list of the sources they have accumulated so far. Have the partner examine the notes and point out which ones appear complete and which appear incomplete or listed incorrectly. Suggest that students use the sample source notes as a guide. This activity helps students focus on the required elements for each source notation and encourages them to be as careful as possible when recording sources in the future. For the present, it gives them the opportunity to update their source notes so that they are accurate and complete.

**TEKS** 10.21B

**List sources.** Remind students to keep their list of sources secure or keep a second copy. If they lose it, it will be quite difficult to re-create, or at least very time consuming. **DIFFERENTIATE INSTRUCTION ↘**

---

 **TEKS** 10.21B

## Prewriting Keeping Track of Your Sources

As you conduct your research, keep track of the sources you use so that you can correctly cite them in your final report. You'll need the following information:

- **Book:** Author's last name, Author's first name. *Book title.* City of publication: Publisher's name, year of publication. Medium of publication.
- **Magazine:** Author's last name, Author's first name. "Article Title." *Magazine Name* day Month year: page number or numbers. Medium of publication.
- **Newspaper:** Author's last name, Author's first name. "Article Title." *Newspaper Name* day Month year: page number or numbers. Medium of publication.
- **Internet:** Author's last name, Author's first name (if known). "Document Title." *Title of Web site* Name of Sponsoring Institution, date of publication (or last update). Medium of publication (Web). Day Month year of access.
- **Videocassette or DVD:** *Film Title.* Director's first and last names. Distributor, year released. Medium of publication.

### Source Notes

> **Source Notes**
>
> **Book**
> Parks, Peggy J. The Aswan High Dam. San Diego: Blackbirch Press, 2008. Print.
>
> **Magazine**
> Sorkin, Michael. "Deciphering Greater Cairo." Architectural Digest. 9 Apr. 2007: Pages 82–87. Print.
>
> **Internet**
> "Aswan Dam." STC-Link. University of Colorado at Denver. 15 Apr. 2004. Web. 7 Feb. 2011.
>
> **Newspaper**
> Shenon, Philip. "Digging Up the Ancient Past: Before the Deluge." New York Times 10 Sept. 2004, morning ed: Section A, page 2. Print.
>
> **Interview**
> Lewis, Polly. Personal interview, E-mail. 28 Feb. 2011.
>
> **Video**
> Building Big: Dams. WGBH Boston Video, 2006. VHS.

Prewrite

**List sources. Keep a list of each of your sources with the information shown above. Whenever you find a new source, add it to the list.**

---

⚡ TEKS 10.13A, 10.15A(iii)

## Writing Your Thesis Statement

With your research completed, you'll be able to write a thesis statement. This statement identifies the controlling idea of your paper and serves as its focus. The rest of your report should explain and support the controlling idea. Use this formula to help you write your thesis statement.

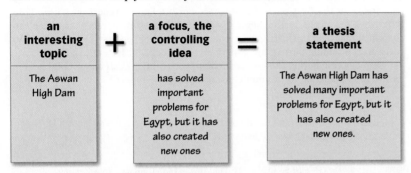

### Other Possible Thesis Statements

The Aswan High Dam (an interesting, complex topic) **is an important accomplishment in Egypt's use of the Nile** (a focus).

Constructing the Aswan High Dam (an interesting, complex topic) **was a politically charged issue involving many nations** (a focus).

The builder of the first Aswan Dam (an interesting, complex topic) **was an engineer who believed the dam was unnecessary** (a focus).

**Form your thesis statement.** Review your research notes and choose a main point about your topic to emphasize in your paper. Using the formula above, write a thesis statement for the controlling idea. Revise your thesis statement until it says exactly what you want it to say.

Prewrite

Research

## Writing Your Thesis Statement

Practice creating two-part thesis statements together as a class. Re-create the graphic on the board, using the same headers (an interesting subject, a focus, a thesis statement). Invite students to share their report topics and focuses, and then have the class work together to create two or three thesis statements, based on these ideas, using the formula. If students seem reluctant to offer ideas, point out the following benefits:

- Sharing ideas gives them an opportunity to articulate the focus of their essays.
- Using or modifying the thesis statements that the class creates from their reports gives them a bit of a head start.

⚡ TEKS 10.13A, 10.15A(iii)

**Form your thesis statement.** Have students practice drafting their thesis statement on their own and checking with a partner or with you to verify completeness.

✳ For more about writing effective thesis statements, see SE page 630.

---

⚡ ELPS 1B, 3A, 3E, 4C, 5B

## Differentiated Instruction: English Language Learners

| ELP Level **Beginning** | ELP Level **Intermediate** | ELP Level **Advanced/Advanced High** |
|---|---|---|
| Have students draw and label examples of each type of source and practice sounding out the words of the information with a partner; encourage students to correct their pronunciation. | Form groups of five; have each student find one example of the listed sources, write and label the source information, and then share with the group. | Have students list their own source information and then work with a partner to correct/confirm each partner's work. |

⚡ TEKS 10.13A Plan a first draft by developing a thesis or idea; 10.15A(iii) Write an analytical essay that includes an idea or thesis; ELPS 1B Monitor oral language and employ self-corrective techniques or other resources; 3A Practice producing sounds of newly acquired vocabulary; 3E Share information in cooperative learning interactions; 4C Comprehend vocabulary used in written classroom materials; 5B Write using content-based grade-level vocabulary

## Prewriting
### Outlining Your Ideas

Explain that a sentence outline is preferable to a topic outline for writing a long research report because it provides a framework for each paragraph in the report. Sometimes students can create their first draft by adding transitions between the sentences. **DIFFERENTIATE INSTRUCTION ↘**

⭐ **TEKS** 10.13B, 10.21B

❋ For more about creating an outline, see SE pages 626–627.

**Create your outline.** Some word-processing programs have a built-in outline feature or a template for creating an outline. Encourage students to find out whether such a feature is available with the program they use.

## Prewriting Outlining Your Ideas

One way to organize your research report is to make an outline. An outline maps the ideas you plan to include in your paper and helps organize ideas in a structured, persuasive manner. A topic outline lists ideas as words or phrases; a sentence outline lists them as full sentences.

Below is the first part of a sentence outline for the report on pages 373–379. Notice that the writer begins with the thesis statement. Next, after the Roman numerals (I., II., III., . . .), she lists the major points that she plans to cover in the middle part of her report. After the capital letters (A., B., C., . . .), she includes the details that support the major points. (Each major point serves as the topic sentence for a middle paragraph in the report.)

### Sentence Outline

Remember, in an outline, if you have a I, you must have at least a II. If you have an A, you must have at least a B.

> **Thesis Statement**
>
> **THESIS STATEMENT:** The Aswan High Dam has solved many important problems for Egypt, but it has also created new ones.
>
> **Major Points (I., II.)**
>
> I. Before the dam was built, Egyptians had to live with annual floods along the Nile.
>    A. Flooding came after the rainy season in the highlands.
>    B. This annual flooding helped to fertilize the land, but sometimes there was too much water.
>    C. A dam was needed.
>
> **Supporting Ideas (A., B., C.)**
>
> II. In years with little rain, Egypt had less flooding, but that also meant less water for irrigation.
>    A. Egypt is mainly desert, so crops are watered by irrigation.
>    B. Before the dam, Egyptians stored floodwater for irrigation after the flood season.

**Prewrite**

**Create your outline.** Write a sentence outline for your report, using the details you have gathered. Be sure that each topic sentence (I., II., III., . . . ) supports the thesis statement and that each detail (A., B., C., . . . ) supports the topic sentence. Use your outline as a guide for writing your first draft.

## Developing Your Ideas

With your research completed, you will need to organize your note cards and the data you have collected. This will help you see if you have chosen a variety of authoritative sources and consulted enough sources so that you have a thorough understanding of both sides of controversial issues and a variety of viewpoints on the major debates involving your topic.

Isabel chose to create a chart based on her outline so that she could easily see which sources she had consulted for each topic.

| Idea | Sources to Support Idea |
|---|---|
| Annual flooding of the Nile | Parks: The Aswan High Dam, 12 |
| Years with little or no rain; lack of irrigation | Parks: The Aswan High Dam, 11 |
| Erosion | Parks: The Aswan High Dam, 12 |

Isabel saw that too much information on this particular topic was coming from a single print source. She was then able to include other sources on the same topic. A greater variety of information meant that she could knowledgeably discuss major debates about this topic.

## Keeping a Computer Log

You may find it useful to create a computer log to organize information from the sources that you have used. This will enable you to enter data and notes about each source that you consulted. If you choose to develop a computer log, be sure to include a complete citation of the source and detailed summaries or paraphrases of the information and date you gathered. It is easy to include quotes in a computer log. Be sure to enter quotations carefully and correctly. Put them in quotation marks, and provide detailed citations for them. In essence, the computer log becomes a form of electronic note card.

Remember that with any kind of graphic or form that you use to organize information, any and all text that directly uses another writer's ideas must be credited, even if it is not a direct quote. This applies to both print and electronic sources, note cards, and logs.

 **Organize your information.** Create a chart, graphic, or computer log to organize information from all of the sources you have used. Be sure to include complete citations for each of the sources you consulted in your research.

### Developing Your Ideas

Point out to students that the chart presented on this page includes a third idea, Erosion, which was not listed on the outline on SE page 392. One reason for this could be that Isabel's outline may not have been completed yet.

Remind students that what they've written on their outlines can still be changed, added to, and deleted at this point if it will improve the overall writing of their paper.

Also point out that each of their ideas, or paragraphs, should reference at least two to three different sources in order to provide enough depth of knowledge about their topic.

However, they should be cautious about making too many changes. Planning and organizing well now will lead to less frustration later in the writing process.

### Keeping a Computer Log

If students have access to computers in the classroom, you could make this a required part of their paper to be printed and turned in.

**Organize your information.** If students do not have regular access to computers in your school, they should be encouraged to create a chart or graphic in their notebook.

**TEKS** 10.21B

**Differentiated Instruction: English Language Learners**   **ELPS** 1E, 2C, 2I, 3E, 5B, 5E, 5F

| ELP Level **Beginning** | ELP Level **Intermediate** | ELP Level **Advanced/Advanced High** |
|---|---|---|
| Provide students with a pre-taught word bank for their topic(s). Model by thinking aloud and gesturing, then guide students through creating an outline. | Have students work with their group/partner to create simple (using only I, II and A, B) word/phrase outlines for their topics. | Encourage students to write three major points and two or three supporting ideas for each major point using a variety of grade-appropriate sentence lengths and patterns. |

 **TEKS** 10.21B Organize information from multiple sources to create graphics and forms; **ELPS** 1E Internalize new basic and academic language by using and reusing it/writing; 2C Learn basic vocabulary heard during classroom instruction/interactions; 2I Demonstrate listening comprehension in increasingly complex spoken language by following directions; 3E Share information in cooperative learning interactions; 5B Write using newly acquired basic and content-based grade-level vocabulary; 5E Employ increasingly complex grammatical structures in content area writing such as using correct verbs, tenses, and pronouns/possessive case/negatives and contractions; 5F Write using a variety of grade-appropriate sentence lengths and patterns in increasingly accurate ways

## Modifying Your Thesis

Reassure students that this section serves as a guidepost for their writing, ensuring that they take the time to reflect before writing their final draft. Most students will not need to rewrite their outlines or their theses extensively, although they may need to make adjustments.

Students may still be apprehensive about this process, but assure them that if they have been actively monitoring, adjusting, and revising their thesis statements up to this point, major changes will not be necessary.

**TEKS** 10.22A

## Evaluating Your Research

Advise students that through their focused and organized research, they have already eliminated much extraneous information. However, it will become more apparent to them as they construct their drafts which collected pieces of information will be useful and relevant and which will not. Encourage students to analyze their information closely and delete obviously irrelevant data.

**TEKS** 10.22B

**Re-evaluate your data.** As students review their material, encourage them to literally cross out obviously irrelevant data. If students are unsure whether a piece of information will be important, have them indicate (draw parentheses around the information) to ignore for now but not toss out.

## Modifying Your Thesis

After you have conducted your research and gathered data, it is important to step back and re-evaluate both your thesis statement and your outline. You may have uncovered important data that will lead you to modify your major research question. As a result, you may need to refocus your research plan, and then rewrite your thesis statement. When this occurs, all or parts of your outline will need to be revised as well.

After you have finished your research, ask yourself the following questions:

- Does my research support the controlling idea and thesis statement?
- If not, what steps should I take to refocus my research plan?
- Do I need to conduct further research?
- How should I revise my thesis statement?

## Evaluating Your Research

When you conduct research on a complex, multi-faceted topic, you will learn a great deal about many aspects of the topic. As you gather data, all these aspects and details may seem relevant and important to the topic. After you have re-evaluated the data and modified your thesis, you will be able to distinguish between those details that are relevant to your topic and those that are not.

In conducting her research on the Aswan High Dam, Isabel learned about the archaeological riches of the Nile region in which the dam was to be built. She gathered data about the pharaohs and ancient history of Egypt. As she developed her thesis statement and her outline, she realized that much of the information about the history of Egypt was not relevant to the controlling idea of her research.

Prewrite

**Re-evaluate your data.** Take time to review the data you have gathered. Ask yourself whether or not it supports your major research questions. If not, modify your thesis and your outline. Then evaluate your research so that you include only the information that is relevant to your topic.

# Drafting

With your research and planning completed, you are ready to write your first draft. Don't worry about getting everything perfect in this draft. For now, just get your ideas on paper in a way that makes sense to you.

Keys to Effective Drafting

1. Use your first paragraph, your introduction, to get your reader's attention. Introduce your controlling idea and present your thesis statement.

2. In the next section, explain why the work of engineering was built.

3. After that, describe the story of the building process.

4. In the final section, your conclusion, spend a paragraph or more revealing the effects the work has had.

5. Remember to cite, within your report, the sources of any ideas you paraphrase or quote; also list those sources alphabetically on a works-cited page.

Research

---

## Drafting

### Keys to Effective Drafting

Remind students that this stage is when they make the first draft of their report.

The Keys to Effective Drafting list explains the process students will be guided through on SE pages 396–409. Review and explain each point on the list, as needed.

**TEKS** 10.15A(i), 10.15A(iii)

Have students review their prewriting materials one last time to make sure that they are complete, organized, and easily accessible. Ideally, students should have space to spread out their materials as they write. Their outlines should be clearly visible and their note cards should be within reach. ✔ DIFFERENTIATE INSTRUCTION

---

## Differentiated Instruction: English Language Learners

**ELPS** 3H, 5B, 5E, 5F, 5G

| ELP Level **Beginning** | ELP Level **Intermediate** | ELP Level **Advanced/Advanced High** |
|---|---|---|
| Use pictures and shared writing to have students narrate a paragraph about a famous engineering marvel to a scribe. | You may wish to abbreviate the report, having students write only one to two paragraphs for each section of the report. | As students draft their papers, review and remind them to use connecting words and phrases and a variety of sentence lengths and patterns. |

 **TEKS** **10.15A(i)** Write an analytical essay that includes an introductory and concluding paragraph; **10.15A(iii)** Write an analytical essay that includes an idea or thesis; **ELPS** **3H** Narrate with increasing specificity and detail; **5B** Write using content-based grade-level vocabulary; **5E** Employ increasingly complex grammatical structures in content area writing such as using correct verbs, tenses, and pronouns/possessive case/negatives and contractions; **5F** Write using a variety of grade-appropriate sentence lengths, patterns, and connecting words/combine in increasingly accurate ways; **5G** Describe and explain with increasing specificity and detail/writing

## Citing Sources in Your Report

Address any questions or problems students may have regarding citations within their reports. Have students look through their sources to see which ones have complete information and which ones are missing elements. Tell students to put red check marks next to the latter so that they will know at a glance that they will have to refer to them differently in the report and on the works-cited page.

**TEKS** 10.21C, 10.23E

### Try It!
### Answers

**Possible Answer**

In an article, "Deciphering Greater Cairo," for *Architectural Record,* Michael Sorkin says that modern Cairo's riverfront—with numerous high-rise buildings on very expensive tracts of land—looks very much like Chicago's famous riverfront (82). **DIFFERENTIATE INSTRUCTION ↘**

 **TEKS** 10.21C, 10.23E

## Citing Sources in Your Report

Credit the sources of ideas and facts you use in your report.

### When You Have All the Information

- The most common type of citation lists the author's last name and page number.

  **Rising groundwater is causing the temples of Luxor to crumble from the bottom up (Brown 22).**

- If you name the author in your report, just include the page number in parentheses.

  **The town of Aswan, according to Peggy J. Parks, had to be prepared to host the thousands of workers needed for the project (27).**

### When Some Information Is Missing

- If a source does not list an author, use the title and page number.

  **These far-reaching changes indicate the great impact the dam has had on Cairo since 1970** (*Giant and Wonderful Dams* **18).**

- If neither the author nor a page number is available, use the title alone.

  **In all, 23 were rescued before the reservoir was filled, though many more were lost** (*Building Big: Dams*).

- Some sources (especially Internet sites) do not use page numbers. In those cases, include just the author (or, if the author is not listed, the title).

  **Now they flourish year-round, making the disease seven times more common (Larrson).**

### Try It!

Rewrite the following sentence, citing Michael Sorkin's article "Deciphering Greater Cairo" from *Architectural Record,* page 82.

**In some ways, modern Cairo's riverfront is similar to Chicago's, with numerous high-rise buildings crowding expensive tracts of land.**

**TEKS** **10.21C** Accurately cite researched information; **10.23E** Synthesize research into a presentation that uses a style manual to document sources

## Evaluating the Relevance of Sources

As Isabel did her research, she found articles, books, and online sources related to the Aswan High Dam. She knew that she wanted to focus on her major research question, or controlling idea: problems the dam solved and created for Egypt. Besides *Building Big: Dams,* Isabel found another video, *Egypt: Land of Archaeological Riches.* Based on the title, Isabel thought the video might deal with the potential destruction of archaeological sites. She read a review of the video, which said it was a travel documentary produced by Egypt's tourism council. She realized the video would not be a relevant source.

The following tips will help you decide whether or not a resource is relevant.

- Read reviews about the source. Look for an overview or summary.
  **Does the content pertain to your topic?**
- Examine the Table of Contents.
  **How many chapters or pages pertain to your topic?**
- Examine the Index.
  **Can you find the specific topics that you are looking for? How many pages are devoted to those topics?**

## Choosing Reliable Sources

After determining the relevance of your sources, you should check their reliability. Reliability means the information is verifiable and accurate. A general rule is that if data can be verified in two sources, the information is reliable and authoritative. When using Web sites, it is critical to check for reliability and accuracy.

As Isabel gathered data, she looked for sources from experts. She also chose data from well-respected sources. Isabel found a travel diary from a tourist who had visited the construction site, but she realized that a tourist would be not be a reliable source about the dam's construction.

To choose reliable sources, look for authors that are well respected. Articles from journals such as *Scientific American* and *National Geographic* are reliable and authoritative. National newspapers such as the *Wall Street Journal, The New York Times,* and *The Washington Post* are considered authoritative and objective. If you have questions about a source, read reviews about the source and its author. You can also check with your teacher or librarian.

**Prewrite**

**Review your sources for relevance and reliability.** Use the guidelines and tips on this page to evaluate your sources. Make sure that you have chosen relevant sources of information and that each source is reliable and authoritative.

Research

### Evaluating the Relevance of Sources

Advise students that, although completing this step may seem time consuming at first, taking the time to evaluate the relevance of sources will save them time in the end. Reading the review of the video most likely took Isabel much less time than it would have for her to watch the video, which would have proved itself irrelevant in the end, thereby saving her time to devote to relevant sources.

### Choosing Reliable Sources

Emphasize to students that determining both the relevance and reliability of sources is necessary. Reliable sources may not be relevant and relevant sources may not be reliable.

Remind students that the Internet is especially susceptible to nonreliable sources, although many Web pages may look authoritative.

★ **TEKS** 10.22B

**TEKS** **10.22B** Evaluate the relevance of information to the topic/determine the reliability of sources by examining their objectivity and authority; **ELPS** **1E** Internalize new basic language by using and reusing it/speaking; **2C** Learn new language structures and expressions heard during classroom instruction; **2D** Monitor understanding of spoken language during classroom instruction; **2E** Use linguistic support to enhance and confirm understanding of increasingly complex spoken language; **2G** Understand the general meaning and main points of spoken language/topics, languages, and contexts are familiar to unfamiliar; **3B** Expand vocabulary by learning and using routine language needed for classroom communication; **3C** Speak using a variety of grammatical structures/sentence lengths and types/connecting words with increasing accuracy and ease; **4I** Expand reading skills; **5B** Write using content-based grade-level vocabulary; **5E** Employ increasingly complex grammatical structures in content area writing

**Evaluating the Validity of Sources**

Have students read the chart and point out problems with the validity of sources:

- Matthew Malin's online article had no data to support or validate the claim; ownership and authorship of the online magazine are questionable.
- Jonathan Baker's online article seems biased because there is no validation from authoritative source; Web site ownership is nebulous/undefined.

 **TEKS** 10.22B

**Review your sources for validity.** Because it is often difficult for students to evaluate sources objectively, encourage students to work in groups, scanning and evaluating each other's sources and asking questions about the author, Web site ownership, definition of terms, etc.

**DIFFERENTIATE INSTRUCTION ↘**

  **TEKS** 10.22B

## Evaluating the Validity of Sources

Sources can be relevant and the data within them may be reliable, but they may still contain bias. Valid sources will contain information on both sides of the issue. For Isabel, this meant that sources should discuss both the problems and the advantages of building the dam.

| Source/Detail | Data/Details in article |
|---|---|
| Malin, Matthew. "Consequences of the Aswan High Dam" *Egypt Today* March 2010: page 25. Online. | "Dam will ruin fertility of fields forever." No data provided to support or validate claim. Online magazine provides little information about ownership or authorship of articles. |
| Parks, Peggy J. *The Aswan High Dam.* pages 39–41. | Agriculture benefits, but there are problems. Farmers use chemical fertilizers, but Egypt can irrigate two million more acres of land than they could before dam was built. Author is well respected in field and provides scholarly footnote for facts. |
| Baker, Jonathan. "Losing Egypt's Treasures." *Modern Archaeological Disasters.* 18 February 2009. Web. October 15 2010. | Egypt has lost "innumerable monuments and others are at high risk." Terms not defined. Argument not defended with any authoritative sources. No name listed for sponsoring institution of the Web site. |
| Brown, Jeff. "Researchers Unravel Mystery of Eroding Egyptian Monuments." *Civil Engineering.* page 22. Print. | Rising groundwater and added moisture causing structures to crumble from bottom up. Details added to explain and defend claim. Supported with authoritative, scholarly footnotes. *Civil Engineering* is a well respected journal in the field. |

**Prewrite**

**Review your sources for validity.** Look again at the data you have collected. Does each source present an honest, unbiased view of the topic? If not, conduct further research to find valid, relevant, and reliable sources.

# Evaluating the Accuracy of Sources

Accurate sources contain information that can be verified by more than one source. For example, as Isabel began her research she read entries in two encyclopedias to gain an overview of the history of the dam. She saw that each encyclopedia gave the same dates for beginning and ending the construction. This was the same date that she found in several other scholarly sources. When she saw different dates in an online article, she knew that those dates were inaccurate. In another instance, Isabel noted a 1995 copyright date on one book about the environmental impact of the dam. This meant that the source was dated and would not contain the recent information she needed to complete her research.

The following guidelines will help you as you evaluate the accuracy of your sources.

## Nonfiction Books

Examine the copyright date. Check the copyright notice. Look for terms such as revised edition and updated edition on the copyright page or cover. If the book has gone through updates, it is likely to be highly accurate. Checking the copyright date will also tell you if the material is out-of-date.

Look for a bibliography. Examine the sources the author used to write. Some books and articles will also include an appendix—a collection of additional material about the subject. Look for footnotes, endnotes, and cross-references. These will help you determine the accuracy of the information.

## Magazines and Periodicals

Is the publication well known and respected? Most large-circulation newspapers and national magazines are reliable and verify the accuracy of the information. Articles in scholarly journals go through a review process to ensure the accuracy of the information.

Was the article originally published in another source? If so, make sure the original source is reliable. For example, articles from news services such as Associated Press might be published in a small newspaper. The source is AP, a reliable news source.

Finally, determine if the facts in the article can be verified. Consult other sources, print or online, to check factual data.

**Check for accuracy.** Examine your sources. Are the authors experts in their fields? Are the publications authoritative and current? Make notes about the objectivity and authority of each of the sources you have used. Replace sources that are not authoritative or that lack objectivity.

Prewrite

Research

## Evaluating the Accuracy of Sources

As a class, develop an accuracy checklist, then encourage students to use it as they evaluate their own sources for accuracy. Example items should include:

- All sources—information supported by two other sources
- Nonfiction books —information as current as possible
- Magazines and periodicals

⭐ **TEKS** 10.22B

**Check for accuracy.** Remind students that a copyright date may be old but the information may still be accurate, depending on the subject. For example, a publication about the building of Fallingwater, constructed by famed architect Frank Lloyd Wright, can be considered accurate if written in 1934 because that is when the house was built. However, if the content is focused on modern architectural methods, that same copyright year should be considered out of date.

---

**TEKS** **10.22B** Determine the accuracy of sources by examining their objectivity and authority; **ELPS 1C** Use strategic learning techniques to acquire basic and grade-level vocabulary; **1E** Internalize new basic and academic language by using and reusing it/speaking; **3B** Expand vocabulary by learning and using routine language needed for classroom communication; **3D** Speak using grade-level content area vocabulary/new words and academic language proficiency; **3E** Share information in cooperative learning interactions; **3F** Give information/ranging from using a limited high-frequency vocabulary to using abstract and content-based vocabulary during speaking; **3G** Express opinions ranging from communicating short phrases to participating in discussions; **4C** Develop and comprehend basic sight vocabulary used in written classroom materials; **4D** Use prereading supports to enhance comprehension of written text/graphic organizers, illustrations, and topic-related vocabulary

## Implementing Changes

Emphasize to students that writing is an ongoing and circular process of drafting, evaluating, analyzing, revising, and editing. It is not a linear process of steps to be followed to the finish.

**Critique your research process.** Students should continually re-evaluate their sources, thesis, outline, and information.

**TEKS** 10.22A , 10.22C

---

## Implementing Changes

As you check your research sources for reliability, validity, and accuracy, you may find that you need to do more research. It is critical to pause before you begin writing to evaluate the information in your sources. Replace any sources that have bias or that do not meet the criteria for reliability, validity, and accuracy.

As you continue your research, ask yourself if your initial inferences and conclusions about the topic are still valid. Often times, as you probe deeper into a topic, you will discover new information that will require a revision of your major research question. When this occurs, you need to refocus your research plan and revise your thesis statement.

As part of the evaluation process, ask yourself the following questions.

- Do I need to implement changes in my research process?
- Do I need to discard any potential source from my research?
- Do I need to find additional reliable, accurate, and valid sources?
- Do I need to change my thesis?
- Do I need to expand a section in my outline, based on my research?

When Isabel began critiquing her research, she was able to apply the lessons that she learned as she conducted new research and evaluated sources. As Isabel went through the process, she realized some of her sources had biases and had not dealt with the health consequence of the dam. After reading several print and online articles about schistosomiasis, Isabel found the following scholarly article and added the information to her research report and listed the information about her new source in her source notes.

### Source Notes

> **Journal Article:**
> Larsson, Birgitta. "Aquaculture and schistosomiasis."
> Three Overviews on Environment and Aquaculture in the Tropics and Sub-Tropics.
> Food and Agriculture Organization of the United Nations. December 1994. Web.
> 12 Feb. 2011.
>
> Disease and the health problems in Egypt resulting from construction of dam.

**Critique your research process.** Critique each step of your research process and implement needed changes. Modify your research question as needed and refocus your research plan.

**TEKS** 10.13B, 10.15A(i), 10.23A

> "Never underestimate your reader's intelligence
> or overestimate his or her information."
>
> —Anonymous

# Drafting Starting Your Research Report

The opening paragraph of your essay should grab the reader's attention, introduce your topic, and present your thesis statement. Here are some examples of rhetorical devices and strategies you can use to convey meaning and create an effective introduction.

- **Start with an interesting fact.**

  Humans have been building dams for thousands of years. One of the oldest is the Saad El Kafara, built in Egypt around 2700 B.C.E.

- **Use a rhetorical device such as a simile or an analogy.**

  Like the industrious beavers of the world, humans have built dams for thousands of years.

- **Start with a quotation.**

  "The Aswan High Dam is known as one of the greatest engineering marvels of the twentieth century," says Peggy J. Parks.

## Beginning Paragraph

This beginning paragraph starts with an interesting fact and ends with the thesis statement (underlined). Writer synthesizes information from a variety of sources to create an effective introduction.

> Humans have been building dams for thousands of years. One of the oldest examples is the Saad El Kafara, built in Egypt around 2700 B.C.E. Its main purpose was to stop catastrophic flooding during wet years, but its water storage also allowed for increased irrigation of croplands. While most dams over the ages have been built for these two purposes, huge new dams in the past century have provided the added benefit of hydroelectric power for the world's growing population. However, people are discovering that these large dams also have many detrimental effects on the environment. Egypt's High Dam at Aswan illustrates this critical trade-off. <u>The Aswan High Dam has solved many important problems for Egypt, but it has also created new ones.</u>

Draft

**Write your opening paragraph.** Be sure to grab the reader's interest. Use rhetorical devices to introduce your topic and controlling idea and to present your thesis statement.

Research

# Drafting
## Starting Your Research Report

Students probably took notes for the following two reasons: (1) because ideas about the topic really grabbed their attention, and (2) to record important facts. Point out that if an idea grabbed their attention, it will probably grab their readers' attention, too. Tell students to think back to when they were taking notes for their reports.

- What were their initial questions about the topic?
- What ideas or facts did they learn that interested or surprised them the most?
- What quotations did they copy because they provided unusual or surprising perspectives on the topic?

**Write your opening paragraph.** Suggest that students use one of the techniques on SE page 401 to begin their report. Remind them that they may decide to change their beginning later. For now, getting started is the most important thing.

Remind students to use the thesis statements that they created during prewriting and place them appropriately in their opening paragraphs.

**⬏ DIFFERENTIATE INSTRUCTION**

**TEKS** 10.15A(i), 10.23A

---

## Differentiated Instruction: English Language Learners

**ELPS** 1A, 3B, 4I, 5F

| ELP Level **Beginning** | ELP Level **Intermediate** | ELP Level **Advanced/Advanced High** |
|---|---|---|
| Use the paragraphs that students dictated earlier to read to a partner. Encourage them to add an interesting fact to their paragraph. | With a partner, have students practice writing each type of opener by using a variety of sentence patterns and then choose one to use in their introductions. | Encourage students to write an introduction using one of the types of opening statements, a variety of sentence patterns and lengths, and their thesis statements. |

 **TEKS** **10.15A(i)** Write an analytical essay that includes an introductory paragraph; **10.23A** Synthesize research into a presentation in support of a clear thesis; **ELPS 1A** Use prior knowledge and experience to understand meanings; **3B** Expand vocabulary by learning and using high-frequency words for identifying and describing; **4I** Demonstrate comprehension by employing basic reading skills; **5F** Write using a variety of grade-appropriate sentence lengths and patterns in increasingly accurate ways

## Drafting
### Developing the Middle Part

Writing the middle paragraphs of a long report can seem daunting. However, it may help if students can see that their reports have a clear direction and that all they have to do is basically follow their outlines. Use the following suggestions to help students.

- If students created their outlines on a computer and are writing on a computer, suggest that they copy and paste the topic sentences (I, II, III, . . .) from their outlines into their drafts. Tell them to underline each topic sentence and to insert a place marker between them (for example, middle paragraph I, middle paragraph II). They can remove the underlining later.

- Students who are drafting their reports by hand can do the same thing. Tell them to write each topic sentence on a separate page and to number the pages to follow their outlines.

- Students can now go back and write each paragraph with details from their outlines and note cards that support each topic sentence.

**TEKS** 10.23A, 10.23B

---

## Drafting Developing the Middle Part

The middle part of your report should show evidence that supports or explains your thesis statement. Start by explaining why this work of engineering was necessary. Then discuss its development in detail.

Each middle paragraph should cover one major point. Use your sentence outline to guide your writing.

### Middle Paragraphs

**The first middle paragraphs explain why the dam was built. Writer cites evidence.**

<u>Before the dam was built, Egyptians had to live with annual floods along the Nile.</u> Each year, after the rainy season in the highlands, the river would spill over its banks onto the Egyptian countryside. While this annual flooding helped to fertilize the land, sometimes there was just too much water. For example, "between 1860 and 1880, there were four major floods that forced people to flee to higher ground" (Parks 12). They desperately needed a dam to help prevent this recurring damage.

**All the details in each paragraph support the topic sentence (underlined). Writer continues to cite evidence.**

<u>In years with little rain, Egypt had less flooding, but that also meant less water for irrigation.</u> Egypt is mainly desert, so crops grown there must be watered by irrigation. Before the dam was built, the Egyptians captured floodwater and stored it in pools for irrigation use during the rest of the year. In dry years, however, they could not capture enough water to last. The result was drought and famine (11).

<u>By building a dam, the people of Egypt hoped to accomplish several things.</u> A dam would help to stop catastrophic floods during wet years. It would also prevent Egypt from running out of water during dry years. In fact, it would store enough water to allow even more land to be irrigated. This was important because Egypt's population started to outgrow its crop production during the twentieth century (Building Big: Dams).

**Ideas progress logically. The next middle paragraphs tell about how the dam was built.**

<u>The first Aswan Dam was built between 1898 and 1902, while Egypt was a colony of Great Britain.</u> It was designed by William Willcocks, a British engineer who was very familiar with traditional Egyptian irrigation. Willcocks built a dam that would let the silt-laden water of each year's early rains pass through to fertilize the croplands below. The dam then stored

---

later rainwater to be used for irrigation during the rest of the year (Pearce 50). Unfortunately, Willcock's dam didn't hold enough water to last through dry years, even after being raised twice, once in 1912 and again in 1933. Also, the dam almost overflowed in 1946, which happened to be a very wet year (Parks 14).

In 1952, Egypt became independent from Britain, and its new government decided to build a dam that could hold enough water for three years of irrigation. The project quickly became a touchy subject, because Egypt didn't want to hire British engineers to design the dam. As a gesture of friendship, Germany donated plans to the new government. In 1956, the World Bank, Great Britain, and the United States offered to fund the project, but they cancelled those plans when Egypt bought Soviet weapons to fight Israel (17–20). The Soviet Union agreed to fund the dam if Egypt agreed to use only Soviet engineers and equipment. By 1959, plans were complete and the project began ("Aswan Dam").

First, the valley that the dam would flood had to be cleared. This meant moving more than 100,000 Nubian people to new lands. Also, the new lake would cover many ancient temples and other monuments. In 1960, the United Nations Educational, Scientific, and Cultural Organization (UNESCO) asked governments around the world to help move these monuments. In all, 23 were rescued before the reservoir was filled, though many more were lost (Building Big: Dams).

Next, preparations had to be made for the dam's actual construction. New roads and railroads had to be built to carry men and equipment to the construction site. In addition, an electrical station had to be built at the old Aswan Dam to supply power for the project. Also, the town of Aswan had to be prepared to host the thousands of workers that would be needed (Parks 27).

Once building began, the construction team faced very harsh conditions. The terrain was extremely rugged, rapidly wearing out tires on construction equipment. Daytime temperatures reached 135 degrees Fahrenheit in the shade, so most work had to be done at night. Under these conditions, the

**Writer includes** sources in parentheses and formats them following an accepted style manual. Citations show evaluation of the quality of research.

**Arrangement** of information ensures that the reader can easily follow all ideas and understand the author's point of view.

Research

Have students point out transition words and phrases in the middle paragraphs on SE pages 402–403. Point out that the writer uses them to create a smooth flow from one paragraph to the next or to show a specific pattern of organization. (Possible choices: *Before, In 1952, First, Next, Once, finally* [chronological order]; *Also, however, in addition* [order of importance]; *Because, As a result* [cause and effect]) Remind students to use transitions in their middle paragraphs to create a smooth flow, to show how ideas are organized, and to make the writer's point of view clear. ✔ DIFFERENTIATE INSTRUCTION

Also point out the source citations used in the draft paper. Have students explain the rules for various citations.

TEKS 10.21C, 10.23A, 10.23B, 10.23D, 10.23E

## Differentiated Instruction: English Language Learners

ELPS 1H, 3A, 3B, 3D, 3E, 4C, 4F, 4I, 5B

| ELP Level **Beginning** | ELP Level **Intermediate** | ELP Level **Advanced/Advanced High** |
|---|---|---|
| Provide a copy of the sample paragraphs to partners and have them work together to find, sound out, and circle transition words indicating time. | Have students read the sample paragraphs aloud with a partner and then find, identify, and classify transition words and phrases using a graphic organizer. *Use pages 624-625* | Using the outlines they created earlier, have students compose their body paragraphs, inserting transition words and phrases where appropriate or needed. |

TEKS **10.21C** Accurately cite researched information; **10.23A** Synthesize research into a presentation in support of related claims; **10.23B** Synthesize research into a presentation that reflects a progression of ideas and a stated point of view; **10.23D** Synthesize research into a presentation that uses evaluative tools to examine the research; **10.23E** Synthesize research into a presentation that uses a style manual to document sources; **ELPS 1H** Develop learning strategies/reasoning, looking for patterns in language, and analyzing sayings and expressions; **3A** Practice producing sounds of newly acquired vocabulary; **3B** Expand vocabulary by learning and using routine language needed for classroom communication; **3D** Speak using grade-level content area vocabulary; **3E** Share information in cooperative learning interactions; **4C** Develop basic sight vocabulary/comprehend vocabulary and language structures used in written classroom materials; **4F** Use visual and contextual support to develop vocabulary and grasp of language structures; **4I** Demonstrate comprehension by employing basic reading skills; **5B** Write using newly acquired basic and content-based grade-level vocabulary

⭐ **TEKS** 10.21A, 10.21C,
10.23A, 10.23B, 10.23E

As students write the middle paragraphs of their reports, they may discover that they are missing a vital statistic or a detail that they feel is essential to telling the whole story about their topic. If students feel that they cannot continue writing without this piece of information, they can stop and do the necessary research. However, this will interrupt the natural flow of ideas and distract students from their immediate goal—to create their first drafts. It is preferable to leave a place marker (draw a line or brackets) to indicate where the missing information belongs. After students complete their drafts, they can do the research and easily insert the statistics or details as they revise.

⭐ **TEKS** 10.21A, 10.21C, 10.23A, 10.23B, 10.23E

> Soviet equipment broke down five times faster than expected. This caused expensive delays while replacement parts were shipped from the Soviet Union or equipment was sent back there for repair. In 1961, with little progress made, the Egyptian government brought in Egyptian construction experts to replace the Soviet engineers, and it began using equipment from Sweden and Great Britain (28–29).
>
> <u>The dam was finally completed in July 1970, ten years after the project began.</u> It was by far the largest engineering work of its time, costing over $1 billion (Building Big: Dams). More than 50,000 people worked on the dam, using 17 times more material than was used to build the Great Pyramid. The finished dam stretches two miles wide and 364 feet high. The reservoir (holding the water) covers an area larger than the state of Delaware (Parks 35).
>
> <u>The Aswan High Dam immediately helped control flooding.</u> Before the Nile was dammed, floods sometimes forced evacuation of the Nile Valley and its delta, with a great loss of life and property. With the dam in place, however, flooding became a thing of the past. As a result, cities like Cairo, which used to be limited to high ground near the river, have expanded all the way to the Nile's banks. As Michael Sorkin puts it, "By stabilizing the river's banks, the dam not only rescued Egyptian agriculture from historic cycles of flood and drought, but enabled extensive urban development along the shore" (82).
>
> <u>The vast reservoir behind the dam makes more irrigation possible in Egypt.</u> In the past, the people could grow crops only as long as their stored water lasted each year. Now the dam provides irrigation throughout the entire year. In fact, Egyptians are able to irrigate two million more acres of land than they could before the dam was built (Parks 41).
>
> Also, <u>the Aswan High Dam provides 50 percent of Egypt's electricity.</u> Once the dam was built, thousands of villages that had never had electricity before were "plugged in." The power station has been important for the swelling populations in Egypt's larger cities (Building).
>
> <u>However, there are some significant environmental problems related to the dam.</u> For one thing, without the annual

**Statistics provide important information for the reader.**

**The remaining middle paragraphs explain both good and bad effects of the dam. Ideas progress logically, and evidence supports each point.**

**Writer quotes, summarizes, and paraphrases source material. Writer clearly communicates her own point of view.**

⭐ **TEKS** **10.21A** Follow the research plan to compile data that identifies major issues and debates; **10.21C** Paraphrase, summarize, and quote researched information; **10.23A** Synthesize research into a presentation in support of related claims; **10.23B** Synthesize research into a presentation that reflects a progression of ideas and a stated point of view; **10.23E** Synthesize research into a presentation that uses a style manual to document sources

**TEKS** 10.13B, 10.23A, 10.23B

The writer shows interest in the subject and point of view through the voice and word choice.

deposit of silt to enrich their fields, Egyptian farmers now have to use tons of chemical fertilizers each year. This has changed the chemistry of the waterways, leading to an excess of waterweeds and a decrease in fish and shrimp. Even the nearby sardine population in the Mediterranean Sea has suffered. The loss of silt has also caused the Nile delta to erode severely (Parks 39–40). Furthermore, industrial building closer to the Nile itself has caused more water pollution. As a result, the soil of the Nile delta, whose crops feed 40 million people, is becoming dangerously contaminated with toxins such as heavy metals (Penvenne 17).

The writer continues to structure ideas in a sustained, persuasive way. Writer provides evidence for thesis statement and for related claims.

<u>Because the irrigation canals no longer dry up each year, Egyptians suffer from more waterborne diseases than before.</u> One example is schistosomiasis, an intestinal and urinary disease transmitted by microscopic worms that live on snails in the waterways. Before the dam was built, these snails died every year during the dry season. Now they flourish year-round, making the disease seven times more common (Larrson). Besides the snails, there are more mosquitoes carrying malaria and other diseases in Egypt since the dam was built (Louria).

In addition, the dam continues to threaten some of Egypt's most important monuments. Year-round irrigation has led to rising groundwater, and this moisture is causing ancient structures like the temples of Luxor to crumble from the bottom up (Brown 22). If this problem isn't corrected, these historical treasures will be destroyed as surely as those that lie beneath the waters of the reservoir.

Draft

**Write your middle paragraphs.** Keep these tips in mind as you write.

- Use a topic sentence for each paragraph. Support it with evidence.
- Refer to your outline for direction. (See page 392.)
- Give credit to all your sources. (See page 396.)

Research

---

Remind students that the *body* of the research report should reflect their interest in the topic. Make sure students know the difference between statements that express opinions (*it's terrible that Egyptian farmers now have to use tons of chemical fertilizers each year*) and sentences that show interest (. . . *without the annual deposit of silt to enrich their fields, Egyptian farmers now have to use tons of chemical fertilizers each year*).

Review the entire first paragraph of SE page 405, and ask students whether they have a sense of how the writer feels about the environmental problems and how students know this. Ask them to point out specific words or phrases that may reveal how the writer feels (*significant . . . problems; tons of chemical fertilizers; excess of waterweeds; decrease in fish; suffered; erode severely; dangerously contaminated*).

Point out that students may state their opinions or reasons for their research in their introductions or conclusions. **✔ DIFFERENTIATE INSTRUCTION**

**TEKS** 10.13B, 10.23A, 10.23B

**Write your middle paragraphs.** Direct students to the bulleted items and reiterate the need to cite sources for all information that is not their own.

**TEKS** **10.13B** Structure ideas in a sustained and persuasive way; **10.23A** Synthesize research into a presentation in support of related claims; **10.23B** Synthesize research into a presentation that reflects a progression of ideas and a stated point of view; **ELPS 1A** Use prior knowledge and experience to understand meanings; **1E** Internalize new basic and academic language by using and reusing it/writing; **1F** Use accessible language and learn new and essential language in the process; **3B** Expand vocabulary by learning and using high-frequency words for identifying and describing; **3D** Speak using grade-level content area vocabulary/academic language proficiency; **3E** Share information in cooperative learning interactions; **4H** Read silently with increasing ease and comprehension for longer periods; **4I** Demonstrate comprehension by employing and expanding basic reading skills/understanding of supporting ideas and details, summarizing text, and distinguishing main ideas from details; **4J** Demonstrate comprehension and expand reading skills by employing inferential skills; **4K** Demonstrate comprehension and expand reading skills by employing analytical skills/evaluating written information and performing critical analyses

---

## Differentiated Instruction: English Language Learners

**ELPS** 1A, 1E, 1F, 3B, 3D, 3E, 4H–4K

| ELP Level **Beginning** | ELP Level **Intermediate** | ELP Level **Advanced/Advanced High** |
|---|---|---|
| Ask students to think of words they use when they experience different emotions and have them draw and label those emotions on paper. | Show students a series of pictures that stir emotions: happy, sad, ominous, etc. Have students list words they could use to describe the feeling of the pictures. | Students should read silently to analyze the text for specific words that show how the writer feels. Ask students to then think-pair-share their findings. |

## Drafting
### Ending Your Research Report

Have students work with partners to analyze Isabel's use of all three strategies in the sample ending.

- Remind the reader of the thesis of the report: *No one can deny that the Aswan High Dam has benefited Egypt.*
- Summarize the main points: the benefits of flood control, year-round irrigation, electrical power; the problems of human interference with the environment.
- Leave the reader with a final thought about the topic: *The building of the Aswan High Dam teaches humans that they have to learn to modernize with caution, and to predict and prepare for the consequences of their actions.*

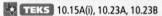 10.15A(i), 10.23A, 10.23B

**Write your ending paragraph and review your first draft.** Encourage students to use one or more of these strategies in their ending paragraphs. If possible, have students set aside their drafts for a day before reviewing them. **DIFFERENTIATE INSTRUCTION**

### Tip

Encourage students to underline the words and phrases in their reports that show how they feel about the topic. Tell students that they can examine these underlined words as they revise their reports and make improvements as needed.

---

TEKS 10.15A(i), 10.23A, 10.23B

## Drafting Ending Your Research Report

Your ending paragraph, your conclusion, should sum up your research report by doing these three things.

- Remind the reader of the thesis of the report.
- Summarize the main points.
- Leave the reader with a final thought about the topic.

### Ending Paragraph

> The report's conclusion summarizes the main points and refers back to the thesis statement.

> The report ends with a final thought for the reader. Writer shares her viewpoint.

No one can deny that the Aswan High Dam has benefited Egypt. Its flood control has prevented loss of life and property in wet years. Year-round irrigation and the expansion of croplands have helped supply food and other goods for Egypt's booming population. The electrical power it provides has helped the country to build and modernize. However, the dam also demonstrates that whenever people change their environment, they introduce new problems that must be dealt with. The building of the Aswan High Dam teaches humans that they have to learn to modernize with caution, and to predict and prepare for the consequences of their actions.

Draft

**Write your ending paragraph and review your first draft.** Draft your ending paragraph using the guidelines above. Then read your draft to make sure it is complete. Check your research notes and outline to be sure you haven't forgotten any important details. In the margins and between the lines, make notes about anything you should change.

### Tip

Present your ideas honestly and clearly. Allow your writing voice to engage the reader by showing how you feel about the topic and the ideas you've synthesized.

---

TEKS 10.23E

# Creating Your MLA Works-Cited Page

The purpose of a works-cited page is to allow the reader to locate the sources you used. The next four pages give standard MLA formats for common types of sources following MLA documentation style. (Your own sources may not always match these formats exactly. In that case, give as much information as possible, in the correct order.)

## Books

**Author or editor** (last name, first name). **Title** (in italics). **City of publication:**
**Publisher's name, year of publication. Medium of publication.**

### One Author

> Parks, Peggy J. *The Aswan High Dam.* San Diego: Blackbirch, 2008. Print.

If a book has two or three authors, list them in the order they appear on the title page. Reverse only the name of the first author. (Example: Brentano, Margaret, and Nicholson Baker.) For a book with four or more authors, list only the first author, followed by "et al."

### A Single Work from an Anthology

To list an essay or a short story from an anthology, include the title of that work in quotation marks, followed by the title of the anthology and the editor.

> Eisenman, Peter. "Post-Functionalism." *Theorizing a New Agenda for Architecture:*
> *An Anthology of Architectural Theory.* Ed. Kate Nesbitt. New York: Princeton
> Architectural, 2006. 60–68. Print.

### An Article in a Familiar Reference Work

It is not necessary to list the editor of familiar reference books, such as dictionaries and encyclopedias. If the article is signed, give the author's name first. If not, give the title first.

**Author** (if available). **Article title** (in quotation marks). **Reference book title** (in
italics). **Edition number** (if available), **year published. Medium of publication.**

> "Aswan High Dam." *Columbia Encyclopedia.* 2010 ed. Print.

Research

---

# Creating Your MLA Works-Cited Page

Suggest that students gather all of their source information together and determine which format on SE pages 407–409 best applies to each of their sources.

TEKS 10.23E

## Books

With students, review the various ways to format a book as a reference.

---

## Differentiated Instruction: English Language Learners

ELPS 1D, 2I, 4G, 5B, 5C, 5E

| ELP Level **Beginning** | ELP Level **Intermediate** | ELP Level **Advanced/Advanced High** |
|---|---|---|
| Have students dictate their concluding sentences to a scribe, employing nonverbal cues and conveying ideas by defining or describing. | Have students work with a partner to help summarize each other's main points for their conclusion, using grade-level vocabulary and employing proper spelling. | Have students compose their ending paragraphs independently, paying special attention to using correct verbs, tenses, pronouns, negatives, and contractions. |

TEKS **10.23E** Synthesize research into a presentation that uses a style manual to document sources and format written materials; ELPS **1D** Speak using learning strategies/request assistance, employ non-verbal cues, and convey ideas by defining or describing; **2I** Demonstrate listening comprehension in increasingly complex spoken language/summarizing spoken messages and collaborating with peers; **4G** Demonstrate comprehension of increasingly complex English/summarizing material; **5B** Write using content-based grade-level vocabulary; **5C** Spell familiar words/employ spelling patterns and rules with increasing accuracy; **5E** Employ increasingly complex grammatical structures in content area writing such as using correct verbs, tenses, and pronouns/possessive case/negatives and contractions

## Periodicals

Point out to students that the MLA standard formats described here are separated into categories of sources (books, periodicals, online sources, other) to make it easier for them to find a format that applies to the different types of sources they may have used in their reports. It is unlikely that they will have used every type of source shown on these pages.

 DIFFERENTIATE INSTRUCTION ↘ DIFFERENTIATE INSTRUCTION ↘

TEKS 10.23E

 TEKS 10.23E

## Periodicals

Periodicals are publications issued on a regular, scheduled basis. This includes magazines, scholarly journals, and newspapers. Again, follow the style guide to document sources and format your works-cited list.

### A Magazine

If a magazine is published weekly or biweekly, include the full date (day, month, year). If it is published monthly, bimonthly, or less often, include only the month and year. If the article isn't printed on consecutive pages, list the first page followed by a "+" sign.

**Author** (last name, first name). **Article title** (in quotation marks). **Title of the magazine** (in italics) **Date** (day, Month, year): **page numbers. Medium of publication.**

> Penvenne, Laura Jean. "The Disappearing Delta." *Earth* Aug. 2004: 16-17. Print.

### A Scholarly Journal

Scholarly journals are identified by volume number rather than by full date of publication.

**Author** (last name, first name). **Article title** (in quotation marks). **Journal title** (in italics) **volume number. issue number** (year of publication): **inclusive page numbers. Medium of publication.**

> Sorkin, Michael. "Deciphering Greater Cairo." *Architectural Record* 189.4 (2007): 82-87. Print.

### A Newspaper

**Author** (if available, last name, first name). **Article title** (in quotation marks). **Title of the newspaper** (in italics) **Date** (day, Month, year), **edition** (if listed): **section and page number or numbers. Medium of publication.**

> Rider, Mary. "'Singing' Bridge to Lose Its Song." *Erie Times-News* 22 Nov. 2009: B11. Web.

## Online Sources

Online sources include Web pages, documents in Internet databases, and e-mail messages. Follow the style guide to format your Works Cited list.

### A Web Page

**Author** (if known, last name, first name). **Document Title** (in quotation marks). **Title of Web site** (in italics). **Name of Sponsoring Institution,** date of publication (or last update). **Medium of publication** (Web). day Month year of access.

> "Aswan Dam." *STC-Link* 15 Dec. 2000. University of Colorado at Denver, 15 Dec. 2000. Web. 17 May 2011.

### An Article in an Online Database

Libraries often subscribe to online databases where articles are kept. To cite such an article, first give any details about the original print version. (See "Periodicals" on page **408**.) Then list the title of the database, the medium of publication, and the date of access.

> Walton, Susan. "Egypt After the Aswan Dam." *Environment* May 1981: 30+. *MasterFILE Premier.* Web. 2 Feb. 2011.

### E-Mail to the Author (Yourself)

**Writer** (last name, first name). **Title of message** (taken from the e-mail "Subject" line). **Description** (Message to the author). **Date received** (day, Month, year). **Medium of delivery.**

> Mythe, Lewis. "Re: Your Experience at the Aswan Dam." Message to the author. 31 Jan. 2011. E-mail.

*Research*

## Online Sources

There are various types of online sources that students can access such as Web pages, online databases, and e-mails. Because these sources of information are becoming more prevalent, carefully review how to format online sources.

TEKS 10.23E

✱ Refer students to SE pages 519–522 for more information on using reference books.

---

### Differentiated Instruction: English Language Learners

ELPS 1C, 3A, 4A, 4C, 5A, 5C

| ELP Level **Beginning** | ELP Level **Intermediate** | ELP Level **Advanced/Advanced High** |
| --- | --- | --- |
| Use actual examples of each type of source listed to teach the names of the types of sources. Have students copy and sound out the terms. | Have students match each item in a list of example sources to the correct type of publication or online source from which it most likely originated. | Have students work with a partner to correctly compose and format their works-cited page, double-checking for accuracy of spelling and punctuation. |

TEKS **10.23E** Synthesize research into a presentation that uses a style manual to document sources and format written materials; **ELPS 1C** Use strategic learning techniques to acquire basic and grade-level vocabulary; **3A** Practice producing sounds of newly acquired vocabulary; **4A** Learn relationships between sounds and letters/sound out words using a combination of skills; **4C** Develop basic sight vocabulary/comprehend vocabulary used in written classroom materials; **5A** Learn relationships between sounds and letters to represent sounds when writing in English; **5C** Spell familiar words/employ spelling patterns and rules with increasing accuracy

## Other Sources

Emphasize the importance of spelling the names of authors and experts correctly when students do their research. **DIFFERENTIATE INSTRUCTION ↘**

Make sure students understand that sources on a works-cited page are arranged alphabetically. Have students look at the sample works-cited page on SE page 379.

**Format your sources.** If students are working on a computer, they can use their software's Sort feature to automatically alphabetize their sources. This assumes that they have recorded their sources correctly according to MLA standard formatting.

 10.23E

---

## Other Sources

Your research may include other sources, such as television programs, video documentaries, and personal interviews.

### A Television or Radio Program

Episode title, if given (in quotation marks). **Program title** (in italics). **Title of the Series** (if any). **Network Name. Call letters, City of the local station. Broadcast day Month year. Medium of reception.**

> "The High Renaissance." *Art of the Western World.* PBS. WMVS, Milwaukee. 29 Nov. 2010. Television.

### Video, DVD, Slide Program

**Title** (in italics). **Director's first and last name, if known. Distributor, year released. Medium of reception.** (DVD, Video, slide program)

> *Building Big: Dams.* WGBH Boston Video, 2006. Videocassette.

### An Interview by the Author (Yourself)

**Person interviewed** (last name, first name). **Description** (Personal interview). **day Month year of interview.**

> Mythe, Lewis. Personal interview. 31 Jan. 2011.

 **Format your sources.** Check your report and your list of sources (page 390) to see which sources you actually used. Then follow these directions.

1. Write out the information for your sources using the guidelines on pages 407–410.
2. Put your sources in alphabetical order.
3. Create your works-cited page. Check the format of each citation on the list to make sure you have followed MLA guidelines. (See the example on page 379.)

---

### Differentiated Instruction: Advanced Learners

Encourage students to make a poster for the class or computer lab, depicting and explaining how to properly list sources for a works-cited page.

 **TEKS** **10.23E** Synthesize research into a presentation that uses a style manual to document sources and format written materials

**TEKS** 10.13C

# Revising

The first draft of a research report is all about getting your thoughts on paper in a logical order. During the revising step, you make changes to ensure that your ideas are clear and interesting, your organization smooth, your voice confident and knowledgeable, your words specific, and the sentences varied.

### Keys to Effective Revising

1. Read your entire draft to get an overall sense of your research report. Think about your audience, the purpose, and the genre of your writing.

2. Review your thesis statement to be sure that it clearly states your main point about the topic.

3. Be certain that your beginning engages the reader and that your ending offers an insightful final thought.

4. Check that the middle part clearly and completely supports the thesis statement. Check to see that you have used a variety of sentence types.

5. Review and adjust your voice to sound knowledgeable and interested in the topic. Make sure you have conveyed subtlety of meaning.

6. Check for effective word choice and sentence fluency.

Research

## Revising
### Keys to Effective Revising

Remind students that the revising stage is when writers have an opportunity to make improvements to their first drafts. At this stage, they can think about refinements they might not have considered when they were drafting.

The Keys to Effective Revising list explains the process that guides students on SE pages 412–420. Suggest that students refer to this checklist throughout the revising process.

If students have set aside their first drafts for a day or two, they can return to them refreshed and with a better perspective for recognizing where changes are needed. ☑ **DIFFERENTIATE INSTRUCTION**

**TEKS** 10.13C

---

**TEKS** **10.13C** Revise drafts/improve style, word choice, sentence variety, and subtlety of meaning and rethink how well the purpose, audience, and genre have been addressed; **ELPS 2I** Demonstrate listening comprehension in increasingly complex spoken language by summarizing spoken messages and collaborating with peers; **3A** Practice producing sounds of newly acquired vocabulary; **3D** Speak using grade-level content area vocabulary/academic language proficiency; **3E** Share information in cooperative learning interactions; **3F** Ask for and give information/ranging from using a limited high-frequency vocabulary to using abstract and content-based vocabulary during speaking; **4F** Use support from peers/teachers to read grade-appropriate text, enhance understanding, and develop vocabulary; **4I** Demonstrate comprehension by employing basic reading skills

**Revising for Focus and Coherence**

Emphasize that students will revise for both *focus* (thesis statement) and *coherence* (sentences connecting and making sense together).

### Is my thesis clearly stated?

Students should work in pairs or groups of three or four, using the questions as guidelines and making suggestions about how to make thesis statements stronger or add missing elements.

### Does my research report support my thesis?

Students should read and evaluate each topic sentence and supporting sentences in their middle paragraphs, asking: *Does this sentence relate to my thesis statement? Does it provide supporting evidence for my thesis statement?*

### Exercise
### Answers

Students should

- underline: *In years with little rain, Egypt had less flooding.*
- cross out: *In times of old, Egyptians expected that pharaohs and the gods would send rain to help crops grow.*
- cross out: *This did not always happen, and people suffered.*
- cross out: *Before the dam was built, Egyptians captured floodwater and stored it in pools for irrigation.*

**Revise your essay for focus and coherence.** Suggest that students underline each topic sentence, making sure it supports the main thesis, and then cross out any sentences that do not support that topic sentence. **DIFFERENTIATE INSTRUCTION** ⬎

 **TEKS** 10.13C

---

 **TEKS** 10.13C

 ## Revising for Focus and Coherence

When you revise for *focus and coherence,* be sure that your thesis statement is clear and complete. Your research and evidence should support the thesis throughout the essay.

### Do I clearly state my thesis?

Your thesis statement should provide your audience with the controlling idea of your research and clearly explain the focus of your research. Here are some guidelines to help you determine if your thesis is clearly stated.

1. Does my thesis explain the direction, or focus, the paper will take?
2. Have I given an overview of the topic and narrowed the controlling idea for my audience?
3. Have I clearly conveyed the purpose for my research?
4. Have I chosen the correct genre for my purpose and audience?

### Do my middle paragraphs support my thesis?

Re-read your middle paragraphs. Does each relate to and provide supporting evidence for the thesis statement? If not, review your research notes and revise your middle paragraphs as needed.

### Exercise

Read the following paragraph and underline the topic sentence. Cross out the sentences that do not relate to or provide supporting evidence for the topic sentence.

> In years with little rain, Egypt had less flooding. That also meant less water for irrigation. In times of old, Egyptians expected that pharaohs and the gods would send rain to help crops grow. This did not always happen, and people suffered. Egypt is mainly desert, so crops grown there must be watered by irrigation. Before the dam was built, Egyptians captured floodwater and stored it in pools for irrigation.

 **Revise your essay for focus and coherence.** Re-read your thesis statement and your middle paragraphs to make sure that the evidence in each paragraph supports the thesis.

---

 **TEKS** **10.13C** Revise drafts/rethink how well the purpose, audience, and genre have been addressed

⭐ **TEKS** 10.13C

## Are my paragraphs coherent?

Each paragraph in your research paper should be coherent, ideas fitting together to form a whole. Each paragraph should have a topic sentence and the rest of the sentences in the paragraph should relate directly to the topic sentence and provide evidence to support it.

- **Check that the evidence is relevant.**
  The details that you use should relate directly to the topic sentence. All the details and supporting evidence should support the controlling idea of your research.
- **Check for unity.**
  Re-read your paper to check for unity. Remember your purpose for writing and look for ways to improve your subtlety of meaning.

### Try It!

Read the paragraph below. Revise it so that the paragraph will be coherent and form a unified whole.

1    Egypt was once a colony of Great Britain. It was still a colony when the
2    first Aswan Dam was built. That happened between 1898 and 1902. Annual
3    flooding during the rainy season meant that the Nile spread over its banks
4    onto the Egyptian countryside. Sometimes there was just too much water. The
5    first dam was designed by William Willcocks, a British engineer who was very
6    familiar with traditional Egyptian irrigation.

**Review your first draft for coherence.** Review each paragraph to make sure that it has coherence and unity. Paragraphs should convey your subtlety of meaning. Revise your draft as needed.

Revise

> **Focus and Coherence**
> Writer deletes a sentence that does not support topic.
>
> There are some significant environmental problems related to the dam. Without the annual deposit of silt to enrich their fields, Egyptian farmers now have to use tons of chemical fertilizers each year. ~~Chemical fertilizers are imported, and this has cost Egypt a good deal of money that the country did not expect to spend.~~ This has changed the chemistry of the waterways, leading to an excess of waterweeds and a decrease in fish and shrimp.

Research

### Are my paragraphs coherent?

Students should ask themselves
- Does my writing have a clear focus?
- Have I included specific ideas and details that support my topic (thesis)?
- Do my sentences make sense together?
- Do my sentences relate directly to the topic (thesis)?

Point out that although the deleted sentence in the sample paragraph mentioned the cost associated with using chemical fertilizers, the sentence was deleted because the paragraph's focus was not about the fertilizers themselves or Egypt's economy but about the environmental impact of the dam. Therefore, the sentence does not support the topic.

### Try It!
Answers

**Possible Answer**

Egypt was once a colony of Great Britain. It was still a colony when the first Aswan Dam was built. The first dam was designed by William Willcocks, a British engineer who was very familiar with traditional Egyptian irrigation.

**Review your first draft for coherence.** Encourage students to have a partner read their paragraphs. It can be very difficult to find problems in coherence and unity in one's own writing. Professional writers very often seek out the objective and unbiased suggestions of others.

⭐ **TEKS** 10.13C

---

⭐ **TEKS** **10.13C** Revise drafts/improve subtlety of meaning and rethink how well the purpose has been addressed; **ELPS** **1H** Develop and expand learning strategies/reasoning, looking for patterns in language, and analyzing sayings and expressions; **3F** Give information/ranging from using a limited high-frequency vocabulary to using abstract and content-based vocabulary during speaking; **3G** Express opinions ranging from communicating short phrases to participating in discussions; **3H** Explain with increasing specificity and detail; **4B** Recognize directionality of English reading such as left to right and top to bottom; **4G** Demonstrate comprehension of increasingly complex English/responding to questions; **4J** Demonstrate comprehension and expand reading skills by employing inferential skills; **4K** Demonstrate comprehension and expand reading skills by employing analytical skills

**Revising** for Organization

As a class, brainstorm a list of transition words and phrases that link ideas and information in terms of location, time, and logic. Possible answers could include these kinds of transitions:

- Location: *among, beyond, inside, throughout*
- Time: *as soon as, during, first, finally*
- Comparison: *also, in the same way, likewise*
- Conclude: *all in all, finally, in summary*
- Add information: *additionally, for example*
- Clarify: *for instance, in other words, that is*

**DIFFERENTIATE INSTRUCTION** ⬎

## Do my paragraphs flow smoothly?

Students should ask themselves:

- Is my writing easy to follow?
- Is each sentence and paragraph logically linked to the ones that come before?
- Do I use effective transitions?

 **TEKS** 10.13B, 10.15A(iv), 10.15C(ii)

### Exercise
**Answers**

**Possible Answer**

In 1952, the government decided to build a dam. By 1959, plans were complete and the project began.

**First**, the valley that the dam would flood had to be cleared. This meant moving more than 100,000 Nubian people to new lands. **Additionally**, the new lake would cover many ancient temples and other monuments. **For this reason**, UNESCO asked governments around the world to help move the 23 monuments that were saved. In all, 23 were rescued, but many more were lost.

**Second**, preparations had to be made for the dam's actual construction. New roads had to be built to carry men and equipment to the construction site. **Next**, an electrical station had to be built at the old Aswan Dam. **Finally**, the town of Aswan had to be prepared to host the thousands of workers that would be needed.

**Review your first draft.** Remind students to add transitions and to identify transitional words and phrases that link sentences.

**TEKS 10.13B** Develop drafts in open-ended situations that include transitions; **10.15A(iv)** Write an analytical essay that includes a structure appropriate to the purpose, audience, and context; **10.15C(ii)** Write a response to expository text that addresses writing skills for an analytical essay

---

 **TEKS** 10.13B, 10.15A(iv), 10.15C(ii)

 **Revising** for Organization

When you revise for *organization* in a research paper, it is critical that the ideas be presented in a logical order. Your paragraphs should flow smoothly from one to the next, and the ideas within each paragraph should be presented logically. Use transitions to ensure that the reader can easily follow the progression of ideas.

## Do my paragraphs flow smoothly from one to the next?

Your paragraphs will flow smoothly if opening sentences include a transitional phrase or a link to the preceding paragraph.

### Exercise

Copy the paragraphs below. Add transitions to make the paragraphs flow smoothly and to help the reader follow the progression of ideas. If needed, reorder the ideas so that they flow in a logical pattern.

> In 1952, the government decided to build a dam. By 1959, plans were complete and the project began.
>
> The valley that the dam would flood had to be cleared. This meant moving more than 100,000 Nubian people to new lands. The new lake would cover many ancient temples and other monuments. In all, 23 were rescued, but many more were lost. UNESCO asked governments around the world to help move the 23 monuments that were saved.
>
> Preparations had to be made for the dam's actual construction. New roads had to be built to carry men and equipment to the construction site. An electrical station had to be built at the old Aswan Dam. The town of Aswan had to be prepared to host the thousands of workers that would be needed.

 **Review your first draft.** Check each paragraph to make sure ideas flow logically. Check for transitions within paragraphs. Make sure that transitions between paragraphs help the reader follow the flow of information. Revise accordingly.

**Differentiated Instruction: Advanced Learners**

Advanced students may enjoy creating a poster for the classroom or computer lab illustrating the use of transitional words and phrases.

**TEKS** 10.13B, 10.15A(iv), 10.15C(ii)

## Revising for Organization within Paragraphs

In a research paper, embedded quotations are often used as supporting evidence. Introducing the quotation and then returning to the paragraph or summary will also require transitions. A good organizational pattern will make this process seem seamless to the reader and fit well into the context and purpose for your writing.

**Revise** **Review your first draft for organization.** Be sure that each paragraph is logically structured. Check that quotations are introduced and integrated into the flow of the paragraph.

**Organization**
Writer moves a sentence to make the paragraph more coherent. An added transitional sentence introduces the quote and integrates it into the paragraph.

With the dam in place, flooding became a thing of the past.

The Aswan High Dam immediately helped control the flooding.

Before the Nile was dammed, floods sometimes forced
evacuation of the Nile Valley. ...As Michael Sorkin put it,
Cities like Cairo have expanded to the Nile's banks.

"By stabililzing the river's banks, the dam not only rescued

Egyptian agriculture from historic cycles of flood and drought,

but enabled extensive urban development along the shore" (82).

### Revising for Organization in Paragraphs

Have students read the sample paragraph aloud as it was written before the revision. Then have students read it in its revised form. Discuss ways in which the paragraph is more coherent after the revision.

■ The first sentence was moved to more logically follow the organizational pattern of the paragraph (chronological).

■ A sentence was added to introduce and integrate the quote naturally into the paragraph.

**Review your first draft for organization.** Before working on their own revisions, have students work in groups to brainstorm various ways to effectively transition into a direct quotation. When each group has listed three to five transitional phrases, have them share their ideas with the rest of the class. ✔DIFFERENTIATE INSTRUCTION

**TEKS** 10.13B, 10.15A(iv), 10.15C(ii)

---

### Differentiated Instruction:
### English Language Learners

**ELPS** 1F, 1H, 2I, 4C, 4F

| ELP Level **Beginning** | ELP Level **Intermediate** | ELP Level **Advanced/Advanced High** |
|---|---|---|
| Preteach necessary vocabulary. Use transition words to give multi-step directions (*First, go to the board . . .*) for students to follow. | Provide a list of transition words and have students work in pairs to place terms into the various categories using a graphic organizer. | Provide students with a list of transition words and phrases, and have them list the terms in the various categories and create a poster for the classroom. |
| | Use pages 624–625 | |

**TEKS** **10.13B** Develop drafts in open-ended situations that include transitions; **10.15A(iv)** Write an analytical essay that includes a structure appropriate to the purpose, audience, and context; **10.15C(ii)** Write a response to expository text that addresses writing skills for an analytical essay and using embedded quotations; **ELPS** **1F** Use accessible language and learn new and essential language in the process; **1H** Develop and expand learning strategies/reasoning, looking for patterns in language, and analyzing sayings and expressions; **2I** Demonstrate listening comprehension in increasingly complex spoken language by following directions and collaborating with peers; **4C** Develop and comprehend basic sight vocabulary used in written classroom materials; **4F** Use visual/contextual support and support from peers/teachers to develop vocabulary

Research

**Revising for** Development of Ideas

Students should ask themselves
- Have I included enough details to give my writing depth?
- Does each sentence add meaning to the one before it?
- Have I included enough of my own original ideas?

### Try It!
**Answers**

**Possible Answers**

Revised paragraphs will vary, but students should have
- Revised to include all source information
- Revised word choice to third person to sound more objective
- Revised facts to show knowledge of the subject
- Deleted the sentence about the Great Pyramid in Egypt (irrelevant)
- Deleted the sentences about health problems and consequences (do not support the topic sentence)
- Revised the last sentence to be more effective in summarizing the paragraph

**TEKS** 10.13C, 10.15C(ii), 10.22C

**Check for well-developed ideas.** Encourage students to create a checklist using the suggested points for revision.

---

 **TEKS** 10.13C, 10.15C(ii), 10.22C

 **Revising for** Development of Ideas

When you revise for *development of ideas,* check to make sure that the evidence you have provided to support your ideas is relevant, accurate, and reliable. In a research paper, it is critical to defend or support each point you make with authoritative data and factual, verifiable evidence. Embedded quotations and cited evidence are ways to show that you have used authoritative evidence.

As you re-read and revise your research paper, look at your word choice. Make sure that your words accurately and clearly convey your viewpoint and your subtlety of meaning. At this point, too, it is important to critique your research process to make sure that your research supports your thesis statement.

### Try It!

The paragraph below sometimes fails to show clear development of ideas. On your own paper, rewrite the paragraph so that each idea is clearly developed. As you rewrite, keep in mind the purpose, audience, and genre for the writing.

> According to one source, the Aswan High Dam was completed in July 1970. It seems to have been the largest engineering project of its time, and it may have cost around $1 billion. A lot of people worked on the dam, and it must have taken a lot of material. We know that it took a lot of material to build the Great Pyramid in Egypt, and that must have taken a lot of workers, too. The finished dam is a couple of miles wide. One of the health problems from the dam is schistosomiasis and it has affected a lot of people. There were other consequences, too, including the need for chemical fertilizers. But, overall I think the dam is a good thing for Egypt.

 **Check for well-developed ideas.** Read your draft. Make sure that you have supported each idea with evidence. Make sure that your work incorporates factual data and that the data is accurate and reliable. Cite your sources, and embed appropriate quotations to support your thesis and paragraph topic sentences. As you revise, consult your outline or other graphics you created to help you better develop your ideas.

---

**TEKS** **10.13C** Revise drafts/improve word choice and subtlety of meaning and rethink how well the purpose, audience, and genre have been addressed; **10.15C(ii)** Write a response to expository text that addresses writing skills for an analytical essay and using embedded quotations; **10.22C** Critique the research process to implement changes as need is identified

## Revising for Drawing Ideas to a Conclusion

The conclusion is a critical component of a research paper. You will provide a final summation of your research and give final support to your thesis statement. The conclusion is the last impression you will leave with your reader. Therefore, all the ideas in your paper need to be pulled together. The conclusion is also your last opportunity to present your own viewpoint on the topic. In a lengthy research paper, the conclusion may be more than one paragraph long.

- **Be direct.** Summarize the ideas and support the thesis statement clearly.
- **Use active verbs.** Leave your reader with strong support for the thesis statement.

### Try It!

Rewrite this conclusion so that the reader is left with a strong final impression and a clear idea of the thesis statement.

> There were a lot of reasons to build the Aswan High Dam. Egypt needed a dam to help control flooding and help its agriculture. The country also wanted to preserve monuments along the Nile River. Egypt also needed more land for cities to grow.

 **Check your conclusion.** Re-read your essay. Is the conclusion effective? Does it summarize your research and clearly support the thesis statement? Revise as needed.

**Development of Ideas**

Writer needs more information to support thesis statement and summarize information in middle paragraphs. Final thought also needs to be fleshed out.

> No one can deny that the Aswan High Dam has benefited Egypt. ∧Flood control has prevented loss of life and property.
>
> Irrigation and the expansion of croplands have helped supply food and other goods. The electrical power it provides has helped Egypt build and modernize. ~~There have been problems,~~ However, the dam also demonstrates that whenever humans change their environment, they ~~too. I think that overall, the dam has been a good thing for~~ introduce new problems that must be dealt with. The building ~~Egypt.~~ of the Aswan High Dam teaches people that they have to learn to modernize with caution, and to predict and prepare for the consequences of their actions.

*Research*

---

## Revising for Drawing Ideas to a Conclusion

Explain to students that, just as a movie or story needs a strong ending to be effective, so does a research paper. Even if the rest of the paper is focused, organized, developed, and strong, the conclusion leaves the reader with a lasting overall impression of the paper. So if the ending is weak, the paper will be remembered as such as well.

### Try It!
**Answers**

Read the sample paragraph revision aloud with students and discuss how the revisions improve the paragraph's strength and overall impression on the reader. Responses will vary, but students should include strong, active verbs and sentences that summarize the main points of the essay. ✔**DIFFERENTIATE INSTRUCTION**

⭐ **TEKS** 10.13C, 10.15A(i), 10.15C(ii), 10.22C

**Check your conclusion.** Encourage students to use the revised sample paragraph as a model for their own revision.

⭐ **TEKS** **10.13C** Revise drafts/improve word choice and subtlety of meaning and rethink how well the purpose, audience, and genre have been addressed; **10.15A(i)** Write an analytical essay that includes a concluding paragraph; **10.15C(ii)** Write a response to expository text that addresses writing skills for an analytical essay and using embedded quotations; **10.22C** Critique the research process to implement changes; **ELPS 3B** Expand vocabulary by learning/using high-frequency words for identifying and describing/retelling information supported by pictures/learning and using routine language for classroom communication; **3F** Give information/ranging from using a limited high-frequency vocabulary to using abstract and content-based vocabulary during speaking; **3G** Express opinions and ideas ranging from communicating short phrases to participating in discussions; **3H** Narrate, describe, and explain with increasing specificity and detail as more English is acquired; **4F** Use visual/contextual support and support from peers/teachers to read grade-appropriate text, enhance understanding, and develop vocabulary and grasp of language structures; **5F** Write using a variety of grade-appropriate sentence lengths, patterns, and connecting words/combine in increasingly accurate ways; **5G** Narrate, describe, and explain with increasing specificity and detail to fulfill content area writing needs as more English is acquired

---

**Differentiated Instruction: English Language Learners**

⭐ **ELPS** 3B, 3F–3H, 4F, 5B, 5F, 5G

| **ELP Level** **Beginning** | **ELP Level** **Intermediate** | **ELP Level** **Advanced/Advanced High** |
|---|---|---|
| To teach this concept, use a scenic picture and have students, in turns, narrate what is happening as you scribe on the board, guiding the development of ideas. | Provide a copy of the paragraph to students and, as a class, find and underline examples of weak word choice, i.e., ideas that need further development. | Using another paragraph, model how you would revise the paragraph. Then use shared writing to guide students though revising the sample paragraph. |

## Revising for Voice

Discuss with students the importance of using the proper voice for their topic.

**Do I maintain an objective, third-person point of view throughout?**

Ask students why they think it is important to maintain a third-person point of view in their analyses. Students should recognize that the third-person point of view enables them to remain objective and sound authoritative.

 **TEKS** 10.13C

### Try It!
**Answers**

**Possible Answer**

*The valley that the dam would flood had to be cleared, resulting in the need to move more than 100,000 Nubian people to new lands. These people's lives were completely disrupted by the building of the dam. Furthermore, many monuments were going to be lost when the valley was flooded, an effect similar to a terrible archaeological disaster. In all, however, 23 monuments were rescued before the reservoir was filled.* **DIFFERENTIATE INSTRUCTION** ↘

**Check for objectivity and third-person point of view.** Encourage students to look for and revise any incidence of first-person point of view and editorializing.

---

## Revising for Voice

When you revise for *voice* in a research report, you want to make sure that you sound knowledgable about the topic. You want to show that you have conducted careful research and that you understand the topic thoroughly. Through your voice, you will show that you have synthesized the information and can present it so that your reader can understand it, as well.

### Do I maintain an objective, third-person point of view throughout my research essay?

You have maintained an objective point of view if you accurately and honestly discuss both sides of the topic you have chosen. While you will provide your reader with your own viewpoint, that viewpoint should be formed by the evidence from your research.

In a research paper, it is also important to maintain a third-person point of view throughout. Avoid personal pronouns, *I*, and *my*, and use third-person pronouns, *he, she, they*, and *his, her, their*.

### Try It!

The paragraph below sometimes drifts away from an objective, third-person point of view. On your own paper, rewrite the paragraph so that the voice is consistently third person and objective. In places, you will need to completely change the sentence structure.

> The valley that the dam would flood had to be cleared. I was surprised and horrified to learn that this meant moving more than 100,000 Nubian people to new lands. That is a lot of people whose lives were completely disrupted by the building of the dam. Then I learned that many monuments were going to be lost when the valley was flooded. To me, this seemed like a terrible archaeological disaster. In all, however, 23 monuments were rescued before the reservoir was filled.

Revise

**Check for objectivity and third-person point of view.** Re-read your research paper to see if you have maintained an objective viewpoint and a third-person point of view throughout. Make any necessary revisions.

---

**TEKS** 10.13C

## Do I sound knowledgeable about the topic?

Your voice will sound knowledgeable if you show a clear understanding of the topic and write with confidence about it. Keep these tips in mind.

- **Avoid casual, inappropriate words.** Expressions such as "The Aswan High Dam was the bomb!" would not be appropriate for the purpose, audience, or context for the writing.
- **Define technical terms.** Your audience may not be familiar with the terms you are using. Show your knowledge by defining or explaining special terminology.
- **Support details with specific data.** Words such as *kind of, sort of, in a way* should be replaced with precise, factual data.

### Try It!

Rewrite the following sentences to make them sound more knowledgeable. Use the strategies given above.

It seems like there were problems with flooding and with drought. In about 20 years there were several floods that forced people to flee to higher ground. Then when there was a drought, it led to famine and some people died.

**Check your essay for voice.** Re-read your essay, marking any places that do not sound knowledgeable. Consult your research notes and revise as needed.

> **Voice**
> Writer defines technical terms and uses precise data to support claim.

> Because the irigation canals no longer dry up every year, Egyptians suffer from more waterborne diseases than before. One example is schistosomiasis. These snails flourish year-round making the disease ~seven times~ more common. There are also more mosquitos carrying diseases in Egypt since the dam was built (Louria 3). , an intestinal and urinary disease transmitted by microscopic worms that live on snails in the waterways.

Research

## Do I sound knowledgeable about the topic?

Refer students to the bulleted items and suggest that they ask several classmates to read their papers in search of the issues listed.

### Try It!
**Answers**

Revisions will vary but should include formal expressions, definitions of technical terms, and specific data to support details.

**Check your essay for voice.** Encourage students to use the revised sample paragraph as a model for their own revision.

 **TEKS** 10.13C

---

**Differentiated Instruction:**
**English Language Learners**

**ELPS** 1A, 1C, 1E, 2C, 2H, 2I, 3D, 3E, 5E

| ELP Level **Beginning** | ELP Level **Intermediate** | ELP Level **Advanced/Advanced High** |
|---|---|---|
| Use pictures, gestures, and a pronoun chart to teach the concepts of first and third person. | Review point of view by having students take turns dictating a story in first person to a partner. Partners should then rewrite the story using third-person point of view. | Review third-person pronouns and then have students work with a partner to revise the sample paragraph. |

**TEKS** 10.13C Revise drafts/improve style, word choice, and subtlety of meaning; **ELPS** 1A Use prior knowledge and experience to understand meanings; 1C Use strategic learning techniques to acquire basic and grade-level vocabulary; 1E Internalize new academic language by using and reusing it/speaking and writing; 2C Learn academic vocabulary heard during classroom instruction/interactions; 2H Understand information in increasingly complex spoken language; 2I Demonstrate listening comprehension in increasingly complex spoken language by collaborating with peers; 3D Speak using grade-level content area vocabulary/academic language proficiency; 3E Share information in cooperative learning interactions; 5E Employ increasingly complex grammatical structures in content area writing such as using correct verbs, tenses, and pronouns/possessive case/negatives and contractions

## Revising

**Improving Your Writing**

Tell students that now is the time to fine-tune their research papers. Explain to students that, much like packing for a trip, single items are often overlooked during revision. Encourage them to use the checklist as a final stage in the revision process, as any good traveler uses a checklist before closing the suitcase to ensure that all items are present. **DIFFERENTIATE INSTRUCTION ↘**

**420**

*Texas Traits*

## Revising Improving Your Writing

On a piece of paper, write the numbers 1 to 13. If you can answer "yes" to a question, put a check mark after that number. If not, continue to revise your report for that trait.

### Revising Checklist

#### Focus and Coherence

_____ **1.** Is my thesis statement clearly presented?

_____ **2.** Does my research support the thesis statement?

_____ **3.** Is each paragraph coherent and related to the controlling idea?

#### Organization

_____ **4.** Does my beginning paragraph capture the reader's interest and introduce my topic?

_____ **5.** Do my transitions lead to a smooth flow of ideas?

_____ **6.** Have I introduced and integrated quotations smoothly?

_____ **7.** Do I draw my ideas into an effective conclusion?

#### Development of Ideas

_____ **8.** Have I chosen an interesting work of engineering to write about?

_____ **9.** Do I include enough relevant, accurate details to support my thesis?

_____ **10.** Do I give credit for ideas that I have paraphrased or quoted?

_____ **11.** Do I clearly support each idea with reliable, authoritative evidence?

#### Voice

_____ **12.** Does my voice sound knowledgeable and engaging?

_____ **13.** Do I consistently maintain an objective, third-person point of view?

**Differentiated Instruction: Struggling Learners**

Students may feel overwhelmed by the number of items on the checklist. If necessary, instruct them to focus on one to two items in each category.

Prewrite — Draft — Revise — Edit — Publish

# Editing

When you have finished revising your research paper, all that remains is checking for conventions in grammar, sentence structure, capitalization, punctuation, and spelling.

---

**Keys to Effective Editing**

1. Read your essay out loud and listen for words or phrases that may be incorrect.

2. Use a dictionary, a thesaurus, your computer's spell-checker, and the "Proofreader's Guide" in the back of this book.

3. Look for errors in grammar, sentence structure, capitalization, punctuation, and spelling.

4. Check your report for proper formatting. (See pages 372–379.)

5. If you use a computer, edit on a printed copy. Then enter your changes on the computer.

6. Use the editing and proofreading marks inside the back cover of this book. Check all citations for accuracy.

Research

---

After going through the extensive revision process, students may be hesitant to begin the editing stage. Assure them that all of their hard work and diligence are worth the effort they have put forth and that editing their writing adds the final touches that will make the reader take their writing seriously. Remind them that, just like they wouldn't want to purchase a brand new car with scratches and dirty wheels, their audience is looking for a polished piece of writing. ✓ **DIFFERENTIATE INSTRUCTION**

Remind students that during the editing stage, they have a chance to find and correct errors in
- grammar,
- sentence structure,
- punctuation,
- capitalization,
- spelling, and
- formatting.

---

**Differentiated Instruction:**
**English Language Learners**

⭐ ELPS 1B, 3A, 3D, 3E, 4A, 4B, 4F, 4G, 4H

| ELP Level **Beginning** | ELP Level **Intermediate** | ELP Level **Advanced/Advanced High** |
|---|---|---|
| Have students read the Keys to Effective Editing with an English-proficient partner, making adjustments to their pronunciation by employing self-corrective techniques. | Have students work with a partner to read aloud and summarize each key. | Have students read all keys silently and then summarize and discuss each point with a partner. |

**ELPS 1B** Monitor oral language and employ self-corrective techniques or other resources; **3A** Practice producing sounds of newly acquired vocabulary; **3D** Speak using grade-level content area vocabulary/new words and academic language proficiency; **3E** Share information in cooperative learning interactions; **4A** Sound out words using a combination of skills; **4B** Recognize directionality of English reading such as left to right and top to bottom; **4F** Use support from peers/teachers to read grade-appropriate text, enhance understanding, and develop vocabulary; **4G** Demonstrate comprehension of increasingly complex English/participating in shared reading and summarizing material; **4H** Read silently with increasing ease and comprehension for longer periods

**Editing** for Conventions

## Grammar

Introduce or review restrictive and nonrestrictive phrases and clauses.

### Have I correctly used restrictive and nonrestrictive clauses and phrases?

Direct students to the bulleted items on SE page 422, and provide some examples of both restrictive and nonrestrictive clauses.

**TEKS** 10.13D, 10.17A(ii)

### Exercise
#### Answers

1. Restrictive – *that is in this particular journal* identifies where information is found and is essential to the meaning of the sentence
2. Nonrestrictive – *which I think you will find useful* adds meaning but not essential information to the sentence
3. Nonrestrictive – *which had been home to just a few thousand people* is not essential to the meaning of the sentence
4. Nonrestrictive – *which used to be limited to high ground near the river* is not essential to the meaning of the sentence
5. Restrictive – *that supports my point* identifies which quotation and is essential to the meaning of the sentence

**Check for restrictive and nonrestrictive clauses.** Encourage students to revise for correct use of restrictive and nonrestrictive clauses in their research reports.

### ★ Conventions Connections

**Grammar: Restrictive and Nonrestrictive Phrases and Clauses**
- *Proofreader's Guide* pages 650, 768–770
- *SkillsBook* pages 14–15

✦ *Write Source Online* **GrammarSnap**

---

**422**

 **TEKS** 10.13D, 10.17A(ii)

 **Editing** for Conventions

## Grammar

In a research paper, you will undoubtedly use complex sentences that contain restrictive and nonrestrictive phrases and clauses.

### Have I correctly used restrictive and nonrestrictive clauses and phrases?

As you paraphrase information from your research or embed quotations into your work, it is important to understand the difference between restrictive and nonrestrictive clauses. Here are some tips to guide you.

- A restrictive clause is essential to the meaning of the sentence.
- A nonrestrictive clause or phrase adds information that is not necessary to the basic meaning of the sentence. In other words, the clause could be deleted from the sentence and the meaning would not be changed.
- Use the word *that* to introduce restrictive clauses. Use the word *which* to introduce nonrestrictive clauses.

### Exercise

Copy the following sentences onto your own paper. Identify whether the clauses are restrictive or nonrestrictive and explain your answer.

1. The information that is in this particular journal gives details about the dam's construction.
2. This information, which I think you will find useful, is about the UNESCO efforts to save the monuments.
3. The town of Aswan, which had been home to just a few thousand people, experienced incredible growth.
4. Cities like Cairo, which used to be limited to high ground near the river, have expanded.
5. I would like to use a quotation from Michael Sorkin that supports my point about urban development.

 **Check for restrictive and nonrestrictive clauses.** As you edit your paraphrases and quotations, check for correct use of restrictive and nonrestrictive clauses.

---

 **TEKS** **10.13D** Edit drafts for grammar; **10.17A(ii)** Use and understand restrictive and nonrestrictive relative clauses

**TEKS** 10.13D, 10.17A(i)
**ELPS** 5E

## Should I Avoid the Passive Voice?

In a research paper, you should try to use verbs in the active voice. Particularly as you write summaries and paraphrases of the research you have done, think about your word choice and how to convey your ideas so that you can use the active voice. The active voice is stronger and will capture your reader's interest. In a paraphrase you should also try to capture the writer's original voice and communicate to your reader the original writer's opinions.

### Try It!

Compare the following sentences from the research paper on the Aswan Dam. The sentences written in active voice are stronger and more engaging to the reader.

In the heat, the Soviet equipment broke down five times faster than expected.

The Soviet equipment was often broken by the heat.

As was reported by Michael Sorkin, "By stabilizing the river's banks, extensive urban development could take place along the river's banks."

As Michael Sorkin puts it, "By stabilizing the river's banks, extensive urban development could take place along the river's banks."

 **Edit for active and passive voice.** Review your essay for active and passive voice. When possible, rewrite sentences so that the verbs are in the active voice.

## LEARNING LANGUAGE

Compare the following examples of active and passive voice. Remember that active and passive voice occur in present, past, and future tenses. Explain to a partner how the passive voice is formed. Take turns with your partner saying three verbs in the passive voice and changing them into the active voice. Then say three different verbs in the passive voice and have your partner change them into the active voice.

| Active Voice | Passive voice |
| --- | --- |
| Engineers observed that | It was observed that |
| Nubians moved | Nubians were moved |
| The construction team faced | The construction team was faced with |

*Research*

## Should I Avoid the Passive Voice?

Explain to students that, although passive voice is appropriate in formal writing to help vary sentence structure, it can come across as weak when used too often.

### Try It!
**Answers**

Direct students to identify the sentences as being written in either passive or active voice and discuss why the sentences written in active voice are more engaging to the reader.

*In the heat, the Soviet equipment broke down five times faster than expected.* **Active**

*The Soviet equipment was often broken by the heat.* **Passive**

*As was reported by Michael Sorkin, "By stabilizing the river's banks, extensive urban development could take place along the river's banks."* **Passive**

*As Michael Sorkin puts it, "By stabilizing the river's banks, extensive urban development could take place along the river's banks."* **Active**

 **TEKS** 10.13D, 10.17A(i); **ELPS** 5E

**Edit for active and passive voice.** Encourage students to revise to use mainly active voice.

### LEARNING LANGUAGE

Encourage students to write their own sentences and then identify them as being active or passive.

**✔ DIFFERENTIATE INSTRUCTION**

 **Conventions Connections**

**Grammar: Passive Voice**
- *Proofreader's Guide* pages 750–751
- *SkillsBook* page 95

⚡ *Write Source Online* **GrammarSnap**

**TEKS** 10.13D Edit drafts for grammar; **10.17A(i)** Use and understand more complex active and passive tenses; **ELPS 1C** Use strategic learning techniques to acquire basic and grade-level vocabulary; **1E** Internalize new basic and academic language by using and reusing it/speaking and writing; **1H** Develop and expand learning strategies/reasoning, looking for patterns in language, and analyzing sayings and expressions; **2C** Learn new language structures heard during classroom instruction/interactions; **2H** Understand implicit ideas and information in increasingly complex spoken language; **2I** Demonstrate listening comprehension in increasingly complex spoken language by collaborating with peers; **3E** Share information in cooperative learning interactions; **5E** Employ increasingly complex grammatical structures in content area writing such as using correct verbs, tenses, and pronouns/possessive case/negatives and contractions

**Differentiated Instruction:**
**English Language Learners**

**ELPS** 1C, 1E, 1H, 2C, 2H, 2I, 3E, 5E

| ELP Level **Beginning** | ELP Level **Intermediate** | ELP Level **Advanced/Advanced High** |
| --- | --- | --- |
| Write four to six sentences on the board using active and passive voice. Have students identify the subject of each sentence so they understand the difference between active/passive voice. | Encourage students to create complete sentences in active and passive voice and then have their partner identify which is which. | Have students complete the **Try It!** activity using examples of passive and active verbs in all three tenses (past, present, future). |

## Sentence Structure

Review each sentence type with students, having students identify the independent and dependent clauses of each example sentence. Below, dependent clauses are bold and independent clauses are italicized.

- simple: *The Aswan High Dam stretches for two miles.*
- compound: *The dam cost over $1 billion, and more than 50,000 people worked on it.*
- complex: *Cities like Cairo,* **which used to be limited to higher ground near the river,** *have expanded all the way to the Nile's banks.*
- complex-compound: **Once the dam was built,** *thousands of villages gained electricity, and the power station,* **which has been enlarged several times,** *has been important to the growing population.*

To visualize the difference in sentence types, you may wish to show a diagram of each example sentence on the board. DIFFERENTIATE INSTRUCTION ↘

⭐ **TEKS** 10.13C, 10.17C

### Try It!
### Answers

**Possible Answer**

*The dam, begun in 1960 and completed in 1970, took 10 years to complete. It was the largest engineering work of its time, spanning two miles, rising 365 feet high, and covering an area larger than the state of Delaware. It cost over $1 billion to build, and more than 50,000 people worked on the dam.*

**Check for sentence variety.** Encourage students to revise their papers to include a variety of sentence structures.

⭐ **ELPS** 5F

⭐ **Conventions Connections**

**Mechanics: Sentence Types for Variety**
- *Student Edition* pages 585–591
- *SkillsBook* pages 140–144

⚡ *Write Source Online* **GrammarSnap**

---

⭐ **TEKS** 10.13C, 10.17C

## Sentence Structure

There are four main types of sentences: simple, compound, complex, and complex-compound. It is important to use a variety of these sentence types in your research paper. It is also important to avoid lengthy compound or complex-compound sentences. Keep your reader in mind as you edit your sentences, and be sure to use correct punctuation.

- A **simple sentence** can have a single subject or a compound subject. It can have a single predicate or a compound predicate. It has no dependent clauses.

  The Aswan High Dam stretches for two miles.

- A **compound sentence** consists of two independent clauses.

  The dam cost over $1 billion, and more than 50,000 people worked on it.

- A **complex sentence** contains one independent clause and one or more dependent clauses.

  Cities like Cairo, which used to be limited to higher ground near the river, have expanded all the way to the Nile's banks.

- A **complex-compound sentence** contains one or more independent clauses and one or more dependent clauses.

  Once the dam was built, thousands of villages gained electricity, and the power station, which has been enlarged several times, has been important to the growing population.

### Try It!

Rewrite the following paragraph so that it contains a variety of sentence structures.

The dam was begun in 1960. It was completed in 1970. It took ten years to complete. It was the largest engineering work of its time. It cost over $1 billion. More than 50,000 people worked on the dam. The dam is two miles wide. It is 364 feet high. The reservoir covers an area larger than the state of Delaware.

**Check for sentence variety.** Use the information above as a guide to ensure that you have used a variety of sentence structures in your research paper.

---

⭐ **TEKS** **10.13C** Revise drafts to improve sentence variety; **10.17C** Use a variety of correctly structured sentences; **ELPS** **5F** Write using a variety of grade-appropriate sentence lengths, patterns, and connecting words/combine in increasingly accurate ways

**TEKS** 10.18B(i), 10.19

# Mechanics

## How do I punctuate nonrestrictive clauses?

When you edit for *mechanics,* you check for punctuation and capitalization. The punctuation of restrictive and nonrestrictive clauses is different. Knowing how to punctuate clauses and phrases in your research paper will help the reader follow your ideas without distractions.

Always use a comma to set off nonrestrictive clauses. Remember that these are clauses that contain information that is not essential to the meaning of the sentence. In addition, nonrestrictive clauses are introduced by the word *which.*

**Austin, which is the capital of Texas, is a vibrant, growing city.**

## What punctuation do I use with quotations?

To introduce a quotation into your work, use a comma before the quotation marks. Always place commas and periods inside the quotation marks. If you are citing material, however, the period goes after the citation.

**As Michael Sorkin puts it, "The dam enabled extensive urban development along the shore" (82).**

**Check for mechanics.** As you edit for mechanics, check the punctuation you have used with embedded quotations and with restrictive and nonrestrictive clauses.

### Try It!

Rewrite the following paragraph, inserting punctuation as needed for quotations and clauses.

**According to Peggy Parks "between 1860 and 1880, there were four major floods that forced people to flee to higher ground" Egypt desperately needed a dam that would replace the old dam and prevent recurring damage. In dry years, the problems suffered by Egypt were quite different. Without irrigation "the result was drought and famine" problems that could be solved by building a new dam. The Aswan High Dam which was in the planning process for decades seemed to be the perfect solution.**

Research

---

# Mechanics

## How do I punctuate nonrestrictive clauses?

Have students refer to SE page 422 to review the punctuation of the example sentences using restrictive and nonrestrictive clauses.

## What punctuation do I use with quotations?

Have a variety of published research writing (magazines, Web articles, etc.) available and have students scan articles, finding examples of how those authors used punctuation with quotations.

**Check for mechanics.** Encourage students to revise their papers to include correct punctuation for embedded quotations and with restrictive and nonrestrictive clauses.

**TEKS** 10.18B(i), 10.19

### Try It!
### Answers

*According to Peggy Parks, "between 1860 and 1880, there were four major floods that forced people to flee to higher ground" (insert page #). Egypt desperately needed a dam that would replace the old dam and prevent recurring damage. In dry years, the problems suffered by Egypt were quite different. Without irrigation, "the result was drought and famine," (insert page #) problems that could be solved by building a new dam. The Aswan High Dam, which was in the planning process for decades, seemed to be the perfect solution.*

 **Conventions Connections**

### Mechanics: Punctuating Quotations
- ***Proofreader's Guide*** pages 668–670
- ***SkillsBook*** pages 31–33

✦ **Write Source Online  GrammarSnap**

---

**Differentiated Instruction: English Language Learners**    **ELPS** 1B, 1C, 1E, 2C, 3E

| ELP Level **Beginning** | ELP Level **Intermediate** | ELP Level **Advanced/Advanced High** |
|---|---|---|
| Have students practice writing simple sentences on the board. Model for students how to combine them into compound sentences. Label each type of sentence. | Write examples of each type of sentence on the board. Think aloud how to identify independent and dependent clauses. Have students label each sentence. | Encourage students to write an example for each type of sentence with a partner. Then share and analyze sentences with the class. |

**TEKS** **10.18B(i)** Use commas in nonrestrictive phrases and contrasting expressions and in clauses; **10.19** Spell correctly using resources to determine and check correct spelling; **ELPS 1B** Monitor written language and employ self-corrective techniques or other resources; **1C** Use strategic learning techniques to acquire basic and grade-level vocabulary; **1E** Internalize new academic language by using and reusing it/writing; **2C** Learn new language structures and academic vocabulary heard during classroom instruction/interactions; **3E** Share information in cooperative learning interactions

## Editing
**Checking for Conventions**

### Using a Checklist

Have students exchange their reports with partners who can use the Editing Checklist to check for mistakes in grammar, sentence structure, capitalization, punctuation, and spelling. Writers should check their reports one final time after their partners edit them.

DIFFERENTIATE INSTRUCTION ↘ DIFFERENTIATE INSTRUCTION ↘

### MLA Research Papers

Make students aware of other formats, such as APA, and reiterate which format they are to use for their research papers.

---

## Editing Checking for Conventions

### Using a Checklist

On a piece of paper, write the numbers 1 to 12. If you can answer "yes" to a question, put a check mark after that number. Continue editing until you can answer "yes" to all of the questions.

#### Editing Checklist

#### Conventions

**GRAMMAR**

_____ 1. Do I use the correct forms of verbs *(he saw,* not *he seen)*?

_____ 2. Do I use active voice whenever possible?

**SENTENCE STRUCTURE**

_____ 3. Have I used a variety of sentence structures, including complex and compound sentences?

_____ 4. Have I avoided run-ons and sentences that are too lengthy?

**MECHANICS (Capitalization and Punctuation)**

_____ 5. Have I capitalized proper nouns and adjectives?

_____ 6. Do I correctly punctuate compound and complex sentences?

_____ 7. Have I correctly cited sources in my research paper?

_____ 8. Do I use quotation marks around all quoted words?

_____ 9. Do I correctly punctuate nonrestrictive clauses?

_____ 10. Have I correctly formatted a works-cited page?

**SPELLING**

_____ 11. Have I spelled all my words correctly?

_____ 12. Have I double-checked the words my spell-checker may have missed?

### MLA Research Papers

In high school English and language arts classes, research papers are usually written in MLA (Modern Language Association) format. However, always follow your teacher's instructions with regard to formatting.

---

**Differentiated Instruction: Struggling Learners**

Provide a copy of the checklist to struggling students and have them literally check off each item after working with a partner to edit their papers.

## Research Report

Titles and title pages are important parts of your research report. Ask your teacher what he or she wants included in the title page. After you have that information, consider including a title before you share your research report.

Writer Randall VanderMey says that a title, like good fish bait, should entice the reader. Each of the following approaches will help you write an effective title:

- Provide a creative hook:
  **Egypt's Modern Marvel**

- Focus on a theme that runs through your paper:
  **A Trade-Off of Monumental Size**

- Highlight a key point of your report:
  **Modernize with Caution**

- Use alliteration or some other literary device:
  **Providing Power to the People**

If you are having trouble choosing a title for your research paper, use the following tips to help.

- Brainstorm and consult with others to get ideas.

- When you have decided on possible titles, discuss them with a classmate or friends. Ask for feedback.

- Review possible titles with your teacher and ask for feedback.

- Review your research, your thesis statement, and your outline. Your title should capture the essence of your research and your writing.

- Write down several ideas, think about them overnight or for a few days, and then select the one that best fits your research paper.

Research

### Editing
#### Creating a Title

Based on the approaches described here, have students write four different titles for their reports. Then have them take a poll to find out which titles appeal to readers the most.

---

**Differentiated Instruction:**
**English Language Learners**

 **ELPS** 1G, 2I, 5A, 5B, 5C, 5D

| **ELP Level** **Beginning** | **ELP Level** **Intermediate** | **ELP Level** **Advanced/Advanced High** |
|---|---|---|
| Students should write several short phrases using newly acquired basic vocabulary, then peer-edit the writing for spelling and formal English use. | Students should edit their research paragraph(s) using content-related vocabulary, then peer-edit for spelling, standard grammar and usage, and formal English use. | Students should peer-edit their research paper for spelling, standard grammar and usage, variety of sentence structure, verb tense, and clarity. |

**ELPS 1G** Demonstrate increasing ability to distinguish between formal/informal English and an increasing knowledge of when to use each one; **2I** Demonstrate listening comprehension in increasingly complex spoken language by collaborating with peers; **5A** Learn relationships between sounds and letters of the English language to represent sounds when writing in English; **5B** Write using newly acquired basic and content-based grade-level vocabulary; **5C** Spell familiar words/employ spelling patterns and rules with increasing accuracy; **5D** Edit writing for standard grammar and usage/subject-verb and pronoun agreement and appropriate verb tenses

## Publishing
### Sharing Your Report

Explain to students that professional writers write to be published. Before they publish their work, however, they share it with editors and others for final feedback.

**TEKS** 10.13E

**Make your final copy.** Have students read the bulleted items under Focusing on Presentation at the bottom of the page before they make their clean final copies. **DIFFERENTIATE INSTRUCTION** ↘

### Focusing on Presentation

Remind students that incorporating visuals (tables, illustrations, charts, and graphs) can enhance their reports.

---

# Publishing Sharing Your Report

When you finish revising, editing, and proofreading the final copy of your research report, make a neat final copy to share. Be sure to ask your teacher to review your final draft. She or he will be able to provide you with helpful feedback and provide useful ideas for making improvements. Share your report with friends and family. Ask them for ways to improve your report, and incorporate their feedback as well. After you have listened carefully to all the feedback you have been given, make any needed final changes to your report. You are now ready to share your report with others.

A research report can serve as an effective starting point for a speech or a multimedia presentation. (See pages **429–441**.)

 **Make your final copy.** Use the following guidelines to format your report. (Also see pages 72–74 for instructions about designing on a computer.) Create a clean final copy and share it with your classmates and family.

## Focusing on Presentation

- Use blue or black ink and double-space the entire paper.
- Write your name, your teacher's name, the class, and the date in the upper left corner of page 1.
- Skip a line and center your title; skip another line and start your writing.
- Indent every paragraph and leave a one-inch margin on all four sides.
- For a research paper, you should write your last name and the page number in the upper right corner of every page of your report.
- If a title page and outline are required, follow your teacher's instructions. (See page **372**.)

---

# Making Presentations

If the very idea of making a presentation in front of a group makes you feel woozy, you're not alone. The fear of speaking in public is probably the most common anxiety around. But you can conquer that fear if you follow the tips and guidance provided in this chapter. Then with preparation and practice, you can make strong, effective presentations that inform and engage your listeners.

In this chapter you will learn to prepare and give a presentation based on a research report you have written. You will then learn how to turn your presentation into a multimedia report.

- Planning Your Presentation
- Creating Note Cards
- Considering Visual Aids
- Practicing Your Speech
- Delivering Your Presentation
- Evaluating a Presentation
- Preparing a Multimedia Report

"Be sincere; be brief; be seated."
—Franklin D. Roosevelt

**429**

## Making Presentations

### Objectives

- transform a research report into an oral presentation
- plan, write, revise, and edit an oral report
- prepare an interactive report

Ask students to share their greatest concerns about speaking in front of a group. Then encourage them to suggest ways to make the prospect of having to deliver a live speech less intimidating. Some students are bound to make humorous suggestions, and this will only help to lighten the mood. Other possible suggestions may include the following:

- being well prepared
- allowing time to practice
- feeling comfortable with the environment
- feeling comfortable with the audience

## Differentiated Instruction: English Language Learners

**ELPS** 1B, 2A, 2G, 2I, 4C

| ELP Level **Beginning** | ELP Level **Intermediate** | ELP Level **Advanced/Advanced High** |
|---|---|---|
| Echo read the bulleted items with the class while writing and modeling how the finished report should look on an overhead. Students should follow your spoken directions. | Have students take turns reading the bulleted items aloud, pausing to monitor their language and to clarify understanding, before working independently to format their reports. | Challenge students to read the bulleted items silently, stopping only to seek clarification and to format their reports independently. |

 **ELPS** **1B** Monitor oral/written language and employ self-corrective techniques or other resources; **2A** Distinguish sounds/intonation patterns with increasing ease; **2G** Understand the general meaning, main points, and important details of spoken language/topics, languages, and contexts are familiar to unfamiliar; **2I** Demonstrate listening comprehension in increasingly complex spoken language by following directions; **4C** Comprehend vocabulary used in written classroom materials

## Planning Your Presentation

Introduce the process to be followed to transform a report into a presentation.

### Considering Your Purpose and Your Audience

Students should review their past writing (portfolio) for the various types of essays and research papers they've written to help them identify the purpose, audience, and type of presentation to prepare.

### Conveying Your Point of View

Encourage students to brainstorm some questions the audience might have about their topic. Remind them that even though they should use their own words, word choice should be appropriate for the topic and audience.

### Reviewing Your Report

Encourage students to consider the bulleted questions as they review their reports.

**TEKS** 10.15D, 10.23A, 10.23B, 10.23C

### Try It!

If students have recently completed their reports on a work of engineering, they will probably choose it for their oral presentations. The ideas are still fresh in their minds, and they probably still have all of their research materials and source information on hand. Be clear, however, that students can choose to transform any other research report they have written in the past if they are still interested in the topic and if they think the report will make an effective oral presentation. Ask students who choose other reports to show them to you before proceeding so that you can check their appropriateness.

**DIFFERENTIATE INSTRUCTION ↘**

---

**TEKS** 10.15D, 10.23A–10.23C

# Planning Your Presentation

To transform a research report into a presentation, you need to consider your purpose, your audience, and the content of your report.

## Considering Your Purpose and Your Audience

Your purpose is your reason for giving a presentation. Your audience is all those who will listen to your presentation. As you think about your purpose and audience, keep the following points in mind.

- **Informative** speeches educate by providing valuable information.
- **Persuasive** speeches argue for or against something.
- **Demonstration** speeches show how to do or make something.
- **Be clear.** Listeners should understand your main points immediately.
- **Engage the listeners** through thought-provoking questions, revealing anecdotes, interesting details, and effective visuals.

## Conveying Your Point of View

- **Anticipate questions** the audience might have and answer them. This helps keep the audience connected.
- **Speak in your own words.** This helps you convey your own point of view about the topic. It will also keep the audience engaged.

## Reviewing Your Report

During a report, your audience obviously cannot go back and listen again to anything you have said, so you must be sure to share your ideas clearly from beginning to end. Review your report to see how the different parts will work in a presentation. Use the following questions as a review guide.

- Will my opening grab the listeners' attention?
- What are my thesis and main points? Is my thesis clearly stated?
- How does my evidence support my claims?
- What visual aids, including graphics and illustrations, can I use to create interest in my topic? (See page **434**.)
- Will the ending have the proper impact on the listeners?

### Try It!

Choose a research report to present. Rework any parts that need to be adjusted. Pay special attention to the beginning and ending. Make sure your ideas follow logically and your point of view is clear. (See the next page for example adaptations.)

---

**TEKS** **10.15D** Produce a multimedia presentation with graphics, images, and sound that conveys a point of view and appeals to a specific audience; **10.23A** Synthesize research into a presentation in support of a clear thesis and related claims; **10.23B** Synthesize research into a presentation that reflects a progression of ideas and a stated point of view; **10.23C** Synthesize research into a presentation that uses graphics and illustrations to explain concepts

**TEKS** 10.15D, 10.23A, 10.23B

# Making Presentations

You may need to rewrite certain parts of your report. The new beginning below grabs the listeners' attention by using short, punchy phrases. The thesis is clearly stated for the audience. The new ending makes a more immediate connection to the thesis statement and ties back to the beginning.

## Written Introduction (page 373)

> Humans have been building dams for thousands of years…main purpose was to stop catastrophic flooding…people are discovering that these large dams also have many detrimental effects on the environment. Egypt's High Dam at Aswan illustrates this critical trade-off. The Aswan High Dam has solved many important problems for Egypt, but it has also created new ones.

### Oral Introduction

> Dams stop flooding; they provide irrigation; they generate hydroelectric power. In general, dams have proven to be a good thing. But the Aswan High Dam in Egypt is a prime example of how dams, while built to serve humanity, can also have a negative impact on our world.

## Written Conclusion (page 378)

> No one can deny that the Aswan High Dam has benefited Egypt. . . . However, the dam also demonstrates that whenever humans change their environment, they introduce new problems that must be dealt with. The building of the Aswan High Dam teaches people that they have to learn to modernize with caution, and to predict and prepare for the consequences of their actions.

### Oral Conclusion

> It's tempting and exciting to find new ways to dominate the physical world. Yet, as the Aswan High Dam has shown, people must modernize with caution. The natural world has a balance of its own, and humans run the risk of destroying their own future when they tamper with that balance.

Making Presentations

## Reworking Your Report

Previously written reports should contain helpful teacher feedback. Suggest that students refer to this feedback as they rethink and rewrite their material.

Emphasize how important it is for students to keep their listening audience in mind as they rework their introductions. Point out that speakers have a very brief time to gain the full attention of an audience.

Have students try out different beginnings to see which one works the best.

**TEKS** 10.15D, 10.23A, 10.23B

---

## Differentiated Instruction: English Language Learners

**ELPS** 1A, 1G

| ELP Level **Beginning** | ELP Level **Intermediate** | ELP Level **Advanced/Advanced High** |
|---|---|---|
| Show videos of different types of speeches, and help students choose a topic and presentation style for a group presentation. | Show videos of example speeches, and have students choose a topic with which they are very familiar and a suitable presentation style for the report. | Challenge students to choose a topic or report that will require them to expand their speaking skills and use formal English usage. |

**TEKS** **10.15D** Produce a multimedia presentation with graphics, images, and sound that conveys a point of view and appeals to a specific audience; **10.23A** Synthesize research into a presentation in support of a clear thesis; **10.23B** Synthesize research into a presentation that reflects a stated point of view; **ELPS** **1A** Use prior knowledge and experiences to understand meanings; **1G** Demonstrate increasing ability to distinguish between formal/informal English and an increasing knowledge of when to use each one

## Creating Note Cards

If students will be using a presentation software for their presentation, review how to use embedded notes in their slides.

### Following Note-Card Guidelines

Emphasize that note cards should be used as prompts, not as reading material. Except for the introduction and ending, students should not write what they will say word for word. Audiences prefer a speaker to make eye contact and talk to them.

✱ Have students refer to the sample note cards on SE page 433 as you review the guidelines.

### Considering the Three Main Parts

Encourage students to review the information and example note cards on the SE pages listed.

**TEKS** 10.15D, 10.23A, 10.23B, 10.23C, 10.23E

### Try It!

Remind students to write short phrases and use lettering large enough to be easily seen. Also encourage students to number their note cards in order to be easily reassembled into the correct order should they fall or scatter.

**DIFFERENTIATE INSTRUCTION ↘**

---

"To be listened to is, generally speaking, a nearly unique experience for most people. It is enormously stimulating."

—Robert C. Murphy

## Creating Note Cards

If you are giving a prepared speech rather than an oral reading of your report, you should use note cards or slides with embedded notes to help you remember your ideas. The guidelines below will help you make effective cards.

### Following Note-Card Guidelines

Write out your entire introduction and conclusion on separate note cards. For the body of your speech, write one point per card, along with specific details. Clearly number your cards.

- Place each main point at the top of a separate note card.
- Write supporting evidence on the lines below the main idea, using key words and phrases to help you remember specific details.
- Number each card in a logical sequence.
- Highlight any ideas you especially want to emphasize.
- Mark cards that call for visual aids.
- Cite your sources on your note cards.

### Considering the Three Main Parts

As you prepare your note cards, keep the following points in mind about the three parts of your oral presentation: introduction, body, and conclusion.

- **The introduction** should grab the listeners' attention, clearly state the thesis, and provide any essential background information about the topic. (See pages **430–431**.)
- **The body** should contain the main points and supporting evidence from your report. Present these points in a way that impacts listeners. Also jot down the visual aids that you plan to use. (See the bold notes on the sample cards on page **433**.)
- **The conclusion** should restate your focus and leave the listener with a final thought about your topic. (See pages **430–431**.)

### Try It!

Create your note cards. Review those on the following page. Then prepare cards for your introduction, main points, and conclusion. Make notes on the cards about where to use visual aids.

---

**TEKS** **10.15D** Produce a multimedia presentation with graphics, images, and sound that conveys a point of view and appeals to a specific audience; **10.23A** Synthesize research into a presentation in support of a clear thesis and related claims; **10.23B** Synthesize research into a presentation that reflects a progression of ideas and a stated point of view; **10.23C** Synthesize research into a presentation that uses graphics and illustrations to explain concepts; **10.23E** Synthesize research into a presentation that uses a style manual to document sources

TEKS 10.15D, 10.23A–10.23C, 10.23E

## Sample Note Cards

Below are the note cards Isabel used for her presentation.

**433**

**Introduction**     1

    Dams stop flooding; they provide irrigation; they generate hydroelectric power. In general, dams have proven to be a good thing. But the Aswan High Dam in Egypt is a good example of how dams, while built to serve humanity, can also have a huge, negative impact on our world.

**Reasons to Build**     2

 – flooding
 – water for dry spells
 – irrigation

    ✱ **Photos of Nile Valley before the dam**

**History: Source: Parks**     3

 – 1898-1902, Britain's   ✱ **Drawing of** William Willcocks    **early workers**
 – Not big enough, raised in 1912 and 1933
 – 1952—Egyptian independence meant new dam
 – Germany gave plans

**Preparations for Second Dam: Source: Building Big: Dams**     4

 – support for machines and workers
 – difficult weather and terrain temperatures up to 135° in shade
 – 1961—Egyptians took over from the Soviets
 – equipment came from Sweden and Great Britain

**Completed: Source: "Aswan Dam"**     5

 – July 1970    ✱ **Photos of**
 – over $1 billion    **finished dam**
 – more than 50,000 people worked on two-mile-wide, 364-foot-high dam
 – reservoir larger than Delaware

**Effects**    ✱ **Show Chart**     6

 – Positive: Stabilized banks, controlled irrigation, expanded urban development, electricity for all
 – Negative: river pollution, industrial waste, erosion, waterborne diseases, ancient statues crumbling

**Conclusion**     7

    It's tempting and exciting to find new ways to control our physical world. Yet, as the Aswan High Dam has shown, people must modernize very carefully. The natural world has a balance of its own, and humans run the risk of destroying their own future if they tamper with that balance.

Making Presentations

## Sample Note Cards

Have students compare the sample note cards with the written research report on SE pages 372–379. What do students notice? Have students discuss the differences noted and the reasons for those differences.

 TEKS 10.15D, 10.23A, 10.23B, 10.23C, 10.23E.

### Differentiated Instruction: English Language Learners

ELPS 1E, 1G, 5A, 5B, 5C

| ELP Level **Beginning** | ELP Level **Intermediate** | ELP Level **Advanced/Advanced High** |
|---|---|---|
| Have students work with their groups to create note cards, sounding out and correctly spelling simple words or phrases. | Encourage students to use newly acquired vocabulary in their presentations and on their note cards. | Encourage students to use newly acquired vocabulary and formal English word choice in their presentations and on their note cards. |

TEKS **10.15D** Produce a multimedia presentation with graphics and images that conveys a point of view and appeals to a specific audience; **10.23A** Synthesize research into a presentation in support of a clear thesis and related claims; **10.23B** Synthesize research into a presentation that reflects a progression of ideas; **10.23C** Synthesize research into a presentation that uses graphics and illustrations to explain concepts; **10.23E** Synthesize research into a presentation that uses a style manual to document sources and format written materials; **ELPS 1E** Internalize new basic and academic language by using and reusing it/speaking and writing; **1G** Demonstrate increasing ability to distinguish between formal/informal English and an increasing knowledge of when to use each one; **5A** Learn relationships between sounds and letters to represent sounds when writing in English; **5B** Write using newly acquired basic and content-based grade-level vocabulary; **5C** Spell familiar words/employ spelling patterns and rules with increasing accuracy

## Considering Visual and Audio Aids

Provide examples, if possible, for each of the items in the table as you begin the discussion.

### Indicating When to Present Visuals

Encourage students to test the effectiveness of their visual aids well in advance of making their oral presentations. This will help them see whether their visuals will be easy to use and visible to the entire audience.

⭐ **TEKS** 10.15D, 10.23C

### Try It!

Direct students to read the bulleted items at the bottom of the page for tips about creating effective visual aids. DIFFERENTIATE INSTRUCTION ⬊

---

 ⭐ **TEKS** 10.15D, 10.23C

## Considering Visual and Audio Aids

Consider using visual and audio aids during your presentation. They can make your presentation clearer, more meaningful, and more appealing to your audience. They can also convey a distinct point of view.

| | |
|---|---|
| **Posters** | include words, pictures, or both. |
| **Photographs** | help people see what you are talking about. |
| **Charts and Graphs** | explain points, compare facts, or show statistics. |
| **Maps** | identify or locate specific places being discussed. |
| **Objects** | show the audience important items related to your topic. |
| **Audio and Visual clips and slides** | project your photographs, charts, and maps onto a screen and turn your speech into a multimedia presentation. (See pages 438–439.) |

### Indicating When to Present Visuals

Write notes in the margins of your note cards to indicate where a visual aid would be helpful. Isabel considered the following visuals for her presentation.

- Photos of Nile Valley before the dam and of the finished dam
- An illustration of workers on the first dam
- An audio clip of an interview
- A chart comparing the pros and cons of the dam

### Try It!

List possible visual aids. Identify two or three visual aids you could use in your presentation. Explain how and when you would use each one.

### Tip

When creating visual aids, keep these points in mind.

- **Make them big.** Your visuals should be large enough for everyone in the audience to see.

- **Keep them simple.** Use labels and short phrases rather than full sentences.

- **Make them eye-catching.** Use color, bold lines, and simple shapes to attract the audience.

---

⭐ **TEKS** **10.15D** Produce a multimedia presentation with graphics, images, and sound that conveys a point of view and appeals to a specific audience; **10.23C** Synthesize research into a presentation that uses graphics and illustrations to explain concepts

★ TEKS 10.23A–10.23C

# Practicing Your Presentation

Practice is the key to giving an effective presentation. Knowing what to say and how to say it will help eliminate those "butterflies" speakers often feel. Here are some hints for an effective practice session.

- **Arrange your note cards and visual aids in the proper order.**
  This will eliminate any confusion as you practice.
- **Practice in front of a mirror.** Check your posture and eye contact and be sure your visual aids are easy to see.
- **Practice in front of others.** Friends and family can help you identify parts that need work.
- **Record or videotape a practice presentation.** Do you sound interested in your topic? Are your voice and message clear?
- **Time yourself.** If your teacher has set a time limit, practice staying within it.
- **Speak clearly.** Do not rush your words, especially later when you are in front of your audience.
- **Work on eye contact.** Look down only to glance at a card.
- **Speak up.** Your voice will sound louder to you than it will to the audience. Rule of thumb: If you sound *too* loud to yourself, you are probably sounding just right to your audience.
- **Look interested and confident.** This will help you engage the listeners.

## Practice Checklist

To review each practice session, ask yourself the following questions.

_____ **1.** Did I appear at ease and convey my point of view?

_____ **2.** Could my voice be heard and my words understood?

_____ **3.** Did I sound like I enjoyed and understood my topic?

_____ **4.** Did my visual aids help explain the concepts? Were the visuals interesting and used effectively?

_____ **5.** Did I clearly convey my thesis and supporting evidence? Did my ideas follow a logical progression?

## Try It!

Practice your presentation. Practice your speech in front of family or friends. Also consider videotaping your speech.

Making Presentations

## Practicing Your Presentation

While practice is important and necessary to help reduce anxiety, the truth is that some presenters experience "butterflies" no matter how much they practice.

Search the Internet and print resources looking for stories related to anxiety that famous entertainers, politicians, and athletes experience when they perform or have to give a speech. Students may be surprised to learn that so many people whom they admire aren't as comfortable as they seem in front of a crowd. Students can also benefit from any useful tips and hints these personalities have to offer about overcoming anxiety.

### Try It!

Encourage students to videotape their practice session and then use the Practice Checklist on SE page 435 to review and fine tune their presentation.

★ TEKS 10.23A, 10.23B, 10.23C

---

**Differentiated Instruction:**
**English Language Learners**
★ ELPS 1A, 2F, 3D, 3E, 3F, 3G, 4C

| ELP Level **Beginning** | ELP Level **Intermediate** | ELP Level **Advanced/Advanced High** |
| --- | --- | --- |
| Have students use posters, objects, and other environmental print to make their visuals meaningful. Emphasize colors, shapes, and size. | Have students work in groups, taking turns asking for and giving suggestions for visual aid ideas. | Challenge students to use more than posters with simple words and sayings. Students should review and use a variety of media in their presentations. |

**TEKS** **10.23A** Synthesize research into a presentation in support of a clear thesis and related claims; **10.23B** Synthesize research into a presentation that reflects a progression of ideas and a stated point of view; **10.23C** Synthesize research into a presentation that uses graphics and illustrations to explain concepts; **ELPS 1A** Use prior knowledge and experiences to understand meanings; **2F** Listen to and derive meaning from a variety of media to build and reinforce concept and language attainment; **3D** Speak using grade-level content area vocabulary/academic language proficiency; **3E** Share information in cooperative learning interactions; **3F** Ask for and give information/ranging from using a limited high-frequency vocabulary to using abstract and content-based vocabulary during speaking; **3G** Express opinions and ideas ranging from communicating short phrases to participating in discussions; **4C** Derive meaning of environmental print

## Delivering Your Presentation

Consider having each student conduct a full "dress rehearsal" in front of two classmates before they deliver their oral presentations to the entire class.

- Speakers should apply all of the guidelines for voice control and body language listed on this page in their run-throughs.
- After a speaker has delivered the presentation, the two listeners can offer feedback and advice.
- Students can alternate roles so that all three students have a chance to deliver their speeches.

 **TEKS** 10.23C

### Controlling Your Voice

The first listener should focus on the speaker's volume, tone, and pace.

### Considering Your Body Language

The other listener should focus on the speaker's body language.

### Try It!

To keep the student audience engaged, provide them with copies of the peer evaluation sheet found on the next page or have them create their own. Encourage students to give positive and constructive feedback to the presenter.

**DIFFERENTIATE INSTRUCTION** ↘

✱ For additional guidelines and tips for speaking and listening, see SE pages 515–518.

---

**TEKS** 10.23C

# Delivering Your Presentation

When you deliver a speech, concentrate on your voice and body language. Voice quality and body language communicate as much as your words do.

## Controlling Your Voice

*Volume, tone,* and *pace* are three aspects of your formal speaking voice. If you can control these three aspects of voice, your listeners will be able to follow your ideas.

- **Volume** is the loudness of your voice. Imagine that you are speaking to someone in the back of the room and adjust your volume accordingly.
- **Tone** expresses your feelings. Be enthusiastic about your topic and let your voice show that.
- **Pace** is the speed at which you speak. For the most part, speak at a relaxed pace. Slow down or pause to make important points.

## Considering Your Body Language

Your body language (*posture, gestures,* and *facial expressions*) plays an important role during a speech. Follow the suggestions given below to communicate effectively.

- **Assume a straight but relaxed posture.** This tells the audience that you are confident and prepared. If you are using a podium, let your hands rest lightly on the surface.
- **Pause before you begin.** Take a deep breath and relax.
- **Look at your audience.** Try to look toward every section of the room at least once during your speech.
- **Think about what you are saying** and let your facial expressions reflect your true feelings.
- **Point to your visual aids** or use natural gestures to make a point. Graphics and illustrations play an important role in explaining ideas. Prepare visual aids carefully and practice using them. Make sure any technology is working before you give your presentation so that you will be relaxed as you present the visual aids.

### Try It!

Deliver your presentation. As you deliver your speech, make sure to control your voice and exhibit the proper body language. Use technology efficiently. Give the audience time to examine your visual aids and listen to audio clips.

---

**TEKS** **10.23C** Synthesize research into a presentation that uses graphics and illustrations to explain concepts

**TEKS** 10.15D, 10.23A, 10.23B

# Evaluating a Presentation

Evaluate a presentation using the following evaluation sheet. Circle the descriptions that best fit each assessed area. Then offer two comments: one positive comment and one helpful suggestion.

---

**Peer Evaluation Sheet**

Speaker _____     Evaluator _____

### 1. Vocal Presentation

**Volume:**
Clear and loud, loud enough, a little soft, mumbled

**Pace:**
Relaxed, a little rushed/slow, rushed/slow, hard to follow

**Comments:**

   a. _____

   b. _____

### 2. Physical Presentation

**Posture:**
Relaxed, straight, a bit stiff, fidgeted a lot, slumped

**Eye contact:**
Excellent contact, made some contact, quick glances, none

**Comments:**

   a. _____

   b. _____

### 3. Information

Thought provoking, interesting, logical, a few good points, no ideas

**Comments:**

   a. _____

   b. _____

### 4. Visual Aids

Interesting, supporting ideas well, not clear, none used

**Comments:**

   a. _____

   b. _____

---

Making Presentations

## Evaluating a Presentation

Students can create their own peer evaluation sheets, similar to the one shown here. Tell them to use their personal responses to the speeches to form their evaluations. They can also use the following information:

- the descriptions for volume, tone, pace, and body language on SE page 518
- the tips at the bottom of SE page 434 for evaluating visual aids

**TEKS** 10.15D, 10.23A, 10.23B

---

## Differentiated Instruction: English Language Learners

**ELPS** 3B, 3C, 3D, 3F, 3G, 3H, 3I

| ELP Level **Beginning** | ELP Level **Intermediate** | ELP Level **Advanced/Advanced High** |
|---|---|---|
| Have students present in groups, with each student contributing one or two short phrases or sentences using content area vocabulary. | If students do not feel comfortable speaking in front of their peers, arrange a time and date when they make their presentations to a small group. | Presentations should encompass a variety of sentence structures and content-area vocabulary and use formal English usage. |

 **TEKS** **10.15D** Produce a multimedia presentation with graphics, images, and sound that conveys a point of view and appeals to a specific audience; **10.23A** Synthesize research into a presentation in support of a clear thesis and related claims; **10.23B** Synthesize research into a presentation that reflects a progression of ideas and a stated point of view; **ELPS** **3B** Expand vocabulary by learning and using high-frequency words for identifying and describing/retelling information supported by pictures/learning and using routine language for classroom communication; **3C** Speak using a variety of grammatical structures/sentence lengths and types/connecting words with increasing accuracy and ease; **3D** Speak using grade-level content area vocabulary/ new words and academic language proficiency; **3F** Give information/ ranging from using a limited high-frequency vocabulary to using abstract and content-based vocabulary during speaking; **3G** Express opinions, ideas, and feelings ranging from communicating short phrases to participating in discussions; **3H** Describe and explain with increasing specificity and detail; **3I** Adapt spoken language for formal and informal purposes

## Preparing a Multimedia Report

Review the common purposes for multimedia reports with students and guide them through completing the various activities listed on the page.

### Planning and Preproduction

Encourage students to ask questions about anything they don't understand. Suggest that they also review the Multimedia Report Checklist on SE page 441 for a clear idea of what a multimedia report should include.

 **TEKS** 10.15D

### Try It!

If some students have prepared research reports on the same topic, they may benefit from working together to create and present a multimedia report.

**TEKS** 10.15D

# Preparing a Multimedia Report

You can enhance an oral report by turning it into a multimedia report. In a multimedia report, graphics, images, video, and sound are used to help convey your ideas. They also appeal to the audience and help convey a distinctive point of view or voice.

Some of the common purposes for multimedia reports include the following: to entertain or to express a theme, observation, or point of view. Audiences could include classmates and teacher, audio/visual program members, Internet video viewers, or community or business leaders. Typical genres or formats include screening for classmates or younger students, online video or podcasts, oral presentations for a class, club, or business or community organizations.

## Planning and Preproduction

As you begin to plan your multimedia presentation, it is important to consider the following.

### Brainstorming

Consider the potential story resources that you have on hand, such as photographs or illustrations.

- **Gather technological tools.** A multimedia presentation depends upon technological resources. Look for these resources at home or at school.
- **Choose your visual format.** Think about which visual format lends itself best to your presentation.

### Developing an Outline

Write a brief synopsis or summary of your report. Refer to the outline you prepared for your first draft. Then create a story outline.

### Creating a Storyboard

Use your outline to create a storyboard—a visual script that includes descriptions of images, sounds, video, and audio clips. Think about what the audience will see as they hear the words.

### Writing a Script

Use your storyboard to create a script. The script will contain the narration that the audience will hear. Be sure to include notes about the graphics, images, and sound clips that you plan to include.

### Try It!

Use your research report to develop an outline and a storyboard. Then write a script for your multimedia presentation.

# Producing Your Presentation

The following information explains the technological steps involved in producing a multimedia presentation.

## Shoot, Scan and Import Images

If you plan to create new photographs or video, shoot in a well-lit location. Scan or import all images—old and new—into your editing software.

## Record Sound Effects and Audio

Choose a quiet place in which to record. Adjust the computer's input and output sound settings. Follow software instructions for recording sound. Perform a sound check and adjust the volume as necessary. Record your narration in parts. Stop, save, and play each part. Re-record if needed.

## Edit Video

Use the time line in your editing software to place images and sounds. Put compatible images and sound files together on the time line as you work through your presentation. As you work, edit images and sound for timing and pacing by replaying segments.

## Add Music and Graphics

Add music to your presentation to support concepts or to create mood. You can collect music files through Web sites that offer royalty-free music.

Add on-screen graphics such as titles, headings, captions, or credits to provide clarity.

### Try It!

Choose one of the media listed above and make a rough cut of your multimedia presentation.

## Indicating When to Present Visuals

Write notes in the margins of your note cards to indicate where a visual aid would be helpful. Isabel considered the following visuals for her presentation about the Aswan High Dam.

- Photos of Nile Valley before the dam
- A drawing of workers on the first dam
- A photo of the finished dam
- A chart comparing the pros and cons of the dam

List possible visual aids. Identify two or three visual aids you could use in your presentation. Explain how and when you would use each one.

*Making Presentations*

## Producing Your Presentation

Ensure that your school has the necessary technology for students to use. Prepare ahead of time if you need to sign up for a computer room or the school's audio/visual room for a number of days.

Review each step listed for producing the presentations and encourage students to ask questions about items that are unfamiliar to them.

TEKS 10.15D

### Try It!

Allow time for students to find or create graphics and sound effects to support their main ideas.

✔ DIFFERENTIATE INSTRUCTION

### Indicating When to Present Visuals

Have students work in pairs or groups to brainstorm and decide how and where to present visuals. Remind them to indicate the use of visuals in their note cards.

**TEKS** 10.15D Produce a multimedia presentation with graphics, images, and sound that conveys a point of view and appeals to a specific audience; **ELPS 1G** Demonstrate increasing ability to distinguish between formal/informal English and an increasing knowledge of when to use each one; **2I** Demonstrate listening comprehension in increasingly complex spoken language by collaborating with peers; **3B** Expand vocabulary by learning and using high-frequency words for identifying and describing/retelling information supported by pictures/learning and using routine language for classroom communication; **3E** Share information in cooperative learning interactions; **3F** Give information/ranging from using a limited high-frequency vocabulary to using abstract and content-based vocabulary during speaking; **3G** Express opinions, ideas, and feelings ranging from communicating short phrases to participating in discussions; **3H** Narrate/describe/explain with increasing specificity and detail; **3I** Adapt spoken language for formal and informal purposes; **3J** Respond orally to information presented in a variety of media to build and reinforce concept and language attainment

Direct students to the bulleted items and encourage them to create a checklist for

- revising,
- editing, and
- publishing.

**Try It!**

Encourage students to use the checklist they created (above) or the one on the following page as a guideline for discussion with their partner.

DIFFERENTIATE INSTRUCTION ↘

 TEKS 10.15D

---

 TEKS 10.15D

### Revising

As you revise your rough cut, consider how successfully you have combined words, images, sounds, and graphics to support your thesis statement.

The goal is to determine if you have achieved your purpose and effectively communicated your ideas and distinct point of view to your audience. The following questions will help guide your revision.

- Do the visuals support the thesis without distracting from my main points?
- Is the pacing appropriate?
- Is the presentation logically organized with a smooth flow of visuals?
- Have I used transitional techniques that continue the flow of ideas?
- Does the presentation hold the interest of the audience?
- Is my point of view distinct and clear?

### Editing

As you revise your rough cut, check for errors in conventions, especially in grammar. Listen carefully to your presentation to check for errors. Ask yourself the following questions.

- Have I used correct grammar throughout?
- Have I used verb tenses consistently and correctly?
- Do I have any other errors in conventions that detract from my presentation?

### Publishing

As you have revised and edited your presentation, it is time to hold a screening. Consider one of these ideas.

- Hold a classroom screening of your presentation.
- Host a home screening of your presentation for family and friends.
- Upload your presentation to the Internet.

### Try It!

View your rough cut with a partner. As you discuss the presentation, focus on the images, sounds, and graphics. Ask for concrete suggestions for improvement.

---

 **TEKS 10.15D** Produce a multimedia presentation with graphics, images, and sound that conveys a point of view and appeals to a specific audience

TEKS 10.15D

# Making Presentations

*Texas Traits* Use the following checklist to help you improve your multimedia report. When you can answer "yes" to all of the questions, your report is ready.

### Revising Checklist

## Focus and Coherence

_____ **1.** Is the controlling idea clearly expressed?

_____ **2.** Do all the graphics and other visual elements support the thesis statement?

_____ **3.** Have I chosen the best audio and video for my purpose and audience?

## Organization

_____ **4.** Do I state the topic in my introduction?

_____ **5.** Do I include the important main points in the body?

_____ **6.** Have I included transitions to ensure a smooth flow of ideas?

_____ **7.** Do I restate my focus in the conclusion?

## Development of Ideas

_____ **8.** Have I included the main ideas of my written report in my multimedia report?

_____ **9.** Have I effectively supported my main ideas with evidence?

_____ **10.** Do my visuals provide relevant details about the topic?

_____ **11.** Does my report flow smoothly from point to point?

## Voice

_____ **12.** Do I sound interested and enthusiastic?

_____ **13.** Is my voice clear, relaxed, and expressive?

_____ **14.** Do I convey a clear and distinct point of view?

Making Presentations

## Multimedia Report Checklist

Have students discuss ways to improve their multimedia reports with a partner. When students have completed the checklist and are ready to present their reports, schedule the time and day for them to present their reports to the class.

Make sure that each piece of technical equipment that students need to present their reports is in good working order and that students know how to operate it.

Students who ordinarily are not comfortable speaking to a group may find they enjoy presenting a multimedia report because the focus is on the technical features and style of the presentation.

TEKS 10.15D

---

### Differentiated Instruction: English Language Learners

ELPS 2G, 2H, 2I, 3B, 3E, 3F, 3G, 3H, 3J

| ELP Level **Beginning** | ELP Level **Intermediate** | ELP Level **Advanced/Advanced High** |
|---|---|---|
| Have students view their rough cut with their groups and use the checklist to discuss what elements to revise in their presentation. | Have students view their rough cut their partner and ask for and give suggestions about what elements to revise and how to revise them. | Have students ask for feedback from peers about their presentations and use the checklist to then revise their presentation. |

 **TEKS** **10.15D** Produce a multimedia presentation with graphics, images, and sound that conveys a point of view and appeals to a specific audience; **ELPS** **2G** Understand the general meaning, main points, and important details of spoken language/topics, languages, and contexts are familiar to unfamiliar; **2H** Understand implicit ideas and information in complex spoken language; **2I** Demonstrate listening comprehension in increasingly complex spoken language/following directions, responding to questions, and collaborating with peers; **3B** Expand vocabulary by learning and using routine language needed for classroom communication; **3E** Share information in cooperative learning interactions; **3F** Ask for and give information/ranging from using a limited high-frequency vocabulary to using abstract and content-based vocabulary during speaking; **3G** Express opinions and ideas ranging from communicating short phrases to participating in discussions; **3H** Describe and explain with increasing specificity and detail; **3J** Respond orally to information presented in a variety of media to build and reinforce concept and language attainment

# Writing Across the Curriculum

## Recording Your Learning (pages 443–448)

Students learn how to record their learning. They learn how to take classroom and reading notes, as well as how to keep a learning log.

## Writing in Science (pages 449–458)

This section covers writing that will help students write about what they learn in lectures and laboratories. They learn how to deepen their knowledge of the subject and share that understanding with others.

## Writing in Social Studies (pages 459–470)

This section models two types of writing students may be asked to complete in their social studies classes. It addresses the descriptive report and responding to a series of documents.

## Writing in Math (pages 471–482)

Although math focuses on numbers, equations, and so on, there are times when math students are called upon to read and write as well. This section shows students how to write a math article summary, how to create a written estimate, how to make a statistical argument, and how to respond to a math prompt.

## Writing in the Applied Sciences (pages 483–490)

In applied sciences, writing exercises often complement the hands-on part of a project. Writing can help students plan projects, remember procedures, reflect on successes and failures, and propose new projects for the future. This section models how writing empowers hands-on learning, as students write a descriptive essay and an essay of analysis.

## Writing in the Arts (pages 491–504)

Writing about the arts can help students capture the power of art. This section helps students write esays and create presentations about the arts.

## Writing in the Workplace (pages 505–513)

Most careers require some form of writing. Workplace communications have the same purpose: to get the reader's attention and prompt some action. This section provides basic information about workplace communication, including how to write a business letter, an e-mail message, and a description of work.

# Writing Across the Curriculum Reference Guide

| *Write Source Student Edition* | |
| --- | --- |
| **Writing in Science**<br>• Lab Report<br>• Science Script<br>• Science-Article Summary<br>• Other Forms of Writing in Science | 449–458 |
| **Writing in Social Studies**<br>• Descriptive Report<br>• Report on Social Studies Research | 459–470 |
| **Writing in Math**<br>• Article Summary<br>• Written Estimate<br>• Statistical Argument<br>• Response to a Math Prompt<br>• Other Forms of Writing in Math | 471–482 |
| **Writing in the Applied Sciences**<br>• Descriptive Essay<br>• Essay of Analysis<br>• Other Forms of Practical Writing | 483–490 |
| **Writing in the Arts**<br>• Response to an Art Prompt<br>• Research Report in the Arts<br>• Other Forms of Writing in the Arts | 491–504 |
| **Writing in the Workplace**<br>• Business Letter<br>• E-Mail Message<br>• Description of Work | 505–513 |

## Writing Focus

- Recording Your Learning
- Writing in Science
- Writing in Social Studies
- Writing in Math
- Writing in the Applied Sciences
- Writing in the Arts
- Writing in the Workplace

## Learning Language

Read aloud the definitions and descriptions as students follow along in their texts. Scaffold understanding by further explaining key words. Break down body language into its separate words, explaining that we express ideas, or "talk," with the way we use our bodies (pointing) and the faces we make (frowning). Then demonstrate the body language described in item 1 and invite volunteers to answer the question.

Organize students into pairs to ask and answer the remainder of the questions.

 **DIFFERENTIATE INSTRUCTION** ↘

**ELPS** 1E, 2C, 3B, 3D, 3E, 4G

## Minilessons

| **Recording Your Learning** | Journaling |
|---|---|

- **REVIEW** the basic and academic vocabulary you learned in the Learning Language activity.

- **RECORD** notes about the new words and ideas you learned by completing the activity.

**ELPS** 4G

 **ELPS 1D** Speak using learning strategies/request assistance, employ non-verbal cues, and convey ideas by defining or describing; **1E** Internalize new basic and academic language by using and reusing it/speaking; **2C** Learn new expressions and basic/academic vocabulary heard during classroom instruction/interactions; **3B** Expand vocabulary by learning and using routine language needed for classroom communication; **3D** Speak using grade-level content area vocabulary/new words and academic language proficiency; **3E** Share information in cooperative learning interactions; **4F** Use visual and contextual support to enhance and confirm understanding; **4G** Demonstrate comprehension of increasingly complex English/responding to questions and taking notes

---

**ELPS** 1E, 2C, 3B, 3D, 3E, 4G

www.hmheducation.com/tx/writesource

# Writing Across the Curriculum

## Writing Focus

## Learning Language

Work with a partner. Read the definitions below and share your answers to the questions that follow.

1. Body language includes posture and facial expressions.
   **If someone is pointing at another person and frowning, what might that body language tell you?**

2. A hypothesis is an explanation that accounts for a set of facts and that can be tested.
   **Why is it important to test a hypothesis?**

3. The term first-rate refers to something that is judged to be of high quality.
   **What are some examples of first-rate cars?**

---

**Differentiated Instruction:**
**English Language Learners**                              **ELPS** 1D, 4F

| ELP Level **Beginning** | ELP Level **Intermediate** | ELP Level **Advanced/Advanced High** |
|---|---|---|
| Have small groups choose ideas from a hat (*excited, hurried, frustrated*). Have groups use body language to express ideas as students guess the meanings of the actions. | Provide descriptions of body language (*raised eyebrows, looking at watch, hand over mouth*) and have pairs identify the meaning, using short phrases. | Have students create and present a brief mime skit in small groups. Have them use body language to express the main ideas. Allow students to share their skits with the class. |

# Recording Your Learning

Writing is central to all of your classes, and to your overall success in school and later in life. Writing about what you learn in your classes can deepen your knowledge of the subjects. Writing about each of your classes will give you a strong structure to help you remember what you have learned. Writing will allow you to share your understanding with others.

Learning to take good classroom notes is another skill that will help you in all your classes. Taking notes while you read will help increase your understanding of reading assignments and provide a framework for review. Finally, keeping a learning log will help you connect new material to material you already know.

This chapter explains ways for you to record your learning. The information will help you succeed in all your classes.

- **Taking Classroom Notes**
- **Taking Reading Notes**
- **Keeping a Learning Log**

"He listens well who takes notes." —Dante Alighieri

**443**

## Recording Your Learning

### Objectives
- learn to take classroom notes
- learn to take reading notes
- learn to keep a learning log

Recording your learning can take many forms. Explain to students that to begin, they must be able to identify and record the main ideas of classroom lectures and of reading assignments. Doing so will solidify their understanding and provide a basis for learning-log entries. Explain that learning logs provide students with an opportunity to review what they have learned as well as identify the questions they have about a topic.

## Resources

### Copy Masters (TE Appendix)

- 5 W's chart (TE p. 445)
- T-chart (TE p. 445)
- Details chart (TE p. 445)

## Taking Classroom Notes

Tell students that, in class, teachers often provide outlines—on the board or on transparencies—of their lectures. Students can use these outlines as a basis for their notes. Discuss other techniques that students use to help with taking classroom notes.

Review the sample notes on SE page 444, or project a two-column chart of notes for students to view and discuss. If possible, show sample notes that include questions. Remind students that when they review their notes, they should find and record the answers to any questions.

**DIFFERENTIATE INSTRUCTION ⬊**

⭐ **ELPS** 1C, 2E, 2G, 2H, 2I

---

⭐ ELPS 1C, 2C, 2E, 2G–2I

## Taking Classroom Notes

Taking good notes helps you focus on a lecture, remember key points, and understand new material. Here are a few tips on taking good notes in class.

### Before you take notes . . .

- **Set up your notes.** Use a three-ring binder so you can add handouts to your notes, or use a notebook with a folder in the back.
- **Date each entry** in your notebook and write down the topic.
- **Organize each page.** Consider using the two-column format, with lecture information on the left and questions on the right.

### As you take notes . . .

- **Write information your teacher puts on the board** or on an overhead. This is often the most important material.
- **Use your own words** as much as possible.
- **Write questions** in the second column of your notebook.
- **Draw pictures.** Use quick sketches to capture complex ideas.

### After you've taken notes . . .

- **Re-read your notes** after class. Add information to make the notes clear.
- **Research the answers** to any questions you wrote.
- **Review your notes** before the next class to be ready for discussions.
- **Study your notes** to prepare for quizzes and tests.

The date and topic are noted.

Main points are underlined.

Dashes set off details.

March 6, 2010—Simple Machines

Simple machines make work easier.
– Use force (push or pull) to move heavy loads.
– Convert low forces into high forces or vice versa.
Compound or complex machine = Two or more simple machines together

Examples of simple machines:
– Inclined plane
– Wedge
– Screw
– Wheel

force
– Lever
– Pulley
force
fulcrum

---

### Differentiated Instruction: Struggling Learners

Introduce the 5 W's and H to students. Explain that when they listen to a lecture, they should record ideas about who, what, when, where, why, and how. Write these key questions on the board, and then have partners practice note-taking on your discussion about Taking Classroom Notes. Tell them to try to answer each question in their notes.

⭐ **ELPS** 2C, 2I

---

⭐ **ELPS 1C** Use strategic learning techniques to acquire basic and grade-level vocabulary; **2C** Learn new expressions and basic/academic vocabulary heard during classroom instruction/interactions; **2E** Use visual support to enhance and confirm understanding of increasingly complex spoken language; **2G** Understand the general meaning, main points, and important details of spoken language/topics are familiar to unfamiliar; **2H** Understand information in increasingly complex spoken language; **2I** Demonstrate listening comprehension in increasingly complex spoken language by responding to questions and taking notes

ELPS 4C, 4D, 4G, 4I

Recording Your Learning  445

# Taking Reading Notes

**Note taking** can increase your understanding of reading assignments. Here are some tips on taking reading notes.

### Before you take notes . . .

- **Write the date, chapter, book, and topic** before each entry.
- **Organize each page.** Try a two-column format with wide margins. Put your notes on the left and your thoughts and questions on the right.
- **Quickly skim the assigned text.** Read the title, introduction, headings, and summaries. Look at the graphics and charts.

### As you take notes . . .

- **Write down headings or subtopics.** Note important details under each. Record any questions or thoughts that you have.
- **Use your own words** to help you understand the material.
- **Summarize graphics.** Make a sketch, note the main ideas, or create your own graphic with notes.
- **List vocabulary words.** You can look up definitions later.

### After you've taken notes . . .

- **Review your notes.** Then write down any other questions you may have. Find answers and add them to your notes.

---

Questions and thoughts are listed in the second column.

Sept. 29, 2010: Exploring Chemistry, chapter 2, section 1
Periodic Table of the Elements*

\* The periodic table is a way of classifying elements: a universal language for chemistry.

Q: How did the periodic table start?

Elements
— sorted by rows and columns
— organized by similarities in their properties
— ordered by increasing atomic numbers
— grouped in columns
— are liquid, gas, or solid

A: Russian professor Dmitry Mendelyev pioneered a chart to organize elements.

---

### Try It!

Take notes as you complete your next reading assignment.

---

## Taking Reading Notes

Suggest that as students take reading notes, they pause at the end of each paragraph to restate the topic sentence in their own words and summarize the materials. Tell students that when they complete a reading assignment, they should take the time to write a brief summary paragraph, including only main ideas.

Explore with students how graphic organizers can be used to take reading notes. Provide reproducible organizers, such as the 5 W's chart, the T-chart, and the details chart (see TE Appendix) and have students use each on upcoming reading assignments. Discuss how each organizer can be effectively used for taking notes on certain kinds of reading materials.

### Try It!

Have students take notes on SE pages 444–445 or other instruction within the text, if they don't have other reading assignments to complete.

ELPS 4C, 4D, 4G, 4I

---

## Differentiated Instruction: English Language Learners

ELPS 3E, 4D. 4G

| ELP Level **Beginning** | ELP Level **Intermediate** | ELP Level **Advanced/Advanced High** |
|---|---|---|
| Provide an example of reading notes in a T-chart, with key ideas in the left column and questions/comments in the right as students attempt the **Try It!** activity. | Organize students into pairs and provide them with an outline of the reading assignment. Tell them to take notes on the text under the correct headings you have provided. | Have partners take notes and write a summary on a reading assignment of one or two paragraphs. Invite partners to discuss the readings and try to answer one another's questions. |

ELPS **3E** Share information in cooperative learning interactions; **4C** Comprehend vocabulary used in written classroom materials; **4D** Use prereading supports to enhance comprehension of written text/graphic organizers, illustrations, and topic-related vocabulary; **4G** Demonstrate comprehension of increasingly complex English/summarizing material, responding to questions, and taking notes; **4I** Demonstrate comprehension by employing and expanding basic reading skills/understanding of supporting ideas and details, summarizing text, and distinguishing main ideas from details

## Keeping a Learning Log

Emphasize the idea that a learning log contains a student's *personal* responses to information he or she is studying, including making connections to prior knowledge and experience. Remind students that their classroom and reading notes will contain facts and explanations that need not be repeated in their learning logs except when they are useful for explaining and clarifying their ideas. Learning logs can focus on:

- trying to understand complicated information,
- forming new insights about learning material, and
- considering how topics apply to daily life.

 ELPS 1A, 2H, 2I

### Tip

Encourage students to try various techniques in their learning logs, including freewriting, making lists, drawing pictures, using graphic organizers, and so on. DIFFERENTIATE INSTRUCTION ›

### Try It!

If students have trouble beginning a learning-log entry, suggest that they try one or more of the following sentence starters:

- The most important thing I learned today about _____ is . . .
- I was amazed to learn about _____
- The hardest thing for me to understand about _____ is . . .

ELPS 4G, 4I

---

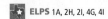 ELPS 1A, 2H, 2I, 4G, 4I

# Keeping a Learning Log

A **learning log** is a specialized journal that lets you reflect on the material you are learning in class. In a learning log, you write about new concepts and connect them to previous knowledge or experiences. Here are some tips for keeping a learning log.

### Before you make an entry . . .

- **Set up your learning log** in a binder or notebook. If you use the same binder for different classes, divide it into sections.
- **Write the topic and date of each entry** so you can find it easily.
- **Leave wide margins** for writing thoughts and questions that occur to you later.

### As you make an entry . . .

- **Summarize key concepts** and develop meaningful comparisons.
- **Apply new ideas** to what you already know.
- **Write down any questions** you have about the subject.
- **Predict how the new ideas** may prove helpful in the future.
- **Write about** what the ideas mean to you.

### After you've made an entry . . .

- **Review your entries** so you can better understand what you are learning.
- **Research any questions** you have and write down the answers.
- **Continue your reflections** by writing new observations or questions in the margins.

### Tip

Most topics are like packed suitcases. You can grab the topic by the handle and carry it around without really understanding what's inside it. Writing helps you "unpack" a complicated topic. What are the main ideas? How do these ideas relate to each other? What do these ideas mean to me? When you write answers to questions such as these, you make learning personal—and you begin to understand what is inside the topic you are carrying around.

### Try It!

Follow the guidelines above to set up your own learning log. When you have a few minutes during or after class, write about the day's topic in order to "unpack the ideas."

---

**ELPS 1A** Use prior knowledge and experiences to understand meanings; **2H** Understand information in increasingly complex spoken language; **2I** Demonstrate listening comprehension in increasingly complex spoken language by summarizing spoken messages and taking notes; **4G** Demonstrate comprehension of increasingly complex English/summarizing material, responding to questions, and taking notes; **4I** Demonstrate comprehension by employing basic reading skills

★ ELPS 3I

Recording Your Learning  **447**

# Learning-Log Entries

Here are sample learning-log entries for three classes. The student thinks about the ideas discussed in class, analyzes them, and tries to apply them to current issues and to his own life.

## Sample Learning Log: Chemistry

> *After recording the date and topic, the student reviews ideas from his class.*

> *He writes questions about the topic in the margin.*

> *He reflects on the complex issues.*

> *He finds answers to his questions.*

### February 18—Chemical Pollution

The class discussion today was about chemicals in the environment. Mrs. Marshall said that fuels, pesticides, paints, cleaners, and other chemicals can cause a lot of harm.

Sometimes natural disasters are to blame. After Hurricane Katrina, many chemicals mixed with floodwaters. When the water drained away, chemicals got into the soil and air. Chlorine, benzene, and gasoline caused huge problems.

Sometimes ignorance is the problem. People pour oil or chemicals into street drains and pollute the water. They dump paint cans in the woods and burn plastics that pollute the air. These actions are as much a problem as natural disasters.

**Q:** How can polluted soil be cleaned up?

**A:** The EPA Web site said contaminated soil and sediment would have to be removed, and clean fill would have to be added.

### February 22—Exxon Valdez

Mrs. Marshall showed a documentary about the Exxon Valdez oil spill, which occurred when a tanker ran aground in Alaska. Biologists continue to study the long-term effects on area habitats.

Cleaning up after an accident or a disaster is important, but it's more important to prevent these things from happening. One way is to switch to alternative energy sources like wind power.

Another way is to use "green chemistry" to develop environmentally friendly compounds. For example, in Australia, researchers use the genes of pests to make pesticides that target only one creature. Also, natural, nonpolluting cleansers like lemon juice (citric acid) and vinegar (acetic acid) work as well as chemicals do.

**Q:** What can the government do about spills?

**A:** Oil doesn't dissolve in water, allowing some spills to be contained. Police and fire departments have "haz-mat" teams for hazardous material spills.

## Learning-Log Entries

Point out that the writer identifies important ideas and poses interesting questions in the sample entries. Set aside 5 to 10 minutes at the end of class or after students complete an assignment for creating entries. Suggest that students review their entries later to informally ask and answer questions.

★ ELPS 3I, 5G

---

## Differentiated Instruction: English Language Learners

★ ELPS 2E, 2G

| ELP Level **Beginning** | ELP Level **Intermediate** | ELP Level **Advanced/Advanced High** |
|---|---|---|
| Fill a suitcase or bag with items related to a topic such as a science book, a magnifying glass, and a picture of an insect. Have students explain how items are related. | Simplify the sentence starters to require one- or two-word answers: *I learned about ____ . I think ____ is____* . Guide students as they complete the sentences. | Have students work with partners to create a learning log by taking notes on the information and then taking turns recording questions/ comments in their log. |

**ELPS 2E** Use visual support to enhance and confirm understanding of increasingly complex spoken language; **2G** Understand the main points of spoken language/topics are familiar to unfamiliar; **3I** Adapt spoken language for informal purposes; **5G** Describe and explain with increasing specificity and detail/writing

## Learning-Log Entries

Review the instruction and the sample learning log entries. Point out how the use of diagrams can help clarify ideas and concepts.

⭐ ELPS 4I

## Try It!

Suggest that students make a habit of recording information in their learning logs at the end of each class.

---

 ELPS 4I

## Learning-Log Entries

As with the chemistry sample, the student dated these social studies and math entries, listed the topics, summarized concepts, and made connections.

### Sample Learning Log: Social Studies

| The date and topic are given. | November 11, 2010    Veterans Day |
|---|---|

Today we learned the history of Veterans Day. Uncle James is a veteran, but until today I never gave the holiday any thought.

*New information is reviewed.*

The holiday was established to honor soldiers who died in World War I, but later it was changed to honor all soldiers. Talking about the holiday made me think more about the men and women who have made sacrifices to defend our country.

*A personal connection is made.*

It also made me curious about how my town celebrated the first Veterans Day. I think I'll do some research about that topic and write about it for my *descriptive report assignment*.

### Sample Learning Log: Math

November 3, 2010  Pythagorean Theorem

A Greek named Pythagoras developed a formula to calculate the lengths of the sides of a right triangle (a triangle with an angle of 90°).

leg — hypotenuse (across from the right angle)

leg

Pythagorean Theorem Formula: $a^2 + b^2 = c^2$
"c" is the side across from right angle (hypotenuse).

Another way to state the formula:
(length one leg)$^2$ + (length other leg)$^2$ = (length of hypotenuse)$^2$

Which side is a, and which side is b?

c
a
b

Or is it like this?

b
c
a

Either one—as long as c is the hypotenuse

### Try It!

Try to update your entries and review your class notes every day.

---

## Differentiated Instruction: English Language Learners

⭐ ELPS 1A, 4D, 4F

| ELP Level **Beginning** | ELP Level **Intermediate** | ELP Level **Advanced/Advanced High** |
|---|---|---|
| Return students to SE page 442 to review the definition of *hypotheses*. Introduce the cognates *observación* and *conclusión* to help students understand the text. | Have students begin a glossary of science terms (*hypotheses*, *observations*, and *laboratories*). Have pairs use a dictionary or science book to record definitions in their glossary. | Organize students into small groups. Have them discuss their prior knowledge and experience with writing in science to prepare them for the upcoming writing tasks. |

 **ELPS 1A** Use prior knowledge and experiences to understand meanings; **4D** Use prereading supports to enhance comprehension of written text/graphic organizers, illustrations, and topic-related vocabulary; **4F** Use support from peers/teachers to enhance and confirm understanding; **4I** Demonstrate comprehension by employing and expanding basic reading skills/understanding of supporting ideas and details, summarizing text, and distinguishing main ideas from details

449

# Writing in Science

Writing is central to science. It allows scientists to express their hypotheses, to record their observations, and to communicate their conclusions. In that way, writing gives structure to the scientific method.

Science classes—whether biology, chemistry, physics, geology, astronomy, or life sciences—take you on a journey of discovery into the natural world. Writing lets you chart your course.

This chapter covers the types of writing that will help you in your science classes. Writing about what you learn in lectures and laboratories can deepen your own knowledge of the subject and allow you to share your understanding with others.

- ■ **Writing Guidelines: Lab Report**
- ■ **Writing Guidelines: Science Script**
- ■ **Writing Guidelines: Science-Article Summary**
- ■ **Other Forms of Writing in Science**

"Science is organized knowledge."
—Herbert Spencer

## Objectives

- • learn writing guidelines for lab reports, science scripts, and science-article summaries
- • learn about other forms of writing in science

Writing in science includes writing narrative passages as well as recording data and statistics. Explain to students that guidelines for writing language arts essays transfer to other disciplines. Just as summaries of stories or news articles include only main ideas, so do science-article summaries, for example. Explain that one of the major hurdles of writing in science is learning the terminology of the discipline. ✔ DIFFERENTIATE INSTRUCTION

## Resources

### Copy Masters (TE Appendix)

- • Sensory chart (TE p. 450)
- • T-chart (TE p. 456)

## Writing Guidelines
### Lab Report

Read the introduction and then point out the headings that name the steps in the writing process. Explain that even in science, writers follow these steps. Then review each of the bulleted ideas under the steps. Consider providing a reproducible sensory chart (see TE Appendix) for students to use in recording their observations. **DIFFERENTIATE INSTRUCTION ↘**

Answer any questions students might have about the process. Suggest that students make their own checklists using the questions about the writing traits included in the "Improve your writing" bullet point.

Show students examples of analogies related to science topics. As a class, discuss how the use of analogies and metaphors can help explain difficult concepts. Be sure to also discuss the limitations of these rhetorical devices.

**TEKS** 10.13A, 10.13B, 10.15A(ii), 10.15A(iii), 10.15A(v); **ELPS** 5G

---

**450**

**TEKS** 10.13A, 10.13B, 10.15A(ii), 10.15A(iii), 10.15A(v)
**ELPS** 5G

## Writing Guidelines Lab Report

A **lab report** outlines the scientific method by stating a hypothesis, setting up a method for testing it, recording observations, and offering conclusions.

### Prewriting

- **Select a topic and plan the experiment.** Follow your teacher's assignment. Use a range of strategies (if given a choice) to select a topic. If you have selected the experiment, use a range of strategies to plan it, gather materials, and be sure you understand each step.
- **Follow the proper format.** Use the lab-report format provided by your teacher or follow the lab-report model on page **451**.

### Drafting

- **Lay the groundwork.** State the purpose (what the experiment is designed to prove), list materials, and note variables. Then write your hypothesis—what you expect the experiment will prove. Organize your ideas in a sustained, logical manner. Use rhetorical devices to engage the reader.
- **Describe procedures.** Use specific language to make each step clear.
- **Record your observations.** Describe what you see, hear, smell, and so forth, in chronological order exactly as it happens. Be sure to use transitions and include only relevant evidence and details.
- **Write a conclusion.** Tell whether your hypothesis was correct or not. Explain why.

### Revising

- **Improve your writing.** Review your first draft for *focus and coherence, organization, development of ideas,* and *voice.* Ask these questions: *Have I clearly stated my hypothesis and conclusion? Have I described the experiment in chronological order? Have I included enough details and relevant evidence?*
- **Improve your style.** Check your *word choice* and *sentence fluency.* Ask: *Have I correctly used and explained scientific terms? Have I used transitions to connect my ideas?*

### Editing

- **Check for conventions and prepare a final copy.** Proofread and correct errors in grammar, sentence structure, mechanics, and spelling. Make a neat final copy of your lab report.

---

### Differentiated Instruction: Struggling Learners

Provide guidance for using different strategies to identify a topic for the lab report. Give students the choice of free writing, concept webbing, or listing. When students finish this stage in the process, have them meet in small groups or with partners to discuss questions they can pose about the listed topics. Once they have decided on a question that is answerable through an experiment, they can then proceed to plan the experiment with partners.

**TEKS** 10.13A; **ELPS** 3E, 5G

---

**TEKS** **10.13A** Plan a first draft by determining topics through a range of strategies and developing a thesis or idea; **10.13B** Structure ideas in a sustained way; **10.15A(ii)** Write an analytical essay that includes rhetorical devices; **10.15A(iii)** Write an analytical essay that includes an idea or thesis; **10.15A(v)** Write an analytical essay that includes relevant evidence and details; **ELPS** **3E** Share information in cooperative learning interactions; **5G** Explain with increasing specificity and detail/writing

Science

# Lab Report

This lab report describes an experiment on suspensions and emulsions.

## Sample Lab Report

### Suspensions and Emulsions

The **beginning** states the purpose, the materials, the variables, and the hypothesis.

**Purpose:** To find out which liquids combine and which do not

**Materials:** 20 ml oil, 20 ml vinegar, egg yolk, two large beakers

**Variables:** Ingredients

**Hypothesis:** Oil and vinegar won't mix. When shaken up together, they will form a suspension, but the two parts will separate again. The egg yolk will mix with the vinegar but not with the oil.

The well-organized **middle** outlines the procedure and records observations. Details are relevant to the hypothesis.

**Procedure:** In the first step, I poured 10 ml of oil into a beaker and added 10 ml of vinegar. Then I shook the liquids and waited for several minutes. I observed the results. In the second step, I combined 10 ml of oil, 10 ml of vinegar, and an egg yolk and shook the liquids. Again, I observed the results.

**Observations:** When I mixed the oil and vinegar together, the oil and vinegar looked as though they had dissolved. However, minutes later, the oil and vinegar separated. When I combined the oil, vinegar, and egg yolk and shook the beaker, the liquid didn't separate.

The **conclusion** tells whether the hypothesis was right or not, and why.

**Conclusions:** My hypothesis that oil and vinegar would not mix was right. They are immiscible. The oil and vinegar made a suspension, but then they separated again.

However, my hypothesis about the egg yolk was wrong. I thought it would mix with the vinegar but not with the oil. The yolk actually mixed with both substances and made them join.

The yolk must be an emulsifier, which allows immiscible substances to blend. The egg yolk, vinegar, and oil form a colloid, which is a stable system of particles dispersed in something else.

## Try It!

Perform your science experiment. Describe the experiment and analyze the results completely in a lab report. Make you sure have a clearly stated hypothesis, relevant details and evidence, and a conclusion.

---

## Lab Report

Read aloud the Sample Lab Report, stopping to read the side notes that apply to each section. Point out the format that includes the heads *Purpose*, *Materials*, *Variables*, *Hypothesis*, *Procedure*, *Observations*, and *Conclusions*.

✔ DIFFERENTIATE INSTRUCTION

## Try It!

Remind students that their lab reports must present ideas in a sustained way while using relevant evidence and well-chosen details to support their conclusions.

TEKS 10.13B, 10.15A(i), 10.15(v); ELPS 5G

---

## Differentiated Instruction: English Language Learners

ELPS 3E, 4D, 4F, 5F, 5G

| ELP Level **Beginning** | ELP Level **Intermediate** | ELP Level **Advanced/Advanced High** |
| --- | --- | --- |
| To increase comprehension, identify each heading and help students define the word. Use synonyms, such as *purpose/reason/goal*, or cognates, such as *material*. | Have students continue building their science terms glossary. Make sure partners begin by using context clues within the report to determine meaning. | Connect writing a lab report to writing a procedural text. Tell students to be sure to order the descriptions of their procedures in sequential order using clear transitions. |

TEKS **10.13B** Structure ideas in a sustained way; **10.15A(i)** Write an analytical essay that includes a concluding paragraph; **10.15A(v)** Write an analytical essay that includes relevant evidence and details; ELPS **3E** Share information in cooperative learning interactions; **4D** Use prereading supports to enhance comprehension of written text/graphic organizers, illustrations, and topic-related vocabulary; **4F** Use support from peers/teachers to develop vocabulary; **5F** Write using a variety of grade-appropriate connecting words in increasingly accurate ways; **5G** Describe and explain with increasing specificity and detail/writing

## Writing Guidelines
### Science Script

Read the introduction aloud and explain to students that writing a script for a presentation will help students focus their deliveries and ensure that they have included all information about their experiments. As needed, guide students through the steps in the writing process. **DIFFERENTIATE INSTRUCTION ↘**

After students have drafted their scripts, use a peer response process to suggest revisions. The questions associated with the "Review your writing" bullet point can be used to create peer response sheets.

⭐ **TEKS** 10.13A, 10.13B, 10.14C, 10.15D; **ELPS** 5G

---

**452**

⭐ **TEKS** 10.13A, 10.13B, 10.14C, 10.15D
**ELPS** 5G

# Writing Guidelines Science Script

You may be asked to give a presentation for a science topic, such as a famous discovery, and it might be most effectively presented in the form of a play. You can be creative in your use of setting and dialogue, but remember to keep your script as true as possible to the discovery or moment being dramatized.

## Prewriting

- **Select a topic.** As you consider topics, keep your audience in mind. Choose an event or discovery that will engage your audience.
- **Gather details.** Research your topic. Remember that your script must have a theme. In your research, find answers to the *who, what, when, where,* and *how* questions. Look for discussions or conflicts about scientific findings. Note events that will add interest and make your characters come alive.
- **Outline your script.** List characters, conflict, and resolution. Decide on organization. Usually scripts are chronological, but to provide background information, you may decide to include a flashback. Remember to establish theme, mood, and tone.

## Drafting

- **Connect your ideas.** Remember your audience and purpose. Your script should be engaging and present factual information. Try to make your dialogue realistic. Characters will convey action, so they need to come alive for your audience. Include details that support your focus and help the audience relate to the characters and topic.

## Revising

- **Review your writing.** Check your draft for *focus and coherence, organization, development of ideas,* and *voice.* Ask: *Can the audience recognize the topic and follow the dialogue? Do I have a clear beginning and ending? Is the script appropriately organized? Do the characters come alive? Is the dialogue authentic?*
- **Improve your style.** Check your *word choice* and *sentence fluency.* Ask these questions: *Have I correctly defined and used scientific terms? Is my language appropriate for the characters?*

## Editing

- **Check for conventions.** Proofread for errors in grammar, sentence structure, mechanics, and spelling. Make a neat final copy.

---

⭐ **TEKS** **10.13A** Plan a first draft by determining topics through a range of strategies and developing a thesis or idea; **10.13B** Structure ideas in a sustained way; **10.14C** Write a script with an explicit/implicit theme and details that contribute to the mood and tone; **10.15D** Produce a multimedia presentation with graphics, images, and sound that conveys a point of view and appeals to a specific audience; **ELPS** **3E** Share information in cooperative learning interactions; **5G** Explain with increasing specificity and detail/writing

---

### Differentiated Instruction: Struggling Learners

Organize students into pairs to revise their scripts. Before students meet with their partners, suggest that they take time to read the script aloud, making any corrections needed to help the script sound natural. Then have partners take turns reading aloud and making suggestions for revisions.

⭐ **ELPS** 3E

Science

# Sample Science Script

In a science script, you have some room to be creative, but you must present factual information about events and the people involved. Remember that the action will be carried through dialogue between characters. The script below dramatizes the discovery of penicillin by Alexander Fleming in 1928.

---

**FLEMING DISCOVERS PENICILLIN**

[SCENE: laboratory, London, 1928; lab table, stacks of petri dishes]

[CHARACTERS: Alexander Fleming; colleague Merlin Price]

PRICE: Dr. Fleming, glad to see you back in your lab, but it looks terrible. I don't know how you can find anything in this mess. Trying to straighten it up after your vacation?

FLEMING: Price, old chap, look at this! Who would have thought that a blue mold would have started to grow in this? It is completely different than anything that has grown in my lab before.

PRICE: Fleming, I find molds rather disgusting. Honestly, all molds look the same to me, but you always seem to notice details. In all this mess, things are bound to grow! But you are a careful scientist and an acute observer. I don't think that bit of blue mold would have caught anyone else's eye. You treat research like a game!

FLEMING: Why not play in the lab and have some fun? I am going to keep studying this mold. You never know—it might lead to something big.

PRICE: Like a great discovery and the Nobel Prize?

FLEMING (laughing): That's pretty unlikely, but I am going to try to grow some more and see what happens. I have a spot of meat broth here, some good "mold juice" that will preserve this bit of mold and let it continue to grow. If I can grow enough, I will run it through a few tests and track the results. It almost looks as if this mold might inhibit the growth of bacteria. Lots more work to do, but it might prove to be worth a bit of study.

---

## Try It!

Using the sample above, write a science script about a famous discovery or moment in science. Try to make your characters come alive.

## Sample Science Script

Read the introduction and the science script aloud as students follow along in their texts. Point out the clearly stated introduction and focus, as well as the formal yet easily understood language of the script. Remind students that if they use the script to give their presentations, they need to maintain eye contact with the audience as much as possible and not simply read from the script.

Direct students to notice the use of the first person pronouns (I, me, my). Explain that the use of first person is appropriate in this formal writing because the student is explaining his or her own experiences in conducting an experiment.

## Try It!

Tell students that their task is to turn their lab reports into science scripts. Explain that they will need to use a formal tone yet present information that the audience will need to comprehend ideas. For example, they should define or provide examples of scientific terminology. ✓ DIFFERENTIATE INSTRUCTION

TEKS 10.14C; ELPS 5G

---

**Differentiated Instruction:**
**English Language Learners**

ELPS 3I, 5B, 5G

| **ELP Level** Beginning | **ELP Level** Intermediate | **ELP Level** Advanced/Advanced High |
|---|---|---|
| Provide frames for students to write a script: *Today I will talk about my experiment with ____. My purpose was to find out ____.* Continue the frames for students to copy. | Give examples of informal language: *Hey guys! I did this great science experiment! I'm gonna talk about my project.* Have students adapt the sentences to formal language. | Have students work with partners to create scripts, using headings in the sample to organize their ideas. Remind students to include specific details to support conclusions. |

TEKS **10.14C** Write a script with an explicit/implicit theme and details that contribute to the mood and tone; **ELPS 3I** Adapt spoken language for formal purposes; **5B** Write using content-based grade-level vocabulary; **5G** Describe and explain with increasing specificity and detail/writing

## Delivering Your Presentation

### Controlling Your Voice

Discuss with the class how volume, tone, and pace in a spoken presentation contribute to setting the mood and tone for the presentation. Consider having students with some acting experience read the same paragraph varying volume, tone, and pace. Then discuss how these differences affected how the audience connected to the material in the paragraph.

### Considering Your Body Language

Discuss with students their concerns about public speaking. In addition to the tips given on SE page 454, add tips that you have learned from your own public speaking experiences.

### Try It!

Consider having each student conduct a full "dress rehearsal" in front of two classmates before delivering the oral presentation to the entire class.

- Speakers should apply all of the guidelines for voice control and body language listed on this page in their run-throughs.
- The first listener should focus on the speaker's volume, tone, and pace.
- The other listener should focus on the speaker's body language.
- After a speaker has delivered the presentation, the two listeners can offer feedback and advice.
- Students can alternate roles so that all three students have a chance to deliver their speeches. **DIFFERENTIATE INSTRUCTION ⟍**

**TEKS** 10.14C, 10.15D; **ELPS** 3G, 3H, 3I

✱ For additional guidelines and tips for speaking and listening, see SE pages 515–516.

---

# Delivering Your Presentation

When you deliver an oral presentation in science, even one written as a play, concentrate on your voice and body language. This will convey a mood and set a definite tone. This will also convey your point of view about the topic. Voice quality and body language communicate as much as your words do.

You may also decide to turn your script into a multimedia presentation. As you incorporate graphics, images, and sound into your report, it is still important to consider your audience, mood, and tone.

## Controlling Your Voice

*Volume, tone,* and *pace* are three aspects of your formal speaking voice. If you can control these three aspects of voice, your listeners will be able to follow your ideas.

- **Volume** is the loudness of your voice. Imagine that you are speaking to someone in the back of the room and adjust your volume accordingly.
- **Tone** expresses your feelings. Be enthusiastic about your topic and let your voice show that.
- **Pace** is the speed at which you speak. For the most part, speak at a relaxed pace.

## Considering Your Body Language

Your body language (*posture, gestures,* and *facial expressions*) plays an important role during a speech. Follow the suggestions given below to communicate effectively.

- **Assume a straight but relaxed posture.** This tells the audience that you are confident and prepared.
- **Pause before you begin.** Take a deep breath and relax.
- **Look at your audience.** Try to look toward every section of the room at least once during your presentation.
- **Think about what you are saying** and let your facial expressions reflect your true feelings.
- **Point to your visual aids** or use natural gestures to make a point.

### Try It!

Deliver your presentation. As you deliver your presentation or script, control your voice and exhibit the appropriate body language and posture.

---

 **TEKS** **10.14C** Write a script with an explicit/implicit theme and details that contribute to the mood and tone; **10.15D** Produce a multimedia presentation with graphics, images, and sound that conveys a point of view and appeals to a specific audience; **ELPS** **3G** Express ideas ranging from communicating short phrases to participating in discussions; **3H** Describe and explain with increasing specificity and detail; **3I** Adapt spoken language for formal purposes

Science

# Preparing a Multimedia Report

You can enhance an oral science report by including electronic aids such as slides, graphics, images, and sound. In order to use these effectively, you must plan exactly where each slide or sound bite will fit into your presentation.

In addition, keep in mind that your graphics, images, and sounds must be appropriate for the topic and audience. Your graphics, images, and sounds must also appeal to your audience and convey a distinct point of view.

Here is a planning script for a multimedia presentation on an experiment about suspensions and emulsions. What will be *seen* appears in the "Video" column, and what will be *heard* appears in the "Audio" column. Note that the directions for the speaker are general, not the actual words to be spoken.

## Planning Script

| Video | Audio |
|---|---|
| 1. **Title Screen:** "Suspensions and Emulsions" | 1. SPEAKER: Introduction and Hypothesis |
| 2. **Slide 2:** Materials on lab bench: oil, vinegar, beakers, egg yolk in dish | 2. SPEAKER: Explains materials needed for experiment |
| 3. **Slide 3:** Student mixing oil and vinegar into beaker | 3. SPEAKER: Explains procedure for first step<br>SOUND: Liquids being poured into beaker |
| 4. **Slide 4:** Student shaking the liquids | 4. SPEAKER: Continues explanation of procedure, revisits hypothesis<br>SOUND: Liquids being shaken and/or upbeat music |
| 5. **Slide 5:** Student mixing and shaking oil, vinegar, and egg yolk. | 5. SPEAKER: Explains materials used, revisits hypothesis |
| 6. **Slide 6:** Student examining results | 6. SPEAKER: Explains results<br>SOUND: suspenseful music |
| 7. **Slide 7:** Student examining both beakers | 7. SPEAKER: Presents conclusions |

## Try It!

Follow the guidelines above and add graphics, images, and sounds to your science report to create a multimedia presentation.

## Preparing a Multimedia Report

If possible, play an example of a complete multimedia presentation to help students conceptualize the task. Then review the planning script with students, allowing them to ask questions that arise.

 TEKS 10.14C, 10.15D

### Try It!

If multimedia equipment is not available, have students complete a planning script instead. If it is available, have students work with partners to improve their presentations with added graphics, images, and sounds. Schedule time for each student to present his or her multimedia report to the class.

TEKS **10.14C** Write a script with an explicit/implicit theme and details that contribute to the mood and tone; **10.15D** Produce a multimedia presentation with graphics, images, and sound that conveys a point of view and appeals to a specific audience; **ELPS 2I** Demonstrate listening comprehension in increasingly complex spoken language by collaborating with peers; **3E** Share information in cooperative learning interactions; **3G** Express ideas ranging from communicating short phrases to participating in discussions; **3H** Describe and explain with increasing specificity and detail

## Writing Guidelines
### Science-Article Summary

Remind students that a summary is a brief description of an article's main ideas. If necessary, review main ideas and supporting details before students begin the writing process. **DIFFERENTIATE INSTRUCTION ↘**

Review the bullet points under each step of the writing process. Consider supplying a reproducible T-chart (see TE Appendix) on which students write the main idea of the article at the top, the important details in the left column, and any questions they have about the article or its details in the right column.

Remind students of the importance of revising their draft paragraphs. Revisions should focus on improvements in focus and coherence, organization, development of ideas, and voice. Editing for all writing conventions is a highly important step, so continue providing editing checklists for students to use as they edit their work.

**⭐ TEKS** 10.13A, 10.13B, 10.13C, 10.13D, 10.17C, 10.18A, 10.18B(ii), 10.18B(iii), 10.19, 10.21C; **ELPS** 4G , 4I, 5C, 5G

---

## Writing Guidelines Science-Article Summary

You may be asked to write a summary of a supplied science article in a timed test. Here are some guidelines to help you summarize science articles.

### Prewriting

- **Find an article.** Browse through science magazines looking for articles that relate to your class work. Page through your science textbook or visit reliable Internet sites such as *www.nasa.gov.*
- **Read the article.** Quickly read the article you select to get its overall message. Then reread it more carefully for details.
- **Focus on the summary.** Write down the main idea of the article.
- **Gather details.** Select only the most important details that support the main idea of the article. Your summary should be no more than one-third the length of the original article.

### Drafting

- **Connect your ideas.** Write your topic sentence, add details to support it. Organize your thoughts logically. Create a closing sentence that wraps up your summary.
- **Paraphrase information.** Use your own words. Avoid plagiarism.

### Revising

- **Improve your writing.** Review your first draft for *focus and coherence, organization, development of ideas,* and *voice.* Ask these questions: *Have I identified the main idea of the article? Have I included only important details? Have I used a topic sentence, body sentences, and a closing sentence?*
- **Improve your style.** Check on your *word choice* and *sentence fluency.* Ask these questions: *Have I used transitions so that my summary reads smoothly? Have I used rhetorical devices to convey my meaning? Have I put the ideas in my own words?*

### Editing

- **Check for conventions.** Proofread your revised summary for errors in grammar, sentence structure, capitalization, punctuation, and spelling. Be sure that you have used commas correctly in phrases, clauses, and contrasting expressions. Be sure to use quotation marks and dashes correctly.
- **Prepare a final copy.** Make a neat final copy of your summary.

---

**⭐ TEKS** **10.13A** Plan a first draft by determining topics through a range of strategies; **10.13B** Structure ideas in a sustained and persuasive way/develop drafts in timed situations that include transitions and rhetorical devices; **10.13C** Revise drafts to improve style; **10.13D** Edit drafts for grammar, mechanics, and spelling; **10.17C** Use a variety of correctly structured sentences; **10.18A** Use conventions of capitalization; **10.18B(ii)** Use commas in nonrestrictive phrases and in clauses; **10.18B(iii)** Use dashes to emphasize parenthetical information; **10.19** Spell correctly using resources to determine and check correct spelling; **10.21C** Summarize researched information; **ELPS** **4G** Demonstrate comprehension of increasingly complex English/summarizing material; **4I** Demonstrate comprehension by employing and expanding basic reading skills/understanding of supporting ideas and details, summarizing text, and distinguishing main ideas from details; **5C** Spell familiar words with increasing accuracy; **5G** Describe and explain with increasing specificity and detail/writing

## Science-Article Summary

The following professional article from a science news magazine is summarized in the student paragraph below.

### Tapping the Earth's Heat

Scientists and environmentalists are increasingly concerned about the limited supply of fossil fuels and the impact of fuel emissions on global warming. As a result, scientists and inventors are looking for alternative sources of energy. One such low-cost, renewable resource—geothermal energy—may be right under our feet.

Geothermal energy has a long history. Early Roman builders and engineers tapped into underground hot springs to help heat homes. Pioneers used underground caves, cooler than the outside air in summer, to store ice and perishable products.

Today, geothermal energy can be used even in areas where there are no hot springs or caves. Modern geothermal systems take advantage of the earth's relatively constant temperature a few feet below ground. Depending on latitude, temperatures underground range from 45 to 75 degrees Fahrenheit.

Geothermal heating and cooling systems exchange heat with the earth rather than with outside air and thus require less energy. These systems often pipe air or water underground (or underwater), where a heat exchanger raises or lowers the temperature. Then a pump transfers the heat from the earth into the building in winter and discharges excess heat from the building into the ground in summer. In summer, the excess heat may also be used to heat the water in the water heater.

Geothermal heating systems may initially cost more to install than fossil fuel systems. However, according to the Environmental Protection Agency (EPA), they save money in operating and maintenance costs. They are also environmentally clean and cost effective.

### Sample Summary

**Topic Sentence**

**Body Sentences**

**Closing Sentence**

> **Geothermal Energy**
>
> *Geothermal energy can be a low-cost, renewable energy source to heat or cool homes using the earth's own temperature.* Geothermal energy works by drawing heat from the earth or underground water using underground pipes and a heat pump. Because the earth's underground temperature is pretty constant, the underground air or water doesn't have to be heated or cooled as much. **That's how geothermal systems can save money and conserve energy.**

### Try It!

Write a summary of an assigned article or one of your own choosing in the time allotted. Follow the writing guidelines on the previous page.

## Science-Article Summary

Before students write their own summaries, review the guidelines on SE page 456, the sample article, and the sample summary.

### Try It!

Provide students with a selection of suitable science articles to use for the **Try It!** activity.

TEKS 10.13B; ELPS 4G, 4I, 5G

---

TEKS **10.13B** Structure ideas in a sustained way; ELPS **4G** Demonstrate comprehension of increasingly complex English/ summarizing material, responding to questions, and taking notes; **4I** Demonstrate comprehension by employing and expanding basic reading skills/understanding of supporting ideas and details, summarizing text, and distinguishing main ideas from details; **4J** Demonstrate comprehension and expand reading skills by employing inferential skills/ predicting, making connections between ideas, drawing conclusions from text, and finding supporting evidence; **5G** Describe and explain with increasing specificity and detail/writing

## Other Forms of Writing in Science

Review the other forms of writing in science, and explain to students that each form requires them to complete all stages of the writing process—prewriting, drafting, revising, editing, and publishing.

**458**

# Other Forms of Writing in Science

### Cause-Effect Essay

*Chemistry*—Explain the effect of automobile emissions on the atmosphere. Then discuss the effect that hydrogen-powered vehicles would have on the environment.

### Classification Essay

*Geology, Earth Science,* or *Chemistry*—Write a classification essay describing three types of igneous rocks. Describe their appearance, hardness, and composition, and tell how each type of rock is formed.

### Definition Essay

*Biology or Earth Sciences*—Write a definition essay in which you thoroughly explain a concept that you have just learned about. Examine the concept from four or five different points of view.

### Process Essay

*Chemistry or Geology*—Write a process essay describing how scientists create synthetic diamonds. Discuss how synthetic diamonds are used.

### Opposing-Views Essay

*Physics, Biology,* or *Chemistry*—Write an opposing-views essay about a controversial proposal, such as replacing gasoline with ethanol (made from corn). Explain both sides of the argument.

### Position Essay

*Any Science*—Read about controversial new theories in biology, earth-space science, physics, chemistry, or any other area of science that interests you. Choose one theory and write a position essay that provides support for the theory and defends it against opposing viewpoints.

## Differentiated Instruction: English Language Learners

ELPS 1A, 4D, 4F

| ELP Level **Beginning** | ELP Level **Intermediate** | ELP Level **Advanced/Advanced High** |
| --- | --- | --- |
| Before introducing *Writing in Social Studies*, preteach content-area vocabulary: *societies, diversity, survey, criteria.* Read aloud the introduction as students follow along. | Write *analyze* on the board. Explain that to analyze is to break something into parts, then explain how the parts work together. Prepare students for writing by sharing an analysis. | Organize students into groups; have them discuss their prior experiences with writing in social studies to prepare them for the upcoming writing tasks. |

**ELPS 1A** Use prior knowledge and experiences to understand meanings; **4D** Use prereading supports to enhance comprehension of written text/graphic organizers, illustrations, and topic-related vocabulary; **4F** Use support from peers/teachers to read grade-appropriate content area text and develop background knowledge

459

# Writing in Social Studies

No two human beings are the same, and no two human societies are either. Social studies focuses on this diversity. As a student of social studies, you may need to survey a variety of documents (speeches, graphs, maps, photos, reports, and so on) and respond to them in writing. You'll need to analyze the documents, summarize and organize the information, and create a response that satisfies the criteria of the assignment.

This chapter models two types of writing you may be asked to do in your social studies classes. It addresses writing a descriptive report and responding to a series of documents.

- **Writing Guidelines: Descriptive Report**
- **Writing Guidelines: Report on Social Studies Research**

"History will be kind to me, for
I intend to write it."
—Winston Churchill

## Writing in Social Studies

### Objective

- learn and apply writing guidelines to a descriptive report and a report on social studies research

The lessons on the following pages provide samples of the kinds of writing students might do in social studies. Assigning these forms of writing will depend on:

- the skill level of your students,
- the subject matter they are studying in different social studies courses, and
- the writing goals of your school, district, or state.

Point out to students that they already have some familiarity with writing in social studies. Research reports are a required form of writing in many social studies classes.

**↙ DIFFERENTIATE INSTRUCTION**

### Resources

**Copy Masters (TE Appendix)**

- Sensory chart (TE p. 460)
- Time line (TE p. 460)

## Writing Guidelines
### Descriptive Report

Remind students that selecting a strong topic that interests them is an important first step in writing a descriptive report. Students could begin by listing events, eras, and places that interest them in a three-column chart. They can conduct some preliminary research to narrow their selections.

Discuss the different graphic organizers that students could use during prewriting to gather details for a descriptive report. Distribute photocopies of the reproducible sensory chart and time line (see TE Appendix).

■ Have students use the sensory chart to note any sensory details related to their topics.

■ If their details should be arranged chronologically, students can use the time line.

■ If the details work best arranged spatially, encourage them to draw a diagram of the object or place and then write the details on the diagram in the appropriate places.

**DIFFERENTIATE INSTRUCTION ↘**

Discuss the revising and editing process students will use for this report. Have partners review revising and editing checklists they have used for other writing assignments. Have them adapt or expand these checklists to create a list that both can use for this writing assignment.

**TEKS** 10.13A, 10.13B, 10.13C, 10.13D, 10.17C, 10.18A, 10.18B(ii), 10.19; **ELPS** 5C, 5G

---

 **TEKS** 10.13A–10.13D, 10.17C, 10.18A, 10.18B(ii), 10.19
**ELPS** 5C, 5G

## Writing Guidelines Descriptive Report

Often in social studies, you will need to describe an event or a location. Use the following guidelines to create a descriptive report.

### Prewriting

■ **Select a topic.** A topic may be assigned by your teacher. If not, use a range of strategies to choose a specific event, time, or place —something you would like to know more about.

■ **Gather details.** Learn all you can about your topic. Read books and Web-site articles. Study maps, graphs, and charts. This information will help you write a clear and interesting essay.

■ **Outline your essay.** Organize your notes logically to put related details together. If you are describing an event, consider organizing your details in chronological order. If you are describing a place, consider organizing your details by order of location.

### Drafting

■ **Connect your ideas.** Introduce your topic. Capture your reader's attention with a few interesting details and then write your thesis statement. In the middle paragraphs, describe your topic, one main point at a time. Write an ending that sums up your thesis.

### Revising

■ **Improve your writing.** Review your first draft for *focus and coherence, organization, development of ideas,* and *voice.* Make sure that you have included relevant details that help the reader clearly understand what you are describing.

■ **Improve your style.** Check for *transitions, rhetorical devices, sentence fluency,* and *word choice.* Ask: *Have I correctly used and explained new terms? Do my sentences flow smoothly?*

### Editing

■ **Check for conventions.** Proofread and correct any errors in grammar, sentence structure, capitalization, punctuation, and spelling. Use quotation marks to indicate irony or sarcasm.

■ **Prepare a final copy.** Make a neat final copy of your descriptive report. Proofread this copy and make corrections before sharing it.

---

 **TEKS** 10.13A Plan a first draft by determining topics through a range of strategies and developing a thesis or idea; **10.13B** Structure ideas in a sustained way; **10.13C** Revise drafts to improve style and word choice; **10.13D** Edit drafts for grammar, mechanics, and spelling; **10.17C** Use a variety of correctly structured sentences; **10.18A** Use conventions of capitalization; **10.18B(ii)** Use quotation marks to indicate sarcasm and irony; **10.19** Spell correctly using resources to determine and check correct spelling; **ELPS 5C** Spell familiar words with increasing accuracy; **5G** Describe with increasing specificity and detail/writing

# Descriptive Report

In this essay, a student writer describes the first Veterans Day celebrated in his hometown.

## Sample Report

### Morrisville's First Veterans Day

On November 11, 1921, ceremonies in Washington, Paris, and London recognized the sacrifice of soldiers killed in World War I. On that same day, residents of Morrisville also honored their fallen soldiers. That was the first Armistice Day, a holiday that later became Veterans Day.

Armistice Day got its name from the treaty that ended World War I. The day honored the veterans who had lost their lives in the First World War. According to the records of the Carle County Clerk's Office, 83 men from Morrisville served in the United States Expeditionary Force during World War I. Of those 83 men, 14 died serving their country. In a town as small as Morrisville, most people knew at least a few if not all of those men, so it's little wonder that the whole town turned out for the memorial.

Photographs in the archives of the Morrisville Historical Society show the buildings on the town's main street draped with red, white, and blue bunting. Similar decorations covered the horse-drawn wagons and the few automobiles present. The people who gathered in Parish Park, 1,200 according to the *Morrisville Daily Examiner,* dressed in their finest clothing.

The focus of the day's ceremonies was the dedication of the sculpture *Fallen Heroes.* The granite carving, created by Morrisville sculptor Henry O'Brien, depicts a World War I soldier carrying a wounded comrade. The names of Morrisville citizens who died in the war are carved in the statue's base.

Morrisville's mayor, a 50-year-old businessman named Andrew Harrington, dedicated the statue with a stirring speech. In his talk, he called for the citizens to remember "those noble men of our town who set aside the cares of farm, home, and family to serve the greater good of their nation and of the world." He then asked the crowd to observe a minute of silence in honor of the fallen.

In 1954, the holiday was changed to Veterans Day, in memory of U.S. soldiers who died in all wars. Even so, reminders of the first Armistice Day remain in Parish Park. Though worn by time and weather, Henry O'Brien's sculpture still stands, as do a row of memorial oak trees planted by the town's children that day. They still provide shade to park visitors, and a place to pause and remember.

## Descriptive Report

After students read the descriptive report, have them comment on it. Use the following questions to guide the discussion:

- *How does the writer go about describing the celebration?*
  - ☐ In the opening, he provides background about Veterans Day.
  - ☐ The middle paragraphs describe how the town looked and the events that took place.
- *What types of transitions does the writer use?*
  - ☐ He uses transitions showing time (*On November 11, then, In 1954*) for the history of Veterans Day and the description of the events at the celebration.
- *How does the closing paragraph relate to the opening one?*
  - ☐ It explains how the change from Armistice Day to Veterans Day—introduced in the first paragraph—affected the meaning of the celebration.

✱ For more about transitions, see SE pages 628–629.

## Differentiated Instruction: English Language Learners

ELPS 2I, 3E, 5B, 5G

| ELP Level **Beginning** | ELP Level **Intermediate** | ELP Level **Advanced/Advanced High** |
|---|---|---|
| Remind students that sensory details appeal to sight, hearing, taste, touch, and smell. Write sensory words on the board; work with students to put them in a sensory chart. | Have students work with partners to plan a descriptive report. Once partners agree on a topic, they can work together to identify sensory details to include in the chart. | Have students complete sensory charts independently, then work with partners to discuss details they chose and add/subtract details before organizing. |
| Use page 625. | Use page 625. | Use page 625. |

ELPS **2I** Demonstrate listening comprehension in increasingly complex spoken language by collaborating with peers; **3E** Share information in cooperative learning interactions; **5B** Write using newly acquired basic and content-based grade-level vocabulary; **5G** Explain with increasing specificity and detail/writing

## Writing Guidelines
### Report on Social Studies Research

Read the introduction and clarify any unfamiliar terms for students, such as *authoritative sources*. If necessary, explain that research reports are longer than regular essays and that they require students to make valid inferences about the topic and support or defend those inferences with reliable evidence. Remind students that good research also explores the debates and issues related to the topic.

### Selecting a Topic

Read aloud the instruction. Tell students that as they brainstorm, they might list ideas, free write, or draw a concept web.

 **TEKS** 10.13A

### Forming a Research Question

Tell students that the answers to their research questions will be the thesis or controlling idea of the report. **DIFFERENTIATE INSTRUCTION ↘**

**TEKS** 10.20A

### Forming a Research Plan

Explain that a research plan not only includes the sources of information students will investigate—such as the Internet or the library—but also the time line for their work. Suggest that students chart their research plan on a calendar, assigning a specific portion of research to each day.

**TEKS** 10.20B

**TEKS** **10.13A** Plan a first draft by determining topics through a range of strategies and developing a thesis or idea; **10.20A** Brainstorm, consult with others, and decide on a research topic/formulate a research question to the research topic; **10.20B** Formulate a plan for research on a complex, multi-faceted topic; **ELPS** **3E** Share information in cooperative learning interactions

 **TEKS** 10.13A, 10.20A, 10.20B

## Writing Guidelines Report on Social Studies Research

In social studies classes, you will often be asked to write a research report on a particular topic or time period. You may be assigned a large, general topic and be asked to narrow it down to a specific focus. Your job is to conduct research and to write an extended essay that thoroughly covers the topic.

The first step in the process is planning and prewriting. In this phase, you will select a topic, form a research question, develop a plan for your research, and conduct research using reliable, authoritative sources.

### Selecting a Topic

- **Brainstorm.** Think freely about all the social studies topics that interest you. Make a list of your ideas.
- **Consult with others.** When you have finished your own brainstorming, ask classmates or your teacher what they think about the ideas on your list. They may be able to add ideas and point out ideas that will not work. Listen openly and carefully to what they have to say.
- **Choose your topic.** After you have consulted with others and reviewed or revised your list, choose a topic. Make sure that your topic is broad enough to write a report, but not so broad that you cannot cover it adequately.

### Forming a Research Question

- **Narrow your topic.** Remember that your social studies topic must not be so broad that you cannot cover it. One of the strategies that you might use in your planning is to create a general categories list or a cluster diagram about the broad, general topic. Put asterisks next to the particular topics that interest you the most.
- **Conduct initial research.** Use the categories that interest you the most and conduct initial research to learn more about each one.
- **Formulate a major research question.** Using your initial research, formulate a question that will be the focus of your essay.

### Forming a Research Plan

- **Gather information.** As you conduct your research, focus on your major research question. Consult a variety of sources that are valid, reliable, and accurate.

### Differentiated Instruction: Struggling Learners

Assist students as they narrow their topics and formulate major research questions. Write *When? Where? Why? Who? What? How?* on the board. Have students work with partners to develop three questions about their chosen topics beginning with one of these question words. Then have partners discuss the scope of the research questions, determining whether they need to narrow or broaden the question.

**TEKS** 10.20A; **ELPS** 3E

## Following Your Research Plan

- **Compile your data.** One way to organize the data you have collected is to create a gathering grid like the one shown here. On one side of the grid, list questions you have about the topic. In the other columns, list sources where you found answers to the questions. For answers that are too long to fit on a grid, use note cards.

| ASWAN DAM | Building Big: Dams (video) | The Aswan High Dam (book) | "Aswan Dam" (Web site) | "Deciphering Greater Cairo" (magazine article) |
|---|---|---|---|---|
| 1. Why was the Aswan Dam built? | To provide year-round irrigation | | | British cotton mill owners wanted more cotton. |
| 2. How was the dam built? | | See note card #1. | All local material Rock: 28.6 million cubic yards Sand: 20 million cubic yards Clay: 4 million cubic yards | |
| 3. What are the effects of the dam? | Doubled agricultural production Damage to environment | | Lake Nasser holds 1.99 trillion cubic yards of water. The lake is 6 miles wide and 310 miles long. | See note card #2. |

- **Identify and research major issues and debates in your field of inquiry.** As you conduct your research, be sure to find valid, reliable, and accurate sources that address both sides of the major issues and debates that involve your topic.

- **Cite your sources.** As you gather information, keep track of the sources you have used so that you can correctly cite them in your essay. Follow the style guide recommended by your teacher to cite and format your sources.

## Paraphrasing, Summarizing, and Using Quotations

- **Paraphrasing means to put ideas that you find during your research into your own words.** You must give credit to the source of the ideas.

- **Summarizing means to present the most important ideas from a longer piece of writing.** You must also give credit to the source of the ideas.

- **Using quotations means using the exact words of a source to add authority to your paper.** Enclose those words in quotation marks and give credit to the source.

**Social Studies**

### Following Your Research Plan

Tell students that they might choose to use note cards or record their notes electronically. Review good note-taking practices. Then remind students of the importance of citing sources. Provide example citations following the MLA style.

TEKS 10.21A, 10.21B, 10.21C; ELPS 4G

### Paraphrasing, Summarizing, and Using Quotations

Point out that even when students use their own words to present ideas they found during research, they still need to accurately cite the sources of information. Review paraphrasing and summarizing with students, reminding them that they need to change more than just a few words from an original sentence. They must change the structure as well as some of the vocabulary. ✔DIFFERENTIATE INSTRUCTION

TEKS 10.21C

---

**Differentiated Instruction: English Language Learners**    ELPS 3E, 4G, 5G

| ELP Level Beginning | ELP Level Intermediate | ELP Level Advanced/Advanced High |
|---|---|---|
| Write on the board: *Instead of celebrating all American soldiers' lives, Armistice Day celebrated the heroes of World War I.* Have students work with partners to paraphrase the idea. | Have students work with partners to read and summarize each paragraph of the sample descriptive report on SE page 461. | Distribute an article to students. Have partners work together to summarize the entire article, using their own words to express the main ideas. |

TEKS **10.21A** Follow the research plan to compile data that identifies major issues and debates; **10.21B** Organize information from multiple sources to create graphics and forms; **10.21C** Paraphrase, summarize, quote, and accurately cite researched information; ELPS **3E** Share information in cooperative learning interactions; **4G** Demonstrate comprehension of increasingly complex English/summarizing material; **5G** Describe and explain with increasing specificity and detail/writing

## Prewriting

### Developing Your Thesis Statement

Read the introduction aloud, pausing at the end of each subhead to provide further direction. Have students review their major research questions and consider whether the information they have found addresses these questions. Tell students that their thesis statements, or controlling ideas, should answer their research questions. Explain that once they have a thesis, they can use that as a basis for evaluation of the relevance of the research. After evaluating authority of sources and critiquing the research process, students can fine-tune their theses and use the revised version as a basis for their outlines. **DIFFERENTIATE INSTRUCTION ↘**

**TEKS** 10.13A, 10.13B, 10.22A, 10.22B, 10.22C; **ELPS** 4J, 4K

---

## Prewriting

### Developing Your Thesis Statement

- **Write your initial thesis statement.** With your initial research complete, you can write a controlling idea, or focus, for your report. Using your controlling idea, write an initial thesis statement for your report.

- **Evaluate the relevance of your research.** With your thesis statement in mind, look back at your research. Is it all relevant to the thesis statement? Have your sources identified and addressed major issues and debates within your topic?

- **Evaluate your sources for reliability, accuracy, and validity.** Check to make sure that you used unbiased, well-respected works and authors as the sources for your research. Examine each source for authority and objectivity. You may need to do more research to replace sources that do not meet these criteria.

- **Critique your research process.** Evaluate your research process at each step. Make any changes, adjustments, or revisions that are needed.

- **Review and revise your initial thesis statement.** With your research complete and evaluated for relevance, accuracy, and validity, you should review your initial thesis statement. Revise it as needed so that it reflects the major research question, and then, if needed, write a new thesis statement.

- **Create an outline.** Use your thesis statement and your research to create an outline for your report. It will help you organize your details in a logical fashion. Also note if and where you might include graphics or visuals to enhance your report.

---

**TEKS** **10.13A** Plan a first draft by developing a thesis or idea; **10.13B** Structure ideas in a sustained way; **10.22A** Modify the major research question to refocus the research plan; **10.22B** Evaluate the relevance of information to the topic/determine the reliability, validity, and accuracy of sources by examining their objectivity and authority; **10.22C** Critique the research process to implement changes as need is identified; **ELPS** **3E** Share information in cooperative learning interactions; **4J** Demonstrate comprehension and expand reading skills by employing inferential skills/predicting, making connections between ideas, drawing conclusions from text, and finding supporting evidence; **4K** Demonstrate comprehension and expand reading skills by employing analytical skills/evaluating written information and performing critical analyses; **5G** Describe and explain with increasing specificity and detail/writing

### Differentiated Instruction: Struggling Learners

Before students formulate their theses, review the criteria of a thesis statement. Remind students that a thesis is not a simple restatement of information. Instead, it must express the writer's interpretation of information. Have students develop their thesis by completing this frame: *In my opinion, ____.* After students complete the frame about their topics, have them work with partners to revise the thesis to eliminate references to *my*.

**ELPS** 3E, 5G

★ **TEKS** 10.13B,
10.23A–10.23C, 10.23E

## Drafting

- **Write your introductory paragraph.** Write an introductory paragraph that contains background information about your topic and clearly presents your thesis statement.

- **Develop your middle paragraphs in a logical order.** Follow or revise your outline so that your essay progresses in a logical way for the reader.

- **Provide relevant, reliable, and accurate details and valid evidence to support the thesis statement.**

- **Clearly state your point of view, based on the research that you have done.**

- **As appropriate, include graphs, charts, illustrations, and other visuals to emphasize or demonstrate your points.** Each visual you include should enhance your meaning and help the reader understand the concepts and points you are making.

- **Connect your ideas with transitions so that your ideas flow smoothly from one to the next.**

- **Follow an approved style guide.** Be sure to cite and format sources correctly within your report and in your works-cited page.

Social Studies

## Drafting

### Developing the First Draft

Read aloud the instruction. Remind students that as they draft, they should be primarily concerned with getting the information on the page. Once they have completed drafting, they will have the opportunity to revisit their work to refine ideas, reorganize information, and correct errors in conventions. ✔**DIFFERENTIATE INSTRUCTION**

Discuss the importance of point of view in research writing. Their theses, the report's organization, and the supports given in the body of the report for the theses contribute to a distinctive point of view.

Show students a report with and without graphics. Have students evaluate the usefulness of graphics in communicating information in descriptive reports.

★ **TEKS** 10.13B, 10.23A, 10.23B, 10.23C, 10.23E

---

### Differentiated Instruction:
### English Language Learners

🔊 **ELPS** 3E, 5G

| **ELP Level Beginning** | **ELP Level Intermediate** | **ELP Level Advanced/Advanced High** |
| --- | --- | --- |
| Work with each student to formulate a thesis statement, using the Struggling Learners activity on TE page 464. Add support to each student's frame to allow them to express ideas clearly. | Define *authority*. Explain that for a work to have authority, it must be from an expert. Tell students to look at URLs for authority: *.edu* and *.gov* are often reputable. | Draw an outline on the board with the labels *Thesis, Main reason, Supporting detail*. Explain how an outline links to a thesis. Have students work in pairs to complete outlines. |

★ **TEKS** **10.13B** Structure ideas in a sustained way; **10.23A** Synthesize research into a presentation in support of a clear thesis and related claims; **10.23B** Synthesize research into a presentation that reflects a progression of ideas and a stated point of view; **10.23C** Synthesize research into a presentation that uses graphics and illustrations to explain concepts; **10.23E** Synthesize research into a presentation that uses a style manual to document sources and format written materials; **ELPS** **3E** Share information in cooperative learning interactions; **5G** Describe and explain with increasing specificity and detail/ writing

## Revising

### Improving Your Writing

Read aloud the instruction and questions. Clarify any confusing terms or ideas. Tell students to read through their essays independently and address any issues in their writing related to the questions. Then have students exchange papers with partners and read their partners' papers, asking and answering the same questions. Finally, have partners reconvene to discuss their findings. Students can then make the suggested revisions.

As a class, discuss the research process. Focus on how the prewriting efforts, especially the development of thesis statements and the research efforts aided students during drafting and revising. Have students freewrite in their journals changes they would like to make in planning and organizing their research for future reports.

**TEKS** 10.13C, 10.22C, 10.23D; **ELPS** 5F

## Editing

### Checking Your Writing

Read aloud the instruction and provide minilessons on troublesome grammar, mechanics, or spelling rules. Repeat the peer conferencing process above, only this time students should check their own and then their partners' papers for errors in conventions. Provide access to dictionaries and grammar handbooks. **DIFFERENTIATE INSTRUCTION** ↘

**TEKS** 10.13D, 10.17C, 10.18A, 10.18B,10.19; **ELPS** 5C

---

## Revising: Improving Your Writing

Review and revise your essay for *focus and coherence, organization, development of ideas,* and *voice.* Use these questions to guide you.

- Is your thesis statement clear to the reader?
- Does your conclusion tie back to the thesis statement and leave the reader with a final thought?
- Do your ideas follow a logical pattern so that the essay forms a cohesive whole?
- Have you used transitions so that ideas flow smoothly from paragraph to paragraph and within paragraphs?
- Does each paragraph have a topic sentence, and are the topic sentences supported with valid, accurate evidence and well-chosen details?
- Have you used a variety of evaluative tools to examine the quality of the research?
- Do you sound knowledgeable and interested in the topic?
- Have you used a more formal tone that is appropriate for the audience and the genre?

## Editing: Checking Your Writing

Check for errors in grammar, sentence structure, mechanics, and spelling. Correct as needed.

- Correct any errors in grammar, including verb tenses. Try to use the active voice whenever possible.
- Check your sentence structure and sentence fluency. Try to use a variety of sentence types.
- Check all your mechanics, especially use of commas, quotations marks, and end punctuation. Make sure that proper nouns are correctly capitalized,
- Recheck your spelling to make sure that all words, especially technical terms and specialized vocabulary, are spelled correctly.

---

**TEKS** **10.13C** Revise drafts/improve word choice and sentence variety and rethink how well the genre has been addressed; **10.13D** Edit drafts for grammar, mechanics, and spelling; **10.17C** Use a variety of correctly structured sentences; **10.18A** Use conventions of capitalization; **10.18B** Use correct punctuation marks; **10.19** Spell correctly using resources to determine and check correct spelling; **10.22C** Critique the research process to implement changes as need is identified; **10.23D** Synthesize research into a presentation that uses evaluative tools to examine the research; **ELPS 5C** Spell familiar words/employ spelling patterns and rules with increasing accuracy; **5F** Write using a variety of grade-appropriate sentence lengths, patterns, and connecting words/combine in increasingly accurate ways

⭐ **TEKS** 10.13B, 10.23A, 10.23B, 10.23E

## Research Report

After thinking carefully about the writing prompt assigned by the teacher, which was to describe one major current global problem and the ways it is being addressed today, one student wrote the following report about the Grameen Bank and microloans.

### Sample Report

> **Thesis statement is clearly stated and background information is provided.**

> **Sources are correctly cited following the style guide.**

> **Transitions are used. Writer uses logical organizational pattern and shows evidence to support thesis.**

#### Ending Poverty One Cent at a Time

In 1976, economics professor Muhammad Yunus was trying to figure out how to reduce poverty in the village near his university in Bangladesh. He spoke to a woman who was so poor that she and her family lived on two cents a day. She made bamboo stools, but had to borrow money from a trader for the material she needed. To pay back the money she owed, she had to sell the stools to the trader, who paid her the two cents for her labor. The trader could then sell the stools for any profit he could make.

Yunus asked the woman how much she needed to buy her own materials. The amount came out to 22 cents. If she could afford her own materials, she could sell the stools herself and make more money. Yunus was shocked that such a small amount might be all a person needed to escape a life of poverty. He realized that because she did not have the cash to buy her raw materials, "Her life was a form of bonded labor, or slavery. The trader made sure certain that he paid Sufiya a price that barely covered the cost of the materials and was just enough to keep her alive. She could not break free of her exploitative relationship with him" (Yunus 48).

The next day, Yunus asked a student to help find other people in the village who had the same sort of arrangement as Sufiya, the woman who made the stools. They found 42 people. The total amount borrowed by all these people came out to less than $27. Yunus donated the amount himself. He hoped that by lending the villagers the money, they could earn more for their labor. They wouldn't have to pay back a trader or moneylender and could sell their products to anyone. It would give the family more money for food and other necessities and maybe help them break out of their cycle of poverty.

## Research Report

Tell students that they will be reading a sample research report. They can use this report as a paradigm for their own writing. Then read each paragraph and stop to review the side notes and connect the ideas in these notes to the text of the report.

⭐ **TEKS** 10.13B, 10.23A, 10.23B, 10.23E; **ELPS** 4J

---

### Differentiated Instruction: English Language Learners

⭐ **ELPS** 5C, 5D, 5E

| ELP Level **Beginning** | ELP Level **Intermediate** | ELP Level **Advanced/Advanced High** |
|---|---|---|
| To help students with their editing, review common spelling rules, such as *i before e except after c.* Have students check their papers for all *ie* and *ei* spellings and make any needed corrections. | Review past, present, and future tenses. Remind students that they need to be careful to use tenses correctly; then, have students check tenses in their reports. | Review active and passive voice. Write: *I opened the door. The door was opened by me.* Discuss how the focus changes. Have students change passive to active tense where possible in their own writing. |

⭐ **TEKS** **10.13B** Structure ideas in a sustained way; **10.23A** Synthesize research into a presentation in support of a clear thesis and related claims; **10.23B** Synthesize research into a presentation that reflects a progression of ideas; **10.23E** Synthesize research into a presentation that uses a style manual to document sources and format written materials; **ELPS** **4J** Demonstrate comprehension and expand reading skills by employing inferential skills/predicting, making connections between ideas, drawing conclusions from text, and finding supporting evidence; **5C** Spell familiar words/employ spelling patterns and rules with increasing accuracy; **5D** Edit writing for standard grammar and usage/subject-verb agreement and appropriate verb tenses; **5E** Employ increasingly complex grammatical structures in content area writing such as using correct verbs, tenses, and pronouns/possessive case/negatives and contractions

Continue reading the research report as students follow along in the text. Review the side notes and connect the ideas to the research report writing.

Have students identify the topic sentence in each paragraph and discuss how it relates to the report's thesis.

⭐ **TEKS** 10.13B, 10.23A, 10.23B

Eventually, Yunus's idea led to his creation of the Grameen Bank in Bangladesh. Grameen means "rural" or "village" in the Bengali language. Unlike other banks, the Grameen Bank provided only small loans, or microloans. Borrowers, who were usually illiterate, didn't need to fill out paperwork or prove that they could repay the loan. It was all based on trust. People were expected to pay back the loans in very small amounts every week, and the full amount had to be repaid in a year. This made repayment easier and even allowed people to put some money away to save.

> Writer continues to synthesize research and develop controlling idea with specific details.

Yunus added another important element to his banking system that also helped make it successful. In order to get loans from Grameen, borrowers had to form a group with five members. These small groups would then be part of a larger "center" composed of up to eight groups that met weekly in the village with a bank worker. Yunus and his colleagues realized that a group acted as support for its members. It also put peer pressure on each member to follow the rules of the program. "Because the group approves the loan request of each member, the group assumes moral responsibility for the loan. If any member of the group gets into trouble, the group usually comes forward to help" (Yunus 63).

> Writer addresses major issues involved in the research topic and continues to cite research.

Despite some trouble recruiting the first borrowers, Grameen's model was soon successful. More and more people began to take out small loans, and almost one hundred percent of the loans were repaid on time. Many borrowers ended up taking out more loans for bigger amounts as their businesses grew. Grameen also found that lending to women was more likely to lead to success. In Bangladesh, women were second-class citizens and the loans were their only chance to make a better life for themselves and their children. Today, over ninety-five percent of Grameen loans are made to women. The group found that "women are more comfortable with the group lending model, are more likely to repay their loans, and are more likely to direct their earnings to providing better clothing, housing, nutrition, health care and education to their families" ("Grameen Lending Model").

> Writer uses precise data to support topic sentence.

The Grameen Bank eventually spread to millions of borrowers and thousands of villages in Bangladesh. Its success led to interest from other countries. In the late 1980s and

⭐ **TEKS** **10.13B** Structure ideas in a sustained way; **10.23A** Synthesize research into a presentation in support of a clear thesis and related claims; **10.23B** Synthesize research into a presentation that reflects a progression of ideas

Social Studies

early 1990s, Grameen-style programs began in Malaysia and the Philippines. By the mid 1990s, more programs were developed in India, Nepal, Vietnam, and China. Latin American and Africa started their own programs too. Even the United States became interested.

In 1985, when Bill Clinton was governor of Arkansas, he invited Yunus to discuss ways that he could create new economic opportunities for the low-income people in the state. Yunus helped set up a program called the Good Faith Fund. Very slowly, the new program grew in Arkansas and was adopted in other parts of the United States. At first, it only was aimed at rural people, but some of Grameen's supporters wanted to take the program to urban areas.

Chicago was the first city to start a micro-credit group, called the Full Circle Fund (FCF). Many social activists, community leaders, and economists didn't think that the Grameen model would work in this environment. "They claimed that Chicagoans needed jobs, training, health care, and protection from drugs and violence, not microloans, and that self-employment was a primitive concept lingering only in the Third World. Low-income people in Chicago needed money for rent and food, not for investment. They had no skills anyway" (Yunus 184). They were also skeptical that Americans would take part in the five-person group idea because they were too independent.

Not only was the FCF successful, but many other micro-credit programs sprang up in cities throughout the United States. Not all of these operate using Grameen principles, but in 2008, Yunus founded Grameen America in New York. The United States may be the world's richest country, but nearly 40 million people live in poverty. Around 28 million people do not use banks. They can't borrow money because they don't have the education, collateral, or the credit ratings they need. Often they turn to other sources such as payday lenders or check cashing services, who might charge over 700% interest ("Poverty in the United States"). In a little over a year, Grameen America lent over $2.9 million to over 1,350 borrowers. People used the money to pay for rental space, sewing machines, food carts, beauty parlor supplies, and other

> **Writer continues to synthesize and summarize research to support thesis statement.**

Continue reading the research report as students follow along in the text. Review the side note and connect the ideas to the research report writing.

↙ **DIFFERENTIATE INSTRUCTION**

TEKS 10.13B, 10.23A, 10.23D

---

## Differentiated Instruction: English Language Learners

ELPS 4G, 4I, 4J, 5G

| ELP Level **Beginning** | ELP Level **Intermediate** | ELP Level **Advanced/Advanced High** |
|---|---|---|
| Remind students of their knowledge of main ideas and details. Read a paragraph from the sample report and have students identify its main idea. | Read aloud the second complete paragraph on this page. Have students identify the topic sentence and supporting details and then create an outline for their work. | Review paragraph structure with students. Have students use the sample report as a model as they fashion their own paragraphs following this structure. |

TEKS **10.13B** Structure ideas in a sustained way; **10.23A** Synthesize research into a presentation in support of a clear thesis and related claims; **10.23D** Synthesize research into a presentation that uses evaluative tools to examine the research; **ELPS 4G** Demonstrate comprehension of increasingly complex English/summarizing material; **4I** Demonstrate comprehension by employing and expanding basic reading skills/understanding of supporting ideas and details, summarizing text, and distinguishing main ideas from details; **4J** Demonstrate comprehension and expand reading skills by employing inferential skills/predicting, making connections between ideas, drawing conclusions from text, and finding supporting evidence; **5G** Describe with increasing specificity and detail/writing

Continue reading the research report as students follow along in the text. Review the side notes and connect the ideas to the research report writing.

Review the MLA style used to cite sources within the report and to format the Works Cited page of the report.

⭐ **TEKS** 10.13B, 10.23E

### Try It!

Remind students that the research report instruction applies to research in any discipline. Clarify any questions that students have about the process. If possible, work with social studies teachers to assign a dual-purpose descriptive research report.

business start-up costs. The repayment rate is over 99%. New branches are starting to open across the United States.

In 2006, Muhammad Yunus and the Grameen Bank won the Nobel Peace Prize. The concept of microloans has caught on globally, and many organizations use Yunus's ideas to help poor people in different cultures and situations. Even individuals can now provide their own microloans to small entrepreneurs throughout the world by using online sites like Kiva.org. Although, unfortunately, no program has been able to eliminate poverty, Yunus's organizations have provided a way for millions of people to break the chain of poverty and lead lives of respect and dignity. And it all started with twenty-two cents.

> Conclusion ties back to the thesis statement and leaves reader with a final thought. Writer gives distinct point of view.

**Works Cited**

"The Grameen Lending Model." *Grameen America*.
    Grameen America. 2008. Web. 16 March 2011.
"Poverty in the United States." *Grameen America*.
    Grameen America. 2008. Web. 17 March 2011.
Yunus, Muhammad, with Alan Jolis. *Banker to the Poor*.
    New York: PublicAffairs. 2003. Print.

> Works Cited list includes all sources actually used and cited in essay.

### Try It!

The next time you have to write a research report for your social studies class, follow the guidelines on pages **462–466** to conduct and present your research.

## Differentiated Instruction: English Language Learners

⭐ **ELPS** 1A, 3E, 3F, 3G, 5B

| ELP Level **Beginning** | ELP Level **Intermediate** | ELP Level **Advanced/Advanced High** |
| --- | --- | --- |
| Define the words *summary, prompt,* and *estimate*. Have students use them to complete sentences: *A __ tells what to write. A __ includes only main ideas. __ is an informed guess.* | Organize students into small groups and have them discuss good strategies for summarizing, estimating, and arguing. Invite groups to share main ideas with the class. | With students in small groups, ask questions such as the following to prepare for this chapter: *How might a summary of a math article be different from that of a newspaper article about a local event?* |

⭐ **TEKS** **10.13B** Structure ideas in a sustained way; **10.23E** Synthesize research into a presentation that uses a style manual to document sources and format written materials; **ELPS** **1A** Use prior knowledge and experiences to understand meanings; **3E** Share information in cooperative learning interactions; **3F** Give information/ ranging from using a limited high-frequency vocabulary to using abstract and content-based vocabulary during speaking; **3G** Express ideas ranging from communicating short phrases to participating in discussions; **5B** Write using content-based grade-level vocabulary

471

# Writing in Math

Some people think in numbers. They have no trouble solving quadratic equations or figuring out logarithms. Other people think in words. They have no trouble diagramming complex sentences or writing research reports.

Most of us, though, are somewhere in the middle. We need words to help us with our numbers, and we need numbers to help us with our words. When a kindergartner struggles to solve a story problem, words and numbers have to work together. The same is true when Stephen Hawking writes a mathematical description of the universe.

This chapter will help you understand the different ways writing can help you in math class.

- **Writing Guidelines: Article Summary**
- **Writing Guidelines: Written Estimate**
- **Writing Guidelines: Statistical Argument**
- **Writing Guidelines: Response to a Math Prompt**
- **Other Forms of Writing in Math**

"Nature's great book is written in mathematics."

—Galileo

## Writing in Math

### Objective

- learn and apply writing guidelines to an article summary, a written estimate, a statistical report, and a response to a math prompt

The lessons on the following pages provide samples of the kinds of writing students might do in math classes. Assigning these forms of writing will depend on:

- the skill level of your students,
- the subject matter they are studying in math courses, and
- the writing goals of your school, district, or state.

Point out that students are familiar with argumentative essays, responding to prompts, and summaries in other disciplines.

**✔ DIFFERENTIATE INSTRUCTION**

---

### Resources

#### Copy Masters (TE Appendix)

- Venn diagram (TE p. 482)
- T-chart (TE p. 482)

## Writing Guidelines
### Article Summary

Before students write their own summaries, review the guidelines and the sample article and summary on SE page 473.

Review the importance of the writing process for every kind of writing. Also review the traits of writing and how they apply to writing summaries. Suggest that students reuse revising and editing checklists from earlier writing assignments.

### Try It!

Provide students with a selection of suitable articles containing math data to use for the **Try It!** activity. DIFFERENTIATE INSTRUCTION ↘

TEKS 10.13A, 10.13B, 10.13C, 10.13D, 10.17C, 10.18A, 10.18B(i), 10.19, 10.21C; **ELPS** 4G, 4I, 5C, 5G

---

TEKS 10.13A–10.13D, 10.17C, 10.18A, 10.18B(i). 10.19, 10.21C
ELPS 4G, 4I, 5C

# Writing Guidelines Article Summary

Many magazine articles, books, and news stories include statistics and mathematical concepts. Use the following guidelines to summarize a math-related article.

## Prewriting

- **Find an article.** Choose a newspaper or magazine article that uses mathematics to support a story, a position, or an issue.
- **Read the article.** Read the selection first to get its overall message. Then reread it carefully, paying attention to details.
- **Find the focus.** Write down the main idea of the article.
- **Gather details.** Select only the most important details that support the main idea of the article.

## Drafting

- **Write your first draft.** Write your topic sentence, putting the main idea of the article in your own words. Supply supporting details. Close with a sentence that summarizes your thoughts.

## Revising

- **Improve your writing.** Review your first draft for *focus and coherence, organization, development of ideas,* and *voice.* Ask these questions: *Have I identified the main idea of the article? Have I included only the most important details? Have I explained the math concepts in clear language?*
- **Improve your style.** Check your *word choice* and *sentence fluency.* Ask these questions: *Does my summary read smoothly? Do I sound knowledgeable about the topic?*

## Editing

- **Check for conventions.** Proofread your summary for errors in grammar, sentence structure, capitalization, punctuation, and spelling.
- **Prepare a final copy.** Make a neat final copy of your summary.

### Try It!

Find an article containing math data. Write a summary and create a graph to illustrate the data. Follow the tips above.

---

TEKS **10.13A** Plan a first draft by determining topics through a range of strategies; **10.13B** Structure ideas in a sustained way; **10.13C** Revise drafts to improve style and word choice; **10.13D** Edit drafts for grammar, mechanics, and spelling; **10.17C** Use a variety of correctly structured sentences; **10.18A** Use conventions of capitalization; **10.18B(i)** Use commas in nonrestrictive phrases and contrasting expressions and in clauses; **10.19** Spell correctly using resources to determine and check correct spelling; **10.21C** Summarize researched information; **ELPS 4G** Demonstrate comprehension of increasingly complex English/summarizing material; **4I** Demonstrate comprehension by employing and expanding basic reading skills/understanding of supporting ideas and details, summarizing text, and distinguishing main ideas from details; **5C** Spell familiar words with increasing accuracy; **5G** Describe and explain with increasing specificity and detail/writing

Writing in Math **473**

TEKS 10.21C, 10.23C
ELPS 4G

## Math Article and Summary

A student read the following article in the newspaper and wrote a brief summary, including a graph to illustrate the statistics in the article.

### Where Is All That Money Going?

Every parent of teenagers knows that they are spending quite a bit of money. A recent mall survey shows that suburban teenage boys are spending more than $70 per week on themselves and suburban teenage girls are spending more than $60 per week on themselves. The money is mainly coming from adults in the form of allowance, gifts, or just handouts. However, some teens are earning their own money by working part time.

Since the survey was conducted in a mall, it is not surprising that mall spending figured high for both genders. However, mall spending was nearly matched by online purchases and downloads. The respondents indicated that they engaged in "social" spending at the mall, but often bought "necessities" on the Internet.

So how are teens spending their money? The survey found that the biggest category for teen spending was fashion, which accounted for 41

percent of female spending and 34 percent of male spending. The next biggest category was electronics, including computer programs, video games and players, CD and MP3 players, and other gadgetry. In this category, young men spent 30 percent of their income, and young women spent 26 percent. As for the third biggest category—music—the genders spent nearly evenly, with males spending 21 percent and females spending 20 percent. Both genders tended to save about 10 percent of their income, and they also reported a few "other" purchases (females at 3 percent and males at 5 percent).

Should parents be worried about these spending habits? Some say these spending habits are a concern due to the rising number of bankruptcies filed by those 25 years and younger. Others say it makes sense that teenagers are spending more than saving in the years before they have more financial responsibility. Both groups, however, are asking for better financial lessons in school.

### Sample Summary

#### Tracking Teen Spending

The article "Where Is All That Money Going?" tracks teen spending. Male suburban teens spend about $70 a week while females spend $60.

Although some work part time for the money, most of it comes from adults. Teens spend the most, at malls and online, for fashion, electronics, and music. Males spend slightly more on electronics and females slightly more on fashion. Music spending is nearly identical, and both genders save about 10 percent of their income. Some adults are concerned, and many feel that schools should do more to teach financial responsibility. (Johnson, *Orange County Times*, 7 Jan. 2010)

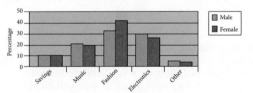

---

## Math Article and Summary

Discuss the benefits of including a graph or chart in a math-article summary.

- A graphic allows the writer to present all numbers mentioned in the article in a clear, concise form.
- A graphic presents information visually.
- A graphic adds variety to a summary.

Review the various ways to present statistical information visually. Encourage students to consider using graphs or charts in their summaries.

TEKS 10.21C, 10.23C; ELPS 4G

---

TEKS **10.21C** Summarize researched information; **10.23C** Synthesize research into a presentation that uses graphics and illustrations to explain concepts; **ELPS 4E** Read linguistically accommodated content area material with a decreasing need for linguistic accommodations as more English is learned; **4F** Use support from peers/teachers to enhance and confirm understanding; **4G** Demonstrate comprehension of increasingly complex English/summarizing material; **5G** Describe and explain with increasing specificity and detail/writing

## Writing Guidelines
### How to Manage Money

Read the introduction and clarify any unfamiliar terms, such as *income, expenditures, evaluations, explanations, calculations,* and *budget.* Guide students through each step in the writing process, providing further instruction as needed. Remind students that following language conventions is necessary even in math writing. Tell them to be sure to check punctuation, spelling, and capitalization. Also, have them check for variety in sentence length and grammatical structure. **DIFFERENTIATE INSTRUCTION ↘**

**DIFFERENTIATE INSTRUCTION ↘**

⭐ **TEKS** 10.13A, 10.13B, 10.13C, 10.13D, 10.17C, 10.18A, 10.18B(i), 10.19; **ELPS** 5C, 5F

### Try It!

Preview the prompt given in the **Try It!** activity. Have students note the givens: (1) 11 people—10 friends and the writer—must eat sandwiches; (2) the total cost of food will be $25; (3) the writer has $10 to spend.

---

## Writing Guidelines Written Estimate

Part of learning how to manage money includes estimating income and expenses. If you are saving for something you want to buy, making a cost estimate and a budget are critical. Making an estimate requires several steps.

- **Weekly or Monthly Income:** (actual amount of money earned)
- **Expenditures:** (rent, food, utilities, car payment, gasoline, insurance, replacing a broken cell phone, hosting a party)
- **Evaluations and Explanations:** (step-by-step calculations involved in making an estimate and clarification of the information)

### Prewriting

- **Select a topic.** Think about a situation in your own life that requires budgeting and estimating expenses.
- **Make assumptions.** Write down the givens as well as the variables of the situation and estimate the costs involved.
- **Plan the steps.** Find a way to arrive at a final cost. Use transitions like *next* and *last* to signal the order of steps.

### Drafting

- **Write your first draft.** Introduce the situation and the costs involved. Explain the steps you took to arrive at a final cost and the amount of your estimate. Clarify your information.

### Revising

- **Improve your writing.** Review your *focus and coherence, organization, development of ideas,* and *voice.* Ask these questions: *Do I identify the situation and explain the budget process clearly? Do I sound knowledgeable?*
- **Improve your style.** Check your *word choice* and *sentence fluency.*

### Editing

- **Check for conventions.** Correct errors in grammar, sentence structure, capitalization, punctuation, and spelling.
- **Prepare a final copy.** Make a neat final copy of your work.

### Try It!

Ten friends are coming over to watch movies. You will buy sub sandwiches to feed them and yourself, but you only have $10. Sandwiches cost $5.50 and are not big enough to share. One friend, however, is going to bring food for himself and one other person. Estimate how many subs you will need and how much money your other friends will have to contribute.

---

⭐ **TEKS** **10.13A** Plan a first draft by determining topics through a range of strategies; **10.13B** Structure ideas in a sustained way/develop drafts in open-ended situations that include transitions; **10.13C** Revise drafts to improve style and word choice; **10.13D** Edit drafts for grammar, mechanics, and spelling; **10.17C** Use a variety of correctly structured sentences; **10.18A** Use conventions of capitalization; **10.18B(i)** Use commas in nonrestrictive phrases and contrasting expressions and in clauses; **10.19** Spell correctly using resources to determine and check correct spelling; **10.21C** Summarize researched information; **ELPS** **1A** Use prior experiences to understand meanings; **5C** Spell familiar words/employ spelling patterns and rules with increasing accuracy; **5F** Write using a variety of grade-appropriate sentence lengths, patterns, and connecting words/combine in increasingly accurate ways

---

### Differentiated Instruction: Struggling Learners

Guide students through prewriting. Suggest a concept web to identify possible topics. Ask questions to assist students' brainstorming:

- *What might you want to save money to buy?*
- *When might you need money to spend?*
- *What have you had to budget in the past?*

⭐ **TEKS** 10.13A; **ELPS** 1A

## Written Estimate

The following estimate was written for a pizza party.

### Sample Estimate

Math

> You and your friends want to watch the basketball game together next weekend. Your mother has agreed to allow you to invite five friends to your house. You have saved $20 to spend on pizza to eat during the game. That is all the money that you can afford to spend on the party. Write an estimate of the amount of money each person should contribute to provide pizza for everyone.
>
> Assumptions:
> The situation has two given quantities.
>   Given 1: Five friends will come to eat pizza.
>   Given 2: I can afford to spend $20 on pizza.
> The situation has three variables that need to be defined.
>   Variable A: The average number of pieces each person will eat, estimated to be 4
>   Variable B: The number of pieces in a pizza, estimated to be 8
>   Variable C: The cost of each large pizza, with tax, delivery, and tip, estimated to be $14
> Evaluations:
>   The total number of pieces = Variable A × Given 1
>     4 pieces × 6 people = 24 pieces of pizza needed
>   The total number of pizzas = 24 ÷ Variable B
>     24 pieces of pizza ÷ 8 pieces per pizza = 3 pizzas
>   The total cost of pizzas needed = 3 × Variable C
>     3 pizzas X $14 = $42
>   The total amount we need to pay = $42 − Given 2
>     $42 - $20 = $22
>   The amount each person needs to pay = $22 ÷ Given 1
>     $22 ÷ 5 = $4.40 per person
> Explanations:
> If my friends and I each eat 4 pieces of pizza, and if I contribute $20, each of my friends should pay $4.40. The cost could be higher if the pizzas have multiple toppings. The cost could be lower if we can use a coupon.

**Given quantities and variables are provided.**

**Each step of the calculation is shown.**

**The estimate is explained and clarified.**

### Managing Money

Go through the sample estimate with the class, pointing out important characteristics and items to keep in mind.

- Note that the Assumptions, Evaluations, and Explanations sections generally correspond to the beginning, middle, and end of the estimate, respectively.
- Have students examine and discuss how the writer defines the givens and variables in the Assumptions section and then uses them in the calculations for the Evaluation section (for example, *Total number of pieces = Variable A x Given 1*).
- Point out that the first two sections of the estimate resemble an outline. Emphasize, however, that students are free to tailor the language and format as they desire as long as they include the required information.
- The Explanation is written in informal prose.

TEKS 10.13B; ELPS 4J

---

### Differentiated Instruction: English Language Learners

ELPS 2E, 3B, 3E

| ELP Level **Beginning** | ELP Level **Intermediate** | ELP Level **Advanced/Advanced High** |
| --- | --- | --- |
| Tell students: Income *means* money "comes in." Ex *means* "out." Expenditure *means* money going out. Have students identify examples (*paycheck, bill, tip*) as one or the other. | Write, define, and give examples of *givens, variables, assumptions*. Help students identify a situation, its givens and variables, as well as assumptions they can make. | Have students list situations and topics independently, then discuss ideas with others to come up with the best topic. Allow students to consult partners as they write. |

TEKS **10.13B** Structure ideas in a sustained way; ELPS **2E** Use linguistic support to enhance and confirm understanding of increasingly complex spoken language; **3B** Expand vocabulary by learning and using routine language needed for classroom communication; **3E** Share information in cooperative learning interactions; **4J** Demonstrate comprehension and expand reading skills by employing inferential skills/predicting, making connections between ideas, drawing conclusions from text, and finding supporting evidence

# Writing Guidelines
## Statistical Argument

Explain to students that statistics refer to information presented in numbers. Explain that even though the numbers may be factual, writers' interpretations of these facts are not. In order to present a statistical argument, the writer must use the numerical facts to build a case for his or her argument.

⭐ **TEKS** 10.13A

## Prewriting

Guide students through the brainstorming process, having them use lists, webs, or free writing to come up with ideas. Then organize students into pairs to discuss and choose an idea. Explain to students that when writing an argumentative essay that requires research, they will need to formulate a plan for research and spend time conducting research. After they have done so, they should identify their interpretation or opinion about the statistics, explaining what the numbers reflect and mean.

⭐ **TEKS** 10.16A, 10.16B; **ELPS** 3E, 5G

## Drafting

Remind students that they will have the opportunity to revisit their drafts in order to revise organization and word choice, as well as edit for errors in conventions. Suggest that students create a graphic organizer or outline to visually depict the structure of their arguments and maintain a clear focus on the thesis.

⭐ **TEKS** 10.13A, 10.13B, 10.16C, 10.16D, 10.17C, 10.18A, 10.19, 10.23C; **ELPS** 5C, 5G

---

**476**

⭐ **TEKS** 10.13A–10.13E, 10.16A–10.16D, 10.17C, 10.18A, 10.18B(i), 10.19, 10.23C
**ELPS** 5C

# Writing Guidelines Statistical Argument

Mathematical statistics are often used—and abused—to argue and prove a point. In an argumentative essay, it is important to include a clear thesis or position that is based on logical reasons and supported by precise, relevant evidence. In statistical arguments, writers must consider the whole range of information on the topic and use statistics to provide an accurate and honest representation of the views on the topic. Often, various kinds of graphics are included to explain concepts and to support points the writer is making.

## Prewriting

- **Select a topic.** Use a range of strategies, including brainstorming, as you think about selecting a topic. You might consider statistics related to your school or community: graduation and dropout rates, SAT scores, crime rates, hours spent watching television, attendance rates, and so forth. Choose a topic that interests you.
- **Gather information.** Research the issue, gathering as many facts and figures as you can. Use reliable, valid, and accurate sources of information. Make sure that your sources cover the whole range of information about the topic and that they provide an honest and accurate representation of the viewpoints surrounding the topic.
- **Form an opinion.** After reviewing the research and data, form your opinion about the issue. Write a position statement that is based on logical reasons and that you can support with precise and relevant data from your research.

## Drafting

- **Decide on an organizational pattern.** Consider your audience, the purpose of your writing, and the context. Then choose an appropriate organizational pattern for your essay. Structure your ideas in a persuasive, sustained way.
- **Create a first draft.** Write a beginning that introduces the topic and clearly states your position. In your middle paragraphs, support your position with logical reasons and with precise, relevant evidence and data. Show that you have considered the whole range of information and views on the topic and that you have accurately and honestly represented those views. In addition, include counter-arguments that you identified and that are based on your research. Anticipate and address objections raised by the counter-arguments. Include graphics to help explain concepts. Your conclusion should reinforce and tie back to the position statement.

---

**TEKS** **10.13A** Plan a first draft by determining topics through a range of strategies and developing a thesis or idea; **10.13B** Structure ideas in a sustained and persuasive way; **10.13C** Revise drafts to improve word choice; **10.13D** Edit drafts for grammar, mechanics, and spelling; **10.13E** Publish written work; **10.16A** Write an argumentative essay supported by precise and relevant evidence; **10.16B** Write an argumentative essay that includes the range of information and views on the topic and an accurate/honest representation of views; **10.16C** Write an argumentative essay that includes counter-arguments to address objections; **10.16D** Write an argumentative essay that includes a structure appropriate to the purpose, audience, and context; **10.17C** Use a variety of correctly structured sentences; **10.18A** Use conventions of capitalization; **10.18B(i)** Use commas in nonrestrictive phrases and contrasting expressions and in clauses; **10.19** Spell correctly using resources to determine and check correct spelling; **10.23C** Synthesize research into a presentation that uses graphics and illustrations to explain concepts; **ELPS** **3E** Share information in cooperative learning interactions; **5C** Spell familiar words with increasing accuracy; **5G** Explain with increasing specificity and detail/writing

⭐ **TEKS** 10.13C, 10.13D, 10.16A–10.16F, 10.15A(i), 10.15A(ii), 10.17A(i), 10.17C, 10.18A, 10.18B(i), 10.19
**ELPS** 5C–5F

## Revising

- **Improve your argument.** Consider *focus and coherence, organization, development of ideas,* and *voice.* Ask these questions: *Is my position statement clear? Do the middle paragraphs connect to and support the position statement? Have I identified and addressed counter-arguments? Is my conclusion effective? Is the organization pattern logical and easy for the reader to follow and understand? Have I developed a convincing argument using statistics? Have I used precise, relevant details and data to support my thesis and cited my sources correctly? Have I varied my sentence structure? Do I sound assured, confident, and knowledgeable?*

- **Improve your style.** Check your *word choice* and *sentence fluency.* Ask these questions: *Have I defined any unfamiliar terms? Is my word choice appropriate for the audience, purpose, and context of the writing? Have I used transitions to connect ideas? Have I used rhetorical devices to convey meaning and engage the reader?*

## Editing

- **Check for conventions.** Correct any errors in grammar, sentence structure, capitalization, punctuation, and spelling. Ask yourself these questions: *Have I correctly used verb tenses and active and passive voice? Have I used complex passive voice correctly, but kept as much as possible to active voice? Have I used verbals, including gerunds, infinitives, and participles correctly? Have I correctly punctuated clauses and phrases? Have I checked end punctuation of sentences? Have I correctly used quotation marks and used correct punctuation to introduce quotations? Have I carefully checked my spelling, especially for technical terms and specialized vocabulary? Have I correctly cited, documented, and formatted my sources and sources-cited list following an approved style manual, such as the MLA Handbook?*

- **Prepare a final copy.** After you have checked for all the conventions and answered the questions above, make a neat final copy of your argument and proofread it.

### Try It!

Follow the guidelines on these two pages to select a topic and write a statistical argument. Consider the whole range of information and give an honest representation of those views. Include counter-arguments to anticipate and address objections. Be sure to revise and edit your work.

## Revising

Use the revising questions on SE page 477 to have students evaluate the sample essay on SE pages 478–479 or another statistical essay. Be sure students can identify the thesis, arguments, and counter-arguments in the essay. Then set up peer conferencing for students to revise their writing. Have students first complete an independent revision and then present their writing to an assigned peer group. Each group member should read the essay and complete a revising checklist.

## Editing

Have students work independently to complete the editing step for their own essays. Encourage them to use the questions on SE page 477 to create their own editing checklist. Remind students that they will likely need to review their essay several times, each time looking for specific types of errors. ✎ **DIFFERENTIATE INSTRUCTION**

⭐ **TEKS** 10.13C, 10.13D, 10.15A(i), 10.15A(ii), 10.16A, 10.16B, 10.16C, 10.16D, 10.16F, 10.17C, 10.18A, 10.18B(i), 10.19; **ELPS** 5C, 5D, 5E, 5F

### Try It!

Encourage students to use the steps on SE page 476 to plan and draft their statistical argument essay. Then have them use the questions on SE page 477 to create their revising and editing checklists.

**Differentiated Instruction: English Language Learners**     ⭐ **ELPS** 4F, 5F

| ELP Level<br>**Beginning** | ELP Level<br>**Intermediate** | ELP Level<br>**Advanced/Advanced High** |
|---|---|---|
| Review simple and complex sentences. Have students use a highlighter to identify each in their writing. Help them combine sentences to achieve variety. | Before students begin peer conferences, review the revising questions and clarify unfamiliar concepts. Then have students work in mixed-level groups to complete the conferences. | Assign advanced students to native English-speaking groups for conferences. As advanced learners evaluate the group's writing, be available to answer questions. |

 **TEKS** **10.13C** Revise drafts/improve style, word choice, and sentence variety and rethink how well the purpose/audience have been addressed; **10.13D** Edit drafts; **10.15A(i)** Write an analytical essay/variety of sentence structures; **10.15A(ii)** Write an analytical essay/transitions; **10.16A–10.16F** Write an argumentative essay; **10.17A(i)** Use and understand more complex active and passive tenses; **10.17C** Use a variety of correctly structured sentences; **10.18A** Use conventions of capitalization; **10.18B(i)** Use commas in nonrestrictive phrases and contrasting expressions and in clauses; **10.19** Spell correctly using resources to determine and check correct spelling; **10.23C** Synthesize research into a presentation that uses graphics and illustrations to explain concepts; **ELPS** **4F** Use support from peers/teachers to enhance understanding and develop vocabulary; **5C** Spell familiar words with increasing accuracy; **5D** Edit writing for standard grammar and usage/subject-verb and pronoun agreement and appropriate verb tenses; **5E** Employ increasingly complex grammatical structures in content area writing; **5F** Write using a variety of grade-appropriate sentence lengths and connecting words in increasingly accurate ways

## Statistical Argument

Review the sample essay and the side notes. Guide students to connect the elements and techniques noted in the side notes to specific portions of the text. Discuss the organization and the content that support the thesis. Ask questions such as: *What evidence does the writer give to support each topic sentence? What appeals does the writer make to a youthful audience? Is the organizational pattern the most useful for the writer's position?*

**TEKS** 10.13B, 10.16A, 10.16B, 10.16D, 10.16E, 10.16F

 **TEKS** 10.13B, 10.16A, 10.16B, 10.16D–10.16F

## Statistical Argument

The following persuasive essay uses statistics about young voter turnout to argue a point of view about voter apathy.

### Sample Statistical Argument

#### Courting the Youth Vote

In the 1960s, the armed services drafted thousands of 18-year-olds to fight in Vietnam, but none of those draftees had the right to vote. Many young people protested this situation. As a result, the minimum voting age was lowered in 1971. That change showed the power of the youth vote in the 1972 elections. Fifty two percent of those 18 to 24 years of age voted, and in order to woo these young voters, candidates had to demonstrate their commitment to ending the war. Although he was unpopular, Nixon still won the election. By 1973 he had withdrawn all American troops from Vietnam and ended the draft. The newest group of voters was obviously an important influence on political policy.

Despite that promising start, over the next 30 years voter turnout among young people slowly declined. By 2000, only 36 percent of young voters went to the polls—a year when their votes could have easily swayed the election. In comparison, 66 to 72 percent of people over the age of 45 voted ("Voting and Registration"). A survey in colleges conducted that year found that "only a quarter of the students said they discussed political issues as often as three or four times a week. A third said government had no influence on their lives" (Clymer).

Why did young voters become so apathetic? According to the U.S. Census, the people who are most likely to go to the polls are people with the biggest stakes in society: older individuals, homeowners, married couples, and people with more schooling, higher incomes, and good jobs ("Voting and Registration"). Since young people usually don't own property, pay much tax, or have children in public schools, they feel they have less economic stake in the political process.

Often, the issues voters 18 to 24 do care about are not addressed. "The chief reason that young voters give for not voting is that they think nobody is listening to them," writes Jack Doppelt, author of *Nonvoters: America's No-Shows*. This theory was supported by the brief surge in the youth vote in 1992, which spiked to 48 percent. Young people felt someone

**Side notes:**

**Background** introduces topic and uses statistics to help build an argument. The position statement is given.

**Middle paragraphs** support thesis with reliable, authoritative evidence. Sources are cited. Writer provides analogies and case studies to support thesis.

**TEKS** **10.13B** Structure ideas in a sustained way; **10.16A** Write an argumentative essay supported by precise and relevant evidence; **10.16B** Write an argumentative essay that includes the range of information and views on the topic and an accurate/honest representation of views; **10.16D** Write an argumentative essay that includes a structure appropriate to the purpose, audience, and context; **10.16E** Write an argumentative essay that includes analysis of specific data, facts, and ideas; **10.16F** Write an argumentative essay that includes a range of appeals

Math

**Middle paragraphs** continue to build support for the thesis statement. Precise, relevant evidence is presented. Writer considers whole range of views on topic and provides honest representation of views. Writer also provides analysis of relative value of facts, ideas, and data.

was listening. Bill Clinton was a young man who played saxophone on the Tonight Show, appeared on MTV, and answered questions about "guns or butter" and "boxers or briefs."

After Clinton's election, however, the youth vote slid again. Then, in 2004, an even bigger spike occurred. Turnout at the polls for young voters jumped 11 points to 47 percent. This time, the reason was not a charismatic candidate but an issue that young people cared about, specifically the war in Iraq. Political strategists tapped into the growing interest and concern. They began to campaign harder at colleges and targeted potential young voters through organizations like Rock the Vote.

Although the youth vote did not have a significant effect on the 2004 elections, the 2008 elections again saw a rise in voters from 18 to 24. It was the only age group that showed a statistically significant increase in turnout, climbing 2 points from 2004 to reach 49 percent (over 2 million votes). Among young voters, African Americans had the highest turnout rate—55 percent, which was an 8 percent increase from the previous election ("Voter Turnout"). This time, candidates went all out to court the young, spreading their message through new media such as Facebook and YouTube.

It helped that the presidential candidate, Barack Obama, was not only charismatic, but also a potent symbol of change. His ideas reflected a new direction away from the anger that had divided the country after 2004. His ethnicity also represented the often overlooked racial and ethnic populations of the country. Compared to his older rivals, the youthful Obama was more like a peer than a parent—not only someone who listened and was "cool," but also someone who addressed their concerns and understood them.

"Young voters helped form the backbone of the Obama campaign, volunteering in their home towns and on college campuses across the country . . . President-elect Obama acknowledged their contribution in his victory speech . . . He said his campaign 'grew strength from the young people who rejected the myth of their generation's apathy, who left their homes and their families for jobs that offered little pay and less sleep'" (Falcone). Once again, the youngest group of voters made a difference.

**The conclusion** restates the position. Writer's viewpoint is clearly stated.

After students have read the sample, talk about how the supporting statistics are presented.

- The writer provides a context by clearly establishing in the opening that the statistics cited apply to people *18 to 24 years of age*. Whenever a statistic is given, the writer also provides the respective year (*By 2000, only 20 percent of young voters went to the polls*).
- Strong verbs (such as *declined, spiked, jumped*) help clarify the meaning of the numbers.
- The writer uses numbers and words according to the style guidelines. The writer expresses numbers higher than nine as figures, spells out *percent* instead of using *%*, and uses *to* instead of a dash in ranges (*18 to 24*, instead of *18–24*). ☑ DIFFERENTIATE INSTRUCTION

TEKS 10.13B, 10.16B, 10.16D, 10.16E

✱ For more about the preferred number style, see SE page 692.

see SE page 692.

---

## Differentiated Instruction: English Language Learners

ELPS 4C, 5B, 5G

| ELP Level **Beginning** | ELP Level **Intermediate** | ELP Level **Advanced/Advanced High** |
|---|---|---|
| Review number style guidelines. Write some cloze sentences on the board and say the number to be inserted. Have students tell whether to write out number or use a numeral. | Write the verbs *increased, spiked, jumped* on the board. Have students rate the impact of each from 1 (most impact) to 3. Lead a class discussion of their ratings. | Have students identify strong verbs in the sample essay and then incorporate at least three of them in their own writing. Invite students to share their sentences with the class. |

TEKS **10.13B** Structure ideas in a sustained way; **10.16B** Write an argumentative essay that includes the range of information and views on the topic and an accurate/honest representation of views; **10.16D** Write an argumentative essay that includes a structure appropriate to the purpose, audience, and context; **10.16E** Write an argumentative essay that includes analysis of specific data, facts, and ideas; ELPS **4C** Develop and comprehend basic sight vocabulary used in written classroom materials; **5B** Write using newly acquired basic vocabulary; **5G** Explain with increasing specificity and detail/writing

## Writing Guidelines
### Response to a Math Prompt

Read the introduction and the writing process instructions. Organize students into pairs and have them summarize each step in the process. Tell them they can consult their summaries as they complete the **Try It!** activity.

**TEKS** 10.13B, 10.13D; **ELPS** 4G, 5C

### Try It!

Provide students with several prompts of various levels from which to choose. Consider working with math teachers at your school on a cross-curricular assignment. Have students begin by identifying the information the prompt asks for and the information it provides. From there, they can complete their writing assignments.

**DIFFERENTIATE INSTRUCTION ↘** **DIFFERENTIATE INSTRUCTION ↘**

---

**TEKS** 10.13B, 10.13D, 10.17C, 10.18A, 10.18B(i), 10.19
**ELPS** 4G, 5C

# Writing Guidelines Response to a Math Prompt

A math prompt is a problem that is solved by writing as well as by mathematics. To answer a prompt, you need to analyze it, decide what you are supposed to do, and then respond to it, working one step at a time. Follow these guidelines.

### Prewriting

- **Read the prompt.** Read carefully, paying attention to the directions. Watch for key words such as *find, solve, justify, demonstrate,* or *compare,* and respond only to the questions asked. Also be aware that some prompts have more than one part.
- **Gather details and data.** Write down any values, assumptions, or variables provided in the prompt.

### Drafting

- **Build your solution.** Respond to each part of the prompt. Set up formulas or equations, and use diagrams if they will help solve the problem. Perform the necessary calculations to get an answer. Show all of your work.

### Revising

- **Improve your response.** Reread the prompt after you do your calculations. If the problem has more than one part, be sure you have answered every part. Work the problem in another way to check that your solution is correct.

### Editing

- **Check for conventions.** Check your solution for errors in grammar, sentence structure, capitalization, punctuation, and spelling.
- **Prepare a final copy.** Make a neat final copy of your solution.

### Try It!

Find a math prompt and write a response. Choose a practice prompt from your textbook or one recommended by your teacher. Follow the tips above to write your solution.

---

### Differentiated Instruction: Struggling Learners

Provide adapted prompts for struggling learners to complete. Also provide revising and editing checklists for them to use. Allow them to work with partners to complete the prompt. Have partners each take a turn rereading the work at both the revising and editing steps of the writing process.

Remind students to check grammar, sentence structure, punctuation, capitalization, and spelling carefully.

**TEKS** 10.17C, 10.18A, 10.18B(i), 10.19; **ELPS** 5C.

---

**TEKS** **10.13B** Structure ideas in a sustained way; **10.13D** Edit drafts for grammar, mechanics, and spelling; **10.17C** Use a variety of correctly structured sentences; **10.18A** Use conventions of capitalization; **10.18B(i)** Use commas in nonrestrictive phrases and contrasting expressions and in clauses; **10.19** Spell correctly using resources to determine and check correct spelling; **ELPS 4G** Demonstrate comprehension of increasingly complex English/summarizing material and responding to questions; **5C** Spell familiar words with increasing accuracy

# Response to a Math Prompt

The following math prompt contains three parts. The writer provides a solution using words, mathematics, and a diagram.

## Sample Prompt and Response

1. Explain this formula: $(a + b)^2 = a^2 + 2ab + b^2$
   a. Using geometry
   b. Using algebra

2. Then show how your two explanations are related.

Trevor Hughes
Math 10, period 6

1a. Geometry
   The area of the large square below is the length x the width.

The area = $(a + b)(a + b)$ or $(a + b)^2$
The area is also the sum of smaller boxes:
$(a)(a) + (a)(b) + (b)(a) + (b)(b) =$
$a^2 + ab + ab + b^2 = a^2 + 2ab + b^2$

The area is the same, so
$(a + b)^2 = a^2 + 2ab + b^2$

1b. Algebra
   $(a + b)^2 = (a + b)(a + b) =$
   $(a)(a) + (a)(b) + (b)(a) + (b)(b) = a^2 + 2ab + b^2$
   So $(a + b)^2 = a^2 + 2ab + b^2$

2. Relation
   The geometric solution comes from calculating area, while the algebraic solution comes from symbol manipulation. Even so, both solutions have the same middle stage: $(a)(a) + (a)(b) + (b)(a) + (b)(b)$. The underlying math is the same.

## Response to a Math Prompt

Have students read the sample response, and then discuss it in depth. Begin by having students identify the three things called for in the prompt:

- explain the formula using geometry,
- explain the formula using algebra, and
- compare the explanations.

Point out that the writer labeled each part of the response to match the corresponding part of the prompt (1a, 1b, 2). Then discuss what the writer needed to know to answer each part:

- 1a. Recognize that $(a + b)^2$ is the formula for the area of a square with sides of length $(a + b)$; decide how to draw the diagram of the square so it demonstrates $a^2 + 2ab + b^2$.
- 1b. Know how to perform polynomial multiplication.
- 2. Note similarities between the two mathematical expressions.

TEKS 10.13B

## Differentiated Instruction: English Language Learners

ELPS 3E, 4F, 5G

| ELP Level **Beginning** | ELP Level **Intermediate** | ELP Level **Advanced/Advanced High** |
|---|---|---|
| Have students complete the math portion of the prompt. Then provide frames for students to complete the prose explanations required by the prompt. | Tell students that an *explanation* in math can take the form of prose or of calculations. Help students determine which is the best to use for their given prompts. | Have students collaborate with partners to complete the **Try It!** activity. Remind students that they will need to explain their responses using specific details. |

TEKS **10.13B** Structure ideas in a sustained way; ELPS **3E** Share information in cooperative learning interactions; **4F** Use support from peers/teachers to enhance and confirm understanding; **5G** Explain with increasing specificity and detail/writing

## Other Forms of Writing in Math

Suggest that students who keep math learning logs consult SE page 482 for entry ideas. In particular, the prompts for the description (a type of expository writing) and narrative essays may be helpful in getting them thinking about the role math plays in their lives.

✱ For more about expository and narrative writing, see SE pages 136–186 and 78–128, respectively.

The position essay (a form of persuasive writing) and research essay are longer-term writing projects. If possible, assign one of these writing projects to give students practice thinking about math in terms of words and explanations.

✱ For more about persuasive writing and research reports, see SE pages 194–251 and 358–428, respectively.

Consider providing reproducible graphic organizers to help students with their prewriting. For example, the Venn diagram (see TE Appendix) could be used in planning a classification essay, while a T-chart (see TE Appendix) could be used to help plan a position essay.

**482**

# Other Forms of Writing in Math

**Definition**

*Algebra*—Write an expository paragraph on the definition of the word *algebra*.

**Description**

*Geometry*—Describe a nature scene using geometry.

**Narrative**

*Any Math*—Write a narrative essay about a time when you used math in daily life.

**Classification**

*Geometry*—Write an essay comparing and contrasting the different types of triangles.

**Position**

*Any Math*—Read about new theories in math or economics that interest you. Choose one theory and write a position essay that supports the theory and defends it against opposing viewpoints.

**Process**

*Algebra*—Write a process paragraph about the details needed to solve a linear equation.

**Research**

*Any Math*—Write a report on a famous mathematician. In your report, include at least one interesting fact about the person's life, describe the time period in which she or he lived, and briefly explain the work or discoveries that made the person famous.

**Differentiated Instruction: English Language Learners**

ELPS 3B, 3G, 3H

| ELP Level **Beginning** | ELP Level **Intermediate** | ELP Level **Advanced/Advanced High** |
|---|---|---|
| Engage students in a discussion about completing tasks they enjoy, using frames: *I am good at ___. I have to ___ first. Then, I ___.* | Discuss with students that when they use their knowledge of a process to complete a task, like cooking or fixing things, that is applied science. | Review descriptive essays and essays of analysis. Ask these questions: *What is the purpose of each form? What might you learn from each?* |

**ELPS 3B** Expand vocabulary by learning and using high-frequency words for identifying and describing; **3G** Express ideas ranging from communicating short phrases to participating in discussions; **3H** Explain with increasing specificity and detail

**483**

# Writing in the Applied Sciences

Classes in the applied sciences provide hands-on learning. For example, in a textile arts class, you may learn about fabrics by sewing. In a machine shop, you may learn about internal combustion engines by taking one apart and putting it back together.

Writing is also important in the applied sciences. It can help you plan projects, remember procedures, reflect on successes and failures, and propose new projects for the future.

In this chapter, you will learn about writing essays in the applied sciences. You will discover how writing empowers hands-on learning.

- **Writing Guidelines: Descriptive Essay**
- **Writing Guidelines: Essay of Analysis**
- **Other Forms of Practical Writing**

"Jump into the middle of things, get your hands dirty, fall flat on your face, and then reach for the stars."

—Ben Stein

## Resources

**Copy Masters (see Appendix)**

- Sensory chart (TE p. 484)
- Time line (TE p. 490)
- Details chart (TE p. 490)

# Writing in the Applied Sciences

## Objective

- learn and apply the writing guidelines to a descriptive essay and an essay of analysis

The lessons on the following pages provide samples of the types of writing students might do in a family and consumer science or technical education class. Assigning these forms of writing will depend on:

- the skill level of your students,
- the subject matter they are studying in different applied sciences courses, and
- the writing goals of your school, district, or state.

Point out to students that they already have some familiarity with writing in the applied sciences. Examples of "how-to" writing belong to this category. **✔ DIFFERENTIATE INSTRUCTION**

## Writing Guidelines
**Descriptive Essay**

### Prewriting

For this writing assignment, students should choose a topic rich with details that they can describe using a variety of sensory words.

Discuss the different graphic organizers that students could use during prewriting for a descriptive essay. Distribute photocopies of the reproducible sensory chart (TE Appendix).

■ Have students use the sensory chart to note any sensory details related to their topics.

■ If the details work best arranged spatially, encourage students to draw a diagram of the object or place and then write the details on the diagram in the appropriate places.

### Drafting

Discuss various organizational patterns for a descriptive essay. Encourage students to include sensory words and phrases in some of their transitions.

### Revising

Encourage students to use the revising questions on SE page 484 to review and revise their drafts. You might have students circle all the descriptive words they have used. Encourage them to find synonyms for any descriptive words that seem overused.

### Editing

Remind students that using a variety of sentence structures will add interest to their essays. As always, students should also edit for grammar, punctuation, capitalization, and spelling.

★ **TEKS** 10.13A, 10.13B, 10.13C, 10.13D, 10.17C, 10.18A, 10.18B(i), 10.18B(ii), 10.18B(iii), 10.19; **ELPS** 2E, 5C, 5F

---

★ **TEKS** 10.13A–10.13D, 10.17C, 10.18A, 10.18B(i)–18B(iii), 10.19
**ELPS** 5C, 5F

# Writing Guidelines Descriptive Essay

A descriptive essay describes a person, place, or thing. The goal is to create a clear mental picture for the reader.

## Prewriting

■ **Select a topic.** If your teacher does not assign a specific topic, review your notes, journal, or textbook to find ideas.

■ **Gather details.** Freewrite about the topic using sensory details. Also research the purpose and history of your topic.

■ **Plan and organize.** Choose an organizational pattern. If you are describing something physical, consider using spatial organization: front to back, top to bottom, inside to outside, or the whole to the parts. If you are describing something that changes, consider using chronological organization.

## Drafting

■ **Connect your ideas.** Write a beginning paragraph that introduces your topic and provides your thesis or focus. Then begin your description, following the organizational pattern you selected. Connect your ideas with transitions.

## Revising

■ **Improve your writing.** Review your first draft for *focus and coherence, organization, development of ideas,* and *voice.* Ask these questions: *Is my thesis or focus clear? Have I chosen the correct organizational pattern for my topic, my audience, and my purpose? Are my ideas fully developed? Have I included details that create a clear mental picture for the reader? Is my level of language appropriate to my audience and topic?* Ask someone else to read your essay and make comments.

■ **Improve your style.** Check your *word choice* and *sentence fluency.* Ask these questions: *Have I used vivid descriptive words? Have I used transitions so that my sentences flow from one to the next?*

## Editing

■ **Check for conventions.** Correct all errors in grammar, sentence structure, capitalization, punctuation, and spelling.

■ **Prepare a final copy.** Make a neat final copy of your essay.

---

★ **TEKS** **10.13A** Plan a first draft by determining topics through a range of strategies; **10.13B** Structure ideas in a sustained way/develop drafts in open-ended situations that include transitions; **10.13C** Revise drafts to improve style and word choice; **10.13D** Edit drafts for grammar, mechanics, and spelling; **10.17C** Use a variety of correctly structured sentences; **10.18A** Use conventions of capitalization; **10.18B(i)** Use commas in nonrestrictive phrases and contrasting expressions and in clauses; **10.18B(ii)** Use quotation marks to indicate sarcasm and irony; **10.18B(iii)** Use dashes to emphasize parenthetical information; **10.19** Spell correctly using resources to determine and check correct spelling; **ELPS 2E** Use visual support to enhance and confirm understanding of increasingly complex spoken language; **5C** Spell familiar words with increasing accuracy; **5F** Write using a variety of grade-appropriate connecting words in increasingly accurate ways

## Descriptive Essay

In her Home Living class, Andrea described her plan for furnishing a family room.

**The beginning** introduces the topic and leads to a thesis statement (underlined).

**The middle** presents each area and describes its arrangement. Organization is logical.

**The ending** reflects on the arrangement of the room.

### Furnishing a Family Room

A family room should be comfortable and inviting—a place that brings the family together. Let's imagine a room 16 feet wide by 20 feet long, with a fireplace on one end and a large bay area on one side. It's a nice space, but it won't be a family room until it is properly furnished.

Creating a gathering spot near the fireplace is the initial focus. On either side of the fireplace should stand two armchairs, with a coffee table between them. Track lighting above the table lights up games and snacks.

Next, it's time to turn the bay area into a quiet place for study. A comfortable chair, a table, and a lamp create a reading nook on one side of the bay. On the other side, a small desk provides a good place for doing homework.

The rest of the room is perfect for larger gatherings. An entertainment center, a couch, and a chair are great for watching TV or listening to music.

Desk

Fire

CD's

TV

The family room is complete. The furnishings make the space comfortable and inviting for individuals, couples, and the whole family. Whether people want to play cards by the fire, read a book by the window, or watch the Cowboys in the play-offs, this room is waiting for them.

### Try It!

Write a descriptive essay about a room or an area you know well. Use spacial organization and follow the guidelines on page **484**.

---

### Descriptive Essay

After students read the descriptive essay, have them comment on it. Use the following questions to guide the discussion:

■ *How does the writer go about describing the room?*
  □ In the opening, she tells its dimensions and shape.
  □ The middle paragraphs describe how the room should be furnished, starting with the fireplace at left and moving clockwise around the room.
■ *What types of transitions does the writer use?*
  □ She uses transitions showing location, such as *On either side* and *On the other side.*
  □ She also uses transitions showing time (*We begin by, Next, At last*) for the process of furnishing the room.
■ *How does the closing paragraph relate to the opening one?*
  □ It restates the idea that the room should be *comfortable and inviting.*
  □ In the opening paragraph, the room is unfurnished. By the closing paragraph, it is complete, and the writer suggests activities to enjoy there.

TEKS 10.13B; ELPS 3F, 4G

✱ For more about transitions, see SE pages 628–629.

### Try It!

Suggest that students describe how they would like to decorate the room they chose. Tell students to be sure to connect ideas logically and use transitions to clearly show organization. ✔ DIFFERENTIATE INSTRUCTION

TEKS 10.13B

---

TEKS **10.13B** Structure ideas in a sustained way; ELPS **3C** Speak using a variety of connecting words with increasing accuracy and ease; **3E** Share information in cooperative learning interactions; **3F** Give information/ranging from using a limited high-frequency vocabulary to using abstract and content-based vocabulary during speaking; **4G** Demonstrate comprehension of increasingly complex English/responding to questions; **5F** Write using a variety of grade-appropriate connecting words in increasingly accurate ways; **5G** Describe with increasing specificity and detail/writing

## Writing Guidelines
**Essay of Analysis**

Explain that understanding a complicated issue takes time—and that deciding how to explain it clearly can take even longer. Suggest to students that they:

- do as much research as possible about their topics, and
- take good reading notes during the process.

Remind students that an essay of analysis is a form of expository writing that often includes research.

✱ For detailed guidance in expository writing, refer students to SE pages 136–186.

### Prewriting

To ensure that students write about suitable topics that are neither too simple nor too complex:

- suggest a list of topics for students to choose from, or
- have students meet with you or another content-area teacher to describe their topic idea before conducting research.

**TEKS** 10.13A

### Drafting

Before students begin their essays, have them read and discuss the sample on SE pages 408–409.

**TEKS** 10.13B, 10.15A(ii), 10.15A(iii), 10.15A(v); **ELPS** 5G

---

## Writing Guidelines Essay of Analysis

An essay of analysis breaks down a topic into its parts and shows how they are related. Complex issues make the best topics for essays of analysis.

### Prewriting

- **Select a topic.** If you are not given a topic, think about complex issues related to your class work. Brainstorm, consult with others, and review your class notes or your learning log. For example, in Family and Consumer Science, you could analyze the factors that affect the rising of yeast. In wood shop class, you could analyze the design and function of a piece of furniture.
- **Gather details.** Create a cluster diagram to break down your topic into different components, aspects, and reasons. Think of how each part of the topic connects to other parts.
- **Write your thesis statement.** Using your controlling idea, or focus, and the information you have collected about your topic, create a clear hypothesis for your essay.
- **Plan and organize.** Select an organizational pattern that is appropriate for your purpose, audience, and context for writing. Using the pattern that you have selected, outline your essay. First explain the topic. Use specific, clear language, and then write your hypothesis. Write a topic sentence about one part of the topic for each middle paragraph. Plan ways in which you will present your conclusion.

### Drafting

- **Write your introduction.** Write a beginning that introduces your topic and leads to your hypothesis. Develop middle paragraphs by following your outline. Show how the different parts of the topic are related and use transitions to connect your ideas.
- **Write your middle paragraphs.** Follow your outline to develop your middle paragraphs. Show how the different parts of the topic are related. Include relevant, well-chosen details to support your thesis. Be sure to use transitions to connect within paragraphs and to connect one paragraph to the next. Transitional phrases and words might include *next, moreover,* and *finally*. Use rhetorical devices to enhance your writing and engage the reader. Certain rhetorical devices, such as analogies and rhetorical questions, are helpful in explaining scientific concepts and maintaining reader interest.

---

**TEKS** **10.13A** Plan a first draft by determining topics through a range of strategies and developing a thesis or idea; **10.13B** Structure ideas in a sustained way; **10.15A(ii)** Write an analytical essay that includes rhetorical devices; **10.15A(iii)** Write an analytical essay that includes an idea or thesis; **10.15A(v)** Write an analytical essay that includes relevant evidence and details; **ELPS** **5G** Explain with increasing specificity and detail/writing

**TEKS** 10.13C, 10.13D, 10.15A(i), 10.15A(ii), 10.17A(i), 10.17C, 10.18A, 10.18B(i)–18B(iii), 10.19
ELPS 5C–5F

Applied Sciences

## Revising

- **Improve your writing.** Review your analysis for *focus and coherence, organization, development of ideas,* and *voice.* Ask these questions: *Does my introduction explain the topic? Is my hypothesis clear? After thinking more about my purpose and audience, how I can revise my draft to better fit each one? Does each middle paragraph focus on one part of the topic? Do all the details in each paragraph support the main point of the paragraph? Are the details that I have chosen relevant to the topic, and do they support my hypothesis? Do I show how the parts of the topic are connected?*

- **Improve your style.** Check your word choice and be sure that you have varied the structure of your sentences, from your introduction through your conclusion. (See **774.1** for sentences classified by structure.) Ask these questions: *Have I used appropriate word choices for my audience, purpose, and context? Have I used transitions so that my sentences flow smoothly and ideas are connected from one paragraph to the next? Have I defined terms associated with my topic? Have I used correct voice in my verbs and shown that I understand the difference between active and passive voice and can use the both correctly? (See page **750** for information on active and passive voice.) Have I used the correct tenses and been consistent in my use of verb tenses? Do my sentences vary in length and structure?*

## Editing

- **Check for conventions.** Look for and correct errors in grammar, sentence structure, capitalization, punctuation, and spelling. Check your essay carefully for subject-verb agreement. Make sure that your sentences are correctly structured and all punctuation is correct. Ask these questions: *Have I correctly used commas in phrases and clauses? Have I correctly used quotation marks and used correct punctuation to introduce quotations? Have I correctly used quotation marks to indicate irony and sarcasm? Have I used dashes to emphasize parenthetical information? Have I used various resources, including dictionaries or a computer spell-checker, to check and correct spelling?*

- **Prepare a final copy.** Make a neat final copy of your essay. Proofread it one more time, and make any needed final corrections.

## Revising

Use the revising questions on SE page 487 to have students evaluate the sample essay on SE pages 488–489 or another analysis essay. Be sure students can identify the hypothesis, organizational pattern, and supports provided to the hypothesis by each of the middle paragraphs. Then set up peer conferencing for students to revise their own writing. Have students first complete an independent revision and then present their writing to an assigned peer group. Each group member should read the essay and complete a revising checklist.

## Editing

Have students work independently to complete the editing step for their own essays. Encourage them to use the questions on SE page 487 to create their own editing checklist. Remind students that they will likely need to review their essay several times, each time looking for specific types of errors. **✔ DIFFERENTIATE INSTRUCTION**

**TEKS** 10.13C, 10.13D, 10.15A(i), 10.15A(ii), 10.17A(i), 10.17C, 10.18A, 10.18B(i), 10.18B(ii), 10.18B(iii), 10.19; **ELPS** 3E, 5C, 5D, 5E, 5F

---

## Differentiated Instruction: English Language Learners

**ELPS 5D**

| ELP Level Beginning | ELP Level Intermediate | ELP Level Advanced/Advanced High |
|---|---|---|
| Review subject and object pronouns. Have students complete frames with pronouns: *The couch is blue. ___ is by the window. Jose wants to decorate ___ room.* | Review subject-verb agreement. Provide examples: *The lamp lights the room. The lamps light the room.* Have students focus on subject-verb agreement as they edit. | Review present and past tenses of regular and irregular verbs. Have students check their use of past-tense verbs, using a dictionary to find the correct past forms of irregular verbs. |

**TEKS** **10.13C** Revise drafts/improve style, word choice, and sentence variety and rethink how well the purpose and audience have been addressed; **10.13D** Edit drafts for grammar, mechanics, and spelling; **10.15A(i)** Write an analytical essay that includes a variety of sentence structures; **10.15A(ii)** Write an analytical essay that includes transitions; **10.17A(i)** Use and understand more complex active and passive tenses; **10.17C** Use a variety of correctly structured sentences; **10.18A** Use conventions of capitalization; **10.18B(i)** Use commas in nonrestrictive phrases and contrasting expressions and in clauses; **10.18B(ii)** Use quotation marks to indicate sarcasm and irony; **10.18B(iii)** Use dashes to emphasize parenthetical information; **10.19** Spell correctly using resources to determine and check correct spelling; **ELPS 5C** Spell familiar words/employ spelling patterns and rules with increasing accuracy; **5D** Edit writing for standard grammar and usage/subject-verb and pronoun agreement and appropriate verb tenses; **5E** Employ increasingly complex grammatical structures in content area writing such as using correct verbs, tenses, and pronouns/possessive case/negatives and contractions; **5F** Write using a variety of grade-appropriate sentence lengths, patterns, and connecting words/combine in increasingly accurate ways

## Essay of Analysis

Read aloud and discuss the sample essay and related side notes to provide students with direction for their own writing.

Focus especially on the middle paragraphs. Ask students to explain how the organization of these paragraphs helps clarify the information.

- Each middle paragraph has a strong topic sentence.
- Each topic sentence is well supported with details.
- The writer uses transitions (*As supplies drop, As a result*) to indicate how one event leads to another.
- The writer lists examples. (For instance, *derivative products such as cooking oil, cereals, and baked goods* clarifies what products are made with grains.)

■ **TEKS** 10.13B, 10.15A(i), 10.15A(iv)

---

## Essay of Analysis

In Consumer Economics, Nina wrote about the impact of severe weather on consumers. As she planned her essay and wrote her draft, Nina kept in mind her purpose, audience, and context.

**The beginning** presents the topic and provides the thesis statement (underlined).

**The middle** paragraphs analyze the main parts of the topic and show how they are related. Organization is appropriate for audience, purpose, and context.

Precise, relevant evidence supports thesis. Sources are cited.

### Weathering High Prices

Most people aren't concerned about bad weather when it happens in another part of the country. A cold snap in Florida, however, or heavy rains in Iowa might end up hurting everyone, no matter where he or she lives. <u>Severe weather can directly affect prices of food, oil, and other consumer goods.</u> When these prices go up, they have ripple effects that can be surprising.

Poor weather can have an effect on food supplies. A sudden freeze in Florida, Texas, or California can ruin the citrus crops in these states. Floods in the midwest can destroy fields of grain or corn. As supplies drop, the prices of these products rise. When there are fewer oranges, grapefruits and lemons in the market, consumers end up paying more for the fruits themselves, for the juice that's made from them, and even for lemon-scented cleaners. If wheat costs more, so does bread, cereal, flour, and even pizza. If farmers pay more for corn to feed their livestock, then the price of meat, leather, and milk can also go up.

In 2005, Hurricane Katrina and a series of hurricanes slammed into the Gulf Coast. This area is one of the major energy producers for the entire country. The hurricanes damaged oil refineries and offshore drilling platforms in the Gulf of Mexico. Some were shut down for weeks and even months. As a result, gasoline prices nationwide skyrocketed (Hermaning 36). Higher gas prices can have a widespread effect. People pay more to drive their cars and heat their houses, which has an impact on family budgets and spending. The cost of airplane flights goes up. Products that are transported by truck or boat cost more to ship. That includes food, mail, and retail products like clothing, toys, and electronic goods. Also, many products are made from oil, including plastic, which is used in everything from zippers to medical equipment. Higher oil prices can cause consumers to pay more for a wide range of products and services (Werner 109).

---

Applied Sciences

The **middle** paragraphs continue to sustain thesis with relevant evidence.

Severe weather can spread its economic effects across the nation. According to Nicholas Grierson, "Weather problems and disasters related to weather cost billions each year. Between 1990 and 2008, insurers paid $300 billion for weather-related problems" ("Economic Impact of the Weather"). When disasters hit a community, agencies could spend billions to get things running again. Often the government has to step in to help. Citizens pay for these costs through taxes, insurance hikes, and higher prices. Fortunately, many communities recover quickly after a weather-related disaster.

The **ending** restates the thesis and leaves the reader with a final thought.

Next time you pay more for a pizza, think about the long chain that caused the increase. It could be due to tomato crops damaged by weather. Maybe the delivery driver paid more for gas because oil production slowed. None of us should take for granted the weather report from across the country. When it rains a thousand miles away, we may not have to take an umbrella to work, but when the weather is bad, everyone pays.

**Works Cited**

Hermaning, Charles. *The Economic Impact of Katrina.* New

York: Heath and Sons. 2009. Print.

Werner, Erica. *The High Cost of Oil: Will It Ever Come*

*Down?* Dallas: Midway Press. 2010. Print.

Grierson, Nicholas. "Economic Impact of the Weather:

Unplanned Disasters." *Applied Science News* July

2010. Web. 15 March 2011.

## Try It!

Write an essay of analysis about a complex issue. Follow the guidelines on pages **486–487**.

---

Review the qualities of a strong ending. Have students identify how the thesis (or hypothesis) is restated. Also, review the importance of using a variety of sources and of citing these sources correctly.

### Try It!

Be sure to give students ample time to research, draft, revise, and edit. If possible, schedule a class session in the library to reinforce the research process. Provide a classroom copy of the *MLA Handbook* or the style guide of your preference. Invite students to share their completed reports with the class.

☑ DIFFERENTIATE INSTRUCTION

TEKS 10.13B, 10.15A(i), 10.15A(v)

---

## Differentiated Instruction: English Language Learners

ELPS 2I, 3E, 4F, 4G

| ELP Level **Beginning** | ELP Level **Intermediate** | ELP Level **Advanced/Advanced High** |
|---|---|---|
| Work with students to develop a list of accessible topics for their essays. Then help them identify possible sources of adapted information about their topics. | Have students work with partners to identify key words for their chosen topics. Once students choose key words, encourage them to use the library or the Internet to start their research. | Review the rules for parenthetical citations. Remind students that even when they paraphrase, they need to cite the unique ideas of others. |

**TEKS** **10.13B** Structure ideas in a sustained way; **10.15A(i)** Write an analytical essay that includes a concluding paragraph; **10.15A(v)** Write an analytical essay that includes details;

**ELPS** **2I** Demonstrate listening comprehension in increasingly complex spoken language by collaborating with peers and taking notes; **3E** Share information in cooperative learning interactions; **4F** Use support from peers/teachers to enhance and confirm understanding; **4G** Demonstrate comprehension of increasingly complex English/taking notes

## Other Forms of Practical Writing

Read aloud the different kinds of writing and the prompts. Invite students to choose one of the prompts to respond to using the writing process. Review organizational structures associated with certain kinds of writing:

- Narrative essay: chronological order
- Process essay: sequential order
- Compare-and-contrast essay: point-by-point or block organization

Also provide reproducible graphic organizers such as the time line or details chart (see TE Appendix) for students to use in their prewriting activities.

**490**

# Other Forms of Practical Writing

**Narrative Essay**

*Child Care*—Write an account of your first babysitting experience. Include mistakes you made and techniques that worked best.

**Process Essay**

*Drafting*—Explain the steps to create an accurate floor plan of your classroom. Include each step in order, using imperative sentences.

**Letter of Application**

*Career Explorations*—Write a cover letter to accompany a résumé. Include an introductory paragraph, a brief background and experience paragraph, and a personal statement about why you want the job.

**Classification Essay**

*Textile Arts*—Define and explain the different types of stitches used in needlework. Tell what each is used for and the effect it can create.

**Problem-Solution Essay**

*Machine Shop*—Write a problem-solution essay about a motor that isn't working. Explain the cause of the problem and explore possible solutions. Indicate which solution is the best and why.

**Proposal**

*Wood Shop*—Design a piece of furniture meant for a specific place or function (for example, a bench along a garden path or a coatrack in a hallway). Write a proposal that explains your design and persuades your teacher to let you build it.

**Compare-Contrast Essay**

*Cooking Class*—Write a compare-contrast essay explaining the various leavening agents (yeast, baking powder, baking soda) and their effects on baked goods.

---

**Differentiated Instruction: English Language Learners**

⭐ **ELPS** 1A, 2E, 3B, 3E, 3G, 4D

| ELP Level **Beginning** | ELP Level **Intermediate** | ELP Level **Advanced/Advanced High** |
|---|---|---|
| Draw a web on the board with *art* in the center. Show pictures of different art forms. Have students name them, then write each in an outlying circle. Tell students they will now analyze art. | Write: *Color, Subject, Spatial Relationships, Brushstrokes*. Tell students these are elements of a painting they will analyze. Provide descriptions as needed. | Explain that students can read a painting the way they read a story. Have groups discuss a Miro painting: how it makes them feel and what they think Miro was trying to say. |

**ELPS 1A** Use prior knowledge to understand meanings; **2E** Use visual support to enhance and confirm understanding of increasingly complex spoken language; **3B** Expand vocabulary by retelling information represented or supported by pictures; **3E** Share information in cooperative learning interactions; **3G** Express ideas and feelings ranging from communicating short phrases to participating in discussions; **4D** Use prereading supports to enhance comprehension of written text/graphic organizers, illustrations, and topic-related vocabulary

# Writing in the Arts

Artists have special powers. A sculptor's chisel can turn rock into skin and cloth, a composer's pen can create landscapes out of sound, and a painter's brush can make a woman immortal. From ancient cave paintings to modern light shows, art empowers human beings to express thoughts and emotions that otherwise would go unspoken.

One way to capture the power of art is to write about it. When you translate paint and stone and notes into words, you understand art more deeply. This chapter will help you write essays and create presentations about the arts.

- ■ Writing Guidelines: Response to an Art Prompt
- ■ Writing Guidelines: Research Report in the Arts

"I try to apply colors like words
that shape poems, like notes
that shape music."

—Joan Miro

# Writing in the Arts

### Objectives

- practice responding to an art prompt
- learn and apply writing guidelines to a research presentation

### Descriptive Essay

The lessons on the following pages provide samples of writing students might do in an art or music class. Assigning these forms of writing will depend on:

- ■ the skill level of your students,
- ■ the arts-related subjects they are studying, and
- ■ the writing goals of your school, district, or state.

Talk with students about the meaning of the quotation on this page, and invite those who enjoy art or music to talk about whether they see parallels between creating art and writing.

To provide added background, briefly explain that Joan Miro was a Spanish artist (note that *Joan* is pronounced *Juan*), and show examples of his work. Many are available on the Internet or in print surveys of modern art.

✔ DIFFERENTIATE INSTRUCTION

## Resources

### Copy Masters (TE Appendix)

- Sensory chart (TE p. 504)
- 5 W's chart (TE p. 504)
- Details chart (TE p. 504)

## Writing Guidelines
### Response to an Art Prompt

Review the STRAP method of analyzing an expository writing prompt. Then have students apply the categories to the sample prompt.

- Subject—the importance of Frank Lloyd Wright's masterpiece, Fallingwater
- Type—multiparagraph essay
- Role—student interested in architecture
- Audience—teacher
- Purpose—to explain (expository writing)

**DIFFERENTIATE INSTRUCTION ↘**

✱ For more about applying the STRAP questions to expository writing prompts, see SE page 130.

Review with students all the bullet points on SE page 492. Tell students that arts writing prompts often ask them to explore the mood or tone of a work of art. As they examine the mood of a piece during prewriting, they might want to list a variety of adjectives that describe the mood. Encourage students to use a Thesaurus to identify additional synonyms for the words on their lists.

After students have completed their drafts, have them use revising and editing checklists to refine their essays. Alternately, have them use a peer response process to get and give feedback.

**TEKS** 10.13A, 10.13D, 10.13C, 10.13D, 10.17C, 10.18A, 10.18B(i), 10.18B(ii), 10.18B(iii), 10.19, 10.21C; **ELPS** 4C, 4F, 5C

---

**TEKS** 10.13A–10.13D, 10.17C, 10.18A, 10.18B(i)–10.18B(iii), 10.19, 10.21C
**ELPS** 5C

## Writing Guidelines Response to an Art Prompt

Responding to a prompt allows you to apply what you know about a specific work. Here are guidelines for planning and writing a response for the arts.

### Prewriting

- **Choose the appropriate genre, or form.** Identify your audiences. Read through the prompt and focus on what it is asking you to do. Is the purpose to explain, compare, describe, persuade?
- **Gather your details.** Go through your notes and any research materials you are allowed to use. Highlight or jot down the details you will use in your response. Be sure to record and accurately cite the sources of any quotations or facts you use.
- **Organize your details.** Check the prompt for clues about organizing your response. For example, if the prompt asks you to "describe Cezanne's painting *Girl at the Piano* and tell how the color choices affect the mood," you might begin with a general description of the painting, then zero in on the main figures, and end with a discussion of colors and mood. Make an outline or a graphic organizer to help organize your thoughts.

### Drafting

- **Write freely.** Use your notes, outline or graphic organizer as a guide. Some short-response essays are one paragraph long. However, if a prompt calls for several main points, write a separate paragraph for each. Cite and format your sources correctly.

### Revising

- **Improve your writing.** Read your draft and cut any details that don't fit the prompt. Also add information that will clarify the ideas in your response. Be as complete as possible.
- **Improve your style.** Check your *word choice* and *sentence fluency* to make sure that your response reads smoothly.

### Editing

- **Check for conventions and prepare your final copy.** Look for and correct errors in grammar, sentence structure, capitalization, punctuation, and spelling. Use quotations to set off sarcasm and irony, and use dashes to emphasize parenthetical information. Copy your response paper, and proofread it a final time.

---

**TEKS** **10.13A** Plan a first draft by selecting the correct genre and determining topics through a range of strategies; **10.13B** Structure ideas in a sustained way; **10.13C** Revise drafts to improve style and word choice; **10.13D** Edit drafts for grammar, mechanics, and spelling; **10.17C** Use a variety of correctly structured sentences; **10.18A** Use conventions of capitalization; **10.18B(i)** Use commas in nonrestrictive phrases and contrasting expressions and in clauses; **10.18B(ii)** Use quotation marks to indicate sarcasm and irony; **10.18B(iii)** Use dashes to emphasize parenthetical information; **10.19** Spell correctly using resources to determine and check correct spelling; **10.21C** Accurately cite researched information; **ELPS** **4C** Comprehend vocabulary used in written classroom materials; **4F** Use support from peers/teachers to enhance and confirm understanding; **5C** Spell familiar words with increasing accuracy

Arts

## Response to an Art Prompt

Maria wrote this response to a prompt about architecture.

### Prompt

> *Why is Frank Lloyd Wright's house Fallingwater so important to American architecture? Cite the design's special features and techniques and discuss the public's early response to it in a multiparagraph answer.*

### Sample Response

**The writer provides background and her main point. She correctly used quotation marks.**

**Writer supports main point by citing particular details. She summarizes information from her source.**

**The writer uses specific examples and details to demonstrate her understanding.**

> Architect Frank Lloyd Wright designed Fallingwater in 1936 as a country retreat for a Pennsylvania family. In this house, Wright spotlighted his key principle of designing "organic" houses, letting people live in harmony with nature.
>
> The house stands on top of a waterfall and seems like part of the rock formation. Its central core of stacked sandstone rises out of the rock, and terraces of reinforced concrete mimic the ledges over the waterfall. Glass walls on three sides open the house to the woods around it, and windows framed in a warm red offset the neutral sandstone.
>
> Fallingwater was immediately famous, even appearing on the cover of <u>Time</u> magazine in 1938. The house's design renewed Frank Lloyd Wright's career and shifted the direction of modern architecture back toward natural materials. Critics and fans agree that Fallingwater is a revolutionary design.
>
> Many of the features of Fallingwater are still used in home building today. For example, Wright's idea of making walls of glass is popular in modern homes. The natural wood and stone in the home's interior are seen today in stone walls and fireplaces and in wood flooring, paneling, and trim. Wright's idea of making a home part of the natural setting also carries through in much of modern architecture.

### Try It!

Respond to a short-essay prompt your teacher will supply about a topic you are studying. Write a multiparagraph answer. Be sure to follow all guidelines for prewriting, drafting, revising, and editing.

---

### Response to an Art Prompt

Ask students to describe how the writer addressed the prompt in each part of the essay. Possible responses:

- **Beginning**—The writer explains what Fallingwater is and why Wright designed it that way.
- **Middle paragraph 1**—The writer describes the features of the house in detail.
- **Middle paragraph 2**—The writer describes the public response to Fallingwater and how American architecture began to change as a result.
- **End**—The writer refers to the idea of harmony with nature mentioned in the opening; describes the house's effect on architecture today.

**ELPS** 4I, 4J

✱ For more about writing thesis statements, see SE page 630.

### Try It!

Remind students to be sure to choose the correct genre for the given prompt and provide summaries, paraphrases, and quotes to support their ideas. If you decide to make this a timed writing assignment, remind students of the need to plan and manage their time effectively.

**TEKS** 10.13A, 10.21C, 10.23E; **ELPS** 5G

---

## Differentiated Instruction: English Language Learners

**ELPS** 2E, 3F, 4F, 4G

| ELP Level **Beginning** | ELP Level **Intermediate** | ELP Level **Advanced/Advanced High** |
|---|---|---|
| Show students pictures of Fallingwater. Ask: *What makes this house special? Do you like the house? Why?* Provide frames for responses if necessary. | Help students analyze the prompt by connecting its text to the response. For example, ask: *In which paragraph is the question answered? (last)* | Explain that when students read a prompt, they should look for key words and ideas. Guide students to name the topic of the writing, the length, and what to include. |

**TEKS** **10.13A** Plan a first draft by selecting the correct genre; **10.21C** Paraphrase, quote, and accurately cite researched information; **10.23E** Synthesize research into a presentation that uses a style manual to document sources; **ELPS** **2E** Use visual and contextual support to enhance and confirm understanding of increasingly complex spoken language; **3F** Give information/ranging from using a limited high-frequency vocabulary to using abstract and content-based vocabulary during speaking; **4F** Use support from peers/teachers to enhance and confirm understanding; **4G** Demonstrate comprehension of increasingly complex English/responding to questions; **4I** Demonstrate comprehension by employing basic reading skills; **4J** Demonstrate comprehension and expand reading skills by employing inferential skills/predicting, making connections between ideas, drawing conclusions from text, and finding supporting evidence; **5G** Explain with increasing specificity and detail/writing

## Writing Guidelines
### Research Report in the Arts

Reiterate that art can be "read" like literature. Instead of words, artists use color, composition, and detail to express themes, tones, and mood.

### Selecting a Topic

Tell students to use the strategy that works best for them to come up with topics. They might browse the Internet, make a list from their own prior knowledge, or talk with partners to come up with ideas.

 10.13A, 10.20A

### Forming a Research Question

After students narrow their topics and conduct initial research, discuss what they would like to find out about their topics. Tell students to consider what aspects of the topics interest them most and use these aspects as springboards for forming research questions.

**DIFFERENTIATE INSTRUCTION ↘**

 10.20A

### Forming a Research Plan

Tell students that their research plans should include not only possible sources of information but also a time line for students to complete the research.

**TEKS** 10.20B

---

**TEKS** 10.13A, 10.20A, 10.20B

## Writing Guidelines Research Report in the Arts

At some point, you may be asked to write a research report in an art or music class. Your topic may be a famous sculptor, painter, composer, or specific style of art or music. The following guidelines will help you with such an assignment.

### Selecting a Topic

- **Brainstorm.** Think freely about topics in art or music that interest you. Make a list of your ideas that pertain to the class.
- **Consult with others.** When you have finished your own brainstorming, ask classmates or your teacher what they think about the ideas on your list. They may be able to add ideas and point out ideas that will not work. Listen openly and carefully to what they have to say.
- **Choose your topic.** After you have consulted with others and reviewed or revised your list, choose a topic. Make sure that your art or music topic is broad enough to write a report, but not so broad that you cannot cover it adequately.

### Forming a Research Question

- **Narrow your topic.** Remember that your topic must not be so broad that you cannot cover it. One of the strategies that you might use in your planning is to create a general categories list or a cluster diagram about the broad, general topic. Put asterisks next to the particular topics that interest you the most.
- **Conduct initial research.** Use the categories that interest you the most and conduct initial research to learn more about each one.
- **Formulate a major research question.** Using your initial research, formulate a question that will be the focus of your essay.

### Forming a Research Plan

- **Gather information.** Use well-known and well-respected authoritative sources in the arts. As you conduct your research, focus on your major research question, which will be a complex, multi-faceted topic. Consult sources that are valid, reliable, and accurate. Plan to use a variety of sources for your research.

---

**Differentiated Instruction: Struggling Learners**

Draw a KWL chart on the board. Show how to use it to form research questions. Tell students to record information from research and their prior knowledge under Know, then form questions about what they Want to learn. Finally, they fill in the Learned column from their research.

**TEKS** 10.20A; **ELPS** 1A

---

 **TEKS** **10.13A** Plan a first draft by determining topics through a range of strategies; **10.20A** Brainstorm, consult with others, and decide on a research topic/formulate a research question to the research topic; **10.20B** Formulate a plan for research on a complex, multi-faceted topic; **ELPS 1A** Use prior knowledge to understand meanings

Arts

## Following Your Research Plan

- **Compile your data.** Use a gathering grid like the one shown here. In the left column, list your questions about the topic. In the others, list sources of your answers. For long answers, use note cards.

### Gathering Grid

| TUVAN THROAT SINGING | Edmonds, Curtis. Rev. of *Genghis Blues.* | Leighton, Ralph. *Tuva or Bust: Richard Feynman's Last Journey.* |
|---|---|---|
| 1. What is throat singing? | Vocal technique from Central Asia | Single vocalist; two or more distinct pitches simultaneously |
| 2. What does it sound like? | Human bagpipe | |

- **Identify and research major issues and debates.** Find valid, reliable, accurate sources that address all sides of the issue.
- **Cite your sources.** Keep track of and correctly cite sources in your essay. Follow the style guide recommended by your teacher.

## Paraphrasing, Summarizing, and Using Quotations

- **Paraphrasing means to put ideas in your own words.** You must give credit to the source of the ideas.
- **Summarizing means to present the most important ideas.** You must also give credit to the source of the ideas.
- **Using quotations means using the exact words of a source.** Enclose those words in quotation marks and give credit to the source. Expressions of irony and/or sarcasm may also be set off with quotation marks.

## Following Your Research Plan

Review the way the Gathering Grid organizes information. Point out that each source is identified clearly. Tell students that they need to collect publication information for all their sources and that they need to credit these sources within their reports even when they summarize or paraphrase ideas.
✔ DIFFERENTIATE INSTRUCTION

Note for students the major issues that the writer plans to address in the essay. Remind students that identifying the major issues and debates related to their research questions is an important part of all research report writing.
TEKS 10.21A, 10.21B, 10.21C

 **TEKS** 10.21A Follow the research plan to compile data that identifies major issues and debates; **10.21B** Organize information from multiple sources to create graphics and forms; **10.21C** Paraphrase, summarize, quote, and accurately cite researched information; **ELPS 2E** Use visual support to enhance and confirm understanding of increasingly complex spoken language; **3B** Expand vocabulary by learning and using routine language needed for classroom communication; **3E** Share information in cooperative learning interactions; **4G** Demonstrate comprehension of increasingly complex English/ summarizing material

## Prewriting

Review each step in the prewriting process. Explain that there are more prewriting steps for research writing because the report is longer and more in depth than an essay.

Explain that a sentence outline is preferable to a topic outline for writing a long research report because it provides a framework for each paragraph in the report. Sometimes students can create their first drafts by adding transitions between the sentences.

⭐ **TEKS** 10.13A, 10.13B, 10.22A, 10.22B, 10.22C

✱ For more about creating an outline, SE pages 626–627.

Some word-processing programs have a built-in outline feature or a template for creating an outline. Encourage students to find out if such a feature is available with the program they use.

---

## Prewriting

- **Write your initial thesis statement.** With your initial research complete, you can write a controlling idea, or focus, for your report. Using your controlling idea, write an initial thesis statement for your report.

- **Evaluate the relevance of your research.** With your thesis statement in mind, look back at your research. Is it all relevant to the thesis statement? Have your sources identified and addressed major issues and debates within your topic?

- **Evaluate your sources for reliability, accuracy, and validity.** Check to make sure that you used unbiased, well-respected works and authors in the arts as the sources for your research. Examine each source for authority and objectivity. You may need to do more research to replace sources that do not meet these criteria.

- **Critique your research process.** Evaluate your research process at each step. Make any changes, adjustments, or revisions that are needed.

- **Review and revise your initial thesis statement.** With your research complete and evaluated for relevance, accuracy, and validity, you should review your initial thesis statement. Revise it as needed so that it reflects the major research question, and then, if needed, write a new thesis statement.

- **Create an outline.** Use your thesis statement and your research to create an outline for your report. It will help you organize your details in a logical fashion. Also note where you might include illustrations, graphics, or other visuals to enhance your report.

---

⭐ **TEKS** **10.13A** Plan a first draft by developing a thesis or idea; **10.13B** Structure ideas in a sustained way; **10.22A** Modify the major research question to refocus the research plan; **10.22B** Evaluate the relevance of information to the topic/determine the reliability, validity, and accuracy of sources by examining their objectivity and authority; **10.22C** Critique the research process to implement changes as need is identified

TEKS 10.13B, 10.23A–10.23C, 10.23E

Arts

## Drafting

- **Write your introductory paragraph.** Write an introductory paragraph that contains background information about your topic and clearly presents your thesis statement.
- **Develop your middle paragraphs in a logical order.** Follow or revise your outline so that the ideas in your essay progress in a logical way for the reader.
- Provide relevant, reliable, and accurate details and valid evidence to support the thesis statement. Remember to cite your sources correctly.
- Clearly state your point of view, based on the research that you have done.
- As appropriate, include graphs, illustrations, and other visuals to emphasize or demonstrate your points. Each visual you include should enhance your meaning and help the reader understand the points you are making.
- Connect your ideas with transitions so that your ideas flow smoothly from one to the next.
- Follow an approved style guide, such as the MLA Style Guide. Be sure to cite and format sources correctly within your report and in your works-cited page.

## Drafting

Remind students to consult the outlines they created during prewriting to clearly express their thesis statements and sustain ideas through logical organization. Encourage students to develop a distinctive point of view throughout the report.

Have students brainstorm ideas for graphics and illustrations to use in their reports. Brainstorming can be effectively accomplished using small groups of students who are writing on similar topics.

Tell students to consult the *MLA Handbook* or other resources you supply for information about formatting and documenting sources. Remind students of the need to cite sources for graphics and illustrations created by others.

✔ **DIFFERENTIATE INSTRUCTION**

TEKS 10.13B, 10.23A, 10.23B, 10.23C, 10.23E; **ELPS** 5G

---

## Differentiated Instruction: English Language Learners

**ELPS** 3E, 4F, 5F, 5G

| **ELP Level** Beginning | **ELP Level** Intermediate | **ELP Level** Advanced/Advanced High |
|---|---|---|
| Help students access English vocabulary needed to express their findings. Have students identify a quote and then work with them to properly paraphrase, using students' own words. | Have students independently write their thesis statements, then meet with small groups to share and discuss them, making suggestions for improvement. | Have students in groups collaborate on the introductory paragraph and assign supporting reasons to different writers, then reconvene and work to add transitions. |

**TEKS** **10.13B** Structure ideas in a sustained way; **10.23A** Synthesize research into a presentation in support of a clear thesis and related claims; **10.23B** Synthesize research into a presentation that reflects a progression of ideas and a stated point of view; **10.23C** Synthesize research into a presentation that uses graphics and illustrations to explain concepts; **10.23E** Synthesize research into a presentation that uses a style manual to document sources and format written materials; **ELPS** **3E** Share information in cooperative learning interactions; **4F** Use support from peers/teachers to enhance understanding and develop vocabulary; **5F** Write using a variety of grade-appropriate connecting words in increasingly accurate ways; **5G** Explain with increasing specificity and detail/writing

## Revising

Use the revising questions on SE page 498 to have students evaluate the sample report on SE pages 499–500 or another research report. Be sure students can identify the thesis, organizational pattern, and the topic sentences and details that support the thesis in each middle paragraph. Also have students evaluate the effectiveness of the writer's voice and use of a formal tone.

Then set up peer conferencing for students to revise their own writing. Have students first complete an independent revision and then present their writing to an assigned peer group. Each group member should read the report and complete a revising checklist.

## Editing

Have students work independently to complete the editing step for their own essays. Encourage them to use the questions on SE page 498 to create their own editing checklist. Remind students that they will likely need to review their essay several times, each time looking for specific types of errors. **DIFFERENTIATE INSTRUCTION ⇘**

**TEKS** 10.13C, 10.13D, 10.17C, 10.18A, 10.18B(i), 10.18B(ii), 10.18B(iii), 10.19, 10.22C, 10.23D; **ELPS** 3E, 5C, 5D, 5E, 5F

---

**TEKS** 10.13C, 10.13D, 10.17C, 10.18A, 10.18B(i)–10.18B(iii), 10.19, 10.22C, 10.23D
**ELPS** 5C, 5F

## Revising

- **Review and revise your essay.** Review and revise your essay for *focus and coherence, organization, development of ideas,* and *voice.* Use the following questions to guide you.

  1. Is your thesis statement clear to the reader?
  2. Does your conclusion tie back to the thesis statement and leave the reader with a final thought?
  3. Do your ideas follow a logical pattern so that the essay forms a cohesive whole?
  4. Have you used transitions so that ideas flow smoothly from paragraph to paragraph and within paragraphs?
  5. Does each paragraph have a topic sentence, and are the topic sentences supported with valid, accurate evidence and well-chosen details?
  6. Have you used a variety of evaluative tools to examine the quality of the research?
  7. Do you sound knowledgeable and interested in the topic?
  8. Have you used a more formal tone that is appropriate for the audience and the genre?

## Editing: Checking Your Writing

- **Check for errors in grammar, sentence structure, capitalization, punctuation, and spelling.** Correct all your errors.

  1. Correct any errors in grammar, including verb tenses. Try to use the active voice whenever possible.
  2. Check your sentence structure and sentence fluency. Try to use a variety of sentence types.
  3. Check all your mechanics, especially use of commas, quotations marks, and end punctuation. Make sure that proper nouns are correctly capitalized. Check to make sure that you have introduced and punctuated quotations correctly and set off sarcasm or irony in quotation marks. Dashes should be used to emphasize parenthetical information.
  4. Recheck your spelling to make sure that all words, especially technical terms and specialized vocabulary, are spelled correctly.

- **Prepare a final copy.** Make a neat final copy of your essay.

---

**TEKS** **10.13C** Revise drafts to improve word choice and sentence variety; **10.13D** Edit drafts for grammar, mechanics, and spelling; **10.17C** Use a variety of correctly structured sentences; **10.18A** Use conventions of capitalization; **10.18B(i)** Use commas in nonrestrictive phrases and contrasting expressions and in clauses; **10.18B(ii)** Use quotation marks to indicate sarcasm and irony; **10.18B(iii)** Use dashes to emphasize parenthetical information; **10.19** Spell correctly using resources to determine and check correct spelling; **10.22C** Critique the research process to implement changes as need is identified; **10.23D** Synthesize research into a presentation that uses evaluative tools to examine the research; **ELPS** **3E** Share information in cooperative learning interactions; **5C** Spell familiar words/employ spelling patterns and rules with increasing accuracy; **5D** Edit writing for standard grammar and usage/subject-verb and pronoun agreement and appropriate verb tenses; **5E** Employ increasingly complex grammatical structures in content area writing such as using correct verbs, tenses, and pronouns/possessive case/negatives and contractions; **5F** Write using a variety of grade-appropriate sentence lengths, patterns, and connecting words/combine in increasingly accurate ways

## Research Report

Sean wrote the following report about Tuvan throat singing. After listening to a CD, he had became curious about how this unusual music developed. He decided to research Tuva, its people, and its music.

### Sample Report

| |
|---|
| The introduction presents the thesis statement for the report. |

| |
|---|
| The body of the report explains what throat singing is and how and where it developed. Ideas are fully developed and supported with precise, relevant details. Organization is logical. Sources are cited. |

### Tuvan Throat Singing: A Unique Vocal Art

The throat singers of Tuva, a remote area of Central Asia, bring a unique musical heritage into the twenty-first century. Throat singing is a vocal technique in which a single vocalist produces two or more distinct pitches simultaneously. One reviewer described the sound as a human bagpipe (Edmonds). This singing technique reflects the lifestyle and the surrounding natural world of the singers.

For many years, throat singing was not well known in the Western world. That's because this technique developed and flourished in places with little contact with the outside world. Tuva is a small Russian republic bordering Mongolia. The remote location and Soviet-era travel restrictions limited visitors but also allowed Tuvans to preserve their musical traditions (Leighton 45).

Throat singing developed among the seminomadic herders who make up much of the area's population. Tuvans herd their horses, sheep, and yaks across dry steppe lands and in the taiga, a cold, mountainous, forested area. Because throat singing produces a musical sound that carries over long distances, the music became a way for shepherds and horsemen to entertain each other and communicate. Variations of throat singing are also found in nearby areas of Mongolia, the Altai region, and other parts of Asia ("Types of Throat Singing").

In Tuva, throat singers use their voices to include the sounds of the natural world—whistling birds, bubbling streams, and blowing wind—in their songs. Because the horse is such an important part of Tuvan culture, many traditional songs have a rhythm that sounds like a cantering horse.

*Khoomei,* from the Mongolian word for throat singing, is the general name for Tuvan throat singing and also

---

## Research Report

Read aloud the sample report and the side notes. Guide students to connect the elements and techniques noted in the side notes to specific portions of the text. Discuss the organization and the content that supports the thesis.

TEKS 10.13B, 10.23A, 10.23B, 10.23E; **ELPS** 4J

---

## Differentiated Instruction: English Language Learners

ELPS 3E, 5A, 5C, 5F

| ELP Level **Beginning** | ELP Level **Intermediate** | ELP Level **Advanced/Advanced High** |
|---|---|---|
| Remind students that *ough* can represent several sounds: *through, dough, ought, rough.* Have students read their writing to partners, checking spelling and pronunciation of *ough* words. | Have students use two colors of highlighters to mark every other sentence, then examine their lengths. Students can then work to achieve variety in sentence lengths. | Have students edit for variety in sentence patterns. Suggest students read aloud their writing to identify repetitiveness; then use phrases/clauses to vary patterns. |

TEKS **10.13B** Structure ideas in a sustained way; **10.23A** Synthesize research into a presentation in support of a clear thesis and related claims; **10.23B** Synthesize research into a presentation that reflects a progression of ideas and a stated point of view; **10.23E** Synthesize research into a presentation that uses a style manual to document sources and format written materials; **ELPS 3E** Share information in cooperative learning interactions; **4J** Demonstrate comprehension and expand reading skills by employing inferential skills/predicting, making connections between ideas, drawing conclusions from text, and finding supporting evidence; **5A** Learn relationships between sounds and letters to represent sounds when writing in English; **5C** Spell familiar words/employ spelling patterns and rules with increasing accuracy; **5F** Write using a variety of grade-appropriate sentence lengths and patterns in increasingly accurate ways

Continue to read aloud the sample essay and the side notes. Guide students to connect the elements and techniques noted in the side notes to specific portions of the text. Discuss the organization and the content that support the thesis. Discuss how the conclusion relates to the introduction. Then review the Works Cited and point out the format that the writer followed.

**TEKS** 10.13B, 10.23A, 10.23B, 10.23E; **ELPS** 4J

---

 **TEKS** 10.13B, 10.23A, 10.23B, 10.23E

> Sources are cited in the report. Writer continues to support thesis with well-chosen, relevant evidence. Research sources are accurate, valid, and reliable.

refers to a specific type of simple throat singing. Other styles of throat singing include *sygyt,* which features a whistling tone; *kargyraa,* which uses flaps (the so-called false vocal chords) in the throat to produce notes an octave below the sung note; and *ezengileer,* which incorporates a horseback-riding rhythm ("Types of Throat Singing").

Throat singers perform alone or in groups, often accompanied by traditional Tuvan instruments. Common instruments include the *igil,* a two-stringed fiddle; the *dosh-poluur,* a guitarlike instrument; and the *xomus,* a type of mouth harp ("Types of Throat Singing").

In recent years, scholars, musicians and even tourists have discovered Tuva and its music. An Academy-award-nominated documentary, *Genghis Blues,* brought international attention to Tuva (Edmonds). Tuvan musicians now regularly tour in Europe and the United States as well as in Russia. Tuvan music is even online.

> The essay concludes with information on recent developments.

Large music festivals and throat singing competitions each summer bring hundreds of international musicians and fans to Tuva. Tuvan organizations such as the Tuvan Institute for Humanities work with Tuvan musicians and scholars to preserve the country's unique musical form and encourage young singers to learn it (Leighton 55).

---

> Turn to pages **407–410** for more on creating a "Works Cited" page.

### Works Cited

Edmonds, Curtis. Rev. of *Ghenghis Blues* by Paul Penn. *TXReviews* 11 July 2006. Web. 16 Jan. 2011.

Leighton, Ralph. *Tuva or Bust: Richard Feynman's Last Journey.* New York: W. W. Norton, 2000. Print.

"Types of Throat Singing." *LandofTuva.com.* Foreign Languages and Education Association. 12 February 2009. Web. 17 Jan. 2011.

---

**TEKS** **10.13B** Structure ideas in a sustained way; **10.23A** Synthesize research into a presentation in support of a clear thesis and related claims; **10.23B** Synthesize research into a presentation that reflects a progression of ideas and a stated point of view; **10.23E** Synthesize research into a presentation that uses a style manual to document sources and format written materials; **ELPS 4J** Demonstrate comprehension and expand reading skills by employing inferential skills/predicting, making connections between ideas, drawing conclusions from text, and finding supporting evidence

# Creating a Multimedia Presentation

To transform your written art or music report into a multimedia presentation, you must first consider your purpose, your audience, and the context for your presentation.

## Determining Your Purpose

Your purpose is your reason for giving the multimedia presentation.

- **Informative presentations** educate by providing valuable, accurate information about the topic.
- **Demonstration presentations** show your audience how to do or how to make something.

## Considering Your Audience and Context

As you think about the audience that will see and hear your presentation, keep the following points in mind.

- **Be clear.** Your audience should understand your main points immediately. They should also be able to see and to hear the presentation easily. Creating good visuals and sound will enable your audience to focus on and understand the key points.
- **Anticipate questions.** As you develop your script and your presentation, think about questions your audience might ask and how you will answer them. This will help keep your audience engaged. It will also show that you are knowledgeable about the topic.

## Reviewing Your Report

In a multimedia report, your audience cannot go back to clarify information, re-read paragraphs, or re-examine graphics or illustrations. It is critical to plan visual aids and sounds that will help explain concepts. They should also create interest in the topic.

In a multimedia presentation, you will control the pacing. Your multimedia presentation should move quickly enough to keep the audience engaged, but it should also enable audience members to understand key ideas and concepts.

Arts

## Creating a Multimedia Presentation

Research reports about subjects related to the arts are especially suitable for multimedia presentations because the visual or auditory elements are inherent to the topics. Showing a picture or playing music is often the best way to demonstrate key ideas to a variety of audiences. ✔DIFFERENTIATE INSTRUCTION

### Determining Your Purpose

Tell students that they will be creating an informative presentation from their research reports.

### Considering Your Audience and Context

Tell students that once they determine purpose, they will need to fashion their presentations to appeal to their particular audience—in this case, classmates and teacher.

### Reviewing Your Report

Tell students to keep their content and their audiences in mind as they prepare reports by adding graphics, images, and sound. Explain that these additions need to support the information in the report, not distract the audience.

★ TEKS 10.15D

---

**TEKS 10.15D** Produce a multimedia presentation with graphics, images, and sound that conveys a point of view and appeals to a specific audience; **ELPS 3B** Expand vocabulary by learning and using high-frequency words for identifying and describing/ retelling information supported by pictures/learning and using routine language for classroom communication; **3D** Speak using grade-level content area vocabulary/new words and academic language proficiency; **3E** Share information in cooperative learning interactions; **3H** Explain with increasing specificity and detail

## Reworking Your Report

### Writing Your Script

Read the instruction and have students read the sample script to structure their own writing for the **Try It!** activity.

### Try It!

Help students search the library or Internet to find images to support their presentations. Suggest that students create their own graphics and write descriptions of the sounds or music that will help them set the mood and tone for their presentations.  DIFFERENTIATE INSTRUCTION ↘

⭐ **TEKS** 10.14C, 10.15D

---

 **TEKS** 10.14C, 10.15D

## Reworking Your Report

When you create a multimedia presentation, you must focus on your message: conveying your thesis statement and supporting ideas. You must also concentrate on the visual and sound elements.

### Writing Your Script

- **Transform your written report into a script.** Your written report will serve as the basis for your script. Make sure that you follow a logical pattern for your audience and purpose. Make sure that your ideas in the script are fully developed. Develop graphics, images, and sounds for your presentation. In your script, note where each of these elements will go and give a brief description of each.

- **Develop graphics, images, and sounds.** As you create your script, remember that this is a multimedia presentation. Develop graphics, images, and sounds that are relevant to the topic and that are appropriate for the audience. Make sure that these elements will appeal to your audience.

- **Convey a distinctive point of view.** As you develop your graphics, images, and sounds, make sure that they convey a distinctive point of view. While your report should present an honest and unbiased view of the topic, you should still convey your own point of view. Use your graphics and sound to help accomplish this objective.

- **Convey your theme, or thesis, mood, and tone.** As you write your script and plan your multimedia presentation, clearly establish your thesis, or theme. Set a definite mood. Finally, use details that will contribute to a definite tone. Adding graphics, images, and sounds to your multimedia presentation will enable you to do this. Remember to keep your audience and purpose in mind.

#### Try It!

Use the guidelines above to develop a script for your multimedia presentation.

---

**Differentiated Instruction: Advanced Learners**

As students create their multimedia presentations, invite them to jot down procedures they follow in order to make sure that things are working smoothly. After they have finished, have them use their notes to create a troubleshooting guide to help other students produce their multimedia presentations.

# Preparing a Multimedia Report

Once your script is completed, you can make an outline for the multimedia presentation. In order to use graphics, images, and sound effectively, you must plan exactly where each slide or sound bite will fit into your speech. Remember that your visuals must appeal to your audience and convey your point of view.

Here is a planning script for a multimedia report on Tuvan throat singing. What will be *seen* appears in the "Video" column, and what will be *heard* appears in the "Audio" column. Note that the directions for the speaker are general, not the actual words to be spoken.

## Planning Script

| Video | Audio |
|---|---|
| 1. **Title Screen:** "Tuvan Throat Singing: A Unique Vocal Art" | 1. SPEAKER: Introduction<br>SOUND: Sample of throat singing begins |
| 2. **Slide 2:** "Where is Tuva" map of Russia, China, Mongolia, Kazakhstan, zoom in on Tuva | 2. SPEAKER: Explain location of Tuva<br>SOUND: Babble of language spoken in Tuva |
| 3. **Slide 3:** "History of Tuvan throat singing" images of Tuvans herding horses, sheep, and yak | 3. SPEAKER: provide history of Tuvan throat singing, how it developed<br>SOUND: somber, lonely music |
| 4. **Slide 4:** "Throat Singers Perform" image of Tuvan throat singers | 4. SPEAKER: Singers use voices to includes sounds of nature<br>SOUND: Tuvan thoat song of birds and bubbling stream |
| 5. **Slide 5:** "Different types of throat singing" Chart explaining types | 5. SPEAKER: Explains differences<br>SOUND: sygyt and ezengileer |
| 6. **Slide 6:** "Instruments" chart showing different types of instruments used in throat singing | 6. SPEAKER: Explains instruments<br>SOUND: mucic from each instrument |
| 7. **Slide 7:** "Come hear the music!" Pictures/Illustrations of touring Tuvan music groups in U.S. | 7. SPEAKER: Discusses how in the U.S. people can hear Tuvan music performed live.<br>SOUND: Tuvan singers; audience clapping |
| 8. **Slide 8:** Tuvan singers performing | 8. SPEAKER: Conclusion<br>SOUND: Music up and out |

Arts

## Preparing a Multimedia Report

Review the sample Planning Script with students carefully before asking them to create their own multimedia reports. Encourage students to ask questions about anything they don't understand. Suggest that they also review the Multimedia Report Checklist on SE page 441 for a clear idea of what a multimedia report should include.

If some students have prepared oral reports on the same topic, they may benefit from working together to create and present a multimedia report. Allow time for students to find or create graphics and sound effects to support their main ideas. ✔ DIFFERENTIATE INSTRUCTION

TEKS 10.15D

TEKS **10.15D** Produce a multimedia presentation with graphics, images, and sound that conveys a point of view and appeals to a specific audience; **ELPS 3E** Share information in cooperative learning interactions; **3G** Express opinions and ideas ranging from communicating short phrases to participating in discussions; **3H** Explain with increasing specificity and detail

## Other Forms of Writing in the Arts

Point out that every type of writing presented on this page is addressed elsewhere in this book. Have students flag this page for topics for future writing assignments or for ideas about what to write in their content-area learning logs.

Point out that the prompts listed under Creative Writing would be especially useful in learning logs because they encourage personal, in-depth responses to topics.

Also consider providing reproducible graphic organizers such as the sensory chart (see TE Appendix) for a descriptive writing assignment, the 5 W's chart (see TE Appendix) for a narrative writing assignment, or a details chart (see TE Appendix) for a persuasive writing assignment. Encourage students to use graphic organizers during prewriting to organize their ideas.

**504**

# Other Forms of Writing in the Arts

### Descriptive Writing

- Describe the use of texture, composition, and color in Vincent van Gogh's *Starry Night*.
- Describe your response to Miles Davis's rendition of "Take Five."
- Describe the varied activity inside a theater from the time you enter until the curtain goes up on a play.

### Expository Writing

- Develop a list of tips for making the most of practice time when you're learning a musical instrument.
- Explain how a computer program can turn a digital photo into a new piece of art.
- Explain how origami is created.

### Narrative Writing

- Research and write the story of the self-taught quilters of Gee's Bend, Alabama.
- Write about the first time you played a musical instrument.
- Write about a time you viewed a piece of art that really moved you.

### Persuasive Writing

- Write an editorial for the school newsletter explaining how dance, art, and music help students learn other subjects.
- Write a letter to the PTA to convince them to sponsor a fund-raiser for new uniforms for the marching band.
- Write a letter to the editor to convince readers that electronic music should be included in the music program.

### Creative Writing

- Write a poem inspired by Beethoven's *Moonlight Sonata*.
- Create a short story based on one of the characters in the diner in Edward Hopper's painting *Nighthawks*.
- Write an imaginary letter from Antonin Dvorak to a friend in which he discusses what inspired him to write the *New World Symphony*.
- Pretend you are the girl in Andrew Wyeth's painting *Christina's World*. Write about what you are thinking as you sit in the field.

505

# Writing in the Workplace

Every bit of correspondence in the workplace reflects the business and the professionalism of the people who work there. Memos, e-mail messages, business letters, and procedural documents are common forms of workplace writing. Memos and e-mail messages are brief and quickly composed forms of business writing. Business letters are formal in tone and more carefully worded. Procedural documents usually explain processes or how to accomplish a task.

Effective business communications, no matter what kind, have the same purpose: to get the reader's attention and prompt some action—a meeting, an agreement, a contract, or a solution to a problem. You, too, can use these types of business communications to get things done—both in and out of school. For example, you can write an e-mail requesting information for a school project, write a letter of application for a job, explain procedures, or describe a step-by-step process,

This chapter will give you the basic information about communication in the workplace.

- **Writing Guidelines: Business Letter**
- **Writing Guidelines: E-mail Message**
- **Writing Guidelines: Description of Work**

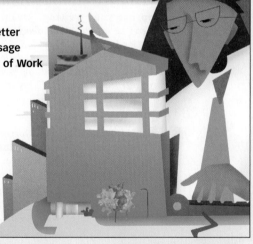

"The word that is heard perishes, but the letter that is written remains."

—Proverb

## Writing in the Workplace

### Objective
- learn and apply writing guidelines to a business letter, an e-mail, and a description of work

The lessons on the following pages provide samples of the types of writing students might do in a workplace. Assigning these forms of writing will depend on
- the skill level of your students, and
- the writing goals of your school, district, or state.

Point out to students that they already have some familiarity with writing in the workplace. Examples of business letters belong to this category. ✔ DIFFERENTIATE INSTRUCTION

---

## Differentiated Instruction: English Language Learners

⭐ **ELPS** 1A, 1G, 2D, 2E, 3E

| ELP Level **Beginning** | ELP Level **Intermediate** | ELP Level **Advanced/Advanced High** |
|---|---|---|
| Draw a web on the board with *business writing* in the center. Read SE page 505; have students raise hands when they hear a kind of business writing. Stop and record in the web. | Write: *Hey, Gary. You making the meeting?* And *Gary, The meeting is at 3 p.m. today. Will you be able to attend?* Ask students to say which would suit business correspondence best. | Have students in small groups discuss their knowledge of business writing. Have them tell about a time when they wrote various kinds of business correspondence. |

 **ELPS 1A** Use prior knowledge and experiences to understand meanings; **1G** Demonstrate increasing ability to distinguish between formal/informal English; **2D** Monitor understanding of spoken language during classroom instruction/interactions; **2E** Use contextual and linguistic support to enhance and confirm understanding of increasingly complex spoken language; **3E** Share information in cooperative learning interactions

## Writing Guidelines
### Business Letter

Tell students that they can write business letters to inquire about work, to file a complaint, or to report information. Remind students that they need to follow the steps of the writing process for business letters just as they do for other kinds of writing.

Emphasize the importance of writing a concise letter that clearly organizes and accurately conveys information.

### Prewriting

Students should think of the purpose as being like the thesis of an essay by asking questions such as: *What is the focus of my letter? What do I want it to accomplish? What information will be important to support this purpose?*

### Drafting

Remind students of the importance of considering how the reader will receive and process the information in the letter.

### Revising

Unlike some other types of writing, business writing does not typically need lots of figurative and sensory language. Students should make sure that their words and sentences are concise and straightforward. Ideas should be very clear and accurately conveyed.

### Editing

In addition to the normal conventions, have students focus on proper formatting. Remind students that spelling and grammatical errors can destroy a business letter's knowledgeable voice and effectiveness.

**TEKS** 10.13B, 10.13C, 10.13D, 10.15B(i), 10.15B(ii), 10.17C, 10.18A, 10.18B(i), 10.18B(ii), 10.18B(iii), 10.19; **ELPS** 5C, 5G

---

**TEKS** 10.13B–10.13D, 10.1
10.15B(ii), 10.17C, 10.18A,
10.18B(i)–10.18B(iii), 10.19
**ELPS** 5C

## Writing Guidelines Business Letter

A business letter is an effective way to ask for information, resources, or a recommendation. The following tips will help you write a successful letter.

### Prewriting

- **Determine your purpose.** Know exactly what you want, need, or intend to ask.
- **Consider your audience.** Word choice, style, and tone should be appropriate for your reader.
- **Gather and organize your information.** Carefully gather details and information. You must also organize the information so that your reader can easily follow and understand your letter.

### Drafting

- **State your purpose clearly.** Keep in mind your purpose, and structure your ideas persuasively. Draft a short, concise letter.
- **Format your letter correctly.** Follow the appropriate conventions and correct format for a reader-friendly business letter.
- **Convey information accurately.** Explain clearly what results you expect from the letter. Make sure that you have the exact name of the company and its correct address. Anticipate questions your reader might have and answer them in your letter.

### Revising

- **Improve your writing.** Review your essay for *focus and coherence, organization, development of ideas,* and *voice*. Ask these questions: *Have I clearly and accurately stated my purpose? Have I organized and formatted my letter so that it is reader-friendly? Have I used a formal tone and appropriate word choice? Have I varied my sentence structure? Do my ideas flow smoothly?*

### Editing

- **Check for conventions.** Correct any errors in grammar, sentence structure, capitalization, punctuation, and spelling, Remember that in business letters, using correct grammar and punctuation, including commas, dashes, and end punctuation is essential.
- **Prepare a final copy.** Make a neat final copy of your letter.

---

 **TEKS** **10.13B** Structure ideas in a persuasive way; **10.13C** Revise drafts to improve word choice; **10.13D** Edit drafts for grammar, mechanics, and spelling; **10.15B(i)** Write procedural and work-related documents that include organized and accurately conveyed information; **10.15B(ii)** Write procedural and work-related documents that include formatting; **10.17C** Use a variety of correctly structured sentences; **10.18A** Use conventions of capitalization; **10.18B(i)** Use commas in nonrestrictive phrases and contrasting expressions and in clauses; **10.18B(ii)** Use quotation marks to indicate sarcasm and irony; **10.18B(iii)** Use dashes to emphasize parenthetical cinformation; **10.19** Spell correctly using resources to determine and check correct spelling; **ELPS 5C** Spell familiar words with increasing accuracy; **5G** Explain with increasing specificity and detail/writing

Workplace

# Parts of a Business Letter

Every business letter is made up of the following six parts. Each part follows a specific form and has a specific function within the letter. Follow this format to help ensure that your reader can follow and understand your letter.

1. The **heading** includes the writer's complete address and the date. Write the heading at least one inch from the top of the page, at the left margin.

2. The **inside address** includes the recipient's name, company name, street address or post office box number, city, state, and ZIP code.

   ■ If the recipient has a short title, include it on the same line as the name, preceded by a comma. If the title is long, write it on the next line.

3. The **salutation** is the greeting. For business letters, use a colon after the salutation, not a comma.

   ■ If you know the recipient's name, use it in your greeting.
   Dear Dr. Bauer:

   ■ If you don't know the name of the person who will read your letter, use a salutation such as one of these:
   Dear Veterinarian:

   Dear Sir or Madam:

4. The **body** is the main part of the letter. It is organized into three parts. The beginning states why you are writing, the middle provides the needed details, and the ending focuses on what should happen next. Organize the information in a sustained manner so that your reader can easily follow your letter. Double-space between the paragraphs; do not indent.

5. The **complimentary closing** follows the body of the letter. Use *Sincerely* or *Yours truly* to close a business letter. Capitalize only the first word of the closing and place a comma at the end.

6. Your **signature** ends the letter. If you are typing, leave four blank lines under the closing; then type your name. Write your signature in the space between the closing and your typed name.

## Tip

The word-processing program on your computer may have templates that will help you set up your business letters. Be sure the template you choose closely follows the format of the letter on the next page.

---

## Parts of a Business Letter

Review the parts of a business letter, using the sample letter on SE page 508 as a model.

If students use a classroom or school computer to write letters, take time to review the business-letter templates that are provided with the available word-processing programs. Most should have a template that conforms to the format shown on SE page 508 or one that students can quickly and easily modify. Word-processing programs also may allow users to create their own templates. ✔ DIFFERENTIATE INSTRUCTION

⭐ **TEKS** 10.13B, 10.15B(i), 10.15B(ii)

---

## Differentiated Instruction:
## English Language Learners

⭐ **ELPS** 1C, 3F, 4F, 4G

| ELP Level **Beginning** | ELP Level **Intermediate** | ELP Level **Advanced/Advanced High** |
|---|---|---|
| Display a sample business letter. Write: *heading, inside address, salutation, body, closing,* and *signature* on the board. Have students identify each part as you point to it. | Use cognates for letter parts to enhance understanding: *salutación, signatura.* Then display a business letter and ask students to name each part. | Have students read the text on SE page 507 in pairs, connect parts to the sample letter on SE page 508, and then list unfamiliar terms or confusing ideas to discuss with partners. |

 **TEKS** **10.13B** Structure ideas in a sustained way; **10.15B(i)** Write procedural and work-related documents that include organized information; **10.15B(ii)** Write procedural and work-related documents that include formatting; **ELPS** **1C** Use strategic learning techniques to acquire basic and grade-level vocabulary; **3F** Give information/ranging from using a limited high-frequency vocabulary to using abstract and content-based vocabulary during speaking; **4F** Use support from peers/teachers to enhance and confirm understanding; **4G** Demonstrate comprehension of increasingly complex English/taking notes

## Business Letter

Read the letter and connect ideas in the side notes to the text. Point out that students will use this same reader-friendly format as they write their letters. Tell students that they need not always write three paragraphs. Sometimes the letter will be shorter and sometimes longer; however, the order of the content will stay the same.

⭐ **TEKS** 10.13B, 10.15B(i), 10.15B(ii)

⭐ **TEKS** 10.13B, 10.15B(i), 10.15B(ii)

## Business Letter

The following is an example of a properly formatted business letter. The writer, Katie Mathews, clearly states her purpose, and her reader. She presents accurate information and has carefully organized her information.

> The letter is organized and correctly formatted according to the guidelines on page **507**. (The numbers at the right correspond to the guidelines.)

**1** 617 Crabtree Lane
Plano, Texas  75023
April 15, 2011

**2** Mr. Alan DeRosa
Waterloo High School
1123 South Spring Street
Austin, Texas  78702

**3** Dear Mr. DeRosa:

> The **beginning** introduces the writer.

I am a sophomore at Rio Mesa High School in Plano. I play first trombone in the band and have been involved in the school music programs since I was 10. My goal is to become a band director someday, and I would like to teach and direct at the middle school level.

> The **middle** is well organized and conveys important information.

**4** Ms. Simenek, our band director, mentioned that you are starting a junior marching band this summer. Would you be interested in hiring an intern? I would appreciate the opportunity to work with younger students.

The new band sounds very exciting, and I would like to know more about your plans. You can reach me at (214) 555-1234 or at my family's e-mail address <tmathews@ourhomeemail.com>.

> The **ending** expresses thanks.

Thank you for considering my request. If you could create an internship for me, I would be very grateful.

**5** Sincerely,

*Katie Mathews*

**6** Katie Mathews

### Differentiated Instruction: Struggling Learners

Help students structure the bodies of their letters by answering these questions: *What background information does the reader need? What is the main point or problem? What do you want the reader to do?*

⭐ **ELPS** 5G

**TEKS** 10.13B–10.13D, 10.15B(i), 10.15B(ii), 10.17C, 10.18A, 10.18B(i)–10.18B(iii), 10.19
**ELPS** 5C

Workplace

# Sending a Letter

Letters will arrive faster if they are properly addressed and stamped. A typed envelope or one with printed address labels is preferred for a business letter. Always include a ZIP Code. If you do not know the ZIP Code, check with the Post Office.

## Addressing the Envelope

Place the writer's name and address in the upper left-hand corner of the envelope and the recipient's name and address in the center. Use correct postage.

> KATIE MATHEWS
> 617 CRABTREE LANE
> PLANO, TEXAS 75023
>
>
> Earth Day USA ¢
>
>          MR. ALAN DEROSA
>          Central High School
>          1123 South Pine Street
>          Austin, TEXAS 78702

There are two acceptable forms for addressing an envelope: the older form, often hand-written, and the new form preferred by the postal service.

| Traditional Form | Postal Service Form |
|---|---|
| Mr. Alan DeRosa | MR. ALAN DEROSA |
| Waterloo High School | WATERLOO HIGH SCHOOL |
| 1123 South Spring Street | 1123 S SPRING ST |
| Austin, Texas 78702 | AUSTIN TX 78702 |

Use the list of common address abbreviations on page **694**. Use numerals rather than words for numbered streets and avenues (9TH AVE NE. 3RD ST SW). If you know the ZIP + 4 code, use it.

### Try It!

Write a business letter asking for information about summer educational programs or internships. Follow all the guidelines on these pages. Be sure to organize your information and format your letter correctly.

## Sending a Letter
### Addressing the Envelope

After reading the instruction and discussing the example, connect the addresses and names on the envelope to the addresses in the letter. Tell students that they can use this cross check to make sure they have used the correct address.

### Try It!

Suggest several organizations for students to write to, or have them search the Internet. If they choose the latter, make sure you check the reliability and validity of the chosen organization or company. ✔ DIFFERENTIATE INSTRUCTION

Explain to students that this letter is a form of persuasive writing. Have them identify what action they want the recipient to take. Then consider the best way to communicate to achieve the desired result.

**TEKS** 10.13B, 10.13C, 10.13D, 10.15B(i), 10.15B(ii), 10.17C, 10.18A, 10.18B(i), 10.18B(ii), 10.18B(iii), 10.19; **ELPS** 5C

---

**TEKS** **10.13B** Structure ideas in a persuasive way; **10.13C** Revise drafts to improve word choice; **10.13D** Edit drafts for grammar, mechanics, and spelling; **10.15B(i)** Write procedural and work-related documents that include organized and accurately conveyed information; **10.15B(ii)** Write procedural and work-related documents that include formatting; **10.17C** Use a variety of correctly structured sentences; **10.18A** Use conventions of capitalization; **10.18B(i)** Use commas in nonrestrictive phrases and contrasting expressions and in clauses; **10.18B(ii)** Use quotation marks to indicate sarcasm and irony; **10.18B(iii)** Use dashes to emphasize parenthetical information; **10.19** Spell correctly using resources to determine and check correct spelling; **ELPS** **3E** Share information in cooperative learning interactions; **5C** Spell familiar words with increasing accuracy; **5D** Edit writing for standard grammar and usage/subject-verb and pronoun agreement and appropriate verb tenses; **5G** Explain with increasing specificity and detail/writing

## Writing Guidelines
### E-Mail Messages

### Prewriting

Emphasize the importance of using standard format and proper tone in e-mail messages that are sent for business or school-related purposes. Tell students that:

- formal e-mail messages should not contain the kind of shorthand that has developed among users of text or instant messaging, and
- formal messages should not contain playful icons. These are appropriate only for casual communications.

### Drafting

Point out that students most likely already know the importance of keeping e-mails short and to the point. Ask them what they typically do when they receive an e-mail with three or more lengthy paragraphs. Chances are, they skim the message or don't read it at all. Discuss with students various goals for writing e-mail messages (to inform, to persuade, to entertain, etc.)

### Revising

On the whole, students should revise in the same way they would for a business letter to be sent through the postal service. The exception is that an e-mail does not need to be as formal.

### Editing

Students want to avoid spelling mistakes as well as other errors in writing conventions when writing a business e-mail. These errors can cause a message to sound unprofessional. Also note the importance of precision in the recipient's e-mail address. An error in the address means the recipient won't receive the message.

**TEKS** 10.13B, 10.13C, 10.13D, 10.15B(i), 10.15B(ii), 10.17C, 10.18A, 10.18B(i), 10.18B(ii), 10.18B(iii), 10.19; **ELPS** 5C

---

**TEKS** 10.13B–10.13D, 10.15B(i), 10.15B(ii), 10.17C, 10.18A, 10.18B(i)–10.18B(iii), 10.19 **ELPS** 5C

## Writing Guidelines E-Mail Message

E-mail is a very common form of business communication. It is used to send information inside and outside a company. While e-mail is less formal than business letters, e-mail still requires formal language and a respectful tone. E-mails must follow all the conventions of writing.

### Prewriting

- **Jot down your purpose and your main points.** E-mails are short and concise. It is important to state your purpose succinctly and present your ideas clearly and concisely.
- **Organize your ideas.** Organize your ideas, information, or requests so that your reader can quickly grasp your message.
- **Complete the e-mail heading.** Fill in the address line by typing in each character of the address or use your address book's automatic fill-in feature. Check to make sure you have the correct person and the correct address. Then write a subject line that clearly indicates the purpose of the message.

### Drafting

- **Format your e-mail.** Format your e-mails so that your reader can quickly and easily grasp your message. Greet your reader and state your reason for writing. Be clear, complete, and accurate. Include only the most important information. Anticipate questions and address them in your e-mail. Close with your name and contact information.
- **Use a proper tone.** Be respectful. Use a formal tone and appropriate word choice.

### Revising

- **Improve your writing.** Review and revise your e-mail for *focus and coherence, organization, development of ideas,* and *voice.* Then check for *accuracy, word choice, tone,* and *sentence fluency.*

### Editing

- **Check for conventions.** Correct any errors in grammar, sentence structure, capitalization, punctuation, and spelling,
- Proofread one more time and send your e-mail.

---

**TEKS** **10.13B** Structure ideas in a persuasive way; **10.13C** Revise drafts to improve word choice; **10.13D** Edit drafts for grammar, mechanics, and spelling; **10.15B(i)** Write procedural and work-related documents that include organized and accurately conveyed information; **10.15B(ii)** Write procedural and work-related documents that include formatting; **10.17C** Use a variety of correctly structured sentences; **10.18A** Use conventions of capitalization; **10.18B(i)** Use commas in nonrestrictive phrases and contrasting expressions and in clauses; **10.18B(ii)** Use quotation marks to indicate sarcasm and irony; **10.18B(iii)** Use dashes to emphasize parenthetical information; **10.19** Spell correctly using resources to determine and check correct spelling; **ELPS** **5C** Spell familiar words with increasing accuracy

# E-Mail Message

E-mail has become an important, quick communication tool in the business world. Workers e-mail colleagues within their company. They also send e-mail to people outside their company. It takes time to draft a good, clear message. In the following e-mail message, an employee asks for information and help.

> **New Message**
>
> To: mchavez@PAJscompany.com
>
> Cc:
>
> Subject: Information concerning next TXS project
>
> Dear Miguel,
>
> As you know I have just been assigned to the upcoming TXS project. I learned from Mark Curtis that a full project description had been prepared. Mark also told me that project precedures and schedules have also been completed.
>
> Could you tell me where these documents have been posted or could you send me a copy of all the available information about the project? I would like to read and digest the information before our project meeting, which has been scheduled for next Tuesday.
>
> In addition, I was hoping to schedule a meeting with you to review my responsibilities on this project. Would you be available to meet with me tomorrow or Thursday at 10 a.m.? I look forward to your response. Thank you very much.
>
> Sincerely,
> Hillary Markham
> Building 203

**The heading** includes the recipient's correct address and concise subject line.

**The beginning** greets the reader. Information is well organized, tells the reason for the e-mail message. Writer anticipates question about the project meeting.

**The ending** has a request and thanks the reader.

## Try It!

Follow the guidelines and write a business-related e-mail asking for information.

## E-Mail Message

Read and discuss the sample e-mail, answering any questions students have about format, organization, or content.

### Try It!

Have students compose an e-mail message to a teacher and ask for a response. They should save it as a draft. After making changes and checking conventions, have them send it. This will provide students with additional practice writing, receiving, and sending formal e-mail messages. ✔ **DIFFERENTIATE INSTRUCTION**

**TEKS** 10.13B, 10.15B(i), 10.15B(ii), 10.15B(iii); **ELPS** 5G

---

## Differentiated Instruction: English Language Learners

**ELPS** 3E, 4F, 5G

| ELP Level **Beginning** | ELP Level **Intermediate** | ELP Level **Advanced/Advanced High** |
|---|---|---|
| Work with students to access the English vocabulary needed to question a teacher and construct an e-mail. If necessary, provide a frame for students to complete. | Work with students to come up with questions about one of their classes. Students then work in pairs to write a formal e-mail with those questions as its basis. | Have students write drafts, then send to partners for revision suggestions. Allow time for pairs to discuss responses and for individuals to make suggested corrections. |

**TEKS** **10.13B** Structure ideas in a sustained way; **10.15B(i)** Write procedural and work-related documents that include organized and accurately conveyed information; **10.15B(ii)** Write procedural and work-related documents that include formatting; **10.15B(iii)** Write procedural and work-related documents that include anticipation of questions; **ELPS** **3E** Share information in cooperative learning interactions; **4F** Use support from peers/teachers to develop vocabulary and grasp of language structures; **5G** Explain with increasing specificity and detail/writing

## Writing Guidelines
### Description of Work

Tell students that instructions for completing a task, guidelines for behavior or work, and written rules are all procedural documents. Have students review the sample before beginning the writing process.

### Prewriting

Explain that some more complicated procedures might require diagrams or graphics. These visual aids can help a reader better understand the text.

### Drafting

Emphasize that only necessary information should be included. Also, emphasize the importance of formatting. If someone is looking for one important piece of information, he or she does not want to pore through long paragraphs of information.

### Revising

One good way to check the clarity of a procedural document is for the classmates to trade documents and read the instructions carefully, suggesting changes in wording and formatting for clarity.

### Editing

Students should continue to edit for all of the writing conventions, including grammar, capitalization, punctuation, spelling, and sentence structure.

★ **TEKS** 10.13B, 10.13C, 10.13D, 10.15B(i), 10.15B(ii), 10.17C, 10.18A, 10.18B(i), 10.18B(ii), 10.18B(iii), 10.19; **ELPS** 5C, 5F

---

## Writing Guidelines Description of Work

Procedural or process documents, either for a volunteer organization or a job, might include a written description of rules and regulations for an organization or company or instructions for coworkers or customers. The following tips will help you write procedural documents.

### Prewriting

- **Think about your purpose and audience.** Ask yourself why you are writing this document and who your intended readers are. This will help determine your word choice and tone.
- **Gather all the information you will need.** Process documents are complex. Verify that the information you have gathered is accurate. Choose an organizational pattern that works best for conveying the information.
- **Decide on a format.** Choose a format that will show your organization and be reader-friendly.

### Drafting

- **State your purpose clearly.** Keep in mind your purpose for writing, and structure your ideas persuasively.
- **Include needed, relevant, and accurate information.** Explain each detail clearly. Make sure that the information is accurate. Be concise and specific so that readers have no difficulty understanding the information. Show your knowledge of the topic.

### Revising

- **Improve your writing.** Review your document for *focus and coherence, organization, development of ideas,* and *voice.* Ask these questions: *Have I explained the purpose or process? Have I organized and formatted my information to make it reader-friendly? Have I used the appropriate tone and word choice? Have I varied my sentence structure?*

### Editing

- **Check for conventions.** Correct errors in grammar, sentence structure, capitalization, punctuation, and spelling. Remember that in process documents, correct grammar and punctuation are essential.
- **Prepare a final copy.** Make a neat final copy of your document.

---

★ **TEKS** **10.13B** Structure ideas in a persuasive way; **10.13C** Revise drafts to improve word choice and improve the subtlety of meaning; **10.13D** Edit drafts for grammar, mechanics, and spelling; **10.15B(i)** Write procedural and work-related documents that include organized and accurately conveyed information; **10.15B(ii)** Write procedural and work-related documents that include formatting; **10.17C** Use a variety of correctly structured sentences; **10.18A** Use conventions of capitalization; **10.18B(i)** Use commas in nonrestrictive phrases and contrasting expressions and in clauses; **10.18B(ii)** Use quotation marks to indicate sarcasm and irony; **10.18B(iii)** Use dashes to emphasize parenthetical information; **10.19** Spell correctly using resources to determine and check correct spelling; **ELPS 5C** Spell familiar words with increasing accuracy; **5F** Write using a variety of grade-appropriate connecting words in increasingly accurate ways

**TEKS** 10.13B–10.13D, 10.15B(i), 10.15B(ii), 10.17C, 10.18A, 10.18B(i)–10.18B(iii), 10.19
**ELPS** 5C, 5F

## Description of Work

Pablo and Thomas decided to organize a community astronomy club. There was sufficient interest, and the two were asked to write bylaws that would include a description of the organization and detailed information about how the club would operate. They began each section with a heading so that readers could easily find information. They were also very specific so that readers would not misunderstand the rules.

---

### Northwood Community Astronomy Club Bylaws

**PURPOSE**

1. To understand astronomy
2. To make science enjoyable
3. To inform the community about astronomy

**MEMBERSHIP REQUIREMENTS**

1. Be a resident of Northwood or a student in a Northwood school
2. Participate in 80 percent of club meetings and club activities

**MEETINGS AND RULES OF ORDER**

1. Meetings will be held on the third Tuesday of every month.
2. Meetings will be held in the Northwood Library Community Room.
3. All meetings will be conducted according to Robert's Rules of Order.
4. A quorum of ten members must be present for discussion of business items and voting.
5. All officers are voting members of the astronomy club; however, the president votes only when there is a tie.

**OFFICERS**

1. Officers will be elected at the first meeting of each year.
2. Elected officers will consist of president, vice president, secretary, and treasurer.
3. Officers will meet twice a month.

---

### Try It!

Think of a work-related or volunteer situation that requires a procedural document. Develop the document following the guidelines on page 512. Make sure to choose an appropriate organizational pattern and format. Check your document for all writing conventions, and correct any errors.

## Description of Work

Read and discuss the sample bylaws with students. Explain that bylaws describe the purpose and operating structure of an organization. Point out the organizational structure and the headings the students chose.

### Try It!

Read aloud the instruction and have students prewrite and draft their procedural documents. Then set up peer conferencing for students to revise and edit their writing. Have students first complete an independent revision and then present their writing to an assigned peer group. Each group member should read, answer the revision questions from a revising checklist, and edit the text for conventions errors. Finally, peer groups should meet and share feedback on individuals' essays. ✔DIFFERENTIATE INSTRUCTION

**TEKS** 10.13B, 10.13C, 10.13D, 10.15B(i), 10.15B(ii), 10.17C, 10.18A, 10.18B(i), 10.18B(ii), 10.18B(iii), 10.19; **ELPS** 5C, 5D, 5E, 5F

---

**Differentiated Instruction: English Language Learners**  **ELPS** 2D, 4F, 5D

| ELP Level **Beginning** | ELP Level **Intermediate** | ELP Level **Advanced/Advanced High** |
|---|---|---|
| In conferences, lead each student through the prewriting, drafting, revising, and editing process. Clarify instructions and help students clearly explain steps. | Reread the revising questions on SE page 512 as students track the text. Allow students to ask for clarification as needed. Have them use these questions as they participate in peer groups. | Remind students to edit for agreement with subjects and verbs, as well as pronouns and antecedents. Review each before students participate in editing conferences. |

**TEKS** 10.13B Structure ideas in a persuasive way; 10.13C Revise drafts to improve word choice and improve the subtlety of meaning; 10.13D Edit drafts for grammar, mechanics, and spelling; 10.15B(i) Write procedural and work-related documents that include organized and accurately conveyed information; 10.15B(ii) Write procedural and work-related documents that include formatting; 10.17C Use a variety of correctly structured sentences; 10.18A Use conventions of capitalization; 10.18B(i) Use commas in nonrestrictive phrases/contrasting expressions/clauses; 10.18B(ii) Use quotation marks to indicate sarcasm and irony; 10.18B(iii) Use dashes to emphasize parenthetical information; 10.19 Spell correctly using resources to determine and check correct spelling; **ELPS** 2D Monitor understanding of spoken language during classroom interactions and seek clarification; 4F Use support from peers/teachers to develop vocabulary and grasp of language structures; 5C Spell familiar words/employ spelling patterns and rules with increasing accuracy; 5D Edit writing for standard grammar and usage/subject-verb and pronoun agreement and appropriate verb tenses; 5E Employ increasingly complex grammatical structures in content area writing; 5F Write using a variety of grade-appropriate sentence lengths, patterns, and connecting words

# The Tools of Language

## Listening and Speaking (pages 515–518)

These pages provide tips and strategies that help students improve their speaking and listening skills.

## Using Reference Materials (pages 519–522)

These pages help students focus on language resources that will help them understand words, expressions, and language structures.

## Language Strategies (pages 524–525)

These pages provide English language learners with several language-learning strategies for speaking and listening that students can use to develop their academic English.

## Language of the Writing Process (pages 526–529)

These pages support English language learners as they delve into The Writing Process (pages 6–32) by giving them a foundation for understanding the process through instruction in key vocabulary and concepts.

## Language of the Writing Traits (pages 530–531)

These pages support English language learners as they learn about the writing traits (pages 46–89) by giving them a foundation for understanding the traits through instruction in key vocabulary and concepts.

## Language of the Writing Forms (pages 532–567)

This section supports English language learners by introducing them to vocabulary and concepts for each writing form as well as the student writing models.

# The Tools of Language Reference Guide

| The Tools of Language | | Corresponding Core Unit | |
|---|---|---|---|
| **Write Source Student Edition** | | | |
| Listening and Speaking | TL 515–518 | | |
| Using Reference Materials | TL 519–522 | | |
| Learning Language | TL 523–567 | **All Core Units** | 6–441 |
| • Language Strategies | TL 524–525 | | |
| • Language of the Writing Process | TL 526–529 | Using the Writing Process | 6–32 |
| • Language of the Writing Traits | TL 530–531 | Using the Writing Process | 33–77 |
| • Language of Narrative Writing | TL 532–537 | **Narrative Writing** | 78–135 |
| • Language of Expository Writing | TL 538–544 | **Expository Writing** | 136–193 |
| • Language of Persuasive Writing | TL 545–549 | **Persuasive Writing** | 194–251 |
| • Language of Interpretive Response | TL 550–555 | **Interpretive Response** | 252–319 |
| • Language of Creative Writing | TL 556–561 | **Creative Writing** | 320–357 |
| • Language of Research Writing | TL 562–567 | **Research Writing** | 358–441 |

## The Tools of Language

### Writing Focus

- Listening and Speaking
- Using Reference Materials
- Learning Language

### Learning Language

Read aloud the definitions and descriptions as students follow along in their texts. Scaffold understanding by further explaining key words. For example, tell students that *prewriting* is made up of the prefix *pre-*, which means "before," and the base word *writing*. Therefore, *prewriting* takes place before writing. Explain that *sensory details* appeal to the five senses—sight, smell, taste, touch, hearing. Finally, read the questions. Model answering the first question: *I am learning to divide and multiply in math. The words* divide *and* multiply *are examples of academic language.*

Divide students into small groups to ask and answer the remainder of the questions.

**DIFFERENTIATE INSTRUCTION ↘**

**ELPS** 1E, 2C, 3B, 3D, 3E, 4G

### Minilessons

**Call to Action**                                 Persuasion

- **THINK** of an issue that is important to you. Consider your opinion on the issue and what you might ask an audience to do to show their support for your opinion.

- **WRITE** a one-paragraph editorial that clearly states your opinion about a specific topic. Include a call to action.

**ELPS** 5G

---

**ELPS** 1E, 2C, 3B, 3D, 3E, 4G

www.hmheducation.com/tx/writesource

# The Tools of Language

## Writing Focus

## Learning Language

**Learning these words and expressions will help you understand this unit.**

1. Academic language is the vocabulary used in learning and education.
   **Name two examples of academic language used in math.**

2. Prewriting is the planning you do as you think about your purpose for writing, your audience, and the genre that best suits your topic.
   **What prewriting strategies work best for you when planning a research report?**

3. Sensory details help your reader visualize sights, hear sounds, and understand smells.
   **What sensory details would you use to describe a garden on a spring day?**

4. A call to action is what you make when you ask people to take action to support your position.
   **Why do editorials often end with a call to action?**

---

**ELPS 1E** Internalize new basic and academic language by using and reusing it/speaking; **2C** Learn new expressions and basic/academic vocabulary heard during classroom instruction/interactions; **3B** Expand vocabulary by learning and using routine language needed for classroom communication; **3D** Speak using grade-level content area vocabulary/new words and academic language proficiency; **3E** Share information in cooperative learning interactions; **4G** Demonstrate comprehension of increasingly complex English/responding to questions; **5G** Explain with increasing specificity and detail/writing

# Listening and Speaking

In his book *The Poet at the Breakfast Table*, Oliver Wendell Holmes stated, "It is the province of knowledge to speak, and it is the privilege of wisdom to listen." This famous nineteenth-century poet understood the importance of strong speaking and listening skills. Effective speaking does, in fact, require that you plan what you say, and meaningful listening clearly requires concentration.

This chapter provides tips and strategies that will help you improve your speaking and listening skills. Mastering these skills will make you a better student, leader, coworker, and companion. But remember that true mastery will come only with effort and practice.

- **Listening in Class**
- **Speaking in Class**
- **A Closer Look at Listening and Speaking**

"There is only one rule for being a good talker: learn how to listen."

—Christopher Morley

## Listening and Speaking

515

### Objectives
- learn to listen in class and take appropriate notes
- learn to speak in class and express ideas clearly
- improve listening and speaking skills through practice

Listening and speaking both require a strong grasp of both basic and academic vocabulary. In order to understand or express ideas, the listener and speaker must expand his or her vocabulary and practice concentrating, note-taking, and public speaking.

---

## Differentiated Instruction: English Language Learners

**ELPS** 1E, 5B, 5G

| ELP Level **Beginning** | ELP Level **Intermediate** | ELP Level **Advanced/Advanced High** |
|---|---|---|
| Read item 3 and draw a five-column sense chart on the board. Write: *sweet, red, smooth, loud, flowery.* Work with students to place each word in the proper sense column. | Augment the Beginning activity by having students record the words they chose to describe a garden on a spring day in the sense chart. | Challenge students to write a brief description of a garden in spring using details that appeal to the senses. Invite students to share their descriptions. |

**ELPS 1E** Internalize new basic language by using and reusing it/speaking and writing; **5B** Write using newly acquired basic and content-based grade-level vocabulary; **5G** Describe with increasing specificity and detail/writing

## Listening in Class

Tell students that in class, teachers often provide outlines of their lectures. Students can use these outlines as a basis for their notes. They can elaborate on the outlines and jot down questions about the information or the vocabulary.

After you review the tips for listening, allow students to ask questions to clarify their understanding. Divide students into pairs to summarize the key steps to listening in class.

⭐ **ELPS** 2C, 2D, 2I

## Try It!

Choose a brief newspaper or magazine article to read aloud to the class. Have students practice taking notes as you read. Tell students that the key to note-taking is to record only main points. They should not write so much that they are distracted from listening. **DIFFERENTIATE INSTRUCTION ↘**

⭐ **ELPS** 2I

---

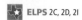

# Listening in Class

When you really listen, you concentrate. You do more than simply hear what is being said. The following tips will help you become a better listener.

- **Know why you're listening.** What is the speaker trying to tell you? Will there be a test? Are you being given an assignment?
- **Listen for the facts.** Listening for the 5 W and H questions—*Who? What? When? Where? Why?* and *How?*—will help you identify the most important information.
- **Take notes.** When you hear important information, write it down in your notebook. In the margins, write down any new vocabulary, expressions, or questions you may have. Review and complete your notes as soon after class as possible.
- **Put the speaker's ideas into your own words.** Summarize the speaker's key points as you take notes. Add your own comments.

## Try It!

The next time you take notes in class, use your own words to record your teacher's ideas. Add comments in the margins.

| The Marshall Plan (1947) | |
|---|---|
| known as the European Recovery Program (ERP) | |
| in effect from 1948-1951 | *What does* |
| | *in effect mean?* |
| designed by George C. Marshall | |
| – army chief of staff during WWII | |
| – secretary of state under President Truman | |
| gave economic aid to parts of Europe | |
| devastated by WWII | *devastated:* |
| – provided about $13 billion | *destroyed* |
| – Europe mostly used the money to buy goods from | |
| America. | *Benefited* |
| – During Korean War, some of the money helped | *the U.S. and* |
| rebuild the militaries of Western Europe. | *Europe.* |

---

## Differentiated Instruction: Struggling Learners

Structure students' note-taking by having them record these questions before note-taking. They can then answer the questions, using these answers as their notes.

- *Who is this about? Who is involved?*
- *What happened? What was the result?*
- *Where did it happen?*
- *Why did it happen? Why did the people do what they did?*
- *How does this change things? How did people make this happen? How can it be addressed?*

⭐ **ELPS** 2C, 2I

---

⭐ **ELPS 2C** Learn new expressions and basic/academic vocabulary heard during classroom instruction/interactions; **2D** Monitor understanding of spoken language during classroom instruction/interactions and seek clarification of spoken language as needed; **2I** Demonstrate listening comprehension in increasingly complex spoken language/following directions, summarizing spoken messages, responding to questions, collaborating with peers, and taking notes

# Speaking in Class

Speaking in class is a skill everyone should master. A good classroom discussion depends on cooperation. These basic strategies will help you and your classmates become better speakers.

## Before you speak . . .

- **Listen** carefully and take notes.
- **Think** about what others are asking or saying.
- **Wait** until it's your turn to speak.
- **Plan** how you can add something positive to the discussion.

## As you speak . . .

- **Use a loud, clear voice.**
- **Stick to the topic.**
- **Express your opinions, ideas, and feelings** with examples, facts, and anecdotes.
- **Narrate, describe, and explain your ideas** with details.
- **Maintain eye contact** with others in the group or class.

### Tip

- Summarize what's been agreed upon in the discussion.
- Mention another person's comments and expand on them constructively.

### Try It!

Play "Where will you be?" Warm up your impromptu speaking skills by interacting in the following activity.

1. Pair up with a classmate. Take turns interviewing each other about this topic: What do you plan to do after high school?
   - As the interviewer, ask specific questions and get as much information as you can. Take notes as you go along.
   - As the interviewee, answer the questions clearly and completely. Include important facts and interesting details.
2. Exchange roles after the first interview is complete.
3. In a mini-speech, present your partner's future plans to the class. Quickly organize your notes into a beginning, a middle, and an ending. Then follow the "As You Speak" strategies above.

Language

## Speaking in Class

Tell students that as they listen to a class discussion, in addition to noting their ideas, they should jot down any questions they have about the topic or other students' comments. Review the speaking tips and establish rules for participating in class discussions, such as the rule that students must raise their hands to speak.

ELPS 2D, 2I, 3G

## Try It!

As students conduct interviews, remind them to take the time to orally summarize partners' answers before recording them. Tell students that they should include specific details in the descriptions of their future plans as they answer the interview questions. ✔ DIFFERENTIATE INSTRUCTION

ELPS 2I, 3E, 3H

## Differentiated Instruction: English Language Learners

ELPS 1D, 3E, 3G, 3H

| ELP Level **Beginning** | ELP Level **Intermediate** | ELP Level **Advanced/Advanced High** |
|---|---|---|
| Pair beginners with English speakers to conduct interviews. Beginners should be the interviewee, answering with short phrases, nonverbal cues, and defining or describing. | After partners have conducted interviews and organized notes, create small groups of students to share and discuss responses. Students should include specific details. | Challenge students to present a summary of their partners' plans from brief notes. Students should not read the notes, but use them as a guide to remind them of their ideas as they speak. |

**ELPS 1D** Speak using learning strategies/request assistance, employ non-verbal cues, and convey ideas by defining or describing; **2D** Monitor understanding of spoken language during classroom instruction/interactions and seek clarification of spoken language as needed; **2I** Demonstrate listening comprehension in increasingly complex spoken language/collaborating with peers and taking notes; **3E** Share information in cooperative learning interactions; **3G** Express opinions, ideas, and feelings ranging from communicating short phrases to participating in discussions; **3H** Narrate/describe/explain with increasing specificity and detail

## A Closer Look at Listening and Speaking

After you read and review the bulleted lists with students, allow them time to seek clarification as needed by requesting assistance and asking questions.

 **ELPS** 1D, 2C, 2D

### Try It!

After reading the directions to students, have them divide into groups of three and number off to complete the activity. Suggest that the listening students take notes on the paragraph and consult these notes as they summarize. Tell students that even though they should include specific details in their summaries, they need only include main ideas and important details.

**DIFFERENTIATE INSTRUCTION ↘**

**ELPS** 2I, 3E, 3G, 3H

---

 **ELPS** 1D, 2C, 2D, 2I, 3E, 3G, 3H

# A Closer Look at Listening and Speaking

Improving your listening and speaking skills will increase your confidence in and out of the classroom. Follow these basic guidelines to carry on productive conversations and discussions.

| Good Listeners . . . | Good Speakers . . . |
|---|---|
| ■ think about what the speaker is saying.<br>■ take notes of important words, ideas, and expressions.<br>■ pay attention to the speaker's tone of voice, gestures, and facial expressions.<br>■ ask for clarification.<br>■ prepare to respond thoughtfully. | ■ speak loudly and clearly.<br>■ maintain eye contact with their listeners.<br>■ express their opinions, ideas, and feelings by changing the tone and volume of their voice.<br>■ use details to describe, explain, narrate, and clarify information.<br>■ use gestures and body language effectively. |

### Try It!

Focus on speaking and listening skills with this activity.

1. Pick two classmates and number yourselves 1, 2, and 3.
2. Ask person 1 to take person 2 aside and read the paragraph below.
3. Then ask person 2 to take person 3 aside and try to retell or summarize the paragraph.
4. Finally, ask person 3 to retell or summarize the paragraph to the first two classmates.
5. Compare the original paragraph to what person 3 reports.

In the early 1920s, Roy Chapman Andrews, an explorer from Wisconsin, proposed studying geologic formations in Mongolia. Many fellow scientists felt that this trip would be a waste of time because the shifting sands of the desert would make such research difficult, if not impossible. Even Andrews began to wonder about the wisdom of his proposal, given the distance and the political uncertainties in Asia. Fortunately, he decided to go through with his plan. The scientific community was rewarded with the discovery of many unique fossils in the Gobi Desert of Mongolia. The most important find was a clutch of dinosaur eggs, the first ever discovered.

---

**ELPS 1D** Speak using learning strategies/request assistance, employ non-verbal cues, and convey ideas by defining or describing; **2C** Learn new expressions and basic/academic vocabulary heard during classroom instruction/interactions; **2D** Monitor understanding of spoken language during classroom instruction/ interactions and seek clarification of spoken language as needed; **2I** Demonstrate listening comprehension in increasingly complex spoken language/summarizing spoken messages, responding to questions, collaborating with peers, and taking notes; **3E** Share information in cooperative learning interactions; **3G** Express opinions, ideas, and feelings ranging from communicating short phrases to participating in discussions; **3H** Narrate/describe/explain with increasing specificity and detail

# Using Reference Materials

Since the late 1980s, the use of computers and the Internet has led people to say that we live in the "Information Age." This term refers to the idea that all sorts of information is easily available to anyone who wants to find it. The key is knowing where to look!

When you need to gather information, knowing which print and electronic reference materials are likely to be helpful can save you time and aggravation. You are probably familiar with many common references, such as encyclopedias, newspapers, and atlases. Do you need facts about a specific topic? Do you need to look at maps or read about current events? One of those common references will probably suit your needs.

This chapter will focus on language references that may be useful to you—resources that will help you understand words, expressions, and language structures. The first section provides details about the information found in a dictionary, and the second describes other types of helpful language resources. When you are able to use these kinds of reference materials well, your ability to write clear, engaging, and informative pieces will grow and grow.

- ■ **Checking a Dictionary**
- ■ **Using Other Language Resources**

"Proper words in proper places make the true definition of a style."
—Jonathan Swift

## Using Reference Materials

### Objectives
- learn how a dictionary is formatted and how to access information in it
- learn when and how to use other language reference materials

Tell students that reference books provide information about a variety of things. Language reference books range from dictionaries of many kinds to grammar and usage instruction. From reference sources, readers can find out how to spell words properly, what words and phrases mean, how words translate from one language to another, and much more.

---

### Differentiated Instruction: English Language Learners

⭐ ELPS 2D, 2I, 4G

| ELP Level **Beginning** | ELP Level **Intermediate** | ELP Level **Advanced/Advanced High** |
|---|---|---|
| Instead of completing the **Try It!** activity, students can work in pairs to fluently read aloud one or two basic sentences: *Scientists studied the earth in Asia. They found dinosaur eggs.* | Scaffold the activity by providing an adapted version of the paragraph for students to summarize and retell. Allow listeners time to ask questions of the speaker. | Allow all three group members to begin by reading the paragraph. Then, have students take turns summarizing and retelling. |

**ELPS 2D** Seek clarification of spoken language as needed; **2I** Demonstrate listening comprehension in increasingly complex spoken language by summarizing spoken messages; **4G** Demonstrate comprehension of increasingly complex English/participating in shared reading

## Checking a Dictionary

After you read and define each boldfaced word, point out the example in the Sample Dictionary Page on SE page 521. To make sure students comprehend the feature, ask questions pertaining to the sample. For example:

- What part of speech is *circularize*? (*transitive verb*)
- Which word could appear on this page—*circulate, circus, circuity*? (*circuity*)
- How many syllables are in the word *circuitous*? (*four*)

⭐ **TEKS** 10.19; **ELPS** 2I

### Try It!

To abbreviate the activity, have students choose words from the **Try It!** paragraph on SE page 518. Have students work with partners to complete the activity. **DIFFERENTIATE INSTRUCTION** ⬊

**DIFFERENTIATE INSTRUCTION** ⬊

⭐ **ELPS** 2I, 3E, 4I

---

# Checking a Dictionary

A dictionary gives many types of information:

- **Guide words:** These are the first and last words on the page. Guide words show whether the word you are looking for will be found alphabetically on that page.
- **Entry words:** Each word defined in a dictionary is called an entry word. Entry words are listed alphabetically.
- **Etymology:** Many dictionaries give etymologies (word histories) for certain words. An etymology tells what language an English word came from, how the word entered our language, and when it was first used.
- **Syllable divisions:** A dictionary tells where to divide a word.
- **Pronunciation and accent marks:** A dictionary tells you how to pronounce a word and also provides a key to pronunciation symbols, usually at the bottom of each page.
- **Illustrations:** Some entries provide an illustration or a photograph.
- **Parts of speech:** A dictionary tells you what part(s) of speech a word is, using these abbreviations:

| | | | | | |
|---|---|---|---|---|---|
| *n.* | **noun** | *intr. v.* | **intransitive verb** | *adj.* | **adjective** |
| *pron.* | **pronoun** | *tr. v.* | **transitive verb** | *adv.* | **adverb** |
| *conj.* | **conjunction** | *interj.* | **interjection** | *prep.* | **preposition** |

- **Spelling and capitalization:** The dictionary shows the acceptable spelling, as well as capitalization, for words. (For some words, more than one spelling is given.)
- **Definitions:** Some dictionaries are large enough to list all of the meanings for a word. Most standard-size dictionaries, however, will list only three or four of the most commonly accepted meanings. Take time to read all of the meanings to be sure that you are using the word correctly.

## Try It!

Find an article on a topic that interests you and select three words that are unfamiliar to you. Look them up in the dictionary.

1. Identify the part(s) of speech for each word.
2. Give the first two meanings for the word.
3. Explain the etymology (if given) for each word.

---

⭐ **TEKS** 10.19 Spell correctly using resources to determine and check correct spelling; **ELPS** 2I Demonstrate listening comprehension in increasingly complex spoken language/responding to questions and collaborating with peers; **3E** Share information in cooperative learning interactions; **4I** Demonstrate comprehension by employing and expanding basic reading skills/understanding of supporting ideas and details, summarizing text, and distinguishing main ideas from details

---

**Differentiated Instruction: Struggling Learners**

Review *etymology* and have students use a dictionary to identify abbreviations for languages. Have students choose a word from the **Try It!** activity and identify its etymology. Once they identify the root word, have them write a list of other words with the same root. Invite students to share their word families with the rest of the class.

## Sample Dictionary Page

Guide words — 

Entry word — 

Etymology — 

Syllable divisions — 

Pronunciation and accent marks — 

Illustration — 

Part of speech — 

Spelling — 

Definitions — 

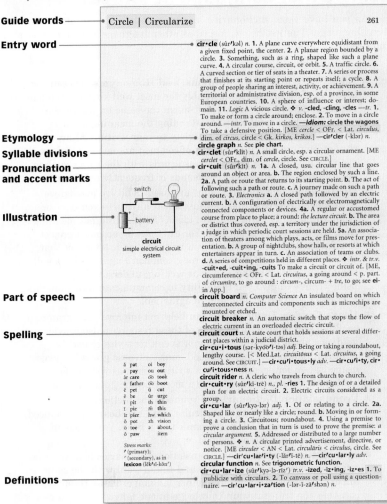

**Language**

Allow students several minutes to review the Sample Dictionary Page and jot down any questions they might have about the format or content. Then lead a class discussion based on students' queries. Allow students to respond to others' questions if they are certain of the answers.

⭐ **ELPS** 3F

---

## Using Other Language Resources

Review each kind of resource and its uses with students. If possible, provide students with copies of each kind of resource or access to the Internet to investigate these resources. Tell English learners that dictionaries of idioms, as well as pronunciation and translation dictionaries, are especially useful to them as they immerse themselves in the English language. **DIFFERENTIATE INSTRUCTION ⌐**

**522**

## Using Other Language Resources

As you have seen, dictionaries are an excellent source of information about language. The list below describes other language resources you may find useful.

- **Books of Synonyms, Antonyms, and Homonyms** Thesauruses, or books of synonyms, are probably the most well-known language resource. Synonyms—words that mean the same or almost the same—can be helpful for understanding the meaning of an unfamiliar word, and can add variety to your writing. Many of these resources also include lists of common antonyms (words with opposite meanings) and homonyms (words with the same spelling but different meanings) for thousands of frequently used words.

- **Dictionaries of Idioms** Idioms are used in books, magazines, newspapers, everyday speech—just about anywhere you hear or read language. Phrases that are idioms have a different meaning than the actual words suggest. For example, if you put a project "on the back burner" it means you will work on it later, not that you've placed it on a stove. Learning common English idioms will help you in your reading and your writing; understanding and using them will give you the ability to communicate your thoughts and ideas with expression and imagination.

- **Usage Guides** Usage guides can help you improve your grammar, spelling, and punctuation. Many of these resources also provide guidance about different writing or speaking styles to use for different audiences. Choose a good, multi-purpose guide for general usage issues; for specific types of writing, such as writing for a newspaper, you may want to use a more specific guide as well.

- **Pronunciation Dictionaries** Pronunciation dictionaries allow you to type in or look up a particular word and hear it pronounced, either online or on a CD accompanied by a book. Variations in pronunciation are often included as well.

- **Translation Dictionaries** Translation dictionaries help you take a familiar word in one language and find a word with the same or almost the same meaning in another language. These resources can help you transfer your knowledge in one language into a new language, making your ideas and your writing clearer for your audience.

**523**

# Learning Language

Has this ever happened to you? You read a page or a chapter in a textbook, put the book down, and say, "I can't remember a thing I just read!" Unfortunately, many students have that experience. The good news, however, is that you can remember the information you read. The way to do it is by reading critically.

Reading for academic success involves a number of steps, including surveying a reading assignment, questioning what the text is about, taking notes as you read, and so on. If you keep these tips in mind and have a tested reading plan, you will be in control of your reading. This chapter gives you an effective critical-reading method to follow.

- **Learning Language: Language Strategies**
- **Language of the Writing Process**
- **Language of the Writing Traits**
- **Language of the Writing Forms**

"Language is the dress of thought."

—Samuel Johnson

# Learning Language

**Objectives**

- learn to use critical reading strategies to comprehend and retain information
- learn and apply the language of the writing process, including steps, traits, and forms

Learning language is key to developing understanding and expressing ideas. Tell students that through simple activities such as vocabulary building, reviewing and monitoring, summarizing, and writing, they can increase comprehension and practice expressing their own ideas.

## Language Strategies

Lead a class discussion about the strategies students use to comprehend and remember new vocabulary and language structures.

**DIFFERENTIATE INSTRUCTION ↘**

⭐ **ELPS** 2C, 2D, 4C

### Use Language Patterns

Read the example. Explain that the pattern gives the time frame to begin and follows with a future-tense verb—*will practice* or *will hold*.

### Try It!

Have students turn to their neighbors. Tell the first student to say two sentences using the future tense and the second to add to the information using the same pattern.

### Look for the Context

Tell students that they can use the environmental context—a sign in a doctor's office—as well as their knowledge of word parts—*co-* means "with" or "together"—to determine meaning.

### Try It!

Have students look at the emergency exit sign or map in your classroom. Discuss as a class what the sign means. Point out that students use the map and the symbols to derive meaning from environmental print.

⭐ **ELPS** 4C

### Use Academic Language

Tell students that they will often have the chance to ask teachers what a word means. Point out that they can use context clues to discern a general meaning. In the example, *overall health* provides a clue that *circulatory* refers to something in the body.

### Try It!

Read a few sentences to the class and have them record unfamiliar words. Help them use context clues and consult a dictionary to determine meaning.

⭐ **ELPS 2C** Learn new language structures and basic/academic vocabulary heard during classroom instruction/interactions; **2D** Monitor understanding of spoken language during classroom instruction/interactions; **3C** Speak using a variety of grammatical structures with increasing accuracy and ease; **4C** Derive meaning of environmental print/comprehend language structures used in written classroom materials

---

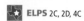 

## Language Strategies

You hear and read new words every day. Here are some strategies to help you understand, remember, and use the new language correctly.

### Use Language Patterns

Listen for patterns others use when speaking English.

You hear: **This morning,** you will practice your presentations. **After school,** the soccer team will hold practice.
You say: **Tomorrow,** I will go on a field trip with my science class.

#### Try It!

Turn to a partner. Say three sentences that tell what will happen. Start with a word that tells when, as in the examples above.

### Look for the Context

You can find the meaning of an unfamiliar word by examining its context, or what surrounds the word.

You read a sign: Pay your co-pay before you see the doctor.
You can conclude that a co-pay is part of the bill you must pay.

#### Try It!

The next time you read unfamiliar words on a sign, try to identify the meaning of the words by the context in which they appear.

### Use Academic Language

Teachers may sometimes use unfamiliar words in class. If your teacher uses a word you don't know, repeat it to yourself and write it down. When you get a chance, look up the word in a dictionary.

You hear: A strong circulatory system is an important part of overall health.
You say and write down: "circulatory."

#### Try It!

Listen for words you don't understand. Repeat them and write them down. Check with your teacher if you are unsure how to write them.

---

**Differentiated Instruction: Struggling Learners**

To help struggling learners identify and emulate patterns in language, provide sentence frames for them to complete the **Try It!** activity:
*Tomorrow, I will _____.*
*After that, I will _____.*
*_____, I will _____.*

⭐ **ELPS** 3C

Language

## Say It Again

When your teacher makes an assignment, retell what you have heard so that you can be sure that you fully understand it.

You hear: Your essay must include a works-cited page that follows MLA style.

You can say: I will need to prepare a list of sources that I used in my essay that follows the MLA style guide.

### Try It!

Retell the details of a recent assignment to your teacher or another classmate. Listen to any clarifications and retell the clarification.

## Look for Word Parts You Know

Many words share prefixes, suffixes, or roots, even across different languages. For example, the prefix *bio-* means "life" in many languages, including French, Spanish, and German.

### Try It!

If you hear a word you don't know, try writing it down. See if you recognize any of its parts. If so, use that part to help you determine the meaning of the whole word.

## Learn Words in Different Ways

You may hear a word that you know used in a way that is unfamiliar to you. Finding the connection to what you know can help you understand the new use of the word.

You think: Suki has to parallel park on her driving test. In geometry, parallel lines are ones that go in the same direction and never meet. Parallel parking must mean that the car is parallel to the curb, going in the same direction.

### Try It!

Listen for familiar words used in unfamiliar ways. Try to find the logical connection between the two uses.

## Say It Again

Students can use this technique for both oral and written directions. If given a writing prompt, they can circle the important words, the form they are to write, and the length of the assignment, and then explain the assignment in their own words. ✔ DIFFERENTIATE INSTRUCTION

### Try It!

Read aloud an assignment or writing prompt. Have pairs take turns restating the assignment in their own words. Tell students to ask questions to clarify the assignment.

⭐ ELPS 2C, 2D, 2I, 3E, 3F

## Look for Word Parts You Know

Provide students with a list of prefixes and their definitions, such as *bio-, im-, re-, co-,* and *un-.* Reiterate the importance of learning the meanings of word parts.

### Try It!

Give pairs a brief list of words to break into parts: *undo, reread, impossible.* Have pairs determine meaning based on the meanings of the words' parts.

## Learn Words in Different Ways

Tell students that along with using the same word in a different way, words within the same family can be used in different contexts. If students know the word *circle,* they can determine the meanings of *encircle* and *circulate.*

### Try It!

Read a paragraph aloud that includes jargon related to computers, math, or science. Have pairs discuss their thought processes used to determine meanings.

## Differentiated Instruction: English Language Learners

⭐ ELPS 2C, 2I, 4C, 4D

| ELP Level **Beginning** | ELP Level **Intermediate** | ELP Level **Advanced/Advanced High** |
|---|---|---|
| Review verb tenses with students. List "future" introductory words: *later, tomorrow, Saturday, next week.* Then review the formation of the future tense. | Have students construct a glossary of common word parts, listing prefixes, meanings, and examples of words. | Have each student in a pair construct a writing prompt. Then have students read their prompts as their partners take notes, restating the prompt in their own words. |

**ELPS 2C** Learn new language structures/expressions and basic/academic vocabulary heard during classroom instruction/interactions; **2D** Monitor understanding of spoken language during classroom instruction/interactions and seek clarification of spoken language as needed; **2I** Demonstrate listening comprehension in increasingly complex spoken language/following directions, summarizing spoken messages, and collaborating with peers; **3E** Share information in cooperative learning interactions; **3F** Give information/ranging from using a limited high-frequency vocabulary to using abstract and content-based vocabulary during speaking; **4C** Develop basic sight vocabulary used in written classroom materials; **4D** Use prereading supports to enhance comprehension of written text/graphic organizers, illustrations, and topic-related vocabulary

## Language of the Writing Process

Tell students that the steps in the writing process will occur frequently in their English classes. They need to familiarize themselves with these terms and their meanings. Write on the board and discuss the tasks to be completed at each step:

- Prewrite
- Draft
- Revise
- Edit
- Publish

Explain that when students complete a process, they need to follow steps in a specific order. As they practice the writing process, they will need to follow these steps in the given order.

**ELPS** 4C

---

 **ELPS** 4C

# Language of the Writing Process

Read the terms below that identify the steps in the writing process. Then read the description of what you will accomplish at each step.

**Prewrite** The first step in the writing process is prewriting, or planning your writing. During prewriting, you will think about your purpose for writing and identify your genre, or form, of writing. You will also plan a topic that will interest your audience. Once you have identified your topic, audience, and genre, you will write your thesis statement, or controlling idea. Finally, you will generate ideas related to your thesis by brainstorming or by using a graphic organizer.

**Draft** When you write a first draft, you should write freely to get all your ideas on paper. Use your prewriting as a guide and always keep your thesis statement in mind. Organize your basic ideas into paragraphs. Since this is a draft, you don't have to worry that it is exactly right. Include everything you think is important. Always keep your audience and purpose in mind.

**Revise** Now it is time to read your draft and revise, or make changes, to it. Consider the first four key writing traits: *focus and coherence, organization, development of ideas,* and *voice.* When you revise, you make sure that all the parts of your writing support the thesis, that your ideas are fully developed, and that the information is organized to flow well. Finally, check to see that your voice is right for your purpose, genre, and audience.

**Edit** When you edit, you look for mistakes in your writing. You check for correct use of conventions—grammar, sentence structure, capitalization, punctuation, and spelling. Correct any errors and then proofread your copy. Print or write a neat copy.

**Publish** Get feedback from your teacher or classmates and make final revisions. Then make a neat final copy that you can share with others.

---

**ELPS** 2D, 2I, 3A, 3E, 3G, 3H, 4C, 4G

# Vocabulary: Writing Process

| draft | edit | feedback |
|---|---|---|
| freewrite | organize | prewrite |
| proofread | publish | revise |
| traits | | |

1. **Say the word.** Listen actively and carefully as your teacher reads the words aloud. Pay special attention to your teacher's pronunciation of long and short vowel sounds, silent letters, and consonant clusters. Then repeat the words. Which of these words have you heard before? Which do you already know?

2. **Discover the meaning.** Working with a partner, make a four-column chart. List the vocabulary word, the pronunciation, and the meanings in the first three columns and a sample sentence in the fourth column. Start with the words you already know. Discuss how you can fill in the chart as you find the meanings and pronunciations for any words you do not know.

3. **Learn more.** Listen as your teacher explains each word. Take notes by listening for key words or phrases that help you understand what each word means. Check your understanding by looking each word up in a dictionary or other reference book.

4. **Think about it.** Work with a partner to share ideas and answer the questions below.
   - When might it be good to write more than one draft?
   - When is it important to think about your audience? Why?
   - How could a graphic organizer or outline help organize your thoughts? Explain.
   - What should you think about when you edit your work?

5. **Show your understanding.** Practice explaining how each word in the vocabulary box above fits into the writing process. Then, share your explanation with a partner. Work together to add specific details in order to create an accurate explanation for each word.

Language

## Vocabulary: Writing Process

As students complete the activities, walk around the room and monitor partners' work. Allow students to ask you questions to clarify understanding. Make sure that all students are explaining and describing with increasing specificity and detail as they complete the activities. Remind students of the Writing Process vocabulary they learned on SE page 526 and have encountered throughout their English classes. Monitor students' responses to the questions presented in the text.

**✔ DIFFERENTIATE INSTRUCTION**

**ELPS** 2D, 2I, 3A, 3E, 3G, 3H, 4C, 4G, 5G

---

## Differentiated Instruction: English Language Learners

**ELPS** 3D, 3E, 3G

| ELP Level **Beginning** | ELP Level **Intermediate** | ELP Level **Advanced/Advanced High** |
|---|---|---|
| For item 2, draw a four-column chart on the board and work with students in a group to complete the chart. Provide frames for students to complete the fourth column. | Scaffold item 4 by simplifying questions: *Is it good to write more than one draft? Why? Why do audiences matter? What does* edit *mean? What do you check when you edit?* | Have advanced learners work in groups of four to complete the activities and answer the questions. |

**ELPS** **2D** Monitor understanding of spoken language during classroom instruction/interactions and seek clarification of spoken language as needed; **2I** Demonstrate listening comprehension in increasingly complex spoken language by collaborating with peers; **3A** Practice producing sounds of newly acquired vocabulary; **3D** Speak using grade-level content area vocabulary/new words and academic language proficiency; **3E** Share information in cooperative learning interactions; **3G** Express opinions and ideas ranging from communicating short phrases to participating in discussions; **3H** Describe and explain with increasing specificity and detail; **4C** Develop basic sight vocabulary/comprehend vocabulary and language structures used in written classroom materials; **4G** Demonstrate comprehension of increasingly complex English/responding to questions and taking notes; **5G** Narrate/describe/explain with increasing specificity and detail to fulfill content area writing needs

## The Writing Process in Action

### Prewrite

Write a prompt on the board: *Think about something you would like to change at school. Write a persuasive essay to convince teachers or the principal to make the change. Be sure to clearly state your opinion and provide supporting details.*

Read the prompt and then pose the Prewrite questions on SE page 528. If necessary, clarify the academic language *genre, purpose, controlling idea,* and *thesis statement.* **DIFFERENTIATE INSTRUCTION ↘**

**ELPS** 2C, 2I, 3E

### Draft

Review topic sentences and transitions. Tell students to use their graphic organizers as a way to order their essays.

---

**528**

 ELPS 2I, 3E

# The Writing Process in Action

Now that you have learned the language of the writing process, it's time to see and experience the process in action. Your teacher will begin by demonstrating each step of the writing process. Then, you and your classmates will go through the steps of the writing process together. Use the questions below as a guide.

## Prewrite

1. What is your topic? Select a topic that interests you or that you know something about.

2. What genre will you use? Sometimes you will be assigned a genre; other times you will be given a prompt, and you must determine the correct genre. Look for clue words in the prompt, such as *describe, explain,* and *give an opinion*, that will help you identify the correct genre, or form.

3. Who is your audience? Will they be interested in your topic? What do they already know about your topic?

4. What is your purpose for writing? Are you writing for a class assignment, for enjoyment, to express an opinion, for a test, and so on.

5. What is your controlling idea or thesis statement? Make sure it is broad enough that you have related ideas to develop and narrow enough to effectively address the thesis statement in the space you have available.

6. How will you generate ideas about your thesis? What graphic organizers can you use to gather and organize your ideas?

## Draft

1. Are all your ideas included? Write freely about your topic so that everything you want to write about your topic is included.

2. Are your ideas organized into paragraphs? While your first draft is not polished writing, it is best to keep related ideas in the same paragraph. You may want to start your draft by writing the topic sentences for your paragraphs and then building your paragraphs with the ideas that support those sentences. Remember to use transitions so that your ideas will flow smoothly from one paragraph to the next.

3. Did you consider your audience and purpose as you wrote your draft?

---

**Differentiated Instruction: Advanced Learners**

Instead of having advanced learners write to a prompt, allow them to write about a topic of their choosing. Encourage them to be creative in their presentation of ideas while still establishing and adhering to a controlling idea.

**ELPS** 5G

---

**ELPS 2C** Learn academic vocabulary heard during classroom instruction/interactions; **2I** Demonstrate listening comprehension in increasingly complex spoken language by responding to questions and collaborating with peers; **3E** Share information in cooperative learning interactions; **5G** Narrate/describe/explain with increasing specificity and detail to fulfill content area writing needs

ELPS 2I, 3E, 3G

Language

## Revise

1. Do you maintain focus on your thesis throughout your writing?
2. Do all your paragraphs support your thesis?
3. Is your writing organized with a beginning, a middle, and an ending?
4. Is your organizational pattern effective for your purpose and your audience?
5. Are your ideas fully developed?
6. Do your transitions help your readers move from paragraph to paragraph and from idea to idea smoothly?
7. Does your voice seem knowledgeable and engaging? Your word choices should indicate that you understand your topic well. Your voice should reflect your interest in the topic.

## Edit

1. Did you check that there is agreement between subjects and verbs?
2. Did you use the correct form of words with more than one spelling, such as *two, to,* and *too*?
3. Did you use a variety of sentence structures?
4. Did you capitalize the correct words, such as the start of sentences and proper nouns?
5. Did you use correct end punctuation for each sentence?
6. Did you use commas correctly?
7. Are all your words spelled correctly?

## Publish

1. Did you leave even margins?
2. Did you indent each paragraph?
3. Did you get feedback from your teacher or classmates? Use this feedback to make final improvements before publishing.

 **Turn and Talk and Listen**

**Take turns talking with a classmate about what you learned as you used the writing process.**

What was easy and what was hard about the writing process?
What do you like about your writing?
What will you do differently the next time you write an essay?
It is important to proofread because _____.

## Revise

Read through the questions with students and clarify any confusing ideas or unfamiliar words. Then have them apply the questions to their writing. When students finish and make the first round of revisions, instruct them to exchange papers and repeat the process for their partners' papers. Partners can then meet and provide oral feedback based on the revision questions.

ELPS 2I

## Edit

Once students incorporate partners' feedback, have them review their work for errors in grammar, usage, and mechanics.

✔ DIFFERENTIATE INSTRUCTION

ELPS 5D

## Publish

Allow students time to make a clean copy, written legibly or typed, of their final drafts. Provide feedback for students based on the content and presentation of their essays.

 **Turn and Talk and Listen**

Divide students into pairs to ask and answer the questions. Have partners take turns reading the questions and providing answers.

ELPS 3D, 3E, 3G

---

**TEKS** ELPS **2I** Demonstrate listening comprehension in increasingly complex spoken language by responding to questions and collaborating with peers; **3D** Speak using grade-level content area vocabulary/new words and academic language proficiency; **3E** Share information in cooperative learning interactions; **3G** Express opinions, ideas, and feelings ranging from communicating short phrases to participating in discussions; **5D** Edit writing for standard grammar and usage/subject-verb and pronoun agreement and appropriate verb tenses

## Language of the Writing Traits

Explain that writing traits are qualities that all good writing possesses. When students prewrite, draft, revise, and edit, they should try to incorporate all of these traits.

 ELPS 4C

### Focus and Coherence

Relate the focus of writing to focusing one's eyes. Tell students to focus their eyes on an object in the classroom. Point out that when they focus on something, they aren't looking at anything else. Explain that focus in writing involves writing about one main idea, not many ideas.

Explain that *cohere* means to "stick" or "hold together" and that coherence in writing is similar in that all ideas "stick" or "hold together" to support the main idea, or focus, of an essay.

### Organization

Explain that organization is the ordering of ideas. Review different types of organization, such as time/sequence or compare and contrast.

### Development of Ideas

Tell students that when something is *developed*, it is planned, built, and expanded upon. When students have an idea for writing, they need to plan how to express it and determine which details to add to expand and support the idea.

### Voice

Relate a person's voice—the sound made while speaking—to voice in writing. Because each person sounds different, they can be identified based on that sound. In the same way, voice in writing expresses who the writer is and is particular to his or her personality.

### Conventions

As students advance in their writing skills, conventions will become second nature to them. However, they will always need to edit writing for correct grammar, usage, and mechanics.

---

**530**

ELPS 4C

 # Language of the Writing Traits

Read each of these terms. Then read about what they mean.

### Focus and Coherence

**Focus** means that everything in your writing supports the main idea. Your main idea is usually expressed in your thesis statement. **Coherence** means the sentences connect and make sense together. Your writing should always have a clear focus. Include specific ideas and details to support the focus of your topic. Any sentences that don't relate directly to the topic weaken the writing. Remember, everything you write should contribute to the readers' understanding of the topic.

### Organization

Your writing should be organized to make it easy to follow from beginning to end. It should have a distinct beginning, middle, and end. Each sentence and paragraph should be logically linked to the ones that come before and after it. Details should support the topic.

### Development of Ideas

Include enough details to give your writing depth. **Depth** means you "layer" and "flesh out" ideas so that each sentence adds meaning to the one before it. Good development must also be original. You can't just repeat what someone else has done before you.

### Voice

Your writing should express your own voice. It should genuinely express your personality or viewpoint to engage the reader. Voice gives your writing a "face," which establishes a relationship between you and the reader.

### Conventions

Think about the basic rules of grammar, sentence structure, punctuation, spelling, and word choice. Edit your work to be sure there are no errors. Writing that has errors is difficult to read and may cause you to lose your reader.

**ELPS 4C** Develop and comprehend basic sight vocabulary used in written classroom materials

# Vocabulary: Writing Traits

| coherence | conventions | depth |
|---|---|---|
| development of ideas | focus | organization |
| thesis statement | voice | |

1. **Say the word.** Listen actively and carefully as your teacher reads each word. Pay special attention to your teacher's pronunciation of long and short vowel sounds, silent letters, and consonant clusters. Then repeat the words. Which of these words have you heard before? Which do you already know?

2. **Discover the meaning.** Work with a partner. Write the vocabulary words you already know, and their meanings. Discuss the words with your partner, teaching each other the words you know. Some of these words have more than one meaning. If you are not sure of the correct meaning in this context, list the word with the meaning you know.

3. **Learn more.** Listen as your teacher explains each word. Work with your partner to restate the meaning of each word by putting the meaning in your own words.

4. **Think about it.** Work with a partner to answer the questions below.
   - How do you decide on a thesis statement?
   - How can you be sure that your writing has depth?
   - How can you tell if your writing has coherence?
   - Why is organization important to your purpose?
   - How can you tell if your writing reflects your voice?
   - What conventions are most difficult for you?

5. **Show your understanding.** Use your vocabulary journal to write what you know about each word. Work with a partner to understand each of the words better. When words connect to each other, show the connections with explanations or descriptions. Include sample sentences. You may wish to read your sample sentences to your partner.

## Vocabulary: Writing Traits

As students complete the activities, walk around the room and monitor partners' work. Allow students to ask you questions to clarify understanding. Make sure that all students are explaining and describing with increasing specificity and detail as they complete the activities. Remind students of the Writing Traits vocabulary they learned on SE page 530 and have encountered throughout their English classes. Monitor students' responses to the questions presented in the text.

**DIFFERENTIATE INSTRUCTION**

**ELPS** 2D, 2I, 3A, 3E, 3G, 3H, 4C, 4G

---

## Differentiated Instruction: English Language Learners

**ELPS** 2I, 3D, 3E, 4C

| ELP Level **Beginning** | ELP Level **Intermediate** | ELP Level **Advanced/Advanced High** |
|---|---|---|
| Use Spanish cognates (*coherence/ coherencia, idea/ idea, voice/voz, organization/ organización*) to help students understand the Vocabulary of Writing Traits. | Have students take notes as you describe the meaning of each word (item 3). Then organize students into pairs and have them summarize your definitions as they consult their notes. | Have students answer the questions in item 4 with partners: *What is a thesis statement? What does depth mean in the context of writing? What is your purpose?* |

**ELPS 2D** Monitor understanding of spoken language during classroom instruction/interactions and seek clarification of spoken language as needed; **2I** Demonstrate listening comprehension in increasingly complex spoken language/following directions, summarizing spoken messages, responding to questions, collaborating with peers, and taking notes; **3A** Practice producing sounds of newly acquired vocabulary; **3D** Speak using grade-level content area vocabulary/new words and academic language proficiency; **3E** Share information in cooperative learning interactions; **3G** Express opinions and ideas ranging from communicating short phrases to participating in discussions; **3H** Describe and explain with increasing specificity and detail; **4C** Develop and comprehend basic sight vocabulary used in written classroom materials; **4G** Demonstrate comprehension of increasingly complex English/responding to questions

## Narrative Essays

Tell students that a narrative essay is a story from a person's life. Explain that when students think of stories to tell, they need to consider why the story might interest an audience and what effect the events had on them as people.

Review the organizational structure of narrative essays. Point out that they usually use time order and are structured with a beginning, middle, and ending.

 **Turn and Talk**

Divide students into pairs for the activity. Walk around the room and monitor students' discussions. [DIFFERENTIATE INSTRUCTION ↘]

**ELPS** 2I, 3D, 3E, 3F

---

# Narrative Essays

A narrative essay is writing that tells a true story. A personal narrative essay tells the writer's audience about an important experience in the writer's life. The experience might be one that extended over a period of time and one that changed the writer in some way. Narrative essays have the same basic organization: a beginning that gets the reader's attention and identifies the topic, middle paragraphs that tell about the experience in time order, and an ending paragraph that concludes the story.

**Narrative Essay Organization**

 **Turn and Talk**
Talk with a partner about the purpose of each paragraph in a narrative essay as shown in the graphic organizer.

---

### Differentiated Instruction: Struggling Learners

To scaffold struggling learners' Turn and Talk discussions, write these questions for students to answer:

- *What do readers learn from the beginning of a narrative essay?*
- *What is described in the three middle paragraphs of a narrative essay?*
- *What order is used to tell about events?*
- *What information is included in the conclusion?*

---

**ELPS** **2I** Demonstrate listening comprehension in increasingly complex spoken language/responding to questions and collaborating with peers; **3D** Speak using grade-level content area vocabulary/academic language proficiency; **3E** Share information in cooperative learning interactions; **3F** Ask for and give information/ranging from using a limited high-frequency vocabulary to using abstract and content-based vocabulary during speaking

ELPS 2C, 3A, 3B, 3G, 4C, 5B, 5G

# Vocabulary: Narrative Form

| | | |
|---|---|---|
| action | chronological order | dialogue |
| experience | narrative | narrator |
| phase autobiography | sensory details | situation |
| suspense | | |

1. **Say the word or phrase.** Listen actively and carefully as your teacher reads the words aloud. Pay special attention to your teacher's pronunciation of long and short vowel sounds, silent letters, and consonant clusters. Then repeat each word.

2. **Discover the meaning.** Work with a partner and make notes about the words you know. Use each of these words in a sentence. Make a list of words that you do not yet know.

3. **Learn more.** Listen as your teacher explains the meaning of each word or phrase. Work with your partner to check and correct your earlier notes. Write the meanings for additional words.

4. **Show your understanding.** Use your notebook to answer the questions below.
   - Where in the narrative does the writer usually reflect upon the situation? Tell why.
   - Why would a narrative be less interesting without suspense?
   - Why is using dialogue important in a narrative essay?
   - Why is chronological order useful in narrative writing?
   - How do sensory details help show the audience what the experience was like?

5. **Write it, explain it.** In your vocabulary journal, list the words that you have learned. Add synonyms, or words that means the same thing, to the right of the word. For example, next to **narrator** you could write "the person who tells a story or a gives a report."

6. **Write about it.** Write a brief paragraph explaining how to write a narrative essay. Use at least three of the vocabulary words above in your paragraph.

*Language*

## Vocabulary: Narrative Form

As students complete the activities, walk around the room and monitor partners' work. Allow students to ask you questions to clarify understanding. Make sure that all students are explaining and describing with increasing specificity and detail as they complete the activities. Monitor students' responses to the questions presented in the text.

**✔ DIFFERENTIATE INSTRUCTION**

⭐ ELPS 2C, 2D, 2I, 3A, 3B, 3E, 3G, 3H, 4C, 4G, 5B, 5G

---

## Differentiated Instruction: English Language Learners

⭐ ELPS 3A, 3B, 3C, 4A

| ELP Level **Beginning** | ELP Level **Intermediate** | ELP Level **Advanced/Advanced High** |
|---|---|---|
| Tell students to track the text as you read each word aloud. Have students repeat the words at least three times to attain fluency. Clarify pronunciation as needed. | For completing item 2, provide students with frames to identify words: *I know the word _____. It means _____.* | After you define words for the class (item 3), have advanced students use each word in an original sentence. Ask partners to provide feedback. |

⭐ **ELPS 2C** Learn new expressions and basic/academic vocabulary heard during classroom instruction/interactions; **2D** Monitor understanding of spoken language during classroom instruction/interactions and seek clarification of spoken language as needed; **2I** Demonstrate listening comprehension in increasingly complex spoken language by collaborating with peers; **3A** Practice producing sounds of newly acquired vocabulary; **3B** Expand vocabulary by learning and using routine language needed for classroom communication; **3C** Speak using a variety of grammatical structures with increasing accuracy and ease; **3E** Share information in cooperative learning interactions; **3G** Express ideas ranging from communicating short phrases to participating in discussions; **3H** Describe and explain with increasing specificity and detail; **4A** Sound out words using a combination of skills; **4C** Develop and comprehend basic sight vocabulary used in written classroom materials; **4G** Demonstrate comprehension of increasingly complex English/responding to questions; **5B** Write using newly acquired basic and content-based grade-level vocabulary; **5G** Narrate/describe/explain with increasing specificity and detail to fulfill content area writing needs

## The Language of Narrative Essays

### What Do You Know?

Lead a class discussion in response to the questions. If necessary, clarify key terms such as *animal shelter*, *volunteer*, and *community*.

 ELPS 2C, 2G, 2I, 4C, 4G

### Build Background

Tell students that building background and accessing their own prior knowledge and experiences will prepare them for reading. Taking the time to build background will help them better comprehend writing. Have students monitor their understanding of the information by asking questions to clarify ideas and background information.

ELPS 1A, 2D, 4F

### Listening

Read aloud the instruction and questions as students track the text. Review the literary terms *images* and *narrator*. Remind students that writers use sensory details to create effective images, or pictures.

### Key Words

Read each word aloud. Have students raise their hands if they know the word. Ask a volunteer to tell what the word means and use it in a sentence. Explain that learning vocabulary before reading a selection will help their reading go smoothly and increase comprehension.

**DIFFERENTIATE INSTRUCTION** ↘

ELPS 4D

---

ELPS 2C, 2G, 2I, 4C, 4G

## The Language of Narrative Essays

### What Do You Know?

Next you will read a sample personal narrative essay about an experience volunteering at an animal shelter. Have you ever done any volunteer work? How can you describe it? Why did you do it? How did you feel? What do you know about animal shelters? Are there any in your community? Tell what you know.

### Build Background

When people do volunteer work, they offer their time and services for no pay. Volunteering has many benefits to both the community and the volunteers. When you volunteer, you help others in need. Volunteering is also a way to get to know more about people and their life situations. It also allows you to explore what interests you and learn what you can accomplish.

### Listening

Listen as your teacher or a classmate reads aloud "In the Doghouse." As you listen, make notes about the order of events. Be prepared to answer the questions below.
1. What are two ways the writer creates effective images for the reader?
2. What challenges does the narrator face and how does he meet them?
3. Why does the writer say, "I thought this would be great preparation"?

### Key Words

| | | |
|---|---|---|
| adoptable | challenge | incompetent |
| instinctively | ordinary | preparation |
| responsibilities | shelter | volunteers |

Look at the words and phrases in the box. You will see these words and phrases when you read the writing sample. Use the words to tell a partner, in chronological order, about an experience that changed you in some way.

---

### Differentiated Instruction: Struggling Learners

Modify the Key Words activity for struggling learners by having them create a glossary of the selection words. Distribute note cards and have students write each word on its own card. Then have students work with partners to record a definition and use the word in an original sentence. Encourage students to write sentences that express a personal context. For example, *Algebra is a challenge for me.*

---

**ELPS 1A** Use prior knowledge and experiences to understand meanings; **2C** Learn new expressions and basic vocabulary heard during classroom instruction/interactions; **2D** Monitor understanding of spoken language during classroom instruction/interactions and seek clarification of spoken language as needed; **2G** Understand the general meaning of spoken language/topics, languages, and contexts are familiar to unfamiliar; **2I** Demonstrate listening comprehension in increasingly complex spoken language/following directions, responding to questions, and collaborating with peers; **4C** Develop basic sight vocabulary/comprehend vocabulary and language structures used in written classroom materials; **4D** Use prereading supports to enhance comprehension of written text/graphic organizers, illustrations, and topic-related vocabulary; **4F** Use support from peers/teachers to enhance understanding and develop vocabulary and background knowledge; **4G** Demonstrate comprehension of increasingly complex English/participating in shared reading, responding to questions, and taking notes

**ELPS** 2C, 2G, 2I, 4C, 4G, 4I–4K

## Read Along

Now it's your turn to read. Turn to pages 83–84 in this book. Read the writing model as your teacher or a classmate reads it aloud.

## After Reading

Copy the following chart and fill it in with information about the narrative. Use your chart to summarize the writing model with a partner.

| Actions or events | Sensory details | Your thoughts |
|---|---|---|
| First: | | |
| Next: | | |
| Next: | | |
| Next: | | |
| Last: | | |

### Differentiated Instruction: English Language Learners

 **ELPS** 2C, 2G, 2I, 4J, 4K

| ELP Level **Beginning** | ELP Level **Intermediate** | ELP Level **Advanced/Advanced High** |
|---|---|---|
| Read the first model paragraph aloud, clarifying unfamiliar terms. Have students identify sensory words, record them in the chart, and use gestures to show their reactions. | Have students copy a five-column sensory chart and record sensory details from the model paragraph under the correct heading: *sight, sound, smell, taste, touch, hearing.* | Have students discuss and answer the Listening activity questions (SE page 534) with partners. Invite students to share their responses with the class. |

## Read Along

Read aloud the writing model as students track the text in their books. Or, organize students into pairs and have them alternate reading aloud, paragraph by paragraph.

## After Reading

Have students copy the chart and revisit the text to identify each event. Then have them record their responses, questions, and ideas about the events in the right column. Finally, organize students into pairs and instruct them to review and discuss their charts before they write their summaries. Invite pairs to share their collaborative summaries with the class.

✔ **DIFFERENTIATE INSTRUCTION**

**ELPS** 2C, 2G, 2I, 3E, 4C, 4G, 4I, 4J, 4K

**ELPS 2C** Learn new language structures/expressions and basic vocabulary heard during classroom instruction/interactions; **2G** Understand the general meaning, main points, and important details of spoken language/topics, languages, and contexts are familiar to unfamiliar; **2I** Demonstrate listening comprehension in increasingly complex spoken language/following directions, summarizing spoken messages, and collaborating with peers; **3E** Share information in cooperative learning interactions; **4C** Comprehend vocabulary and language structures used in written classroom materials; **4G** Demonstrate comprehension of increasingly complex English/participating in shared reading, summarizing material, and taking notes; **4I** Demonstrate comprehension by employing and expanding basic reading skills; **4J** Demonstrate comprehension and expand reading skills by employing inferential skills; **4K** Demonstrate comprehension and expand reading skills by employing analytical skills

## Oral Language

Remind students that as they prewrite and draft, they need to keep their audience in mind. Explain that tone is the attitude that a speaker or writer takes toward his or her subject. The tone of a piece of writing might be serious or funny, thoughtful, or flippant. Tell students that a writer might use formal language to express a serious tone and appeal to an adult audience. On the other hand, informal language might have more appeal to a teenaged audience.

**ELPS** 1G

### Try It!

Read the directions to students and then organize them into pairs to complete the activity. Make sure students understand the situation and the audiences. Have students take turns describing the situation while their partners take on the roles of the varied audiences. Remind students to use formal or informal language to express tone and appeal to particular audiences.

**ELPS** 3G, 3H, 3I

---

 ELPS 3G, 3I

## Oral Language

The person or people who will listen to you or read your writing are called your **audience.** When you speak or write, it is important to choose just the right words that will reach your audience. When you write, the **tone,** or the way you write, will be different for each audience.

### Try It!

Read about the situation below. Then choose two audiences from the list below. With a partner, discuss how the words you choose might be different for each audience.

**Situation**

Your friend has just finished his campaign to run for class president. He told you about the experience, including why he decided to run, the tactics he used to try to win votes, the day of the election, and what he learned from the experience. You will retell his story.

**Audiences**

■ a classmate, an aunt or uncle, an experienced politician

---

**ELPS** **1G** Demonstrate increasing knowledge of when to use formal/informal English; **3G** Express ideas ranging from communicating short phrases to participating in discussions; **3H** Describe with increasing specificity and detail; **3I** Adapt spoken language for formal and informal purposes

# Let's Talk!

When you answer a question, you might use one word, a few words, a sentence, or a few sentences.

Example: What was it like to run for class president?

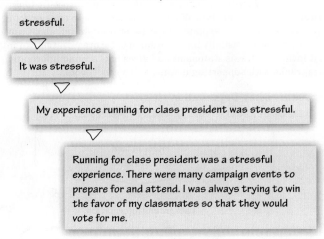

stressful.

▽

It was stressful.

▽

My experience running for class president was stressful.

▽

Running for class president was a stressful experience. There were many campaign events to prepare for and attend. I was always trying to win the favor of my classmates so that they would vote for me.

In the first box, there is only a one-word answer. In the other boxes, the writer includes more information. The last box shows the most information. When you use more details to tell about something, the listener will understand it better.

## Try It!

Choose a new question that you would like to talk about with a partner. First make notes about details that would make your answer entertaining. Then use your notes to tell your story to your partner.

Here are some ideas to get you started.

1. Have you had an experience, like campaigning for something, from which you learned an important life lesson? Tell what happened and the lesson you learned.

2. Describe a time when you learned something for the first time.

## Let's Talk

Read the example and discuss the information that is added to each answer. Make sure students understand the information as the response increases in complexity.

⭐ ELPS 2H

## Try It!

Have students begin by jotting down questions for their partners. Then have them record notes that would allow them to answer their own questions. Finally, have partners take turns asking and answering questions.

☑ **DIFFERENTIATE INSTRUCTION**

⭐ ELPS 3E, 3G, 3H

---

| **Differentiated Instruction: English Language Learners** | | ⭐ ELPS 2I, 3G, 3H |
|---|---|---|
| **ELP Level**<br>**Beginning** | **ELP Level**<br>**Intermediate** | **ELP Level**<br>**Advanced/Advanced High** |
| Write simple questions. Provide sentence frames for answers: *What new thing have you learned? I learned to _____. What was it like? It was _____.* | Have partners answer these questions: *What important lesson did you learn this year? How did you learn it?* Tell students to answer in complete sentences. | After each student responds to the question and shares a narrative, have them take time to ask questions to clarify the main ideas and events of the responses. |

⭐ **ELPS 2H** Understand information in increasingly complex spoken language; **2I** Demonstrate listening comprehension in increasingly complex spoken language by responding to questions; **3E** Share information in cooperative learning interactions; **3G** Express ideas and feelings ranging from communicating short phrases to participating in discussions; **3H** Narrate/describe/explain with increasing specificity and detail

# Language of Expository Writing

Tell students that expository writing explains something. When students write expository essays, their purpose is to give information and help the audience understand more about the topic.

Review the organizational structure of expository essays. Tell students that expository essays use different kinds of organization within the structure to make ideas clear. For example, if a writer wanted to explain the reasons that an event occurred, he or she would use cause-and-effect organization.

## Turn and Talk and Listen

Before students discuss the prompt, review the Language of the Writing Traits on SE page 530. Review Focus and Coherence and Development of Ideas to inform students' discussions.

Organize students into pairs for the activity. Walk around the room and monitor students' discussions. **DIFFERENTIATE INSTRUCTION ↘**

⭐ **ELPS** 2I, 3E, 4D

---

# Language of Expository Writing

Expository writing explains something about a specific topic to the writer's audience. This type of writing might explain one particular subject, compare two subjects, explain a process, or it might tell about cause and effect. Expository essays usually have the same basic organization: an introduction that includes a thesis statement and gives background information, body paragraphs with supporting details, and a conclusion.

**Expository Essay Organization**

**Turn and Talk and Listen**
Talk with a partner about why it is important that all parts of the essay work together.

---

## Differentiated Instruction: Struggling Learners

To improve struggling learners' comprehension, introduce fundamental academic vocabulary for expository writing in logical pairs. Explain:

- A *cause* is a reason something happens. An *effect* is the result of a cause.

- When you *compare*, you look at how things are alike. When you *contrast*, you look at how things are different.

---

**ELPS 2I** Demonstrate listening comprehension in increasingly complex spoken language/following directions, responding to questions, and collaborating with peers; **3E** Share information in cooperative learning interactions; **4D** Use prereading supports to enhance comprehension of written text/graphic organizers, illustrations, and topic-related vocabulary

**ELPS** 2C, 2I, 3A, 3G, 3H, 4C, 4G, 5B, 5G

Learning Language **539**

Language

# Vocabulary: Expository Writing

| | | |
|---|---|---|
| background | cause | effect |
| explanation | expository | fact |
| paraphrase | quotation | source |
| thesis statement | | |

1. **Say the word or phrase.** Listen actively and carefully as your teacher reads the words aloud. Pay special attention to your teacher's pronunciation of long and short vowel sounds, silent letters, and consonant clusters. Then repeat each word.

2. **Discover the meaning.** Work with a partner. Identify the words you already know. Write notes about their meanings. Review the definitions of terms that you have already heard. Discuss with your partner possible meanings of words you do not yet know.

3. **Learn more.** Listen as your teacher explains the meaning of each word or phrase. Ask for clarification if needed. Work with your partner to review meanings, and correct any misunderstandings.

4. **Think about it.** Use your notebook to answer the questions below.
   - Where should you state your thesis? Why?
   - When and why should you paraphrase and when use quotations?
   - What is the difference between a cause and an effect?
   - Why is the word *opinion* usually not part of expository writing?

5. **Show your understanding.** In your journal, create a graphic organizer that shows the basic structure of an expository essay. Write the vocabulary words in the organizer where they apply. You may wish to add synonyms, or words that mean the same thing. For example, near *paraphrase* you could write *say in your own words*.

6. **Write about it.** Write a brief paragraph explaining how to write an expository essay. Use at least three of the vocabulary words above in your paragraph.

## Vocabulary: Expository Writing

As students complete the activities, walk around the room and monitor partners' work. Allow students to ask you questions to clarify understanding. Make sure that all students are explaining and describing with increasing specificity and detail as they complete the activities. Monitor students' responses to the questions presented in the text.

**✔ DIFFERENTIATE INSTRUCTION**

 **ELPS** 2C, 2D, 2I, 3A, 3B, 3E, 3G, 3H, 4C, 4G, 5B, 5G

---

### Differentiated Instruction: English Language Learners

**ELPS** 2C, 3E, 3G

| **ELP Level** **Beginning** | **ELP Level** **Intermediate** | **ELP Level** **Advanced/Advanced High** |
|---|---|---|
| Tell students that *explain* is the base of the word *explanation*. Have students complete the frame: *If I explain something, I give an _____.* | Give students frames for item 4 responses: *Your thesis should be stated in the _____. You should paraphrase/ use quotations when _____ because _____.* | Have pairs copy and complete a three-row chart labeled *Introduction, Body,* and *Conclusion.* Tell students that some of the vocabulary words might appear in more than one section. |

**ELPS 2C** Learn new expressions and basic/academic vocabulary heard during classroom instruction/interactions; **2D** Monitor understanding of spoken language during classroom instruction/interactions and seek clarification of spoken language as needed; **2I** Demonstrate listening comprehension in increasingly complex spoken language/collaborating with peers; **3A** Practice producing sounds of newly acquired vocabulary; **3B** Expand vocabulary by learning and using routine language needed for classroom communication; **3E** Share information in cooperative learning interactions; **3G** Express opinions and ideas ranging from communicating short phrases to participating in discussions; **3H** Describe and explain with increasing specificity and detail; **4C** Develop and comprehend basic sight vocabulary used in written classroom materials; **4G** Demonstrate comprehension of increasingly complex English/taking notes; **5B** Write using newly acquired basic and content-based grade-level vocabulary; **5G** Narrate/describe/explain with increasing specificity and detail to fulfill content area writing needs

## Reading the Expository Model

### What Do You Know?

Lead a class discussion in response to the questions. Then organize students into pairs to discuss their prior knowledge and experiences gaining that knowledge.

⭐ **ELPS** 1A, 2I, 3E, 3G, 4K

### Build Background

Tell students that building background and accessing their own prior knowledge and experiences will prepare them for reading. Clarify unfamiliar terms and concepts such as *emperor, Middle Ages, stabilizing, economy, trade,* and *commerce.* **DIFFERENTIATE INSTRUCTION ↘**

⭐ **ELPS** 2C, 4C, 4F

### Listening

Read aloud the instruction and questions as students track the text. Remind students that background information provides a basis for readers' understanding.

### Key Words

Read each word or phrase aloud. Have students raise their hands if they know what each means. Ask a volunteer to explain the meaning and use the word or phrase in a sentence. Explain that learning vocabulary before reading a selection will help students' reading go smoothly and increase comprehension.

⭐ **ELPS** 2G, 3H, 4D

 ⭐ ELPS 2C, 2G, 2I, 3E, 3G, 3H

# Reading the Expository Model

## What Do You Know?

Next you will read a sample expository essay about Charlemagne. Have you ever heard of Charlemagne? What do you already know about him? When and where did he live? What did he do? Talk to a partner about what you know and where you learned it.

## Build Background

Charlemagne, or "Charles the Great," was an emperor in Europe during the Middle Ages. He is famous for bringing together many nations into one great empire—the Holy Roman Empire. Charlemagne is known for stabilizing the European economy by balancing trade and commerce. He is also known for his efforts to promote education and learning across the empire.

## Listening

Listen as your teacher or a classmate reads aloud "Charlemagne." As you listen, make a note about the thesis statement. Be prepared to answer the questions below.

1. What are two pieces of background information the writer gives?
2. According to the writer, why did Charlemagne stabilize the economy?
3. With what final thought does the writer leave the reader?

## Key Words

| ability | by the sword or the cross | due to |
|---------|---------------------------|--------|
| in order to | peace | stability |
| trust | when | |

Look at the words and phrases in the box. You will see these when you read the writing model. With a partner, discuss what the words **by the sword or the cross** mean. Use the other words to talk about the effects of another event in history or the effects of an event in your own life, such as an imposed curfew.

---

 **ELPS 1A** Use prior knowledge and experiences to understand meanings; **2C** Learn new expressions and basic/academic vocabulary heard during classroom instruction/interactions; **2G** Understand the general meaning of spoken language/topics, languages, and contexts are familiar to unfamiliar; **2I** Demonstrate listening comprehension in increasingly complex spoken language/responding to questions, collaborating with peers, and taking notes; **3E** Share information in cooperative learning interactions; **3G** Express ideas ranging from communicating short phrases to participating in discussions; **3H** Explain with increasing specificity and detail; **4C** Comprehend vocabulary used in written classroom materials; **4D** Use prereading supports to enhance comprehension of written text/graphic organizers, illustrations, and topic-related vocabulary; **4F** Use support from peers/teachers to enhance understanding and develop background knowledge; **4K** Demonstrate comprehension and expand reading skills by employing analytical skills/ evaluating written information and performing critical analyses

---

### Differentiated Instruction: Struggling Learners

Write on the board: *Charlemagne built his empire by the sword and the cross.* Ask students what they think about when they picture a sword. Guide them to understand that the sword represents war. Ask the same question about the cross. Explain that the cross represents religion. Therefore, Charlemagne built his empire by conquering peoples and converting them to Christianity.

Learning Language **541**

⭐ ELPS 4G, 4I

## Read Along

Now it's your turn to read. Turn to pages 141–142 in this book. Read the writing model as your teacher or a classmate reads it aloud.

## After Reading

Copy the following chart on a piece of paper. Fill it in with the most important details of each effect of Charlemagne's unification of Europe. Use your chart to summarize the writing model with a partner.

|  | EFFECTS | DETAILS |
|---|---|---|
| peace |  |  |
| stabilized economy |  |  |
| education |  |  |

## Read Along

Read aloud the writing model as students track the text in their books. Or, organize students into pairs and have them alternate reading aloud, paragraph by paragraph.

## After Reading

Have students copy the chart and revisit the text to identify each cause and its effects. Then have them record details about the causes and effects. Finally, organize students into pairs and instruct them to review and discuss their charts before they write their summaries. Invite pairs to share their collaborative summaries with the class. ✔ DIFFERENTIATE INSTRUCTION

⭐ ELPS 3E, 4C, 4G, 4I

---

### Differentiated Instruction: English Language Learners

⭐ ELPS 4G, 4I, 4J, 4K

| ELP Level **Beginning** | ELP Level **Intermediate** | ELP Level **Advanced/Advanced High** |
|---|---|---|
| Have students copy a cause-and-effect chart in their notebooks. Guide students to record one- or two-word answers in the effects column. | Tell students that the first column is a list of causes. Guide students through the model, paragraph by paragraph, to identify the results of each idea listed. | After finishing their charts, have students discuss and answer the Listening activity (SE page 546) questions with partners. Invite students to share their responses with the class. |

**ELPS 3E** Share information in cooperative learning interactions; **4C** Comprehend vocabulary and language structures used in written classroom materials; **4G** Demonstrate comprehension of increasingly complex English/participating in shared reading, summarizing material, and taking notes; **4I** Demonstrate comprehension by employing and expanding basic reading skills/understanding of supporting ideas and details, summarizing text, and distinguishing main ideas from details; **4J** Demonstrate comprehension and expand reading skills by employing inferential skills/predicting, making connections between ideas, drawing conclusions from text, and finding supporting evidence; **4K** Demonstrate comprehension and expand reading skills by employing analytical skills/evaluating written information and performing critical analyses

## Oral Language: Expository Writing

Remind students that as they prewrite and draft, they need to keep their audience in mind. Explain that word choice not only depends on a writer's purpose, but also on his or her audience. For example, if students were to address a principal, they would likely use formal language. If addressing a friend or a younger sibling, informal language would be appropriate.

⭐ **ELPS** 1G

### Try It!

Read the directions to students and then organize them into pairs to complete the activity. Make sure students understand the situation and the audiences. Have students take turns describing the situation while their partners take on the roles of the varied audiences. Remind students to use formal or informal language to appeal to particular audiences.

⭐ **ELPS** 2I, 3G, 3I

---

## Oral Language: Expository Writing

The person or people who will listen to you or read your writing are called the **audience.** When you speak or write, it is important to choose just the right words that will reach your audience. Use sentence structures that are appropriate for expressing your ideas. In writing and speaking, the **word choice** that you use will be different for each audience.

### Try It!

Read about the situation below. Then choose two audiences from the list below. With a partner, discuss how the words you choose might be different for each audience.

**Situation**

The students at your school would like to have more after-school activities. The student council discussed ways to convince the school board to offer more activities. They decided to focus on benefits by explaining three positive effects of after-school activities on students. You will explain these effects.

**Audiences**

■ a member of the school board, the school principal, a classmate, a younger sibling

---

**ELPS** **1G** Demonstrate increasing knowledge of when to use formal/informal English; **2I** Demonstrate listening comprehension in increasingly complex spoken language by following directions; **3G** Express ideas and feelings ranging from communicating short phrases to participating in discussions; **3I** Adapt spoken language for formal and informal purposes

## Let's Talk!

When you answer a question, you might use one word, a few words, a sentence, or a few sentences.

Example: Why should your school offer more after-school activities?

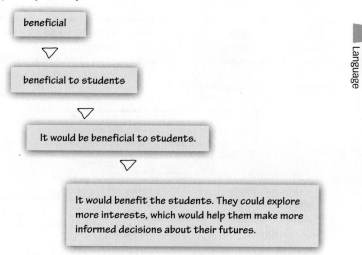

beneficial

▽

beneficial to students

▽

It would be beneficial to students.

▽

It would benefit the students. They could explore more interests, which would help them make more informed decisions about their futures.

In the first box, there is only a one-word answer. In the other boxes, the writer includes more information. The last box shows the most information. When you use more details to tell about something, the other person will understand it better.

### Try It!

Choose a new question that you would like to talk about with a partner. First make notes about details that would give your partner more information about your ideas. Then use your notes to describe your ideas to your partner.

Here are some ideas to get you started.

1. What are the reasons for a school dress code?
2. Why should your school offer more after-school activities?
3. Should your school offer after-school tutoring?

## Let's Talk

Read the example and discuss the information that is added to each answer. Make sure that students understand the information as the response increases in complexity.

## Try It!

Have students begin by jotting down questions pertaining to school for their partners. Then have them record notes that explain their answers to their own questions. Finally, have partners take turns asking and answering questions. ◢DIFFERENTIATE INSTRUCTION

ELPS 2H, 3C, 3E, 3G, 3H

---

### Differentiated Instruction: English Language Learners

ELPS 2I, 3G, 3H

| ELP Level **Beginning** | ELP Level **Intermediate** | ELP Level **Advanced/Advanced High** |
|---|---|---|
| Write: *Chorus or Baseball* and ask students: *Who likes chorus? Who likes baseball?* Have students read the frame for their responses: *I like _____ because it is _____.* | Draw an idea web on the board with *school* in the center. Add *dress code* and *after-school activities.* Have students add other ideas to refer to as they write original questions. | Have students ask their partners questions about their responses. Encourage students to jot down notes as their partners speak. |

**ELPS 2H** Understand information in increasingly complex spoken language; **2I** Demonstrate listening comprehension in increasingly complex spoken language by responding to questions; **3C** Speak using a variety of sentence lengths with increasing accuracy and ease; **3E** Share information in cooperative learning interactions; **3G** Express opinions and ideas ranging from communicating short phrases to participating in discussions; **3H** Narrate/describe/explain with increasing specificity and detail

## The Language of Persuasive Essays

Read aloud the instruction and review the organization of a persuasive essay. Clarify terms such as *logical reasons, arguments, opinion, counterarguments,* and *call to action.* Make sure students understand that persuasive essays follow the structure of introduction, body, and conclusion. **DIFFERENTIATE INSTRUCTION ⬎**

 **Turn and Talk and Listen**

Before partners discuss the prompt, activate prior knowledge by discussing recent local or national political campaigns. If possible, play a tape of a political speech for students. Then have partners complete the activity.

**ELPS** 1A, 3E, 4D

---

**544**

 ELPS 3E

# The Language of Persuasive Essays

Persuasive essays have a common purpose: to convince the reader to support a position on a topic. The writer uses logical reasons, or arguments, to defend his or her opinion. The writer must also identify and address counter-arguments with logic and reason. The final paragraph usually includes a summary of the reasons to support the writer's position and a call to action.

Persuasive Essay Organization

The beginning engages the audience and includes a position statement.

| Middle paragraphs give reasons and evidence to support the position. | Middle paragraphs include information on relevant perspectives. | Middle paragraphs refute opposing positions. |

The ending restates the position and adds a final thought.

Beginning
Middle
Ending

 **Turn and Talk and Listen**
Talk with a partner about how speeches and debates you might hear during a political campaign are like persuasive essays.

---

## Differentiated Instruction: Struggling Learners

To improve struggling learners' comprehension, use a relevant example of persuasion to complete a chart.

The writer's position: Teen curfews should be extended.

Reason 1: Teens must rely on parents to drive them home from late sports and band practices.

Reason 2: Often movies get out later than the curfew.

Counterargument: Parents think it makes teens safer, but teens are often driving faster to get home in time.

Conclusion: An extension of the curfew would save parents time, allow teens to enjoy movies, and keep them safe on the way home.

ELPS 2B, 3A, 3B, 3C, 3E, 3G, 3H, 5B, 5G

# Vocabulary: Persuasive Writing

| | | |
|---|---|---|
| argument | call to action | counterargument |
| evidence | objection | opinion |
| persuade | position | problem |
| solution | support | |

**Language** (vertical tab)

1. **Say the word.** Listen actively and carefully as your teacher reads the words. Pay special attention to your teacher's pronunciation of long and short vowel sounds, silent letters, and consonant clusters. Repeat the words. What part of speech are all of the words? Try to make nouns into verbs and verbs into nouns. Say each word again.

2. **Discover the meaning.** Work with a partner. Define two of the words for your partner. Your partner should then use those words in sentences. Discuss whether or not your partner has used the word correctly.

3. **Clarify.** Listen as your teacher explains the meaning of each word. Work with your partner to find synonyms, words or phrases that mean the same thing, and antonyms, words or phrases that mean the opposite.

4. **Think about it.** Answer the questions below.
   - Which words relate to what the writer thinks?
   - Which word means "to convince"?
   - Which word means "proof or confirmation"?
   - Which word means "the answer to a problem"?
   - Which two words have opposite meanings?

5. **Show your understanding.** Use your vocabulary journal. Write a few sentences about a problem at school and what you think should be done about it and why. Then label parts of your writing with the vocabulary words. Create a graphic organizer that shows the connections among the words. Then write a phrase or give an example of each word from your own writing.

6. **Write about it.** Write a brief paragraph explaining how to write a persuasive essay. Use at least three of the vocabulary words above in your paragraph.

## Vocabulary: Persuasive Writing

As students complete the activities, walk around the room and monitor partners' work. Allow students to ask you questions to clarify understanding. Make sure that all students are explaining and describing with increasing specificity and detail as they complete the activities. Monitor students' responses to the questions presented in the text.

**✔ DIFFERENTIATE INSTRUCTION**

 ELPS 2B, 3A, 3B, 3C, 3E, 3G, 3H, 4C, 4G, 5B, 5G

---

## Reading the Persuasive Model

### What Do You Know?

Lead a class discussion in response to the questions. Then, organize students into pairs to discuss their prior knowledge and opinions.

⭐ ELPS 1A, 2G, 2I, 3E, 3G

### Build Background

Tell students that building background will prepare them for reading. Clarify unfamiliar terms and concepts such as *oil, fuel, supply, demand,* and *economic crisis.*

⭐ ELPS 1A, 1E, 2C, 4C, 4F

### Listening

Read aloud the instruction and questions as students track the text. Remind students that the writer's position is the argument he or she makes. In the essay, the writer will argue for the proposed solution.

⭐ ELPS 2C, 2I, 4C, 4G

### Key Words

Read each word or phrase aloud. Have students raise their hands if they know what each means. Ask a volunteer to explain the meaning and use the word or phrase in a sentence. Explain that learning vocabulary before reading a selection will help students' reading go smoothly and increase comprehension. **DIFFERENTIATE INSTRUCTION ↘**

⭐ ELPS 2G, 4D

⭐ **ELPS 1A** Use prior knowledge and experiences to understand meanings; **1E** Internalize new basic language by using and reusing it/writing; **2C** Learn new expressions and basic/academic vocabulary heard during classroom instruction/interactions; **2G** Understand the general meaning, main points, and important details of spoken language/topics, languages, and contexts are familiar to unfamiliar; **2I** Demonstrate listening comprehension in increasingly complex spoken language/responding to questions, collaborating with peers, and taking notes; **3E** Share information in cooperative learning interactions; **4C** Comprehend vocabulary used in written classroom materials; **4D** Use prereading supports to enhance comprehension of written text/graphic organizers, illustrations, and topic-related vocabulary; **4F** Use visual and contextual support to develop vocabulary/use support from peers and teachers to enhance understanding and develop background knowledge; **4G** Demonstrate comprehension of increasingly complex English/participating in shared reading and responding to questions

---

## Reading the Persuasive Model

### What Do You Know?

What do you and your friends argue about? Are they local or global problems? Think about the issues, and then think of arguments and counterarguments that support and oppose your opinions. What have you learned recently learn about the energy crisis? Do you think it is a serious problem? What are some possible solutions? Talk to your partner, and listen carefully to what your partner has to say, as well.

### Build Background

People in America and people around the world use a lot of oil. As well as using oil as fuel, many of the things we use on a daily basis are made from oil. Cleaning supplies, auto parts, eye glasses, and electrical wiring are just a few of the things made from oil. The problem is that there isn't enough oil to supply this huge, growing demand. Running out of oil would cause a world-wide economic crisis. There is a way to avoid this happening—using less oil!

### Listening

Listen as your teacher or a classmate reads "Conservation Can Prevent an Oil Crisis" aloud. As you are listening, make notes about the problem and facts that explain the problem. Jot down the solution and three reasons for the solution. Write another solution that the writer doesn't agree with and tell why. What does the writer ask the reader to think about at the end of the essay? Be ready to answer the questions below.

1. What is the writer's position?
2. Name four reasons the writer gives for the proposed solution.
3. What solution to the problem does the writer not agree with? Why?

### Key Words

| | | |
|---|---|---|
| conserve | economists | estimates |
| exceed | gas-guzzling | global warming |
| short-term | trends | worry |

Look at the words and phrases in the box. You will see them when you read the writing model. With a partner, discuss connections among the words.

---

### Differentiated Instruction: Struggling Learners

Instead of having students discuss connections, provide cloze sentences for students to complete with the Key Words.

- Students should _____ about passing a test if they don't study. *(worry)*
- If you _____ expectations, you do better than expected. *(exceed)*
- Sarah read fashion magazines to keep up with the latest clothing _____. *(trends)*
- Turning off the lights when we leave the room helps us _____ electricity. *(conserve)*

⭐ ELPS 1E, 4C, 4F

**ELPS** 2C, 2G, 2I, 4C, 4G, 4I–4K

## Read Along

Now it's your turn to read. Turn to page 199 in this book. Read the writing model as your teacher or classmate reads it aloud.

## After Reading

Look at the key words in the box. With a partner, choose a social or environmental problem to discuss. Agree about three solutions. Then discuss the problem and solutions. Use the words in the box in your discussion.

On a separate piece of paper, respond to the following questions about the writing model. Share your answers with your partner or in a small group.

1. Why does the writer say that people could struggle in the future to heat their homes and buy gas for their cars?
2. What does the writer say will happen if people don't learn how to conserve?
3. How does the writer say the U.S. could save millions of barrels of oil every day?
4. What is the economic benefit to consumers of conserving oil?
5. Why does the writer of the writing model think it is better to conserve oil than to drill more oil wells?

---

## Read Along

Read aloud the writing model as students track the text in their books. Or, organize students into pairs and have them alternate reading aloud, paragraph by paragraph.
 **ELPS** 4C

## After Reading

Organize students into pairs and have them decide on an environmental or social problem. Have students independently think, jot down ideas, and propose three possible solutions. Then have pairs reconvene to share ideas and come to an agreement on the best possible solution.

Before students answer the questions, clarify difficult or unfamiliar terms such as *economic, benefit,* and *consumers.* Have students independently answer the questions about the text and then meet with their partners to share and discuss answers. ✓ **DIFFERENTIATE INSTRUCTION**
**ELPS** 2C, 2G, 2I, 3E, 4C, 4G, 4I, 4J, 4K

---

**ELPS 2C** Learn new language structures/expressions and basic vocabulary heard during classroom instruction/interactions; **2G** Understand the general meaning, main points, and important details of spoken language/topics, languages, and contexts are familiar to unfamiliar; **2I** Demonstrate listening comprehension in increasingly complex spoken language/following directions, summarizing spoken messages, responding to questions, collaborating with peers, and taking notes; **3E** Share information in cooperative learning interactions; **4C** Comprehend vocabulary used in written classroom materials; **4G** Demonstrate comprehension of increasingly complex English/participating in shared reading, responding to questions, and taking notes; **4I** Demonstrate comprehension by employing and expanding basic reading skills; **4J** Demonstrate comprehension and expand reading skills by employing inferential skills; **4K** Demonstrate comprehension and expand reading skills by employing analytical skills

## Oral Language

Review the instruction with students. Provide students with examples of formal and informal language: *How are you today, sir? What's up?* Ask students to identify which would be more appropriate for addressing a doctor and a friend.

⭐ **ELPS** 1G, 3I

### Try It!

Read the directions to students and then organize them into pairs to complete the activity. Make sure students understand the situation and the audiences. Have students take turns describing the situation while their partners take on the roles of the varied audiences. Remind students to use formal or informal language to appeal to particular audiences.

⭐ **ELPS** 3G, 3I

## Oral Language

When you speak or write, the words you choose depend on your audience. Your goal is to create a persuasive message that will influence your audience to support your position. While your persuasive message will stay the same, you should tailor your tone and your language to the audience you are addressing.

### Try It!

Read the situation and then select two audiences from the list below. With your partner, discuss how you would vary your persuasive message for two very different audiences. What changes would you make for each audience in tone, voice, and word choice? What arguments and words would you use to convince each audience to support your position?

**Role-Play**

Imagine that your school doesn't recycle. You and your partner are members of the student council and want to persuade your audience that your school needs to start recycling soda cans, plastic bottles, and paper. Convince your audience that this change is important and that they should support your efforts.

**Audiences**

- school principal, community member who wants to help the school, parent, teacher, classmates

Learning Language **549**

**ELPS** 2H, 3E, 3G, 3H

## Let's Talk!

When you answer a question, you might use one word, a few words, a sentence, or a few sentences. Below are possible answers to the question **What is one problem in your community?**

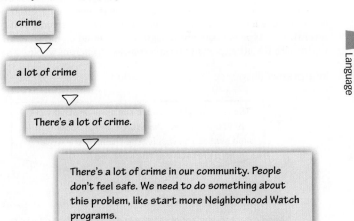

crime

↓

a lot of crime

↓

There's a lot of crime.

↓

There's a lot of crime in our community. People don't feel safe. We need to do something about this problem, like start more Neighborhood Watch programs.

### Try It!

Choose an issue that interests you. Answer these questions about the issue: What is my position? What logical solution or call to action can I propose? What arguments can I use to support my position? What are some counterarguments and how can I address them?

Brainstorm words and details that describe your position and your arguments. Use a graphic organizer to rank your arguments from most to least important.

 **Turn and Talk and Listen**

Tell a partner about a problem in your community that concerns you. Remember to use as much detail as you can. You can use the sentence frames below.

_____ is a problem. One way to solve this problem is _____.

Language

### Let's Talk

Read the example and discuss the information that is added to each answer. Make sure that students understand the information as the response increases in complexity.

 **ELPS** 2H

### Try It!

Have students begin by freewriting for five minutes about issues they find interesting or that cause them to have big reactions. After students finish freewriting, instruct them to respond to the questions in the text and organize their ideas in graphic organizers.

**Turn and Talk and Listen**

Organize students into pairs and have them share their ideas from the **Try It!** activity. Tell students to use their graphic organizers as a structure for discussion. Remind students to explain each idea and support it with details.

✔ DIFFERENTIATE INSTRUCTION

**ELPS** 3E, 3G, 3H

---

### Differentiated Instruction: English Language Learners

**ELPS** 3E, 3G

| ELP Level **Beginning** | ELP Level **Intermediate** | ELP Level **Advanced/Advanced High** |
|---|---|---|
| Draw an idea web with *Stop Crime* written in the center. Ask students to volunteer ideas in short phrases and then vote on which one they think is the best idea. | Students work in pairs to complete the **Try It!** activity. Review content-area vocabulary before students begin: *argument, counterargument, position, solution.* | Before completing the **Turn and Talk and Listen** activity, have students evaluate each solution based on the ease of implementing it, the cost, and the possible effects. |

 **ELPS 2H** Understand information in increasingly complex spoken language; **3E** Share information in cooperative learning interactions; **3G** Express opinions and ideas ranging from communicating short phrases to participating in discussions; **3H** Describe and explain with increasing specificity and detail

## Interpretive Response

Read aloud the instruction and review *theme*. Explain that when students *analyze*, they break things down into parts and explain what they think the parts mean as a whole. Tell students that an *interpretation* is an explanation of the meaning of something. DIFFERENTIATE INSTRUCTION ↘

### Turn and Talk and Listen

Before partners discuss the prompt, activate prior knowledge by discussing a story or novel students have recently read. Have them provide their interpretations of the theme. Then have partners complete the activity.

★ ELPS 1A, 3E, 4J

---

 ELPS 3E

# Interpretive Response

An interpretive response is writing that tells about something you have read, usually a novel, short story, poem, or essay. In an interpretive response to a work of literature, you should analyze at least one theme, often two. A theme is the writer's message. A novel or play may have one theme, or it may have several. This type of essay has a beginning, a middle, and an ending. Each part works with the other parts to form a cohesive, coherent whole.

Interpretive Response Essay Organization

The beginning introduces the novel or other work of literature and the author. The introduction also states the thesis. The thesis is the writer's interpretation of the work and its theme.

Middle paragraphs are organized in a logical order and give specific details from the work to support the thesis statement. Embedded quotations are used to support the writer's interpretation of the theme and to add support for the thesis statement.

The ending analyzes the themes.

| Beginning |
| Middle |
| Ending |

### Turn and Talk and Listen
Talk with a partner about how to organize an interpretive response essay and how to determine the themes in a literary work.

---

### Differentiated Instruction: Struggling Learners

Provide a brief minilesson on *theme* before students complete the **Turn and Talk and Listen** activity. Remind them not to confuse a topic with a theme. Give them an example:

- Topic: *love*
- Theme: *Love conquers all*

Tell students that the message of a text is often expressed through the lessons learned by a character.

Divide students into pairs and have them suggest a theme based on the following descriptions:

- *A bully finds himself in trouble and no one will help him.*
- *One man tries to make money quickly and cheats people in order to do it. Another works hard and is honest. In the end, the honest man is wealthy and the other is alone and poor.*

---

★ **ELPS** **1A** Use prior knowledge to understand meanings; **3E** Share information in cooperative learning interactions; **4J** Demonstrate comprehension and expand reading skills by employing inferential skills/predicting, making connections between ideas, drawing conclusions from text, and finding supporting evidence

Learning Language **551**

⭐ ELPS 2C, 3A, 3B, 4C, 5B, 5G

# Vocabulary: Interpretive Response

| | | |
|---|---|---|
| analyze | annotate | cohesive |
| interpretation | plot | quotations |
| response | summarize | theme |

1. **Say the word.** Listen actively and carefully as your teacher reads each word. Pay special attention to your teacher's pronunciation of long and short vowel sounds, silent letters, and consonant clusters. Repeat the words.

2. **Discover the meaning.** Work with a partner. Find some of the vocabulary words on page 550. Write notes about what you think each of the words means. Use the context in which the words appear on page 550 as clues.

3. **Learn more.** Listen as your teacher explains the meaning of each word. Then work with a partner to review the meanings you just heard. Write down any words that you still don't understand. Ask clarifying questions and discuss your questions with your teacher if you do not understand completely.

4. **Think about it.** Use your notebook to answer the questions below.
   - Why is it important for your essay to be cohesive?
   - How does the plot relate to the theme?
   - What is the difference between an analysis and a summary?
   - When does a writer analyze the theme?
   - How can quotations help support the thesis statement and clarify the theme?

5. **Show your understanding.** Use your vocabulary journal. Outline a response to a literature essay using as many vocabulary words as you can. Write a few sentences about any other vocabulary words. Add notes to help you remember and understand the words.

6. **Write about it.** Write a brief paragraph explaining how to write an interpretive response essay. Use at least three of the vocabulary words above in your paragraph.

Language

## Vocabulary: Interpretive Response

As students complete the activities, walk around the room and monitor partners' work. Allow students to ask you questions to clarify understanding. Make sure that all students are explaining and describing with increasing specificity and detail as they complete the activities. Monitor students' responses to the questions presented in the text.

✔ DIFFERENTIATE INSTRUCTION

⭐ ELPS 2C, 3A, 3B, 3E, 4C, 5B, 5G

---

**Differentiated Instruction:**
**English Language Learners**

⭐ ELPS 1E, 2C, 3E, 4C

| **ELP Level** **Beginning** | **ELP Level** **Intermediate** | **ELP Level** **Advanced/Advanced High** |
|---|---|---|
| To establish meaning, provide students with the following cognates: *analyze/analizar*, *interpretation/interpretación*, *theme/tema*, and *response/respuesta*. | Scaffold item 4 with a response frame that includes as many of the literature vocabulary words as possible to increase understanding. | Have students work with partners to discuss and answer the questions in item 3. Suggest that students record answers in complete sentences. |

 **ELPS 1E** Internalize new academic language by using and reusing it/writing; **2C** Learn new expressions and basic/academic vocabulary heard during classroom instruction/interactions; **3A** Practice producing sounds of newly acquired vocabulary; **3B** Expand vocabulary by retelling information supported by pictures/learning and using routine language for classroom communication; **3E** Share information in cooperative learning interactions; **4C** Develop basic sight vocabulary/comprehend language structures used in written classroom materials; **5B** Write using newly acquired basic and content-based grade-level vocabulary; **5G** Narrate/describe/explain with increasing specificity and detail to fulfill content area writing needs

## Reading the Interpretive Response Model

### What Do You Know?

Lead a class discussion in response to the questions. Then organize students into pairs to discuss their prior knowledge and answer the questions.

⭐ ELPS 1A, 2I, 3E, 3G

### Build Background

Tell students that building background will prepare them for reading. Explain that the "monster" Frankenstein creates really isn't evil, but he reacts violently as he is shunned by society because of his differences.

⭐ ELPS 1A, 2G

### Listening

Read aloud the instruction and questions before reading the model. After reading, have students respond to the questions in a group discussion.

**DIFFERENTIATE INSTRUCTION ↘**

⭐ ELPS 2G, 2I, 4G

### Key Words

Read each word or phrase aloud. Have students raise their hands if they know what each means. Reread sentences with the words in context. Ask a volunteer to explain the meaning and use the word or phrase in a sentence. Then organize students into pairs to complete the activity.

⭐ ELPS 2C, 2G

---

# Reading the Response to Literature Model

## What Do You Know?

Next you will read a sample response to a literature essay about a scientist who creates a superhuman being. What stories and movies have you seen that have superhuman beings or monsters? How are they treated by others?

## Build Background

For centuries, scientists have been intrigued with the idea of creating life. We know that some of that is possible today. However, when Mary Shelley wrote *Frankenstein,* the idea of actually creating life was true science fiction.

Shelley finished writing *Frankenstein* when she was just 19. Her first edition was published anonymously in 1818 in London. The main character, Victor Frankenstein, is a scientist who learns how to create life. He creates a being in the likeness of man, but larger than average and more powerful.

## Listening

Listen as your teacher or a classmate reads aloud "Monsters are Made, Not Born." As you listen, make notes about what decisions Victor Frankenstein made. Think about what the consequences were. Be prepared to answer the questions below.

1. Why does Shelley say the lives of Frankenstein and his monster are "tragic"?
2. Why is Victor relieved that the monster escapes? How does that feeling change later?
3. If Victor Frankenstein were to start over, what do you think he would have done differently?

## Key Words

| | | |
|---|---|---|
| barbarity of man | deformed | eerie |
| monster | outcasts | tortured |
| unhallowed arts | vicious | |

Look at the key words in the box. These words appear in the sample. Write a sentence for each word or phrase using the meaning from the essay. Trade sentences with a partner. Discuss how your understandings of each word are the same or different. Consider another meaning for some of the words. Write sentences to reflect those meanings.

---

**Differentiated Instruction: Struggling Learners**

After reading aloud the questions and the model, reread the Listening questions as students follow along. Work with struggling students to answer each question, guiding them to specific portions of text that contain answers. Challenge students to paraphrase answers from the information given in the text.

---

**ELPS 1A** Use prior knowledge to understand meanings; **2C** Learn new language structures/expressions and basic/academic vocabulary heard during classroom instruction/interactions; **2G** Understand the general meaning, main points, and important details of spoken language/topics, languages, and contexts are familiar to unfamiliar; **2I** Demonstrate listening comprehension in increasingly complex spoken language/responding to questions and collaborating with peers; **3E** Share information in cooperative learning interactions; **3G** Express ideas ranging from communicating short phrases to participating in discussions; **4G** Demonstrate comprehension of increasingly complex English/responding to questions

## Read Along

Now it's your turn to read. Turn to pages 257–258 in this book. Read the writing model as your teacher or classmate reads it aloud.

## After Reading

Copy the table below and use some of the key words to describe the actions of Victor Frankenstein. Use other words to describe the monster and how people reacted to him.

| Victor Frankenstein | Monster |
|---|---|
|  |  |
|  |  |
|  |  |

## Read Along

Read aloud the writing model as students track the text in their books. Or, organize students into pairs and have them alternate reading aloud, paragraph by paragraph.

⭐ **ELPS** 4C

## After Reading

Make sure students understand the task. Tell students they should not limit their descriptions to the Key Words. When students finish, invite them to share their responses with the class.

**⟋ DIFFERENTIATE INSTRUCTION**

⭐ **ELPS** 2C, 2G, 2I, 4C, 4G, 4I, 4J, 4K

---

**Differentiated Instruction: English Language Learners**

⭐ ELPS 3G, 4G, 4J, 4K

| ELP Level **Beginning** | ELP Level **Intermediate** | ELP Level **Advanced/Advanced High** |
|---|---|---|
| Draw the chart on the board and have students indicate each Key Word's appropriate column. Have students copy the chart when you finish. | In addition to listing Key Words in the chart, have students paraphrase explanations and descriptions from the model. | After completing their charts, organize students into small groups to discuss their responses. Pose various questions for discussion regarding the story. |

⭐ **ELPS 2C** Learn new language structures/expressions and basic vocabulary heard during classroom instruction/interactions; **2G** Understand the general meaning of spoken language when topics and languages are familiar to unfamiliar/understand the main points of spoken language when topics are familiar to unfamiliar/understand the important details of spoken language/topics, languages, and contexts are familiar to unfamiliar; **2I** Demonstrate listening comprehension in increasingly complex spoken language/summarizing spoken messages and taking notes; **3G** Express opinions, ideas, and feelings ranging from communicating short phrases to participating in discussions; **4C** Develop basic sight vocabulary/comprehend vocabulary used in written classroom materials; **4G** Demonstrate comprehension of increasingly complex English/participating in shared reading and responding to questions; **4I** Demonstrate comprehension by employing and expanding basic reading skills; **4J** Demonstrate comprehension and expand reading skills by employing inferential skills; **4K** Demonstrate comprehension and expand reading skills by employing analytical skills

## Oral Language

Review the instruction with students. Remind students that their word choice is the basis of their message in speaking and writing. Word choice expresses tone, or the writer's attitude toward a subject; is essential to voice; and presents the author's viewpoint through shades of meaning. Tell students to consider their audience and purpose carefully as they decide whether to use formal or informal language to express their ideas.

⭐ **ELPS** 3I

### Try It!

Read the directions to students and then organize them into pairs to complete the activity. Make sure students understand the situation and the audiences. Have students take turns describing the situation while their partners take on the roles of the varied audiences. Remind students to use formal or informal language to appeal to particular audiences.

⭐ **ELPS** 3G, 3I

---

 **ELPS** 3G, 3I

## Oral Language

The person or people who will listen to you or read your writing are called the **audience.** When you speak or write, it is important to choose just the right words that will reach your audience. In writing and speaking, choose words that express your own opinions, ideas, and feelings, and participate in discussions about the literature.

### Try It!

Read about the situation below. Then choose two audiences from the list. With a partner, discuss how the words you choose might be different for each audience.

**Situation**

You read a novel where the main character has an argument with her father. She wants to move to France to be an artist, and her father is against it. She moves to France anyway, but while there, she learns an important lesson, which is one theme of the book. She also learns more about the importance of friends and family, both young and old. Use your imagination to fill in details of the story. Then tell about the book's themes.

**Audiences**

- teacher or parent, third-grade child, classmate, grandparent

**ELPS 3G** Express opinions, ideas, and feelings ranging from communicating short phrases to participating in discussions; **3I** Adapt spoken language for formal and informal purposes

## Let's Talk!

When you answer a question, sometimes one word will do. Most often, more details are needed to communicate to your audience.

Example: What is one theme of the novel?

argument

▽

argument about her future

▽

The main character and her dad argue, and she moves to France.

▽

The main character wants to be an artist in France. Her father disagrees, and they argue. She moves to France, but later realizes how much she misses her family and friends.

In the first box, there is only a one-word answer. In the other boxes, the writer includes more information. The last box shows the most information. The more details you add to your story, the better the reader or listener will be able to understand and visualize what you mean.

### Try It!

Work with a partner. Choose a story that you have both recently read. Choose a new question that you would like to talk about. Make notes about details that would give your partner more information about your ideas. Then use your notes to describe your ideas to your partner.

Here are some ideas to get you started.

1. How can you describe the main character?
2. What is the main theme of the book?
3. What lessons does the main character learn?

## Let's Talk

Read the example and discuss the information that is added to each answer. Make sure that students understand the information as the response increases in complexity.

ELPS 2H

## Try It!

Have students begin by deciding on a story together. Then they can write their questions and jot down notes independently before reconvening with partners to discuss ideas.

✔ **DIFFERENTIATE INSTRUCTION**

ELPS 3E, 3G, 3H

---

### Differentiated Instruction: English Language Learners

ELPS 3E, 3G, 4K

| ELP Level **Beginning** | ELP Level **Intermediate** | ELP Level **Advanced/Advanced High** |
|---|---|---|
| Invite students to act out scenes from a story in small groups. Allow students to practice and then present their performances for the class. | Provide sentence starters for students to use in response to the questions on SE page 555, such as: *1. The main character is _____. 2. The theme of the story is _____.* | Have pairs summarize a story together. Students can then ask analytical questions and discuss answers. Tell students to make sure they express their ideas clearly. |

**ELPS 2H** Understand information in increasingly complex spoken language; **3E** Share information in cooperative learning interactions; **3G** Express opinions and ideas ranging from communicating short phrases to participating in discussions; **3H** Describe and explain with increasing specificity and detail; **4K** Demonstrate comprehension and expand reading skills by employing analytical skills/ evaluating written information and performing critical analyses

## Creative Writing

Read aloud the instruction and then review The Shape of Stories on SE pages 322–323. Help students merge the ideas from the Plot Line with the Beginning-Middle-Ending graphic on SE page 556.

 **Turn and Talk and Listen**

As a variation of the activity, organize students into small groups and assign each group a different story part: *exposition, rising action, climax, falling action,* or *resolution.* Have groups discuss the purpose and importance of each section and arrive at a brief summary of ideas to share with the remainder of the class. Lead a class discussion about the ways in which parts build upon one another. **DIFFERENTIATE INSTRUCTION** ↘

**ELPS** 2I, 3E

**TEKS** **ELPS 2C** Learn academic vocabulary heard during classroom instruction/interactions; **2I** Demonstrate listening comprehension in increasingly complex spoken language/ summarizing spoken messages and collaborating with peers; **3E** Share information in cooperative learning interactions; **3F** Give information/ ranging from using a limited high-frequency vocabulary to using abstract and content-based vocabulary during speaking

---

**556** **ELPS** 3E

# Creative Writing

Creative writing often tells a fictional story. This type of writing can take the form of a story, a play, or even a poem. Most often, creative writing that tells a story has the same basic organization: an introduction of the characters, conflict, and setting; action that rises, climaxes, and falls; and a resolution. Look at this graphic organizer. It shows what is in each part of a piece of creative writing.

Creative Writing Organization

Introduces the main character, conflict, and setting

The rising action includes important actions of the main character and develops his or her problem. This part also builds suspense in the story.

The climax of the story is the most exciting part when the main character confronts his or her problem head-on.

The falling action includes what happens after the climax as the main character begins to deal with life after the moment of truth.

The resolution brings the story to a conclusion.

Beginning
Middle
Ending

 **Turn and Talk and Listen**
Talk with a partner about one important part of the graphic organizer. Discuss how the parts of a story build on each other to form a whole.

---

**Differentiated Instruction: Struggling Learners**

Review literary terms with students to improve comprehension:

- characters: *who the story is about*
- conflict: *the main problem a character faces. It can be inside the character or between the character and an outside force, such as a person or the weather.*
- setting: *where and when the story takes place*

- suspense: *the feeling of anticipation or of wondering what will happen next*

Choose a familiar story and have students identify its *characters, conflict,* and *setting.*

**ELPS** 2C, 3F

ELPS 2C, 3A, 3B, 4C, 5B, 5G

# Vocabulary: Creative Writing

| climax | complication | conflict |
|--------|--------------|----------|
| exposition | falling action | plot |
| resolution | rising action | tension |

1. **Say the word or phrase.** Listen actively and carefully as your teacher reads the words and phrases aloud. Pay special attention to your teacher's pronunciation of long and short vowel sounds, silent letters, and consonant clusters. Then repeat each word or phrase.

2. **Discover the meaning.** Think about what you know about creative writing. Working with a partner, write notes about what you think the words and phrases mean.

3. **Learn more.** Listen carefully as your teacher explains the meaning of each word. Ask questions to ensure that you understand the meaning and use of each word. Work with your partner to make changes and additions to your notes about what the words mean.

4. **Think about it.** Use your notebook to answer the questions below.
   - Which happens first in creative writing—a climax or the falling action? Explain why.
   - How does the conflict or complication add to a story?
   - Why would a writer place the climax near the end of a story?
   - Which term best describes the part of a fairy tale that ends with the words "and they lived happily ever after"?

5. **Show your understanding.** In your vocabulary journal, write short sentences to help you remember the meaning of each of the words and phrases. Where appropriate, list examples or synonyms to show the meaning of the word.

6. **Write about it.** Write a brief paragraph explaining how to write a story, play, or narrative poem (a poem that tells a story). Use at least three of the vocabulary words above in your paragraph.

Language

## Vocabulary: Creative Writing

As students complete the activities, walk around the room and monitor partners' work. Allow students to ask you questions to clarify understanding. Make sure that all students are explaining and describing with increasing specificity and detail as they complete the activities. Monitor students' responses to the questions presented in the text.

**✓ DIFFERENTIATE INSTRUCTION**

ELPS 2C, 3A, 3B, 3E, 4C, 5B, 5G

---

## Differentiated Instruction: English Language Learners

ELPS 1E, 2C, 3E, 5G

| ELP Level **Beginning** | ELP Level **Intermediate** | ELP Level **Advanced/Advanced High** |
|---|---|---|
| Have students make a creative writing glossary, including synonyms or brief definitions. Have students identify *plot/story*; *conflict/problem*; *exposition/introduction*. | Have students copy a three-column chart with the heads *Vocabulary Word, Meaning,* and *Example*. Have pairs complete the *Example* column by listing examples from stories. | Have students use at least four creative writing vocabulary words to write a paragraph or brief essay describing a story or book they have read. |

**ELPS 1E** Internalize new academic language by using and reusing it/writing; **2C** Learn new expressions and basic/academic vocabulary heard during classroom instruction/interactions; **3A** Practice producing sounds of newly acquired vocabulary; **3B** Expand vocabulary by retelling information supported by pictures/learning and using routine language for classroom communication; **3E** Share information in cooperative learning interactions; **4C** Develop basic sight vocabulary/comprehend vocabulary used in written classroom materials; **5B** Write using newly acquired basic and content-based grade-level vocabulary; **5G** Narrate/describe/explain with increasing specificity and detail to fulfill content area writing needs

## Reading the Creative Writing Model

### What Do You Know?

Lead a class discussion in response to the questions. Then organize students into pairs to discuss their opinions and answer the questions.

⭐ ELPS 2I, 3E

### Build Background

Tell students that building background will prepare them for reading. Ask students what other benefits working part time might have.

**DIFFERENTIATE INSTRUCTION ↘**

⭐ ELPS 1A, 3F

### Listening

Read aloud the instruction and questions before reading the model. After reading, have students respond to the questions in a group discussion.

⭐ ELPS 2G, 2I, 3E, 4G

### Key Words

Read aloud the terms in the box as students follow along. Tell students that they will see these terms when they read the writing model. Point out the basic sight words *some* and *well* and have students repeat them several times. Then help students as they complete the activity.

⭐ ELPS 2C

---

⭐ **ELPS 1A** Use prior knowledge to understand meanings; **2C** Learn new language structures/expressions and basic/academic vocabulary heard during classroom instruction/interactions; **2G** Understand the general meaning, main points, and important details of spoken language/topics, languages, and contexts are familiar to unfamiliar; **2I** Demonstrate listening comprehension in increasingly complex spoken language/responding to questions and collaborating with peers; **3E** Share information in cooperative learning interactions; **3F** Give information/ranging from using a limited high-frequency vocabulary to using abstract and content-based vocabulary during speaking; **4G** Demonstrate comprehension of increasingly complex English by participating in shared reading, retelling or summarizing material, responding to questions, and taking notes commensurate with content area and grade level needs; **5B** Write using newly acquired basic and content-based grade-level vocabulary

---

## Reading the Creative Writing Model

### What Do You Know?

Next you will read a creative writing script about a boy who is interviewing for a part-time job. Do you think appearances matter when interviewing for a job? Would your opinion change depending on the kind of job it was? Tell what you think.

### Build Background

Many students have part-time jobs after school or on the weekends. Not only do these students earn money, but they learn the importance of showing up at work on time and doing a job effectively. If students are interested, they have the opportunity to learn how businesses are run. They may be mopping up in a restaurant, but they can see what the waiters, cooks, and even managers do each day.

### Listening

Listen as your teacher or a classmate reads aloud *Suiting Up*. As you listen, make notes about the interchanges between the characters and how the story resolves itself. Be prepared to answer the questions below.

1. How is the format of a script different than a story?
2. Why did Wesley have similar encounters with Luke and Tori?
3. Do you think Wesley got the job in the end?

### Key Words

| | | |
|---|---|---|
| competition | down payment | earn some bucks |
| executive position | frozen | impression |
| shoot some hoops | stocking shelves | suited up |
| well groomed | | |

Look at the words and phrases in the box. You will see these words when you read the writing sample. With a partner, use the words to talk about jobs and money.

---

### Differentiated Instruction: Struggling Learners

Explain that an *idiom* is a phrase that has a meaning different from the sum of its parts. Tell students they can use context to determine the meanings of idioms. They can also look up idioms in a dictionary of idioms. Help students use context to determine the meanings of *shoot some hoops,* *earn some bucks,* and *suited up.* Have students work with partners to write a sentence using each idiom.

⭐ ELPS 5B

ELPS 2C, 2G, 2I, 4C, 4G, 4I–4K

Learning Language **559**

## Read Along

Now it's your turn to read. Turn to pages 334–336 in this book. Read the writing model as your teacher or a classmate reads it aloud.

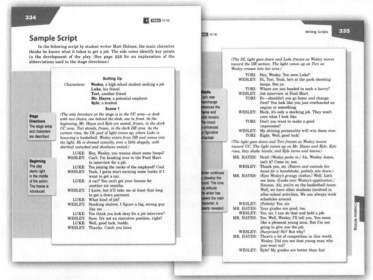

## After Reading

Copy the table below. In one column, write phrases that describe Mr. Hayes's impression of Wesley. In the second column, write some of the phrases that Tori uses to tell Wesley that he is not dressed appropriately for a job interview.

Use the information in your chart to summarize the script, explaining what lesson Wesley learned.

| Mr. Hayes | Tori |
|---|---|
|  |  |

## Read Along

Read aloud the writing model as students track the text in their books. Or, organize students into pairs and have them alternate reading aloud, paragraph by paragraph.

ELPS 4C

## After Reading

Expand the activity to include other characters. Have students add a column to the chart for each. When students finish, invite them to share their responses with the class.

✔ DIFFERENTIATE INSTRUCTION

ELPS 2C, 2G, 2I, 4C, 4G, 4I, 4J, 4K

---

### Differentiated Instruction: English Language Learners

ELPS 2C, 2G, 4G, 4J, 4K

| ELP Level **Beginning** | ELP Level **Intermediate** | ELP Level **Advanced/Advanced High** |
|---|---|---|
| Ask guiding questions and model finding answers in the text. Have students record the words and phrases in the chart. | Have student pairs draw a plot line with the major parts of stories and then write a summary of each part of the model at the appropriate point in the diagram. | Have student pairs complete the chart and summary. Ask them to identify the theme and discuss how the author used events to express the theme. |

**ELPS 2C** Learn new language structures/expressions and basic/academic vocabulary heard during classroom instruction/interactions; **2G** Understand the general meaning and important details of spoken language when topics, languages, and contexts are familiar to unfamiliar/understand the main points of spoken language when topics are familiar to unfamiliar; **2I** Demonstrate listening comprehension in increasingly complex spoken language/summarizing spoken messages; **4C** Develop basic sight vocabulary/comprehend vocabulary used in written classroom materials; **4G** Demonstrate comprehension of increasingly complex English/participating in shared reading, summarizing material and responding to questions; **4I** Demonstrate comprehension by employing and expanding basic reading skills/understanding of supporting ideas and details, summarizing text, and distinguishing main ideas from details; **4J** Demonstrate comprehension and expand reading skills by employing inferential skills; **4K** Demonstrate comprehension and expand reading skills by employing analytical skills

## Oral Language: Creative Writing

Review the instruction with students. Remind students that tone is the attitude a writer takes toward his or her subject. A writer uses word choice to express tone. Tell students to consider their audience and purpose carefully as they decide whether to use formal or informal language to express tone.

⭐ ELPS 3I

### Try It!

Read the directions to students and then organize them into pairs to complete the activity. Make sure students understand the situation and the audiences. Have students take turns describing the situation while their partners take on the roles of the varied audiences. Remind students to use formal or informal language to appeal to particular audiences.

⭐ ELPS 3G, 3H, 3I

---

## Oral Language: Creative Writing

The person or people who will listen to you or read your writing are called the **audience.** When you speak or write, it is important to think about the right words to use so your audience will understand your ideas and opinions. The **tone,** or the way you write, will be different for each audience.

### Try It!

Read about the situation below. Then choose two audiences from the list that follows. With a partner, discuss how the words you choose might be different for each audience.

**Situation**

Everyone knows that Roberta is the best player on the basketball team. She is the one the team turns to when there is a big game. However, Roberta is always late for practice. She misses a lot of games if she knows she isn't going to start as center. The playoffs are beginning, and the team is playing their archrival. The coach asks Stephanie to start as center. Roberta is furious, but the coach tells Roberta that Stephanie is a team player. You will retell the story.

**Audiences**

■ classmate, basketball coach, elementary school student

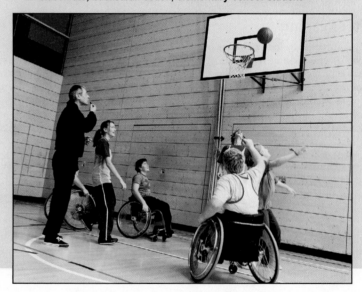

---

**ELPS 3G** Express opinions and ideas ranging from communicating short phrases to participating in discussions; **3H** Narrate with increasing specificity and detail; **3I** Adapt spoken language for formal and informal purposes

## Let's Talk!

When you answer a question, you might use one word, a few words, a sentence, or a few sentences.

Example: What problem does the coach have with Roberta?

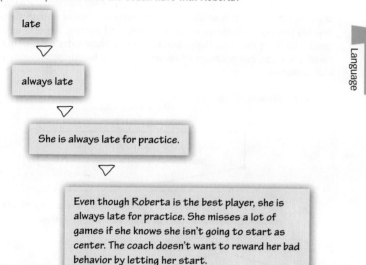

late

△

always late

△

She is always late for practice.

△

Even though Roberta is the best player, she is always late for practice. She misses a lot of games if she knows she isn't going to start as center. The coach doesn't want to reward her bad behavior by letting her start.

In the first box, there is only a one-word answer. In the other boxes, the writer includes more information. The last box shows the most information. It lets you understand what the writer is thinking. When you use more details to tell about something, the person you are addressing will have a much better understanding of what you mean.

## Try It!

Choose a new question that you would like to talk about with a partner. Make notes about details that would give your partner more information. Then use your notes to describe your ideas to your partner.

Here are some ideas to get you started.

**1.** What problem might you have working on a group class project?
**2.** What problem might you have as a server in a restaurant?

Language

---

## Let's Talk

Read the example and discuss the information that is added to each answer. Make sure that students understand the information as the response increases in complexity.

⭐ **ELPS** 2H

## Try It!

Have students begin by deciding on a general topic. Then they can write their questions and jot down notes independently before reconvening with partners to discuss ideas.

✔ DIFFERENTIATE INSTRUCTION

⭐ **ELPS** 3C, 3E, 3G, 3H

---

| **Differentiated Instruction:** **English Language Learners** | | ⭐ ELPS 3C, 3E, 3G, 3H |
|---|---|---|
| **ELP Level** **Beginning** | **ELP Level** **Intermediate** | **ELP Level** **Advanced/Advanced High** |
| Build on responses of students to question 1, using a variety of sentence types. Example: *getting along; trouble getting along; They might have trouble getting along.* | Provide sentence starters for students to use in response to the questions, such as: *Servers in a restaurant might have a problem with _____.* | Have student partners create a brief story based on the conflict they chose to discuss. Invite students to share their stories with the rest of the class. |

⭐ **ELPS** **2H** Understand information in increasingly complex spoken language; **3C** Speak using a variety of grammatical structures/sentence lengths and types/connecting words with increasing accuracy and ease; **3E** Share information in cooperative learning interactions; **3G** Express opinions and ideas ranging from communicating short phrases to participating in discussions; **3H** Narrate/describe/explain with increasing specificity and detail

## Research Writing

Read aloud the instruction and clarify related terminology, such as *topic, sources, issues, debates, thesis statement, supporting evidence and details, conclusion,* and *works cited.* Review the organization and remind students that a research report has an introduction, a body that provides main reasons and supporting evidence, and a conclusion. **DIFFERENTIATE INSTRUCTION ↘**

 **ELPS** 2C

 ### Turn and Talk and Listen

Before partners begin the activity, share a sample research report with students. After students discuss their ideas, invite volunteers to share them with the class.

 **ELPS** 3E, 3G, 3H

---

562

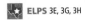 ELPS 3E, 3G, 3H

# Research Writing

Research involves exploring a topic of interest in detail using multiple sources and identifying important issues and debates about the topic. Research writing is the presentation of that knowledge to an audience. Research reports need an introduction that includes the thesis statement and sections that develop the topic with supporting evidence and details. Reports end with a conclusion that sums up the paper and leaves the reader with a final thought about the topic. Sections are often separated by headings. A works-cited page is also included.

Research Writing Organization

Beginning introduces the topic and the thesis statement.

The middle sections develop the topic using a clear organization pattern. Evidence is cited to support thesis. Sections are separated by headings.

Ending summarizes the paper and leaves reader with final thought.

Separate sheet for sources.

Beginning
Middle
Ending

### Turn and Talk and Listen
Talk with a partner about why it is important for a research paper to include plenty of supporting details.

---

### Differentiated Instruction: Advanced Learners

Review crediting sources with students. Explain that within a research report, students need to give credit to the sources of information. Tell students they can either credit a source within a sentence or use a parenthetical citation. Explain that the latter refers to a full credit in the works-cited page. Provide examples of each kind of credit and have students discuss with partners why they would vary the kinds of citations in a research report.

 **ELPS** 3G, 3H

---

**ELPS 2C** Learn academic vocabulary heard during classroom instruction/interactions; **3E** Share information in cooperative learning interactions; **3G** Express ideas ranging from communicating short phrases to participating in discussions; **3H** Describe and explain with increasing specificity and detail

ELPS 2C, 3A, 3B, 4C, 5B, 5G

# Vocabulary: Research Writing

| authoritative | headings | outline |
|---|---|---|
| paraphrase | plagiarism | quotation |
| reliable | source cited | supporting details |
| transitions | valid | |

1. **Say the word or phrase.** Listen actively and carefully as your teacher reads each word or phrase aloud. Pay special attention to your teacher's pronunciation of long and short vowel sounds, silent letters, and consonant clusters. Then repeat each word or phrase.

2. **Discover the meaning.** Work with a partner to discuss meanings of the words that you know. Write notes about what you and your partner think the words mean in the context of research writing.

3. **Learn more.** Listen as your teacher explains each word or phrase. Work with your partner to correct your earlier notes. Ask questions if you still do not understand the words or how they relate to research writing.

4. **Think about it.** Use the information in your notebook to help you answer the questions below.
   - How are headings useful in a research report?
   - What role do transitions play in a research report?
   - When might you paraphrase instead of using an exact quote?
   - Why must you cite sources and create a sources-cited page?
   - What is the difference between paraphrasing and plagiarism?
   - What does it mean when a source is authoritative and valid?

5. **Show your understanding.** In your vocabulary journal, add related words to help you remember what each word means. For example, write **alphabetical order** and **indented** next to **source cited** to remember how sources are listed.

6. **Write about it.** Write a paragraph or two explaining how to write a research essay. Use at least three of the vocabulary words above in your paragraphs.

## Vocabulary: Research Writing

As students complete the activities, walk around the room and monitor partners' work. Allow students to ask you questions to clarify understanding. Make sure that all students are explaining and describing with increasing specificity and detail as they complete the activities. Monitor students' responses to the questions presented in the text.

**✓ DIFFERENTIATE INSTRUCTION**

ELPS 2C, 3A, 3B, 3E, 4C, 5B, 5G

---

## Differentiated Instruction: English Language Learners

ELPS 2C, 3E, 4G, 5G

| ELP Level **Beginning** | ELP Level **Intermediate** | ELP Level **Advanced/Advanced High** |
|---|---|---|
| Have students construct a research writing glossary, writing each vocabulary word, its pronunciation, and a brief definition or explanation. Provide frames as needed. | Write: *According to a majority of students at our school, research writing is both challenging and interesting.* In pairs, students should paraphrase the sentence. | Pair students and give them copies of a news article. Have them paraphrase three ideas from the article, then compare to the original to be sure they have paraphrased effectively. |

 **ELPS 2C** Learn new expressions and academic vocabulary heard during classroom instruction/interactions; **3A** Practice producing sounds of newly acquired vocabulary; **3B** Expand vocabulary by retelling information supported by pictures/learning and using routine language for classroom communication; **3E** Share information in cooperative learning interactions; **4C** Develop and comprehend basic sight vocabulary used in written classroom materials; **4G** Demonstrate comprehension of increasingly complex English/summarizing material; **5B** Write using newly acquired basic and content-based grade-level vocabulary; **5G** Narrate/describe/explain with increasing specificity and detail to fulfill content area writing needs

## Reading the Research Writing Model

### What Do You Know?

Lead a class discussion in response to the questions. Then, organize students into pairs to discuss their answers to the questions.

⭐ ELPS 2I, 3E, 3G

### Build Background

Tell students that building background will prepare them for reading. Clarify unfamiliar terms, such as *engineering feats* and *reservoir*, to increase comprehension.

⭐ ELPS 1A, 2C, 2G

### Listening

Read aloud the instruction and questions before reading the model. After reading, have students respond to the questions in a group discussion.

⭐ ELPS 2G, 2I, 4G

### Key Words

Read each word or phrase. Have students raise their hands if they know what each means. Reread sentences from the model with the words in context. Ask a volunteer to explain the meaning and use the word or phrase in a sentence. Then, divide students into pairs to complete the activity. DIFFERENTIATE INSTRUCTION ↘

⭐ ELPS 2C, 2G

---

# Reading the Research Writing Model

## What Do You Know?

Next you will read a research report about the Aswan High Dam in Egypt. What do you know about dams? Why are they built? How do they help the people who live near them? What problems might they cause?

## Build Background

Dams have been around for thousands of years. They are built to prevent flooding and to allow communities to store excess water in rainy years. Some dams provide electric power as well. Modern dams are complicated engineering feats. One of the best-known dams in the United States is the Hoover Dam, completed in 1936. By diverting the water from the Colorado River, the largest reservoir in the United States, Lake Mead, was created.

## Listening

Listen as your teacher or a classmate reads aloud "The Aswan High Dam." As you listen, make notes about the dam. Be prepared to answer the questions below.

1. Why was the Aswan High Dam created?
2. Under what conditions did the construction team work? Explain.
3. What is one benefit of the Aswan High Dam to Egypt?

## Key Words

| | | |
|---|---|---|
| catastrophic | contaminated | detrimental effects |
| fertilize | forced evacuation | hydroelectric power |
| irrigation | reservoir | toxins |
| urban development | | |

Look at the words in the box. You will see these words when you read the writing sample. With a partner, use the words to talk about consequences that may occur when people build dams. Think about whether the benefits always outweigh the problems.

---

⭐ **ELPS 1A** Use prior knowledge to understand meanings; **2C** Learn new language structures/expressions and basic/academic vocabulary heard during classroom instruction/interactions; **2G** Understand the general meaning, main points, and important details of spoken language/topics, languages, and contexts are familiar to unfamiliar; **2I** Demonstrate listening comprehension in increasingly complex spoken language/responding to questions and collaborating with peers; **3E** Share information in cooperative learning interactions; **3G** Express ideas ranging from communicating short phrases to participating in discussions; **4F** Use visual/contextual support to read grade-appropriate text, enhance understanding, and develop vocabulary; **4G** Demonstrate comprehension of increasingly complex English/responding to questions; **5B** Write using newly acquired basic and content-based grade-level vocabulary

---

### Differentiated Instruction: Struggling Learners

Support comprehension of advanced vocabulary by providing synonyms or basic meanings for students. Have students create vocabulary note cards by writing each word at the top of the card. Then work as a class to record synonyms or understandable descriptions. Have students independently write notes or draw pictures that will help them remember the words. Suggest that they write sentences using the words in a way that shows their meanings. Give students an example:

**catastrophic**: awful, terrible, disastrous. Tornadoes and hurricanes can be catastrophic.

⭐ ELPS 2C, 4F, 5B

## Read Along

⭐ ELPS 2G, 2I, 4C, 4G, 4I

Now it's your turn to read. Turn to pages 373–379 in this book. Read the writing model as your teacher or a classmate reads it aloud.

## After Reading

On a separate piece of paper, write answers to these questions about the writing model.

1. Why is it a problem if water and soil get contaminated?
2. How can dams help urban development?
3. When would it be necessary to have a forced evacuation?
4. How can dams help protect against both flooding and drought?
5. What are some of the health problems associated with the Aswan High Dam? Explain your answer.

Work with a partner to compare the outline on page 392 to the research report. Then discuss with your partner how you think the outline helped the writer create a clear organization pattern for the report.

## Read Along

Read aloud the writing model as students track the text in their books. Or, organize students into pairs and have them alternate reading aloud, paragraph by paragraph.

⭐ ELPS 4C

## After Reading

Read aloud the questions before students begin. After students have answered the questions, allow them time to share and discuss their answers with the class. Organize students into pairs for the final activity. ✔DIFFERENTIATE INSTRUCTION

⭐ ELPS 2G, 4C, 4G, 4I, 4J

---

### Differentiated Instruction: English Language Learners

⭐ ELPS 4D, 4F, 4G, 5B

| **ELP Level** **Beginning** | **ELP Level** **Intermediate** | **ELP Level** **Advanced/Advanced High** |
|---|---|---|
| To aid comprehension, provide photographs of the Aswan High Dam area. If your class has computer access, have students search the Web for the photographs. | Before students answer the questions, define content-area vocabulary: *contaminated, forced evacuation, drought.* Allow students to answer questions orally with partners. | Have students work with partners to answer the questions in complete sentences, including a restatement of the question to start the sentence. |

---

 **ELPS 2G** Understand the general meaning, main points, and important details of spoken language/topics and languages are familiar to unfamiliar; **2I** Demonstrate listening comprehension in increasingly complex spoken language by following directions; **4C** Comprehend vocabulary used in written classroom materials; **4D** Use prereading supports to enhance comprehension of written text/graphic organizers, illustrations, and topic-related vocabulary; **4F** Use visual and contextual support to read grade-appropriate text, enhance and confirm understanding, and develop background knowledge; **4G** Demonstrate comprehension of increasingly complex English/participating in shared reading and responding to questions; **4I** Demonstrate comprehension by employing and expanding basic reading skills/understanding of supporting ideas and details, summarizing text, and distinguishing main ideas from details; **4J** Demonstrate English comprehension and expand reading skills by employing inferential skills such as predicting, making connections between ideas, drawing inferences and conclusions from text and graphic sources, and finding supporting text evidence commensurate with content area needs; **5B** Write using newly acquired basic and content-based grade-level vocabulary

## Oral Language: Research Report Writing

Review the instruction with students. Tell students that research reports will use formal language because no matter whom the audience is, the purpose of the writing is to provide factual information. Explain, however, that the facts they include will vary depending on the audience.

⭐ **ELPS** 3I

### Try It!

Read the directions to students and then organize them into pairs to complete the activity. Make sure students understand the situation and the audiences. Have students take turns describing the situation while their partners take on the roles of the varied audiences. Remind students to use formal language and adjust information to appeal to particular audiences.

⭐ **ELPS** 3E, 3G, 3H, 3I

---

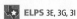

## Oral Language: Research Report Writing

The person or people who will listen to you or read your writing are called the **audience.** When you speak or write, it is important to think about the right words to use so your audience will relate to and understand your thesis. The **tone,** or the way you write, will be different for each audience and for different types of writing. Research reports should have a more formal tone than many other types of writing.

### Try It!

Read about the research topic below. Then choose two audiences from the list that follows the paragraph. Think about what each audience would be interested in knowing about your topic if you had to retell it. With a partner, discuss how the words and examples you choose might be different for each audience.

**Topic**

Cowboys Stadium in Arlington, Texas, has a retractable roof. As home of the Dallas Cowboys, it has 80,000 permanent seats and can expand seating to 100,000 for all kinds of concerts, including band concerts. It is the largest domed stadium in the world. The architects put in a retractable roof so the stadium could be air conditioned in the hot summer and keep people dry in wet weather.

**Audiences**

■ middle-school student, architect, teen football fan, college band director, construction foreman

---

**ELPS 3E** Share information in cooperative learning interactions; **3G** Express ideas ranging from communicating short phrases to participating in discussions; **3H** Describe with increasing specificity and detail; **3I** Adapt spoken language for formal and informal purposes

## Let's Talk!

When you answer a question, you might use one word, a few words, a sentence, or a few sentences.

Example: What do you like best about the new Cowboys Stadium?

roof

▽

retractable, domed roof

▽

The retractable, domed roof can be opened if weather permits.

▽

The roof is retractable, so it is kept closed when it is very hot or raining. When weather permits, the roof is left open. Since the roof is domed, balls won't hit the ceiling, even when thrown by professional football players.

In the first box, there is only a one-word answer. In the other boxes, the writer tells more. The last box shows the most information. When you use more details to tell about something, the other person will have a better idea of what you are talking about. They are more interested in what you have to say.

## Try It!

Choose a famous work of engineering that you would like to research. Make notes about what you want to know about the project and its designers. Then use your notes to describe your ideas to your partner.

Here are some ideas to get you started.

**1.** How was the Brooklyn Bridge designed and built?

**2.** How were some of the world's tallest buildings, such as the Willis Tower in Chicago, built?

Language

## Let's Talk!

Read the example and discuss the information that is added to each answer. Make sure that students understand the information as the response increases in complexity.

⭐ ELPS 2G, 2H

## Try It!

Provide students with a list of famous engineering works for research, such as the Empire State Building, Golden Gate Bridge, Hoover Dam, Erie Canal, and so on. Tell students to form research and inquiry questions from their ideas before they meet and discuss with partners. ✔ DIFFERENTIATE INSTRUCTION

⭐ ELPS 3C, 3E, 3G, 3H

### Differentiated Instruction: English Language Learners

⭐ ELPS 3C, 3E, 3G, 3H

| ELP Level **Beginning** | ELP Level **Intermediate** | ELP Level **Advanced/Advanced High** |
|---|---|---|
| Show a picture of a structure to students. Identify it and have students repeat: *This is the [name of structure].* Guide students to form questions, such as *Who made it? When?* | Write the 5Ws and H on the board. Tell students to use these starters to complete the **Try It!** activity. Once students decide on a structure, they can ask the questions. | After students discuss their ideas and questions, have them work with their partners to list possible sources of information on their chosen topics. |

⭐ **ELPS 2G** Understand the general meaning of spoken language/topics and languages are familiar to unfamiliar; **2H** Understand implicit ideas and information in increasingly complex spoken language; **3C** Speak using a variety of grammatical structures/sentence lengths and types with increasing accuracy and ease; **3E** Share information in cooperative learning interactions; **3G** Express ideas ranging from communicating short phrases to participating in discussions; **3H** Describe and explain with increasing specificity and detail

# Resource Units

**BGW** *"Basic Grammar and Writing"* **WR** *"A Writer's Resource"* **PG** *"Proofreader's Guide"*

# Basic Grammar and Writing

## ⬤ UNIT TEKS

**10.13A** Plan a first draft; **10.13B** Structure ideas and develop drafts; **10.13C** Revise drafts; **10.13D** Edit drafts; **10.13E** Revise final draft and publish work; **10.14A** Write an engaging story; **10.15A** Write an analytical essay; **10.15B(i)** Write procedural and work-related documents/convey information; **10.17A(i)** Use and understand tenses and verbals; **10.17C** Use correctly structured sentences; **10.18A** Use capitalization; **10.18B(i)** Use commas; **10.18B(ii)** Use quotation marks; **10.18B(iii)** Use dashes; **10.19** Spell correctly

## ⬤ UNIT ELPS

**1E** Internalize new language/speaking and writing; **3E** Share information; **4C** Develop sight vocabulary/derive meaning of environmental print/comprehend written class materials; **4I** Employ and expand reading skills; **4J** Employ inferential skills; **4K** Employ analytical skills; **5F** Write using a variety of sentence lengths/patterns/connecting words; **5G** Narrate, describe, and explain with increasing specificity/content-area writing

### Using Words Effectively

**(pages 569–584)**

These pages discuss the parts of speech.

### Understanding Sentence Style

**(pages 585–596)**

These pages give guidelines for writing well-crafted sentences.

### Writing Strong Paragraphs

**(pages 597–615)**

These pages give guidelines for writing effective paragraphs.

###  Technology Connections

 *Write Source Online*
www.hmheducation.com/tx/writesource

- *Net-text*
- *Writing Network*
- *Portfolio*
- *GrammarSnap*
- *Essay Scoring*
- *File Cabinet*

*Interactive Whiteboard Lessons*

# A Writer's Resource

## ⬤ UNIT TEKS

**10.13A** Plan a first draft; **10.13B** Structure ideas and develop drafts; **10.13D** Edit drafts; **10.14A** Write an engaging story; **10.15A** Write an analytical essay; **10.15C(iii)** Write a response to expository and literary text/address writing skills and use quotations; **10.16A** Write an argumentative essay/clear thesis; **10.18A** Use capitalization; **10.18B(i)** Use commas; **10.18B(ii)** Use quotation marks; **10.18B(iii)** Use dashes; **10.19** Spell correctly

## ⬤ UNIT ELPS

**1E** Internalize new language/speaking and writing; **2C** Learn new structures/expressions/vocabulary; **3B** Expand and internalize initial vocabulary; **3D** Speak using content-area vocabulary; **3E** Share information; **4G** Demonstrate comprehension of language/shared reading, summarizing, responding to questions, taking notes; **5C** Spell and employ spelling patterns/rules with increasing accuracy; **5E** Employ complex grammatical structures; **5F** Write using a variety of sentence lengths/patterns/connecting words

### A Writer's Resource (pages 617–641)

These pages contain writing tips and guidelines to help students complete any writing assignment creatively and effectively.

###  Technology Connections

 *Write Source Online*
www.hmheducation.com/tx/writesource

- *Net-text*
- *Writing Network*
- *Portfolio*
- *GrammarSnap*
- *Essay Scoring*
- *File Cabinet*

 *Interactive Whiteboard Lessons*

### A Note About Style Guides

Style guides vary in their recommendations for certain issues, including questions of grammar, usage, spelling, punctuation, and formatting. For example, the *Texas Write Source* Proofreader's Guide calls for an apostrophe and an *s* in the plurals of numbers, letters, and words used as words. The *MLA Handbook* calls only for the *s*. As developing writers, students will encounter differences among style guides. Use these encounters to teach that style guides differ and that students should find out their instructor's preferred style guide.

# Proofreader's Guide

Checking Mechanics
(pages 643–703)

Understanding Idioms
(pages 704–709)

Using the Right Word
(pages 710–729)

Parts of Speech (pages 730–763)

Understanding Sentences
(pages 764–787)

## Technology Connections

 **Write Source Online**
www.hmheducation.com/tx/writesource
- **Net-text**
- **Writing Network**
- **Portfolio**
- **GrammaSnap**
- **Essay Scoring**
- **File Cabinet**

 **Interactive Whiteboard Lessons**

# Writing Paragraphs

| Day | Writing and Grammar Instruction | Basic Grammar and Writing | Proofreader's Guide | SkillsBook | Write Source Online |
|---|---|---|---|---|---|
| 1–3 | **Writing Strong Paragraphs**<br>The Parts of a Paragraph | 598–599 | | | |
| | Skills Activities:<br>•Spelling | | 698–703 | | |
| | •Using the Right Word | | 710–729 | 61–68 | |
| | •Constructing Sentences | | 764–771 | 125–138 | GrammarSnap |
| | •Sentence Variety | | 772–777 | 167–177 | GrammarSnap |
| 4 | Types of Paragraphs | 600–606 | | | |
| 5 | Patterns of Organization | 607–610 | | | |

(WEEK 1)

⊕ ELPS 1E, 2C, 3B, 3D, 3E, 4G

TEXAS
WRITE
SOURCE
Online
www.hmheducation.com/tx/writesource

# Basic Grammar and Writing

## Writing Focus

| | |
|---|---|
| Using Words Effectively | **569** |
| Understanding Sentence Style | **585** |
| Writing Strong Paragraphs | **597** |

## Learning Language

**Work with a partner. Read the definitions below and share your answers to the questions that follow.**

1. A modifier is a word, a phrase, or a clause that changes or limits the meaning of other words.
   **Why are adjectives and adverbs common modifiers?**

2. An anecdote is a short account of an interesting or humorous incident.
   **How can an anecdote help engage your reader? Explain.**

3. To classify means to arrange or organize by class or category, based on common characteristics.
   **What characteristics would you use to classify bicycles?**

4. The idiom "to hit a home run" means to succeed or to do well.
   **When did you last hit a home run? Describe the incident.**

# Using Words Effectively

Just as atoms are the fundamental building blocks of matter, words are the building blocks of communication. And like atoms, words have power. Think about the word *yes*. That one little word can change your life forever—for better or for worse. So can the tiny word *no*. And what about the word *ridiculous*? Try shouting that word in just about any situation, and you'll see how powerful a word can be.

English has many types of words: nouns, pronouns, verbs, adjectives, adverbs, prepositions, and conjunctions. This chapter explores these parts of speech, helping you unlock the power each one has to offer.

- Nouns
- Pronouns
- Verbs
- Adjectives
- Adverbs
- Prepositions
- Conjunctions
- Checking Your Word Choice

"Give me the right word and the right accent, and I will move the world."
—Joseph Conrad

## Learning Language

Use this collaborative speaking and listening activity on SE page 568 to help students internalize new basic and academic language; share and understand new expressions, basic vocabulary, and academic vocabulary; expand vocabulary by learning and using routine language; speak using grade-level content area vocabulary; share information; and demonstrate comprehension by responding to questions.

## Using Words Effectively

Read the section introduction on SE page 569 with students. Invite volunteers to paraphrase the quotation at the bottom of the page.

**ELPS 1E** Internalize new basic and academic language by using and reusing it in meaningful ways in speaking and writing activities that build concept and language attainment; **2C** Learn new language structures, expressions, and basic and academic vocabulary heard during classroom instruction and interactions; **3B** Expand and internalize initial English vocabulary by learning and using high-frequency English words necessary for identifying and describing people, places, and objects, by retelling simple stories and basic information represented or supported by pictures, and by learning and using routine language needed for classroom communications; **3E** Share information in cooperative learning interactions; **4G** Demonstrate comprehension of increasingly complex English by participating in shared reading, retelling or summarizing material, responding to questions, and taking notes commensurate with content area and grade level needs; **5F** Write using a variety of grade-appropriate sentence lengths, patterns, and connecting words to combine phrases, clauses, and sentences in increasingly accurate ways as more English is acquired

## Nouns Using General and Specific Nouns

Since some nouns are general (*man, rock*) and some are specific (*Barnum Brown, sandstone*), they can affect the focus of your writing. As with a camera lens, you can start with general nouns and zoom in to specific nouns, or you can start with specific nouns and zoom out to general ones.

### Zooming In (from general nouns to specific nouns)

In the wide *desert*, a *man* crouched under a blazing *sun* and dug. He spent most of his *time* kneeling in the *dirt* holding a small *tool*. Slowly he chipped *sandstone* away from what looked like a *vertebra*. *Stroke* by *stroke*, the paleontologist *Barnum Brown* was uncovering the *skeleton* of a *Tyrannosaurus rex*.

This paragraph starts with general nouns, which paint a broad picture and invite the reader to imagine the scene. Then it zooms in to specific nouns, which provide detailed information.

### Zooming Out (from specific nouns to general nouns)

In early *July 1905*, *Barnum Brown* discovered the *skeleton* of a *Tyrannosaurus rex*. An avid *hunter* of dinosaur *bones*, *Barnum* had come to *Hell Creek, Montana*, in hopes of finding something special. However, he could not have suspected that his *discovery* would soon visit the *imaginations* of *children* everywhere.

This paragraph starts with specific nouns, providing exact information up front. Then it zooms out to general nouns to reflect on the importance of the discovery.

### Try It!

Think of a topic that interests you. Then brainstorm a list of general and specific nouns about the topic. (See the sample chart below.) Afterward, write a paragraph, using the nouns to zoom in or zoom out.

| Topic: Dinosaur Hunting | | | |
|---|---|---|---|
| **General** | | **Specific** | |
| dinosaur | bones | Tyrannosaurus rex | vertebra |
| man | desert | paleontologist | Hell Creek, Montana |

## Creating Metaphors

A **metaphor** is a comparison of two unlike things in which no word of comparison (*as* or *like*) is used. A metaphor represents a high level of thinking and is a powerful writing technique.

### Basic Metaphors

A basic metaphor can be a simple noun equation: Noun A = Noun B. In basic metaphors, the nouns are equated using a linking verb such as *is, am, are, was,* or *were.*

Janice **is a** human calculator.      Life **is a** banquet.
(Janice = calculator)      (life = banquet)

### Advanced Metaphors

Some advanced metaphors *imply* the equation between the nouns. In this example, the highlighted nouns are equated without linking verbs.

The gears in Janice's mind grind through any math test.
(The word *gears* implies that Janice's *mind* is a machine.)

### Tip

Create an advanced metaphor by substituting Noun B for Noun A.

Her **lasers** scan problems while her **processor** builds solutions.

| Noun A | | Noun B |
|---|---|---|
| eyes | = | lasers |
| brain | = | processor |

### Extended Metaphors

Sometimes an author extends a metaphor, creating a series of pictures for the reader.

Bill's mind is a locker, with his letter jacket hanging from a hook in the center, pictures of his girlfriend covering the inside of the door, and textbooks lying, forgotten, at the bottom.

### Try It!

Equate the name of a friend (Noun A) with another noun (Noun B). Then write one basic, one advanced, and one extended metaphor about this person.

*Word Style*

---

## Using General and Specific Nouns

Discuss general and specific nouns with the class, including the capitalization rules for some specific nouns.

### Try It! Answers

Answers will vary, but students should show an ability to use specific nouns related to their chosen topics.

## Creating Metaphors

Discuss with students the types of metaphors listed on SE page 571 to help them comprehend language structures, employ increasingly complex grammatical structures, write using a variety of grade-appropriate sentence patterns, and describe with specificity in their writing. Have students contribute other examples for each type of metaphor.

### Try It! Answers

Answers will vary. Students should demonstrate their ability to form an extended metaphor.

---

**TEKS** 10.18A Use conventions of capitalization; **ELPS** 4C Comprehend language structures used in written classroom materials; 5E Employ increasingly complex grammatical structures in content area writing such as using correct verbs, tenses, and pronouns/possessive case/negatives and contractions; 5F Write using a variety of grade-appropriate sentence patterns in increasingly accurate ways; 5G Describe with increasing specificity and detail/writing

ELPS 5E, 5F, 5G

## Pronouns Engaging Your Reader

Most often, a pronoun should clearly refer to a specific noun (its *antecedent*). However, one special use of pronouns delays mentioning the antecedent, making the reader wonder who or what you are talking about. This technique can work on a sentence level or in a whole paragraph.

### Sentence Hook

In the following examples, notice how the pronouns turn the sentences into riddles, causing the reader to wonder, "Who?"

When he did a screen test for Paramount, he was told, "[You] can't sing, can't act, but you can dance a little." Still, Fred Astaire was in more than 40 films.

Though she was fired from her first Broadway show after one night, and though Hollywood producers labeled her "box office poison," Katharine Hepburn became a leading lady of twentieth-century film.

### Paragraph Hook

In this paragraph, the reader doesn't discover who *he* is until the end of the paragraph.

He was a short, unassuming comedian from New York, but he sat on a train bound for the Soviet Union in 1933. The tools of his trade were simple—a rumpled hat, a curly red wig, a worn-out coat, and a bicycle horn. The young pantomimist was traveling to the Soviet Union to open up a new market to American performers. Arriving in Moscow, he was greeted with suspicion, and when he performed, his audiences were afraid to laugh. In utter frustration, the young American was about to give up, but then the United States and the Soviet Union officially recognized each other. That changed everything. Suddenly, Soviet crowds went wild for Harpo Marx. He later wrote that he had never before played for an audience so desperate to laugh.

### Try It!

Make a list of favorite performers—musicians, actors, comedians, dancers, or friends. Choose one, and think of (or learn) interesting anecdotes about his or her life and career. Write a paragraph about one of these anecdotes, using pronouns to withhold the person's identity until the end.

---

 ELPS 5E

Word Style

## Persuading Your Reader

In persuasive writing, you can unite people, instruct them, or divide them, depending on the person of the pronouns you use.

| Person of Pronouns | | |
|---|---|---|
| **First Person** (Unite) | **Second Person** (Instruct) | **Third Person** (Divide) |
| we   us   our | you   your | they   them   their |

### Selecting the Person of a Pronoun

Notice the effect that is created by changing the person of pronouns in the following sentence:

These pronouns **unite** the writer and the reader: "We're all in this together."

When we buy a car, van, truck, or SUV, we must consider how our consumption of gasoline will affect us in the future.

These pronouns **instruct** the reader.

When you buy a car, van, truck, or SUV, you must consider how your consumption of gasoline will affect you in the future.

These pronouns **divide** the reader from those being written about.

When they buy a car, van, truck, or SUV, they must consider how their consumption of gasoline will affect them in the future.

In persuasive writing, use pronouns carefully. Use first-person pronouns to create common ground with your reader. Use second-person pronouns (or the implied "you") to instruct the reader. Use third-person pronouns sparingly, perhaps to point an accusing finger.

### Try It!

Check a newspaper opinion/editorial page to find an editorial that uses personal pronouns. Are they first-, second-, or third-person pronouns? Change the pronouns in one of the paragraphs, switching to another person. Then explain how the changes make the paragraph more or less persuasive.

---

## Engaging Your Reader

Discuss how pronouns can be used to engage the reader in order to help students learn how to employ complex grammatical structures in content area writing; to write using a variety of grade-appropriate sentence lengths, sentence patterns, and connecting words; and to narrate with specificity in their writing.

### Try It! Answers

Answers will vary. Students should write an interesting anecdote about their favorite performer.

## Persuading Your Reader

Discuss how pronouns can be used to unite, instruct, or divide in order to teach students to employ complex grammatical structures in their content area writing.

### Try It! Answers

Answers will vary. Students should demonstrate an ability to analyze how the change in person affects the persuasiveness of an opinion article.

---

 **ELPS 5E** Employ increasingly complex grammatical structures in content area writing such as using correct verbs, tenses, and pronouns/possessive case/negatives and contractions; **5F** Write using a variety of grade-appropriate sentence lengths, patterns, and connecting words/combine in increasingly accurate ways; **5G** Narrate with increasing specificity and detail/writing

ELPS 5G

## Verbs Affecting the Sense of Time

Verbs and verb tenses can affect the sense of time in a piece of writing. For example, they help express whether an event took place in the past, takes place in the present, or will occur in the future.

### Past Tense in Essays

Past-tense verbs work best for most of your writing, showing that events are completed. Past-tense verbs help you to express and analyze solid facts.

> Throughout history, women have made major contributions to science. For example, in the fourth century C.E., Hypatia of Alexandria created an astrolabe, an instrument for tracking the position of stars and planets. It revolutionized astronomy and navigation.

### Present Tense in Narratives

Present-tense verbs work well for certain narratives. These verbs make action seem immediate, as if it were happening right now.

> Lise Mitner glances down from the face of Albert Einstein and stares at the paper before her. On it, she has laid out the secrets of the atom. Always shy, Lise covers the equations with her hand. Einstein clucks, shaking his head. "Don't hide your work. You should trumpet it from the rooftops. Don't you know, my dear: You are the German Madame Curie."

### Present Tense in Process Essays

Present-tense verbs also work well for essays that describe action that happens routinely.

> Every year, more young women decide to study mathematics and science; every year, more female researchers and doctors start their practices; every year, more women make the discoveries that advance human knowledge.

### Try It!

Pull out a recent expository essay or narrative you have written. What verb tense did you use? Choose a paragraph and replace the verbs in it with verbs of a different tense. How does the change affect the sense of time and action?

---

ELPS 5G

## Creating Verbal Metaphors

Though most metaphors are based on nouns (Noun A = Noun B), some metaphors can be created using verbs.

### Verbal Metaphors

**My heart** galloped **in my chest.**
(The heart is equated to a running horse.)

**The letter** ignited **my mind.**
(The letter is equated to a fire.)

**Dad's junker** staggered **into the driveway,** bled **transmission fluid, and** gasped **its last breath.**
(The junker car is equated to a dying animal.)

**Note:** In these examples, verbs that are usually used with one type of noun (the *horse* galloped) are used with nouns of a completely different type (my *heart* galloped).

### Try It!

Study the bank of verbs below. Each is strongly associated with a specific noun. Select five verbs and write a sentence for each, creating metaphors by pairing the verb with a completely different type of noun.

**Example:** The gray sky frowned on our picnic plans.

| | | | |
|---|---|---|---|
| anchored | eroded | hurdled | rotted |
| baked | flew | joked | sizzled |
| bucked | frowned | kindled | sprinted |
| burned | gargled | laughed | snored |
| catapulted | groomed | muttered | stomped |
| danced | hacked | punted | thundered |
| drummed | hollered | raced | tripped |

### FYI

When a metaphor implies that a nonhuman thing is performing a human action, the technique is called *personification*.

> The day **snored** along, occasionally **muttering** empty promises of adventure before **rolling over** and **drowsing** again.

*Word Style*

---

## Affecting the Sense of Time

Discuss with students the use of verb tenses in order to help them narrate with specificity and detail.

### Try It! Answers

Answers will vary. Students should demonstrate an ability to change verb tenses and recognize the effects such changes have on the time and action of the paragraph.

---

## Creating Verbal Metaphors

Discuss with students how verbs are used to create metaphors in order to help them write descriptions with specificity and detail.

### Try It! Possible Answers

1. The pouring rain drummed across the top of the old picnic shelter.
2. When Jamie saw his assignment, his confidence quickly eroded.
3. The wind sprinted past the window, throwing leaves everywhere.
4. Blaine hurdled through the math problems, astounding all of us.
5. The bathtub gargled as the water drained out.

---

## Adjectives Making a Precise Point

Some writers use adjectives like frosting, slathering their nouns as if the adjectives will make them tastier. You will do better to consider how adjectives subtract from a noun, rather than adding to it, by limiting its meaning and making it more precise.

> **DON'T Write**
> I had a big, beautiful party.
> (The adjectives do not make *party* more precise.)
>
> **DO Write**
> I had a sweet-sixteen birthday party.
> (The adjectives tell precisely what *kind* of party.)

### Adjective Phrases and Clauses

Phrases and clauses that function as adjectives also need to be precise.

**The house rocked like a dryer** filled with shoes.
(The phrase *filled with shoes* tells precisely what kind of *dryer*.)

**We played a game** of truth or dare that resulted in a pillow fight.
(The phrase *of truth or dare* and the clause *that resulted in a pillow fight* tell exactly what kind of *game*.)

### Try It!

Think of a special event that you have attended, and make a list of nouns related to it. Add one adjective and one adjective phrase or clause that would make the noun's meaning precise. (See the examples below.) Write a paragraph about the event, using some of the nouns and modifiers from your list. Share and discuss your paragraph with a classmate.

| Nouns | Adjectives | Adjective Phrases or Clauses |
|---|---|---|
| pool | above-ground | with a ten-foot-deep end |
| diving board | squeaky | which got a workout |
| dives | ridiculous | such as the "Spider" |
| belly flop | blistering | that nearly emptied the pool |

## Emphasizing the Quality of a Noun

One way to emphasize the quality of a given noun is to use a series of adjectives to describe it.

### Series of Adjectives

The sentences below contain adjectives in a series. The first series is separated with commas and the word *and*. The second series is separated without commas, using only the word *and*. This provides special emphasis.

**My friend Eva is** smart, quirky, funny, **and** driven.

**She says I am** kind **and** patient **and totally** infuriating.

### Series of Phrases or Clauses

Phrases or clauses that function as adjectives can also be used in a series.

Sitting in her living room, propping her feet on the radiator, **and** balancing a notepad on her lap, **Eva writes stories.** (Three participial phrases describe *Eva*.)

**Eva writes stories about places** that she has seen, that she wishes to see, **and** that she knows don't even exist. (Three relative clauses describe *places*.)

### FYI

The quickest way to know whether a phrase or clause is functioning as an adjective is to decide whether it answers one of the adjective questions—*which? what kind of? how many?* or *how much?*

### Try It!

Write down the name of a person. Beside the name, write two nouns you associate with that person. Under each noun, list descriptive words, phrases, or clauses. (See the sample chart below.) Then create a sentence that uses an adjective series.

| Eva | apartment | places |
|---|---|---|
| smart | on the eighth floor | that she has seen |
| funny | with a view of the alley | that she wishes to see |
| quirky | in the old downtown | that she knows don't even exist |
| driven | in Bloomington | |

*Word Style*

---

## Making a Precise Point

Have students brainstorm additional correct and incorrect examples of adjective use in order to give them practice sharing information cooperatively.

### Try It! Answers

Answers will vary. As students discuss their paragraphs, encourage them to make suggestions for improvements in the choice of modifiers.

## Emphasizing the Quality of a Noun

Discuss the use of a series of adjectives or adjectival phrases/clauses in order to help students learn to narrate with specificity and detail in their writing.

### Try It! Answers

Answers will vary. Make sure students first create their charts, then write the sentence. Students may create additional sentences based on the information in their charts.

Word Style

## Adverbs Writing Strong Beginnings

Adverbs make great sentence starters because they help create a context. Before the reader knows *what* happens in the sentence, the adverb can tell *how, when,* or *where* it happens. Single-word adverbs (as well as phrases and clauses that act as adverbs) answer these questions: *how? when? where? why? to what degree?* and *how often?*

### Adverb Beginnings

**Gradually,** the glowing twilight surrendered to spangled night. *(How?)*

**Afterward,** the Perseid meteor shower began. *(When?)*

**In the northern sky,** meteors were flashing overhead. *(Where?)*

**One by one,** shooting stars streaked across the sky. *(To what degree?)*

**Every few minutes,** a new fireball left its fleeting signature. *(How often?)*

**Because the earth was passing through the path of a comet,** there were hundreds of shooting stars. *(Why?)*

### Try It!

Read and then rewrite each sentence below, moving the adverb (or adverbial phrase or clause) to the beginning of the sentence.

1. Dust particles often made slim dashes of light.
2. Marble-sized chunks of matter created bright shooting stars as they crossed the whole sky before burning out.
3. Fist-sized meteorites crossed the sky burning, spinning, and flaming.
4. Earth passes through this cloud of debris every August.

### FYI

The regular subject-verb order may be reversed when an adverb starts a sentence.

**At the top of the hill** lay a clearing. *(A clearing lay at the top of the hill.)*
**Overhead** were the dancing stars. *(The dancing stars were overhead.)*

### Try It!

Think about a natural phenomenon you've witnessed and write a paragraph about what you saw. Try starting a few sentences with adverbs.

## Avoiding Adverb Props

Avoid propping up a weak verb with an adverb. Often, the two words can be replaced with a single verb that tells exactly what is happening.

### Adverb Props

| DON'T Write | DO Write |
|---|---|
| ran quickly | charged, darted, dashed, scurried, sprinted |
| walked heavily | marched, plodded, slogged, stomped, trudged |
| said angrily | growled, hissed, shouted, snarled |

## Avoiding Redundant Adverbs

A strong verb doesn't need an adverb. When you fix an adverb prop by replacing the weak verb with a stronger one, you can omit the unnecessary adverb.

### Redundant Adverbs

| DON'T Write | DO Write |
|---|---|
| dashed quickly (no one dashes slowly) | dashed |
| plodded heavily (no one plods lightly) | plodded |
| growled angrily (no one growls happily) | growled |

### Try It!

Read the passage below and identify the adverb props and redundant adverbs. Suggest how each adverb problem could be corrected.

> Afghan refugees staggered unsteadily up the hill. Their world had been changed completely by the war, and now it was rocked deeply by an earthquake. "We are weary," an old man said quietly. Abdullah al Ibin had worked hard to survive the Taliban regime. He thought wishfully that things would become easier. They did not. He put up with robbers until he gave up and escaped away from his hometown. "Now, with this earthquake, even the mountains aren't safe," he murmured sadly.

---

## Writing Strong Beginnings

Discuss adverb beginnings to help students comprehend language structures and use a variety of grammatical and sentence structures.

### Try It! Answers

1. Often, dust particles made slim dashes of light.
2. Before burning out, marble-sized chunks of matter created bright shooting stars as they crossed the whole sky.
3. Burning, spinning, and flaming, fist-sized meteorites crossed the sky.
4. Every August, Earth passes through this cloud of debris.

### Try It! Answers

Answers will vary.

## Avoiding Adverb Props

Discuss adverb props and revising drafts to avoid them and improve word choice.

### Try It! Answers

Adverb props

changed completely→turned upside down
thought wishfully→hoped, dreamed

Redundant adverbs

staggered unsteadily→staggered
rocked deeply→rocked
escaped away→escaped

---

 **TEKS** 10.13C Revise drafts to improve word choice; **ELPS** 4C Comprehend language structures used in written classroom materials; 5E Employ increasingly complex grammatical structures in content area writing such as using correct verbs, tenses, and pronouns/possessive case/negatives and contractions; 5F Write using a variety of grade-appropriate sentence patterns in increasingly accurate ways

## Prepositions Creating Similes

The preposition *like* allows you to compare two things, creating a simile. For a simile to be effective, it should point out an unexpected similarity.

> **DON'T Write**
> Rain is like water that falls from the sky.
> (Rain *is* water.)
>
> **DO Write**
> Spring rain is like a mother's voice whispering to the world, "Wake up."

Use similes as good cooks use spices—sparingly to enhance the flavor of the sentence. A simile pushed too far may become tiresome.

> **DON'T Write**
> Spring rain is like a mother's voice whispering to the world, "Wake up," and the winds of March are like the rustle of covers drawn back from the slumbering planet.

### Try It!

For each of the terms listed below, write a one-sentence simile that shows a surprising similarity. Use the words *is like* or *are like*.

1. lightning    3. a bird's song    5. spring flowers
2. warm winds    4. new leaves    6. umbrellas

### FYI

Many similes use the preposition *like* to introduce a prepositional phrase that functions as an adjective.

> The winter sky was **like a woolen blanket.**
> (The simile modifies the noun *sky*.)

Other similes use the subordinating conjunction *as* to introduce a subordinate clause that functions as an adverb.

> Spring draws away the clouds **as a mother draws back a woolen blanket.**
> (The simile modifies the verb *draws*.)

---

## Using Prepositional Phrases as Adjectives

Prepositions can turn nouns into modifiers. By placing a preposition before a noun, you can create a phrase that acts as an adjective, answering the questions *which? what kind?* or *how many?*

> **The proposal** with the blue cover **is mine.**
> *Which proposal?*
>
> **Calculations** for the construction costs **were inaccurate.**
> *What kind of calculations?*
>
> **Letters** from two hundred constituents **stopped the bill from passing.**
> *How many?*

Prepositional phrases can be used to revise an awkward sentence that strings too many adjectives together.

> **The** city budget debate's **end finally came.** (awkward)
>
> **The end** of the debate over the city budget **finally came.**

### Try It!

Rewrite each sentence below, turning at least one of the adjectives into a prepositional phrase. Be sure the new sentence makes sense.

1. The **mayor's hilltop** house needs painting.
2. The **busy street's anxious** residents spoke to the city council.
3. The **school board budget** referendum passed the vote.
4. An **environmental activist student** organization opposes the bypass.
5. The council passed the **2006 property tax reassessment** bill.

### FYI

Prepositional phrases also can function as adverbs, answering the questions *how? when? where? why? to what degree?* and *how often?* However, these prepositional phrases can often be replaced by a single adverb—or by a stronger verb.

> The mayor replied **with a firm voice** that the budget had been approved.
>
> The mayor replied **firmly** that the budget had been approved.
> (adverb)
>
> The mayor **asserted** that the budget had been approved.
> (strong verb)

*Word Style*

---

### Try It! Possible Answers

1. The television is like lightning, flickering bright light into the darkness.
2. His plans to solve the disagreement are like the warm winds of spring.
3. The chirping tune on his cell phone is like a bird's song.
4. The color of the paint was like the color of new leaves on an oak tree.
5. After several unnerving minutes in complete darkness, the candles are like the first spring flowers, blooming through the snow.
6. Their floppy hats are like umbrellas, blocking the sun.

---

### Using Prepositional Phrases as Adjectives

Discuss the use of prepositional phrases in order to help students comprehend language structures that are used in classroom materials.

### Try It! Possible Answers

1. The mayor's house on the hilltop needs painting.
2. The anxious residents of a busy street spoke to the city council.
3. The referendum for the school board budget passed the vote.
4. A student organization of environmental activists opposes the bypass.
5. The council passed the reassessment bill for 2006 property taxes.

---

 **ELPS 4C** Comprehend language structures used in written classroom materials

## Conjunctions Creating Tension

As a writer, you can create tension in a sentence by using certain subordinating conjunctions. The following conjunctions tell the reader that your train of thought will soon shift directions.

| | | | |
|---|---|---|---|
| although | though | unless | while |
| even though | whereas | until | |

### Present a Contrast

In the following examples, ideas pull in opposite directions, building a powerful contrast.

> Although the French Revolution was meant to provide "liberty, equality, and brotherhood" to all, it actually resulted in repression, inequality, and war.

> While royal oppression had been cruel, the mob's remedy for it—gauntlets and guillotines—proved crueler still.

### Create Irony

In this example, the conjunction *even though* sets up a contrast that creates *irony*. Irony is when a writer's actual words say the opposite of what is meant. The writer uses quotation marks to indicate irony.

> Even though the French thought they had escaped from King Louis XVI's "divine right" to rule France, they found themselves stuck with Emperor Napoleon I's divine right to rule the world.

### Try It!

Select four of the conjunctions listed at the top of the page and use each one at the start of a sentence. Work to create tension and irony in your sentences. Use quotation marks to indicate irony.

### FYI

Another way to create tension is to use correlative conjunctions.

| | |
|---|---|
| not only . . . but also | neither . . . nor |
| either . . . or | both . . . and |
| if . . . then | whether . . . or |

---

## Creating Pivot Points

The coordinating conjunctions *but* and *yet* can provide pivot points in an essay. They allow the writer to present one line of thought and then create a reversal. In an expository essay, *but* or *yet* can show a shift from background information to the real issue. The technique also works in persuasive writing.

### Expository Excerpt

> This paragraph gives background and conventional wisdom.

> *But* signals the shift to new information.

> Our climate should be a self-righting system. After all, the main greenhouse gas, carbon dioxide, is also the main food for plants. More carbon dioxide should cause more plant growth. More plants should mean less carbon dioxide and more oxygen. The levels of greenhouse gases should self-regulate.
>
> **But** experiments have shown otherwise. Increased levels of carbon dioxide increase plant growth, but not enough to reduce carbon-dioxide levels. In addition, with global warming, arctic tundras that once were "carbon sinks," absorbing more carbon dioxide than they lost, are becoming "carbon pumps"—accelerating the rise in greenhouse gases.

*Word Style*

### Persuasive Excerpt

> The opposing position is presented.

> *Yet* signals the shift to the writer's opinion.

> The politicians are right in this: The world economy is driven by oil, and capitalism is driven by consumption. To keep the economy and capitalism strong, the world needs a great deal of oil now—and an even greater amount in the future.
>
> **Yet** this argument breaks down. Yes, oil is needed now, but alternative energy sources will reduce the future demands. The standard argument fails to account for one great resource—human ingenuity.

### Try It!

Read the paragraphs above, and think of an issue with two sides. Write a paragraph that explains one side. Then write a second paragraph, beginning with *but* or *yet*, to explain the other side of the issue.

---

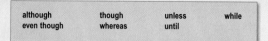

## Conjunctions

Discuss conjunctions that set up a contrast and the use of quotation marks to indicate irony.

### Try It! | Answers

Answers will vary.

## Creating Pivot Points

Discuss the use of *but* and *yet* as pivot points in order to help students comprehend language structures that are used in classroom materials.

### Try It! | Answers

Answers will vary. Share the most successful uses of conjunctions to create tension and irony with the class.

---

**TEKS** **10.15A(ii)** Write an analytical essay that includes rhetorical devices; **10.18B(ii)** Use quotation marks to indicate irony; **ELPS** **4C** Comprehend language structures used in written classroom materials

584

⭐ TEKS 10.13C

585

## Word Choice Using a Checklist

After you finish a writing assignment, you can check your word choice by using the following checklist.

### Word-Choice Checklist

_____ 1. Have I used nouns to set my focus (zooming in or out)?

_____ 2. Have I included any metaphors? List examples: The Calcutta massacre was a last gasp of the dying imperial beast.

_____ 3. Have I used pronouns occasionally to create suspense? List examples: He was a small man of noble birth, but Mohandas Gandhi became a titan who fought for the common people.

_____ 4. Have I used pronouns persuasively? List examples:

To unite: We wonder if the world holds more Gandhis.

To instruct: "Live as if you were to die tomorrow. Learn as if you were to live forever."

To divide: Though some may say passive resistance cannot stand up to armies and bombs, they have forgotten the lessons of Gandhi.

_____ 5. Have I used verb tense to establish time?

_____ 6. Have I used adjectives to make precise points?

_____ 7. Have I used an adjective series?

_____ 8. Have I started any sentences with adverbs?

_____ 9. Have I used any similes? List examples: Gandhi's heart was like a magic box, larger on the inside than on the outside.

_____ 10. Have I used prepositional phrases as adjectives?

_____ 11. Have I used subordinating conjunctions to create contrast or irony where needed?

_____ 12. Have I used *but* or *yet* to create pivot points in my writing?

# Understanding Sentence Style

Close your eyes, and imagine a carefully handwoven scarf or shawl. Try to visualize how each stitch works with the next one to create a unique design. Now imagine that the sentences you write are like those stitches. As you weave them together, your design—your message—takes form, leaving a lasting impression on your reader.

Good writing holds sentences that are clear, creative, and effective. To become sentence-smart, look for well-crafted sentences as you read. Then write sentences of your own modeled after some of these published gems. If you read and write often, your writing style will continue to improve—one sentence at a time. The guidelines in this chapter will help.

- Sentence Patterns
- Sentence Length
- Sentence Variety
- Sentence Combining
- Sentence Problems
- Sentence Agreement
- Sentence Modeling

"The best advice on writing I've ever received is: 'Knock 'em dead with the lead sentence.' "
—Whitney Balliet

## Word Choice

Discuss the use of the word choice checklist so that students can revise their drafts to improve word choice.

## Understanding Sentence Style

Read the section introduction on SE page 585 aloud. Point out the suggestion to read and write regularly as the best way to understand what makes a well-written sentence and to improve personal writing style.

ELPS 4C, 5E

## Sentence Patterns Understanding the Basics

In the English language, sentences follow basic patterns. Combining a variety of sentence patterns adds interest to your writing.

**1. Subject + Action Verb**

> S    AV
> **Armin coughed.** (Some action verbs, like *coughed*, are intransitive. They *do not need* a direct object to express a complete thought. See **744.1**.)

**2. Subject + Action Verb + Direct Object**

> S    AV    DO
> **Omaya directs the play.** (Some action verbs, like *directs* in this sentence, are transitive. They *do need* a direct object to express a complete thought. See **744.2**.)

**3. Subject + Action Verb + Indirect Object + Direct Object**

> S    AV    IO    DO
> **The teacher read the students a description of the test.** (The direct object *description* names who or what receives the action; the indirect object *students* names to whom or for whom the action is done. See **744.2**.)

**4. Subject + Action Verb + Direct Object + Object Complement**

> S    AV    DO    OC
> **The class found the presentation entertaining.** (The object complement *entertaining* describes the direct object.)

**5. Subject + Linking Verb + Predicate Noun**

> S    LV    PN
> **Serafina is a dancer.** (The predicate noun *dancer* renames the subject. See **732.3**.)

**6. Subject + Linking Verb + Predicate Adjective**

> S    LV    PA
> **Our parents are interested in contributing to the fund.** (The predicate adjective *interested* describes the subject. See **756.1**.)

**Note:** In the patterns below, the subject comes after the verb.

> LV    S    PN
> **Is Dominic a sports fan?** (A question)

> LV    S
> **There were three limousines in the parking lot.** (A sentence beginning with *there*)

---

*"Whatever sentence will bear to be read twice, we may be sure was thought twice."*
—Henry David Thoreau

## Sentence Length Varying Sentence Lengths

Using sentences of different lengths adds interest to your writing. If too many of your sentences have the same number of words, your writing may sound monotonous.

In this paragraph, all of the sentences have the same basic length.

> Being a veterinarian is hard work. Sometimes the veterinarian has to handle heavy animals. Some dogs can weigh more than 100 pounds. Rural veterinarians must care for large farm animals on-site. That means they must travel from farm to farm. Of course, there are also late-night emergencies. Still, there are many rewards. Veterinarians know the joy of helping animals. They have the satisfaction of relieving their pain.

The same paragraph has been improved below because the sentences now vary in length. The writer added and deleted words as needed.

> Being a veterinarian is hard work. A veterinarian must be able to handle heavy animals, including dogs that can weigh more than 100 pounds. In addition, rural veterinarians must care for large animals on-site, which means they must travel from farm to farm. Of course, there are also late-night emergencies to deal with. Still, there are many rewards, especially knowing the joy and satisfaction of helping animals and relieving their pain.

### Try It!

Read and then rewrite the following paragraph using a variety of sentence lengths.

> Thad is starting an internship as an audio/video technician. Technicians are part of the production crew for television shows. Thad will work on both live and taped television events. He is very excited about learning some new job skills. He will set up sound and video equipment. Thad's math and science skills will help him set up complicated productions. It is Thad's job to regulate and monitor audio levels. He is also responsible for setting up television video signals. Thad would like to work as an audio engineer.

Sentence Style

---

## Sentence Patterns

Review the sentence patterns on SE page 586 with students to help them comprehend language structures and employ increasingly complex grammatical structures in their content area writing.

## Sentence Length

In addition to the activity on SE page 587, have students rewrite one of their own paragraphs specifically looking for opportunities to vary their sentence lengths.

**Try It!** Possible Answer

Thad is starting an internship as an audio/video technician. Technicians are part of the production crew for television shows. Thad will work on both live and taped television events, and he is very excited about learning some new job skills. Thad's math and science skills will help him set up complicated productions using sound and video equipment. It is Thad's job to regulate and monitor audio levels and set up television video signals. Thad would like to work as an audio engineer.

---

**TEKS** 10.13C Revise drafts to improve style; 10.17C Use a variety of correctly structured sentences; **ELPS 4C** Comprehend language structures used in written classroom materials; 5E Employ increasingly complex grammatical structures in content area writing such as using correct verbs, tenses, and pronouns/possessive case/negatives and contractions; 5F Write using a variety of grade-appropriate sentence lengths and patterns in increasingly accurate ways

TEKS 10.17C
ELPS 4C, 5F

## Sentence Variety Using Sentences for Effect

Short and long sentences can be used for special effect in your writing. Short sentences build tension and speed while longer ones add meaning in a paced way.

### Using Short Sentences

- Short sentences grouped together build tension.
  **The TV screen was lying. It couldn't be true. I blinked once, twice. The trail of puffy smoke remained.** *The Challenger,* **its crew, hope—were all gone.**

- Short sentences pick up the pace of the action.
  **The finish line lay just ahead. We ran close enough to smell each other's sweat. Four arms pumped hard. Four feet slapped the ground. We breathed only to win.**

### Using Long Sentences

- A long sentence builds layers of meaning.
  **We hauled out the boxes of food and set up the camp stove, all the time battling the hot wind that would not stop, even when we screamed to the sky.**

- Long sentences slow down the pace and facilitate reflection.
  **Although I have no memory of the ordeals I faced during my first years of life, I shall always bear the orthopedic deformities that I was handed at birth. These deformities have been difficult to accept, but they have provided me with a unique life and greatly influenced the development of my character.**

- A long sentence with a central idea forms a complex thought.
  **"To those peoples in the huts and villages across the globe struggling to break the bonds of mass misery, we pledge our best efforts to help them help themselves, for whatever period is required—not because the Communists may be doing it, not because we seek their votes, but because it is right."**

  —President John F. Kennedy

### Try It!

Carefully read the examples above. Then write a series of short sentences that build tension. Write a long sentence that builds layers of meaning or slows down the pace.

---

"How can we combine the old words in new order so that they survive, so that they create beauty, so that they tell the truth?"

—Winston Weathers

## Writing Loose Sentences

A loose sentence expresses the main idea near the beginning and adds details as needed. In loose sentences, the thoughts seem to be presented as they occur to the writer. When used effectively, this type of sentence can add a special style and rhythm to your writing. In the examples below, the main ideas are underlined. (See page 776.)

### Example Loose Sentences

<u>**Sam was studying at the kitchen table**</u>, memorizing a list of vocabulary words, completely focused, intent on acing tomorrow's Spanish quiz.

<u>**"They are wonderfully built homes**</u>, aluminum skin, double-walled, with insulation, and often paneled with walls of hardwood."

—John Steinbeck, *Travels with Charley*

<u>**"Jeff couldn't see the musician clearly**</u>, just a figure on a chair on the stage, holding what looked like a misshapen guitar."

—Cynthia Voight, *A Solitary Blue*

### Tip

Remember these important points when writing loose sentences.

1. Structure the sentence carefully. If a sentence begins to ramble, the reader will lose track of the main idea.

2. Avoid using too many long, loose sentences. Remember that varying your sentence lengths will keep the reader interested.

### Try It!

Read the examples and the tip above. Then write four loose sentences using these brief sentences as starting points.

1. Nayara gasped.
2. Storm clouds surged through the sky.
3. Ari wrote a free-verse poem.
4. Mr. Groves sauntered away.

*Sentence Style*

---

## Using Sentences for Effect

Discuss the use of long and short sentences in order to help students comprehend language structures and write using a variety of grade-appropriate sentence patterns. Then have students find examples in both fiction and nonfiction of several authors' use of short and long sentences.

**Try It!** **Answers**

Answers will vary.

## Writing Loose Sentences

Discuss the use of loose sentences to help students comprehend language structures and write using a variety of grade-appropriate sentence lengths and patterns.

**Try It!** **Possible Answers**

1. Nayara gasped, sucking in all the air around her, shaking uncontrollably, staring into the bulging eyes of a vampire bat.
2. Storm clouds surged through the sky, folding over the rooftop terraces as people below flicked up their collars, sprinting for an awning.
3. Ari wrote a free-verse poem, scribbling for hours, the paper under his stubby pencil becoming stained with coffee rings and smeared with eraser dust.
4. Mr. Graves sauntered away, perhaps a little smug, and unaware of his customer's reaction.

---

 **TEKS 10.17C** Use a variety of correctly structured sentences; **ELPS 4C** Comprehend language structures used in written classroom materials; **5F** Write using a variety of grade-appropriate sentence lengths and patterns in increasingly accurate ways

TEKS 10.15A(i), 10.17A(i), 10.17C
ELPS 5F

# Sentence Combining
## Using Infinitive and Participial Phrases

Ideas from shorter sentences can be combined into one sentence using an infinitive phrase or a participial phrase.

### Using an Infinitive Phrase

An infinitive phrase is a group of related words introduced by the word *to* plus a verb form—*to conquer* my fears. (See page **768**.)

- **Short Sentences:**
  Annetta searched the Internet. She needed information about the Serengeti Plain.
  I would really like to go to Africa. That's my dream vacation.

- **Combined Sentence:**
  Annetta searched the Internet to find information about the Serengeti Plain.
  To go to Africa is my dream vacation.

### Using a Participial Phrase

A participial phrase is a group of related words introduced by a participle (a verb form ending in *–ing* or *–ed*)—*circling* the date. (See page **768**.)

- **Short Sentences:**
  Kyle walked barefoot in the garden. He stepped on a hornets' nest.
  Shannon covered her ears. She was annoyed by the sound of the air hammer.

- **Combined Sentence:**
  Kyle, walking barefoot in the garden, stepped on a hornets' nest.
  Annoyed by the sound of the air hammer, Shannon covered her ears.

### Try It!

Combine these sentences using an infinitive or a participial phrase.

1. Marcus went to the ballet. He did it to please his mother.
2. The ring was locked in a safety deposit box. It was safe for many years.
3. A cold front swept through Michigan. It sent temperatures plummeting below zero.
4. The tornado swept through a small town. It left a trail of death and destruction.

---

 TEKS 10.17C
ELPS 4C, 5F

# Creating Complex Sentences

Ideas from shorter sentences can also be combined into a complex sentence. A complex sentence is made up of two clauses that are not equal in importance. The more important idea should be included in the *independent clause*, which can stand alone as a single sentence. The less important idea should be included in the *dependent clause*, which cannot stand alone. (See pages **770** and **774**.)

The two clauses in a complex sentence can be connected with a subordinate conjunction (*after, although, because, before, even though, until, when,* and so on) or a relative pronoun (*who, whose, which,* or *that*).

- Even though LeBron sprained his ankle, **he sunk the winning free throw.**
  [dependent clause, independent clause]

- **It isn't funny** when a practical joke continues until someone's feelings are hurt. [independent clause, two dependent clauses]

### Using a Complex Sentence

- **Two Short Sentences:**
  Mt. McKinley rises 20,320 feet above sea level.
  It is the highest peak in the United States.

- **Combined Sentence:**
  Mt. McKinley, which rises 20,320 feet above sea level, is the highest peak in the United States.

### Try It!

Read the sentences below. Combine each set of short sentences into a complex sentence using the subordinating conjunction or relative pronoun in parentheses.

1. Mrs. Lopez returned to work.
   School lunch tasted good again. (because)
2. We found a village called "Pity Me."
   The village is located in County Durham. (which)
3. I want my sister to proofread my report.
   I will give it to Ms. Belmont. (before)
4. My aunt loves to travel.
   She is planning a trip to France. (who)
5. We had to leave the golf course.
   The storm finally started. (when)

Sentence Style

---

## Using Infinitive and Participial Phrases

Discuss the use of infinitive and participial phrases in order to help students write with a variety of grade-appropriate sentence lengths and patterns.

**Try It!** **Possible Answers**

1. Marcus went to the ballet to please his mother.
2. The ring was locked in a safety deposit box to keep it safe for many years.
3. A cold front, sweeping through Michigan, sent temperatures plummeting below zero.
4. The tornado swept through a small town, leaving a trail of death and destruction.

## Creating Complex Sentences

Discuss how to create complex sentences in order to help students comprehend language structures and write using a variety of grade-appropriate sentence lengths.

**Try It!** **Possible Answers**

1. Because Mrs. Lopez returned to work, school lunch tasted good again.
2. We found a village called "Pity Me," which is located in County Durham.
3. I want my sister to proofread my report before I give it to Ms. Belmont.
4. My aunt, who loves to travel, is planning a trip to France.
5. When the storm finally started, we had to leave the golf course.

---

 **TEKS** **10.15A(i)** Write an analytical essay that includes a variety of sentence structures; **10.17(i)** Use and understand verbals (infinitives and participles); **10.17C** Use a variety of correctly structured sentences; **ELPS** **4C** Comprehend language structures used in written classroom materials; **5F** Write using a variety of grade-appropriate sentence lengths and patterns in increasingly accurate ways

**TEKS** 10.17C, 10.18B(i)
ELPS 5F

## Sentence Problems Avoiding Sentence Errors

Avoid sentence problems as you write—or correct them when you revise.

### Correcting Run-On Sentences

Run-on sentences occur when two sentences are joined without punctuation or without a connecting word (and, but, or, so).

- **Run-on Sentence:** Lightweight cookware soon came on the market the idea of casserole cooking became popular.
- **Corrected as Two Sentences:** Lightweight cookware soon came on the market. The idea of casserole cooking became popular.
- **Corrected as a Compound Sentence:** Lightweight cookware soon came on the market, so the idea of casserole cooking became popular.

### Eliminating Comma Splices

Comma splices occur when two independent clauses are connected with a comma and no conjunction.

- **Comma Splice:** Casseroles took little preparation time, women's magazines began promoting easy-to-prepare meals.
- **Corrected as Two Sentences:** Casseroles took little preparation time. Women's magazines began promoting easy-to-prepare meals.
- **Corrected as a Compound Sentence:** Casseroles took little preparation time, and women's magazines began promoting easy-to-prepare meals.

### Try It!

On your own paper, rewrite the following paragraph, correcting the run-ons and comma splices.

(1) The word "soup" comes from the Old English word "sopp" it means a slice of bread over which roast drippings are poured. (2) Soup was eaten even in ancient times the first evidence of it dates back to around 6000 B.C.E. (3) The main ingredient of "ancient" soup may surprise you it was hippopotamus bones. (4) Soup is easily digested, so it is often prescribed as a nutritious meal for sick people. (5) Many families eat a lot of soup, most often it comes in cans and boxes and can be quickly heated.

### Fixing Fragments

A fragment is not a sentence because it does not form a complete thought. In a sentence fragment, a subject, a predicate, or both are missing.

**Fragment:** Was introduced in 4 B.C.E. (The subject is missing.)
The mathematical decimal system was introduced in 4 B.C.E.

**Fragment:** Roman emperors many lighthouses. (A predicate is missing.)
Roman emperors built many lighthouses.

**Fragment:** Including schools. (A subject and predicate are missing.)
All public institutions, including schools, were closed.

### Try It!

Rewrite each fragment as a complete sentence.

1. Under the Golden Gate Bridge.
2. About 200 feet deep.
3. Served in Iraq.
4. Steven Spielberg.
5. Is celebrated on November 11th.
6. John Philip Sousa his own band.

### Rewriting Rambling Sentences

Rambling sentences seem to go on and on. Their parts are connected by coordinating conjunctions. While not grammatically incorrect, these sentences can be hard to read. As a rule, if a sentence links more than two complete ideas with and, but, or so, try to divide it into shorter sentences.

**Rambling:** I saw my band director, Mr. Sandoval, at the jazz concert, and I called to him but he didn't hear me and then he disappeared into the crowd.

**Better:** I saw my band director, Mr. Sandoval, at the jazz concert. I called to him, but he didn't hear me. Then he disappeared into the crowd.

### Try It!

Rewrite this rambling sentence by eliminating one or more of the connecting words. Punctuate the new sentences correctly.

I wanted to be on the prom committee so I went to the first meeting and I knew I was on time and in the right place and I waited around for almost an hour but nobody showed up.

---

## Avoiding Sentence Errors

Discuss ways to correct run-on sentences and comma splices. Focus on various approaches to correcting sentence problems, including the use of connecting words to eliminate problems.

### Try It! Possible Answer

The word "soup" comes from the Old English word "sopp," which means a slice of bread over which roast drippings are poured. Soup was eaten even in ancient times. The first evidence of it dates back to 6000 B.C.E. The main ingredient may surprise you. It was hippopotamus bones. Soup is easily digested, so it is often prescribed as a nutritious meal for sick people. Many families eat a lot of soup. Most often it comes in cans and boxes, and it can be quickly heated.

### Try It! Possible Answers

1. Marlin likes to take pictures of ships passing under the Golden Gate Bridge.
2. The old shipwreck was found in water that was about 200 feet deep.
3. The Second Marine Division served in Iraq.
4. Steven Spielberg created many excellent science-fiction films.
5. Veterans Day is celebrated on November 11th.
6. John Philip Sousa directed his own band.

### Try It! Possible Answer

I wanted to be on the prom committee, so I went to the first meeting. I knew I was on time and in the right place. I waited around for almost an hour, but nobody showed up.

---

**TEKS** **10.17C** Use a variety of correctly structured sentences; **10.18B(i)** Use commas in nonrestrictive phrases and contrasting expressions and in clauses; **ELPS** **5F** Write using a variety of grade-appropriate connecting words in increasingly accurate ways

ELPS 5E

## Correcting Double Subjects

Be careful not to use a pronoun immediately after the subject. The result is usually a double subject.

**Double Subject:** The Presidential election it is this Tuesday.

**Corrected:** The Presidential election is this Tuesday.

**Double Subject:** Barry he plays college football.

**Corrected:** Barry plays college football.

## Correcting Double Negatives

Avoid sentences that contain double negatives. Double negatives occur when two negative words are used together in the same sentence (*not never, barely nothing, not no,* and so on). Double negatives also occur if you use contractions ending in *n't* with a negative word (*didn't never, can't not*).

### Negative Words

| nothing | nowhere | neither | never | not | barely | hardly | nobody | none |

**Double Negative:** I could not go nowhere.

**Corrected Sentence:** I could not go anywhere.

### Negative Contractions

| don't | can't | won't | shouldn't | wouldn't | couldn't | didn't | hadn't |

**Double Negative:** He didn't hear nothing unusual.

**Corrected Sentence:** He didn't hear anything unusual.

### Try It!

Rewrite each sentence below, correcting the double-subject or double-negative errors.

1. King Richard he was known as "Richard the Lionhearted."
2. I didn't do nothing about the mistake on my application.
3. Why don't you never listen to hip-hop?
4. I hadn't never heard of The Hanging Gardens of Babylon. The gardens they are one of the Seven Wonders of the Ancient World.
5. We can't go nowhere without Steve's brother coming along.
6. Oscar and I we went to the rock concert on Friday night.

---

ELPS 5E

## Sentence Agreement
### Making Subjects and Verbs Agree

A verb must agree in number (singular or plural) with its subject. The basic rules for subject-verb agreement are listed below.

■ A **singular subject** needs a singular verb, and a plural subject needs a plural verb.

**Singular Subject and Verb:** Los Angeles is the second-most populated city in the United States.

**Plural Subject and Verb:** Most Los Angeles beaches provide plenty of sun.

■ A **compound subject connected by the word *and*** usually needs a plural verb.

**Compound Subject and Verb:** Ty and Janelle are going to Europe.

■ A **compound subject connected by the word *or*** needs a verb that agrees in number with the subject nearest to the verb.

**Compound Subject and Verb:** Either the pool managers or a Red Cross volunteer teaches the lifeguard class.

■ An **indefinite pronoun** can be singular or plural when used as a subject. (See **780.2**.)

**Singular Subject and Verb:** Almost everyone in school likes the new coach.

**Plural Subject and Verb:** Many of the parents appreciate his approach.

### Try It!

Number your paper from 1 to 5. Write the correct verb choice for each of these sentences.

1. Some sodas or a juice container (*remains, remain*) in the refrigerator.
2. Kindra and Lawson (*is, are*) my friends from Mahone High School.
3. Vegetarians (*has, have*) some great recipe ideas.
4. Two coffee shops on our block (*sells, sell*) fair-trade coffee.
5. Each of the tourists (*has, have*) moved to another hotel.

Draft

**Write a sentence using each of the subjects below. Remember to use verbs that agree in number with the subjects.**

1. drivers
2. musician
3. Washington and Lincoln
4. the principal or counselors
5. everyone
6. all

Sentence Style

---

## Avoiding Sentence Errors

Discuss how to correct double subjects and double negatives so students will be able to write with increasingly complex grammatical structures.

### Try It! Possible Answers

1. King Richard was known as "Richard the Lionhearted."
2. I did nothing about the mistake on my application.
3. Why don't you ever listen to hip-hop?
4. I had never heard of The Hanging Gardens of Babylon. The gardens are one of the Seven Wonders of the Ancient World.
5. We can't go anywhere without Steve's brother coming along.
6. Oscar and I went to the rock concert on Friday night.

### Try It! Answers

1. remains
2. are
3. have
4. sell
5. has

Draft

### Answers

Answers will vary, but should include verbs that agree in number, as indicated here.

1. plural verb
2. singular verb
3. plural verb
4. plural verb
5. singular verb
6. singular or plural verb, depending on the number of the object of the preposition

---

**ELPS 5E** Employ increasingly complex grammatical structures in content area writing such as using correct verbs, tenses, and pronouns/possessive case/negatives and contractions

**TEKS** 10.17C
ELPS 5E, 5F

## Sentence Modeling Writing Stylish Sentences

Many painters learn to paint by copying famous works of art. Student writers, too, can learn to write better by modeling sentence patterns used by professional writers.

**Model:** Eventually, all things merge into one, and a river runs through it.

—Norman Maclean, *A River Runs Through It*

**New Sentence:** Slowly, new players develop into a unit, and a team forms among them.

### Try It!

Choose three of the sentences below and write your own sentences, modeling the sentence structure as closely as possible.

**1.** I neither marched up to the stage like a conquering Amazon, nor did I look in the audience for Bailey's nod of approval.

—Maya Angelou, *I Know Why the Caged Bird Sings*

**2.** A leftover smile of moon hides in the bottom branches of the sugar maple, teasing her to smile back.

—Barbara Kingsolver, *Pigs in Heaven*

**3.** Then from behind the black and wavy line of the forests a column of golden light shot up into the heavens and spread over the semicircle of the eastern horizon.

—Joseph Conrad, "The Lagoon"

**4.** I awoke that morning from a bizarre dream in which I had climbed down the stairs in our house, lifted the piano high above my head, then dropped it onto my right big toe.

—Joel Ben Izzy, *The Beggar King and the Secret of Happiness*

**5.** If General Jackson hadn't run the Creeks up the creek, Simon Finch would never have paddled up the Alabama, and where would we be if he hadn't?

—Harper Lee, *To Kill a Mockingbird*

**6.** I came, I saw, I conquered, as the first baby in the family always does.

—Helen Keller, *The Story of My Life*

597

# Writing Strong Paragraphs

In the real world of literature, the paragraph is not considered a form of writing. You wouldn't, for example, head to the local bookstore to buy a book of paragraphs. Nor would you pursue a writing career because you wanted to write award-winning paragraphs.

But paragraphs are very important as building blocks for other kinds of writing. When you write an essay, for instance, you develop paragraphs to organize your thoughts into manageable units. The paragraphs work together to build a clear, convincing argument or explanation. Learning how to write effective paragraphs will give you control of all your academic writing—from essays to articles to research papers.

- **The Parts of a Paragraph**
- **Types of Paragraphs**
- **Writing Guidelines**
- **Types of Details**
- **Patterns of Organization**
- **Modeling Paragraphs**
- **Connecting Paragraphs in Essays**
- **Paragraph Traits Checklist**

"Excellence is doing ordinary things extraordinarily well."

—John W. Gardner

---

### Try It! **Possible Answers**

1. I neither danced across the stage like a giddy maniac, nor did I trip on the bleachers and fall flat on my face.
2. A wisp of smoke rises from the large pile of leaves on the driveway, suggesting an ember deep within.
3. From behind the faraway shape of the barn the startling sound of the tractor's engine grew to a deep rumble and swept across the fields.
4. I surfaced from an eventful dive during which I'd become tangled in seaweed, broken free, and then found myself face to face with a hammerhead shark.
5. If the fireman hadn't found the short circuit, the landlord would not have known to repair it, and then what would have happened to us?
6. I walked, I jogged, I ran, as I got closer to shelter from the storm.

### **Writing Strong Paragraphs**

Discuss the section introduction on SE page 597 with students, including the importance of learning to write effective paragraphs. Invite volunteers to talk about how the quotation at the bottom of the page relates to writing strong paragraphs.

---

 **TEKS** **10.17C** Use a variety of correctly structured sentences; **ELPS 5E** Employ increasingly complex grammatical structures in content area writing such as using correct verbs, tenses, and pronouns/possessive case/negatives and contractions; **5F** Write using a variety of grade-appropriate sentence patterns in increasingly accurate ways

ELPS 4G, 4I

# The Parts of a Paragraph

A typical paragraph consists of three main parts: a **topic sentence**, the **body sentences**, and a **closing sentence**. A paragraph can develop an explanation, an opinion, a description, or a narrative. Whatever form a paragraph takes, it must contain enough information to give the reader a complete picture of the topic. The following expository paragraph provides information about a remarkable ancient sculpture. As you read, notice how each detail in the body supports the topic sentence.

**Topic Sentence**

**Body**

**Closing Sentence**

### Power and Glory

The huge, leonine sculpture known as the Great Sphinx prompts feelings of awe and curiosity from visitors to Giza, Egypt. At 200 feet long and 65 feet high, the statue, depicting a lion's body with the head of a man, is the world's earliest known sculpture. The man was probably the pharaoh Kahfre, who also built the nearby pyramids around 2500 B.C.E. No records or building plans of the Great Sphinx have been found, and scientists are not sure what tools would have been used to create such a huge sculpture. Because the body consists of soft limestone, wind and sand have caused terrible erosion. Several attempts have been made to save it, including restoration work done by ancient Egyptians and, later, by Roman invaders. The 13-foot-wide head was sculpted from a harder rock, so it is in better shape, although it is missing its nose. Scientists also believe the head may have included a plume and a curled beard. Because of the blowing desert sand, the body of the Sphinx has been covered and dug out several times over the centuries, with the latest excavation occurring in 1905. The world seems to agree that this statue is just too magnificent and mysterious to hide beneath shifting sands.

 **Respond to the reading.** What main idea about the topic does this paragraph communicate? What specific details are included to support this idea? Name two or three of them.

## A Closer Look at the Parts

Whether a paragraph stands alone or is part of an extended piece of writing, it contains three elements.

### The Topic Sentence

A **topic sentence** tells the reader what your paragraph is about. The topic sentence should do two things: (1) name the specific topic of the paragraph and (2) identify a particular feeling or feature about the topic. Here is a simple formula for writing a topic sentence.

> a specific topic
> + a particular feeling or feature about the topic
> = an effective topic sentence
>
> The huge, leonine sculpture known as the Great Sphinx
> + prompts feelings of awe and curiosity from visitors
> = **The huge, leonine sculpture known as the Great Sphinx prompts feelings of awe and curiosity from visitors to Giza, Egypt.**

**Tip**

The topic sentence is *usually* the first sentence in a paragraph. However, it can also be located elsewhere. For example, you can present details that build up to an important summary topic sentence at the end of a paragraph.

### The Body

The sentences in the **body** of the paragraph should all support the topic sentence. Each sentence should add new details about the topic.

- Use specific details to make your paragraph interesting.
  **At 200 feet long and 65 feet high, the statue, depicting a lion's body with the head of a man, is the world's earliest known sculpture.**

- Organize your sentences in the best possible order: time order, order of importance, classification, and so on. (See pages **607–610**.)

### The Closing Sentence

The **closing sentence** comes after all the body details have been presented. This sentence can remind the reader of the topic, summarize the paragraph, or link the paragraph to the next one.

**The world seems to agree that this sculpture is just too magnificent and mysterious to hide beneath shifting sands.**

Paragraphs

---

## The Parts of a Paragraph

Review basic reading skills and have students apply these skills to the example reading on SE page 598. After students read the first paragraph, ask them questions that reveal students' comprehension of what they have read.

 **Possible Answer**

### Respond to the reading.

The main idea is that the Great Sphinx causes feelings of awe and curiosity. The body is 200 feet long, and the head is 13 feet wide. The Sphinx has been dug out of the sand a number of times over the centuries.

 **ELPS 4G** Demonstrate comprehension of increasingly complex English/responding to questions; **4I** Demonstrate comprehension by employing and expanding basic reading skills/ understanding of supporting ideas and details, summarizing text, and distinguishing main ideas from details

TEKS 10.13B
ELPS 4G, 4I, 4J, 5G

## Types of Paragraphs

There are four basic types of paragraphs: *narrative, descriptive, expository,* and *persuasive*.

### Narrative Paragraph

A **narrative paragraph** tells a story. It may draw from the writer's personal experience or from other sources of information. A narrative paragraph is almost always organized chronologically, or according to time.

**Topic Sentence**

**Body**

**Closing Sentence**

#### My First Driving Lesson

I began my first driving lesson thinking I would hit a home run my first time in the car. I got into the car and immediately turned the key. The instructor made a mark on his clipboard because in my excitement, I hadn't buckled my seat belt. After buckling up, I put the car into gear, which led to another mark. I hadn't checked my mirrors or looked to see if someone else was coming. After looking around, I stepped on the gas, and we sort of lunged to the practice area marked by orange highway cones. As I started through the practice course, I jerked the wheel to avoid one cone and knocked down two others. Then, in my panic, I hit the gas pedal instead of the brake! Two more cones went down before my instructor slammed on his master brake pedal. Unfortunately, the rest of my lesson didn't go any smoother. My instructor's pencil scratched noisily as he wrote on the clipboard. I figured I would never get my license. But when we finally stopped, he just handed me a copy of the checklist and said we would work on all my mistakes. I was relieved to know that they didn't expect perfection right away. Suddenly, I couldn't wait for my second lesson.

 **Respond to the reading.** What transitional words or phrases does the writer use to indicate the passage of time? Find three. What tone does the writer use—serious, entertaining, or surprising? Explain.

 **Write a narrative paragraph.** Share your first driving experience or some other "first" experience. (Follow the guidelines on page 604.)

---

### Descriptive Paragraph

A **descriptive paragraph** provides a detailed picture of a person, a place, an object, or an event. This type of paragraph should contain a variety of sensory details—specific sights, sounds, smells, tastes, and textures.

**Topic Sentence**

**Body**

**Closing Sentence**

#### The Northside Youth Center

The Northside Youth Center is the perfect place to spend time after school and on weekends. When entering the multipurpose room, one's eyes are immediately drawn to the bank of six computers along the left wall. There, students play games or do homework on the softly humming machines, while nearby a teacher/supervisor sits at a desk, ready to help. Beneath the tall, narrow windows on the back wall is the art area, with glow-in-the-dark metal cabinets that contain art supplies. To the right of the cabinets are several vending machines, their flashy windows offering fruit, sandwiches, and juice. A table with a microwave oven sits next to the machines, and the inviting scent of a warming sandwich or popping popcorn often fills the air. A large door on the wall to the right is open, and echoing shouts mixed with a chorus of bouncing basketballs spill in from the gym. Games of a quieter nature are played at tables stacked with colorful board games along this wall. Next to the tables, an area dominated by a bookshelf sprawling behind comfortable chairs spreads out into the middle of the room. This is a favorite spot. Students usually occupy these chairs, reading, studying, or talking with a friend. The Northside Youth Center provides many positive opportunities for students, all in a safe, inviting environment.

Paragraphs

 **Respond to the reading.** What senses are covered in this paragraph? Which two or three details seem especially descriptive?

 **Write a descriptive paragraph.** Write a paragraph that describes a place that is important to you. Use sensory details in your description and structure your ideas in a sustained way. (Follow the guidelines on page 604.)

---

## Narrative Paragraph

Work through the activities on SE page 600 to help students demonstrate comprehension, employ reading skills, employ inferential skills, and narrate with specificity.

 ### Answers

**Respond to the reading.**

Answers will vary. Words indicating time passage are *after, as, then,* and *when*. The tone is entertaining. The writer tells about all the mistakes he made while taking his first driving lesson, but he does so in a way that is meant to be encouraging.

**Write a narrative paragraph.**

Answers will vary.

## Descriptive Paragraph

Discuss descriptive paragraphs and work through the activities on SE page 601 with students to help them demonstrate comprehension, employ and expand basic reading skills, and describe with specificity.

 ### Answers

**Respond to the reading.**

Answers will vary.

Senses: sight, sound

Details: softly humming, glow-in-the-dark, flashy windows, echoing shouts, sprawling

**Write a descriptive paragraph.**

Answers will vary.

---

 **TEKS** 10.13B Structure ideas in a sustained way; **ELPS** 4G Demonstrate comprehension of increasingly complex English/responding to questions; 4I Demonstrate comprehension by employing and expanding basic reading skills/understanding of supporting ideas and details, summarizing text, and distinguishing main ideas from details; 4J Demonstrate comprehension and expand reading skills by employing inferential skills; 5G Narrate and describe with increasing specificity and detail/writing

TEKS 10.13B
ELPS 4G, 4I, 5G

## Expository Paragraph

An **expository paragraph** shares information about a specific topic. Expository writing presents facts, gives directions, defines terms, explains a process, and so forth. It should clearly inform the reader.

**Topic Sentence**

**Body**

**Closing Sentence**

### Step, Toe, Heel

There are many types of dance shoes, but three of the most popular types are specially designed for ballet, jazz, and tap. Ballet shoes are soft, leather-soled slippers that have an adjustable tie to help them fit the foot. They often have ribbons sewn on to wrap around the leg for an elegant look. Some ballet slippers are designed especially for *pointe,* which is dancing on the tips of the toes. These have a more structured toe box that is heavily padded at the base to prevent damage to the toes. Jazz shoes, which lace on and look like street shoes, are generally made of leather with a rubber sole and heel. The sole might be whole or split to offer more flexibility. Jazz shoes may be boot height to give the dancer firmer ankle support. Tap shoes also vary in style and construction, but they usually include a layer of fiberboard glued and stapled to the leather sole. The extra layer provides a hard surface for the screws holding the metal taps. Men's tap shoes can be almost any style, while those for women generally have a stacked heel and a strap. A rubber pad is sometimes attached to the bottom of the sole to prevent slipping. Whether a dancer chooses to leap, glide, or tap, there is a shoe that will help get the "pointe" across.

 **Respond to the reading.** What is the specific topic of this paragraph? What supporting facts or examples does the writer include? Name at least three of them.

 **Write an expository paragraph.** Write a paragraph that shares information about a specific topic. Be sure to include plenty of supporting details and structure your ideas in a sustained way. (Follow the guidelines on page 604.)

---

TEKS 10.13B
ELPS 4G, 4I

Writing Strong Paragraphs

Paragraphs

## Persuasive Paragraph

A **persuasive paragraph** expresses an opinion and tries to convince the reader that the opinion is valid. To be persuasive, a writer must include effective supporting reasons and facts.

**Topic Sentence**

**Body**

**Closing Sentence**

### Helping One Child Helps the World

The Midtown High School Spanish Club should sponsor a needy child in a Spanish-speaking country, working through the Save the Children Foundation. Such sponsorship would be extremely beneficial to all. Club members would be encouraged to communicate with the child. Sending and receiving letters in Spanish would enhance our Spanish reading and writing skills. In addition, we could ask questions and receive information about the child's city and country, further expanding our understanding of another culture. Finally, we would be doing something important. Offering humanitarian aid is one of the most selfless and beneficial things a person can do, and sponsoring a child could even prove to be life saving. Our sponsorship would help assure the child's nutritional and educational needs are met, giving that child a better life. Some members have said that our club could not afford to sponsor a child, but the cost of $18 a month could easily be covered for an entire year by our club's treasury. We could also do additional fund-raising to send extra materials and supplies to our adopted child. This shared sense of purpose would draw club members closer together, creating a family feeling. The Spanish Club sponsoring a needy child would benefit everyone and should begin as soon as possible.

 **Respond to the reading.** What is the writer's opinion in the paragraph? What reasons does the writer include to support the opinion? Name two.

 **Write a persuasive paragraph.** Write a paragraph expressing your opinion about an event or an activity. Include at least two or three strong reasons that support your opinion. Be sure to structure your ideas in a sustained, persuasive way. (Follow the guidelines on page 604.)

---

## Expository Paragraph

Discuss expository paragraphs and work through the activities on SE page 602 with students to help them demonstrate comprehension, employ and expand basic reading skills, and explain with specificity in their writing.

### Answers

**Respond to the reading.**

Answers will vary.

Specific topic: types of dance shoes

Examples: ballet shoes, jazz shoes, tap shoes

**Write an expository paragraph.**

Answers will vary.

## Persuasive Paragraph

Work through the activities on SE page 603 with students to help them demonstrate comprehension.

### Answers

**Respond to the reading.**

Answers will vary.

Opinion: Sponsoring a child in a Spanish-speaking country would benefit all involved.

Reasons: Club members can improve their Spanish, learn more about another culture, and benefit from doing humanitarian work.

**Write a persuasive paragraph.**

Answers will vary.

---

 **TEKS** 10.13B Structure ideas in a sustained way; **ELPS** 4G Demonstrate comprehension of increasingly complex English/responding to questions; 4I Demonstrate comprehension by employing and expanding basic reading skills/understanding of supporting ideas and details, summarizing text, and distinguishing main ideas from details; 5G Explain with increasing specificity and detail/writing

**604-605** Basic Grammar and Writing

604

 10.13A–10.13D, 10.17C, 10.18B(i)–10.18B(iii), 10.19
ELPS 5C

 10.13B, 10.15A(ii)
ELPS 4C

Writing Strong Paragraphs **605**

# Writing Guidelines Developing a Paragraph

Before you begin your writing, make sure you understand the requirements of the assignment. Then follow the steps listed below.

## Prewriting Planning Your Writing

- Select a specific topic that meets the assigned requirements.
- Collect facts, examples, and other details about your topic.
- Write a topic sentence stating what your paragraph will be about. (See page 599.)
- Decide on the best way to organize the supporting details. (See pages 607–610.)

## Drafting Developing Your Ideas

- Start your paragraph with the topic sentence.
- Follow with sentences that support your topic. Use your details and organizational plan as a general guide.
- Connect your ideas and sentences with transitions.
- Close with a sentence that restates your topic, gives a final thought, or, in the case of an essay, leads into the next paragraph.

## Revising Improving Your Writing

- Add information if you need to say more about your topic or better convey your subtlety of meaning.
- Move sentences that aren't in the best order.
- Delete sentences that don't support the topic.
- Rewrite any sentences that are unclear.

## Editing Checking for Conventions

- Check the revised draft for grammar, sentence structure, capitalization, punctuation, and spelling. Correct all errors.
- Write a neat final copy and proofread it one last time.

### Tip

When you write a paragraph, remember that the reader wants to . . .

- learn something new and interesting and hear the writer's voice. (*Let your personality come through in the writing.*)

# Types of Details

There are many types of details you can include in paragraphs (and in longer forms of writing). The purpose of your writing determines which details you should use. The key types are explained below and on the following page.

**Facts** are *details that can be proven.*

> The Great Chicago Fire began on October 8, 1871.
> Eating blueberries helps lower cholesterol and prevent infections.

**Statistics** present *numerical information* (numbers) about a specific topic.

> In 2010, more than 400 people in the United States were hit by lightning, and on average, lightning strikes result in approximately 50 deaths per year in our country. (National Safety Council; CNN.com)

**Examples** are *statements that illustrate a main point.*

> A pancake may not always be called a pancake (*main point*). In Wales, pancakes are called Welshcakes and might be served flat or split and spread with jam. France has its crepes, and Italy, its cannelloni. In the Middle East, you'll find sweet wedding pancakes called ataif. In Russia or Poland, you can enjoy delicious blini, but if you're hungry in Hungary, ask for palacsinta.

**Anecdotes** are *brief stories* that help to make a point about a topic. They can be much more effective than a matter-of-fact list of details.

> Members of the media might try to influence us, but they often find that they should not underestimate the American voter. Perhaps the best example of this occurred during the presidential election of 1948. Harry Truman was running for re-election against Thomas Dewey, the popular governor of New York. All the polls and commentators had predicted a landslide victory for Dewey, and even Truman's wife, Bess, felt her husband could not win.
>
> Truman refused to give up, and set off on a "whistle stop" campaign, traveling the country to talk to the people face-to-face. The night of the election, Truman went to bed early, convinced he would lose. Dewey's victory seemed such a sure thing, the *Chicago Tribune* even printed the next day's headline early: "Dewey Defeats Truman." But in the morning, the results showed that Truman had won. The American people had ignored the polls and had made the decision for themselves.

## Developing a Paragraph

Review and discuss the steps in the writing process, highlighting key points in each, such as the need for students to spell familiar words accurately.

## Types of Details

Discuss and define the types of details given on SE page 606, and check that students comprehend the meaning of each term.

**TEKS** **10.13A** Plan a first draft by determining topics through a range of strategies; **10.13B** Structure ideas in a sustained way/develop drafts in open-ended situations that include transitions and rhetorical devices; **10.13C** Revise drafts to improve the subtlety of meaning; **10.13D** Edit drafts for grammar, mechanics, and spelling; **10.15A(ii)** Write an analytical essay that includes rhetorical devices; **10.17C** Use a variety of correctly structured sentences; **10.18B(i)** Use commas in nonrestrictive phrases and contrasting expressions and in clauses; **10.18B(ii)** Use quotation marks to indicate sarcasm and irony; **10.18B(iii)** Use dashes to emphasize parenthetical information; **10.19** Spell correctly using resources to determine and check correct spelling; **ELPS 4C** Comprehend vocabulary used in written classroom materials; **5C** Spell familiar words with increasing accuracy

ELPS 4C

**Quotations** are *people's statements* repeated word for word. Quotations can provide powerful supporting evidence.

> Hunger is a great motivator for change, as witnessed by the French Revolution and by the rise of Nazi Germany. Both governmental changes were precipitated by the poverty of the common people, who resorted to violence to improve their lives. As O. Henry wrote, "Love and business and family and religion and art and patriotism are nothing but shadows of words when a man's starving." People who are fed and comfortable will accept the status quo, while those who are in need often demand violent change.

**Definitions** give the *meaning* of unfamiliar terms. Definitions of technical terms are especially important for the reader. Defining such terms makes your writing clear.

> Chiaroscuro—the play of light and shade—to create mood was used effectively in films by Orson Welles and Alfred Hitchcock.

**Reasons** answer *why* and can explain or justify ideas.

> Carpeting the school would be an excellent idea. A good indoor-outdoor carpet would muffle noise in hallways and classes, creating an atmosphere conducive to learning. Carpeting creates a more formal feel, subtly encouraging better behavior and reducing litter. Carpeting is also easier to repair than hard flooring, as a damaged or stained area can simply be cut out and a new patch set in.

**Comparisons** address the *similarities* or *differences* between two things. It is especially helpful to compare something new or unknown to something your reader understands.

> Regular broadcast television and satellite television both depend on radio waves to deliver the signal to your TV. Broadcast television is limited because the waves transmitted follow a straight path, eventually heading into space. Satellite TV, however, uses a fixed-location space satellite to catch the waves and bounce them back, allowing for a greater number of signals and, consequently, a larger choice of TV stations.

### Try It!

Find examples in this book's writing samples of any four types of details listed on the previous two pages. On your own paper, write the examples and the pages where you found them.

---

TEKS 10.13B, 10.15B(i)

## Patterns of Organization

On the following four pages, sample paragraphs show basic patterns of organization. Reviewing these samples can help you organize your own writing.

### Chronological Order

**Chronological** (time) **order** is effective for explaining a process or sharing a story. The paragraph below, from a procedural document written for customers, explains how to change the oil and the oil filter in a car.

**Graphic Organizer: Time Line**

| | | Changing the Oil Time Line | | | |
|---|---|---|---|---|---|
| prepare car: raise and brake | place large container under oil pan | drain old oil | replace old filter | refill with new oil to the proper level | dispose of old oil |

Paragraphs

**Topic Sentence**

**Body**

**Closing Sentence**

> **Change Is Good**
>
> Changing the oil and oil filter in a car is easy. First, put several newspapers under the engine to catch any oil accidentally spilled while the oil is drained. Then place a large container under the oil pan to catch the old oil. Lie on some newspaper and use a wrench to loosen the plug. Wear rubber gloves and use your fingers to gently unscrew the plug and pull it quickly away, allowing the old oil to pour into the container beneath. When all the oil has drained, replace the plug, tightening it with the wrench. Next, loosen the old oil filter with a filter wrench. Finish removing the filter by hand and empty the contents into the used-oil container. Spread a small amount of oil around the new filter's gasket to create a good seal and hand-turn the new filter into place. Finally, remove the engine's oil cap and pour in the new oil to the proper level. Be sure to properly dispose of the old oil at a recycling center. With a little care and regular oil changes, an engine will continue to run smoothly for a long time.

---

## Types of Details

Discuss and define the types of details given on SE page 606, and check that students comprehend the meaning of each term.

### Try It! Answers

Answers will vary.

## Chronological Order

Discuss the chronological order pattern of organization and how it can be used to structure ideas and write procedural and work-related documents.

---

 **TEKS** **10.13B** Structure ideas in a sustained way; **10.15B(i)** Write procedural and work-related documents that include organized information; **ELPS** **4C** Comprehend vocabulary used in written classroom materials

TEKS 10.13B
ELPS 3E, 3H

## Cause and Effect

**Cause-effect** paragraphs can take on a variety of forms: one cause with many effects (as in the sample below), many causes that create one final effect, and other variations. When writing about cause-and-effect relationships, you can use an organizer like the one below to arrange details.

Cause-Effect Organizer

**Topic Sentence**

**Body**

**Closing Sentence**

### The Dust of the Earth

House dust, if considered at all, is usually dismissed as an unavoidable inconvenience; but for allergy sufferers, it can mean total misery. The allergic reaction to dust can include chronic year-round rhinitis, or runny nose. Other symptoms may include sneezing and a stuffy nose. The sufferer may have itchy, teary eyes, or even develop a rash or hives. Dust allergies can mimic major health problems such as asthma or emphysema, with wheezing or shortness of breath, accompanied by coughing. People who already have these diseases could find their conditions aggravated by dust. Many people who suffer from dust allergies may face significant expenses because they must dust-proof their homes with special air filters and substitute existing building materials with nonallergenic ones. A little dust doesn't seem so bad, but in extreme cases, it can lead to major health issues and heavy financial costs.

**Try It!**

Work with a classmate and re-read the paragraph above. Take turns explaining and describing to each other the effects of house dust on people who suffer from allergies. Use specific details in your description.

---

TEKS 10.13B
ELPS 4G, 4I

## Classification

**Classification** is a technique used to break down a topic into categories. The following paragraph classifies the different types of pyramids. The writer used a line diagram to plan her writing.

Line Diagram

**Topic Sentence**

**Body**

**Closing Sentence**

### Types of Pyramids

Three distinct styles of pyramids were created in ancient Egypt: the step pyramid, the bent pyramid, and the more commonly recognized straight-sided pyramid. The step pyramid actually evolved from the earliest burial chambers, the *mastabas,* which were low, flat structures built of mud brick. Around 2780 B.C.E., the architect Imhotep stacked six successively smaller mastabas, creating the first step pyramid as a burial chamber for King Djoser. This pyramid can be seen near Saqqara, south of Cairo. The next attempt at a pyramid came in Dashur, also south of Cairo, during the reign of Pharaoh Snefru. The limestone-faced sides were straight, but they changed angle and cut sharply inward about halfway up, creating a bent, squashed-looking top. Not satisfied with this design, Snefru ordered another pyramid to be built, this time with straight sides that met at a tip. The result was the first straight-sided pyramid, called the red pyramid because the sun gave it a reddish tint. Snefru's son, Khufru, also known as Cheops, perfected the pyramid, creating the magnificent Great Pyramid of Giza, today known as one of the Seven Wonders of the Ancient World. Whether step, bent, or straight-sided, the pyramids of Egypt are magnificent reminders of a great ancient nation.

 **Respond to the reading.** What facts or details did you learn about the straight-sided pyramid? Name three.

---

## Cause and Effect

As a class, discuss the organizer and its usefulness, giving students the opportunity to share ideas cooperatively and to describe the organizer with specificity and detail.

**Try It! Possible Answers**

Effects: cold-like symptoms, breathing problems, expense

Details: chronic runny nose; sneezing; itchy, teary eyes; hives; wheezing; shortness of breath; etc.

## Classification

Discuss classification and the example paragraph on SE page 609, guiding students by asking questions to check their comprehension of the text.

**Possible Answers**

**Respond to the reading.**

The first straight-sided pyramid was called the red pyramid because of the reddish tint of the sun on the pyramid's surface. Snefru built the first of these pyramids. His son, Cheops, perfected the pyramid, creating the Great Pyramid of Giza.

---

 **TEKS 10.13B** Structure ideas in a sustained way; **ELPS 3E** Share information in cooperative learning interactions; **3H** Describe with increasing specificity and detail; **4G** Demonstrate comprehension of increasingly complex English/responding to questions; **4I** Demonstrate comprehension by employing and expanding basic reading skills/understanding of supporting ideas and details, summarizing text, and distinguishing main ideas from details

## Comparison and Contrast

Organizing by **comparison** shows the similarities or differences between two subjects. To compare trolleys with modern buses, one student used a Venn diagram. After organizing her details, she found the two modes of transportation had key similarities, which became the focus of her paragraph.

### Venn Diagram

|  | Trolleys | Both | City Buses |
|---|---|---|---|
|  | needed a track | mass transit | ride on any roadway |
|  | nonpolluting | cost-effective | pollution emissions |
|  | closed or open | specific routes | windows, air conditioning |
|  | within city limits | reliable | city to city |
|  |  | adaptable for comfort |  |

**Trolley Cars and Buses**

**Topic Sentence**

**Body**

**Closing Sentence**

Today's buses might seem like a huge improvement over the trolley cars of a century ago, but in some ways the old mode of transportation was very similar to its modern counterpart. Trolleys were an early form of mass transportation, and, like modern buses, they were able to move large numbers of people across cities in an efficient, cost-effective manner. Like buses, trolleys had established routes with specific schedules, making both modes of transportation convenient and reliable for commuters. Today's buses provide air-conditioned relief from hot weather and comfortable heat when the weather is cold. Similarly, trolleys also adapted for rider comfort, though they had to rely on removable wooden panels to let in cool summer breezes or to shut out cold winter winds. So while modern buses offer comfortable, efficient transportation, trolleys served well as a moving force of yesterday. The two really aren't that different after all, showing, perhaps, that the more things change, the more they stay the same.

## Modeling Paragraphs

When you come across paragraphs that you really like, practice writing examples of your own that follow the author's pattern of writing. This process is called **modeling**. Follow these guidelines:

### Guidelines for Modeling

- **Find a paragraph** you would like to model.
- **Think of a topic** for your practice writing.
- **Follow the pattern** of the paragraph.
- **Build your paragraph** one sentence or idea at a time.
- **Review your work** and change any parts that seem confusing.

### Using an Anecdote

An anecdote is a brief story that can be used to illustrate a point. The following paragraph uses an anecdote in this way.

I had always thought I lacked the genes for artistic expression. My artwork was chaotic and my sculptures misshapen. Even coloring inside the lines when I was little was an exercise in futility. Then I had an art class with Ms. Edelman. She laughed at my mistakes and encouraged me to try again. I learned to carefully follow her directions, but also to experiment with new ideas. Sometimes the results were awful, but Ms. Edelman said that failure is only a stepping-stone to success. She taught me to look at art not as a finished product, but as a creative process, and that I should value and have confidence in my efforts. Most important, I learned that everyone has the ability for creative expression, even if that expression is unconventional or unappreciated. Ms. Edelman taught me that a good, caring teacher can make a huge difference in a student's life.

 **Respond to the reading.** What is the topic of the above paragraph? In which sentence is the topic identified? Which main points provide the strongest support of the topic? Name two.

**Try It!**

Write a paragraph modeled on the sample above. Consider your audience and refer to the modeling guidelines to help you complete your writing.

Paragraphs

---

## Comparison and Contrast

Discuss the comparison and contrast diagram and the example paragraph on SE page 610. Explain how the use of organizational tools such as graphic organizers can aid students in structuring their ideas in a sustained way when they are drafting paragraphs and essays.

## Using an Anecdote

Discuss the use of modeling as a tool to help students narrate with specificity in their writing.

### Answers

**Respond to the reading.**

Topic: A good, caring teacher can make a difference in a student's life.

The topic is identified in the last sentence.

Main points: Mrs. Edelman encouraged the writer to try. She taught that art is a process.

**Try It!** ### Answers

Answers will vary.

 **TEKS** **10.13A** Plan a first draft by determining topics through a range of strategies; **10.13B** Structure ideas in a sustained way; **10.13C** Revise drafts to improve the subtlety of meaning; **10.13E** Publish written work; **10.14A** Write a story with literary strategies and devices to enhance the plot; **ELPS 5G** Narrate with increasing specificity and detail/writing

ELPS 4I, 4K

"Good writing has an aliveness that keeps the reader reading from one paragraph to the next."
—William Zinsser

## Creating a List Paragraph

A creative way to develop a paragraph is to provide supporting sentences, one after another, almost in list form. In the following paragraph, the writer "lists" her friends like a lineup of television programs.

Lunchtime with my friends is like watching television—with a complete lineup of television programs. Drew supplies the news and commentary, advising us all of the latest school happenings, along with his sometimes sarcastic "editorials." Keisha provides us with our own private sitcom, as she hilariously describes her ups and downs of the morning, along with some dead-on impersonations of teachers and other students. Gabriel is our public service announcer, serenely reminding us of the importance of our music and drama departments, and trying to get us involved. Meanwhile, Yolanda rattles off sports anecdotes and updates for the current teams, including who is starting, injured, or benched because of grades. Squeezed in between all these formidable conversations, Leanne manages to give us a celebrity update, dropping in gossipy little tidbits about the social life of various CHS students. So what is my function while all this chatter is going on? I serve as the audience, appreciating the array of friends who offer me such varied programming.

 **Respond to the reading.** What is the topic of this paragraph? What do all of the sentences in the body have in common?

### Try It!

Write your own list paragraph modeled after the sample above. Refer to the guidelines for modeling on page **611** to help you complete your writing.

---

## Connecting Paragraphs in Essays

To write strong essays, you must organize the ideas within each paragraph and then organize the paragraphs within the essay. The guidelines that follow will help you connect the paragraphs in your essay.

- **Be sure that your paragraphs are complete.** Each one should contain an effective topic sentence and supporting details.
- **Identify the topic and thesis (focus) of your essay** in the beginning paragraph. Start with some interesting details to get the reader's attention. Then share the focus of your writing.
- **Develop your ideas** in the middle paragraphs. Each middle paragraph should include information that explains and supports your focus. Often, the paragraph that contains the most important information comes right after the beginning paragraph or right before the final paragraph.
- **Review one or more of the main points in your essay** in the closing paragraph. The last sentence usually gives the reader a final interesting thought about the topic.
- **Use transition words or phrases** to connect the paragraphs. Transitions help the reader follow an essay from one paragraph to the next. In the sample below, the transitions are shown in red.

. . . Suddenly, sports enthusiasts discovered they did not need a boat to go sailing.
In addition to skateboard sailing, people started adding sails when they went skiing, snowboarding, or roller-skating. Using the principles of water sailing, they were able to increase their speed and skills, moving rapidly across the landscape. . . .
Because of several factors, wind sports have gained in popularity through the past decade. For one, wind power is free, and all the sailor needs is a sail and something to slide or glide on. Another reason for the popularity of wind sports is the availability of places to practice. Any snowy area, flat or hilly, works for winter sailing, while parking lots and quiet streets offer excellent summer conditions. . . .

### Try It!

Turn to pages **628–629** to see examples of transition words and phrases. Find one or two writing samples that use some of these transitions.

*Paragraphs*

---

## Creating a List Paragraph

Discuss the example paragraph on SE page 612 so students can demonstrate comprehension by employing analytical skills.

###  Answers

The topic of the paragraph is lunchtime conversation. The sentences show how each lunchtime conversation gives information similar to that given on various television shows.

### Try It! Answers

Answer will vary.

## Connecting Paragraphs in Essays

Discuss how best to connect paragraphs in an essay to help students write using a variety of grade-appropriate connecting words.

### Try It! Answers

Answers will vary.

---

**TEKS** 10.13B Structure ideas in a sustained way/develop drafts in open-ended situations that include transitions; **ELPS** 4I Demonstrate comprehension by employing and expanding basic reading skills/understanding of supporting ideas and details, summarizing text, and distinguishing main ideas from details; 4K Demonstrate comprehension and expand reading skills by employing analytical skills/evaluating written information and performing critical analyses; 5F Write using a variety of grade-appropriate connecting words in increasingly accurate ways

TEKS 10.13B, ELPS 4G, 4I, 4J

 TEKS 10.13C, 10.13D, 10.17C, 10.18A, 10.18B(i)–10.18B(iii), 10.19 ELPS 5C, 5F

## Sample Essay

Read this sample essay about coffee production. Notice how the three parts—the beginning, the middle, and the ending—work together.

### Java Crisis

The production of coffee beans is a huge, profitable business, but, unfortunately, full-sun production is taking over the industry and leaving destruction in its wake. The change in how coffee is grown endangers the very existence of certain animals and birds, and even alters the world's environmental equilibrium.

On a local level, the devastation of the forest required by full-sun fields affects the area's birds and animals. The forest canopy of shade trees provides a home for migratory birds and other species that depend on the trees' flowers and fruits. Full-sun coffee growers destroy this forest home. Many species have already become extinct due to deforestation, and many more are quickly dying out.

On a more global level, the destruction of the rain forest for full-sun coffee fields also threatens human life. Medical research often makes use of the forests' plant and animal life, and the destruction of such species could prevent researchers from finding cures for certain diseases. In addition, new coffee-growing techniques are contributing to toxic runoff that is poisoning the water locally—a poison that could eventually find its way into much of the world's groundwater.

Both locally and globally, the continued spread of full-sun coffee plantations could mean the ultimate destruction of the rain-forest ecology. The loss of shade trees is already causing a slight change in the world's climate, and studies show that the loss of oxygen-giving trees also contributes to air pollution and global warming. In addition, the new growing techniques are contributing to acidic soil conditions and erosion.

It is obvious that the way much coffee is grown affects many aspects of life, from the local environment to the global ecology. But consumers do have a choice. They can purchase shade-grown coffee whenever possible, although at a higher cost. The future health of the planet and its inhabitants is surely worth more than an inexpensive cup of coffee.

**Look at the transitions.** What specific words does the author use to move from one paragraph to the next? Identify them.

## Paragraph Traits Checklist

Use the checklist below as a basic guide when you review your paragraphs. If you answer "no" to any of the questions, continue to work with that part of your paragraph.

### Revising and Editing Checklist

#### Focus and Coherence

_____ **1.** Do I have a clear topic sentence and an effective conclusion?

_____ **2.** Does the body of my paragraph or essay support the thesis?

_____ **3.** After I have thought more about the purpose for my writing, do I need to revise my writing?

#### Organization

_____ **4.** Is my organizational pattern appropriate for my audience and topic?

_____ **5.** Have I used transitions to connect my ideas?

#### Development of Ideas

_____ **6.** Have I included specific, relevant details to support both my topic sentences and my thesis statement?

_____ **7.** Have I fully developed each of my ideas?

#### Voice

_____ **8.** Do I sound interested in and knowledgeable about my topic?

_____ **9.** Does my voice fit the assignment and my audience?

_____ **10.** Is my word choice appropriate for my topic and audience?

#### Conventions

_____ **11.** Have I checked for and corrected errors in grammar, sentence structure, capitalization, and punctuation?

_____ **12.** Have I checked carefully for spelling errors using a dictionary or my computer spell-checker?

Paragraphs

---

## Sample Essay

Discuss the sample essay on SE page 614, allowing students to demonstrate comprehension by responding to your questions, by employing and expanding reading skills, and by employing inferential skills.

 ## Answers

**Look at the transitions.**
on a local level, on a more global level, both locally and globally, it is obvious

## Paragraph Traits Checklist

Review the five writing traits with students, highlighting specific aspects of each one, such as fully developing their ideas, spelling familiar words accurately, and using a variety of grade-appropriate sentence patterns.

---

**TEKS** **10.13B** Develop drafts in open-ended situations that include transitions; **10.13C** Revise drafts/improve style, word choice, and sentence variety and rethink how well the purpose has been addressed; **10.13D** Edit drafts for grammar, mechanics, and spelling; **10.17C** Use a variety of correctly structured sentences; **10.18A** Use conventions of capitalization; **10.18B(i)** Use commas in nonrestrictive phrases and contrasting expressions and in clauses; **10.18B(ii)** Use quotation marks to indicate sarcasm and irony; **10.18B(iii)** Use dashes to emphasize parenthetical information; **10.19** Spell correctly using resources to determine and check correct spelling; **ELPS** **4G** Demonstrate comprehension of increasingly complex English/responding to questions; **4I** Demonstrate comprehension by employing and expanding basic reading skills; **4J** Demonstrate comprehension and expand reading skills by employing inferential skills; **5C** Spell familiar words with increasing accuracy; **5F** Write using a variety of grade-appropriate sentence patterns in increasingly accurate ways

616

# A Writer's Resource

## Writing Focus

## Learning Language

Work with a partner. Read the definitions below and share your answers to the questions that follow.

1. A commitment is a pledge or an agreement to do something.
**What commitments have you made for the coming week?**

2. To incorporate means to combine into an organized whole.
**What is one of the ways to incorporate evidence into an essay?**

3. Subsequent means following in time or order.
**What are your plans subsequent to graduating from high school?**

4. A "red-letter day" is an important or very good day.
**Why is the first day of high school considered a red-letter day?**

617

# A Writer's Resource

Personal narratives, persuasive essays, short stories, poetry, reports—writing assignments come in all shapes and sizes. Some assignments come together quite easily because you know a lot about the topic; others are more challenging because they require thoughtful planning and research. Whatever the situation, you should approach *all* writing assignments in the same way—with a commitment to do your best work.

This chapter contains tips and guidelines to help you complete any writing assignment creatively and effectively. Once you become familiar with this material, you'll find it easier to write essays, articles, research papers, and more.

- **Finding a Topic**
- **Knowing the Different Forms**
- **Collecting and Organizing Details**
- **Creating an Outline**
- **Using Transitions**
- **Writing Thesis Statements**
- **Writing Great Beginnings and Endings**
- **Integrating Quotations**
- **Learning Key Writing Terms**
- **Using Writing Techniques**
- **Adding Graphics to Your Writing**

"When everything seems to be going against you, remember the airplane takes off against the wind, not with it."

—Henry Ford

## Learning Language

Use this collaborative speaking and listening activity on SE page 616 to help students internalize new basic and academic language; share and understand new expressions, basic vocabulary, and academic vocabulary; expand vocabulary by learning and using routine language; speak using grade-level content area vocabulary; share information; and demonstrate comprehension by responding to questions.

**ELPS** **1E** Internalize new basic and academic language by using and reusing it/speaking; **2C** Learn new expressions and basic/academic vocabulary heard during classroom instruction/interactions; **3B** Expand vocabulary by learning and using routine language needed for classroom communication; **3D** Speak using grade-level content area vocabulary/new words and academic language proficiency; **3E** Share information in cooperative learning interactions; **4G** Demonstrate comprehension of increasingly complex English/responding to questions

## Finding a Topic

Searching for a topic can be a challenge even if the teacher provides a general writing subject. For example, you might be asked to write about the westward development of the United States in the 1800s. This subject is too broad to cover well in one paper. It would be necessary to narrow the focus to find a manageable topic. Here are some ideas to help you.

### Using a Cluster Diagram

A cluster diagram can help you identify a topic. Place the general subject in the center and then break it down into categories. Break each category into yet smaller topics. Choose one that has enough information and is the most interesting to you.

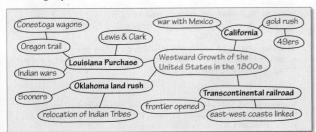

### Trying Freewriting

Freewriting can help you identify a topic. Take a few minutes to write what you can remember about a general subject. Incorporate questions and ideas that occur to you as you write. The freewriting below led one student to write about the relocation of Native American tribes.

The book Bury My Heart at Wounded Knee really made me think. I knew that people came from other countries to start a new life here and that the transcontinental railroad made it much easier to open the West to settlement. But why couldn't Native Americans and settlers share the land? The ownership of land seemed to make cooperation impossible. Were reservations the only answer? How long did it take to settle the West?

## Reviewing a "Basics of Life" List

Most people find they need a few basic things in order to live a full life. The list below, a "Basics of Life" list, could help you focus on a topic. For example, choosing "trade/money" might lead you to explore and write about ranching and cattle drives.

| | | | |
|---|---|---|---|
| family | warmth | food | shelter |
| friends | work | community | art/music |
| faith/religion | love | machines | natural resources |
| tools | education | clothing | health |
| hobbies | identity | trade/money | literature |
| water | rules/laws | freedom | government |

## Studying Visual Images

Paintings and visuals can give you topic ideas as well. The paintings and photographs of the Old West by nineteenth-century artists could prompt you to write about changes brought to the West by the transcontinental railroad.

Resource

---

## Finding a Topic

Lead students through the strategies given on SE pages 618–620 for determining topics so that they can effectively plan their first drafts. Discuss the importance of discovering topics that interest the student.

## Using Writing Prompts

Every day is full of experiences that make you think. You do things that you feel good about. You hear things that make you angry. You wonder how different things work. You are reminded of a past experience. These everyday thoughts can make excellent starting points for writing. As you write about one of these prompts, a number of specific topics will come to mind.

### Best and Worst

My most memorable day in school
My best hour
My encounter with a bully

### It could only happen to me!

A narrow escape from trouble
I was so shocked when . . .
My life began in this way.
My strangest phone conversation
If only I had done that differently
Whatever happened to my . . .

### Quotations

"Someone who makes no mistakes does not usually make anything."
"When people are free to do as they please, they usually imitate each other."
"More is not always better."
"It is easier to forgive an enemy than a friend."
"Never give advice unless asked."
"Honesty is the best policy."
"Know thyself."
"Like mother, like daughter."
"Like father, like son."

### I was thinking.

Everyone should know . . .
Where do I draw the line?
Is it better to laugh or cry?
Why do people like to go fast?
I don't understand why . . .

### First and Last

My first game or performance
My last day of _____
My last visit with _____

### School, Then and Now

The pressure of tryouts
Grades—are they the most important part of school?
Finally, a good assembly
What my school really needs is . . .
A teacher I respect
I'm in favor of more . . .

### People and Places

Who knows me best? What does he or she know?
Getting along with my brother, sister, or friend
A person I admire
My grandparents' house
The emergency room
A guided tour of my neighborhood

---

## Using Sample Topics

People, places, experiences, and information you encounter all offer springboards for writing. Here are some topic ideas for descriptive, narrative, expository, and persuasive writing.

### Descriptive

**People:** friend, cousin, favorite uncle, minister, boss, cashier, waiter, parent, bus driver, librarian, professional athlete

**Places:** store, diner, river, amusement park, religious building, train station, airport, city center, zoo, cemetery

**Things:** video game, CD, bike, wrench, skateboard, basketball, warehouse, movie, shoes, spoon, book, bench, kiosk, postcard

**Animals:** elephant, walrus, pigeon, zebra, mouse, spider, moth, poodle, penguin, cat, lobster, rat, raccoon, squirrel

### Narrative

**Stories:** entering an abandoned building, saving an injured bird, helping a lost child, attending the ballet, entering a contest, attending a concert, riding on the train, visiting a museum

### Expository

**Comparison-Contrast:** private school and public school, taxis and buses, apartments and condominiums, butterfly and moth, mopeds and motorcycles, two different city neighborhoods

**Cause/Effect:** thunder, street potholes, echo, sonic boom, hurricane, sunburn, erosion, capillary action, flooding

**Classification:** types of volcanoes, kinds of television shows, groups of invertebrates, types of birds, branches of the military, kinds of cameras

### Persuasive

**School:** banning the use of cell phones in school, keeping cars out of the school bus loading area, eliminating all carbonated drinks

**Home:** getting an electric guitar, negotiating rules about visitors when parents aren't around, sleeping in on Saturdays, taking the bus by yourself, getting a job, going downtown with friends

**Community:** relocating the stop sign by the library, creating a skateboard park, closing the city center to cars, setting up a teen advisory board for the city

---

## Using Writing Prompts

Lead students through the various writing prompts on SE page 620 that can be used to help determine a topic. Have students contribute additional ideas for the various categories.

## Using Sample Topics

Lead students through the various topic ideas listed on SE page 621 to help them find effective starting points for various genres of writing. Encourage students to contribute additional ideas for each genre.

# Knowing the Different Forms

Finding the right form, or genre, for your writing is just as important as finding the right topic. When you are selecting a form, be sure to ask yourself who you're writing for (your *audience*) and why you're writing (your *purpose*).

| | |
|---|---|
| **Anecdote** | A brief story that helps to make a point |
| **Autobiography** | A writer's story of his or her own life |
| **Biography** | A writer's story of someone else's life |
| **Book review** | An essay offering an opinion about a book, not to be confused with *literary analysis* |
| **Cause and effect** | A paper examining an event, the forces leading up to that event, and the effects following the event |
| **Character sketch** | A brief description of a specific character showing some aspect of that character's personality |
| **Descriptive writing** | Writing that uses sensory details that allow the reader to clearly visualize a person, a place, a thing, or an idea |
| **Editorial** | A letter or an article offering an opinion, an idea, or a solution |
| **Essay** | A thoughtful piece of writing in which ideas are explained, analyzed, or evaluated |
| **Expository writing** | Writing that explains something by presenting its steps, causes, or kinds |
| **Eyewitness account** | A report giving specific details of an event or a person |
| **Fable** | A short story that teaches a lesson or moral, often using talking animals as the main characters |
| **Fantasy** | A story set in an imaginary world in which the characters usually have supernatural powers or abilities |
| **Historical fiction** | An invented story based on an actual historical event |
| **Interview** | Writing based on facts and details obtained through speaking with another person |
| **Journal writing** | Writing regularly to record personal observations, thoughts, and ideas |

| | |
|---|---|
| **Literary analysis** | A careful examination or interpretation of some aspect of a piece of literature |
| **Myth** | A traditional story intended to explain a mystery of nature, religion, or culture |
| **Novel** | A book-length story with several characters and a well-developed plot, usually with one or more subplots |
| **Personal narrative** | Writing that shares an event or experience from the writer's personal life |
| **Persuasive writing** | Writing intended to persuade the reader to follow the writer's way of thinking about something |
| **Play** | A form that uses dialogue to tell a story, usually meant to be performed in front of an audience |
| **Poem** | A creative expression that may use rhyme, rhythm, and imagery |
| **Problem-solution** | Writing that presents a problem followed by a proposed solution |
| **Process paper** | Writing that explains how a process works, or how to do or make something |
| **Profile** | An essay that reveals an individual or re-creates a time period |
| **Proposal** | Writing that includes specific information about an idea or a project that is being considered for approval |
| **Research report** | An essay that shares information about a topic that has been thoroughly researched |
| **Response to literature** | Writing that is a reaction to something the writer has read |
| **Science fiction** | Writing based on real or imaginary science and often set in the future |
| **Short story** | A short fictional piece with only a few characters and one conflict or problem |
| **Summary** | Writing that presents the most important ideas from a longer piece of writing |
| **Tall tale** | A humorous, exaggerated story about a character or an animal that does impossible things |
| **Tragedy** | Literature in which the hero fails or is destroyed because of a serious character flaw |

Resource

## Knowing the Different Forms

Direct students to read the different forms listed on SE pages 622–623, and discuss the importance of selecting the correct genre, or form. Explain that this sets the purpose for writing.

# Collecting and Organizing Details

## Using Graphic Organizers

**Graphic organizers** can help you gather, organize, and structure your ideas and details for writing. Clustering is one method (see page **618**). These two pages show other useful organizers.

### Cause-Effect Organizer

Use to collect and organize details for cause-effect essays.

### Problem-Solution Web

Use to map out problem-solution essays.

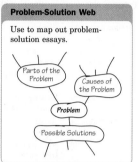

### Time Line

Use for personal narratives to list actions or events in the order they occurred.

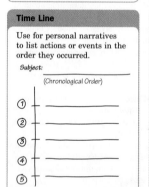

### Evaluation Collection Grid

Use to collect supporting details for essays of evaluation.

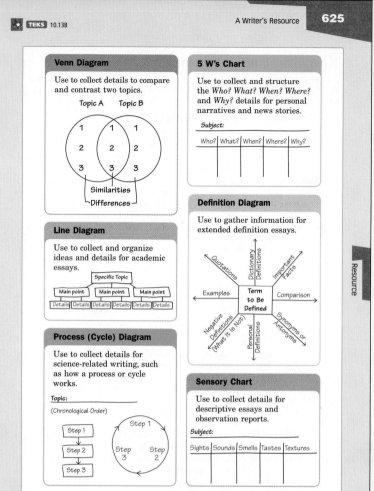

### Venn Diagram

Use to collect details to compare and contrast two topics.

### 5 W's Chart

Use to collect and structure the *Who? What? When? Where?* and *Why?* details for personal narratives and news stories.

### Line Diagram

Use to collect and organize ideas and details for academic essays.

### Definition Diagram

Use to gather information for extended definition essays.

### Process (Cycle) Diagram

Use to collect details for science-related writing, such as how a process or cycle works.

### Sensory Chart

Use to collect details for descriptive essays and observation reports.

Resource

---

## Using Graphic Organizers

Review the various graphic organizers provided on SE pages 624–625. Discuss how the organizers aid in structuring ideas as students plan and write their first drafts.

TEKS **10.13B** Structure ideas in a sustained way

# Creating an Outline

An **outline** organizes a set of facts or ideas by listing main points and subpoints. An effective outline shows how topics or ideas fit together. A well-designed outline helps you structure your ideas in a sustained way, and it serves as a frame for an effective essay. There are two types of outlines: *topic outlines* and *sentence outlines*. (See the samples below and on the next page.)

## A Topic Outline

In a **topic outline**, main points and details appear as phrases rather than as complete sentences. Topic outlines are useful for short essays, including essay-test answers. The information after the Roman numerals (I., II., III., and so on) identifies the main points in the essay. The information after the capital letters (A., B., C., and so on) identifies the details that support the main points.

### Sample Topic Outline

I. Effects of malnutrition on the body
  A. Extreme weight loss and stunted growth
  B. Frequent infections
  C. Lower resistance to life-threatening diseases
II. Marasmus—a form of malnutrition
  A. Extremely underweight
  B. Lack of body fat or defined muscles
  C. Puppet-like appearance
  D. Increased internal problems
III. Kwashiorkor—another form of malnutrition
  A. Badly swollen bellies
  B. Pale or red skin
  C. Thinning hair
IV. Effects of malnutrition on development
  A. Limited ability to walk and to talk
  B. Stunted intellectual development
  C. Ongoing effects into adulthood

**Note:** Information for the opening and closing paragraphs is not included in this outline for an essay on malnutrition.

### Tip

In an outline, if you have a "I.," you must have at least a "II." If you have an "A.," you must have at least a "B.," and so on.

## A Sentence Outline

A **sentence outline** is a detailed plan for writing. In this type of outline, the ideas are explained in complete sentences. This type of outline is useful for longer writing assignments like research reports and formal essays.

### Sample Sentence Outline

I. Malnutrition limits the physical development of children.
  A. Malnutrition causes extreme weight loss and stunted growth.
  B. It can result in children suffering from frequent infections.
  C. It can lower children's resistance to diseases.
II. Marasmus is one form of malnutrition.
  A. Children with this condition lack body fat and muscle.
  B. They appear puppet-like.
  C. This condition causes the skin to sag and wrinkle.
  D. It also decreases the size of internal organs.
III. Kwashiorkor is another form of malnutrition.
  A. Children with this condition have swollen bellies.
  B. Kwashiorkor causes pale or red skin and thinning hair.
  C. This condition causes growth to stop.
IV. Malnutrition limits the mental development of children.
  A. It hinders toddlers' ability to walk and to talk.
  B. Iron and iodine deficiencies stunt intellectual development.
  C. Malnutrition in early childhood affects ongoing learning.

## A Quick List

Use a **quick list** when there is no time for an outline. A quick list organizes ideas in the most basic way, but it will still help you organize or structure your writing.

### Sample Quick List

Malnutrition
  • effects on body (physical)
  • marasmus
  • kwashiorkor
  • effects on development (mental)

Resource

## Creating an Outline

Review the various types of outlines shown on SE pages 626–627. Discuss how an outline can aid in structuring ideas during prewriting. Explain that the outline can help free students to focus on writing solid first drafts. The outline serves as a type of road map—not a road block—for their writing.

TEKS **10.13B** Structure ideas in a sustained way

## Using Transitions

**Transitions** can be used to connect one sentence to another sentence within a paragraph, or to connect one paragraph to another within a longer essay or report. The lists below show a number of transitions and how they are used.

Each colored list below is a group of transitions that could work well together in a piece of writing.

### Words used to show location

| above | around | between | inside | outside |
|-------|--------|---------|--------|---------|
| across | behind | by | into | over |
| against | below | down | near | throughout |
| along | beneath | in back of | next to | to the right |
| among | beside | in front of | on top of | under |

| | | |
|-------|-------|-------|
| Above | In front of | On top of |
| Below | Beside | Next to |
| To the left | In back of | Beneath |
| To the right | | |

### Words used to show time

| about | during | yesterday | until | finally |
|-------|--------|-----------|-------|---------|
| after | first | meanwhile | next | then |
| at | second | today | soon | as soon as |
| before | to begin | tomorrow | later | in the end |

| | | | | |
|--------|-------------|------------|--------|------------|
| First | To begin | Now | First | Before |
| Second | To continue | Soon | Then | During |
| Third | To conclude | Eventually | Next | After |
| Finally | | | In the end | Subsequent |

### Words used to compare things

| likewise | as | in the same way | one way |
|----------|------|-----------------|---------|
| like | also | similarly | both |

| | |
|-----------------|-------------|
| In the same way | One way |
| Also | Another way |
| Similarly | Both |

### Words used to contrast (show differences)

| but | still | although | on the other hand |
|---------|-----|----------|-------------------|
| however | yet | otherwise | even though |

| | |
|-------------------|-------------|
| On the other hand | Although |
| Even though | Yet |
| Still | Nevertheless |

### Words used to emphasize a point

| again | truly | especially | for this reason |
|-----------|---------|-------------|-----------------|
| to repeat | in fact | to emphasize | |

| | | |
|----------------|--------------|------------|
| For this reason | Truly | In fact |
| Especially | To emphasize | To repeat |

### Words used to conclude or summarize

| finally | as a result | to sum it up | in conclusion |
|---------|-------------|--------------|---------------|
| lastly | therefore | all in all | because |

| | | | |
|--------------|-------------|--------------|-----------|
| Because | As a result | To sum it up | Therefore |
| In conclusion | All in all | Because | Finally |

### Words used to add information

| again | another | for instance | for example |
|---------|---------|--------------|-------------|
| also | and | moreover | additionally |
| as well | besides | along with | other |
| next | finally | in addition | |

| | | | |
|-------------|--------------|----------|------------|
| For example | For instance | Next | Another |
| Additionally | Besides | Moreover | Along with |
| Finally | Next | Also | As well |

### Words used to clarify

| in other words | for instance | that is | for example |
|----------------|--------------|---------|-------------|

| | |
|----------------|-----------------|
| For instance | For example |
| In other words | Equally important |

## Using Transitions

Discuss the importance of developing drafts that include transitions, and review how specific transitions are used in order to help students use a variety of grade-appropriate connecting words in their writing.

## Using Transitions

Review how specific transitions are used in order to help students use a variety of grade-appropriate connecting words in their writing. If possible, show various examples of how great writers have effectively used transitions.

# Writing Thesis Statements

An effective thesis statement tells the reader specifically what you plan to write about. In a longer essay or research report, your thesis statement generally comes at the end of the opening paragraph. It serves as a guide to keep you on track as you develop your writing. You will be supporting your thesis statement with logical reasons and relevant evidence as your write your essay.

## The Process at Work

A thesis statement usually takes a stand or expresses a specific feeling about, or feature of, your topic. Write as many versions as it takes to hit upon the statement that sets the right tone for your writing. The following formula can be used to form your thesis statements.

A specific topic *(The Lincoln Memorial)*
+ a particular stand, feeling, or feature *(is being damaged by pollution.)*
= an effective thesis statement.

## Sample Thesis Statements

**Writing Assignment:** Research report about aviation
**Specific Topic:** The DC-3 airplane
**Thesis Statement:** The DC-3 airplane established many structural standards for propeller aircraft.

**Writing Assignment:** Expository essay on cooking
**Specific Topic:** Gourmet meal
**Thesis Statement:** A gourmet meal results from careful preparation.

**Writing Assignment:** Analysis of a poem
**Specific Topic:** "Old Ironsides" by Oliver Wendell Holmes
**Thesis Statement:** Oliver Wendell Holmes wrote "Old Ironsides" to support the restoration of a historic warship.

### Thesis Checklist

Be sure that your thesis statement . . .

_____ identifies a limited, specific topic,
_____ focuses on a particular feature or feeling about the topic,
_____ is stated in one or more clear sentences,
_____ can be supported with logical reasons, convincing facts and details, and meets the requirements of the assignment.

# Writing Great Beginnings

There are a variety of rhetorical devices you can use as you write your opening paragraph. Try one of these approaches to grab the reader's attention, introduce your topic, and present your thesis.

- **Start with an important or an interesting fact.**
  A catalytic converter is a key component in reducing automobile exhaust emissions.

- **Ask an interesting question.**
  How many people know that the internal temperature of a catalytic converter can reach 1,200 degrees Fahrenheit?

- **Start with a quotation.**
  George Wilson, a technician at Miller Motors, warned us, "A badly timed engine can raise catalytic temperatures to more than 1,200 degrees Fahrenheit!"

## Trying a Beginning Strategy

If you have trouble writing your first paragraph, follow the example below.

**First sentence—Grab the reader's attention.**
Write a sentence that will draw the reader into the topic. (See above.)

Did you know that the internal temperature of a catalytic converter can reach 1,200 degrees Fahrenheit?

**Second sentence—Give some background information.**
Supporting information will add clarity and interest to your paper.

A catalytic converter is enclosed in stainless steel, so it should last a long time.

**Third sentence—Introduce the specific topic of the essay.**
Introduce the topic in a way that builds up to the thesis statement.

Car companies have installed this device in automobiles to meet emission standards.

**Fourth sentence—Give the thesis statement.**
Clearly present the thesis statement. (See page **630**).

Fortunately, the installation of catalytic converters has greatly reduced exhaust emissions in cars.

Resource

---

**Writing Thesis Statements**

Discuss thesis statements with the class, including their importance in staying on track and on topic as students develop their drafts.

**Writing Great Beginnings**

Explore the beginning strategies on SE page 631 with students. Invite volunteers to give examples of great first sentences that grab the reader's attention.

 **TEKS** **10.13A** Plan a first draft by developing a thesis or idea; **10.13B** Structure ideas in a sustained way/develop drafts in open-ended situations that include rhetorical devices; **10.15A(ii)** Write an analytical essay that includes rhetorical devices; **10.16A** Write an argumentative essay supported by relevant evidence

TEKS 10.13B

TEKS 10.21C

## Developing Great Endings

The closing paragraph of a paper should summarize your thesis and leave the reader with something to think about. When writing your closing paragraph, use two or more of the following ideas.

- Reflect on the topic.
- Restate your thesis.
- Review your main supporting points.
- Emphasize the special importance of one main point.
- Answer any questions the reader may still have.
- Draw a conclusion and put the information in perspective.
- Provide a final significant thought for the reader.

### Trying an Ending Strategy

If you have trouble coming up with an effective closing paragraph, follow the step-by-step example below. Remember that in your conclusion, as in the body of your essay, you must structure your ideas in a sustained way.

**First sentence—Reflect on the topic.**
Start by reflecting on the material presented previously about the topic.

Emission controls have greatly improved air quality in major cities.

**Second sentence—Add another point.**
Include a significant point of interest that you didn't mention before.

Along with clearer skies, catalytic converters have also offered the bonus of greater fuel economy.

**Third sentence—Emphasize the most important point.**
Stress the importance of one or more key points that support the thesis.

Continued improvements of the catalytic converter will mean longer equipment life and increased pollution control.

**Fourth sentence—Wrap up the topic or draw a conclusion.**
Add one final thought about the topic or draw a conclusion from the points you've presented in the writing.

Although the cost of developing the catalytic converter may be substantial, there is no price too high to pay for cleaner, breathable air.

## Integrating Quotations

Always choose quotations that are clear and appropriate for your writing. Quotations should *support* your ideas, not replace them.

### Trying Strategies for Using Quotations

Use the strategies below to get the most from quoted material in your writing.

- **Use quotations to support your own thoughts and ideas.**
  Effective quotations can support your main points and arguments.
  Doing what you know to be right will build your self-esteem. As Mark Twain noted, "A man cannot be comfortable without his own approval." That is why it is so important to let your conscience guide your actions.

- **Use quotations to lend authority to your writing.**
  Quoting an expert shows that you have researched your topic and understand its significance.
  Albert Einstein observed the growth of nuclear power with concern, stating, "I know not with what weapons World War III will be fought, but World War IV will be fought with sticks and stones." His disturbing comment reminds people that a nuclear war would result in unthinkable destruction.

- **Use quotations that are succinct and powerful.**
  Any quotation that you use must add value to your writing.
  Clearly, the education provided for today's students will determine the success of the future. As Benjamin Franklin put it, "An investment in knowledge always pays the best interest." A well-funded education system greatly benefits and enriches society.

### Common Quotation Problems to Avoid

Keep these problems in mind when you consider using quotations.

- **Don't plagiarize.**
  Accurately cite sources for all quotations (and paraphrases). Follow an approved style guide for your citations.

- **Don't use long quotations.**
  Keep quotations brief and to the point.

- **Don't overuse quotations.**
  Use a quotation only if you can't share the idea as powerfully or effectively in another way.

Resource

## Developing Great Endings

Review the information on developing great endings on SE page 632, and model the ending strategy for students. Discuss the importance for effective writing to be sustained from beginning to ending.

## Integrating Quotations

Discuss the importance of selecting appropriate quotations and providing accurate citations for them. Review the examples on SE page 633 for integrating quotations smoothly into students' writing.

**TEKS 10.13B** Structure ideas in a sustained way; **10.21C** Paraphrase, quote, and accurately cite researched information

## Learning Key Writing Terms

Here's a glossary of terms that describe aspects of the writing process.

| | |
|---|---|
| **Balance** | Arranging words or phrases in a way to give them equal importance |
| **Body** | The main part of a piece of writing, containing details that support or develop the thesis statement |
| **Brainstorming** | Collecting ideas by thinking freely about all the possibilities; used most often with groups |
| **Central idea** | The main point of a piece of writing, often stated in a thesis statement or a topic sentence |
| **Closing sentence** | The summary or final part in a piece of writing |
| **Coherence** | The logical arranging of ideas so they are clear and easy to follow |
| **Dialogue** | Written conversation between two or more people |
| **Emphasis** | Giving great importance to a specific idea in a piece of writing |
| **Exposition** | Writing that explains and informs |
| **Figurative language** | Language that goes beyond the normal meaning of the words used, often called "figures of speech" |
| **Focus (thesis)** | The specific part of a topic that is written about in an essay |
| **Generalization** | A general statement that gives an overall view, rather than focusing on specific details |
| **Grammar** | The rules that govern the standard structure and features of a language |
| **Idiom** | A phrase or an expression that means something different from what the words actually say <br> **That answer was really** out in left field. (This means the answer was not even close to being correct.) <br> **Next year you'll** sing a different tune. (This means you'll think differently.) |
| **Jargon** | The special language of a certain group or occupation <br> **The weaver pointed out the fabric's unique** warp **and** weft. <br> Computer jargon:   byte   icon   server   virus |

| | |
|---|---|
| **Limiting the subject** | Narrowing a general subject to a more specific one |
| **Literal** | The actual dictionary meaning of a word; a language that means exactly what it appears to mean |
| **Loaded words** | Words slanted for or against the subject <br> **The new tax bill** helps the rich **and** hurts the poor. |
| **Logic** | Correctly using facts, examples, and reasons to support a point |
| **Modifiers** | Words, phrases, or clauses that limit or describe another word or group of words |
| **Objective** | Writing that gives factual information without adding feelings or opinions (See *subjective*.) |
| **Poetic license** | A writer's freedom to bend the rules of writing to achieve a certain effect |
| **Point of view** | The position or angle from which a story is told (See page 332.) |
| **Prose** | Writing in standard sentence form |
| **Purpose** | The specific goal of the writing |
| **Style** | The author's unique choice of words and sentences |
| **Subjective** | Writing that includes the writer's feelings, attitudes, and opinions (See *objective*.) |
| **Supporting details** | Facts or ideas used to sustain the main point |
| **Syntax** | The order and relationship of words in a sentence |
| **Theme** | The main point or unifying idea of a piece of writing |
| **Thesis statement** | A statement of the purpose, or main idea, of an essay |
| **Tone** | The writer's attitude toward the subject |
| **Topic** | The specific subject of a piece of writing |
| **Topic sentence** | The sentence that carries the main idea of a paragraph |
| **Transitions** | Words or phrases that connect or tie ideas together |
| **Unity** | A sense of oneness in writing in which each sentence helps to develop the main idea |
| **Usage** | The way in which people use language (*Standard language* follows the rules; *nonstandard language* does not.) |
| **Voice** | A writer's unique personal tone or feeling that comes across in a piece of writing |

Resource

## Learning Key Writing Terms

Define and explain the terms on SE pages 634–635 to help students comprehend the vocabulary of writing. Encourage them to use these terms in classroom discussions.

TEKS 10.13B, 10.14A, 10.15A(ii), 10.15C(iii)
ELPS 4C

TEKS 10.13B, 10.14A, 10.15A(ii), 10.15C(iii)
ELPS 4C

## Using Writing Techniques

Become familiar with these common literary and rhetorical devices. Experiment with some of these techniques in your own essays and stories.

| | |
|---|---|
| **Allusion** | A reference to a familiar person, place, thing, or event<br>**Mario threw me my mitt.** "Hey, Babe Ruth, you forgot this!" |
| **Analogy** | A comparison of similar ideas or to help aid clarification.<br>"There is no frigate like a book, to take us lands away."<br>—Emily Dickinson |
| **Anecdote** | A brief story used to illustrate or make a point<br>It is said that the last words John Adams uttered were "Thomas Jefferson survives." Ironically, Jefferson had died just a few hours earlier. Both deaths occurred on July 4, 1826—the 50th anniversary of the Declaration of Independence. (This anecdote intensifies the importance of both men.) |
| **Colloquialism** | A common word or phrase suitable for everyday conversation but not for formal speech or writing<br>"Cool" and "rad" are colloquialisms suggesting approval. |
| **Exaggeration** | An overstatement or a stretching of the truth to emphasize a point (See *hyperbole* and *overstatement*.)<br>We opened up the boat's engine and sped along at a million miles an hour. |
| **Flashback** | A technique in which a writer interrupts a story to go back and relive an earlier time or event<br>I stopped at the gate, panting. Suddenly I was seven years old again, and my brother was there, calling me "chicken" from the edge of the stone well. Then I opened my eyes and heard only the crickets chirping. |
| **Foreshadowing** | Hints about what will happen next in a story<br>As Mai explained why she had to break their date, she noticed Luke looking past her. Turning, she saw Meg smiling—at Luke. |
| **Hyperbole** | (hi-púr-bə-lē) Exaggeration used to emphasize a point<br>The music was loud enough to make your ears bleed. |
| **Irony** | An expression in which the author says one thing but means just the opposite<br>As we all know, students love nothing better than homework. |

| | |
|---|---|
| **Juxtaposition** | Putting two words or ideas close together to create a contrasting of ideas or an ironic meaning<br>Ah, the sweet smell of fuel emissions! |
| **Local color** | The use of details that are common in a certain place |
| **Metaphor** | A figure of speech that compares two things without using the words *like* or *as*<br>The sheep were dense, dancing clouds scuttling across the road. |
| **Overstatement** | An exaggeration or a stretching of the truth (See *exaggeration* and *hyperbole*.)<br>On this red-letter day, if I eat one more piece of pie, I will burst! |
| **Oxymoron** | Connecting two words with opposite meanings<br>small fortune, cruel kindness, original copy |
| **Paradox** | A true statement that says two opposite things<br>As I crossed the finish line dead last, I felt a surge of triumph. |
| **Parallelism** | Repeating similar grammatical structures (words, phrases, or sentences) to give writing rhythm<br>We cannot undo, we will not forget, and we should not ignore the pain of the past. |
| **Personification** | A figure of speech in which a nonhuman thing is given human characteristics<br>The computer spit out my disk. |
| **Pun** | A phrase that uses words that sound the same in a way that gives them a funny effect<br>I call my dog Trousers because he pants so much. |
| **Simile** | A figure of speech that compares two things using *like* or *as*<br>Her silent anger was like a rock wall, hard and impenetrable. |
| **Slang** | Informal words or phrases used by a particular group of people<br>cool it     hang out     shoot the curl |
| **Symbol** | A concrete object used to represent an idea |
| **Understatement** | The opposite of exaggeration; using very calm language to call attention to an object or an idea<br>The car broke down, we were stranded for two days, and missed the wedding. Other than that we had a great trip. |

Resource

## Using Writing Techniques

Define and explain the terms on SE pages 636–637 to help students comprehend vocabulary that may be used in written classroom materials. Encourage students to find examples of these writing techniques to share with the class.

 **TEKS** **10.13B** Develop drafts in open-ended situations that include rhetorical devices; **10.14A** Write a story with literary strategies and devices to enhance the plot; **10.15A(ii)** Write an analytical essay that includes rhetorical devices; **10.15C(iii)** Write a response to expository and literary text that extends beyond a summary; **ELPS** **4C** Comprehend vocabulary used in written classroom materials

# Adding Graphics to Your Writing

Graphics and illustrations can enhance your writing by explaining your ideas in a visual manner. You can create graphics and illustrations by hand or design them on a computer and paste them into your document. Be sure to refer to the graphic in the text of your paper, either in the body of a paragraph or in a parenthetical reference.

## Line Graphs

Line graphs show change or trends across a period of time. A line graph is drawn as an L-shaped grid. The horizontal axis shows time, and the vertical axis denotes quantity. Dots are plotted and connected to show changes. The stages are clearly labeled as well as the quantity figures.

Concentrations of $CO_2$

## Bar Graphs

United States Population in 2005

Bar graphs use columns representing the subjects of the graph. Unlike the line graph, it does not show how things change over time but is used to show comparisons. The bars may run horizontally or vertically. Label each axis clearly so the reader can easily see and understand the information.

## Pie Graphs

Pie graphs show all the proportions and percentages of a whole, along with how those percentages relate to each other. Use a different color for each section. You can either add a key explaining each color or label the graph itself if the graph is large enough.

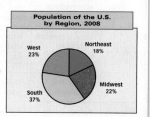

Population of the U.S. by Region, 2008

## Tables

Tables can organize information in a convenient manner. Most tables have rows (going across) and columns (going down). Rows contain one set of details, while columns contain another. At the right is a sample flight table, showing how far it is from one place to another. Check one place's column against the other's row.

Air Miles Between Major Cities

## Diagrams

Diagrams are drawings that show how something is constructed, how it works, or how its parts relate to each other. A diagram may leave out parts to show you only what you need to learn.

The Brain

## Maps

Maps can be used to illustrate many different things, from political boundaries to population issues to weather conditions. Use color or patterns to show differences.

U.S. Weather Map

# Adding Graphics to Your Writing

Review the material on SE pages 638–639 with the class. Discuss how graphics and illustrations can help explain concepts even better than words, in some cases. Remind students that unnecessary graphics can be distracting, though. Every graphic should have a purpose.

TEKS 10.13D, 10.18A,
10.18B(i)–10.18B(iii), 10.19
ELPS 5C, 5E

## Using Editing and Proofreading Marks

You may be asked to review the work of peers or to mark corrections on a draft of your own work. As you edit for grammar, sentence structure, capitalization, punctuation, and spelling, you should mark your suggested changes clearly and consistently using the proofreader's marks on the next page.

Editing requires that you read every word of an essay carefully, looking specifically for errors. You may want to read the draft several times, looking for a different type of mistake each time. Use the following questions to help you identify and mark errors.

- Have I found and marked for correction any errors in subject-verb agreement?
- Have I found and marked for correction any errors in pronoun-antecedent agreement?
- Are the correct verb tenses used? If not, have I marked corrections?
- Have I found any run-on sentences and sentence fragments and marked changes?
- Are any errors in capitalization marked for correction?
- Have I identified and marked for correction any errors in ending punctuation?
- Have I identified and marked for correction any errors in punctuation within sentences?
- Have I used quotation marks and dashes correctly?

### Tip

If possible, let your writing sit overnight before proofreading it. When you return to your writing, it will be easier to identify and correct mistakes.

### Try It!

Work with a partner. Exchange a piece of writing that you have recently drafted. Edit your partner's work for grammar, sentence structure, mechanics, and spelling. Use the proofreader's marks shown on the next page. Then, correct your writing following the proofreader's marks and changes indicated by your partner.

## Editing and Proofreading Marks

Use these symbols and letters to show where and how your writing needs to be changed. Your teachers may also use these symbols to point out errors in your writing. (This chart also appears inside the back cover of your book.)

| Symbols | Meaning | Example | Corrected Example |
|---|---|---|---|
| = | Capitalize a letter. | Willa Cather wrote _my_ Antonia. | Willa Cather wrote _My_ Antonia. |
| / | Make a capital letter lowercase. | Her novel tells the story of a Pioneer woman. | Her novel tells the story of a pioneer woman. |
| ⊙ | Insert (add) a period. | The story focuses on the right thing to do⊙Antonia is . . . | The story focuses on the right thing to do. Antonia is . . . |
| ◯ or sp. | Correct spelling. | Jim Burden (narates) the story. | Jim Burden narrates the story. |
| ℓ | Delete (take out) or replace. | Jim he tells about his relationship with Antonia. | Jim tells about his relationship with Antonia. |
| ∧ | Insert here. | Antonia represents ∧western Jim's childhood on the∧ frontier. | Antonia represents Jim's childhood on the western frontier. |
| ∧ ∧ ∧ | Insert a comma, a colon, or a semicolon. | Antonia's family, the Shimerdas∧came from Bohemia. ∧ | Antonia's family, the Shimerdas, came from Bohemia. |
| V̇ V̇ V̇ | Insert an apostrophe or quotation marks. | They are friends with Jim∨s family on the frontier. | They are friends with Jim's family on the frontier. |
| ? ! ∧ ∧ | Insert a question mark or an exclamation point. | Why is Antonia condescending toward Jim∧? | Why is Antonia condescending toward Jim? |
| ¶ | Start a new paragraph. | ¶ Their friendship changes when . . . | Their friendship changes when . . . |
| ∼ | Switch words or letters. | Jim goes away to college∼attend. | Jim goes away to attend college. |

---

## Using Editing and Proofreading Marks

Discuss editing strategies with students to help them learn to edit writing for standard grammar and usage (subject-verb agreement, pronoun agreement, and verb tenses) and to use complex grammatical structures correctly in their own writing.

## Editing and Proofreading Marks

Review the proofreading marks on SE page 641 and model how they can be used to mark corrections to grammar, usage, mechanics, and spelling.

### Try It! Answers

Answers will vary. Use the peer response part of this activity to demonstrate the importance of using standard proofreader's marks to communicate effectively.

**TEKS** **10.13D** Edit drafts for grammar, mechanics, and spelling; **10.18A** Use conventions of capitalization; **10.18B(i)** Use commas in nonrestrictive phrases and contrasting expressions and in clauses; **10.18B(ii)** Use quotation marks to indicate sarcasm and irony; **10.18B(iii)** Use dashes to emphasize parenthetical information; **10.19** Spell correctly using resources to determine and check correct spelling; **ELPS** **5C** Spell familiar words with increasing accuracy; **5E** Employ increasingly complex grammatical structures in content area writing such as using correct verbs, tenses, and pronouns/possessive case/negatives and contractions

ELPS 1E, 2C, 3B, 3D, 3E, 4G

# Proofreader's Guide

## Writing Focus

| | |
|---|---|
| Checking Mechanics | **643** |
| Understanding Idioms | **704** |
| Using the Right Word | **710** |
| Parts of Speech | **730** |
| Understanding Sentences | **764** |

## Learning Language

**Learning these words and expressions will help you understand this unit.**

1. An acronym is a word formed by the first letter or the first few letters of words in a phrase.
   **Explain what the letters in the acronym "NASA" represent.**

2. Function refers to the purpose or role of a person or thing.
   **What is the function of a hospital emergency room?**

3. The idiom on board means to agree or to be on the job.
   **Describe a recent group project in which all the members were on board with the idea for the project.**

---

# Checking Mechanics

## Period

### 643.1 At the End of a Sentence

Use a **period** at the end of a sentence that makes a statement, requests something, or gives a mild command.

(Statement) **The man who does not read good books has no advantage over the man who can't read them.**

—Mark Twain

(Request) **Please bring your folders and notebooks to class.**

(Mild command) **Listen carefully so that you understand these instructions.**

**NOTE:** It is not necessary to place a period after a statement that has parentheses around it and is part of another sentence.

**My dog Bobot** (I don't quite remember how he acquired this name) **is a Chesapeake Bay retriever—a hunting dog—who is afraid of loud noises.**

### 643.2 After an Initial or an Abbreviation

Place a period after an initial or an abbreviation (in American English).

Ms.    Sen.    D.D.S.    M.F.A.    M.D.    Jr.    U.S.    p.m.    a.m.
Edna St. Vincent Millay    Booker T. Washington    D. H. Lawrence

**NOTE:** When an abbreviation is the last word in a sentence, use only one period at the end of the sentence.

**Valerie eyed each door until she found the name Fletcher B. Gale, M.D.**

### 643.3 As a Decimal Point

A period is used as a decimal point.

**New York City has a budget of $59 billion to serve its 8.4 million people.**

## Exclamation Point

### 643.4 To Express Strong Feeling

Use the **exclamation point** (sparingly) to express strong feeling. You may place it after a word, a phrase, or a sentence.

**Imagine the sheer joy of shouting "Finished!" when you turn in your last assignment of the school year.**

---

## Learning Language

Use the collaborative speaking and listening activity on SE page 642 to help students share, understand, and expand new language structures, expressions, basic vocabulary, and general meaning of spoken language; demonstrate listening comprehension; and demonstrate comprehension of increasingly complex English.

## Period and Exclamation Point

Discuss with students the uses of periods to help them use appropriate punctuation conventions in their compositions. Have students contribute other examples for each use.

## Related Skills Activities

- **SkillsBook**
  Pretest: Punctuation, pp. 3–4
  End Punctuation, p. 5

---

**TEKS** 10.18B Use correct punctuation marks; **ELPS 1E** Internalize new basic and academic language by using and reusing it/speaking; **2C** Learn new expressions and basic/academic vocabulary heard during classroom instruction/interactions; **3B** Expand vocabulary by learning and using routine language needed for classroom communication; **3D** Speak using grade-level content area vocabulary/new words and academic language proficiency; **3E** Share information in cooperative learning interactions; **4G** Demonstrate comprehension of increasingly complex English/responding to questions

TEKS 10.18B

## Question Mark

### 644.1 Direct Question

Place a **question mark** at the end of a direct question.

> Where do I go now? I wondered. Do I climb the stairs or take the elevator? Why is there no escalator in this building? Why should I be discouraged by the sound of ringing in my ears?

When a question ends with a quotation that is also a question, use only one question mark, and place it within the quotation marks.

> On road trips, do you remember driving your parents crazy by asking, "Are we there yet?"

**NOTE:** Do *not* use a question mark after an indirect question.

> While I was crossing through the park, I found a friendly looking woman and asked her where nearest the bus stop was.

### 644.2 To Show Uncertainty

Use a question mark within parentheses to show uncertainty.

> This summer marks the 20th season (?) of the American Players Theatre.

### 644.3 Short Question Within a Sentence

Use a question mark for a short question within parentheses.

> We crept so quietly (had they heard us?) past the kitchen door and back to our room.

Use a question mark for a short question within dashes.

> Maybe somewhere in the pasts of these humbled people, there were cases of bad mothering or absent fathering or emotional neglect—what family surviving the '50s was exempt?—but I couldn't believe these human errors brought the physical changes in Frank.
> —Mary Kay Blakely, *Wake Me When It's Over*

---

TEKS 10.18B

Mechanics

## Practice

### Periods and Question Marks

 Write a period where it is needed to end a sentence and after an abbreviation. Write a question mark where it is needed to end a sentence or for a short question within parentheses.

**Example:** Ms Henson is teaching a course in forensic science this year
     Ms.      year.

1. With the popularity of television shows featuring forensic science (isn't *CSI* one), many high schools have begun offering classes in the subject

2. What is forensic science

3. It's any area of science that could be used in a court of law

4. For instance, a forensic psychologist (Dr Sam Waters of *Profiler* is a TV example) studies a crime scene to determine clues to the criminal's personality

5. Have you heard of a *criminalist*

6. A criminalist, who uses chemical and microscopic techniques to examine physical evidence, can identify an individual through DNA analysis

7. A forensic pathologist is an MD and examines samples removed from the body to establish the time and cause of death

8. He or she might also be able to determine if a death was a homicide or a suicide

9. Ms Henson asked me if I'd like to be a forensic pathologist someday

---

### Model

Model the following sentences to practice using the correct punctuation for direct and indirect questions.

> Have you given any consideration to joining the military?
> I asked him why he wants to join the armed forces.

---

## Question Mark

Discuss with students the uses of question marks in direct questions and to show uncertainty to help them use appropriate punctuation conventions in their compositions. Have students contribute other examples for each use. Also, have students complete the Grammar Practice on SE page 645 individually. Review the answers with the class.

## Related Skills Activities

■ *SkillsBook*
End Punctuation, p. 5

## Answers

1. ...one?), subject.
2. science?
3. court of law.
4. Dr. Sam Waters, personality.
5. *criminalist*?
6. analysis.
7. M.D., death.
8. suicide.
9. Ms. Henson, someday.

646

## Comma

### 646.1 Between Two Independent Clauses

Use a **comma** between two independent clauses that are joined by a coordinating conjunction (*and, but, or, nor, for, yet, so*).

> I wanted to work in the garden, but it was raining too hard.

**NOTE:** Do not confuse a sentence containing a compound verb for a compound sentence.

> I decided to plant flower bulbs and then mow the yard.

### 646.2 To Separate Adjectives

Use commas to separate two or more adjectives that *equally* modify the same noun. (Note: Do not use a comma between the last adjective and the noun.)

> Miriam saw the kind, curious look in her grandmother's eyes as they discussed her plans for the future.

—Julio Namente, student writer

### A Closer Look

To determine whether adjectives modify equally—and should, therefore, be separated by commas—use these two tests:

1. Shift the order of the adjectives; if the sentence is clear, the adjectives modify equally. (In the example below, *hot* and *smelly* can be shifted and the sentence is still clear; *usual* and *morning* cannot.)

2. Insert *and* between the adjectives; if the sentence reads well, use a comma when the *and* is omitted. (The word *and* can be inserted between *hot* and *smelly*, but *and* does not make sense between *usual* and *morning*.)

> Matty was tired of working in the hot, smelly kitchen and decided to take her usual morning walk.

### 646.3 To Separate Contrasted Elements

Use commas to separate contrasted elements within a sentence. Often the word or phrase that is set off is preceded by *not*.

> Since the book was about children and their antics, and not the problems that teenagers face, I was not that interested.

---

 **Practice**

### Commas 1

- To Separate Adjectives
- To Separate Contrasted Elements

Indicate where commas are needed in the following sentences by writing the commas along with the words that surround them.

**Example:** Marianna was very smart though not a genius.
  smart, though

1. One of her favorite things was learning unfamiliar interesting words.

2. Marianna unlike many of her friends could solve tough word puzzles with little effort.

3. Putting together challenging complex word puzzles was her favorite pastime.

4. Marianna created her puzzles for personal satisfaction not for financial gain.

5. The puzzles she made had thought-provoking entertaining themes.

6. They included fascinating little-known facts about countries of the world.

7. Books of her puzzles were published overseas not in the United States.

8. She was pleasantly surprised when her hobby became a serious profitable business.

9. Now Marianna is a busy successful business owner.

### Model

Model the following sentences to practice using commas to separate contrasted elements.

> Be a first-rate version of yourself, not a second-rate version of someone else.
> —Judy Garland

> Strive not to be a success, but rather to be of value.
> —Albert Einstein

---

## Comma

Discuss with students the uses of commas to help them use appropriate comma placement in contrasting expressions in their compositions. Have students contribute other examples for each use. Then have students complete the Grammar Practice on SE page 647 individually.

## Related Skills Activities

- **Basic Grammar and Writing**
  Eliminating Comma Splices, p. 592

- *SkillsBook*
  Commas Between Independent Clauses, p. 7
  Commas to Separate Adjectives, p. 8
  Commas to Set Off Contrasted Elements and
    Appositives, p. 12

---

 **Answers**

1. unfamiliar, interesting
2. Marianna, unlike...friends,
3. challenging, complex
4. satisfaction, not
5. thought-provoking, entertaining
6. fascinating, little-known
7. overseas, not
8. serious, profitable
9. busy, successful

---

TEKS 10.18B(i)

## Comma (continued)

### 648.1 To Set Off Appositives

A specific kind of explanatory word or phrase called an **appositive** identifies or renames a preceding noun or pronoun.

**Benson**, our uninhibited and enthusiastic Yorkshire terrier, **joined our family on my sister's fifteenth birthday.**

—Chad Hockerman, student writer

**NOTE**: Do not use commas with *restrictive appositives*. A restrictive appositive is essential to the basic meaning of the sentence.

Sixteen-year-old student Ray Perez **was awarded an athletic scholarship.**

### 648.2 Between Items in a Series

Use commas to separate individual words, phrases, or clauses in a series. (A series contains at least three items.)

**Dad likes** meat, vegetables, and a salad **for dinner.** (words)

**I took her for walks, read her stories, and made up games** for her to play. (phrases)

—Anne Moody, *Coming of Age in Mississippi*

**NOTE**: Do not use commas when all the words in a series are connected with or, nor, or and.

**We washed the car** and **waxed the car** and **changed the oil.**

### 648.3 After Introductory Phrases and Clauses

Use a comma after an introductory participial phrase.

Determined to finish the sweater by Friday, **my grandmother knit night and day.**

Use a comma after a long introductory prepositional phrase or after two or more short ones.

In the oddest places and at the strangest times, **my grandmother can be found knitting madly away.**

**NOTE**: You may omit the comma if the introductory phrase is short.

Before breakfast **my grandmother knits.**

Use a comma after an introductory adverb (subordinate) clause.

After the practice was over, **Tina walked home.**

**NOTE**: A comma is not used if an adverb clause follows the main clause and is needed to complete the meaning of the sentence.

**Tina practiced hard** because she feared losing.

However, a comma is used if the adverb clause following the main clause begins with *although, even though, while,* or another conjunction expressing a contrast.

**Tina walked home,** even though it was raining very hard.

---

 TEKS 10.18B(i)

Mechanics

 **Practice**

## Commas 2

- To Set Off Appositives
- Between Items in a Series
- After Introductory Phrases and Clauses

Indicate where commas are needed in the following paragraph by writing the commas along with the words that surround them.

**Example:** Sharks probably the oldest predators in the sea live in every ocean in the world.

Sharks, probably          sea, live

1   Sharks belong to a family that includes dogfish skates and
2   rays. They are distinguished from other fish by their cartilaginous
3   skeletons. Besides this unusual feature the skin of a shark feels
4   much like sandpaper. Throughout the world's seas sharks search for
5   something to eat. Sharks bite off chunks of food and then swallow
6   the pieces whole. A tiny seven-inch-long shark the pygmy is dwarfed
7   by the fifty-foot-long variety the whale shark within this intriguing
8   group. Though there are more than 360 species most people have only
9   heard of the great white the tiger the hammerhead and the mako.
10  Although it is foolish to ignore them most sharks are not interested
11  in eating every person who steps into the sea.

### Model

Model the following sentences to practice using commas in a series, after an introductory phrase, and to set off an appositive.

**Only through experience of trial and suffering can the soul be strengthened, ambition inspired, and success achieved.**

—Helen Keller

**If you don't know where you are going, any road will take you there.**

—Lewis Carroll

**What we're all striving for is authenticity, a spirit-to-spirit connection.**

—Oprah Winfrey

---

## Comma

Discuss with students the uses of commas with appositives, between items in a series, and after introductory phrases and clauses to help them use appropriate comma placement in their compositions. Have students contribute other examples for each use. Also have students complete the Grammar Practice on SE page 649 and review the answers as a class.

### Related Skills Activities

- **SkillsBook**
  Commas in a Series, p. 8
  Commas After Introductory Phrases and Clauses, pp. 9–10
  Commas to Set Off Contrasted Elements and Appositives, p. 12

---

 **Answers**

*line 1:* dogfish, skates, and
*line 3:* feature, the
*line 4:* seas, sharks
*line 6:* tiny, seven-inch-long shark, the pygmy, is
*line 7:* variety, the whale shark, within
*line 8:* species, most
*line 9:* white, the tiger, the hammerhead, and
*line 10:* them, most

---

TEKS 10.18B(i)

## Comma (continued)

### 650.1  To Enclose Parenthetical Elements

Use commas to separate parenthetical elements, such as an explanatory word or phrase, within a sentence.

**The two children played together on the sand,** away from the high, rough waves that were crashing onto the shore, **and they laughed as their sand castles grew higher and higher.**

**Allison meandered into class,** late as usual, **and sat down.**

### 650.2  To Set Off Nonrestrictive Phrases and Clauses

Use commas to set off **nonrestrictive** (unnecessary) clauses and participial phrases. A nonrestrictive clause or participial phrase adds information that is not necessary to the basic meaning of the sentence. For example, if the clause or phrase (in red) were left out in the two examples below, the meaning of the sentences would remain clear. Therefore, commas are used to set them off.

**The Altena Fitness Center and Visker Gymnasium,** which were built last year, **are busy every day.** (nonrestrictive clause)

**Students and faculty,** improving their health through exercise, **use both facilities throughout the week.** (nonrestrictive phrase)

Do not use commas to set off a **restrictive** (necessary) clause or participial phrase, which helps to define a noun or pronoun. It adds information that the reader needs to know in order to understand the sentence. For example, if the clause and phrase (in red) were dropped from the examples below, the meaning wouldn't be the same. Therefore, commas are *not* used.

**The handball court** that has a sign-up sheet by the door **must be reserved.** The clause identifies which handball court must be reserved. (restrictive clause)

**Individuals** wanting to use this court **must sign up a day in advance.** (restrictive phrase)

### A Closer Look: *That* and *Which*

Use *that* to introduce restrictive (necessary) clauses; use *which* to introduce nonrestrictive (unnecessary) clauses. When the two words are used in this way, the reader can quickly distinguish necessary and unnecessary information.

The treadmill that monitors heart rate is the one you must use. (The reader needs the information to find the right treadmill.)

This treadmill, which we got last year, is required for your program. (The main clause tells the reader which treadmill to use; the other clause gives additional, unnecessary information.)

---

TEKS 10.18B(i)    Checking Mechanics

## Practice

### Commas 3

- To Enclose Parenthetical Elements
- To Set Off Nonrestrictive Phrases and Clauses

Indicate where commas are needed in the following sentences by writing the commas along with the words that surround them. If no commas are needed, write "none."

**Example:** Patrick who loves science tried to get me interested in astronomy.
 *Patrick, who loves science, tried*

**1.** He has a Dobsonian telescope which he built from a kit.

**2.** Last July having time on my hands I stayed at his country home.

**3.** With Patrick's telescope we spotted the International Space Station which I was surprised to be able to see.

**4.** The "Dob" as my cousin affectionately calls it is popular among amateur astronomers.

**5.** When I got home, my dad helped me buy a telescope that is similar to the Dobsonian.

**6.** Patrick attempting to help me put it together accidentally broke one of the legs.

**7.** Dad's coworker whose experience with telescopes is amazing fixed it easily.

**8.** Next month armed with my new telescope I'll be searching the heavens for new planets and moons.

### Model

Model the following sentences to reinforce the difference between restrictive and nonrestrictive phrases and clauses and their correct punctuation.

Those who don't believe in magic will never find it.    —Roald Dahl

The hardest thing to explain is the glaringly evident, which everybody has decided not to see.
 —Ayn Rand

---

## Comma

Discuss with students the mechanics of comma usage with nonrestrictive phrases and clauses in their compositions. Have students contribute other examples for each use. Also have students complete the Grammar Practice on SE page 651 and review the answers as a class.

## Related Skills Activities

- **SkillsBook**
  Commas with Nonrestrictive Phrases and Clauses 1 and 2, pp. 14–15

---

## Answers

1. telescope, which
2. July, having time on my hands, I
3. Station, which
4. "Dob," as my cousin affectionately calls it, is
5. none
6. Patrick, attempting to help me put it together, accidentally
7. coworker, whose experience with telescopes is amazing, fixed
8. month, armed with my new telescope, I'll

---

**TEKS  10.18B(i)** Use commas in nonrestrictive phrases and in clauses

## Comma (continued)

### 652.1 To Set Off Dates

Use commas to set off items in a date.

**On September 30, 2010, my little sister entered our lives.**

**He began working out on December 1, 2010, but quit by May 1, 2011.**

However, when only the month and year are given, no commas are needed.

**He began working out in December 2010 but quit by May 2011.**

When a full date appears in the middle of a sentence, a comma follows the year.

**On June 7, 1938, my great-grandfather met his future wife.**

### 652.2 To Set Off Items in Addresses

Use commas to set off items in an address. (No comma is placed between the state and ZIP code.)

**Mail the box to Friends of Wildlife, Box 402, Spokane, Washington 20077.**

When a city and state (or country) appear in the middle of a sentence, a comma follows the last item in the address.

**Several charitable organizations in Fort Worth, Texas, pool their funds.**

### 652.3 In Numbers

Use commas to separate numerals in large numbers in order to distinguish hundreds, thousands, millions, and so forth.

**1,101        25,000        7,642,020**

### 652.4 To Enclose Titles or Initials

Use commas to enclose a title or initials and names that follow a surname (a last name).

**Letitia O'Reilly, M.D., is our family physician.**

**Hickok, J. B., and Cody, William F., are two popular Western heroes.**

## Practice

### Commas 4

- To Set Off Dates
- To Set Off Items in Addresses
- To Enclose Titles or Initials

Indicate where commas are needed in the following sentences by writing the commas along with the words that surround them.

**Example:** Thomas Bonnicksen Ph.D. has written extensively about the forests that grew after the last ice age.
*Bonnicksen, Ph.D., has*

1. Professors in Austin Texas answered some questions about the role of carbon dioxide in warming the atmosphere.

2. Although many think the world is going to warm up considerably, Chronis Tzedakis Ph.D. believes we may be headed into a new ice age.

3. On April 30 2011 a science magazine reported the earth's climate has changed dramatically over the last 9,000 years.

4. You can get information about glaciers and ice ages by writing to World Data Center for Glaciology University of Colorado Campus Box 449 Boulder Colorado 80309.

5. The coldest temperature on record for North America—81 degrees below zero Fahrenheit—occurred near the town of Beaver Creek Yukon Territory on February 3 1947.

6. John Margolies CPA counsels against buying investment property in the Yukon.

### Model

Model the following sentences to practice using commas to enclose titles or initials.

**Richard Swenson, D.D.S., advises his patients to put their toothbrushes in the dishwasher.**

**For his daughter's graduation gift, Mr. Blade had her office door painted with her new title: Miranda K. Blade, J.D.**

Mechanics

---

## Comma

Discuss with students the additional uses of commas listed on SE page 652 to help them use appropriate comma placement in their compositions. Have students contribute other examples for each use. Then have students complete the Grammar Practice on SE page 653, and review the answers as a class.

### Related Skills Activities

- ***SkillsBook***
  Other Uses of Commas, p. 13

## Answers

1. Austin, Texas, answered
2. Chronis Tzedakis, Ph.D., believes
3. April 30, 2011, a science
4. Glaciology, University of Colorado, Campus Box 449, Boulder, Colorado
5. Beaver Creek, Yukon Territory, on February 3, 1947
6. John Margolies, CPA, counsels

---

TEKS 10.18B(i)

## Comma *(continued)*

### 654.1 To Set Off Dialogue

Use commas to set off the speaker's exact words from the rest of the sentence. (It may be helpful to remember that the comma is always to the left of the quotation mark.)

"It's as if people no longer care about the problems of city life," added Monica Torres, an urban studies student.

### 654.2 To Set Off Interjections

Use a comma to separate an interjection or a weak exclamation from the rest of the sentence.

Hey, how am I to know that a minute's passed?
—Nathan Slaughter and Jim Schweitzer, *When Time Dies*

### 654.3 To Set Off Interruptions

Use commas to set off a word, a phrase, or a clause that interrupts the movement of a sentence. Such expressions usually can be identified through the following tests: (1) They may be omitted without changing the meaning of a sentence. (2) They may be placed nearly anywhere in the sentence without changing its meaning.

For most of the students, well, it was just another normal day at school.
The safest way to cross this street, as a general rule, is with the light.

### 654.4 In Direct Address

Use commas to separate a noun of direct address from the rest of the sentence. A *noun of direct address* is the noun that names the person(s) spoken to.

I don't think you understand, my friend, how important it is for me to do well in school and create a successful life for myself.

### 654.5 For Clarity or Emphasis

You may use a comma for clarity or for emphasis. There will be times when none of the traditional rules call for a comma, but one will be needed to prevent confusion or to emphasize an important idea.

Those who can see tomorrow, can find the energy to continue. (emphasis)
What the crew does, does affect our voyage. (clarity)

---

TEKS 10.18B(i)  Checking Mechanics **655**

Mechanics

## Practice

### Commas 5

- To Set Off Dialogue
- To Set Off Interjections
- In Direct Address

 Indicate where commas are needed in the following sentences by writing the commas along with the words that surround them.

**Example:** Hey do you have a hero?
Hey, do

1. "My hero" said Jolene "is the science-fiction author Ray Bradbury."
2. In his introduction to *The Circus of Dr. Lao,* Bradbury stated "Science fiction balances you on the cliff. Fantasy shoves you off."
3. Writer Miriam Allen de Ford said "Science fiction deals with improbable possibilities."
4. Mr. Castillo says "Science fiction entertains and provides insights into sciences and society."
5. The main elements in science fiction may be real or imagined Jolene.
6. People often attribute the following words to the television show *Star Trek:* "Beam me up Scotty!"
7. Well did you know it was never said on the show?
8. Hey are you sure about that?

### Model

Model the following sentences to practice using commas to set off dialogue and interjections.

"I need to rake the leaves again," I inanely said to my old friend.
—Patricia Cornwell, *Black Notice*

Oh, life is a glorious cycle of song . . .
—Dorothy Parker

---

## Comma

Discuss with students the additional uses of commas listed on SE page 654 to help them use appropriate comma placement in their compositions. Have students contribute other examples for each use. Then have students complete the Grammar Practice on SE page 655, and review the answers as a class.

## Related Skills Activities

- **SkillsBook**
Other Uses of Commas, p. 13

## Answers

1. hero," said Jolene, "is
2. stated, "Science
3. said, "Science
4. says, "Science
5. imagined, Jolene
6. up, Scotty
7. Well, did
8. Hey, are

 TEKS 10.18B(i) Use commas in nonrestrictive phrases

TEKS 10.18B

## Semicolon

### 656.1 To Join Two Independent Clauses

Use a **semicolon** to join two or more closely related independent clauses that are not connected with a coordinating conjunction. (Independent clauses can stand alone as separate sentences.)

> A heart attack is a medical emergency; immediate attention and care is required.

> Silence coated the room like a layer of tar; not even the breathing of the 11 Gehad made any sound.

> —Gann Bierner, "The Leap"

**NOTE:** When independent clauses are especially long or contain commas, a semicolon may punctuate the sentence, even though a coordinating conjunction connects the clauses.

> We waited all day in that wide line, tired travelers pressing in from all sides; and when we needed drinks or sandwiches, I would squeeze my way to the cafeteria and back.

### 656.2 With Conjunctive Adverbs

A semicolon is used *before* a conjunctive adverb (with a comma after it) when the word connects two independent clauses in a compound sentence. (Common conjunctive adverbs are *also, besides, finally, however, indeed, instead, meanwhile, moreover, nevertheless, next, still, then, therefore,* and *thus*.)

> I know that I need to finish the research for my essay; however, our Internet service is down and the library is closed on Sunday.

### 656.3 To Separate Groups That Contain Commas

A semicolon is used to separate groups of words that already contain commas.

> Every Saturday night my little brother gathers up his things—goggles, shower cap, and snorkel; bubble bath, soap, and shampoo; tapes, stereo, and rubber duck—and heads for the tub.

Checking Mechanics **657**

Mechanics

## Practice

### Semicolons

- To Join Two Independent Clauses
- To Separate Groups That Contain Commas

Indicate where a semicolon is needed in the following sentences by writing the semicolon along with the words that surround it.

**Example:** "It's not what I can do it's what I *will* do." —Kyle Maynard

> do; it's

1. Kyle Maynard has a rare disorder called "congenital amputation" he has been limbless since birth.

2. He wrestles, swims, and plays baseball competes in athletic contests and has written a book.

3. Kyle is a normal young man despite having no elbows or hands and no knees or legs below them, he has become an outstanding role model.

4. He stands only three feet tall and weighs 120 pounds those who know him hardly notice his unique proportions.

5. Kyle has traveled cross-country as a motivational speaker won an ESPN ESPY Award, a Courage Award, and wrestling awards and modeled for Vanity Fair and Abercrombie & Fitch.

6. What makes Kyle different isn't his body it's his heart.

7. His story goes way beyond athletics his story serves as an inspiration to anyone who must overcome huge odds.

8. Kyle's book is titled *No Excuses* it is a revealing autobiography.

### Model

Model the following sentence to practice using a semicolon to join two independent clauses.

> His brows came together; his mouth became a thin line.
> —Harper Lee, *To Kill a Mockingbird*

## Semicolon

Discuss with students the uses of semicolons listed on SE page 656 to help them use appropriate punctuation conventions in their compositions. Have students contribute other examples for each use. Then have students complete the Grammar Practice on SE page 657 individually, and review the answers as a class.

## Related Skills Activities

## Answers

1. amputation"; he
2. baseball; competes contests; and
3. 19-year-old; despite
4. pounds; those
5. speaker; won awards; and
6. body; it's
7. athletics; his
8. *Excuses*; it

TEKS 10.18B

## Colon

### 658.1 After a Salutation

Use a **colon** after the salutation of a business letter.

**Dear Judge Parker:      Dear Governor Whitman:**

### 658.2 Between Numerals Indicating Time

Use a colon between the hours, minutes, and seconds of a number indicating time.

**8:30 p.m.      9:45 a.m.      10:24:55**

### 658.3 For Emphasis

Use a colon to emphasize a word, a phrase, a clause, or a sentence that explains or adds impact to the main clause (also see **684.3**).

**The newest candidates announced their platforms today: Lower taxes and more efficient services are the consistent themes.**

### 658.4 To Introduce a Quotation

Use a colon to formally introduce a quotation, a sentence, or a question.

**Directly a voice in the corner rang out wild and clear: "I've got him! I've got him!"**
                                                    —Mark Twain, *Roughing It*

### 658.5 To Introduce a List

A colon is used to introduce a list.

**I got all the proper equipment: scissors, a bucket of water to keep things clean, some cotton for the stuffing, and needle and thread to sew it up.**
                                                    —Joan Baez, *Daybreak*

### A Closer Look

Do not use a colon between a verb and its object or complement, or between a preposition and its object.

**Incorrect:** Min has: a snowmobile, an ATV, and a canoe.
**Correct:** Min has plenty of toys: a snowmobile, an ATV, and a canoe.
**Incorrect:** I watch a TV show about: cooking wild game.
**Correct:** I watch a TV show about a new subject: cooking wild game.

### 658.6 Between a Title and a Subtitle

Use a colon to distinguish between a title and a subtitle, volume and page, and chapter and verse in literature.

**Encyclopedia Americana IV: 211      Psalm 23:1–6**

---

TEKS 10.18B

## Practice

### Colons

- Between Numerals Indicating Time
- For Emphasis
- To Introduce a Quotation

Indicate where a colon is needed in the following sentences by writing the colon along with the words that surround it.

**Example:** The Orloj is a glorious old clock tower in Prague, unique for this reason It dates back to medieval times.
*reason:* It

1. The clock was built in 1410 by Mikulas of Kadan, royal clock maker under the reign of a familiar ruler King Wenceslas IV.

2. Whether it's 1200 midnight, 1200 noon, or any hour between, the Orloj will astound you with its moving statues.

3. After "The Walk of the Apostles," a rooster flaps and crows, and the clock chimes 900, 1000, 1100 . . .

4. Other moving figures include a Turk shaking his head, a miser watching his bag, and an individual admiring his reflection in a mirror Vanity himself.

5. The clock also has a calendar dial and an astronomical dial that displays the current state of the heavens sort of an ancient planetarium.

6. Otakar Zamecnik, a keeper of the Orloj, relates "The Orloj will soon be 600 years old, and I'm proud to be continuing the work of some 100 Orloj keepers before me."

### Model

Model the following sentence to practice using a colon for emphasis.

**Humanity's true moral test, its fundamental test, consists of its attitude toward those who are at its mercy: animals.**
                                                    —Milan Kundera, *The Unbearable Lightness of Being*

---

## Colon

Discuss with students the uses of colons listed on SE page 658 to help them use appropriate punctuation conventions in their compositions. Have students contribute other examples for each use. Then have students complete the Grammar Practice on SE page 659 individually, and review the answers as a class.

## Related Skills Activities

■ **SkillsBook**
Colons 1 and 2, pp. 18–19
Review: Semicolons and Colons, p. 21

## Answers

1. ruler: King
2. 12:00 midnight, 12:00 noon
3. 9:00, 10:00, 11:00
4. mirror: Vanity
5. heavens: sort
6. relates: "The

**660**

## Hyphen

**660.1 In Compound Words**

Use the **hyphen** to make some compound words.

great-great-grandfather     maid-in-waiting     three-year-old

**660.2 To Create New Words**

Use a hyphen to form new words beginning with the prefixes *self-, ex-, all-,* and *half-*. Also use a hyphen to join any prefix to a proper noun, a proper adjective, or the official name of an office. Use a hyphen before the suffix *-elect.*

self-**contained**     ex-**governor**     all-**inclusive**     president-**elect**
pre-**Cambrian**     mid-**December**     half-**painted**

Use a hyphen to join the prefix *great-* only to the names of relatives.

great-**aunt**, great-**grandfather** (correct)     great-**hall** (incorrect)

**660.3 To Form an Adjective**

Use a hyphen to join two or more words that serve as a single adjective (a single-thought adjective) before a noun.

When I am on the field, I see myself as a tall, well-built quarterback armed with magic plays and an incredible ability to throw the ball.

Use common sense to determine whether a compound adjective might be misread if it is not hyphenated. Generally, hyphenate a compound adjective that is composed of . . .

- a phrase     heat-and-serve **meal**     off-and-on **relationship**
- a noun + adjective     oven-safe **handles**     book-smart **student**
- a noun + participle (*ing* or *ed* form of a verb)     bone-chilling **story**

### A Closer Look

When words forming the adjective come after the noun, do not hyphenate them.

In real life I am large and big boned.

When the first of these words is an adverb ending in *-ly*, do not use a hyphen.

delicately prepared **pastry**

Also, do not use a hyphen when a number or a letter is the final element in a single-thought adjective.

class B **movie**

**660.4 To Join Letters and Words**

Use a hyphen to join a capital letter or lowercase letter to a noun or participle. (Check your dictionary if you're not sure of the hyphenation.)

T-**shirt**     Y-**turn**     G-**rated**     x-**axis**

---

 **Practice**

### Hyphens 1

- In Compound Words
- To Create New Words
- To Join Letters and Words

For each sentence below, write the words that should be hyphenated.

**Example:** Robert Ripley is best known for his vast collection of mind boggling artifacts.
*mind-boggling*

1. Ripley was a self taught artist who won fame as a cartoonist.

2. As a so called world traveler, Ripley collected innumerable oddities.

3. Each year, thousands take self guided tours through his 27 "odditoriums."

4. Each odditorium, or museum, contains improbable, far flung rarities.

5. The museums are filled with eye popping exhibits.

6. A miniature Rolls Royce made of 1,016,711 matchsticks took 4,609 man hours to complete over a fifteen month period.

7. A close up of *Self Portrait in Front of Easel,* 1888, reveals that this work of art is made up of thousands of postcards.

8. Most of the exhibits are G rated, but some visitors might find a few of them disturbing.

### Model

Model the following sentences to practice using a hyphen to create new words.

"Slumgullion" was the name given by the miners to a certain soft, half-liquid mud . . .
—Bret Harte, *The Queen of the Pirate Isle*

"The spring of 1885 a new wave of settlers broke and spread over the hard-land table of the upper Niobrara."
—Mari Sandoz, *Old Jules*

*Mechanics*

---

## Hyphen

Discuss with students the uses of hyphens listed on SE page 660 to help them use appropriate punctuation conventions in their compositions. Have students contribute other examples for each use. Invite volunteers to share their answers to the Grammar Practice on SE page 661.

### Related Skills Activities

- **SkillsBook**
Hyphens 1 and 2, pp. 22–23

---

 **Answers**

1. self-taught
2. so-called, world-traveler
3. self-guided
4. far-flung
5. eye-popping
6. man-hours, fifteen-month
7. close-up, *Self-Portrait*
8. G-rated

---

**662**

## Hyphen (continued)

### 662.1 Between Numbers and Fractions

Use a hyphen to join the words in compound numbers from *twenty-one* to *ninety-nine* when it is necessary to write them out (see 692.3).

Use a hyphen between the numerator and denominator of a fraction, but not when one or both of those elements are already hyphenated.

forty-five       five-sixteenths       seven thirty-seconds (7/32)

### 662.2 In a Special Series

Use hyphens when two or more words have a common element that is omitted in all but the last term.

The ship has lovely two-, four-, or six-person cabins.

### 662.3 To Join Numbers

Use a hyphen to join numbers indicating the life span of a person or the score in a contest or a vote.

We can thank Louis Pasteur (1822–1895) for pasteurized milk.

In the 2009 Fiesta Bowl, Texas defeated Ohio State 24–21.

### 662.4 To Prevent Confusion

Use a hyphen with prefixes or suffixes to avoid confusion or awkward spelling.

re-create (not *recreate*) the image       re-cover (not *recover*) the sofa

### 662.5 To Divide a Word

Use a hyphen to divide a word, only between its syllables, at the end of a line of print. Always place the hyphen after the syllable at the end of the line—never before a syllable at the beginning of the following line.

#### Guidelines for Dividing with Hyphens

1. Always divide a compound word between its basic units: **sister-in-law**, not **sis-ter-in-law**.
2. Avoid dividing a word of five or fewer letters: **paper, study, July.**
3. Avoid dividing the last word in a paragraph.
4. Never divide a one-syllable word: **rained, skills, through.**

5. Never divide a one-letter syllable from the rest of the word: **omit-ted**, not **o-mitted.**
6. When a vowel is a syllable by itself, divide the word after the vowel: **epi-sode**, not **ep-isode.**
7. Never divide abbreviations or contractions: **shouldn't**, not **should-n't.**
8. Never divide the last word in more than two lines in a row.

---

**663**

Mechanics

### Practice

## Hyphens 2

- In a Special Series
- To Divide a Word

 In the sentences below, write the numerals or words that should be hyphenated.

**Example:** The golfers received first, second, and third place trophies.
*first-, second-, and third-place*

1. Asra found fabric remnants in two, three, and four yard lengths.
2. The assignment requires 4, 8, and 16 ounce measuring cups.
3. The department store is hiring both full and part time employees for the holidays.
4. We heard pro and anti war speeches at the convention.
5. Both English and Spanish speaking citizens attended the rally.

 Use a slash (/) as shown below to indicate where each word should be divided at the end of a line of print. If the word should not be divided, explain.

**Example:**  mass-produced
      *mass- / produced*

6. gasoline
7. duty
8. father-in-law
9. marched
10. haven't

### Model

Model the following sentence to practice using hyphens in a special series.

Goran was curious about the Russian Revolution as well as pre- and post-war history.

—Jean Fischer, *Vladimir's Reign*

---

## Hyphen

Discuss with students the uses of hyphens listed on SE page 662 to help them use appropriate punctuation conventions in their compositions. Have students contribute other examples for each use after they have completed the Grammar Practice on SE page 663. Review the answers to the Grammar Practice with the class.

### Related Skills Activities

- **SkillsBook**
  Hyphens 1 and 2, pp. 22–23

## Answers

1. two-, three-, and four-yard
2. 4-, 8-, and 16-ounce
3. full- and part-time
4. pro- and anti-war
5. English- and Spanish-speaking
6. gaso- / line
7. should not be divided; fewer than five letters
8. father- / in-law OR  father-in- / law
9. should not be divided; one-syllable word
10. should not be divided; contraction

## Apostrophe

### 664.1 In Contractions

Use an **apostrophe** to show that one or more letters have been left out of a word group to form a contraction.

hadn't — *o* is left out     they'd — *woul* is left out     it's — *i* is left out

**NOTE:** Use an apostrophe to show that one or more numerals or letters have been left out of numbers or words in order to show special pronunciation.

class of '99 — *19* is left out     g'day — *ood* is left out

### 664.2 To Form Singular Possessives

Add an apostrophe and *s* to form the possessive of most singular nouns.

Spock's **ears**     Captain Kirk's **singing**     the ship's **escape plan**

**NOTE:** When a singular noun ends with an *s* or a *z* sound, you may form the possessive by adding just an apostrophe. When the singular noun is a one-syllable word, however, you usually add both an apostrophe and an *s* to form the possessive.

San Carlos' **government** (or) San Carlos's **government** (two-syllable word)
Ross's **essay** (one-syllable word)     The class's **field trip** (one-syllable word)

### 664.3 To Form Plural Possessives

The possessive form of plural nouns ending in *s* is usually made by adding just an apostrophe.

students' **homework**     bosses' **orders**

For plural nouns not ending in *s*, an apostrophe and *s* must be added.

children's **book**     men's **department**

### A Closer Look

It will help you punctuate correctly if you remember that the word immediately before the apostrophe is the owner.

girl's **guitar** (*girl* is the owner)     boss's **order** (*boss* is the owner)
girls' **guitar** (*girls* are the owners)     bosses' **order** (*bosses* are the owners)

### 664.4 To Show Shared Possession

When possession is shared by more than one noun, use the possessive form for the last noun in the series.

Hoshi, Linda, and Nakiva's **water skis** (All three own the same skis.)
Hoshi's, Linda's, and Nakiva's **water skis** (Each owns her own skis.)

---

## Practice

### Apostrophes 1

- To Form Singular Possessives
- To Form Plural Possessives

 Correctly write the words from the following sentences that need apostrophes.

**Example:** An ice climbers helmet is an essential piece of equipment.
*climber's*

1. For some, a mountains icy walls or frozen waterfalls are a real test.
2. A climbers tools include crampons, hard boots, an ice pick, ice screws, cold-weather clothes, and goggles.
3. Although articles in mens magazines focus on men who lead the sport of ice climbing, many women love the challenge as well.
4. An ice climber must make sure his or her crampons spikes are strong and sharp.
5. Enthusiasts also depend upon each ice screws holding power.
6. These screws give climbers a measure of safety on a walls icy face.
7. The American Alpine Institute is one of North Americas best climbing schools.
8. The Institutes programs teach beginners as well as seasoned climbers.
9. Marchs longer days and slightly higher temperatures make it an ideal month for ice climbing.

### Model

Model the following sentences to practice using apostrophes in contractions.

Twenty years from now you will be more disappointed by the things that you didn't do than by the ones you did do.
—Mark Twain

If you wait to do everything until you're sure it's right, you'll probably never do much of anything.
—Win Borden

---

## Apostrophe

Discuss with students the uses of apostrophes in contractions and to show possession to help them use appropriate punctuation conventions in their compositions. Have students contribute other examples for each use. Invite students to bring in examples of errors in apostrophe usage in printed materials and signage for the class to correct. Also have students work with partners to complete and check the Grammar Practice on SE page 665.

## Related Skills Activities

■ *SkillsBook*
Apostrophes to Form Possessives 1, 2, and 3, pp. 26–28

## Answers

1. mountain's
2. climber's
3. men's
4. crampons'
5. screw's
6. wall's
7. North America's
8. Institute's
9. March's

## Apostrophe (continued)

### 666.1 To Show Possession with Indefinite Pronouns

Form the possessive of an indefinite pronoun by placing an apostrophe and an *s* on the last word (see 734.1 and 736.3).

**everyone's** **anyone's** **somebody's**

### 666.2 To Show Possession in Compound Nouns

Form the possessive of a compound noun by placing the possessive ending after the last word.

the secretary of the interior's (singular) **agenda**
her lady-in-waiting's (singular) **day off**

If forming a possessive of a plural compound noun creates an awkward construction, you may replace the possessive with an *of* phrase. (All four forms below are correct.)

their fathers-in-law's (plural) **birthdays**
or the birthdays of their fathers-in-law (plural)
the ambassadors-at-large's (plural) **plans**
or the plans of the ambassadors-at-large (plural)

### 666.3 To Express Time or Amount

Use an apostrophe and an *s* with an adjective that is part of an expression indicating time or amount.

a penny's worth      today's business      this morning's meeting
yesterday's news      a day's wage      a month's pay

### 666.4 To Form Certain Plurals

Use an apostrophe and *s* to form the plural of a letter, a number, a sign, or a word discussed as a word.

B — B's      C — C's      8 — 8's      + — +'s      *and* — *and*'s

Ms. D'Aquisto says our conversations contain too many *like*'s and *no way*'s.

**NOTE:** If two apostrophes are called for in the same word, omit the second one.

Follow closely the *do*'s and *don't*s (not *don't*'s) on the checklist.

---

## Practice

### Apostrophes 2

- To Show Possession with Indefinite Pronouns
- To Express Time or Amount

Write the possessive form of the underlined words in the following sentences.

**Example:** Who will succeed Coach Marshall is <u>anyone</u> guess.
*anyone's*

1. This <u>morning</u> paper included a story about the Animal Rescue League.

2. At times, it is best to keep <u>one</u> opinions confidential.

3. Kendra found <u>somebody</u> gym shoes on the bench near Mr. Mariano's office.

4. <u>Today</u> advanced geometry exam was easier than I'd expected.

5. Rob is <u>everyone</u> first choice as a geometry tutor.

6. When I get this <u>week</u> paycheck, I'll have enough to buy a new CD.

7. Latisha and Petra usually share <u>each other</u> oil paints.

8. It was <u>nobody</u> fault but my own.

9. <u>Yesterday</u> chemistry lab turned out better than I expected it would.

10. Because of the tough competition, <u>no one</u> artwork from our school won an award.

### Model

Model the following sentences to practice using apostrophes to express time or amount.

After a day's walk, everything has twice its usual value.
—George Macauley Trevelyan

A single conversation with a wise man is worth a month's study of books.
—Chinese Proverb

---

## Apostrophe

Discuss with students the additional uses of apostrophes listed on SE page 666 to help them use appropriate punctuation conventions in their compositions. Have students contribute other examples for each use. Then have students complete the Grammar Practice on SE page 667, and review the answers as a class.

## Related Skills Activities

- ***SkillsBook***
  Apostrophes to Form Possessives 1, 2, and 3, pp. 26–28
  Other Uses for Apostrophes, p. 30

## Answers

1. morning's
2. one's
3. somebody's
4. Today's
5. everyone's
6. week's
7. each other's
8. nobody's
9. Yesterday's
10. no one's

## Quotation Marks

**668.1 To Set Off Direct Quotations**

Place **quotation marks** before and after the words in direct quotations.

"Come with me to the concert tonight," Michaela suggested. "You'll come away with a totally different opinion about classical music."

In a quoted passage, put brackets around any word or punctuation mark that is not part of the original quotation. (See 680.1.)

If you quote only part of the original passage, be sure to construct a sentence that is both accurate and grammatically correct.

Much of the restructuring of the Postal Service has involved "turning over large parts of its work to the private sector."

**668.2 Placement of Punctuation**

Always place periods and commas inside quotation marks.

"Dr. Slaughter wants you to have liquids, Will," Mama said anxiously. "He said not to give you any solid food tonight."

—Olive Ann Burns, *Cold Sassy Tree*

Place an exclamation point or a question mark *inside* quotation marks when it punctuates the quotation and *outside* when it punctuates the main sentence.

"Am I dreaming?"    Had she heard him say, "Here's the key to your new car"?

Always place semicolons or colons outside quotation marks.

I wrote about James Joyce's "The Dead"; I found it thought provoking.

**668.3 For Long Quotations**

If you quote more than one paragraph, place quotation marks before each paragraph and at the end of the last paragraph (Example A). If a quotation has more than four lines on a page, you may set it off from the text by indenting 10 spaces from the left margin (block form). Do not use quotation marks either before or after the quoted material, unless they appear in the original (Example B).

**Example A**

**Example B**

## Practice

### Quotation Marks 1

- To Set Off Direct Quotations
- Placement of Punctuation

**Write the following conversation, placing quotation marks correctly.**

**Example:** Calvin, would you please get that? his mom asked.
*"Calvin, would you please get that?" his mom asked.*

The phone had already rung four times; Calvin picked it up.

Hello? he greeted the caller. He listened for a bit, and then said, Yes, I think so. What's the problem?

Calvin's mom came into the room and asked, Who is it?

Calvin gestured to his mom to wait a second and continued to speak into the phone. No, we'd prefer the black one. . . . Right. OK, hold on, please. He covered the mouthpiece and said to his mom, It's the repair shop. They can't fix our car by this weekend, but they have a rental car for us.

Calvin's mom said, Ask them when our car will be ready.

Calvin talked again to the mechanic. Did Calvin hear him right? Did he say, It won't be ready for at least a week?

We have to special order a part, the mechanic explained. I wish I had better news for you.

**Exercise**

Continue the phone conversation between Calvin and the mechanic. Use quotation marks correctly.

## Quotation Marks

Discuss with students the uses of quotation marks listed on SE page 668 to help them use appropriate punctuation conventions in their compositions. Have students contribute other examples for each use. Also, have students complete the Grammar Practice on SE page 669 individually, and review the answers as a class.

### Related Skills Activities

- ***SkillsBook***
  Quotation Marks with Dialogue, p. 31
  Quotation Marks with Direct Quotations, p. 32

## Answers

The phone had already rung four times; Calvin picked it up.

"Hello?" he greeted the caller. He listened for a bit, and then said, "Yes, I think so. What's the problem?"

Calvin's mom came into the room and asked, "Who is it?"

Calvin gestured to his mom to wait a second and continued to speak into the phone. "No, we'd prefer the black one. . . . Right. OK, hold on, please." He covered the mouthpiece and said to his mom, "It's the repair shop. They can't fix our car by this weekend, but they have a rental car for us."

Calvin's mom said, "Ask them when our car will be ready."

Calvin talked again to the mechanic. Did Calvin hear him right? Did he say, "It won't be ready for at least a week"?

"We have to special order a part," the mechanic explained. "I wish I had better news for you."

TEKS 10.18B(ii)

## Quotation Marks (continued)

### 670.1 Quotation Marks Within Quotations

Use single quotation marks to punctuate a quotation within a quotation. Use double quotation marks in order to distinguish a quotation within a quotation within a quotation.

> "For tomorrow," said Mr. Botts, "read 'Unlighted Lamps.'"
> Sue asked, "Did you hear Mr. Botts say, 'Read "Unlighted Lamps"'?"

### 670.2 For Special Words

You may use quotation marks (1) to distinguish a word that is being discussed, (2) to indicate that a word is unfamiliar slang, or (3) to point out that a word is being used in a special way, i.e., to indicate irony or sarcasm.

> (1) If I had to choose a word to describe his attitude, it would be "stoic."
> (2) The next time I hear a New Zealander say "ta," I will know that I am being thanked.
> (3) Tom pushed the wheelchair across the street, showed the lady his "honest" smile . . . and stole her purse.

**NOTE:** You may use italics (underlining) in place of quotation marks in each of these three situations. (See 672.3.)

### 670.3 To Punctuate Titles

Use **quotation marks** to punctuate titles of songs, poems, short stories, one-act plays, lectures, episodes of radio or television programs, chapters of books, unpublished works, electronic files, and articles found in magazines, newspapers, encyclopedias, or online sources. (For punctuation of other titles, see 672.2.)

> "Santa Lucia" (song)
> "The Chameleon" (short story)
> "Twentieth-Century Memories" (lecture)
> "Affordable Adventures" (magazine article)
> "Dire Prophecy of the Howling Dog" (chapter in a book)
> "Dancing with Debra" (television episode)
> "Miss Julie" (one-act play)

**NOTE:** Punctuate one title within another title as follows:

> "Clarkson's 'Breakaway' Hits the Waves"
> (title of a song in title of an article)

---

TEKS 10.18B(ii)

## Practice

### Quotation Marks 2

- Quotation Marks Within Quotations
- For Special Words
- To Punctuate Titles

 Write the word or words that should be enclosed in quotation marks in the following sentences.

**Example:** The players stood on the sidelines as Olivia sang the Star-Spangled Banner.
"Star-Spangled Banner."

1. Ms. Rupka said, "The exam will include Hills like White Elephants and other short stories by Hemingway."

2. He called himself benevolent, but everyone knew he was exaggerating his measly donations.

3. Hazim was featured in the *Trumpet* magazine article Flags to Riches.

4. No one answered correctly when asked to define the word pidgin.

5. I like Usher's new song Truth Hurts.

6. The coach shouted, "I called Ty, and he said, Madison West won 28–10!"

7. Merina asked, "Who sings Happy Ever After?"

8. My three-year-old nephew calls dogs oggies.

9. According to the newspaper, gasoline prices are expected to increase just twenty-five percent this summer..

### Model

Model the following sentence to practice using quotation marks within quotations.

> "'The Duke's Daughter' paid the butcher's bill, 'A Phantom Hand' put down a new carpet, and the 'Curse of the Coventrys' proved the blessing of the Marches in the way of groceries and gowns."
> —Louisa May Alcott, *Little Women*

---

## Quotation Marks

Discuss with students the uses of quotation marks listed on SE page 670 to help them use quotation marks to indicate sarcasm or irony, among other uses, in their compositions. Invite volunteers to give their answers to the Grammar Practice on SE page 671.

## Related Skills Activities

- **SkillsBook**
  Double and Single Quotation Marks, p. 33

##  Answers

1. 'Hills like White Elephants'
2. "benevolent,"
3. "Flags to Riches."
4. "pidgin."
5. "Truth Hurts."
6. 'Madison West won 28–10'
7. 'Happy Ever After'
8. "oggies."
9. no quotation marks needed; not a direct quotation

---

 **TEKS** **10.18B(ii)** Use quotation marks to indicate sarcasm and irony

TEKS 10.18B

## Italics (Underlining)

### 672.1 Handwritten and Printed Material

**Italics** is a printer's term for a style of type that is slightly slanted. In this sentence, the word *happiness* is printed in italics. In material that is handwritten or typed on a machine that cannot print in italics, underline each word or letter that should be in italics.

**My Ántonia is the story of a strong and determined pioneer woman.**
(printed)

**Willa Cather's My Ántonia describes pioneer life in America.**
(typed or handwritten)

### 672.2 In Titles

Use italics to indicate the titles of magazines, newspapers, pamphlets, books, full-length plays, films, videos, radio and television programs, book-length poems, ballets, operas, paintings, lengthy musical compositions, sculptures, cassettes, CD's, legal cases, and the names of ships and aircraft. (For punctuation of other titles, see 670.3.)

*Newsweek* (magazine)          *Cold Sassy Tree* (book)
*X-Men Origins: Wolverine* (film)     *Law & Order* (television program)
*Caring for Your Kitten* (pamphlet)   *Hedda Gabler* (full-length play)
*Chicago Tribune* (newspaper)      *The Thinker* (sculpture)

### 672.3 For Special Uses

Use italics for a number, letter, or word that is being discussed or used in a special way. (Sometimes quotation marks are used for this reason. See 670.2.)

**I hope that this letter *I* on my report card stands for *incredible* and not *incomplete*.**

### 672.4 For Foreign Words

Use italics for foreign words that have not been adopted into the English language; also use italics for scientific names.

**The voyageurs—tough men with natural *bonhomie*—discovered the shy *Castor canadensis*, or North American beaver.**

---

TEKS 10.18B

Mechanics

## Practice

### Italics (Underlining)

- In Titles
- For Special Uses
- For Foreign Words

Write and underline the word or words that should be italicized in the following sentences.

**Example:** Kelly's embroidered jeans were très chic.
<u>très chic</u>

1. Jennifer Aniston was in last month's issue of People magazine.

2. We are studying Antigone, a Greek tragedy by Sophocles.

3. Sodium aluminum sulfate, also known as soda alum, is used in baking powder.

4. In the 1857 legal case Dred Scott v. Sandford, the Supreme Court claimed that African Americans were not considered United States citizens.

5. The first episode of The Real World aired on MTV in 1992.

6. When did the word props become slang?

7. My brother was stationed on the United States Navy ship the USS Richard Bonhomme.

8. The workshop featured an art technique called trompe l'oeil, which means "trick of the eye."

### Model

Model the following sentence to practice using italics (underlining) for special uses.

**I had no faith in pie charts or diagrams of humanity wherein the wicked were divided from the good and the *forever after* was in direct opposition to the *here and now*.**
—Alice Hoffman, *The Ice Queen*

---

## Italics (Underlining)

Discuss with students the uses of italics (underlining) listed on SE page 672 to help them use appropriate punctuation conventions in their compositions. Have students contribute other examples for each use. Also have students complete the Grammar Practice on SE page 673, and review the answers as a class.

## Related Skills Activities

- *SkillsBook*
  Italics (Underlining) and Quotation Marks 1 and 2, pp. 42–43

## Answers

1. People
2. Antigone
3. soda alum
4. Dred Scott v. Sandford
5. The Real World
6. props
7. USS Richard Bonhomme
8. trompe l'oeil

---

TEKS 10.18B

## Parentheses

### 674.1 To Set Off Explanatory Material

You may use **parentheses** to set off explanatory or added material that interrupts the normal sentence structure.

**Benson** (our dog) **sits in on our piano lessons** (on the piano bench), **much to the teacher's surprise and amusement.**
— Chad Hockerman, student writer

**NOTE:** Place question marks and exclamation points within the parentheses when they mark the added material.

**Ivan at once concluded** (the rascal!) **that I had a passion for dances, and . . . wanted to drag me off to a dancing class.**
— Fyodor Dostoyevsky, "A Novel in Nine Letters"

### 674.2 With Full Sentences

When using a full sentence within another sentence, do not capitalize it or use a period inside the parentheses.

**Since the judging has already begun** (the judges have narrowed their selection to the top six), **you'll have to wait until next year to enter your apple pie in the contest.**

When the parenthetical sentence comes after the period of the main sentence, capitalize and punctuate it the same way you would any other complete sentence.

**Register for the event by completing this application.** (Use blue or black ink.)

**NOTE:** For unavoidable parentheses within parentheses ( . . . [ . . . ] . . . ), use brackets. Avoid overuse of parentheses by using commas instead.

## Diagonal

### 674.3 To Show a Choice

Use a **diagonal** (also called a *slash* or forward *slash*) between two words, as in *and/or*, to indicate that either is acceptable.

**Press the** load/eject **button.**
**Don't worry; this is** indoor/outdoor **carpet.**

### 674.4 When Quoting Poetry

When quoting more than one line of poetry, use a diagonal to show where each line of poetry ends. (Insert a space on each side of the diagonal.)

**"In Venice behind, / Fall the leaves, / Brown, / And yellow streaked with brown."**
— Amy Lowell, "The City of Falling Leaves"

---

Mechanics

## Practice

### Parentheses and Diagonals

 Write the word or words that should be enclosed in parentheses or divided by a diagonal. (Use the correct punctuation.)

**Example:** I tried tekka maki a kind of sushi at the restaurant.
*(a kind of sushi)*

1. Julia Alvarez she wrote *How the Garcia Girls Lost Their Accents* is my favorite author.

2. Push the up down button on the control panel to change the time.

3. Captain Chuck Yeager made famous as a test pilot was also a World War II flying ace.

4. Pizza and or lasagna will be served at the open house.

5. Raymond our Chihuahua likes to sleep in the bathroom sink.

6. Aunt Jo she's not really my aunt but a family friend is coming for a visit.

### Model

Model the following sentence to practice using parentheses with full sentences.

**"One day he brought the teacher a dead chicken snake in a burlap sack, and a chicken was still in the snake's belly (or whatever snakes call bellies).**
— Willie Morris, *Good Old Boy*

### Model

Write the lyrics to a favorite song to practice using diagonals when quoting poetry.

**Tell them at home I long to be there, / While thro this wide world ever I roam; / Only to meet my darling so fair, / Only to see the dear folks at home.**

---

## Parentheses and Diagonal

Discuss with students the uses of parentheses and diagonals listed on SE page 674 to help them use appropriate punctuation conventions in their compositions. Invite volunteers to give their answers to the Grammar Practice questions on SE page 675.

## Related Skills Activities

■ *SkillsBook*
Parentheses, Ellipses, and Brackets, p. 38

## Answers

1. (she wrote *How the Garcia Girls Lost Their Accents*)
2. up/down
3. (made famous as a test pilot)
4. and/or
5. (our Chihuahua)
6. (she's not really my aunt but a family friend)

---

## Dash

**676.1** To Indicate a Sudden Break

Use a **dash** to indicate a sudden break or change in the sentence.

**Near the semester's end**—and this is not always due to poor planning—**some students may find themselves in a real crunch.**

**NOTE:** Dashes are often used in place of commas. Use dashes when you want to give special emphasis; use commas when there is no need for emphasis.

**676.2** To Set Off an Introductory Series

Use a dash to set off an introductory series from the clause that explains the series.

**A good book, a cup of tea, a comfortable chair**—these things always saved my mother's sanity.

**676.3** To Set Off Parenthetical Material

You may use a dash to set off parenthetical material—material that explains or clarifies a word or a phrase.

**A single incident**—a tornado that came without warning—**changed the face of the small town forever.**

**676.4** To Indicate Interrupted Speech

Use a dash to show interrupted or faltering speech in dialogue.

**Why**—why are you doing this to me?

**676.5** For Emphasis

Use a dash to emphasize a word, a series, a phrase, or a clause.

**After years of trial and error, Belther made history with his invention**—the unicycle.

**After several hours of hearing the high-pitched yipping, Petra finally realized what it was**—coyote pups.

---

### Practice

## Dashes

- To Indicate a Sudden Break
- To Set Off Parenthetical Material
- For Emphasis

 A word, a phrase, or a clause follows each sentence below. Write the sentences to include those words, set off by one or two dashes.

**Example:** The ingredients he cooked with were strange and unfamiliar. (mustard oil and fenugreek seeds)

*The ingredients he cooked with—mustard oil and fenugreek seeds—were strange and unfamiliar.*

1. This machine was destined to change the world. (the computer)

2. Suddenly I realized exactly what he was telling me. (a lie)

3. The tsunami came without any warning. (caused by an underwater earthquake)

4. In the distance, a mournful cry echoed through the woods. (and this is not to say that it was miles away)

5. *The Greensboro Gazette* is doing a feature article on Blaine High School senior Todd Davis. (winner of the Langston Hughes Poetry Award)

6. Tears filled his eyes as he recognized the ring in the pawnshop window. (the emerald ring he had given Tamara)

---

### Model

Model the following sentences to practice using a dash to show emphasis.

**The ancient sea-faring cultures**—the Phoenician, the Greek, and the Roman—**all used ships driven by three sets of oars.**

**The manager of the hotel**—I can't remember his name—**switched us to a room with a view of the ocean.**

---

## Dash

Discuss with students the uses of dashes to help them correctly employ dashes to emphasize parenthetical information in their compositions. Have students contribute other examples for each use. Also have students complete the Grammar Practice on SE page 677 individually, and review the answers as a class.

### Related Skills Activities

- **SkillsBook**
  Dashes, p. 24

## Answers

Answers will vary. Possible answers:

1. This machine—the computer—was destined to change the world.

2. Suddenly I realized exactly what he was telling me—a lie.

3. The tsunami—caused by an underwater earthquake—came without any warning.

4. In the distance—and this is not to say that it was miles away—a mournful cry echoed through the woods.

5. *The Greensboro Gazette* is doing a feature article on Blaine High School senior Todd Davis—winner of the Langston Hughes Poetry Award.

6. Tears filled his eyes as he recognized the ring—the emerald ring he had given Tamara—in the pawnshop window.

TEKS 10.18B

## Ellipsis

**678.1** To Show Omitted Words

Use an **ellipsis** (three periods with one space before and after each period) to show that one or more words have been omitted in a quotation.

(Original)

**We the people of the United States, in order to form a more perfect Union, establish justice, insure domestic tranquility, provide for the common defense, promote the general welfare, and secure the blessings of liberty to ourselves and our posterity, do ordain and establish this Constitution for the United States of America.**

—Preamble, *U.S. Constitution*

(Quotation)

**"We the people . . . in order to form a more perfect Union . . . establish this Constitution for the United States of America."**

**678.2** At the End of a Sentence

If words from a quotation are omitted at the end of a sentence, place the ellipsis after the period that marks the conclusion of the sentence.

**"Standing at the entrance were small groups of students. . . . As Will walked by, he could not help but overhear the murmurs of discontent as they continued to wait for the signal to return to classes."**

—Pamela Brown, student writer

**NOTE:** If the quoted material is a complete sentence (even if it was not complete in the original), use a period, then an ellipsis.

(Original)

**I am tired; my heart is sick and sad. From where the sun now stands I will fight no more forever.**

—Chief Joseph of the Nez Percé

(Quotation)

**"I am tired. . . . From where the sun now stands I will fight no more forever."**

or

**"I am tired. . . . I will fight no more. . . ."**

**678.3** To Show a Pause

Use an ellipsis to indicate a pause.

**I brought my trembling hand to my focusing eyes. It was oozing, it was red, it was . . . it was . . . a tomato!**

—Laura Baginski, student writer

---

 TEKS 10.18B

Marking Punctuation **679**

Mechanics

## Practice

### Ellipses

- To Show Omitted Words
- At the End of a Sentence
- To Show a Pause

For each of the following paragraphs, select the least important information to replace with ellipses. Write the shortened paragraphs on your paper.

**Example:**  Joseph Geissman, a local deputy sheriff who has been on the force for five years, was honored for his bravery during the recent flood.

*Joseph Geissman, a local deputy sheriff . . . was honored for his bravery during the recent flood.*

1. Plan now to land a part-time summer job. First, decide on what kind of job you want in terms of location, hours, and pay. Then think about what you have to offer—in particular, your skills and past experience. Next, write a résumé using one of the many online or printed guides. Then look for suitable jobs: Ask around, read newspaper job ads. Apply for any jobs that interest you. Finally, prepare for your interviews. Decide how you will make a great impression on potential employers.

2. Ancient Olympic events were different from modern games. For example, one of the most popular events was chariot racing. There were two-horse races and four-horse races. There were other types of races as well—with foals and mules, for example. The course was 9 miles long (12 laps around the track). Only rich people could afford the horses, equipment, and jockey. It was the owners, and not the winning jockey, who received the olive wreath of victory.

### Model

Model the following sentence to practice using an ellipsis to show a pause.

**When the student is ready . . . the lesson appears.**   —Gene Oliver

---

## Ellipsis

Discuss with students the uses of ellipses listed on SE page 678 to help them use appropriate punctuation conventions in their compositions. Have students contribute other examples for each use. Also have students share their answers to the Grammar Practice on SE page 679 with the class.

## Related Skills Activities

- ***SkillsBook***
  Parentheses, Ellipses, and Brackets, p. 38

---

 **Answers**

1. Plan now to land a part-time summer job. First, decide on what kind of job you want in terms of location, hours, and pay. Then think about what you have to offer. . . . Next, write a résumé. . . . Apply for any jobs that interest you. Finally, prepare for your interviews. Decide how you will make a great impression on potential employers.

2. Ancient Olympic events were different from modern games. For example, one of the most popular events was chariot racing. . . . The course was 9 miles long. . . . It was the owners, and not the winning jockey, who received the olive wreath of victory.

---

## Brackets

**680.1 To Set Off Clarifying Information**

Use **brackets** before and after words that are added to clarify what another person has said or written.

**"Those annoying pests** [the mosquitoes] **ruined our day fishing at the lake."**
—Will Shepherd, student writer

**NOTE:** The brackets indicate that the words *the mosquitoes* are not part of the quotation but were added for clarification.

**680.2 Around an Editorial Correction**

Place brackets around an editorial correction inserted within quoted material.

**"Brooklyn alone has 8 percent of lead poisoning** [victims] **nationwide," said Marjorie Moore.**
—Donna Actie, student writer

**NOTE:** The brackets indicate that the word *victims* replaced the author's original word.

Place brackets around the letters *sic* (Latin for "as such"); the letters indicate that an error appearing in the material being quoted was made by the original speaker or writer.

**"When I'm queen," mused Lucy, "I'll show these blockheads whose** [sic] **got beauty and brains."**

**680.3 To Set Off Added Words**

Place brackets around comments that have been added to a quotation.

**"Congratulations to the astronomy club's softball team, which put in, shall we say, a 'stellar' performance."** [groans]

### Punctuation Marks

| | | | | | |
|---|---|---|---|---|---|
| ´ | Accent, acute | , | Comma | ( ) | Parentheses |
| ` | Accent, grave | † | Dagger | . | Period |
| ' | Apostrophe | — | Dash | ? | Question mark |
| * | Asterisk | / | Diagonal/Slash | " " | Quotation marks |
| { } | Brace | ¨ (ü) | Dieresis | § | Section |
| [ ] | Brackets | ... | Ellipsis | ; | Semicolon |
| ^ | Caret | ! | Exclamation point | ~ | Tilde |
| (ç) | Cedilla | - | Hyphen | ___ | Underscore |
| ^ | Circumflex | ... | Leaders | | |
| : | Colon | ¶ | Paragraph | | |

---

## Practice

### Brackets

- To Set Off Clarifying Information
- Around an Editorial Correction
- To Set Off Added Words

 Follow the directions for each activity below.

**Example:** In the following quotation, the speaker is talking about the English Industrial Revolution. Use words in brackets to clarify the quotation.

"The productive capacity of England was changed dramatically," Dr. Bates said. "Every class of people was touched by it."

. . . was touched by it [the English Industrial Revolution]."

**1.** In the following quotation, the speaker is talking about satellites. Use words in brackets to clarify the quotation.

"There has been some damage to them," the astrophysicist explained. "For the most part, it has been minor."

**2.** In the following quotation, replace the speaker's use of the word *repartee* with *witty reply*.

Mr. Daly reported, "She responded to my commentary with a repartee."

**3.** Quote the following statement and show that the error was made by the original writer, Joy Thayer.

James Monroe's secratary of state was John Quincy Adams.

**4.** Add the comment *sigh* to the following quotation.

"I'm so tired that I can't concentrate."

### Model

Model the following sentence to practice using brackets to set off clarifying information.

Nobody thought that it [the airline strike] would last as long as it did.

---

## Brackets

Discuss with students the uses of brackets listed on SE page 680 to help them use appropriate punctuation conventions in their compositions. Invite student volunteers to provide examples for some of the less common punctuation marks in the blue box. Also invite students to share their answers to the Grammar Practice on SE page 681 with the class.

## Related Skills Activities

- **SkillsBook**
  Parentheses, Ellipses, and Brackets, p. 38
  Review: Hyphens and Dashes, p. 25
  Review: Apostrophes, p. 30
  Review: Quotation Marks and Italics (Underlining), pp. 36–37

## Answers

1. . . . damage to them [satellites]."
2. . . . with a [witty reply]."
3. According to Joy Thayer, "James Monroe's secratary [sic] of state was John Quincy Adams."
4. "I'm so tired that I can't concentrate." [sigh]

TEKS 10.18A

## Capitalization

**682.1** Proper Nouns and Adjectives

**Capitalize** proper nouns and proper adjectives (those derived from proper nouns). The chart below provides a quick overview of capitalization rules. The pages following explain some specific rules of capitalization.

### Capitalization at a Glance

| | |
|---|---|
| Names of people | Alice Walker, Matilda, Jim, Mr. Roker |
| Days of the week, months | Sunday, Tuesday, June, August |
| Holidays, holy days | Thanksgiving, Easter, Hanukkah |
| Periods, events in history | Middle Ages, the Battle of Bunker Hill |
| Official documents | Declaration of Independence |
| Special events | Elgin Community Spring Gala |
| Languages, nationalities, religions | French, Canadian, Islam |
| Political parties | Republican Party, Socialist Party |
| Trade names | Oscar Mayer hot dogs, Pontiac Vibe |
| Official titles used with names | Mayor John Spitzer, Senator Feinstein |
| Formal epithets | Alexander the Great |

*Geographical names*

| | |
|---|---|
| Planets, heavenly bodies | Earth, Jupiter, the Milky Way |
| Continents | Australia, South America |
| Countries | Ireland, Grenada, Sri Lanka |
| States, provinces | Ohio, Utah, Nova Scotia |
| Cities, towns, villages | El Paso, Burlington, Wonewoc |
| Streets, roads, highways | Park Avenue, Route 66, Interstate 90 |
| Landforms | the Rocky Mountains, the Sahara Desert |
| Bodies of water | Yellowstone Lake, Pumpkin Creek |
| Buildings, monuments | Elkhorn High School, Gateway Arch |
| Public areas | Times Square, Sequoia National Park |

---

TEKS 10.18A

## Capitalization 1

- Proper Nouns and Adjectives

 **For each sentence below, write the words that should be capitalized.**

**Example:** On tuesday, mayor henke declared that all city offices would be closed on martin luther king day.
Tuesday, Mayor Henke, Martin Luther King Day

1. Edward the confessor ruled england from 1042 to 1066.

2. Admittance to the independence ball required a ticket from the presidential inaugural committee.

3. When sylvie attended carlton college, she learned to speak greek and latin.

4. I wish stores would not decorate for christmas until after thanksgiving.

5. A severe earthquake hit san francisco on april 18, 1906.

6. The missouri river flows from its source in the rocky mountains to the mississippi river near st. louis.

7. Ancient greeks called mercury, venus, mars, jupiter, and saturn "wandering stars."

8. The teachings of the chinese philosopher confucius (551 to 479 B.C.E.) are called confucianism.

### Model

Model the following sentences to practice capitalizing proper nouns and adjectives.

> Though Africa and Egypt were popular destinations, Carlos decided to travel to Chile, the country where his father was born.

> While in Rome, Larissa saw the Colosseum, the Vatican, the Arch of Constantine, and the Roman Forum.

---

## Capitalization

Discuss with students the uses of capitalization listed on SE page 682 to help them use appropriate capitalization conventions in their compositions. Have students contribute other examples for each use. Also invite students to share their answers to the Grammar Practice on SE page 683 with the class.

### Related Skills Activities

■ *SkillsBook*
Pretest: Capitalization, pp. 39–40
Capitalization 1, 2, and 3, pp. 49–51

---

## Answers

1. Confessor, England
2. Independence Ball, Presidential Inaugural Committee
3. Sylvie, Carlton College, Greek, Latin
4. Christmas, Thanksgiving
5. San Francisco, April
6. Missouri River, Rocky Mountains, Mississippi River, St. Louis
7. Greeks, Mercury, Venus, Mars, Jupiter, Saturn
8. Chinese, Confucius, Confucianism

---

Mechanics

TEKS 10.18A

## Capitalization (continued)

### 684.1 First Words

Capitalize the first word of every sentence, including the first word of a full-sentence direct quotation.

> The crowd was quiet. A girl whispered, "I hope it's not Nancy," and the sound of her whisper reached the edges of the crowd.
> —Shirley Jackson, "The Lottery"

### 684.2 Sentences in Parentheses

Capitalize the first word in a sentence enclosed in parentheses, but do not capitalize the first word if the parenthetical appears within another sentence.

> In a bygone era, a fortunate New Orleans visitor could be entertained by a young Louis Armstrong playing the cornet. (A cornet is a kind of small trumpet with a mellower sound.)
> Damien's aunt (she's a wild woman) plays bingo every Saturday night.

### 684.3 Sentences Following Colons

Capitalize the first word in a complete sentence that follows a colon when (1) you want to emphasize the sentence or (2) the sentence is a quotation.

> When we quarreled and made horrible faces at one another, Mother knew what to say: "Your faces will stay that way, and no one will marry you."

### 684.4 Sections of the Country

Capitalize words that indicate particular sections of the country; do not capitalize words that simply indicate direction.

> Mr. Johnson is from the Southwest. (section of the country)
> After moving north to Montana, he had to buy winter clothes. (direction)

### 684.5 Certain Religious Words

Capitalize nouns that refer to the Supreme Being, the word *Bible*, the books of the Bible, and the names for other holy books.

> God   Jehovah   the Lord   the Savior   Allah   Bible   Genesis

### 684.6 Titles

Capitalize the first word of a title, the last word, and every word in between except articles (*a, an, the*), short prepositions, and coordinating conjunctions. Follow this rule for titles of books, newspapers, magazines, poems, plays, songs, articles, films, works of art, photographs, and stories.

> *Washington Post*   "The Diary of a Madman"   *Nights of Rain and Stars*

Mechanics

## Practice

### Capitalization 2

- Sentences Following Colons
- Certain Religious Words
- Titles

For the paragraphs below, write the line number along with the words that should be capitalized.

**Example:** 2. What

1 When my grandfather was young, everyone asked the same
2 question: what would he be when he grew up? Hans was interested
3 in many things. He studied the bible and the torah. He considered
4 becoming a religious philosopher. When he read *a tale of two cities,*
5 *for whom the bell tolls,* and other great novels, he decided to be an
6 author. He also wanted to be an architect, an engineer, and even a
7 horse trainer! So what profession did my grandfather finally choose?
8 He became a typesetter!
9 Hans thought typesetting was a way to be a part of great events
10 in the world. He set type for some amazing headlines: "Pearl Harbor
11 attacked," "Yankees win the Series." He set articles about coronations
12 and the first astronauts' ventures into space. Yes, Hans was there
13 for all the great happenings. Shortly before he died, he summed it up
14 this way: "if it happened in the last 40 years, I was there—a mere
15 shadow, perhaps, but that was me."

### Model

Model the following sentences to practice capitalizing certain religious words, titles, and sentences following colons.

> Allah, Jehovah, Jah, and the Lord are different names for God.
> The class was stunned by the teacher's statement: "We'll be reading *Notes from the House of the Dead, Crime and Punishment,* and *The Idiot* this semester."

## Capitalization

Discuss with students the uses of capitalization listed on SE page 684 to help them use appropriate capitalization conventions in their compositions. Have students contribute other examples for each use. Also invite students to share their answers to the Grammar Practice on SE page 685 with the class.

## Related Skills Activities

- ***SkillsBook***
  Capitalization 1, 2, and 3, pp. 49–51

## Answers

*line 2:*   What
*line 3:*   Bible, Torah
*line 4:*   *A Tale of Two Cities*
*line 5:*   *For Whom the Bell Tolls*
*line 11:*   Attacked, Win
*line 14:*   If

TEKS 10.18A

## Capitalization (continued)

### 686.1 Words Used as Names

Capitalize words like *father, mother, uncle,* and *senator* when they are used as titles with a personal name or when they are substituted for proper nouns (especially in direct address).

**We've missed you, Aunt Lucinda!** (*Aunt* is part of the name.)
**I hope Mayor Bates arrives soon.** (*Mayor* is part of the name.)

### A Closer Look

To test whether a word is being substituted for a proper noun, simply read the sentence with a proper noun in place of the word. If the proper noun fits in the sentence, the word being tested should be capitalized; otherwise, the word should not be capitalized.

**Did Mom (Sue) say we could go?** (*Sue* works in this sentence.)
**Did your mom (Sue) say you could go?** (*Sue* does not work here.)

**NOTE:** Usually the word is not capitalized if it follows a possessive —*my, his, your*—as it does in the second sentence above.

### 686.2 Letters

Capitalize the letters used to indicate form or shape.

**U-turn    I-beam    S-curve    T-shirt    V-shaped**

### 686.3 Organizations

Capitalize the name of an organization, an association, or a team.

**Lake Ontario Sailors    American Red Cross    Democratic Party**

### 686.4 Abbreviations

Capitalize abbreviations of titles and organizations. (Some other abbreviations are also capitalized. See pages 694–696.)

**AAA    CEO    NAACP    M.D.    Ph.D.**

### 686.5 Titles of Courses

Capitalize words like *sociology* and *history* when they are used as titles of specific courses; do not capitalize these words when they name a field of study.

**Who teaches History 202?** (title of a specific course)
**It's the same professor who teaches my sociology course.** (a field of study)

**NOTE:** The words *freshman, sophomore, junior,* and *senior* are not capitalized unless they are part of an official title.

**Rosa is a senior this year and is in charge of the Senior Class Banquet.**

---

TEKS 10.18A

 **Practice**

## Capitalization 3

■ Words Used as Names
■ Organizations
■ Letters

For each of the following sentences, correctly write any word or word groups that are incorrectly capitalized or lowercased.

**Example:** The a-frame house, popularized by Architect Andrew Geller, was a popular style for vacation homes in the 1960s.
  *A-frame, architect*

**1.** The American institute of architects has more than 74,000 members.

**2.** Last week, vice president Shannon Kraus from that Organization visited our school.

**3.** My Dad wanted to meet her; he was once a member of his high school's Future architects club.

**4.** That, of course, was before his stint on the School's lacrosse team, the Arlington eagles.

**5.** Back then, dad was so good that he was recruited by the Long island lizards.

**6.** He had to put his lacrosse career on hold, however, when he burned his hand while changing an o-ring on grandma's motorcycle.

**7.** Now he and mom own their own Cycle-repair Shop.

**8.** They also belong to the Canadian motorcycle association.

### Model

Model the following sentences to practice capitalizing organizations and words used as names.

**We met Senator Blanche Lincoln at an American Heart Association fund-raiser.**

**After the last election, Uncle Ray said he was going to vote for the Green Party next time.**

---

Mechanics

## Capitalization

Discuss with students the uses of capitalization listed on SE page 686 to help them use appropriate capitalization conventions in their compositions. Have students contribute other examples for each use. Also invite students to share their answers to the Grammar Practice on SE page 687 with the class.

## Related Skills Activities

■ *SkillsBook*
  Capitalization 1, 2, and 3, pp. 49–51
  Review: Capitalization, p. 44

 **Answers**

1. Institute, Architects
2. Vice President, organization
3. dad, Architects Club
4. school's, Eagles
5. Dad, Island Lizards
6. O-ring, Grandma's
7. Mom, cycle-repair shop
8. Motorcycle Association

## Plurals

**688.1 Most Nouns**

Form the **plurals** of most nouns by adding *s* to the singular.
cheerleader — cheerleaders wheel — wheels crate — crates

**688.2 Nouns Ending in *sh, ch, x, s,* and *z***

Form the plurals of nouns ending in *sh, ch, x, s,* and *z* by adding *es* to the singular.
lunch — lunches dish — dishes mess — messes fox — foxes

**Exception:** When the final *ch* sounds like *k*, add an *s* (*monarchs*).

**688.3 Nouns Ending in *y***

The plurals of common nouns that end in *y* (preceded by a consonant) are formed by changing the *y* to *i* and adding *es*.
fly — flies jalopy — jalopies

Form the plurals of nouns that end in *y* (preceded by a vowel) by adding only an *s*.
donkey — donkeys monkey — monkeys

**NOTE:** Form the plurals of all proper nouns ending in *y* by adding *s* (*Kathys*).

**688.4 Nouns Ending in *o***

The plurals of nouns ending in *o* (preceded by a vowel) are formed by adding an *s*.
radio — radios rodeo — rodeos studio — studios duo — duos

The plurals of most nouns ending in *o* (preceded by a consonant) are formed by adding *es*.
echo — echoes hero — heroes tomato — tomatoes

**Exception:** Musical terms always form plurals by adding *s*.
alto — altos banjo — banjos solo — solos piano — pianos

**688.5 Nouns Ending in *ful***

Form the plurals of nouns that end in *ful* by adding an *s* at the end of the word.
two tankfuls three pailfuls four mouthfuls

**NOTE:** Do not confuse these examples with *three pails full* (when you are referring to three separate pails full of something) or *two tanks full*.

**688.6 Compound Nouns**

Form the plurals of most compound nouns by adding *s* or *es* to the important word in the compound.
brothers-in-law maids of honor secretaries of state

## Practice

### Plurals 1

- Regular Nouns
- Nouns Ending in *sh, ch, x, s,* and *z*
- Nouns Ending in *y, o,* and *ful*

Write the correct plural of the underlined word in each sentence.

**Example:** The art <u>portfolioes</u> of seven students were on display.
*portfolios*

1. The <u>keyes</u> for the table saw are in the industrial arts office.
2. Lila poured five <u>cansful</u> of water into the kettle and carefully stirred the soup.
3. We followed our guide across three mountain <u>pass's</u> to get to Blaine's Ridge.
4. The landscaping staff will plant lilac <u>bushs</u> along the walk to the main entrance.
5. The Wilmores looked at five different <u>patioes</u> before picking out a design they liked.
6. Harbor <u>authoritys</u> reported that ship traffic increased by 50 percent during the last quarter of 2005.
7. The home economics class used six different cake <u>mixs</u> to make one large cake.
8. A cow does not have four <u>stomaches</u>; it has one stomach with four parts.
9. No one can explain all the <u>mysterys</u> of the universe.
10. Use this paint to make 20 <u>dashs</u> across the wall.
11. Jayleen and Francine found five dust-covered <u>piccoloes</u> in the band's storage room.

### Exercise

Write a sentence for the plural of each of the following words.
ray, tress, glassful, territory

## Plurals

Discuss with students the uses of plurals listed on SE page 688 to help them spell correctly. Have students contribute other examples for each use. Also have students complete the Grammar Practice on SE page 689 individually, and review the answers as a class.

### Related Skills Activities

- **SkillsBook**
  Pretest: Plurals and Spelling, pp. 49–50
  Plurals 1 and 2, pp. 51–52

## Answers

1. keys
2. canfuls
3. passes
4. bushes
5. patios
6. authorities
7. mixes
8. stomachs
9. mysteries
10. dashes
11. piccolos

## Plurals *(continued)*

### 690.1 Nouns Ending in *f* or *fe*

Form the plurals of nouns that end in *f* or *fe* in one of two ways: if the final *f* sound is still heard in the plural form of the word, simply add *s;* but if the final *f* sound becomes a *v* sound, change the *f* to *ve* and add *s.*

**Plural ends with *f* sound:** roof — roofs;  chief — chiefs
**Plural ends with *v* sound:** wife — wives;  loaf — loaves

**NOTE:** Several words are correct with either ending.

**Plural ends with either sound:** hoof — hooves/hoofs

### 690.2 Irregular Spelling

A number of words form a plural by taking on an irregular spelling.

crisis — crises        child — children    radius — radii
criterion — criteria    goose — geese      die — dice

**NOTE:** Some of these words are acceptable with the commonly used *s* or *es* ending.

index — indices/indexes    cactus — cacti/cactuses

Some nouns remain unchanged when used as plurals.

deer      moose      sheep      salmon      aircraft      series

### 690.3 Words Discussed as Words

The plurals of symbols, letters, numbers, and words being discussed as words are formed by adding an apostrophe and an *s.*

Dad yelled a lot of *wow's* and *yippee's* when he saw my A's and B's.

**NOTE:** You may omit the apostrophe if it does not cause any confusion.

the three R's or Rs      YMCA's or YMCAs

### 690.4 Collective Nouns

A collective noun may be singular or plural depending upon how it's used. A collective noun is singular when it refers to a group considered as one unit; it is plural when it refers to the individuals in the group.

**The class was on its best behavior.** (group as a unit)
**The class are preparing for their final exams.** (individuals in the group)

If it seems awkward to use a plural verb with a collective noun, add a clearly plural noun such as *members* to the sentence, or change the collective noun into a possessive followed by a plural noun that describes the individuals in the group.

**The class members are preparing for their final exams.**
**The class's students are preparing for their final exams.**

---

## Practice

### Plurals 2

- Irregular Spelling
- Words Discussed as Words
- Collective Nouns

 For each sentence below, write the plural form of the word in parentheses.

**Example:** How many (child) attend the Bayshore Science School?
*children*

1. When Diego opened the musty trunk, he was startled to see four (mouse) staring back at him.

2. It was disturbing to me to hear the president continue his incorrect pronunciation of all the *(nuclear)* in his speeches.

3. Isle Royale, an island in Lake Superior, supports a population of about 550 (moose).

4. Many of the university's (alumnus) donate money to help keep the school competitive both academically and athletically.

5. Mr. Lake pointed out that the writer had used six *(and)* in quite a rambling sentence.

6. Scientists count the number of protons and neutrons to distinguish between the (nucleus) of atoms.

7. Kev plans to ask the five (W) during the interview.

8. Najib and Sylvia were pleased with their catch of 15 (fish).

### Model

Model the following sentences to practice using collective nouns correctly.

Make sure you have finished speaking before your audience has finished listening.
—Dorothy Sarnoff

After their honeymoon was interrupted by a hurricane, the couple were happy to be back home.

---

## Plurals

Discuss with students the uses of plurals listed on SE page 690 to help them spell correctly. Have students contribute other examples for each use. Also invite students to share their answers to the Grammar Practice on SE page 691 with the class.

## Related Skills Activities

- ***SkillsBook***
Plurals 1 and 2, pp. 51–52

## Answers

1. mice
2. nuclear's
3. moose
4. alumni
5. and's
6. nuclei
7. W's or Ws
8. fish

## Numbers

### 692.1 Numerals or Words

**Numbers** from one to nine are usually written as words; numbers 10 and over are usually written as numerals. However, numbers being compared or contrasted should be kept in the same style.

**8 to 11 years old      eight to eleven years old**

You may use a combination of numerals and words for very large numbers.

**1.5 million      3 billion to 3.2 billion      6 trillion**

If numbers are used infrequently in a piece of writing, you may spell out those that can be written in no more than two words.

**ten      twenty-five      two hundred      fifty thousand**

### 692.2 Numerals Only

Use numerals for the following forms: decimals, percentages, chapters, pages, addresses, phone numbers, identification numbers, and statistics.

| | | | |
|---|---|---|---|
| **26.2** | **8 percent** | **Highway 36** | **chapter 7** |
| **pages 287–89** | **July 6, 1945** | **44 B.C.E.** | **a vote of 23 to 4** |

Always use numerals with abbreviations and symbols.

**8%      10 mm      3 cc      8 oz      90° C      24 mph      6' 3"**

### 692.3 Words Only

Use words to express numbers that begin a sentence.

**Fourteen students "forgot" their assignments.**

**NOTE:** Change the sentence structure if this rule creates a clumsy construction.

**Clumsy:** *Six hundred thirty-nine* teachers were laid off this year.

**Better: This year, 639 teachers were laid off.**

Use words for numbers that come before a compound modifier if that modifier includes a numeral.

**They made twelve 10-foot sub sandwiches for the picnic.**

### 692.4 Time and Money

If time is expressed with an abbreviation, use numerals; if it is expressed in words, spell out the number.

**4:00 A.M., 4:00 a.m., (or) four o'clock**

If an amount of money is spelled out, so is the currency; use a numeral if a symbol is used.

**twenty dollars (or) $20**

## Practice

### Numbers

- Numerals or Words
- Numerals Only
- Words Only
- Time and Money

 For each sentence below, write the underlined numbers the correct way. If a number is already correctly presented, write "correct."

**Example:** In <u>1</u> year, an acre of trees produces enough oxygen for <u>eighteen</u> people.
*one, 18*

**1.** In that same year, those trees can absorb as much carbon as is produced by a car driven up to <u>8,700</u> miles.

**2.** A tree does not reach its most productive stage of carbon storage until it is <u>ten</u> years old.

**3.** Over its life, a <u>seventy</u>-year-old tree absorbs over three tons of carbon.

**4.** Trees that provide shade and shelter reduce yearly heating and cooling costs by <u>$2.1 billion dollars</u>.

**5.** A giant redwood in California, the world's tallest tree, measures <u>378</u> feet high.

**6.** The largest tree in the world, a sequoia in California, has a volume of <u>fourteen hundred eighty-seven</u> cubic meters.

**7.** Found in the White Mountains of California, bristlecone pines are the world's oldest trees at more than <u>four thousand, eight hundred</u> years old!

**8.** The *Apollo 14* mission of <u>January thirty-first, 1971</u>, had tree seeds among its cargo.

### Exercise

Complete these sentences with your own numbers.

**Please read chapter _____ in your science book. Remember, the test next week will count for _____ percent of your grade.**

## Related Skills Activities

- ### *SkillsBook*
  Numbers 1 and 2, pp. 45–46

## Answers

1. correct
2. 10
3. 70
4. $2.1 billion OR 2.1 billion dollars
5. correct
6. 1,487
7. 4,800
8. January 31, 1971,

# Abbreviations

### 694.1 Formal and Informal Abbreviations

An **abbreviation** is the shortened form of a word or phrase. Some abbreviations are always acceptable in both formal and informal writing:

Mr.  Mrs.  Jr.  Ms.  Dr.  a.m. (A.M.)  p.m. (P.M.)

**NOTE:** In most of your writing, you do not abbreviate the names of states, countries, months, days, or units of measure. However, you may use the abbreviation *U.S.* after it has been spelled out once. Do not abbreviate the words *street, company,* and similar words, especially when they are part of a proper name. Also, do not use signs or symbols (%, &, #, @) in place of words. The dollar sign, however, is appropriate with numerals ($325).

### 694.2 Correspondence Abbreviations

**United States**

| | Standard | Postal |
|---|---|---|
| Alabama | Ala. | AL |
| Alaska | Alaska | AK |
| Arizona | Ariz. | AZ |
| Arkansas | Ark. | AR |
| California | Calif. | CA |
| Colorado | Colo. | CO |
| Connecticut | Conn. | CT |
| Delaware | Del. | DE |
| District of Columbia | D.C. | DC |
| Florida | Fla. | FL |
| Georgia | Ga. | GA |
| Guam | Guam | GU |
| Hawaii | Hawaii | HI |
| Idaho | Idaho | ID |
| Illinois | Ill. | IL |
| Indiana | Ind. | IN |
| Iowa | Iowa | IA |
| Kansas | Kan. | KS |
| Kentucky | Ky. | KY |
| Louisiana | La. | LA |
| Maine | Maine | ME |
| Maryland | Md. | MD |
| Massachusetts | Mass. | MA |
| Michigan | Mich. | MI |
| Minnesota | Minn. | MN |
| Mississippi | Miss. | MS |
| Missouri | Mo. | MO |
| Montana | Mont. | MT |
| Nebraska | Neb. | NE |
| Nevada | Nev. | NV |
| New Hampshire | N.H. | NH |
| New Jersey | N.J. | NJ |
| New Mexico | N.M. | NM |
| New York | N.Y. | NY |
| North Carolina | N.C. | NC |
| North Dakota | N.D. | ND |
| Ohio | Ohio | OH |
| Oklahoma | Okla. | OK |
| Oregon | Ore. | OR |
| Pennsylvania | Pa. | PA |
| Puerto Rico | P.R. | PR |
| Rhode Island | R.I. | RI |
| South Carolina | S.C. | SC |
| South Dakota | S.D. | SD |
| Tennessee | Tenn. | TN |
| Texas | Texas | TX |
| Utah | Utah | UT |
| Vermont | Vt. | VT |
| Virginia | Va. | VA |
| Virgin Islands | V.I. | VI |
| Washington | Wash. | WA |
| West Virginia | W.Va. | WV |
| Wisconsin | Wis. | WI |
| Wyoming | Wyo. | WY |

**Canadian Provinces**

| | Standard | Postal |
|---|---|---|
| Alberta | Alta. | AB |
| British Columbia | B.C. | BC |
| Labrador | Lab. | NL |
| Manitoba | Man. | MB |
| New Brunswick | N.B. | NB |
| Newfoundland | N.F. | NL |
| Northwest Territories | N.W.T. | NT |
| Nova Scotia | N.S. | NS |
| Nunavut | | NU |
| Ontario | Ont. | ON |
| Prince Edward Island | P.E.I. | PE |
| Quebec | Que. | QC |
| Saskatchewan | Sask. | SK |
| Yukon Territory | Y.T. | YT |

**Addresses**

| | Standard | Postal |
|---|---|---|
| Apartment | Apt. | APT |
| Avenue | Ave. | AVE |
| Boulevard | Blvd. | BLVD |
| Circle | Cir. | CIR |
| Court | Ct. | CT |
| Drive | Dr. | DR |
| East | E. | E |
| Expressway | Expy. | EXPY |
| Freeway | Fwy. | FWY |
| Heights | Hts. | HTS |
| Highway | Hwy. | HWY |
| Hospital | Hosp. | HOSP |
| Junction | Junc. | JCT |
| Lake | L. | LK |
| Lakes | Ls. | LKS |
| Lane | Ln. | LN |
| Meadows | Mdws. | MDWS |
| North | N. | N |
| Palms | Palms | PLMS |
| Park | Pk. | PK |
| Parkway | Pky. | PKY |
| Place | Pl. | PL |
| Plaza | Plaza | PLZ |
| Post Office Box | Box | BOX |
| Ridge | Rdg. | RDG |
| River | R. | RV |
| Road | Rd. | RD |
| Room | Rm. | RM |
| Rural | R. | R |
| Rural Route | R.R. | RR |
| Shore | Sh. | SH |
| South | S. | S |
| Square | Sq. | SQ |
| Station | Sta. | STA |
| Street | St. | ST |
| Suite | Ste. | STE |
| Terrace | Ter. | TER |
| Turnpike | Tpke. | TPKE |
| Union | Un. | UN |
| View | View | VW |
| Village | Vil. | VLG |
| West | W. | W |

### 695.1 Other Common Abbreviations

**abr.** abridged; abridgment
**AC, ac** alternating current
**ack.** acknowledge; acknowledgment
**acv** actual cash value
**A.D.** in the year of the Lord (Latin *anno Domini*)
**AM** amplitude modulation
**A.M., a.m.** before noon (Latin *ante meridiem*)
**ASAP** as soon as possible
**avg., av.** average
**BBB** Better Business Bureau
**B.C.** before Christ
**B.C.E.** before the Common Era
**bibliog.** bibliographer; bibliography
**biog.** biographer; biographical; biography
**C** 1. Celsius 2. centigrade 3. coulomb
**c.** 1. circa (about) 2. cup
**cc** 1. cubic centimeter 2. carbon copy
**CDT, C.D.T.** central daylight time
**C.E.** of the Common Era
**chap.** chapter
**cm** centimeter
**c.o., c/o** care of
**COD, C.O.D** 1. cash on delivery 2. collect on delivery
**co-op.** cooperative
**CST, C.S.T.** central standard time
**cu., c** cubic
**D.A.** district attorney
**d.b.a.** doing business as
**DC, dc** direct current
**dec.** deceased
**dept.** department
**DST, D.S.T.** daylight saving time
**dup.** duplicate
**DVD** digital video disc
**ea.** each
**ed.** edition; editor
**EDT, E.D.T.** eastern daylight time
**e.g.** for example (Latin *exempli gratia*)
**EST, E.S.T.** eastern standard time
**etc.** and so forth (Latin *et cetera*)
**ex.** example
**F** Fahrenheit
**FM** frequency modulation
**F.O.B., f.o.b.** free on board
**ft** foot
**g** 1. gram 2. gravity
**gal.** gallon
**gloss.** glossary
**GNP** gross national product
**hdqrs, HQ** headquarters
**HIV** human immunodeficiency virus
**Hon.** Honorable (title)
**hp** horsepower
**HTML** hypertext markup language
**Hz** hertz
**ibid.** in the same place (Latin *ibidem*)
**id.** the same (Latin *idem*)
**i.e.** that is (Latin *id est*)
**illus.** illustration
**inc.** incorporated
**IQ, I.Q.** intelligence quotient
**IRS** Internal Revenue Service
**ISBN** International Standard Book Number
**Jr., jr.** junior
**K** 1. kelvin (temperature unit) 2. Kelvin (temperature scale)
**kc** kilocycle
**kg** kilogram
**km** kilometer
**kn** knot
**kW** kilowatt
**l** liter
**lat.** latitude
**lb., lb.** pound (Latin *libra*)
**l.c.** lowercase
**lit.** literary; literature
**log** logarithm
**long.** longitude
**Ltd., ltd.** limited
**m** meter
**M.A.** master of arts (Latin *Magister Artium*)
**Mc, mc** megacycle
**M.C., m.c.** master of ceremonies
**M.D.** doctor of medicine (Latin *medicinae doctor*)
**mdse.** merchandise
**mfg.** manufacturing
**mg** milligram
**mi.** 1. mile 2. mill (monetary unit)
**misc.** miscellaneous
**ml** milliliter
**mm** millimeter
**mpg, m.p.g.** miles per gallon
**mph, m.p.h.** miles per hour
**MS** 1. manuscript 2. Mississippi 3. multiple sclerosis
**Ms., Ms** title of courtesy for a woman
**MST, M.S.T.** mountain standard time
**neg.** negative
**N.S.F., n.s.f.** not sufficient funds
**oz, oz.** ounce
**PA** 1. public-address system 2. Pennsylvania
**pct.** percent
**pd.** paid
**PDT, P.D.T.** Pacific daylight time
**PFC, Pfc.** private first class
**pg., p.** page
**P.M., p.m.** after noon (Latin *post meridiem*)
**P.O.** 1. personnel officer 2. purchase order 3. postal order; post office 4. (also **p.o.**) petty officer
**pop.** population
**POW, P.O.W.** prisoner of war
**pp.** pages
**ppd.** 1. postpaid 2. prepaid
**PR, P.R.** 1. public relations 2. Puerto Rico
**P.S.** post script
**psi, p.s.i.** pounds per square inch
**PST, P.S.T.** Pacific standard time
**PTA, P.T.A.** Parent-Teacher Association
**qt.** quart
**RF** radio frequency
**RN** registered nurse
**R.P.M., rpm** revolutions per minute
**R.S.V.P., r.s.v.p.** please reply (French *répondez s'il vous plaît*)
**SASE** self-addressed stamped envelope
**SCSI** small computer system interface
**SOS** 1. international distress signal 2. any call for help
**Sr.** 1. senior (after surname) 2. sister (religious)
**ST** standard time
**St.** 1. saint 2. strait 3. street
**std.** standard
**syn.** synonymous; synonym
**TBA** to be announced
**tbs, tbsp** tablespoon
**TM** trademark
**tsp** teaspoon
**UHF, uhf** ultra high frequency
**UPC** universal product code
**UV** ultraviolet
**V** 1. *Physics:* velocity 2. *Electricity:* volt 3. volume
**V.A., VA** Veterans Administration
**VHF, vhf** very high frequency
**VIP** *Informal:* very important person
**vol.** 1. volume 2. volunteer
**vs.** versus
**W** 1. *Electricity:* watt 2. *Physics:* (also **w**) work 3. west
**whse., whs.** warehouse
**wkly.** weekly
**w/o** without
**wt.** weight
**yd** yard (measurement)

## Related Skills Activities

■ *SkillsBook*
Abbreviations, p. 47

## Acronyms and Initialisms

**696.1** Acronyms

An **acronym** is a word formed from the first (or first few) letters of words in a phrase. Even though acronyms are abbreviations, they require no periods.

| | |
|---|---|
| radar | radio detecting and ranging |
| CARE | Cooperative for American Relief Everywhere |
| NASA | National Aeronautics and Space Administration |
| VISTA | Volunteers in Service to America |
| LAN | local area network |

**696.2** Initialisms

An **initialism** is similar to an acronym except that the initials used to form this abbreviation are pronounced individually.

| | |
|---|---|
| CIA | Central Intelligence Agency |
| FBI | Federal Bureau of Investigation |
| FHA | Federal Housing Administration |

**696.3** Common Acronyms and Initialisms

| | | | |
|---|---|---|---|
| ADD | attention deficit disorder | MADD | Mothers Against Drunk Driving |
| AIDS | acquired immunodeficiency syndrome | MRI | magnetic resonance imaging |
| AKA | also known as | NASA | National Aeronautics and Space Administration |
| ATM | automatic teller machine | NATO | North Atlantic Treaty Organization |
| BMI | body mass index | OPEC | Organization of Petroleum-Exporting Countries |
| CD | compact disc | OSHA | Occupational Safety and Health Administration |
| DMV | Department of Motor Vehicles | | |
| ETA | expected time of arrival | PAC | political action committee |
| FAA | Federal Aviation Administration | PDF | portable document format |
| FCC | Federal Communications Commission | PETA | People for the Ethical Treatment of Animals |
| FDA | Food and Drug Administration | PIN | personal identification number |
| FDIC | Federal Deposit Insurance Corporation | PSA | public service announcement |
| FEMA | Federal Emergency Management Agency | ROTC | Reserve Officers' Training Corps |
| FTC | Federal Trade Commission | SADD | Students Against Destructive Decisions |
| FYI | for your information | | |
| GPS | global positioning system | SUV | sport utility vehicle |
| HDTV | high-definition television | SWAT | special weapons and tactics |
| IRS | Internal Revenue Service | TDD | telecommunications device for the deaf |
| IT | information technology | | |
| JPEG | Joint Photographic Experts Group | VA | Veterans Administration |
| LCD | liquid crystal display | | |
| LLC | limited liability company | | |

### Practice

**Abbreviations, Acronyms, and Initialisms**

For each abbreviation, acronym, or initialism below, write out what it stands for. Then write whether it is an abbreviation, acronym, or initialism. (Do as many as you can before referring to the previous pages.)

**Example:** MI
　　　　　*Michigan, abbreviation*

| *States/Provinces* | *Addresses* | *Miscellaneous* |
|---|---|---|
| **1.** NC | **10.** PKY | **15.** OPEC |
| **2.** AK | **11.** CT | **16.** B.C.E. |
| **3.** QC | **12.** LK | **17.** d.b.a. |
| **4.** MA | **13.** HTS | **18.** PETA |
| **5.** MS | **14.** RV | **19.** DVD |
| **6.** VI | | **20.** i.e. |
| **7.** IA | | **21.** IRS |
| **8.** ON | | **22.** PIN |
| **9.** PR | | **23.** lb. |
| | | **24.** POW |
| | | **25.** pct. |
| | | **26.** UPC |
| | | **27.** avg. |
| | | **28.** SWAT |

### Model

Model the following acronyms and initialisms to come up with your own abbreviations. (Write at least one acronym and one initialism.)

HTML – hypertext markup language
HRH – Her Royal Highness
PERT – program evaluation review technique
MERCAD – measurement electronically recorded computer-aided design

### Related Skills Activities

■ *SkillsBook*
　Review: Numbers and Abbreviations, p. 48

### Answers

1. North Carolina, abbreviation
2. Alaska, abbreviation
3. Quebec, abbreviation
4. Massachusetts, abbreviation
5. Mississippi, abbreviation
6. Virgin Islands, abbreviation
7. Iowa, abbreviation
8. Ontario, abbreviation
9. Puerto Rico, abbreviation
10. Parkway, abbreviation
11. Court, abbreviation
12. Lake, abbreviation
13. Heights, abbreviation
14. River, abbreviation
15. Organization of Petroleum-Exporting Countries, acronym
16. before the Common Era, abbreviation
17. doing business as, abbreviation
18. People for the Ethical Treatment of Animals, acronym
19. digital video disc, abbreviation
20. that is (Latin *id est*), abbreviation
21. Internal Revenue Service, initialism
22. personal identification number, acronym
23. pound (Latin *libra*), abbreviation
24. prisoner of war, abbreviation
25. percent, abbreviation
26. universal product code, abbreviation
27. average, abbreviation
28. special weapons and tactics, acronym

## Spelling Rules

### 698.1 Write *i* before *e*

Write *i* before *e* except after *c*, or when sounded like *a* as in *neighbor* and *weigh*.

relief   receive   perceive   reign   freight   beige

**Exceptions:** There are a number of exceptions to this rule, including these: *neither, leisure, seize, weird, species, science.*

### 698.2 Words with Consonant Endings

When a one-syllable word *(bat)* ends in a consonant *(t)* preceded by one vowel *(a)*, double the final consonant before adding a suffix that begins with a vowel *(batting)*.

sum — summary       god — goddess

**NOTE:** When a word with more than one syllable *(control)* ends in a consonant *(l)* preceded by one vowel *(o)*, the accent is on the last syllable *(con trol´)*, and the suffix begins with a vowel *(ing)*, the same rule holds true: double the final consonant *(controlling)*.

prefer — preferred    begin — beginning
forget — forgettable   admit — admittance

### 698.3 Words with a Silent *e*

If a word ends with a silent *e*, drop the *e* before adding a suffix that begins with a vowel. Do not drop the *e* when the suffix begins with a consonant.

state — stating — statement    like — liking — likeness
use — using — useful           nine — ninety — nineteen

**Exceptions:** *judgment, truly, argument, ninth*

### 698.4 Words Ending in *y*

When *y* is the last letter in a word and the *y* is preceded by a consonant, change the *y* to *i* before adding any suffix except those beginning with *i*.

fry — fries — frying   hurry — hurried — hurrying   lady — ladies
ply — pliable          happy — happiness            beauty — beautiful

When *y* is the last letter in a word and the *y* is preceded by a vowel, do not change the *y* to *i* before adding a suffix.

play — plays — playful   stay — stays — staying   employ — employed

**Important reminder:** Never trust your spelling even to the best spell-checker. Use an online or print dictionary to determine or check the spelling of words your spell-checker does not cover.

---

## Practice

### Spelling 1

Find the 11 words that are misspelled in the following paragraph and write them correctly. (Several of the misspelled words are in the "Commonly Misspelled Words" list on pages 700–701. Use an online or print dictionary to help you identify and correctly spell the others.)

**Example:** 1. wholly

The Kyoto Protocol is an international agreement to avert climate change caused by greenhouse gases. Enforcement began in February 2005. More than 150 countries are wholey on board with this effort to aleviate global warming. Among those countries not joining are Australia and the United States. These two priviledged countries, with approximitely 5 percent of the world's population, account for more than 20 percent of the world's fossil fuel emissions. Yet leaders in niether of these two industreal nations agree with the Protocol's approach. They claim that the effort would cost too much money and would hurt the economy. In addision, these leaders believe China and India should not be exempt from emisions' controls because China alone will soon become the largest emitter of greenhouse gases. Many other government leaders beleive the costs of the Kyoto Protocol are affordable, but no one relly knows if the Protocol will make any differince.

### Learning Language

Work with a partner and re-read aloud the spelling rules on the previous page. Take turns retelling each rule in your own words. Ask your partner to listen carefully and correct any errors you might have made as you retold the rules. With your partner, identify and discuss patterns in the spelling rules. Ask questions that you have about any of the rules and answer any questions your partner might have. Ask your teacher for clarification, if needed. Finally, work with your partner to summarize each of the spelling rules. Provide your own examples of each rule, and be sure to spell each of your own words correctly.

---

## Spelling Rules

Use the collaborative speaking and listening activity on SE page 699 to help students share and demonstrate comprehension by participating in shared reading, retelling or summarizing material, and responding to questions; and employ English spelling patterns and rules.

## Learning Language

Have students work in pairs and take turns reading and summarizing material to demonstrate comprehension of complex English. Have students share their summaries with the class.

## Related Skills Activities

■ *SkillsBook*
Plurals and Spelling Pretest, pp. 49–50
Spelling 1, 2, 3, and 4, pp. 53–58

## Answers

1. alleviate (line 4)
2. privileged (line 5)
3. approximately (line 6)
4. neither (line 7)
5. industrial (line 8)
6. addition (line 10)
7. emissions (line 11)
8. believe (line 13)
9. really (line 13)
10. difference (line 14)

---

**TEKS** 10.19 Spell correctly using resources to determine and check correct spelling; **ELPS** 4G Demonstrate comprehension of increasingly complex English/participating in shared reading and summarizing material; 5C Spell familiar words/employ spelling patterns and rules with increasing accuracy

## Commonly Misspelled Words

### A
abbreviate
abrupt
absence
absolute (ly)
absurd
abundance
academic
accelerate
accept (ance)
accessible
accessory
accidentally
accommodate
accompany
accomplish
accumulate
accurate
accustom (ed)
ache
achieve (ment)
acknowledge
acquaintance
acquired
across
address
adequate
adjustment
admissible
admittance
adolescent
advantageous
advertisement
advisable
aggravate
aggression
alcohol
alleviate
almost
alternative
although
aluminum
amateur
analysis
analyze
anarchy
ancient
anecdote
anesthetic
annihilate
announce
annual
anonymous
answer
anxious
apologize
apparatus
apparent (ly)
appearance
appetite
applies
appreciate
appropriate
approximately
architect
arctic
argument
arithmetic
arrangement
artificial
ascend
assistance
association
athlete
attendance
attire
attitude
audience
authority
available

### B
balance
balloon
bargain
basically
beautiful
beginning
believe
benefit (ed)
biscuit
bought
boycott
brevity
brilliant
Britain
bureau
business

### C
cafeteria
caffeine
calculator
calendar
campaign
canceled
candidate
catastrophe
category
caught
cavalry
celebration
cemetery
certificate
changeable
chief
chocolate
circuit
circumstance
civilization
colonel
colossal
column
commercial
commitment
committed
committee
comparative
comparison
competitively
conceivable
condemn
condescend
conference
conferred
confidential
congratulate
conscience
conscientious
conscious
consequence
consumer
contaminate
convenience
cooperate
correspondence
cough
coupon
courageous
courteous
creditor
criticism
criticize
curiosity
curious
cylinder

### D
dealt
deceitful
deceive
decision
defense
deferred
definite (ly)
definition
delicious
descend
describe
description
despair
desperate
destruction
development
diameter
diaphragm
diarrhea
dictionary
dining
disagreeable
disappear
disappoint
disastrous
discipline
discrimination
discuss
dismissal
dissatisfied
dissect
distinctly
dormitory
doubt
drought
duplicate
dyeing
dying

### E
earliest
efficiency
eighth
elaborate
eligible
eliminate
ellipse
embarrass
emphasize
employee
enclosure
encourage
endeavor
English
enormous
enough
enrichment
enthusiastic
entirely
entrance
environment
equipment
equipped
equivalent
especially
essential
eventually
exaggerate
examination
exceed
excellent
excessive
excite
executive
exercise
exhaust (ed)
exhibition
exhilaration
existence
expensive
experience
explanation
exquisite
extinguish
extraordinary
extremely

### FG
facilities
familiar
fascinate
fashion
fatigue (d)
feature
February
fiery
financially
flourish
forcible
foreign
forfeit
fortunate
forty
fourth
freight
friend
fulfill
gauge
generally
generous
genuine
glimpse
gnarled
gnaw
government
gradual
grammar
gratitude
grievous
grocery
guard
guidance

### H
happiness
harass
harmonize
height
hemorrhage
hereditary
hindrance
hoping
hopping
hospitable
humorous

### IJ
ignorance
illiterate
illustrate
imaginary
immediately
immense
incidentally
inconvenience
incredible
indefinitely
independence
indispensable
industrial
industrious
inevitable
infinite
inflation
innocence
inoculation
inquiry
installation
instrumental
intelligence
interesting
interfere
interrupt
investigate
irregular
irresistible
issuing
itinerary
jealous (y)
jewelry
journal
judgment

### KL
knowledge
laboratory
laugh
lawyer
league
legacy
legalize
legitimate
leisure
hygiene
hymn
hypocrisy
liaison
license
lightning
likable
likely
liquid
literature
loneliness

### MN
maintenance
maneuver
manufacture
marriage
mathematics
medieval
memento
menagerie
merchandise
merely
mileage
miniature
miscellaneous
mischievous
misspell
moat
mobile
mortgage
multiplied
muscle
musician
mustache
mutual
mysterious
naive
nauseous
necessary
neither
neurotic
nevertheless
ninety
nighttime
noticeable
nuclear
nuisance

### OP
obstacle
obvious
occasion
occupant
occupation
occurred
occurrence
official
often
omitted
opinion
opponent
opportunity
opposite
optimism
ordinarily
organization
original
outrageous
pamphlet
parallel
paralyze
partial
particularly
pastime
patience
peculiar
pedestal
performance
permanent
permissible
perseverance
personal (ly)
personality
perspiration
persuade
petition
phenomenon
physical
physician
picnicking
planned
playwright
plead
pneumonia
politician
ponder
positively
possession
practically
precede
precious
preference
prejudice
preparation
presence
prevalent
primitive

### QR
privilege
probably
proceed
professional
professor
prominent
pronounce
pronunciation
protein
psychology
puny
purchase
pursuing
qualified
quality
quantity
questionnaire
quiet
quite
quizzes
recede
receipt
receive
recipe
recognize
recommend
reference
referred
regard
regimen
religious
repel
repetition
residue
responsibility
restaurant
rheumatism
rhythm
ridiculous
robot
roommate

### S
sacrifice
salary
sandwich
satisfactory
scarcely
scenic
schedule
scholar
science
secretary
seize
separate
sergeant
several
severely
sheriff
shrubbery
siege
signature
signify
silhouette
similar
simultaneous
sincerely
skiing
skunk
society
solar
sophomore
souvenir
spaghetti
specific
specimen
statue
stomach
stopped
strength
strictly
submission
substitute
subtle
succeed
success
sufficient
supersede
suppose
surprise
suspicious
symbolism
sympathy
synthetic

### TU
tariff
technique
temperature
temporary
tendency
thermostat
thorough (ly)
though
throughout
tongue
tornado
tortoise
tragedy
transferred
tremendous
tried
trite
truly
unanimous
undoubtedly
unfortunately
unique
unnecessary
until
urgent
usable
usher
usually

### V
vacuum
vague
valuable
variety
vengeance
versatile
vicinity
villain
visibility
visual

### W
waif
Wednesday
weird
wholly
width
women
wrath
wreckage

### Y
yesterday
yield
yolk

---

## Commonly Misspelled Words

Discuss with students the commonly misspelled words listed on SE pages 700–701. Explore strategies to help them spell with accuracy and employ English spelling patterns and rules.

## Related Skills Activities

■ **SkillsBook**
Spelling 1, 2, 3, and 4, pp. 53–58
Review: Plurals and Spelling, pp. 59–60

**702**

## Steps to Becoming a Better Speller

**1. Be patient.**
Becoming a good speller takes time.

**2. Check the correct pronunciation of each word you are attempting to spell.**
Knowing the correct pronunciation of a word can help you remember its spelling.

**3. Note the meaning and history of each word as you are checking the dictionary for pronunciation.**
Knowing the meaning and history of a word provides you with a better notion of how the word is properly used, and this can help you remember its spelling and pronunciation.

**4. Before you close the dictionary, practice spelling the word.**
Look away from the page and try to "see" the word in your mind. Then write it on a piece of paper. Check your spelling in the dictionary; repeat the process until you are able to spell the word correctly.

**5. Learn some spelling rules.**
For four of the most useful rules, see page 698.

**6. Make a list of the words that you often misspell.**
Select the first 10 and practice spelling them.

**STEP A:** Read each word carefully; then write it on a piece of paper. Check to see that you've spelled it correctly. Repeat this step for the words that you misspelled.

**STEP B:** When you have finished your first 10 words, ask someone to read them to you as you write them again. Then check for misspellings. If you find none, congratulations! (Repeat both steps with your next 10 words, and so on.)

**7. Write often.**

---

**703**

### Spelling 2

 Find the 10 words that are misspelled in the following paragraphs and write them correctly. (Each misspelled word is in the "Commonly Misspelled Words" list on pages 700–701.)

**Example:** 1. scenic

In the early part of the twentieth century—before air travel, before the interstate highway system, before cars—people took the train to travel long distances. Rail service provided passengers with a comfortable, seenic trip accross the country. Slowly, however, private railroads were dieing as ridership decreased.

In 1970, the goverment agreed to subsidize the passenger rail service that became Amtrak. A network of 23,000 miles of track connected 314 communities with 184 trains. The number of trains and cities served by them has grown since then, but skedules are always subject to change. Maintainance of the aging equippment has also become a problem. Allthough the railroad has always struggled finantially (it has never made a profit), it remains a prominint part of many Americans' transportation options.

#### Model

Model the following sentences to practice using the "words with a silent *e*" spelling rule. (Use the underlined words in your sentences, too.)

Behind every underline{argument} is someone's ignorance. —Louis D. Brandeis

Journal underline{writing} is a voyage to the interior. —Christina Baldwin

---

Mechanics

---

## Steps to Becoming a Better Speller

Discuss with students the steps to becoming a better speller listed on SE page 702 to help them employ English spelling patterns and rules to spell accurately and to learn relationships between sounds and letters and decode (sound out) words using a combination of skills.

## Related Skills Activities

■ *SkillsBook*

 **Answers**

1. scenic (line 4)
2. across (line 4)
3. dying (line 5)
4. government (line 6)
5. schedules (line 9)
6. maintenance (line 10)
7. equipment (line 10)
8. although (line 11)
9. financially (line 12)
10. prominent (line 12)

---

 **TEKS 10.19** Spell correctly using resources to determine and check correct spelling; **ELPS 4A** Learn relationships between sounds and letters; **5C** Spell familiar words/employ spelling rules with increasing accuracy

ELPS 1H, 2C

ELPS 1H, 2C

## Understanding Idioms

Idioms are phrases that are used in a special way. You can't understand an idiom just by knowing the meaning of each word in the phrase. You must learn it as a whole. For example, the idiom *bury the hatchet* means "to settle an argument," even though the individual words in the phrase mean something much different. This section will help you learn some of the common idioms in American English.

| | |
|---|---|
| apple of his eye | **Eagle Lake is the** apple of his eye. (something he likes very much) |
| as plain as day | **The mistake in the ad was** as plain as day. (very clear) |
| as the crow flies | **New London is 200 miles from here** as the crow flies. (in a straight line) |
| at a snail's pace | **My last hour at work passes** at a snail's pace. (very, very slowly) |
| axe to grind | **The manager has an** axe to grind **with that umpire.** (disagreement to settle) |
| bad apple | **There are no** bad apples **in this class.** (a bad influence) |
| beat around the bush | **Don't** beat around the bush; **answer the question.** (avoid getting to the point) |
| benefit of the doubt | **Everyone has been given the** benefit of the doubt **at least once.** (another chance) |
| beyond the shadow of a doubt | Beyond the shadow of a doubt, **this is my best science project.** (for certain) |
| blew my top | **When I saw the broken statue, I** blew my top. (showed great anger) |
| bone to pick | **Alison had a** bone to pick **with the student who copied her paper.** (problem to settle) |
| brain drain | Brain drain **is a serious problem in some states.** (the best students moving elsewhere) |
| break the ice | **The nervous ninth graders were afraid to** break the ice. (start a conversation) |
| burn the midnight oil | **Ryan had to** burn the midnight oil **to finish his report.** (work late into the night) |

| | |
|---|---|
| bury the hatchet | **My sisters were told to** bury the hatchet **immediately.** (settle an argument) |
| by the skin of her teeth | **Diana avoided an accident** by the skin of her teeth. (just barely) |
| champing at the bit | **The skiers were** champing at the bit **to get on the slopes.** (eager, excited) |
| chicken feed | **The prize was** chicken feed **to some people.** (not worth much money) |
| chip off the old block | **Frank's just like his father. He's a** chip off the old block. (just like someone else) |
| clean as a whistle | **My boss told me to make sure the place was as** clean as a whistle **before I left.** (very clean) |
| cold shoulder | **I wanted to fit in with that group, but they gave me the** cold shoulder. (ignored me) |
| crack of dawn | **Tony delivers his papers at the** crack of dawn. (first light of day, early morning) |
| cry wolf | **If you** cry wolf **too often, no one will believe you.** (say you are in trouble when you aren't) |
| dead of night | **Hearing a loud noise in the** dead of night **frightened Bill.** (middle of the night) |
| dirt cheap | **A lot of clothes at that store are** dirt cheap. (inexpensive, costing very little money) |
| doesn't hold a candle to | **That award** doesn't hold a candle to **a gold medal.** (is not as good as) |
| drop in the bucket | **The contributions were a** drop in the bucket. (a small amount compared to what's needed) |
| everything from A to Z | **That catalog lists** everything from A to Z. (a lot of different things) |
| face the music | **Mario had to** face the music **when he broke the window.** (deal with the punishment) |
| fish out of water | **He felt like a** fish out of water **in the new math class.** (someone in an unfamiliar place) |
| fit for a king | **The food at the athletic banquet was** fit for a king. (very special) |

Idioms

## Understanding Idioms

Discuss with students the uses of idioms listed on SE pages 704–705 to help them develop and expand their repertoire of learning strategies and to learn new language structures, expressions, and basic vocabulary. Allow classroom interaction so students can ask about other idioms they may have heard or read.

**ELPS 1H** Develop learning strategies/reasoning, looking for patterns in language, and analyzing sayings and expressions; **2C** Learn new expressions heard during classroom instruction/interactions

⭐ ELPS 1H, 2C

⭐ ELPS 1H, 2C

| | |
|---|---|
| flew off the handle | Bill flew off the handle when he saw a reckless driver near the school. (became very angry) |
| floating on air | Celine was floating on air at the prom. (feeling very happy) |
| food for thought | The boys' foolish and dangerous prank gave us food for thought. (something to think about) |
| get down to business | After sharing several jokes, Mr. Morales said we should get down to business. (start working) |
| get the upper hand | The wrestler moved quickly on his opponent in order to get the upper hand. (gain the advantage) |
| give their all | Student volunteers give their all to help others. (work as hard as they can) |
| go fly a kite | Rosa stared at her nosy brother and said, "Go fly a kite." (go away) |
| has a green thumb | Talk to Mrs. Lopez about your sick plant. She has a green thumb. (is good at growing plants) |
| has a heart of gold | Joe has a heart of gold. (is very kind and generous) |
| hit a home run | Rhonda hit a home run with her speech. (succeeded, or did well) |
| hit the ceiling | When my parents saw my grades, they hit the ceiling. (were very angry) |
| hit the hay | Exhausted from the hike, Jamal hit the hay without eating supper. (went to bed) |
| in a nutshell | Can you, in a nutshell, tell us your goals for this year? (in summary) |
| in one ear and out the other | Marcella, concerned about her pet, let the lecture go in one ear and out the other. (without really listening) |
| in the black | My aunt's gift shop is finally in the black. (making money) |
| in the nick of time | Anna caught the falling vase in the nick of time. (just in time) |
| in the red | Many businesses start out in the red. (in debt) |
| in the same boat | The new tax bill meant everyone would be in the same boat. (in a similar situation) |

| | |
|---|---|
| iron out | Martin will meet with the work crew to iron out their complaints. (solve, work out) |
| it goes without saying | It goes without saying that saving money is a good idea. (it is clear) |
| it stands to reason | It stands to reason that your stamina will increase if you run every day. (it makes sense) |
| keep a stiff upper lip | Keep a stiff upper lip when you visit the doctor. (be brave) |
| keep it under your hat | Keep it under your hat about the pop quiz. (don't tell anyone) |
| knock on wood | My uncle knocked on wood after he said he had never had the flu. (did something for good luck) |
| knuckle down | After wasting half the day, we were told to knuckle down. (work hard) |
| learn the ropes | It takes every new employee a few months to learn the ropes. (get to know how things are done) |
| leave no stone unturned | The police plan to leave no stone unturned at the crime scene. (check everything) |
| lend someone a hand | You will feel good if you lend someone a hand. (help someone) |
| let the cat out of the bag | Gabe let the cat out of the bag during lunch. (told a secret) |
| let's face it | Let's face it. You don't like rap. (let's admit it) |
| look high and low | We looked high and low for Jan's dog. (looked everywhere) |
| lose face | In some cultures, it is very bad to lose face. (be embarrassed) |
| needle in a haystack | Trying to find a person in New York is like trying to find a needle in a haystack. (something impossible to find) |
| nose to the grindstone | With all of these assignments, I have to keep my nose to the grindstone. (work hard) |
| on cloud nine | After talking to my girlfriend, I was on cloud nine. (feeling very happy) |
| on pins and needles | Elizabeth was on pins and needles during the championship game. (feeling nervous) |

Idioms

## Understanding Idioms

Discuss with students the uses of idioms listed on SE pages 706–707 to help them develop and expand their repertoire of learning strategies and to learn new language structures, expressions, and basic vocabulary. Have students contribute other examples.

**ELPS** **1H** Develop learning strategies/reasoning, looking for patterns in language, and analyzing sayings and expressions; **2C** Learn new expressions heard during classroom instruction/interactions

| | |
|---|---|
| out the window | Once the rain started, our plans were out the window. (ruined) |
| over and above | Over and above the required work, Will cleaned up the lab. (in addition to) |
| pain in the neck | Mark knew the report would be a pain in the neck. (very annoying) |
| pull your leg | Cassie was only pulling your leg. (telling you a little lie as a joke) |
| put his foot in his mouth | Alex put his foot in his mouth when he answered the question. (said something embarrassing) |
| put the cart before the horse | Tonya put the cart before the horse when she sealed the envelope before inserting the letter. (did something in the wrong order) |
| put your best foot forward | When applying for a job, you should put your best foot forward. (do the best that you can do) |
| red-letter day | Taylor had a red-letter day because she did so well on her math test. (very good day) |
| rock the boat | I was told not to rock the boat. (cause trouble) |
| rude awakening | Jake will have a rude awakening when he sees the bill for his computer. (sudden, unpleasant surprise) |
| save face | His gift was clearly an attempt to save face. (fix an embarrassing situation) |
| see eye to eye | We see eye to eye about the need for a new school. (are in agreement) |
| shake a leg | I told Enrique to shake a leg so that we wouldn't be late. (hurry) |
| shift into high gear | Greg had to shift into high gear to finish the test in time. (speed up, hurry) |
| sight for sore eyes | My grandmother's smiling face was a sight for sore eyes. (good to see) |
| sight unseen | Liz bought the coat sight unseen. (without seeing it first) |
| sink or swim | Whether you sink or swim in school depends on your study habits. (fail or succeed) |

| | |
|---|---|
| spilled the beans | Suddenly, Kesia realized that she had spilled the beans. (revealed a secret) |
| spring chicken | Although Mr. Gordon isn't a spring chicken, he sure knows how to talk to kids. (young person) |
| stick to your guns | Know what you believe, and stick to your guns. (don't change your mind) |
| sweet tooth | Chocolate is often the candy of choice for those with a sweet tooth. (a love for sweets, like candy and cake) |
| take a dim view | My sister will take a dim view of that movie. (disapprove) |
| take it with a grain of salt | When you read that advertisement, take it with a grain of salt. (don't believe everything) |
| take the bull by the horns | It's time to take the bull by the horns so the project gets done on time. (take control) |
| through thick and thin | Those two girls have remained friends through thick and thin. (in good times and in bad times) |
| time flies | Time flies as you grow older. (time passes quickly) |
| time to kill | Grace had time to kill, so she read a book. (extra time) |
| to go overboard | The class was told not to go overboard. A $50.00 donation was fine. (to do too much) |
| toe the line | The new teacher made everyone toe the line. (follow the rules) |
| tongue-tied | He can talk easily with friends, but in class he is usually tongue-tied. (not knowing what to say) |
| turn over a new leaf | He decided to turn over a new leaf in school. (make a new start) |
| two peas in a pod | Ever since kindergarten, Lil and Eva have been like two peas in a pod. (very much alike) |
| under the weather | Mike was feeling under the weather this morning. (sick) |
| wallflower | Maria knew the other girls thought she was a wallflower. (a shy person) |
| word of mouth | Joseph learns a lot about his favorite team by word of mouth. (talking with other people) |

Idioms

## Understanding Idioms

Discuss with students the uses of idioms listed on SE pages 708–709 to help them develop and expand their repertoire of learning strategies and to learn new language structures, expressions, and basic vocabulary.

TEKS 10.19
ELPS 1C, 4C, 5C

## Using the Right Word

**a lot** ■ *A lot* (always two words) is a vague descriptive phrase that should be used sparingly.

> "You can observe a lot just by watching."
>
> — Yogi Berra

**accept, except** ■ The verb *accept* means "to receive" or "to believe"; the preposition *except* means "other than."

> The principal accepted the boy's story about the broken window, but she asked why no one except him saw the ball accidentally slip from his hand.

**adapt, adopt** ■ *Adapt* means "to adjust or change to fit"; *adopt* means "to choose and treat as your own" (a child, an idea).

> After a lengthy period of study, Malcolm X adopted the Islamic faith and adapted to its lifestyle.

**affect, effect** ■ The verb *affect* means "to influence"; the verb *effect* means "to produce, accomplish, complete."

> Ming's hard work effected an A on the test, which positively affected her semester grade.

The noun *effect* means the "result."

> Good grades have a calming effect on parents.

**aisle, isle** ■ An *aisle* is a passage between seats; an *isle* is a small island.

> Many airline passengers on their way to the Isle of Capri prefer an aisle seat.

**all right** ■ *All right* is always two words (not *alright*).

**allusion, illusion** ■ *Allusion* is an indirect reference to someone or something; *illusion* is a false picture or idea.

> My little sister, under the illusion that she's movie-star material, makes frequent allusions to her future fans.

**already, all ready** ■ *Already* is an adverb meaning "before this time" or "by this time." *All ready* is an adjective meaning "fully prepared."

**NOTE:** Use *all ready* if you can substitute *ready* alone in the sentence.

> Although I've already had some dessert, I am all ready for some ice cream from the street vendor.

---

## Practice

### Using the Right Word 1

**accept, except; affect, effect; all right; allusion, illusion; already, all ready**

Write the correct word if the underlined word is not used correctly. If it is, then write "OK."

**Example:** 1. *already*

The small group of people staggering across the hot sand had **(1)** <u>all ready</u> been without water for a day. One said, "I refuse to **(2)** <u>except</u> this situation! We must find water!"

They forced themselves to continue—**(3)** <u>accept</u> for one man, who was **(4)** <u>all ready</u> to give up. The other members of the group persuaded the despairing man to keep up. If he stayed behind, surely his loss would **(5)** <u>effect</u> the others negatively. A woman said, "This is not Gilligan's Island, you know, where we could survive in huts." He didn't quite get the **(6)** <u>illusion</u>, but he went along anyway.

Soon the lack of water would begin to have an adverse **(7)** <u>affect</u> on them. Many times, of course, they would "see" water—only to realize that it was just an **(8)** <u>illusion</u>. They knew that if they could only find water, they'd be **(9)** <u>all right</u>.

### Model

Model the following sentences to practice using *allusion* and *illusion* correctly.

> I think we must quote whenever we feel that the allusion is interesting or helpful or amusing.
>
> —Clifton Fadiman
>
> If power was an illusion, wasn't weakness necessarily one also?
>
> —Lois McMaster Bujold, *A Civil Campaign*

*Right Word*

---

## Using the Right Word

Discuss with students the uses of the words listed on SE page 710 to help them spell with accuracy, use strategic learning techniques to acquire basic and grade-level vocabulary, and comprehend vocabulary used in written classroom materials. Invite students to share their answers to the Grammar Practice on SE page 711 with the class.

## Related Skills Activities

■ **SkillsBook**
Pretest: Using the Right Word, p. 61
Using the Right Word 1, 2, 3, 4, and 5, pp. 62–66
Review: Using the Right Word, pp. 67–68

## Answers

1. already
2. accept
3. except
4. OK
5. affect
6. allusion
7. effect
8. OK
9. OK

---

712

**altogether, all together** ■ *Altogether* means "entirely." The phrase *all together* means "in a group" or "all at once."

> "There is altogether too much gridlock," complained the Democrats. All together, the Republicans yelled, "No way!"

**among, between** ■ *Among* is typically used when speaking of more than two persons or things. *Between* is used when speaking of only two.

> The three of us talked among ourselves to decide between going out or eating in.

**amount, number** ■ *Amount* is used for bulk measurement. *Number* is used to count separate units. (See also *fewer, less*.)

> A substantial amount of honey spilled all over a number of my CD's.

**annual, biannual, semiannual, biennial, perennial** ■ An *annual* event happens once every year. A *biannual* or *semiannual* event happens twice a year. A *biennial* event happens every two years. A *perennial* event is one that is persistent or constant.

> Dad's annual family reunion gets bigger every year.
> We're going shopping at the department store's semiannual white sale.
> Due to dwindling attendance, the county fair is now a biennial celebration.
> A perennial plant persists for several years.

**anyway** ■ Do not add an *s* to *anyway*.

**ascent, assent** ■ *Ascent* is the act of rising or climbing; *assent* is "to agree to something after some consideration" (or such an agreement).

> We completed our ascent of the butte with the assent of the landowner.

**bad, badly** ■ *Bad* is an adjective. *Badly* is an adverb.

> This apple is bad, but one bad apple doesn't always ruin the whole bushel.
> In today's game, Ross passed badly.

**base, bass** ■ *Base* is the foundation or the lower part of something. *Bass* (pronounced like *base*) is a deep sound. *Bass* (pronounced like *class*) is a fish.

**beside, besides** ■ *Beside* means "by the side of." *Besides* means "in addition to."

> Mother always grew roses beside the trash bin. Besides looking nice, they also gave off a sweet smell that masked odors.

---

## Practice

### Using the Right Word 2

**among, between;** amount, number; **anyway;** bad, badly; **base, bass;** beside, besides

 Write the correct choice from those given in parentheses.

**Example:** The team talked *(among, between)* themselves as they watched Lamar being carried off the field.
> among

**1.** Lamar was hurt *(bad, badly)* when he was tackled during the game.

**2.** A cut near the *(base, bass)* of his skull caused concern.

**3.** *(Beside, Besides)* the cut, Lamar had also fractured his leg.

**4.** *(Anyway, Anyways)*, he had to stay in the hospital for several days.

**5.** His classmates sent him a huge *(amount, number)* of get-well cards.

**6.** Lamar spotted a letter *(beside, besides)* his water pitcher.

**7.** It was from the player who tackled him—he felt *(bad, badly)* about the incident.

**8.** The player suggested that he and Lamar go *(base, bass)* fishing when Lamar felt better.

**9.** Now, *(beside, besides)* getting out of the hospital, Lamar had something else to look forward to.

**10.** *(Among, Between)* the medical treatment and the good *(number, amount)* of support from his friends, he knew he would be well soon.

### Model

Model the following sentences to practice using the words *among* and *between*.

> And in the midst of it, out sprang from among the trees and bushes the great white body of a man, who dashed into the stream and swam like a dolphin.
> —Frances Hodgson Burnett, *His Grace of Osmonde*

> The shortest distance between two points is under construction.
> —Noelie Altito

Right Word

---

## Using the Right Word

Discuss with students the uses of the words listed on SE page 712 to help them spell with accuracy, use strategic learning techniques to acquire basic and grade-level vocabulary, and comprehend vocabulary used in written classroom materials. Invite volunteers to give their answers to the Grammar Practice on SE page 713.

## Related Skills Activities

■ *SkillsBook*
Pretest: Using the Right Word, p. 61
Using the Right Word 1, 2, 3, 4, and 5, pp. 62–66
Review: Using the Right Word, pp. 67–68

## Answers

1. badly
2. base
3. Besides
4. Anyway
5. number
6. beside
7. bad
8. bass
9. besides
10. Between, amount

TEKS 10.19
ELPS 1C, 4C, 5C

**board, bored** ■ *Board* is a piece of wood. *Board* is also an administrative group or council.

**The school board approved the purchase of fifty 1- by 6-inch pine boards.**

*Bored* is the past tense of the verb "bore," which may mean "to make a hole by drilling" or "to become weary out of dullness."

**Watching television bored Joe, so he took his drill and bored a hole in the wall where he could hang his new clock.**

**brake, break** ■ *Brake* is a device used to stop a vehicle. *Break* means "to separate or to destroy."

**I hope the brakes on my car never break.**

**bring, take** ■ *Bring* suggests the action is directed toward the speaker; *take* suggests the action is directed away from the speaker.

**Bring home some garbage bags so I can take the trash outside.**

**can, may** ■ *Can* suggests ability while *may* suggests permission.

**"Can I go to the mall?" means "Am I physically able to go to the mall?"**
**"May I go to the mall?" asks permission to go.**

**capital, capitol** ■ The noun *capital* refers to a city or to money. The adjective *capital* means "major or important." *Capitol* refers to a building.

**The state capital is home to the capitol building for a capital reason. The state government contributed capital for its construction.**

**cent, sent, scent** ■ *Cent* is a coin; *sent* is the past tense of the verb "send"; *scent* is an odor or a smell.

**For forty-four cents, I sent my girlfriend a mushy love poem in a perfumed envelope. She adored the scent but hated the poem.**

**cereal, serial** ■ *Cereal* is a grain, often made into breakfast food. *Serial* relates to something in a series.

**Daniel enjoys reading serial novels while he eats a bowl of cereal.**

**chord, cord** ■ *Chord* may mean "an emotion" or "a combination of musical tones sounded at the same time." A *cord* is a string or a rope.

**The guitar player strummed the opening chord to the group's hit song, which struck a responsive chord with the audience.**

**chose, choose** ■ *Chose* (chōz) is the past tense of the verb *choose* (chōoz).

**Last quarter I chose to read Chitra Divakaruni's *The Unknown Errors of Our Lives*—a fascinating book about Indian immigrants.**

---

TEKS 10.19
ELPS 1C, 4C, 5C

## Using the Right Word 3

brake, break; bring, take; can, may; chord, cord; chose, choose

 Write the correct choice from those given in parentheses.

**Example:** The *(chord, cord)* on these blinds doesn't work right.
cord

**1.** *(Can, May)* I get you something to drink?

**2.** Cheng wants to *(brake, break)* the old school record for consecutive free throws.

**3.** Make sure we *(bring, take)* some sunscreen with us to the beach.

**4.** Wilson *(choose, chose)* a bright blue, sparkling sweater for his girlfriend's birthday present.

**5.** At the first *(chord, cord)*, the audience knew the song and went wild.

**6.** This printer *(can, may)* make two-sided copies.

**7.** I would not *(choose, chose)* a career as a septic-tank cleaner.

**8.** Tristan should *(bring, take)* his suit to the cleaners on his way to the concert.

**9.** Most often, a vehicle does not come to an immediate stop when the *(brake, break)* is applied.

**10.** You *(can, may)* leave the room when you are done with the test.

### Model

Model the following sentences to practice using *brake* and *break* correctly.

**Even though you may want to move forward in your life, you may have one foot on the brake. In order to be free, you must learn how to let go.**
—Mary Manin Morrissey

**A hole is nothing at all, but you can break your neck in it.**
—Austin O'Malley

Right Word

---

## Using the Right Word

Discuss with students the uses of the words listed on SE page 714 to help them spell correctly, use strategic learning techniques to acquire basic and grade-level vocabulary, and comprehend vocabulary used in written classroom materials. Have students contribute other examples for each use. Also invite students to share their answers to the Grammar Practice on SE page 715 with the class.

## Related Skills Activities

■ **SkillsBook**
Pretest: Using the Right Word, p. 61
Using the Right Word 1, 2, 3, 4, and 5, pp. 62–66
Review: Using the Right Word, pp. 67–68

 **Answers**

1. May
2. break
3. bring
4. chose
5. chord
6. can
7. choose
8. take
9. brake
10. may

**TEKS** 10.19 Spell correctly using resources to determine and check correct spelling; **ELPS 1C** Use strategic learning techniques to acquire basic and grade-level vocabulary; **4C** Comprehend vocabulary used in written classroom materials; **5C** Spell familiar words with increasing accuracy

⭐ **TEKS** 10.19
ELPS 1C, 4C, 5C

**coarse, course** ■ *Coarse* means "rough or crude"; *course* means "a path or direction taken." *Course* also means "a class or a series of studies."

> Fletcher, known for using coarse language, was barred from the golf course until he took an etiquette course.

**complement, compliment** ■ *Complement* refers to that which completes or fulfills. *Compliment* is an expression of admiration or praise.

> Kimberly smiled, thinking she had received a compliment when Carlos said that her new Chihuahua complemented her personality.

**continual, continuous** ■ *Continual* refers to something that happens again and again with some breaks or pauses; *continuous* refers to something that keeps happening, uninterrupted.

> Sunlight hits Texas on a continual basis; sunlight hits Earth continuously.

**counsel, council** ■ When used as a noun, *counsel* means "advice"; when used as a verb, it means "to advise." *Council* refers to a group that advises.

> The student council counseled all freshmen to join a school club. That's good counsel.

**desert, dessert** ■ The noun *desert* (dĕz′ərt) refers to barren wilderness. *Dessert* (dĭ zûrt′) is food served at the end of a meal.

> The scorpion tiptoed through the moonlit desert, searching for dessert.

The verb *desert* (dĭ zûrt′) means "to abandon"; the noun *desert* (dĭ zûrt′) means "deserved reward or punishment."

> The burglar's hiding place deserted him when the spotlight swung his way; his subsequent arrest was his just desert.

**die, dye** ■ *Die* (dying) means "to stop living." *Dye* (dyeing) is used to change the color of something.

**different from, different than** ■ Use *different from* in a comparison of two things. *Different than* should be used only when followed by a clause.

> Barry is quite different from his brother.
> Life is different than it used to be.

**farther, further** ■ *Farther* refers to a physical distance; *further* refers to additional time, quantity, or degree.

> Alaska extends farther north than Iceland does. Further information can be obtained in an atlas.

**fewer, less** ■ *Fewer* refers to the number of separate units; *less* refers to bulk quantity.

> Because we have fewer orders for cakes, we'll buy less sugar and flour.

---

## Practice

### Using the Right Word 4

complement, compliment; counsel, council; desert, dessert; farther, further

 Write the correct choice from those given in parentheses.

**Example:** Saaid needs *(farther, further)* information for his essay.
> further

1. Nadia's energy *(deserted, desserted)* her as she approached the end of the triathlon.

2. The student *(council, counsel)* sponsored this year's food drive.

3. Dylan *(complemented, complimented)* Renee on her new hairstyle.

4. Zach can punt the ball *(farther, further)* than any of his teammates.

5. Mr. Garcia *(counciled, counseled)* our class on the SAT tests.

6. Jorge's sly smile was a *(complement, compliment)* to his secretive disposition.

7. Mrs. Lang's *(deserts, desserts)* were first to go at the bake sale.

8. Soo got her just *(deserts, desserts)* when she missed the last bus.

9. To *(complement, compliment)* her costume, Yvette dyed her hair an outrageous purple.

10. My Panhandle town is a *(desert, dessert)* compared to a rain forest.

### Model

Model the following sentences to practice using the words *further* and *farther* correctly.

> Gratitude is merely the secret hope of further favors.
> —Francois de La Rochefoucauld

> Men came from the east and built these American towns because they wished to go no farther, and the towns they built were shaped by the urge to go onward.
> —Rose Wilder Lane, *Old Home Town*

Right Word

---

## Using the Right Word

Discuss with students the uses of the words listed on SE page 716 to help them spell correctly, use strategic learning techniques to acquire basic and grade-level vocabulary, and comprehend vocabulary used in written classroom materials. Have students contribute other examples for each use. Also invite students to share their answers to the Grammar Practice on SE page 717 with the class.

## Related Skills Activities

■ ***SkillsBook***
Pretest: Using the Right Word, p. 61
Using the Right Word 1, 2, 3, 4, and 5, pp. 62–66
Review: Using the Right Word, pp. 67–68

 **Answers**

1. deserted
2. council
3. complimented
4. farther
5. counseled
6. complement
7. desserts
8. deserts
9. complement
10. desert

---

 **TEKS** 10.19 Spell correctly using resources to determine and check correct spelling; **ELPS** 1C Use strategic learning techniques to acquire basic and grade-level vocabulary; 4C Comprehend vocabulary used in written classroom materials; 5C Spell familiar words with increasing accuracy

TEKS 10.19
ELPS 1C, 4C, 5C

**flair, flare** ■ *Flair* refers to style or natural talent; *flare* means "to light up quickly" or "burst out" (or an object that does so).

> Ronni was thrilled with Jorge's flair for decorating—until one of his strategically placed candles flared, marring the wall.

**good, well** ■ *Good* is an adjective; *well* is nearly always an adverb. (When *well* is used to describe a state of health, it is an adjective: He was happy to be *well* again.)

> The MP3 player works well.
>
> Our team looks good this season.

**heal, heel** ■ *Heal* means "to mend or restore to health." A *heel* is the back part of a foot.

> Achilles died because a poison arrow pierced his heel and caused a wound that would not heal.

**healthful, healthy** ■ *Healthful* means "causing or improving health"; *healthy* means "possessing health."

> Healthful foods build healthy bodies.

**hear, here** ■ You *hear* with your ears. *Here* means "the area close by."

**heard, herd** ■ *Heard* is the past tense of the verb "hear"; *herd* is a large group of animals.

**hole, whole** ■ A *hole* is a cavity or hollow place. *Whole* means "complete."

**idle, idol** ■ *Idle* means "not working." An *idol* is someone or something that is worshipped.

> The once-popular actress, who had been idle lately, wistfully recalled her days as an idol.

**immigrate, emigrate** ■ *Immigrate* means "to come into a new country or environment." *Emigrate* means "to go out of one country to live in another."

> Martin Ulferts immigrated to this country in 1882. He was only three years old when he emigrated from Germany.

**imply, infer** ■ *Imply* means "to suggest or express indirectly"; *infer* means "to draw a conclusion from facts." (A writer or speaker implies; a reader or listener infers.)

> Dad implied by his comment that I should drive more carefully, and I inferred that he was concerned for both me and his new car.

---

TEKS 10.19
ELPS 1C, 4C, 5C

Right Word

 **Practice**

### Using the Right Word 5

good, well; heard, herd; idle, idol; immigrate, emigrate; imply, infer

 Choose the correct words from the list above to fill in the blanks.

**Example:** Let the engine _____ for a few minutes.
*idle*

1. Have you _____ the latest news?

2. My little sister's _____ is Blue of Blue's Clues.

3. Some people think the government should tighten restrictions on those wishing to _____ to the United States.

4. Everyone agrees that Dena has a _____ head on her shoulders.

5. If Yadira declined Al's invitation, she would _____ that she didn't want to spend time with him.

6. Victims of civil wars have every reason to _____ from their countries.

7. I had never seen a _____ of any kind of animal until we saw the buffalo in South Dakota's Custer State Park.

8. I _____ from your silence that you do not agree.

9. Granddad actually plays the violin quite _____, but he calls it "fiddling."

10. Dallas was suffering from the flu last week, but he is _____ again.

### Model

Model the following sentences to practice using *imply* and *infer* correctly.

> The fact that some geniuses were laughed at does not imply that all who are laughed at are geniuses.
>
> —Carl Sagan

> That man is the noblest creature may also be inferred from the fact that no other creature has yet contested this claim.
>
> —G. C. Lichtenberg

---

## Using the Right Word

Discuss with students the uses of the words listed on SE page 718 to help them spell correctly, use strategic learning techniques to acquire basic and grade-level vocabulary, and comprehend vocabulary used in written classroom materials. Have students contribute other examples for each use. Also invite students to share their answers to the Grammar Practice on SE page 719 with the class.

## Related Skills Activities

■ *SkillsBook*
Pretest: Using the Right Word, p. 61
Using the Right Word 1, 2, 3, 4, and 5, pp. 62–66
Review: Using the Right Word, pp. 67–68

 **Answers**

1. heard
2. idol
3. immigrate
4. good
5. imply
6. emigrate
7. herd
8. infer
9. well
10. well

---

 **TEKS** **10.19** Spell correctly using resources to determine and check correct spelling; **ELPS** **1C** Use strategic learning techniques to acquire basic and grade-level vocabulary; **4C** Comprehend vocabulary used in written classroom materials; **5C** Spell familiar words with increasing accuracy

TEKS 10.19
ELPS 1C, 4C, 5C

**insure, ensure** ■ *Insure* means "to secure from financial harm or loss." *Ensure* means "to make certain of something."

To ensure that you can legally drive that new car, you'll have to insure it.

**it's, its** ■ *It's* is the contraction of "it is." *Its* is the possessive form of "it."

It's hard to believe, but the movie *Shrek* still holds its appeal for many kids.

**later, latter** ■ *Later* means "after a period of time." *Latter* refers to the second of two things mentioned.

Later that year we had our second baby and adopted a stray kitten. The latter was far more welcomed by our toddler.

**lay, lie** ■ *Lay* means "to place." *Lay* is a transitive verb. (See 744.1.)

Lay your books on the big table.

*Lie* means "to recline," and *lay* is the past tense of *lie*. *Lie* is an intransitive verb. (See 744.1.)

In this heat, the children must lie down for a nap. Yesterday they lay down without one complaint. Sometimes they have lain in the hammocks to rest.

**lead, led** ■ *Lead* (lēd) is the present tense of the verb meaning "to guide." The past tense of the verb is *led* (lĕd). The noun *lead* (lĕd) is a metal.

We were led along the path that leads to an abandoned lead mine.

**learn, teach** ■ *Learn* means "to acquire information." *Teach* means "to give information."

I learn better when people teach with real-world examples.

**leave, let** ■ *Leave* means "to allow something to remain behind." *Let* means "to permit."

Would you let me leave my bike at your house?

**lend, borrow** ■ *Lend* means "to give for temporary use." *Borrow* means "to receive for temporary use."

I told Mom I needed to borrow $18 for a CD, but she said she could only lend money for school supplies.

**like, as** ■ When *like* is used as a preposition meaning "similar to," it can be followed only by a noun, pronoun, or noun phrase; when *as* is used as a subordinating conjunction, it introduces a subordinate clause.

You could become a gymnast like her, as you work and practice hard.

**medal, meddle** ■ *Medal* is an award. *Meddle* means "to interfere."

Some parents meddle in the awards process to be sure that their kids get medals.

---

TEKS 10.19
ELPS 1C, 1E, 2I, 3E, 3H, 4C, 5C

## Using the Right Word 6

it's, its; lay, lie; lead, led; learn, teach; leave, let; like, as

 Write the correct choice from those given in parentheses.

**Example:** Let your mind wander *(like, as)* a bird searching for food.
    like

**1.** In my opinion, an apple is a snack at *(it's, its)* best.

**2.** After dinner, Grandpa *(leaves, lets)* scraps on the porch for our cat.

**3.** The mountain guide *(lead, led)* the inexperienced campers down a winding path.

**4.** Mia wants Ms. Benke to *(learn, teach)* her how to play the flute.

**5.** Just as I *(lay, lie)* my head on the pillow, the smoke alarm went off.

**6.** I wish I could fly on my own *(like, as)* the birds do.

**7.** The dogs enjoy being out this time of year; they *(lay, lie)* in the shade of the maple tree.

**8.** Children can *(learn, teach)* a foreign language more easily than adults can.

### Learning Language

With a partner, re-read the information on the previous page. Note the differences in each word pair. Choose four pairs and tell a story with the words. Have your partner write the story as you narrate it and then retell it to you. When you have finished, discuss and correct the retelling. Check the spelling in the written story; discuss and correct any errors. Have your partner choose a different set of words and tell another story with clear, precise details. Follow the same process as your partner tells the new story.

Right Word

---

## Using the Right Word

Discuss with students the uses of the words listed on SE page 720 to help them spell correctly, use strategic learning techniques to acquire vocabulary, comprehend vocabulary used in written classroom materials, and develop basic sight vocabulary. Have students contribute other examples for each use. Also invite students to share their answers to the Grammar Practice on SE page 721 with the class.

## Learning Language

Use this collaborative speaking and listening activity on SE page 721 to help students internalize new basic language by using and reusing it in meaningful ways, demonstrate listening comprehension, and narrate with increasing specificity and detail.

 **Answers**

1. its
2. leaves
3. led
4. teach
5. lay
6. as
7. lie
8. learn

## Related Skills Activities

■ **SkillsBook**
Pretest: Using the Right Word, p. 61
Using the Right Word 1, 2, 3, 4, and 5, pp. 62–66
Review: Using the Right Word, pp. 67–68

---

**TEKS** **10.19** Spell correctly using resources to determine and check correct spelling; **ELPS 1C** Use strategic learning techniques to acquire basic and grade-level vocabulary; **1E** Internalize new basic language by using and reusing it/speaking; **2I** Demonstrate listening comprehension in increasingly complex spoken language by summarizing spoken messages; **3E** Share information in cooperative learning interactions; **3H** Narrate with increasing specificity and detail; **4C** Comprehend vocabulary used in written classroom materials; **5C** Spell familiar words with increasing accuracy

**722**

**metal, mettle** ■ *Metal* is a chemical element like iron or gold. *Mettle* is "strength of spirit."

> Grandad's mettle during battle left him with some metal in his shoulder.

**miner, minor** ■ A *miner* digs for valuable ore. A *minor* is a person who is not legally an adult. A *minor* problem is one of no great importance.

**moral, morale** ■ A *moral* is a lesson drawn from a story; as an adjective, it relates to the principles of right and wrong. *Morale* refers to someone's attitude.

> Ms. Ladue considers it her moral obligation to go to church every day.
> The students' morale sank after their defeat in the forensics competition.

**passed, past** ■ *Passed* is a verb. *Past* can be used as a noun, an adjective, or a preposition.

> That old pickup truck passed my sports car! (verb)
> Many senior citizens hold dearly to the past. (noun)
> Tilly's past life as a circus worker must have been . . . interesting. (adjective)
> Who can walk past a bakery without looking in the window? (preposition)

**peace, piece** ■ *Peace* means "tranquility or freedom from war." *Piece* is a part or fragment.

> Grandma sits in the peace and quiet of the parlor, enjoying a piece of pie.

**peak, peek, pique** ■ A *peak* is a high point. *Peek* means "brief look" (or "look briefly"). *Pique*, as a verb, means "to excite by challenging"; as a noun, it is a feeling of resentment.

> The peak of Dr. Fedder's professional life was his ability to pique children's interest in his work. "Peek at this slide," he said to the eager students.

**pedal, peddle, petal** ■ A *pedal* is a foot lever; as a verb, it means "to ride a bike." *Peddle* means "to go from place to place selling something." A *petal* is part of a flower.

> Don Miller paints beautiful petals on his homemade birdhouses. Then he pedals through the flea market every weekend to peddle them.

**personal, personnel** ■ *Personal* means "private." *Personnel* are people working at a particular job.

**plain, plane** ■ *Plain* means "an area of land that is flat or level"; it also means "clearly seen or clearly understood."

> It's plain to see why settlers of the Great Plains had trouble moving west.

*Plane* means "flat, level"; it is also a tool used to smooth the surface of wood.

> I used a plane to make the board plane and smooth.

---

 **Practice**

### Using the Right Word 7

moral, morale; passed, past; peak, peek, pique; plain, plane

 Write the correct word if the underlined word is not used correctly. If it is, then write "OK."

**Example:** 1. *passed*

The jet from Boston **(1)** <u>past</u> the mid-Atlantic states and crossed the Great **(2)** <u>Plains</u> on its way to Denver. After another short ride, we finally reached our **(3)** <u>plane</u> yet beautiful mountain lodge, greatly improving our **(4)** <u>morale</u>. An elderly gentleman spoke to some children gathered about him. "A ghost named Ahote lives on the mountain **(5)** <u>peek</u>," he said. I didn't catch much else of his speech, but it **(6)** <u>peaked</u> my curiosity, so I decided to do some research upon my return home.

I was not able to find much. An Internet search led me to a book about Native Americans of the **(7)** <u>passed</u> century. I found a copy at the city library and took a **(8)** <u>pique</u>. Yes, there was an Ahote—meaning "restless one"—from the area where we vacationed. He guided non-natives across the mountain. When he died, his grave was placed at the highest mountain pass. Pioneers knew they were headed in the right direction when they came upon it. I thought of this **(9)** <u>morale</u>: A guiding spirit can make its presence known in more ways than one.

### Model

Model the following sentences to practice using *peak* and *peek* correctly.

> Simplicity is the peak of civilization.
> —Jessie Sampter

> I've stayed in the front yard all my life.
> I want a peek at the back
> Where it's rough and untended and hungry weed grows.
> —Gwendolyn Brooks, "A Street in Bronzeville"

*Right Word*

---

## Using the Right Word

Discuss with students the uses of the words listed on SE page 722 to help them spell correctly, use strategic learning techniques to acquire basic and grade-level vocabulary, and comprehend vocabulary used in written classroom materials. Have students complete the Grammar Practice on SE page 723 individually, and review the answers with the class.

## Related Skills Activities

■ **SkillsBook**
Pretest: Using the Right Word, p. 61
Using the Right Word 1, 2, 3, 4, and 5, pp. 62–66
Review: Using the Right Word, pp. 67–68

 **Answers**

1. passed
2. OK
3. plain
4. OK
5. peak
6. piqued
7. past
8. peek
9. moral

---

TEKS 10.19
ELPS 1C, 4C, 5C

**poor, pour, pore** ■ *Poor* means "needy or pitiable." *Pour* means "to cause to flow in a stream." A *pore* is an opening in the skin.

> **Tough exams on late spring days make my poor pores pour sweat.**

**principal, principle** ■ As an adjective, *principal* means "primary." As a noun, it can mean "a school administrator" or "a sum of money." *Principle* means "idea or doctrine."

> **His principal concern is fitness. (adjective) The principal retired. (noun)**
> **During the first year of a loan, you pay more interest than principal. (noun)**
> **The principle of *caveat emptor* is "Let the buyer beware."**

**quiet, quit, quite** ■ *Quiet* is the opposite of "noisy." *Quit* means "to stop." *Quite* means "completely or entirely."

**quote, quotation** ■ *Quote* is a verb; *quotation* is a noun.

> **The quotation I used was from Woody Allen. You may quote me on that.**

**real, really, very** ■ Do not use *real* in place of the adverbs *very* or *really*.

> **Mother's cake is usually very (not *real*) tasty, but this one is really stale!**

**right, write, wright, rite** ■ *Right* means "correct or proper"; it also refers to that which a person has a legal claim to, as in copyright. *Write* means "to inscribe or record." A *wright* is a person who makes or builds something. *Rite* refers to a ritual or ceremonial act.

> **Write this down: It is the right of the shipwright to perform the rite of christening—breaking a bottle of champagne on the stern of the ship.**

**ring, wring** ■ *Ring* means "encircle" or "to sound by striking." *Wring* means "to squeeze or twist."

> **At the beach, Grandma would ring her head with a large scarf. Once, it blew into the sea, so she had me wring it out.**

**scene, seen** ■ *Scene* refers to the setting or location where something happens; it also may mean "sight or spectacle." *Seen* is a form of the verb "see."

> **Serena had seen her boyfriend making a scene; she cringed.**

**seam, seem** ■ *Seam* (noun) is a line formed by connecting two pieces. *Seem* (verb) means "to appear to exist."

> **The ragged seams in his old coat seem to match the creases in his face.**

**set, sit** ■ *Set* means "to place." *Sit* means "to put the body in a seated position." *Set* is transitive; *sit* is intransitive. (See 744.1.)

> **How can you just sit there and watch as I set all these chairs in place?**

Right Word

 **Practice**

## Using the Right Word 8

**principal, principle; real, really, very; ring, wring; set, sit**

 In each sentence, a word is misused. Write the correct word.

**Example:** My parents are trying to pay down the principle on their mortgage.
*principal*

1. I am real excited about my sister's engagement ring.

2. In this game, you must find something to set on when you hear a bell ring.

3. "That is a very interesting painting," remarked the principle to the art student.

4. Reina's hair is really long—she has to ring it out one section at a time when she washes it.

5. My ears are starting to wring; I think I'd better sit down.

6. Rosa Parks was a real hero who adhered to the principal of fairness.

7. Don't sit that candle on the wooden table . . . it could lead to a very bad situation.

8. The principle reason to recycle is really quite simple: it saves natural resources.

### Model

Model the following sentences to practice using *real* and *really* correctly.

> **A man always has two reasons for doing anything—a good reason and the real reason.**
> —J. P. Morgan

> **All that is really necessary for survival of the fittest, it seems, is an interest in life—good, bad, or peculiar.**
> —Grace Paley

---

## Using the Right Word

Discuss with students the uses of the words listed on SE page 724 to help them spell correctly, use strategic learning techniques to acquire basic and grade-level vocabulary, and comprehend vocabulary used in written classroom materials. Have students contribute other examples for each use. Also invite students to share their answers to the Grammar Practice on SE page 725 with the class.

## Related Skills Activities

■ *SkillsBook*
Pretest: Using the Right Word, p. 61
Using the Right Word 1, 2, 3, 4, and 5, pp. 62–66
Review: Using the Right Word, pp. 67–68

 **Answers**

1. really or very
2. sit
3. principal
4. wring
5. ring
6. principle
7. set
8. principal

 **TEKS** **10.19** Spell correctly using resources to determine and check correct spelling; **ELPS** **1C** Use strategic learning techniques to acquire basic and grade-level vocabulary; **4C** Comprehend vocabulary used in written classroom materials; **5C** Spell familiar words with increasing accuracy

**TEKS** 10.19
**ELPS** 1C, 4C, 5C

**sight, cite, site** ■ *Sight* means "the act of seeing"; a *sight* is what is seen. *Cite* means "to quote" or "to summon," as before a court. *Site* means "location."

> In her report, the general contractor cited several problems at the downtown job site. For one, the loading area was a chaotic sight.

**sole, soul** ■ *Sole* means "single, only one"; *sole* also refers to the bottom surface of the foot. *Soul* refers to the spiritual part of a person.

> As the sole inhabitant of the island, he put his heart and soul into his farming.

**stationary, stationery** ■ *Stationary* means "not movable"; *stationery* refers to the paper and envelopes used to write letters.

**steal, steel** ■ *Steal* means "to take something without permission"; *steel* is a type of metal.

**than, then** ■ *Than* is used in a comparison; *then* tells when.

> Abigail shouted that her big brother was bigger than my big brother. Then she ran away.

**their, there, they're** ■ *Their* is a possessive personal pronoun. *There* is an adverb used to point out location. *They're* is the contraction for "they are."

> They're a well-dressed couple. Do you see them there, with their matching jackets?

**threw, through** ■ *Threw* is the past tense of "throw." *Through* means "from beginning to end."

> Through seven innings, Janelle threw just seven strikes.

**to, too, two** ■ *To* is a preposition that can mean "in the direction of." *To* is also used to form an infinitive. (See 754.2.) *Too* means "also" or "very." *Two* is a number.

**vain, vane, vein** ■ *Vain* means "valueless or fruitless"; it may also mean "holding a high regard for oneself." *Vane* is a flat piece of material set up to show which way the wind blows. *Vein* refers to a blood vessel or a mineral deposit.

> The vain prospector, boasting about the vein of silver he'd uncovered, paused to look up at the turning weather vane.

**vary, very** ■ *Vary* means "to change." *Very* means "to a high degree."

> Though the weather may vary from day to day, generally, it is very pleasant.

---

**TEKS** 10.19
**ELPS** 1C, 1E, 3B, 3E, 3H, 4C, 5C

### Using the Right Word 9

sole, soul; than, then; *vain, vane, vein;* vary, very

 **Read the following paragraphs. If the underlined word is used incorrectly, write the correct word. If it's correct as is, write "OK."**

How do credit cards work? Essentially, you (the card user) borrow money to buy something. The card issuer, a bank, agrees to the loan and **(1)** <u>than</u> deposits the money into the merchant's bank account.

If you cannot pay the full amount of the bill, the bank charges interest on the unpaid balance. Interest rates typically **(2)** <u>vary</u> from 11 to 23 percent. The next bill will be for the unpaid amount plus interest. The amount owed, even if you don't borrow a dollar more, keeps going up! It can be **(3)** <u>vary</u> difficult to pay off a balance. You may begin to think that you're making payments in **(4)** <u>vein</u>. You may even feel you owe your heart and **(5)** <u>sole</u> to the credit card company.

Banks also charge credit card users fees for cash advances and late payments. Anyone who uses credit cards should be aware of how easy it is to incur more debt **(6)** <u>then</u> he or she can comfortably repay. List your charges on some paper. **(7)** <u>Than</u> learn to use credit responsibly to build a positive credit record.

### Learning Language

Work with a partner and re-read the information on the previous page. Discuss the differences in meaning among the words. Then choose four words from different groups and use them to describe a particular person or thing. Be sure to include specific details in your narration. Have your partner retell the description to you. Have your partner tell which words you used and how those words would be spelled. Then have your partner choose a different set of words, and repeat the activity.

---

## Using the Right Word

Discuss with students the uses of the words listed on SE page 726 to help them spell familiar words accurately, use strategic learning techniques to acquire basic and grade-level vocabulary, and comprehend vocabulary used in written classroom materials. Invite students to share their answers to the Grammar Practice on SE page 727 with the class.

## Learning Language

Use the collaborative speaking and listening activity on SE page 727 to help students expand and internalize vocabulary by using high-frequency English words to describe a particular person or thing.

 ## Answers

1. then
2. OK
3. very
4. vain
5. soul
6. than
7. Then

## Related Skills Activities

■ *SkillsBook*
Pretest: Using the Right Word, p. 61
Using the Right Word 1, 2, 3, 4, and 5, pp. 62–66
Review: Using the Right Word, pp. 67–68

---

**TEKS** **10.19** Spell correctly using resources to determine and check correct spelling; **ELPS 1C** Use strategic learning techniques to acquire basic and grade-level vocabulary; **1E** Internalize new basic language by using and reusing it/speaking; **3B** Expand vocabulary by learning and using high-frequency words for identifying and describing; **3E** Share information in cooperative learning interactions; **3H** Describe with increasing specificity and detail; **4C** Comprehend vocabulary used in written classroom materials; **5C** Spell familiar words with increasing accuracy

TEKS 10.19
ELPS 1C, 4C, 5C

**vial, vile** ■ A *vial* is a small container for liquid. *Vile* is an adjective meaning "foul, despicable."

It's a vile job, but someone has to clean these lab vials.

**waist, waste** ■ *Waist* is the part of the body just above the hips. The verb *waste* means "to spend or use carelessly" or "to wear away or decay"; the noun *waste* refers to material that is unused or useless.

Her waist is small because she wastes no opportunity to exercise.

**wait, weight** ■ *Wait* means "to stay somewhere expecting something." *Weight* refers to a degree or unit of heaviness.

**ware, wear, where** ■ *Ware* refers to a product that is sold; *wear* means "to have on or to carry on one's body"; *where* asks "in what place?" or "in what situation?"

The designer boasted, "Where can anybody wear my ware? Anywhere."

**way, weigh** ■ *Way* means "path or route." *Weigh* means "to measure weight" or "to have a certain heaviness."

My dogs weigh too much. The best way to reduce is a daily run in the park.

**weather, whether** ■ *Weather* refers to the condition of the atmosphere. *Whether* refers to a possibility.

Due to the weather, the coach wondered whether he should cancel the meet.

**which, that** ■ Use *which* to refer to objects or animals in a nonrestrictive clause (set off with commas). Use *that* to refer to objects or animals in a restrictive clause. (For more information about these types of clauses, see 650.2.)

The birds, which stay in the area all winter, know where the feeders are located. The food that attracts the most birds is sunflower seed.

**who, whom** ■ Use *who* to refer to people. *Who* is used as the subject of a verb in an independent clause or in a relative clause. *Whom* is used as the object of a preposition or as a direct object.

To whom do we owe our thanks for these pizzas? And who ordered anchovies?

**who's, whose** ■ *Who's* is the contraction for "who is." *Whose* is a pronoun that can show possession or ownership.

Cody, whose car is new, will drive. Who's going to read the map?

**your, you're** ■ *Your* is a possessive pronoun. *You're* is the contraction for "you are."

Take your boots if you're going out in that snow.

---

## Practice

### Using the Right Word 10

vial, vile; ware, wear, where; **weather, whether;** which, that; **who, whom**

 In each numbered paragraph below, some words are used incorrectly. Write the correct word for each.

**Example:** This is my dad, Emerson Whitley, who you probably recognize from his work in commercials.
who—whom

**1.**  Willis had been feeling a bit under the weather lately. He went to the doctor, whom ordered some tests. The doctor told him wear the blood lab was because Willis needed to provide a vile or two of blood to be tested.

**2.**  "I don't know weather you're aware of this or not, but there is a vile odor coming from the science lab," Lupe informed Ms. Yiel.

"I'll have to talk to Dario, who I allowed to perform an experiment," Ms. Yiel said. "He must have used the sodium chloride instead of the potassium chloride, which I *did* warn him about!"

**3.**  Aunt Yolanda's utensils are agate wear, that is not agate at all but enameled steel. Her plates are real china, and she uses the glasses which she got in Ireland. Mom thinks Aunt Yolanda's table settings are very beautiful, so she makes us where nice clothes whenever we eat there.

### Model

Model the following sentences to practice using *who* and *whom* correctly.

A jury consists of twelve persons chosen to decide who has the better lawyer.
—Robert Frost

We cannot really love anybody with whom we never laugh.
—Agnes Repplier, *Americans and Others*

---

## Using the Right Word

Discuss with students the uses of the words listed on SE page 728 to help them spell familiar words accurately, use strategic learning techniques to acquire basic and grade-level vocabulary, and comprehend vocabulary used in written classroom materials. Have students contribute other examples for each use. Also have students complete the Grammar Practice on SE page 729 individually, and review the answers as a class.

## Related Skills Activities

■ *SkillsBook*
Pretest: Using the Right Word, p. 61
Using the Right Word 1, 2, 3, 4, and 5, pp. 62–66
Review: Using the Right Word, pp. 67–68

## Answers

**1.** whom—who
wear—where
vile—vial
**2.** weather—whether
who—whom
**3.** wear—ware
what—which
which—that
where—wear

---

 **TEKS 10.19** Spell correctly using resources to determine and check correct spelling; **ELPS 1C** Use strategic learning techniques to acquire basic and grade-level vocabulary; **4C** Comprehend vocabulary used in written classroom materials; **5C** Spell familiar words with increasing accuracy

# Parts of Speech

Words in the English language are used in eight different ways. For this reason, there are eight parts of speech.

**730.1** Noun

A word that names a person, a place, a thing, or an idea
> Governor Smith-Jones   Oregon   hospital   religion

**730.2** Pronoun

A word used in place of a noun
> I   you   she   him   who   everyone   these   neither
> theirs   themselves   which

**730.3** Verb

A word that expresses action or state of being
> float   sniff   discover   seem   were   was

**730.4** Adjective

A word that describes a noun or a pronoun
> young   big   grim   Canadian   longer

**730.5** Adverb

A word that describes a verb, an adjective, or another adverb
> briefly   forward   regally   slowly   better

**730.6** Preposition

The first word or words in a prepositional phrase (which functions as an adjective or an adverb)
> away from   under   before   with   for   out of

**730.7** Conjunction

A word that connects other words or groups of words
> and   but   although   because   either, or   so

**730.8** Interjection

A word or phrase that shows strong emotion or surprise
> Oh no!   Yipes!   Good grief!   Well, . . .

# Parts of Speech

## Noun

A **noun** is a word that names something: a person, a place, a thing, or an idea.
governor   Oregon   hospital   Buddhism   love

### Classes of Nouns

The five classes of nouns are *proper, common, concrete, abstract,* and *collective.*

**731.1** Proper Noun

A **proper noun** names a particular person, place, thing, or idea. Proper nouns are always capitalized.
> Jackie Robinson   Brooklyn   World Series
> Christianity   Ebbets Field   Hinduism

**731.2** Common Noun

A **common noun** does not name a particular person, place, thing, or idea. Common nouns are not capitalized.
> person   woman   president   park   baseball   government

**731.3** Concrete Noun

A **concrete noun** names a thing that is tangible (can be seen, touched, heard, smelled, or tasted). Concrete nouns are either proper or common.
> child   Grand Canyon   music   aroma   fireworks   Becky

**731.4** Abstract Noun

An **abstract noun** names an idea, a condition, or a feeling—in other words, something that cannot be touched, smelled, tasted, seen, or heard.
> New Deal   greed   poverty   progress   freedom   awe

**731.5** Collective Noun

A **collective noun** names a group or a unit.
> United States   choir   team   crowd   community

Parts of Speech

---

## Related Skills Activities

■ *SkillsBook*
Pretest: Nouns, p.73

ELPS 4C

## Forms of Nouns

Nouns are grouped according to their *number, gender,* and *case.*

### 732.1 Number of a Noun

**Number** indicates whether the noun is singular or plural.

A **singular noun** refers to one person, place, thing, or idea.

actor   stadium   Canadian   bully   truth   child   person

A **plural noun** refers to more than one person, place, thing, or idea.

actors   stadiums   Canadians   bullies   truths   children   people

### 732.2 Gender of a Noun

**Gender** indicates whether a noun is masculine, feminine, neuter, or indefinite.

**Masculine:** uncle   brother   men   bull   rooster   stallion
**Feminine:** aunt   sister   women   cow   hen   filly
**Neuter** (without gender): tree   cobweb   garage   closet
**Indefinite** (masculine or feminine): president   plumber   doctor   parent

### 732.3 Case of a Noun

**Case** tells how nouns are related to other words used with them. There are three cases: *nominative, possessive,* and *objective.*

■ A **nominative case** noun can be the subject of a clause.

Andrew's jacket was soaking wet. . . . His new umbrella had broken in the wind and was useless in the pouring rain.

A nominative noun can also be a predicate noun (or predicate nominative), which follows a "be" verb (*am, is, are, was, were, be, being, been*) and renames the subject. In the sentence below, *type* renames *Mr. Cattanzara.*

Mr. Cattanzara was a different type than those in the neighborhood.
—Bernard Malamud, "A Summer's Reading"

■ A **possessive case** noun shows possession or ownership.

Unlike John's new baseball mitt, mine is old and dirty, but it still serves me very well each time we take the field.

■ An **objective case** noun can be a direct object, an indirect object, or an object of the preposition.

Keisha always gives Mylo science-fiction books for his birthday.

(*Mylo* is the indirect object and *books* is the direct object of the verb "gives." *Birthday* is the object of the preposition "for.")

---

 ELPS 3E, 3G, 3F                                        Parts of Speech   **733**

## Grammar Practice

### Nouns

■ Classes of Nouns
■ Number of a Noun
■ Case of a Noun

For each underlined noun, write its class (there will be at least two classes for each), number, and case.

**Example:** The Bill of Rights refers to the first ten amendments of the United States Constitution.

Class: proper, concrete; Number: singular; Case: nominative

1. Checks and balances in the United States government allow Congress to override a presidential veto.

2. During the American Revolution, George Washington was commander of the Continental army.

3. The tax laws imposed on the colonists by the British government were viewed as unfair.

4. The Civil War began when the Confederates shelled Fort Sumter.

5. Frederick Douglass made the argument that African Americans should be allowed to serve in the army.

6. The Great Wall of China formed a boundary between China and Mongolia.

7. In feudal Japan, a shogun had more military power than an emperor.

8. A megalopolis is an area made up of adjoining cities and suburbs.

### Learning Language

Working with a partner, re-read the information on the two previous pages. Take turns describing a concept or a particular process using at least one proper, one common, one concrete, and one abstract noun. Have your partner listen carefully, name the nouns, and identify the classification of each.

Parts of Speech

---

## Nouns

Discuss with students the forms of nouns listed on SE page 732 to help develop and comprehend basic vocabulary and language structures. Have students contribute other examples for each use.

## Learning Language

Use the cooperative speaking and listening activity on SE page 733 to help students express ideas by asking for and giving information.

## Related Skills Activities

■ **Basic Grammar and Writing**
General and Specific Nouns, p. 570

■ *SkillsBook*
Types of Nouns, p. 74
Singular and Plural Nouns, p. 75
Functions of Nouns, p. 76
Nominative, Possessive, Objective Cases of Nouns, p. 77
Gender of Nouns, p. 78

## Answers

1. Class: proper, abstract, collective
   Number: singular, Case: objective
2. Class: proper, concrete
   Number: singular, Case: nominative
3. Class: common, concrete
   Number: plural, Case: objective
4. Class: proper, concrete
   Number: singular, Case: objective
5. Class: common, abstract
   Number: singular, Case: objective
6. Class: common, concrete
   Number: singular, Case: objective
7. Class: common, abstract
   Number: singular, Case: objective
8. Class: common, concrete
   Number: plural, Case: objective

 **ELPS 3E** Share information in cooperative learning interactions; **3F** Give information/ranging from using a limited high-frequency vocabulary to using abstract and content-based vocabulary during speaking; **3G** Express ideas ranging from communicating short phrases to participating in discussions; **4C** Comprehend language structures used in written classroom materials

TEKS 10.17A(iii)
ELPS 4C, 5E

## Pronoun

A **pronoun** is a word used in place of a noun.

I, you, she, it, which, that, themselves, whoever, me, he, they, mine, ours

The three types of pronouns are *simple, compound,* and *phrasal.*

Simple:   I, you, he, she, it, we, they, who, what
Compound:   myself, someone, anybody, everything, itself, whoever
Phrasal:   one another, each other

All pronouns have **antecedents**. An antecedent is the noun that the pronoun refers to or replaces.

Ambrosch was considered the important person in the family. Mrs. Shimerda and Ántonia always deferred to him, though he was often surly with them and contemptuous toward his father. —Willa Cather, *My Ántonia*

(*Ambrosch* is the antecedent of *him, he,* and *his.*)

**NOTE:** Each pronoun must agree with its antecedent. (See page 782.)

**734.1** Classes of Pronouns

The seven classes of pronouns are *personal, reflexive and intensive, reciprocal, relative, indefinite, interrogative,* and *demonstrative.*

### Personal
I, me, my, mine / we, us, our, ours
you, your, yours / they, them, their, theirs
he, him, his, she, her, hers, it, its

### Reflexive and Intensive
myself, yourself, himself, herself, itself, ourselves, yourselves, themselves

### Reciprocal
each other, one another

### Relative
what, who, whose, whom, which, that

### Indefinite
| | | | | |
|---|---|---|---|---|
| all | both | everything | nobody | several |
| another | each | few | none | some |
| any | each one | many | no one | somebody |
| anybody | either | most | nothing | someone |
| anyone | everybody | much | one | something |
| anything | everyone | neither | other | such |

### Interrogative
who, whose, whom, which, what

### Demonstrative
this, that, these, those

---

ELPS 4C, 5E

## Grammar Practice

### Pronouns 1

■ Antecedents

 For the following paragraphs, write the antecedent of each underlined pronoun.

**Example:** 1. Marian Anderson

In the early 1900s, nobody imagined that "Baby Contralto" would grow up to be the first African American to sing a leading role with the Metropolitan Opera. "Baby Contralto" is what the Baptist parishioners called Marian Anderson when **(1)** she began singing at **(2)** their church at age six.

Marian's family had a piano, but **(3)** they could not afford lessons, so Marian taught **(4)** herself. Soon she became a popular singer in her community. After graduating from high school, she applied to a local music school. **(5)** It coldly rejected Marian because of her color.

Prejudice did not stop her. She stalwartly pursued a successful singing career, and in 1930, **(6)** she became the first black female to perform at Carnegie Hall. Famed composer Jean Sibelius was so moved by her work that **(7)** he dedicated a song to her. Marian went on to perform all over the world. Audiences loved her, and **(8)** they demanded even more performances. In 1955, at the age of 58, she performed at the New York Metropolitan Opera as Ulrica in Guiseppe Verdi's *The Masked Ball.*

### Model

Model the following sentence to practice using a pronoun and an antecedent in the same sentence.

There are many persons ready to do what is right because in their hearts, they know it is right.

—Marian Anderson

---

## Pronoun

Discuss with students the uses of pronouns listed on SE page 734 to help them comprehend language structures used in written classroom materials, and employ complex grammatical structures. Have students contribute other examples for each use. Also invite students to share their answers to the Grammar Practice on SE page 735 with the class.

### Related Skills Activities

■ **Basic Grammar and Writing**
Pronouns, pp. 572–573

■ *SkillsBook*
Pretest: Pronouns, p. 80

##  Answers

1. Marian Anderson
2. parishioners
3. family
4. Marian
5. school
6. Marian
7. Jean Sibelius
8. audiences

---

 **TEKS** 17A(iii) Use and understand reciprocal pronouns; **ELPS 4C** Comprehend language structures used in written classroom materials; **5E** Employ increasingly complex grammatical structures in content area writing such as using correct verbs, tenses, and pronouns/possessive case/negatives and contractions

TEKS 10.17A(ii), 10.17A(iii) ELPS 4C, 5E, 5F

### 736.1 Personal Pronouns

A **personal pronoun** can take the place of any noun.

Our coach made her point loud and clear when she raised her voice.

- A **reflexive pronoun** is formed by adding -self or -selves to a personal pronoun. A reflexive pronoun can be a direct object, an indirect object, an object of the preposition, or a predicate nominative.

   Miss Sally Sunshine loves herself. (direct object of *loves*)
   Tomisha does not seem herself today. (predicate nominative)

- An **intensive pronoun** is a reflexive pronoun that intensifies, or emphasizes, the noun or pronoun it refers to.

   Leo himself taught his children to invest their lives in others.

### 736.2 Relative Pronouns

A **relative pronoun** relates or connects a relative clause to the noun or pronoun it modifies.

   Students who study regularly get the best grades. Surprise!
   The dance, which we had looked forward to for weeks, was canceled.

(The relative pronoun *who* relates the restrictive relative clause to *students*; *which* relates the nonrestrictive relative clause to *dance*.)

### 736.3 Reciprocal Pronouns

A **reciprocal pronoun** refers to the individual parts of a plural antecedent and expresses mutual actions or relationships between the parts.

   The students decided not to exchange holiday cards with one another this year.
   John and Toby often do favors for each other.

### 736.4 Indefinite Pronouns

An **indefinite pronoun** refers to unnamed or unknown people or things.

   I have never known anybody that well. (antecedent of *anybody* is unknown)

### 736.5 Interrogative Pronouns

An **interrogative pronoun** asks a question.

   Who are you? What do you want? What do you expect to find here?

### 736.6 Demonstrative Pronouns

A **demonstrative pronoun** points out people, places, or things without naming them.

   This shouldn't be too hard. That looks about right.
   These are the best ones. Those ought to be thrown out.

**NOTE:** When one of these words precedes a noun, it functions as an adjective, not a pronoun. (See 756.1.)

   That movie bothers me. (*That* is an adjective.)

---

 TEKS 10.17A(iii) ELPS 4C, 5E

## Grammar Practice

### Pronouns 2

- Indefinite Pronouns
- Interrogative Pronouns
- Demonstrative Pronouns
- Reciprocal Pronouns

 Identify each underlined pronoun as *indefinite, interrogative, reciprocal,* or *demonstrative.*

**Example:** Whom do you think is the funniest woman in America?
   *interrogative*

1. Many of today's actresses have been cast in comedy roles.

2. These are a few well-known women comedians: Ellen DeGeneres, Rosie O'Donnell, Tina Fey, and Lucille Ball.

3. They all seem to know one another quite well.

4. Which of the above-named comedians was the voice of Dory in *Finding Nemo*?

5. Who would have guessed that *I Love Lucy* would still be on the air 50 years after it was made?

6. This is a famous quotation from comedian Gilda Radner: "I base most of my fashion taste on what doesn't itch."

7. Those are my favorite kind of clothes, too.

8. None of the women believed that they would grow up to be famous.

9. All of them became famous for their ability to make people laugh.

10. I wonder if Ellen and Tina correspond with each other about comedy routines.

### Model

Model the following sentence to practice using indefinite and interrogative pronouns.

   Who is rich? He that is content. Who is that? Nobody.
   —Benjamin Franklin

Parts of Speech

---

## Pronouns

Discuss with students the uses of pronouns listed on SE page 736 to help them comprehend language structures such as the classes of pronouns, and employ complex grammatical structures in content area writing. Have students write sentences showing other examples for each class of pronouns. Also invite students to share their answers to the Grammar Practice on SE page 737 with the class.

## Related Skills Activities

■ *SkillsBook*
Functions of Pronouns, p. 82
Relative Pronouns, p. 85
Indefinite, Interrogative, and Demonstrative Pronouns, p. 86
Reciprocal Pronouns, p. 88

 ## Answers

1. indefinite
2. demonstrative
3. reciprocal
4. interrogative
5. interrogative
6. demonstrative
7. demonstrative
8. indefinite
9. indefinite
10. reciprocal

---

 **TEKS** 17A(ii) Use and understand restrictive and nonrestrictive relative clauses; **10.17A(iii)** Use and understand reciprocal pronouns; **ELPS** **4C** Comprehend language structures used in written classroom materials; **5E** Employ increasingly complex grammatical structures in content area writing such as using correct verbs, tenses, and pronouns/possessive case/negatives and contractions; **5F** Write using a variety of grade-appropriate sentence patterns in increasingly accurate ways

ELPS 4C, 5E

## Forms of Personal Pronouns

The form of a personal pronoun indicates its *number* (singular or plural), its *person* (first, second, third), its *case* (nominative, possessive, or objective), and its *gender* (masculine, feminine, or neuter).

### 738.1 Number of a Pronoun

Personal pronouns are singular or plural. The singular personal pronouns include *my, him, he, she, it.* The plural personal pronouns include *we, you, them, our.* (*You* can be singular or plural.) Notice in the caption below that the first *you* is singular and the second *you* is plural.

**"Larry, you need to keep all four tires on the road when turning. Are you still with us back there?"**

### 738.2 Person of a Pronoun

The **person** of a pronoun indicates whether the person, place, thing, or idea represented by the pronoun is speaking, is spoken to, or is spoken about.

- **First person** is used in place of the name of the speaker or speakers.
  I went to the movies with some friends, but when we arrived at the theatre, we realized the movie we wanted to see was not playing.
- **Second-person** pronouns name the person or persons spoken to.
  "If you hit your duck, you want me to go in after it?" Eugie said.
  —Gina Berriault, "The Stone Boy"
- **Third-person** pronouns name the person or thing spoken about.
  He did not understand what was happening to him. It wasn't even noon, and here he was in the hospital with a broken leg.

---

## Grammar Practice

### Pronouns 3

- Number of a Pronoun
- Person of a Pronoun

 **Identify the person and number of each underlined pronoun in the paragraphs below.**

**Example:** 1. second person, plural

"Mom and Dad!" Greg yelled. "Are **(1)** you ready yet?" Greg, his sister, and **(2)** their folks were going to a football game; they were late. Greg was almost ready to say **(3)** he would leave without **(4)** them. The kickoff was less than an hour away, and Greg would be mad if he missed **(5)** it.

When they were finally on their way, Greg's dad said, "Uh-oh, I forgot **(6)** our tickets. We'll have to go back."

"**(7)** I can't believe it," Greg sighed, shaking his head.

"Why are **(8)** you so worried?" Greg's mom asked **(9)** him.

Before Greg could answer **(10)** her, his sister said, **(11)** "We don't have to turn around. I have the tickets."

### Model

Model the following sentences to practice using first-, second-, and third-person pronouns.

Computers are useless; they can only give you answers.
—Pablo Picasso

We are so vain that we even care for the opinion of those we don't care for.
—Marie Ebner von Eschenbach

---

## Personal Pronouns

Discuss with students the uses of pronouns listed on SE page 738 to help them comprehend language structures used in written classroom materials and employ complex grammatical structures in content area writing. Have students complete the Grammar Practice on SE page 739 with a partner.

## Related Skills Activities

- **SkillsBook**
  Number and Person of Personal Pronouns, p. 81

## Answers

1. second person, plural
2. third person, plural
3. third person, singular
4. third person, plural
5. third person, singular
6. first person, plural
7. first person, singular
8. second person, singular
9. third person, singular
10. third person, singular
11. first person, plural

 **ELPS 4C** Comprehend language structures used in written classroom materials; **5E** Employ increasingly complex grammatical structures in content area writing such as using correct verbs, tenses, and pronouns/possessive case/negatives and contractions

**740**

ELPS 4C, 5E

### 740.1 Case of a Pronoun

The **case** of each pronoun tells how it is related to the other words used with it. There are three cases: *nominative, possessive,* and *objective.*

- A **nominative case** pronoun can be the subject of a clause. The following are nominative forms: *I, you, he, she, it, we, they.*

  I like life when things go well. You must live life in order to love life.

A nominative pronoun is a *predicate nominative* if it follows a "be" verb (*am, is, are, was, were, be, being, been*) or another linking verb (*appear, become, feel,* etc.) and renames the subject.

  "Oh, it's only she who scared me just now," said Mama to Papa, glancing over her shoulder.
  "Yes, it is I," said Mai in a superior tone.

- **Possessive case** pronouns show possession or ownership. Apostrophes, however, are not used with personal pronouns. (Pronouns in the possessive case can also be classified as adjectives.)

  But as I placed my hand upon his shoulder, there came a strong shudder over his whole person.
  —Edgar Allan Poe, "The Fall of the House of Usher"

- An **objective case** pronoun can be a direct object, an indirect object, or an object of the preposition.

  The kids loved it! We lit a campfire for them and told them old ghost stories. (*It* is the direct object of the verb *loved. Them* is the object of the preposition *for* and the indirect object of the verb *told.*)

#### Number, Person, and Case of Personal Pronouns

| | Nominative | Possessive | Objective |
|---|---|---|---|
| First Person Singular | I | my, mine | me |
| Second Person Singular | you | your, yours | you |
| Third Person Singular | he | his | him |
| | she | her, hers | her |
| | it | its | it |
| | Nominative | Possessive | Objective |
| First Person Plural | we | our, ours | us |
| Second Person Plural | you | your, yours | you |
| Third Person Plural | they | their, theirs | them |

### 740.2 Gender of a Pronoun

**Gender** indicates whether a pronoun is masculine, feminine, or neuter.

Masculine: **he him his**       Feminine: **she her hers**
Neuter (without gender): **it its**

---

ELPS 4C, 4F, 4G, 5E

Parts of Speech **741**

## Grammar Practice

### Pronouns 4

- Case of a Pronoun

 Identify each underlined pronoun as *nominative, possessive,* or *objective.*

**Example:** 1. *possessive*

Mr. Lee, a neighbor, was taking out **(1)** his garbage. **(2)** He saw **(3)** me beginning to rake our yard and asked, "Do you need any help, Maria?"

Not one to turn down such an offer, **(4)** I accepted. The next thing I knew, he came from his garage with a new "toy." **(5)** It was a noisy, smelly leaf blower.

"Have **(6)** you ever seen one of these things?" he asked. He demonstrated **(7)** its powerful wind, aiming **(8)** it at a pile of leaves I had just raked.

"Well, I've seen people use them," I admitted, "but **(9)** we only have rakes at **(10)** our house. I guess we're a little old-fashioned that way."

### Learning Language

With a partner, review the information about pronouns on the previous page. As you re-read the information, take notes about each case and the corresponding pronouns. This will help you remember the information. In your notes use your own words to write a brief definition of the word *case* and an explanation of its function. Write new example sentences, and share and explain your sentences. Listen as your partner reads his or her sentences to you. If you have questions about pronoun cases, ask your teacher for clarification.

Parts of Speech

---

## Forms of Personal Pronouns

Discuss with students the uses of pronouns listed on SE page 740 to help them comprehend language structures and employ complex grammatical structures in content area writing. Have students contribute other examples for each use. Also invite students to share their answers to the Grammar Practice on SE page 741 with the class.

## Learning Language

Use the collaborative speaking and listening activity on SE page 741 to help students use support from peers and teachers to enhance and confirm understanding and develop grasp of the case of pronouns. Students will also demonstrate comprehension of complex English by taking notes.

## Answers

1. possessive
2. nominative
3. objective
4. nominative
5. nominative
6. nominative
7. possessive
8. objective
9. nominative
10. possessive

## Related Skills Activities

- **SkillsBook**
  Nominative, Possessive, and Objective Cases of Pronouns, p. 83
  Reflexive and Intensive Pronouns, p. 87

---

 **ELPS 4C** Comprehend language structures used in written classroom materials; **4F** Use support from peers/teachers to enhance understanding and develop grasp of language structures; **4G** Demonstrate comprehension of increasingly complex English/taking notes; **5E** Employ increasingly complex grammatical structures in content area writing such as using correct verbs, tenses, and pronouns/possessive case/negatives and contractions

ELPS 4C, 5E

## Verb

A **verb** is a word that expresses action (*run, carried, declared*) or a state of being (*is, are, seemed*).

### Classes of Verbs

**742.1** Linking Verbs

A **linking verb** links the subject to a noun or an adjective in the predicate.

In the outfield, the boy felt confident.
He was the best fielder around.

| Common Linking Verbs | | | | | | |
|---|---|---|---|---|---|---|
| is | are | was | were | be | been | am |

**Additional Linking Verbs**

| smell | seem | grow | become | appear | sound |
|---|---|---|---|---|---|
| taste | feel | get | remain | stay | look | turn |

**742.2** Auxiliary Verbs

**Auxiliary verbs,** or helping verbs, are used to form some of the **tenses** (746.3), the **mood** (752.1), and the **voice** (750.2) of the main verb. (In the example below, the auxiliary verbs are in red; the main verbs are in blue.)

The mud had flowed quickly down the mountain, covering everything in its path. By the time the rain had stopped, the rescue crews were faced with the daunting task of slogging through the mud to help those who had survived.

| Common Auxiliary Verbs | | | | | | | |
|---|---|---|---|---|---|---|---|
| is | was | being | did | have | would | shall | might |
| am | were | been | does | had | could | can | must |
| are | be | do | has | should | will | may | |

---

## Grammar Practice

### Verbs 1

■ Linking and Auxiliary Verbs

 Write whether each underlined word is a linking verb or an auxiliary verb.

**Example:** The earth's solid inner core <u>is</u> surrounded by a fluid outer core about 4,200 miles across.
auxiliary

1. Researchers <u>have</u> recently discovered that the core spins 1/4 to 1/2 of a degree faster than the rest of the planet.

2. Magnetic interaction <u>is</u> the most likely reason for the different spin rates.

3. The researchers <u>had</u> arrived at their discovery by studying the travel times of earthquake waves through the earth.

4. There <u>are</u> differences not only in the times but also in the shapes of the waves.

5. The researchers theorized there must <u>be</u> differences in the core as the waves pass through it.

6. The small difference in the rotation speed means that it <u>would</u> take 700 to 1,400 years for the core to get one full revolution ahead.

7. The rate, however, <u>could</u> vary from one decade to the next.

8. The inner core <u>appears</u> to spin slower than the outer core at other times.

### Model

Model the following sentences to practice using linking and auxiliary verbs.

Thought is only a flash between two long nights, but this flash is everything.
—Henri Poincare

A loud voice cannot compete with a clear voice, even if it's a whisper.
—Barry Neil Kaufman

---

## Verb

Discuss with students the uses of verbs listed on SE page 742 to help them comprehend English language structures and employ complex grammatical structures in content area writing. Invite volunteers to share their answers to the Grammar Practice on SE page 743 with the class.

### Related Skills Activities

■ **SkillsBook**
Pretest: Verbs, p. 90
Types of Main Verbs, p. 91
Auxiliary (Helping Verbs), p. 92
Linking Verbs, p. 93

## Answers

1. auxiliary
2. linking
3. auxiliary
4. linking
5. linking
6. auxiliary
7. auxiliary
8. linking

744                                              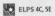 ELPS 4C, 5E

### 744.1 Action Verbs: Transitive and Intransitive

An **intransitive verb** communicates an action that is complete in itself. It does not need an object to receive the action.

> The boy flew on his skateboard. He jumped and flipped and twisted.

A **transitive verb** (red) is an action verb that needs an object (blue) to complete its meaning.

> The city council passed a strict noise ordinance.

While some action verbs are only transitive *or* intransitive, some can be either, depending on how they are used.

> He finally stopped to rest. (intransitive)
> He finally stopped the show. (transitive)

### 744.2 Objects with Transitive Verbs

- A **direct object** receives the action of a transitive verb directly from the subject. Without it, the transitive verb's meaning is incomplete.

  > The boy kicked his skateboard forward. (*Skateboard* is the direct object.)
  > Then he put one foot on it and rode like a pro.

- An **indirect object** also receives the action of a transitive verb, but indirectly. An indirect object names the person *to whom or for whom* something is done. (An indirect object can also name the thing *to what or for what* something is done.)

  > Ms. Oakfield showed us pictures of the solar system.
  > (*Us* is the indirect object.)
  > She gave Tony an A on his project.

**NOTE:** When the word naming the indirect receiver of the action is in a prepositional phrase, it is no longer considered an indirect object.

> Ms. Oakfield showed pictures of the solar system to us.
> (*Us* is the object of the preposition *to*.)

---

 ELPS 4C, 5E                        Parts of Speech    745

## Grammar Practice

### Verbs 2

- Transitive and Intransitive Verbs

 Write whether each underlined verb is transitive or intransitive. For a transitive verb, also write the direct object and, if present, the indirect object.

**Example:**  The customer <u>provided</u> the cash.
            *transitive — direct object: cash*

1. Nasha <u>jogs</u> around the track every day after school.

2. My dad <u>found</u> the map under the front passenger seat.

3. <u>Look</u> at the sky!

4. Simone <u>guessed</u> correctly.

5. Veronica <u>guessed</u> the answer exactly.

6. We <u>bought</u> my mom a new leather briefcase.

7. Kumar <u>allowed</u> me the use of his cell phone for one afternoon.

8. I'm not feeling well; I should <u>lie</u> down.

9. Juana <u>opened</u> the jar of pickles quite easily after Alex couldn't.

10. Mario <u>sent</u> his brother an autographed program from the game.

### Model

Model the following sentences to practice using transitive and intransitive verbs.

> I don't like to write, but I love to have written.
> —Michael Kanin

> Life shrinks or expands in proportion to one's courage.
> —Anaïs Nin

---

## Verb

Discuss with students the uses of verbs listed on SE page 744 to help them comprehend language structures and employ complex grammatical structures in content area writing. Have students contribute other examples for each use. Also invite students to share their answers to the Grammar Practice on SE page 745 with the class.

### Related Skills Activities

- **SkillsBook**
  Transitive and Intransitive Verbs, p. 99
  Direct and Indirect Objects, p. 100

## Answers

1. intransitive
2. transitive — direct object: map
3. intransitive
4. intransitive
5. transitive — direct object: answer
6. transitive — direct object: briefcase; indirect object: mom
7. transitive — direct object: use; indirect object: me
8. intransitive
9. transitive — direct object: jar
10. transitive — direct object: program; indirect object: brother

## 746

### Forms of Verbs

A verb has different forms depending on its *number, person, tense, voice,* and *mood.*

**746.1 Number of a Verb**

**Number** indicates whether a verb is singular or plural. In a clause, the verb (in blue below) and its subject (in red) must both be singular or both be plural.

- **Singular**
  One large island floats off Italy's "toe."
  Italy's northern countryside includes the spectacular Alps.
- **Plural**
  Five small islands float inside Michigan's "thumb."
  The Porcupine Mountains rise above the shores of Lake Superior.

**746.2 Person of a Verb**

**Person** indicates whether the subject of the verb is first, second, or third person (is speaking, is spoken to, or is spoken about). The form of the verb usually changes only when a present-tense verb is used with a third-person singular pronoun.

|  | Singular | Plural |
|---|---|---|
| First Person | I sniff | we sniff |
| Second Person | you sniff | you sniff |
| Third Person | he/she/it sniffs | they sniff |

**746.3 Tense of a Verb**

**Tense** indicates time. Each verb has three principal parts: the *present, past,* and *past participle.* All six tenses are formed from these principal parts. The past and past participle of regular verbs are formed by adding *ed* to the present form. For irregular verbs, the past and past participle are usually different words; however, a few have the same form in all three principal parts (see page **748.2**).

**746.4 Simple Tenses**

- **Present tense** expresses action that is happening at the present time, or action that happens continually, regularly.
  In September, sophomores smirk and joke about the "little freshies."
- **Past tense** expresses action that was completed at a particular time in the past.
  They forgot that just ninety days separated them from freshman status.
- **Future tense** expresses action that will take place in the future.
  They will recall this in three years when they will be freshmen again.

---

## Grammar Practice

### Verbs 3

- Person of a Verb
- Simple Tenses

Write the verb or verbs in the sentences below. Then identify the person and tense of each.

**Example:** Every year sophomores plan a scuba diving trip.
plan: third person, present tense

1. Jacques-Yves Cousteau invented the Aqua-Lung® in 1942.
2. One day scientists will make artificial gills for divers.
3. Today, no one believes that is possible.
4. Scuba divers enjoy the freedom to dive without restraints.
5. If you dive deep into the ocean, make a series of timed stops on your way back to the surface.
6. Otherwise, nitrogen in your air mixture dissolves under pressure and enters your blood stream.
7. Rising directly to the surface will result in nitrogen narcosis.
8. Without special treatment in a decompression chamber, this dangerous condition will almost always lead to death.
9. A diver who follows proper diving protocol is in no danger.
10. Thousands of people safely dived last year with scuba gear and experienced the marvels of the undersea world.

### Model

Model the following sentence to practice using past-tense verbs effectively.

In a sky of iron the points of the Dipper hung like icicles, and Orion flashed his cold fires.
—Edith Wharton, *Ethan Frome*

---

### Verb

Discuss with students the forms and uses of verbs listed on SE page 746 to help them comprehend language structures used in written classroom materials and employ complex grammatical structures in content area writing. Have students contribute other examples for each use. Also invite students to share their answers to the Grammar Practice on SE page 747 with the class.

### Related Skills Activities

- **Basic Grammar and Writing**
  Verb Tenses, p. 574

- *SkillsBook*
  Present Tense Verbs and Third-Person Pronouns, p. 94
  Present, Past, and Future Verb Tenses, p. 96

### Answers

1. invented: third person, past tense
2. will make: third person, future tense
3. believes: third person, present tense
4. enjoy: third person, present tense
5. dive: second person, present tense; make: second person, present tense
6. dissolves: third person, present tense; enters: third person, present tense
7. will result: third person, future tense
8. will lead: third person, future tense
9. follows: third person, present tense; is: third person, present tense
10. dived: third person, past tense; experienced: third person, past tense

---

**ELPS 4C** Comprehend language structures used in written classroom materials; **5E** Employ increasingly complex grammatical structures in content area writing such as using correct verbs, tenses, and pronouns/possessive case/negatives and contractions

TEKS 10.17A(i)
ELPS 4C, 5E

## Forms of Verbs (continued)

### 748.1 Perfect Tenses

- **Present perfect tense** expresses action that began in the past but continues in the present or is completed in the present.

  Our boat has weathered worse storms than this one.

- **Past perfect tense** expresses an action in the past that occurred before another past action.

  They reported, wrongly, that the hurricane had missed the island.

- **Future perfect tense** expresses action that will begin in the future and be completed by a specific time in the future.

  By this time tomorrow, the hurricane will have smashed into the coast.

### 748.2 Irregular Verbs

#### Common Irregular Verbs and Their Principal Parts

| Present Tense | Past Tense | Past Participle | Present Tense | Past Tense | Past Participle | Present Tense | Past Tense | Past Participle |
|---|---|---|---|---|---|---|---|---|
| am, be | was, were | been | go | went | gone | shrink | shrank | shrunk |
| begin | began | begun | grow | grew | grown | sing | sang, sung | sung |
| bite | bit | bitten | hang | hanged | hanged | sink | sank, sunk | sunk |
| blow | blew | blown | (execute) | | | sit | sat | sat |
| break | broke | broken | hang | hung | hung | slay | slew | slain |
| bring | brought | brought | (suspend) | | | speak | spoke | spoken |
| buy | bought | bought | hide | hid | hidden, hid | spring | sprang, | sprung |
| catch | caught | caught | know | knew | known | | sprung | |
| choose | chose | chosen | lay | laid | laid | steal | stole | stolen |
| come | came | come | lead | led | led | strive | strove | striven |
| dive | dove | dived | leave | left | left | swear | swore | sworn |
| do | did | done | lie | lay | lain | swim | swam | swum |
| draw | drew | drawn | (recline) | | | swing | swung | swung |
| drink | drank | drunk | lie | lied | lied | take | took | taken |
| drive | drove | driven | (deceive) | | | teach | taught | taught |
| eat | ate | eaten | lose | lost | lost | tear | tore | torn |
| fall | fell | fallen | make | made | made | throw | threw | thrown |
| fight | fought | fought | ride | rode | ridden | wake | waked, | waked, |
| flee | fled | fled | ring | rang | rung | | woke | woken |
| fly | flew | flown | rise | rose | risen | wear | wore | worn |
| forsake | forsook | forsaken | run | ran | run | weave | weaved, | weaved, |
| freeze | froze | frozen | see | saw | seen | | wove | woven |
| get | got | gotten | shake | shook | shaken | wring | wrung | wrung |
| give | gave | given | show | showed | shown | write | wrote | written |

These verbs are the same in all principal parts: *burst, cost, cut, hurt, let, put, set,* and *spread.*

---

TEKS 10.17A(i)
ELPS 4C, 5E

## Grammar Practice

### Verbs 4

- Irregular Verbs
- Perfect Tenses

Write the correct form (past tense or past participle) of the verb shown in parentheses to complete each sentence. Decide if any perfect tenses have been created. If not, write *simple.*

**Example:** Thirty-five students had _____ the bus to the wrestling match. *(ride)*
had ridden = past perfect

1. Salina _____ off her cold by getting lots of rest. *(fight)*

2. Nadia discovered that her backpack had been _____. *(steal)*

3. Owen _____ to get a perfect score on his algebra exam. *(strive)*

4. Rajan _____ to taste the egg roll, but it was too hot. *(begin)*

5. The fastest swimmers had _____ in the first heat. *(dive)*

6. Dontriece _____ at the assembly about the upcoming tournament. *(speak)*

7. My mom has a blanket that my great-great-grandmother _____ on a loom. *(weave)*

8. Martin had _____ the book on the shelf and forgotten about it. *(lay)*

9. He knew he had _____ a good story by the look on his teacher's face. *(write)*

10. I liked the suit that my cousin _____ to my brother's wedding. *(wear)*

### Model

Model the following sentence and perfect tenses to practice using irregular verbs.

He has chosen to run many marathons, and he has run with the best.

---

## Verb

Discuss with students the perfect-tense verbs and irregular verbs listed on SE page 748 to make sure they comprehend basic vocabulary and language structures. To ensure that students can employ complex grammatical structures in content area writing, have students contribute other examples for each use. Also have students complete the Grammar Practice on SE page 749 with a partner.

## Related Skills Activities

- **SkillsBook**
  Perfect Tense Verbs, p. 97
  Irregular Verbs 1 and 2, pp. 102–103

## Answers

1. fought = simple
2. stolen = past perfect
3. strove = simple
4. began = simple
5. dived = past perfect
6. spoke = simple
7. wove = simple
8. laid = past perfect
9. written = past perfect
10. wore = simple

 **TEKS** **10.17A(i)** Use and understand more complex active tenses; **ELPS** **4C** Comprehend language structures used in written classroom materials; **5E** Employ increasingly complex grammatical structures in content area writing such as using correct verbs and tenses

TEKS 10.17A(i)
ELPS 4C, 5E

## 750.1 Continuous Tenses

- A **present continuous tense** verb expresses action that is not completed at the time of stating it. The present continuous tense is formed by adding *am, is,* or *are* to the *-ing* form of the main verb.

  **Scientists** are learning **a great deal from their study of the sky.**

- A **past continuous tense** verb expresses action that was happening at a certain time in the past. This tense is formed by adding *was* or *were* to the *-ing* form of the main verb.

  **Astronomers** were beginning **their quest for knowledge centuries ago.**

- A **future continuous tense** verb expresses action that will take place at a certain time in the future. This tense is formed by adding *will be* to the *-ing* form of the main verb.

  **Someday astronauts** will be going **to Mars.**

  This tense can also be formed by adding a phrase noting the future *(are going to)* plus *be* to the *-ing* form of the main verb.

  **They** are going to be performing **many experiments.**

## 750.2 Voice of a Verb

**Voice** indicates whether the subject is acting or being acted upon.

- **Active voice** indicates that the subject of the verb is, has been, or will be doing something.

  **For many years Lou Brock** held **the base-stealing record.**

  Active voice makes your writing more direct and lively.

- **Passive voice** indicates that the subject of the verb is being, has been, or will be acted upon.

  **For many years the base-stealing record** was held **by Lou Brock.**

**NOTE:** Passive verbs also have tense—the same simple, perfect, and continuous tenses as active verbs. (The chart below shows simple tenses.)

  **The ordinance** had been overturned. (passive past perfect)

| Tense | Active Voice Singular | Plural | Passive Voice Singular | Plural |
|---|---|---|---|---|
| Present | I see<br>you see<br>he/she/it sees | we see<br>you see<br>they see | I am seen<br>you are seen<br>he/she/it is seen | we are seen<br>you are seen<br>they are seen |
| Past | I/he saw<br>you saw | we/they saw<br>you saw | I/it was seen<br>you were seen | we/they were seen<br>you were seen |
| Future | I/you/he will see | we/you/they will see | I/you/it will be seen | we/you/they will be seen |

## Grammar Practice

### Verbs 5

- Active and Passive Voice
- Continuous Tenses

 If a sentence below is in the passive voice, rewrite it in the active voice. If it is already in the active voice, write "active."

**Example:** By then, the pizzas will have been eaten by my brothers.
*By then, my brothers will have eaten the pizzas.*

1. The announcement was heard by only half of the students.
2. My geometry textbook has been lost.
3. The student council is considering action on the proposal.
4. Most of the class is going to the afternoon assembly.
5. Winners' names will be published in the next issue of *The Bugle.*
6. The new menu was tested last week by the cooks.
7. A fossil of an unknown dinosaur was recently discovered by scientists in a remote area of New Mexico.
8. Stefan will perform his composition at the fall concert.
9. Since we hadn't missed any school all semester, we had been given movie passes by the attendance office.
10. You may use my computer today after school.

### Learning Language

Although the active voice is more direct and forceful, the passive voice is appropriate in some situations. Read and think about the following sentence.

**It was learned that Patrick was being followed by a detective.**

Explain to a partner why you think the passive voice and the past continuous tense are or are not appropriate in this sentence. Then ask your partner to share his or her opinions.

## Verb

Discuss with students the tenses and voices of verbs in order to help them employ increasingly complex grammatical structures in content area writing. Invite students to share their answers to the Grammar Practice on SE page 751.

## Learning Language

Use the collaborative speaking and listening activity on SE page 751 to help students ask for and give information, share information with peers, express ideas verbally, explain with detail, and demonstrate listening comprehension.

## Related Skills Activities

- ***SkillsBook***
  Active and Passive Voice, p. 95

## Answers

1. Only half of the students heard the announcement.
2. I lost my geometry textbook.
3. active
4. active
5. The Bugle will publish winners' names in the next issue.
6. The cooks tested the new menu last week.
7. Scientists recently discovered a fossil of an unknown dinosaur in a remote area of New Mexico.
8. active
9. Since we hadn't missed any school all semester, the attendance office gave us movie passes.
10. active

 **TEKS** 10.17A(i) Use and understand more complex active tenses; **ELPS** **2I** Demonstrate listening comprehension in increasingly complex spoken language/following directions, responding to questions and collaborating with peers; **3E** Share information in cooperative learning interactions; **3F** Ask for and give information/ranging from using a limited high-frequency vocabulary to using abstract and content-based vocabulary during speaking; **3G** Express ideas ranging from communicating short phrases to participating in discussions; **3H** Explain with increasing specificity and detail; **4C** Comprehend language structures used in written classroom materials; **5E** Employ increasingly complex grammatical structures in content area writing such as using correct verbs and tenses

752

### 752.1 Mood of a Verb

The **mood** of a verb indicates the tone or attitude with which a statement is made.

- **Indicative mood** is used to state a fact or to ask a question.

   Sometimes I would ride my old bicycle to school, but my friends would laugh and ask, "What's the matter? Your parents bought you a car for your birthday." The answer was simple: I wanted the exercise I got from riding the bike.

- **Imperative mood** is used to give a command.

"Whatever you do, don't fly your kite during a storm."
—Mrs. Abiah Franklin

- **Subjunctive mood** is used to express a condition that is contrary to fact or highly doubtful, a wish, a possibility, a suggestion, or a necessity.

   Use the subjunctive *were* to express a condition that is contrary to fact or highly doubtful.

   If I were finished with my report, I could go to the movie.

   The young lady looked as if she were at least 14 years old, but her childish behavior suggested otherwise.

   Use the subjunctive *were* to express a wish or a possibility.

   Oh, how I wish I were rich!

   Were your circumstances to change, you could reapply for admission.

   Use the subjunctive *be* in "that" clauses to express a suggestion or a necessity.

   Carlos suggested that we be ready to go when he arrives."

   It is essential that everyone be seated by the time the bell rings.

---

## Grammar Practice

### Verbs 6

- Mood of a Verb

 Write whether each statement shows *indicative*, *imperative*, or *subjunctive* mood.

**Example:** Mr. Cerminera closes the windows, even on the nicest days.
   *indicative*

1. He moved as if he were a deer running from a hunter.

2. Don't forget to read chapters eight and nine before the test tomorrow.

3. What is wrong with Lamont's car?

4. The city councilwoman amended the proposal to include schools in our district.

5. Whatever happens, don't forget to call me tonight.

6. She acted as though the exam weren't important.

7. Everyone must attend the meeting.

8. Sarena arrived on time.

9. Where in Kansas is Cottonwood Falls?

10. Katrina would have gotten the part if she were a Redford or an Eastwood.

11. Will your family plan a trip to New York City next summer?

12. If it were to rain, we will have to change the plans for the outdoor concert.

### Model

Model the following sentence to practice using the subjunctive mood.

When there is no news, [newscasters] give it to you with the same emphasis as if there were.
—David Brinkley

---

## Verb

Discuss with students the moods of verbs listed on SE page 752. In particular, help them identify and use the subjunctive mood to express doubts, wishes, and possibilities and to help in comprehension of increasingly grammatical structures. Invite students to share their answers to the Grammar Practice on SE page 753 with the class.

## Related Skills Activities

- *SkillsBook*
  Verb Moods, pp. 104–105

## Answers

1. subjunctive
2. imperative
3. indicative
4. indicative
5. imperative
6. subjunctive
7. imperative
8. indicative
9. indicative
10. subjunctive
11. indicative
12. subjunctive

---

 **TEKS** **10.17B** Identify and use subjunctive mood to express doubts, wishes, and possibilities; **ELPS 4C** Comprehend language structures used in written classroom materials; **5E** Employ increasingly complex grammatical structures in content area writing such as using correct verbs and tenses

TEKS 10.17A(i)
ELPS 4C, 5E

## Verbals

A **verbal** is a word that is derived from a verb but acts as another part of speech. There are three types of verbals: *gerunds*, *infinitives*, and *participles*. Each is often part of a verbal phrase.

### 754.1 Gerunds

A **gerund** is a verb form that ends in *ing* and is used as a noun.

Swimming **is my favorite pastime.** (subject)
**I began** swimming **at the age of six months.** (direct object)
Swimming in chlorinated pools **makes my eyes red.** (gerund phrase used as a subject)

### 754.2 Infinitives

An **infinitive** is a verb form that is usually introduced by *to*; the infinitive may be used as a noun, an adjective, or an adverb.

**Most people find it easy** to swim. (adverb modifying an adjective)
To swim the English Channel **must be a thrill.** (infinitive phrase as noun)
**The urge** to swim in tropical waters **is more common.** (infinitive phrase as adjective)

### 754.3 Participles

A **participle** is a verb form ending in *ing* or *ed* that acts as an adjective.

**The workers** raking leaves **are tired and hungry.** (participial phrase modifies *workers*)
**The bags full of** raked **leaves are evidence of their hard work.** (participle modifies *leaves*)

---

TEKS 10.17A(i)
ELPS 4C, 5E

Parts of Speech   **755**

## Grammar Practice

### Verbs 7

- Gerunds
- Infinitives
- Participles

 Write whether each underlined word or phrase is a *gerund*, a *participle*, or an *infinitive*.

**Example:** 1. gerund

(1) Playing the piano is an acquired skill. The piano is a popular instrument because it is relatively easy (2) to learn. Most people enjoy the piano's (3) inviting sound.

Many great pianists had excellent teachers. Franz Liszt, the famous pianist and composer, enjoyed (4) teaching young students. (5) Studying with Carl Czerny, an accomplished student of Beethoven, Liszt became a very capable teacher.

Usually, learning how (6) to play the piano involves (7) taking lessons from an (8) experienced professional. A good teacher knows how (9) to make practice fun. First, you will practice scales and chords and learn simple melodies. Before long, you will read music and learn (10) to create your own compositions.

### Model

Model the following sentences to practice using infinitives, gerunds, and participles.

The best way to live is by not knowing what will happen to you at the end of the day.
—Donald Barthelme

Good communication is just as stimulating as black coffee, and just as hard to sleep after.
—Anne Morrow Lindbergh

*Parts of Speech*

---

## Verbals

Discuss with students the uses of verbals listed on SE page 754 to help them use and understand verbals in the context of reading, writing, and speaking and to comprehend and employ increasingly complex vocabulary, language, and grammatical structures. Invite volunteers to share their answers to the Grammar Practice on SE page 755 with the class.

## Related Skills Activities

- **SkillsBook**
  Verbals: Gerunds, Infinitives, and Participles, p. 101
  Review: Verbs 1, p. 98
  Review: Verbs 2, p. 106

## Answers

1. gerund
2. infinitive
3. participle
4. gerund
5. participle
6. infinitive
7. gerund
8. participle
9. infinitive
10. infinitive

---

 **TEKS** 10.17A(i) Use and understand verbals (gerunds, infinitives, participles); **ELPS 4C** Comprehend language structures used in written classroom materials; **5E** Employ increasingly complex grammatical structures in content area writing such as using correct verbs, tenses, and pronouns/possessive case/negatives and contractions

## Adjective

An **adjective** describes or modifies a noun or a pronoun. The articles *a*, *an*, and *the* are also adjectives.

> The young **driver** peeked through the big **steering wheel.**
>
> (*The* and *young* modify *driver*; *the* and *big* modify *steering wheel.*)

### 756.1 Types of Adjectives

A **proper adjective** is created from a proper noun and is capitalized.

> In Canada (proper noun), you will find many cultures and climates.
>
> Canadian (proper adjective) winters can be harsh.

A **predicate adjective** follows a form of the "be" verb (or other linking verb) and describes the subject.

> Late autumn seems grim **to those who love summer.** (*Grim* modifies *autumn.*)

**NOTE:** Some words can be either adjectives or pronouns (*that, these, all, each, both, many, some,* and so on). These words are adjectives when they come before the nouns they modify; they are pronouns when they stand alone.

> Jiao made both **goals.** (*Both* modifies *goals*; it is an adjective.)
>
> Both **were scored in the final period.** (*Both* stands alone; it is a pronoun.)

### 756.2 Forms of Adjectives

Adjectives have three forms: *positive, comparative,* and *superlative.*

- The **positive form** describes a noun or a pronoun without comparing it to anyone or anything else.

  > The first game was long **and** tiresome.

- The **comparative form** (*-er, more,* or *less*) compares two persons, places, things, or ideas.

  > The second game was longer **and** more tiresome **than the first.**

- The **superlative form** (*-est, most,* or *least*) compares three or more persons, places, things, or ideas.

  > The third game was the longest **and** most tiresome **of all.**

**NOTE:** Use *more* and *most* (or *less* and *least*)—instead of adding a suffix—with many adjectives of two or more syllables.

| Positive | Comparative | Superlative |
|----------|-------------|-------------|
| big | bigger | biggest |
| helpful | more helpful | most helpful |
| painful | less painful | least painful |

---

## Grammar Practice

### Adjectives

- Forms of Adjectives

For each sentence below, write the adjective and its form (positive, comparative, or superlative). Some sentences contain more than one adjective. (For this activity, ignore any proper adjective.)

**Example:** Odysseus is one of the most famous characters in Greek mythology.

> most famous (superlative)

1. Also known as Ulysses, he was king of a smaller Greek island called Ithaca.

2. He was a suitor of Helen of Troy, the most beautiful woman on earth.

3. Some believe that he was more resourceful than other Greek warriors.

4. It was his idea to build a huge, hollow horse made of wood to sneak Greek soldiers into the city of Troy.

5. When the Trojans saw the big horse, they believed that it would bring them good luck.

6. The Trojan horse gave the Greeks an easier way to enter and destroy the city.

7. Odysseus is probably most renowned for his long journey back from Troy.

8. The trip was more difficult than Odysseus could ever have imagined.

### Learning Language

Work with a partner to make a list of at least six adjectives. Take turns describing objects using the comparative form of the adjectives on your list. Have your partner change the adjective from comparative to superlative form. Listen carefully to make sure that the correct form of each adjective has been used. Discuss and correct as needed.

Parts of Speech

---

## Adjective

Discuss with students the uses of adjectives listed on SE page 756 to help them comprehend vocabulary and language structures used in written classroom materials.

## Learning Language

Use the collaborative speaking and listening activity on SE page 757 to help students expand and internalize new language structures; speak with increasing ease using a variety of grammatical structures; ask for and give information; describe with detail; and demonstrate listening comprehension.

## Answers

1. smaller (comparative)
2. most beautiful (superlative)
3. more resourceful (comparative)
4. huge, hollow (positive)
5. big (positive), good (positive)
6. easier (comparative)
7. most renowned (superlative), long (positive)
8. more difficult (comparative)

## Related Skills Activities

- **Basic Grammar and Writing**
  Adjective Phrases and Clauses, p. 576

- **SkillsBook**
  Types of Adjectives, p. 108
  Forms of Adjectives to Compare, p. 109

---

 **ELPS 2C** Learn new language structures and basic vocabulary heard during classroom instruction/interactions; **2I** Demonstrate listening comprehension in increasingly complex spoken language by collaborating with peers and taking notes; **3B** Expand vocabulary by learning and using high-frequency words and routine language; **3C** Speak using a variety of grammatical structures with increasing accuracy and ease; **3E** Share information in cooperative learning interactions; **3F** Give information; **3H** Describe with increasing specificity and detail; **4C** Comprehend language structures used in written classroom materials

ELPS 4C, 5E

ELPS 4C, 5E

## Adverb

An **adverb** describes or modifies a verb, an adjective, or another adverb.

**She sneezed** loudly. (*Loudly* modifies the verb *sneezed*.)

**Her sneezes are really dramatic.** (*Really* modifies the adjective *dramatic*.)

**The sneeze exploded very noisily.** (*Very* modifies the adverb *noisily*.)

An adverb usually tells *when, where, how,* or *how much*.

### 758.1 Types of Adverbs

Adverbs can be cataloged in four basic ways: *time, place, manner,* and *degree*.

**Time** (These adverbs tell *when, how often,* and *how long*.)

   today, yesterday   daily, weekly   briefly, eternally

**Place** (These adverbs tell *where, to where,* and *from where*.)

   here, there   nearby, beyond   backward, forward

**Manner** (These adverbs often end in *ly* and tell *how* something is done.)

   precisely   effectively   regally   smoothly   well

**Degree** (These adverbs tell *how much* or *how little*.)

   substantially   greatly   entirely   partly   too   much

**NOTE:** Some adverbs can be written with or without the *ly* ending. When in doubt, use the *ly* form.

   slow, slowly   loud, loudly   fair, fairly   tight, tightly   quick, quickly

### 758.2 Forms of Adverbs

Adverbs of manner have three forms: *positive, comparative,* and *superlative*.

- The **positive form** describes a verb, an adjective, or another adverb without comparing it to anyone or anything else.

   **Model X vacuum cleans** well **and runs** quietly.

- The **comparative form** (*-er, more,* or *less*) compares how two things are done.

   **Model Y vacuum cleans** better **and runs** more quietly **than model X does.**

- The **superlative form** (*-est, most,* or *least*) compares how three or more things are done.

   **Model Z vacuum cleans** best **and runs** most quietly **of all.**

| Irregular Forms | | |
|---|---|---|
| Positive | Comparative | Superlative |
| well | better | best |
| fast | faster | fastest |
| remorsefully | more remorsefully | most remorsefully |

## Grammar Practice

### Adverbs

- Types of Adverbs

 For each sentence below, write the adverb as well as its type (time, place, manner, degree). The number of adverbs in each sentence is given in parenthesis.

**Example:** Today, all new cars are equipped with air bags. *(1)*
   today (time)

1. An air bag's inflation system is much like a solid rocket booster. *(1)*

2. The system has a device inside that tells the bag when to inflate. *(1)*

3. A solid propellant burns extremely rapidly to create a large amount of hot gas. *(2)*

4. It quickly inflates the bag, causing it to explode from its container at speeds up to 200 mph. *(1)*

5. The purpose of the air bag is to restrain the driver or passenger immediately with little or no damage to his or her body. *(1)*

6. They prevent a person from moving forward too fast in a collision. *(3)*

7. After the air bag is entirely inflated, the gas escapes through tiny holes. *(1)*

8. Used air bags should always be replaced by factory technicians. *(1)*

### Model

Model the sentence below to practice using types of adverbs.

**He lay down low to the race, whining eagerly, his splendid body flashing forward, leap by leap, in the wan white moonlight.**

—Jack London, *Call of the Wild*

---

## Adverb

Discuss with students the uses of adverbs listed on SE page 758 to help them comprehend and employ complex grammatical and language structures. Have students contribute other examples for each use. Also have students complete the Grammar Practice on SE page 759 individually, and review the answers as a class.

## Related Skills Activities

- **Basic Grammar and Writing**
  Adverbs, pp. 578–579

- *SkillsBook*
  Types of Adverbs 1 and 2, pp. 111–112
  Forms of Adverbs, p. 113
  Review: Adverbs, p. 114

 **Answers**

1. much (degree)
2. inside (place)
3. extremely (degree), rapidly (manner)
4. quickly (manner)
5. immediately (time)
6. forward (place), too (degree), fast (manner)
7. entirely (degree)
8. always (time)

 **ELPS 4C** Comprehend language structures used in written classroom materials; **5E** Employ increasingly complex grammatical structures in content area writing such as using correct verbs, tenses, and pronouns/possessive case/negatives and contractions

## Preposition

A **preposition** is the first word (or group of words) in a prepositional phrase. It shows the relationship between its object (a noun or a pronoun that follows the preposition) and another word in the sentence. The first noun or pronoun following a preposition is its object.

> **To make a mustache, Natasha placed the hairy caterpillar** under **her** nose.
> (*Under* shows the relationship between the verb, *placed*, and the object of the preposition, *nose*.)
>
> **The drowsy insect clung obediently** to **the girl's upper** lip.
> (The first noun following the preposition *to* is *lip; lip* is the object of the preposition.)

### 760.1 Prepositional Phrases

A **prepositional phrase** includes the preposition, the object of the preposition, and the modifiers of the object. A prepositional phrase functions as an adverb or as an adjective.

> **Some people** run **away** from caterpillars.
> (The phrase functions as an adverb and modifies the verb *run*.)
>
> **However, little** kids with inquisitive minds **enjoy their company.**
> (The phrase functions as an adjective and modifies the noun *kids*.)

**NOTE:** A preposition is always followed by an object; if there is no object, the word is an adverb, not a preposition.

> **Natasha never** played **with caterpillars** before. (The word *before* is not followed by an object; therefore, it functions as an adverb that modifies *played*, a verb.)

### Common Prepositions

| | | | | |
|---|---|---|---|---|
| aboard | before | from | of | save |
| about | behind | from among | off | since |
| above | below | from between | on | subsequent to |
| according to | beneath | from under | on account of | through |
| across | beside | in | on behalf of | throughout |
| across from | besides | in addition to | onto | till |
| after | between | in back of | on top of | to |
| against | beyond | in behalf of | opposite | together with |
| along | by | in front of | out | toward |
| alongside | by means of | in place of | out of | under |
| along with | concerning | in regard to | outside of | underneath |
| amid | considering | inside | over | until |
| among | despite | inside of | over to | unto |
| apart from | down | in spite of | owing to | up |
| around | down from | instead of | past | upon |
| aside from | during | into | prior to | up to |
| at | except | like | regarding | with |
| away from | except for | near | round | within |
| because of | for | near to | round about | without |

## Grammar Practice

### Prepositions

 Write the prepositional phrases from the sentences below.

**Example:** According to some people, the creature called Bigfoot lives in the forests of Washington and Oregon.
*according to some people, in the forests, of Washington and Oregon*

**1.** Since a 1959 magazine article, people have searched for solid evidence of this hairy humanoid creature's existence.

**2.** In 1967, Roger Patterson saw and filmed what he called a Sasquatch.

**3.** The animal moved over a riverbank and disappeared into the trees.

**4.** Many people around the world say they have seen a similar beast.

**5.** In Asia, this being, called a Yeti, is usually seen at 10,000 feet.

**6.** Presumably, a man standing beside a Bigfoot would look small.

**7.** Serious Bigfoot searchers say the animal remains elusive because it moves during the night.

**8.** Despite all the sightings, no solid proof of such a creature has ever been found.

### Model

Model the following sentences to practice using prepositional phrases as adjectives.

> **Love is like an hourglass, with the heart filling up as the brain empties.**
> —Jules Renard

> **Life isn't a matter of milestones but of moments.**
> —Rose Fitzgerald Kennedy

Parts of Speech

## Preposition

Discuss with students the uses of prepositions listed on SE page 760 to help them comprehend and employ complex vocabulary and grammatical structures. Have students contribute other examples for each use. Also invite students to share their answers to the Grammar Practice on SE page 761 with the class.

## Related Skills Activities

■ **Basic Grammar and Writing**
Prepositional Phrases, p. 581

■ *SkillsBook*
Pretest: Prepositions, Conjunctions, and Interjections, p. 115
Prepositions and Interjections, p. 116

## Answers

1. since a 1959 magazine article, for solid evidence, of this hairy humanoid reature's existence
2. in 1967
3. over a riverbank, into the trees
4. around the world
5. in Asia, at 10,000 feet
6. beside a Bigfoot
7. during the night
8. despite all the sightings, of such a creature

 **ELPS 4C** Comprehend language structures used in written classroom materials; **5E** Employ increasingly complex grammatical structures in content area writing such as using correct verbs, tenses, and pronouns/possessive case/negatives and contractions

## Conjunction

A **conjunction** connects individual words or groups of words. There are three kinds of conjunctions: *coordinating, correlative,* and *subordinating.*

### 762.1 Coordinating Conjunctions

**Coordinating conjunctions** usually connect a word to a word, a phrase to a phrase, or a clause to a clause. The words, phrases, or clauses joined by a coordinating conjunction are equal in importance or are of the same type.

> I could see from the look on my sister's face that she was disappointed and wanted to come with me, but my parents said she had to stay home.

(*And* connects the two parts of a compound predicate; *but* connects two independent clauses that could stand on their own.)

### 762.2 Correlative Conjunctions

**Correlative conjunctions** are conjunctions used in pairs.

> They were not only exhausted by the day's journey but also sunburned.

### 762.3 Subordinating Conjunctions

**Subordinating conjunctions** connect two clauses that are *not* equally important, thereby showing the relationship between them. A subordinating conjunction connects a dependent clause to an independent clause in order to complete the meaning of the dependent clause.

> A brown trout will study the bait before he eats it. (The clause *before he eats it* is dependent. It depends on the rest of the sentence to complete its meaning.)

> ### Kinds of Conjunctions
> Coordinating: and, but, or, nor, for, yet, so
> Correlative: either, or; neither, nor; not only, but also; both, and; whether, or
> Subordinating: after, although, as, as if, as long as, as though, because, before, if, in order that, provided that, since, so that, that, though, till, unless, until, when, where, whereas, while

**NOTE:** Relative pronouns (see 734.1 and 736.2) and conjunctive adverbs (see 656.2) can also connect clauses.

## Interjection

An **interjection** communicates strong emotion or surprise. Punctuation—a comma or an exclamation point—sets off an interjection from the rest of the sentence.

> Oh no! The TV broke. Good grief! I have nothing to do! Yipes, I'll go mad!

---

## Grammar Practice
### Conjunctions

 Number your paper from 1 to 11. Write the conjunctions you find in the following paragraph and label them *coordinating, subordinating,* or *correlative.* (Write both correlative conjunctions as one answer.)

**Example:** 1. *although; subordinating*

The Afrikaans language is attributed to the Dutch, although many other languages influenced it over time. Words and phrases of shipwrecked sailors found their way into the language, and when slaves arrived from eastern regions, they contributed an Oriental dialect. Soon, the language was neither Dutch nor any other known language. It had become unique after the new accents, dialects, and words were added. Today, Afrikaans is the first language of almost 60 percent of South Africa's whites, but it is spoken by more than 90 percent of the mixed-race population. Afrikaans is spoken not only in South Africa but also in the Republic of Namibia and in Zimbabwe. Afrikaans is the only language in the world that has a monument dedicated to it (in Paarl, Western Cape Province, South Africa), yet it is not the only official language of South Africa—there are nine others!

### Model
Model the following sentences to practice using interjections effectively.

> With a disgusted look on her face, Lakendra exclaimed, "Ugh! I can't eat this!"

> Crikey, is that all?
> —Alan Grayson, *Mile End*

---

## Conjunction

Discuss with students the uses of conjunctions shown on SE page 762 to help them comprehend and employ complex language and grammatical structures. Have students contribute other examples for each use. Invite students to share their answers to the Grammar Practice on SE page 763 with the class.

## Related Skills Activities

■ **Basic Grammar and Writing**
Conjunctions, p. 582

■ *SkillsBook*
Coordinating Conjunctions, p. 117
Correlative Conjunctions, p. 118
Subordinating Conjunctions, p. 119
Prepositions and Interjections, p. 116
Review: Prepositions, Conjunctions, and Interjections, p. 120

##  Answers

1. although; subordinating
2. and; coordinating
3. and; coordinating
4. when; subordinating
5. neither, nor; correlative
6. after; subordinating
7. and; coordinating
8. but; coordinating
9. not only, but also; correlative
10. and; coordinating
11. yet; coordinating

 **ELPS 4C** Comprehend language structures used in written classroom materials; **5E** Employ increasingly complex grammatical structures in content area writing such as using correct verbs, tenses, and pronouns/possessive case/negatives and contractions

TEKS 10.17C
ELPS 4E, 5E, 5F

## Understanding Sentences

### Constructing Sentences

A **sentence** is made up of one or more words that express a complete thought. Sentences begin with a capital letter; they end with a period, a question mark, or an exclamation point.

**What should we do this afternoon? We could have a picnic. No, I hate the ants!**

### Using Subjects and Predicates

A sentence usually has a *subject* and a *predicate*. The subject is the part of the sentence about which something is said. The predicate, which contains the verb, is the part of the sentence that says something about the subject.

We write **from aspiration and antagonism, as well as from experience.**

—Ralph Waldo Emerson

#### 764.1 The Subject

The **subject** is the part of the sentence about which something is said. The subject is always a noun; a pronoun; or a word, clause, or phrase that functions as a noun (such as a gerund or a gerund phrase or an infinitive).

Wolves **howl.** (noun)
They **howl for a variety of reasons.** (pronoun)
To establish their turf **may be one reason.** (infinitive phrase)
Searching for "lost" pack members **may be another.** (gerund phrase)
That wolves and dogs are similar animals **seems obvious.** (noun clause)

- A **simple subject** is the subject without its modifiers.
  Most wildlife biologists **disapprove of crossbreeding wolves and dogs.**
- A **complete subject** is the subject with all of its modifiers.
  Most wildlife biologists **disapprove of crossbreeding wolves and dogs.**
- A **compound subject** is composed of two or more simple subjects.
  Wise breeders and owners **know that wolf-dog puppies can display unexpected, destructive behaviors.**

#### 764.2 Delayed Subject

In sentences that begin with *There* or *It* followed by a form of the "be" verb, the subject comes after the verb. The subject is also delayed in questions.

**There was** nothing **in the refrigerator.** (The subject is *nothing*; the verb is *was*.)
**Where is my** sandwich? (The subject is *sandwich*; the verb is *is*.)

---

TEKS 10.17C
ELPS 4E, 5E, 5F

## Practice

### Constructing Sentences 1

- Simple, Complete, and Compound Subjects
- Delayed Subjects

 Write the complete subject of each sentence. Circle the simple subject or subjects.

**Example:** There is an art fair on the county grounds this weekend.
an art (fair)

1. Various artists are setting up their tents near the Picasso statue.
2. The Lakefront Art Fair is the best festival of the summer.
3. Colorful hot-air balloons float in the air, inviting people to the visit the event.
4. The bands and food tents are popular with the crowd.
5. There is a children's play area near the restrooms.
6. The fair, consisting of more than 100 vendors, attracts thousands of visitors each year.
7. The chamber of commerce spends a lot of time to put it together.
8. Pottery, paintings, and sculpture are featured items at the fair.
9. Is your sister-in-law looking for a special piece of art?
10. Most visitors come away with several purchases.

### Model

Model the following sentences to practice using delayed subjects.

**There was such a glory over everything.**
—Harriet Tubman

**Hasn't the fine line between sanity and madness gotten finer?**
—George Price

Sentences

---

## Constructing Sentences: Subject

Discuss with students the types and structures of subjects listed on SE page 764 to help them use a variety of correctly structured sentences and comprehend complex language structures. In order to show that they can write using grade-appropriate sentence patterns with accuracy, have students contribute other examples of subjects for each use. Then have students complete the Practice activity on SE page 765 with a partner.

## Related Skills Activities

- **Basic Grammar and Writing**
  Sentence Patterns, p. 586
  Subject/Verb Agreement, p. 595

- **SkillsBook**
  Subjects and Predicates 1 and 2, pp. 126–127

## Answers

1. Various (artists)
2. The (Lakefront Art Fair)
3. Colorful hot-air (balloons)
4. The (bands) and food (tents)
5. a children's play (area)
6. The (fair), consisting of more than 100 vendors,
7. The (chamber of commerce)
8. (Pottery), (paintings), and (sculpture)
9. your (sister-in-law)
10. Most (visitors)

---

 **TEKS** **10.17C** Use a variety of correctly structured sentences; **ELPS** **4C** Comprehend language structures used in written classroom materials; **5E** Employ increasingly complex grammatical structures in content area writing such as using correct verbs, tenses, and pronouns/possessive case/negatives and contractions; **5F** Write using a variety of grade-appropriate sentence patterns in increasingly accurate ways

**TEKS** 10.17C
ELPS 4E, 5E, 5F

**766.1** Predicates

The **predicate** is the part of the sentence that shows action or says something about the subject.

> Giant squid do exist.

- A **simple predicate** is the verb without its modifiers.
  > One giant squid measured nearly 60 feet long.

- A **complete predicate** is the simple predicate with all its modifiers.
  > One giant squid measured nearly 60 feet long.
  > (*Measured* is the simple predicate; *nearly 60 feet long* modifies *measured*.)

- A **compound predicate** is composed of two or more simple predicates.
  > A squid grasps its prey with tentacles and bites it with its beak.

**NOTE:** A sentence can have a **compound subject** and a **compound predicate.**
> Both sperm whales and giant squid live and occasionally clash in the deep waters off New Zealand's South Island.

- A **direct object** is part of the predicate and receives the action of the verb. (See **744.2.**)
  > Sperm whales sometimes eat giant squid.
  > (The direct object *giant squid* receives the action of the verb *eat* by answering the question *whales eat what*?)

**NOTE:** The **direct object** may be compound.
> In the past, whalers harvested oil, spermaceti, and ambergris from slain sperm whales.

**766.2** Understood Subjects and Predicates

Either the subject or the predicate may be "missing" from a sentence, but both must be clearly **understood.**

Who is in the hot-air balloon?
(*Who* is the subject; *is in the hot-air balloon* is the predicate.)

No one.
(*No one* is the subject; the predicate *is in the hot-air balloon* is understood.)

Get out of the way!
(The subject *you* is understood; *get out of the way* is the predicate.)

---

## Practice

### Constructing Sentences 2

- Simple, Complete, and Compound Predicates

 Write the complete predicate of each sentence. Circle the simple predicate or predicates.

**Example:** The flatness of the Great Plains allows dry, cold air to collide with warm, moist air.
(allows) dry, cold air to collide with warm, moist air

1. Most tornadoes form along the front between these air masses.

2. Meteorologists call this "Tornado Alley" and include in it parts of Texas, Oklahoma, Kansas, and Nebraska.

3. Many cities in Tornado Alley enforce stronger building codes.

4. States in Tornado Alley can experience millions of dollars in damage each year.

5. Who is responsible for paying for the damage?

6. The federal government often provides disaster aid.

7. Storm chasers travel throughout Tornado Alley and search for storms.

8. The chasers sometimes find themselves in dangerous situations.

9. Spotters used binoculars, barometers, and other simple forecasting methods to predict a tornado's proximity.

10. The sophisticated computer systems in current use accurately predict and pinpoint a storm.

### Model

Model the following sentence to practice using a compound predicate.

> We learn and grow and are transformed not so much by what we do but by why and how we do it.
> —Sharon Salzberg, "The Power of Intention"

Sentences

---

## Constructing Sentences: Predicate

Discuss with students the use of predicates listed on SE page 766 to help them use a variety of correctly structured sentences, employ complex grammatical structures, and write using a variety of grade-appropriate sentence patterns. Have students contribute other examples of predicates for each use. Also invite students to complete the Practice activity on SE page 767 individually, and review the answers with the class.

## Related Skills Activities

- **SkillsBook**
  Subjects and Predicates 1 and 2, pp. 126–127
  Review: Subjects and Predicates, p. 128

## Answers

1. (form) along the front between these air masses

2. (call) this "Tornado Alley" and include in it parts of Texas, Oklahoma, Kansas, and Nebraska

3. (enforce) stronger building codes

4. (can experience) millions of dollars in damage each year

5. (is) responsible for paying for the damage

6. often (provides) disaster aid

7. (travel) throughout Tornado Alley and search for storms

8. sometimes (find) themselves in dangerous situations

9. (used) binoculars, barometers, and other simple forecasting methods to predict a tornado's proximity

10. accurately (predict) and pinpoint a storm

---

 **TEKS** 10.17C Use a variety of correctly structured sentences; **ELPS** 4C Comprehend language structures used in written classroom materials; 5E Employ increasingly complex grammatical structures in content area writing such as using correct verbs, tenses, and pronouns/possessive case/negatives and contractions; 5F Write using a variety of grade-appropriate sentence patterns in increasingly accurate ways

**TEKS** 10.17A(i)
ELPS 4C, 5E

## Using Phrases

A **phrase** is a group of related words that function as a single part of speech. The sentence below contains a number of phrases.

*Finishing the race will require running up some steep slopes.*

**finishing the race** (This gerund phrase functions as a subject noun.)

**will require** (This phrase functions as a verb.)

**running up some steep slopes** (This gerund phrase acts as an object noun.)

### 768.1 Types of Phrases

■ An **appositive phrase,** which follows a noun or a pronoun and renames it, consists of a noun and its modifiers. An appositive adds new information about the noun or pronoun it follows.

**The Trans-Siberian Railroad,** the world's longest railway, **stretches from Moscow to Vladivostok.** (The appositive phrase renames *Trans-Siberian Railroad* and provides new information.)

■ A **verbal phrase** is a phrase based on one of the three types of verbals: *gerund, infinitive,* or *participle.* (See 754.1, 754.2, and 754.3.)

■ A **gerund phrase** consists of a gerund and its modifiers. The whole phrase functions as a noun.

*Spotting the tiny mouse* **was easy for the hawk.**
(The gerund phrase is used as the subject of the sentence.)

**Dinner escaped by** *ducking under a rock.*
(The gerund phrase is the object of the preposition *by.*)

■ An **infinitive phrase** consists of an infinitive and its modifiers. The whole phrase functions either as a noun, an adjective, or an adverb.

*To shake every voter's hand* **was the candidate's goal.**
(The infinitive phrase functions as a noun used as the subject.)

**Your efforts** *to clean the chalkboard* **are appreciated.**
(The infinitive phrase is used as an adjective modifying *efforts.*)

**Please watch carefully** *to see the difference.*
(The infinitive phrase is used as an adverb modifying *watch.*)

■ A **participial phrase** consists of a past or present participle and its modifiers. The whole phrase functions as an adjective.

*Following his nose,* **the beagle took off like a jackrabbit.**
(The participial phrase modifies the noun *beagle.*)

**The raccoons,** *warned by the rustling,* **took cover.**
(The participial phrase modifies the noun *raccoons.*)

---

## Practice

## Constructing Sentences 3

■ Appositive Phrases
■ Verbal Phrases

Identify each underlined phrase as an *appositive, gerund, infinitive,* or *participial phrase.*

**Example:** Ice fishing on the lake at this time of year is dangerous.
*gerund phrase*

**1.** Lucinda's goal of becoming class president was finally accomplished.

**2.** John Steinbeck, the famous American author, never graduated from college.

**3.** Dirk postponed cleaning the garage so he could go to the movies.

**4.** When he got his driver's license, Geoff wanted to buy a used car.

**5.** Refusing to accept defeat, Luis limped over the finish line.

**6.** The student chosen to compete will travel to Washington, D.C.

**7.** To continue his education, Reggie borrowed money from his uncle.

**8.** Working hard usually pays off.

**9.** Keleigh kept the secret to prevent anyone from telling Mr. Bain.

**10.** *Araucaria heterophylla,* the Norfolk Island pine, is a popular houseplant.

### Model

Model the following sentence to practice using appositive phrases.

**Everyone agreed that my father, my Baba, had built the most beautiful house in the Wazir Akbar Khan district, a new and affluent neighborhood in the northern part of Kabul.**
—Khaled Hossein, *The Kite Runner*

*Sentences* (side tab)

---

## Using Phrases

Discuss with students the types of phrases listed on SE page 768 to help them comprehend and employ complex vocabulary and language structures. Have students contribute other examples of phrases for each use. Also have students complete the Practice activity on SE page 769 with a partner.

## Related Skills Activities

■ *SkillsBook*
Pretest: Phrases, p. 129
Verbal Phrases, p. 130
Prepositional and Appositive Phrases, p. 131

## Answers

**1.** gerund phrase
**2.** appositive phrase
**3.** gerund phrase
**4.** infinitive phrase
**5.** participial phrase
**6.** participial phrase
**7.** infinitive phrase
**8.** gerund phrase
**9.** gerund phrase
**10.** appositive phrase

---

 **TEKS** 10.17A(i) Use and understand verbals (gerunds, infinitives, participles); **ELPS** 4C Comprehend language structures used in written classroom materials; 5E Employ increasingly complex grammatical structures in content area writing such as using correct verbs, tenses, and pronouns/possessive case/negatives and contractions

## Using Phrases *(continued)*

- A **verb phrase** consists of a main verb preceded by one or more helping verbs.

  **Snow has been falling for days.** (*Has been falling* is a verb phrase.)

- A **prepositional phrase** is a group of words beginning with a preposition and ending with a noun or a pronoun. Prepositional phrases function mainly as adjectives and adverbs.

  **Reach for that catnip ball behind the couch.** (The prepositional phrase *behind the couch* is used as an adjective modifying *catnip ball*.)

  **Zach won the wheelchair race in record time.** (*In record time* is used as an adverb modifying the verb *won*.)

- An **absolute phrase** consists of a noun and a participle (plus the participle's object, if there is one, and any modifiers). An absolute phrase functions as a modifier that adds information to the entire sentence. Absolute phrases are always set off with commas.

  **Its wheels clattering rhythmically over the rails, the train rolled into town.** (The noun *wheels* is modified by the present participle *clattering*. The entire phrase modifies the rest of the sentence.)

## Using Clauses

A **clause** is a group of related words that has both a subject and a predicate.

### 770.1 Independent and Dependent Clauses

An **independent clause** presents a complete thought and can stand alone as a sentence; a **dependent clause** (also called a *subordinate clause*) does not present a complete thought and cannot stand alone as a sentence.

  **Sparrows make nests in cattle barns** (independent clause) **so that they can stay warm during the winter** (dependent clause).

### 770.2 Types of Dependent Clauses

There are three basic types of dependent clauses: *adverb, noun,* and *adjective.*

- An **adverb clause** is used like an adverb to modify a verb, an adjective, or an adverb. Adverb clauses begin with a subordinating conjunction. (See **762.3**.)

  **If I study hard, I will pass this test.** (The adverb clause modifies the verb *will pass*.)

- A **noun clause** is used in place of a noun.

  **However, the teacher said that the essay questions are based only on the last two chapters.** (The noun clause functions as a direct object.)

- An **adjective clause** modifies a noun or a pronoun.

  **Tomorrow's test, which covers the entire book, is half essay and half short answers.** (The adjective clause modifies the noun *test*.)

---

## Practice

### Constructing Sentences 4

- Verb Phrases
- Prepositional Phrases
- Absolute Phrases

Identify the underlined part of each sentence as a *prepositional phrase*, an *absolute phrase*, or a *verb phrase*.

**Example:** <u>All things considered</u>, the Wildcats were headed for the finals.
  *absolute phrase*

1. I could hear Min and Lissa whispering <u>in the next room</u>.

2. We <u>will meet</u> at Gerald's Diner at 4:30.

3. <u>The full moon lighting his way</u>, my brother followed the tracks through the field.

4. Once her speech was over, Heather <u>did feel</u> more relaxed.

5. <u>His heart pounding like a jackhammer</u>, Ty slam-dunked the ball.

6. Stuart reviewed his notes <u>before the test</u>.

7. <u>Her hands and feet stinging from the cold</u>, Danielle left the bleachers and went inside.

8. The baby clinging to the old woman <u>had been making</u> mewling noises for at least half an hour.

### Learning Language

Work with a partner and take turns reading aloud the information about clauses and phrases on pages **768** and **770**. Listen carefully as your partner reads one section. Take notes and then summarize the information. Ask your partner to listen carefully and take notes as you read. Your partner should then summarize those sections. Ask each other questions as you finish reading each section to ensure that you both understand the text and the summaries. When you have finished, copy each other's summaries and check them against the text.

---

## Using Phrases and Using Clauses

Discuss with students the types of phrases and clauses listed on SE page 770 to help them comprehend vocabulary and language structures. Have students contribute other examples for each use. Then have students complete the Practice activity on SE page 771 individually, and review the answers with the class.

## Learning Language

Use the collaborative speaking and listening activity on SE page 771 to help students learn new language structures and academic vocabulary, and to demonstrate listening comprehension by summarizing spoken messages, collaborating with peers, participating in shared reading, and taking notes.

## Answers

1. prepositional phrase
2. verb phrase
3. absolute phrase
4. verb phrase
5. absolute phrase
6. prepositional phrase
7. absolute phrase
8. verb phrase

## Related Skills Activities

- **Basic Grammar and Writing**
  Adjective Phrases and Clauses, p. 576
  Prepositional Phrases, p. 581

- *SkillsBook*
  Absolute Phrases, p. 132
  Effective Phrases, p. 133
  Clauses, pp. 136, 137

---

**ELPS 2C** Learn academic vocabulary heard during classroom instruction/interactions; **2I** Demonstrate listening comprehension in increasingly complex spoken language by summarizing spoken messages and taking notes; **4C** Comprehend language structures used in written classroom materials; **4G** Demonstrate comprehension of increasingly complex English/participating in shared reading, summarizing material, and taking notes

TEKS 10.17C
ELPS 4C, 5E, 5F

## Using Sentence Variety

A **sentence** may be classified according to the type of statement it makes, the way it is constructed, and its arrangement of words.

### 772.1 Kinds of Sentences

Sentences can make five basic kinds of sentences: *declarative, interrogative, imperative, exclamatory,* or *conditional.*

- **Declarative sentences** make statements. They tell us something about a person, a place, a thing, or an idea.

    The Statue of Liberty stands in New York Harbor.

    For over a century, it has greeted immigrants and visitors to America.

- **Interrogative sentences** ask questions.

    Did you know that the Statue of Liberty is made of copper and stands more than 150 feet tall?

    Are we allowed to climb all the way to the top?

- **Imperative sentences** make commands. They often contain an understood subject *(you)* as in the examples below.

    Go see the Statue of Liberty.

    After a few weeks of physical conditioning, climb its 168 stairs.

- **Exclamatory sentences** communicate strong emotion or surprise.

    Climbing 168 stairs is not a dumb idea!

    Just muster some of that old pioneering spirit, that desire to try something new, that never-say-die attitude that made America great!

- **Conditional sentences** express wishes ("if . . . then" statements) or conditions contrary to fact.

    If I could design a country's flag, I would use six colors behind a sun, a star, and a moon.

    I would feel as if I were representing many cultures in my design.

TEKS 10.17C
ELPS 4C, 5E, 5F

## Practice

### Kinds of Sentences

■ Sentence Variety

Write the kind of statement each sentence in the following paragraph makes: *declarative, interrogative, imperative, exclamatory,* or *conditional.*

**Example:** 1. *declarative*

(1) The earth's magnetic field has flipped many times in geologic history, and scientists think it is poised to flip again. (2) Think about what that means. (3) Compasses will point to the South Pole instead of to the North Pole. (4) What other effects would a flip have? (5) It most likely would confuse many types of migratory birds and sea creatures who use the earth's magnetic fields to find their way. (6) It would also leave the earth temporarily unprotected from some of the solar wind filtered out by the current magnetic field. (7) A solar flare could then disrupt communications and damage the ozone layer. (8) There is a trade-off, though. (9) If there were no magnetic field, people would be lucky enough to see auroras almost every night. (10) That would be cool!

### Model

Model the following conditional sentences.

If you cannot convince them, confuse them.
—Harry S. Truman

If you aren't fired with enthusiasm, you will be fired with enthusiasm.
—Vince Lombardi

Sentences

---

## Using Sentence Variety

Discuss with students the kinds of sentences listed on SE page 772 to help them use a variety of correctly structured sentences, comprehend vocabulary and language structures, and write using a variety of grade-appropriate sentence patterns. Also invite students to share their answers to the Practice activity on SE page 773 with the class.

## Related Skills Activities

- **Basic Grammar and Writing**
  Sentence Variety, p. 588
  Combining Sentences, p. 590

- *SkillsBook*
  Pretest: Sentences, p. 139
  Kinds of Sentences, p. 140

## Answers

1. declarative
2. imperative
3. declarative
4. interrogative
5. declarative
6. declarative
7. declarative
8. declarative
9. conditional
10. exclamatory

TEKS 10.17C
ELPS 4C, 5E, 5F

**774.1** Types of Sentence Constructions

A sentence may be *simple, compound, complex,* or *compound-complex.* It all depends on the relationship between independent and dependent clauses.

- A **simple sentence** can have a single subject or a compound subject. It can have a single predicate or a compound predicate. However, a simple sentence has only one independent clause, and it has no dependent clauses.

    **My** back aches.
    (single subject; single predicate)

    **My** teeth **and my** eyes hurt.
    (compound subject; single predicate)

    **My** throat **and** nose feel **sore and** look red.
    (compound subject; compound predicate)

    I must have caught the flu **from the sick kids in class.**
    (independent clause with two phrases: *from the sick kids* and *in class*)

- A **compound sentence** consists of two independent clauses. The clauses must be joined by a comma and a coordinating conjunction or by a semicolon.

    I usually don't mind missing school, **but** this is not fun.

    I feel too sick to watch TV; I feel too sick to eat.

**NOTE:** The comma can be omitted when the clauses are very short.

    I wept **and** I wept.

- A **complex sentence** contains one independent clause (in black) and one or more dependent clauses (in red).

    When I get back to school, I'm actually going to appreciate it.
    (dependent clause; independent clause)

    I won't even complain about math class, although I might be talking out of my head because I'm feverish.
    (independent clause; two dependent clauses)

- A **compound-complex sentence** contains two or more independent clauses (in black) and one or more dependent clauses (in red).

    Yes, I have a bad flu, and because I need to get well soon, I won't think about school just yet.
    (two independent clauses; one dependent clause)

TEKS 10.17C
ELPS 4C, 5E, 5F

## Practice

### Types of Sentence Constructions

- Types of Sentences

Identify each of the following sentences as a *simple, compound, complex,* or *compound-complex* sentence.

**Example:** 1. simple

(1) How do auroras form? (2) The solar wind contains charged particles that make the air glow when they blast into Earth's atmosphere. (3) The aurora borealis (or northern lights) and the aurora australis (southern lights) can take many different forms. (4) Sometimes simple lines appear across the sky, or pillars form at different points in the sky. (5) These lines or pillars can broaden into curtains of light, which wave back and forth overhead. (6) Lucky observers see more exotic forms. (7) Some aurora forms are petal shapes like giant blooming flowers, and others expand across the sky like slow-motion fireworks. (8) White aurora lights are most common, but when the solar wind is especially favorable, more vibrant colors such as purple, violet, green, and orange may appear. (9) Whatever colors they display or form they take, the lights of the aurora are always a sight to behold. (10) People who live in extreme north or south locales know this; they can see auroras almost 200 days a year!

### Model

Model the following complex sentences.

When we blame ourselves, we feel that no one else has a right to blame us.
—Oscar Wilde, *The Picture of Dorian Gray*

Forgive me my nonsense as I also forgive the nonsense of those who think they talk sense.
—Robert Frost

Sentences

---

## Using Sentence Variety

Discuss with students the types of sentence constructions listed on SE page 774 to help them use a variety of correctly structured sentences and comprehend language structures used in written classroom materials. Have students contribute other examples for each use to demonstrate their abilities to write using grade-appropriate sentence patterns. Invite students to share their answers to the Practice activity on SE page 775 with the class.

## Related Skills Activities

- ***SkillsBook***
    Types of Sentences 1 and 2, pp. 141–142

## Answers

1. simple
2. complex
3. simple
4. compound
5. complex
6. simple
7. compound
8. compound-complex
9. complex
10. compound-complex

 **TEKS** 10.17C Use a variety of correctly structured sentences; **ELPS 4C** Comprehend language structures used in written classroom materials; **5E** Employ increasingly complex grammatical structures in content area writing such as using correct verbs, tenses, and pronouns/possessive case/negatives and contractions; **5F** Write using a variety of grade-appropriate sentence patterns in increasingly accurate ways

**TEKS** 10.17C
ELPS 4C, 5E, 5F

### 776.1 Arrangements of Sentences

Depending on the arrangement of the words and the placement of emphasis, a sentence may also be classified as *loose, balanced, periodic,* or *cumulative.*

- A **loose sentence** expresses the main thought near the beginning and adds explanatory material as needed.

  > We hauled out the boxes of food and set up the camp stove, **all the time battling the hot wind that would not stop, even when we screamed into the sky.**

  > Jet airplanes do the seemingly impossible—**moving us across countries and over oceans, transporting us to new continents, all within just a few hours.**

- A **balanced sentence** is constructed so that it emphasizes a similarity or a contrast between two or more of its parts (words, phrases, or clauses).

  > **The wind in our ears** drove us crazy **and** pushed us on.
  > (The similar wording emphasizes the main idea in this sentence.)

  > **Experience is not** what happens to you; **it is what you do with** what happens to you.
  >
  > —Aldous Huxley

- A **periodic sentence** is one that postpones the crucial or most surprising idea until the end.

  > Following my mother's repeated threats to ground me for life, **I decided it was time to propose a compromise.**

  > There is only one way to achieve happiness on this terrestrial ball—**and that is to have either a clear conscience or no conscience at all.**
  >
  > —Ogden Nash, *I'm a Stranger Here Myself*

- A **cumulative sentence** places the general idea in the middle of the sentence with modifying clauses and phrases coming before and after.

  > With careful thought and extra attention to detail, **I wrote out my plan for being a model teenager,** a teen who cared about neatness and reliability.

  > With careful planning and diligence, **students who finish high school and graduate from college will end up in high-paying, satisfying jobs,** an accomplishment we all admire and to which we all aspire.

---

 **Practice**

### Arrangements of Sentences

- Sentence Arrangements

Classify each of the following sentences as *loose, balanced, periodic,* or *cumulative.*

**Example:** From Chicago to Milwaukee it was cloudy, but north of Milwaukee it was clear.
*balanced*

1. The restaurant was nice, but the food was terrible.

2. The three of us climbed to the top of the hill and found the best spot, all the while darkness falling upon us, and then the fireworks began.

3. Suddenly, without a word and for no reason, Joshua bolted out the open door.

4. The energetic horses ran hard, following each other through the tall grass, occasionally slowing to catch their breath and then hurrying on toward the horizon.

5. With grass in his hair, dirt between his fingers, and mud all over his face, Oscar triumphantly held up the football.

6. After the ice storm, the woods looked hauntingly beautiful, as though diamonds had melted on the trees.

7. Although we were hungry, exhausted, and covered in mud, we continued to follow the moose tracks.

8. Some students study at home; others study at the public library.

9. Maria considered William a good friend—one who was trustworthy, honest, and reliable.

### Model

Model the following balanced sentence.

**We may brave human laws, but we cannot resist natural ones.**
—Jules Verne, *20,000 Leagues Under the Sea*

Sentences

---

## Using Sentence Variety

Discuss with students the types of sentence constructions listed on SE page 776 to help them use a variety of correctly structured sentences and comprehend vocabulary and language structures used in written classroom materials. Have students contribute other examples for each use to demonstrate their abilities to write using grade-appropriate sentence patterns. Invite students to share their answers to the Practice activity on SE page 777 with the class.

## Related Skills Activities

- **SkillsBook**
  Sentence Modeling 1 and 2, pp. 143–144
  Review: Sentences, p. 145

 **Answers**

1. balanced
2. periodic
3. periodic
4. loose
5. periodic
6. cumulative
7. balanced
8. balanced
9. loose

---

 **TEKS** 10.17C Use a variety of correctly structured sentences; **ELPS 4C** Comprehend language structures used in written classroom materials; **5E** Employ increasingly complex grammatical structures in content area writing such as using correct verbs, tenses, and pronouns/possessive case/negatives and contractions; **5F** Write using a variety of grade-appropriate sentence patterns in increasingly accurate ways

ELPS 4C, 5E

## Getting Sentence Parts to Agree

### Agreement of Subject and Verb

A verb must agree in number (singular or plural) with its subject.

**The** student **was proud of her quarter grades.**

**NOTE:** Do not be confused by words that come between the subject and verb.

**The** manager, **as well as the players,** is **required to display good sportsmanship.** (*Manager,* not *players,* is the subject.)

#### 778.1 Compound Subjects

**Compound subjects** joined by *or* or *nor* take a singular verb.

**Neither** Bev **nor** Kendra is **going to the street dance.**

**NOTE:** When one of the subjects joined by *or* or *nor* is singular and one is plural, the verb must agree with the subject nearer the verb.

**Neither** Miguel **nor his** friends **are singing in the band anymore.** (The plural subject *friends* is nearer the verb, so the plural verb *are* is correct.)

**Compound subjects** connected with *and* require a plural verb.

**Strength and** balance **are necessary for gymnastics.**

#### 778.2 Delayed Subjects

**Delayed subjects** occur when the verb comes before the subject in a sentence. In these inverted sentences, the delayed subject must agree with the verb.

**There** are **many hardworking** students **in our schools.**

**There** is **present among many young people today a** will **to succeed.**

(*Students* and *will* are the true subjects of these sentences, not *there.*)

#### 778.3 "Be" Verbs

When a sentence contains a form of the "be" verb—and a noun comes before and after that verb—the verb must agree with the subject, not the *complement* (the noun coming after the verb).

**The** cause **of this problem** was **the bad** brakes.

**The bad** brakes were **the** cause **of this problem.**

#### 778.4 Special Cases

Some nouns that are **plural in form but singular in meaning** take a singular verb: *mumps, measles, news, mathematics, economics, gallows, shambles.*

**Measles** is **still considered a serious disease in many parts of the world.**

Some nouns that are plural in form but singular in meaning take a plural verb: *scissors, trousers, tidings.*

**The** scissors are **missing again.**

---

## Practice

### Agreement of Subject and Verb 1

■ Subject-Verb Agreement

 For each sentence, write the correct verb from the choice given in parentheses.

**Example:** The problem with both computers *(was, were)* their memory cards.

was

1. Mr. Valero *(are, is)* planning a quiz for this Friday.

2. There *(are, is)* rumors circulating that David will be the starting quarterback on Friday.

3. *(Do, Does)* this skin cream really prevent acne?

4. The result of last week's drills *(was, were)* a seminar on fire safety.

5. Either Serena or Kim and Tyler Garcia *(take, takes)* the gerbils home over holiday breaks.

6. The news of his accident *(was, were)* not surprising.

7. There *(are, is)* remaining one medium-sized sweatshirt with the team logo.

8. Dale Earnhardt, Jr., and Kyle Bush *(are, is)* popular race-car drivers.

9. Neither DeWayne nor Kevin *(are, is)* going with us to the stadium.

10. *(Have, Has)* the fireworks started yet?

### Model

Model the following sentences to practice subject-verb agreement with special-case nouns.

**Your glasses need a good cleaning.**

**The mathematics is not there until we put it there.**

—Sir Arthur Eddington

Sentences

---

## Agreement of Subject and Verb

Discuss with students the agreement of subject and verb explained on SE page 778 to help them comprehend language structures used in classroom materials and employ complex grammatical structures. Have students contribute other examples for each use. Also invite students to share their answers to the Practice activity on SE page 779 with the class.

## Related Skills Activities

■ **SkillsBook**
Subject-Verb Agreement 1, p. 147
Subject-Verb Agreement 2 (Delayed and Compound Subjects), p. 148

## Answers

1. is
2. are
3. Does
4. was
5. take
6. was
7. is
8. are
9. is
10. Have

---

 **ELPS 4C** Comprehend language structures used in written classroom materials; **5E** Employ increasingly complex grammatical structures in content area writing such as using correct verbs, tenses, and pronouns/possessive case/negatives and contractions

ELPS 4C, 5E

## Agreement of Subject and Verb (continued)

### 780.1 Collective Nouns

**Collective nouns** (*faculty, committee, team, congress, species, crowd, army, pair, squad*) take a singular verb when they refer to a group as a unit; collective nouns take a plural verb when they refer to the individuals within the group.

> The favored **team is losing, and the** crowd **is getting ugly.** (Both *team* and *crowd* are considered units in this sentence, requiring the singular verb *is*.)
> The pair were **finally reunited after 20 years apart.**
> (Here, *pair* refers to two individuals, so the plural verb *were* is required.)

### 780.2 Indefinite Pronouns

Some **indefinite pronouns** are singular: *each, either, neither, one, everybody, another, anybody, everyone, nobody, everything, somebody,* and *someone.* They require a singular verb.

> Everybody **is** invited to the cafeteria for refreshments.

Some **indefinite pronouns** are plural: *both, few, many,* and *several.*

> Several like **chocolate cake.** Many ask **for ice cream, too.**

Some **indefinite pronouns** are singular or plural: *all, any, most, none,* and *some.*

**NOTE:** Do not be confused by words or phrases that come between the indefinite pronoun and the verb.

> One **of the participants** is (not *are*) **going to have to stay late to clean up.**

### A Closer Look

As stated above, some **indefinite pronouns** can be either singular or plural: *all, any, most, none,* and *some.* These pronouns are singular if the number of the noun in the prepositional phrase is singular; they are plural if the noun is plural.

> Most **of the food complaints** are **coming from the seniors.**
> (*Complaints* is plural, so *most* is plural.)
> Most **of the tabletop** is **sticky with melted ice cream.**
> (*Tabletop* is singular, so *most* is singular.)

### 780.3 Relative Pronouns

When a **relative pronoun** (*who, which, that*) is used as the subject of a clause, the number of the verb is determined by the antecedent of the pronoun. (The antecedent is the word to which the pronoun refers.)

> This is one **of the books** that are **required for class.** (The relative pronoun *that* requires the plural verb *are* because its antecedent, *books,* is plural.)

**NOTE:** To test this type of sentence for agreement, read the "of" phrase first.

> Of the books **that are** required for geography class, **this is one.**

---

 ELPS 4C, 5E

Understanding Sentences **781**

## Practice

### Agreement of Subject and Verb 2

- Subject-Verb Agreement

For each underlined verb, state the reason it does not agree with its subject.

**Example:** 1. *Were* is plural, and its subject, *one*, is singular.

One of Edna Ferber's most popular works **(1)** were the novel *So Big.* (This is one book that **(2)** are required reading for literature class.) Some students **(3)** wonders about the author's reasons for writing the book. In one interview, Ferber answered: "I wrote my book because I wanted to write it more than anything in the world."

Many readers are aware that *So Big* won a Pulitzer Prize for literature. The main characters, Selina Peake DeJong and her son, Dirk "So Big" DeJong, **(4)** makes the story memorable. The pair **(5)** faces many challenges. Selina is a widow who **(6)** are forced to make her way in a male-dominated world. Dirk experiences many changes as he grows into a young man.

The novels *Showboat* and *Giant* **(7)** is other well-known works by Edna Ferber. Some of her fans **(8)** believes that she was the greatest novelist of her day.

### Model

Model the following sentence to practice subject-verb agreement.

> He had preconceived ideas about everything, and his idea about Americans was that they should be engineers or mechanics.
> —Willa Cather, *Alexander's Bridge*

Sentences

---

## Agreement of Subject and Verb

Discuss with students the agreement of subject and verb explained on SE page 780 to help them comprehend vocabulary and language structures and employ complex grammatical structures in content area writing. Have students contribute other examples for each use. Then have students complete the Practice activity on SE page 781 with a partner.

## Related Skills Activities

- **SkillsBook**
  Subject-Verb Agreement 3
  (Indefinite Pronouns and Collective Nouns), p. 149

## Answers

1. Were is plural, and its subject, one, is singular.
2. Are is plural, and its subject, book, is singular.
3. Wonders is singular, and its subject, students, is plural.
4. Makes is singular, and its subject, characters, is plural.
5. Faces is singular, and its subject, pair, is plural.
6. Are is plural, and its subject, who (antecedent, widow), is singular.
7. Is is singular, and its subject, novels, is plural.
8. Believes is singular, and its subject, some, is plural.

---

 **ELPS 4C** Comprehend language structures used in written classroom materials; **5E** Employ increasingly complex grammatical structures in content area writing such as using correct verbs, tenses, and pronouns/possessive case/negatives and contractions;

## Agreement of Pronoun and Antecedent

A pronoun must agree in number, person, and gender with its *antecedent*. (The *antecedent* is the word to which the pronoun refers.)

**Cal brought his gerbil to school.** (The antecedent of *his* is *Cal*. Both the pronoun and its antecedent are singular, third person, and masculine; therefore, the pronoun is said to "agree" with its antecedent.)

### 782.1 Agreement in Number

Use a **singular pronoun** to refer to such antecedents as *each, either, neither, one, anyone, anybody, everyone, everybody, somebody, another, nobody,* and *a person.*

**Neither of the brothers likes his (not their) room.**

Two or more singular antecedents joined by *or* or *nor* are also referred to by a **singular pronoun.**

**Either Connie or Sue left her headset in the library.**

If one of the antecedents joined by *or* or *nor* is singular and one is plural, the pronoun should agree with the nearer antecedent.

**Neither the manager nor the players were crazy about their new uniforms.**

Use a **plural pronoun** to refer to plural antecedents as well as compound subjects joined by *and.*

**Jared and Carlos are finishing their assignments.**

### 782.2 Agreement in Gender

Use a **masculine** or **feminine pronoun** depending upon the gender of the antecedent.

**Is either Connor or Gloria bringing his or her baseball glove?**

When *a person* or *everyone* is used to refer to both sexes or either sex, you will have to choose whether to offer optional pronouns or rewrite the sentence.

**A person should be allowed to choose her or his own footwear.**
(optional pronouns)

**People should be allowed to choose their own footwear.**
(rewritten in plural form)

## Practice

### Agreement of Pronoun and Antecedent

- **Pronoun-Antecedent Agreement**

For each sentence below, first write the antecedent of the pronoun that appears later in the sentence. Then replace the incorrect pronoun with one that agrees with the antecedent. If the pronoun is correct as is, write "C."

**Example:** Should students always know the basics about how to maintain her computers?
students, their

1. Everyone should know how to delete files and save his documents to the network drive.
2. Tamyra and Ricardo know a lot about maintaining her computers.
3. Both of them keep his computers running smoothly.
4. The computer lab tech helps students with problems they can't fix.
5. Neither Tamyra nor Ricardo could help Arturo with their problem.
6. Arturo's computer was freezing up, and the lab tech fixed them.
7. The tech said that Arturo probably needs a new monitor for his computer.
8. Ricardo just got a new flat-screen monitor for their computer at home.
9. Most students at our school know how to fix his computers when something minor goes wrong.

### Model

Model the following sentence to practice pronoun-antecedent agreement.

My parents gave up entirely their wandering life and fixed themselves in their native country.
—Mary Shelley, *Frankenstein*

## Agreement of Pronoun and Antecedent

Discuss with students the agreement of pronoun and antecedent explained on SE page 782 to help them comprehend vocabulary and language structures and employ complex grammatical structures in content area writing. Invite students to share their answers to the Practice activity on SE page 783 with the class.

## Related Skills Activities

- **SkillsBook**
  Pretest: Pronoun-Antecedent Agreement, p. 151
  Pronoun-Antecedent Agreement 1 and 2, pp. 152–153

## Answers

1. everyone, his or her
2. Tamyra and Stan, their
3. both, their
4. students, C
5. Arturo, his
6. computer, it
7. Arturo, C
8. Ricardo, his
9. students, their

784

## Diagramming Sentences

A **graphic diagram** of a sentence is a picture of how the words in that sentence are related and how they fit together to form a complete thought.

### 784.1 Simple Sentence with One Subject and One Verb

Chris fishes.

### 784.2 Simple Sentence with a Predicate Adjective

Fish are delicious.

### 784.3 Simple Sentence with a Predicate Noun and Adjectives

Fishing is my favorite hobby.

**NOTE:** When possessive pronouns (*my, his, their, etc.*) are used as adjectives, they are placed on a diagonal line under the word they modify.

### 784.4 Simple Sentence with an Indirect and Direct Object

My grandpa gave us a trout.

**NOTE:** Articles (*a, an, the*) are adjectives and are placed on a diagonal line under the word they modify.

---

 **Practice**

## Sentence Diagramming 1

■ Diagramming Sentences

 **Diagram the following sentences.**

**Example:** Wind is powerful.

1. Wind turbines generate electricity.
2. This power is a clean energy source.
3. The turbine blades are huge.
4. My uncle made us a small wind turbine.
5. Our neighbors are glad.
6. We give them our excess power.
7. No wind means no power.
8. Wind is supplementary power.

### Model

Model the following sentences to practice writing sentences with a direct object and with an indirect object.

> Never give a party if you will be the most interesting person there.
> —Mickey Friedman

> Beauty is in the eye of the beholder, and it may be necessary from time to time to give a stupid or misinformed beholder a black eye.
> —Miss Piggy

*Sentences*

---

## Sentence Diagramming

Discuss with students the diagrammed sentences shown on SE pages 784 and 786 to help them comprehend vocabulary and language structures and employ complex grammatical structures in content area writing. Have students complete the Practice activity on SE page 785, and review the answers as a class.

## Answers

---

 **TEKS 10.17C** Use a variety of correctly structured sentences; **ELPS 4C** Comprehend language structures used in written classroom materials; **5E** Employ increasingly complex grammatical structures in content area writing such as using correct verbs, tenses, and pronouns/possessive case/negatives and contractions; **5F** Write using a variety of grade-appropriate sentence patterns in increasingly accurate ways

TEKS 10.17C
ELPS 4C, 5E, 5F

## Diagramming Sentences (continued)

**786.1** Simple Sentence with a Prepositional Phrase

I like fishing by myself.

**786.2** Simple Sentence with a Compound Subject and Verb

The team and fans clapped and cheered.

**786.3** Compound Sentence

The team scored, and the crowd cheered wildly.

**786.4** Complex Sentence with a Subordinate Clause

Before Erin scored, the crowd sat quietly.

TEKS 10.17C
ELPS 4C, 5E, 5F

## Practice

### Sentence Diagramming 2

■ Diagramming Sentences

Diagram the following sentences.

**Example:** The small boy on the swing emitted a squeal of delight.

1. After the hawk landed, the rabbit ran across the field.
2. I put three new batteries in the silver flashlight.
3. Gene and Valeria planned and completed the school's mural.
4. My school won the state tournament, and my cousin's school captured third place.
5. The police and firefighters pushed and pulled the damaged crate.
6. All the students were gone, so the janitor locked the door.
7. Although the book was long, everyone wanted a copy.
8. The girl on the snowboard flew down the hill.

### Model

Model the following sentences to practice writing compound and complex sentences.

Stay committed to your decisions, but stay flexible in your approach.
—Tom Robbins

The whole world opened to me when I learned to read.
—Mary McLeod Bethune

Sentences

## Answers

1.
2.
3.
4.

5.
6.
7.
8.

**TEKS** 10.17C Use a variety of correctly structured sentences; **ELPS 4C** Comprehend language structures used in written classroom materials; **5E** Employ increasingly complex grammatical structures in content area writing such as using correct verbs, tenses, and pronouns/possessive case/negatives and contractions; **5F** Write using a variety of grade-appropriate sentence patterns in increasingly accurate ways

# How Does *Texas Write Source* Teach the Forms of Writing?

*T*exas Write Source provides numerous models and assignments for each major form of writing: **narrative**, **expository**, **persuasive**, **interpretive response**, **creative**, and **research**.

## Writing Assignments

Each integrated core writing unit provides students with a comprehensive, research-based exploration of a particular form. Every unit includes the following writing lessons:

- a **start-up paragraph assignment**—complete with a writing sample and step-by-step writing guidelines;
- two or more **multiparagraph essay assignments**—complete with writing samples, in-depth step-by-step guidelines, and integration of Texas traits and grammar instruction; and
- one **assessment writing assignment**—complete with a sample response to a prompt plus writing tips.

A separate section—Writing Across the Curriculum—provides students with authentic writing assignments from the major content areas and the world of work. Each assignment includes step-by-step instruction and annotated models.

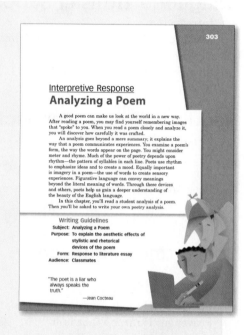

## Writing Skills and Strategies

As students develop the writing in each unit, they will gain valuable experience working with the following skills or strategies:

- reading and responding to literature (writing models)
- **working with the writing process integrated with the Texas traits**
- using graphic organizers
- developing beginnings, middles, and endings
- **practicing grammar skills in context**
- publishing (presenting) writing
- reflecting on writing
- **responding to a prompt for assessment**

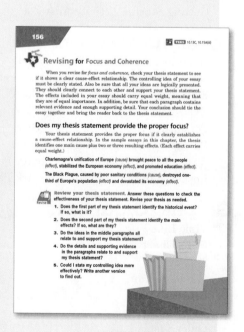

# How Does the Program Integrate the Writing Process and the Traits of Writing?

Throughout each core writing unit, the Texas traits of writing are integrated into the steps of the writing process. As students develop their writing in each unit, they will develop an understanding of, and appreciation for, each trait of writing. In addition, checklists, guidelines, and activities are used to ensure that each piece of writing is completely traits-based.

## The Process and the Texas Traits in the Core Units

### Understanding Your Goal

The beginning of each core essay assignment helps students understand the goal of their writing. A chart listing the traits of writing helps students meet that goal.

### Focus on the Traits

As students develop their essays, they will find valuable discussions of the Texas traits at different points during the writing process.

### Revising and Editing for the Traits

When students are ready to revise and edit, they will find step-by-step instruction, guidelines, and strategies to help them improve their writing for each of the traits of writing.

### Model Essays and Holistic Scoring

Each core unit contains example essays for each score on the Holistic Scoring Guide, from 4 ("highly effective") to 1 ("not effective"). These annotated examples will help students gauge the effectiveness of their own writing and better understand how holistic scoring works.

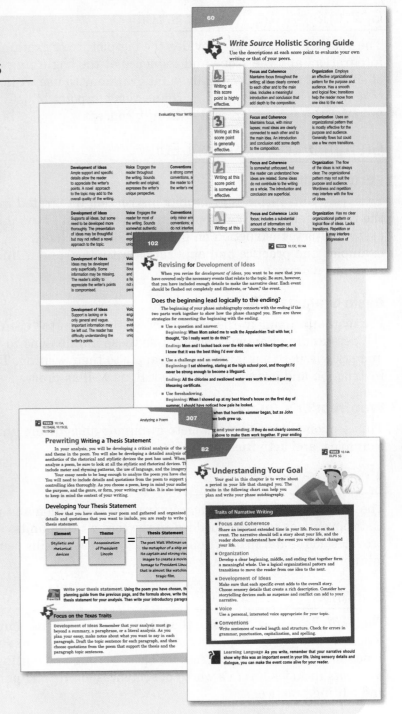

# How Is Grammar Presented?

**If you follow the suggested yearlong timetable, you will cover all the key grammar skills, including those listed in the TEKS.** The program includes grammar instruction integrated into the core writing units. This allows students to learn about grammar in context when they are working on their own writing. If students have trouble with a particular concept, you can refer to a wealth of print and online resources for additional support.

## Grammar in the Teacher's Edition

The yearlong timetable provides the big picture of grammar integration, and the scope and sequence at the beginning of each unit shows specifically what grammar to use while teaching writing. Conventions connections at point of use pinpoint the time to present each new concept.

## Grammar in the Student Edition

### Forms of Writing

Each core unit includes grammar instruction integrated into the revising and editing steps in the development of the main essay or story. Instruction on grammar skills includes examples and practice and application activities, and it links to students' writing.

### Basic Grammar and Writing

For more grammar in the context of writing, turn to "Using Words Effectively" and "Understanding Sentence Style." Use these minilessons to workshop specific grammar and style issues that students can apply to their writing. These pages include instruction and examples of each skill, as well as practice activities.

### Proofreader's Guide

This section serves as a complete grammar and editing guide, providing rules, examples, and activities.

## ⚡Write Source Online

The *Write Source* **Net-text** offers interactive instruction and practice for the grammar and conventions topics embedded in the core writing units. *Write Source* **GrammarSnap** provides additional instruction, practice, and basic skills reinforcement through videos, minilessons, games, and quizzes.

## Grammar in Other Program Components

The *SkillsBook* provides more than 130 punctuation, mechanics, spelling, usage, sentence, and parts-of-speech activities. *Texas Assessment Preparation* contains pretests, benchmark tests, and post-tests for basic writing and editing skills. *Daily Language Workouts* includes a year's worth of sentences (daily) and paragraphs (weekly) for writing and editing practice.

## Planning Grammar Instruction

### Should I implement *all* of the suggested basic grammar activities?

In the course of the year, if you assigned every grammar exercise listed in the daily lesson schedules (located in the unit overviews of your TE), your students would complete **all** of the "Basic Grammar and Writing," "Proofreader's Guide," *SkillsBook*, and GrammarSnap activities.

Because the most effective grammar instruction happens in context, daily lesson schedules call for these exercises at appropriate times during revising and editing in the core writing units. As the teacher, you must choose the type and number of exercises that will best meet the needs of your students.

### How are all the grammar resources related?

*Texas Write Source SkillsBook* activities parallel and expand on the rules and exercises found in the "Proofreader's Guide." In "Basic Grammar and Writing," the brief exercises function well as minilessons and may be assigned on an as-needed basis. GrammarSnap offers additional support for key editing topics in an engaging, interactive format.

### How do I use the unit scope and sequence chart?

The sample below from the "Persuasive Writing" unit is followed by two points that explain how to read and use the daily lesson schedules.

Persuasive Writing **194B**

| | Day | Writing and Conventions Instruction | Write Source Student Edition | | | Daily Language Workouts | Skills-Book | Write Source Online |
| | | | Core Unit | Tools of Language | Resource Units | | | |
|---|---|---|---|---|---|---|---|---|
| WEEK 2 | 6–7 | Prewriting | 201–204 | TL 526–529 | WR 618–627 | 54–57 | | Net-text |
| | 8–10 | Drafting | 205–210 | | WR 628–633 | | | Net-text |
| | 11–12 | Revising | 211–220 | TL 526–529 | | 58–61 | | Net-text |
| | | Skills Activities:<br>•Fragments | | | BGW 594–595<br>PG 772–773 | | 161–165 | |
| | | •Adverbs | | | BGW 578–579<br>PG 766–767 | | 111–114 | GrammarSnap |
| | 13–14 | Editing and Publishing | 221–227 | | | | | Net-text |
| | | Skills Activities:<br>•Subjunctive and Indic... | | | PG 752–753 | | 104–105 | GrammarSnap |

1. The Resource Units and column indicates the SE pages that cover rules, examples, and exercises for each "Skills Activity" item.
2. The *Daily Language Workouts, SkillsBook,* and **Write Source** Online columns indicate pages and information from those particular resources, not from the SE.

### How do I use *Daily Language Workouts*?

*Daily Language Workouts* is a teacher resource that provides a high-interest sentence for each day of the year and weekly paragraphs for additional editing and proofreading practice. This regular practice helps students develop the objectivity they need to effectively edit their own writing.

# How is Writing Across the Curriculum Addressed?

*Texas Write Source* program provides a wide variety of writing across the curriculum activities and assignments. It promotes *writing to show learning, writing to learn new concepts,* and *writing to reflect on learning.*

## Writing to Show Learning

Writing to show learning is the most common type of writing that content-area teachers assign. The following forms of writing covered in the program are commonly used for this purpose.

- Descriptive paragraph and essay
- Narrative paragraph and essay
- Expository paragraph and essay
- Persuasive paragraph and essay
- Response paragraph and book review
- Response to nonfiction
- Summary paragraph
- Research report

## Specific Writing Across the Curriculum Assignments

Specific content-area assignments let students show learning.

### Writing in Science

    Writing a Lab Report
    Writing a Science Script
    Writing a Science Article Summary

### Writing in Social Studies

    Writing a Descriptive Report
    Writing a Document-Based Research Report

### Writing in Math

    Writing a Math Article Summary
    Writing a Statistical Argument
    Responding to a Math Prompt

### Writing in the Arts

    Responding to an Art Prompt
    Writing a Research Report

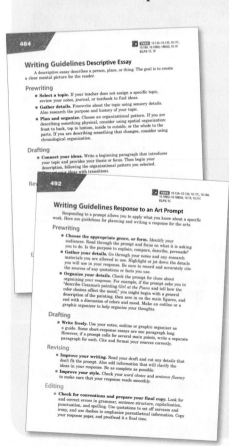

# How Does *Texas Write Source* Incorporate Technology?

*T*exas Write Source includes a number of digital resources to help you provide each student the scaffolding—and challenges—he or she needs.

## Interactive Whiteboard Lessons

**Interactive Whiteboard Lessons** provide an engaging means of introducing the major forms of writing. Whether used for whole class or small group instruction, these interactive lessons help you generate interest, promote discussion, and build background in the foundational concepts needed for success in writing.

## Net-text

Designed as a digital worktext, the **Net-text** serves as an online alternative to key instruction found in the core print units. The **Net-text** features interactive instruction, online document creation, peer-to-peer commenting, additional grammar support, and more—all supported by simple yet powerful tools that help you monitor progress and give feedback.

## GrammarSnap

**GrammarSnap** offers a suite of flexible resources that reinforce and extend the applied grammar instruction embedded in the core units of Write Source. Videos, practice exercises, and games make learning about parts of speech, sentences, and mechanics fun. Follow-up quizzes measure understanding.

## Online Portfolio

The *Write Source* **Online Portfolio** gives students an authentic resource for publication, reflection, and discussion. In addition, it provides you with a flexible vehicle for ongoing, formative assessment as well as a handy tool for parent-teacher conferences.

## Assignment Manager

A productivity tool for both you and your students, the **Assignment Manager** simplifies the complex task of managing daily work. Once you have created an assignment, automatic notifications give students directions, due dates, and reminders. When an assignment has been completed, notifications provide you with linked access to student work for comment and grading.

# How Can I Implement a Writing Workshop?

*Texas Write Source* complements implementation of a writing workshop through both print and technology resources. The program includes minilessons for instruction, high-quality models to encourage individual writing, support for whole-class sharing, and much more.

## Integrated Minilessons

As a starting point, **Interactive Whiteboard Lessons** provide short, focused teaching opportunities designed to lay a foundation in key concepts. Students build on this foundation as they move through the core units, where each step in the writing process presents additional opportunities for minilessons targeting individual need. Both the print book and the **Net-text** lessons teach students to:

- preview the Texas trait-based goal of a writing project
- select a topic and gather details using a graphic organizer
- create a focus (thesis) statement
- organize details using a list or an outline
- create a strong beginning, a coherent middle, and an effective ending
- receive (and provide) peer responses
- revise for the Texas traits
- edit and proofread for conventions
- publish a finished piece
- use Texas traits-based rubrics

| Mon | Tues | Wed | Thurs | Fri |
|---|---|---|---|---|
| **Writing Minilessons** (10 minutes as needed) | | | | |
| **Status Checks** (2 minutes) Find out what students will work on for the day. | | | | |
| **Individual Work** (30 minutes) Drafting, Revising, Editing, Conferencing, or Publishing | | | | |
| **Whole-Class Sharing Session** (5 minutes) | | | | |

### Graphic Organizers

*Texas Write Source* contains a wealth of graphic organizers that can serve as the subject of minilessons. The graphic organizers modeled in print and technology include the following:

| | | | | |
|---|---|---|---|---|
| Pie graph | Sensory chart | Process diagram | "Why" chart | Topic list |
| Web | Plot chart | Venn diagram | Basics of life list | Character chart |
| Cluster | Storyboard | Circle graph | 5 W's chart | Picture diagram |
| T-chart | Bar graph | Cycle diagram | Cause-effect chart | Comparison-contrast chart |
| Outline | KWL chart | Gathering grid | Problem-solution chart | Time line |

## High-Quality Models

Each core unit begins with a high interest model, complete with annotations pointing out key features. The **Net-text** provides additional tools for exploring each model, including the ability for students to interact with their classroom peers online as they rate and comment on the model. Once students have read and analyzed each model, they will be ready—and excited—to begin their own writing. Other models and examples throughout each unit offer specific techniques that students can use in their own writing.

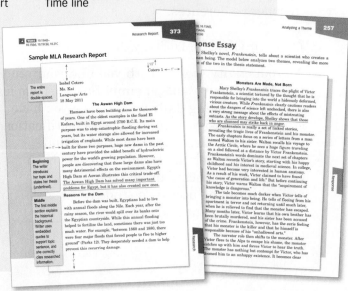

## Individual Writing

*Texas Write Source* makes it easy for writing-workshop students to work on their own. It also provides specific help whenever students have questions about their writing. Here are some of the areas that are addressed:

- catching the reader's interest
- providing background information
- developing strong paragraphs
- elaborating on ideas
- organizing ideas by time, location, importance, logic
- quoting, paraphrasing, and summarizing
- using transitions
- drawing conclusions
- calling the reader to act

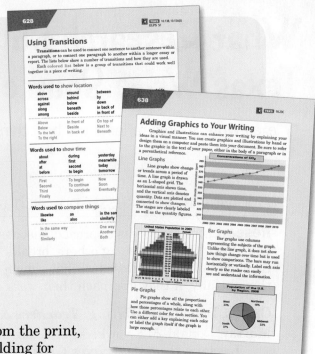

In addition to supporting these and other key concepts from the print, the *Write Source* **Net-text** provides an extra layer of scaffolding for independent writing, including exercises with immediate feedback; at-a-click support for grammar and conventions concepts; ready access to resources such as a dictionary and thesaurus; and an application for creating and managing work online.

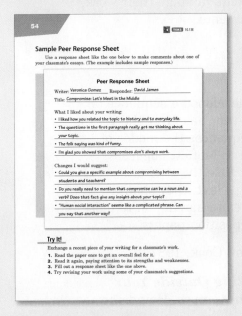

## Peer and Teacher Response

*Texas Write Source* reviews peer responding and provides a peer response sheet. Consistent integration of the traits in the writing process allows students and teachers to speak a common language as they conduct responding sessions. Traits-based checklists and rubrics help pinpoint just what is working—and what could work better—in each piece of writing. The *Write Source* **Net-text** provides additional support for teacher-to-student and student-to-student response, including a commenting tool and notifications.

## Whole-Class Sharing

*Texas Write Source* helps students complete their work, preparing it for whole-class sharing—whether in a traditional presentation or in the public section of the **Online Portfolio**. In addition, the program provides a wealth of suggestions for publishing student work in a variety of forms and for a variety of audiences.

Every writing unit ends with evaluation using traits-based rubrics. Even the evaluation process is modeled with sample essays and assessments. A reflection sheet also helps students think about what they have learned and internalize the lessons to use in the future.

# What Research Supports Texas Write Source?

*Texas Write Source* reflects the best thinking and research on writing instruction.

## Applying the Process Approach to Writing

**Research:** The process approach, discussed by educators Donald M. Murray and Donald H. Graves, among others, breaks writing down into a series of steps—prewriting through publishing. Research has shown that students write more effectively, and more thoughtfully, if they approach their work as a process rather than as an end product.

Graves, Donald. H. *Writing: Teachers & Children at Work.* Heinemann, 2003.

Murray, Donald. M.; Newkirk, Thomas; Miller, Lisa C. *The Essential Don Murray Lessons from America's Greatest Writing Teacher.* Boynton/Cook Heinemann, 2009.

***Texas Write Source:*** All writing units and assignments are arranged according to the steps in the writing process. This arrangement helps students manage their work, especially in the case of longer essay or research report assignments.

## Sequencing Assignments

**Research:** Writing instructor and researcher James Moffett developed a sequence of writing assignments—known as the "Universe of Discourse"—that has, over the years, served countless English/language arts classrooms. Moffett sequences the modes of writing according to their connection or immediacy to the writer. Moffett suggests that students first develop descriptive and narrative pieces because the students have an immediate, personal connection to this type of writing. Next, they should develop informational pieces that require some investigation before moving on to more challenging, reflective writing, such as persuasive essays and position papers.

Moffett, James. *Teaching the Universe of Discourse.* Boynton/Cook, 1987.

**Related Title:** Fleischer, Cathy; Andrew-Vaughn, Sarah. *Writing Outside Your Comfort Zone: Helping Students Navigate Unfamiliar Genres.* Heinemann, 2009.

***Texas Write Source:*** The writing units and assignments in the *Texas Write Source* texts are arranged according to the "Universe of Discourse," starting with descriptive and narrative writing, moving on to expository writing, and so on. These assignments are designed to be used in a sequence that supports an existing writing curriculum or integrated reading/language arts program.

## Implementing a Writing Workshop

**Research:** Countless respected writing instructors and researchers have touted the importance of establishing a community of writers in the classroom. Teachers can establish such a community by implementing a writing workshop. In a writing workshop, students are immersed in all aspects of writing, including sharing their work with their peers.

Atwell, Nancie. ***In the Middle: New Understandings About Writing, Reading, and Learning.*** Heinemann, 1998.

**Texas Write Source:** The units in *Texas Write Source* are so clearly presented that most students can work independently on their writing in a workshop. In addition, the core units contain innumerable opportunities for workshop minilessons.

## Producing Writing with Detail

**Research:** Rebekah Caplan learned through her teaching experience that students don't automatically know how to add details to their personal, informational, and persuasive writing. She discovered with her students that adding detail to writing is a skill that must be practiced regularly. To address this problem, Caplan came up with the "show-me" sentence strategy in which students begin with a basic idea—"My locker is messy"—and create a brief paragraph that shows rather than tells the idea.

Caplan, Rebekah. ***Writers in Training: A Guide to Developing a Composition Program.*** Dale Seymour Publications, 1984.

**Related Title:** Bernabei, Gretchen S.; Hover, Jayne; Candler, Cynthia. ***Crunchtime: Lessons to Help Students Blow the Roof Off Writing Tests—and Become Better Writers in the Process.*** Heinemann, 2009.

**Texas Write Source:** *Daily Language Workouts* contain a series of show-me sentences that teachers can implement as a regular classroom warm-up.

## Meeting Students' Diverse Needs

**Research:** Many students in today's classrooms struggle with writing and learning. For struggling students, following the writing process is not enough. According to the research done by James L. Collins, struggling students need specific strategies and aids to help them become better writers. Collins found that these students benefit from the following: *skills instruction integrated into the process of writing, color coding and signposts in the presentation of instructional material, the use of graphic organizers, instructions presented in discreet chunks of copy,* and so on.

Collins, James L. ***Strategies for Struggling Writers.*** Guilford Press, 1998.

**Related Title:** Cruz, M. Colleen; Calkins, Lucy; ***A Quick Guide to Researching Struggling Writers, K–5.*** FirstHand/Heinemann, 2008.

**Texas Write Source:** The core writing units contain all the key features from Collins's work. As a result, the units are well suited for struggling learners and English language learners.

# Language Transfer Support

## Introduction

Students learning English come to us with myriad backgrounds, both culturally and linguistically. These backgrounds serve as marvelous resources for learning another language. For instance, all spoken languages are made up of sounds that comprise words that comprise sentences that comprise communication. We use the wealth of knowledge provided to us by our first language as a roadmap for interpreting all aspects of a second language—grammar (syntax), phonics (sounds and writing symbols), and vocabulary. This knowledge is an asset and a valuable tool in accelerating the acquisition of a second language. Just think how much harder language learning would be if a learner didn't know to look for words among the endless string of babble!

Because English language learners rely on their primary language experiences to guide their acquisition of English, transfer issues—language learning areas in which the primary language influences English production—arise. There are three types of transfer between languages.

The first is **positive transfer.** Cognates are an excellent example of positive transfer. If a student speaks Spanish and knows the word *teléfono,* he or she will have little trouble learning the word *telephone* in English. The two words sound similar and even have a similar spelling to a certain extent. The transfer from Spanish to English, in this case, has a positive effect. Another example of positive transfer can occur in the realm of phonics. If a student speaks Spanish and has learned that the letter *m* represents /m/, that knowledge will transfer readily to English phonics, in which the letter represents the same sound.

The second type of language transfer is **zero transfer.** Zero transfer occurs when something is encountered in English that is not present in the primary language. For some languages, such as Chinese, the writing system of English is a zero transfer situation. Because these languages rely on different writing systems, a student from one of these language backgrounds will not mistake the letter *j* for another sound because he or she has never encountered that writing symbol in the primary language. In a sense, the slate is clean, and while there is no assistance from the primary language as in positive transfer, there is no impediment either.

The last type of language transfer is **negative transfer.** In these situations, an element of the primary language conflicts with an element of English and causes difficulty in acquiring that specific element of English. A simple example is that Spanish speakers who know the word *librería* might be tempted to use their knowledge to interpret the English word *library* as a bookstore instead of as an institution that lends books to the public. In the realm of grammar, that same Spanish speaker might be tempted to place an adjective after the noun (*house big* as in *casa grande*) when constructing English sentences. And when he or she encounters the letter *j* while learning to read, the reader with a Spanish language background might substitute /h/ for the English *j* sound because that is the Spanish letter-sound correspondence.

Because each primary language has unique characteristics, there are unique language transfer issues for all of the languages represented in our classrooms. This resource guide focuses on providing teachers valuable information about zero and negative Language Transfer Support that affect the English acquisition of our students. As part of this introduction, background information for the ten languages highlighted in this guide is provided. The first chart that follows provides grammar transfer issues for the top ten primary languages found among English language learners in U.S. schools. The second chart provides phonics transfer issues for the top seven primary languages. A final section highlights word study transfer issues for five languages.

Teachers should use this wealth of information to help them identify possible areas of difficulty for students in their classrooms during instruction and to modify expectations accordingly. For instance, when teaching third-person agreement to Vietnamese students, it's helpful to know that the group may not be able to produce a final *s* sound. Therefore, while they might be able to listen to and absorb the grammar lesson passively, the teacher should be aware that Vietnamese speakers may have difficulty producing the sentence *That hurts me* with accurate third-person agreement.

The phonics transfer chart is divided into two sections: sound transfer (phonology) and sound-symbol transfer (phonics). Acquiring the sound-symbol system of English phonics relies on two elements for an English language learner—first, the learner's ability to produce the English sound accurately and second, his or her ability to associate the sound produced with the correct symbol. Therefore, both the sound system and the writing system of the primary language can affect a student's English language acquisition. The sound-symbol correspondence chart includes only those languages that use the Roman alphabet because other languages have zero transfer for the entire English writing system.

Best instructional practice proceeds from the known to the unknown. Therefore, with a group of language learners with a single language background, elements of positive transfer are taught first, followed by zero transfer elements, and finally by negative transfer elements.

> Because each primary language has unique characteristics, there are unique language transfer issues for all of the languages represented in our classrooms.

When encountering an element of negative transfer in a young learner's ability to produce the sounds of English, teachers often find that overt correction can raise children's anxiety, resulting in an overall negative effect for language learning. Because children who learn a second language before the age of 12 will generally acquire the sound system perfectly over time, spending instructional time on pronunciation is not necessary. Rather, modeling correct pronunciation back to students while validating their English approximations is the best course to follow.

It can also be beneficial to use knowledge about negative transfer issues to inform an instructional approach to a specific language element. For instance, when teaching the letters *b* and *v* to Spanish-speaking students (these two sounds are variants of a single phoneme, or distinctive sound, in Spanish), an approach that contrasts the English sounds and symbols of these two letters will probably yield the best results. Similarly, raising the awareness of intermediate language learners to the cause of their errors can help them learn to self-correct. For example, a teacher might say, "Lupita, I see that you wrote *country large* in this assignment. I know that's how you say it in Spanish, but we always say *large country* in English. Next time you write a paper, maybe you can proofread for that type of mistake." Metacognitive language learning strategies, those in which students are actively engaged in analyzing and improving their learning process, can accelerate language learning.

> **Best instructional practice proceeds from the known to the unknown.**

Good instruction is anchored in a well-rounded knowledge of students and their learning needs. Because teachers of English language learners cannot possibly speak all the primary languages that represent the backgrounds of each of their students, we have brought together expert language consultants in order to provide important information that can inform classroom instruction.

# Background Information for Ten Primary Languages

The following background information is provided to help you understand the linguistic and cultural heritage of the students in your classroom. The list is ordered according to size of population in U.S. schools.

## Spanish

The largest group of English language learners in the United States is comprised of Spanish-speaking students whose families have come from Mexico, Central America, South America, and the Caribbean. Immigrants come to the United States seeking economic opportunity, education, or refuge from political unrest. Spanish colonial conquest led to the dominance of Spanish as the official language in much of the Americas. Over 70 percent of Spanish-speaking immigrants come to the United States from Mexico. Other Spanish-speaking countries and territories are Argentina, Bolivia, Chile, Colombia, Costa Rica, Cuba, Dominican Republic, Ecuador, El Salvador, Guatemala, Honduras, Nicaragua, Panama, Paraguay, Peru, Puerto Rico, Spain, Uruguay, and Venezuela. This great diversity is reflected in the different regional variations of Spanish spoken by different groups. There can be several different words (lexical variants) to refer to the same thing or express the same action. However, Spanish speakers from different regions can still communicate with each other. Given that Spanish is a language derived from Latin and that English also contains many words of Latin origin, English and Spanish share many cognates with a common Latin root. These cognates are words with a common origin that have a similar meaning and spelling in both languages.

# Vietnamese

Vietnamese is one of approximately 150 languages belonging to the Austro-Asiatic family of languages. It is spoken in Vietnam, on the eastern portion of the Indo-Chinese Peninsula in Southeast Asia. The official language of Vietnam, Vietnamese is a tonal language made up of six distinct tones. Vietnamese is written with the Roman alphabet and employs diacritical markings to depict tones. Many Vietnamese speakers immigrated to the United States in 1975 after the end of the Vietnam War and the reunification of North and South Vietnam, and, most recently, from 1985 to 1991 through family reunification programs.

# Hmong

The Hmong language is one of a group of closely related languages of Southeast Asia and Southern China often referred to as the Miao-Yao languages. It is the tonal language of an ethnic group called *Hmong* that is spread among several countries: China, Thailand, Laos, and Vietnam. Hmong is predominantly monosyllabic. It is made up of eight different tones, and each syllable has a particular tone associated with it. Many Hmong speakers immigrated to the United States in 1975 as refugees after the Vietnam War. Today Hmong people can be found in China, Thailand, Laos, and Vietnam as well as the United States, France, French Guiana, Argentina, Canada, Germany, and Australia.

# Cantonese

Cantonese is a tonal language belonging to the Sino-Tibetan language family. It is one of the major dialects of Chinese spoken in both the Zhujiang delta, in South China's Guangdong Province, and in Hong Kong. Other major dialects of Chinese include Mandarin, Hakka, Wu, and Min. Although these Chinese dialects share a common writing system, speakers of the various dialects cannot necessarily understand one another. Chinese is traditionally written top to bottom rather than left to right, and text starts from what we usually consider the back of a book. Mandarin, the official language of the People's Republic of China, is used in education in Guangdong rather than Cantonese. An influx of Cantonese speakers came into the United States after World War II and again in the late 1960s after the passage of the Immigration and Naturalization Act of 1965. A further impetus occurred in the 1970s, when the United States offered educational opportunities to Chinese immigrants.

# Korean

Korean is a non-tonal Asian language spoken in the Korean Peninsula in Northeast Asia. There are seven Korean dialects: Ham-Kyung, Pyung-Yang, Choong-Chung, Kyung-Sang, Chul-La, Che-Joo, and Central, which is spoken in Seoul and Kyung-Gui. Korean speakers can be found in both North and South Korea, China, Japan, and Russia. Many immigrated to the United States after the liberation of Korea from Japanese colonization in 1945 and again after the passage of the 1965 Immigration and Naturalization Act. Koreans continue to immigrate to the United States seeking a higher standard of living, better educational opportunities, and political stability.

# Haitian Creole

An official language of Haiti and the sole language
of much of the population of Haiti, Haitian Creole
is a language that developed out of contact between
the French colonists and West African languages
of the plantation workers. As a result, it contains
elements of all of these languages. While much of its
vocabulary is similar to French, other elements of the
language, such as grammar, differ dramatically. Since 1940 three
different writing systems, all based on the Roman alphabet, have
been introduced for the language, resulting in widespread use of
hybrid elements of each of these systems despite the Haitian government's
adoption of a standard writing system in 1979. Speakers of Haitian Creole
come to the United States seeking economic opportunity. Between 1981 and
1996, almost one million people left Haiti.

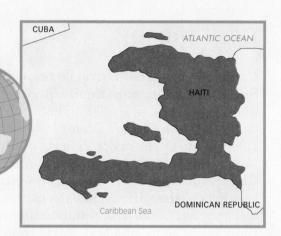

# Arabic

Arabic belongs to the Semitic language family. It is
spoken in an area stretching from Morocco in the
west to the Persian Gulf in the east. There are
many varieties, including Classical Arabic, Eastern
Arabic, Western Arabic, and Maltese, not all of
which can be mutually understood. A Modern
Standard Arabic also exists and is used in literature,
education, and the media. Unlike most European languages,
Arabic is written from right to left, and text starts from what we
usually consider the back of a book. Its alphabet consists of 28 letters, mainly consonants,
with vowels that are indicated by marks above or below the letters. Most speakers of
Arabic immigrated to the United States from the nations of Syria, Lebanon, Egypt,
Yemen, and Jordan. A large influx of Arabic speakers occurred after the passage of the
1965 Immigration and Naturalization Act.

# Russian

As a member of the Indo-European language family, the same language family as English, Russian shares some cognates with English. Cognates are words of similar meaning that sound similar between two languages. Russian is written in a left-to-right format, with the Cyrillic alphabet, however, not the Roman one. The first influx of Russian-speaking immigrants to the United States occurred during the first decades of the last century and consisted of those seeking religious and political freedom and an escape from war. A second wave of immigration to the United States from Russia occurred in the 1970s, when dissidents were exiled from the Soviet Union, many of them choosing the United States as their new country of residence. After the demise of the Soviet Union in the 1990s, more Russian immigrants have come to the United States seeking better economic opportunities and social stability.

# Tagalog

Tagalog (pronounced tah-GAH-lug) is one of over 300 languages that belong to the Malayo-Polynesian family of languages spoken in the Philippines, a set of islands off the southeast coast of mainland China. Tagalog (also called *Filipino*) and English have been the two official languages of the Philippines since 1973, while Tagalog remains the sole national language of the Philippines. There is a great diversity of languages in the Philippines. Some of the major languages other than Tagalog include Cebuano, Ilocano, Hiligaynon, Bicol, and Waray. Tagalog speakers immigrated to the United States mainly after 1946, when they achieved independence after being a U.S. territory for 46 years.

# Khmer (Cambodian)

The word *Khmer* (pronounced kuh-MIE, rhymes with *pie*) refers to both the national language and the people of Cambodia, located in Southeast Asia. Khmer, a non-tonal language, is spoken by 90 percent of the population in Cambodia and also by many people in northeast Thailand and southern Vietnam. Cambodian immigrants arrived in the United States in two waves. The first wave consisted of a small number who escaped Cambodia just before the Khmer Rouge takeover in 1975. The second wave consisted of a much larger number of refugees who fled the country after the 1979 invasion of Cambodia by Vietnam, ending the reign of the Khmer Rouge. Between 1975 and 1987, over 140,000 Cambodian refugees resettled in the United States. Refugee resettlement came to an end in the late 1980s, but Cambodian immigrants continue to arrive as Cambodian Americans sponsor family members who had been left behind.

THAILAND    LAOS

CAMBODIA

VIETNAM

Gulf of Thailand

# Grammar Transfer Support

The following chart identifies areas in which speakers of various primary languages may have some difficulty in acquiring English grammar (syntax). The type of transfer error and its cause is outlined for each grammatical category.

## NOUNS

| Grammar Point | Type of Transfer Error in English | Language Background | Cause of Transfer Difficulty |
|---|---|---|---|
| **Plural forms** | omission of plural marker *–s* <br><br>*I have 5 book.* | Cantonese, Haitian Creole, Hmong, Khmer, Korean, Tagalog, Vietnamese | Nouns do not change form to show the plural in the primary language. |
| **Possessive forms** | avoidance of *'s* to describe possession <br><br>*the children of my sister* instead of *my sister's children* | Haitian Creole, Hmong, Khmer, Spanish, Tagalog, Vietnamese | The use of a prepositional phrase to express possession reflects the only structure or a more common structure in the primary language. |
| | no marker for possessive forms <br>*house my friend* instead of *my friend's house* | Haitian Creole, Khmer, Vietnamese | A noun's owner comes after the object in the primary language. |
| **Count versus noncount nouns** | use of plural forms for English noncount nouns <br><br>*the furnitures, the color of her hairs* | Haitian Creole, Russian, Spanish, Tagalog | Nouns that are count and noncount differ between English and the primary language. |

## ARTICLES

| Grammar Point | Type of Transfer Error in English | Language Background | Cause of Transfer Difficulty |
|---|---|---|---|
| **Placement of articles** | omission of article <br><br>*He has job.* <br>*His dream is to become lawyer, not teacher.* | Cantonese, Haitian Creole, Hmong, Khmer, Korean, Russian, Tagalog, Vietnamese | Articles are either lacking or the distinction between *a* and *the* is not paralleled in the primary language. |
| | omission of articles in certain contexts, such as to identify a profession <br><br>*He is teacher.* | Spanish | The article is not used in Spanish in this context, but it is needed in English. |
| **Use of articles** | overuse of articles <br><br>*The honesty is the best policy.* <br>*This food is popular in the Japan.* <br>*I like the cats.* | Arabic, Haitian Creole, Hmong, Spanish, Tagalog | The article is used in the primary language in places where it isn't used in English. |
| | use of *one* for *a/an* <br><br>*He is one engineer.* | Haitian Creole, Hmong, Vietnamese | Learners sometimes confuse the articles *a/an* with *one* since articles either do not exist in the primary language or serve a different function. |

# PRONOUNS

| Grammar Point | Type of Transfer Error in English | Language Background | Cause of Transfer Difficulty |
|---|---|---|---|
| **Personal pronouns, gender** | use of pronouns with inappropriate gender<br><br>*He is my sister.* | Cantonese, Haitian Creole, Hmong, Khmer, Korean, Tagalog | The third person pronoun in the primary language is gender free. The same pronoun is used where English uses masculine, feminine, and neuter pronouns, resulting in confusion of pronoun forms in English. |
| | use of pronouns with inappropriate gender<br><br>*He is my sister.* | Spanish | In Spanish, subject pronouns are dropped in everyday speech and the verb conveys third-person agreement, effectively collapsing the two pronouns and causing transfer difficulty for subject pronouns in English. |
| | use of inappropriate gender, particularly with neuter nouns<br><br>*The house is big. She is beautiful.* | Russian, Spanish | Inanimate nouns have feminine and masculine gender in the primary language, and the gender may be carried over into English. |
| **Personal pronoun forms** | confusion of subject and object pronoun forms<br><br>*Him hit me.*<br>*I like she.*<br>*Let we go.* | Cantonese, Hmong, Khmer | The same pronoun form is used for *he/him, she/her,* and in some primary languages for *I/me* and *we/us.* |
| | use of incorrect number for pronouns<br><br>*I saw many yellow flowers. It was pretty.* | Cantonese, Korean | There is no number agreement in the primary language. |
| | omission of subject pronouns<br><br>*Michael isn't here. Is in school.* | Korean, Russian, Spanish | Subject pronouns may be dropped in the primary language and the verb ending supplies information on number and/or gender. |
| | omission of object pronouns<br><br>*That man is very rude, so nobody likes.* | Korean, Vietnamese | Direct objects are frequently dropped in the primary language. |
| | omission of pronouns in clauses<br><br>*If not have jobs, they will not have food.* | Cantonese, Vietnamese | A subordinate clause at the beginning of a sentence does not require a subject in the primary language. |
| | use of pronouns with subject nouns<br><br>*This car it runs very fast.*<br><br>*Your friend he seems so nice.*<br><br>*My parents they live in Vietnam.* | Hmong, Spanish, Vietnamese | This type of redundant structure reflects the popular "topic-comment" approach used in the primary language: The speaker mentions a topic and then makes a comment on it. |

## PRONOUNS *continued*

| Grammar Point | Type of Transfer Error in English | Language Background | Cause of Transfer Difficulty |
|---|---|---|---|
| **Pronoun use** | avoidance of pronouns by repetition of nouns<br><br>*Sara visits her grandfather every Sunday, and Sara makes a meal.* | Korean, Vietnamese | It is common in the primary language to repeat nouns rather than to use pronouns. |
| **Pronoun *one*** | omission of the pronoun *one*<br><br>*I saw two nice cars, and I like the small.* | Russian, Spanish, Tagalog | Adjectives can be used on their own in the primary language, whereas English often requires a noun or *one*. |
| **Possessive forms** | confusion of possessive forms<br><br>*The book is my.* | Cantonese, Hmong, Vietnamese | Cantonese and Hmong speakers tend to omit final *n*, creating confusion between *my* and *mine*. |

## ADJECTIVES

| Grammar Point | Type of Transfer Error in English | Language Background | Cause of Transfer Difficulty |
|---|---|---|---|
| **Placement of adjective** | position of adjectives after nouns<br><br>*I read a book interesting.* | Haitian Creole, Hmong, Khmer, Spanish, Vietnamese | Adjectives commonly come after nouns in the primary language. |
| | position of adjectives before certain pronouns<br><br>*This is interesting something.* | Cantonese, Korean | Adjectives always come before words they modify in the primary language. |
| **Comparison** | omission of markers for comparison<br><br>*She is smart than me.* | Khmer | Since there are no suffixes or inflections in Khmer, the tendency is to omit them in English. |
| | avoidance of *-er* and *-est* endings<br><br>*I am more old than my brother.* | Hmong, Khmer, Korean, Spanish | Comparative and superlative are usually formed with separate words in the primary language, the equivalent of *more* and *most* in English. |
| **Confusion of *-ing* and *-ed* forms** | confusion of *-ing* and *-ed* forms<br><br>*The movie was bored.*<br>*I am very interesting in sports.* | Cantonese, Khmer, Korean, Spanish | The adjective forms in the primary language that correspond to the ones in English do not have active and passive meanings. In Korean, for many adjectives, the same form is used for both active and passive meanings, such as *boring* versus *bored*. |

# VERBS

| Grammar Point | Type of Transfer Error in English | Language Background | Cause of Transfer Difficulty |
|---|---|---|---|
| **Present tense** | omission of *s* in present tense, third person agreement<br><br>*She go to school every day.* | Cantonese, Haitian Creole, Hmong, Khmer, Korean, Tagalog, Vietnamese | There is no subject-verb agreement in the primary language. |
| | problems with irregular subject-verb agreement<br><br>*Sue and Ed has a new house.* | Cantonese, Hmong, Khmer, Korean, Tagalog | Verb forms do not change to indicate the number of the subject in the primary language. |
| **Past tense** | omission of tense markers<br><br>*I study English yesterday.*<br>*I give it to him yesterday.* | Cantonese, Haitian Creole, Hmong, Khmer, Korean, Tagalog, Vietnamese | Verbs in the primary language do not change form to express tense. |
| | confusion of present form and simple past of irregular verbs<br><br>*I give it to him yesterday.* | Cantonese, Spanish | Speakers of the primary language have difficulty recognizing that merely a vowel shift in the middle of the verb, rather than a change in the ending of the verb, is sufficient to produce a change of tense in irregular verbs. |
| | incorrect use of present for the future<br><br>*I come tomorrow.* | Cantonese, Korean | The primary language allows the use of present tense for the future. |
| **In negative statements** | omission of helping verbs in negative statements<br><br>*I no understand.*<br>*I not get into university.* | Cantonese, Korean, Russian, Spanish, Tagalog | Helping verbs are not used in negative statements in the primary language. |
| **Perfect tenses** | avoidance of present perfect where it should be used<br><br>*I live here for two years.* | Haitian Creole, Russian, Tagalog, Vietnamese | The verb form either doesn't exist in the primary language or has a different function. |
| | use of present perfect where past perfect should be used<br><br>*Yesterday I have done that.* | Khmer, Korean | In the primary language a past marker, e.g., *yesterday*, is inserted to indicate a completed action and no other change is necessary. In English when a past marker is used, the verb form must change to past perfect instead of present perfect. |
| **Past continuous** | use of past continuous for recurring action in the past<br><br>*When I was young, I was studying a lot.* | Korean, Spanish, Tagalog | In the primary language, the past continuous form can be used in contexts in which English uses the expression *used to* or the simple past. |
| **Verb as a noun** | omission of infinitive marker *to*<br><br>*Criticize people is not good.* | Cantonese | Unlike English, Cantonese does not require an infinitive marker when using a verb as a noun. |

# VERBS *continued*

| Grammar Point | Type of Transfer Error in English | Language Background | Cause of Transfer Difficulty |
|---|---|---|---|
| **Two verbs in a sentence** | Use of two or more main verbs in one clause without any connectors<br><br>*I took a book studied at the library.* | Hmong | In Hmong verbs can be connected without *and* or any other conjunction (serial verbs). |
| **Linking verbs** | Omission of linking verb<br><br>*He hungry.* | Cantonese, Haitian Creole, Hmong, Khmer, Russian, Vietnamese | The verb *be* is not required in all sentences. In some primary languages, it is implied in the adjectival form. In others, the concept is expressed as a verb. |
| **Passive voice** | Omission of helping verb *be* in passive voice<br><br>*The food finished.* | Cantonese, Vietnamese | Passive voice in the primary language does not require a helping verb. |
| | Avoidance of passive constructions<br><br>*They speak Creole here.*<br>*One speaks Creole here.*<br>avoiding the alternate<br>*Creole is spoken here.* | Haitian Creole | Passive constructions do not exist in Haitian Creole. |
| **Transitive verbs versus intransitive verbs** | confusion of transitive and intransitive verbs<br><br>*He married with a nice girl.* | Cantonese, Korean, Russian, Spanish, Tagalog | Verbs that do and do not take a direct object differ between English and the primary language. |
| **Phrasal verbs** | confusion of related phrasal verbs<br><br>*I look after the word in the dictionary.*<br>instead of *I look up the word in the dictionary.* | Korean, Russian, Spanish | Phrasal verbs do not exist in the primary language. There is often confusion over their meaning in English. |
| *have* **versus** *be* | use of *have* instead of *be*<br><br>*I have hunger.*<br>*I have right.* | Spanish | Some Spanish constructions use *have* where English uses *be*. |

# ADVERBS

| Grammar Point | Type of Transfer Error in English | Language Background | Cause of Transfer Difficulty |
|---|---|---|---|
| **Use of adverbs** | use of adjective form where adverb form is needed<br><br>*Walk quiet.* | Haitian Creole, Hmong, Khmer | There are no suffix-derived adverb forms in the primary language, and the adjective form is used after the verb. |
| **Placement of adverbs** | placement of adverbs before verbs<br><br>*At ten o'clock this morning my plane landed.*<br>avoiding the alternate, *My plane landed at ten o'clock this morning.* | Cantonese, Korean | Adverbs usually come before verbs in the primary language, and this tendency is carried over into English. |

# PREPOSITIONS

| Grammar Point | Type of Transfer Error in English | Language Background | Cause of Transfer Difficulty |
|---|---|---|---|
| **Preposition use** | omission of prepositions<br><br>*Money does not grow trees.* | Cantonese | There are no exact equivalents of English prepositions in Cantonese although there are words to mark location and movement. |

# COMPLEX SENTENCES

| Grammar Point | Type of Transfer Error in English | Language Background | Cause of Transfer Difficulty |
|---|---|---|---|
| **Relative clauses** | omission of relative pronouns<br><br>*My grandfather was a generous man helped everyone.* | Vietnamese | Relative pronouns are not required in Vietnamese. |
| | incorrect pronoun used to introduce a relative clause<br><br>*the house <u>who</u> is big* | Hmong | Hmong uses the same forms of relative pronouns for both personal and inanimate antecedents. |
| **Adverbial clauses** | inclusion of additional connecting word<br><br>*Because he was reckless, <u>so</u> he caused an accident.*<br>*Although my parents are poor, <u>but</u> they are very generous.* | Cantonese, Korean, Vietnamese | The primary language sometimes uses a "balancing word" in the main clause. |
| | use of inconsistent tenses in sentences with multiple clauses<br><br>*She <u>speaks</u> French before she <u>studied</u> English.*<br>*After she <u>comes</u> home, it <u>was</u> raining.*<br>*We <u>will go</u> to the beach if the weather <u>will be</u> nice.* | Cantonese, Hmong, Tagalog, Vietnamese | The primary language lacks tense markers so that matching the tenses of two verbs in one sentence correctly can be difficult. Learners may also try to analyze the tense needed in English according to meaning, which in some cases can result in the use of an incorrect tense. |
| ***If* versus *when*** | Confusion of *if* and *when*<br><br>*If you get there, call me!* instead of *When you get there, call me!* | Korean | The primary language has one expression that covers the use of English *if* and *when* for the future. |

# INFINITIVES AND GERUNDS

| Grammar Point | Type of Transfer Error in English | Language Background | Cause of Transfer Difficulty |
|---|---|---|---|
| **Infinitive and gerund use** | use of present tense verbs in places where gerunds or infinitives are used in English<br><br>*Stop walk.*<br>*I want go there.* | Haitian Creole, Khmer, Korean | Either the *–ing* form does not exist in the primary language, or learners tend to use present tense verbs instead of gerunds even if they do exist [Haitian Creole]. |
| | use of *for* in infinitive phrases<br><br>*They went for to see the movie.* | Spanish | Spanish uses a prepositional form in similar constructions, which is carried over into English and translated as *for*. |

# SENTENCE STRUCTURE

| Grammar Point | Type of Transfer Error in English | Language Background | Cause of Transfer Difficulty |
|---|---|---|---|
| **Objects** | omission of object<br><br>*He dyed [his hair].*<br>*Yes, I want [some].* | Korean | Korean tends to omit objects and noun phrases after verbs. |
| **Variety** | lack of variety in the position of clauses<br><br>*Because you weren't at home and I couldn't find you, I left.*<br>avoiding the alternate,<br>*I left because you weren't at home and I couldn't find you.* | Korean | Since main clauses always come last in Korean, there is a tendency to put the main clause last in English. This is not an error in English, but it leads to a lack of sentence variety. |
| **Sequential action** | clauses that describe earlier actions come first<br><br>*After I finish my homework, I will watch TV.*<br>avoiding the alternate,<br>*I will watch TV after I finish my homework.* | Cantonese, Korean | The pattern in the primary language is to describe what happens first while later occurrences follow. This is not an error in English, but it leads to a lack of sentence variety. |
| **Placement issues** | placement of phrase with the indirect object before the direct object<br><br>*They gave to the girl the book.* | Spanish | The phrase with the indirect object can come before the direct object in Spanish. |
| | placement of modifiers between verb and direct object<br><br>*She speaks very well English.* | Korean, Spanish | Word order, including the placement of adverbials, is freer in the primary language than in English. |
| **Usage issues** | use of double negatives<br><br>*I no see nobody.* | Spanish | Spanish requires double negatives in many sentence structures. |
| | use of clauses for other structures<br><br>*I want that you help me.* | Russian, Spanish | Verbs that take direct objects versus those that require clauses differ in the primary language and English. |

# QUESTIONS

| Grammar Point | Type of Transfer Error in English | Language Background | Cause of Transfer Difficulty |
|---|---|---|---|
| **Subject-verb order** | lack of subject-verb inversion in questions with helping verbs<br><br>*When she will be home?*<br>*Where you are going?* | Cantonese, Hmong, Russian, Tagalog | In the primary language, word order is the same in some questions and statements, depending on the context. |
| *Do* **and** *did* | omission of *do* or *did* in questions<br><br>*Where you went?* | Haitian Creole, Hmong, Khmer, Korean, Russian, Spanish, Tagalog | In the primary language, there is no exact counterpart to the *do/did* verb in questions. |
| **Yes/no questions** | avoidance of English inverted question forms in yes/no questions in favor of tag questions or intonation<br><br>*You come tomorrow, OK?*<br>*He goes to school with you?* | Cantonese, Haitian Creole, Khmer, Korean, Russian, Tagalog, Vietnamese | The primary language doesn't use subject-verb inversion in questions. |
| | incorrect answer form for yes/no questions<br><br>*A: Do you want more food?*<br>*B: I want.*<br>*A: Do you have a pen?*<br>*B: I not have.* | Cantonese, Hmong, Khmer, Korean, Russian | In the primary language, learners tend to answer *yes* by repeating the verb in the question. They tend to say *no* by using *not* and repeating the verb. |
| | positive answer to negative question<br><br>*A: Aren't you going?*<br>*B: Yes. (when the person is not going)* | Cantonese, Korean, Russian | The appropriate response pattern differs between the primary language and English. |
| **Tag questions** | incorrect tag questions<br><br>*You want to go home, are you?* | Cantonese, Khmer, Korean, Vietnamese | The primary language has no exact counterpart to a tag question, forms them differently, or does not add *do/did* to questions. |

# Phonics Transfer Support for Seven Languages

## Sound Transfer (Phonology)

The symbol ■ identifies areas in which these primary language speakers may have some difficulty pronouncing and perceiving spoken English. The sound may not exist in the primary language, may exist but be pronounced somewhat differently, or may be confused with another sound. Sound production and perception issues affect phonics instruction.

### CONSONANTS

| Sound | Spanish | Vietnamese | Hmong | Cantonese | Haitian Creole | Korean | Khmer |
|---|---|---|---|---|---|---|---|
| /b/ as in bat | | | ■ | ■ | | ■ | |
| /k/ as in cat and kite | | | ■ | | | | |
| /d/ as in dog | | | | ■ | | ■ | |
| /f/ as in fan | | | | | | ■ | |
| /g/ as in goat | | | ■ | ■ | | ■ | ■ |
| /h/ as in hen | | | | | ■ | | |
| /j/ as in jacket | ■ | ■ | ■ | ■ | | ■ | |
| /l/ as in lemon | | | | | | ■ | |
| /m/ as in money | | | | | | | |
| /n/ as in nail | | | | | | | |
| /p/ as in pig | | | ■ | | | | |
| /r/ as in rabbit | ■ | | ■ | ■ | ■ | ■ | |
| /s/ as in sun | | | ■ | | | | |
| /t/ as in teen | | ■ | ■ | | | | |
| /v/ as in video | ■ | | | ■ | | ■ | ■ |
| /w/ as in wagon | ■ | | ■ | | | | ■ |
| /y/ as in yo-yo | | | | | | | |
| /z/ as in zebra | ■ | | ■ | ■ | | ■ | ■ |
| /kw/ as in queen | | | ■ | | | | |
| /ks/ as in X ray | | | ■ | ■ | | | |

### SHORT VOWELS

| Sound | Spanish | Vietnamese | Hmong | Cantonese | Haitian Creole | Korean | Khmer |
|---|---|---|---|---|---|---|---|
| short *a* as in hat | ■ | ■ | | ■ | | ■ | |
| short *e* as in set | ■ | | ■ | ■ | ■ | ■ | |
| short *i* as in sit | ■ | ■ | ■ | ■ | ■ | ■ | |
| short *o* as in hot | ■ | | ■ | | | ■ | |
| short *u* as in cup | ■ | | ■ | ■ | ■ | ■ | |

## LONG VOWELS

| Sound | Spanish | Vietnamese | Hmong | Cantonese | Haitian Creole | Korean | Khmer |
|---|---|---|---|---|---|---|---|
| long *a* as in d**a**te | | | ■ | ■ | | | |
| long *e* as in b**e** | | | | ■ | | ■ | |
| long *i* as in **i**ce | | | | ■ | | | |
| long *o* as in r**oa**d | | | ■ | ■ | | | |
| long *u* as in tr**u**e | | | | ■ | | ■ | |

## VOWEL PATTERNS

| Sound | Spanish | Vietnamese | Hmong | Cantonese | Haitian Creole | Korean | Khmer |
|---|---|---|---|---|---|---|---|
| *oo* as in b**oo**k | ■ | ■ | ■ | | ■ | ■ | ■ |
| *aw* as in s**aw** | ■ | | | | | ■ | |

## DIPHTHONGS

| Sound | Spanish | Vietnamese | Hmong | Cantonese | Haitian Creole | Korean | Khmer |
|---|---|---|---|---|---|---|---|
| *oy* as in b**oy** | | | ■ | | | | |
| *ow* as in h**ow** | ■ | | | | | | |

## *R*-CONTROLLED VOWELS

| Sound | Spanish | Vietnamese | Hmong | Cantonese | Haitian Creole | Korean | Khmer |
|---|---|---|---|---|---|---|---|
| *ir* as in b**ir**d | ■ | ■ | ■ | ■ | ■ | ■ | ■ |
| *ar* as in h**ar**d | ■ | ■ | ■ | ■ | ■ | ■ | ■ |
| *or* as in f**or**m | ■ | ■ | ■ | ■ | ■ | ■ | ■ |
| *air* as in h**air** | ■ | ■ | ■ | ■ | ■ | ■ | ■ |
| *ear* as in h**ear** | ■ | ■ | ■ | ■ | ■ | ■ | ■ |

## CONSONANT DIGRAPHS

| Sound | Spanish | Vietnamese | Hmong | Cantonese | Haitian Creole | Korean | Khmer |
|---|---|---|---|---|---|---|---|
| *sh* as in **sh**oe | ■* | ■ | | ■ | | | ■ |
| *ch* as in **ch**ain | | ■ | ■ | | | | |
| *th* as in **th**ink | ■ | ■ | ■ | ■ | | ■ | ■ |
| *ng* as in si**ng** | ■ | | ■ | | ■ | | |

## CONSONANT BLENDS

| Sound | Spanish | Vietnamese | Hmong | Cantonese | Haitian Creole | Korean | Khmer |
|---|---|---|---|---|---|---|---|
| *bl, tr, dr,* etc. (start of words) as in **bl**ack, **tr**ee, **dr**ess | | ■ | ■ | ■ | | ■ | |
| *ld, nt, rt,* etc. (end of words) as in co**ld**, te**nt**, sta**rt** | | ■ | ■ | ■ | ■ | ■ | ■ |

* Spanish speakers from Mexico or Central America who also speak Nahuatl or a Mayan language will be familiar with this sound, written as an x in words like *mixteca* (pronounced *mishteca*).

# Sound-Symbol Transfer (Phonics)

The following chart identifies sound-symbol transfer issues for four languages that use the roman alphabet. (The remaining three do not.) The symbol ■ identifies symbols which do not represent the corresponding sound in the writing system of the primary language.

## CONSONANTS

| Sound | Spanish | Vietnamese | Hmong | Haitian Creole |
|---|---|---|---|---|
| b as in bat | | | ■ | |
| c as in cat | | ■ | ■ | ■ |
| as in cent | | ■ | ■ | |
| d as in dog | | | | |
| f as in fish | | | | |
| g as in goat | | | ■ | |
| as in giant | ■ | | ■ | |
| h as in hen | ■ | | | |
| j as in jacket | ■ | ■ | ■ | |
| k as in kite | | | ■ | |
| l as in lemon | | | | |
| m as in moon | | | | |
| n as in nice | | | | |
| p as in pig | | | | |
| qu as in queen | ■ | | ■ | ■ |
| r as in rabbit | ■ | | ■ | |
| s as in sun | | | ■ | |
| t as in teen | | | ■ | |
| v as in video | ■ | | | |
| w as in wagon | | ■ | ■ | |
| x as in X ray | | ■ | ■ | ■ |
| y as in yo-yo | ■ | | | |
| z as in zebra | ■ | ■ | ■ | |

## CONSONANT DIAGRAPHS

| Sound | Spanish | Vietnamese | Hmong | Haitian Creole |
|---|---|---|---|---|
| sh as in shoe | ■ | | | |
| ch as in chair | | | | ■ |
| th as in think / as in that | ■ | | | ■ |

# VOWELS AND VOWEL PATTERNS

| Sound | Spanish | Vietnamese | Hmong | Haitian Creole |
|---|:---:|:---:|:---:|:---:|
| *a* as in b<u>a</u>t | ■ | | ■ | |
| *aCe* as in d<u>a</u>te | ■ | ■ | | |
| *ai* as in r<u>ai</u>n | ■ | ■ | ■ | ■ |
| *ay* as in d<u>ay</u> | ■ | | ■ | ■ |
| *au* as in <u>au</u>thor | ■ | ■ | ■ | ■ |
| *aw* as in s<u>aw</u> | ■ | ■ | ■ | ■ |
| *e* as in b<u>e</u>t | ■ | | ■ | ■ |
| *ee* as in s<u>ee</u>d | ■ | ■ | ■ | ■ |
| *ea* as in t<u>ea</u> | ■ | ■ | ■ | ■ |
| *ew* as in f<u>ew</u> | ■ | ■ | ■ | ■ |
| *i* as in s<u>i</u>t | ■ | | ■ | ■ |
| *iCe* as in p<u>i</u>pe | ■ | ■ | ■ | ■ |
| *o* as in h<u>o</u>t | ■ | | ■ | ■ |
| *o* as in r<u>o</u>de | ■ | ■ | ■ | ■ |
| *oo* as in m<u>oo</u>n | ■ | ■ | ■ | ■ |
| *oo* as in b<u>oo</u>k | ■ | | ■ | ■ |
| *oa* as in b<u>oa</u>t | ■ | ■ | ■ | ■ |
| *ow* as in r<u>ow</u> | ■ | ■ | ■ | ■ |
| *ow* as in h<u>ow</u> | ■ | ■ | ■ | ■ |
| *ou* as in s<u>ou</u>nd | ■ | ■ | ■ | ■ |
| *oi* as in b<u>oi</u>l | | | ■ | ■ |
| *oy* as in b<u>oy</u> | | ■ | ■ | ■ |
| *u* as in c<u>u</u>p | ■ | ■ | | ■ |
| *uCe* as in J<u>u</u>ne | ■ | ■ | | |
| *ui* as in s<u>ui</u>t | ■ | ■ | ■ | ■ |
| *ue* as in bl<u>ue</u> | ■ | ■ | ■ | ■ |
| *y* as in tr<u>y</u> | ■ | ■ | ■ | ■ |
| *ar* as in st<u>ar</u> | | | ■ | ■ |
| *er* as in f<u>er</u>n | ■ | | ■ | ■ |
| *ir* as in b<u>ir</u>d | ■ | | ■ | ■ |
| *or* as in t<u>or</u>n | ■ | | ■ | |
| *ur* as in b<u>ur</u>n | ■ | | ■ | |

# Word Study Transfer Support

## Spanish

English and Spanish share some basic linguistic characteristics, such as using word parts like prefixes and suffixes and changing verb forms. The example words below are not intended to be cognates, but words that illustrate the similar meaning of the word parts. Note that Haitian Creole, Cantonese, Hmong, and Vietnamese do not use word parts to construct new words in the same way that English does.

## PREFIXES

| English Word Part or Parts | English Example Words | Spanish Word Part or Parts | Spanish Example Words | Word Part Purpose |
|---|---|---|---|---|
| un-, non-, in-, dis- | unhappy<br>nonstop<br>incorrect<br>dislike | in-, des-/dis-<br>no plus the verb<br>sin plus the noun<br>or verb | infeliz, incorrecto<br>desconocido<br>disparejo<br>no gustar<br>sin parar | Means "not" |
| re- | redo | re- | rehacer | Means "again" |
| pre- | preteen | pre- | preescolar | Means "before" |

## SUFFIXES

| English Word Part or Parts | English Example Words | Spanish Word Part or Parts | Spanish Example Words | Word Part Purpose |
|---|---|---|---|---|
| -ful | powerful | -oso/a | poderoso/a | Means "with"; turns a noun into an adjective |
| -able | readable<br>likeable | -ible<br>-able | legible<br>agradable | Turns a verb into an adjective |
| -less | fearless<br>careless | sin plus the noun<br>prefix des- | sin miedo<br>descuidado | Means "without"; turns a noun into an adjective |
| -ness | happiness | -idad | felicidad | Turns an adjective into a noun |
| -ion/-tion, -ment | reaction<br>payment<br>amazement | -ción/-sión<br>verb stem + -o | reacción<br>conclusión<br>pago<br>asombro | Turns a verb into a noun |
| -ly | quickly | -mente | rápidamente | Turns an adjective into an adverb |

# Reading-Writing Connection

The literary works listed on pages A-36–43 provide high-interest **mentor texts** that you can use to inspire your students as you teach the different forms of writing. Use these texts to accentuate **writer's craft**:

- Read **strong beginnings** or **strong endings** to inspire students as they create their own beginnings and endings.
- Read paragraphs that **develop ideas** or demonstrate **strong organization**.
- Read from two different examples to **contrast voice** and **word choice**.
- Read from different authors to examine their **sentence style**.

## Narrative Books for Grades 9–10

***We Are All the Same: A Story of a Boy's Courage and a Mother's Love***
Jim Wooten, 2004

***Persepolis: The Story of a Childhood***
Marjane Satrapi, 2004

***The Catcher in the Rye***
J. D. Salinger, 1951

***The Burn Journals***
Brent Runyon, 2004

***Finding Their Stride: A Team of Young Runners and Their Season of Triumph***
Sally Pont, 2001

***Life of Pi: A Novel***
Yann Martel, 2002

***Crow Lake: A Novel***
Mary Lawson, 2003

***Truth and Bright Water: A Novel***
Thomas King, 2000

***The Secret Life of Bees***
Sue Monk Kidd, 2003

***Damage***
A. M. Jenkins, 2001

***A Painted House***
John Grisham, 2001

***Peace Like a River***
Leif Enger, 2002

***Grayson***
Lynne Cox, 2006

***My Losing Season***
Pat Conroy, 2002

***Hacker Cracker: A Journey from the Mean Streets of Brooklyn to the Frontiers of Cyberspace***
David Chanoff, Ejovi Nuwere, 2002

***March***
Geraldine Brooks, 2005

***The Road from Coorain***
Jill Ker Conway, 1989

***A Separate Peace***
John Knowles, 1959

***She Said Yes: The Unlikely Martyrdom of Cassie Bernall***
Misty Bernall, 1999

***A Killing in Plymouth Colony***
Carol Otis Hurst, Rebecca Otis, 2003

**Legend Days: Part 1 of the Ghost Horse Cycle**
Jamake Highwater, 1984

**No Promises in the Wind**
Irene Hunt, 1970

**Abraham Lincoln: Letters from a Slave Girl (Dear Mr. President)**
Andrea Davis Pinkney, 2001

**The Examination**
Malcolm Bosse, 1994

**Cleopatra VII: Daughter of the Nile, Egypt, 57 B.C. (The Royal Diaries)**
Kristiana Gregory, 1999

**The Shining Company**
Rosemary Sutcliff, 1992

**My Brother Sam Is Dead**
James Lincoln Collier, 1984

**Notes From the Midnight Driver**
Jordan Sonnenblick, 2006

**Over a Thousand Hills I Walk with You**
Hanna Jansen, Elizabeth D. Crawford, 2006

**Growing Up in Slavery: Stories of Young Slaves as Told by Themselves**
Yuval Taylor, 2005

**That Was Then, This Is Now**
S. E. Hinton, 1971

**Between a Rock and a Hard Place**
Aron Ralston, 2004

**Lost Moon: the Perilous Voyage of Apollo 13**
Jim Lovell, 1994

**Pilgrim at Tinker Creek**
Annie Dillard, 1974

**Shoeless Joe**
W. P. Kinsella, 1982

**Teen Angst? Naaah . . . A Quasi-autobiography**
Ned Vizzini, 2000

**Rosa Parks: My Story**
Rosa Parks, Jim Haskins, 1992

**Bruce Lee: The Celebrated Life of the Golden Dragon**
Bruce Lee, John R. Little, 2000

**Barrio Boy**
Ernesto Galarza, 1971

**Shabanu: Daughter of the Wind**
Suzanne Fisher Staples, 1989

## Expository Books for Grades 9–10

**Police Lab: How Forensic Science Tracks Down and Convicts Criminals**
David Owen, 2002

**Vietnam: A War on Two Fronts**
Sidney Lens, 1990

**The Race to Save the Lord God Bird**
Phillip Hoose, 2004

**Getting Away with Murder**
Chris Crowe, 2003

**Photo by Brady: A Picture of the Civil War**
Jennifer Armstrong, 2005

**In the Land of White Death**
Valerian Albanov, 2000

**When I Was Puerto Rican**
Esmeralda Santiago, 1993

**Zarafa: A Giraffe's True Story, from Deep in Africa to the Heart of Paris**
Michael Allin, 1998

**The Endurance: Shackleton's Legendary Antarctic Expedition**
Caroline Alexander, 1998

**George Washington, Spymaster: How the Americans Outspied the British and Won the Revolutionary War**
Thomas B. Allen, 2004

**With Courage and Cloth: Winning the Fight for a Woman's Right to Vote**
Ann Bausum, 2004

**Wake Up Our Souls: A Celebration of African American Artists**
Tonya Bolden, 2004

**Flags of Our Fathers: Heroes of Iwo Jima (Young Reader's Abridged Edition)**
James Bradley, Ron Powers, Michael French, 2003

**Close to Shore: The Terrifying Shark Attacks of 1916**
Michael Capuzzo, 2003

**Counting Coup: A True Story of Basketball and Honor on the Little Big Horn**
Larry Colton, 2000

**Out of Harm's Way**
Terry Crisp, 1997

**The Day the World Came to Town: 9/11 in Gander, Newfoundland**
Jim DeFede, 2002

**Seeing in the Dark: How Backyard Stargazers Are Probing Deep Space and Guarding Earth from Interplanetary Peril**
Timothy Ferris, 2002

**Ben Franklin's Almanac: Being a True Account of the Good Gentleman's Life**
Candace Fleming, 2003

**In Defense of Liberty: The Story of America's Bill of Rights**
Russell Freedman, 2003

**Coal: A Human History**
Barbara Freese, 2003

**Hole in My Life**
Jack Gantos, 2002

**Meltdown: A Race Against Nuclear Disaster at Three Mile Island: A Reporter's Story**
Wilborn Hampton, 2001

**Fields of Fury: The American Civil War**
James M. McPherson, 2002

**Stiff: The Curious Lives of Human Cadavers**
Mary Roach, 2003

**Working Fire: The Making of an Accidental Fireman**
Zac Unger, 2004

**The Hot Zone**
Richard Preston, 1994

**Motorcycle: Evolution, Design, Passion**
Mick Walker, 2006

**Buzz: The Intimate Bond Between Humans and Insects**
Josie Glausiusz, Volker Steger, 2004

**Streetball: All the Ballers, Moves, Slams, & Shine**
Chris Palmer, 2004

**Dream Job Profiles**
Donna Hayden Green, 2006

**The Driving Book: Everything New Drivers Need to Know but Don't Know to Ask**
Karen Gravelle, Helen Flook, 2005

**Making the Most of High School: Success Secrets for Freshmen**
Carol Carter, 2004

**Yes Yes Y'All: The Experience Music Project Oral History of Hip-Hop's First Decade**
Jim Fricke, Charlie Ahearn, 2002

**Teens Cook: How to Cook What You Want to Eat**
Megan Carle, Jill Carle, Judi Carle, Jessica Boone, 2004

**Chess (From First Moves to Checkmate)**
Daniel King, 2001

**In a Different Light**
Carolyn Meyer, 1996

**We Just Want to Live Here: A Palestinian Teenager, an Israeli Teenager--An Unlikely Friendship**
Amal Rifa'i, Odelia Ainbinde, Sylke Tempel, 2003

**They Broke the Law—You Be the Judge: True Cases of Teen Crime**
Thomas A. Jacobs, 2003

**How Rude! The Teenagers' Guide to Good Manners, Proper Behavior, and Not Grossing People Out**
Alex J. Packer, 1997

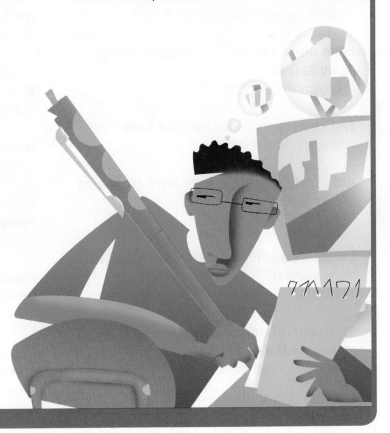

## Persuasive Books for Grades 9–10

*You Can Save the Animals: 251 Simple Ways to Stop Thoughtless Cruelty*
Ingrid Newkirk, 1999

*Save Our Land, Save Our Towns: A Plan for Pennsylvania*
Thomas Hylton, Blair Seitz, 2000

*Eating to Save the Earth: Food Choices for a Healthy Planet*
Linda Riebel, Ken Jacobsen, 2002

*Inside Dope: How Drugs Are the Biggest Threat to Sports, Why You Should Care, and What Can Be Done About Them*
Richard W. Pound, 2006

*Tons of Trash: Why You Should Recycle and What Happens When You Do*
Joan Rattner Heilman, Nancy Schill, 1992

*101 Reasons to Love the Red Sox: And 10 Reasons to Hate the Yankees*
David Green, 2005

*Let's Clear the Air: 10 Reasons Not to Start Smoking*
Lobster Press, 2007

*The Loch Ness Monster: The Evidence*
Steuart Campbell, 2004

*AIDS (Introducing Issues with Opposing Viewpoints)*
Andrea C. Nakaya, 2005

*Gangs (Introducing Issues with Opposing Viewpoints)*
Scott Barbour, 2005

*Gun Control (Introducing Issues With Opposing Viewpoints)*
Beth Rosenthal, 2006

*Stop Global Warming: The Solution Is You!*
Laurie David, 2006

*50 Ways to Save the Ocean*
David Helvarg, Philippe Cousteau, Jim Toomey, 2006

*Ultimate Weight Solution for Teens: The 7 Keys to Weight Freedom*
Jay McGraw, Phil McGraw, 2003

*Pollution: Problems & Solutions*
National Wildlife Federation, 1998

*Conflict Resolution: The Win-Win Solution*
Carolyn Casey, 2001

*Cosmetic Surgery for Teens: Choices and Consequences*
Kathleen Winkler, 2003

*Teens Can Make It Happen: Nine Steps for Success*
Stedman Graham, 2000

*Friends, Cliques, and Peer Pressure: Be True to Yourself*
Christine Wickert Koubek, 2002

*Teen Fads: Fun, Foolish, or Fatal?*
Ray Spangenburg, Kit Moser, 2003

*Propaganda: Understanding the Power of Persuasion*
Ray Spangenburg, Kit Moser, Diane Moser, 2002

*Tattooing and Body Piercing: Understanding the Risks*
Kathleen Winkler, 2002

*The Debate over Human Cloning: A Pro/Con Issue*
David Goodnough, 2003

## Books About Responding to Literature—Grades 9–10

**American Indian Themes in Young Adult Literature**
Paulette F. Molin, 2005

**Theme-Sets for Secondary Students: How to Scaffold Core Literature**
Jeannine D. Richison, Anita C. Hernandez, Marcia J. Carter, 2006

**The Most Wonderful Books: Writers on Discovering the Pleasures of Reading**
Michael Dorris, Emilie Buchwald, 1997

**Books I Read When I Was Young: The Favorite Books of Famous People**
M. Jerry Weiss, Bernice E. Cullinan, and National Council of Teachers of English Commission on Literature, 1980

**Characters in Children's Literature**
Raymond E. Jones, 1997

**Characters in Young Adult Literature**
John T. Gillespie, 1997

**Traveling Literary America: A Complete Guide to Literary Landmarks**
B. J. Welborn, 2005

**Words About Pictures: The Narrative Art of Children's Picture Books**
Perry Nodelman, 1989

**The Young Actor's Book of Improvisation: Dramatic Situations Based on Literature, Plays, and Films: Ages 12-16**
Sandra Caruso, Susan Kosoff, 1998

**Romeo & Juliet: The Contemporary Film, The Classic Play**
William Shakespeare, 1996

**Guts: The True Stories Behind Hatchet and the Brian Books**
Gary Paulsen, 2001

**Brian's Song (Screenplay)**
William Blinn, 1983

**Drama for Reading and Performance: Collection 1**
Aurand Harris, Horton Foote, Gary Soto, and Wendy Wasserstein, 2000

**Classic Readers Theatre for Young Adults**
Suzanne I. Barchers, Jennifer L. Kroll, 2002

**Building Literature Circles**
Jimmie Aydelott, 2003

**Making Literature Circles Come Alive: A Time-Saving Resource**
Amy Hamra, 2003

**Discovering Florida through Literature**
Elizabeth Knowles, Martha Smith, 2002

**Sketching Stories, Stretching Minds: Responding Visually to Literature**
Phyllis Whitin, 1996

**Ready-To-Tell Tales (American Storytelling)**
David Holt, 1995

**The Annotated Night Before Christmas: A Collection Of Sequels, Parodies, And Imitations Of Clement Moore's Immortal Ballad About Santa Claus**
Martin Gardner, 2005

**Fact, Fiction, and Folklore in Harry Potter's World: An Unofficial Guide**
George W. Beahm, Tim Kirk, Britton McDaniel, 2005

**Beauty: A Retelling of the Story of Beauty and the Beast**
Robin McKinley, 1978

**Dear Author: Students Write About the Books That Changed Their Lives**
Weekly Reader's Read Magazine, 1995

## Books About Creative Writing—Grades 9–10

**Whatcha Mean, What's a Zine?**
Esther Pearl Watson, Mark Todd, 2006

**The DC Comics Guide to Writing Comics**
Dennis O'Neil, 2001

**Prepare to Board! Creating Story and Characters for Animation Features and Shorts**
Nancy Beiman, 2007

**A Teen's Guide to Getting Published: Publishing for Profit, Recognition And Academic Success**
Jessica Dunn, Danielle Dunn, 2006

**Teen Ink Love and Relationships (Teen Ink Series)**
Stephanie Meyer, 2002

**Twice Told: Original Stories Inspired by Original Artwork**
Scott Hunt, 2006

**Be a Writer: Your Guide to the Writing Life (Be a Writer)**
Steve Peha, 2006

**Be a Better Writer: Power Tools for Young Writers! Essential Tips, Exercises and Techniques for Aspiring Writers**
Steve Peha, 2006

**Beyond Roses Are Red Violets Are Blue: A Practical Guide for Helping Students Write Free Verse**
Benjamin Green, Anita Punla, 1996

**Image to Word: Art and Creative Writing**
Kathleen Walsh-Piper, 2003

**Like It Was: A Complete Guide to Writing Oral History**
Cynthia Stokes Brown, 1988

**Nonstandardized Quests: 500+ Writing Prompts That Matter**
David E. LeCount, 2002

**Web Design for Teens**
Maneesh Sethi, 2004

**A Fire in My Hands: Revised and Expanded Edition**
Gary Soto, 2006

**Out Of The Dust**
Karen Hesse, 1997

**Names Will Never Hurt Me**
Jaime Adoff, 2004

**Fe-Vers: Feeling Verses for Teens**
Cynthia Blomquist Gustavson, 2006

**Red Hot Salsa: Bilingual Poems on Being Young and Latino in the United States**
Lori Marie Carlson, 2005

**I Am the Darker Brother: An Anthology of Modern Poems by African Americans**
Arnold Adoff, Benny Andrews, 1997

**Necessary Noise: Stories About Our Families as They Really Are**
Michael Cart, 2006

**An Island Like You: Stories of the Barrio**
Melanie Kroupa, 1995

**Big City Cool: Short Stories About Urban Youth**
M. Jerry Weiss, Helen S. Weiss, 2002

**No Easy Answers: Short Stories About Teenagers Making Tough Choices**
Donald R. Gallo, 1999

**America Street: A Multicultural Anthology of Stories**
Anne Mazer, 1993

## Reference Books for Grades 9–10

**The American Heritage High School Dictionary: Fourth Edition**
Houghton Mifflin, 2007

**The American Heritage Essential Student Thesaurus**
Houghton Mifflin, 2003

**100 Research Topic Guides for Students**
Barbara Wood Borne, 1996

**100 More Research Topic Guides for Students**
Dana McDougald, 1999

**On Speaking Well**
Peggy Noonan, 1999

**Painless Speaking**
Mary Elizabeth, 2003

**The New York Public Library Student's Desk Reference**
Frommer's, New York Public Library, Press Stonesong, 1995

**An Encyclopedia of the History of Technology**
Ian McNeil, 1996

**Building the World, Volumes 1 and 2: An Encyclopedia of the Great Engineering Projects in History**
Frank Davidson, Kathleen Lusk-Brooke, 2006

**Mightier Than the Sword: How the News Media Have Shaped American History**
Rodger Streitmatter, 1998

**The New York Public Library Amazing African American History: A Book of Answers for Kids**
The New York Public Library and Diane Patrick, 1997

**American Heritage Science Dictionary**
Houghton Mifflin, 2005

**Technology in World History**
Oxford, 2005

**Encyclopedia of American Folklife**
Ed. J. Simon Bronner, 2006

**Unexplained: An Encyclopedia of Curious Phenomena, Strange Superstitions, and Ancient Mysteries**
Judy Allen, 2006

**National Geographic Atlas of the World**
National Geographic, 2005

**Atlas of the United States**
Oxford, 2006

**Opposing Viewpoints in American History: Volumes 1 and 2**
William Dudley, 2007

**The World Book Encyclopedia of People and Places**
Ed. Thomas S. Richardson, 2007

**Timelines of History**
Grolier, 2005

**Encyclopedia of Architectural and Engineering Feats**
Donald Langmead, Christine Garnaut, 2001

**You Are Here: High School Internet Guide**
Eric Leebow, 2001

**Find It Online, Fourth Edition: The Complete Guide to Online Research**
Alan M. Schlein, 2004

**The New York Times Almanac 2007**
John W. Wright, 2006

# Scope and Sequence

| | Grades 2 | 3 | 4 | 5 | 6 | 7 | 8 | 9 | 10 | 11 | 12 |
|---|---|---|---|---|---|---|---|---|---|---|---|
| **FORMS OF WRITING** | | | | | | | | | | | |
| **Descriptive Writing** | | | | | | | | | | | |
| paragraph | ■ | ■ | ■ | ■ | ■ | ■ | ■ | | | | |
| essay | | ■ | ■ | ■ | ■ | ■ | ■ | | | | |
| **Narrative Writing** | | | | | | | | | | | |
| paragraph | ■ | ■ | ■ | ■ | ■ | ■ | ■ | | | | |
| personal narrative | ■ | ■ | ■ | ■ | ■ | ■ | ■ | ■ | ■ | ■ | ■ |
| biographical narrative | | | | | ■ | | ■ | ■ | | | |
| phase autobiography | | | | | | ■ | | | | ■ | |
| historical narrative | | | | | | | | | | ■ | |
| reflective narrative | | | | | | | | | | ■ | |
| college entrance essay | | | | | | | | | | | ■ |
| **Expository Writing** | | | | | | | | | | | |
| paragraph | ■ | ■ | ■ | ■ | ■ | ■ | ■ | | | | |
| letter | ■ | | | | | | | | | | |
| essay | | ■ | ■ | ■ | | | | | | | |
| classification essay | | | | | ■ | | ■ | | | | |
| how-to/process essay | | | | | ■ | | ■ | | | | |
| cause-and-effect essay | | | | | | ■ | | | ■ | | |
| comparison-contrast essay | | | | | | ■ | ■ | | | ■ | |
| comparison essay | | | | | | | | ■ | | | |
| concept definition essay | | | | | | | | | ■ | | |
| informative article | | | | | | | | | | ■ | |
| opposing ideas essay | | | | | | | | | | | ■ |
| analysis essay | | | | | | | | | | | ■ |
| **Persuasive Writing** | | | | | | | | | | | |
| paragraph | ■ | ■ | ■ | ■ | ■ | ■ | ■ | | | | |
| letter | ■ | ■ | | | | | ■ | | | | |
| essay | | | ■ | ■ | ■ | | | | | | |
| promote a cause | | | | | ■ | | | | | | |
| problem-solution essay | | | | | | ■ | | ■ | | | |

| | Grades 2 | 3 | 4 | 5 | 6 | 7 | 8 | 9 | 10 | 11 | 12 |
|---|---|---|---|---|---|---|---|---|---|---|---|
| **Persuasive Writing (continued)** | | | | | | | | | | | |
| editorial | | | | | | ■ | | | ■ | ■ | ■ |
| personal commentary | | | | | | | ■ | | | | |
| argumentative essay | | | | | | | | ■ | ■ | ■ | ■ |
| **Response to Texts** | | | | | | | | | | | |
| paragraph | ■ | ■ | ■ | ■ | ■ | ■ | ■ | | | | |
| book review | ■ | ■ | ■ | ■ | ■ | ■ | | | | | |
| respond to a poem | ■ | ■ | ■ | ■ | | | | ■ | ■ | ■ | |
| respond to a nonfiction article | | | ■ | ■ | | | | | ■ | | |
| respond to a biography | | | ■ | | | | | | | | |
| respond to a textbook | | | ■ | | | | | | | | |
| respond to a tall tale | | | ■ | | | | | | | | |
| respond to a quotation | | | | ■ | | | | | | | |
| respond to an anecdote | | | | ■ | | | | | | | |
| respond to a magazine article | | | | | ■ | | | | | | |
| respond to an expository text | | | | | | ■ | ■ | | | | ■ |
| analysis of a theme | | | | | | | ■ | | ■ | ■ | ■ |
| respond to an essay | | | | | | | | ■ | | | |
| respond to a short story | | | | | | | | ■ | | ■ | |
| respond to a novel | | | | | | | | | | | ■ |
| **Creative Writing** | | | | | | | | | | | |
| story | ■ | ■ | ■ | ■ | ■ | ■ | ■ | ■ | ■ | ■ | ■ |
| poem | ■ | ■ | ■ | ■ | ■ | ■ | ■ | ■ | ■ | ■ | ■ |
| play/script | ■ | ■ | ■ | ■ | | | | | ■ | ■ | ■ |
| **Research Writing** | | | | | | | | | | | |
| research report | ■ | ■ | ■ | ■ | ■ | ■ | ■ | | | | |
| MLA research paper | | | | | | | | ■ | ■ | ■ | ■ |
| multimedia presentation | ■ | ■ | ■ | ■ | ■ | ■ | ■ | ■ | ■ | ■ | ■ |
| oral presentation | ■ | ■ | ■ | ■ | ■ | ■ | ■ | ■ | ■ | ■ | ■ |
| **Writing for Assessment** | | | | | | | | | | | |
| narrative writing | ■ | ■ | ■ | ■ | ■ | ■ | ■ | ■ | ■ | ■ | ■ |
| expository writing | ■ | ■ | ■ | ■ | ■ | ■ | ■ | ■ | ■ | ■ | ■ |
| persuasive writing | ■ | ■ | ■ | ■ | ■ | ■ | ■ | ■ | ■ | ■ | ■ |
| response writing | | | | | | ■ | ■ | ■ | ■ | ■ | ■ |

| | Grades | 2 | 3 | 4 | 5 | 6 | 7 | 8 | 9 | 10 | 11 | 12 |
|---|---|---|---|---|---|---|---|---|---|---|---|---|

## THE WRITING PROCESS

### Prewriting

**Select a Topic**

| | 2 | 3 | 4 | 5 | 6 | 7 | 8 | 9 | 10 | 11 | 12 |
|---|---|---|---|---|---|---|---|---|---|---|---|
| make a list | ■ | ■ | ■ | ■ | ■ | ■ | ■ | ■ | ■ | ■ | ■ |
| create a cluster/web | ■ | ■ | ■ | ■ | ■ | ■ | ■ | ■ | ■ | ■ | ■ |
| brainstorm | ■ | ■ | ■ | ■ | ■ | ■ | ■ | ■ | ■ | ■ | ■ |
| use sentence starters | | ■ | ■ | ■ | ■ | ■ | ■ | ■ | | | |
| freewrite | | ■ | ■ | ■ | ■ | ■ | ■ | ■ | ■ | ■ | ■ |
| create a line diagram | | | ■ | ■ | | ■ | | | | | |
| take notes | | | ■ | ■ | | ■ | | | | | |
| create a people chart | | | | ■ | | | | ■ | | ■ | |
| create a media grid | | | | | ■ | | ■ | | | | |

**Gather Details**

| | 2 | 3 | 4 | 5 | 6 | 7 | 8 | 9 | 10 | 11 | 12 |
|---|---|---|---|---|---|---|---|---|---|---|---|
| draw | ■ | ■ | | | | | | | | | |
| use sentence starters | ■ | | ■ | | | ■ | | | | | |
| create a sensory/details chart | ■ | ■ | ■ | ■ | ■ | ■ | ■ | ■ | | | |
| use a map | ■ | ■ | | | | | | | | ■ | |
| create a time line | ■ | ■ | ■ | ■ | ■ | ■ | ■ | ■ | ■ | ■ | |
| create a 5 *W*s chart/list | ■ | ■ | ■ | ■ | ■ | ■ | ■ | ■ | ■ | | |
| answer questions | ■ | ■ | ■ | ■ | ■ | ■ | ■ | ■ | ■ | ■ | |
| create a T-chart | ■ | ■ | | ■ | | | | ■ | ■ | ■ | ■ |
| create a gathering grid/chart | ■ | ■ | ■ | ■ | ■ | ■ | ■ | ■ | ■ | ■ | ■ |
| create a chart/cluster | ■ | ■ | ■ | ■ | ■ | ■ | ■ | ■ | ■ | ■ | ■ |
| list topics/ideas | ■ | ■ | ■ | ■ | ■ | ■ | ■ | ■ | ■ | ■ | ■ |
| create a character chart | | ■ | ■ | | | ■ | | ■ | | | |
| freewrite | | ■ | ■ | | | ■ | | ■ | ■ | ■ | |
| take notes | | ■ | ■ | ■ | ■ | ■ | ■ | ■ | ■ | ■ | ■ |
| create a table diagram | | | ■ | ■ | ■ | ■ | ■ | | | | |
| create a cause-effect chart | | | | | | ■ | | ■ | ■ | | |
| create a problem-solution chart | | | | | | ■ | | ■ | | | |
| create a before-and-after chart | | | | | | | ■ | ■ | ■ | | |

| Grades | 2 | 3 | 4 | 5 | 6 | 7 | 8 | 9 | 10 | 11 | 12 |
|---|---|---|---|---|---|---|---|---|---|---|---|
| **Use Research Skills** | | | | | | | | | | | |
| understand the parts of a book | ■ | ■ | ■ | ■ | ■ | ■ | ■ | ■ | ■ | ■ | ■ |
| use diagrams, charts, time lines, maps | ■ | ■ | ■ | ■ | ■ | ■ | ■ | ■ | ■ | ■ | ■ |
| take notes/summarize | ■ | ■ | ■ | ■ | ■ | ■ | ■ | ■ | ■ | ■ | ■ |
| use computer catalogs | ■ | ■ | ■ | ■ | ■ | ■ | ■ | ■ | ■ | ■ | ■ |
| use periodicals | ■ | ■ | ■ | ■ | ■ | ■ | ■ | ■ | ■ | ■ | ■ |
| interview experts | ■ | ■ | ■ | ■ | ■ | ■ | ■ | ■ | ■ | ■ | ■ |
| conduct online research | ■ | ■ | ■ | ■ | ■ | ■ | ■ | ■ | ■ | ■ | ■ |
| use reference texts | ■ | ■ | ■ | ■ | ■ | ■ | ■ | ■ | ■ | ■ | ■ |
| use a library | ■ | ■ | ■ | ■ | ■ | ■ | ■ | ■ | ■ | ■ | ■ |
| formulate open-ended questions | ■ | ■ | ■ | ■ | ■ | ■ | ■ | ■ | ■ | ■ | ■ |
| create a works cited list/bibliography | ■ | ■ | ■ | ■ | ■ | ■ | ■ | ■ | ■ | ■ | ■ |
| evaluate sources | ■ | ■ | ■ | ■ | ■ | ■ | ■ | ■ | ■ | ■ | ■ |
| use primary vs. secondary sources | | | | ■ | ■ | ■ | ■ | ■ | ■ | ■ | ■ |
| **Organize Details** | | | | | | | | | | | |
| create a sequence chart | ■ | ■ | | | | ■ | | | | | |
| create a cluster/details web | ■ | ■ | | | ■ | | | | | ■ | ■ |
| list topics/ideas | | ■ | ■ | ■ | ■ | ■ | ■ | ■ | ■ | ■ | ■ |
| outline topics/ideas | ■ | ■ | ■ | ■ | ■ | ■ | ■ | ■ | ■ | ■ | ■ |
| create a chart | ■ | ■ | ■ | ■ | ■ | ■ | ■ | ■ | ■ | ■ | ■ |
| put events/ideas in time order | ■ | ■ | ■ | ■ | ■ | ■ | ■ | ■ | ■ | ■ | ■ |
| create a plot/setting/character chart | | ■ | ■ | ■ | | | ■ | | ■ | ■ | |
| create a Venn diagram | | ■ | | | | ■ | | ■ | | ■ | ■ |
| create a story/plot line | | ■ | | | | | ■ | ■ | ■ | ■ | ■ |
| create a sensory chart | | | ■ | | ■ | | | | | | |
| create a collection sheet/grid | | | ■ | ■ | | | | ■ | ■ | | |
| use note cards | | | ■ | ■ | ■ | ■ | ■ | ■ | ■ | ■ | ■ |
| create a table diagram | | | | ■ | ■ | ■ | | | | | |
| create a line diagram | | | | | ■ | | | ■ | | | |
| **Drafting** | | | | | | | | | | | |
| **Beginning Paragraphs** | | | | | | | | | | | |
| connect with the reader | ■ | ■ | ■ | ■ | ■ | ■ | ■ | ■ | ■ | ■ | ■ |
| write a main idea/topic sentence | ■ | ■ | ■ | ■ | ■ | ■ | ■ | ■ | ■ | ■ | ■ |
| write a position statement | ■ | ■ | ■ | ■ | ■ | ■ | ■ | ■ | ■ | ■ | ■ |

| Grades | 2 | 3 | 4 | 5 | 6 | 7 | 8 | 9 | 10 | 11 | 12 |
|---|---|---|---|---|---|---|---|---|---|---|---|
| **Beginning Paragraphs (continued)** | | | | | | | | | | | |
| incorporate dialogue | ■ | ■ | ■ | ■ | ■ | ■ | ■ | ■ | ■ | ■ | ■ |
| write a focus statement | | ■ | ■ | ■ | ■ | ■ | ■ | ■ | ■ | ■ | ■ |
| write a thesis statement | | ■ | ■ | ■ | ■ | ■ | ■ | ■ | ■ | ■ | ■ |
| incorporate a quotation | | | | | | ■ | ■ | ■ | ■ | | |
| ask a question | ■ | ■ | ■ | ■ | | ■ | ■ | ■ | ■ | ■ | |
| include an interesting fact | ■ | | ■ | ■ | | ■ | ■ | ■ | ■ | ■ | |
| specify time and place | ■ | | | ■ | | ■ | ■ | | ■ | ■ | |
| include background information | | ■ | | | | ■ | ■ | ■ | ■ | ■ | |
| begin with a surprising statement | | | | ■ | ■ | | | | ■ | ■ | |
| include an anecdote | | | | | | ■ | | ■ | ■ | ■ | |
| **Middle Paragraphs** | | | | | | | | | | | |
| make comparisons | ■ | ■ | ■ | ■ | ■ | ■ | ■ | ■ | ■ | ■ | ■ |
| incorporate dialogue | ■ | ■ | ■ | ■ | ■ | ■ | ■ | ■ | ■ | ■ | ■ |
| include supporting details/reasons | ■ | ■ | ■ | ■ | ■ | ■ | ■ | ■ | ■ | ■ | ■ |
| include sensory details | ■ | ■ | ■ | ■ | ■ | ■ | ■ | ■ | ■ | ■ | ■ |
| incorporate personal feelings/details | ■ | ■ | ■ | ■ | ■ | ■ | ■ | ■ | ■ | ■ | ■ |
| include specific details | ■ | ■ | ■ | ■ | ■ | ■ | ■ | ■ | ■ | ■ | ■ |
| write topic sentences | ■ | ■ | ■ | ■ | ■ | ■ | ■ | ■ | ■ | ■ | ■ |
| use action words | ■ | ■ | ■ | ■ | ■ | ■ | ■ | ■ | ■ | ■ | ■ |
| use transitions | ■ | ■ | ■ | ■ | ■ | ■ | ■ | ■ | ■ | ■ | ■ |
| include facts | ■ | ■ | ■ | ■ | | ■ | ■ | ■ | ■ | ■ | |
| include a point-by-point discussion | | ■ | | ■ | | ■ | ■ | ■ | ■ | | |
| counter objections | | ■ | | ■ | | ■ | ■ | ■ | ■ | ■ | ■ |
| paraphrase information | | ■ | ■ | ■ | ■ | ■ | ■ | ■ | ■ | ■ | ■ |
| build to a climax/high point | | ■ | ■ | ■ | ■ | ■ | ■ | ■ | ■ | ■ | ■ |
| incorporate quotations | | | ■ | ■ | ■ | ■ | ■ | ■ | ■ | ■ | ■ |
| show, don't tell | | | ■ | | | ■ | ■ | ■ | ■ | | |
| explain terms | | | | | | | ■ | ■ | ■ | | |
| include anecdotes | | | | | | | ■ | ■ | ■ | ■ | ■ |
| build suspense | | | | | | | | ■ | ■ | ■ | ■ |
| incorporate statistics | | | | | | | | ■ | ■ | ■ | ■ |

| | Grades | 2 | 3 | 4 | 5 | 6 | 7 | 8 | 9 | 10 | 11 | 12 |
|---|---|---|---|---|---|---|---|---|---|---|---|---|

## Ending Paragraphs

| | 2 | 3 | 4 | 5 | 6 | 7 | 8 | 9 | 10 | 11 | 12 |
|---|---|---|---|---|---|---|---|---|---|---|---|
| include interesting facts | ■ | | ■ | ■ | | ■ | ■ | ■ | | | |
| include a call to action | ■ | ■ | ■ | ■ | ■ | ■ | ■ | ■ | ■ | ■ | |
| write a concluding statement | ■ | ■ | ■ | ■ | ■ | ■ | ■ | ■ | ■ | ■ | ■ |
| add a final thought/insight | ■ | ■ | ■ | ■ | ■ | ■ | ■ | ■ | ■ | ■ | ■ |
| reflect on experiences | ■ | ■ | ■ | ■ | ■ | ■ | ■ | ■ | ■ | ■ | ■ |
| restate a thesis/focus statement | | ■ | ■ | ■ | ■ | ■ | ■ | ■ | ■ | ■ | ■ |
| revisit a theme | | ■ | | | | | ■ | ■ | | | |
| refer to the beginning | | ■ | | ■ | | ■ | ■ | | ■ | ■ | |
| include a direct quotation | | ■ | ■ | ■ | ■ | ■ | ■ | ■ | ■ | ■ | ■ |
| restate a position | | ■ | ■ | ■ | ■ | ■ | ■ | ■ | ■ | ■ | |
| summarize ideas | | ■ | ■ | ■ | ■ | ■ | ■ | ■ | ■ | ■ | ■ |
| propose a solution | | | | | ■ | ■ | ■ | ■ | ■ | | |
| include a final scene | | | | | | ■ | ■ | ■ | | ■ | |
| emphasize a key idea | | | | | | ■ | ■ | | ■ | | ■ |
| add new information | | | | | | | ■ | ■ | | | |

## Revising

### Focus and Coherence

| | 2 | 3 | 4 | 5 | 6 | 7 | 8 | 9 | 10 | 11 | 12 |
|---|---|---|---|---|---|---|---|---|---|---|---|
| focus on one main idea | ■ | ■ | ■ | ■ | ■ | ■ | ■ | ■ | ■ | ■ | ■ |
| eliminate unnecessary information | ■ | ■ | ■ | ■ | ■ | ■ | ■ | ■ | ■ | ■ | ■ |
| connect ideas | | ■ | ■ | ■ | ■ | ■ | ■ | ■ | ■ | ■ | ■ |
| clarify supporting information | | ■ | ■ | ■ | ■ | ■ | ■ | ■ | ■ | ■ | ■ |
| improve coherence | | ■ | ■ | ■ | ■ | ■ | ■ | ■ | ■ | ■ | ■ |
| revise the thesis statement | | ■ | ■ | ■ | ■ | ■ | ■ | ■ | ■ | ■ | ■ |
| include a clear introduction/conclusion | | ■ | ■ | ■ | ■ | ■ | ■ | ■ | ■ | ■ | ■ |

### Organization

| | 2 | 3 | 4 | 5 | 6 | 7 | 8 | 9 | 10 | 11 | 12 |
|---|---|---|---|---|---|---|---|---|---|---|---|
| order ideas/details | ■ | ■ | ■ | ■ | ■ | ■ | ■ | | | | |
| check time order | ■ | ■ | ■ | ■ | ■ | ■ | ■ | | | | |
| check order of importance | | ■ | ■ | ■ | ■ | ■ | ■ | ■ | ■ | | |
| check logical order | ■ | ■ | ■ | ■ | ■ | ■ | ■ | ■ | | ■ | ■ |
| check overall organization | ■ | ■ | ■ | ■ | ■ | ■ | ■ | ■ | ■ | ■ | ■ |
| use transitional words and phrases | ■ | ■ | ■ | ■ | ■ | ■ | ■ | ■ | ■ | ■ | ■ |
| include a clear beginning/middle/ending | ■ | ■ | ■ | ■ | ■ | ■ | ■ | ■ | ■ | ■ | ■ |
| include line breaks/indents | | ■ | | | | | | ■ | ■ | ■ | |

| | Grades | 2 | 3 | 4 | 5 | 6 | 7 | 8 | 9 | 10 | 11 | 12 |
|---|---|---|---|---|---|---|---|---|---|---|---|---|

**Organization (continued)**

| | 2 | 3 | 4 | 5 | 6 | 7 | 8 | 9 | 10 | 11 | 12 |
|---|---|---|---|---|---|---|---|---|---|---|---|
| use clear topic sentences | | ■ | | | | ■ | ■ | | ■ | ■ | ■ |
| build to a high point | | | | | | ■ | ■ | ■ | ■ | ■ | |
| use key ideas | | | | | | | | | ■ | ■ | ■ |

**Development of Ideas**

| | 2 | 3 | 4 | 5 | 6 | 7 | 8 | 9 | 10 | 11 | 12 |
|---|---|---|---|---|---|---|---|---|---|---|---|
| write clear topic sentences | ■ | ■ | ■ | ■ | ■ | ■ | ■ | | | | |
| add supporting details | ■ | ■ | ■ | ■ | ■ | ■ | ■ | | | | |
| add sensory details | ■ | ■ | ■ | ■ | ■ | ■ | ■ | | ■ | ■ | ■ |
| add dialogue | | ■ | ■ | ■ | ■ | ■ | ■ | | | | |
| delete unnecessary details | | ■ | ■ | ■ | ■ | ■ | ■ | | | | |
| show, don't tell | | ■ | | | | ■ | ■ | ■ | ■ | | |
| add specific reasons | | ■ | | | | ■ | | | ■ | ■ | ■ |
| write clear focus statements | | | ■ | ■ | ■ | ■ | ■ | | | | |
| write a clear thesis statement | | | | | | ■ | | | ■ | ■ | ■ |
| use sources | | | | | | ■ | ■ | ■ | ■ | | |
| include a conflict | | | | | | ■ | ■ | ■ | ■ | ■ | ■ |

**Voice**

| | 2 | 3 | 4 | 5 | 6 | 7 | 8 | 9 | 10 | 11 | 12 |
|---|---|---|---|---|---|---|---|---|---|---|---|
| sound confident | ■ | ■ | | | | ■ | | | | | |
| use formal/informal language | ■ | | ■ | ■ | ■ | ■ | ■ | | | | |
| match voice to writing purpose | ■ | | ■ | ■ | ■ | ■ | ■ | ■ | ■ | | |
| sound interested | ■ | ■ | ■ | ■ | ■ | ■ | ■ | ■ | ■ | ■ | |
| sound convincing | ■ | ■ | ■ | ■ | ■ | ■ | ■ | ■ | ■ | | ■ |
| sound natural | ■ | ■ | ■ | ■ | ■ | ■ | ■ | ■ | ■ | ■ | ■ |
| sound knowledgeable | | | ■ | ■ | ■ | ■ | ■ | ■ | ■ | ■ | ■ |
| add dialogue | | | ■ | ■ | ■ | ■ | ■ | ■ | ■ | ■ | ■ |
| engage readers | | ■ | | | | | ■ | ■ | ■ | ■ | ■ |
| match voice to topic | | | | | | ■ | ■ | ■ | ■ | ■ | ■ |

**Editing**

| | 2 | 3 | 4 | 5 | 6 | 7 | 8 | 9 | 10 | 11 | 12 |
|---|---|---|---|---|---|---|---|---|---|---|---|
| use correct grammar rules | ■ | ■ | ■ | ■ | ■ | ■ | ■ | ■ | ■ | ■ | ■ |
| use correct usage rules | ■ | ■ | ■ | ■ | ■ | ■ | ■ | ■ | ■ | ■ | ■ |
| use correct punctuation rules | ■ | ■ | ■ | ■ | ■ | ■ | ■ | ■ | ■ | ■ | ■ |
| use correct capitalization rules | ■ | ■ | ■ | ■ | ■ | ■ | ■ | ■ | ■ | ■ | ■ |
| use correct sentence structure | ■ | ■ | ■ | ■ | ■ | ■ | ■ | ■ | ■ | ■ | ■ |

| | Grades | 2 | 3 | 4 | 5 | 6 | 7 | 8 | 9 | 10 | 11 | 12 |
|---|---|---|---|---|---|---|---|---|---|---|---|---|

### Editing (continued)

| | 2 | 3 | 4 | 5 | 6 | 7 | 8 | 9 | 10 | 11 | 12 |
|---|---|---|---|---|---|---|---|---|---|---|---|
| use spelling rules | ■ | ■ | ■ | ■ | ■ | ■ | ■ | ■ | ■ | ■ | ■ |
| use rubrics | ■ | ■ | ■ | ■ | ■ | ■ | ■ | ■ | ■ | ■ | ■ |

### Publishing

| | 2 | 3 | 4 | 5 | 6 | 7 | 8 | 9 | 10 | 11 | 12 |
|---|---|---|---|---|---|---|---|---|---|---|---|
| create a final copy | ■ | ■ | ■ | ■ | ■ | ■ | ■ | ■ | ■ | ■ | ■ |
| use a self assessment | ■ | ■ | ■ | ■ | ■ | ■ | ■ | ■ | ■ | ■ | ■ |
| create a portfolio | ■ | ■ | ■ | ■ | ■ | ■ | ■ | ■ | ■ | ■ | ■ |
| evaluate writing models | | ■ | ■ | ■ | ■ | ■ | ■ | ■ | ■ | ■ | ■ |

## WRITING ACROSS THE CURRICULUM

### Descriptive Writing

| | 2 | 3 | 4 | 5 | 6 | 7 | 8 | 9 | 10 | 11 | 12 |
|---|---|---|---|---|---|---|---|---|---|---|---|
| math | ■ | | | | ■ | ■ | ■ | | ■ | | |
| practical/workplace | ■ | | | | ■ | ■ | ■ | | ■ | | |
| science | ■ | | ■ | ■ | ■ | ■ | ■ | | | | |
| social studies | | ■ | ■ | ■ | ■ | ■ | ■ | ■ | ■ | | |

### Narrative Writing

| | 2 | 3 | 4 | 5 | 6 | 7 | 8 | 9 | 10 | 11 | 12 |
|---|---|---|---|---|---|---|---|---|---|---|---|
| art | | ■ | | | | | | | | | |
| math | | ■ | ■ | ■ | ■ | ■ | | | | | |
| music | ■ | | | | | | | | | | |
| practical/workplace | ■ | ■ | ■ | ■ | ■ | ■ | ■ | | | | |
| science | | | | ■ | | ■ | ■ | ■ | | | |
| social studies | ■ | ■ | | ■ | ■ | ■ | ■ | | | | |

### Expository Writing

| | 2 | 3 | 4 | 5 | 6 | 7 | 8 | 9 | 10 | 11 | 12 |
|---|---|---|---|---|---|---|---|---|---|---|---|
| math | | | | ■ | ■ | ■ | ■ | ■ | ■ | ■ | ■ |
| music/arts | | ■ | | | | | | ■ | ■ | ■ | ■ |
| practical/workplace | ■ | ■ | ■ | ■ | ■ | ■ | ■ | ■ | ■ | ■ | ■ |
| science | ■ | ■ | ■ | | ■ | ■ | ■ | ■ | ■ | ■ | ■ |
| social studies | | ■ | | ■ | ■ | ■ | ■ | ■ | ■ | ■ | ■ |

### Persuasive Writing

| | 2 | 3 | 4 | 5 | 6 | 7 | 8 | 9 | 10 | 11 | 12 |
|---|---|---|---|---|---|---|---|---|---|---|---|
| health | | ■ | | | | | | | | | |
| math | | | | ■ | | ■ | ■ | ■ | ■ | ■ | ■ |
| practical/workplace | | | ■ | ■ | ■ | ■ | ■ | ■ | ■ | | |
| science | ■ | ■ | ■ | ■ | ■ | ■ | ■ | ■ | | | |
| social studies | ■ | | | ■ | ■ | ■ | ■ | | | | |

| | Grades | 2 | 3 | 4 | 5 | 6 | 7 | 8 | 9 | 10 | 11 | 12 |
|---|---|---|---|---|---|---|---|---|---|---|---|---|
| **Response to Texts** | | | | | | | | | | | | |
| art | | | | | | | | | ■ | ■ | | ■ |
| math | | | | | | | | | | ■ | ■ | ■ |
| practical/workplace | | | | | | ■ | ■ | ■ | | | | |
| science | | | | | | ■ | ■ | ■ | ■ | | | |
| social studies | | | | | | ■ | ■ | ■ | | | | |
| **TOOLS OF LANGUAGE** | | | | | | | | | | | | |
| language strategies | | ■ | ■ | ■ | ■ | ■ | ■ | ■ | ■ | ■ | ■ | ■ |
| language of writing | | ■ | ■ | ■ | ■ | ■ | ■ | ■ | ■ | ■ | ■ | ■ |
| informal/formal language | | ■ | ■ | ■ | ■ | ■ | ■ | ■ | ■ | ■ | ■ | ■ |
| listening/speaking skills | | ■ | ■ | ■ | ■ | ■ | ■ | ■ | ■ | ■ | ■ | ■ |
| idioms | | ■ | ■ | ■ | ■ | ■ | ■ | ■ | ■ | ■ | ■ | ■ |
| shared reading | | ■ | ■ | ■ | ■ | ■ | ■ | ■ | ■ | ■ | ■ | ■ |
| reference materials | | ■ | ■ | ■ | ■ | ■ | ■ | ■ | ■ | ■ | ■ | ■ |
| **GRAMMAR** | | | | | | | | | | | | |
| **Understanding Sentences** | | | | | | | | | | | | |
| word order | | ■ | ■ | | | | | | | | | |
| run-on sentence | | ■ | ■ | ■ | ■ | ■ | ■ | ■ | | | | |
| simple subject/predicate | | ■ | ■ | ■ | ■ | ■ | ■ | ■ | | | | |
| compound sentence | | ■ | ■ | ■ | ■ | ■ | ■ | ■ | | | | |
| complete subject/predicate | | ■ | ■ | ■ | ■ | ■ | ■ | ■ | | | | |
| prepositional phrase | | ■ | ■ | ■ | ■ | ■ | ■ | ■ | | | | |
| subject-verb agreement | | ■ | ■ | ■ | ■ | ■ | ■ | ■ | ■ | ■ | ■ | ■ |
| complete sentence | | ■ | ■ | ■ | ■ | ■ | ■ | ■ | ■ | ■ | ■ | ■ |
| sentence variety | | ■ | ■ | ■ | ■ | ■ | ■ | ■ | ■ | ■ | ■ | ■ |
| declarative/exclamatory/ interrogative/imperative sentence | | ■ | ■ | ■ | ■ | ■ | ■ | ■ | ■ | ■ | ■ | ■ |
| compound subject/predicate | | | ■ | ■ | ■ | ■ | ■ | ■ | | | | |
| modeling | | | ■ | ■ | ■ | ■ | ■ | ■ | | ■ | ■ | ■ |
| appositive phrase | | | | ■ | ■ | ■ | ■ | ■ | | | | |
| direct object | | | | ■ | ■ | ■ | ■ | ■ | | | | |
| indirect object | | | | ■ | ■ | ■ | ■ | ■ | | | | |
| double negative | | | | ■ | ■ | ■ | ■ | ■ | | | | |
| independent clause | | | | ■ | ■ | ■ | ■ | ■ | | | | |
| dependent clause | | | | | ■ | ■ | ■ | ■ | | | | |

| | Grades | 2 | 3 | 4 | 5 | 6 | 7 | 8 | 9 | 10 | 11 | 12 |
|---|---|---|---|---|---|---|---|---|---|---|---|---|

## Understanding Sentences (continued)

| | 2 | 3 | 4 | 5 | 6 | 7 | 8 | 9 | 10 | 11 | 12 |
|---|---|---|---|---|---|---|---|---|---|---|---|
| complex sentence | | | ■ | ■ | ■ | ■ | ■ | ■ | ■ | ■ | ■ |
| noun/verb phrase | | | ■ | ■ | ■ | ■ | ■ | ■ | ■ | ■ | ■ |
| sentence diagramming | | | | | | ■ | | | | ■ | ■ |

## Understanding the Parts of Speech

### Nouns

| | 2 | 3 | 4 | 5 | 6 | 7 | 8 | 9 | 10 | 11 | 12 |
|---|---|---|---|---|---|---|---|---|---|---|---|
| possessive | | ■ | ■ | ■ | ■ | ■ | ■ | ■ | | | |
| specific | | ■ | ■ | ■ | ■ | ■ | ■ | ■ | | | |
| singular/plural | | ■ | ■ | ■ | ■ | ■ | ■ | ■ | | ■ | ■ |
| common/proper | | ■ | ■ | ■ | ■ | ■ | ■ | ■ | ■ | ■ | ■ |
| singular/plural possessive | | ■ | ■ | ■ | ■ | ■ | ■ | ■ | ■ | ■ | ■ |
| appositive | | | | | ■ | ■ | ■ | | | | |
| compound | | | | ■ | ■ | ■ | ■ | | | | |
| object | | | | ■ | ■ | ■ | ■ | | | | |
| predicate | | | | ■ | ■ | ■ | ■ | | | | |
| subject | | | | ■ | ■ | ■ | ■ | | | | |
| abstract/concrete | | | | ■ | ■ | ■ | ■ | ■ | ■ | ■ | ■ |
| collective | | | | ■ | ■ | ■ | ■ | ■ | ■ | ■ | ■ |
| case | | | | | | | | ■ | ■ | ■ | ■ |

### Verbs

| | 2 | 3 | 4 | 5 | 6 | 7 | 8 | 9 | 10 | 11 | 12 |
|---|---|---|---|---|---|---|---|---|---|---|---|
| contractions with *not* | | ■ | ■ | ■ | ■ | ■ | ■ | ■ | | | |
| subject-verb agreement | | ■ | ■ | ■ | ■ | ■ | ■ | ■ | | | |
| helping | | ■ | ■ | ■ | ■ | ■ | ■ | ■ | | | |
| past, present, future tense | | ■ | ■ | ■ | ■ | ■ | ■ | ■ | ■ | ■ | ■ |
| action | | ■ | ■ | ■ | ■ | ■ | ■ | ■ | ■ | ■ | ■ |
| linking | | ■ | ■ | ■ | ■ | ■ | ■ | ■ | ■ | ■ | ■ |
| singular/plural | | ■ | ■ | ■ | ■ | ■ | ■ | ■ | ■ | ■ | ■ |
| irregular | | ■ | ■ | ■ | ■ | ■ | ■ | ■ | ■ | ■ | ■ |
| simple tense | | | | | ■ | ■ | ■ | ■ | | | |
| perfect tense | | | | | ■ | ■ | ■ | ■ | | | |
| transitive/intransitive | | | | | ■ | ■ | ■ | ■ | ■ | ■ | ■ |
| active/passive voice | | | | ■ | ■ | ■ | ■ | ■ | ■ | ■ | ■ |
| participle | | | | ■ | ■ | ■ | ■ | | | | |
| continuous tense | | | | | | ■ | ■ | | | | |

| Grades | 2 | 3 | 4 | 5 | 6 | 7 | 8 | 9 | 10 | 11 | 12 |
|---|---|---|---|---|---|---|---|---|---|---|---|
| **Verbs (continued)** | | | | | | | | | | | |
| gerund | | | | | ■ | ■ | ■ | | | | |
| infinitive | | | | | ■ | ■ | ■ | | | | |
| auxiliary | | | | | | | ■ | ■ | ■ | ■ | ■ |
| verbal | | | | | | | ■ | ■ | ■ | ■ | ■ |
| complex tense | | | | | | | ■ | ■ | ■ | ■ | ■ |
| mood | | | | | | | ■ | ■ | ■ | ■ | |
| person | | | | | | | ■ | ■ | ■ | ■ | ■ |
| **Pronouns** | | | | | | | | | | | |
| possessive | ■ | ■ | ■ | ■ | ■ | ■ | ■ | | | | |
| personal | ■ | ■ | ■ | ■ | ■ | ■ | ■ | ■ | ■ | ■ | ■ |
| antecedent | ■ | ■ | ■ | ■ | ■ | ■ | ■ | ■ | ■ | ■ | ■ |
| singular/plural | ■ | ■ | ■ | ■ | ■ | ■ | ■ | ■ | ■ | ■ | ■ |
| subject/object | ■ | ■ | ■ | ■ | ■ | ■ | ■ | ■ | | | |
| intensive/reflexive | | | ■ | ■ | ■ | ■ | ■ | ■ | ■ | ■ | ■ |
| demonstrative/interrogative | | | ■ | ■ | ■ | ■ | ■ | ■ | ■ | ■ | ■ |
| indefinite | | | ■ | ■ | ■ | ■ | ■ | ■ | ■ | ■ | ■ |
| relative | | | ■ | ■ | ■ | ■ | ■ | ■ | ■ | ■ | ■ |
| gender | | | ■ | | ■ | ■ | ■ | ■ | ■ | ■ | ■ |
| person | | | | | ■ | | | ■ | ■ | ■ | ■ |
| case | | | | | | | ■ | ■ | ■ | ■ | ■ |
| **Adjectives** | | | | | | | | | | | |
| comparative/superlative | ■ | ■ | ■ | ■ | ■ | ■ | ■ | ■ | ■ | ■ | ■ |
| article | ■ | ■ | ■ | ■ | ■ | ■ | ■ | ■ | ■ | ■ | ■ |
| compound | | ■ | ■ | ■ | ■ | ■ | ■ | ■ | ■ | ■ | ■ |
| positive | | ■ | ■ | ■ | ■ | ■ | ■ | ■ | ■ | ■ | ■ |
| proper | | ■ | ■ | ■ | ■ | ■ | ■ | ■ | ■ | ■ | ■ |
| demonstrative | | | ■ | ■ | ■ | ■ | ■ | ■ | ■ | ■ | ■ |
| equal | | | ■ | ■ | ■ | ■ | ■ | | | | |
| indefinite | | | ■ | ■ | ■ | ■ | ■ | | | | |
| predicate | | ■ | ■ | ■ | ■ | ■ | ■ | ■ | ■ | ■ | ■ |
| **Interjections** | ■ | ■ | ■ | ■ | ■ | ■ | ■ | ■ | ■ | ■ | ■ |

| | Grades | 2 | 3 | 4 | 5 | 6 | 7 | 8 | 9 | 10 | 11 | 12 |
|---|---|---|---|---|---|---|---|---|---|---|---|---|

### Adverbs

| | 2 | 3 | 4 | 5 | 6 | 7 | 8 | 9 | 10 | 11 | 12 |
|---|---|---|---|---|---|---|---|---|---|---|---|
| of manner | ■ | ■ | ■ | ■ | ■ | ■ | ■ | ■ | ■ | ■ | ■ |
| of place | ■ | ■ | ■ | ■ | ■ | ■ | ■ | ■ | ■ | ■ | ■ |
| of time | ■ | ■ | ■ | ■ | ■ | ■ | ■ | ■ | ■ | ■ | ■ |
| to modify verbs | ■ | ■ | ■ | ■ | ■ | ■ | ■ | ■ | ■ | ■ | ■ |
| of degree | | | ■ | ■ | ■ | ■ | ■ | ■ | ■ | ■ | ■ |
| to modify adjectives/adverbs | | | ■ | ■ | ■ | ■ | ■ | ■ | ■ | ■ | ■ |
| comparative/superlative | | | ■ | ■ | ■ | ■ | ■ | ■ | ■ | ■ | ■ |
| positive | | | ■ | ■ | ■ | ■ | ■ | ■ | ■ | ■ | ■ |

### Conjunctions

| | 2 | 3 | 4 | 5 | 6 | 7 | 8 | 9 | 10 | 11 | 12 |
|---|---|---|---|---|---|---|---|---|---|---|---|
| coordinating | ■ | ■ | ■ | ■ | ■ | ■ | ■ | ■ | ■ | ■ | ■ |
| correlative | | | ■ | ■ | ■ | ■ | ■ | ■ | ■ | ■ | ■ |
| subordinating | | | ■ | ■ | ■ | ■ | ■ | ■ | ■ | ■ | ■ |

### Prepositions

| | 2 | 3 | 4 | 5 | 6 | 7 | 8 | 9 | 10 | 11 | 12 |
|---|---|---|---|---|---|---|---|---|---|---|---|
| common | ■ | ■ | ■ | ■ | ■ | ■ | ■ | ■ | ■ | ■ | ■ |
| prepositional phrase | ■ | ■ | ■ | ■ | ■ | ■ | ■ | ■ | ■ | ■ | ■ |

## Mechanics

### Capitalization

| | 2 | 3 | 4 | 5 | 6 | 7 | 8 | 9 | 10 | 11 | 12 |
|---|---|---|---|---|---|---|---|---|---|---|---|
| pronoun I | ■ | ■ | | | | ■ | ■ | ■ | | | |
| beginning of a quotation | ■ | ■ | ■ | ■ | ■ | ■ | ■ | | | | |
| name of a day, month, holiday | ■ | ■ | ■ | ■ | ■ | ■ | ■ | ■ | ■ | ■ | ■ |
| first word of a sentence | ■ | ■ | ■ | ■ | ■ | ■ | ■ | ■ | ■ | ■ | ■ |
| name of a person | ■ | ■ | ■ | ■ | ■ | ■ | ■ | ■ | ■ | ■ | ■ |
| proper noun | ■ | ■ | ■ | ■ | ■ | ■ | ■ | ■ | ■ | ■ | ■ |
| title used with a name | ■ | ■ | ■ | ■ | ■ | ■ | ■ | ■ | ■ | ■ | ■ |
| title | | ■ | ■ | ■ | ■ | ■ | ■ | ■ | ■ | ■ | ■ |
| geographical name/place | ■ | ■ | ■ | ■ | ■ | ■ | ■ | ■ | ■ | ■ | ■ |
| abbreviation, acronym | ■ | ■ | ■ | ■ | ■ | ■ | ■ | ■ | ■ | ■ | ■ |
| proper adjective | | | ■ | ■ | ■ | ■ | ■ | ■ | ■ | ■ | ■ |
| word used as a name | | | ■ | ■ | ■ | ■ | ■ | ■ | ■ | ■ | ■ |
| name of a historical event or period | | ■ | ■ | ■ | ■ | ■ | ■ | ■ | ■ | ■ | ■ |
| name of a religion, nationality | | | ■ | ■ | ■ | ■ | ■ | ■ | ■ | ■ | ■ |
| name of an organization | | | ■ | ■ | ■ | ■ | ■ | ■ | ■ | ■ | ■ |
| particular section of a country | | | ■ | ■ | ■ | ■ | ■ | ■ | ■ | ■ | ■ |

| | Grades | 2 | 3 | 4 | 5 | 6 | 7 | 8 | 9 | 10 | 11 | 12 |
|---|---|---|---|---|---|---|---|---|---|---|---|---|
| **Capitalization (continued)** | | | | | | | | | | | | |
| trade name/official name | | | | ■ | ■ | ■ | ■ | ■ | ■ | ■ | ■ | ■ |
| names of a language, ethnicity | | | ■ | ■ | | | | ■ | ■ | ■ | ■ | ■ |
| letter to indicate form or direction | | | | | | ■ | ■ | ■ | ■ | ■ | ■ | ■ |
| specific course name | | | | | | ■ | ■ | ■ | ■ | ■ | ■ | ■ |
| sentence following a colon | | | | | | | | | ■ | ■ | ■ | ■ |
| sentence in parentheses | | | | | | | | | ■ | ■ | ■ | ■ |
| **Plurals** | | | | | | | | | | | | |
| common noun | | ■ | ■ | ■ | ■ | ■ | ■ | ■ | | | | |
| noun with irregular spelling | | ■ | ■ | ■ | ■ | ■ | ■ | ■ | ■ | ■ | ■ | ■ |
| noun ending with *sh, ch, x, s,* or *z* | | ■ | ■ | ■ | ■ | ■ | ■ | ■ | ■ | ■ | ■ | ■ |
| noun ending in *y* | | ■ | ■ | ■ | ■ | ■ | ■ | ■ | ■ | ■ | ■ | ■ |
| adding *'s* | | | ■ | ■ | ■ | ■ | ■ | ■ | ■ | ■ | ■ | ■ |
| compound noun | | | ■ | ■ | ■ | ■ | ■ | ■ | ■ | ■ | ■ | ■ |
| noun ending with *f* or *fe* | | | ■ | ■ | ■ | ■ | ■ | ■ | ■ | ■ | ■ | ■ |
| noun ending with *ful* | | | ■ | ■ | ■ | ■ | ■ | ■ | ■ | ■ | ■ | ■ |
| noun ending with *o* | | | ■ | ■ | ■ | ■ | ■ | ■ | ■ | ■ | ■ | ■ |
| word discussed as a word | | | | | | | | ■ | ■ | ■ | ■ | ■ |
| collective noun | | | | | | | | | ■ | ■ | ■ | ■ |
| **Abbreviations** | | | | | | | | | | | | |
| day and month | | ■ | ■ | ■ | ■ | ■ | ■ | ■ | | | | |
| title of a person | | ■ | ■ | ■ | ■ | ■ | ■ | ■ | | | | |
| address | | ■ | ■ | ■ | ■ | ■ | ■ | ■ | | | | |
| state postal abbreviation | | | ■ | ■ | ■ | ■ | ■ | ■ | | | | |
| acronym/initialism | | | ■ | ■ | ■ | ■ | ■ | ■ | ■ | ■ | ■ | ■ |
| correspondence abbreviation | | | | | | | | ■ | ■ | ■ | ■ | ■ |
| **Numbers** | | | | | | | | | | | | |
| numbers 1 to 9 | | | ■ | ■ | ■ | ■ | ■ | ■ | | | | |
| sentence beginning | | | ■ | ■ | ■ | ■ | ■ | ■ | | | | |
| numeral only | | | ■ | ■ | ■ | ■ | ■ | ■ | ■ | ■ | ■ | ■ |
| very large number | | | ■ | ■ | ■ | ■ | ■ | ■ | ■ | ■ | ■ | |
| time/money | | | | | ■ | | ■ | ■ | ■ | ■ | ■ | ■ |
| in a compound modifier | | | | | | ■ | ■ | ■ | ■ | ■ | ■ | |
| word only | | | | | | | | ■ | ■ | ■ | ■ | ■ |
| numeral or word | | | | | | | | ■ | ■ | ■ | ■ | ■ |

| | Grades | 2 | 3 | 4 | 5 | 6 | 7 | 8 | 9 | 10 | 11 | 12 |
|---|---|---|---|---|---|---|---|---|---|---|---|---|
| **Punctuation** | | | | | | | | | | | | |
| **Periods** | | | | | | | | | | | | |
| after an initial or abbreviation | | ■ | ■ | ■ | ■ | ■ | ■ | ■ | ■ | ■ | ■ | ■ |
| end of a sentence | | ■ | ■ | ■ | ■ | ■ | ■ | ■ | ■ | ■ | ■ | ■ |
| as a decimal point | | | ■ | ■ | ■ | ■ | ■ | ■ | ■ | ■ | ■ | ■ |
| after an indirect question | | | | | | ■ | ■ | ■ | | | | |
| **Question Marks** | | | | | | | | | | | | |
| end of a question | | ■ | ■ | ■ | ■ | ■ | ■ | ■ | | | | |
| after a tag question | | | ■ | ■ | ■ | ■ | | | | | | |
| to show doubt | | | ■ | ■ | ■ | ■ | ■ | ■ | ■ | ■ | ■ | ■ |
| end of a direct/indirect question | | | | | | | | ■ | ■ | ■ | ■ | ■ |
| short question within a sentence | | | | | | | | | ■ | ■ | ■ | ■ |
| **Exclamation Points** | | | | | | | | | | | | |
| for a word, phrase, sentence | | ■ | ■ | ■ | ■ | ■ | ■ | ■ | | | | |
| for an interjection | | ■ | ■ | ■ | ■ | ■ | ■ | ■ | | | | |
| to express strong feelings | | ■ | ■ | ■ | ■ | ■ | ■ | ■ | ■ | ■ | ■ | ■ |
| **Commas** | | | | | | | | | | | | |
| in greeting of friendly letter | | ■ | ■ | ■ | ■ | ■ | ■ | ■ | | | | |
| after an introductory word or phrase | | ■ | ■ | ■ | ■ | ■ | ■ | ■ | | | | |
| in a series | | ■ | ■ | ■ | ■ | ■ | ■ | ■ | ■ | ■ | ■ | ■ |
| in a date and address | | ■ | ■ | ■ | ■ | ■ | ■ | ■ | ■ | ■ | ■ | ■ |
| with an interjection | | ■ | ■ | ■ | ■ | ■ | ■ | ■ | ■ | ■ | ■ | ■ |
| in a compound sentence | | ■ | ■ | ■ | ■ | ■ | ■ | ■ | ■ | ■ | ■ | ■ |
| to set off dialogue | | ■ | ■ | ■ | ■ | ■ | ■ | ■ | ■ | ■ | ■ | ■ |
| in a direct address | | ■ | ■ | ■ | ■ | ■ | ■ | ■ | ■ | ■ | ■ | ■ |
| in a number | | | ■ | ■ | ■ | ■ | ■ | ■ | ■ | ■ | ■ | ■ |
| to separate equal adjectives | | | ■ | ■ | ■ | ■ | ■ | ■ | ■ | ■ | ■ | ■ |
| to set off a phrase | | | | ■ | ■ | ■ | ■ | ■ | | | | |
| to set off an appositive | | | | ■ | ■ | ■ | ■ | ■ | ■ | ■ | ■ | ■ |
| to set off an interruption | | | | ■ | ■ | ■ | ■ | ■ | ■ | ■ | ■ | ■ |
| to separate nonrestrictive/ introductory clauses and phrases | | | | | | ■ | | | ■ | ■ | ■ | ■ |
| to set off a title of person | | | | | | | ■ | ■ | ■ | ■ | ■ | ■ |
| to enclose parenthetical elements | | | | | | | | | ■ | ■ | ■ | ■ |
| to separate contrasted elements | | | | | | | | ■ | ■ | ■ | ■ | ■ |

| | Grades | 2 | 3 | 4 | 5 | 6 | 7 | 8 | 9 | 10 | 11 | 12 |
|---|---|---|---|---|---|---|---|---|---|---|---|---|
| **Apostrophes** | | | | | | | | | | | | |
| in a contraction | | ■ | ■ | ■ | ■ | ■ | ■ | ■ | ■ | ■ | ■ | ■ |
| to form a plural possessive noun | | ■ | ■ | ■ | ■ | ■ | ■ | ■ | ■ | ■ | ■ | ■ |
| to form a singular possessive noun | | ■ | ■ | ■ | ■ | ■ | ■ | ■ | ■ | ■ | ■ | ■ |
| to form certain plurals | | | | ■ | ■ | ■ | ■ | ■ | ■ | ■ | ■ | ■ |
| to replace an omitted number/letter | | | | ■ | ■ | ■ | ■ | ■ | ■ | ■ | ■ | ■ |
| with an indefinite pronoun | | | | ■ | ■ | ■ | ■ | ■ | ■ | ■ | ■ | ■ |
| to show shared possession | | | | ■ | ■ | ■ | ■ | ■ | ■ | ■ | ■ | ■ |
| in a possessive with compound nouns | | | | | | | ■ | ■ | ■ | | | |
| to express time or amount | | | | | | ■ | ■ | ■ | ■ | ■ | ■ | ■ |
| **Quotation Marks** | | | | | | | | | | | | |
| for a direct quotation | | ■ | ■ | ■ | ■ | ■ | ■ | ■ | ■ | | ■ | ■ |
| for a title | | | ■ | ■ | ■ | ■ | ■ | ■ | ■ | ■ | ■ | ■ |
| for a special word | | | | ■ | ■ | ■ | ■ | ■ | ■ | ■ | ■ | ■ |
| for a quotation within a quotation | | | | | | ■ | ■ | ■ | ■ | ■ | ■ | ■ |
| **Colons** | | | | | | | | | | | | |
| after a salutation of business letter | | | ■ | ■ | ■ | ■ | ■ | ■ | ■ | ■ | ■ | ■ |
| between hour and minutes | | | ■ | ■ | ■ | ■ | ■ | ■ | ■ | ■ | ■ | ■ |
| to introduce a list of items | | | ■ | ■ | ■ | ■ | ■ | ■ | ■ | ■ | ■ | ■ |
| to introduce a quotation | | | | | | ■ | | | ■ | ■ | ■ | ■ |
| to introduce a sentence | | | | | | ■ | ■ | ■ | ■ | ■ | ■ | ■ |
| for emphasis | | | | | | ■ | ■ | ■ | ■ | ■ | ■ | ■ |
| between a title and a subtitle | | | | | | | ■ | | ■ | ■ | ■ | ■ |
| **Hyphens** | | | | | | | | | | | | |
| in word division | | | ■ | ■ | ■ | ■ | ■ | ■ | ■ | ■ | ■ | ■ |
| in a compound word | | | | ■ | ■ | ■ | ■ | ■ | ■ | ■ | ■ | ■ |
| in a fraction | | | | ■ | ■ | ■ | ■ | ■ | ■ | ■ | ■ | ■ |
| to create a new word | | | | ■ | ■ | ■ | ■ | ■ | ■ | ■ | ■ | ■ |
| to join letters and words | | | | ■ | ■ | ■ | ■ | ■ | ■ | ■ | ■ | ■ |
| to avoid confusion or awkward spelling | | | | | | ■ | ■ | ■ | ■ | ■ | ■ | ■ |
| to make an adjective | | | | | | ■ | ■ | ■ | ■ | ■ | ■ | ■ |
| **Parentheses** | | | | | | | | | | | | |
| to add information | | | ■ | ■ | ■ | ■ | ■ | ■ | ■ | ■ | ■ | ■ |

| Grades | 2 | 3 | 4 | 5 | 6 | 7 | 8 | 9 | 10 | 11 | 12 |
|---|---|---|---|---|---|---|---|---|---|---|---|
| **Dashes** | | | | | | | | | | | |
| for emphasis | | | ■ | ■ | ■ | ■ | ■ | ■ | ■ | ■ | ■ |
| to show a sentence break | | | ■ | ■ | ■ | ■ | ■ | ■ | ■ | ■ | ■ |
| to show interrupted speech | | | ■ | ■ | ■ | ■ | ■ | ■ | ■ | ■ | ■ |
| **Ellipses** | | | | | | | | | | | |
| to show a pause | | | ■ | ■ | ■ | ■ | ■ | ■ | ■ | ■ | ■ |
| to show omitted words | | | ■ | ■ | ■ | ■ | ■ | ■ | ■ | ■ | ■ |
| **Semicolons** | | | | | | | | | | | |
| in a compound sentence | | | ■ | | ■ | ■ | ■ | ■ | ■ | ■ | ■ |
| to separate groups (that have commas) in a series | | | ■ | ■ | ■ | ■ | ■ | ■ | ■ | ■ | ■ |
| to join two independent clauses | | | | ■ | ■ | ■ | ■ | ■ | ■ | ■ | ■ |
| with a conjunctive adverb | | | | ■ | ■ | ■ | ■ | ■ | ■ | ■ | ■ |
| **Brackets** | | | | | | | | | | | |
| to set off clarifying information | | | | | ■ | | | ■ | ■ | ■ | ■ |
| to set off added words | | | | | ■ | | ■ | ■ | ■ | ■ | ■ |
| around an editorial correction | | | | | | | | ■ | ■ | ■ | ■ |
| **Underlining and Italics** | | | | | | | | | | | |
| for a title | ■ | ■ | ■ | ■ | ■ | ■ | ■ | ■ | ■ | ■ | ■ |
| for a special word | | ■ | ■ | ■ | ■ | | | | | | |
| for special uses | | | | ■ | | | | ■ | ■ | ■ | ■ |
| in handwritten and printed material | | | | | | ■ | | ■ | ■ | ■ | ■ |
| for scientific and foreign words | | | | | | ■ | ■ | ■ | ■ | ■ | ■ |
| **Using the Right Word** | ■ | ■ | ■ | ■ | ■ | ■ | ■ | ■ | ■ | ■ | ■ |
| **Improving Spelling** | ■ | ■ | ■ | ■ | ■ | ■ | ■ | ■ | ■ | ■ | ■ |

# Scavenger Hunt 1: Find It!

**Directions** Find the following information in your book by turning to the pages listed in parentheses.

**1.** Which traits to focus on during each step of the writing process (page 12)

_____

_____

_____

_____

**2.** What STRAP stands for (page 130, 134, 188, 246, 250)

_____

_____

**3.** How to vary sentence beginnings (page 110)

_____

**4.** What the mood of a verb indicates (page 752)

_____

**5.** Types of details you can include in your writing (pages 605–606)

_____

**6.** How to check and revise an interpretive response essay for voice (pages 278–279)

_____

**7.** An alternative way of writing about a scientific discovery or principle (page 452)

_____

_____

**8.** A formula that can be used to write thesis statements (page 630)

_____

_____

**9.** Places to which you can send your writing for publication (page 77)

_____

_____

**10.** How to form the plural of words ending in *ful* (page 688)

_____

# Scavenger Hunt 2: What Is It?

**Directions** Find the answers to the following questions using the index in the back of the book. The underlined words below tell you where to look in the index.

1. What is an <u>absolute phrase</u>?

   _____

   _____

2. What <u>figures of speech</u> can you use to make your writing more engaging?

   _____

3. What can <u>graphic elements</u> do to enhance your writing?

   _____

4. What is a <u>diagonal</u>?

   _____

   _____

5. What do <u>prepositions</u> do?

   _____

   _____

6. What is a <u>gerund</u>?

   _____

7. What are the three <u>forms of adjectives</u>?

   _____

8. What is a <u>phase autobiography</u>?

   _____

   _____

9. What are the three principal parts of the <u>irregular verb</u> *rise*?

   _____

10. What is an <u>adverb prop</u>?

    _____

    _____

11. What does the <u>idiom</u> *nose to the grindstone* mean?

    _____

12. What is a <u>lune</u>?

    _____

# Getting to Know *Write Source*

**Directions** Locate the pages in *Write Source* where answers to the following learning tasks can be found. Both the index and the table of contents can help you.

_____ 1. You want to invite a well-known author who lives locally to visit your school. You need to know how to write a business letter.

_____ 2. A child you are caring for after school asks you why DVD's are called that. You need to know what the common abbreviation DVD stands for.

_____ 3. Your teacher announces an assignment in which you must write a skit or script dramatizing a famous scientific discovery. You need to find help for such an assignment.

_____ 4. When your teacher assigns a research report, she asks that you include a title page and an outline. You need to see examples of a title page and an outline.

_____ 5. You have to write an autobiographical free-verse poem, and during Prewriting, your teacher tells you to choose a focus. You need some strategies for choosing a focus.

_____ 6. You need some ideas about creating verbal metaphors to make your writing come alive.

_____ 7. Your teacher points out places in your writing where you could use an ellipsis to show a pause. You need to know what an ellipsis is.

_____ 8. Your essays have good "meat" in the middle, but you need help writing good beginnings and endings.

_____ 9. You are supposed to use both primary and secondary sources for your research report. You need to understand what each one is.

_____ 10. Your teacher tells you that you can use a holistic scoring guide to direct your writing as well as to assess it. You need to understand more about using a scoring guide.

# Getting Started Activity Answers

## Scavenger Hunt 1: Find It!

1. Prewriting focuses on focus and coherence, organization, and development of ideas. Drafting incorporates focus and coherence, organization, development of ideas, and voice. Revising also uses focus and coherence, organization, development of ideas, and voice. Editing focuses on conventions, and publishing uses all of these traits.

2. STRAP stands for Subject, Type, Role, Audience, and Purpose.

3. Sentence beginnings vary if some sentences begin with a subject, some with a phrase, and some with a clause.

4. The mood of a verb indicates the tone or attitude with which a statement is made.

5. Types of details include facts, statistics, examples, anecdotes, quotations, definitions, reasons, and comparisons.

6. Reread your essay. Mark any places that don't maintain a consistent point of view or don't sound direct or positive.

7. A script or play may be an alternative and interesting way to write about a scientific discovery or idea.

8. A specific topic + a particular stand, feeling, or feature = an effective thesis statement.

9. Your writing may be sent to various publications (magazines, etc.) and writing contests.

10. Form the plural of words ending in ful by adding an s at the end of the word.

## Scavenger Hunt 2: What Is It?

1. An absolute phrase consists of a noun and a participle (plus the participle's object, if there is one, and any modifiers) (p. 770).

2. Figures of speech that can enhance your writing include similes, metaphors, personification, and hyperbole (p. 340–341).

3. Graphic elements can explain ideas in a visual manner (pp. 638–639).

4. A diagonal (slash) is a punctuation mark used (a) to indicate either of two words is acceptable or (b) to quote poetry (p. 674).

5. A preposition, the first word in a prepositional phrase, shows the relationship between the word's object (a noun or pronoun) and another word in the sentence (p. 760).

6. A gerund is a verb that ends in ing and is used as a noun (p. 754).

7. The three forms of adjectives are the positive form, the comparative form, and the superlative form (p. 756).

8. A phase autobiography describes or re-creates an extended period in the writer's life that changed the writer in some way (p. 79).

9. The three principal parts of the irregular verb rise are rise, rose, and risen (p. 748).

10. An adverb prop is an unnecessary adverb added to a weak verb in an attempt to strengthen the verb (p. 579).

11. Nose to the grindstone means work hard (p. 707).

12. A lune is a poem written in three lines containing 13 syllables in a 5-3-5 pattern (p. 356).

## Getting to Know *Write Source*

| | | | |
|---|---|---|---|
| **1.** | 507–508 | **6** | 575 |
| **2.** | 695 | **7.** | 678 |
| **3.** | 452–455 | **8.** | 595–596 |
| **4.** | 372, 392 | **9.** | 360 |
| **5.** | 349 | **10.** | 56–68 |

# Narrative Writing

## The Game

1   The rain hit my helmet lightly, like a soft tapping on the door. I

2   pulled my chin strap tightly around my face and snapped it on the

3   other side. Forty-three teammates standing beside me started to jog,

4   workhorses on the move, the clip-clop of our spikes the only sound.

5       As we approached the field the rain picked up. I looked at my

6   teammates after hearing the cheer from our fans. I said to myself,

7   'This is why I play football; this is what it's all about." As we burst

8   through the gate the roar of the crowd engulfed us. Our coach

9   gathered us together on the sidelines and barked the game plan to

10  us. Forty-four sets of eyes locked on his as if we were hypnotized. We

11  broke the huddle and the receiving team trotted out onto the field.

12      The ball was kicked. It soared high above our heads as the two

13  teams ran full charge at each other. I found my man and fixed on him

14  like a missile locking onto its target. The return man was hit hard

15  and brought down around the 50-yard line.

16      The crowd was yelling; the cheerleaders were pumped. I heard

17  the chanting fade into the background as the game progressed. Two

18  quarters passed then three. Hard-hitting crunches and cracks could

19  be heard play after play. Each team traded scores.

20      With less than a minute left in the game we had a 24-to-17 lead.

21  The rain was running down my helmet like an overflowing gutter.

22  With time running out the opposing quarterback dropped back.

# Narrative Writing *(cont.)*

23  The crowd was silent and he passed to an open receiver in the end

24  zone. Everything seemed to go into slow motion as the ball dropped

25  securely into his hands. I stood openmouthed, dumbfounded, and

26  barely breathing. They made the extra point so the score was tied,

27  which meant overtime.

28      The opposing team won the coin toss and went first. The

29  official put the ball on the 10-yard line. In three short plays, they

30  scored again, putting them ahead by six. I felt like I was in a bad

31  dream. After the extra point, it was our turn. Our first two plays

32  were stopped cold by their tenacious defense. On third down our

33  quarterback dropped back and connected with the tailback a yard

34  short of the end zone. I snapped my helmet anticipating heading out

35  onto the field for the extra point.

36      Fourth down in overtime . . . this is the stuff dreams are made of.

37  A quarterback sneak was our money play, a play we had executed to

38  perfection at least 30 times throughout the season. How could it go

39  wrong?

40      Eleven men broke the huddle and slowly walked to the line. The

41  center placed his hands on the ball, keeping the laces up for luck.

42  The quarterback broke his cadence like a general shouting orders.

43  Eyes were locked; the crowd was silent. At the snap of the ball, their

44  linemen charged us, trying to crack the wall. Our quarterback took a

45  hit and fumbled before he could cross the line. The game was over. We

46  lost by inches.

# Narrative Writing *(cont.)*

47    I went still and fell to my knees. Our quarterback sat in the end

48    zone, alone. I could hear sobs from the crowd. Tears ran down my face

49    or maybe it was just the rain. I couldn't tell. Some teammates were

50    consoled by their families or hugged by their friends. Our last game

51    was not supposed to end in this way.

52    Heads down, our team walked slowly back to the locker room, the

53    once thunderous footsteps now silent. For the first time that night, I

54    felt the cold.

# Narrative Writing
# Benchmark Paper Comments

*Title: The Game*                    Holistic Score: **4**

In this highly effective response, the writer clearly and concisely takes the reader through the events and emotions experienced while playing in a football game. Strong sensory details (*the clip-clop of our spikes, hard-hitting crunches and cracks could be heard*) and similes (*as if we were hypnotized, like a general shouting orders*) allow the reader to picture events and appreciate the writer's unique perspective. The writer's thoughts and feelings (*For the first time that night, I felt the* cold) help provide voice and depth of ideas. Lack of transitions and minor errors in punctuation do not interfere with fluency.

| | Focus and Coherence | Organization | Development of Ideas | Voice | Conventions |
|---|---|---|---|---|---|
| **4** | focused and connected | flows smoothly | ideas deeply supported | highly engaging and original | strong command of conventions |
| **3** | mostly focused and connected | generally flows smoothly | ideas thoughtfully supported | mostly engaging and original | few errors |
| **2** | somewhat focused | flows somewhat smoothly | ideas adequately supported | somewhat engaging and original | some errors |
| **1** | unfocused, disconnected | does not flow | ideas unsupported | not engaging or original | major errors |

# Narrative Writing

## Just Another Day at the Beach

1    I sliced through the calm California waters off the shore of Goleta

2    Beach. The only thing I could think about as I moved more and more

3    far away was getting to that buoy. I began my journey pretty slowly

4    so as not to alert my Mom. She would never willingly let me go. I was

5    pretty far out when mid stroke I stopped, to hear the frantic calls

6    of my Mom as she screamed for me to come back to shore. "Melissa,

7    what do you think you are doing?" You are too far out. I want you to

8    come back right now!" I could hear the anger, and frustration in her

9    voice. My response to her order was simply, "I'm swimming out to the

10   buoys," and I continued my swim, moving more far out, completely

11   ignoring her. I heard her say, "John go with her." My Dad had no

12   choice but to catch up to me, because I wasn't stopping until I reached

13   the buoy. He reached me and by now my Mom had become a dot on

14   the shoreline. My Dad and I treaded water and dog paddled and we

15   were surrounded by a mixture of browns, greens, and blues that make

16   up the ocean. There was no excape from the smell of salt water. Or

17   the taste of salt water. It stayed on my lips from the waves crashing

18   against my Dad and I. All the while the shoreline got more and more

19   small, the shoreline blended into the horizon only to vanish from

20   sight. I had never been that far from the shore in my entire life. I was

21   eight years old. My Dad turned and asked, "Melissa can you touch?"

22   I wiggled my feet underneath me to try and find some of the soft,

# Narrative Writing *(cont.)*

23   squishy sand that I was familiar with along the shoreline. However

24   there was nothing below me, I was floating in the middle of the ocean,

25   as the waves rocked my Dad and I toward our destination and I was

26   frightened, yet exhilarated. I had no idea how deep the water was, I

27   could be floating highest above any sand, their could be fish or sharks

28   in the waters below me. I felt like I was in a seen from one of those

29   shark movies. I was half way there. I wanted to know how my baby-

30   sitter Julie and her sister Susie felt after they got to the buoy, and

31   jumped off it. After swimming forever, we finally reached the buoys ,

32   they were smaller then I thought and made of plastic. I didn't jump

33   off them I just wanted to go back to shore. I was a little disapointed

34   with the buoys. They were not what I had expected. They were just

35   these floating pieces of plastic. Getting there was the cool part. I had

36   the bragging rights, and I couldn't wait to share on Monday at school.

37   What I did over the weekend.

# Narrative Writing
# Benchmark Paper Comments

*Title: Just Another Day at the Beach*                Holistic Score: **2**

The writer of this unfocused composition relates the experience of swimming far out into the ocean to reach a buoy. Although the use of dialogue and a determined voice are present (*"Melissa, what do you think you are doing?"*), the frequent use of both run-on and incomplete sentences (*I was pretty far out when mid stroke I stopped, to hear the frantic calls of my Mom as she screamed for me to come back to shore. What I did over the weekend.*) and mistakes in punctuation confuse the reader and slow the progression of ideas. In addition, details that do not belong (*I wanted to know how my baby-sitter Julie and her sister Susie felt...*) contribute to making this response only somewhat effective.

| | Focus and Coherence | Organization | Development of Ideas | Voice | Conventions |
|---|---|---|---|---|---|
| **4** | focused and connected | flows smoothly | ideas deeply supported | highly engaging and original | strong command of conventions |
| **3** | mostly focused and connected | generally flows smoothly | ideas thoughtfully supported | mostly engaging and original | few errors |
| **2** | **somewhat focused** | **flows somewhat smoothly** | ideas adequately supported | **somewhat engaging and original** | some errors |
| **1** | unfocused, disconnected | does not flow | **ideas unsupported** | not engaging or original | **major errors** |

# Expository Writing

## No Escape for Malnourished Children

1      Hunger and malnutrition are tremendous problems in our world

2 today. According to the magazine *Population Reports,* about 18 million

3 people, mostly children, die each year from starvation, malnutrition,

4 and related causes. This magazine also states that nearly 200 million

5 children under the age of five—40 percent of all children this age—

6 lack sufficient nutrition to develop fully. Tragically, children suffering

7 from malnutrition have little chance of living long, productive lives.

8      Malnutrition can lead to death, but long before that happens,

9 poorly nourished children suffer from a number of physical problems.

10 Extreme weight loss, stunted growth, and frequent infections are just

11 a few of the physical problems resulting from poor nutrition. Because

12 the immune system often begins to shut down in malnourished

13 children, they are also very susceptible to life-threatening diseases

14 such as tuberculosis, measles, and diarrhea. According to Dr. Hiroshi

15 Nakajima, Director-General of the World Health Organization, "Much

16 of the sickness and death attributed to major communicable diseases

17 is, in fact, caused by malnutrition" (81).

18      One form of malnutrition is called *marasmus.* It occurs when

19 children are weaned too soon and receive very few nutrients. Children

20 with marasmus are extremely underweight. They lack any body fat

21 or defined muscles. They look almost puppet-like—with large heads,

22 small bodies, and thin arms and legs. Their skin sags and their faces

# Expository Writing *(cont.)*

23   wrinkle. Their body organs get small. Their intestines fail. Their pulse

24   rate gets slow. Marasmus causes the child's body to waste away.

25        Another form of malnutrition is called *kwashiorkor*. It occurs

26   when children are weaned later than normal and do not receive

27   enough protein and nutrients. Children with this disease have badly

28   swollen bellies that make them look healthy. Their stomachs look

29   large because their muscles are loose and weak. Their skin is often

30   pale or red and their hair becomes very thin. Children who suffer

31   from this form of malnutrition simply stop growing.

32        In terms of their mental development, children lacking proper

33   food may become sleepy, dull, and withdrawn. As a result, their ability

34   to learn decreases. Because these children have no energy, it's difficult

35   for them to even learn how to walk and talk. According to the *Public*

36   *Health News and Notes,* iron and iodine deficiencies in children often

37   impairs their intellectual development. Even a small deficiency in

38   iodine can reduce a child's development by as much as 10 percent.

39   Studies have shown that poor nutrition in early childhood can

40   continue to hinder development well into adulthood.

41        Malnutrition is a serious problem for people of all ages, but it

42   takes its greatest toll on innocent children. The problem is not likely

43   to go away soon. New methods of farming, food distribution, and

44   health care are needed. Those changes are just now beginning to take

45   place.

# Expository Writing
# Benchmark Paper Comments

*Title: No Escape for Malnourished Children*     Holistic Score: **3**

The writer of this generally effective response explains the reasons which make malnutrition a serious world problem. The organization is mostly focused with a smooth progression of thought. The main idea of each paragraph (*Malnutrition can lead to death...One form of malnutrition is ...*) is well developed except for the final one, which introduces several new thoughts. The use of statistics, published sources, and expert quotes are for the most part used effectively. Excellent word choice (*tragically, very susceptible*) and comparisons (*They look almost puppet-like...*) along with a good command of conventions add to the strength of this composition.

| | Focus and Coherence | Organization | Development of Ideas | Voice | Conventions |
|---|---|---|---|---|---|
| **4** | focused and connected | flows smoothly | ideas deeply supported | highly engaging and original | strong command of conventions |
| **3** | mostly focused and connected | generally flows smoothly | ideas thoughtfully supported | mostly engaging and original | few errors |
| **2** | somewhat focused | flows somewhat smoothly | ideas adequately supported | somewhat engaging and original | some errors |
| **1** | unfocused, disconnected | does not flow | ideas unsupported | not engaging or original | major errors |

# Expository Writing

## The Manatee

1     What do the bald eagle, gray whale, manatee, tiger, American

2 crocodile, and a hundred more animals have in common? There

3 endangered species. They have all become this way for many of the

4 same reasons. Destruction of habitat, pollution, and capturing animals

5 for amusement and use of their fur and other body parts.

6     Destruction of habitat is probably the number one cause of

7 endangered species. We just can't see that every time we build a condo

8 or mall we are taking the home of many plants and animals. I don't

9 think we would like it very much if someone just came and bulldozed

10 our houses down and poured concrete. We would get very upset. Our

11 human nature would probably come out strong. We would demand

12 to know who and why this was done. Since animals accept human

13 weren't given the gift of speech. They can't let people know how they

14 feel. They need someone to do that for them. Loggers take thousands

15 of animal's homes from them everyday. The number of people in a

16 place grows. Dams are needed. They make energy from them. Sea

17 levels change. Animals have to deel with the change. They can't do it

18 quick enough. Manatees are one of those animals. They have to move

19 away from what they know. They may not be able to find food to feed

20 their young. So, some can die. This is bad. All because of things done

21 by humans.

22     Carelessness is another cause of endangering animals. Humans

# Expository Writing *(cont.)*

23  are careless. They drive boats near the shore, pollute, and litter.

24  Boaters could save hundreds of manatees a year by simply staying

25  out of the manatees territory. The blades in the engines of motor boats

26  cut deep into the backs of manatees. They can bleed to death. Or

27  become weak. They can't eat enough food to survive. They cannot feed

28  themselves. They cannot feed their offspring. They starve, too. Another

29  main cause is the endangerment of animals. Large corporations

30  put huge amounts of toxic chemicals in streams, rivers, and oceans

31  everyday. Plants that pollute the air are also polluting the water.

32  Oil spills are an additional way that water is polluted. They trap

33  animals and cause fires. Humans also have a problem with littering.

34  It destroys the land. It changes habitats. Animals can't live their

35  anymore.

36       Another reason for animals being endangered is humans. Capture

37  them for the entertainment of others. Animals are captured for zoos,

38  amusement parks, and for the use of their body parts. Manatees are

39  captured for their hides. They make leather, meat, and blubber oil.

40  Other animals are used for their fur and meat. Elephants tusks are

41  used for ivory. Many cheetahs are killed so rich women can have fur

42  coats. Sea turtles are endangered because some featherbrained people

43  decide to walk down to the beach and collect eggs. This is done more

44  often than you think. Crocodiles are butchered for their skin to make

45  shoes and pocketbooks. The Indian bat is endangered because people

46  visit caves.

# Expository Writing *(cont.)*

47         Animals are important to us for many reasons. Manatees clear

48   channels. They are thick with water plants. Boats need to move

49   through these places. Also, if one thing dies out the entire food chain

50   will be hurt. Animals also provide beauty and entertainment in just

51   watching them in nature. If we don't take care of our endangered

52   species or try to get there population total up we won't have them to

53   enjoy anymore.

# Expository Writing
# Benchmark Paper Comments

Title: *The Manatee*                    Holistic Score: **2**

The writer of this expository composition focuses on three reasons that animals are endangered (*destruction of habitat, pollution, humans capturing animals*), and develops each reason in a paragraph. However, the supporting details are often disconnected thoughts in short, choppy sentences (*Dams are needed. Sea levels change.*). A sense of voice is evident (*If we don't take care of our endangered species or try to get there population total up we won't have them to enjoy anymore.*), but the superficial development and weak control of conventions interfere with the reader's understanding of the writer's ideas and cause this response to be only somewhat effective.

|   | Focus and Coherence | Organization | Development of Ideas | Voice | Conventions |
|---|---|---|---|---|---|
| **4** | focused and connected | flows smoothly | ideas deeply supported | highly engaging and original | strong command of conventions |
| **3** | mostly focused and connected | generally flows smoothly | ideas thoughtfully supported | **mostly engaging and original** | few errors |
| **2** | **somewhat focused** | **flows somewhat smoothly** | **ideas adequately supported** | somewhat engaging and original | some errors |
| **1** | unfocused, disconnected | does not flow | ideas unsupported | not engaging or original | **major errors** |

# Persuasive Writing

## Group Work: A Good Idea?

1     Jane has her head buried in her books, finding information for

2 our project. Tom and Joe are talking about the dates they had last

3 weekend. Mary and Anne are catching up on the latest gossip. George

4 is memorizing his plays for tonight's football game. I'm just sitting

5 here counting the minutes on the clock until I can get out of this class

6 and satisfy my growling stomach. This is usually how most groups act

7 when assigned a project. Students enjoy group work for this reason,

8 and I don't blame them. Anyone likes to have a break and relax a

9 little during the school day. A break from lectures and note taking to

10 catch up on the latest rumors is always accepted by students.

11     Despite the popularity of group work among students, in my

12 opinion, group work discourages responsibility and wastes both the

13 students' and teachers' time. In the example above, Jane will have

14 done most of the work, if not all of it. The project and paper will be

15 handed in with everyone's name on it, and everyone will receive the

16 same grade, although the other members of the group may not even

17 know what the project was about.

18     The students who have actually done the work are the only

19 ones who benefit from the project. For this reason, students who are

20 assigned a group project and work on it alone receive a higher grade

21 and learn more than students who are assigned to do a project with a

# Persuasive Writing *(cont.)*

22    group. Individual work is a more accurate measure of knowledge. The

23    information turned in is a true test of what the student knows.

24        There are other reasons why I think group work is a bad idea.

25    Group work discourages responsibility and gives students the idea

26    that they can "slack off" and not do any of the work. A group usually

27    consists of one or two hard workers like Jane, leaving the rest of

28    the group without responsibility. The work is almost never evenly

29    divided. It becomes habit to let someone else do everything, someone

30    who wants to take over and do the work, just do it all. Students

31    should learn from the other group projects throughout the class, but

32    since group projects are poorly done, they only learn about the topic

33    their group was assigned, if even that. What students really learn

34    is laziness while in group work; that's why most kids ask to work

35    in groups. Only one person needs to take charge, and the rest of the

36    group can do what they want. Most students goof off when they are

37    put in groups, and they see it as an opportunity to talk with friends.

38    The example that I used earlier shows that Tom and Joe aren't even

39    thinking about their assignment; they're too busy talking about

40    girls. George is not only oblivious to the work, but to everyone and

41    everything besides football.

42        Another problem with group work involves time. Since most

43    group work requires work outside of class, students have to find

44    time to get together. This becomes almost impossible because of the

# Persuasive Writing *(cont.)*

45    student's conflicting schedules. Between jobs and sports, it's nearly

46    impossible to get a whole group to find a time to meet. Once again

47    the responsibility and work is put on only one or two people who

48    make the time and care enough to get the project done and in on

49    time. Yes, teachers become more flexible when it comes to group work.

50    They understand that kids can't find time to get together outside of

51    class because of conflicts. But some teachers don't realize that if time

52    wasn't wasted in class talking about other things besides the work,

53    students would have a majority of the project done and not need

54    so much time outside of class. Teachers often extend the deadlines

55    and give more class time to finish the project. This wastes time and

56    pushes back what the teacher has already planned.

57       A final problem with group work is clashing personalities. People

58    don't always click. Not all students get along the way it is, and having

59    to do assigned work together makes it even more difficult. Everyone

60    should be accountable for his own portion of the work. If all but one

61    person turns in his or her part, the grade goes down and makes

62    others in the group upset. Cooperation doesn't come easily when the

63    students can't work together or get along. So groups that are assigned

64    by the teacher, instead of students picking their own groups, often

65    have a difficult time getting along.

## Persuasive Writing *(cont.)*

66      How much is learned from group work? Group work can be a
67  positive thing if students learn to work well with others, and they
68  are able to successfully combine their ideas. In a perfect situation,
69  responsibility and "team work" can be learned and benefit the
70  students. But in most situations, group work teaches irresponsibility,
71  and it is a bad experience for the teachers and students. Group work
72  should not be a waste of time but a great learning experience.

# Persuasive Writing
# Benchmark Paper Comments

*Title: Group Work: A Good Idea?*                    Holistic Score: **3**

This generally effective persuasive response is focused on the problems that arise when students work in groups. The writer begins with an anecdote and engages the reader with a strong sense of voice (*...in my opinion, group work ...wastes both the students' and teachers' time.*). The progression and development of ideas is generally smooth and effective even though some of the supporting details are rambling and repetitive (*...gives students the idea that they can "slack off"...Most students goof off...*) and some ideas don't belong (*...students who are assigned a group project and work on it alone receive a higher grade*). Sustained focus and strong conventions also contribute to the effectiveness of this composition.

| | Focus and Coherence | Organization | Development of Ideas | Voice | Conventions |
|---|---|---|---|---|---|
| **4** | **focused and connected** | flows smoothly | ideas deeply supported | highly engaging and original | **strong command of conventions** |
| **3** | mostly focused and connected | **generally flows smoothly** | **ideas thoughtfully supported** | **mostly engaging and original** | few errors |
| **2** | somewhat focused | flows somewhat smoothly | ideas adequately supported | somewhat engaging and original | some errors |
| **1** | unfocused, disconnected | does not flow | ideas unsupported | not engaging or original | major errors |

# Persuasive Writing

## Letter to the Editor: Grading Students on Effort

1    Dear Editor,

2    I just want to say a few things about the talk that's been going on

3    around this school abot changing the ways were graded.

4    School would not be more easy if grades were based on effort

5    instead of by how many a student got wrong or write. Sure it sounds

6    like a good idea. It isn't really a good idea.

7    If grades were based only on you're effort, students would not

8    have to get the answers write. It would make the work a hole lot more

9    easy, but how would a student ever learn how to do it? Doing your

10   work would have no point. They will need to know how to do things

11   the right way if a person does have the skills, they probably won't

12   hold a job very long. Students have to learn that their is a write way

13   and a wrong way. If they can work which ever way they want, they

14   will not be doing it write and they will not learn how to be succesful.

15   This way of grading would be difficult. Both for students and

16   teachers. There is no real definite way of measuring how much

17   effort a student has put in. The teachers would have to get used to a

18   hole new method. They would have to figure out some way to grade

19   students based on effort. It would also not be fair to the students. Plus

20   one teacher would have a hard time watching everyone in the class

21   work all at once.

## Persuasive Writing *(cont.)*

22        So you can see that if this did happen, both the students and the

23    teachers would have a really harder time. It would not help anyone

24    who planned to get a job. Because it does not teach the students how

25    to do things the write way. Next time you think that this would be a

26    better way of gradeing, think again.

27    Thanks, Sean T.

# Persuasive Writing
# Benchmark Paper Comments

*Title: Letter to the Editor: Grading Students on Effort*     Holistic
Score: **1**

In this ineffective composition, the writer uses a letter format strategy to explain why grading on effort is a bad idea. The writer's voice is evident in the two reasons (*teach students how to do things the right way, no real definite way of measuring effort*) with some supporting details, but the overall development is superficial and confusing. Serious errors in word usage (*more easy, on you're effort*) and spelling (*abot, gradeing*) interfere with the effective communication of the author's ideas and with fluency.

| | Focus and Coherence | Organization | Development of Ideas | Voice | Conventions |
|---|---|---|---|---|---|
| **4** | focused and connected | flows smoothly | ideas deeply supported | highly engaging and original | strong command of conventions |
| **3** | mostly focused and connected | generally flows smoothly | ideas thoughtfully supported | mostly engaging and original | few errors |
| **2** | **somewhat focused** | flows somewhat smoothly | ideas adequately supported | **somewhat engaging and original** | some errors |
| **1** | unfocused, disconnected | **does not flow** | **ideas unsupported** | not engaging or original | **major errors** |

# Interpretive Response

## *Watership Down:* More Than Another Bunny Tale

1   At one level, *Watership Down* is an entertaining story about a

2   group of rabbits on a quest to start a new warren. On another level,

3   however, the story serves as an allegory exploring the different ways

4   that governing bodies function. An allegory is a story in which people,

5   things, and events have symbolic meaning, often intended to be

6   instructive.

7       The first rabbit community that is introduced is the Sandleford

8   Warren, led by the powerful, but inactive, chief rabbit, the Threrah. In

9   this warren there seem to be different classes of rabbits, starting with

10  the Outskirters. The Outskirters are ordinary young rabbits without

11  aristocratic parentage or unusual size or strength, who often get sat

12  on by their elders. Outskirters, such as Hazel and Fiver, are forced to

13  live out in the open at the very edge of the warren.

14      Higher up in this society is the Owsla, a group of strong, clever

15  rabbits who exercise authority and protect the Chief Rabbit and

16  his doe. The Owsla receive many privileges and have access to the

17  best food. Highest of all is that Chief Rabbit, who in Sandleford

18  Warren is very complacent and not open to change. In this system of

19  government, similar to that which was found in the early twentieth

20  century in Great Britain, rabbits lead a pretty normal, peaceful life.

# Interpretive Response (cont.)

21    They know where they stand and there is no hope of advancement for

22    smaller rabbits like Fiver.

23        Cowslip's Warren, found near a large grassy meadow, is far

24    different from the Sandleford Warren. In this system there is no Chief

25    Rabbit. The rabbits' needs are met by a farmer who supplies the

26    warren with good food and protection from their enemies. In return,

27    he snares a few rabbits here and there for his own use. The good thing

28    about this arrangement is that all the rabbits' needs are met without

29    expending any energy. Unfortunately, they must sacrifice their

30    freedom and their lives. All of these rabbits have become rather tame

31    and have given up on life, for they all know how it will end and they

32    accept their fate. This is similar to how many European Jews seemed

33    to react during the Holocaust.

34        Efrafa, another rabbit society, is run like a totalitarian state,

35    not unlike Nazi Germany. It is controlled by a cruel rabbit named

36    General Woundwort and by an unbending council of elders. They go to

37    measures to insure security by implementing wide patrols, by giving

38    every rabbit a distinguishing mark and group they must stay in, and

39    by strongly enforcing strict rules and regulations. The Efrafan rabbits

40    believe that they have total security from enemies and their basic

41    needs like food and shelter are met. But they obtain these things at

42    the expense of their freedom. The rabbits are not allowed to socialize

43    with others not in their group, burrow, have litters, or even leave

## Interpretive Response *(cont.)*

44   Efrafa. These regulations cause many rabbits, especially does, to be

45   unhappy and dissatisfied, and many attempts at escape are made.

46   The last rabbit society is the one founded by Hazel and his

47   followers on Watership Down. It was their wish that a warren be

48   created where everyone would be equal and would have a chance

49   for his or her opinion to be heard. It was formed on a large hill,

50   called Watership Down. It allows the rabbits to spot predators from

51   far away. It is a sort of hybrid of other warrens, utilizing protection

52   techniques from the Efrafans and structural features such as a large

53   open burrow in which rabbits can congregate such as those found in

54   Cowslip's Warren. The rabbits of Watership Down have also worked

55   to eliminate key problems found in other warrens. Here, rabbits have

56   many personal freedoms and are free to leave at any time. The only

57   disadvantages are that the rabbits are responsible for finding their

58   own food and for protecting themselves. This warren parallels the

59   development of the American form of government, a government in

60   which the founding fathers, who were not happy with the way things

61   were going, created a new government according to their beliefs and

62   ideals.

63   When understood at this level, *Watership Down* becomes much

64   more than an adventure story about rabbits; it becomes a grand

65   allegory about the pros and cons of different governmental systems.

66   That this story can be read on two such different levels is a sign of its

67   greatness.

# Interpretive Response
# Benchmark Paper Comments

*Title:* **Watership Down:** *More Than Another Bunny Tale*
Holistic Score: **4**

This highly effective interpretive response examines the idea that *Watership Down* is an allegory about governing bodies. The writer's strong opening presents the thesis statement, while the following paragraphs present a clear and concise organizational strategy of main points (*The first rabbit community... ,The last rabbit society...*), supporting details, and final analysis. The overall depth of development with specific examples (*Efrafa, another rabbit society, is run like a totalitarian state, not unlike Nazi Germany.*) along with excellent use of conventions and knowledgeable voice contribute to the effectiveness of this composition.

|   | Focus and Coherence | Organization | Development of Ideas | Voice | Conventions |
|---|---|---|---|---|---|
| **4** | focused and connected | flows smoothly | ideas deeply supported | highly engaging and original | strong command of conventions |
| **3** | mostly focused and connected | generally flows smoothly | ideas thoughtfully supported | mostly engaging and original | few errors |
| **2** | somewhat focused | flows somewhat smoothly | ideas adequately supported | somewhat engaging and original | some errors |
| **1** | unfocused, disconnected | does not flow | ideas unsupported | not engaging or original | major errors |

# Interpretive Response

## *Medea:* Portrait of a Villain

1  Villains are very bad characters. A good example of a villain is in

2  Euripides' *Medea*. The mean character is Medea herself. She weaves

3  a web of lies and destruction. She does not let anyone get in her way.

4  Medea hurts many to get her desires. Medea is a true villain in every

5  sense of the word.

6  First, Medea wants Jason. She wants him to the point of obsesion.

7  She will not let anyone get in her way. After she wins Jason, they

8  have to flee to Corinth. Once there, Jason leaves her for the princess.

9  Medea is in a lot of pain. Now she only wants Jason to suffer. She

10  comes up with a plan and causes Jason a lot of suffering. The fact that

11  all of what she does to get what she wants is done for her own intrest

12  makes her more horrible with every action.

13  Medeas interests were unstabel and unpredictable. When she

14  marries Jason her interests are to have a home and gain social

15  position. Her interests are changed when Jason leaves her. She has

16  been made a fool of. Her top priority is to get even with Jason so he

17  can know her suffering. She also wants to gain her pride back. Trying

18  to suit all of her interests and trying to get what she wants, she hurts

19  many people.

20  Medeas constant pursuit of happiness causes her to hurt anyone

21  in her path. No matter who it is. First to win Jason by helping him to

22  get the Golden Fleece. She kills her brother and then tricks her father.

## Interpretive Response *(cont.)*

23  She then gets Pelias' daughters to kill their father. This is so Jason

24  can be the king. They are forced to go to Corinth because the people

25  were angry that their king had been killed. Once there Jason leaves

26  her. Medeas pain is great. She takes revenge on him. To get what she

27  wants she kills Jason's bride to be and her father, Creon, the king of

28  Corinth. She even kills her own two children to give him more pain.

29  She does everything just to hurt others.

30      In conclusion, Medea is a villain. She sees something she wants

31  and does not let anything get in her way. She does not care who she

32  hurts and even kills six people. All of which Medea does for her own

33  good.

# Interpretive Response
# Benchmark Paper Comments

*Title:* ***Medea:*** *Portrait of a Villain*              Holistic Score: **2**

The writer of this response to literature focuses on examples from the text to support the thesis statement that Medea can be classified as a villain. Some effective word choice (*to the point of obsesion, top priority*) and details show that the writer knows the selection, but the progression of the paper is slowed because the middle paragraphs often restate the same events (Medea wants Jason, gets him, loses him, punishes all around her). Along with some errors in conventions, the overall development is superficial and only somewhat effective.

|  | Focus and Coherence | Organization | Development of Ideas | Voice | Conventions |
|---|---|---|---|---|---|
| **4** | focused and connected | flows smoothly | ideas deeply supported | highly engaging and original | strong command of conventions |
| **3** | mostly focused and connected | generally flows smoothly | ideas thoughtfully supported | mostly engaging and original | few errors |
| **2** | **somewhat focused** | **flows somewhat smoothly** | ideas adequately supported | somewhat engaging and original | **some errors** |
| **1** | unfocused, disconnected | does not flow | **ideas unsupported** | **not engaging or original** | major errors |

© Houghton Mifflin Harcourt Publishing Company

# Time Line

Topic: _____

# 5 W's Chart

Topic: _____

| | |
|---|---|
| Who? | |
| What? | |
| When? | |
| Where? | |
| Why? | |
| How? | |

# T-Chart

Topic:

# Venn Diagram

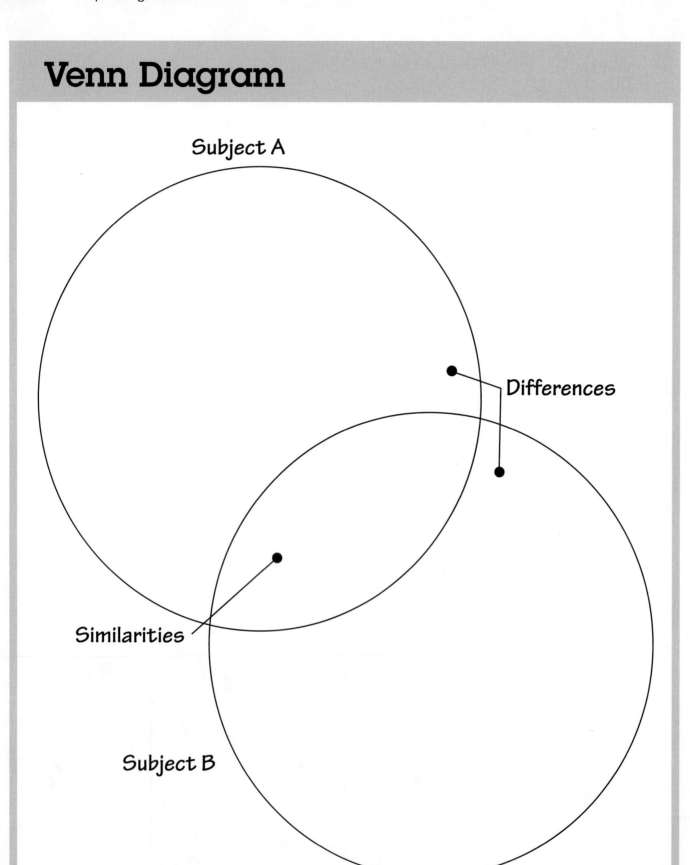

Subject A

Differences

Similarities

Subject B

# Sensory Chart

Subject: _____

| Sights | Sounds | Smells | Tastes | Textures |
|--------|--------|--------|--------|----------|
|        |        |        |        |          |

# Details Chart

# Quick List

1. First Point:

   ■

   ■

2. Second Point:

   ■

   ■

3. Third Point:

   ■

   ■

# Index